Fodor's 2009

MEXICO

Where to Stay and Eat for All Budgets

Must-See Sights and Local Secrets

Ratings You Can Trust

Fodor's Travel Publications New York, Toronto, London, Sydney, Auckland
www.fodors.com

FODOR'S MEXICO 2009

Editor: Kelly Lack

Editorial Contributors: Christina Knight, Mark Sullivan
Writers: Carissa Bluestone, Grant Cogswell, Larry Dunmire, Robin Goldstein, John Hecht, Alexis Herschkowitsch, Michele Joyce, Marlise Kast, Coco Krumme, Jonathan J. Levin, Maribeth Mellin, Jane Onstott, Claudia Rosenbaum

Editorial Production: Evangelos Vasilakis
Maps & Illustrations: David Lindroth, *cartographer*; Additional cartography provided by Henry Colomb, Mark Stroud, and Ali Baird, Moon Street Cartography, and Dr. Ed Barnhart, director, Maya Exploration Center (map of Palenque), *cartographers*; William Wu, *information graphics*; Bob Blake and Rebecca Baer, *map editors*
Design: Fabrizio LaRocca, *creative director*; Guido Caroti, Siobhan O'Hare, *art directors*; Tina Malaney, Chie Ushio, Ann McBride, *designers*; Melanie Marin, *senior picture editor;* Moon Sun Kim, *cover designer*
Cover Photo: (Ballet Folklorico de Mexico, Mexico City): Lindsay Hebberd/Corbis
Production/Manufacturing: Steve Slawsky/Amanda Bullock

ISBN 978-1-4000-1946-5

ISSN 0196-5999

SPECIAL SALES
This book is available at special discounts for bulk purchases for sales promotions or premiums. Special editions, including personalized covers, excerpts of existing books, and corporate imprints, can be created in large quantities for special needs. For more information, write to Special Markets/Premium Sales, 1745 Broadway, MD 6-2, New York, New York 10019, or e-mail specialmarkets@randomhouse.com.

AN IMPORTANT TIP & AN INVITATION
Although all prices, opening times, and other details in this book are based on information supplied to us at press time, changes occur all the time in the travel world, and Fodor's cannot accept responsibility for facts that become outdated or for inadvertent errors or omissions. So **always confirm information when it matters,** especially if you're making a detour to visit a specific place. Your experiences—positive and negative—matter to us. If we have missed or misstated something, **please write to us.** We follow up on all suggestions. Contact the Mexico editor at editors@fodors.com or c/o Fodor's at 1745 Broadway, New York, NY 10019.

PRINTED IN THE UNITED STATES OF AMERICA

10 9 8 7 6 5 4 3 2 1

Be a Fodor's Correspondent

Your opinion matters. It matters to us. It matters to your fellow Fodor's travelers, too. And we'd like to hear it. In fact, we need to hear it.

When you share your experiences and opinions, you become an active member of the Fodor's community. That means we'll not only use your feedback to make our books better, but we'll publish your names and comments whenever possible. Throughout our guides, look for "Word of Mouth," excerpts of your unvarnished feedback.

Here's how you can help improve Fodor's for all of us.

Tell us when we're right. We rely on local writers to give you an insider's perspective. But our writers and staff editors—who are the best in the business—depend on you. Your positive feedback is a vote to renew our recommendations for the next edition.

Tell us when we're wrong. We're proud that we update most of our guides every year. But we're not perfect. Things change. Hotels cut services. Museums change hours. Charming cafés lose charm. If our writer didn't quite capture the essence of a place, tell us how you'd do it differently. If any of our descriptions are inaccurate or inadequate, we'll incorporate your changes in the next edition and will correct factual errors at fodors.com immediately.

Tell us what to include. You probably have had fantastic travel experiences that aren't yet in Fodor's. Why not share them with a community of like-minded travelers? Maybe you chanced upon a beach or bistro or B&B that you don't want to keep to yourself. Tell us why we should include it. And share your discoveries and experiences with everyone directly at fodors.com. Your input may lead us to add a new listing or highlight a place we cover with a "Highly Recommended" star or with our highest rating, "Fodor's Choice."

Give us your opinion instantly at our feedback center at www.fodors.com/feedback. You may also e-mail editors@fodors.com with the subject line "Mexico Editor." Or send your nominations, comments, and complaints by mail to Mexico Editor, Fodor's, 1745 Broadway, New York, NY 10019.

You and travelers like you are the heart of the Fodor's community. Make our community richer by sharing your experiences. Be a Fodor's correspondent.

¡Buen Viaje!

Tim Jarrell, Publisher

CONTENTS

MEXICO IN FOCUS

CONTENTS

MAPS

ABOUT THIS BOOK

Our Ratings

Sometimes you find terrific travel experiences and sometimes they just find you. But usually the burden is on you to select the right combination of experiences. That's where our ratings come in.

As travelers we've all discovered a place so wonderful that its worthiness is obvious. And sometimes that place is so unique that superlatives don't do it justice: you just have to be there to know. These sights, properties, and experiences get our highest rating, **Fodor's Choice,** indicated by orange stars throughout this book. Black stars highlight sights and properties we deem **Highly Recommended**, places that our writers, editors, and readers praise again and again for consistency and excellence.

By default, there's another category: any place we include in this book is by definition worth your time, unless we say otherwise. And we will.

Disagree with any of our choices? Care to nominate a place or suggest that we rate one more highly? Visit our feedback center at www.fodors.com/feedback.

Budget Well

Hotel and restaurant price categories from ¢ to $$$$ are defined in the opening pages of each chapter. For attractions, we always give standard adult admission fees; reductions are usually available for children, students, and senior citizens. Want to pay with plastic? **AE, D, DC, MC, V** following restaurant and hotel listings indicate whether American Express, Discover, Diner's Club, MasterCard, and Visa are accepted.

Restaurants

Unless we state otherwise, restaurants are open for lunch and dinner daily. We mention dress only when there's a specific requirement and reservations only when they're essential or not accepted—it's always best to book ahead.

Hotels

Hotels have private bath, phone, TV, and air-conditioning and operate on the European Plan (aka EP, meaning without meals), unless we specify that they use the Continental Plan (CP, with a Continental breakfast), Breakfast Plan (BP, with a full breakfast), or Modified American Plan (MAP, with breakfast and dinner) or are all-inclusive (AI, including all meals and most activities). We always list facilities but not whether you'll be charged an extra fee to use them, so when pricing accommodations, find out what's included.

Many Listings

- ★ Fodor's Choice
- ★ Highly recommended
- ⊠ Physical address
- ✣ Directions
- Mailing address
- ☎ Telephone
- Fax
- ⊕ On the Web
- E-mail
- Admission fee
- ⊙ Open/closed times
- Ⓜ Metro stations
- ▭ Credit cards

Hotels & Restaurants

- Hotel
- Number of rooms
- Facilities
- Meal plans
- ✕ Restaurant
- Reservations
- Smoking
- BYOB
- ✕ Hotel with restaurant that warrants a visit

Outdoors

- Golf
- Camping

Other

- Family-friendly
- ⇨ See also
- Branch address
- ☞ Take note

WHEN TO GO

Mexico is sufficiently large and geographically diverse that you can find a place to visit any time of year. October through May are generally the driest months; during the peak of the rainy season (June–September) it usually rains for a few hours daily, especially in the late afternoon. But the sun often shines for the rest of the day.

From December through the second week after Easter the resorts—where most people go—are the most crowded and expensive. This also holds true for July and August, school-vacation months, when Mexican families fill hotels. To avoid the masses, the highest prices, and the worst rains, consider visiting Mexico during November, April, or May.

Mexicans travel during summertime school vacations, during traditional holiday periods—Christmas through January 6 (Three Kings Day), Semana Santa (Holy Week, the week before Easter), and the week after Easter—as well as over extended national holiday weekends, called *puentes* (bridges). Festivals play a big role in Mexican national life. If you plan to travel during a major national event, reserve both lodgings and transportation well in advance.

Climate

Mexico's coasts and low-lying sections of the interior are often very hot if not actually tropical. The high central plateau, home to Mexico City, Guadalajara, and many of the country's colonial cities, tends to be springlike year-round—days may be downright hot, however, and evenings chilly or even cold.

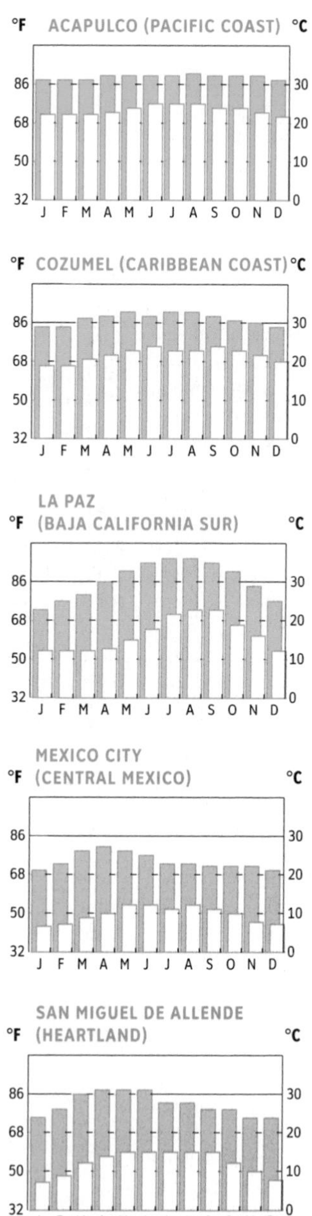

WHAT'S NEW IN MEXICO

Despite causing minor backups at the border, stricter U.S. reentry requirements have done little to slow Mexico tourism. As the weak dollar makes Europe a budget-busting destination, many are seeking out the bargains Mexico still offers, and increased air service from U.S. carriers and domestic airlines has made getting here that much easier.

Papers, Please

Gone are the days when a loud declaration of U.S. citizenship was enough to get you back across the border after a weekend of doing shots in Tijuana. In early 2007, the first part of the Western Hemisphere Travel Initiative (WHTI) went into effect, and now all people traveling by air must present a valid passport to reenter the United States. Eventually, the same will be true for those traveling by sea or land—at this writing, phase two of WHTI is set for June 2009—but for now, you must present the following: (a) passport or passport card, or (b) a combination of a government-issued photo ID, and another form of proof of citizenship, such as a birth certificate.

Flight Options Galore

Hartford to Cancún? Atlanta to Queretaro? Albuquerque to Puerto Vallarta? There seems to be no end to direct-flight options these days, as the major players like Delta and Continental and the smaller airlines like Frontier have added many new routes. In addition, the low-cost airline trend has reached Mexico; new carriers include Click Mexicana, Vivaaerobus, InterJet, Alma de Mexico, and Volaris. Because these airlines' hubs are located in lesser-visited cities like Monterrey and Guadalajara, it's hard to predict just how much the low-cost fliers will benefit the average traveler.

Coastal Shake-up

Whether it's due to the bad rep west-coast Cancún received from cranky tourists stuck there when Hurricane Wilma hit or the influence of all the baby boomers building condos where only RVers and surfers used to tread, the Pacific Coast is the place to be these days. It's nearly impossible to snag a room in Puerto Vallarta in high season and even tired old Mazatlán is receiving press as a "destination to watch," with several new megaprojects like the Diamond Beach development underway. Interest in Oaxaca's coast, particularly Puerto Escondido, has been renewed now that its main gateway, Oaxaca City, has fully recovered from the protests of 2006. And way up north, Puerto Penasco is poised for a boom thanks to the construction of a new airport.

Going Off the Beaten Path Gets Chic Again

Though many people head to Mexico's shores to hole up in all-inclusives, the country's smaller beach communities are all the rage these days. Sayulita, north of Puerto Vallarta, and Troncones, north of Zihuatanejo, both former surfing enclaves, are current obsessions. On the Caribbean Coast, tiny Isla Holbox, northwest of Cancún, is getting a lot of attention for its serene, car-free streets and snorkeling expeditions among whale sharks.

Puebla Gains Hipster Cred

This pleasant colonial city two hours from Mexico City has always been a place for foodies, but with the opening of La Purificadora hotel (part of the super-stylish Habita chain), Puebla now stands to draw a creative, fashion-forward crowd. It has already ensnared Enrique Olvera, chef-owner of vaunted Mexico City eat-

Experience Mexico

Women in traditional dress holding pottery, Chiapa de Corzo, Chiapas.

WORD OF MOUTH

"Chiapas is a wonderful option . . . In the same vicinity you can travel to San Cristobal de las Casas, in my opinion, one of the greatest little towns on earth . . . My next suggestion would be Tabasco. Villahermosa is the main part, but you can also travel to the outskirts to see beautiful jungles . . . Next on my list would be Oaxaca. The city is one of the most beautiful I've seen, with little (if any) tourist influence."

–tanita12

www.fodors.com/forums

ery Pujol, known for its innovative takes on traditional classics, who will be overseeing the hotel's restaurant.

Mexico City Gets Spruced Up

Adding to its already formidable list of world-class museums, the capital is poised for the summer 2008 opening of the University Museum of Contemporary Art on the main campus of the Universidad Nacional Autónoma de México; it will be the largest contemporary-art space in the city. The museum will undoubtedly draw more attention to the campus itself, which was awarded UNESCO World Heritage Site status in 2007 for its modernist buildings. Meanwhile, the city's foremost attraction, its historic center, has been getting a bit of a makeover as part of a "quality of life" program by Mayor Marcelo Ebrard; improvements included repaving, clearing illegal street vendors from congested sidewalks, and turning avenues over to pedestrians and cyclists on Sunday.

Celebrities Venture Beyond Baja

With its proximity to L.A. and its posh spa-resorts, Baja (especially Los Cabos) has been the go-to vacation spot for celebrities. But the A-listers have begun to branch out. The up-and-coming Riviera Nayarit north of Puerto Vallarta gets a wide spectrum of stars from Robert de Niro to Britney Spears. Many of them end up at the Four Seasons Punta Mita, which is able to accommodate "entourage travel." La Casa que Canta and The Tides in Zihuatanejo have recently become prime celebrity-spotting resorts for the likes of Steve Martin and Meg Ryan. Acapulco is back on the map thanks to its upscale Las Brisas and Diamond Point neighborhoods, pricey nightclubs, and trendy fusion restaurants. On the Caribbean Coast, there have been a few random sightings along the Riviera Maya—Maroma Resort and Spa seems to be the resort of choice for those who are oh-so-fabulous.

Green Travel Battles

In 2007 President Felipe Calderón made some progress with a wildlife protection law to save coastal mangrove forests, which have been greatly affected by tourism development, a plan to plant nearly 250 million trees, and a pledge of $4.6 million dollars to promote Michoacan's monarch butterfly reserve in the hopes that increased tourism would deter the illegal logging practices that threaten their migratory corridor. In other news, the World Heritage Alliance (WHA; a partnership between Expedia, Inc. and the United Nations Foundation) is working with the Mexico Tourism Board to promote sustainable tourism around the country's UNESCO World Heritage sites. Unfortunately, coastal overdevelopment continues to undermine these efforts. Baja real-estate ventures threaten a lagoon that is a breeding ground for gray whales; beachfront resorts on the Pacific Coast continually pipe wastewater directly into the sea; and all coastal areas are dealing with the environmental consequences of the shantytowns that spring up to house hotel workers. What's more, following Calderón's legislation, more than a dozen state governors declared they would ignore the new provisions to protect the development of tourism infrastructure in their regions.

WHAT'S WHERE

Numbers correspond to chapter numbers.

2 Mexico City. Mexico's sprawling capital isn't for everyone (the crime, the smog), but its cultural vibrancy attracts hip globe-trotters. You can sample the city in a day or two by strolling the streets around the central square or enjoying downtown's high-rises and galleries.

3 Around Mexico City. Within a few hours of Mexico City you'll find ruins, colonial capitals, indigenous villages, and volcanoes. Some sights, like the ancient city of Teotihuacán, are easy day trips, whereas others may require an overnight stay.

4 San Miguel de Allende & the Heartland. San Miguel's cobblestone streets and haciendas continue to provide much romantic fodder for its colony of American artists, writers, and retirees. For a place where people actually speak Spanish, head to any of the surrounding communities.

5 Guadalajara. Mexico's second-largest city has a Centro Histórico lined with many beautiful buildings, and is thoroughly modern everywhere else, which means good restaurants and happening nightlife.

6 Veracruz. Veracruz is often overlooked by foreigners. Its beaches, though not as nice as Cancún's, are popular with Mexican families. Cuban-influenced, seaside Veracruz City is noteworthy, as are the ruins of El Tajín.

7 Oaxaca. Oaxaca has it all: a pretty colonial city, ruins, crafts villages, forest-covered mountains, beaches, and superb Oaxaca City.

8 Chiapas & Tabasco. Isolated, jungle-swathed Chiapas has always been untrammeled, due in part to occasional Zapatista uprisings. What keeps it from falling off the map are the ruins of Palenque—as Mayan cities go, only Tikal in Guatemala and Copán in Honduras compare. Neighboring Tabasco is worth a trip to see the massive heads carved by the Olmecs.

9 Sonora. If you don't live close to the border, getting to Sonora will likely require more effort than it's worth. Its well-maintained highways and mission route, however, make it popular with road-trippers (especially RVers).

10 Barrancas del Cobre. Many people compare the Barrancas del Cobre, or Copper Canyon, to the Grand Canyon—the one that existed a century ago. Most people rely on a stunning 15-hour

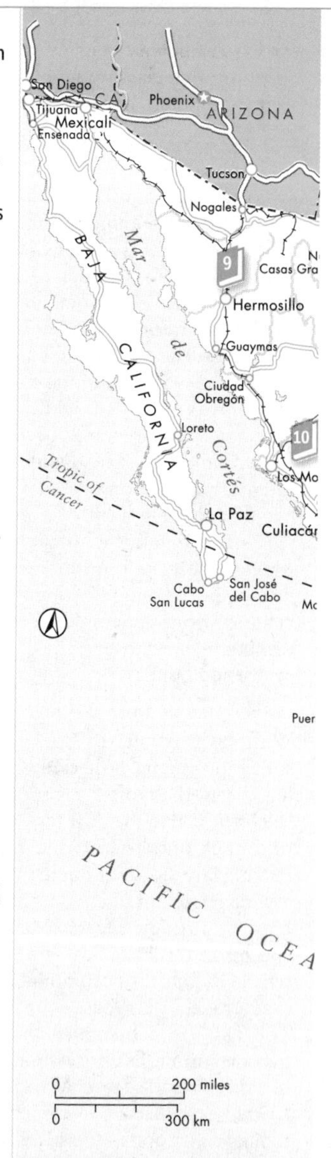

NEW MEXICO
OKLAHOMA
ARKANSAS
TENN.
MISS.
ALA.
TEXAS
LOUISIANA
Oklahoma City
Memphis
Little Rock
Las Cruces
El Paso
Ciudad Juárez
Dallas
Fort Worth
Jackson
Austin
San Antonio
Mobile
Baton Rouge
New Orleans
Río Grande
Río Bravo
Chihuahua
SIERRA MADRE OCCIDENTAL
SIERRA MADRE ORIENTAL
SIERRA MADRE DEL SUR
Gómez Palacio
Torreón
Monterrey
Saltillo
Reynosa
Brownsville
Matamoros
Durango
Fresnillo
Ciudad Victoria
Gulf of Mexico
Zacatecas
Ciudad Mante
Túxpan
Aguascalientes
Tampico
Tropic of Cancer
Tepic
San Luis Potosí
León
Guadalajara
San Miguel de Allende
Querétaro
Poza Rica
El Tajín
Isla Mujeres
Puerto Progreso
Cancún
Mérida
Tizimin
Colima
Tula
Teotihuacán
Manzanillo
Toluca
Morelia
Mexico City
Veracruz
Chichén Itzá
Uxmal
Cozumel
Xel-Há
Cobá
Campeche
Puebla
YUCATAN
Tulum
Bahía de Campeche
Ciudad del Carmen
Ixtapa/ Zihuatanejo
Coatzacoalcos
Chetumal
Caribbean Sea
Chilpancingo
Minatitlan
Villahermosa
Monte Albán
Acapulco
Oaxaca
Palenque
Tuxtla Gutiérrez
Bonampak
BELIZE
Tehuantepec
San Cristóbal de las Casas
Huatulco
Golfo de Tehuantepec
GUATEMALA
Tapachula
HONDURAS
1
2
3
4
5
6
7
8

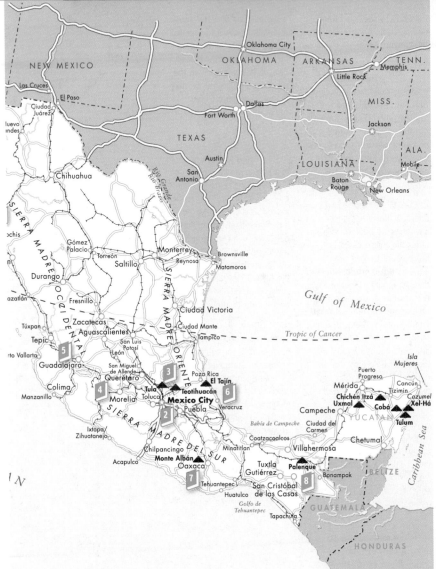

WHAT'S WHERE

train ride to see this region, perhaps doing a day hike into the canyon.

11 Los Cabos & the Baja Peninsula. There are two Bajas, literally and figuratively. Baja Norte is still slightly rugged, with boulder-strewn deserts, mountain ranges, and long beaches. Baja Sur is where you'll find Los Cabos and expensive spa-resorts.

12 Puerto Vallarta & the Pacific Coast Resorts. Puerto Vallarta occupies a nice niche between the other big resort cities—it's more sophisticated than Cancún, but more laid-back than Acapulco. North of PV is Mazatlán, a former spring-break spot that now attracts families and retirees. South of PV are miles of untouched beaches reached by dirt roads and linked by the port town of Manzanillo and the twin resort towns of Ixtapa and Zihuatanejo.

13 Acapulco. You've got to give Acapulco credit for staying power. After falling out of favor with the international jet set, this city with an undeniably beautiful bay is heating up again.

14 Cancún & Isla Mujeres. There are reasons why so many Americans flock to Spring Break Land—stunning beaches, tons of water sports, and, admittedly, a fun scene. Though there's no escaping how horribly overdeveloped Cancún is, it's low-key in the off-season and a few swanky lounges and hotels now offset the rowdy bars and all-inclusives.

15 Cozumel & the Riviera Maya. The island of Cozumel is a kinder, gentler version of Cancún. Many reefs and the 8-mi channel just off the coast make this a top snorkeling and diving destination. Playa del Carmen, a charming beach town on the mainland, acts as the unofficial capital of the Riviera Maya, a string of beaches quickly becoming the next big destination.

16 Mérida & Environs. Chances are you've heard of Chichén Itzá. The ruins are in Yucatan State and pretty far inland—in fact they're so close to the neighboring state of Quintana Roo, the home of Cancún and Cozumel, that many people prefer to do their day trips from there. But Yucatán also holds the colonial city of Merida, which is one of those places that seems to cast a spell.

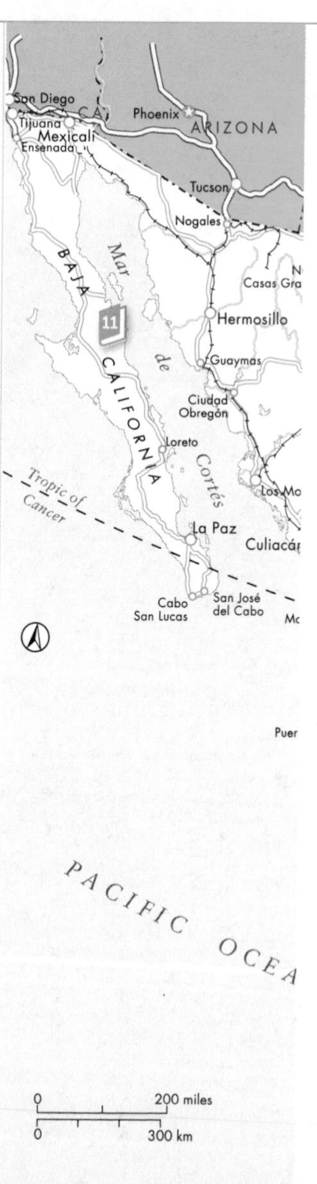

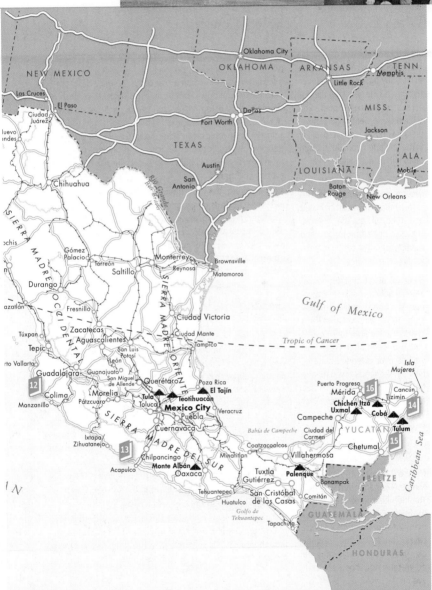

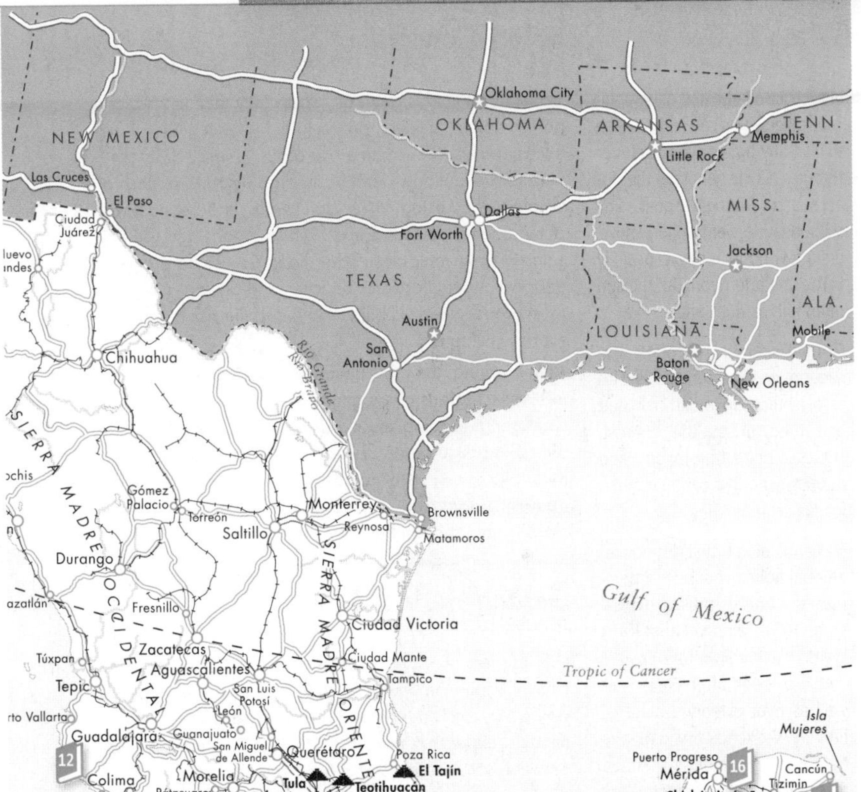

NEW MEXICO
OKLAHOMA
ARKANSAS
TENN.
Oklahoma City
Memphis
Little Rock
Las Cruces
El Paso
Ciudad Juárez
Dallas
Fort Worth
MISS.
Jackson
TEXAS
ALA.
Austin
LOUISIANA
Mobile
San Antonio
Baton Rouge
New Orleans
Chihuahua
Río Grande
Río Bravo
SIERRA MADRE OCCIDENTAL
Gómez Palacio
Torreón
Monterrey
Brownsville
Reynosa
Matamoros
Saltillo
SIERRA MADRE ORIENTE
Durango
Fresnillo
Ciudad Victoria
Gulf of Mexico
Zacatecas
Ciudad Mante
Túxpan
Aguascalientes
Tropic of Cancer
Tepic
San Luis Potosí
Tampico
León
Isla Mujeres
Guadalajara
Guanajuato
San Miguel de Allende
Querétaro
Poza Rica
Puerto Progreso
12
16
Colima
Morelia
Tula
Teotihuacán
El Tajín
Mérida
Cancún
Manzanillo
Pátzcuaro
Toluca
Mexico City
Veracruz
Chichén Itzá
Tizimin
Uxmal
Cobá
14
Puebla
Campeche
SIERRA MADRE DEL SUR
Cuernavaca
Bahía de Campeche
Ciudad del Carmen
YUCATÁN
Tulum
Ixtapa/ Zihuatanejo
Coatzacoalcos
Chetumal
15
13
Minatitlán
Villahermosa
Caribbean Sea
Chilpancingo
Monte Albán
Acapulco
Oaxaca
Tuxtla Gutiérrez
Palenque
BELIZE
Bonampak
Tehuantepec
San Cristóbal de las Casas
Comitán
Huatulco
Golfo de Tehuantepec
GUATEMALA
Tapachula
HONDURAS

MEXICO PLANNER

When to Go

Mexico is so large and geographically diverse you can find a region to visit any time of year. October through May is generally the driest season. During the peak rainy season (June–September) showers a few hours a day, especially in the late afternoon. But the sun often shines right after.

From December through the second week after Easter the resorts are the most crowded and their prices the highest. This also holds true for July and August, school-vacation months for Mexican families.

Mexicans also travel during traditional holiday periods—Christmas through January 6 (Three Kings Day), Semana Santa (Holy Week, the week before Easter), and the week after Easter—as well as over extended national holiday weekends. If you plan to travel during one of these times, reserve well in advance. Your best bet is to visit Mexico during November, April, or May.

CLIMATE

Mexico's coasts and its low-lying interior are often very hot. The high central plateau, home to Mexico City, Guadalajara, and many of the country's colonial cities, tends to be spring-like year-round—days may be downright hot, however, and evenings chilly.

Safety Concerns

Travel in Mexico is generally safe. Petty theft is the biggest threat to travelers, particularly in Mexico City, though occasionally serious crimes do occur. Overall, just take normal precautions: don't flash large amounts of cash and be alert when using ATMs; don't walk on deserted beaches at night; don't accept drinks from strangers; and use hotel safes to stow valuables. Other hazards include strong undertows on lifeguard-less beaches and driving at night in rural areas, when visibility is low and the risk of highway robbery is higher.

At this writing, the most troubling reports were of violence in several regions of the country where President Felipe Calderón is waging war on drug cartels. The violence is aimed at police or the drug cartels, not tourists, and often takes place in cities or rough neighborhoods that are not frequented by travelers. Acapulco has seen its share of clashes, too, though the hotel zone is generally safe.

Getting Here & Around

U.S. carriers provide frequent service to all major Mexican cities. Despite the emergence of low-cost carriers, flying within Mexico is not as easy. Coastal cities aren't well connected—expect layovers in Mexico City—although travel between some major points has been facilitated.

Bus travel is the most economical way to get around the country and air-conditioned deluxe- and first-class buses provide very comfortable rides. Many long-distance routes are stunning, too, winding through mountain passes or past farmland or undeveloped coastline.

Mexico does not have an extensive rail system. The country's only great train ride is through the Copper Canyon.

Driving through the Mexican countryside can be very pleasant, and is usually (and sometimes very!) scenic. Car rentals are available in all major cities and resort towns, though you should only bother with a rental if you plan on making some side trips. Take a taxi in the city.

A Quick Look

White-Sand Beaches: Maroma (Mayan Riviera), Playa del Carmen; Tulum; North Beach, Isla Mujeres

Party Towns: Puerto Vallarta, Acapulco, Cancún, Veracruz City

Colonial Splendor: Oaxaca City, the Heartland (especially Zacatecas and Morelia), Puebla, Mérida

Hiking & Mountain Climbing: Barancas del Cobre, the Heartland, Ajusco outside of Mexico City, Valle de Bravo, Pico de Orizaba in Veracruz

Nature Preserves: Chiapas, Michoacan, Oaxaca Coast, Cozumel, Veracruz

Modern Arts Scene: Mexico City, San Miguel de Allende, Monterrey

Monasteries & Missions: The Mixteca region of Oaxaca, Cuernavaca, Morelos, Sonora, Queretaro

Food: Puebla, Oaxaca City, Mexico City, Acapulco

The Perfect Gift for . . .

The dedicated drinker: Artisanal mezcal, Baja wines, pasita (a liqueur made from the pasa fruit popular in Puebla), almendrados (liqueur or tequila flavored with almonds), or damiana (an herbal liqueur that's great in margaritas).

The collector of kitsch: Lucha libre wrestling masks, Zapatista dolls, Frida Kahlo refrigerator magnets.

The aspiring gourmet: Jars of mole, chunks of dark chocolate, organic coffee, molcajete (three-legged stone bowls with pestles for grinding spices), or brightly decorated cazuelas (clay pots for simmering sauces) and molinillos (wooden sticks for stirring that delectable hot chocolate).

Money Matters

DINING & LODGING PRICE CATEGORIES

¢	$	$$	$$$	$$$$
Restaurants				
under $5	$5–$10	$10–$15	$15–$25	over $25
Hotels				
under $50	$50–$75	$75–$150	$150–$250	over $250

Restaurant prices are per person for a main course at dinner. Hotel prices are for two people in a standard double room, including tax and service.

Trip Planning

If it's too overwhelming to tackle Mexico by state or region, consider looking at the country the way the tour operators do—as a collection of cultural or historical routes. The Ruta del Vino (wine route) is a road through Baja's burgeoning wine region in the Valle de Guadalupe. The Ruta Maya (Mayan route) allows you to trace Mayan history through the southeastern states. The Ruta de los Dioses (Route of the Gods) shows up in one form or another in many tour operators' itineraries and usually starting in Mexico City (and Teotihuacan), heading to Puebla and Cholula, before continuing to Veracruz City or Oaxaca City, hitting ruins along the way.

If you're not ready to commit to the grand Mayan trek, 🌐 www.visitmexico.com has a list of the country's UNESCO World Heritage Sites—picking two or three would easily focus your trip. Similarly, consider building a trip around SECTUR's Pueblos Magicos (Magical Towns), well-preserved towns of historical and/or cultural significance. As of 2008, there were 35 towns on the list including Tepotzotlan and Valle de Bravo, outside Mexico City; Cuetzalan, north of Puebla; Todos Santos in Baja Sur; Alamos in Sonora; Tequila, outside Guadalajara; Papantla and Coatepec in Veracruz; San Miguel de Allende, Dolores Hidalgo, Tepoztlan, and Patzcuaro in the Heartland; Taxco, outside Acapulco; and San Cristobal de las Casas in Chiapas.

MEXICO TODAY

Politics

In September 2006 the conservative National Action Party's candidate, Felipe Calderón, was declared the victor after two months of controversy. The presidential race was perhaps the closest in Mexican history and populist candidate Andres Manuel Lopez Obrador, former mayor of Mexico City, lost to Calderón by less than one percentage point (243,000 votes). Election officials refused Obrador's requests for a total recount, which sparked mass protests.

In the first year of his presidency, Calderón wasted no time making an impression on his divided electorate, thereby separating himself from his predecessor, Vicente Fox, who was largely considered ineffectual, particularly when it came to passing legislation. To date, his administration's most noteworthy moves have included a pension-reform bill and a historic overhaul of the criminal justice system, which would introduce oral trials and speed up the trial and sentencing processes.

He has also decided to take a hard line against the country's warring drug cartels, a type of joint effort with the Bush administration, wherein the United States agrees to crack down on the flow of money and arms headed south and provide $1 billion in aid for Calderón's efforts. Though the crackdown has met with some success, it has also unleashed retaliatory violence that killed 120 police officers in the first year alone.

The Economy

Mexico's economy grew in 2006 and 2007, and although the growth was moderate, it was enough to spark the emergence of a new middle class (as well as pull some citizens out of poverty into lower-middle-class status). That said, with more than 70% of its exports going north of the border, Mexico's economy is tied to that of the United States, so recession could put the brakes on its growth.

In addition, there's been a noticeable dip in the country's invisible economy—remittances, the money that migrant workers send home to Mexico. The flagging U.S. economy (and a construction slump) have meant that workers already in the States have less money to send home, and stricter border enforcement has led some workers to decide against crossing the border at all.

One of the country's biggest economic puzzles is how to deal with its struggling oil monopoly, Pemex, which posted big losses in 2007 even as oil prices soared. President Calderón is pushing for reform that would allow private investment to help Pemex do deep-water drilling in the Gulf of Mexico, which would bolster Mexico's dwindling reserves. This proposition, however, is fiercely opposed by Andres Manuel Lopez Obrador—and nearly half the electorate. The rise of global food prices is another big-picture concern—in 2007 tens of thousands of people protested when the cost of tortillas skyrocketed.

Religion

Mexico has the second-largest Catholic population in the world—roughly 92% of the population. Religion is an important part of daily life for many people, as evidenced the large number of Catholic holidays, the larger number of elaborate churches, and the spectacle surrounding religious events like first communion. Even younger generations who are more

openly critical of the church retain a cultural identification with Catholicism.

That said, confidence in the church's authority has been shaken a bit by clergy sex-abuse scandals, and two recent legislative events in Mexico City point to the growing influence of an urban, less socially conservative population that is willing to break with church opinion. In April 2007 the legislature approved a bill legalizing first-trimester abortion within the federal district. Several months earlier, the city assembly legalized same-sex civil unions.

Cultural Mores

A country with great swaths of rural area and visible indigenous heritage, Mexico is often on the receiving end of behind-the-times barbs. But developments in the past few years suggest that the country is keeping pace with a few Western trends.

For one, hipster irony has made its way to the big cities. Lately there's a demand among urbanites for all things "naco," slang, which roughly translates as "tacky," "kitschy," or "cheesy" depending on whom you ask. It's not unusual to find lucha libre masks decorating the walls of trendy bars or hipsters drinking pulque (essentially Mexican moonshine). A Mexico City boutique, NaCo, is a favorite among the country's hot young actors and musicians.

Mexico has no shortage of smokers, but 2008 brought a nationwide smoking ban (following similar restrictions enacted by Mexico City the previous year), the first such legislation in Latin America. Smoking is prohibited in offices, restaurants, and public spaces, restricting lighting up to special areas where special ventilation equipment has been installed. Of course, it remains to be seen how well any of the new restrictions are enforced. The governors of tobacco-growing states like Nayarit are particularly opposed to the ban and say they will not enforce it.

Sports

Fútbol (soccer) remains an enduring passion of Mexico. The best teams in the top tier (the Primera Division) are Chivas de Guadalajara, Pachuca, Toluca, and Club América, which plays in Mexico City's famous Estadio Azteca. In 2007 the men's national team reached the quarterfinals at the FIFA Under-20 World Cup in Canada. The team's hit a few rough patches since, failing to make the Beijing Olympics and losing to the United States in the 2007 CONCACAF Gold Cup. The combination of events led to the firing of coach and soccer legend Hugo Sanchez. The women's national team has yet to qualify for a World Cup tournament but is still a contender for the Beijing Olympics.

But the biggest developments of the past few years have to do with sports not typically associated with Mexico. Golf star Lorena Ochoa was in 2007 the number-one ranked female golfer in the world, the first Mexican player to earn such a title. Though golf has yet to be widely embraced, Ochoa's emergence as an international star and role model have certainly piqued interest in a sport usually reserved for tourists.

TOP MEXICO ATTRACTIONS

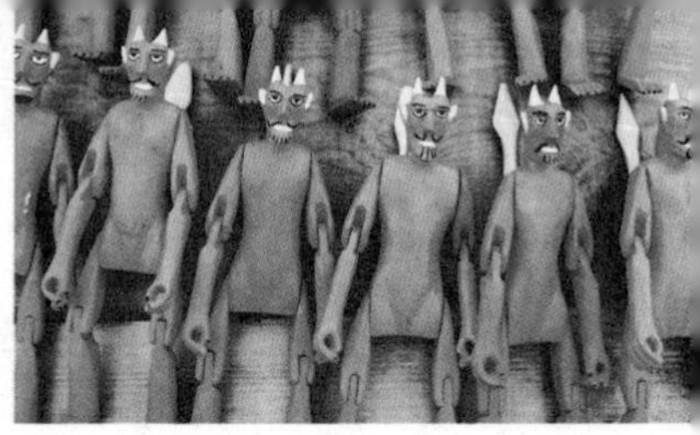

Chichén Itzá

An immense and important Mayan center, this ruined city of sun-baked pyramids and jungle-choked temples was named one of the New Seven Wonders of the World in 2007. Its proximity to Cancún sure doesn't detract from its popularity. Thousands come to Chichén on the vernal equinox (first day of spring).

The Great Maya Barrier Reef

Along the Caribbean Coast lies part of an immense reef system that snakes all the way to Honduras. Cozumel's marine park alone has 25 prime scuba-diving reefs, some of which are accessible to novices. Of course, experienced divers get to see the good stuff: 90-foot coral pinnacles, and giant sponges in all shades.

Finding Frida (and Diego)

Even if you're not an avid fan of Frida Kahlo's vivid and macabre paintings, retracing her and her husband Diego Rivera's steps is one of the best ways to approach Mexico City. Frida's old house in the serene Coyoacan neighborhood and the converted hacienda housing an impressive overview of Diego's work are particularly lovely, not to mention an intimate look at the lives of these two artists.

Monarch-Butterfly Migration

From November to March, 100 million monarchs make the pines of Santuario de Mariposas El Rosario look as though they're deciduous trees cloaked in autumn leaves. This once-in-a-lifetime experience is even more special when you consider how deforestation is destroying much of this habitat.

Pico de Orizaba

It may not be as fierce as its active cousin, Popocatepl, but this dormant volcano holds the distinction of highest mountain in Mexico, making it the third highest in North America. Even if you don't climb the summit, the surrounding national park is worth a visit into the less-visited state of Veracruz, known also for its cuisine.

Guanajuato

As San Miguel de Allende gets all the attention and the expats (artists, poets, and writers flock there), Guanajuato quietly enjoys its hill-ringed beauty—it's a standout in a region with no shortage of stunning colonial cities. A well-known colonial church, a handful of offbeat sights like the mummy museum, and an international Cervantes festival provide entertainment after you're done exploring the city's twisty streets.

Subterranean Swimming Holes

In addition to its sparkling seas, the Yucatán Peninsula has intricate systems of underground rivers connected to the surface by sinkholes called cenotes. Swimmers can take a quick dip in the crystal-clear freshwater, while divers can explore the cave systems.

Barrancas del Cobre

Larger and deeper in parts than the Grand Canyon, the Barrancas del Cobre, or Copper Canyon, is one of the most remote and striking areas in all of Mexico. A comfortable train trundles through it, though with a good guide, you can see the canyon up close through combination of jeep, bicycle, and leg power. In between the railroad's two terminals are a few small mountain towns and an indigenous group that's barely changed in 1,000 years.

FAQ

Can I drink the water?

Some hotels do have purified water—sometimes from a dedicated tap in the bathroom labeled agua purificada—but this is rare and in most cases it's best to rely on bottled water. Many restaurants, particularly in heavily touristed areas, serve purified water and ice, but if you're in doubt, ask or avoid it altogether.

Should I steer clear of Mexico City?

There's no easy answer. Mexico City can be a dangerous place and tourists are targets of petty theft. But Mexico City is also a dynamic city with world-class attractions—an exciting look at modern Mexico you won't find on the coasts or in the heartland. It's also much easier to navigate than it seems.

Mexico travel is super cheap, right?

That all depends on how far off the beaten path you're willing to go. Stay in any of the major resort areas and you will hemorrhage pesos. In midsize cities it's increasingly difficult to accomplish "Mexico on $50 a day" even when sticking with basic accommodations; "Mexico on $25 a day" is impossible unless you're willing to string a hammock between two trees and call it a night. Once you add in compulsory insurance, car rental is as expensive as in the states, though buses and taxis are still very affordable. Airfare from many U.S. cities is surprisingly reasonable, but air travel within Mexico can be expensive. Food and drink remain the real bargains.

Then how can I cut costs in the big resort towns?

Do as much shopping and eating outside the resort as possible—even in Cancún, cheaper restaurants can be found a few blocks from the hotel strip. Do some research before taking an all-inclusive package—you might book a room with a kitchenette so you can shop in the local market and cook. Beware of fixed taxi rates set by the hotel—they are always higher than what you can negotiate when on the street. Always ask for prices when offered the "catch of the day"—otherwise you might end up paying more than $20 for a whole fish. And when at the swim-up bar, ask for local beers and spirits.

Are ATMs plentiful?

Bringing a money belt crammed full of dollars is not necessary—despite popular belief, dollars are not widely accepted outside of border towns and the biggest resorts. All major and midsize cities have numerous ATMs. Most airports, even small regional ones, have at least one ATM. You get the best exchange rate when withdrawing pesos from an ATM, though be careful of high fees from your bank. Villages do not have ATMs, so make sure you have cash on hand before traveling outside a hub city.

Se hablan ingles?

You'll find English-speakers in major resort areas like Los Cabos, Cancún, Cozumel, and Puerto Vallarta, in border towns, and in Mexico City and cities popular with expats like San Miguel. But Spanish is still the official language of the country, so don't expect every bellboy, waiter, shopkeeper, and taxi driver you encounter to speak English. Even in resort areas, if a hotel caters to Mexican clientele, the concierge may only speak Spanish. Outside the resort areas, knowing some key phrases and how to decipher basic signage will make your trip a lot easier, as will carrying a good phrase book.

MEXICO'S TOP EXPERIENCES

Seeing a Baby Whale Breach

Even if you only glimpse it from shore, spotting a pod of whales in the cold blue Pacific is one of Mexico's definitive experiences. If you're lucky, you'll get to watch while a mama whale teaches her young one the not-so-delicate art of breaching. Baja is whale-watching central, with gray whales in the waters from December to April; in particular, three lagoons on the Pacific Coast seem to sing out a siren call to grays, and come in droves they do, congregating in these lagoons—Laguna Ojo de Liebre, Laguna San Ignacio, and Bahía Magdalena—to give birth or mate. Sightings are also good between Puerto Vallarta and Manzanillo.

Catching Live Music in the Zócalo

Nearly every town in Mexico has a main plaza of some sort, great for relaxing with an ice cream and people-watching. And as you read though this book, you're sure to see the word zócalo mentioned over and over again, as they really are the heartbeat of the country. In the larger cities, these shady spots also come with live music: the Caribbean sounds in Veracruz City's square, the folk singers or brass bands of Oaxaca City's zócalo, and the late-night mariachi bacchanalia at Mexico City's Plaza Garibaldi (the original Zócalo).

Watching a Craftsperson at Work

With tacky T-shirts, shot glasses, and picture frames glue-gunned with dyed shells being the default souvenirs, how often do you get to see your mementos made right before your eyes? Many regions have rich crafts traditions, so before you settle on that refrigerator magnet, take a side trip to a village where nearly every house doubles as a workshop: you'll find pottery and delicate wood sculptures in Oaxaca's countryside, ceramics and blown glass outside Guadalajara, hammocks made to order in Mérida. You can even watch Talavera tiles being made at the factory in Puebla. Prices are often better at the source, since you're cutting out the middle man.

Savoring Seafood & a Coco Frio at a Beachfront Palapa

No matter which coast you're on, the beachfront palapa restaurant will be ubiquitous. And there's no greater pleasure after hours of swimming or kayaking than ordering a simple meal of ceviche or fish tacos with a side of rice and beans and washing it down with a coco frio (a cold coconut hacked open just enough to stick a straw into). No matter how much you've fallen in love with your megaresort's elaborate beachfront, make sure you experience this low-brow delight.

Seeking Out Lesser Ruins

The sheer enormity of sites like Teotihuacan, Monte Albán, Chichén Itzá, and Palenque make them must-sees, but after you've taken pictures and shuffled up or around pyramids shoulder to shoulder with other tourists, leave for a lesser monument. Sites like Dainzu in Oaxaca, Yaxchilan in Chiapas, and Coba near Tulum, are small and serene and much more atmospheric. Bring a book, take a nap, or just soak in the scenery. The calm that awaits will allow for a totally different experience than the major sites provide.

De-stressing Simply or In-Style

In the central regions of the country you'll find temazcales, traditional Mayan sweat lodges. These may be simple outbuildings at the end of a trail or reconstructed rooms inside local spas. On the other end of the spectrum are the lavish treatments at the posh spas of Los Cabos, Puerto Vallarta, and Acapulco—look for treatments that incorporate unusual local ingredients (nopales, Corona beer) and massages in oceanfront palapas. Many of these upscale spas have introduced their own temezcal treatments, with special touches like essential oils, perfumed air, and a spa employee who helps along your spiritual journey within the temazcal.

Making Your Own Mole

Every region has its own cuisine, but no dish is more mythic than the mole. (It's said that floating around somewhere in the ether is a recipe for a mole that contains 100 ingredients.) Two of Mexico's gastronomic centers—Oaxaca City and Puebla—excel at this complex sauce, though you'll find them all over the place. Sign up for a cooking class that starts at a local market where you'll get a crash course on Mexican produce and spices before mastering a menu full of regional specialties. We can almost guarantee that this will be one of your most memorable travel experiences.

Marveling at Mexico City from a Rooftop Bar

Spend your first night in town trying to get your bearings in this sprawling city while sipping a specialty cocktail at the Habita Hotel's Area Bar or the W's Terrace Bar, both in the trendy Polanco neighborhood. Casa de las Sirenas restaurant also has a nice view of the historic center from its roof. If on no other night during your trip, let this be the one that you spend $15 on a drink.

QUINTESSENTIAL MEXICO

Day of the Dead

People across the country celebrate El Día de los Muertos, or the Day of the Dead. Some traditions, such as visiting cemeteries, setting up *ofrendas* (altars) in the home, and bestowing sugary *calaveritas* (meaning "little skulls") on children, are observed everywhere. But the holiday, held on November 1–2, will also differ depending on where you go.

In Campeche, families pilgrimage to family members' graves, remove the bones, dust them off, and carefully place them back for another year. Villagers in the most remote regions of Chiapas blanket the burial plots with marigolds, then go home to await a visit from the deceased. In Oaxaca, what begins as a meditative march to the cemetery ends with music and dancing, displays of larger-than-life puppets, and seemingly endless volleys of fireworks.

Mariachi

When Mexicans celebrate weddings, anniversaries, and *quinceañeras* (a "sweet 15" birthday bash), the music of choice is mariachi. Although this type of music hails from Jalisco state, it's popular throughout the country. You'll find men playing folk songs in concert halls, town squares, restaurants, or, as in the Mexico City suburb of Xochimilco, while floating by on flower-covered boats. Their distinctive costumes are adapted from the clothing worn by *charros,* or cowboys of the Jalisco region.

Mariachi music was born in the 19th century. Traditional melodies of various indigenous peoples were adapted to the instruments introduced by the Spanish. This is a music of contrasts, with a highly syncopated rhythm playing below a sweet and sometimes wistful melody.

Tortillas

Mexico's food varies wildly, but one item will appear on the table no matter where you are: the corn tortilla. If tortillas aren't an ingredient in your meal—look closely, as they sometimes masquerade as crispy croutons in soups or as slender noodles in stews—there's always a stack of them in a basket. The average Mexican eats nearly a pound of tortillas every day.

The corn tortilla (not to be confused with the flour tortilla) was a favorite food of the Aztecs. You'll find the staple in all sizes from two inches (stuffed with beans or meat to make *gorditas*) to 10 inches or more (covered with cheese and other ingredients for pizzalike *tlayudas*). Tiny *tortillerias* crank out the goods for busy urbanites, though in villages across Mexico you'll still see women making them by hand.

Virgin of Guadalupe

The Virgin of Guadalupe, who first revealed herself to a barefoot farmer in 1531, continues to appear all over the country. Shrines to her are found in quiet corners of outdoor markets and crowded corridors of bus stations. If you take a taxi, her image may be swinging on the rearview mirror.

Although she always had a following, the popularity of La Guadalupana grew when Padre Miguel Hidalgo emblazoned her image on his flag during Mexico's War of Independence. Thus she became an important religious symbol. Her enduring appeal is due to her adaptability. In the 20th century she was adopted by those demonstrating for the rights of workers, then by women who felt the sting of discrimination.

IF YOU LIKE

Diving & Snorkeling

Cozumel is still considered one of the world's premier diving destinations. Waving sea fans, anemones, moray eels, swooping manta rays, and more than 500 species of fish make their home along the **Maya Reef.** The visibility here can reach 100 feet, so even if you stay on the surface you'll be amazed by what you can see. Thrill-seekers won't want to miss Isla Contoy's extraordinary **Cave of the Sleeping Sharks.** Here you can see otherwise fierce creatures "dozing," a bizarre response to the chemical composition of the water.

There are plenty of dive sites along the Pacific Coast. In Puerto Vallarta the best snorkeling and diving is around the offshore rock formations near **Playa Mismaloya. Punta de Mita,** about 80 km (50 mi) north of Puerto Vallarta, has at least 10 good places to snorkel and dive, including spots for advanced divers. In winter you might spot orcas or humpback whales; the rest of the year, look for manta rays, several species of eel, sea turtles, and colorful fish. In Manzanillo the shallow waters of **Playa la Audiencia** make it a good spot for snorkeling, while an offshore wreck draws divers to **Playa la Boquita.**

At the southern tip of Baja California there are some good sites near La Paz at the coral banks off **Isla Espíritu Santo,** where you'll see parrot fish, manta rays, neons, and angelfish. **Bahía Santa María** is a great place to snorkel. Fish of almost every hue swim through formations of gleaming white coral. **El Arco,** the most spectacular sight near Cabo San Lucas, is also a prime dive area.

Colonial Architecture

Before you leave **Mexico City,** make sure to take a good look at the main square. To crush the spirit of the Aztecs, Cortés built the massive Catedral Metropolitana where their temples had stood. Renaissance and baroque styles mingle in the sections completed in the 17th century, while the bell towers dating from the 18th century show a neoclassical flair.

Within a few hours of Mexico City are some of the country's finest colonial cities, including **Tepotzotlán** and **Tlaxcala.** Both cities have supreme examples of churrigueresque architecture. The Iglesia de San Sebastián y Santa Prisca is the centerpiece of **Taxco,** one of the most perfectly preserved colonial capitals. The church is a memorable shade of pink.

The Heartland's colonial cities were financed by silver from the nearby mines. You may get lost in the labyrinthine streets of **Guanajuato,** but be sure to see La Valenciana—its altars vary in style from baroque to plateresque, the flowing lines resembling the work of a silversmith. The cathedral in nearby **Zacatecas** is thought to be the finest baroque building in Mexico. Beautifully restored mansions dating from the 18th century are the main attraction of **Querétaro.**

Perhaps the loveliest colonial capital is **Oaxaca,** known for the pale green stone used for almost all its landmarks. The architects went for baroque in most of its churches, including the Iglesia de Santo Domingo. In neighboring Chiapas the baroque facade of the cathedral in **San Cristóbal de las Casas** is painted vivid shades of red, yellow, and black—the colors seen most often in the shirts worn by indigenous women.

Ancient Cities & Ruins

Although their civilization was at its height at the time of the conquest, there are surprisingly few Aztec sites left. One of the structures that survived is the **Templo Mayor** in the middle of Mexico City. Discovered in 1978, this temple had been buried beneath a row of colonial-era houses.

Ironically, the best-preserved ruins are often the oldest. North of Mexico City is **Teotihuacán,** which thrived between AD 250 and AD 600. So little is known about the culture that archaeologists don't even know its real name. Its centerpiece, the Pirámide del Sol, is one of the largest pyramids ever built. Not far away is **Tula,** the capital of the Toltec empires. This city controlled the region after the fall of Teotihuacán. Climb to the top of the tallest temple to see the rows of stone warriors.

Other massive monuments are found in the southeastern part of the country. Overlooking Oaxaca is the Zapotec capital of **Monte Albán.** Archaeologists still debate the use of the arrow-shape structure that stands at a strange angle in the central plaza. But the people who left behind the most impressive cities were, of course, the Maya. After their civilization fell about a millennium ago, the jungle closed in around their temples, protecting them from those who would carry off their treasures. In Chiapas you'll marvel at the elegant carvings that distinguish **Palenque,** perhaps the most awe-inspiring of these ancient cities. In the Yucatán is Mexico's most famous monument, the ancient city of **Chichén Itzá,** which is visited often, by many, but still worth a trip.

Roads Less Traveled

The Barrancas del Cobre (Copper Canyon) has grown in popularity as a tourist destination. Get off the train at Cerocahui and head down to **Urique** at the canyon's floor.

The Mixteca is a beautiful region not far from Oaxaca City, but since the major activity here is standing slack-jawed before a massive monastery, most people leave it off their itinerary. The **Oaxaca Coast** is stubbornly low-key despite some stirrings of development. Even the towns that get listed in all the guidebooks are no-frills compared with other resort areas, and a rental car will get you to beaches that don't have so much as a *palapa* on them.

You'll be happy anywhere in the state of Veracruz, which sees more Mexican vacationers than American tourists, but the village of **Xico,** surrounded by natural wonders, feels like a slice of a different era.

In Chiapas, Palenque is truly amazing, but you should also push on to the ruins of **Yaxchilán** on the Guatemalan border. The last hour of the trip has to be done by boat, so you definitely won't see a parking lot full of tour buses here.

The **Santuario de Mariposas el Rosario** is no easy day trip from the city of Morelia (consider going from San Miguel), but where else can you see a grove of 100 million monarch butterflies?

And there's always roadtripping the **Baja Peninsula.** It's easy to access, with its length run through by the Carretera Transpeninsular highway, which connects many small towns you've never heard of.

GREAT ITINERARIES

DAYS 1–3: THE CAPITAL'S WONDERS & BEYOND

Welcome to Mexico City

Can you really know Mexico if you haven't visited its dizzying capital? Once the world's largest metropolis and the primary stomping grounds of the Aztecs, the first city was razed by the conquistadors, who built the city that still stands today.

After you've settled into your hotel, head straight for the city's heart: the immense *Zócalo*. Highlights include the Diego Rivera murals at Palacio Nacional, the Templo Mayor, and the Catedral Metropolitana.

Next up: hop on a red Turibus for a tour of the city. If you're in a walking mood, walk up Calle Madero to the Palacio de Bellas Artes and Alameda Central park. You can catch the Turibus here at the *Hemiciclo a Benito Juárez* monument on Avenida Juárez.

Logistics: When you emerge from the highly efficient immigration and customs facilities at Mexico City's Aeropuerto Internacional Benito Juárez, you can hire a porter to guide you to an official ticket counter marked Transportación Terrestre for a taxi. A taxi ride to a central hotel will cost about $15 and take 30 minutes. You shouldn't purchase a ticket from other vendors or take any other taxis. Keep in mind that the subway is ideal for getting around town but it does not allow luggage.

Beyond the Zócalo

Although the historic center of Mexico City could keep you enthralled for days, you'll enjoy visiting different *colonias,* (neighborhoods) such as the Roma and Condesa, where aging edifices mingle with trendy restaurants and bars. San Angel and Coyoacán channel colonial times with cobblestone streets, elegant homes, and lush gardens. Some of the Diego Rivera and Frida Kahlo museums are here.

Logistics: One of the easiest ways to get around the city is the subway. You can also take a *pesero* (minibus) at just about any point in the city, or the Metrobus, which runs along Avenida Insurgentes. Another fantastic option is the Turibus, which allows you to hop on and off; it runs daily from 9 AM to 9 PM. Or you can take a taxi from the taxi stands (*sitios*). Immediately state your destination to find out the fare (average $5).

Anthropology in the City

A visit to Mexico City simply isn't complete until you've stepped foot in the enormous Museo Nacional de Antropología, located on Paseo de la Reforma and guarded by a large Olmec head of Tlahuac, the rain god.

Logistics: The museum is one of the Turibus stops; the subway stop is Auditorio. After your visit, head over to Colonia Polanco for a stroll along Avenida President Masarik, the Rodeo Drive of Mexico City, where the rich and famous dine and shop. Here the closest subway stop is Polanco.

DAYS 4–6: ESCAPING THE CITY—EASILY

Option #1: The Pyramid of the Sun

One of the most fascinating ruins in the country is 48 km (30 mi) outside the capital: Teotihuacán and its pyramids to the Sun and Moon. If Mexico City is now one of the world's largest cities, Teotihuacán undoubtedly held that title in AD 600. A

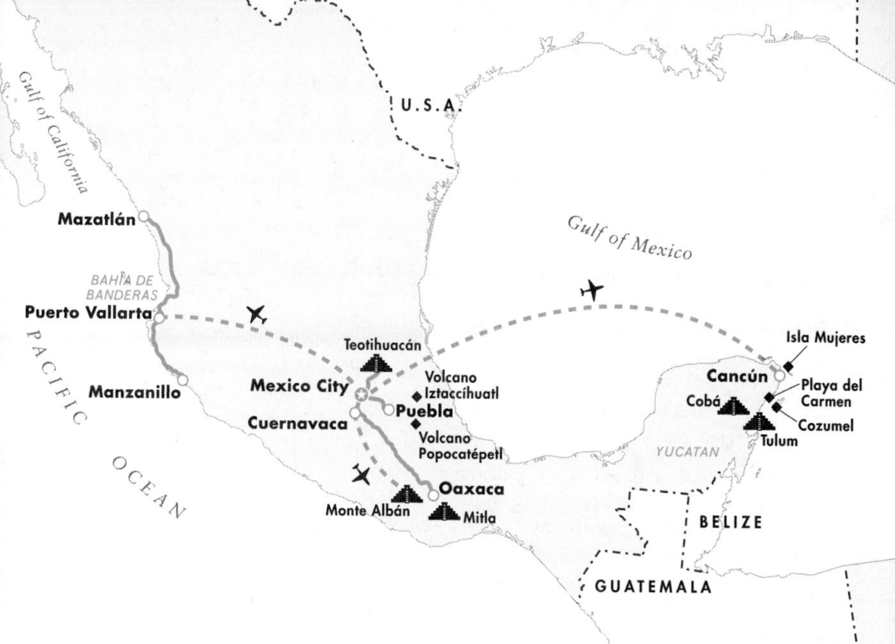

walk around these awe-inspiring grounds will give you insight into the power of the Aztec empire that once ruled most of central Mexico.

Logistics: One of the best ways to view the famous pyramids is via a guided tour on a bus, which will cost $25 to $40, available through most hotels or local travel agencies.

Option #2: City of Eternal Spring

An hour south is the "eternal spring" city of Cuernavaca, where Hernán Cortés once went to get a breather from the city and where the capital's residents flee to enjoy a more relaxed atmosphere. A visit here can include side trips to the ruins at Xochicalco and Tepoztlán.

Logistics: One option is to rent a car and drive to Cuernavaca. It's a little more than 161 km (100 mi) round-trip on a beautiful superhighway; consider an overnight stay. If you decide to rent a car, daily rates at Avis and Hertz are about $60–$75, insurance included. Bear in mind that you'll also have to pay highway tolls. Alternatively, take a bus from the Central de Autobuses del Sur in the capital; the ride takes about 1½ hours and costs about $6.50.

Option #3: Popo, Itza & Puebla

For a spectacular view of the snowcapped volcanoes Popocatépetl and Iztaccíhuatl, head southeast to Puebla, famed for its colonial charms, beautiful Talavera pottery, and numerous ex-convents. Nearby towns include Cholula and Cuetzalan.

Logistics: The bus ride from the capital to Puebla takes about two hours. Thanks to the frequency of buses, this makes a great one-day trip. Driving to Puebla is another easy option and will be a bit quicker. Cholula is a 15-minute cab ride from Puebla.

DAYS 7–14: MOVING ON FROM MEXICO CITY

Option #1: Oaxaca's Wonders

One hour by plane from the capital, Oaxaca is a world of culture unto itself. Observe the magnificence of the ancient Zapotec and Mixtec cultures at the Monte Albán and Mitla ruins. In the nearby vil-

GREAT ITINERARIES

lages, shop for gorgeous black pottery (*barro negro*), handwoven rugs, and *alebrijes* (colorful, carved wooden figurines). Known as "the land of the seven moles," Oaxaca is a gourmet's paradise. Start off with a shot of the local mezcal and some fried grasshoppers.

Logistics: Low-cost airline Click Mexicana (P55/5322–6262 in Mexico City wwww.click.com.mx) offers reasonably priced tickets between the capital and Oaxaca City. First-class buses run direct to Oaxaca from the TAPO bus station and take about 6½ hours. The one-way fare is about $40.

Option #2: Crazy for Cancún

If you're in the mood for sunshine and white, sandy beaches, hop on an eastbound plane and two hours later you'll arrive at Aeropuerto Internacional Cancún. Nearby are the resorts of Cozumel, Playa del Carmen, and Isla Mujeres. Although occasionally battered by hurricanes—Wilma in 2005 was considered the strongest ever—the Riviera Maya is quick to recover. Some of Mexico's priciest resorts and spas are in the vicinity. Keep in mind that Cancún tends to draw party crowds. But there are plenty of escapes, including the nearby Maya ruins, Tulúm and Cobá.

Logistics: Daily flights leave the capital on Aeroméxico and Mexicana. Aviacsa (☎*55/5582–8280*; 🌐*www.aviacsa.com*) has the cheapest nonstop flights with round-trip airfares from $250 to $350. Note that low-cost carrier Volaris flies from Puebla to Cancún for about half that price. If you have the time and patience, buses depart daily from the TAPO terminal. The run takes 23 hours and will cost you $100 on a first-class bus.

TIP

For more detailed travel information, *see* the By Bus and By Air sections of the Travel Smart chapter at the end of this book, as well as the Essentials information in each chapter.

Option #3: Pacific Coast Paradise

Mexico's Pacific coast is easily accessible from Mexico City either by plane or bus. From Mazatlán to Puerto Vallarta to Zihuatanejo, the Pacific Coast is dotted with hundreds of beaches with accommodations for visitors ranging from ritzy to secluded to simple. Puerto Vallarta (PV), an elegant town on the Bahía de Banderas, is the most popular resort in the area.

Logistics: PV is 1½ hours by air from the capital and has its own airport (Aeropuerto Internacional Gustavo Díaz Ordáz). Aeroméxico, Mexicana, Líneas Aéreas Azteca, and AeroCalifornia all fly direct from Mexico City (round-trip $250 and up). Volaris flies for half the cost from nearby Toluca. By bus you depart from the Terminal Norte on a 12-hour first-class bus ride for about $100.

ON THE CALENDAR

	Mexico is the land of festivals, or fiestas—there are more than 10,000 of them. You should reserve lodging well in advance, as they're a golden opportunity to experience Mexico's culture. January is full of long, regional festivals. Notable are the Fiesta de la Inmaculada Concepción (Feast of the Immaculate Conception), which transforms the city of Morelia into a sea of lights and flowers for much of the month; and a series of folkloric dances in Chiapa de Corzo, Chiapas, that culminates in the Fiesta de San Sebastián the third week in January. Several cultural events take place at different times each year. Among these is Cancún's noteworthy Jazz Festival, which happens in the spring or fall and draws a huge international crowd from the United States, South America, and Europe. The Isla Mujeres International Music Festival, during which the island fills with music and dancers from around the world, is another such event. The Festival Internacional Cervantino in Guanajuato in October is one of Mexico's most important cultural events, showcasing performances by orchestras, dance troupes, and theaters from around the world.
WINTER December	On the 12th, during the **Fiesta de la Virgen de Guadalupe** *(Feast of the Virgin of Guadalupe)*, Mexico's patron saint is honored with processions and native folk dances, particularly at her Basilica de Guadalupe shrine in Mexico City, where, at midnight, singers gather to serenade her. In Puerto Vallarta, 12 days of processions and festivities lead up to the night of the 12th. **Navidad** *(Christmas)* and the days leading up to it (roughly the 16th through the 24th) see candlelight processions, holiday parties, and the breaking open of piñatas. Cities and villages alike are brightly decorated.
December 23	The **Noche de Rábanos** *(Radish Night)*, a pre-Christmas tradition in Oaxaca, is one of the most colorful in Mexico: participants carve giant radishes into amusing shapes and display their unusual tableaux in the city's main plaza.
January 1	**Día del Año Nuevo** *(New Year's Day)* is traditionally celebrated with large family gatherings. Shops and restaurants may be closed; agricultural and livestock fairs are held in the provinces.
January 6	The **Día de los Reyes** *(Epiphany, or Three Kings Day)* refers to the day the Three Wise Men brought gifts to the Christ

ON THE CALENDAR

	child; on this day Mexican children are traditionally treated to small gifts (although Santa Claus has made inroads in more cosmopolitan cities and border towns).
February–March	**Día de la Candelaría,** or Candlemas Day, means fiestas, parades, bullfights, and lantern-decorated streets. Festivities include a running of the bulls through the streets of Tlacotalpan, Veracruz. The pre-Lenten **Carnaval** season is celebrated throughout Mexico—most notably in Mazatlán, Veracruz, and Cozumel—with parades of floats, bands, and all-night parties.
SPRING March 21	**Aniversario de Benito Juárez** *(Birthday of Benito Juárez)*, a national holiday, is most popular in Oaxaca, birthplace of the beloved 19th-century Mexican president. This is also the day of Cuernavaca's **Fiesta de la Primavera,** or Spring Festival.
April	**Semana Santa** *(Holy Week)*, the week leading to Easter Sunday, is a moveable feast, observed with parades and passion plays. There are particularly moving ceremonies in Mexico City, Oaxaca, and Taxco.
May 5	**Cinco de Mayo** is a bank holiday, although some towns, especially those in the state of Puebla, celebrate the anniversary of the defeat of French invaders in 1862 with speeches and parades.
SUMMER June 1	**Día de la Marina** *(Navy Day)* is commemorated in all Mexican seaports and is especially colorful in Acapulco, Mazatlán, and Veracruz.
June 24	On the **Fiesta de San Juan Bautista** *(Feast of Saint John the Baptist)*, a popular national holiday, many Mexicans observe a tradition of tossing a "blessing" of water on most anyone within reach.
July	Many towns celebrate the days preceding the **Fiesta de Santiago Apostle** *(Feast of Saint James the Apostle)*, on July 25, with *charredas,* Mexican-style rodeos.
July 16	**Fiesta de Nuestra Señora del Carmen** *(Feast of Our Lady of Mt. Carmel)* is celebrated with fairs, bullfights, fireworks, even a major fishing tournament.

August	The **Fiesta de San Augustine** *(Feast of St. Augustine)* brings a month of music, dance, and fireworks to Puebla. On the 28th it's customary to prepare the famous *chiles en nogada.*
August 15	**Fiesta de la Asunción** *(Feast of the Assumption)* is celebrated nationwide with religious processions. In Huamantla, Tlaxcala, the festivities include a running of the bulls and a carpet of flowers laid out in front of the church.
FALL	
September 16	**Día de la Independencia,** or Independence Day, is celebrated beginning the evening of the 15th. It's marked throughout Mexico with fireworks and parties that out-blast those of New Year's Eve. The biggest celebration takes place in Mexico City's main square.
September 29	Towns with the name San Miguel naturally celebrate the **Fiesta de San Miguel,** honoring their patron saint, St. Michael. Colorful parties are held in San Miguel de Allende with bullfights, folk dances, concerts, and fireworks.
October	The **Fiestas de Octubre** *(October Festival)* means a month of cultural, epicurean, and sporting events in Guadalajara. The **Festival Internacional Cervantino** *(International Cervantino Festival)* in Guanajuato, running throughout the month, is a top cultural event that attracts dancers, singers, and actors from various countries.
October 12	The **Día de la Raza** marks the "discovery" of the Americas from an indigenous perspective. Mexicans get a day off work to contemplate the sociopolitical ramifications of the conquest, or merely to party with their *compadres.*
November	On **Día de Todos los Santos and Día de los Muertos** *(November 1–2)*, the Day of All Saints and Day of the Dead, families pay respects to departed relatives. Customs vary, but in parts of central and southern Mexico, particularly in Patzcuaro, Michoácan, families erect elaborate home altars to welcome the dead, refurbish grave sites, and, in some places, hold all-night cemetery vigils.
November 20	The **Aniversario de la Revolución Mexicana** *(Anniversary of the Mexican Revolution)* is a major national holiday.

Mexico City

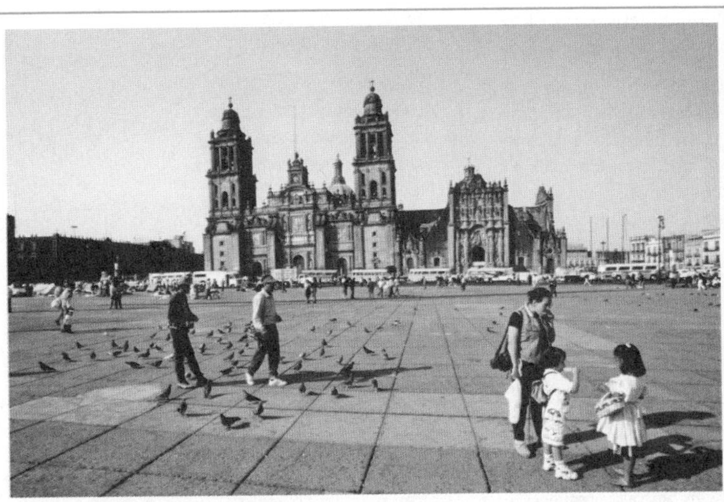

Plaza de la Constitución (the zócalo, the cathedral)

WORD OF MOUTH

"[Mexico City] is about as authentic and you can get. I'd suggest the Hotel Majestic on the Zócalo. Visit the Templo Mayor and its small museum, the National Palace, the Cathedral. Next day see the National Anthropology Museum. Next day Teotihuacan. "

–Fra_Diavolo

WELCOME TO MEXICO CITY

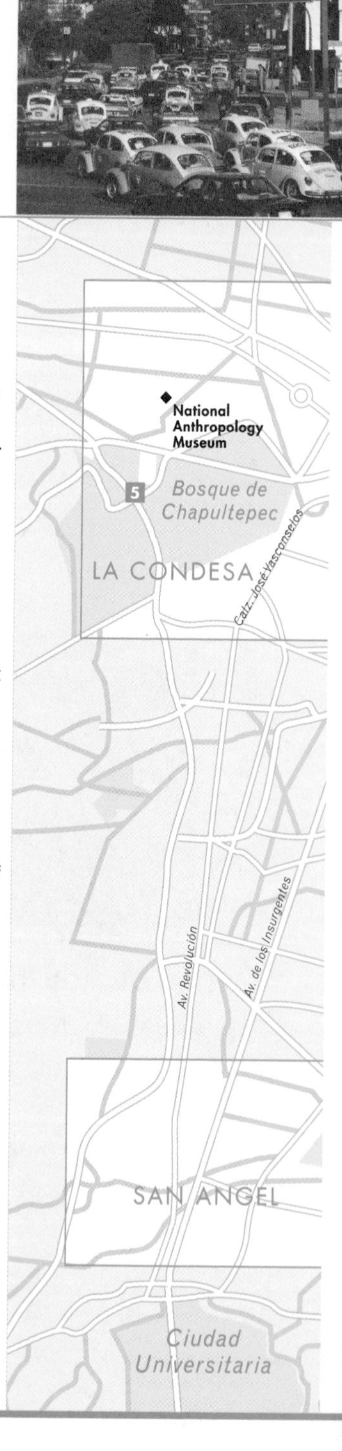

TOP REASONS TO GO

★ **Hitting the hippest spot in the country:** Mexico City is the undisputed cultural capital of Latin America, with a lifestyle as distinct as that of New York or Rio.

★ **Strolling through the Centro Histórico:** Imagine if Washington, D.C. contained Plymouth Rock, Jamestown, Gettysburg, and Hiroshima to understand the atmosphere and historic significance of this 500-year-old neighborhood laid atop—and made of—Aztec ruins.

★ **Sampling *la cocina Mexicana*:** As street vendors offer up traditional snacks, chefs reinvent those recipes with amazing results.

★ **Museum-hopping:** You'll find Frida Kahlo and Diego Rivera all over; the stunning contemporary Museo Antropológico is worth visiting just for the building—a full exploration of its collection would take days.

★ **Mexico's melting pot:** The city's size and status mean you'll see all aspects of Mexican society from fashionistas to farmers.

1 Centro Histórico & Alameda Central. This quickly revamping *vecino* is the heart and soul of the nation and where you'll find the bustling zócalo, the famous Alameda park, the murals of the Palacio Nacional, and the cathedral.

2 San Angel & Coyoacán. San Angel is mostly residential; near the main square are bars and restaurants. Mexico's intellectual community for 100 years, Coyoacán is a slow-paced Aztec market town where you'll find Frida and Diego's Casa Azul and a delightful, low-key market fronting one of the loveliest plazas in the country.

3 La Condesa & La Roma. Quiet La Roma has a slew of galleries, cantinas, and eateries, while trendy Condesa's upscale cafés and bars try to outdo one another; all are trumped by Parque México, a tiny, tropical oasis.

4 Zona Rosa. This tourist and shopping area is a perfect blend of modern and traditional, crass and classy, and is teeming with hotels, restaurants, shops, and bars. It's lost ground to more fashionable neighborhoods, but is still one of city's most vibrant districts.

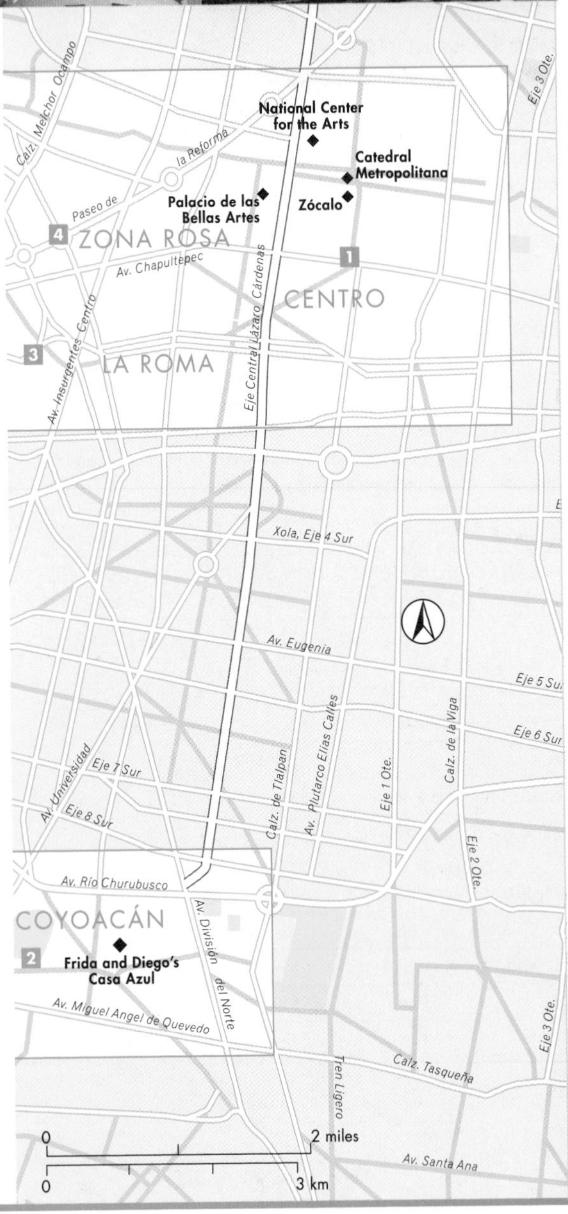

National Center for the Arts
Catedral Metropolitana
Palacio de las Bellas Artes
Zócalo
Calz. Melchor Ocampo
Paseo de la Reforma
4 ZONA ROSA
Av. Chapultepec
1
CENTRO
3 LA ROMA
Av. Insurgentes Centro
Eje Central Lázaro Cárdenas
Eje 3 Ote.
Xola, Eje 4 Sur
Av. Eugenia
Eje 5 Sur
Eje 6 Sur
Eje 7 Sur
Eje 8 Sur
Av. Universidad
Calz. de Tlalpan
Av. Plutarco Elías Calles
Eje 1 Ote.
Calz. de la Viga
Eje 2 Ote.
Av. Río Churubusco
COYOACÁN
2 Frida and Diego's Casa Azul
Av. División del Norte
Av. Miguel Angel de Quevedo
Calz. Tasqueña
Tren Ligero
Av. Santa Ana
0 — 2 miles
0 — 3 km

5 Bosque de Chapultepec. This is Mexico City's Central Park—and a sight for sore eyes in a place plagued with pollution. This enormous park has its own 14th-century castle and a museum row, including the National Anthropology Museum.

GETTING ORIENTED

Mexico City is one sprawling metropolis; it's packed to the gills with both buildings and people (22 million inhabitants). It occupies a high (7,347 feet) dry lakebed in the center of the country—its location and size make it the main hub for bus and air travel. Though the city has more neighborhoods than most cities have streets, the main tourist areas, including the core historic center, are fairly contained and close to one another.

MEXICO CITY PLANNER

Safety

Mexico City has a reputation for danger. However, its well-publicized spate of kidnappings has generally targeted wealthy businesspeople and Las Mil Familias, the Mexican power elite; the average tourist is not likely to be a victim of this type of crime. In recent years, authorities have been cracking down on taxi robberies, but policing a city with an estimated 90,000 cabs is no easy feat. The first rule of Mexico City is *never* hail a taxi on the street, from a tourist attraction, or with your debit card in your pocket. Choose the *sitio* (stationed) cabs that operate out of stands or cabs called for by hotel or restaurant staff.

The zócalo has undergone major changes, including rigorous trash pickup, a ban (sadly) on vendors and street food in the core, lots of guards, and in some places, security cameras. Major tourist areas are generally very safe, but petty theft is still pervasive. To avoid being an easy mark, recognize that Mexico City is quite formal, so things like big cameras, backpacks, shorts, and sandals will only make you stand out. Pickpockets are brazen and unbelievably skilled. If one of them sidles up and you're not holding your wallet in your hand, chances are he or she has it.

Health Concerns

The biggest concerns in Mexico City (besides avoiding Montezuma's Revenge) are the elevation and pollution. It may take a few days for you to acclimate, so take it easy, drink extra fluids, and don't be surprised if you're huffing and puffing a little more than usual. A change in elevation may also affect sleep patterns and digestion. Note that alcohol will have a greater effect on you until you adjust.

The pollution has gotten much better, but if you have respiratory problems, you'll want to limit the amount of time you spend walking along busy streets, especially during rush hour. Some people may experience watery eyes, a runny nose, or a mild sore throat from the fumes, but some big-city dwellers may not notice a difference in air quality at all. The smog is heaviest from mid-November through January, and lightest in September and October.

Travel Times

ONE-WAY FROM MEXICO CITY TO OTHER MAJOR CITIES:

CITY	TIME BY BUS	1ST-CLASS BUS FARES	TIME BY AIR*
Guadalajara	7–8 hrs	$40	1¼ hrs
San Miguel	3½ hrs	$20	45 min
Veracruz City	5 hrs	$28	1 hr
Oaxaca City	6½ hrs	$33	1 hr
Puerto Vallarta	12 hrs	$72	1½ hrs
Acapulco	5–6 hrs	$28	1 hr
San Cristóbal	16 hrs	$72	n/a
Villahermosa	11 hrs	$55	1½ hrs
Cancún	23 hrs	$100	2 hrs
Mérida	19 hrs	$92	1¾ hrs

*One-way airfares for nonstop flights from Mexico City generally range $150–$220.

How's the Weather?

Mexico City has a fairly mild climate all year round. The coldest and, consequently, most smog-infested months are December and January. Although it stays warm during the day, the temperature dips considerably at night during these months, so you'll need to bring a jacket.

The warmest months of the year are April and May, although it never gets too hot thanks to the capital's high altitude.

The rainy season, which brings strong downpours and causes occasional flooding, is from May to October, though you'll often have hours—and sometimes whole days—of sunshine.

How Much Time?

You could spend weeks in Mexico City—there are enough museums, restaurants, and side trips to keep even the most jaded globe-trotter occupied for a long time—but how much time you spend in the capital really depends on your expectations and your tolerance for fast-paced urban living. If you're short on time and anxious to move on to friendlier (or more scenic) climes, you can see a lot in two days, though three would be ideal.

With three days you'll have enough time to tour the historic sights, do a little museum-hopping, have more than a few fabulous meals, and spend at least part of one day on a side trip to nearby ruins (see Chapter 3). Hard-core city travelers will want to spend a week here to feel like they've really covered enough ground.

Money Matters

DINING & LODGING PRICE CATEGORIES

¢	$	$$	$$$	$$$$
Restaurants				
under $5	$5–$10	$10–$15	$15–$25	over $25
Hotels				
under $50	$50–$75	$75–$150	$150–$250	over $250

Restaurant prices are per person for a main course at dinner. Hotel prices are for two people in a standard double room.

Hot Tickets

Sure, a good concierge can work miracles, finding last-minute tickets to sold-out events or the last table for two at the city's hottest restaurant. But if you've only got a few days in the capital, you might not want to leave it all up to them. The following should be booked in advance or as soon as you get to Mexico City.

1. Reservations at the restaurants Fonda del Recuerdo, Au Pied de Cochon, and Izote.

2. Tickets to Ballet Folklórico de México. There are only three shows a week—the Sunday evening show is particularly popular.

3. The VIP treatment at the clubs. If you want a table or bottle service, make reservations one to two days in advance.

4. An English-speaking guide for the Museo Nacional de Antropología. Call the museum one week in advance.

5. Tickets for important soccer games at Estadio Azteca and Estadio Olímpico (get them at least a week in advance).

6. Around holidays, you should buy first-class bus tickets to other destinations at least a week in advance.

2

Updated by Grant Cogswell & Michele Joyce

BY AND LARGE, PEOPLE HAVE the wrong idea about Mexico City. To many the very name summons two words: crime and pollution. No doubt there are areas to be avoided, but the Distrito Federal is packed to the gills with decent people who will usually look out for one another, and for you. Pollution summons visions of unwalkable, megahighway-filled cities jammed with cars, which this is not. The smog is real: the Aztecs built their city of Tenochtitlan in a high (7,347 feet) valley that often waits days for the air to move. But there are a little over 2.5 million cars and buses in the city, just more than one for every 10 of 20-million-something inhabitants (reports vary). Truth is, those living in the capital do so more sustainably than most people in the industrialized world, at high—yet comfortable—densities (though not in high-rises), and move mostly by foot and public transit. (If you are tempted to drive this Gordian knot of merged villages, well, we would recommend that you not.)

Most of Mexico City is aligned on two major intersecting thoroughfares: Paseo de la Reforma and Avenida Insurgentes—at 34 km (21 mi), the longest avenue in the city. Administratively, Mexico City is divided into 16 *delegaciones* (districts) and about 400 *colonias* (neighborhoods), many with street names fitting a given theme, such as rivers, philosophers, or revolutionary heroes. The same street can change names as it goes through different colonias. So, most street addresses include their colonia (abbreviated as Col.). Unless you're going to a landmark, it's important to tell your taxi driver the name of the colonia and, whenever possible, the cross street.

Mexico City's principal sights fall into three areas. Allow a full day to cover each thoroughly, although you could race through them in four or five hours apiece. You can generally cover the first area—the Zócalo and Alameda Central—on foot. Getting around Zona Rosa, Bosque de Chapultepec, and Colonia Condesa may require a taxi ride or two (though the Chapultepec metro stop is conveniently close to the park and museums), as will Coyoacán and San Angel in southern Mexico City.

GETTING HERE & AROUND

Mexico City's airport, Aeropuerto Internacional Benito Juárez (MEX), is the main gateway to the country. Many airlines fly nonstop between major U.S. cities and Mexico City. If you're taking a taxi, purchase your ticket at an official airport taxi counter marked TRANSPORTACIÓN TERRESTRE (ground transportation); never take a *pirata* taxi (unofficial drivers offering their services). Reaching the city center takes 20 minutes to an hour depending on traffic. Within Mexico City, buses are a cheap and convenient way to travel. Leaving the capital, ETN (Enlaces Terrestres Nacionales) serves cities to the west and northwest and ADO buses depart southeast. Buses depart from four outlying stations (*terminales de autobuses*): Terminal de Autobuses del Norte, going north; Terminal de Autobuses del Sur, going south; Terminal Terminal de Autobuses del Oriente, going east; and Terminal de Autobuses del Poniente, going west. It's usually impractical to rent a car for travel within Mexico City, though it may be a good option for trips outside of the city. Within the city, you can also get around by *pesero* (originally six-passenger sedans, now minibuses), which operate on a number of fixed routes and charge a flat rate, or the metro, which is incredibly cheap, but can be super busy at times. ⚠ **Simply do not hail taxis on the street under any circumstances.** If you need a cab but don't speak the Spanish necessary to call one yourself, your best bet is to have a hotel concierge or waiter call you a sitio.

> **WHAT'S IN A NAME?**
>
> Mexico City is rarely referred to as "Mexico City" by its residents, or by anyone in Mexico for that matter. The term "Mexico City" is of course an Anglicization: the official name of the city is Ciudad México; residents often refer to it as "D.F." (pronounced deh-effay), short for Distrito Federal (Federal District). On train and bus schedules and in addresses, you'll often see it listed simply as México. And elsewhere in the country, when anyone refers simply to México, they mean here.

ESSENTIALS

Bus Contacts **ETN** (☎ *01800/800-0386 toll-free in Mexico* 🌐 *www.etn.com.mx*). **Terminal de Autobuses del Norte** (✉ *Av. Cien Metros 4907, Col. Magdalena de las Salinas* ☎ *55/5587-1552 Ext. 102*). **Terminal de Autobuses del Sur** (✉ *Tasqueña 1320* ☎ *55/5689-9745 or 55/5689-4987*). **Terminal de Autobuses del Oriente (TAPO)** (✉ *Ignacio Zaragoza 200, Col. 10 de Mayo* ☎ *55/5522-5400*). **Terminal de Autobuses del Poniente** (aka *"Observatorio"* ✉ *Río Tacubaya and Sur 122, Col. Real del Monte* ☎ *55/5271-0149 or 55/5271-0038*). **Ticketbus** (☎ *55/5133-2424, 55/5133-2444, 01800/702-8000 toll-free in Mexico* 🌐 *www.ticketbus.com.mx*).

Internet **Java Chat Café** (✉ *Génova 44-K, near Hamburgo, Zona Rosa* ☎ *55/5525-6853*).

Medical Assistance **American British Cowdray Hospital** (✉ *Calle Sur 136-116, at Observatorio, Col. las Américas* ☎ *55/5230-8161 emergencies, 55/5230-8000 switchboard* 🌐 *www.abchospital.com*). **Hospital Angeles** (✉ *Camino a Sta. Teresa 1055, Col. Heroes de Padierna* ☎ *55/5449-5500 for switchboard* 🌐 *www.angeles.com.mx/home.htm*). **Hospital Español** (✉ *Ejército Nacional 613, Col. Granada* ☎ *55/5255-9600* 🌐 *www.hespanol.com*).

Rental Cars **Alamo** (✉ *Av. Paseo de la Reforma 157-B, Col. Cuauhtémoc* ✉ *Thiers 195, Col. Verónica Anzures* ☎ *55/5592-8312* 🌐 *www.alamo-mexico.com.mx*). **Avis** (✉ *Atenas 44, Col. Juárez* ✉ *Campos Eliséos 218, Col. Polanco* ✉ *Insurgentes Sur 730, Col. del Valle* ☎ *55/5535-6927 or 55/5591-1994* 🌐 *www.avis.com.mx*). **Budget** (✉ *Campos Eliséos 204, Col. Polanco* ☎ *55/5280-1111* ✉ *Atenas 40, Col. Juárez* ☎ *55/5566-7923* ✉ *Hamburgo 71, Col. Juárez* ☎ *55/5566-6800* 🌐 *www.budget.com.mx*)

Visitor & Tour Info **Mexico City Tourist Office** (✉ *Sala A1, Mexico City Airport, in National Arrivals* ☎ *55/5786-9002* ✉ *Nuevo Leon 56, at Toledo, Hipódromo Condesa* ☎ *55/5212-0259* ✉ *Terminal de Autobuses de Oriente (TAPO), Av. Calle Ignacio Zaragosa 200, Col. 10 de Mayo* ☎ *55/5784-3077* ✉ *Casa Municipal, Plaza Hidalgo 1, ground fl., Coyoacán* ☎ *55/5658-0221* ✉ *Gladiolas 161 Col. Xochimilco, Barrio de San Marcos* ☎ *55/5676-0810 or 55/5676-8879* 🌐 *www.mexicocity.gob.mx*). **Tourism Secretariat (Federal)** (✉ *Av. Presidente Masarik 172, Col. Polanco*

☎55/3002-6300, 55/5250-0027, or 800/482-9832 🌐www.travelguidemexico.com). **Tourism Secretariat (DF)** (✉Av. Nuevo León 56, at Laredo, Col. Condesa ☎55/5212-0260).

CENTRO HISTÓRICO & ALAMEDA CENTRAL

The zócalo, its surrounding Centro Histórico (historic center), and Alameda Central were the heart of both the Aztec and Spanish cities. There's a palpable European influence in this area, which is undergoing a major refurbishment, leaving the streets cleaner and many buildings, particularly around the zócalo, more attractive. Seven hundred years of history lie beneath its jagged thoroughfares. The sidewalks hum with street vendors, hurried office workers, and tourists blinking in wonder. Every block seems energized with perpetual noise and motion, though the area has recently become a bit quieter and much easier to walk. In October 2007, government efforts pushed vendors from the streets at the very heart of the historic center (there are still vendors outside the few surrounding the zócalo). The area has become more easily accessible to tourists, and locals are beginning to enjoy the neighborhood more and more. Several of the streets near the central plaza are also now closed to cars on weekends, so the streets are free for bicyclists and pedestrians.

During the daytime the downtown area is vibrant with this activity. As in any capital, watch out for pickpockets, especially on crowded buses and subways, and avoid deserted streets at night. The zócalo area is quietest on Sunday, when bureaucrats have their day of rest. Shops open around 10 AM on weekends, so go earlier if you prefer to enjoy the area at its quietest. Alameda Park is quieter during the week; on weekends it's jumping with children and their parents.

EXPLORING

MAIN ATTRACTIONS

16 **Alameda Central.** Strolling around this park is a great way to break up sightseeing in the neighborhood. During the week it's lively, but not too busy. You'll be able to find a shaded bench for a few moments of rest before heading off to more museums. There are food vendors throughout the park, selling all kinds of snacks from ice cream to grilled corn on the cob. The park has been an important center of activity since Aztec times, when the Indians held their *tianguis* (market) here. In the early days of the viceroyalty the Inquisition burned its victims at the stake here. Later, national leaders, from 18th-century viceroys to Emperor Maximilian and President Porfirio Díaz, envisioned the park as a symbol of civic pride and prosperity. In fact, the park was enjoyed exclusively by the wealthy during this time, and it was only open to the public after Independence. Still, Life in Mexico, the quintessential book on the country, describes how women donned their finest jewels to take a walk around the park even after Independence. Over the centuries it has been fitted out with fountains, a Moorish kiosk imported from

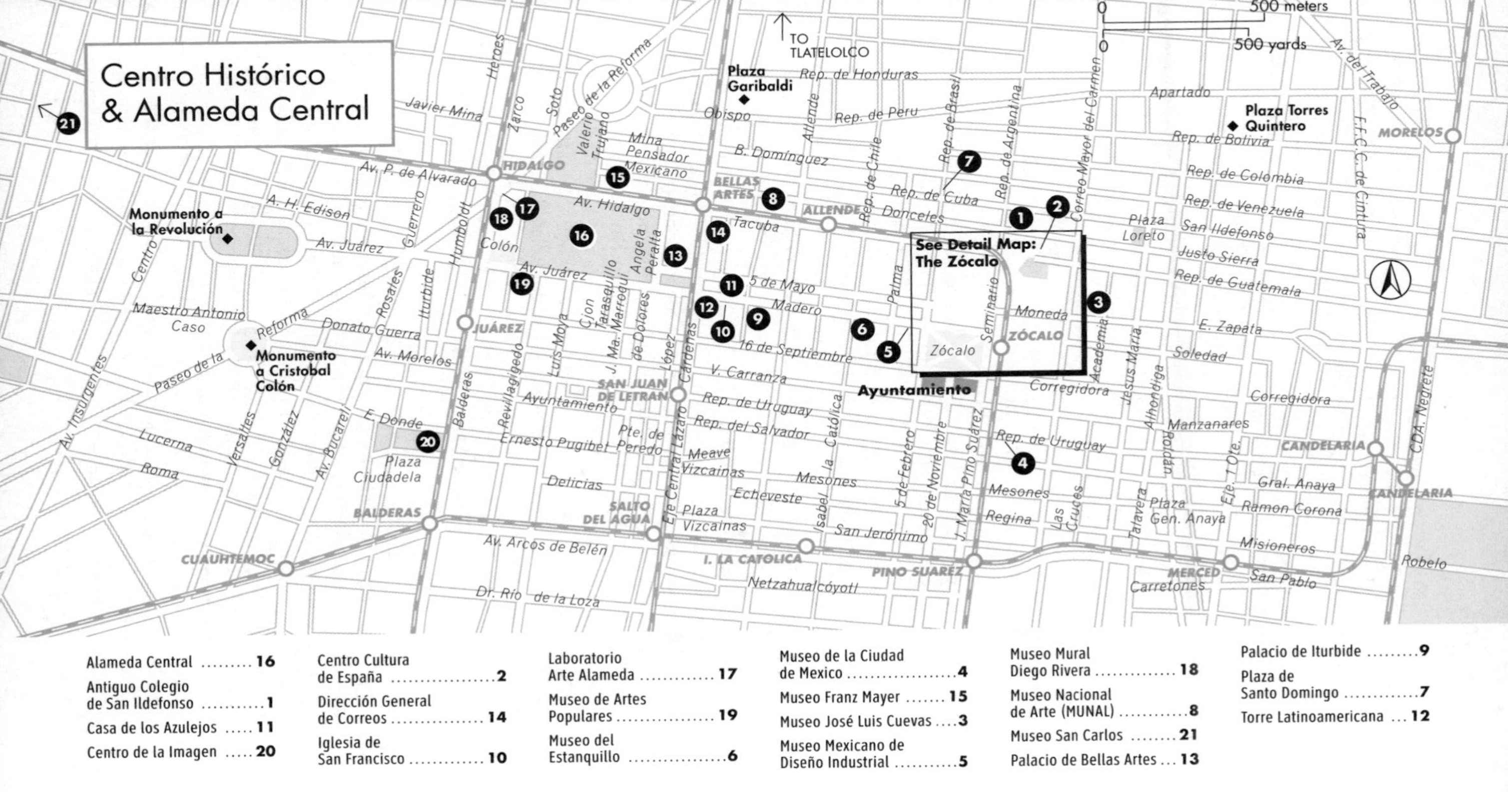
Centro Histórico
& Alameda Central
0
500 meters
0
500 yards
TO
TLATELOLCO
Plaza Garibaldi
Plaza Torres Quintero
Monumento a la Revolución
Monumento a Cristobal Colón
See Detail Map: The Zócalo
Ayuntamiento
Zócalo
Plaza Loreto
Plaza Ciudadela
Plaza Vizcainas
Plaza Gen. Anaya
HIDALGO
BELLAS ARTES
ALLENDE
ZÓCALO
MORELOS
CANDELARIA
JUÁREZ
SAN JUAN DE LETRAN
SALTO DEL AGUA
BALDERAS
CUAUHTEMOC
I. LA CATOLICA
PINO SUAREZ
MERCED
Av. P. de Alvarado
Av. Hidalgo
Av. Juárez
Paseo de la Reforma
Av. Insurgentes
Av. Morelos
Av. Bucareli
Av. Arcos de Belén
Eje Central Lazaro Cardenas
J. Maria Pino Suárez
Av. del Trabajo
F.F.C.C. de Cintura
Alameda Central 16
Antiguo Colegio de San Ildefonso 1
Casa de los Azulejos 11
Centro de la Imagen 20
Centro Cultura de España 2
Dirección General de Correos 14
Iglesia de San Francisco 10
Laboratorio Arte Alameda 17
Museo de Artes Populares 19
Museo del Estanquillo 6
Museo de la Ciudad de Mexico 4
Museo Franz Mayer 15
Museo José Luis Cuevas 3
Museo Mexicano de Diseño Industrial 5
Museo Mural Diego Rivera 18
Museo Nacional de Arte (MUNAL) 8
Museo San Carlos 21
Palacio de Bellas Artes ... 13
Palacio de Iturbide 9
Plaza de Santo Domingo 7
Torre Latinoamericana ... 12

Paris, and ash, willow, and poplar trees. A white-marble monument, **Hemiciclo a Benito Juárez,** stands on the Avenida Juárez side of the park. There's live music on Sunday and holidays. ✉ *Av. Juárez, Eje Central Lázaro Cárdenas, and Av. Hidalgo all surround the plaza* Ⓜ *Bellas Artes or Hidalgo.*

X-MAS MEN

The Alameda Central is particularly festive in December, when dozens of "Santas" will appear with plastic reindeer to take wish lists. Although Mexicans celebrate on the night of December 24, the tradition of giving presents—especially to children—kicks in at dawn on January 6, the Day of the Three Kings, so for about a week beforehand the Three Wise Men replace the Santas in the Alameda.

14 **Dirección General de Correos.** Mexico City's main post office building, designed by Italian architect Adamo Boari and Mexican engineer Gonzalo Garita, is a fine example of Renaissance Revival architecture. Constructed of cream-color sandstone from Teayo, Puebla, and Carrara, Italy, it epitomizes the grand imitations of European architecture common in Mexico during the Porfiriato—the long dictatorship of Porfirio Díaz (1876–1911). For many, it is one of the most beautiful buildings in Mexico. Upstairs, the **Museo del Palacio Postal** shows Mexico's postal history. ✉ *Calle Tacuba and Eje Central Lázaro Cárdenas, Alameda Central* ☎ *55/5510–2999 museum, 55/5521–7394 post office* 🌐 *www.palaciopostal.gob.mx* 🎟 *Free* ⏲ *Museum Tues.–Fri. 9–5:30, weekends 9–3; post office weekdays 8–8, Sat. 9–1* Ⓜ *Bellas Artes.*

8 **Museo Nacional de Arte (MUNAL).** The collections of the National Art Museum, which include more than 800 pieces that fill a neoclassical building (designed by Italian architect Silvio Contri), span nearly every school of Mexican art, with a concentration on work produced between 1810 and 1950. On display are Diego Rivera's portrait of Adolfo Best Maugard, José María Velasco's *Vista del Valle de México desde el Cerro de Santa Isabel (View of the Valley of Mexico from the Hill of Santa Isabel),* and Ramón Cano Manilla's *El Globo (The Balloon). Temporary exhibits are also extremely well planned and presented.* ✉ *Calle Tacuba 8, Col. Centro* ☎ *55/5130–3400* 🌐 *www.munal.com.mx* 🎟 *$3, free Sun.* ⏲ *Tues.–Sun. 10:30–5:30* Ⓜ *Bellas Artes or Allende.*

★ 13 **Palacio de Bellas Artes.** Construction on this colossal white-marble opera house was begun in 1904 by Porfirio Díaz, who wanted to add yet another ornamental building to his accomplishments. The striking structure is the work of Italian Adamo Boari, who also designed the post office; pre-Hispanic motifs trim the art deco facade. In fact, Boari was only present during the construction of the facade. The Revolution brought about an economic crisis, and he left the country in 1916. The opera house was not inaugurated until 1934. Inside the concert hall a Tiffany stained-glass curtain depicts the two volcanoes outside Mexico City. Today the theater serves as a handsome venue for international and national artists, including the Ballet Folklórico de México. For an entrance fee you can see the interior, with its paintings by several celebrated Mexican artists, including Rufino Tamayo and Mexico's most famous trio of muralists: Rivera, Orozco, and Siqueiros. There are interesting temporary art exhibitions as well, plus an elegant cafeteria and a bookshop with a great selection of art books and magazines. Note that when there is no exhibition at the museum, the entry is free, and it is still worth a visit to see both the murals and the building itself. ✉*Eje Central Lázaro Cárdenas and Av. Juárez, Alameda Central* ☎*55/5512–2593* 🌐*www.bellasartes.gob.mx* 🎫*$3.50, free Sun.* ⏲*Tues.–Sun. 10–5; cafeteria 11–6* Ⓜ*Bellas Artes.*

12 **Torre Latinoamericana.** This is Mexico City's version of the Empire State Building. It took eight years to complete; construction began in 1948 and ended in 1956. It has 44 floors and a TV-radio tower, and weighs 25,000 tons; its mass is held up by 361 concrete pylons. You can get a great view of the city from the skyscraper's observation decks or from the cafés on floors 42, 43, and 44. On your way back down, stop in at the cafeteria and the new museum (your entry fee covers this as well), which offers information on the history of the building, on the 37th floor. ✉*Eje Central Lázaro Cárdenas 2 at Calle Madero, Alameda Central* ☎*55/5518–7423* 🌐*www.torrelatino.com* 🎫*$5* ⏲*Deck daily 9 AM–10 PM* Ⓜ*Bellas Artes.*

TLATELOLCO

At Paseo de la Reforma's northern end, about 2 km (1.2 mi) north of Palacio de Bellas Artes, the area known as Tlatelolco (pronounced tla-tel-*ohl*-coh) was the domain of Cuauhtémoc—the last Aztec emperor before the conquest—and the sister city of Tenochtitlán. The center of Tlatelolco is the Plaza de las Tres Culturas, so named because Mexico's three cultural eras—pre-Hispanic, colonial, and contemporary—are present here: the Iglesia de Santiago Tlatelolco (1609); Colegio de la Santa Cruz de Tlatelolco (1535–36); and the modern Ministry of Foreign Affairs (1970).

⇨ **1 Zócalo 2 Catedral Metropolitana** ★ **3 Palacio Nacional** ★ **4 Templo Mayor,** *see The Zócalo.*

IF YOU HAVE TIME

1 **Antiguo Colegio de San Ildefonso.** The college, a colonial building with lovely patios, started out in the 18th century as a Jesuit school for the sons of wealthy Mexicans. Frida Kahlo also famously studied here as an adolescent. It's now a splendid museum that showcases outstanding regional exhibitions. The interior contains murals by Diego Rivera, José Clemente Orozco, and Fernando Leal. ✉*Calle Justo Sierra 16, almost at corner of República de Argentina, 2 blocks north of Zócalo, Col. Centro* ☎*55/5702–6378 or 55/5702–2991* 🌐*www.sanildefonso.org.mx* 🎫*$4.50, free Tues.* ⏲*Tues.–Sun. 10–5:30* Ⓜ*Zócalo.*

11 **Casa de los Azulejos.** This 17th-century masterpiece acquired its name, House of Tiles, from its elaborate tile work. The dazzling designs, along with the facade's iron balconies, make it one of the prettiest baroque structures in the country. The interior is also worth seeing for its Moorish patio, monumental staircase, and mural by Orozco. The house,

Continued on page 50

THE ZÓCALO

It seems no matter how small a Mexican town is, it has a main square. The most famous of these plazas is Mexico City's dizzying Zócalo, the largest main square in Latin America. It's bounded on the south by 16 de Septiembre, on the north by Avenida 5 de Mayo, on the east by Pino Suarez, and on the west by Monte de Piedad.

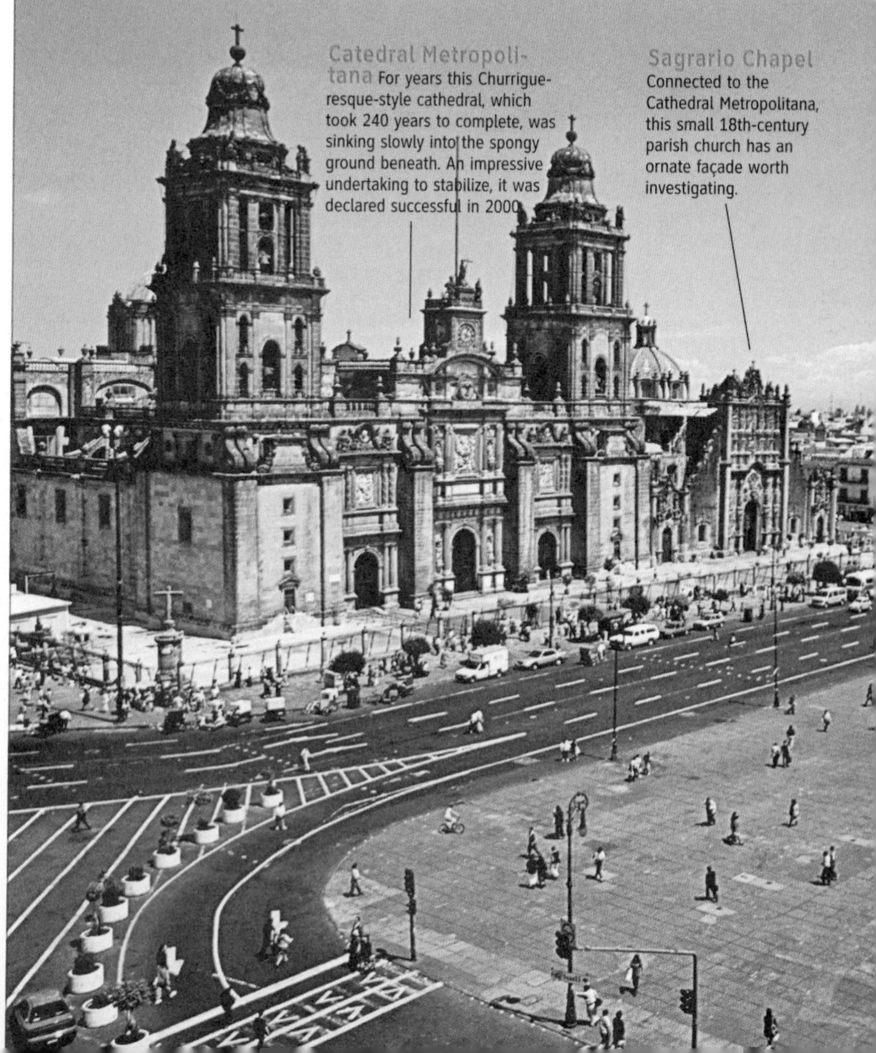

Catedral Metropolitana For years this Churrigueresque-style cathedral, which took 240 years to complete, was sinking slowly into the spongy ground beneath. An impressive undertaking to stabilize, it was declared successful in 2000.
Sagrario Chapel Connected to the Cathedral Metropolitana, this small 18th-century parish church has an ornate façade worth investigating.

❶ **Zócalo** literally means "pedestal" or "base": in the mid-19th century, an independence monument was planned for the square, but it was never built. The term stuck, however, and now the word "zócalo" is applied to the main plazas of most Mexican cities. Mexico City's Zócalo (because it's the original, it's always capitalized) is used for government rallies, protests, sit-ins, and festive events. It's the focal point for Independence Day celebrations on the eve of September 16 and is a maze of lights, tinsel, and traders during the Christmas season. Flag-raising and -lowering ceremonies take place here in the early morning and late afternoon.

Mexico City's historic plaza (formally called the Plaza de la Constitución) and the buildings around it were built by the Spaniards, using local slaves. This enormous paved square occupies the site of the ceremonial center of Tenochtitlán, the capital of the Aztec empire, which

Templo Mayor and Museo del Templo Mayor
A temple dedicated to the Aztec cult of death, this ancient treasure was discovered in 1978 by unsuspecting telephone repairmen. The museum holds some 3,000 archaeological pieces, including an 8-ton carved stone disk depicting the moon goddess Coyolxauhqui, discovered in this very vicinity.
Palacio Nacional
Built on Moctezuma's home, this building has been rebuilt and revamped many times; today, it serves as the seat of government. Nearly 1,200 square feet of astounding murals by Diego Rivera adorn the second floor. Far above still hangs the liberty bell that was rung by Padre Hidalgo in 1810.

A SPECTACULAR VIEW OF THE ZÓCALO

If you want a break, grab a balcony seat at the Hotel Majestic's top-floor restaurant (at the corner of Madero and 5 de Febrero) and enjoy a spectacular view of the plaza below. These seats are reserved months in advance for the Independence Day celebrations, but are easily accessible when there are no events in the Zócalo.

once comprised 78 buildings. Throughout the 16th, 17th, and 18th centuries, elaborate churches and convents, elegant mansions, and stately public edificies were constructed around the square; many of these buildings have long since been converted to other uses.

The Zócalo is the heart of the Centro Histórico, and many of the neighborhood's sights are on the plaza's borders or a few short blocks away. Clusters of small shops, eateries, cantinas, and street stalls, as well as various women in native Indian dress contribute to an inimitably Mexican flavor and exuberance.

❷Catedral Metropolitana. Construction on this, the largest and one of the oldest cathedrals in Latin America, began in the late 16th century and continued intermittently throughout the next three centuries. The result is a medley of Baroque and neo-classical touches. There are five altars and 14 chapels, mostly in the ornate Churrigueresque style, named for Spanish architect José Churriguera (died 1725). Like most Mexican churches, the cathedral itself is all but overwhelmed by innumerable paintings, altarpieces, and statues—in graphic color—of Christ and the saints. Over the centuries, this cathedral began to sink into the spongy subsoil, but a major engineering project to stabilize it was declared successful in 2000. The older-looking church attached to the cathedral is the 18th-century Sagrario chapel. ✉ *Zócalo, Col. Centro* ⏲ *Daily 7–7* Ⓜ *Zócalo.*

★❸Palacio Nacional. The grand national palace was initiated by Cortés on the site of Moctezuma's home and remodeled by the viceroys. Its current form dates from 1693, although a third floor was added in 1926. Now the seat of government, it has always served as a public-function site. In fact, during colonial times, the first bullfight in New Spain took place in the inner courtyard.

Diego Rivera's sweeping, epic murals on the second floor of the main courtyard exert a mesmeric pull. For more than 16 years (1929–45), Rivera and his assistants mounted scaffolds day and night, perfecting techniques adapted from Renaissance Italian fresco painting. The result, nearly 1,200 square feet of vividly painted wall space, is grandiosely entitled *Epica del Pueblo Mexicano en su Lucha por la Libertad y la Independencia* (*Epic of the Mexican People in Their Struggle for Freedom and Independence*). The paintings represent two millennia of Mexican history, filtered through Rivera's imagination. He painted pre-Hispanic times in innocent, almost sugary scenes of Tenochtitlán. Only a few vignettes—a man offering a human arm for sale, and the carnage of warriors—acknowledge the darker aspects of ancient life. As you walk around, you'll pass

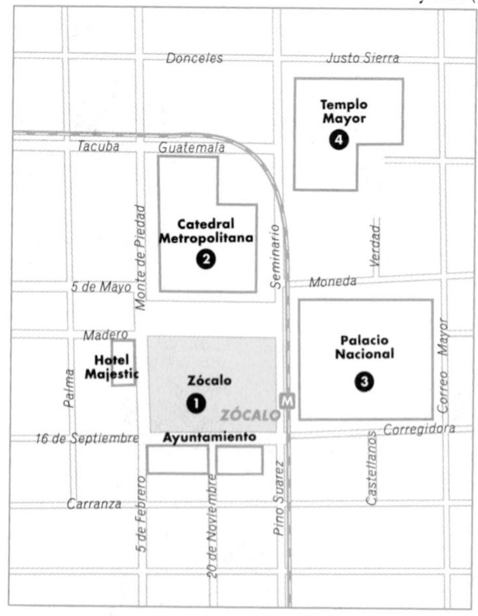

Seven rows of ominous stone skulls adorn one side of Templo Mayor.

images of the savagery of the conquest and the hypocrisy of the Spanish priests, the noble independence movement, and the bloody revolution. Marx appears amid scenes of class struggle, toiling workers, industrialization (which Rivera idealized), bourgeois decadence, and nuclear holocaust. These are among Rivera's finest works—as well as the most accessible and probably most visited. The palace also houses a minor museum that focuses on 19th-century president Benito Juárez and the Mexican Congress.

The liberty bell rung by Padre Hidalgo to proclaim independence in 1810 hangs high on the central façade. It chimes every eve of September 16, while from the balcony the president repeats the historic shout of independence to throngs of *chilangos* (Mexico City residents) below. ✉ *East side of the Zócalo, Col. Centro* 🎫 *Free; you'll be asked to leave an ID at the front desk* ⏲ *Mon.–Sat. 9–6, Sun. 9–2* Ⓜ *Zócalo.*

Fodor's Choice **4 Templo Mayor.** The ruins of the ancient hub of the Aztec empire were unearthed accidentally in 1978 by telephone repairmen and have since been turned into a vast archaeological site and museum. At this, their main temple, dedicated to the Aztec cult of death, captives from rival tribes—as many as 10,000 at a time—were sacrificed to the bloodthirsty god of war, Huitzilopochtli. Seven rows of leering stone skulls adorn one side.

The adjacent **Museo del Templo Mayor** housed in a discreet building designed by the influential Mexican architect Pedro Ramírez Vázquez, contains 3,000 pieces unearthed from the site and from other ruins in central Mexico; they include ceramic warriors, stone carvings and knives, skulls of sacrificial victims, a rare gold ingot, models and scale reproductions, and a room on the Spaniards' destruction of Tenochtitlán. The centerpiece is an 8-ton disk discovered at the Templo Mayor. It depicts the moon goddess Coyolxauhqui, who, according to myth, was decapitated and dismembered by her brother Huitzilopochtli. Call six weeks ahead to schedule free English-language tours by museum staff in the mornings. ✉ *Seminario 8, at República de Guatemala; entrance on the plaza, near Catedral Metropolitana, Col. Centro* ☎ *55/5542–4784, or 55/5542–4785* 🌐 *azteca.conaculta.gob.mx/templomayor* 🎫 *$4.50, free Sun.* ⏲ *Tues.–Sun. 9–5* Ⓜ *Zócalo.*

An ancient stone carving at Museo Del Templo Mayor.

which belonged to the Condes of the Valle de Orizaba, was not originally clad in tile. This took place a few years later when it was covered with tiles from the nearby city of Puebla, where the fifth Countess of Orizaba spent much of her time. The building is currently occupied by Sanborns, a chain store and restaurant, and if you have plenty of time (service is slow) this is a good place to stop for a meal—especially breakfast. Many writers and journalists hang out here, so you might spot important names in Mexican intellectual circles. There is also a store with a pharmacy, bakery, candy counter, and an ATM. ✉ *Calle Madero 4, at Callejón de la Condesa, Col. Centro* ☎ *55/5512–9820 Ext. 103* 🌐 *www.sanborns.com.mx* ⏲ *Daily 7 AM–1 AM* Ⓜ *Bellas Artes.*

2 **Centro Cultural de España.** The Cultural Center of Spain can be found in the heart of the downtown area. It was built in an area that Hernán Cortés himself assigned to his butler, Diego de Soto, though the land changed hands many times and the current building was constructed in the 18th century, well after the years of Cortés. Temporary exhibits housed in the seven exposition rooms often highlight young artists and showcase current artistic trends. While the expositions are worth a look, there are also conferences and workshops offered on a nearly daily basis for those who are interested in art and culture. In a fun twist, on many nights you can catch live jazz at the bar, which is favored by local twentysomethings who flock here to listen. Every weekend, there are also activities for children. Check out the center's Web site for listings. ✉ *Guatemala 18, Col. Centro* ☎ *55/5521–1925* 🌐 *www.ccemx.org* 🎟 *Free* ⏲ *Closed Mon.* Ⓜ *Zócalo.*

20 **Centro de la Imagen.** This pioneering photography center, housed in a former colonial tobacco-processing plant, stages the city's most important photography exhibitions, as well as occasional shows of contemporary sculpture and other art or mixed media. Photography by international artists is often grouped thematically, drawing parallels between various cultures. This is also a good place to pick up some English-language reading material—the center publishes books, catalogs, and a bilingual magazine. ✉ *Plaza de la Ciudadela 2, at Balderas, Col. Centro* ☎ *55/9172–4724 or 55/9172–4729* 🌐 *centrodelaimagen.conaculta.gob.mx* 🎟 *Free* ⏲ *Tues.–Sun. 11–6* Ⓜ *Balderas.*

10 **Iglesia de San Francisco.** On the site of Mexico's first convent (1524), this 18th-century structure in a French neo-Gothic style has served as a barracks, a hotel, a circus, a theater, and a Methodist temple. On Independence Day in 1856 a conspiracy was uncovered here, leading to a temporary banishment of the convent's religious folk. ✉ *Calles Madero and 16 de Septiembre, Alameda Central* ☎ *No phone* ⏲ *Daily 7 AM–8:30 PM* Ⓜ *Bellas Artes.*

17 **Laboratorio Arte Alameda.** The facade of this refurbished building from the 1950s has a colonial air, but inside is one of the most contemporary art museums in town. The name says it all: the aim of this museum is truly to be a laboratory, a place where artists let loose and engage in unbridled experimentation, collaboration, and learning. There is a space for contemporary, often experimental art, a display

area for video and photographs, and room where artists whose works are not displayed in other museums and galleries can exhibit. These are not necessarily young artists, but those who have yet to become truly established. A cafeteria provides grub, and live music often livens up the place on Thursday and Friday nights. *Doctor Mora 7, Centro Histórico 55/5709–9993 www.artealameda.inba.gob.mx Free Mon.–Wed. 10 AM–10 PM, Thurs.–Sat. 10 AM–midnight, or whenever the crowd leaves Hidalgo.*

19 **Museo de Artes Populares.** This ultramodern museum is one of the best places to learn about the popular art of Mexico: you can gawk at art from 31 states in the museum's permanent collection, then buy a few pieces at the beautiful museum store. **TIP→**The museum store has more unique popular art pieces than just about anywhere else in the city. *Revillagigedo at Independencia, Centro Histórico 55/5521–2921 www.map.org.mx Free Tues.–Sun. 10–5. Juárez.*

4 **Museo de la Ciudad de México.** The city museum is on land that was originally owned by Juan Gutiérrez de Altamirano, Cortés' cousin. The original building was destroyed and rebuilt in 1778, and later became home to the Campeche native, Joaquín Clausell (1866–1935), who arrived to Mexico City to study law, but never finished his degree because he was expatriated to Europe for his opposition to the government. While in Europe, he learned to paint, and became one of the most important impressionist painters in Mexican history. The museum displays historical objects from Mexico City, including antique maps. Clausell's studio is also open to the public, and its walls are covered with his work. *Pino Suárez 30, Col. Centro 55/5542–0083 or 55/5542–0671 $2, free Wed. Tues.–Sun. 10–6 Pino Suárez.*

6 **Museo del Estanquillo.** In Mexico, an *estanquillo* is a small store that sells a wide variety of items. You'll find images of colonial life in New Spain, the Mexican Revolution, political life, and other artifacts that document daily life through history to present times. Photographs of Porfirio Díaz are displayed alongside paintings and small sculptures of the *lucha libre wrestlers*. Postcards, stamps, and cartoons are also exhibited near lead miniatures that re-create an early-20th-century afternoon in the Santo Domingo plaza. Additionally, this museum houses Carlos Monsiváis' eclectic collection of more than 10,000 unique pieces relating to the history and popular culture of the country, though the whole of his collection cannot all be displayed at once, and is displayed on a rotating basis. One of the best-known journalists and writers in Mexico, Monsiváis has written extensively on Mexican history, politics, and popular culture. The museum also has a small library, a store, and a rooftop café. *Isabel la Católica 26, at Av. MaderoCol. Centro 55/5521–3052 www.museodelestanquillo.com $3.50, Sun. free Wed.–Mon. 10–6. Zócalo or Allende*

15 **Museo Franz Mayer.** Housed in the 16th-century Hospital de San Juan de Dios, this museum exhibits thousands of works collected by Franz Mayer, which he left to the Mexican people. The permanent collection includes 16th- and 17th-century antiques, such as wooden chests inlaid

CLOSE UP

The Mind of Mexico

Mexican culture in general is a unique hybrid, and its history a long and bloody one. But the political outlook of contemporary Mexico City (and new power dynamics of the country itself) were set in place principally by two recent tragic events. On October 2, 1968, as activists used mass protest to try and force reforms on the 40-year-old, soft-Soviet Partido Revolucionario Institutional regime as the city played host to the Olympic Games, thousands of demonstrators filled the Plaza de Tres Culturas northwest of the Centro. The square was already a memorial to resistance, having been the place where, in 1521, the rebel Aztecs under Cuauhtémoc were massacred making their last stand against the Spanish invaders. Authorities responded to the protest with deadly force, as army men and police officers swept into the square and killed an estimated 300 of those assembled, in what would come to be known as the Tlatelolco massacre. That response (much like that in the Tiananmen Square protests in 1989) more or less ended the nascent democracy movement, and little changed in Mexico for the next 30 years. What finally set the change in motion would be Mother Nature herself.

On the morning of September 19, 1985, the capital was shaken by an earthquake measuring a devastating 8.1 on the Richter scale. Hundreds of buildings collapsed (built at high altitude, on the former bed of Lake Tenochtitlan, the city was particularly vulnerable), with horrible results. Nobody knows how many died then or in the deadly aftershocks, which terrified rescue and medical workers and lasted for the next two days. Citizens organized parties to search for survivors and dispose of the dead, which may have numbered up to 50,000. (A 16-year-old boy named Felipe Fernandez del Paso owned a camera, and so was given the task of photographing the dead for later identification before burial; 18 years later he became the first Mexican to win an Oscar, for the production design of the 2003 film *Frida*.)

When President Miguel de la Madrid appeared in the rubble with his entourage (after three days had passed without any government aid) volunteers jeered him, and the PRI dictatorship suffered a permanent loss of credibility. The neighborhood rescue and sanitation organizations survived and evolved into political organizations, on the right and the left. In 2000, this dynamic produced real change with the election to the presidency of Vicente Fox Quesada, the conservative Partido Acción Nacional governor of Guanajuato state, ending the PRI's 71-year grip on the country's institutions. In 2006 the Interior Secretary (later president) at the time of the Tlatelolco massacre, Luis Echeverria Alvarez, was placed under house arrest under charges of genocide for his role in the killings. That year's (disputed) presidential election was won by a nose by Fox's successor, Felipe Calderón, but his PRD (Partido de la Revolución Democrático) opponent, former Mexico City mayor Andrés Manuel López Obrador, to this day claims the title of legitimate president, heading a leftist movement which leans heavily on memories of Tlatelolco.

CLOSE UP

Take a Tour

Mexico City has a system of red double-decker, open-top buses called the Turibus, which runs 9–9 daily. An excellent option for tourists is the $11 daily pass (purchased on board), which allows passengers to get on and off as many times as desired. Two- and three-day passes cost $15 and $19 each. The bus travels up and down Reforma, passes through the Centro, Plaza Río de Janeiro in the Colonia Roma, Michoacán in the Colonia Condesa (a great place to stop and eat), and Avenida Presidente Masarik in Polanco (a great stop to shop). Most passengers board at the staircase of the Auditorio Nacional, just outside the Auditorio metro stop. Buses leave around a quarter-past and a quarter-till the hour every day except Christmas.

The Paseo por Coyoacán tourist trolleybus goes around the Coyoacán neighborhood, with a guide telling the history of the area in Spanish. It leaves from a stop opposite the Museo Nacional de Culturas Populares whenever there are enough people, so departures are irregular. It costs $4 and runs weekdays 10–5, weekends 11–6. Guided tours in English are available only for large groups; reservations are a must.

A good way to see the historic downtown—if you know some Spanish—is on the Tranvía Turístico Cultural, charming replicas of 20-passenger trolleys from the 1920s. The 45-minute narrated tour ($3) includes Palacio de Bellas Artes, la Casa de los Azulejos, Palacio de Iturbide, Plaza de la Constitución, Antiguo Ayuntamiento, Palacio Nacional, la Catedral and Plaza Manuel Tolsá (location of the Palacio de Minería and Museo Nacional de Arte). Trolleys depart hourly 10–5 daily from the train's offices in front of Alameda Park. There's also a night tour on Tuesday at 8 called Leyendas del Centro Histórico (Legends of the Historic Center) and a cantina tour on Thursday at 8. For the night tours, you'll need to make a reservation.

Information **National Association of Guides and Interpreters** (✉ *Serapio Rendón 95-202A, Col. San Rafael* ☎ *55/5591-0418 or 55/5592-0365*). **National Syndicate of Guides and Tourism Employees** (✉ *Ezequiel Montes 79, Col. Tabacalera* ☎ *55/5535-7787 or 55/5535-5305*). **Paseo por Coyoacán** (✉ *Av. Hidalgo 198, at Calle Allende, Coyoacán* ☎ *55/5559-2433*). **Tranvía Turístico** (✉ *Cultural Av. Juárez 66, near Palacio de Bellas Artes, Col. Centro* ☎ *55/5512-1012 Ext. 0202 or 0230*). **Turibus** (☎ *55/5133-2488* 🌐 *www.turibus.com.mx*)

with ivory, tortoiseshell, and ebony; tapestries, paintings, and lacquerware; rococo clocks, glassware, and architectural ornamentation; and an unusually large assortment of Talavera ceramics. The museum also has more than 700 editions of Cervantes's *Don Quixote*. The old hospital building is faithfully restored, with pieces of the original frescoes peeking through. You can also enjoy a great number of temporary exhibitions, often focused on modern applied arts. ✉ *Av. Hidalgo 45, at Plaza Santa Veracruz, Alameda Central* ☎ *55/5518-2267* 🌐 *www.franzmayer.org.mx* 🎫 *$3.50, free Tues.* ⏲ *Tues. and Thurs.–Sun. 10–5, Wed. 10–7* ☞ *Call 1 wk ahead for an English-speaking guide* Ⓜ *Bellas Artes or Hidalgo.*

3 **Museo José Luis Cuevas.** Installed in a refurbished former Santa Inés convent, this attractive museum displays international modern art as well as work by Mexico's *enfant terrible*, José Luis Cuevas, one of the country's best-known contemporary artists. The highlight is the sensational *La Giganta (The Giantess)*, Cuevas's 8-ton bronze sculpture in the central patio. It represents male-female duality and pays homage to Charles Baudelaire's poem of the same name. There is also a small collection of original Rembrandt and Picasso drawings. Up-and-coming Latin American artists appear in temporary exhibitions throughout the year. No photographs are permitted. ✉*Academia 13, at Calle Moneda, Col. Centro* ☎*55/5522–0156* 🌐*www.museojoseluiscuevas.com.mx* 🎫*$2.00, free Sun.* 🕑*Tues.–Sun. 10–5:30* Ⓜ*Zócalo.*

5 **Museo Mexicano de Diseño Industrial.** This new museum with a big gift shop and café features small expositions of contemporary Mexican design. The goals of the museum are to provide a space for design, to assist local designers, and to offer a location in which designers can make money from their craft. The expositions are shown in a back room made of brick, where you can see the old archways from Cortés's patio, which was built, in part, on top of Moctezuma's pyramid. ✉*Francisco I. Madero 74, Col. Centro* ☎*55/5510–8609* 🌐 *www.mumedi.org* 🎫*$4* 🕑*Tues.–Sun. 11–3 and 4–8* Ⓜ*Zócalo.*

⇨ 17 **Museo Mural Diego Rivera** *see Frida & Diego.*

21 **Museo San Carlos.** The San Carlos collection, housed in a beautiful, 18th-century, neoclassic stone building with a stunning open-air oval courtyard, is one of the most important collections of European art in Latin America, primarily paintings and prints, with a few examples of sculpture and decorative arts. In small rooms off the patio the works are grouped by period and style: Gothic, Renaissance, baroque, rococo, English portraiture, neoclassicism, naturalism, romanticism, impressionism, and realism. The museum offers seminars, workshops, and extraordinary weekend classes for children. ✉*Puente de Alvarado 50, Tabacalera* ☎*55/5566–8342 or 55/5592–3721* 🎫*$2.50, free Sun.* 🕑*Wed.–Mon. 10–6* Ⓜ*San Cosme.*

9 **Palacio de Iturbide.** In 1780 this baroque palace—note the imposing door and its carved-stone trimmings—was built for Mariana de Berrio, a descendent of the Córdoba family, related to one of the original conquistadores. When she married a man who was said to be a poor administrator, her parents constructed this palace for her. This may have helped to preserve the resources that she brought to her marriage. The palace's name comes from Agustín de Iturbide, who stayed here only for a short time in 1822. One of the heroes of the independence movement, the misguided Iturbide proclaimed himself emperor of a country that had thrown off the Habsburg imperial yoke only a year before. He was staying here when he became emperor, though his own empire was short-lived. The house has been incarnated as a school, a café, and a hotel; however it's now owned by Banamex (Banco Nacional de México), which sponsors cultural exhibitions in the atrium. ✉*Calle Madero 17, Col. Centro* ☎*55/1226–0120* 🌐*www.banamex.*

com/esp/filiales/fomento_cultural/palaciocultura.htm *Free* *Inner atrium daily 10–7* M *Bellas Artes.*

7 **Plaza de Santo Domingo.** The Aztec emperor Cuauhtémoc built a palace here, where heretics were later burned at the stake during the Spanish Inquisition. The plaza was the intellectual hub of the city during the colonial era. Today its most charming feature is the **Portal de los Evangelistas,** whose arcades are filled with scribes at old-fashioned typewriters filling in official forms, formatting theses, printing invitations, or composing letters. In the past, people who didn't know how to write would come here for a little help. While there are still those, there are also the people who desire to keep traditions alive. At Christmastime especially, people come to have greeting cards personalized—with their greeting on the inside and return address printed on the envelopes.

The 18th-century baroque **Santo Domingo church,** slightly north of the portal, is all that remains of the first Dominican convent in New Spain. The convent building was demolished in 1861 under the Reform laws that forced clerics to turn over all religious buildings not used for worship to the government. ✉ *Bounded by República de Cuba, República de Brasil, República de Venezuela, and Palma, Col. Centro* ☎ *No phone* M *Zócalo.*

BOSQUE DE CHAPULTEPEC & ZONA ROSA

Bosque de Chapultepec, named for the *chapulines* (grasshoppers) that populated it long ago, is the largest park in the city, a great green refuge from concrete, traffic, and dust. Housing five world-class museums, a castle, a lake, an amusement park, and the Mexican president's official residence, Chapultepec is a saving grace for visitors and locals. If you have time to visit only one of the park's museums, make it the Museo Nacional de Antropología.

Stores, hotels, travel agencies, and restaurants line the avenues of the touristy Zona Rosa, just east of the park—once one of the city's cultural centers, it's a great stop for shopping. There aren't many sights in Zona Rosa, but you can easily combine a meal and some shopping with a day in the park.

You'll find a plethora of restaurants, cafés, galleries, hotels, discos, and shops in the Zona Rosa. The 29-square-block area is bounded by Paseo de la Reforma on the north, Niza on the east, Avenida Chapultepec on the south, and Avenida Floréncia on the west. With the mushrooming of fast-food spots and some tacky bars and stores, the area has lost some of its former appeal. Most of the buildings were built in the 1920s as two- and three-story private homes for the well-to-do. All the streets are named after European cities; some, such as Génova, are garden-lined pedestrian malls accented with contemporary bronze statuary.

You can head right to the park or start your exploration of the Zona Rosa at the junction of Reforma, Avenida Juárez, and Bucareli. The best-known landmark here is the Monumento a la Independencia, also known as El Angel, which marks the western edge of the Zona Rosa. To enjoy the Zona Rosa, walk the lengths of Hamburgo and Londres and some of the side streets, especially Copenhague—a veritable restaurant row. There's a crafts market, Mercado Insurgentes, also known as Mercado Zona Rosa, on Londres. Four blocks southwest of the market, at Avenida Chapultepec, you'll come to the main entrance of the Bosque de Chapultepec.

You can easily spend an hour at each Bosque de Chapultepec museum, with the exception of the Museo Nacional de Antropología, which is huge compared with its sister institutions. There you can have a quick go-through in two hours, but to appreciate the fine exhibits, anywhere from a half day to a full day is more appropriate. Tuesday through Friday are good days to visit the museums and stroll around the park. On Sunday and on Mexican holidays they're often packed with families, and if you get to the Museo Nacional de Antropología after 10 AM, you can expect to spend considerable time there, waiting.

PASEO DE LA REFORMA

Emperor Maximilian built the Paseo de la Reforma in 1865, calling it the Causeway of the Empress, for his wife, Carlotta. It was modeled after the Champs-Elysées in Paris. Its purpose was to connect the Palacio Nacional with his residence, the Castillo de Chapultepec. At Reforma's northeastern end are Tlatelolco, the Lagunilla Market, and Plaza Garibaldi, where mariachis cluster and strut. To the west Reforma winds its leisurely way west into the neighborhoods of Lomas de Chapultepec, where posh estates sit behind stone walls.

EXPLORING

MAIN ATTRACTIONS

❶ **Bosque de Chapultepec.** This 1,600-acre green space, literally the Woods of Chapultepec, draws hordes of families on weekend outings, cyclists, joggers, and horseback riders into its three sections. Its museums rank among the finest in Mexico, if not the world. This is one of the oldest parts of Mexico City, having been considered a sacred place, and inhabited by the Mexica (Aztec) tribe as early as the 13th century. Several Aztec kings had their effigies carved in stone here. The Mexica poet-king Nezahualcóyotl had his palace here and ordered construction of the aqueduct that brought water to Tenochtitlán. Ahuehuete trees (Moctezuma cypress) still stand from that era, when the woods were used as hunting preserves.

At the park's principal entrance, one block west of the Chapultepec metro station, the **Monumento a los Niños Héroes** (Monument to the Boy Heroes) consists of six asparagus-shape marble columns adorned with eaglets. Supposedly buried in the monument are the young cadets who, it is said, wrapped themselves in the Mexican flag and jumped to their deaths rather than surrender to the Americans during the U.S. invasion of 1847. To Mexicans that war is still a troubling symbol of

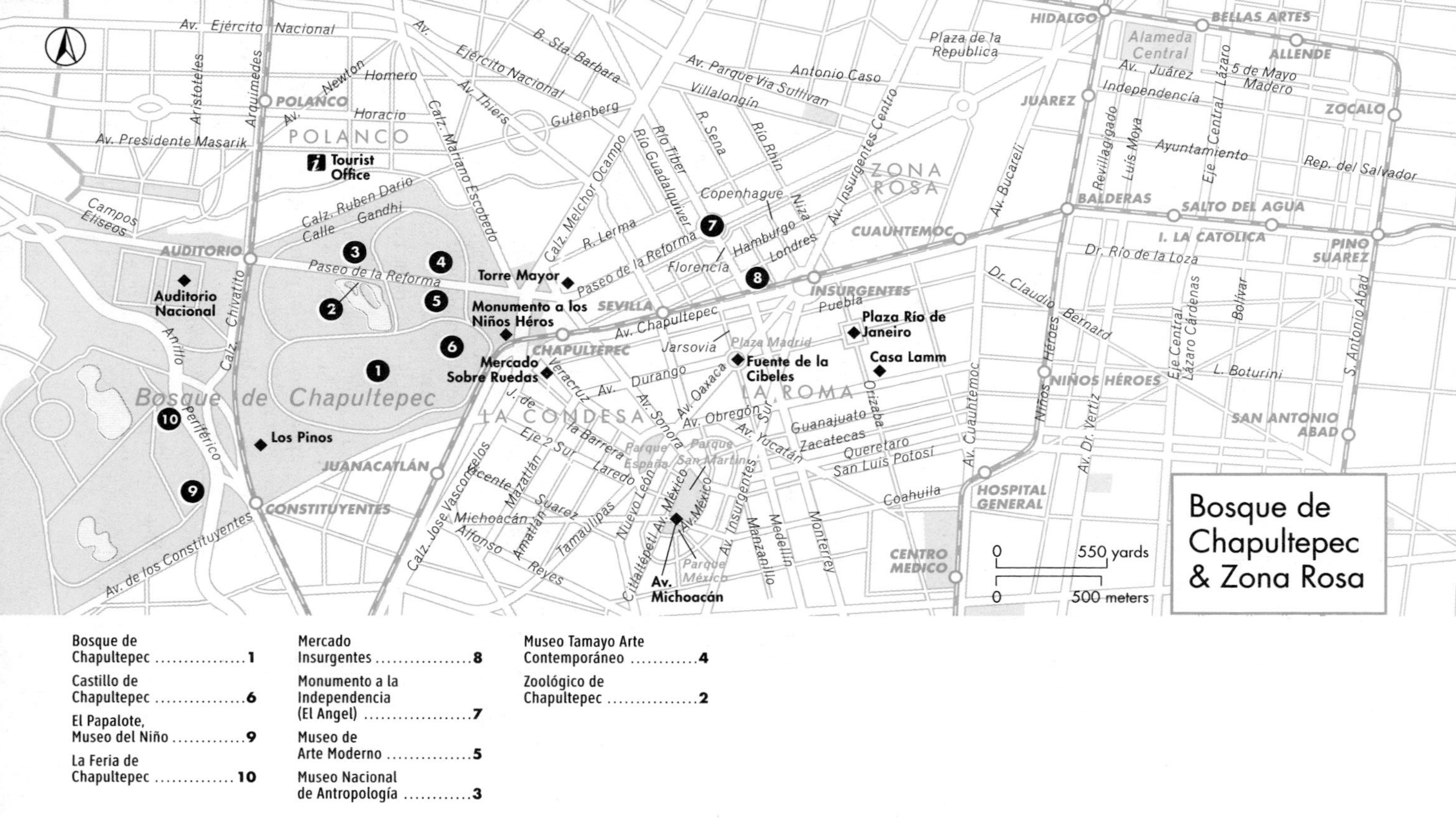
Bosque de Chapultepec & Zona Rosa
0 550 yards
0 500 meters
Bosque de Chapultepec
POLANCO
ZONA ROSA
LA ROMA
LA CONDESA
Tourist Office
Auditorio Nacional
Los Pinos
Torre Mayor
Monumento a los Niños Héros
Mercado Sobre Ruedas
Plaza Río de Janeiro
Casa Lamm
Fuente de la Cibeles
Av. Michoacán
Alameda Central
Plaza de la Republica
Parque España
Parque San Martín
Parque México
Plaza Madrid
HIDALGO
BELLAS ARTES
ALLENDE
ZOCALO
JUAREZ
BALDERAS
SALTO DEL AGUA
I. LA CATOLICA
PINO SUAREZ
CUAUHTEMOC
INSURGENTES
SEVILLA
CHAPULTEPEC
NIÑOS HÉROES
SAN ANTONIO ABAD
HOSPITAL GENERAL
CENTRO MEDICO
AUDITORIO
POLANCO
JUANACATLÁN
CONSTITUYENTES
Paseo de la Reforma
Av. Chapultepec
Av. Insurgentes Centro
Av. Insurgentes
Av. Ejército Nacional
Av. Presidente Masarik
Calz. Mariano Escobedo
Calz. Melchor Ocampo
Calz. Chivatito
Calz. Jose Vasconcelos
Av. de los Constituyentes
Anillo Periférico
Campos Eliseos
Av. Bucareli
Av. Cuauhtemoc
Av. Dr. Vertiz
Eje Central Lázaro Cárdenas
Av. Juárez
5 de Mayo
Madero
Rep. del Salvador
S. Antonio Abad
Dr. Río de la Loza
Dr. Claudio Bernard
Niños Heroes
L. Boturini
Bolívar
Revillagigado
Luís Moya
Ayuntamiento
Independencia
Eje 2 Sur
Av. Oaxaca
Av. Obregón
Av. Sonora
Av. Yucatán
Av. México
Citlaltépetl
Nuevo León
Tamaulipas
Amatlán
Mazatlán
Vicente Suarez
Michoacán
Alfonso Reyes
Laredo
Durango
Jarsovia
Veracruz
Puebla
Orizaba
Guanajuato
Zacatecas
Queretaro
San Luis Potosí
Coahuila
Monterrey
Medellín
Manzanillo
Copenhague
Hamburgo
Londres
Niza
Florencia
R. Lerma
Río Tiber
Río Guadalquiver
R. Sena
Río Rhin
Villalongín
Av. Parque Via Sullivan
Antonio Caso
B. Sta. Barbara
Gutenberg
Av. Thiers
Homero
Horacio
Newton
Arquimedes
Aristoteles
Calz. Ruben Dario
Calle Gandhi
Bosque de Chapultepec 1
Castillo de Chapultepec 6
El Papalote, Museo del Niño 9
La Feria de Chapultepec 10
Mercado Insurgentes 8
Monumento a la Independencia (El Angel) 7
Museo de Arte Moderno 5
Museo Nacional de Antropología 3
Museo Tamayo Arte Contemporáneo 4
Zoológico de Chapultepec 2

their neighbor's aggressive dominance: it cost Mexico almost half its territory—the present states of Texas, California, Arizona, New Mexico, and Nevada.

Other sights in the first section of Bosque de Chapultepec include three small boating lakes, a botanical garden, and the Casa del Lago cultural center, which hosts free plays, cultural events, and live music on weekends. **Los Pinos,** the residential palace of the president of Mexico, is on a small highway called Avenida Constituyentes, which cuts through the park; it's heavily guarded and cannot be visited.

Most visitors enter through the first section of the park, near the Chapultepec metro stop, close to the Museo de Arte Moderno. This is a great place to people-watch, especially on weekends. The less crowded second and third sections of Bosque de Chapultepec contain a fancy restaurant, the national cemetery, and the grounds where Lienzo Charro (Mexican rodeo) is staged on Sunday afternoon.

6 **Castillo de Chapultepec.** The castle on Cerro del Chapulín (Grasshopper Hill) has borne witness to all the turbulence and grandeur of Mexican history. In its earliest form it was an Aztec palace, where the Mexica made one of their last stands against the Spaniards. Later it was a Spanish hermitage, gunpowder plant, and military college. Emperor Maximilian used the castle, parts of which date from 1783, as his residence, and his example was followed by various presidents from 1872 to 1940, when Lázaro Cárdenas decreed that it be turned into the **Museo Nacional de Historia.**

Displays on the museum's ground floor cover Mexican history from the conquest to the revolution. The bathroom, bedroom, tea salon, and gardens were used by Maximilian and his wife, Carlotta, in the 1860s. The ground floor also contains works by 20th-century muralists O'Gorman, Orozco, and Siqueiros, and the upper floor is devoted to temporary exhibitions, Porfirio Díaz's malachite vases, and religious art. ⊠ *Section 1, Bosque de Chapultepec* ☎ *55/5241–3100* 🌐 *mnh.inah.gob.mx* 🎟 *$4.50* ⏲ *Tues.–Sun. 9–4:30.* Ⓜ *Chapultepec.*

7 **Monumento a la Independencia.** Known as El Angel, this Corinthian column topped by a gilt angel is the city's most uplifting monument, built to celebrate the 100th anniversary of Mexico's War of Independence. Beneath the pedestal lie the remains of the principal heroes of the independence movement; an eternal flame burns in their honor. El Angel was renovated in 2006 and became shinier and more magnificent than it had been in years. As you pass by, you may see one or more couples dressed in their wedding apparel, posing for pictures on the steps of the monument. Many couples stop off here before or after they get married, as a tribute to their own personal independence from their parents. ⊠ *Traffic circle bounded by Calle Río Tiber, Paseo de la Reforma, and Calle Florencia, Zona Rosa* Ⓜ *Insurgentes.*

5 **Museo de Arte Moderno.** The Modern Art Museum's permanent collection has many important examples of 20th-century Mexican art, including works by Mexican school painters like Frida Kahlo—her

Las dos Fridas is possibly the most famous work in the collection—Diego Rivera, José Clemente Orozco, David Alfaro Siqueiros, and Olga Costa. There are also pieces by Surrealists Remedios Varo and Leonora Carrington. ✉*Paseo de la Reforma, Section 1, Bosque de Chapultepec* ☎*55/5211–8331 or 55/5211–7827* 🌐*www.bellasartes.gob.mx* *$20, free Sun.* 🕘*Tues.–Sun. 10–5:30* Ⓜ*Chapultepec.*

❸ Fodor's Choice ★ **Museo Nacional de Antropología.** Architect Pedro Ramírez Vázquez's distinguished design provides the proper home for one of the finest archaeological collections in the world. Each salon on the museum's two floors displays artifacts from a particular geographic region or culture. The collection is so extensive—covering some 100,000 square feet—that you could easily spend a day here, and that might be barely adequate. Explanatory labels have been updated, some with English translations, and free tours are available at set times between 3 and 6. ■ TIP→ **You can reserve a special tour with an English-speaking guide by calling the museum a week in advance, or opt for an English audio guide ($4) or the English-language museum guide for sale in the bookshop.**

A good place to start is in the Orientation Room, where a film is shown in Spanish nearly every hour on the hour weekdays and every two hours on weekends. The film traces the course of Mexican prehistory and the pre-Hispanic cultures of Mesoamerica. The 12 ground-floor rooms treat pre-Hispanic cultures by region, in the Sala Teotihuacána, Sala Tolteca, Sala Oaxaca (Zapotec and Mixtec peoples), and so on. Objects both precious and pedestrian, including statuary, jewelry, weapons, figurines, and pottery, evoke the intriguing, complex, and frequently bloodthirsty civilizations that peopled Mesoamerica for the 3,000 years preceding the Spanish invasion.

A copy of the Aztec ruler Moctezuma's feathered headdress (the original is now in Vienna); a stela from Tula, near Mexico City; massive Olmec heads from Veracruz; and vivid reproductions of Mayan murals in a reconstructed temple are other highlights. Be sure to see the magnificent reconstruction of the tomb of 8th-century Mayan ruler Pacal, which was discovered in the ruins of Palenque. The perfectly preserved skeletal remains lie in an immense stone chamber, and the stairwell walls leading to it are beautifully decorated with bas-relief scenes of the underworld. Pacal's jade death mask is on display nearby.

The nine rooms on the upper floor contain faithful ethnographic displays of current indigenous peoples, using maps, photographs, household objects, folk art, clothing, and religious articles. When leaving the museum, take a rest and watch the famous Voladores de Papantla (flyers of Papantla) as they swing by their feet down an incredibly high maypolelike structure just outside the museum entrance. ✉*Paseo de la Reforma at Calle Gandhi, Section 1, Bosque de Chapultepec* ☎*55/5286–2923, 55/5553–6381, 55/5553–6386 for a guide* 🌐*www.mna.inah.gob.mx* *$4.80 (tickets sold until 6), free Sun.* 🕘*Tues.–Sun. 9–7* Ⓜ*Auditorio.*

CLOSE UP

The Sun Stone

The Aztec calendar stone—the original *Piedra del Sol* (Stone of the Sun)—is in the anthropology museum's Room 7 (Sala Mexica). The 12-foot, 25-ton, intricately carved, basalt slab describing Aztec life is one of Mexico's most famous symbols. Nobel Prize–winning poet and essayist Octavio Paz immortalized the stone in his epic poem "Piedra del Sol." The stone was carved in the late 1400s; it was discovered buried beneath the zócalo in 1790. It was originally thought to be a calendar, and, for a brief time, a sacrificial altar. In the stone's center is the sun god Tonatiuh. The rest of the carvings explain the Aztecs' idea of the cosmos: namely, that prior to their existence, the world had endured four periods (called suns) of creation and destruction. Four square panels surrounding the center image represent these four worlds and their destruction (by jaguars, wind, firestorms, and water, respectively). The ring around the panels is filled with symbols representing the 20 days of the Aztec month. Finally, two snakes form an outer ring and point to a date, 1011 AD—the date the fifth sun, or the Aztecs' current world, was created. The Aztecs believed that this fifth sun was the final sun; they believed that one day they would witness a catastrophic end of the world.

IF YOU HAVE TIME

10 **La Feria de Chapultepec.** This children's amusement park has various games and more than 50 rides, including a truly hair-raising haunted house and a *montaña rusa*—"Russian mountain," or roller coaster. Admission prices vary, depending on which rides are covered and whether meals are included. ⊠ *Section 2, Bosque de Chapultepec* ☎ *55/5230–2121 or 55/5230–2112* 🎟 *$5–$25* ⏲ *Weekdays 10–6, weekends 10–7* Ⓜ *Constituyentes.*

8 **Mercado Insurgentes.** Also referred to as either Mercado Zona Rosa or Mercado Londres, this is the neighborhood's large crafts market. Vendors here can be aggressive, calling visitors to their stalls with promises of low prices (which you may or may not find). Opposite the market's Londres entrance is Plaza del Angel, a small, upscale shopping mall, the halls of which are crowded by antiques vendors on weekends. ⊠ *At Londres between Florencia and Amberes Zona Rosa* Ⓜ *Insurgentes*

★ 4 **Museo Tamayo Arte Contemporáneo** *(Rufino Tamayo Contemporary Art Museum).* Within its modernist shell (which earned the National Architecture Prize in 1982), this sleek museum contains paintings by the noted Mexican artist as well as temporary exhibitions of international contemporary art. The selections from Tamayo's personal collection, which he donated to the Mexican people, making the basis for this museum's permanent collection, demonstrate his unerring eye for great art; he owned works by Picasso, Joan Miró, René Magritte, Francis Bacon, and Henry Moore. One Wednesday every month the museum offers live jazz music at night. Check the Web site for dates. ⊠ *Paseo de la Reforma at Calle Gandhi, Section 1, Bosque de Chapultepec* ☎ *55/5286–6519* 🌐 *www.museotamayo.org* 🎟 *$1.50, free Sun.* ⏲ *Tues.–Sun. 10–6* Ⓜ *Chapultepec.*

9 **El Papalote, Museo del Niño.** Five theme sections compose this excellent interactive children's museum: Our World; The Human Body; Con-Sciencia, with exhibits relating to both consciousness and science; Communication, on topics ranging from language to computers; and Expression, which includes art, music, theater, and literature. There are also workshops, an IMAX theater, a store, and a restaurant. Although exhibits are in Spanish, there are some English-speaking staff on hand. ✉*Av. Constituyentes 268, Section 2, Bosque de Chapultepec* ☎*55/5237–1781 or 55/5237–1700* 🌐*www.papalote.org.mx* *$8.50* ⏲*Mon.–Wed. and Fri. 9–6, Thurs. 9–11, weekends 10–7* Ⓜ*Constituyentes.*

2 **Zoológico de Chapultepec.** In the early 16th century Mexico City's zoo, in Chapultepec, housed a small private collection of animals belonging to Moctezuma II; it became quasi-public when he allowed favored subjects to visit it. The current zoo opened in the 1920s, and has the usual suspects, as well as some superstar pandas. A gift from China, the original pair—Pepe and Ying Ying—produced the world's first panda baby born in captivity (much to competitive China's chagrin). In fact, the zoo has one of the world's best mating records for these endangered animals. The zoo includes the Moctezuma Aviary and is surrounded by a miniature train depot, botanical gardens, and lakes where you can go rowing. You'll see the entrance on Paseo de la Reforma, across from the Museo Nacional de Antropología. ✉*Section 1, Bosque de Chapultepec* ☎*55/5553–6263 or 55/5256–4104* 🌐*www.chapultepec.df.gob.mx* *Free* ⏲*Tues.–Sun. 9–4:30* Ⓜ*Auditorio.*

LA CONDESA & LA ROMA

Next to Bosque de Chapultepec, two nearby colonias, known simply as La Condesa and La Roma, are filled with fading 1920s and 1930s architecture, sun-dappled parks, and a wide variety of eateries that cater to the city's young and trendy. The capital's elite were concentrated here at the turn of the 20th century. In the late 1990s a tide of artists, entrepreneurs, and foreigners brought a new wave of energy. La Condesa is the sprucer, hipper area of the two. Grittier La Roma is now home to a group of important art galleries, as well as some of the city's best cantinas, and it is becoming increasingly more trendy. Many say that the Roma is slated to be the next Condesa. That is, it's on the verge of becoming the next big thing for those edgy young things who are always on the lookout.

COLONIA POLANCO

If you want to see how Mexico's upper crust lives, head to the upscale Polanco neighborhood, just north of Bosque de Chapultepec. A mixture of residential and commercial areas with many boutiques and specialty shops, Polanco offers some of the city's best shopping—that is, if you can afford it. The colonia is also home to Mexico's largest Jewish community, so it's not uncommon to see Orthodox Jews on the streets. As for nightlife, there are plenty of restaurants and bars, but be prepared to pay Polanco prices.

Although it's possible to walk to Colonia Condesa from the Bosque de Chapultepec, you'd have to trek along busy, heavily trafficked roads; it's best to take a sitio taxi to the circular Avenida Amsterdam. Loop around Amsterdam until you reach Avenida Michoacán, where you can check out the boutiques and peek down the side streets. On Avenida Michoacán you'll find a sitio taxi stand—hop in for another short cab ride, this time to Colonia Roma's Plaza Río de Janeiro and more atmospheric strolling.

The Condesa's nucleus is the restaurant zone (you can ask your taxi driver to take you to the neighborhood's zona de restaurantes). La Roma and La Condesa border each other along Avenida Insurgentes Sur, so once you're in one, the other's relatively close on foot.

A late-afternoon stroll in La Roma after the museum visits, with dinner in La Condesa, is an excellent way to wind down a visit to the park. Keep in mind that art galleries tend to close on Sunday. The colonias are a must-see in spring, when the jacarandas are in bloom.

EXPLORING

COLONIA CONDESA

Avenida Michoacán. Restaurants, cafés, and hip boutiques radiate along and out from La Condesa's main drag, Avenida Michoacán. It's a great place for a break from a sightseeing slog—just relax at a sidewalk table and watch the hip young world go by. Stop to sip coffee and flip through the magazines at **Coffee Max** (✉ *Tamaulipas 72A, at Av. Michoacán, Col. Condesa* ☎ *55/5553–9563* Ⓜ *Patriotismo*). Just across the street, you can also pick up a quick slice of pizza in inventive combinations (such as ham and fig) at **Pizza Amore** (✉ *Michoacán 78, Col. Condesa* ☎ *55/5286–5126* Ⓜ *Patriotismo*). The tacos at **El Farolito** (✉ *Altata 19 at Alfonso Reyes, Col. Condesa* ☎ *55/5515–2389* 🌐 *www.taqueriaselfarolito.com* Ⓜ *Patriotismo*) are also yummy. Try the costras—tacos in which the meat is wrapped in fried cheese before being wrapped in a tortilla. Wash it down with a delicious juice, like the mango or strawberry-coconut, made fresh in the taquería. If you are craving a more substantial meal, try **Due Amici** (✉ *Fernando Montes de Oca 17* ☎ *55/5286–4043*) for rib-eye steaks, Italian seafood dishes, and great sandwiches.

A snack will fortify you for Avenida Michoacán's other main activity, shopping. The clothing stores often lean toward the trendy; Kulte, for instance, at Atlixco 118, dishes up the latest fads, as does Soho, on Avenida Vicente Suárez between avenidas Michoacán and Tamaulipas. Along the nearby streets you'll find a good mix of temptations—everything from modern furniture to risqué lingerie. As its name (The Open Closet) suggests, the bookstore **El Armario Abierto** (✉ *Agustín Melgar 25, at Pachuca, Col. Condesa* ☎ *55/5286–0895* 🌐 *www.elarmarioabierto.com.mx* Ⓜ *Chapultepec*) gives a rare glimpse of progressive Mexico; it specializes in sexuality-related books, videos, and other resources. **El Péndulo** (✉ *Av. Nuevo León 115, at Av. Vicente Suárez, Col. Condesa* ☎ *55/5286–9493* 🌐 *www.pendulo.com* Ⓜ *Chilpancingo*)

Continued on page 68

Diego Rivera mural, Palacio Nacional, Mexico City

FRIDA & DIEGO

Among Mexico's most provocative artists, Frida Kahlo and Diego Rivera had a relationship that never failed to amaze and astonish. Though they created some of Mexico's most fascinating art, it's the bizarre Beauty-and-the-Beast dynamic that has captivated the world and enshrouded both figures in intrigue. Whether you're an art historian or simply an admirer of this eccentric duo, a visit to Mexico City—where you can tour the homes they once shared, study their work, and even see the shoes they wore and beds they slept in—will compel you to delve even further into their story.

Diego Rivera and Frida Kahlo's relationship was far from placid: they were married in 1929, divorced in 1940, and then married again that same year. Together, these two colorful, larger-than-life artists have endured as vibrant characters in a singularly Mexican drama. You can connect the dots on a journey of discovery in Mexico City, where you'll find numerous sites dedicated to Frida and Diego. These include Museo Dolores Olmedo Patino, the estate of Rivera's longtime model; Museo Mural Diego Rivera; Museo de Frida Kahlo; and Estudio Diego Rivera y Frida Kahlo, which is the home that Rivera and Kahlo shared.

A gifted painter and muralist, Diego Rivera was also a political activist; many of the sumptuous murals he created in Mexico and throughout the world speak of politics, history, and the worker's struggle. Considered one of the 20th century's major artistic figures, Rivera created images—especially those rounded peasant women with braided hair, arms brimful of calla lilies—that have come to typify Mexico. Flamboyant, irreverent, and unforgettable, Frida Kahlo created arresting, and at times disturbing, works of art. Fifty-five of her 143 paintings are self-portraits, which speak of her vivaciousness and personal tragedies.

FRIDA KAHLO: A RIBBON AROUND A BOMB

Born: July 6, 1907, in Coyoacán, Mexico

Died: July 13, 1954, in Mexico City

Favorite medium: Oil paint on canvas, wood, metal, and masonite

Famous works: *Diego on my Mind; What the Water Gave Me; Tree of Hope; The Little Deer; The Two Fridas; The Broken Column; Roots;* and numerous self-portraits

Number of medical operations: 32

Pets: Monkeys, hairless dogs, parrots

Trademarks: Bright Tehuana costumes; bat-wing eyebrows; clunky, colorful jewelry

Famous lie: Kahlo often gave her birth year as 1910 because she wanted her life to begin with the Mexican Revolution.

Rumored Extramarital affairs: Communist exile Leon Trotsky; actress Dolores del Rio; painter Georgia O'Keeffe; actress Paulette Goddard; artist Isamu Noguchi

Quote: "I have suffered two accidents in my life: One in which a streetcar ran over me. The other is Diego." (Kahlo quoted in *Frida Kahlo: Torment and Triumph in Her Life and Art,* by Malka Drucker)

Frida Kahlo's hauntingly beautiful face, broken body, and bright Tehuana costumes have become the trademark of Mexican femininity. Images of her batwing brows, moustache, and clunky ethnic jewelry are as familiar in Mexico as Marilyn's pout and puffed-up white dress are in the U.S. This petite painter has gained international recognition since her death for her colorful but pained self-portraits.

In fact, Kahlo didn't even need to paint to make it into the history books. Controversy surrounded her two marriages to Diego Rivera, including his affair with her younger sister and her own affair with Communist exile Leon Trotsky. It's hard not to become mired in the tragic details of her life—from childhood polio to a tram accident that smashed her pelvis, and a gangrenous foot that resulted in the amputation of a leg.

But Kahlo was also a groundbreaking artist who pioneered a new expressiveness, and her unique iconography of suffering transcended self-pity to create an existential art. Kahlo was the first Latin American woman to have a painting in the Louvre; her work caused a storm in Paris in 1939 (at an exhibition entitled *Méxique*). It was André Breton who described her art as "a ribbon around a bomb."

Frida Kahlo tried hard to be as much the revolutionary as the icon of Mexican femininity. Her last public appearance was 11 days before her death on July 13, 1954, in a wheelchair at Diego's side, protesting the intervention of the United States in Guatemala.

In 2007, to celebrate the 100th anniversary of her birth, there was a mega exposition of her work in Bellas Artes, in Mexico City.

Self portrait

DIEGO RIVERA: REVOLUTIONARY WITH A PAINTBRUSH

Born: December 8, 1886, in Guanajuato, Mexico

Died: November 24, 1957, in Mexico City

Favorite process: Fresco painting

Famous works: *Night of the Rich; Detroit Industry; The Flower Carrier; A Dream of a Sunday Afternoon in Alameda Park*

Early loss: Born a twin, Rivera lost his brother before their second birthday.

Physical traits: At over 6 feet tall and 300 lbs, Rivera towered over his tiny wife.

Most incendiary moment: In 1933, Rivera was commissioned to paint a mural for the RCA building at New York's Rockefeller Center; he included Soviet leader Vladimir Lenin and the mural was destroyed a year later.

Rumored mourning: It is believed that in his intense mourning for Frida Kahlo, Rivera ate some of his wife's ashes.

Extramarital affairs: Model Dolores Olmedo and Frida Kahlo's younger sister Cristina, among many others

Quote: "Too late, I realized the most wonderful part of my life had been my love for Frida."

Diego Rivera was active both in art and politics early in his life, getting expelled from his academy for joining a student strike. In 1907 he won a scholarship to study abroad and left Mexico for Spain. He returned home briefly in 1910 and held a successful exhibition in Mexico City, at which Porfirio Díaz's wife purchased six of the 40 paintings. As auspicious as this event was, Rivera opted to return to Paris in 1911, this time falling in with the Parisian avant garde.

A trip to Italy in 1919 with fellow Mexican artist David Alfaro Siqueiros introduced Rivera to the frescos of the great Italian painters. In 1921, Rivera decided to return to Mexico with a plan to incorporate these techniques into his art—art that would be created for the enjoyment of the public. In the grand murals he created, he addressed Mexican history and humanity's future at large.

Mural Depicting Aztec Life (detail), Palacio Nacional

Rivera's presence—and the controversy that inevitably followed him—had a profound effect on American painting and the American conception of public art. The strong Marxist themes in his work raised eyebrows wherever he went, but no controversy was greater than the one caused in 1933, when he endowed a mural commissioned by the Rockefellers for the lobby of the RCA building in Rockefeller Center with a portrait of Lenin. Rivera refused to remove the portrait from the mural, and the commission was canceled and the whole piece destroyed.

Despite these controversies, Rivera's work proved to be the inspiration for Franklin Delano Roosevelt's Works Progress Administration (WPA) program, which provided many unemployed artists with work during the 1930s. Rivera also continued to play a central role in the development of Mexican national art until his death in Mexico City in 1957.

The Main Sights

Above: Kitchen in Casa Azul

Museo Mural Diego Rivera. Diego Rivera's controversial mural, *Sunday Afternoon Dream in the Alameda Park*, originally was painted on a lobby wall of the Hotel Del Prado in 1947–48. Its controversy grew out of Rivera's Marxist inscription, "God does not exist," which the artist later replaced with the bland "Conference of San Juan de Letrán" to placate Mexico's Catholic population. The 1985 earthquake destroyed the hotel but not the mural, and this museum was built across the street from the hotel's site to house it. ✉ *Colón 7, at Calle Balderas, Alameda Central* ☎ *55/5512–0754* 🌐 *www.arts-history.mx/museomural.html* 🎫 *$1.50* ⏲ *Tues.–Sun. 10–5:40* Ⓜ *Hidalgo.*

★ Fodor's Choice **Museo de Frida Kahlo.** The Casa Azul (blue house) where she was born in 1907 (not 1910, as she wanted people to believe) and died 47 years later, is both museum and shrine. Kahlo's astounding vitality and originality are reflected in the house, from the giant papier-mâché skeletons outside and the *retablos* (small religious paintings on tin) on the staircase to the gloriously decorated kitchen and the bric-a-brac in her bedroom. You can admire her early sketches, diary entries, tiny outfits, wheelchair at the easel, plus her four-poster bed fitted with mirror above. ✉ *Londres 247, at Calle Allende, Coyoacán* ☎ *55/5554–5999* 🎫 *$4.50 (includes admission to Museo del Anahuacalli)* ⏲ *Tues.–Sun. 10–5:45* Ⓜ *Viveros.*

Museo Casa Estudio Diego Rivera y Frida Kahlo. Some of Rivera's last paintings are still resting here on ready easels, and his denim jacket and shoes sit on a wicker chair, waiting. The museum that once was home to Diego and Frida appears as if the two could return at any moment to continue work. Architect and artist Juan O'Gorman, who designed the unique 1931 structure (essentially two houses connected by a bridge), was a close friend of Rivera. The house is now one of the city's architectural landmarks. ✉ *Calle Diego Rivera, at Av. Altavista, San Angel* ☎ *55/5616–0996, 55/5550–1518, or 55/5550–1189* 🎫 *$1* ⏲ *Tues.–Sun. 10–6.*

★ Fodor's Choice **Museo Dolores Olmedo Patino.** In Xochimilco, on the outskirts of the city, is a superb collection of paintings by Frida Kahlo and the largest private collection of works by Diego Rivera. The museum was established by Olmedo, Rivera's lifelong model, patron, and onetime mistress. The lavish display of nearly 140 pieces from his cubist, post-cubist, and mural periods hangs in a magnificent 17th-century hacienda with beautiful gardens. This is also the place to see the strange Mexican hairless dog: Ms. Olmedo shares Rivera's passion for these creatures and keeps a few as pets on the grounds. There is a lovely small café in a glassed-in gazebo. The museum is very easy to reach by public transportation;

Museo Dolores Olmedo Patino

at the Tasqueña metro station, catch the light rail to La Noria (*not* Xochimilco). As you exit the station, cross the street via the the stairway bridge. Walk half a block on 20 de Noviembre until you come to a traffic intersection. Without crossing the street, turn left at this intersection and continue walking down this street for two blocks. ✉ *Av. México 5843* ☎ *55/5555–1016* 🌐 *www.mdop.org.mx* 🎫 *$3, free Tues.* ⏲ *Tues.–Sun. 10–6.*

Museo del Anahuacalli. Diego Rivera built his own museum for the thousands of pre-Columbian artifacts he collected over the years. The third-floor studio that Rivera did not live long enough to use displays sketches for his murals. If you visit between October and late December you'll see one of the city's finest altars to the dead in honor of Rivera himself. ✉ *Calle del Museo 150, Coyoacán, Col. San Pablo Tepetlapa* ☎ *55/5617–4310 or 55/5617–3797* 🎫 *$4.50 (includes admission to Museo de Frida Kahlo)* ⏲ *Tues.–Sun. 10–6.*

Other Sights

The **Museo Nacional de Arte (MUNAL)** in Alameda Central has Rivera's portrait of Adolfo Best Maugard. The **Museo de Arte Moderno** in Bosque de Chapultepec has Frida's *Las dos Fridas,* as well as a few of Rivera's pieces. In San Angel, the **Museo de Arte Carrillo Gil** has early murals by Rivera. And, last, but definitely not least, the **Palacio Nacional** in Centro Historico holds Rivera's epic murals, *Epic of the Mexican People in Their Struggle for Freedom and Independence*, representing two millennia of Mexican history.

Detail of *Dream of a Sunday Afternoon in the Alameda Park,* 1947-48. Hotel del Prado, Mexico City.

acts as a sort of cultural center. The first of what is now a chain of bookstores is stuffed with Spanish-language books and international CDs; classical guitarists and other musicians play on weekends.

The designer shop Carmen Rion caps Michoacán where it meets the **Parque México,** which has a duck pond, plus one of the city's cheapest and best taxi stands. The park used to be a racetrack, which explains the circular roads like the looping Avenida México and the occasional references to the Hipódromo (hippodrome) Condesa. From Michoacán you could also turn north on Tamaulipas and walk up a few blocks to visit smaller **Parque España** for a picnic or stroll. (Note that many locals refer to both parks as "Parque México," as most are unaware that the two parks are actually divided, and each has its own name.)

CULTURE ONLINE

If visiting the galleries has inspired you to learn more about Mexican art and culture, take a look at the following Spanish-language Web sites.

Arte Joven (🌐 *www.artejoven.com*). A directory of young, up-and-coming artists.

Consejo Nacional para la Cultura y las Artes (🌐 *www.ecultura.gob.mx*). Information on history, and events calendars.

Instituto de Cultura de la Ciudad de México (🌐 *www.cultura.df.gob.mx*). Events calendars and listings for many Mexico City venues.

Mexico Desonocido (🌐 *www.mexicodesconocido.com.mx*). A magazine similar to National Geographic, all about Mexico.

If you're in town on a Tuesday, stop by Avenida Pachuca, where vendors set up a charming outdoor market, the **Mercado Sobre Ruedas,** between Avenida Veracruz and Juan de la Barrera, from 9 to 5. Although there are many markets to visit in Mexico, this one is particularly clean and peaceful, since it's set up in a relaxed neighborhood. All tables are draped in pink plastic tablecloths, and identical cloths are hung above the tables for shade; on a sunny day the predominance of pink can be strikingly beautiful. Vendors here sell everything from children's clothes, pirated CDs, and ceramic pots to produce, fresh flowers, and take-away food. Sometimes music groups wander between the stalls, singing and strumming their guitars for tips.

COLONIA ROMA

Adventurous private art galleries, independent artist-run spaces, and a rough-around-the-edges atmosphere are the hallmarks of La Roma. Like its western neighbor La Condesa, La Roma was once an aristocratic enclave with stately homes. Now it's known for its lively cantinas, pool halls, dance clubs, and night haunts of questionable repute. Gentrification creeps slowly but steadily onward, though, so enjoy this up-and-comer before it becomes too respectable. ■ TIP→ **La Roma is divided into Roma Sur (south) and Roma Norte (north). Most of the action takes place in Roma Norte.**

Recently, bookstores and cafés have helped transform this old neighborhood into the capital's full-blown arts district.

The **Galería OMR** (✉ *Plaza Río de Janeiro 54, Col. Roma* ☎ *55/5511–1179* 🌐 *www.galeriaomr.com* Ⓜ *Insurgentes*) is tucked away in a typical Colonia Roma house, with an early-20th-century stone facade and quirkily lopsided exhibition rooms. This active gallery has a strong presence in international art fairs and art magazines. It's open weekdays 10–3 and 4:30–7 and Saturday 10–2. A short walk from OMR, **Galería Nina Menocal** (✉ *Zacatecas 93, at Cordoba, Col. Roma* ☎ *55/5564–7443* 🌐 *www.ninamenocal.com* Ⓜ *Insurgentes*) specializes in work by Cuban artists. The gallery is open weekdays 10–7 and Saturday 10–2, but the small staff is not always particularly welcoming to tourists who just want to take a look around. The **Casa Lamm Cultural Center** (✉ *Av. Alvaro Obregón 99, at Orizaba, Col. Roma* ☎ *55/5525–0019* 🌐 *www.casalamm.com.mx* Ⓜ *Insurgentes*), a small mansion and national monument, nurtures artists and welcomes browsers with three exhibition spaces, a library, a bookstore, a wide range of courses, a superb café, and a great restaurant that offers modern twists on Mexican classics as well as delicious international cuisine. **Galería Pecanins** (✉ *Av. Durango 186 at Plaza Cibeles, Col. Roma* ☎ *55/5514–0621 or 55/5207–5661* Ⓜ *Insurgentes*) may be small, but it's a significant local presence. It's open weekdays 11–2:30 and 4–7:30.

SAN ANGEL & COYOACÁN

Originally separate colonial towns and then suburbs of Mexico City, San Angel and Coyoacán were both absorbed by the ever-growing capital. But they've managed to retain their original tranquillity.

San Angel is a little colonial enclave of cobblestone streets, stone walls, pastel houses, rich foliage, and gardens drenched in bougainvillea. It became a haven for wealthy Spaniards during the viceroyalty period, around the time of the construction of the Ex-Convento del Carmen. The elite were drawn to the area because of its rivers, pleasant climate, and rural ambience, and proceeded to build haciendas and mansions that, for many, were country homes. It is now sliced through by the busy Avenida Revolución; visitors usually focus on the area from the cobblestoned Avenida de la Paz, lined with some excellent eateries, to the Ex-Convento on Avenida Revolución, and up to the Plaza San Jacinto and its famous Saturday market.

Coyoacán was founded by Toltecs in the 10th century and later settled by the Aztecs, or Mexica. Bernal Díaz Castillo, a Spanish chronicler, wrote that there were 6,000 houses at the time of the conquest. Cortés set up headquarters in Coyoacán during his siege of Tenochtitlán and kept his famous Indian mistress La Malinche here. At one point he considered making Coyoacán his capital; many of the Spanish buildings left from the two-year period during which Mexico City was built still stand.

Coyoacán has had many illustrious residents from Mexico's rich and intellectual elite, including Miguel de la Madrid, president of Mexico from 1982 to 1988; artists Diego Rivera, Frida Kahlo, and José Clemente Orozco; Gabriel Figueroa, cinematographer for Luis Buñuel and John Huston; film star Dolores del Río; film director El Indio Fernández; and writers Carlos Monsiváis, Jorge Ibargüengoitia, and Nobel laureate Octavio Paz. It's also the neighborhood where the exiled Leon Trotsky met his violent death. Coyoacán's streets buzz with activity, and it has a popular food market, the **Mercado Xicotencatl.** On weekends families flock to its attractive *Zócalo* (central square), second in importance and popularity only to the Zócalo downtown.

LEGEND HAS IT

Coyoacán means "Place of the Coyotes." According to local legend, a coyote used to bring chickens to a friar who had saved the coyote from being strangled by a snake.

Each neighborhood is accessible by subway, though you'll need to rely on at least one sitio taxi ride to cover them both in one day. San Angel is closer to the subway than Coyoacán. If you get off the metro at M.A. de Quevedo and walk west down Arenal, you'll soon come to the **Monumento al General Alvaro Obregón**—the somber, gray, granite monument is a good neighborhood landmark. From there you can easily walk to all the neighborhood's sights with the exception of **Museo Casa Estudio Diego Rivera y Frida Kahlo** (though if you have the energy, that can technically be reached on foot, too). To start out from the monument, cross Insurgentes to walk up the cobblestoned, restaurant-lined Avenida de la Paz. Next cross Avenida Revolución and take the crooked street that leads upward to the left of the little park until you come to San Angel's center, **Plaza San Jacinto.**

Coyoacán is farther from the Quevedo stop, but you can reach its main attraction, **Museo de Frida Kahlo,** on foot. Most of the other sights are within walking distance of the museum, but you'll need a sitio taxi to get to **Museo del Anahuacalli.**

You'll want to linger in these elegant and beautiful sections of town, especially in Coyoacán. The Frida Kahlo and Leon Trotsky museums give intense, intimate looks at the lives of two famous people who were friends and lovers, and who breathed their personalities into the places where they lived. Allow at least an hour at each. The other museums are much smaller and merit less time. Remember that museums close on Monday. Weekends are liveliest at the Plaza Hidalgo and its neighboring Jardín Centenario (usually referred to as *la plaza* or *el zócalo*), where street life explodes into a fiesta with balloons, clowns, cotton candy, live music, and hypnotic dancing to the sound of drums. On weekends Plaza Hidalgo hosts a crafts market.

EXPLORING

MAIN ATTRACTIONS

❹ **Museo de Arte Carrillo Gil.** The private collection here contains early murals by Orozco (with 50 works, this is one of the best Orozco collections you'll find anywhere), Rivera, and Siqueiros and works by modern European artists such as Klee and Picasso; with its temporary

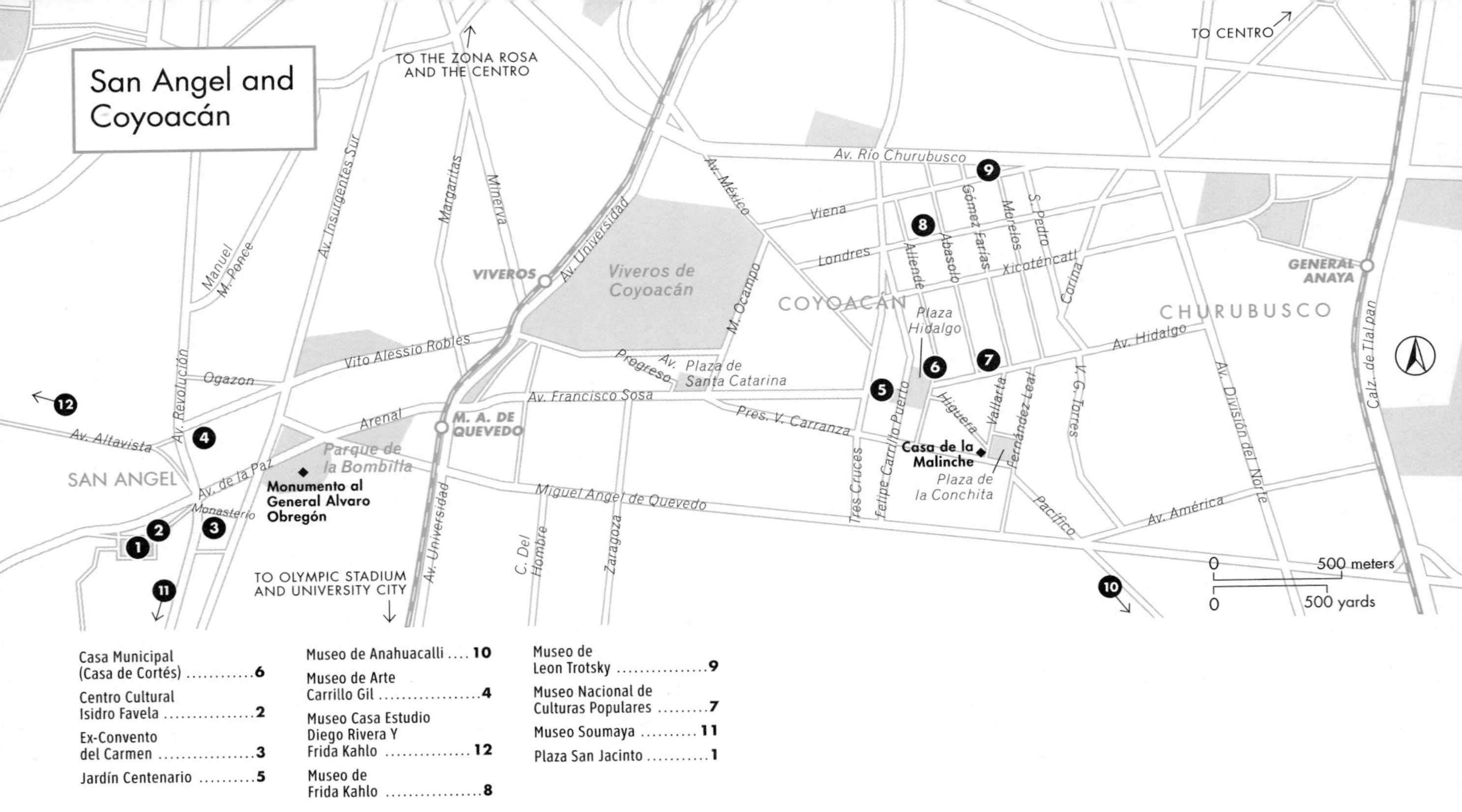

San Angel and Coyoacán
TO THE ZONA ROSA AND THE CENTRO
TO CENTRO
Av. Río Churubusco
Av. México
Viena
Londres
Allende
Abasolo
Gómez Farías
Morelos
S. Pedro
Xicoténcatl
Corina
GENERAL ANAYA
CHURUBUSCO
COYOACÁN
Plaza Hidalgo
Av. Hidalgo
Calz. de Tlalpan
Av. Universidad
VIVEROS
Viveros de Coyoacán
M. Ocampo
Manuel M. Ponce
Av. Insurgentes Sur
Margaritas
Minerva
Vito Alessio Robles
Ogazon
Av. Revolución
Av. Progreso
Plaza de Santa Catarina
Av. Francisco Sosa
Pres. V. Carranza
Tres Cruces
Felipe Carrillo Puerto
Higuera
Vallarta
Fernández Leal
V. G. Torres
Av. División del Norte
Casa de la Malinche
Plaza de la Conchita
Pacífico
Av. América
M. A. DE QUEVEDO
Arenal
Parque de la Bombilla
Av. Altavista
SAN ANGEL
Av. de la Paz
Monasterio
Monumento al General Alvaro Obregón
Miguel Angel de Quevedo
TO OLYMPIC STADIUM AND UNIVERSITY CITY
Av. Universidad
C. Del Hombre
Zaragoza
0 500 meters
0 500 yards
Casa Municipal (Casa de Cortés) 6
Centro Cultural Isidro Favela 2
Ex-Convento del Carmen 3
Jardín Centenario 5
Museo de Anahuacalli 10
Museo de Arte Carrillo Gil 4
Museo Casa Estudio Diego Rivera Y Frida Kahlo 12
Museo de Frida Kahlo 8
Museo de Leon Trotsky 9
Museo Nacional de Culturas Populares 7
Museo Soumaya 11
Plaza San Jacinto 1

exhibitions of contemporary international artists it's often considered the most important contemporary-art center in the city. It's a good place to learn about vanguard art. ■TIP→**This museum is considerably superior in terms of design and natural lighting to the city's better-known Museo Nacional de Arte Moderno.** ✉*Av. Revolución 1608, at Av. Altavista, San Angel* ☎*55/5550–1254 or 55/5550–6260* ⊕*www.macg.inba.gob.mx* 🎟*$1.50, free Sun.* ⏲*Tues.–Sun. 10–6* Ⓜ*M. A. de Quevedo.*

⇨ **Museo Casa Estudio Diego Rivera y Frida Kahlo,** see Frida & Diego.

WORD OF MOUTH

"Walking in the Paseo de la Reforma, I felt almost transported to Paris, except that this boulevard was lined with palms and ornate Nativity scenes. What with the blue skies overhead, the grandeur of the boulevard, and my general comfort level, I felt almost angry at the widespread preconception of 'crime and pollution,' which are the only words some people had to say when I told them I was going to Mexico City."

–Daniel Williams

❶ ★ **Plaza San Jacinto.** This welcoming plaza with a grisly history constitutes the heart of San Angel. In 1847 about 50 Irish soldiers of St. Patrick's Battalion, who had sided with the Mexicans in the Mexican-American War, had their foreheads branded here with the letter *D*—for deserter—and were then hanged by the Americans in this plaza. These men had been enticed to swim the Río Grande, deserting the ranks of U.S. General Zachary Taylor, by appeals to the historic and religious ties between Spain and Ireland. As settlers in Mexican Texas, they felt their allegiance lay with Catholic Mexico, and they were among the bravest fighters in the war. A memorial plaque (on a building on the plaza's west side) lists their names and expresses Mexico's gratitude for their help in the "unjust North American invasion." Off to one side of the plaza the excellent arts-and-crafts market **Bazar Sábado** is held all day Saturday. ✉*Bounded by Miramon, Cda. Santisima, Dr. Galvez, and Calle Madero, San Angel* Ⓜ*M. A. de Quevedo.*

❺ **Jardín Centenario.** The Centenary Gardens are barely separated from the **Plaza Hidalgo** by a narrow slow-moving road; both squares are referred to as Coyoacán's zócalo. The Jardín, with its shading trees, a fountain with two snarling coyotes, and a fringe of outdoor cafés, is the place to sit and people-watch. On weekends from 11 AM until about 10 PM it morphs into a lively, hippie-ish handicrafts market, complete with drummers and palm readings. The larger Plaza Hidalgo hosts children's funfairs, amateur musical and dance performances, clowns, bubble blowers, cotton candy, and balloon sellers on weekends and national holidays. It's studded with an ornate old bandstand and the impressive **Templo de San Juan Bautista,** one of the first churches to be built in New Spain. It was completed in 1582, and its door has a baroque arch. On the afternoon of September 15, before the crowds become suffocating at nightfall, this delightful neighborhood zócalo is probably the best place in the capital to enjoy Independence Day celebrations. ✉ *Bounded by Calle Centenario, Av. Hidalgo, and Caballo Calco, Coyoacán* Ⓜ *Viveros.*

NEED A BREAK?

About a block away from the Jardín Centenario and the Jardín Hidalgo, El Jarocho Cafe (✉ ***Cuauhtémoc 134, at Allende, Coyoacán*** ☎ ***55/5658–5029 or 55/5554–5418*** ✉ ***Av. México 25-C, at Guerrero, Coyoacán*** ✉ ***Centenario 91-B, between Xicotencatl and Malintzin, Coyoacán*** 🌐 ***www.cafeeljarocho.com.mx*****)is a great place to grab a coffee. The Cuauhtémoc branch has been on this corner since 1957, originally selling coffee, mangos, and other produce from Veracruz (in Mexico, *jarocho* means "native of Veracruz"). In recent years demand has grown for this excellent coffee, and this corner has become a favorite spot for locals to get their caffeine fix and as a front-row people-watching seat. If you're lucky enough to find a space on the outside benches on weekends, it's a good place to watch the hip Coyoacán crowd and the vendors who set up shop here, selling jewelry and art crafts in makeshift stands on the street and on the top of their cars. With the success of the original locale, there are now a few other branches, but the original is still the most popular—and the best place to get a feel for Coyoacán.**

⇨★ ❽ **Museo de Frida Kahlo,** *see Frida & Diego.*

IF YOU HAVE TIME

❻ **Casa Municipal (Casa de Cortés).** The place where the Aztec emperor Cuauhtémoc was held prisoner by Cortés is reputed to have been rebuilt in the 18th century from the stones of his original house. Now a sandy color and topped by two coyote figures, it's used for municipal government offices; a small tourist bureau at the entrance offers maps and leaflets publicizing cultural events in the area. Usually you can wander through the wide arches to the pretty tile patio. ✉ *Plaza Hidalgo 1 between Calles Carillo Puerto and Allende, Coyoacán* ☎ *55/5658–0221* ⏲ *Daily 8–8.* Ⓜ *Viveros, then take a taxi.*

❷ **Centro Cultural Isidro Favela.** This 1681 mansion is one of the prettiest houses facing the Plaza San Jacinto. A huge free-form fountain sculpture—exploding with colorful porcelain, tiles, shells, and mosaics—covers the eastern wall of its patio. Although it's not ranked among the city's top museums, it has a splendid collection of 17th- and 18th-century European and colonial Mexican paintings, all donated by the house's last owner, Isidro Favela. Favela also donated

LA MALINCHE

Two blocks east of Plaza Hidalgo on Calle Higuera at Vallarta is a somber-looking residence called Casa de la Malinche. It was the home of La Malinche, Cortés' Indian mistress and interpreter. She aided the conquest by enabling Cortés to communicate with the Nahuatl-speaking tribes he met en route to Tenochtitlán. Today she is a reviled symbol of a traitorous xenophile—hence the term *malinchista,* used to describe a Mexican who prefers things foreign. Legend says that Cortés' wife died in this house, poisoned by the conquistador, and that it's bad luck just to walk by.

CLOSE UP

Mexico City Background

Mexico City is a city of superlatives. It is both the oldest (founded in 1325) and the highest (7,350 feet) metropolis on the North American continent. And with an estimated 22 million inhabitants it's the most populous city in the western hemisphere.

As the gargantuan pyramids of Teotihuacán attest, the area around Mexico City was occupied from early times by a great civilization, probably Nahuatl in origin. The founding farther south of the Aztec capital, Tenochtitlán, did not occur until more than 600 years after Teotihuacán was abandoned, around AD 750. Between these periods, from 900 to 1200, the Toltec Empire controlled the valley of Mexico. As the story goes, the nomadic Aztecs were searching for a promised land in which to settle. Their prophecies announced that they would recognize the spot when they encountered an eagle perched on a prickly pear cactus and holding a snake in its beak. In 1325, the disputed date of Tenochtitlán's founding, they discovered this eagle in the valley of Mexico, the image of which is now emblazoned on the national flag. They settled on what was then an island in shallow Lake Texcoco and connected it to lakeshore satellite towns by a network of *calzadas* (canals and causeways, now freeways). Even then it was the largest city in the western hemisphere and, according to historians, one of the three largest cities on Earth. When he first laid eyes on Tenochtitlán in the early 16th century, Spanish conquistador Hernán Cortés was dazzled by the glistening lacustrine metropolis, which reminded him of Venice.

A combination of factors made the Spanish conquest possible. Aztec emperor Moctezuma II believed the white, bearded Cortés on horseback to be the mighty plumed serpent-god Quetzalcóatl, who, according to prophecy, was supposed to arrive from the east in the year 1519 to rule the land. Thus, Moctezuma welcomed the foreigner with gifts of gold and palatial accommodations. In return, Cortés initiated a massacre. He was backed by a huge army of Indians from other settlements such as Cholula and Tlaxcala, who saw a chance to end their submission to the Aztec empire. With these forces, the European tactical advantages of horses, firearms, and, inadvertently, the introduction of smallpox and the common cold, Cortés succeeded in erasing Tenochtitlán only two centuries after it was founded.

Cortés began building the capital of what he patriotically dubbed New Spain, the Spanish empire's colony that would spread north to cover what is now the southwestern United States, and south to Panama. *Mexico* comes from *Mexica* (pronounced meh-shee-ka), which was the Aztecs' name for themselves. (Aztec is the Spaniards' name for the Mexica.) At the site of Tenochtitlán's demolished ceremonial center—now the 10-acre Zócalo—Cortés started building a church (the precursor of the impressive Metropolitan Cathedral), mansions, and government buildings. He utilized the slave labor—and the artistry—of the vanquished native Mexicans. On top of the ruins of their city, and using rubble from it, they were forced to build what became the most European-style city in North America. But instead of having the random layout of contemporary medieval cities, it followed the grid pattern of the Aztecs. For much of the construction material the Spaniards quarried the local porous, volcanic reddish stone called *tezontle*. The Spaniards also drained the lakes, preferring wheels and horses (which they introduced to Mexico) over canals and canoes for transport. The land-filled lake bed turned out to be a soggy support for the immense buildings that have been slowly sinking into it since they were built.

The city flourished during the colonial period, filling what is now its historic center with architectural treasures. The Franciscans and Dominicans eagerly set about converting the Aztecs to Christianity, but some indigenous customs persisted. Street vending, for instance, is a city signature even today. It is said that the conquering soldiers looked out on them in 1520 and said they had never seen such a market, not even in Rome. In 1571 the Spaniards established the Inquisition in New Spain and burned heretics at its palace headquarters, now a museum in Plaza de Santo Domingo.

It took almost three centuries for Mexicans to rise up successfully against Spain. The historic downtown street 16 de Septiembre commemorates the "declaration" of Independence. On that date in 1810, Miguel Hidalgo, father of the Catholic Church—and of a couple of illegitimate daughters—rang a church bell and cried out his history-making *grito* (shout): "Death to the *gachupines* [wealthy Spaniards living in Mexico]! Long live the Virgin of Guadalupe!" Excommunicated and executed the following year, Hidalgo is one of many independence heroes who fostered a truly popular movement, culminating in Mexico's independence in 1821. The liberty bell that now hangs above the main entrance to the National Palace is rung on every eve of September 16 by the president of the republic, who then shouts a revised version of the patriot's cry: "¡Viva México!"

Flying in or out of Mexico City you get an aerial view of the remaining part of Lake Texcoco on the eastern outskirts of the city. In daylight you'll notice the sprawling flatness of the 1,480-square-km (570-square-mi) Meseta de Anáhuac (Valley of Mexico), completely surrounded by mountains. On its southeastern side, two usually snowcapped volcanoes, Popocatépetl and Iztaccíhuatl, are both well over 17,000 feet high. After a period of relative tranquillity, Popocatépetl, known as El Popo, awoke and began spewing smoke, ash, and some lava in the mid-1990s; it has remained intermittently active since then.

Unfortunately, the single most widely known fact about Mexico City is that its air is polluted. There's no denying the smog and nightmarish traffic, but strict legislation in recent years has led to cleaner air and, especially after the summer rains, the city has some of the clearest, bluest skies anywhere.

If the city's notoriety for smog brings Los Angeles to mind, so might the fault line that runs through the valley. In 1985 a major earthquake—8.1 on the Richter scale—took a tragic toll. The government reported 10,000 deaths, but locally it's said to be closer to 50,000. The last traces of that quake's damage have disappeared with the major renovation project in the capital's historic center, an overhaul that includes the application of the latest earthquake-resistant technology.

books and magazines to a small library behind the museum (by way of a beautiful open patio) that is open to the public. Temporary art exhibitions also rotate through. ✉*Plaza San Jacinto 15, San Angel* ☎*55/5616–2711* 🎫*Free* 🕐*Tues.–Sun. 10–5* Ⓜ*M. A. de Quevedo.*

❸ **Ex-Convento del Carmen.** Erected by Carmelite friars with the help of an Indian chieftain between 1615 and 1628, this church, with its domes, fountains, and gardens, was never actually a convent, despite its name. Though some locals might tell you otherwise, nuns never actually lived here. It is one of the most interesting examples of colonial religious architecture in this part of the city, and it has always been an important place for meeting and socializing. The church still operates, but part of it has been converted to **Museo Regional del Carmen,** with a fine collection of 16th- to 18th-century religious paintings and icons. Another museum area, the well-designed **Novohispana,** illustrates life in New Spain with work by early colonial artisans and trade guilds. This exhibit has a separate entrance at the back. It's also worth visiting the 12 mummified corpses tucked away in the crypt. ✉*Av. Revolución 4, at Monasterio, San Angel* ☎*55/5616–2816 or 55/5616–1177* 🎫*$3.20, free Sun.* 🕐*Tues.–Sun. 10–5* Ⓜ*M. A. de Quevedo.*

⇨ ❿ **Museo del Anahuacalli** *see Frida & Diego.*

㉝ **Museo de Leon Trotsky.** Resembling an anonymous and forbidding fortress, with turrets for armed guards, this house is where Leon Trotsky lived and was murdered. It's difficult to believe that it's the final resting place for the ashes of one of the most important figures of the Russian Revolution, but that only adds to the allure of this austere dwelling, which is owned by Trotsky's grandson. Anyone taller than 5 feet must stoop to pass through doorways to Trotsky's bedroom—with bullet holes still in the walls from the first assassination attempt, in which the muralist Siqueiros was implicated—his wife's study, the dining room, and the study where assassin Ramón Mercader—a man of many aliases—allegedly drove a pickax into Trotsky's head. On his desk, cluttered with writing paraphernalia and an article he was revising in Russian, the calendar is open to that fateful day, August 20, 1940. All informative materials are in Spanish only. ✉*Río Churubusco 410, Coyoacán* ☎*55/5658–8732* 🎫*$3* 🕐*Tues.–Sun. 10–5* Ⓜ*Viveros.*

❼ **Museo Nacional de Culturas Populares.** A huge *arbol de la vida* (tree of life) sculpture stands in the courtyard of this museum devoted to popular culture and regional arts and crafts. Its exhibitions and events are nicely varied, including children's workshops, traditional musical concerts, and dance performances. On weekends the courtyard becomes a small crafts and sweets market with some worthwhile exhibitors displaying their wares from all over the country. The museum shop stocks art books and high-quality crafts. ✉*Av. Hidalgo 289, at Calle Allende, Coyoacán* ☎*55/9172–8840* 🎫*Free* 🕐*Tues.–Thurs. 10–6, Fri.–Sun. 10–8* Ⓜ*Viveros.*

⓫ **Museo Soumaya.** This small private museum is owned by the Slim family, who own a great number of businesses, including Sanborns and Telmex. The museum has four rooms, each with a distinct theme. The first has an exhibit of 18th- and 19th-century Mexican portraiture, the second the art of New Spain, including 18th-century ironwork. The Julián Slim Gallery has more than 100 sculptures by Auguste Rodin in marble, bronze, terra-cotta, and plaster. The last room displays a collection of works from such painters as Pierre Renoir, Camille Claudelle, and Paul Gauguin. The entrance and exit halls feature 1954 murals by Rufino Tamayo. Note that there are big plans in the works for this small museum. A new, ultramodern building has been designed by the Laboratory of Architecture, and is currently under construction. In 2009 the Soumaya collection will be housed in the Polanco neighborhood. Stay tuned for news! ✉ *Av. Revolución at Rio Magdalena, Eje 10 Sur, San Angel* ☎ *55/5616–3731 or 55/5616–6620* 🌐 *www.museosoumaya.com* 🎟 *$1, free Sun. and Mon.* ⏲ *Sun., Mon., and Wed.–Fri. 10:30–6:30, Sat. 10:30–10:30.* Ⓜ *No stop nearby.*

OUTSKIRTS OF MEXICO CITY

As the capital continues to expand, many attractions that used to be side trips are becoming more accessible. To the north of Mexico City stands the Basílica de Guadalupe, a church dedicated to Mexico's patron saint. It can be enjoyed in a half-day tour; if you get an early start, you could combine your visit with a jaunt to the pyramids of Teotihuacán in the afternoon. Xochimilco (pronounced kso-chee-*meel*-co), famous for its floating gardens, lies on the southern outskirts of the city. You can ride in gondolalike boats and get a fleeting sense of a pre-Hispanic Mexico City. The western extremes of the capital offer the popular Parque Nacional Desierto de los Leones—a forested national park with a Carmelite monastery in its center.

EXPLORING

MAIN ATTRACTIONS

La Villa de Guadalupe. "La Villa"—the local moniker of the site of the two basilicas of the Virgin of Guadalupe, north of the Zócalo—is Mexico's holiest shrine. Its importance derives from the miracle that the devout believe occurred here on December 12, 1531: an Aztec named Juan Diego received from the Virgin a cloak permanently imprinted with her image so he could prove to the priests that he had had a holy vision. Although the story of the miracle and the cloak itself has been challenged for centuries, it is hotly defended by clergy and laity alike. As author Gary Wills observed, the story's "authority just grows as its authenticity diminishes." Every December 12, millions of pilgrims arrive, many crawling on their knees for the last few hundred yards, praying for divine favors. Outside the **Antigua Basílica** stands a statue of Juan Diego, who became the first indigenous saint in the Americas with his canonization in 2002. The canonization of Juan Diego was wildly popular among Mexican Catholics, although a vocal minority of critics (both in and out of the Church) argued that, despite the Church's extensive investigation, the validity of Juan Diego's existence is suspect. Many critics see the canonization of this polarizing figure as a strategic move by the Church to retain its position among Mexico's indigenous population. The old basilica dates from 1536; various additions have been made since then. The altar was executed by sculptor Manuel Tolsá. The basilica now houses a museum of ex-votos (hand-painted depictions of miracles, dedicated to Mary or a saint in gratitude) and popular religious, decorative, and applied arts from the 15th through 18th centuries.

Because the structure of the Antigua Basílica had weakened over the years and the building was no longer large enough or safe enough to accommodate all the worshippers, Pedro Ramírez Vázquez, the architect responsible for Mexico City's splendid Museo Nacional de Antropología, was commissioned to design a new shrine, which was consecrated in 1976. In this case, alas, the architect's inspiration failed him: the **Nueva Basílica** is a gigantic, circular mass of wood, steel, and polyethylene that feels like a stadium rather than a church. The famous image of the Virgin is encased high up in its altar at the back and can be viewed from a moving sidewalk that passes below. The holiday itself is a great time to visit if you don't mind crowds; it's celebrated with various kinds of music and dancers. Remember to bring some water with you; you'll need it in the crush.

A PLEASANT PLAZA

If you're taking a sitio taxi from San Angel, have it drop you at Plaza de Santa Catarina on Avenida Francisco Sosa. The pretty 16th-century Iglesia de Santa Catarina dominates this tiny plaza. Across the street is the Casa de Jesús Reyes Heroles—the former home of the ex-minister of education is a fine example of 20th-century architecture on the colonial model. It's now used as a cultural center. Continue east on Francisco Sosa and you'll pass Casa de Diego de Ordaz at the corner of Tres Cruces. This *mudéjar* (Spanish-Arabic) structure was the home of a former captain.

You can reach **La Villa de Guadalupe** by taking the No. 3 metro line from downtown to Deportivo 18 de Marzo. Here, change to line No. 6 in the direction Martin Carrera, getting off at the Villa–Basílica stop. ✉ *Paseo Zumarraga, Atrio de América, Col. Villa de Guadalupe* ☎ *55/5577–3654* ⏲ *Daily* 6 AM–9 PM.

⇨ ★ **Museo Dolores Olmeda Patino,** *see Frida & Diego.*

Xochimilco. When the first nomadic settlers arrived in the Valley of Mexico, now *21 km (13 mi) south of Mexico City center,* they found an enormous lake. As the years went by and their population grew, the land could no longer satisfy their agricultural needs. They solved the problem by devising a system of *chinampas* (floating gardens), rectangular structures akin to barges, which they filled with reeds, branches, and mud. They planted the barges with willows, whose roots anchored the floating gardens to the lake bed, making a labyrinth of small islands and canals on which vendors carried flowers and produce grown on the chinampas to market.

Today Xochimilco is the only place in Mexico where the gardens still exist. Go on a Saturday, when the *tianguis* (market stalls) are most active, or, though it's crowded, on a Sunday. On weekdays the place is practically deserted, so it loses some of its charm. Hire a *trajinera* (flower-painted boat); an arch over each spells out its name in flowers. As you sail through the canals you'll pass mariachis and women selling tacos from other trajineras.

For **Xochimilco** take metro line No. 2 to Tasqueña; here hop on the *tren ligero* (light rail) that continues south to Xochimilco. Expect a bit of a free-for-all outside the station, as several guides—often on bicycles—will be waiting to direct tourists to the gardens. Official tour guides, employed by the government, wear identifying tags; any other guides offering to take people to the gardens take them to a specific *trajinera* rental business that pays them for bringing in clients. You can cast your lot with a guide (official or not) or catch any bus marked Xochimilco; buses usually pick up passengers right outside the train station. To walk to the nearest trajinera *embarcadero* (dock), head down Cuauhtémoc for three blocks, then make a left on Violeta. Continue on Violeta for two blocks (you'll see signs pointing toward "Belen," the embarcadero), and turn right off Violeta at Nezahualcóyotl. Alternatively, you could take a sitio taxi (up to $35). The trip should take between 45 minutes and one hour from the downtown area, depending on traffic.

IF YOU HAVE TIME

Parque Nacional Desierto de los Leones. The "Desert of Lions," 25 km (16 mi) west of Mexico City's center owes its name to a quarrel in colonial days over land ownership by brothers called "León." Several walking trails crisscross this 5,000-acre national park's pine forest at 7,511 feet above sea level. Pack a lunch and enjoy it at one of the picnic tables. The park's focal point is the ruined 17th-century **ex-monastery of the Carmelites,** isolated amid an abundance of greenery; it's open Tuesday through Sunday from 9 to 5 and entrance costs a dollar. Although a few restaurants dot the park entrance, the restaurants near the ex-monastery are better bets. Stores selling candies, backpacks, and baseball caps are nearby. On weekends, which are more crowded with families, you can ride horses. The park played a significant role in the War of Independence: in late October 1810, at a spot called **Las Cruces,** Father Hidalgo's troops trounced the Spaniards but resolved not to go on to attack Mexico City, an error that cost the insurgents 10 more years of fighting.

For **Parque Nacional Desierto de los Leones,** follow Paseo de la Reforma all the way west. It eventually merges with the Carretera Libre at Toluca, and after 20 km (12 mi) you'll see signs for the turnoff; it's another 10 km (six mi) to the park. You can also take a sitio taxi to the park; simply ask to be dropped off in the Desierto de los Leones.

MEXICO CITY'S MODERN-DESIGN MAKER

Casa Luis Barragán. As you travel through the capital, it would be nearly impossible to note all of the architectural styles, since there are just too many. Bold colors, lines, and innovative designs decorate just about everywhere you look. If you are interested in learning more about these modern-architecture nuances, visit the home of architect Luis Barragán. Yes, this museum is far from the typical tourist routes, but if you have a little extra time to spend in the city, this is a good way to do it. Barragán was an influential modernist architect on a world scale, and certainly one of the most influential architects in Mexico in the last century. This house, designated by UNESCO as a World Heritage Center, is quite an accomplishment in itself, but Barragán was also involved in much larger-scale projects that shaped the city you see today. He was instrumental in the design of the Pedregal neighborhood, in the south of the city, and Ciudad Satélite, just north of the capital. It is imperative that you call ahead, since guided tours through the museum are required. Tours are available in English; mention that you'll need English when you call, so they'll be prepared for you. ✉ *General Francisco Ramírez 14, Col. Daniel Garza* ☎ *55/5515–4908* ⏲ *Weekdays 10–2 and 4–6, Sat. 10–1.*

WHERE TO EAT

Mexico City has been a culinary capital ever since the time of Moctezuma. Chronicles tell of the extravagant banquets prepared for the Aztec emperor with more than 300 different dishes served. Today's Mexico City is a gastronomic melting pot, with some 15,000 restaurants. You'll find everything from taco stands on the streets to simple, family-style eateries and world-class restaurants. The number and range of international restaurants is growing and diversifying, particularly in middle- and upper-class neighborhoods like Polanco, San Angel, La Condesa, La Roma, Lomas de Chapultepec, and Del Valle. Argentine, Spanish, and Italian are the most dominant international cuisines; however you'll also find a fair share of Japanese, Korean, Arabic, and French restaurants. Mexico City restaurants open 7–11 AM for breakfast (*el desayuno*) and 1–6 for lunch (*la comida*)—although it's rare for Mexicans to eat lunch before 2 and you're likely to feel lonely if you arrive at a popular restaurant before then. Lunch is an institution in this country, often lasting two hours, and until nightfall on Sunday. Consequently, the evening meal (*la cena*) may often be very light, consisting of sweet bread and coffee, traditional tamales and atole at home, or tacos and appetizers in a restaurant.

When dining, most locals start out at 9 PM for dinner; restaurants stay open until 11:30 during the week and a little later on weekends. Many restaurants are open only for lunch on Sunday. At deluxe restaurants dress is generally formal (jacket at least), and reservations are recommended; see reviews for details. If you're short on time, you can always head to American-style coffee shops or recognizable fast-food chains that offer the tired but reliable fare of burgers, fried chicken, and pizza all over the city. If it's local flavor you're after, go with tacos or the Mexico City fast-food staple, the *torta* (a giant sandwich stacked with the ingredients of your choice for about $2). Eating on the street is part of the daily experience for those on the go, and surprising as it may seem, many people argue that it's some of the best food in the city. Still, even locals can't avoid the occasional stomach illness, so dig in at your own risk.

Also cheap and less of a bacterial hazard are the popular *fondas* (small restaurants). At lunchtime fondas are always packed, as they serve a reasonably priced four-course meal, known as the *comida corrida,* which typically includes soup of the day, rice or pasta, an entrée, and dessert. Asian cuisine is still limited here, but you'll find some decent Japanese, Korean, and Chinese restaurants. There are very few vegetarian restaurants, but you'll have no trouble finding nonmeat dishes wherever you grab a bite. Vegetarians, however, will have a more difficult time, as many dishes are often prepared using lard.

Colonia Polanco, the upscale neighborhood on the edge of the Bosque de Chapultepec, has some of the best and most expensive dining (and lodging) in the city. Zona Rosa restaurants get filled quickly on Saturday night, especially on Saturdays coinciding with most people's paydays: the 1st and 15th of each month. The same is true of San Angel, whereas the Condesa and Roma neighborhoods buzz with a younger crowd Thursday to Saturday.

CENTRO HISTÓRICO

$$$$ MEXICAN ✕**El Cardenal.** In the ground floor of the Centro Histórico Sheraton across Juárez from the elegant Alameda, this upscale venue concentrates on food over atmosphere (you could be in any luxury hotel in any city), and how. Representing a wide array of local Mexican cuisines, the chef nevertheless winds up concentrating on Oaxacan, the most elaborate. Their moles—*colorado, rojo,* and *almendrado* (almond)—are famous all over the city. ✉*Juárez 70, Col. Centro* ☎*55/1866–3332* ▭*AE, MC, V.*

$$$–$$$$ MEXICAN ★ ✕**Hostería de Santo Domingo.** This genteel institution near downtown's Plaza Santo Domingo has been serving colonial dishes in an atmospheric town house since the late 19th century. Feast on stuffed cactus paddles, thousand-flower soup, pot roast, and the house specialty, *chiles en nogada* (stuffed poblano chile peppers bathed in walnut sauce). Among some of the best homemade Mexican desserts in town are the flan and rice pudding. The place is open for breakfast and is always full at lunch; it closes at 10 PM. ✉*Belisario Dominguez 72, Col. Centro* ☎*55/5510–1434 or 55/5526–5276* ▭*AE, MC, V.*

$$–$$$ MIDDLE EASTERN ✕**Al Andalus.** Lebanese restaurant Al Andalus, in a magnificent 16th-century colonial building downtown, makes some of the best Arabic food in the capital. If the extensive menu seems overwhelming, order the *mesa libanesa,* a mixed platter with everything from hummus and

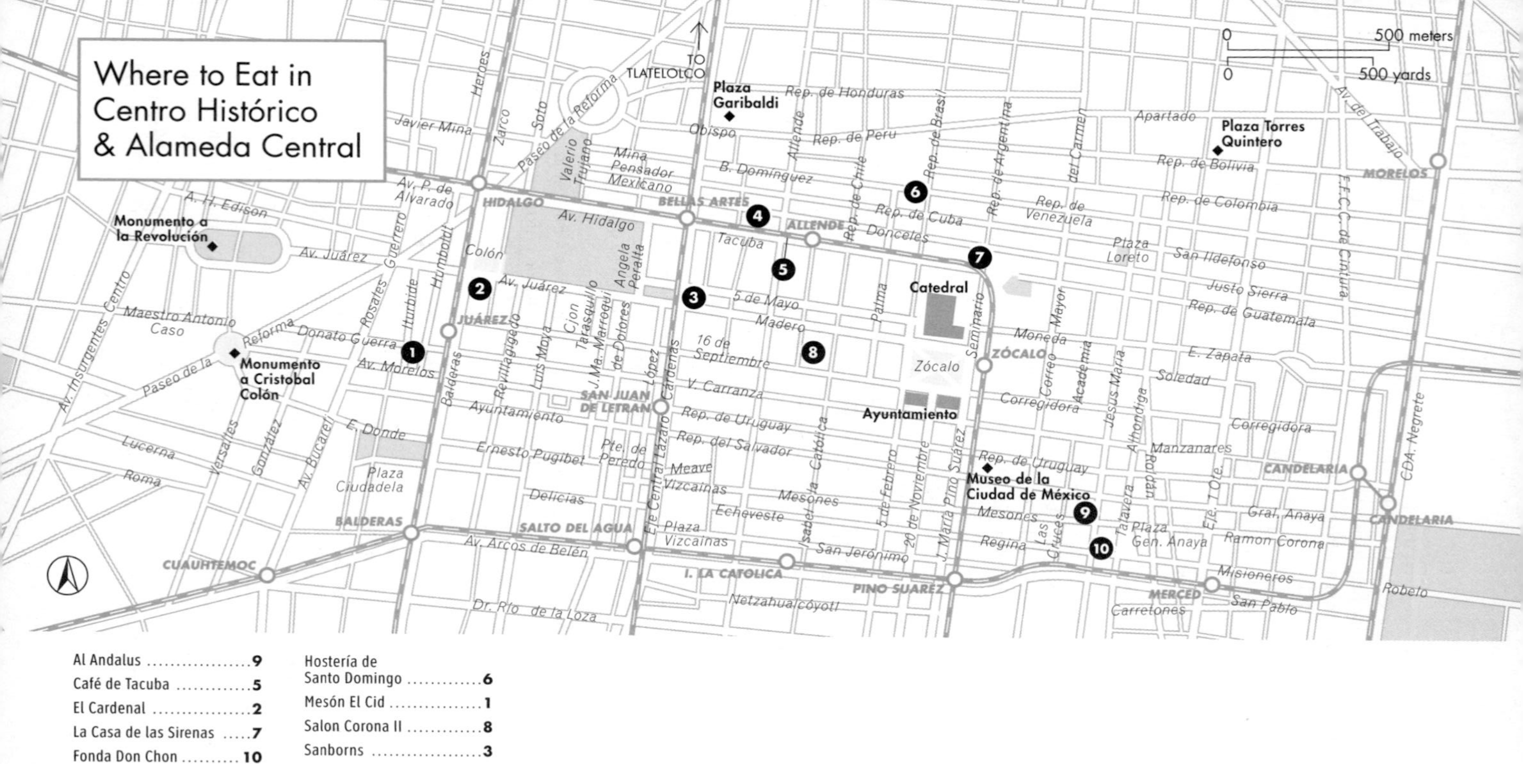

Al Andalus 9
Café de Tacuba 5
El Cardenal 2
La Casa de las Sirenas 7
Fonda Don Chon 10
Los Girasoles 4
Hostería de Santo Domingo 6
Mesón El Cid 1
Salon Corona II 8
Sanborns 3

kebbeh to lamb shwarmas. ✉*Mesones 171, at Cruces, Col. Centro* ☎*55/5522–2528* ▭*AE, MC, V.*

$$–$$$ MEXICAN ✕**Café de Tacuba.** An essential breakfast, lunch, dinner, or snack stop downtown, this Mexican classic has been rewarding the hungry since it opened in 1912 in a section of an old convent. At the entrance to the main dining room are huge 18th-century oil paintings depicting the invention of *mole poblano,* a complex sauce with a variety of chiles and chocolate that was created by the nuns in the Santa Rosa Convent of Puebla. A student group dressed in medieval capes and hats serenades clients Wednesday through Sunday from 3 to 11. ✉*Calle Tacuba 28, at Allende, Col. Centro* ☎*55/5518–4950* ▭*AE, MC, V.*

$$–$$$ MEXICAN ✕**Fonda Don Chon.** This unpretentious family-style restaurant, deep in a downtown working-class neighborhood, is famed for its pre-Hispanic Mexican dishes. A knowledge of zoology, Spanish, and Nahuatl helps in making sense of a menu that includes ingredients from throughout the republic. *Escamoles de hormiga* (red-ant roe) is known as the "caviar of Mexico" for its costliness, but you may have to acquire a taste for it. Among the exotic dishes are armadillo in mango sauce and fillet of wild boar. ✉*Regina 160, near La Merced market, Col. Centro* ☎*55/5542–0873* ▭*No credit cards* ⏲*Closed Sun. No dinner.*

$$–$$$ SPANISH ✕**Mesón El Cid.** This charming *mesón* (tavern) exudes Old Spain with Spanish stained-glass windows and a roaring fireplace. Weekdays, classic dishes such as paella, spring lamb, suckling pig, and Cornish hens with truffles keep customers happy, but on Saturday night this place comes into its own with a four-course medieval banquet, including a procession of costumed waiters carrying huge trays of steaming hot viands for $30 per person. Further entertainment is provided by a student singing group dressed in medieval Spanish capes and hats, a juggler, and a magician. For dessert, a real winner is the *turrón* (Spanish nougat) ice cream. Reservations are recommended. ✉*Humboldt 61, Col. Centro* ☎*55/5512–7629* ▭*AE, MC, V* ⏲*No dinner Sun. and Mon.*

$$ MEXICAN ✕**La Casa de las Sirenas.** The setting is the calling card here—the 16th-century mansion sits at the foot of the Templo Mayor ruins, stones from which were incorporated into the building. The atmospheric second-floor terrace is within sight and sound of numerous Indian dancers below honoring the spirits of the crumbling Aztec temples. On the menu you'll find eclectic pairings, such as Cornish hen with a mango mole sauce, and a plethora of meat and fish dishes. ✉*República de Guatemala 32, Col. Centro* ☎*55/5704–3225 or 55/5704–3465* ▭*AE, DC, MC, V* ⏲*No dinner Sun.*

$–$$ MEXICAN ✕**Los Girasoles.** Two prominent Mexico City society columnists own this downtown spot. Los Girasoles (which means "sunflowers") is on a lovely old square in a restored three-story colonial home and serves light, tasty, and innovative *nueva cocina mexicana.* There are also pre-Hispanic delicacies such as *escamoles* (ant roe), *gusanos de maguey* (chilied worms), and *mini chapulines* (tiny, crispy fried grasshoppers). It closes at 9 PM on Sunday and Monday. ✉*Plaza Manuel Tolsá on Xicoténcatl 1, Col. Centro* ☎*55/5510–0630* ▭*AE, MC, V* ⏲*Open 1–9 Sun. and Mon.*

$-$$ MEXICAN **Salon Corona II.** The longtime, eponymous popular cervezeria went into the restaurant business last year, with this clean, well-lighted upstairs locale overlooking one of the centro's busiest pedestrian streets. The concept was to take street food indoors, clean it up, and serve it (still cheap) with a beer. (Try the bacalao [salted, dried cod] tacos.) The flat-screen TVs tuned to sports are outsized by the room and so don't dominate the place, and if it is warm outside you can sit in the open air under the retractable roof. ✉*Filomeno Mata 18, Col. Centro* ☎*55/5510–0624* ▭*No credit cards* ⏲*Open 1–12 Mon.-Sat., 1–6 Sun.*

WORD OF MOUTH

"Sanborns is an institution—fun people-watching in a beautiful building."

–Matt G., San Francisco

$ MEXICAN **Sanborns.** The Casa de los Azulejos was among the first of the Sanborns in the country, which now populate every major town in Mexico. Though it's not the best food around, the ever-popular restaurant inside the store is perfect for a quick snack or meal—or just a respite from sightseeing. Burgers, soups, salads, and ice creams for American tastes are just as common on the menu as nonspicy Mexican dishes. Mexicans love to meet friends here for coffee. ✉*Calle Madero 4, at Callejón de la Condesa, Col. Centro* ☎*55/5512–7824* ▭*AE, MC, V.*

ZONA ROSA

$$–$$$ CHINESE **El Dragón.** The former ambassador to China was so impressed by El Dragón's lacquered Beijing duck that he left behind a note of recommendation (now proudly displayed on one of the restaurant's walls) praising it as the most authentic in Mexico. The duck is roasted over a fruitwood fire and later brought to your table, where the waiter cuts it into thin, tender slices. Hailing from the Beijing region, the cooks like to mix it up with sweet and spicy sauces like that used in the delicious, spicy, sesame chicken dish. ✉*Hamburgo 97, between Génova and Copenhague, Zona Rosa* ☎*55/5525–2466* ▭*AE, MC, V.*

$$–$$$ ITALIAN **La Lanterna.** The Petterino family has run this two-story restaurant since 1966. The downstairs has the rustic feel of a northern Italian trattoria, with the cramped seating adding to the intimacy. All pastas are made on the premises; the Bolognese sauce is a favorite. Raw artichoke salad, *conejo en Salmi* (rabbit in a wine sauce), and *filete al burro nero* (steak in black butter) are all tasty dishes, served in a very cosmopolitan setting right on elegant Reforma but away from the main flow of traffic. ✉*Paseo de la Reforma 458, at Toledo, Col. Juárez* ☎*55/5207–9969* ▭*AE, DC, MC, V* ⏲*Closed Sun. and Dec. 25–Jan. 1.*

$$–$$$ SPANISH **Tezka.** This Zona Rosa restaurant specializing in *nueva cocina Basque* was created by the acclaimed chef Arzac, who transposed many of his best dishes to Mexico from his restaurant in San Sebastían, Spain. Feast on yellow tuna in a sweet and spicy sauce, or liver prepared with beer, green pepper, and malt. The starters are exquisite; the *caldo de xipiron* (broth of baby squid) is the best in the city. A decent list of Spanish wines includes Cune, Vina Ardanza, and Reserva 904. ✉*Royal Hotel,*

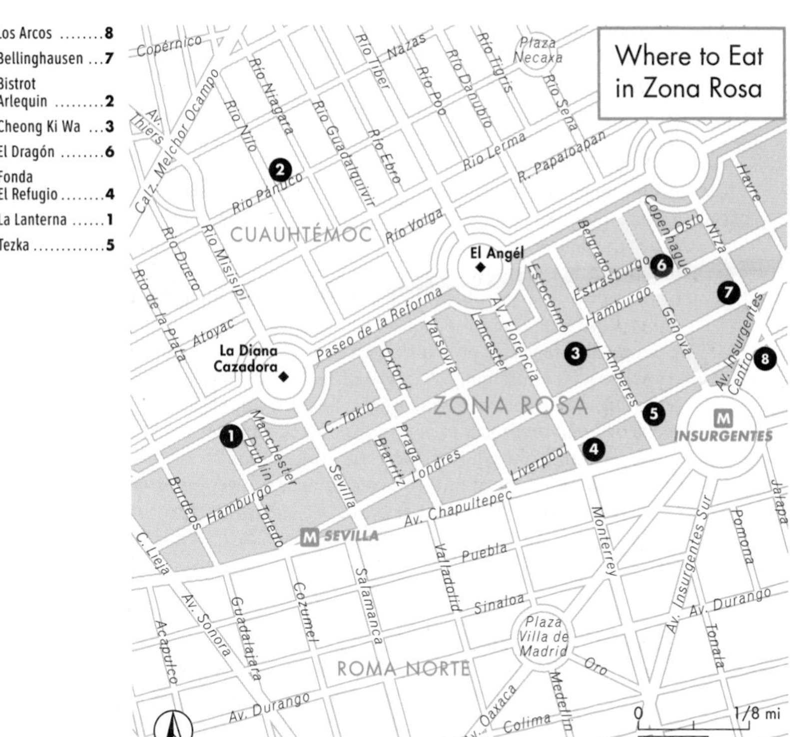

Amberes 78, at Liverpool, Col. Juárez ☎55/9149–3000 Ext. 2250 or 2251 ▭AE, DC, MC, V ⊙Closed Sun. No dinner Sat.

$–$$$ MEXICAN/SEAFOOD ✕ **Los Arcos.** This chain of Pacific Coast–style seafood restaurants has branched out to six states, yet it hasn't compromised on quality. The restaurant's crowning culinary accomplishment is the *corbina a las brasas,* a sweet fish grilled to perfection and seasoned with chipotle, soy sauce, and mustard. For some fish dishes, like the corbina and the pargo, you'll be charged by the kilogram, so don't be surprised if prices vary. ✉*Liverpool 104, at Niza, Zona Rosa* ☎*55/5525–4408* ▭*MC, V.*

$–$$ CONTINENTAL ✕ **Bellinghausen.** This cherished Zona Rosa lunch spot is one of the capital's classics. The partially covered hacienda-style courtyard at the back, set off by an ivy-laden wall, is a midday magnet for executives and tourists. A veritable army of waiters scurries back and forth serving such tried-and-true favorites as *filete chemita* (broiled steak with mashed potatoes). ✉*Londres 95, Zona Rosa* ☎*55/5207–6149* ▭*AE, DC, MC, V* ⊙*No dinner.*

★$–$$ FRENCH ✕ **Bistrot Arlequin.** Here you'll find everything you would expect from a petit bistrot: an intimate setting, comforting food, and excellent French wines. Start off by ordering the house specialty hailing from Lyon, France: fish quenelles in curry sauce with wild rice. A popular main dish is the *carne bourguignonne,* beef cooked in a red wine sauce topped with bacon and mushrooms. If there's room for dessert, try the chocolate mousse. There is no sign—go to the northeast corner of Plaza Juanacatlán and listen for people speaking French. ✉*Rio Nilo 42, at Rio Panuco, Cuauhtémoc, northwest of Zona Rosa* ✣*About 3 blocks from Angel of Independence monument* ☎*55/5207–5616* ▭*MC, V* ⊗*No lunch.*

$–$$ KOREAN ✕ **Cheong Ki Wa.** Of the many Korean restaurants cropping up in the Zona Rosa, this one ranks among the best. Parties of three or more can order the *paquetes,* complete with appetizers, tofu soup, Korean dumplings, and marinated meats, which you cook on a grill in the middle of the table. A word of caution: some dishes are spicy. ✉*Amberes 41, Zona Rosa* ☎*55/5511–6198* ▭*AE, DC, MC, V.*

$–$$ MEXICAN ✕ **Fonda El Refugio.** Expect dishes from each major region of the country when you come here. Along with a varied regular menu, there are tempting daily specials; you might find a mole made with pumpkin seeds or *huachinango a la veracruzana* (red snapper cooked in onions, tomatoes, and olives). Try the refreshing *aguas* (fresh-fruit and seed juices) with your meal and the *café de olla* (clove-flavor coffee sweetened with brown sugar) afterward. ✉*Liverpool 166, at Florencia, Zona Rosa* ☎*55/5207–2732 or 55/5525–8128* ▭*AE, DC, MC, V.*

POLANCO

$$$$ ARGENTINE ✕ **Cambalache.** If you come with friends to this ever-busy beef-lover's dream, try the Super Lomo Cambalache, a steak big enough for three or four people. Or try the Don Ignacio, a boneless chicken breast served in a mushroom sauce with pineapple and fresh sweet peppers. And why not sink your fork into the potato soufflé, a house specialty? ✉*Arquímedes 85, Col. Chapultepec Morales* ☎*55/5280–2080 or 55/5282–2922* ▭*AE, MC, V.*

$$$–$$$$ FRENCH ★ ✕ **Au Pied de Cochon.** Open around the clock inside the Hotel Presidente, this fashionable bistro continues to seduce well-heeled *chilangos* with everything from oysters to oxtail. The roasted leg of pork with béarnaise sauce is the signature dish; the green-apple sorbet with Calvados is a delicate finish. The daily three-course set menu is $23 and includes a glass of house wine; it's served on weekdays from 2 PM to 6 PM. ✉*Campos Elíseos 218, Col. Polanco* ☎*55/5327–7756 or 55/5327–7700* ✍*Reservations essential* ▭*AE, DC, MC, V.*

$$$–$$$$ JAPANESE ✕ **Benkay.** The silk-clad staff includes a sake sommelier in this prestigious restaurant in the Hotel Nikko. *Kaiseki* is the specialty, a series of small, exquisite dishes. Prices are high, but you're getting the best Japanese food in the city. ✉*Campos Elíseos 204, Col. Polanco* ☎*55/5283–8700 Ext. 8600* ▭*AE, DC, MC, V.*

$$$–$$$$ ARGENTINE ✕ **Rincón Argentino.** This established Argentine restaurant is known as much for its decor as for its exquisite cuts of beef. The ceiling is painted to resemble the sky, the bar is covered by a thatch roof, and the dining areas call to mind a stone-and-wood lodge. Most Argentines prefer their beef *bien cocida* (well done), but you can have it any way you like. ✉*Av. Presidente Masarik 177, Col. Polanco* ☎ *55/5254–8775* ▭*AE, MC, V.*

$$$–$$$$ THAI ✕ **Thai Gardens.** Thai artifacts adorn the walls, and a beautiful indoor garden puts even the most stressed-out city slicker at ease. Recommended dishes are the spicy red curry with chicken and the pad thai noodles. If you want to sample a little bit of everything, order the *menú de gustación,* which includes six appetizers, six entrées, and dessert. ✉ *Calderón de la Barca 72, between Emilio Castelar and Av. Presidente Masarik, Col. Polanco Chapultepec* ☎ *55/5281–3850* 💳 *AE, DC, MC, V.*

WORD OF MOUTH

"A sentimental favorite. Hacienda de los Morales is the best restaurant in Mexico. I'm biased, however, since this was the first restaurant I ate in on my first trip to Mexico many years ago. It's perfect in every way: surroundings, food, service. Don't miss it!"

–Lisa, Boca Raton, FL

$$$–$$$$ MEXICAN Fodor's Choice ★ ✕ **La Valentina.** The epitome of good taste in all things Mexican, La Valentina devotes itself to rescuing and promoting traditional native cuisine. It avoids gimmicks with balanced dishes that are soft on the palate, yet fragrant, with blends of chiles, herbs, nuts, and flowers. Starters reflect specialties from across the country, from the Sinaloan Chilorio tacos to the famous *panuchos Yucatecos* (fried tortillas with Yucatán-style spiced chicken or pork). The place is very hard to find, upstairs inside a mall between calles Anatole France and La Fontaine. ✉ *Av. Presidente Masarik 393, Col. Polanco* ☎ *55/5282–2297* 💳 *AE, MC, V.*

$$–$$$$ CHINESE ✕ **Chez Wok.** Above an elegant ladies' boutique on the corner of posh Polanco's Avenida Presidente Masarik and Tennyson, two Chinese chefs trained in Hong Kong prepare an extensive, excellent menu. Start with exotic frogs' legs Mandarin style, served with lychees and shiitake mushrooms and steamed in lotus leaves. Three can share a hot pot of leg of venison with bamboo shoots in oyster sauce. A business crowd generates a lively lunchtime bustle. ✉ *Tennyson 117, Col. Polanco* ☎ *55/5281–3410 or 55/5281–2921* 💳 *AE, MC, V.*

$$–$$$$ MEXICAN ✕ **Hacienda de los Morales.** This Mexican institution, in a former hacienda that dates back to the 16th century, is grandly colonial in style, with dark-wood beams, huge terra-cotta expanses, and dramatic torches. You could start with the delicate walnut soup and follow with one of the chef's highlights, duck in raspberry sauce. The soothing sounds of piano and violin fill the air after 8 PM. A sporty wood-and-brass tequila bar with more than 200 brands is perfect for a predinner cocktail. ✉ *Vázquez de Mella 525, Col. Del Bosque, in Polanco area* ☎ *55/5096–3000 or 55/5096–3054* 💳 *AE, DC, MC, V.*

$$$ MEXICAN ✕ **Los Almendros.** If you can't make it to the Yucatán, try the peninsula's unusual food here. The habañero chiles, red onions, and other native Yucatecan ingredients are a delightful surprise for those not yet in the know. Traditional dishes like a refreshing lime soup share the menu with hard-to-pronounce Mayan cuisine. Especially worth trying is the *pescado tikinxic*—white fish in a mild red marinade of annatto-seed and bitter-orange juice. The branch in Colonia Guadalupe Inn does not serve dinner on Sunday. ✉ *Campos Elíseos 164, Col. Polanco* ☎ *55/5531–6646* ✉ *Av. Insurgentes Sur 1759, Col. Guadalupe Inn* ☎ *55/5663–5151* 💳 *AE, MC, V.*

$$$ MEXICAN ★ **La Fonda del Recuerdo.** This popular fonda has made a name for itself with fish and seafood platters from Veracruz. Sharing their fame is the *torito,* a potent drink made from sugarcane liquor and tropical fruit juices. Every day from 1 to 10, five *jarocho* (Veracruz-style) and mariachi groups provide live entertainment. Between the torito and the music, this place is always full of good cheer. Colonia Veronica Anzures is northwest of the Zona Rosa and east of Polanco. *Bahía de las Palmas 37, Col. Veronica Anzures 55/9112–7476 or 55/9112–7477 AE, MC, V.*

$$–$$$ MEXICAN Fodor'sChoice ★ **Aguila y Sol.** Chef-owner Marta Ortiz Chapa brings considerable experience and creativity to her *nueva cocina mexicana*—she's the author of eight cookbooks on regional Mexican cuisine. Here's your chance to try indigenous produce with a new spin, such as an appetizer of *tortitas de huauzontle* (a green vegetable) with goat cheese, Parmesan, and a *chile pasilla* sauce, or a main course of salmon in a maize crust with clams. Portions are small, so it's a good thing that there's a great dessert selection; we recommend the crème brûlée with a carnation-petal jelly. Also look for traditional drinks such as *flor de jamaica* (hibiscus-flower drink) or, in cold weather, *ponche de manzana* (apple punch). If you are making a return visit, note the recent change of venue. No children under 15 are allowed. *Emilio Castelos 229, Col. Polanco 55/5281–8354 AE, DC, MC, V No dinner Sun.*

$$–$$$ SPANISH **Loyola.** A Basque tour de force, the ample menu with unpronounceable but delicious items includes *kokotxas* (fish cheeks), tapas, black rice simmered in squid ink, oxtail, and many other regional delicacies. Great salads and wines are another welcome feature. Courteous service, stained glass, Basque coats of arms, and the cozy hum of conversation make this an excellent and authentic dining experience. A weekend buffet is $16. *Aristóteles 239, Col. Polanco 55/5250–6756 or 55/5250–9097 AE, MC, V No dinner.*

$–$$$ ECLECTIC **Bistro Charlotte.** You may get addicted to dining at this intimate neighborhood bistro, a tiny spot with only 11 tables. At lunch, regulars flock here for inspired culinary surprises. Most dishes are prepared with French and Mediterranean accents, yet Thai flourishes appear with increasing regularity. You won't go wrong with the risotto and shrimp bathed in white wine and cream sauce. Open daily from noon to 6 PM. *Lope de Vega 341-A, Col. Polanco 55/5250–4180 DC, MC, V.*

$–$$$ MEXICAN ★ **Izote.** A reservation here is one of the hardest to get, as cookbook author Patricia Quintana has won over the capital with her sophisticated take on pre-Hispanic flavors. Even the likes of Hollywood moguls are seeking out seats at this place. Keep an eye out for the unique fish entrées, such as shark fillet sautéed with chile, onion, garlic, and epazote, then steamed in chicken stock and *pulque* (a liquor made from a cactuslike plant). Tender lamb gets steamed as well, in maguey and banana leaves, after being quickly fried with chiles. *Av. Presidente Masarik 513, at Socrates, Col. Polanco 55/5280–1671 Reservations essential AE, DC, MC, V No dinner Sun.*

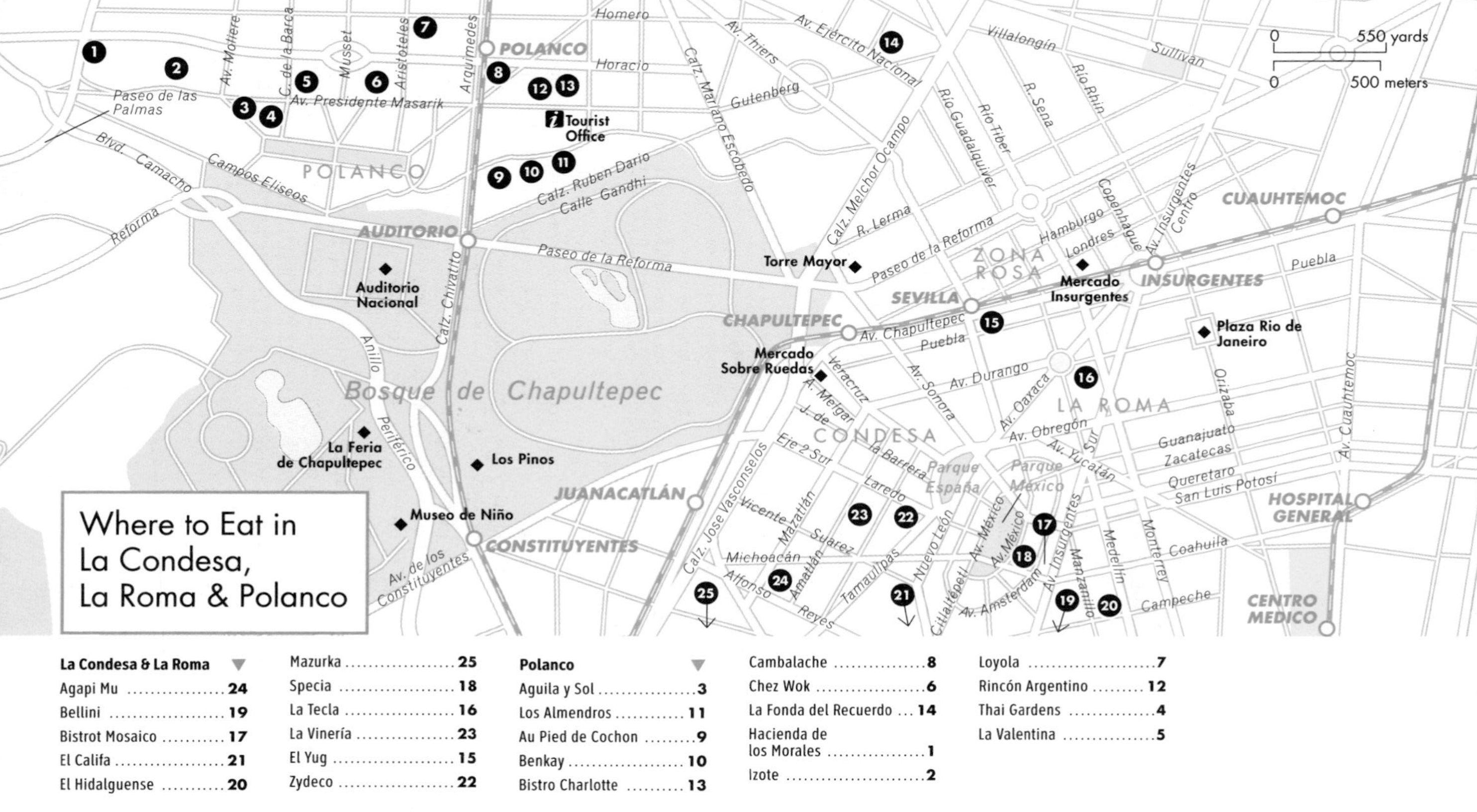

La Condesa & La Roma ▼		Polanco ▼	
Agapi Mu	24	Aguila y Sol	3
Bellini	19	Los Almendros	11
Bistrot Mosaico	17	Au Pied de Cochon	9
El Califa	21	Benkay	10
El Hidalguense	20	Bistro Charlotte	13
Mazurka	25	Cambalache	8
Specia	18	Chez Wok	6
La Tecla	16	La Fonda del Recuerdo	14
La Vinería	23	Hacienda de los Morales	1
El Yug	15	Izote	2
Zydeco	22	Loyola	7
		Rincón Argentino	12
		Thai Gardens	4
		La Valentina	5

LA CONDESA & LA ROMA

$$$$ POLISH Fodor's Choice ★ ✕ **Specia.** One taste of Specia's famous duck and you'll think you've died and gone to heaven—the *pato tin* is a generous portion of roasted duck with an apple-based stuffing, mashed potatoes, and a baked apple bathed in blueberry sauce. Another crowd-pleaser is the mutton goulash, seasoned with paprika and tomato. At lunchtime (between 3 and 5), you'll probably have to wait for a table if you haven't made a reservation. ✉ *Amsterdam 241, at Michoacán, Col. Condesa* ☎ *55/5564–1367* ▭ *AE, MC, V.*

★ $$$$ CONTEMPORARY ✕ **La Vinería.** A welcome addition to La Condesa, this dark, cozy restaurant and wine bar is ideal for a light meal and a sip. Try the *rollos de berenjena* (eggplant rolls) with goat cheese, nuts, and red pepper sauce, or the delicious *hojaldre con hongos* (mushroom pastry). Then indulge in a Chablis, a tasty strudel, or a cigar. ✉ *Av. Fernando Montes de Oca 52-A, at Amatlán, Col. Condesa* ☎ *55/5211–9020* ▭ *AE, MC, V* ⊗ *Closed Sun.*

$$–$$$$ ECLECTIC ✕ **Bellini.** Revolving slowly on the 45th floor of the World Trade Center, Bellini maintains a formal, reserved atmosphere. Any effusiveness will likely be prompted by the spectacular views: romantically twinkling city lights at night and the volcanoes on a clear day. Despite the name, most dishes here aren't Italian but Mexican and international, with lobster as the house specialty. For a real night out on the town, order the Canadian lobster for $100 a pop. Finish in style with a flambéed dessert, such as strawberries jubilee or crêpes suzette. Colonia Napoles is south of La Condesa and La Roma—you'll need to take a sitio (stationed) taxi here. ✉ *Av. de las Naciones 1, World Trade Center, Col. Napoles* ☎ *55/5628–8305* ▭ *AE, DC, MC, V.*

$$$ MEXICAN Fodor's Choice ★ ✕ **El Hidalguense.** This restaurant has mastered the art of preparing Hidalgo-style *barbacoa* (oven-baked mutton slow-cooked over mesquite). The family has been in the barbacoa biz for nearly four decades; its Mexico City restaurant has been going strong for 15 years. Most people order the barbacoa tacos and the consommé. Wash it all down with a potent glass of *pulque* (the fresh, pre-tequila, semi-fermented mulch from the heart of the agave plant). ✉ *Campeche 155, Col. Roma* ☎ *55/5564–0538* ▭ *No credit cards* ⊗ *Closed Mon.–Thurs.*

$$–$$$ POLISH ★ ✕ **Mazurka.** The glowing reputation of this Polish restaurant shone even brighter after people got word that the establishment had prepared food for Pope John Paul II on several of his visits to Mexico City. Settle in with complimentary starters of blini with herring paste and cucumber, dill, and cream salad, as Chopin's polonaises trill and leap in the background. The star of the house is a crispy, oven-baked duck stuffed with bitter apple and blueberries. Or try the juicy, sweet duck and pear with cassis. The generous "Pope's Menu" includes two sets of entrées and is only $23 a head. Colonia Napoles is south of La Condesa and La Roma so the best bet is to take a sitio taxi. ✉ *Nueva York 150, between Calles Texas and Oklahoma, Col. Napoles* ☎ *55/5543–4509 or 55/5523–8811* ▭ *No credit cards* ⊗ *No dinner Sun. and Mon.*

★ $–$$ MEXICAN ✕ **La Tecla.** This see-and-be-seen eatery, with branches in two of the hippest neighborhoods, is a popular veteran of Mexico City's *nueva cocina mexicana* scene. The appetizers are especially intriguing, includ-

CLOSE UP

Cuisine Old & New

The capital may be able to sate your cravings for blini or sushi, but some of the most intriguing dining experiences stem from Mexican chefs looking forward—or far backward. Some newcomers on the restaurant scene are experimenting with established Mexican favorites; others are bringing ancient dishes out of the archives and onto the table.

Until the 15th century, Europeans had never seen indigenous Mexican edibles such as corn, chiles of all varieties, tomatoes, potatoes, pumpkin, squash, avocado, turkey, cocoa, and vanilla. In turn, the colonization brought European gastronomic influence and ingredients—wheat, onions, garlic, olives, citrus fruit, cattle, sheep, goats, chickens, domesticated pigs (and lard for frying)—and ended up broadening the already complex pre-Hispanic cuisine into one of the most multifaceted and exquisite in the world: traditional Mexican.

The last decade has seen the evolution of *nueva cocina mexicana* (nouvelle Mexican cuisine) from a trend to an established and respected restaurant genre. The style emphasizes presentation and intriguing combinations of traditional ingredients and contemporary techniques. In the more serious or purist restaurants that aim to rescue recipes from the pre-Hispanic past, you can enjoy the delicate tastes of regional dishes gleaned from colonial reports, and indigenous cooking techniques such as steaming and baking. And, irrespective of fashion, market eateries offer pre-Hispanic seasonal delicacies such as crunchy fried grasshoppers and fried *maguey* larva.

ing squash flowers stuffed with goat cheese in a chipotle sauce, and a spicy crab-stuffed chile. ✉*Av. Durango 186A, Col. Roma* ☎*55/5525–4920* ✉*Av. Moliere 56, Col. Polanco* ☎*55/5282–0010* ▭*AE, MC, V* ⊗*No dinner Sun.*

$–$$ CAJUN ✕**Zydeco.** Don Bergeron, a Louisiana native and traveling chef for the state tourism office, developed the menu for Zydeco, making it a one-of-a-kind Cajun treat. Popular appetizers include New Orleans crab cakes and blackened chicken tenders served with Jack Daniels barbecue sauce. Next up is the gumbo or the Swamp Pop Jambalaya, a spicy rice dish with chicken, pork, and sausage. Live zydeco, blues, and rock acts play on Tuesday, Wednesday, and Sunday nights. ✉*Tamaulipas 30, at Juan Escutia, Condesa* ☎*55/5553–3329* ▭*AE, MC, V.*

$ GREEK ✕**Agapi Mu.** Rambunctious Greek song and dance enliven this small, friendly bistro Thursday through Saturday nights. Tucked away in a snug room of a converted Colonia Condesa home, you'll hum along as you tear into *paputsáka* (stuffed eggplant), *kalamárea* (fried Greek-style squid), and *dolmades* (stuffed grape leaves). ✉*Alfonso Reyes 96, between Cuatla and Cuernavaca, Col. Condesa* ☎*55/5286–1384* ▭*AE, MC, V.*

$ FRENCH Fodor'sChoice ★ ✕**Bistrot Mosaico.** You may have to wait for a table at this local-favorite restaurant, but one look at the deli case and you'll be hooked: the exquisite breads and chipotle mayonnaise that come to your table are just the start of your reward. Try the signature *terrine de berengena* (eggplant) for a starter. The menu also lists quiche or sausage and lentils, depending on whether it's sweltering or raining outside. ✉ *Av. Michoacán 10, between Avs. Amsterdam and Insurgentes, Col. Condesa* ☎ *55/5584–2932* ▭ *AE, MC, V* ⊙ *No dinner Sun.*

$ VEGETARIAN ✕ **El Yug.** This vegetarian spot offers delicious fare to the accompaniment of New Age music. Homemade soups, and main courses such as chiles rellenos come with whole-grain bread. A daily *comida corrida* (fixed-price menu) is only $6. The sister restaurant in the Zona Rosa is open daily for breakfast, lunch, and dinner. If you can't find the address for the Roma location it's because the entrance is actually three doors down around the corner on Calle Cozumel. ✉ *Puebla 326-6, Col. Roma* ☎ *55/5553–3872* ✉ *Varsovia 3, at Paseo de la Reforma, Zona Rosa* ☎ *55/5525–5330* ▭ *AE, DC, MC, V.*

¢–$ MEXICAN ✕ **El Califa.** For a late-night taco fix, the handmade tortillas, zesty salsas, and choice cuts at this *taqueria* are as good as it gets. The folks at El Califa baste tender fillets with melted butter and herbs. They also make excellent *tacos al pastor,* tacos with thin slices of spit-cooked marinated pork topped with onion, cilantro, and pineapple. ✉ *Altata 22, at Alfonso Reyes, Col. Condesa* ☎ *55/5271–6285* ▭ *AE, MC, V*

¢–$ MEXICAN **Tamales Emporio México** (✉ *Alvaro Obregón 254 ABC, Col. Roma* ☎ *55/574–2078* 🌐 *www.tamales.com.mx*). If you like tamales, this is the place. This small, unassuming restaurant serves up delicious tamales, with recipes from all over the country. There are tamales wrapped with corn husks—the rajas con queso—or the poblano chile with cheese also is delicious. There are also tamales prepared in banana leaves. The recipe from Chiapas which includes green olives, almonds, prunes, egg, red pepper, chicken, and mole is exceptional. Many of these varieties of tamales are hard to come by in other areas of the city. Be sure to get in early, especially on weekends, because the restaurant does sometimes run out of their most popular tamales, even early in the day, because tamales make a wonderful breakfast.

SAN ANGEL & COYOACÁN

$$$$ MEXICAN ★ ✕ **San Angel Inn.** During a meal in this magnificent old ex-convent it may be hard not to fall into gluttony. Dark mahogany furniture, crisp white table linens, and beautiful blue-and-white Talavera place settings strike a note of restrained opulence. For a classic treat, have the *sopa de tortilla* (tortilla soup); note that the *puntas de filete* (sirloin tips) are liberally laced with chiles. Desserts—from crunchy meringues to pastries—are very rich. ✉ *Calle Diego Rivera 50, at Av. Altavista, San Angel* ☎ *55/5616–0537 or 55/5616–2222* ▭ *AE, DC, MC, V.*

$$–$$$ CHINESE ✕ **Mandarin House.** Standing proudly at the head of the eateries that line San Angel's cobbled Avenida de la Paz, this spacious restaurant offers predominantly Mandarin cuisine. The chef's specialties include *pato Pekin* (duck with plum sauce and crepes) and *pollo mo su* (chicken with bamboo, cabbage, mushroom, and hoisin sauce). Though there's no strict dress code, you may feel comfortable in more formal dress. ✉ *Av. de la Paz 57, San Angel* ☎ *55/5616–4410 or 55/5616–4434* ✉ *Cofre de Perote 205-B, Col. Lomas de Chapultepec* ☎ *55/5520–9870 or 55/5540–1683* ▭ *AE, MC, V* ⊙ *No dinner Sun.*

$–$$$ ARGENTINE ✕**El Entrevero.** An Uruguayan may own this friendly eatery on the square of Coyoacán, but all Argentine standards appear on the menu—the scrumptious *provoleta* (grilled provolone cheese with oregano) among them. Entrevero is also one of the few restaurants in the capital where you will find good pizzas and gnocchi. The *crema quemada* (a version of crème brûlée) is sinful. Fair prices and the excellent location guarantee it's always busy, so arrive early on weekends. ✉*Jardín Centenario 14-C, Col. Coyoacán* ☎*55/5659–0066* ▭*AE, MC, V.*

2

$–$$$ ARGENTINE ✕**La Taba.** Smart yet unpretentious, this restaurant in the south of the city is characterized by its generous portions of top-quality beef. The flavorful *chistorra* (a semicured chorizo-type sausage) stands out from the wide range of starters; vegetarians can choose from soups, pastas, and salads. The *bife de chorizo* (rump steak) is unforgettable, and big eaters might find room for one of the traditional desserts. Colonia Guadalupe Inn is a 10-minute taxi ride north from central San Angel, but if you are coming from the north the restaurant is just six blocks from the end of the metro line at Barranca del Muerte. ✉*Av. Revolución 1398, Col. Guadalupe Inn* ☎*55/5662–3165 or 55/5662–2671* ▭*AE, MC, V* ⊙*No dinner Sun.*

$–$$ MEXICAN ✕**El Tajín.** Named after El Tajín pyramid in Veracruz, this elegant lunch spot sizzles with pre-Hispanic influences. Innovative appetizers include *chilpachole,* a delicate crab-and-chile soup with epazote, while main dishes could include octopus cooked in its own ink. Prices are quite moderate for this caliber of cooking, and there's an impressive wine list to boot. Spacious and relaxing with a garden for children to play in, the place has an excellent vibe. Ancient Huastecan faces grinning from a splashing fountain add a bit of levity to the dining experience. ✉*Centro Cultural Veracruzano, Miguel Angel de Quevedo 687, Coyoacán* ☎*55/5659–4447 or 55/5659–5759* ▭*AE, MC, V* ⊙*No dinner.*

OTHER AREAS

$ MEXICAN ✕**El Bajío.** Decorated in bright colors, El Bajío attracts Mexican families and is run by vivacious Carmen "Titita" Ramírez—a culinary expert who has been featured in various U.S. food magazines. The labor-intensive 30-ingredient mole de Xico is a favorite; also excellent are *empanadas de plátano rellenos de frijol* (tortilla turnovers filled with bananas and beans) and *carnitas* (roast pork). You may have to go a little off the beaten track to get here, but it's worth it. ✉*Av. Cuitláhuac 2709, Col. Obrero Popular* ✥*8 blocks north of metro Cuitláhuac* ☎*55/5341–9889* ▭*AE, MC, V* ⊙*No dinner* ✉*Parque Delta, Cuahutemoch 462, Local R03, Col. Navarte* ☎*55/5530–7518* 🌐*www.carnitaselbajio.com.mx* ▭*AE, MC, V.*

WHERE TO STAY

Although the city is huge and spread out, most hotels are clustered in a few neighborhoods. Colonia Polanco has a generous handful of business-oriented hotels; these tend to be familiar major chains. The Zona Rosa has plenty of big, contemporary properties; it's handy to have restaurants and other services right outside the door. The pleasant tourist areas of La Roma, Coyoacán, and San Angel are still poorly furnished with accommodations, but La Condesa is a growing hot spot for new and notable hotels.

Business travelers tend to fill up deluxe hotels during the week; some major hotels discount their weekend rates. Many smaller properties have taken the cue and offer similarly reduced rates as well. If you reserve through the toll-free reservation numbers, you may find rates as much as 50% off during special promotions.

CENTRO HISTÓRICO

$$$ **Gran Hotel de la Ciudad de México.** Ensconced in a former 19th-century department store, this recently renovated hotel has rooms furnished in a modern style. Its distinctive belle epoque lobby—with a striking Parisian stained-glass dome from Jacque Graber's workshop, chandeliers, gilded birdcages, and 19th-century wrought-iron elevators—is worth a visit in its own right. The Terrace breakfast restaurant overlooks the Zócalo. **Pros:** The Restaurant Plaza Mayor restaurant-bar, with some windows facing the Zócalo, is one of Mexico City's best. **Cons:** Hotel often holds parties in lobby, staff can be unhelpful. ✉ *16 de Septiembre 82, at 5 de Febrero, Col. Centro,* ☎ *55/1083–7700* *60 rooms* *In-room: Safe, dial-up. In-hotel: 3 restaurants, room service, bar, gym, spa, concierge, parking (fee)* ▭ *AE, MC, V.*

$$$ **Sheraton Centro Histórico.** The abstract red-and-blue mural in the lobby and cantilevered gray facade add a dramatic flourish to the city's newest hotel gracing the historic center. Geared to conventions, everything is oversize here, from the lobby to the seven food and beverage outlets. Plush Italian furniture, gray-green carpeting, and Spanish marble are features of the guest rooms, which come in one of four different color schemes: vanilla, gray, wine, or blue. Rooms and hallways all feature old photos of the Centro Histórico. **Pros:** Suites with a kichenette and dining area are available for long-term stays, walking distance to several sights. **Cons:** Additional charge for gym and internet. ✉ *Av. Juarez 70, Col. Centro,06010* ☎ *55/5130–5300* 🌐 *www.sheratonmexico.com* *375 rooms, 25 suites, 27 extended-stay suites* *In-room: Safe, dial-up. In-hotel: 3 restaurants, bar, pool, gym, spa, concierge, executive floor, parking (fee), no elevator* ▭ *AE, DC, MC, V.*

$$ **Holiday Inn Zócalo.** This hotel couldn't have a better location—on the Zócalo and close to a gaggle of museums, restaurants, and historic buildings. There's some flavor to the terrace restaurant, which has old-fashioned wrought-iron tables and an amazing view of the Catedral Metropolitana and Palacio Nacional. **Pros:** The location is phenomenal, price is affordable. **Cons:** The building may be historic, but the interior has the feel of a typical Holiday Inn; food so-so at best. ✉ *Av. 5 de Mayo at Zócalo, Col. Centro,* ☎ *55/5130–5130, 55/5521–2121, or 800/990–9999* 🌐 *www.ichotelsgroup.com* *100 rooms, 10 suites* *In-room: Safe, Wi-Fi. In-hotel: 2 restaurants, room service, bar, gym, public Internet, parking (fee)* ▭ *AE, MC, V*

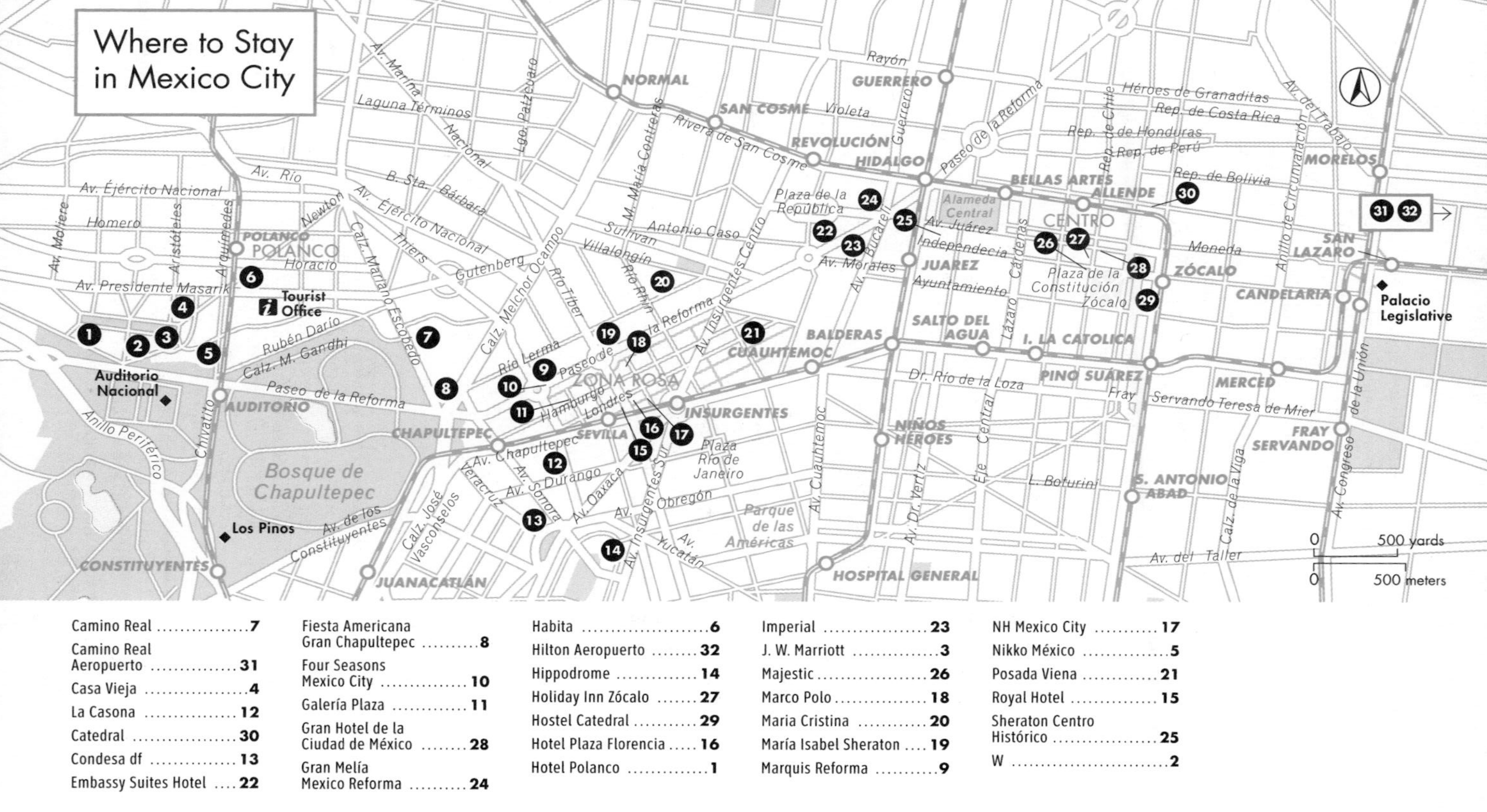
Where to Stay in Mexico City
Camino Real ... 7
Camino Real Aeropuerto ... 31
Casa Vieja ... 4
La Casona ... 12
Catedral ... 30
Condesa df ... 13
Embassy Suites Hotel ... 22
Fiesta Americana Gran Chapultepec ... 8
Four Seasons Mexico City ... 10
Galería Plaza ... 11
Gran Hotel de la Ciudad de México ... 28
Gran Melía Mexico Reforma ... 24
Habita ... 6
Hilton Aeropuerto ... 32
Hippodrome ... 14
Holiday Inn Zócalo ... 27
Hostel Catedral ... 29
Hotel Plaza Florencia ... 16
Hotel Polanco ... 1
Imperial ... 23
J. W. Marriott ... 3
Majestic ... 26
Marco Polo ... 18
Maria Cristina ... 20
María Isabel Sheraton ... 19
Marquis Reforma ... 9
NH Mexico City ... 17
Nikko México ... 5
Posada Viena ... 21
Royal Hotel ... 15
Sheraton Centro Histórico ... 25
W ... 2
NORMAL
SAN COSME
REVOLUCIÓN
HIDALGO
GUERRERO
BELLAS ARTES
ALLENDE
MORELOS
SAN LAZARO
ZÓCALO
CANDELARIA
POLANCO
AUDITORIO
CHAPULTEPEC
SEVILLA
INSURGENTES
CUAUHTEMOC
BALDERAS
JUAREZ
SALTO DEL AGUA
I. LA CATOLICA
PINO SUÁREZ
MERCED
FRAY SERVANDO
NIÑOS HÉROES
S. ANTONIO ABAD
HOSPITAL GENERAL
CONSTITUYENTES
JUANACATLÁN
ZONA ROSA
CENTRO
Bosque de Chapultepec
Auditorio Nacional
Los Pinos
Tourist Office
Palacio Legislative
Plaza de la República
Alameda Central
Plaza de la Constitución Zócalo
Plaza Río de Janeiro
Parque de las Américas
Paseo de la Reforma
Anillo Periférico
0 500 yards
0 500 meters
2

$$ **Majestic.** If you're interested in exploring the historic downtown, the atmospheric, colonial-style Majestic will give you a perfect location. It's also ideal for viewing the Independence Day (September 16) celebrations, for which many people reserve a room one year in advance. Rooms have heavy wooden furniture and bright linens. There is also a restaurant on the top floor with a wonderful view of the Zócalo. **Pros:** Restaurant serves all kinds of well-prepared international food, and it's hard to beat their classic tacos. **Cons:** Although the front units have balconies and a delightful view, they can be noisy with car traffic until about 11 PM. ✉ *Ave. Madero 73, Col. Centro,* ☎ *55/5521–8600 or 800/528–1234* 🌐 *www.hotelmajestic.com.mx* *84 rooms* *In-room: Safe, Wi-Fi. In-hotel: Restaurant, bar, laundry service* *AE, MC, V.*

★ $ **Catedral.** This refurbished older hotel on a busy street in the heart of downtown is a bargain, with many of the amenities of the more upscale hotels at less than half the price. Public areas sparkle with marble and glass. Guest rooms are spacious and clean, if a little generic. You can get a room with a view of the namesake Catedral. If your room doesn't have a view, the small terrace is a great place to watch the sun set over the zócalo. Pros: El Retiro bar attracts a largely Mexican clientele to hear live Latin music. Cons: The Catedral's bells chime every 15 minutes late into the night. ✉ *Donceles 95, Col. Centro,* ☎ *55/5512–8581 or 55/5521–6183* 🌐 *www.hotelcatedral.com* *116 rooms, 8 suites* *In-hotel: Restaurant, room service, bar, laundry service, public Internet, parking (no fee)* *AE, MC, V.*

¢ **Hostel Catedral.** In the heart of downtown Mexico City, just behind the Catedral Metropolitana, this large hostel offers sunny, clean, and comfortable rooms at rock-bottom prices. The café in the entryway, which serves up inexpensive pastas, sandwiches, and salads, is a great place to swap stories with fellow travelers (mostly young vacationers on a budget). The kitchen, sunroof, and TV room are also natural places to strike up a conversation. If you're on a tight budget, ask about the shared rooms. Also be sure to ask about tours and other classes offered at the hostel. There are often weekly excursions and dance classes. ✉ *República de Guatemala No. 4, Col. Centro,* ☎ *55/5518–1726* 🌐 *www.hostelcatedral.com* *42 rooms* *In-room: No a/c, no phone, no TV. In-hotel: Restaurant, laundry facilities, public Internet* *BP.*

MIDTOWN & ALONG THE REFORMA

$$$$ **Embassy Suites Hotel.** This comfortable hotel, on a long undeveloped corner, right in the middle of Reforma Avenue action, is perfectly located to get just about anywhere in the city fast. It is within walking distance to the Zona Rosa, and close to the Monumento a la Revolución. Both the monument (which fills up with politicians and union workers during work hours on weekdays) and Reforma surround the hotel with activity. Rooms are spacious and comfortable, furnished with queen- or king-sized beds, marble bathrooms, and flat-screen TVs. **Pros:** There are also evening receptions with snacks and drinks, where guests can swap stories about the sights; prices are lower on the weekends. **Cons:** Many agree that taxis, when booked through this hotel, are much more expensive than

they otherwise would be. ✉*Paseo de la Reforma 69, Col. Tabacalera,* ☎*55/5061–3050 or 800/800–6868* 🌐*www.embassysuites.com* *123 rooms, 86 suites* *In-room: Safe, dial-up. In-hotel: restaurant, bar, pool, gym, spa, no-smoking rooms* *AE, DC, MC, V.*

> **WORD OF MOUTH**
>
> "Go with a Four Seasons weekend package for a great time. The cultural tour that was part of our package was a bonus. We were even met at the airport and ushered through customs quickly—a truly perfect city experience."
>
> –Howard, London, England

$$$$ Fodor'sChoice ★ **Four Seasons Mexico City.** Among the most luxurious hotels in the capital, this eight-story hotel was modeled after the 18th-century Iturbide Palace—it even has a traditional inner courtyard with a fountain. Half the rooms overlook this courtyard. The rest of the hotel doesn't disappoint: rooms are adorned with palettes of either deep blue and brown or peach and emerald green and the business center is so complete it even has a reference library. The well-stocked tequila bar off the lobby is a perfect predinner option. **Pros:** Excellent cultural tours of the city are offered free to guests on weekends. **Cons:** All amenities are (as expected) expensive. ✉*Paseo de la Reforma 500, Col. Juárez,* ☎*55/5230–1818, 01800/906–7500 toll-free in Mexico, or 888/304–6755* 🌐*www.fourseasons.com/mexico* *200 rooms, 40 suites* *In-room: Dial-up. In-hotel: 2 restaurants, bar, pool, gym, concierge, laundry service, executive floor* *AE, DC, MC, V.*

$$$$ **Gran Melía Mexico Reforma.** Convenient to downtown, the Stock Exchange, and the Zona Rosa, this gorgeous, if a little over-the-top, 22-floor smoked-glass behemoth answers the call of business travelers looking for location, well-appointed rooms, and high-tech business services. The lobby is certainly a great meeting place, with a brass-domed lounge, snug little corners for tête-à-têtes, and a glossy, dove-gray marble floor. Guest rooms are large, with soft blue and auburn colors, oversize TVs, and comfortable sitting areas; the executive floor features butler service. There's also a full-service spa (the largest such spa in a Mexico City hotel). **Pros:** Large guest rooms, friendly staff. **Cons:** Time for a refurbishment. ✉*Reforma 1, Col. Tabacalera,* ☎*55/5128–5000 or 800/901–7100* 🌐*www.solmelia.com* *424 rooms, 30 suites* *In-room: Safe, dial-up. In-hotel: 2 restaurants, gym, spa, concierge, executive floor* *AE, DC, MC, V.*

$$$$ **María Isabel Sheraton.** Don Antenor Patiño, the Bolivian "Tin King," inaugurated this Mexico City classic in 1969 and named it after his granddaughter, socialite Isabel Goldsmith. The stunning marble lobby has gleaming brass fixtures. All guest and public rooms are impeccably maintained; the former have extra comfy Posturepedic mattresses and goose-down pillows. Penthouse suites in the 22-story tower are extra-spacious and have butler service. **Pros:** The location—across from the Angel Monument and the Zona Rosa, with Sanborns next door and the U.S. Embassy a half block away—is prime. **Cons:** Some areas need some TLC, unexpected charges. ✉*Paseo de la Reforma 325, Col. Cuauhtémoc,* ☎*55/5242–5555* 🌐*www.sheraton.com* *681 rooms, 74 suites* *In-room: Safe, dial-up. In-hotel: 3 restaurants, room ser-*

vice, bars, pool, gym, spa, concierge, laundry service, executive floor, parking (fee), no-smoking rooms ⊟*AE, DC, MC, V.*

$$$ **Imperial.** Suiting its name, this hotel occupies a stately late-19th-century, clean, white building with a corner cupola right on the Reforma alongside the Columbus Monument. The hotel's Restaurant Gaudí serves Continental cuisine with some classic Spanish selections. **Pros:** Quiet elegance and personal service are keynotes of this privately owned property. **Cons:** Rooms aren't terribly impressive, though—the pink-and-white furnishings could use some updating. ✉*Paseo de la Reforma 64, Col. Juárez,* ☎*55/5705–4911* 🌐*www.hotelimperial.com.mx* *50 rooms, 10 junior suites, 5 master suites* *In-room: Safe, dial-up. In-hotel: 2 restaurants, bar, laundry service, parking (no fee)* ⊟*AE, MC, V.*

$$$ Fodor's Choice ★ **Marquis Reforma.** This plush, privately owned member of the Leading Hotels of the World is within walking distance of the Zona Rosa. Its striking art nouveau facade combines pink stone and curved glass, and the seventh-floor suites afford picture-perfect views of the Castillo de Chapultepec. An art deco theme defines the rooms. You can enjoy Mexican cuisine at La Jolla restaurant and take advantage of hard-to-find holistic massages at the health club. **Pros:** Rates are lower on weekends, interesting decor. **Cons:** Needs some updating. ✉*Paseo de la Reforma 465, Col. Cuauhtémoc,* ☎*55/5229–1200 or 800/235–2387* 🌐*www.marquisreforma.com* *123 rooms, 86 suites* *In-room: Safe, dial-up. In-hotel: 2 restaurants, bar, pool, gym, spa, no-smoking rooms, Wi-Fi* ⊟*AE, DC, MC, V.*

$$ ★ **María Cristina.** This Spanish colonial–style gem is a Mexico City classic. Impeccably maintained since it was built in 1937, the building surrounds a delightful garden courtyard—the setting for its El Retiro bar. Three apartment-style master suites come complete with hot tubs. In a quiet residential setting near Parque Sullivan, the hotel is close to the Zona Rosa. **Pros:** All in all you get a lot for your money here. **Cons:** The rooms aren't that exciting. ✉*Río Lerma 31, Col. Cuauhtémoc,* ☎*55/5703–1212 or 55/5566–9688* 🌐*www.hotelmariacristina.com.mx* *140 rooms, 8 suites* *In-room: No a/c (some), safe. In-hotel: Room service, bar, parking (no fee)* ⊟*AE, MC, V.*

ZONA ROSA

$$$ **Galería Plaza.** Location gives this ultramodern hotel an edge; it's on a quiet street, but plenty of shops, restaurants, and nightspots are nearby. Service and facilities are faultless; advantages include a heated rooftop pool with sundeck, a secure underground parking lot, and a 24-hour restaurant. **Pros:** All rooms are fresh and bright with small work areas. **Cons:** Many conferences held here. ✉*Hamburgo 195, at Varsovia,* ☎*55/5230–1717 or 888/559–4329* 🌐*www.brisas.com.mx* *420 rooms, 19 suites* *In-room: Safe, dial-up. In-hotel: 2 restaurants, room service, bar, pool, gym, concierge, laundry service, executive floor, parking (fee)* ⊟*AE, DC, MC, V.*

$$$ **Hotel Geneve.** This five-story 1906 hotel, referred to locally as El Génova, has a pleasant lobby with traditional colonial-style carved-wood

chairs and tables. Guest rooms are small but comfortable, with modern furnishings. The attractive Salón Jardín, part of the popular Sanborns restaurant chain, has art deco stained-glass flourishes. **Pros:** It's in the heart of the Zona Rosa. **Cons: Service and decor are only so-so.** ✉*Londres 130,* ☎*55/5080–0800* 🌐*www.hotelescalinda.com.mx* *210 rooms* *In-room: Safe, dial-up. In-hotel: 2 restaurants, room service, bar, gym, spa, laundry facilities, parking (fee)* 💳*AE, DC, MC, V.*

> **WORD OF MOUTH**
>
> "Marco Polo may have the slowest elevator on the planet, but our recent stay was marvelous. The hotel provided a car and driver/guide for trips in the city and to the pyramids. For the price, we have no complaints. One note: the Zona Rosa seems to be on the decline, with many vacant storefronts along Amberes and other streets."
>
> –Ray, Utah

$$$ **NH Mexico City.** The former Krystal Rosa now belongs to the Spanish NH chain and is still a superbly run high-rise hotel. There's a stylish lobby cocktail lounge and a restaurant, Hacienda del Mortero, which serves excellent classic Spanish and international cuisine. Rooms have business travelers in mind, with sober gray and green colors, Scandinavian-style furniture, and hardwood floors. **Pros:** The hotel is in the heart of Zona Rosa, has an excellent view of the neighborhood from the rooftop pool terrace. **Cons:** Very business focused, so seems a little impersonal. ✉*Liverpool 155,* ☎*55/5228–9928 or 800/231–9860* 🌐*www.nh-hotels.com* *267 rooms, 35 suites* *In-room: Safe, dial-up. In-hotel: Restaurant, bar, pool, concierge, laundry service, parking (fee)* 💳*AE, DC, MC, V.*

$$ **Hotel Plaza Florencia.** The lobby of this hotel may be weighted with heavy furniture and dark colors, but the rooms upstairs are bright, modern, and, most important, soundproofed against the traffic noise of the busy avenue below. Some large family suites are available. **Pros:** Higher floors have views of the Angel Monument. **Cons:** A little dark and dated. ✉*Florencia 61,* ☎*55/5242–4700 or 800/717–2983* 🌐*www.qualityinnpf.com* *134 rooms, 8 suites* *In-room: Safe, dial-up (some). In-hotel: 2 restaurants, bar, pool, laundry service* 💳*AE, DC, MC, V.*

$$ ★ **Marco Polo.** Modern and intimate, the central Marco Polo has the amenities and personalized service often associated with a small European hotel. North-facing top-floor rooms have excellent views of Paseo de la Reforma and the Angel Monument, and the U.S. Embassy is close by. Four penthouse suites have terraces, and are normally rented by the month. **Pros:** Good included breakfast, helpful staff. **Cons:** Hard mattresses. ✉*Amberes 27,* ☎*55/5080–0063 or 800/448–8355* 🌐*www.marcopolo.com.mx* *59 rooms, 16 suites* *In-room: Safe, dial-up. In-hotel: Restaurant, bar, gym, laundry service, parking (fee)* 💳*AE, DC, MC, V* *CP.*

$$ **Royal Hotel.** The immaculate marble lobby of the modern Royal Hotel, beloved by travelers from Spain, is filled with plants and the exuberant conversation of its guests. Spacious rooms have large bath-

rooms, well-equipped work areas, and interactive TV. Its Spanish restaurant, Tezka, was founded by award-winning chef Arzac and is known for its extraordinary Basque cuisine. **Pros:** Nice views if you're on one of the top floors. **Cons:** Is a Best Western property, which means that some things are more generic. ✉*Amberes 78,* ☎*55/5228–9918 or 888/740–8314* 🌐*www.hotelroyalzr.com* *161 rooms, 1 suite* *In-room: Safe, refrigerator, Wi-Fi. In-hotel: 2 restaurants, bar, gym, laundry service, parking (no fee)* *AE, MC, V.*

$ **Posada Viena.** Hidden away in a quiet neighborhood three blocks from the hustle and bustle of the Zona Rosa, this hotel is convenient to restaurants, bars, and shops, but much more affordable than some of its more central counterparts. The rooms are fresh and clean, painted with slivers of bright purples, oranges, yellows, and blues. Suites, suitable for up to four people, are ideal for families. The Argentine restaurant offers free tango lessons on Saturday night and delicious steak dishes. **Pros:** The staff couldn't be nicer. **Cons:** Elevator and hallways are a little musty. ✉*Marsella 28, corner of Dinamarca,* ☎*55/5566–0700 or 800/849–8402* *66 rooms, 20 suites* *In-room: No a/c. In-hotel: 2 restaurants, room service, bar, laundry service, parking (no fee)* *AE, MC, V.*

POLANCO

$$$$ **Casa Vieja.** This mansion is simply stunning. Tastefully selected folk art, handsome hand-carved furniture, and gilded wall trimmings complement patios and splashing fountains. Each of the one- and two-bedroom suites are named after an artist and decorated with paintings in that artist's style. The hotel's Mexican restaurant is named after its huge floor-to-ceiling *Arbol de la Vida* (*Tree of Life*) sculpture. The hotel is owned by Lolita Ayala, a prominent journalist who knows how difficult a peaceful stay can be for public personalities. As you might imagine at such a small and exclusive hotel, with advance notice the restaurant can prepare any plate visitors would like. **Pros:** The suites have full kitchens, CD player, VCR, high-speed Internet, and hot tub. **Cons:** Not all staff speaks English, views aren't great. ✉*Eugenio Sue 45,* ☎*55/5282–0067* 🌐*www.casavieja.com* *10 suites* *In-room: No a/c, safe, kitchen, Internet, CD, VCR. In-hotel: Restaurant, bar, concierge, laundry service, parking (no fee), no elevator* *AE, MC, V* *BP.*

$$$$ ★ **Habita.** Characterized by pale colors and a spalike atmosphere, Mexico's first design hotel strikes a harmonious balance between style statements and minimalism. New Age music is piped into the rooms (you can turn it off, of course), and bowls of limes sit by state-of-the-art TVs. The swanky tapas bar, Area, has beautiful open-air views and draws plenty of chic chilangos Thursday to Saturday. **Pros:** Large rooms, nicely decorated, unique concept. **Cons:** Hidden charges, some difference between rooms. ✉*Av. Presidente Masarik 201,* ☎*55/5282–3100* 🌐*www.hotelhabita.com* *32 rooms, 4 suites* *In-room: Safe, dial-up. In-hotel: Restaurant, bar, gym, spa, concierge, parking (no fee)* *AE, MC, V.*

$$$$ **J. W. Marriott.** In keeping with its genteel neighborhood, this high-rise hotel has personalized service and small, clubby public areas; nothing overwhelms here. Rooms have plenty of wood and warm colors. The hotel has a well-equipped 24-hour business center and an ATM machine. **Pros:** Attractive weekend rates for double rooms cost around $265. **Cons:** Rooms are unremarkable in decor. ✉ *Andrés Bello 29, at Campos Elíseos,* ☎ *55/5999–0000* 🌐 *www.marriott.com* *312 rooms* *In-room: Safe, Wi-Fi. In-hotel: 2 restaurants, bar, pool, gym, concierge, laundry service, executive floor* *AE, MC, V.*

$$$$ **Nikko México.** Occupying a prime Polanco position adjacent to the Bosque de Chapultepec, this hotel is a five-minute walk from the anthropology museum. With signage and menus in Japanese, English, and Spanish, it caters especially to business travelers. It's the second-largest hotel in the city and has marvelous views from the top-floor suites. The lobby is filled with paintings by important Mexican artists. There are also several small galleries in the hotel, including a branch of the highly regarded Galería Alberto Misrachi. Each room soothes with subdued earth tones and bamboolike walls; two rooms are done in Japanese style, with tatami mats. Among the restaurants is the excellent Benkay. **Pros:** Considering that this is one of the most elegant places to stay in the city, weekend special rates are very reasonable. **Cons:** Falls short in some aspects of service. ✉ *Campos Elíseos 204,* ☎ *55/5283–8700 or 800/280–9191* 🌐 *www.hotelnikkomexico.com.mx* *744 rooms, 24 suites* *In-room: Safe, dial-up. In-hotel: 4 restaurants, bar, tennis courts, pool, gym, concierge, executive floor, no-smoking rooms* *AE, DC, MC, V.*

$$$$ Fodor's Choice ★ **W.** The first W hotel in Latin America grooves with sassy red, black, and white colors under colorful fluorescent lighting. It manages to be informal and chic at the same time, with the staff clad in casual black rather than the usual stiff uniforms. Guest rooms feature some outside-the-box design: bathrooms are big enough for a dance, strung with hammocks, and feature pressure-point showers; sinks are placed inside the bedroom European-style. Work areas have enormous desks and ergonomic chairs; some rooms are outfitted with faxes and scanners. See and be seen in the red lobby bar or just chill in the Music Lounge. The Away spa has a huge pre-Hispanic *temazcal* (adobe-domed sweat lodge). **Pros:** Special touches, nice place to hang out. **Cons:** More attention is paid to look than comfort. ✉ *Campos Eliseos 252* ☎ *55/9138–1895* 🌐 *www.whotels.com* *229 rooms, 8 suites* *In-room: Safe, DVD, dial-up. In-hotel: Restaurant, bar, gym, spa, laundry service* *AE, DC, MC, V.*

$$$–$$$$ Fodor's Choice ★ **Camino Real.** About the size of Teotihuacán's Pyramid of the Sun, this sleek, minimalist, bright pink-and-yellow, 8-acre megalith was designed by Mexico's modern master, Ricardo Legorreta. Impressive artworks embellishing the public spaces include Rufino Tamayo's mural *Man Facing Infinity* and a Calder sculpture. Rooms have gorgeous marble bathrooms and Legoretta's signature bright yellow on one wall. The fifth-floor executive level has 100 extra-large guest rooms with special amenities. El Centro Castellano restaurant offers free child care for long weekend lunchtimes. There's also a branch of Le Cirque. **Pros:**

Unique in that it's almost a city-within-a-city. **Cons:** Too large for some people's liking, draws a lot of conferences. ✉*Mariano Escobedo 700, Col. Anzures,* ☎*55/5227–7200* 🌐*www.caminoreal.com* *714 rooms, 45 suites* *In-room: Safe, dial-up. In-hotel: 3 restaurants, bar, tennis courts, pools, gym, concierge, laundry service, executive floor, parking (fee), no-smoking rooms* *AE, DC, MC, V.*

$$$ **Fiesta Americana Grand Chapultepec.** Sleek and contemporary, this stylish hotel stands opposite the Bosque de Chapultepec, close to the city's main shopping area, and five minutes from the Auditorio Nacional. Rooms are done in muted olives and browns. The spa, beauty salon, and barbershop guarantee you will be presentable for the ultramodern Asian bar, where you can hang out for sushi and cocktails. **Pros:** Rooms are angled to maximize views. **Cons:** Many amenities cost extra. ✉*Mariano Escobedo 756, Col. Anzures,* ☎*55/2581–1500* 🌐*www.fiestaamericana.com* *189 rooms, 14 suites* *In-room: Wi-Fi. In-hotel: Restaurant, bars, gym, spa, concierge, laundry service, parking (no fee)* *AE, MC, V.*

$$ **Hotel Polanco.** This small favorite right off Polanco park, and not far from Chapultepec park, has many of the amenities of larger hotels, but at a much better price. Marble floors and dark-wood furniture accent the cozy lobby, which leads to five floors of tidy, carpeted rooms with old-fashioned blue-flowered bedspreads and cedar furnishings. **Pros:** A pleasant street-side restaurant serves out-of-the-ordinary Italian cuisine. **Cons:** Rooms are tiny. ✉*Edgar Allan Poe 8,* ☎*55/5280–8082* *hotelpolanco@prodigy.net.mx* *65 rooms, 5 suites* *In-room: No a/c, safe. In-hotel: Restaurant, room service, bar, gym, laundry service, parking (no fee)* *MC, V.*

LA ROMA & LA CONDESA

$$$–$$$$ **La Casona.** This charming hotel is an elegant, understated former mansion, registered as an artistic monument by Mexico's Institute of Fine Arts. From its sunny patios to its sitting rooms, the hotel's interior conveys the spirit of the Porfiriato. The owner loves classical music and has added such whimsical touches as a trumpet turned into a lamp in one room and a portrait of Richard Strauss in another. The two-story hotel building, with its salmon-color facade, looks out onto a quiet tree-lined street. **Pros:** No two rooms are alike, but all have hardwood floors, elegant furniture, and good-size bathtubs. **Cons:** Room decoration a little tacky. ✉*Av. Durango 280, at Cozumel,* ☎*55/5286–3001* 🌐*www.hotellacasona.com.mx* *29 rooms* *In-room: Safe, refrigerator (some), dial-up, Wi-Fi. In-hotel: Restaurant, room service, bar, gym, laundry service, no elevator* *AE, DC, MC, V* *BP.*

$$$–$$$$ **Condesa df.** It's all about the details at this hip hotel, from rooms equipped with flat-screen televisions, DVDs, and iPods to a library of coffee-table books about Mexican history and culture. Room doors are labeled with black, oversize Roman numerals in white corridors surrounding a central patio, where the hotel restaurant serves up a delicious mix of Mexican- and Asian-inspired cuisine. Rooms are buffered from restaurant noise at night by a foldout wall that is as impressively

designed as the hundreds of other details that make a stay here a real experience. **Pros:** There's a sushi bar, hot tub, saunas, and a small spa on the roof, where there's also a great view of the neighborhood. ✉ *Av. Veracruz 102, 06700* ☎ *55/5241–2600* 🌐 *www.condesadf.com* *24 rooms, 16 suites* *In-room: Safe, Wi-Fi. In-hotel: 2 restaurants, gym, spa, no-smoking rooms* *AE, MC, V.*

2

$$$ **Hippodrome.** Housed in a 1930s art deco building near Parque México, this newcomer boutique hotel adds some hip style to the already vibrant Condesa neighborhood. The building was remodeled by architect Nahim Dagdug and Tom Shortt, the hotel owner. All 15 rooms are done up in browns and subdued colors with marble bathrooms. You'll settle in easy with flat-screen TVs and memory-foam beds. Despite these luxuries, some rooms still feel a little low on space. The hotel's restaurant, the Hip Kitchen, with a menu designed by Richard Sandoval, serves up contemporary Mexican fusion food. **Pros:** An added bonus? Guests can use fashionable Qi Fitness health club just blocks away. **Cons:** Rooms are little for what you're paying. ✉ *188 Avenida México, 06100* ☎ *55/1454–4599* 🌐 *www.thehippodromehotel.com* *15 rooms* *In-room: Safe. In hotel: Restaurant, gym, room service, safe, public Wi-Fi* *AE, MC, V.*

AIRPORT

$$$ **Camino Real Aeropuerto.** This sleek hotel can be reached from the airport via a short, covered footbridge. Rooms are light and cheery and have sealed double windows to keep out airport noise. Even if you're only between flights and don't overnight, you can sit in one of the overstuffed chairs in the soothing lobby or catch a meal in the restaurant to get away from the frantic energy of the airport. **Pros:** Linked to airport by walkway, a couple of services, including room service and the business center, run 24 hours, useful for travelers on odd-hours schedules. **Cons:** Some rooms can be noisy. ✉ *Benito Juárez International Airport,* ☎ *55/3003–0000 or 800/228–9290* 🌐 *www.caminoreal.com* *600 rooms, 8 suites* *In-room: Safe, dial-up, Wi-Fi. In-hotel: Restaurant, bar, pool, gym, concierge, parking (fee).* *AE, DC, MC, V.*

$$$ **Hilton Aeropuerto.** Cool and compact—with a distinctive gray marble lobby and a bar with a wide-angle view of landing planes—the Hilton feels like a private club, enhanced by an attentive but unobtrusive staff. You can choose from four different views: airstrip, street, atrium, or "garden" (bamboo plants set along a concrete ledge). **Pros:** Rooms come with full working gear for a traveling executive: two phone lines, modem connection, ergonomic chairs, oversized desk, and coffeemaker. **Cons:** Not as swank as some Hiltons, more convenient to Terminal 1. ✉ *Benito Juárez International Airport,* ✣ *At international terminal* ☎ *55/5133–0505 or 800/774–1500* 🌐 *www.hilton.com* *129 rooms* *In-room: Safe, dial-up, Wi-Fi. In-hotel: Restaurant, bar, gym, parking (fee), no-smoking rooms* *AE, DC, MC, V.*

NIGHTLIFE

> **WHERE IT'S AT**
>
> The most popular neighborhoods for barhopping are Condesa, Roma, the Centro Histórico, Coyoacán, Polanco, and the Zona Rosa. Drink prices fluctuate wildly according to area and establishment.

Night is the key word. People generally take in dinner and a show at 9 or 10 PM, head to bars or nightclubs at midnight, then find a spot for a nightcap or tacos somewhere around 3 AM. (Cantinas are the exception; people start hitting them in the late afternoon and most close by 11 PM.) One way to do this if you don't speak Spanish is on a guided tour. **Gray Line** (☎*55/5583–5533* 🌐*www.grayline.com*) organizes nightlife tours to the mariachi plaza (Plaza Garibaldi) and the zócalo, complete with an English-speaking guide and a complimentary drink. The outings are cheaper if you have a group of 10 or more people; you should make reservations 12 hours in advance. If you set off on your own you should have no trouble getting around, but see the Safety box in the Planner at the start of the chapter about the perils of hailing cabs—if money is no object, take official hotel taxis or call a *sitio* (stationed) taxi (☎*55/5514–7861*).

Condesa, Roma, Centro Histórico, Coyoacán, and Polanco stand out as Mexico City's hippest neighborhoods. If you're looking to do some barhopping and want to foot it, you can do so in La Condesa. The Zona Rosa has lost ground to Condesa and Polanco in the past few years, but it's still packed on Friday and Saturday nights and everything is within walking distance. Niza, Florencia, Londres, and Hamburgo streets are teeming with bars and discos.

BARS

Nice bars to sit and have a few drinks in used to be hard to come by in Mexico City, but the situation is improving. The rougher cantinas are usually noisy and sometimes seedy, with an early closing time (11 PM), but the better cantinas, still full of character, are well worth a visit. The cantinas we list are fairly safe places, but women may get some stares and hellos from time to time. Bars are usually open Tuesday–Saturday 8 PM–3 AM and generally don't charge a cover.

CENTRO HISTÓRICO

Fodor's Choice ★ **Centro Cultural de España** (✉*Guatemala 18, behind Cathedral in Col. Centro* ☎*55/5521–1925* 🌐*www.ccemx.org* ⏲*Closed Mon.*) once housed conquistadors during the 16th century; today the Centro is a Spanish cultural center for art exhibits, plays, and other events. On Thursday, Friday, and Saturday nights, starting at 9, indie rock bands play live music on the terrace of the bar-restaurant.

La Ópera (✉*5 de Mayo 10, at Filomeno Mata, Col. Centro* ☎*55/5512–8959*) is one of the city's most elegant watering holes, and it's brought in top personalities since it opened in 1870. Don't forget to have your waiter point out the bullet hole allegedly left in the ceiling by Mexican revolutionary hero Pancho Villa.

Perhaps because of its proximity to the Zócalo's tourist-friendly west side, the simple and traditional **El Puerto del Sol** (✉ *Corner of 5 de Mayo and Calle Palma, Col. Centro* ☎ *No phone*) always seems to have the only Americans in the neighborhood kicking back a few reasonably priced tequilas.

Not strictly a cantina (a cervezeria) but a popular hangout for local artists, journalists, and photographers, the **Salón Corona** (✉ *Calle Bolívar 24, at Madero, Col. Centro* ☎ *55/5512–5725 or 55/5512–9007*) is one of the friendliest joints in town and is centrally located if you plan to hit other bars in the historic center. In typically fatalistic Mexican fashion the giant photos on the wall show the clientele reacting to the 1986 World Cup at the moment defeat was snatched from the jaws of victory by the national team.

> **CAUTION**
>
> Remember that the capital's high altitude makes liquor extremely potent, even jolting. Imported booze is expensive, so you may want to stick with what the Mexicans order: tequila, cerveza (beer), and rum, usually as a Cuba libre (with Coke). If you order a bottle of hard alcohol (some clubs require this), make sure that the seal hasn't been broken before you're served, as some ill-reputed establishments have been known to sell adulterated booze. Your head will thank you the next day.

ZONA ROSA

Bar Milán (✉ *Milán 18, at General Prim, Col. Juárez* ☎ *55/5592–0031*), northeast of Zona Rosa (a 10-minute walk), is a local favorite with the young and hip. Upon entering you need to change pesos into *milagros* (miracles), which are notes necessary to buy drinks throughout the night. The trick is to remember to change them back before last call.

A perfect getaway spot from the Zona Rosa's loud discos and flashy nightclubs, cantina **El Trompo** (✉ *Hamburgo 87, at Niza, Zona Rosa* ☎ *55/5207–8503*) keeps it simple and cheap with a daily two-for-one drink special from 1 PM to midnight. Just remember that if you ask for two beers, the waiter will automatically bring four.

POLANCO

Perched atop the Habita Hotel, **Area** (✉ *Av. Presidente Masarik 201, at Arquímedes, Col. Polanco* ☎ *55/5282–3100*) offers a magnificent view of the city from a chic open-air bar and terrace.

The Blue Lounge (✉ *Mariano Escobedo 700, Col. Nueva Anzures* ☎ *55/5263–8888 Ext. 8489*) in the Camino Real Hotel southeast of Polanco, has a sophisticated crowd and mellow music.

As the name suggests, **Cosmo** (✉ *Av. Presidente Masarik 410, at Calderón de la Barca, Col. Polanco* ☎ *55/5281–4412*) specializes in designer cocktails for those tired of the cerveza-and-tequila routine. Of course, fancy drinks don't come cheap. DJs here spin acid jazz and house music.

2

LA CONDESA

Fodor'sChoice ★ **The Black Horse** (✉*Mexicali 85, at Tamaulipas, Col. Condesa* ☎*55/5211–8740* 🌐*www.caballonegro.com*) doesn't miss a beat with live funk, jazz, and rock groups jamming throughout the week. On the third Wednesday of each month, the Horse hosts a pub quiz; the winner takes home a bottle of booze. For a late-night nosh, try the all-day breakfast, the curry dish, or bangers (Scottish sausage) with mashed potatoes and gravy. Their Web site lists the bar's weekly events. Open Tuesday–Sunday from 6 PM to 2 AM.

★ **La Botica** (✉*Campeche 396, at Tamaulipas, Col. Condesa* ☎*55/5211–60456*) D.F.'s only *mezcaleza*, serves 20 varieties of mezcal; try the *pechuga* (distilled with fruit, and a chicken breast), the *añejo* (aged), or the *cremas* (liqueurs). Mezcal is not ordinary booze: if you drink it like tequila shots, no matter how much of a pro you are, you will end up literally on the floor. If the tiny space is too crowded, order some bottles to go.

Get your Guinness on at Irish-style pub **Celtics** (✉*Tamaulipas 36, Col. Condesa* ☎*55/5211–9081*)—that is, if you can push your way through the throng to reach the bar.

A good place to start is **El Centenario** (✉*Vicente Suarez 48, at Michoacán, Col. Condesa* ☎*55/5211–0276*), a traditional cantina in the heart of the Condesa's restaurant zone. Tables go fast, so prepare to belly up to the bar. Barhoppers often meet at El Centenario for drinks and song before moving on to late-night haunts nearby.

El Mitote (✉*Amsterdam 53, at Sonora, Col. Condesa* ☎*55/5211–9150*) is one of those rare Mexico City bars where the music doesn't drown out the conversation. The famous vodka sangrias pack a punch. (Closed Sunday and Monday.)

While in the neighborhood, drop by the popular **Pata Negra** (✉*Tamaulipas 30, at Juan Escutia, Col. Condesa* ☎*55/5211–5563*). On weekends this Argentinian hot spot can get pretty crowded, so it's a good idea to get there before 11 PM if you want a table. Sunday through Wednesday, when the bar thins out, local groups play acid jazz, bossa nova, and flamenco.

Another Condesa favorite is **Rioma** (✉*Insurgentes Sur 377, near Michoacán, Col. Condesa* ☎*55/5584–0613*), a basement restaurant-bar formerly owned by renowned Mexican film comedian Cantinflas. Local and foreign DJs spin mostly house music.

Salón Malafama (✉*Michoacán 78, at Tamaulipas, Condesa* ☎*55/5553–5138*) takes the prize for Mexico City's hippest pool hall. Since there's often a wait for the pool tables, the bar area is a popular gathering spot.

NEED A BREAK?

After dinner or after drinks (and usually open very late), Neveria Roxy (✉*Fernando Montes de Ocq 89 Col. Condesa* ☎*No phone*) Condesa's old-style, traditional-Mexican ice-cream parlor packs in hipsters and families until the wee hours.

2

LA ROMA

La Bodeguita del Medio (✉*Cozumel 37, Col. Roma Norte* ☎*55/5553–0246* ✉*Insurgentes Sur 1798, Col. Florida* ☎*55/5662–1671*) is a warmly welcoming sit-down joint full of life, (every surface is splashed with graffiti, but it isn't dirty). One of the most appealing spaces in the city and inspired by the original Havana establishment where Hemingway lapped up mojitos, the place also serves cheap Cuban food.

The grand cantina **La Covadonga** (✉*Puebla 121, at Córdoba, Col. Roma* ☎*55/5533–2922*) has an antique bar and a good restaurant serving up Spanish fare. Nightly it's filled with the sound of exuberant games of dominoes. It's open weekdays from 1 PM to 2 AM.

Fodor'sChoice ★ Part metro stop, part college-dorm commons, part pulqueria, and part debating society, **La Hija de los Apaches** (✉*Corner of Doctor Lavista and Av. Cuauhtémoc, Col. Doctores* ☎*No phone*) is the capital's sloppiest gem. Run by 1950s national middleweight boxing champion and folk hero Epiphanio 'Pifas' Leyva, this upstairs loft (technically in Doctores but really part of Roma/Insurgentes) serves beer and pulque to a young, intellectual crowd who loves to sing and dance to the excellent jukebox of punk and local guacapunk classics. If you want a rowdy afternoon (the bar is usually closed by 10, and always closed on Tuesday), this is the place to go.

The bar within **Ixchel** (✉*Medellín 65, at Colima, Col. Roma* ☎*55/5208–4055*) is a great place for a relaxing sip; it's in a lovely old building.

A fantastic old cantina, **El Portal de Cartagena** (✉*Chiapas 174, at Medellín, Col. Roma* ☎*55/5264–8714 or 55/5584–1113*) is ideal for a long lunch and a few beers.

La Taverna Travazares (✉*Orizaba 127, at Chihuahua, Col. Roma* ☎*55/5264–1421*) is a recent addition to the Atrio, an art gallery and cultural center. It's a quiet and pleasant place, which serves Cosaco on tap, one of Mexico's finest microbrews. A jazz group plays on Wednesday and Saturday nights.

COYOACÁN

A former convent converted into a restaurant-bar, the sights and sounds of **El Convento Fernández** (✉*Leal 96, at Pacífico, Coyoacán* ☎*55/5554–4065*) have certainly changed over the years but the hospitality remains the same. There's live music on Wednesday, Friday, and Saturday.

La Guadalupana (✉*Calle Higuera 2, Coyoacán* ☎*55/5554–6253*), a famous cantina dating from 1932, is always packed. The wall-mounted bulls' heads add a dash of flavor to the bar's bullfighting theme.

Students and hip intellectuals of all ages pack **El Hijo del Cuervo** (✉*Jardín Centenario 17, Coyoacán* ☎*55/5658–5196*) for an interesting mix of rock and protest music, known as *nueva canción*. It also offers the occasional theater show; cover charges vary (up to $7).

DANCE CLUBS

Dance emporiums in the capital run the gamut from cheek-to-cheek romantic to throbbing strobe lights and ear-splitting music. Most places have a cover charge, but it's rarely more than $10. Friday and Saturday are the busiest club nights, while Thursday's a good option if you'd like a bit of elbow room for dancing. The most popular clubs are open Wednesday, too. Some clubs require that reservations be made one to two days in advance if you want a table.

CENTRO

The so-called cathedral of *quebraditas* (a fast-paced country dance), **El Pacífico** (☒*Bucareli 43, at Morelos, Col. Centro* ☎*55/5592–2778*) showcases some of the city's most talented dancers as they toss and swing their partners to northern-style *banda* music. El Pacífico could easily win a prize as the noisiest club in Mexico; it never disappoints. **The Pervert Lounge** (☒*Uruguay 70, between 5 de Febrero and Isabel La Católica, Col. Centro* ☎*55/5510–4454*) may not live up (or down?) to its name, but it's funky and fun if you like electronic music. Open Thursday through Saturday.

To reserve a table at **Salón Baraimas** (☒*Filomeno Mata 7, between Av. 5 de Mayo and Calle Tacuba, Col. Centro* ☎*55/5510–4488*), a serious setting for those who know how to salsa, you have to buy a bottle of rum or tequila. Dancing begins around 9, but live bands start at 11.

Salón Los Angeles (☒*Lerdo 206, Col. Guerrero* ☎*55/5597–8847*) takes you back in time to the 1930s, with a setting straight out of the golden era of Mexican cinema. The grand, open dance floor swings to the rhythms of danzón and salsa. When renowned Latin musicians come to town, this is often where they perform.

Local bands play danzón, cha-cha, and mambo upstairs in a converted factory at **Salón México** (☒*Pensador Mexicano, at San Juan de Dios, Col. Centro* ☎*55/5518–0931*), combining nostalgia with fresh energy. The club also books pop and rock concerts on occasion.

ZONA ROSA

When it seems as though every place in Zona Rosa has shut down, **El Alamo** (☒*Hamburgo 96, Zona Rosa* ☎*55/5525–8352*) is probably just getting started, with live tropical music or jukebox picks.

If Latin music isn't your thing, **El Colmillo** (☒*Versalles 52, Col. Juárez* ☎*55/5592–6164*), northeast of Zona Rosa (10 minutes on foot), spins techno downstairs and has an acid jazz lounge upstairs. Founded by two Englishmen, El Colmillo draws a variety of foreigners and locals.

The Tandem Pub (☒*Río Nazas 73, Río Tigris, Col. Cuauhtémoc* ☎*55/1130–9431*) underwent a makeover of sorts several years ago when a group of local DJs transformed the otherwise quiet pub into a weekend hot spot. It's a five-minute walk north of Zona Rosa.

2

POLANCO

★ So popular you can barely move is the friendly **Mama Rumba** (✉*Querétaro 230, at Medellín, Col. Roma* ☎*55/5264–7823* ✉*Plaza San Jacinto 23, San Angel* ☎*55/5550–8099 or 55/5550–8090*), a 10-minute cab ride from the Zona Rosa. A nondescript Cuban restaurant during the day, it turns on the heat Wednesday through Saturday nights. If the Roma location is too crowded, which it usually is, the San Angel location may give you a little more breathing room.

Many locals consider the tropical sounds at dance hall **La Maraka** (✉*Mitla 410, at Eje 5, Col. Narvarte* ☎*55/5682–0636* ⊙*Wed., Fri., and Sat.* *$5*), south of Roma, among the city's finest in merengue and salsa music.

In recent years the huge **Salón 21** (✉*Moliere, at Andrómaco, Col. Ampliación Granada* ☎*55/5255–1496 or 55/5255–5658*), near Polanco, has hosted the best international salsa and Afro-Caribbean bands to visit Mexico City. The popular venue has become much more diversified lately; acts vary from electronic music and rock gigs to the mainstay Latin ensembles.

ELSEWHERE

Urban cowboy dance club **Rodeo Santa Fe** (✉*Avenida de los Maestros 6, Col. San Andrés Atenco* ☎*55/5361–6491* *$6.50*) caters to wannabe bronco busters with live *grupero* music, a huge dance floor, a mechanical bull, and a rodeo show, all bundled up into one knee-slappin' package. It's open Thursday through Sunday.

DINNER SHOWS

Arroyo (✉*Av. Insurgentes Sur 4003, Col. Tlalpan* ☎*55/5573–4344*) is a huge complex south of Zona Rosa (a 40-minute drive), complete with its own bullring. *Novilleros* (novice bullfighters) try out their skills from August to October. An open kitchen serves traditional Mexican specialties and drinks, such as the potent pulque, from 8 to 8. On weekends, mariachi and jarocho musicians add to the buzz.

The liveliest shows are in clubs downtown and in the Zona Rosa. At **Focolare** (✉*Hamburgo 87, at Niza, Zona Rosa* ☎*55/5207–8257*), you can watch traditional folk and Aztec dances Monday through Saturday nights, and on Sunday you can sit down to a meal with live mariachi music. The show costs $6.50; Mexican dinner and drinks are separate.

FOLK PERFORMANCES

Fodor'sChoice ★ The world-renowned **Ballet Folklórico de México** (✉*Palacio de Bellas Artes, Av. Juárez at Eje Central Lázaro Cárdenas, Centro* ☎*55/5512–2593 box office, 55/5325–9000 Ticketmaster* 🌐*www.balletamalia.com*) is a visual feast of Mexican regional folk dances in whirling colors. Lavish and professional, it's one of the most popular shows in Mexico. Performances are on Wednesday at 8:30 PM and Sunday at

9:30 AM and 8:30 PM at the beautiful Palacio de Bellas Artes—it's a treat to see its Tiffany-glass curtain lowered. You can purchase tickets directly at the Palacio's box office or call Ticketmaster for prices and reservations. Hotels and travel agencies can also secure tickets.

The **Miguel Covarrubias Hall** (✉ *National Autonomous University of Mexico [UNAM], Av. Insurgentes Sur 3000, Ciudad Universitaria* ☎ *55/5622–7137*), home of the university's dance department, frequently sponsors modern dance performances.

Teatro de la Danza (✉ *Centro Cultural del Bosque, off Paseo de la Reforma and Campo Marte, Col. Polanco* ☎ *55/5280–8771*) stages contemporary and classical dance at a reasonable price.

GAY BARS

Gay and lesbian life in the capital is something of a contradiction. In one of the largest cities in the world, and one which has recently legalized same-sex unions, one would expect a thriving, out-and-proud queer community. But Mexico isn't like that, and here the queer demimonde largely still exists in the shadows. Personal freedom of choice in Mexico is the companion of money, and so the majority of gays and lesbians, who lack deep pockets, live a closeted, traditional (heterosexual) family lifestyle. When gathering places do appear, they tend to be down and dirty, and get closed down by authorities or swap locations quickly. The Centro's Calle Republica de Cuba was once the closest (apart from the anything-goes Zona Rosa in general) D.F. had to a gay neighborhood, and its hole-in-the-wall taverns may at times once again take on that character. Apart from the large and established institutions listed below, we recommend looking on the Web for the latest updates.

In a high-ceilinged colonial mansion, **Living Room/Box** (✉ *Paseo de la Reforma 483, Col. Polanco* ☎ *55/5286–0069 or 55/5286–0671*) now hosts two of the most popular gay clubs in town.

LIVE MUSIC

Music thrums throughout the capital, from itinerant trumpeters and drummers playing in the streets to marimba in the marketplaces. Some of the best street musicians can be found at popular lunchtime eateries, especially in markets. It's customary to offer a tip of small change; at least a few pesos will be appreciated. Free concerts are spread through the city's plazas on weekends. Most Mexican music (salsa, son, cumbia, danzón) is for dancing, and you will usually find a succession of great live bands in the dance halls and nightclubs.

CLASSICAL

Another good venue for classical music is in the south of the city, **Auditorio Blas Galindo** (✉ *Av. Río Churubusco 79, at Calz. de Tlalpan* ☎ *55/1253–9400 Ext. 1607*), in the Centro Nacional de las Artes (CNA, the National Arts Center).

For choral performances, look for one of the free performances of **El Coro de Madrigalistas de Bellas Artes** (✉*Calle Moneda 4, Col. Centro* ☎*55/5709–2366*) in the Antiguo Palacio del Arzobispado.

The National Autonomous University of Mexico's Philharmonic (✉*Av. Insurgentes Sur 3000, Ciudad Universitaria* ☎*55/5622–7112 or 55/5606–8933*) orchestra performs at the university.

Classical concerts (often free) are also held at the **National Music Conservatory** (✉*Auditorio Silvestre Revueltas, Av. Presidente Masarik 582, Col. Polanco* ☎*55/5280–6347*).

The top concert hall, often touted as the best in Latin America, is **Ollin Yoliztli** (✉*Periférico Sur 5141, Col. Isidro Favela* ☎*55/5606–0016 or 55/5606–8558*); it hosts the **Mexico City Philharmonic.**

OH, PAQUITA!

If you're up for a few good laughs and want to test your Spanish skills, don't miss male-bashing balladeer Paquita la del Barrio at **La Casa de Paquita la del Barrio** (Zarco 202, near Estrella, Col. Guerrero, 55/5583–1668). The jaded, overweight Paquita sings in the mariachi tradition but her songs, such as "Rata de Dos Patas" ("Two-legged Rat"), are anything but traditional as they poke fun at macho Mexican society. Paquita usually performs on Friday and Saturday at 7:30 PM and 9:30 PM; however, showtimes are subject to change. Arrive about an hour early to avoid long lines.

The primary venue for classical music is the **Palacio de Bellas Artes** (✉*Eje Central Lázaro Cárdenas and Av. Juárez, Col. Centro* ☎*55/5512–2593*), which has a main auditorium and the smaller Manuel Ponce concert hall. The National Opera performs from February through November at the palace. The National Symphony Orchestra stages classical and modern pieces at the palace in spring and fall.

JAZZ & BLUES

Fodor'sChoice ★ Basement lounge **Zinco Jazz Club** (✉*Motolonía 20, at 5 de Mayo, Col. Centro* ☎*55/5518–6369*) toots its horn as the capital's coolest jazz joint. Set in the vault of an art-deco bank in the heart of the revamped Centro Histórico, the club features local and international jazz acts in an intimate, enthusiastic setting that seems to bring out the best in performers. It's open Wednesday through Saturday; entry fee is $10 on Friday and Saturday, and free other days.

MARIACHI

The traditional last stop for nocturnal Mexicans is **Plaza Garibaldi** in Colonia Centro, east of Eje Central Lázaro Cárdenas, between República de Honduras and República de Perú. Here exuberant, and often inebriated, mariachis gather to unwind after evening performances—by performing even more. There are roving mariachis, as well as norteño (country-style) musicians and white-clad jarocho bands (Veracruz-style) peddling songs in the outdoor plaza, where you can also buy beer and shots of tequila. Beware: the alcohol sold in the outdoor square is rotgut. You'll usually find nonadulterated drinks inside the cantinas or clubs surrounding the plaza, where well-to-do Mexicans park themselves and belt out their favorite songs.

■ TIP→ The square was spruced up in the early 1990s to improve its seedy image, but things still get rough late at night. Furthermore, leaving Plaza Garibaldi can be dangerous—be sure to arrange for transportation ahead of time. You may call a tour agency, drive your car and park on the well-lighted ramp below the plaza, or call a safe sitio taxi. It is pretty safe to return to hotels in the Centro via Eje 1 Lazaro Cardenás, but any other streets around the Plaza should be strictly avoided.

ROCK, POP & ALTERNATIVE

The **Auditorio Nacional** (✉ *Paseo de la Reforma 50, across from Nikko México hotel, Col. San Miguel Chapultepec* ☎ *55/5280–9250 or 55/5280–9979* 🌐 *www.auditorio.com.mx*) is smart and modern, with great acoustics.

Bulldog (✉ *Rubens 6, at Av. Revolución, Col. Mixcoac* ☎ *55/5611–8818*), north of Coyoacán, books mostly rock acts. The cover charge varies depending on the headline band; expect to pay at least $25 if a well-known group is playing.

The sound quality may not be the best at the **Circo Volador** (✉ *Calzada de la Viga 146, Col. Jamaica* ☎ *55/5740–9012*), but nobody seems to be complaining at this headbangers' haven. Colonia Jamaica is southeast of the Centro Histórico; it's accessible via subway or sitio taxi.

A choice venue, the **Hard Rock Cafe** (✉ *Campos Elíseos 278, Col. Chapultepec Polanco* ☎ *55/5327–7100 or 55/5327–7101*) is intimate and has state-of-the-art sound.

For the fast and furious, just a short walk from the Cuauhtémoc metro stop, **Multiforo Alicia** (✉ *Cuauhtémoc 91-A, at Durango, Col. Roma* ☎ *55/5511–2100*) headlines foreign and local indie bands playing punk, ska, surf, and garage music. In true punk-rock fashion, the space is poorly ventilated and the sound system leaves much to be desired, but it's a cheap night out and the scene is entertaining.

Palacio de los Deportes (✉ *Av. Río Churubusco and Calle Añil* ☎ *55/5237–9999 Ext. 4264*) has an open-air venue called the Foro Sol where you can catch the glitzy shows of Madonna or the Rolling Stones.

Multi-use venue **Pasagüero** (✉ *Motolinía 33, at 16 de Septiembre, Col. Centro* ☎ *55/5521–6112* 🌐 *www.pasaguero.com*) offers a mixed bag of live indie music, art exhibits, and other cultural events. The concerts start at 10 PM on Thursday, Friday, and Saturday. For a complete listing of upcoming events, visit the Web site.

Though it's in need of an overhaul, the ambience is good at the **Teatro Metropolitano** (✉ *Independencia 90, Col. Centro* ☎ *55/5510–1035 or 55/5510–1045*). It hosts mostly rock concerts.

PUBLIC PARTY

Fodor's Choice ★ There is probably nothing anywhere in the world like a weekend night at **Xochimilco,** the floating gardens that were the breadbasket of the Aztec city of Tenochtitlan. Take the No. 2 metro (blue) line south to its end, in Tasqueña (sometimes written on signs as Taxqueña), and follow the signs across the pedestrian bridge to the *tren ligero*, or light rail, and ride it to its end, at Xochimilco (all this will take less than an hour from the Zócalo). Once in the neighborhood, simply follow the signs saying BARCOS; almost any eastward side street here will lead to a jetty where you can rent a flower-bedecked *trajinera*, with a pilot to push it along (cost is about $16 for three hours). If you go on a warm weekend evening, just before sundown to get the look of the place, you will witness a magical transformation. At dusk canoes pull up with candles, corn, tacos, beer, and tequila shots, and other boats bearing entire mariachi bands pole over to perform while festive locals hail you loudly from their own floating parties. It has been said before by well-traveled individuals that this could be the most beautiful and romantic place on the planet, and you will be hard-pressed to argue otherwise.

THEATER

Good live theater, whether in English or Spanish, is not Mexico City's strong suit. **Centro Cultural Helénico** (☒*Av. Revolución 1500, Col. Guadalupe Inn* ☎*55/5662–2535 or 55/5662–9166*) is one of the most reliable bets.

Centro Cultural Telmex (☒*Av. Cuauhtémoc 19, at Av. Chapultepec, Col. Roma* ☎*55/5514–2300*) stages Spanish-language versions of Broadway plays. Ticket prices range from $18 to $48. Showtimes are Monday, Wednesday, and Friday at 8 PM; Saturday at 5 PM; and Sunday at 1:30 PM and 6 PM.

El Vicio (☒*Madrid 13, Coyoacán* ☎*55/5659–1139*), run by four satirists, puts on lively music, cabaret, and political theater, but you'll need proficient Spanish to understand the performances.

FILM

Besides the mainstream movie theaters offering dubbed Hollywood blockbusters, there are a profusion of small-scale cineclubs in the city, whose location, times, and repertoire vary infinitely. Pick up a copy of Tiempo Libre at a newsstand or look on the paper's Web site at 🌐*www.tiempolibre.com.mx* for times and locations.

Centro Cultural Universitaria (☒*Insurgentes Sur 3000, Ciudad Universitaria* ☎*55/5622–7100*), run by the national university, UNAM, regularly shows an esoteric selection of films.

Cineteca Nacional (☒*Av. México Coyoacán 389, Col. Zoco, Coyoacán* ☎*55/4155–1200*) is the national cinematheque, showing several films a day from all over the world and throughout the complete history of the moving image. Unlike most Coyoacán attractions, it is right near the Coyoacán metro stop.

SHOPPING

The most concentrated shopping area is in the **Zona Rosa,** which is chock-full of boutiques, jewelry stores, leather-goods shops, antiques stores, and art galleries.

Polanco, a choice residential neighborhood along the northeast perimeter of Bosque de Chapultepec, has blossomed into a more upscale shopping area. Select shops line the huge, ultramodern **Plaza Polanco** (✉ *Jaime Balmes 11, Col. Polanco*). You can also head to the **Plaza Masarik** (✉ *Av. Presidente Masarik and Anatole France, Col. Polanco*). **Plaza Moliere** (✉ *Moliere between Calles Horacio and Homero, Col. Polanco*) is another upscale shopping area. **Reforma 222** (✉ *Reforma 222 at Havre, Col. Zona Rosa*) is a new shopping center with an attached apartment building. At the time of this writing, it only has a few department stores that are found in other parts of the city, as well as fast-food restaurants. Several stalls and storefronts are still vacant.

La Condesa, though better known for restaurants and cafés, is sprouting designer boutiques, primarily for a younger crowd. Jewelers, shoe shops, and hip housewares stores are squeezing in as well. Most cluster along avenidas Michoacán, Vicente Suárez, and Tamaulipas.

Hundreds of shops with more modest trappings and better prices are spread along the length of **Avenida Insurgentes** and **Avenida Juárez.**

DEPARTMENT STORES, MALLS & SHOPPING ARCADES

Antara Polanco (✉ *Ejercito Nacional s/n, Col. Polanco* ☎ *55/5280–2954*) is one of the only outdoor malls in the city. The upscale collection of stores includes Carolina Herrera, Kenneth Cole, and American Eagle.

Bazar del Centro (✉ *Isabel la Católica 30, just below Calle Madero, Col. Centro*), in a restored, late-17th-century mansion built around a garden courtyard, houses several chic boutiques and prestigious jewelers such as **Aplijsa** (☎ *55/5521–1923*), known for its fine gold, silver, pearls, and gemstones, and **Ginza** (☎ *55/5518–6453*), which has Japanese pearls, including the prized cultured variety. Other shops sell Taxco silver, Tonalá stoneware, and Mexican tequilas.

Liverpool (✉ *Av. Insurgentes Sur 1310, Col. Guadalupe Inn* ✉ *Mariano Escobedo 425, Col. Polanco* ✉ *Plaza Satélite shopping center* ✉ *Perisur shopping mall* ☎ *55/5262–9999 general customer service, 01800/713–555 toll-free in Mexico* 🌐 *www.liverpool.com.mx*) is the largest retailer in Mexico City and often has bargains on clothes.

Magic Trek (☎ *55/5440–1483* 🌐 *www.magictrek.com*) is a place where children can dress up and play at different kinds of make-believe adventures while their parents shop.

The upscale department store chain **El Palacio de Hierro** (✉ *Av. Durango and Salamanca, Col. Condesa* ✉ *Plaza Moliere, Col. Polanco* ✉ *Plaza Coyoacán, Col. Xoco* 🌐 *www.palaciodehierro.com.mx*)

is noted for items by well-known designers, as well as its seductive advertising campaigns.

LAS HORAS

Department stores are generally open Monday, Tuesday, Thursday, and Friday 10–7, and Wednesday and Saturday 10–8.

Parque Delta (✉*Av. Cuauhtémoc 462, Col. Navarte* ☎*55/5584–3409*) is a new shopping mall in the Roma neighborhood with clothing stores, a movie theater, one of the few Applebee's restaurants in Mexico, and a branch of the celebrated Bajío restaurant.

Perisur shopping mall (✉*Periférico Sur, Perisur* 🌐*www.perisur.com.mx*), on the southern edge of the city, near where the Periférico Expressway meets Avenida Insurgentes, is posh, pricey, and always attractively decorated for the holidays—especially at Christmas.

Piccolo Mondo (☎*55/5395–2335* 🌐*www.piccolomondo.com.mx*) has a wide variety of toys and games, and is a good place to play with the kids, or to leave them while you shop.

Plaza Loreto (✉*Av. Revolución and Río Magdalena, San Angel* ☎*55/5550–6292*) has a strange history. It was built on land that once held a wheat mill owned by Martín Cortés, the son of conqueror Hernán Cortés, and later a paper factory. This small outdoor mall has boutiques, CD stores, a Sanborns, and the Museo Soumaya.

Plaza La Rosa (✉*Between Amberes and Génova, Zona Rosa*), a modern shopping arcade, has 72 prestigious shops and boutiques, including Mango and Diesel. It spans the depth of the block between Londres and Hamburgo, with entrances on both streets.

Portales de los Mercaderes (*Merchants Arcade* ✉*Extending length of west side of Zócalo between Calles Madero and 16 de Septiembre, Col. Centro*) has attracted merchants since 1524. It's lined with jewelry shops selling gold (often by the gram) and authentic Taxco silver at prices lower than those in Taxco, where the overhead is higher. In the middle of the Portales de los Mercaderes is **Tardán** (✉*Plaza de la Constitución 7, Col. Centro* ☎*55/5512–2459*), an unusual shop specializing in fashionable men's hats of every shape and style.

Sanborns (🌐*www.sanborns.com.mx*) is a chain of minidepartment stores with some 70 branches in Mexico City. The most convenient are at Calle Madero 4 (its original store in the House of Tiles, downtown); several along Paseo de la Reforma (including one at the Angel Monument and another four blocks west of the Diana Fountain); in San Angel (on Avenida de la Revolución and Avenida de la Paz); Coyoacán (at the Jardín Centenario); and in the Zona Rosa (one at the corner of Niza and Hamburgo and another at Londres 130 in the Hotel Calinda Geneve). They carry ceramics and crafts (and can ship anywhere), and most have restaurants or coffee shops, a pharmacy, ATMs, and periodical/book departments with English-language publications.

Santa Fe (⊠*Salida a Toluca, Santa Fe*) is the largest mall in Latin America, with 285 stores, a movie theater, an international exhibition center, hotels, and several restaurants. It's in the wealthy Santa Fe district, which in recent years has become the favored office real-estate property in the city. To get here, take the Periférico Expressway south to the exit marked CENTRO SANTA FE.

MARKETS

Fodor'sChoice ★ Open every day about 10–5, the bustling **Mercado Artesanal La Ciudadela** (⊠*Balderas, 1 block south of Parque José María Morelos, Col. Juárez*) bursts with the widest range of wares and the best bargains in the capital. Browse through the crafts, from Talavera pottery, leather belts, guitars, tile-framed mirrors, hammocks, silverware, and papier-mâché skeletons to rugs, trays from Olinalá, and the ubiquitous sombrero. Prices are better than at most other crafts markets, but you can still haggle. Not only are prices good, but this is a fabulous market in which to wander around. If you are in the area on Saturday, head out of the market and watch the dancers across the street. In the open-air Plaza de la Ciudadela, enthusiasts from all over the city gather at around noon to dance danzón every Saturday. A number of casual restaurants serve up hearty set-menu lunches for $3–$5. Covered stalls take up a whole square, a 10–15-minute walk from the Alameda.

★ A must if you're in town on a Saturday is a visit to the **Bazar Sábado** (*[Saturday Bazaar]* ⊠*Plaza San Jacinto, San Angel*). Hundreds of vendors sell tons of crafts, silver, wood carvings, embroidered clothing, leather goods, wooden masks, beads, *amates* (bark paintings), and trinkets at stalls on the network of cobbled streets outside. Inside the bazaar building, a renovated two-story colonial mansion, are the better-quality—and higher-priced—goods, including *alebrijes* (painted wooden animals from Oaxaca), glassware, pottery, jewelry, and papier-mâché flowers. A patio buffet and an indoor restaurant will help you conquer hunger and thirst.

Sunday 10–4, more than 100 artists exhibit and sell their paintings and sculpture at the **Jardín del Arte** (*[Garden of Art]* ⊠*Río Nevada, between Sullivan and Manuel Villalongín, Parque Sullivan, northeast of Reforma-Insurgentes intersection, Col. Cuauhtémoc*). Along the west side of the park is a colorful weekend mercado with scores of food stands.

The **Mercado Insurgentes** (aka *Mercado Zona Rosa* ⊠*Between Florencia and Amberes, Zona Rosa*) is an entire block deep, with entrances on both Londres and Liverpool. This typical public neighborhood market distinguishes itself from others in one noticeable way: most of the stalls (222 of them) sell crafts. You can find all kinds of items—including serapes and ponchos, baskets, pottery, silver, pewter, fossils, and onyx. Expect to pay slightly higher prices here than at the Mercado Artesanal de la Ciudadela.

The enormous market **La Lagunilla** (✉*Libertad, between República de Chile and Calle Allende, Col. Centro*) has been a site for local trade and bartering for more than five centuries. The day to go is Sunday, when flea-market and antiques stands are set up outside, selling everything from antique paintings and furniture to old magazines and plastic toys. Dress down and watch out for pickpockets; it's known affectionately as the Thieves' Market—local lore says you can buy back on Sunday what was stolen from your home Saturday.

SPECIALTY SHOPS

ANTIQUES

Antigüedades Coloniart (✉*Estocolmo 37, at Hamburgo, Zona Rosa* ☎*55/5514–4799*) has good-quality antique paintings, furniture, and sculpture.

Bazar de Antigüedades (✉*Between Londres and Hamburgo, opposite Mercado Insurgentes, Zona Rosa*) is a line of antiques stores along a passageway, at its liveliest on Saturday.

Galería Windsor (✉*Hamburgo 224, at Praga, Zona Rosa* ☎*55/5525–2881 or 55/5525–2996* 🌐*www.galeriawindsor.com.mx*) specializes in 18th- and 19th-century antiques.

Rodrigo Rivera Lake (✉*Campos Elíseos 199-Piso 10, Col. Polanco* ☎*55/5281–5505*) collects high-quality antiques and decorative art. It's open by appointment only.

ART

The **Galeria de Arte Mexicano** (✉*Gob. Rafael Rebollar 43, Col. San Miguel Chapultepec* ☎*55/5272–5696 or 55/5272–5529* 🌐*www.arte-gam.com*), founded in 1935, was the first place in Mexico City dedicated full-time to the sale and promotion of art (before its inception, there were no official galleries in the city). The GAM, as it's often referred to, has played an important role in many Mexican art movements and continues to support many of the most important artists in the country. GAM has also published noteworthy books; these works and catalogs are available at the gallery bookstore.

Collectors won't want to miss the best gallery in the south of the city, the **Galería Kin** (✉*Altavista 92, Col. San Angel* ☎*55/5661–5556*), which exhibits a variety of contemporary Mexican painting and sculpture.

The **Juan Martín Gallery** (✉*Dickens 33-B, Col. Polanco* ☎*55/5280–0277* 🌐*www.arte-mexico.com/juanmartin*) shows avant-garde work.

Misrachi (✉*Av. Presidente Masarik 83, at Taine, Col. Polanco* ☎*55/5281–7456* 🌐*www.misrachi.com.mx* 🏨*Hotel Nikko, Campos Elíseos 204, Col. Polanco* ☎*55/5280–3866 or 55/5280–5728*) promotes well-known Mexican and international artists.

The **Nina Menocal de Rocha Gallery** (✉*Zacatecas 93, Col. Roma* ☎*55/5564–7209* 🌐*www.ninamenocal.com*) specializes in up-and-coming Cuban painters, but the small staff isn't always very welcoming.

The **Oscar Roman Gallery** (✉*Julio Verne 14, Col. Polanco* ☎*55/5280–0436* 🌐*www.arte-mexico.com/romanosc*) is packed with work by good Mexican painters with a contemporary edge.

> **ART SMARTS**
>
> The best group of modern galleries is in La Roma. Before you go, check out www.arte-mexico.com to find out what events are going on.

Praxis Arte International (✉*Arquimedes 175, Col. Polanco* ☎*55/5254–8813 or 55/5255–5700* 🌐*www.praxismexico.com*) also promotes Mexican and Latin American artists. They work with many distinguished artists like Santiago Carbonell and Roberto Cortázar.

The store and gallery of the renowned **Sergio Bustamante** (✉*Nikko México hotel, Campos Elíseos 204, Col. Polanco* ☎*55/5282–2638* 🌐*www.sergiobustamante.com.mx*) displays and sells the artist's wild sculpture and jewelry.

CANDY

Celaya (✉*5 de Mayo 39, Col. Centro* ☎*55/5521–1787* ✉*Orizaba 143, Col. Roma* ☎*55/5514–8438*) was founded in 1874, and has been haven for those with a sweet tooth ever since. It specializes in candied pineapple, guava, and other exotic fruits; almond paste; candied walnut rolls; and *cajeta,* made with thick caramelized milk. These traditional sweets are not available in many other stores in Mexico City.

El Secreto (✉ San Jerónimo 924,*Col. San Jerónimo* ☎*55/ 5595–4727* ✉*Prado Norte 525, Col. Lomas de Chapultepec* ☎*55/5520–8493*) also offers traditional candies. These sweets are not brought in from around the country, like those at Celaya, but are made in Mexico City by the Torres family, the shop owners who are serious about their secret recipes. Their two shops aren't close to most major sights, but worth a trip if you have a sweet tooth.

DESIGNER CLOTHING

At first glance, the linen dresses in **Carmen Ríon** (✉*Av. Michoacán 30-A, at Parque México, Col. Condesa* ☎*55/5264–6179*) may seem classic, but look closely and you'll find innovative ties and fastenings. The jewelry, often combining wood, silver, and seedpods, is equally unique.

The Little Black Dress has a D.F. outpost: **Chanel** (✉*Av. Presidente Masarik 450-2, Col. Polanco* ☎*55/5282–3121* 🌐*www.chanel.com*).

Frattina (✉*Av. Presidente Masarik 420, at Calderón de la Barca and Edgar Allan Poe, Col. Polanco* ☎*55/5281–4036* ✉*Altavista 52, San Angel* ☎*55/5550–6830* 🌐*www.frattina.com.mx*) carries women-only work by international and top Mexican designers.

If the exchange rate goes your way, a trip to **Hermès** (✉*Av. Presidente Masarik 422A, between Calderón de la Barca and Edgar Allan Poe, Col. Polanco* ☎*55/5282–2118* 🌐*www.hermes.com*) may be in order for their legendary silk scarves and leather goods.

INTERIOR DESIGN & UNIQUE GIFTS

Mexico City has several independent furniture stores that offer unique designs and extraordinary gifts.

Over a hundred young designers display work at a small shop in the Colonia Roma. **DIME** (✉ *Álvaro Obregón 185, Col. Roma* ☎ *55/2454–6790* 🌐 *www.dimetienda.com.mx*) is a fun place to browse, and a good place to find original, one-of-a-kind designs. Kitsch is welcome here, and they have a large selection of T-shirts and bags made from plastic tablecloths, and images of the Virgin as well as of the lucha libre.

dupuis (✉ *Fuentes 180B, Pedregal* ☎ *55/5595–4852* ✉ *Palmas 240, Las Lomas* ☎ *55/5540–5349* ✉ *Diego Rivera 50, San Angel* ☎ *55/5550–6178* 🌐 *www.dupuis.com.mx*) is a pricey furniture store with different styles steeped in various traditions, including indigenous Mexican designs, Spanish colonial decorations, and the strong French influence that characterized so much Mexican design at the beginning of the 20th century. They also have unique accessories in subdued colors, including flowerpots, lamps, and picture frames, which make excellent gifts—and dupuis is known for elegant gift presentation.

A new find for the young and trendy in the Condesa neighborhood is **Mob** (✉ *Campeche 322, Col. Condesa* ☎ *55/5286–7239* 🌐 *www.mob.com.mx*), a store with hip accessories for home decoration.

JEWELRY

Cartier (✉ *Av. Presidente Masarik 438, Col. Polanco* ☎ *55/5281–5528* 🌐 *www.cartier.com*) sells the sophisticated jewelry and clothes under the auspices of the French Cartier.

For unusual jewelry, mostly in silver, glass, and stone, look in at **Entenaya** (✉ *Montes de Oca 47, Col. Condesa* ☎ *55/5286–1535*).

Pelletier (✉ *Torcuato Caso 237, Col. Polanco* ☎ *55/5250–8600*) sells fine jewelry and watches.

Plata Real (✉ *Goldsmith 56-D, Col. Polanco* ☎ *55/5281–0818* 🌐 *www.platareal.com.mx*) aims to preserve silversmithing from the colonial period. In addition to creating replicas of colonial pieces, they offer high-quality contemporary sculptures, many by well-respected Mexican artists.

Tane (✉ *Av. Presidente Masarik 430, Col. Polanco* ☎ *55/5281–4775* ✉ *Santa Catarina 207, San Angel* ☎ *55/5616–0165* ✉ *Centro Comercial Perisur, Periférico Sur 4690-363, Col. Pedregal* ☎ *55/5606–7834* ✉ *Casa Lamm, Alvaro Obregón 99, Col. Roma* ☎ *55/5208–0171* 🌐 *www.tane.com.mx*) is a treasure trove of perhaps the best silverwork in Mexico—jewelry, flatware, candelabra, museum-quality reproductions of archaeological finds, and bold new designs by young Mexican silversmiths.

LEATHER

Aries (✉ *Avenida de las Palmas 858, Las Lomas* ☎ *55/5202–7005*) is Mexico's finest purveyor of leather goods, with a superb selection of bags and accessories for men and women; prices are high.

Las Bolsas de Coyoacán (*✉Carrillo Puerto 9, Coyoacán ☎55/5554–2010*) specializes in high-quality leather goods.

Tecnopiel (*✉Londres 158, Local B, Col. Juárez ☎55/5511–0757 🌐www.tecnopiel.com*) sells quality jackets, bags, and luggage at fair prices in the heart of the Zona Rosa.

Via Spiga (*✉Hamburgo 136, Zona Rosa ☎55/5207–9997 or 55/5208–9224*) has a fine selection of shoes, gloves, and handbags.

MEXICAN CRAFTS

A store selling high-quality art-craft at reasonable prices (though prices here really do vary, so check out the competition if you want to make sure you are getting a good deal) is in the heart of the downtown area. Its location makes browsing here a great way to get in both your shopping and sightseeing if you are only in town for a short period. **Arte Mexicano para el Mundo** (*✉Monte de Piedad 11, Col. Centro ☎55/5180–0300 🌐www.arte-mexicano.com.mx*) has a floor with temporary exhibits, a textile shop, a ceramics shop, a bookstore, and a fabulous restaurant on the sixth floor, overlooking the Zócalo. The restaurant would be worth a visit for the view alone, but the food, mainly Mexican with inventive temporary specialties, is also great.

Browse for folk art, sculpture, and furniture in the gallery **Artesanos de México** (*✉Londres 117, Zona Rosa ☎55/5514–7455*).

Under the auspices of the National Council for Culture and Arts, **Fonart** (*National Fund for Promoting Arts and Crafts ✉Juárez 89, Col. Juárez ☎55/5521–0171 ✉ Main store–warehouse ✉Av. Patriotismo 691, Col. Mixcoac ☎55/5563–4060 ✉Av. Paseo de la Reforma 116, Col. Juárez ☎55/5328–5000 🌐www.fonart.gob.mx*) operates three stores in Mexico City and others around the country. Prices are fixed and high, but the diverse, top-quality folk art and handcrafted furnishings from all over Mexico represent some of the best artisans. The best location is downtown, west of Alameda Park. Major sales at near-wholesale prices are held from time to time at the main store–warehouse.

Miniaturas Felguerez (*✉Hamburgo 85, Col. Juárez ☎55/5525–8145*) is a tiny shop filled with tiny things, from dollhouse furniture and lead soldiers to miniature Nativity scenes.

You can find handwoven wool rugs, tapestries, and fabrics with original and unusual designs at **Tamacani** (*✉Av. Insurgentes Sur 1748B, Col. Florida ☎55/5662–7133 🌐www.tamacani.com*).

SPORTS & THE OUTDOORS

Latin sports such as the *fiesta brava* (bullfighting)—brought to Mexico by the Spanish—have enjoyed popularity for more than four centuries in the capital, which attracts the country's best athletes. And although the roots of *fútbol* (soccer) are probably English, a weekend afternoon game at Mexico City's colossal Estadio Azteca makes clear that this is the sport Mexicans are craziest about. Baseball and boxing have strong followings, too, as does the over-the-top *lucha libre* (wrestling). There are plenty of lovely parks for a safe jog or walk. For more challenging activities, seek out an ecotourism or adventure travel agency for a getaway such as white-water rafting in nearby Veracruz, volcano climbing in Puebla, or mountain biking in the Desierto de los Leones. Some city agencies leave much to be desired, though, so you may need to take extra initiative to find the right group.

ADVENTURE TRAVEL & ECOTOURISM

Mexico continues to develop both government offices and private industry groups to promote ecotourism, but these are still nascent. A good starting point for information is the **Asociación Mexicana de Turismo de Aventura y Ecoturismo** ([**AMTAVE**] ✉ *Mariposa 1012-A, Col. General Anaya* ☎ *55/5688–3883, 01800/654–4452 toll-free in Mexico* 🌐 *www.amtave.org*), a group of ecotourism and adventure-travel providers. The association produces an annual catalog and a bilingual (English-Spanish) Web site.

Aventura Vertical (✉ *Juan Bautista 450, Col. La Nopalera* ☎ *55/5863–3363* 🌐 *www.aventuravertical.com*) offers weekend courses and trips for rock climbing, ice climbing, camping, and canyoneering, among other sports, with certified bilingual guides. Equipment is provided or you can bring your own.

A number of adventure-travel agencies have sprouted up to entice both tourists and locals out of the chaos of Mexico City for a weekend of white-water rafting, rappelling, or biking. One of the best is **Río y Montaña Expediciones** (✉ *Guillermo González Camarena 500, at Manuel Chávez, Col. Centro de Ciudad Santa Fe* ☎ *55/5292–5032* 🌐 *www.rioymontana.com*), which organizes trips to the nearby State of Mexico and to other popular states like Veracruz and Oaxaca.

BOXING

The weathered **Arena México** (✉ *Dr. Lavista between Dr. Carmona and Dr. Lucio, Col. Doctores* ☎ *55/5588–0478*) holds amateur boxing events on most Saturdays, starting at around 6 PM.

For top-notch, lightning-quick pugilism, **Salon 21** (✉ *Moliere, at Andrómaco, Col. Ampliación Granada* ☎ *55/5255–5459*), near Polanco, hosts professional and amateur bouts about once every two weeks. Fights are announced one week before the event at 🌐 *www.ticketmaster.com.mx*. Ticket prices are $9 for general admission and $20 for ringside seats. The opening match begins at 8:30 PM.

BULLFIGHTING

The main season for bullfighting is the dry season, around November through March, when celebrated matadors appear at **Plaza México** (✉ *Calle Agusto Rodín 241, at Holbein, Col. Ciudad de los Deportes* ☎ *55/5563–3959* 🌐 *www.plazadetorosmexico.com.mx*), the world's largest bullring (it seats 40,000). Tickets, which range from $4.50 to $55, can be purchased at the bullring's ticket booths (open weekends 9:30–2 and 3–7). The show goes on at 4 PM on Sunday.

LUCHA LIBRE

Wrestling is right up there with soccer as a sport that evokes many emotional outbursts, though it doesn't have as much cachet as the latter. It's been around since the mid-1800s, or at least the early 1900s (there is some debate about how and when it began), but it is growing more and more famous with international children's programs and movies like Nacho Libre (2007). Wrestlers wear masks and dress in costumes depicting good or evil (the devil against the angel, for example), and it's usually good who wins after a couple of acrobatic slams and pitches out of the ring. The debate on whether the fights are fixed rages on—and is a heated debate among aficionados. The good guy wrestlers often become folk heroes, appear in comic books and movies, and are role models for young kids. One of the most famous wrestlers was El Santo (The Saint), whose son continues the legacy. Most wrestlers are from the barrios and the sport attracts their compatriots: it's rowdy and loud. Note that both of the arenas where you can catch the lucha are in parts of town where caution is recommended as you come and go. Be sure to arrange for safe transport (hailing down a cab in the street is not recommended), and go with company whenever possible. Matches take place every Friday night at 8:30 at the **Arena Mexico** (☒*Dr. Lavista between Dr. Carmona and Dr. Lucio, Col. Doctores* ☎*55/5588–0508*). Ringside seats fetch $10. Avoid hailing cabs directly outside the arena.

Matches also take place at the **Arena Coliseo** (☒*Perú 77, Col. Centro* ☎*55/5588–0266*), the oldest arena in Mexico, every Tuesday at 7:30 and Sunday at 5.

NEED A BREAK?

El Cuadrilátero (☒ Luis Moya 73*Col. Centro* ☎ 55/5521–3060) For true lucha libre fans, this little downtown café, decorated with historic photos from the lucha libre and professional masks, is a real treat. The menu was designed with a luchador's appetite in mind. There are plates named after famous fighters, and the enormous size of the plates actually have attracted some famous fighters. With a little luck, if you pass by, you might run in to some

PROFESSIONAL BASEBALL

Thanks to Mexico City's batter-friendly thin air, baseball fans here are usually treated to slugfests at **Foro Sol** (☒*Av. Viaducto Río de la Piedad, at Río Churubusco, Col. Granjas México* ☎*55/5639–8722* 🌐*www.diablos.com.mx*). The regular season runs from March to July; playoffs begin in August. Ticket prices range from $1 to $6. When purchasing tickets, you'll be asked if you want to sit along the baseline of the home team (the Diablos Rojos) or of the visitors.

SOCCER

Fútbol is the sport that Mexicans are most passionate about, which is evident in the size of their soccer stadium, **Estadio Azteca** (✉*Calz. de Tlalpan 3465, Tlalpan* ☎*55/5617–8080*), the second largest in Latin America and home of the Aguilas de América, one of Mexico's top fútbol teams. The World Cup Finals were held here in 1970 and 1986. You can buy tickets outside the stadium in the south of the city on the same day of any minor game. For more important games, buy tickets a week in advance. The Pumas, a popular university-sponsored team, play at Estadio Olímpico, Avenida Insurgentes Sur at Universidad Nacional Autónoma de México, Ciudad Universitaria. Tickets sell fast for Pumas games, so the best bet is to order them through Ticketmaster at 55/5325–9000 or online at www.ticketmaster.com.mx.

Around Mexico City

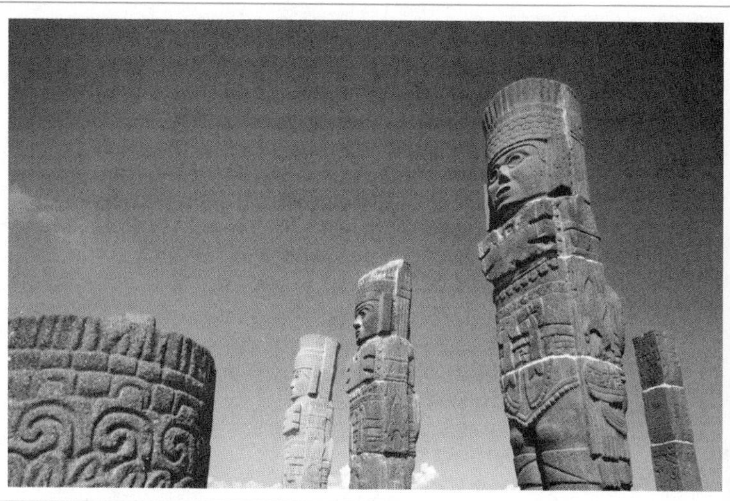

The Atlantes, Tula

WORD OF MOUTH

"Topozlan set in a deep valley is [impressive]. My favorite towns are Tlalpujahua and El Oro on the Michoacan/Estado de Mexico line. Valle del Bravo is . . . an Alpine-like resort town nestled around a beautiful lake. They have wonderful foods . . . including delicious local fresh and smoked trout and morel and chanterelle mushrooms from the forests at five pesos a bag!"

–northerner

www.fodors.com/forums

AROUND MEXICO CITY

TOP REASONS TO GO

★ **Day-tripping to ancient cities:** Spend the day scrambling over ruins and pyramids and be back in Mexico City for dinner.

★ **Experiencing the great outdoors:** Some of the country's highest mountains, such as Iztaccíhuatl, offer challenging climbs for the intrepid or easier trails at their bases.

★ **The chance to eat Puebla's regional cuisine:** The city has made some important contributions to Mexico's culinary heritage, such as mole, a sauce that can use upwards of 30 different ingredients, including chocolate.

★ **Getting a European vacation without having to cross the pond:** Due to its lakeside setting amid pine forests, and popularity with wealthy jet-setters, Valle de Bravo has been likened to the "Switzerland of Mexico."

★ **Putting the guidebook away:** In Tlaxcala and Cuetzalan, you'll run out of sights to see in the first 15 minutes. The real joy is strolling around without an agenda.

1 Valle de Bravo & Environs. Lakeside Valle de Bravo has eclipsed Cuernavaca as the weekend getaway of Mexico City's elite. It's a good spot for sports, both on and off the lake. Parque Nacional Nevado de Toluca has a bunch of trails snaking up its mountain; there's also a scenic drive if you can't make the climb.

2 Cuernavaca & Environs. This is the direction to head in if you want to find a spa or *temazcal, a Mayan sweat lodge.* For centuries Cuernavaca has been the old standby for Mexicans fleeing the capital. Nearby Tepoztlán has become a center for meditation, yoga, and the like, and is cleaner and more peaceful. The ruins of Xochicalco are a good side trip from Cuernavaca.

3 Teotihuacán & Tula. Both sets of ruins are about an hour north of the city. They're outstanding day trips, as there's frequent bus service to both from the capital. Teotihuacán is a must—the view from either of its two pyramids is worth the trip alone. Tula is equally striking and much less crowded with visitors.

4 Puebla & Environs. If you don't have time to visit the Heartland, colonial Puebla and its surrounding towns are a great alternative. Puebla's the hub of the region; from here you can head to the city's smaller, more peaceful counterparts, Cholula and Tlaxcala, or take a four-hour bus ride up winding mountain roads to Cuetzalan, a beautiful town in the Sierra Norte.

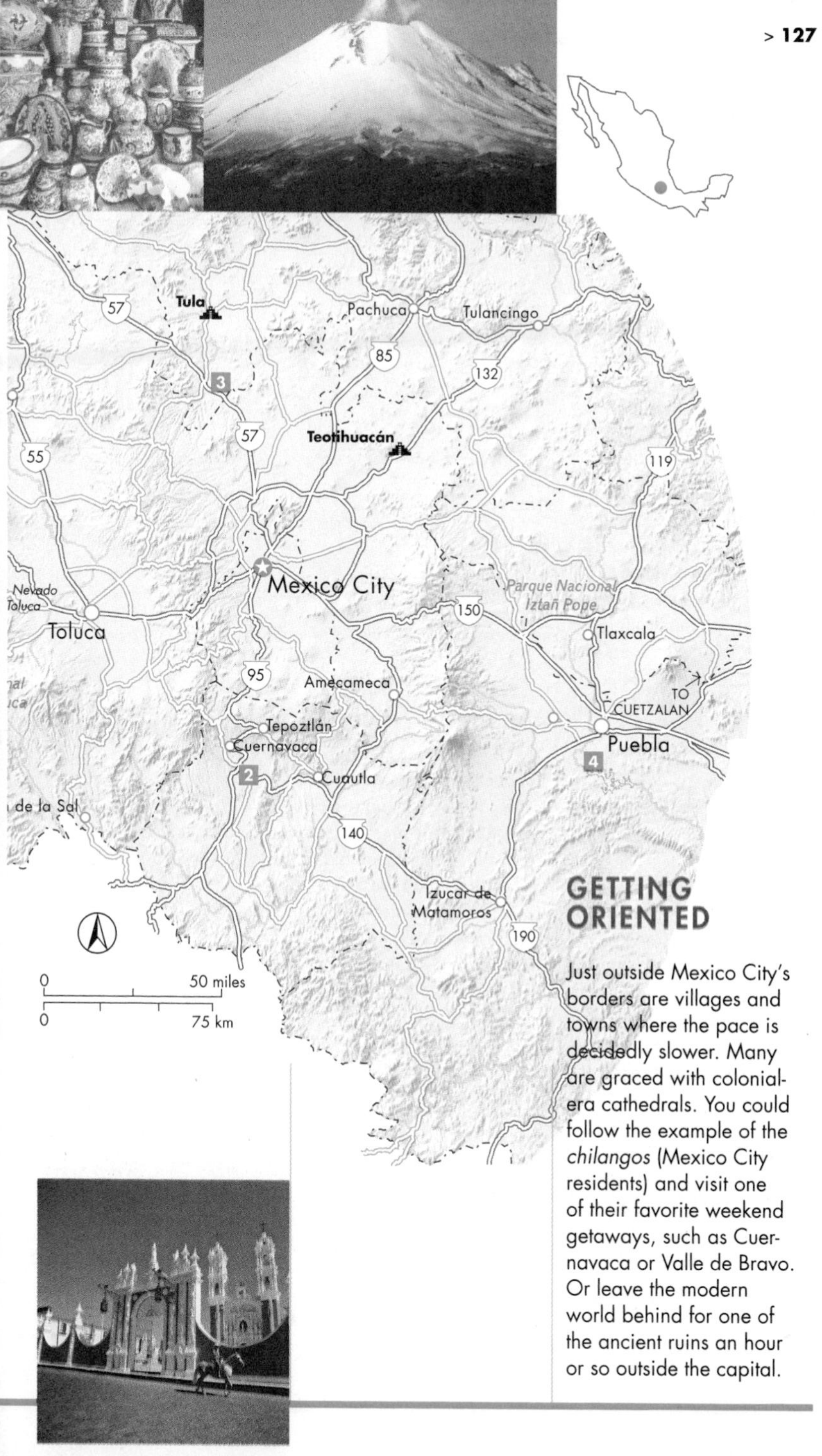

GETTING ORIENTED

Just outside Mexico City's borders are villages and towns where the pace is decidedly slower. Many are graced with colonial-era cathedrals. You could follow the example of the *chilangos* (Mexico City residents) and visit one of their favorite weekend getaways, such as Cuernavaca or Valle de Bravo. Or leave the modern world behind for one of the ancient ruins an hour or so outside the capital.

AROUND MEXICO CITY PLANNER

Day Trips vs. Extended Stays

Mexico City is less than two hours away, so an overnight stay won't be necessary (the exception is Cuetzalan, which is six hours from the capital or four hours from Puebla). If you're going to Cuernavaca or Valle de Bravo, you should plan to overnight. Two nights in either city would allow you to do a side trip to the ruins of Xochicalco (from Cuernavaca) or to the Parque Nacional Nevado de Toluca (from Valle). You can visit Puebla on a day trip, but it would be a shame to rush it. Moreover, the city is lovely at night, when the buildings around the zócalo are floodlit, and the sidewalk cafés along the plaza fill up. If you do overnight, spend the first day seeing the city and the next day in nearby Cholula or at the ruins of Cacaxtla. In addition, you might want to leave some flexibility in your schedule for an overnight stay at the magical Hotel La Escondida in Tlaxcala.

Health Concerns

Even if you don't feel the altitude in Mexico City proper, you're bound to feel it if you head up to Cuetzalan or while attempting to climb the pyramids at Teotihuacán; take it slow and give yourself time to acclimate.

Travel Times

BY BUS FROM MEXICO CITY

City	Time
Tula	1½ hrs
Puebla	2 hrs
Cholula	1¾ hrs
Tlaxcala	1¾ hrs
Cuetzalan	6 hrs (4 hrs from Puebla)
Valle de Bravo	3 hrs

Note that travel times can vary greatly. Traffic snarls, especially at highway exits and tollbooths, can eat up a great deal of time. The easiest way to cut down on time in traffic, especially at city exits, is to plan on traveling when others are not. Head out of the capital early in the morning, for example.

Booking in Advance

Many of these places are popular destinations for Mexican families and may fill up fast during major holidays and festivals. Advance reservations are advised for the Christmas period and Semana Santa. On the long weekend marking Independence Day (September 16) it's often hard to get a room in Cuernavaca or Valle de Bravo. You should also make reservations if you plan to visit Cuetzalan during the town's fair on October 4.

WHAT IT COSTS IN DOLLARS

	¢	$	$$	$$$	$$$$
Restaurants	under $5	$5–$10	$10–$15	$15–$25	over $25
Hotels	under $50	$50–$75	$75–$150	$150–$250	over $250

Restaurant prices are per person for a main course at dinner. Hotel prices are for two people in a standard double room.

Updated by Michele Joyce

PUEBLA, A WELL-PRESERVED COLONIAL TOWN that is the capital of the state of the same name, is a beautiful city and a destination in its own right. You can cover the city in a day trip, but you really should try to stay overnight. You could be drawn onward by nearby Cholula, with its dozens of churches, or Tlaxcala, with a pair of shady plazas perfect for spending a lazy afternoon in. Farther north in Puebla state you'll find the mountain town of Cuetzalan, with its wonderful Sunday market. If you've opted to head this way instead of hitting Teotihuacán and Tula, you can get a ruins fix at Cacaxtla.

PUEBLA

120 km (75 mi) east of Mexico City center.

The city of Puebla fairly bursts with baroque flourishes and the colors of its famed Talavera tiles. The downtown area in particular overflows with religious structures; it probably has more ex-convents and monasteries, chapels, and churches per square mile than anywhere else in the country.

The city center generally follows a tidy grid pattern. The streets are either *avenidas* or *calles*, and most are numbered. Avenidas run east (*oriente*) and west (*poniente*), while calles run north (*norte*) and south (*sur*). Odd-numbered avenidas start south of the *zócalo* (town square) and even-numbered avenidas start from the square's north side. Odd-numbered calles begin on the west of the zócalo, even-numbered calles to the east.

TIP→ Some of the blocks are very long here, so if you get tired or need to save time, hail a taxi. They're safe and should cost no more than $4 for a ride in the city center—just remember to fix the price before you set off.

GETTING HERE & AROUND

Buses bound for Puebla depart several times an hour from Mexico City's TAPO terminal. On ADO, the most reliable company, the two-hour ride costs about $11. From Mexico City's Terminal del Sur, hourly Cristobal Colón buses cost $12. By car, trips on the toll road Route 150D take about 1½ hours; on Route 190, the scenic—and bumpy—free road, the same journey takes three hours.

TIP→ The double-decker Turibus (☎ 55/5563-6693 🌐 web.turibus.com) is a good option for exploring the city. Every day from 10 AM to 5:30 PM, these open-topped buses leave from the zócalo.

ESSENTIALS

Bus Contacts **ADO** (*☎ 55/5133-2424 🌐 www.adogl.com.mx*). **Cristobal Colón** (*☎ 55/5544-9008 in Mexico City, 222/225-9007 in Puebla 🌐 www.ticketbus.com*).

Currency Exchange **Caja Central** (*✉ Portal Hidalgo 6-11, Col. Centro ☎ 222/232 –9691*).

Medical Assistance **Hospital Angeles** (*✉ Av. Kepler 2143, Unidad Territorial ☎ 222/303-6600*).

Post Office **Central Post Office** (⊠*16 de Septiembre 305, Col. Centro*).

Rental Cars **Avis** (⊠*Blvd. Hermanos Serdán 104, Col. Real del Monte* ☎*222/249-6199* ⊕*www.avis.com*). **Hertz** (⊠, *Col. Real del Monte* ☎*222/249 –6199* ⊕*www.hertz.com*).

Visitor & Tour Info **Puebla Municipal Tourist Office** (⊠*Portal Hidalgo 14, Centro Histórico* ☎*222/404-5008* ⊕*www.puebladezaragoza.gob.mx*). **Puebla State Tourism Office** (⊠*Av. 5 Oriente 3, Centro Histórico* ☎*222/777-1506* ⊕*www.puebla.gob.mx*).

EXPLORING

MAIN ATTRACTIONS

12 **Barrio del Artista.** Watch painters and sculptors at work in the galleries in this neighborhood. Farther down Calle 8 Norte you can buy Talavera pottery and other local crafts from the dozens of small stores and street vendors. There are occasional concerts and open-air theater performances. ⊠*Calle 8 Norte and Av. 6 Oriente* ⊙*Daily 10–6.*

6 **La Calle de los Dulces.** Puebla is famous for all kinds of homemade goodies. Calle de Santa Clara, also known as Sweets Street, is lined with shops selling a wide variety of sugary treats in the shape of sacred hearts, guitars, and sombreros. Don't miss the cookies—they're even more delicious than they look. ⊠*Av. 6 Oriente, between Av. 5 de Mayo and Calle 4 Norte* ⊙*Daily 9–8.*

10 **Callejón de los Sapos.** Alley of the Toads cuts diagonally behind the cathedral. The attached square has an up-and-coming antiques market with all sorts of Mexican art, from elaborately carved doors to small paintings on pieces of tin offering thanks to saint for favors. There are also cafés filled with young people listening to live music on Friday and Saturday nights. ⊠*Av. 5 Oriente and Calle 6 Sur* ⊙*Daily 10–7.*

7 **Catedral.** Construction on the cathedral began between 1536 and 1539. Work was completed by Puebla's most famous son, Bishop Juan de Palafox y Mendoza, who donated his personal fortune to build its famous tower, the second-largest in the country. The altar was constructed between 1797 and 1818. Manuel Tolsá, Mexico's most illustrious colonial architect, adorned it with onyx, marble, and gold. ⊠*Calle 2 Sur, south of the zócalo* ☎*No phone* ⊙*Daily 6:30 am –12:30 and 4–7:30.*

5 **Iglesia de Santo Domingo.** The beautiful church of St. Dominic is famous for its overwhelming **Capilla del Rosario** (Chapel of the Rosary), where almost every inch of the walls and ceilings are covered with gilded carvings. Dominican friars arrived here in 1534, barely a dozen years after the Spanish conquered this region. The **Capilla de la Tercera Orden** (Chapel of the Third Order) was originally called the "Chapel of the Dark-Skinned Ones," named for the mixed-race population born a short time later. ⊠*Av. 5 de Mayo at Av. 4 Poniente* ☎*222/232-6264* ⊙*Daily 10–6.*

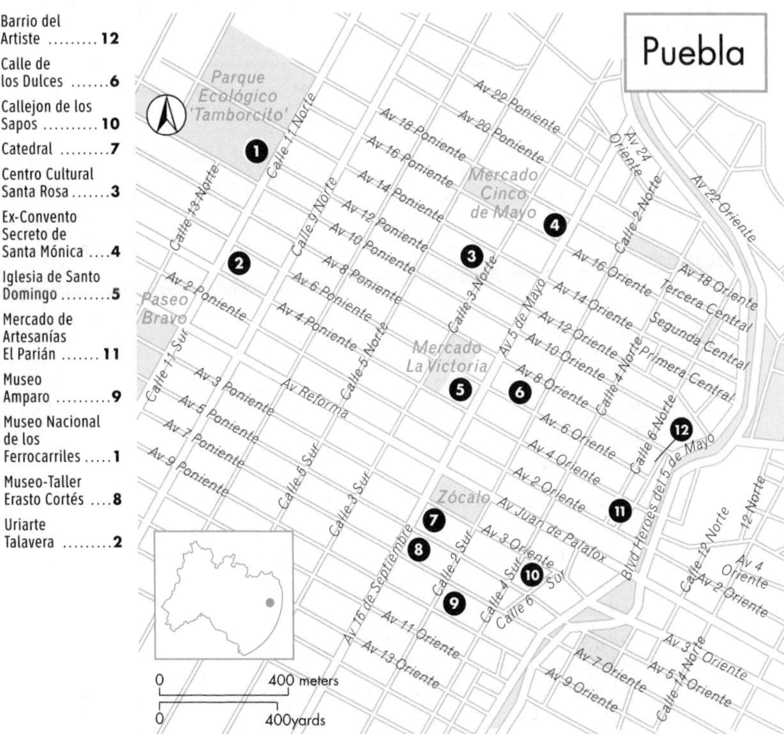

11 **Mercado de Artesanías El Parián.** This market is the place for kitschy versions of such tourist souvenirs as toy guitars and colorful sombreros. Feel free to haggle. For better-quality goods, **La Casa del Artesano,** alongside the market, is the state-sponsored shop for regional craftwork. ✉*Av. 4 Oriente and Calle 6 Norte* ⏲*Daily 10–7:30.*

9 ★ **Museo Amparo.** Home to the private collection of pre-Columbian and Colonial-era art of Mexican banker and philanthropist Manuel Espinoza Yglesias, Museo Amparo is one of the country's most beautiful museums. It exhibits unforgettable pieces from all over Mexico, including nearly 4,800 pre-Hispanic artifacts. The collection includes colonial-era painting, sculpture, and decorative objects and a small modern art section notable for works by Diego Rivera, Frida Kahlo, Miguel Felguérez, and Vicente Rojo. ✉*Calle 2 Sur at Av. 9 Oriente* ☎*222/246–4646 or 222/229–3850* 🌐*www.museoamparo.com* 🎟*$3.50; free Mon.* ⏲*Wed.–Mon. 10–6.*

IF YOU HAVE TIME

3 **Centro Cultural Santa Rosa.** The former convent houses a museum of crafts from the state's seven regions. The museum also contains the intricately tiled kitchen where Puebla's renowned chocolate mole sauce is believed to have been invented by the nuns, as a surprise for their

CLOSE UP

Misty Mountaintops

Leaving Mexico City on Route 150D (known as the Carretera to Puebla or the Puebla Highway), you'll see Mexico's second- and third-highest peaks, **Popocatépetl** and **Iztaccíhuatl,** to your right—if the clouds and climate allow. "Popo," 17,887 feet high, is the pointed volcano farther away, sometimes graced with a plume of smoke; "Izta" is the larger, rugged one covered with snow. Popo has seen a renewed period of activity since the mid-1990s, which come to an end at the beginning of 2003 and was still quiet at this writing.

As legend has it, Aztec warrior Popocatépetl was sent by the emperor—father of his beloved Iztaccíhuatl—to bring back the head of a feared enemy in order to win her hand. He returned triumphantly only to find that Iztaccíhuatl had killed herself, believing him dead. Grief-stricken, Popo laid out her body on a small knoll and lighted an eternal torch that he watches over. Each of Iztaccíhuatl's four peaks is named for a different part of her body, and its silhouette conjures up its nickname, "Sleeping Woman" (although the correct Nahuatl translation is "the white woman").

Popo is strictly off-limits for climbing, but several of Izta's rugged peaks can be explored as long as you are accompanied by recommended guides. You'll be rewarded with sublime views of Popo and other volcanoes, with the Pico de Orizaba (or Citlaltepetl) to the east and the Nevado de Toluca to the west.

TIP→ **Ideally, you won't need it, but the Brigada del Rescate del Socorro Alpino de México (☎55/5392-9299 or 044-55/2698-7557) handles emergencies in the Parque Nacional Izta-Popo.**

The town of **Amecameca** is the most convenient base. Its tourism infrastructure is no-frills but adequate, and the offices of the national park and CONANP (the national commission for protected areas) are both here. The **CONANP** (✉ *Plaza de la Constitución 10-B* ☎ *597/978-3829 or 597/978-3830* 🌐 *www.edomexico.gob.mx*) bureau, near the church on the zócalo, is a rich source of information on the volcanoes. It also makes guiding arrangements for climbing Izta. The best time to visit is from the end of October until May; it's bitterly cold at night in the winter months.

Los Volcanes buses, part of the bus company Cristobal Colón, leave for Amecameca from Mexico City's Terminal del Oriente (TAPO) every 20 minutes daily. The trip takes approximately 1¼ hours and costs less than $2. The buses returning to the capital from Amecameca run just as frequently up to 9:30 PM; they leave from a small bus station behind the old flour factory on the northwest side of the zócalo.

A cobbled road lined with olive trees and cedars leads to the hilltop **Santuario del Sacromonte,** a church and active seminary known for the *Cristo de Sacromonte.* The black Christ figure, made of sugarcane, is said to date from 1527; it's kept in a cavelike space behind the altar. On clear days this perch is one of the best spots for breathtaking views over Amecameca toward the volcanoes. Take a bumpy track even higher up to reach the little Guadalupita chapel. ✉ *Cerro del Sacromonte* ☎ *No phone* ⊙ *Daily 9–5.*

CLOSE UP

A Well-Rounded Hacienda

La Hacienda de Panoaya, also known as Parque de los Venados Acariciables (pettable deer), has plenty of animals for curious kids, with ostriches, emus, and llamas as well as deer (horseback rides are also a possibility). But the menagerie is only part of the game; there are also two museums. The **Museo Internacional de los Volcanes** has some interesting information on volcanoes, but it's primarily a big thrill for kids, who love to scream at the recorded sound of an eruption. Meanwhile, the **Museo Sor Juana Inés de la Cruz** honors its namesake, a nun, scholar, and author who learned to read here and went on to produce some of the most significant poetry and prose of the 17th century. De la Cruz's intellectual accomplishments were truly exceptional in her time, as was her fervent defense of women's rights. The hacienda is a 15-minute walk out of town along the boulevard Iztaccíhuatl. ✉ *Carretera México-Cuautla, Km 58, Amecameca* ☎ *597/978–2670 or 597/978–2813* 🌐 *www.haciendapanoaya.com* 🎫 *$8.50* ⏲ *Zoo daily 10–5; museums weekends 10–6.*

3

demanding bishop. ✉ *3 Norte 1203* ☎ *222/232–7792 or 222/232–3240* 🎫 *$2; free Tues.* ⏲ *Tues.–Sun. 10–5.*

4 **Ex-Convento Secreto de Santa Mónica.** This former convent opened in 1688 as a spiritual refuge for women whose husbands were away on business. Despite the Reform Laws of the 1850s, it continued to function until 1934. It is said that the women here invented the famous dish called *chiles en nogada, a complicated recipe that incorporates the red, white, and green colors of the Mexican flag.* Curiosities include the gruesome display of the preserved heart of the convent's founder and paintings in the *Sala de los Terciopelos (Velvet Room),* in which the feet and faces seem to change position as you view them from different angles. ✉ *Av. 18 Poniente 103, near Av. 5 de Mayo* ☎ *222/232–0178* 🎫 *$2.90; free Sun.* ⏲ *Tues.–Sun. 9–6.*

1 **Museo Nacional de los Ferrocarriles.** Occupying a train station inaugurated by President Juárez in 1869, the National Railway Museum offers a nostalgic treat. Period engines sit on the now-unused platforms, and several cars—including a caboose—can be explored. ✉ *Calle 11 Norte at Av. 12 Poniente* ☎ *222/232–0395* 🎫 *Free* ⏲ *Tues.–Sun. 10–6.*

8 **Museo-Taller Erasto Cortés.** Named for Erasto Cortés Juárez, the city's most important 20th-century artist, this museum displays his vibrant engravings and portraits. It also showcases up-and-coming international artists. ✉ *Av. 7 Oriente 4, between 2 Sur and 16 de Septiembre* ☎ *222/246–6922* 🎫 *$20; free Tues.* ⏲ *Tues.–Sun. 10–5.*

2 **Uriarte Talavera.** Founded in 1824, this is one of the few authentic Talavera workshops left today. To be the real deal, pieces must be hand-painted in intricate designs with natural dyes derived from minerals. That's why only five colors are used: blue, black, yellow, green, and a reddish pink. ■ TIP→ **English-language tours begin weekdays at 11, 12, and 1. If you miss the tour, you can only visit the shop and the patio.** ✉ *Av.*

4 Poniente 911, at Calle 11 Norte ☎222/232–5126 🌐www.uriartetalavera.com.mx ⏲Weekdays 9–6:30, Sat. 10–6:30, Sun. 11–6.

WHERE TO EAT

Lunchtime is when most *poblanos* (people from Puebla) eat out, and restaurants tend to be quiet at night unless it's a Friday or Saturday. There are an increasing number of cafés and fast-food joints around the zócalo that are good for a quick bite between museum visits. At the restaurants under the *portales* (arches) you can tuck into Mexican and international fare while enjoying some prime people-watching.

$$ MEXICAN ✕ **Antigui Merendero Sta. Monica.** Seafood is the specialty here, especially the *acamaya*, a freshwater, prawnlike crustacean. Brought in from Veracruz, this delicacy is served with a chipotle-chile sauce. The one-of-a-kind flavor draws an ever-expanding group of regulars to this simple restaurant. ✉*25 Poniente 506* ☎*222/243–2501* ▭*MC, V.*

$$ MEXICAN ✕ **Mi Ciudad Puebla.** This longtime favorite is the place for a tasty, traditional meal. The decor is typical Puebla—complete with tile floors, colorful murals, and a newspaper stand inside—as is the menu. The mole is as traditional as it comes, and the *sopa poblana (a cream soup with poblano chiles, mushrooms, and corn)* is exceptional. This is also a great place to enjoy grilled meat. ✉*Av. Juárez 2507* ☎*222/231–5326* ▭*AE, MC, V* ⏲*Closed Mon.*

$–$$ MEXICAN ✕ **Las Bodegas del Molino.** This restaurant's setting—an elegant 16th-century hacienda at the edge of town—is matched by its fine cuisine. If you're not sure about mole, give it a try here: the same woman has been making it since 1982, and her seductive, fruity blend will probably win you over. Romantics should book a private dinner in the French Room. **TIP→ Request a tour of the fabulous premises.** ✉*Molino de San José del Puente* ☎*222/249–0483 or 222/249–0399* ▭*AE, MC, V* .

$ MEXICAN ✕ **Fonda de Santa Clara.** Founded in 1965, this popular eatery has two branches in Puebla (and others in Acapulco and Mexico City). Both of the Puebla locations have great settings. The original, near the zócalo, is cozier, but the larger newcomer at Paseo Bravo still manages a nice colonial feel. The food consists of mole, mole, and more mole, but you can also get *nopal* (prickly pear leaf) salad, *sopa de medula* (marrowbone soup), and other hearty regional fare. ✉*Calle 3 Poniente 307* ☎*222/242–2659* 🌐*www.fondadesantaclara.com* ✉*Paseo Bravo, Calle 3 Poniente 307* ☎*222/246–1919* ▭*AE, MC, V.*

MOLE & MORE

Two of Mexico's most popular dishes were supposedly created in Puebla. One specialty is mole (pronounced mo-lay), a sauce with as many as 30 ingredients. The other specialty is *chiles en nogada*, green poblano chiles filled with meats, fruits, and nuts, then covered with a sauce of chopped walnuts and cream, and topped with pomegranate seeds; the colors represent the Mexican flag. Typical snacks are *pelonas*, fried rolls filled with lettuce, beef, cream, and sauce; and *cemita*, which is like a torta but made with a sweeter bread, and filled with avocado, meat, and cheese.

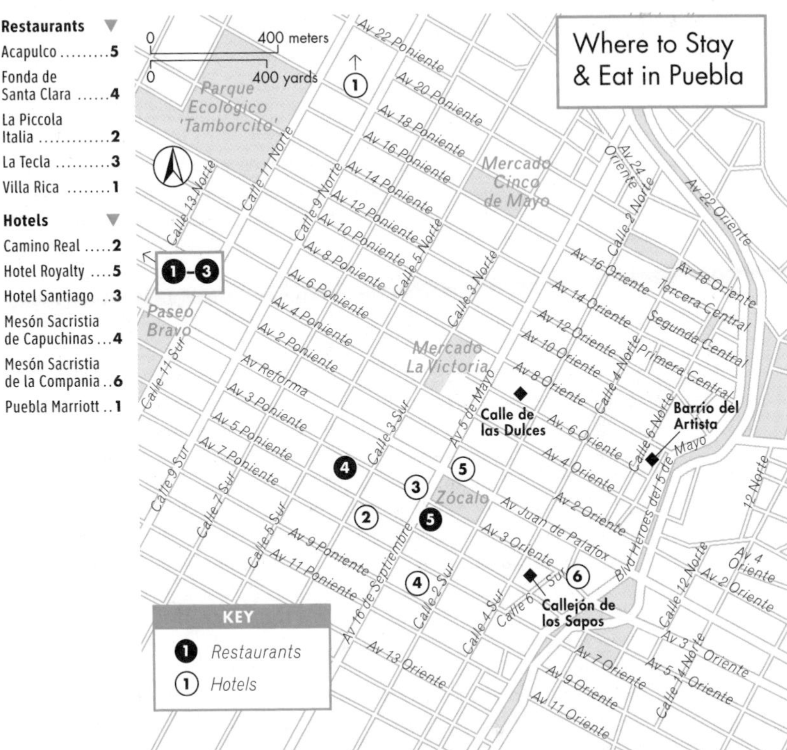

$
MEXICAN

✕**La Tecla.** A modern design and decently priced nouvelle Mexican cuisine have made this place a hit. Try the duck in mango and tamarind sauce, or the chicken breast stuffed with plantains and covered in a deliciously spicy sauce. ✉*Ave. Juárez 1909, between Calles 19 and 21 Sur* ☎*222/246–6066* ▭*AE, MC, V.*

WHERE TO STAY

$$$–$$$$

Casona de la China Poblano. This beautifully renovated colonial building may no longer be a private home, but it still has the same cozy atmosphere. Many of the original details have been preserved, but there are also modern furnishings. The central patio is home to Ekos, which serves well-prepared and beautifully presented traditional Mexican dishes and interesting international fare. Keeping watch over the dining room is a large statue of the place's namesake: China Poblana, the daughter of a Mongol king who was kidnapped and brought to Mexico. **Pros:** Great restaurant, friendly service, easy walk to downtown sights. **Cons:** More expensive than nearby hotels. ✉*4 Norte 2,* ☎*222/242–5621* 🌐*www.casonadelachinapoblana.com* *10 rooms* *In-room: Refrigerator, Wi-Fi. In-hotel: Restaurant, bar, spa* ▭*AE, D, MC, V.*

$$$–$$$$ **La Purificadora.** This is without a doubt one of the hottest places to stay in Puebla. While many historic elements of this former factory have been left untouched, ultramodern materials have been used for the renovation, creating an environment full of interesting contrasts. For example, rough-hewn stone walls are paired with brushed metal and polished glass. The place has a whimsical feel, with wonderful touches like the glass-sided rooftop pool. Rooms, decorated with sleek furnishings, are very modern. The menu at the hotel restaurant, designed by award-winning chef Enrique Olvera, offers many traditional regional options. **Pros:** Attention paid to every detail, interesting architecture, wonderful restaurant. **Cons:** Can be a bit of a scene, pricier than most lodgings. ✉*Callejon de la Norte 802 72000* ☎*222/329–1920* 🌐*www.lapurificadora.com* *26 rooms* *In-room: Safe, refrigerator. In-hotel: Restaurant, room service, pool, gym, spa, no elevator* 💳*AE, MC, V.*

$$$ **Camino Real.** Formerly a convent, this 16th-century building radiates historic character, from its luminous restored frescoes to its wooden shutters. Large white rooms have colonial antique furniture and exposed beams. The junior suite was once the convent's chapel, and the presidential suite has original 16th-century gilded furnishings and carpeting. The staff is warm and professional. **Pros:** Stunning architecture, in the heart of the city, excellent service. **Cons:** Pricier than nearby lodgings. ✉*Av. 7 Poniente 105,* ☎*222/229–0909 or 222/229–0910* 🌐*www.caminoreal.com/puebla* *75 rooms, 9 suites* *In-room: Safe, refrigerator, dial-up. In-hotel: 2 restaurants, room service, bar* 💳*AE, DC, MC, V.*

$$$ **Mesón Sacristía de Capuchinas.** Though this 17th-century building sits in the center of the city, its thick walls make it a calm, quiet sanctuary. Each spacious room has a slightly different, somewhat monastic, decor. Many have beamed ceilings; some have wrought-iron bedsteads or religious icons. The suites are decorated in a more contemporary style. The restaurant ($) is especially popular at lunch. **Pros:** Great service, pleasant restaurant, rooms have attractive antiques. **Cons:** Street noise in the evening. ✉*Av. 9 Oriente 16,* ☎*222/232–8088 or 222/246–6084* 🌐*www.mesones-sacristia.com* *7 suites* *In-room: Safe. In-hotel: Restaurant, bar, parking (no fee)* 💳*AE, MC, V* *BP.*

$$$ **Mesón Sacristía de la Compañía.** If any of the antiques that decorate your rooms strike your fancy, you might consider taking home a souvenir. They are all for sale. Warming touches are both figurative and literal at this converted colonial mansion; you'll be welcomed with a plate of cookies, and if it gets chilly, heaters are brought to your room. The rich colors of folk art pervade the cozy but stylish bar. The attractive restaurant ($$) serves tasty regional dishes such as *carne San Pascual* (steak with corn fungus). There is live music in the evening. **Pros:** Excellent restaurant, top-notch service, good location. **Cons:** Street noise in the evening. ✉*Calle 6 Sur 304, at Callejón de los Sapos,* ☎*222/242–3554* 🌐*www.mesones-sacristia.com* *8 rooms* *In-room: No a/c. In-hotel: Restaurant, room service, bar, parking (no fee), no elevator* 💳*AE, MC, V* *BP.*

$$ **Hotel Casa de la Palma.** In an older building, this newly renovated hotel has a great location in the center of town. Every room has been

lovingly restored and individually decorated by Carlos Olea, an antiquarian who has years of experience working in Puebla. Some rooms are named for artists or animals, but the real showstopper is the room dedicated to former President Porfirio Díaz—with its high ceilings, over-the-top portraits, and original letters signed by the dictator himself. Also popular is the Suite Morisca decorated in a Moorish style complete with tall arches and intricate wall carvings. **Pros:** Great decor, reasonable prices, friendly staff. **Cons:** Not all rooms are created equal, stairs are a little steep. ✉ *3 Oriente 217 72000* ☎ *222/246–1437* 🌐 *www.casadelapalmapuebla.com* *16 rooms* *In-room: Wi-Fi. In-hotel: Gym, no elevator* *AE, MC, V.*

3

$–$$ **Hotel Royalty.** This well-maintained hotel is always busy because of its popular restaurant under the *portales* (arches) on the main square. People stop by for a pleasant breakfast or lunch while watching residents go about their day. The old colonial building is an excellent choice for its central location on the zócalo; the best rooms are the junior suites. **Pros:** On the main square, bargain price. **Cons:** No air-conditioning, no Internet connection. ✉ *Portal Hidalgo 8,* ☎ *222/242–4740* 🌐 *www.hotelr.com* *34 rooms, 11 suites* *In-room: No a/c. In-hotel: Restaurant, room service, bar, parking (fee)* *AE, MC, V* *BP.*

¢ **Hotel Santiago.** One of the cheaper central options, this little no-frills hotel opposite a department store is modern and clean. The double rooms have two double beds. **Pros:** Unbeatable price, comfortable rooms. **Cons:** No air-conditioning, no Internet access. ✉ *Av. 3 Pte. 106 at 16 de Septiembre,* ☎ *222/242–2860* *37 rooms* *In-room: No a/c* *No credit cards.*

NIGHTLIFE

Puebla's nightlife centers on the bars on Avenida Juárez. Mariachis keep the songs coming at **La Cantina de los Remedios** (✉ *Av. Juárez 2504, Col. la Paz* ☎ *222/249–0843*), a good place for after-dinner drinks.

CHOLULA

19 km (12 mi) west of Puebla via Rte. 190, 112 km (70) mi southeast of Mexico City.

Creeping out from under the shadow of Puebla, Cholula is gradually being restored to something of its former greatness. Before the Spanish conquest, the ancient settlement west of Puebla had hundreds of temples and rivaled Teotihuacán as a cultural and ceremonial center. On his arrival, Cortés ordered every temple destroyed and replaced by a church. However, the claim that Cholula has 365 church cupolas, one for every day in the year, is to be taken with a grain of salt.

GETTING HERE & AROUND

Second-class Autobuses Unidos buses depart from Mexico City's Terminal Autobuses Oriente several times daily. The two-hour ride costs $9. You may prefer to take a first-class bus to Puebla and then take a $10 taxi ride to Cholula. By car, trips from Mexico City on the toll road Route 150D take about 1½ hours; on Route 190, the scenic—and bumpy—free road, the same journey takes three hours.

ESSENTIALS

Bus Contacts **Autobuses Unidos** (☎ *55/5133–2424*).

Medical Assistance **Farmacia Sagrado Corazón** (✉ *Av. Hidalgo 103 B* ☎ *222/247–0398*). **Hospital General de Cholula** (✉ Calle 2 Poniente 1504 ☎ *222/247–1800*).

Visitor & Tour Info **San Andrés Cholula Tourist Office** (✉ *Av. 16 de Septiembre 102* ☎ *222/247–8606*). **San Pedro Cholula Tourist Office** (✉ *12 Oriente at 4 Norte* ☎ *222/261–2393*).

EXPLORING

Weekends are the liveliest time to visit Cholula, when you can catch the Sunday market and some live music with dinner. The town's even busier during one of its many festivals, especially the *feria de San Pedro,* during the first two weeks of September.

The town is divided into three municipalities; most of the major sites of interest are divided between San Pedro Cholula and San Andres Cholula.

MAIN ATTRACTIONS

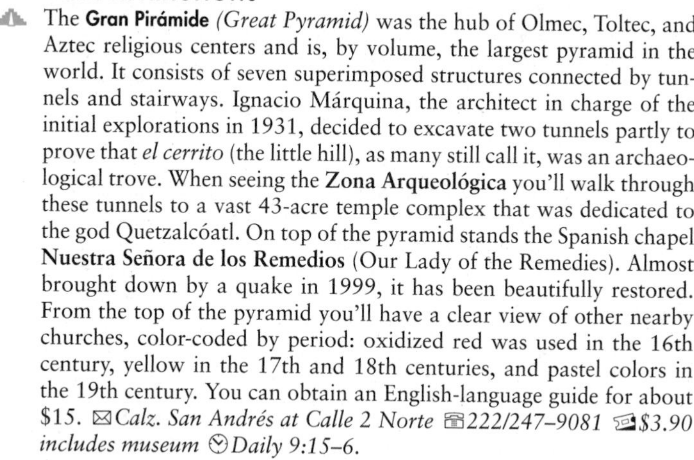

The **Gran Pirámide** *(Great Pyramid)* was the hub of Olmec, Toltec, and Aztec religious centers and is, by volume, the largest pyramid in the world. It consists of seven superimposed structures connected by tunnels and stairways. Ignacio Márquina, the architect in charge of the initial explorations in 1931, decided to excavate two tunnels partly to prove that *el cerrito* (the little hill), as many still call it, was an archaeological trove. When seeing the **Zona Arqueológica** you'll walk through these tunnels to a vast 43-acre temple complex that was dedicated to the god Quetzalcóatl. On top of the pyramid stands the Spanish chapel **Nuestra Señora de los Remedios** (Our Lady of the Remedies). Almost brought down by a quake in 1999, it has been beautifully restored. From the top of the pyramid you'll have a clear view of other nearby churches, color-coded by period: oxidized red was used in the 16th century, yellow in the 17th and 18th centuries, and pastel colors in the 19th century. You can obtain an English-language guide for about $15. ✉ *Calz. San Andrés at Calle 2 Norte* ☎ *222/247–9081* *$3.90 includes museum* ⏲ *Daily 9:15–6.*

The huge, impressive **Ex-Convento de San Gabriel** includes a trio of churches. The most unusual is the Moorish-style **Capilla Real,** with 49 domes. Construction began in the 1540s, and the building was originally open on one side to facilitate the conversion of huge masses of people. About 20 Franciscan monks still live in one part of the premises, so be respectful of their privacy. ✉ *2 Norte s/n, east of Cholula Zócalo* ☎ *No phone* ⏲ *Daily 10–12:30 and 4:30–6.*

IF YOU HAVE TIME

Manuel Toussaint, an expert in colonial art, likened the church of **San Francisco Acatepec** to "a temple of porcelain, worthy of being kept beneath a crystal dome." Construction began in 1590, with the elaborate Spanish baroque decorations added between 1650 and 1750. Multicolored Talavera tiles cover the exceptionally ornate facade. The interior blazes with polychrome plasterwork and gilding; a sun radiates overhead. Unlike the nearby Santa María Tonantzintla, the ornamentation hews to the standard representations of the Incarnation, the Evangelists, and the Holy Trinity. Look for St. Francis, to whom the church is dedicated, between the altarpiece's spiraling columns. ✉*6½ km (4 mi) south of Cholula* ☎*No phone* ⏲*Daily 9–5.*

★ The exterior of the 16th-century church of **Santa María Tonantzintla** may be relatively simple, but inside waits an explosion of color and swirling shapes. To facilitate the conversion of the native population, Franciscan monks incorporated elements recalling the local cult of the goddess Tonantzin in the ornamentation of the chapel. The result is a jewel of the style known as Churrigueresque. The polychrome wood-and-stucco carvings—inset columns, altarpieces, and the main archway—were completed in the late 17th century. The carvings, set off by ornate gold-leaf figures of plant forms, angels, and saints, were made by local craftspeople. Flash photography is not allowed. ✉*Av. Reforma, 5 km (3 mi) south of Cholula* ☎*No phone* ⏲*Daily 9–5.*

WHERE TO EAT & STAY

$ MEXICAN ✕ **La Lunita.** A stone's throw from the Gran Pirámide, this little eatery has bumped up its prices a bit, but it's still a good place to cool off after a sweltering afternoon in the archaeological zone. It's welcoming and cluttered with bric-a-brac. The specialty is *acamayas,* a kind of crayfish. ✉*Av. Morelos at 6 Norte* ☎*222/247–0011* 🌐*www.lalunita.com* ▭*D, MC, V.*

¢–$ MEXICAN ✕ **Restaurant-Bar Los Jarrones.** Simple but smart, Los Jarrones ("The Pitchers") welcomes diners with long wooden tables, comfy cushioned chairs, and white walls accented with green tiles. Starters include onion and garlic soup; the *parrillada* (a variety of grilled meats) is a popular option for sharing. A weekend breakfast buffet is served 9:30 to 1. Live music at night is loud but pleasant. ✉*Portal Guerrero No. 7* ☎*222/247–1098* ▭*AE, MC, V.*

¢ MEXICAN ✕ **Güeros.** This budget eatery to the side of the portales on the zócalo is a favorite for fresh local fare. The menu includes tacos *cecina (filled with salt pork), flautas* (tortillas rolled into tubes and deep-fried), and *pozole* (hominy soup with pork). The *tortas* (sandwiches) are stuffed with anything from breaded chicken to *riñones* (kidneys). The place stays open until around midnight. ✉*Av. Hidalgo 101* ☎*222/247–2188* ▭*MC, V.*

★ $$$–$$$$ 🏨 **Hotel Quinta Luna.** The elegance of this boutique hotel—a five-minute walk from the zócalo—has been crucial in putting Cholula back on the map. The restored 17th-century mansion was built around a central patio with a fountain. Immaculate rooms have natural colors, polished wood furniture and floors, and high, exposed-beam ceilings. King-size beds are wrapped in luscious, down-filled bedding and supplied with more pillows than you could possibly use. The outstanding restaurant ($–$$) offers Mexican and nouvelle dishes and is worth a visit in its own right. **Pros:** Pretty gardens, comfortable rooms, elegant atmosphere. **Cons:** Expensive rates, fills up far in advance. ✉*3 Sur 702, San Pedro Cholula, 72760* ☎*222/247–8915* 🌐*www.laquintaluna.com* *3 rooms, 3 suites* *In-room: DVD, refrigerator, Wi-Fi. In-hotel: Restaurant, bar, no elevator* *AE, MC, V* *BP.*

$$ **Hotel Parador Cholula.** This small hotel is close enough to the pyramids to enjoy a run up all those steps before breakfast (or if you prefer, you can just enjoy the view from the hotel entrance). Rooms are simple, decorated with rustic wood furniture and brightly colored bedspreads; Mexican crafts occupy small niches in the rooms and hallways. The inviting outdoor swimming pool, surrounded by plants, is a great place to relax after a day in the warm sun. **Pros:** Great location near the pyramid, reasonable rates. **Cons:** Cramped rooms, no Internet connection. ✉*2 Poniente 601* ☎*222/273–7900* *37 rooms* *In-hotel: Restaurant, bar, tennis courts, pool, no elevator* *AE, MC, V.*

¢ **Hotel Posada Señorial.** This place has the distinction of being the only hotel on the zócalo; look for the small entrance under the arches by a busy coffee shop. The rooms are comfortable, but some are depressingly dark, so ask to see a few before you settle on one. **Pros:** Great location, bargain price. **Cons:** No air-conditioning, no Internet connection. ✉*Portal de Guerrero 5, San Pedro Cholula* ☎ *222/247–7719* *28 rooms* *In-room: No a/c* *AE, MC, V.*

SPORTS & THE OUTDOORS

Club de Golf La Huerta (✉*Prolongación 15 Sur 219, Privada Juan Blanca* ☎*222/247–3392* 🌐*www.lahuertagolfhotel.com)* is a 9-hole golf course with reasonable greens fees of $40 on weekdays and $50 on weekends.

TLAXCALA

30 km (19 mi) north of Puebla, 120 km (75 mi) east of Mexico City.

Tlaxcala (pronounced tlas-*ca*-la) is a place where you may well find yourself lingering longer than you had planned, lulled by a few hours spent on the Plaza Xicohténcatl or at a café in one of the colonnades near the zócalo. The distinctive terra-cotta roofs gave the state capital the name Ciudad Roja, or Red City. Climb up to one of the hilltop churches and a sea of ruddy roofs will stretch out around you.

EXPLORING

MAIN ATTRACTIONS

Tlaxcala's most famous site isn't in the town at all. At the nearby archaeological site of **Cacaxtla** you'll see some of Mexico's most vividly colored murals. Accidentally discovered in 1975 by a farmer, the main temple at Cacaxtla contains breathtaking scenes of a surprisingly vicious battle between two bands of warriors. The nearly life-size figures wearing jaguar skins clearly have the upper hand against their foes in lofty feathered headdresses.

The site, dating from AD 650 to AD 900, is thought to be the work of the Olmeca-Xicalanca people. Other paintings adorn smaller structures.

The newly restored Templo Rojo, or Red Temple, is decorated with stalks of corn with cartoonlike human faces. Perhaps the most delightful is in the Templo de Venus, or Temple of Venus, where two figures are dancing in the moonlight, their bodies a striking blue.

On a hill about 1½ km (1 mi) north of Cacaxtla is the site of **Xochitécatl,** with four Classic Period pyramids. You can see both sites with the same admission ticket. Head south from Mexico City toward Puebla on Carretera Federal 119. Veer off to the right toward the town of Nativitas. Both sites are near the village of San Miguel del Milagro. ⊠*About 19 km (12 mi) southwest of Tlaxcala on Carretera Federal 119* ☎*246/416–0477* *$3.70* ⊙*Tues.–Sun. 10–4:30.*

3

Bordered by Calle Camargo and Avenida Juárez, Tlaxcala's **zócalo** has a beautifully tiled bandstand shaded by graceful trees.Adjoining the zócalo at its southeast corner is another square, **Plaza Xicohténcatl.** Souvenir shops line its eastern edge. To the north of the zócalo is the **Palacio de Gobierno** (⊠*Between Av. Lira y Ortega and Av. Juárez*). Inside the eastern entrance are murals by local painter Desiderio Hernández Xochitiotzin depicting Tlaxcala's pivotal role in the Spanish conquest. The city aligned itself with Cortés against the Aztecs, thus swelling the conqueror's ranks significantly. The palace is open daily 8–8.

IF YOU HAVE TIME

★ On a hill about 1 km (½ mi) northwest of the center of Tlaxcala stands the ornate **Basilica de Ocotlán.** You can see its Churrigueresque facade, topped with twin towers adorned with the apostles, from just about everywhere in the city. The church is most notable as a pilgrimage site. In 1541 the Virgin Mary appeared to a poor peasant, telling him to cure an epidemic with water from a stream that had suddenly appeared. Franciscan monks, eager to find the source of the miracle, ventured into the forest. There they discovered raging flames that didn't harm one particular pine (*ocotlán*). When they split the tree open, they discovered the wooden image of the Virgen de Ocotlán, which they installed in a gilded altar. Many miracles have been attributed to the statue, which wears the braids popular for indigenous women at the time. Behind the altar is the brilliantly painted Camarín de la Virgen (Dressing Room of the Virgin) that tells the story. At the base of the hill is the charming **Capilla del Pocito de Agua Santa,** an octagonal chapel decorated with images of the Virgen de Ocotlán. The faithful come to draw holy water from its seven fountains. ⊠*Calle Guridi y Alcocer* ☎*246/465–0960* ⊙*Daily 9–6.*

The **Catedral de Nuestra Señora de la Asunción** stands atop a hill one block south of Plaza Xicohténcatl. The cathedral's most unusual feature is its Moorish-style wood ceiling beams, carved and gilded with gold studs. There are only a few churches of this kind in Mexico, as mudéjar flourishes were popular here only during the very early years after the Spanish conquest. Don't miss the view of the city's bullring from the churchyard.

The cathedral's austere monastery, now home to the **Museo Regional de Tlaxcala,** displays 16th- to 18th-century religious paintings as well as a small collection of pre-Columbian pieces. A beautiful outdoor chapel near the monastery has notable Moorish and Gothic traces. ✉ *Calz. de San Francisco* ☎ *No phone* 🎫 *Museum $3.50* ⏲ *Daily 10–5.*

To the west of Plaza Xicohténcatl is the fascinating **Museo de la Memoria,** with a colonial-era facade but a strikingly modern interior. By focusing on the folklore and festivals of various indigenous cultures, the Museum of Memory recounts the region's past and present. ✉ *Av. Independencia 3* ☎ *246/466–0791* 🎫 *$1; free Sun.* ⏲ *Tues.–Sun. 10–5.*

The **Parroquia de San José** (✉ *Av. Lira y Ortega and Calle Lardizábal*), cheerfully decorated in vivid shades of yellow and green. Don't miss the pair of fonts near the entrance that depict Tlaxcalan, a god of war. The church is open daily 9–6.

WHERE TO EAT & STAY

$ MEXICAN ✕ **Fonda del Convento.** In a low stone building on a tree-lined street, this unassuming café is overlooked by most travelers but is always packed with locals. The series of small dining rooms means it won't be hard to find a quiet table. The delicious traditional fare includes such dishes as chicken broth with creamy avocados and strips of cactus flambéed with bits of onion and chiles. The *caldo de habas*, a bean soup with strips of cactus, is not something that you find everywhere, and it is quite tasty. ✉ *Calz. de San Francisco 1* ☎ *246/462–0765* 💳 *AE, MC, V.*

$$ MEXICAN Fodor'sChoice ★ **Hotel Soltepec La Escondida.** Resembling an old castle, this hacienda was made famous as the setting for the 1955 film *La Escondida*. Converted into an elegant and welcoming hotel, it is a true gem in the middle of nowhere. Located 51 km (32 mi) from Tlaxcala, it has pristine views of the Malinche volcano. The stately restaurant ($), watched over by two stuffed bulls, offers delicious regional fare and a cozy fireplace to warm up the chilly winter nights. It is a hive of activity on Sunday when *poblanos* come here to lunch. Best of all, the hotel offers tours to other remote haciendas of Tlaxcala state, an eye-opener into the history of the rural region. **Pros:** Beautiful building, excellent service, great volcano views. Cons: Need a car to get around. ✉ *Carretera Huamantla-Puebla, Km 3, Huamantla* ☎ *247/472–1466 or 247/472–3110* 🌐 *www.haciendasoltepec.com* *12 rooms* *In-room: No a/c, Wi-Fi. In-hotel: Restaurant, tennis courts, pool, gym, parking (no fee), no elevator* 💳 *AE, MC, V.*

CUETZALAN

Fodor'sChoice ★ *182 km (113 mi) north of Puebla, 320 km (198 mi) northeast of Mexico City.*

The colonial town of Cuetzalan in the Sierra Norte region is one of the most precious and unspoiled attractions in the state of Puebla. The Sierra Norte has been referred to as the Sierra Mágica (magical mountain range) for the mystic beliefs held by the pre-Hispanic peoples who inhabited this lush, dramatic swath of land. Cuetzalan's breathtaking landscape is etched with canyons, rushing rivers, and caves, and swaddled in dense, outsize vegetation. Because of its elevation the town is often enveloped in clouds.

At the weekly Sunday market, or *tianguis,* in the town center, local farmers come to sell and trade corn, coffee, beans, spices, and citrus fruits. Most people wear indigenous dress and chatter in Nahuatl, sizing up the cinnamon or bargaining for guavas. The atmosphere, color, and fragrant smells of this lively event are not to be missed.

GETTING HERE & AROUND

Texcoco/Primera Plus buses make the six-hour trip from Mexico City's TAPO terminal only on weekends. The ride costs about $13. For those who wish to visit during the week, the best option is to go to Puebla and transfer to an ADO bus to Cuetzalan. The four-hour trip from Puebla costs $6.

ESSENTIALS

Bus Contacts **ADO** (☎ *55/5133–2424* 🌐 *www.adogl.com.mx*).**Texcoco/Primera Plus** (☎ *233/331–0498 in Cuetzalan*).

Medical Assistance **Hospital Integral** (✉ *Miguel Alvarado 85* ☎ *233/331–0127*).

Vistor & Tour Info **Dirección Municipal de Turismo Cuetzalan** (✉ *Hidalgo 29* ☎ *233/331–0004*).

EXPLORING

MAIN ATTRACTIONS

On the town's **zócalo** you'll find the Renaissance-style church, **La Parroquia de San Francisco,** as well as the **Palacio Municipal.** The bandstand and the municipal clock tower were both built in the early 20th century. As you take in the sights, vendors will offer you everything from flowers to napkin holders. If you are not interested in buying, sometimes saying "*no, gracias*" ("no, thank you") is not sufficient. If you want to get your point across, try "*ya compré*" ("I already bought one").

■ TIP→ **Wear sturdy walking shoes and be prepared for cool and damp weather. The steep, cobblestoned streets can be dangerously slippery when the weather is misty or rainy. Fortunately, taxis here are very cheap.**

IF YOU HAVE TIME

Originally a coffee processing plant, the **Casa de la Cultura** has been revamped to combine a public library, the town archives, and a somewhat haphazard ethnographic museum, which often displays works by local artists. Opposite the building across Avenida Miguel Alvarado is Cuetzalan's daily crafts market, open from noon to 5. ✉ *Av. Miguel Alvarado 18* ☎ *No phone* 🎟 *Free* ⏲ *Daily 10–6.*

The church of **El Santuario de Guadalupe** shows a Gothic strain in its needle-slim tower and the pointed arch of the main door. Its common name, La Iglesia de los Jarritos (Church of the Little Pitchers) refers to its landmark spire, prettily adorned by 80 clay vessels. There is a cemetery in front of the church that is often full of vibrantly colored flowers. ✉ *Calz. de Guadalupe* ☎ *No phone* ⏲ *Daily 9–6.*

About 8 km (5 mi) outside Cuetzalan lies the splendid archaeological zone of **Yohualichan,** founded by the Totonac around AD 400. Partly obscured from the road by an austere stone church, Yohualichan (which means "house of night") consists of a beautiful hilltop grouping of administrative and ceremonial buildings, houses, plazas, and a long ball court. The easiest way to get here is to take a taxi (the ride should cost no more than $6), but *combis* (vans used for public transport) also make regular drop-offs at the top of the road that leads down to the site. To return to Cuetzalan, you can either make arrangements with your taxi driver to wait for you or walk up to the road and hail a combi or taxi. ✉*Carretera a Santiago* ☎*No phone* *$2.50* *Tues.–Sun. 9–5.*

WHERE TO EAT & STAY

¢ CAFE ✕ **Café Te Cuento.** This attractive cafeteria serves pies, cakes, and flans, as well as pizzas, sandwiches, beer, and a range of cocktails and liquors. It's open until 10 PM daily. ✉*Calle Hidalgo 38* ☎*233/331–1259* *No credit cards.*

★ ¢ MEXICAN ✕ **Los Jarritos.** This cavelike restaurant is an unforgettable trove of regional cuisine. Even simple items like the salsas and *frijoles* (small black beans) are intensely flavored. There's an exquisite *sopa de setas* (soup of oyster mushrooms), or you could try the signature dish, *enchiladas de picadillo con mole de olla* (ground beef and raisin enchiladas with a savory local mole). ✉*Plazuela Lopez Mateo 7* ☎*233/331–0558* *MC, V* *Closed Mon.–Thurs. No dinner Sun.*

¢ MEXICAN ✕ **Restaurante Yoloxochilt.** Just above the market, with a view of the main plaza, this plant-filled restaurant offers delicious regional cuisine served by a friendly staff. The *envueltos de mole* (chicken-filled tortillas covered in a thick, smoky mole sauce) are an excellent choice if you want to take a break from walking around the market and enjoy a snack. ✉*2 de Abril 1* ☎*233/331–0335* *No credit cards.*

¢ SEAFOOD ✕ **La Terraza.** Though it's known for its good seafood—like the tasty *pulpos enchipotlados* (octopus in hot chipotle sauce)—this simple, friendly spot caters to various cravings with pastas, hamburgers, and even pancakes for breakfast. This is a great place to try *tlayoyos*, a traditional regional dish like a thick tortilla stuffed with a pea-and-avocado-leaf paste and topped with red or green salsa. ✉*Calle Hidalgo 33* ☎*233/331–0262* *No credit cards.*

$ **Hotel Casa de Piedra.** This fine hotel, with its sunny, cobblestone courtyard and appealing restaurant, tops the rest. Guest rooms have wood furniture and small balconies for views over the town or of the flourishing, overgrown yard with cackling turkeys. The staff will help you hire guides to the nearby waterfall or Yohualichan. The hotel is less than two blocks from the zócalo. **Pros:** Good service, tours available. **Cons:** No room phones, stairs to climb. ✉*Calle Lic. Carlos García 11,* ☎*233/331–0030* *www.lacasadepiedra.com* *19 rooms* *In-room: No a/c, no phone, no TV. In-hotel: Restaurant, parking (no fee), no elevator* *MC, V.*

$ **Hotel Posada Cuetzalan.** Centrally located and well established, this cheerful hotel has colorful rooms, a pair of pretty patio gardens, and a busy restaurant. The staff can help organize cave tours and horseback rides to the pyramids and local waterfalls. **Pros:** Excellent location, friendly staff, nice mountain views. **Cons:** Rooms facing the pool are noisy, rooms in the back are far from the entrance. ✉ *Zaragoza 12,* ☎ *233/331–0154 or 233/331–0395* 🌐 *www.posadacuetzalan.com* *37 rooms* *In-room: No a/c. In-hotel: Pool, restaurant, laundry service, parking (no fee), no elevator* 💳 *MC, V.*

TULA & TEOTIHUACÁN

Little more than an hour north of Mexico City, in Estado de México (Mexico State), are two of the country's most celebrated ancient cities. The pyramids of Teotihuacán can be enjoyed in a day tour. The ruins of Tula, in the state of Hidalgo, known for its battalion of basalt warriors, can be combined with a visit to the nearby colonial city of Tepotzotlán.

3

TULA

Fodor's Choice ★

75 km (47 mi) north of Mexico City center.

The capital of the Toltecs, Tula is one of the most stunning archaeological sites in central Mexico. Much of the great city—known to its inhabitants as Tollán—was ransacked by the Aztecs. What remains, however, makes it worth the trip. From afar you can spot the stone sentinels standing guard atop its magnificent pyramid.

Tula rose to power about the same time as the fall of Teotihuacán. It is bordered on the north and west by carefully reconstructed ball courts. Between the courts sits the **Templo Quemado,** or Burned Palace. Its dozens of ruined columns delineate what was once an important governmental building. Directly to the east is the completely restored **Templo de Tlahuizcalpantecuhtli,** or Temple of the Morning Star. Climb up the uneven steps to reach the cresting row of 15-foot-tall *atlantes,* or warriors. These awe-inspiring figures gaze southward over the main plaza. ☎ *773/732–1183* 🌐 *www.inah.gob.mx* *$3.50* *Tues.–Sun. 9–5.*

GETTING HERE & AROUND

Tula is about 8 km (5 mi) north of Tepotzotlán on Highway 57D. Even though this archaeological site isn't far from the capital, traffic can make getting here a headache. The best way to avoid congestion is to set out early in the morning. Safe and reliable buses leave from Mexico City's Central de Autobuses del Norte every half an hour. The 1½-hour journey costs about $4.50.

ESSENTIALS

Bus Contacts **Autotransportes Valle Mezquital** (☎ *773/732–9600*).

TEPOTZOTLÁN

35 km (22 mi) north of Mexico City center via Autopista México-Querétaro or Highway 57D.

In pre-Hispanic times Tepotzotlán was an important stop along the trade route between Toluca and Texcoco. Tepotzotlán (pronounced teh-po-tzot-*lan*), about an hour's car or bus ride from Mexico City, is still a frequent stop for travelers headed to Tula and environs.

GETTING HERE & AROUND

Tepotzotlán is a 45-minute drive from Mexico City. Safe and reliable buses leave from Mexico City's Central de Autobuses del Norte. You have to change buses at the tollbooth about five minutes from town.

ESSENTIALS

Bus Contacts **Autotransportes Valle Mezquital** (☎ *773/732-9600*).

EXPLORING

In 1580 a group of Jesuit priests arrived in Tepotzotlán, intent on converting the locals. On the main square they built the **Iglesia de San Francisco Javier**, which ranks among the masterpieces of churrigueresque architecture. The unmitigated baroque facade will catch your eye immediately; inside, handsome gilded altars stretch from floor to ceiling. Look for the paintings of angels decorating the church—some are dark-skinned, a nod to the indigenous people forced to help in its construction. The Capilla de la Virgen de Loreto glows with gilding and mirrors.

The church is now part of the massive **Museo Nacional del Virreinato** (✉*Plaza Hidalgo 99* ☎*55/5876–0245 or 55/5876–2771* 🌐*www.munavi.inah.gob.mx* 🎫*$4.70* ⏲*Tues.–Sun. 9:30–6*). You're likely to be overwhelmed by the amount of colonial religious art brought here from churches all around the country. Look for the breathtaking 17th-century Cristo del Arbol (Christ of the Tree), carved from a single piece of wood. For a break, walk outside to the Claustro de los Naranjos, a lovely patio planted with tiny orange trees.

WHERE TO EAT

$ MEXICAN ✕ **Casa Mago.** Across the square from the Museo Nacional del Virreinato you'll find a row of nearly identical outdoor cafés. This one, with a seemingly endless buffet on the weekends, serves up the best regional fare, such as *filete tampiqueña* (finely sliced tender beef fillet) served with guacamole, beans, tortillas, and rice. If you are feeling adventurous, the *escamoles,* a pre-Hispanic delicacy of fried ant eggs and the delicious *cabrito,* or goat, served with flour tortillas, are also worth trying. ✉*Plaza Virreynal 34* ☎*55/5876–0229* ▭*MC, V.*

CUERNAVACA & ENVIRONS

Cuernavaca and the surrounding region have long been a playground for residents of Mexico City. Known as "City of Eternal Spring," Cuernavaca basks in springlike temperatures for most of the year, making it irresistible to the capital's elite. The area's allure has a long history: Aztec emperors came here to enjoy the weather, Cortés built a palace here on the ruins of the Aztec city he destroyed, and Emperor Maximilian retreated here when the pressures of governing a country where he was despised grew too much to bear.

Nearby Tepoztlán is another popular spot, especially with outdoors enthusiasts who enjoy hiking to its famous pyramid. Like Cuernavaca, the town itself has charming architecture and an attractive downtown area with interesting sites for visitors.

CUERNAVACA

85 km (53 mi) south of Mexico City center.

The road to Cuernavaca will likely heighten your anticipation—you'll catch your first glimpse of the city's lush surroundings from a mountain highway, through lacy pine branches. Cuernavaca's perfect weather has made for stunning gardens. The Jardín Borda, where José de la Borda (who made his fortune in Taxco silver) died, is perhaps the most famous. It has been a private garden for centuries, and it is where Emperor Maximilian and his empress came to rest. It is now open to the public.

Of course, many of the best gardens lie behind high walls. And truth be told, Cuernavaca's growth in the last decade has weakened some of its tourist appeal. But the city still has much to recommend it. There are certainly enough museums, palaces, old churches, and other sites to see—many of them concentrated in the downtown area—to keep you busy.

GETTING HERE & AROUND

Buses from Mexico City's Central de Autobuses del Sur depart for Cuernavaca every 10 minutes. The 1½-hour trip costs about $5.50. Both Grupo Pullman and Cristobal Colón offer regular, reliable service. To drive here, the *cuota* (toll road, Route 95D) costs about $10 but takes 1½ hours. The *carretera libre* (free road, Route 95) takes much longer, but has attractive forest scenery.

ESSENTIALS

Buses **Cristobal Colón** (*☎ 55/5544-9008*).**Grupo Pullman de Morelos** (*☎ 55/5549-3505 in Mexico City, 777/318-4638 in Cuernavaca 🌐 www.pullman.com.mx*).

Currency Exchange **Centro Cambiario Morelos** (*✉ Av. Manuel Avila Camacho 274-28, Col. San Jéronimo ☎ 777/372-3003*).

Medical Assistance **Hospital General de Cuernavaca "Dr. José G. Parrés"** (*✉ Av. Domingo Diez s/n, Col. Lomas de la Selva ☎ 777/311-2209 or 777/311-2210*).

Visitor & Tour Info **Cuernavaca Tourist Office** (*✉ Av. Morelos 278, Col. Centro ☎ 777/318-7561 🌐 www.morelostravel.com*).

EXPLORING

MAIN ATTRACTIONS

The **Jardín Borda** is one of the most popular sights in Cuernavaca. It was designed in the late 18th century for Don Manuel de la Borda, son of Don José de la Borda, the wealthy miner who established the beautiful church of Santa Prisca in Taxco. The Borda Gardens were

Continued on page 153

Pirámide de la Luna
(Pyramid of the Moon) dominates the northern end of the city. From the top of this structure you can scan the entire city (pictured left).
The **Calzada de los Muertos**
(Avenue of the Dead), at nearly 4-km (2½-mi) long, was given this name by the Aztecs because they mistook the temples along each side for tombs.

TEOTIHUACÁN

Imagine yourself walking down a pathway called Calzada de los Muertos (Avenue of the Dead). Surrounding you are some of Earth's most mysterious ancient structures, among them the Palace of the Jaguars, the Pyramid of the Moon, and the Temple of the Plumed Serpent. From the top of the awe-inspiring Pyramid of the Sun—at 210 feet, the third tallest pyramid in the world—you begin to appreciate your 242-stair climb as you survey a city that long ago was the seat of a powerful empire. This is Teotihuacán, meaning "place where men became gods."

Pirámide del Sol

At its zenith, around AD 600, Teotihuacán (teh-oh-tee-wa-can) was one of the largest cities in the world and the center of an empire that inhabited much of central Mexico. Many archaeologists believe that Teotihuacán was home to some 100,000 people. The questions of just who built this city, at whose hands it fell, and even its original name remain a mystery, eluding archaeologists and fueling imaginations the world over.

Just 31 miles from the center of Mexico City, Teotihuacán is one of the most significant and haunting archaeological sites in the world. Climbing on the structures that were once painted a bright, glowing red; discovering the etchings of winged creatures at the Palace of the Plumed Butterfly; meandering through the circuitous underground chambers of colorful murals in the Palace of the Jaguars; taking on the invigorating climb up the Pyramid of the Moon—all will transport you to a Mexico of days past.

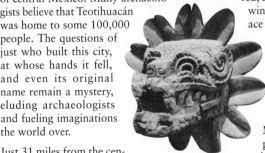

Quetzalcóatl, the Plumed Serpent

View of Avenue of the Dead from Pirámide del Sol

THE MAJOR SIGHTS

The ❶ **Ciudadela** is a massive citadel ringed by more than a dozen temples, with the ❷ **Templo de Quetzalcóatl** (Temple of the Plumed Serpent) as the centerpiece. Here you'll find detailed carvings of the benevolent deity Quetzalcóatl, a serpent with its head ringed by feathers, jutting out of the facade.

One of the most impressive sights in Teotihuacán is the 4-km-long (2½-mi-long) ❸ **Calzada de los Muertos** (Avenue of the Dead), which once held great ceremonial importance. The Aztecs gave it this name because they mistook the temples lining either side for tombs. It leads to the 126-foot-high ❹ **Pirámide de la Luna** (Pyramid of the Moon), which dominates the city's northern end. Some of the most exciting recent finds, including a royal tomb, have been unearthed here. In late 2002 a discovery of jade objects gave new evidence of a link between the Teotihuacán rulers and the Maya.

Facing the Pyramid of the Moon is the ❺ **Palacio del Quetzalpápalotl** (Palace of the Plumed Butterfly); its beautifully reconstructed terrace has columns etched with images of various winged creatures, some still with their original obsidian-set eyes. Nearby is the ❻ **Palacio de los Jaguares** (Palace of the Jaguars), a residence for priests. Spectacular bird and jaguar murals wind through its underground chambers. The stunning ❼ **Pirámide del Sol** (Pyramid of the Sun), the first monumental structure constructed here, stands in the center of the city. With a base as broad as that of the pyramid of Cheops in Egypt, its size takes your breath away, often quite literally, during the climb up its west face. Deep within the pyramid archaeologists have discovered a natural clover-shape cave that they speculate may have had some connection to the city's religion.

Set amidst rich obsidian mines, the city was home to powerful rulers. The city's crafts and goods were traded with distant cities such as Tikal in Guatemala and Copán in Honduras. Not only did the people of Teotihuacán trade with foreigners, but foreigners also lived in this city which archaeologists surmise was incredibly cosmopolitan. The best artifacts uncovered at Teotihuacán are on display at the Museo Nacional de Antropologia in Mexico City. Still, the **8 Museo de la Sitio**, adjacent to the Pirámide del Sol, contains a few good pieces, such as a stone sculpture of the saucer-eyed Tlaloc, some black and green obsidian arrowheads, and the skeletons of human sacrifices arranged as they were when discovered.

More than 4,000 one-story adobe and stone dwellings surround the Calzada de los Muertos; these were occupied by artisans, warriors, and tradesmen. The best example, a short walk from the Pirámide del Sol, is called **9 Tepantitla**. Here you'll see murals depicting a watery realm ruled by the rain god Tláloc. Restored in 2002, its reds, greens, and yellows are nearly as vivid as when they were painted more than 1,500 years ago.

The Aztecs believed the gods created the universe at Teotihuacán; they settled the land here years after the city's collapse. After a walk through the ruins, and perhaps a climb up one of the pyramids, you'll have a profound sense of the importance this landscape held in the pre-conquest world.

Keep in mind that the city stretched beyond what has been excavated, and that most of the living areas lay beyond the ceremonial center of the city.

ARCHAEOLOGY ACCESS

There are five entrances to Teotihuacán, each near one of the major attractions. Around these entrances there are small restaurants and vendors. If you have a car, it's a good idea to drive from one entrance to the next. Seeing the ruins will take several hours, especially if you head to the lesser-known areas. A good English-language guidebook is sold at the site. ☎ *594/956–0052 or 594/956–0276* 🌐 *archaeology.la.asu.edu/teo* 🎫 *$4.*

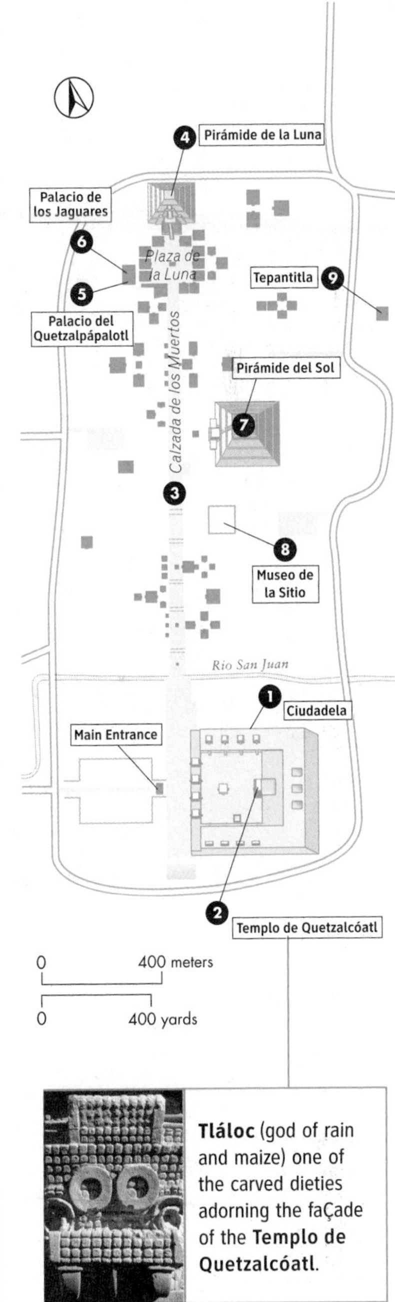

Tláloc (god of rain and maize) one of the carved dieties adorning the faÇade of the **Templo de Quetzalcóatl**.

Pirámide del Sol as seen from Pirámide de la Luna

HOW TO GET HERE

50 km (31 mi) northeast of Mexico City center.

BY BUS: To get to Teotihuacán, take one of the Línea Teotihuacán buses that depart every 15 minutes from the Central de Autobuses del Norte (www.centraldelnorte.com.mx) in Mexico City. (In the bus station, look for signs marked PIRAMIDES; they don't say Teotihuacán.) The hour-long trip costs about $2.50. Buses leave Mexico City from 6 AM–6 PM. The last bus from Teotihuacán leaves at 8 PM.

Bus Companies **Autobus Teotihuacanos** 55/5781-1812 or 55/5587-0501.

BY CAR: To get to Teotihuacán from Mexico City, take Highway 85D, and follow the signs. In general, the ruins have free parking but the parking areas are a short walk from the sites, so be sure not to leave any valuables in your car.

so famous they attracted royalty. Maximilian and Carlotta visited frequently. Here the emperor reportedly dallied with the gardener's wife, called La India Bonita, who was immortalized in a famous portrait. Novelist Malcolm Lowry turned the formal gardens into a sinister symbol in his 1947 novel *Under the Volcano*. A pleasant café and a well-stocked bookstore sit just inside the gates. ✉*Av. Morelos 103, at Hidalgo* ☎*777/318–1050* 🎫*$3* ⏲*Tues.–Sun. 10–5:30.*

CAUTION

Watch out for drunk drivers on the highways surrounding Mexico City, especially around local or national holidays. There's generally heavy traffic on the way back from Tepotzotlán and Tula after 4 PM on Sunday.

North of the Plaza de Armas you'll find the **Museo Regional Cuauhnáhuac,** from the Aztec word for the surrounding valley, also known as the Palacio de Cortés. The fortresslike building was constructed as a stronghold for Hernán Cortés in 1522, as the region had not been completely conquered at that time. His palace sits atop the ruins of Aztec buildings, some of which have been partially excavated. There are plenty of stone carvings from the area on display, but the best way to digest all this history is by gazing at the murals Diego Rivera painted between 1927 and 1930 on the top floor. ✉*Juárez and Hidalgo* ☎*777/312–8171* 🌐*www.inah.gob.mx* 🎫*$3.90; free Sun.* ⏲*Tues.–Sun. 9–6; ticket sales stop at 5:30.*

The city's most traditional square is the **Plaza de Armas,** marked by a hefty, volcanic stone statue of revolutionary hero José María Morelos and a couple of little fountains. On weekdays the square fills with vendors from neighboring villages. On weekends it is crowded with balloon sellers, amateur painters, and stalls for crafts, jewelry, and knickknacks. **TIP→The Tren Turístico (☎777/317–0421 🌐www.morelosweb.com/tren-turistico), a wooden trolleybus for sightseeing, departs from the southeast corner opposite the Palacio de Cortés. 🎫 $3.50 on weekdays and $4.50 on weekends.** To the north of the square is leafy **Jardín Juárez** (Juárez Garden), which hosts Sunday concerts at its bandstand.

★ A trip to the ruins of **Xochicalco** is one of the best reasons to visit Morelos state. Built by the Olmeca-Xicalanca people, the mighty hilltop city reached its peak between AD 700 and 900. It was abandoned a century later after being destroyed, perhaps by its own inhabitants.

With its several layers of fortifications, the city appears unassailable. The most eye-catching edifice is the **Pyrámide de Quetzalcóatl** (Temple of the Plumed Serpent). Carvings of vicious-looking snakes—all in the style typical of the Maya to the south—wrap around the lower level, while figures in elaborate headdresses sit above. Be sure to seek out the **Observatorio** in a man-made cave reached through a tunnel on the northern side of the city. Through a narrow shaft in the ceiling the Xochicalco astronomers could observe the heavens. Twice a year—May 14 and 15 and July 28 and 29—the sun passes directly over the opening, filling the room with light.

Stop in at the museum—a beautifully mounted exhibition of a wide variety of artifacts from Xochicalco are on display—but note that all explanations are in Spanish.

There are dozens of other structures here, including three impressive ball courts. The site's solar-powered museum has six rooms of artifacts, including beautiful sculptures of Xochicalco deities found nearby. ✉*Hwy. 95D, southwest of Cuernavaca* ☎*777/374–3092* 🌐*www.inah.gob.mx* 🎟*$3.80* ⏲*Daily 9–6; tickets are sold until 5.*

IF YOU HAVE TIME

Cortés ordered the construction of the **Catedral de la Asunción,** with work beginning in 1525. Like his palace, the cathedral doubled as a fortress. Cannons mounted above the flying buttresses helped bolster the city's defenses. The facade may give you a sense of foreboding, especially when you catch sight of the skull and crossbones over the door. The interior is much less ominous, though, thanks to the murals uncovered during renovations. ✉*Hidalgo and Av. Morelos* ☎*777/312–1290* ⏲*Daily 8–6.*

On a quiet street south of the Plaza de Armas, the **Robert Brady Museum** shows the collection of the artist, antiquarian, and decorator from Fort Dodge, Iowa. Ceramics, antique furniture, sculptures, paintings, and tapestries fill the restored colonial mansion, all beautifully arranged in rooms painted with bright colors. Note that the building numbers on this street are out of order. The museum is just across the street from numbers 21 and 121. ✉*Calle Netzahuacóyotl 4, between Hidalgo and Abasolo* ☎*777/318–8554* 🌐*www.geocities.com/bradymuseum* 🎟*$3* ⏲*Tues.–Sun. 10–6.*

WHERE TO EAT

$$$$ MEXICAN ✕ **Restaurante Gaia.** In a beautiful old house that once belonged to Mario Moreno, the movie star popularly known as Cantiflas, is one of the most elegant restaurants in Cuernavaca. The chef serves up delicious and beautifully presented lunches and dinners, including tasty twists on old Mexican classics like *chiles rellenos* (peppers stuffed with three cheeses). The *camarones con costar de amaranto* (shrimp with an amaranto crust) is also worth a try. A long lunch is served by the pool, which has a mosaic often attributed to Diego Rivera. The restaurant has a great location two blocks from the Palacio de Cortés. ✉Blvd. Benito Juárez 102 ☎*777/312–3656* 💳*AE, MC, V.*

$$ MEXICAN ✕ **Casa Hidalgo.** The marvelous view of the Palacio de Cortés helped make this restaurant a big hit among the foreigners in town. The menu mixes Mexican and international foods; you might try the *filetón hidalgo* (breaded veal stuffed with serrano ham and manchego cheese). A jazz band plays on Saturday night. ■ TIP→ **Reservations are recommended on weekends—request a table on the small balcony for a great view of the Palacio just across the street.** ✉*Hidalgo 6, Col. Centro* ☎*777/312–2749* 🌐*www.casahidalgo.com* 💳*AE, MC, V.*

$$ CONTEMPORARY ✕ **Casa Tamayo.** This chic restaurant has a startling view over the *barranca* (gulley). For those longing for something fresh and green, the Hesch salad (almonds and Roquefort cheese over mixed greens) will

CLOSE UP

Traditional Medicine Makes a Comeback

Herbal medicine remains an integral part of Mexican life, and still predominates in remote areas where modern medicines are hard to come by or are too expensive for rural laborers. Even in the capital, most markets will have distinctive stalls piled with curative herbs and plants.

The Aztecs were excellent botanists, and their extensive knowledge impressed the Spanish, who borrowed from Mexico's indigenous herbarium and cataloged the intriguing new plants. Consequently, medicine remains one of the few examples of cultural practices and indigenous wisdom that has not been lost to history. Visitors to the capital can find a display of medicinal plants used by the Aztecs in the Museum of Medicine, in the former Palace of the Inquisition, at the northwest corner of Plaza Santo Domingo.

A rich variety of herbs is harvested in the 300 rural communities of the fertile state of Morelos, where *curanderos* (natural healers) flock to the markets on weekends to offer advice and sell their concoctions. Stores in the state capital, Cuernavaca, sell natural antidotes for every ailment imaginable and potions for sexual prowess, lightening the skin, colic in babies, and IQ enhancement.

Chamanes (shamans) and healers abound at the weekend market in the main square of the picturesque mountain village of Tepoztlán. Long known for its *brujas* (witches), Tepoztlán continues to experience a boom in spiritual retreats and New Age shops. Visitors can benefit from the healing overload without getting hoodwinked by booking a session in one of the many good *temazcales* (Aztec sweat lodges) in town.

The temazcal is a "bath of cleansing" for body, mind, and spirit; a session consists of a ritual that lasts at least an hour, ideally (for first-timers) with a guide. Temazcales are igloo-shape clay buildings, round so as not to impede the flow of energy. They usually seat 6 to 12 people, who can participate either naked or in a bathing suit. Each guide develops his own style, under the tutelage of a shaman, so practices vary. In general your aura (or energy field) is cleaned with a bunch of plants before you enter the temazcal, so that you start off as pure as possible. You will have a fistful of the same plants—usually rosemary, sweet basil, or eucalyptus—to slap or rub against your skin. You walk in a clockwise direction and take your place, and water is poured over red-hot stones in the middle to create the steam. Usually silence is maintained, although the guide may chant or pray, often in Nahuatl. The procedure ends with a warm shower followed by a cold one to close the pores.

The experience helps eliminate toxins, cure inflammations, ease pains in the joints, and relieve stress. Consequently, temazcales are growing in popularity, even drawing city executives from the capital on weekends. You can find some of the most outstanding temazcales in Morelos's top spas, such as the Misión del Sol in Jiutepec and Hostería las Quintas in Cuernavaca. Less pricey are El Centro Mayahuel in Ahuacatitlán or the temazcales of Teresa Contreras or Dr. Horacio Rojas in Cuernavaca.

–Barbara Kastelein

be a treat. A favorite main dish is the *pollo pancha*, a chicken breast filled with mozzarella and spinach in a semisweet orange sauce. Reservations are recommended on weekends. ✉*Francisco Leyva 94, Col. Centro* ☎*777/318–9477* ▭*AE, MC, V* ⊙*No dinner Sun.*

WORD OF MOUTH

"Las Mañanitas is certainly worth a visit for at least a drink. I just returned from studying Spanish at Instituto Chac-Mool Spanish school in Cuernavaca and we had an evening excursion to Las Mañanitas for drinks and appetizers. I went back on my own two more times, I found the food quite good and they offer Mexican dishes as well as steaks and seafood. It is such a lovely, peaceful place that I could walk to from my school. Just be sure to stroll through the gardens to see all the sculptures. I'd love to stay at their hotel someday soon."

–Katie2Travel

WHERE TO STAY

$$$$ **Camino Real Sumiya.** Woolworth heiress Barbara Hutton built this monumental hideaway in the 1950s, after her long search for a site with excellent weather and an interesting history. The Japanese theme is pleasingly consistent, flowing seemlessly from the imposing entrance to the lobby and bar. Restaurante Sumiya, which serves international and Japanese food, is so good it draws people who aren't staying at the hotel. The rooms are set in the far part of the garden for privacy, and many have beautiful garden views. To reach the hotel, which is about 15 minutes south of town at Interior del Fraccionamiento Sumiya, take the Civac-Cuauhtla exit on Acapulco Highway. **Pros:** Excellent restaurant, beautiful gardens, unexpected architecture. **Cons:** Frequent events mob the place, prices are high. ✉*Col. José Parres, Jiutepec* ☎*777/329–9888* 🌐*www.caminoreal.com/sumiya* *157 rooms, 6 suites* *In-room: Safe, refrigerator, Wi-Fi. In-hotel: 2 restaurants, bar, tennis courts, pools, concierge, no elevator* ▭*AE, DC, MC, V.*

$$$$ Fodor'sChoice ★ **Las Mañanitas.** An American expat opened this hacienda-style hotel in the 1950s, and it is still one of the best lodgings in Cuernavaca. The ample rooms are outfitted with traditional fireplaces, hand-carved bedsteads, hand-painted tiles in the bathrooms, and gilded crafts. The restaurant ($–$$$), with its spectacular open-air terraces and garden inhabited by flamingos, peacocks, and African cranes, is a beautiful place to spend an afternoon enjoying a leisurely meal. Unfortunately, the quality of the food isn't as reliable as it once was. However, you can't go wrong with traditional dishes like the well-prepared *mole poblano*. **Pros:** Gorgeous setting, stylish rooms. **Cons:** Restaurant has lost a bit of its luster. ✉*Ricardo Linares 107,* ☎*777/314–1466, 01800/221–5299 toll-free in Mexico, 888/413–9199 toll-free in U.S.* 🌐*www.lasmananitas.com.mx* *32 suites* *In-room: No TV, safe, Wi-Fi. In-hotel: Restaurant, room service, bar, pool, no elevator* ▭*AE, MC, V.*

$$$$ **Misíon del Sol.** This exclusive resort and spa was designed with body and spirit in mind, and every detail of the grounds—from the handmade adobe buildings and lush gardens to the exceptional restaurant to the pool with water that somehow feels like silk—invites its adults-only clientele to relax and enjoy. Maybe it's the beauty of the place,

the magnets strategically placed under the beds to promote rest, or the massages offered at the spa, but guests come from this resort and spa happy and rested. Consciousness-expanding events, from yoga and meditation classes to guest speakers like Dr. Deepak Chopra (who has spoken several times here) are always available and listed on the Web site. **Pros:** Peaceful atmosphere, exceptional service, good spa treatments. **Cons:** A bit too quiet at times, not the place for families. ✉*Av. Gral. Diego Días González 31,* ☎*777/321–0999* 🌐*www.misiondelsol.com* *40 rooms, 10 villas* *In-hotel: Restaurant, pool, spa, no elevator, no kids under 18* 💳*AE, MC, V*

★ $$$–$$$$ **Hacienda de Cortés.** This 16th-century former sugar mill once belonged to the famed conquistador. Wandering around the gardens and discovering cascades, fountains, abandoned pillars, and sculptures is an enchanting experience, especially at dusk. Ask for a room in the old part of the building to immerse yourself in the atmosphere. Rooms have traditional Mexican furnishings and lovely patios or balconies. The restaurant ($–$$) is within old fort walls draped with vines—it's like dining inside a ruined castle. **Pros:** Historic building, romantic setting, beautiful bar. **Cons:** Noisy events sometimes take over the hotel. ✉*Plaza Kennedy 90, Col. Atlacomulco, Jiutepec* ☎*777/315–8844* 🌐*www.hotelhaciendadecortes.com* *14 rooms, 6 suites* *In-room: Safe, refrigerator, Wi-Fi. In-hotel: Restaurant, bar, pool, no elevator* 💳*AE, MC, V.*

★ $$$–$$$$ **Hacienda San Gabriel de las Palmas.** A colorful history surrounds this grand hacienda, built in 1529. Now it's a haven of quiet with lush gardens—disturbed only by birdcalls, the splashing of a waterfall, and the ringing of a chapel bell. If you'd like to get even more blissed-out, visit the spa, which includes a traditional temazcal. Antiques fill both the public areas and the spacious guest rooms. Outstanding Mexican food is prepared in an attractive open kitchen close to the pool. The hacienda is 25 minutes outside Cuernavaca. **Pros:** Peaceful atmosphere, easy drive to Cuernavaca and Taxco. **Cons:** Far from main sites, rates are pricey. ✉*Carretera Federal Cuernavaca–Chilpancingo Km 41.8, Amacuzac* ☎*751/348–0636, 01800/508–7923 toll-free in Mexico, 877/278–8018 toll-free from U.S.* 🌐*www.hacienda-sangabriel.com.mx* *5 rooms, 13 suites* *In-room: No a/c, no TV. In-hotel: Restaurant, bar, tennis court, pools, spa, no elevator, public Wi-Fi* 💳*AE, MC, V.*

$$$ **Hotel Posada María Cristina.** This delightful hotel, popular with foreigner travelers, was constructed in the 16th century as a home for one of Cortés's soldiers. It is full of character, with plenty of alcoves, nooks, and crannies to explore. Lush gardens slope down the steep hill toward the pool. The main restaurant serves Mexican and international cuisine, while the poolside restaurant refreshes loungers with Argentine food. **Pros:** Incredible location, historic building, architectural charm. **Cons:** Some rooms are better than others, street noise can be a problem on weekends. < ✉*Leyva 20, at the corner of Abasolo, Col. Centro,* ☎*777/318–5767, 01800/024–5767 toll-free in Mexico* 🌐*www.maria-cristina.com* *16 rooms, 4 suites* *In-room: Dial-up (some). In-hotel: 2 restaurants, bar, pool, no elevator* 💳*AE, DC, MC.*

$$$ **Hotel Villa Rosa.** This very pink hotel has the advantage of being both very central and very tranquil. Although each room is different—you'll find everything from floral patterns to executive-friendly modernity—all have high ceilings with exposed beams and are refreshingly cool, even though only three rooms have air-conditioning. Located at the end of a cobblestone street, with a grassy garden, shaded pool area, and tiny spa, the Villa Rosa makes a good retreat, particularly midweek when prices dip. **Pros:** Central location, lovely shaded pool. **Cons:** Drab decor, not all rooms have air-conditioning, pricey for what you get. ✉*2a Privada de Humboldt 6, Col. Centro,* ☎*777/312–1632 or 777/312–9225* 🌐*www.vrosahotel.com.mx* *11 rooms* *In-room: No a/c (some), dial-up. In-hotel: Restaurant, pool, spa, no elevator* *AE, MC, V.*

$$–$$$ **Hotel Casa Colonial.** This old colonial mansion has been beautifully restored. The rooms are individually decorated, giving them a homey feel. The best part is that you are right in the middle of downtown. You can be at any number of interesting sites in minutes. **Pros:** Incredible location, pleasant accommodations. **Cons:** Neighborhood is noisy on the weekends. ✉*Netzahualcoyotl 37,* ☎*777/312–7033* 🌐*www.casacolonial.com* *15 rooms* *In-room: Wi-Fi. In-hotel: Restaurant, bar, pool, no elevator* *AE, MC, V.*

NIGHTLIFE

Cuernavaca is a great place to be after the sun goes down. Evenings are cool and agreeable throughout the year, which means people venture out to enjoy a drink or listen to live music. The bars draw an interesting mix of locals, weekenders escaping the capital, and international tourists.

Young people crowd the dance floor at**Alebrije** (✉ *Av. Plan de Ayala 405, Col. Teopanzolco* ☎*777/322–4282)* to move to popular English- and Spanish-language tunes every Friday and Saturday night. Men pay $15 to get in the door, while women enter for free.

Juárez 0000(✉ *Blvd. Benito Juárez 4, Col. Centro* ☎*777/312–7984*)is *the* spot for those who are into electronic music. While there is no cover, there's a minimum amount men must spend at the bar. Women, of course, do not have a minimum.

Drawing a more diverse crowd than its competitors,**Taizz**(✉*Bajada Chapultepec 13, Col. Chapultepec* ☎*777/315–4060*, a popular dance club, mixes its musical styles well. You'll hear everything from electronic music to the latest hits in English and Spanish.

SHOPPING

Cuernavaca has shops for all tastes. In the downtown area, vendors are found around the zócalo and along the surrounding streets. You'll find leather shoes, embroidered blouses, beaded necklaces, and other crafts. Some of these are produced in Cuernavaca, but others are brought in from around the country.

Librería Educal Libros y Arte Jardín Borda (✉*Av. Morelos 271* ☎*777/314–3978*), a bookshop at the entrance to the Jardín Borda, has quite a collection of titles, particularly on Mexico and Mexican art. Many titles are in English.

A small bookstore connected to the Palacio de Cortes, **Libros y Arte** (✉*Leyva 100* ☎*777/312–9933*) sells titles on Mexican history, culture, and art, mostly in Spanish.

SPORTS & THE OUTDOORS

With near-perfect weather, Cuernavaca a great place for sports enthusiasts, and there are some good places to play tennis and golf. Remember that you will find more crowds on weekends.

Hacienda San Gaspar (✉*Avenida Emiliano Zapata s/n, Col. Cliserio* ☎*777/323–6015* 🌐 *www.sangaspar.com*) is a golf club with an impressive steel-and-glass clubhouse. The 18-hole course is surrounded by lush gardens. Greens fees are $80.

LAS ESTACAS

Ninety minutes from Mexico City, **Las Estacas** (✉Carretera Jojutla-Tltizapán, Km 7 ☎ 734/345–0077, 55/5563–2428 in Mexico City, 777/312–4412 in Cuernavaca, 🌐 www.lasestacas.com) is an ideal place for a swim in a pool or in a cool, clean river born of an underwater spring. The weather here is almost always sunny, even when it's raining in Mexico City. Large stretches of grass under palm trees are great places to sunbathe. Dive classes and spa services are available. Grab a juicy grilled hamburger at the restaurant. A day pass costs $19.50; the complex is open daily 8 to 6.

TEPOZTLÁN

75 km (47 mi) south of Mexico City, 26 km (16 mi) east of Cuernavaca via Route 95D.

Surrounded by sandstone monoliths that throw off a russet glow at sunset, Tepoztlán is a magical place. No wonder it attracts practitioners of astrology, meditation, yoga, and other New Age pursuits. But you'll still find women selling homegrown produce in the lively weekend market surrounding the main square and traditional celebrations that predate the conquest.

Tepoztlán's temperatures fluctuate, from blistering around midday to bitterly cold at night. Visitors who plan an overnight stay in the winter months should bring warmer clothing and a coat.

GETTING HERE & AROUND

Buses leave Mexico City's Central de Autobuses del Sur. Two reliable bus companies include Grupo Pullman de Morelos and Cristobal Colón. You can easily combine a trip to Cuernavaca and Tepoztlán by taking a bus to Cuernavaca, and another bus or a taxi from Cuernavaca to Tepoztlán. By car, take the Mexico-Cuernavaca *cuota*, or toll highway. It costs about $10. If you want to take the free Route 95D, budget much more time.

3

EXPLORING

★ The town is famous for its tiny **Pirámide de Tepozteco.** Perched on a mountaintop, this temple is dedicated to either the Aztec deity Tepoztécatl or—depending on whose story you believe—Ome Tochtli, the god of the alcoholic drink pulque. The pyramid was part of a city that has not been uncovered, but was of such importance that pilgrims flocked here from as far away as Guatemala. It attracts hikers and sightseers not afraid of the somewhat arduous climb. The view over the valley is terrific. ✉ *North end of Av. Tepoztlán* 🎫 *$3.50* ⏲ *Tues.–Sun. 9:30–5:30.*

Rising above most of Tepoztlán's buildings is the buttressed **Ex-Convento Dominico de la Natividad.** The former convent, dating from the mid-16th century, has a facade adorned with icons dating from before the introduction of Christianity. Many of the walls, especially on the ground floor, have fragments of old paintings in earthen tones on the walls and decorating the arches. It is worth a visit just to see the building, which also houses temporary exhibitions and a complete bookstore with a good selection of books, CDs, and videos. ✉ *Av. Revolución 1910* ☎ No phone ⏲ *Tues.–Sun. 10–5.*

FIREWATER

Pulque, a thick alcoholic beverage made by fermenting juice from the maguey plant, is a dying drink in modern Mexico, but you can still try it at **Alejandro's Pulquería** (✉ Av. del Tepozteco 23 ☎ No phone) from midday to about 8 PM (or whenever the store runs out). Alejandro Gómez offers unusual flavors, including *nuez* (walnut), *apio* (celery), and *guayaba* (guava, yum). A cup costs about 70¢. Alejandro works out of a grimy room open to the street, and there are usually pulque drunkards tottering (harmlessly) about. Watch out: this pre-Hispanic drink causes pounding hangovers.

WHERE TO EAT

$$ MEXICAN ✕ **El Ciruelo.** You'll need to call two or three days in advance to reserve a nice seat—with a view of the pyramid—for the weekend. The rest of the tables at this casual restaurant are centered around a partially open patio. A varied menu includes chicken breast stuffed with *huitlacoche,* an exquisite inky fungus that grows on corn, and spicy shrimp tacos. There is a place for children to play on weekends. ✉ *Zaragoza 17* ☎ *739/395–1037* 💳 *AE, MC, V.*

$ MEXICAN ✕ **Axitla.** This smart establishment in the folds of the mountains is surrounded by ponds and bridges. Among the delicious concoctions are *chile jaral* (ancho chili stuffed with shredded beef and raisins) and lamb in zucchini sauce. You can dine in the pink, high-ceilinged dining room overlooking the trees and river or alfresco. A lone guitar player adds to the atmosphere weekend lunchtimes. ✉ *Av. del Tepozteco, at road to Pyramid* ☎ *739/395–0519 or 739/395–2555* 💳 *MC, V* ⏲ *Closed Mon. and Tues. No dinner.*

★ $ MEXICAN ✕ **Los Colorines.** Hung with colorful *papeles picados* (paper cutouts), this family-friendly restaurant serves great bean soups, stuffed chiles, and grilled meats made in an open kitchen. Special dishes include *huauzontles* (a broccoli-like vegetable you scrape from the stalk with your teeth). Note that the restaurant closes at 9 PM during the week; weekends it's open until 10 or until the crowd leaves. ✉*Av. del Tepozteco 13* ☎*739/395–0198* ▭*No credit cards.*

WHERE TO STAY

$$$–$$$$ **Hostal de la Luz.** An experiment in "holistic tourism" is making waves at the foot of the Quetzalcóatl mountains in the village of Amatlán. The complex, from the traditional adobe structure to the use of feng shui, is designed to blend with the environment and soothe its guests. The guest rooms have wicker meditation chairs set in bay window alcoves from which to absorb the unparalleled views. The resort is roughly a 15-minute drive from Tepoztlán. **Pros:** Secluded setting, excellent spa treatments. **Cons:** Rather pricey, no Internet connections. ✉*Carretera Federal Tepoztlán-Amatlán, Km 4, Amatlán de Quetzalcóatl,* ☎*739/395–3374* 🌐*www.hostaldelaluz.com* *13 rooms* *In-room: No a/c, no TV. In-hotel: Restaurant, pool, spa, no elevator* ▭*AE, MC, V* *BP.*

$$$–$$$$ **Posada del Tepozteco.** Enjoy splendid views of both the village and the pyramid as you stroll through this hotel's terraced gardens. A honeymooners' favorite, the inn is also a good place for children, with its trampoline, swings, and pair of pet rabbits. Most rooms have balconies and hot tubs, and some have beautiful views of the pyramid. Make reservations for weekend stays two weeks in advance. This is also a great place to stop in for a leisurely meal on the patio, where the tables are set around a murmuring stone fountain and circled by vine-covered archways. **Pros:** Unbeatable views, excellent service. **Cons:** Buffet draws big crowds, uphill walk from downtown. **TIP→The weekend buffet breakfast is an excellent time to visit and enjoy the view overlooking the village, even if you are not staying at the hotel.** ✉*Calle del Paraíso 3,* ☎*739/395–0010* 🌐*www.posadadeltepozteco.com* *8 rooms, 12 suites* *In-room: No a/c, no TV. In-hotel: Restaurant, room service, bar, tennis court, pool, no elevator, public Wi-Fi* ▭*AE, MC, V.*

$–$$ **Posada Ali.** With unobstructed views of the mountains from its rooms, this family-run inn draws many repeat customers. No two rooms are exactly alike, and all have charming hand-hewn furniture. There's a tiny pool in back. This is not the most elegant hotel in Tepoztlán, but it is clean and inexpensive. **Pros:** Family-friendly environment, lovely views. **Cons:** Weekends are busy, need to reserve far in advance. ✉*Netzahualcóyotl 2,* ☎*739/395–1971* *13 rooms* *In-room: No a/c. In-hotel: Restaurant, pool, no elevator* ▭*No credit cards.*

SHOPPING

Ceramic Servín (✉*Av. Del Tepoxteco 27* ☎*739/753–1206*) is a standout. You'll find delicately hand-painted ceramics produced by the Servín family.

VALLE DE BRAVO

75 km (47 mi) west of Mexico City.

A few hours here explains why "Valle" is often billed as Mexico's best-kept secret. The pines, clear air, and the Lago Valle de Bravo make it very different from most people's idea—and experience—of Mexico.

This colonial lakeside treasure is peppered with white stucco houses trimmed with wrought-iron balconies and red-tile roofs with long eaves to protect walkers from both the rain and the glaring sun. Connected to Mexico City mostly via a two-lane, winding, mountainous road, the town is visited primarily by wealthy Mexicans—particularly weekenders from the capital—and fans of adventure tourism.

Valle was founded in 1530, but has no significant historical sights to speak of other than the St. Francis of Assisi cathedral on the town square and the church of Santa Maria, with a huge crucified black Christ on its altar. Rather than sightsee, saunter the streets and check out the bazaars, boutiques, galleries, and markets. Valle is famous for its lacelike fabrics called *deshilados* and its earthenware and hand-glazed ceramics.

The town's two major festivals are on May 3 and October 4, and both involve many old Mexican traditional games and dances as well as elaborate fireworks displays. If you plan to come on these dates, over Christmas, or on a weekend, make sure you make hotel reservations well in advance. ■TIP→**To avoid the crowds from the capital and nab lower hotel rates, visit during the week for a quieter experience, more suitable for those who wish to hike and enjoy the pristine views.**

GETTING HERE & AROUND

By car, take Highway 15 toward Toluca. As the highway passes through Toluca it is called Paseo Tollocan. Look for signs on the left for Valle de Bravo. Follow Highway 142 until you reach Francisco de los Ranchos, then bear right to reach Valle de Bravo. Much of the route is a narrow, two-lane road through leafy countryside. Passing slower traffic is impossible, so expect a long ride. Buses for Valle de Bravo leave the Terminal de Autobuses Poniente, at the Observatorio metro station. Todo Valle buses leave Mexico City nearly every hour for Valle de Bravo.

ESSENTIALS

Bus Contacts **Todo Valle** (☎ *726/262–0213*).

Medical Assistance **Farma Pronto** (✉ *Farma Pronto, Pagaza 100, on corner of Plaza Independencia at Bocanegra* ☎ *726/262–1441*). **Hospital General de Valle de Bravo** (✉ *Fray Gregorio Jiménez de la Cuenca s/n* ☎ *726/262–1646*).

Visitor & Tour Info **Mexico State Tourist Office** (✉ *Urawa 100, Gate 110, Toluca* ☎ *722/219–5190* 🌐 *www.edomexico.gob.mx*). **Valle de Bravo Turismo Municipal** (✉ *Presidencia Municipal, 5 de Febrero 100, entrance opposite bell tower* ☎ *726/262–1678*).

WHERE TO EAT

$$$ SEAFOOD ✕ **Los Veleros.** If you want seafood, skip the floating restaurants at the dock (where the food leaves much to be desired and locals say you will likely walk away with a stomachache) and head to Los Veleros, a cozy family restaurant in an old mansion just a block away. Sit out on the terrace overlooking the beautiful garden as you enjoy your meal. It's open on Friday, Saturday, and Sunday until midnight or later,

depending on how many customers are still around. ✉*Salitre No. 104* ☎*726/262–0370* 💳*AE, MC, V.*

$$ MEXICAN ✕ **Mozzarella Restaurant.** People spend hours enjoying their meals at this eatery in a plant-filled courtyard of the Hotel Batucada. Tables are set around a carved stone fountain. The creative plates include black rice, made with shrimp, squid, octopus, clams, and mussels, and the fresh and delicious blue salad, made with different varieties of greens, pears, grapefruit, and beets, topped off with a light blue-cheese dressing. ✉*Bocanegra 201-C* ☎*726/262–1666* 🌐*www.hotelbatucada.com.mx* 💳*AE, MC, V.*

$ MEXICAN ✕ **La Michoacana.** You can gaze out over the lake and the town's red rooftops at the Michoacana, which is just a short walk from the zócalo. It's one of the town's best sources of regional fare and a great place for a family meal. You can't go wrong here—all the typical Mexican plates you'll recognize are available, but the house specialties include pre-Hispanic dishes that you won't find everywhere else, such as venison, *chapulines con cebolla y chile de arbol* (toasted grasshoppers with onion and a spicy red chili sauce), and *escamoles a la mantequilla* (ant eggs lightly fried in butter). ✉*Calle de la Cruz 100* ☎*726/262–1625* 💳*AE, MC, V.*

¢ CAFE ✕ **Paletería La Michoacana.** This is where everyone comes to buy fruity ice pops (made with fruit juice and sometimes milk, but no water), some of the best being *zarzamora* (blackberry) and *zapote* (a sweet, inky black fruit). The custom among weekenders is to enjoy these with a bag of *campechanas* (thin sugary pastries) sold on every corner of the zócalo. There are two Michoacanas in the plaza. Make sure you stop in at number 66, the best option for good service and delicious ice cream. ✉*Plaza Independencia 66* ☎*No phone* 💳*No credit cards.*

WHERE TO STAY

$$$ **Avandaro Golf & Spa Resort.** This former country club morphed into the one of the most upscale resorts in Valle. All guest rooms have fireplaces and great views of the pine forest. If the 18-hole, par-72 golf course doesn't tempt you, perhaps a massage, facial, or yoga class at the high-tech spa will. The property is about 10 minutes from Valle de Bravo, so if you didn't come by car you'll need to take taxis into town. **Pros:** Excellent service, great restaurant, excellent golf. **Cons:** Far from downtown, area gets very cold. ✉*Vega del Río, Fracc. Avándaro,* ☎*726/266–0366, 55/5280–1532 in Mexico City* 🌐*www.grupoavandaro.com.mx* *60 rooms* *In-room: No a/c. In-hotel: Restaurant, room service, bar, golf course, tennis courts, pools, gym, spa, no elevator* 💳*AE, MC, V.*

$$ **Hotel Cueva de Leon.** This cheerful hotel on the corner of Plaza Independencia is an excellent option for its location alone. Rooms are cozy, with brightly colored bedspreads and carved headboards; some have very kitschy hot tubs tucked into a corner. The restaurant ($) is by far the most attractive on the square and has wonderful views of the town. **Pros:** Downtown is steps away, pleasant restaurant. **Cons:** Sparsely decorated rooms. ✉*Plaza Independencia 251200* ☎*726/262–4062* *10 rooms, 3 suites* *In-room: No a/c. In-hotel: Restaurant, bar, no elevator* 💳*MC, V.*

3

$–$$ **Hotel Casanueva.** This small hotel is the best option on Plaza Independencia. There are crafts in every room and hallway, in some of the most unexpected places. The terraced rooms offer great views of the plaza. There are tables in the courtyard, and the hotel calls orders over to Alma Edith, the small restaurant just across the cobblestone street, which serves up typical Mexican food at affordable prices. **Pros: Good service, excellent location, decorated with care. Cons: Noisy neighborhood on weekends.** ⊠*Villagrán 100, at Plaza Independencia 51200* ☎*726/262–1766* *10 rooms* *In-room: No a/c. In-hotel: Restaurant, no elevator* *No credit cards*

SHOPPING

Head to the small shop of **La Canica** (⊠*5 de Mayo 105* ☎ *726/262–1623*) where you can find quality handmade toys, including sweet versions of old classics like dominos. These make great gifts—nobody on your block already has these!

Galería Indigo(⊠*Joaquín A. Pagaza 403* ☎*762/262–5345*) has wonderful exhibits that are worth a visit. The gallery is only open on weekends.

SPORTS & THE OUTDOORS

MOUNTAIN BIKING

Valle is ideal for mountain biking, with readily accessible trails. **Cletas Valle** (⊠*16 de Septiembre 200* ☎*726/262–0291*) offers a very good rate for bikes and helmets, and sells other biking gadgets. Owner Carlos Mejía can recommend places to go. **Pablo's Bikes** (⊠*Joaquín Arcadio Pagaza 103* ⊕*www.pablosbikes.com*) is a good place to rent bikes by the hour or by the day.

PARAGLIDING

Valle is world-famous for paragliding, and competitions are held here early every year. The exhilarating sport is so popular that anyone with a flat, large garden for landing in is prepared for *angelitos* (little angels) to appear out of the sky when winds or misjudgment cause them to miss the standard landing spots. **Vuelos Panorámicos** (⊠*Plaza Valle* ☎*726/262–6382*), across the road from the lake, has certified instructors and is a good place to learn. A 30-minute tandem glide down with an instructor costs $130 on weekends and $100 during the week. Bring a jacket or windbreaker, sneakers, and a camera.

San Miguel de Allende & the Heartland

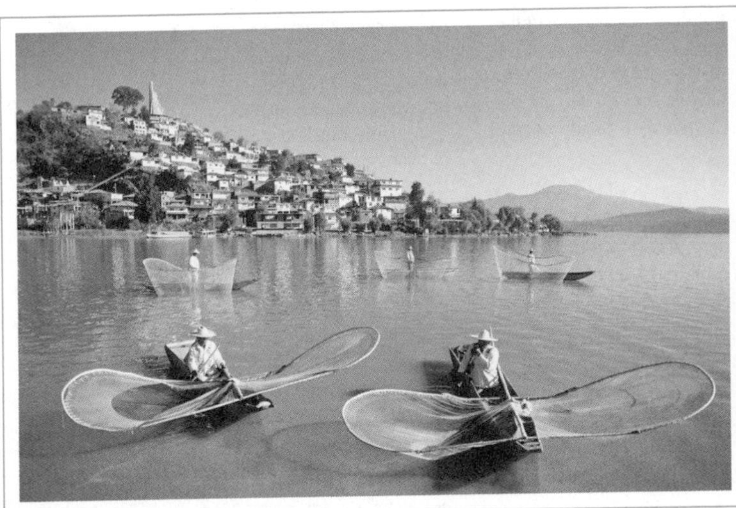

Tarascan fishermen with butterfly nets, Lake Pátzcuaro, Michoacán State.

WORD OF MOUTH

"Querétaro, San Miguel de Allende, and Guanajuato are some of the best colonial cities in all of Mexico."

–juribe31

"Pátzcuaro about 30 minutes from Morelia in Michoacan is the true home of this fête. The Día de los Muertos is best observed on a couple of islands in Pátzcuaro lake, home to indigenous people who to this day refuse to learn/speak Spanish."

–Stewbear

www.fodors.com/forums

WELCOME TO THE HEARTLANDS

TOP REASONS TO GO

★ **Experiencing modern life amid colonial grandeur:** The Heartland's cities preserve the best of colonial Mexico, but they're not stuck in the past. Each has its own restaurant scene, nightlife, and classic zócalo, usually anchored by a grand church.

★ **Enjoying the outdoors:** The region's farmland, lofty volcanoes, lakes, and river valleys afford many opportunities for day hikes, riding, and mountain biking.

★ **A calendar full of festivals:** From jazz in San Miguel de Allende to Pátzcuaro's elaborate Day of the Dead celebration, they're always partying somewhere.

★ **Staying in a hacienda:** Colonial mansions with gracious courtyards are ubiquitous in the Heartland's cities, and many have been restored into gorgeous hotels.

★ **The chance to see millions of butterflies:** Monarchs migrate to the Santuario de Mariposas el Rosario, 115 km (71 mi) east of Morelia, between November and March. The pine forest, layered with orange-and-black butterflies, looks as if it's on fire.

1 Zacatecas. It's slightly off the beaten track, but Zacatecas is a must. The city's not without sophistication—you can dance the night away in a disco buried in a silver mine—but its middle-of-nowhere status has kept it more on the small-town side of things than some of its sprawling sisters.

2 Pátzcuaro. An enchanting colonial town on the shores of Lake Pátzcuaro is the site of important Day of the Dead celebrations. Shops sell folk art and honest and delicious food is turned out at humble food stalls.

3 Morelia. It doesn't have the peaceful charm of its neighbors, but the university town Morelia makes up for it with youthful vivacity, a hopping café scene and nightlife, and a booming economy.

4 Guanajuato. Every inch of this gorgeous town, tucked into a gorge and spilling across the surrounding mountainsides, is covered with brightly colored houses. Add in church spires, twisting streets and alleys, and the fortresslike University of Guanajuato, and it's hard to find a more visually arresting city.

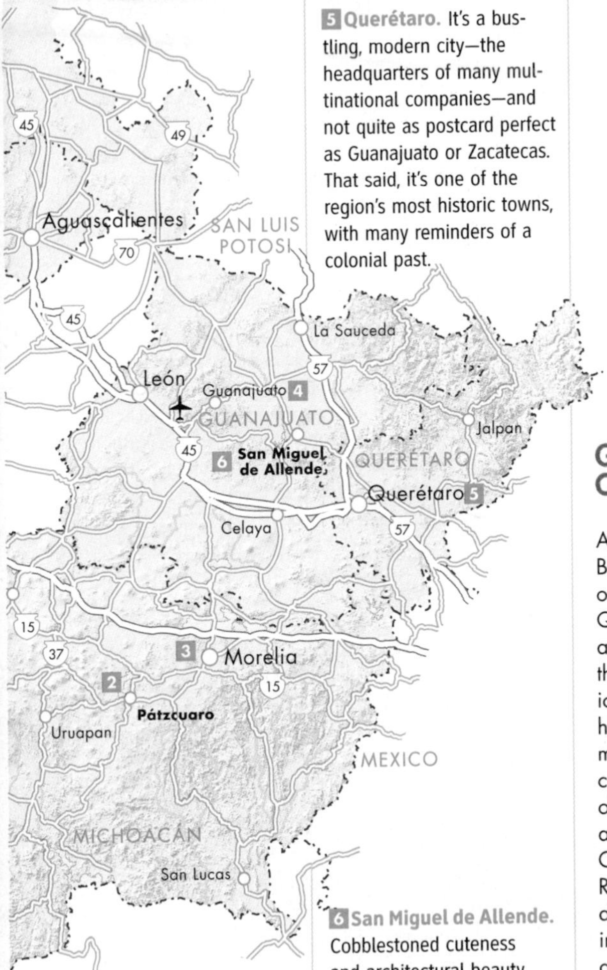

5 Querétaro. It's a bustling, modern city—the headquarters of many multinational companies—and not quite as postcard perfect as Guanajuato or Zacatecas. That said, it's one of the region's most historic towns, with many reminders of a colonial past.

6 San Miguel de Allende. Cobblestoned cuteness and architectural beauty make San Miguel the most-touristed city in the Heartland, even if it lacks an airport. There's a thriving arts and music scene and a renowned language and arts school.

GETTING ORIENTED

Also referred to as the Bajío, this area (parts of the Guanajuato, Querétaro, and Michoacán states) really is the heartland of Mexico—geographically and historically. This is where men fought and died to create the United States of Mexico and where a 60-foot-high statue of Christ the King (Cristo Rey) keeps watch from atop the highest mountain in Guanajuato. The main attraction of the region is a collection of colonial cities, many former silver- and gold-mining centers. Beyond city life, the mountains beckon intrepid bike riders and natural hot springs invite all to relax.

SAN MIGUEL DE ALLENDE & THE HEARTLAND PLANNER

How Much Can You Do?

Travel between the Heartland's major cities is easy; distances are (relatively) short. Even if you only have a few days, you'll still be able to see a lot.

If you have 3 days. Fly into and out of León's airport and base yourself in Guanajuato, enjoying its spectacular architecture, silver mine and church, and memorable funicular ride. Visit San Miguel de Allende on a day trip; it's an easy 1½-hour drive from Guanajuato. Alternatively, fly into Querétaro, visiting the Sierra Gorda missions and Xilitla, and make a day trip to San Miguel.

If you have 5-6 days. Spend the first two nights in Guanajuato, and the third night in San Miguel. Next, head south for a few hours and staying in the bustling university town of Morelia. From there, it's only an hour drive on a superhighway to Pátzcuaro, which for many people is the highlight of the Heartland. On your last day, take a boat ride on Lake Pátzcuaro. Fly back out of Morelia's airport, which is nearby. An alternative route would begin by flying into Zacatecas and spending two nights there, then driving down to Guanajuato and spending the balance of your time there and in San Miguel.

Busing It

Primera Plus, ETN, and Estrella Blanca are the major first-class lines. Aero Plus runs buses between the Mexico City and Querétaro airports. Flecha Amarilla is the second-class branch of Primera Plus, operating along the same routes. Herradura de Plata also has limited second-class service throughout the Bajío.

Hotel Tips

Except for the five-star hotels, most properties in the region aren't heated—bring warm clothes for chilly nights or inquire in advance. Likewise, most haciendas-turned-hotels lack air-conditioning because the thick-walled construction keeps interior temperatures low. Room size and furnishings vary in these restored properties, so if you aren't satisfied with one room, ask to see another.

Tour Companies

GUANAJUATO **Juvenal Díaz López** (☎473/733–3026 or 473/560–1969). **Transporte Exclusivo de Turismo** (☎473/732–5968). **Transportes Turísticos de Guanajuato** (☎473/732–2134, 472/732–2838, or 473/733–1791).

HEARTLAND **Arturo Morales** (☎415/152–5400 🌐www.tasma.info).

MORELIA **Explora Viajes** (☎443/317–5801). **Morelia Operadores de Viajes** (☎443/312–8723 or 443/312–8747).

PÁTZCUARO **Francisco Castilleja** (☎434/344–0167). **Miguel Angel Nuñez** (☎434/344–0108).

ZACATECAS **Operadora Zacatecas** (☎492/924–0050). **Viajes Mazzoco** (☎492/922–0859).

When to Go

The good news is that for the most part, high season is limited to Christmas, Easter, and the weeks around regional festivals. San Miguel's at its busiest in September, when it honors the Mexican Revolution; in mid-August during the International Chamber Music Festival; and in late-November for the International Jazz Festival. Tourism also spikes during the Day of the Dead celebrations in Pátzcuaro on November 1–2; during Morelia's International Organ Festival in May; and during Guanajuato's International Cervantes Festival in October.

Travel Times

Mexico City to:	
San Miguel	3½ hrs
Querétaro	3 hrs
Guanajuato	5 hrs
Morelia	4 hrs
Pátzcuaro	5 hrs
Zacatecas	8 hrs
San Miguel to:	
Querétaro	1 hr
Guanajuato	1½ hrs
León	2½ hrs
Morelia	4½ hrs
Zacatecas	3¾ hrs
Guadalajara	5½ hrs

Money Matters

WHAT IT COSTS IN DOLLARS

¢	$	$$	$$$	$$$$
Restaurants				
under $5	$5–$10	$10–$15	$15–$25	over $25
Hotels				
under $50	$50–$75	$75–$150	$150–$250	over $250

Restaurant prices are per person for a main course at dinner. Hotel prices are for two people in a standard double room.

Getting Around

The Heartland is an accessible destination, easily reached from Mexico City or Guadalajara. A network of superhighways connects many major cities. Although it may be more fun to tour by car, there is frequent and inexpensive bus service between region's cities.

How's the Weather?

Among the Heartland's most pleasing attributes is its superb climate—rarely does it get overly hot, even in midsummer, and although winter days can get nippy, especially in northern Zacatecas, they are generally temperate.

Average temperatures in the southern city of Morelia range from 20°C (68°F) in May to just under 10°C (49°F) in January. Zacatecas is more extreme, with winter temperatures as low as 0°C (32°F) and snow flurries every several years, and summer highs of 28°C–30°C (81°F–85°F). Expect cool nights year-round in most of the region's cities.

The Heartland's rainy season hits between June and October and is generally strongest in July and August. A visit during the rainy season can be delightful, as the semiarid countryside comes to life with pink, yellow, and blue wildflowers, and the area's farmlands offer up fresh vegetables and fruits.

4

SAN MIGUEL DE ALLENDE

Updated by Robin Goldstein & Alexis Herschkowitsch

YOU'VE HEARD SAN MIGUEL DE ALLENDE is an artists' retreat, where the beauty of the surroundings coupled with the inspired bent of those who seem to be drawn here, result in proliferation of all things creative. There are literary readings, art shows, annual chamber music and jazz festivals, as well as yoga classes.

Despite the city's offerings, those who have spent a lot of time in Mexico find it hard to stomach what has now become a never-ending parade of yuppie tourists and a U.S.-dollar-driven economy. For travel novices, San Miguel's Disneyish qualities can make it a painless entry-level experience, a Mexico Lite practically free from concerns about health, safety, culture clash, and language. But even newcomers to Mexico shouldn't make the mistake of spending their whole trip here; there are more authentic, if slightly less cute, Mexican experiences to be had in the Heartland's many other beautiful cities.

The city began luring foreigners in the late 1930s, when American Stirling Dickinson and prominent local residents founded an art school in this mountainous settlement. The school, now called the Instituto Allende, has grown in stature over the years—as has the city's reputation as a writers' and artists' colony. On any cobblestone street you'll run into expats of all nationalities, but particularly Americans and Canadians. Some come to study at the Instituto Allende or the Academia Hispano-Americana, some to escape harsh northern winters, and still others to retire.

San Miguel, declared a national monument in 1926, retains its Mexican characteristics. Eighteenth-century mansions, fountains, monuments, and churches are all reminders of the city's illustrious and sometimes notorious past. At the corner of Calles Hernández Macías and Pila Seca, for example, is the onetime headquarters of the Spanish Inquisition in New Spain. The former Inquisition jail stands across the way.

A great way to get your bearings is to take a spin on San Miguel's trolleybus that departs every two hours from the Municipal Tourism Office in the Jardín from 10 AM to 8 PM. The trolley's route will let you see most of the town, including a stop at the Mirador overlook, where you'll have a spectacular view of San Miguel, especially at sunset. The trolley runs Thursday through Tuesday and the fare is $6.

Bear in mind that the city is more than a mile above sea level, so you might tire quickly during your first few days if you aren't accustomed to high altitudes. Also, the streets are paved with rugged cobblestones, and narrow sidewalks are paved with stones that can get very slippery when wet. Most of San Miguel's sights are in a cluster downtown, which you can visit in a couple of hours.

Independence Day, celebrated on September 15 and 16, is San Miguel's biggest fiesta, with fireworks, dances, and parades; bullfights and cultural events fill out the remainder of the month.

GETTING HERE & AROUND

Querétaro has the closest airport to San Miguel. The 45-minute drive costs about $40 by taxi. Primera Plus and ETN have first-class service from Mexico City's Central Norte station to San Miguel. The trip takes 3½ hours and costs $25. First-class service by Primera Plus from Guadalajara takes 5½ hours and costs $34. First-class bus lines such as Autobuses Americanos offer direct bus service from cities in Texas for under $100. Driving from Mexico City to San Miguel (300 km [186 mi]) takes roughly four hours via the excellent Highway 57 (to Querétaro).

WORD OF MOUTH

"San Miguel is definitely worth a visit. It's one of the most important historical places in Mexico, and the city itself is beautiful, very colonial, with streets lined with cobblestones and colourful architecture. They have a couple of churches worth visiting, like their Parroquia Cathedral at their main plaza, their botanical garden…or just simply stroll through their streets and wander around…"

-diSol

4

ESSENTIALS

Bus Contacts **Autobuses Americanos** (☎ *415/154–8233 in San Miguel, 800/714–9607 in U.S.* 🌐 *www.autobusesamericanos.com.mx*). **ETN** (☎ *01800/800–0386 toll-free in Mexico* 🌐 *www.etn.com.mx*). **Primera Plus** (☎ *415/152–0084, 01800/849–9001 toll-free in Mexico* 🌐 *www.primeraplus.com.mx*).

Medical Assistance **Ambulance–Red Cross** (☎ *415/152–1616*). **Fire Department** (☎ *415/152–2888*). **Hospital de la Fé** (✉ *Libramiento Manuel Zavala 12, Mesa el Malanquín* ☎ *415/152–2233, 415/152–2545, or 415/152–2320*).

Police (☎ *415/152–0022*). **Traffic Police** (☎ *415/152–8420*).

Rental Cars **Hola Rent a Car** (✉ *Plaza Principal 2, Int. 5, El Centro* ☎ *415/152–0198* 🌐 *www.holarentacar.com*).

Visitor & Tour Info **Delegación de Turismo** (☎ *415/152–6565*). **Departamento de Turismo Municipal** (✉ *Plaza Principal 8, El Centro* ☎ *415/152–0900 or 415/152–0001 Ext. 116*).

EXPLORING

MAIN ATTRACTIONS

2 **Casa de Ignacio Allende.** A series of statues will leave no doubt as to this building's former resident: this is the birthplace of Ignacio Allende, one of Mexico's great independence heroes. Allende was a Creole aristocrat from Querétaro who, along with Father Miguel Hidalgo, plotted in the early 1800s to overthrow the Spanish regime. He was captured and executed by the Spanish Royalists in 1811. As a tribute to his brave efforts, San Miguel El Grande was renamed San Miguel de Allende in the 20th century. ✉ *Cuna de Allende 1, El Centro* ☎ *415/152–2499* 🎟 *$3* ⏲ *Tues.–Sun. 9–4.*

4 **Iglesia de la Concepción.** Just behind the Bellas Artes cultural center is this church, which has one of the largest domes in Mexico. The two-

Bellas Artes......3
Biblioteca Pública..........5
Casa de Ignacio Allende..........2
El Charco del Ingenio..........9
Iglesia de la Concepción......4
Iglesia de San Francisco........6
Instituto Allende..........8
El Jardín.........1
Lavaderos Públicos.........7

story dome (completed in 1891) and the elegant Corinthian columns and pilasters gracing its drum are said to have been inspired by Paris's dome of the Hôtel des Invalides. Ceferino Gutiérrez, the architect of La Parroquia, is credited with its design. ✉ *Calle Canal between Calles Hernández Macías and Zacateros, El Centro* ☎ *No phone.*

6 **Iglesia de San Francisco.** This church has one of Guanajuato state's finest Churrigueresque facades. The term for this style refers to José Churriguera, a 17th-century (baroque) Spanish architect noted for his extravagant surface decoration. Built in the late 18th century, the church was financed by donations from wealthy patrons and by bullfight revenues. Topping the elaborately carved exterior is the image of Saint Francis of Assisi. Below, along with a crucifix, are sculptures of Saint John and Our Lady of Sorrows. ✉ *Calle Juárez between Calles San Francisco and Mesones, El Centro* ☎ *No phone.*

1 **El Jardín.** San Miguel's heart, the plaza commonly known as El Jardín (the Garden), is where much of the town's action takes place, from political rallies and live music to dance presentations and fireworks on special occasions. You can get a real feel for the town just by sitting on one of its wrought-iron benches, where locals and expats alike enjoy the early-morning sunshine and share some gossip before attending to the

serious business of the day. The Parroquia bells toll each quarter hour and at dusk. When the sun goes down, thousands of grackles return to roost in the laurel trees, making a fantastic ruckus of what sounds almost like human cries. The square fills with musicians, mothers and their kids, and teenagers taking their ritual evening stroll around the garden. ✉ *Bordered by Correo on south, San Francisco on north, Portal Allende on west, and Portal Guadalupe on east, El Centro.*

NEED A BREAK?

Cafés around El Jardín offer outdoor seating under the *portales* (arcades), with the side streets closed to traffic: La Terraza, next to the Parroquia, has a big terrace perfect for people-watching; Café del Jardín in the Portal Allende is *the* breakfast spot; Mesón de Don Tomás in the Portal Guadalupe is good any time of the day; and the Posada de San Francisco has a sunny restaurant.

IF YOU HAVE TIME

5 **Bellas Artes.** Once the Royal Convent of the Conception, this impressive cloister has been an institute for the study of music, dance, and the visual arts since 1938. It's across the street from the U.S. Consulate and has rotating exhibits and a café. Cultural events are listed on a bulletin board at the entrance. It's swarming with expats. ✉ *Calle Hernández Macías 75, El Centro* ☎ *415/152–0289* 🎫 *Free* ⏲ *Mon.–Sat. 9–8, Sun. 10–2.*

5 **Biblioteca Pública.** Within the library's walls are a lovely courtyard café, the offices of the English-language newspaper *Atención San Miguel*, and reading rooms with back issues of popular publications and books in English. Movies are shown during the week at their Santa Ana Theater. On Sunday at noon a two-hour house-and-garden tour (about $15) of San Miguel leaves from the library. TIP→ **Notices about such things as literary readings and yoga and aerobics classes are posted on the bulletin board in the library's entranceway.** ✉ *Insurgentes 25, El Centro* ☎ *415/152–0293* 🎫 *Free* ⏲ *Weekdays 10–7, Sat. 10–2.*

9 **El Charco del Ingenio.** San Miguel's botanical garden has an extensive collection of Mexican cacti and other plants collected from different parts of the country. The area is protected from encroachment by an ecological reserve of 445 acres and was visited by the Dalai Lama, who declared El Charco one of the five "zones of peace" in Mexico. A new garden area will introduce you to some of the 120 varieties of agaves that grow here. TIP→ **The reserve is huge and has special pathways for walking, running, and mountain biking. You can also rock climb here.** Several times a month they open the *temazcales*, ritual herbal steam baths. If you're driving, turn left past the shopping center on the Salida a Querétaro and follow the signs to the main entrance. A cab will cost about $3. ✉ *Paloma s/n, above Atascadero* ☎ *415/154–4715 or 415/154–8838* 🌐 *www.laneta.apc.org/charco* 🎫 *$3* ⏲ *Daily 9–4.*

8 **Instituto Allende.** Since the school's founding in 1951, thousands of students from around the world have come here to learn Spanish and to take classes in the arts. The gorgeous campus, a former country estate, is open to visitors—even if you don't plan on taking any courses, the

institute is a great place to spend a few peaceful hours. Take a break at El Cafecito coffee bar or enjoy a meal at their excellent Italian restaurant, L'Invito. Their Galería La Pérgola specializes in modern Mexican art. The Institute also provides a complete travel service, hotel bookings, and cultural, adventure, and shopping tours. ✉*Ancha de San Antonio 20, El Centro* ☎*415/152–0226* 🌐*www.institutoallende.com.mx* *Free* *Weekdays 8–6, Sat. 9–1.*

BENITO JUAREZ PARK

This fantastic park in the heart of San Miguel boasts ancient trees, flower-lined paths ideal for a morning jog, a basketball court, and a children's play area with swings and fun things to climb. It's on Calle Aldama in El Centro; it's a short stroll south from El Jardín.

7 **Lavaderos Públicos.** This collection of red concrete tubs above Parque Benito Juárez is a public laundry where local women gather daily to wash clothes and chat as has been done for centuries. Some women claim to have more efficient washing facilities at home, but the lure of the spring-fed troughs and the chance to catch up on the news bring them to this shaded courtyard. ✉*Calle Diezmo Viejo at Calle Recreo, El Centro.*

WHERE TO EAT

$$–$$$ ITALIAN ✕**Da Andrea.** A short drive from the city is chef Andrea's countryside restaurant, connected with the Hacienda La Landeta. Grab an umbrella-shaded table in the hacienda's vast gardens; indoors is decidedly more drab and stuffy, with poor lighting and high ceilings. Service is slow, but you're not in a rush. Start with a salad of octopus, or maybe whole grilled sardines. Follow it with the signature dish: homemade ravioli in a delicate butter-and-sage sauce. Fish and meat mains are less impressive. Reserve ahead, and be prepared to eat on a European schedule; the lunch crowd begins showing up at 2 PM. ✉*Hacienda Landeta, Km 2.5, Carretera A, Dr. Mora* ☎*415/120–3481* ▭*MC, V* *Closed Mon.–Wed.*

$$ MEXICAN ★ ✕**Pueblo Viejo.** Don't let the faux-folksy colonial Mexican murals and synthetic street scenes on the walls scare you into thinking you're at Disney World. There's definitely a tourist bent here, but it's all in good fun. Steamed trout with sesame seeds is a pleasant surprise, as is a chicken breast with cheese and a poblano cream sauce. Guacamole prepared table-side, another fun gimmick, is pulled off with style. Live music accompanies your meal, and when you're done, head upstairs to the wonderful open-air bar at La Azotea. ✉*Umarán 6, El Centro* ☎*415/152–9477* ▭*MC, V.*

$–$$ MEXICAN ✕**Bugambilia.** A beautiful setting in an evocative courtyard and live music played every night make this a favorite with tourists and locals alike—and in a city like San Miguel, it's refreshing to see some locals. Most come for the *chiles en nogada* (poblano peppers with a creamy walnut sauce) with pomegranate seeds sprinkled on top. *Sopa azteca* (tortilla soup) is pleasant, if not the most exciting dish around. There's a good list of local liquors, and the margaritas have a good kick. ✉*Hidalgo 42, El Centro* ☎*415/154–5180* ▭*AE, MC, V.*

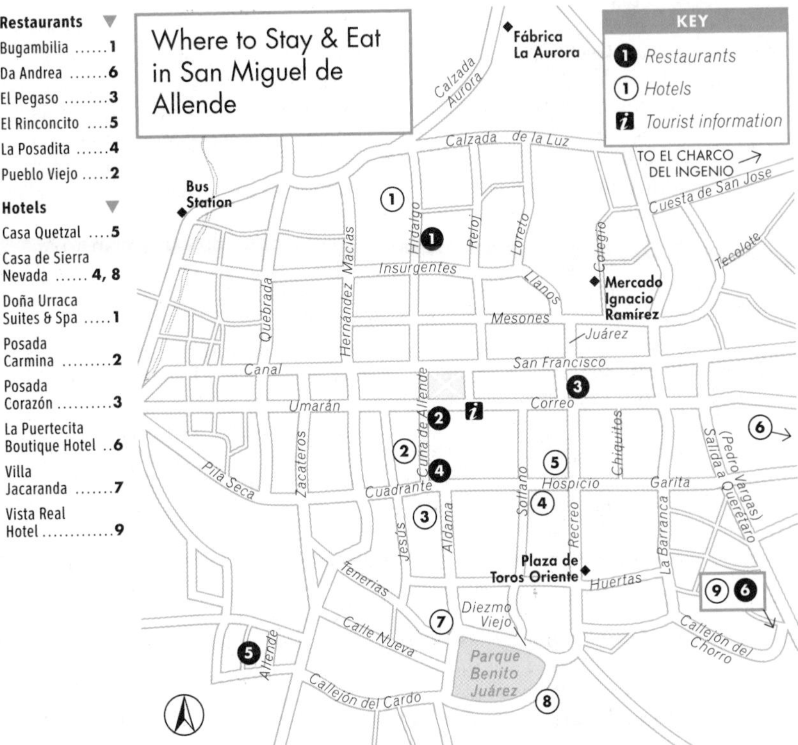

$–$$ MEXICAN Fodor'sChoice ★ **La Posadita.** Here in the shadow of La Parroquia, you'll find what are, by consensus, the best margaritas in the city—or maybe it's just that they taste that much better to the tune of church bells. The sweeping countryside view from one of San Miguel's most romantic rooftop terraces is another enhancement. The guacamole is great, as are the other traditional Mexican dishes such as enchiladas. It's a fantastic local standby. ✉ *Cuna de Allenda 13, El Centro* ☎ *415/154–7588* ▭ *MC, V* ⊙ *Closed Mon.*

$ ECLECTIC **El Pegaso.** This family-owned restaurant wins the award for best service in town. It also has great breakfast options, which are available until noon to aid late risers and hangover victims. At lunch, the menu takes a turn for the worse, with pedestrian, tourist-friendly dishes such as Caesar salad with a grilled chicken breast. Better are the daily specials. Still, it's more about the atmosphere than the food. ✉ *Calle Corregidora 6, El Centro* ☎ *415/152–1351* ▭ *MC, V* ⊙ *Closed Sun.*

$ MEXICAN **El Rinconcito.** The best bargain in town is also the place for the best home-cooked Mexican food, prepared in the immaculate open-air kitchen. Along with tacos and quesadillas, try hamburgers, grilled chicken, or shrimp wrapped in bacon. ✉ *Calle Refugio Norte 7, San Antonio* ☎ *415/154–4809* ▭ *No credit cards* ⊙ *Closed Tues. No dinner Sun.*

WHERE TO STAY

$$$–$$$$ ★ **Casa Quetzal.** Three blocks from the main square, this boutique hotel offers eclectic suites, each with its own characteristic style; for example, you'll find Japanese-inspired touches in the Zen Suite and bold colors in the Mexican-style Frida Suite. Rooms are considerably smaller; a suite is ideal even for a party of just two. A full breakfast is included with your stay. Casa Quetzal can arrange tours to Querétaro and Guanajuato, as well as horseback-riding trips to a nearby canyon. **Pros:** Tranquil setting. **Cons:** Some rooms feel cramped. Breakfast plan leaves a bit to be desired. ✉ *Calle Hospicio 34, El Centro* ☎ *415/152–0501, 888/296–9067 in U.S.* 🌐 *www.casaquetzalhotel.com* *2 rooms, 5 suites* *In-room: Kitchen. In-hotel: Public Wi-Fi, airport shuttle, refrigerator, laundry service, no elevator* *AE, MC, V* *BP.*

$$$–$$$$ **Casa de Sierra Nevada.** Built in 1580 as the archbishop of Guanajuato's residence, this elegant country-style inn still attracts ambassadors, diplomats, film stars, and other luminaries; however, the formerly attentive service has declined. Rooms are distributed throughout a series of small mansions. Lace curtains, handwoven rugs, and chandeliers adorn some of them; fireplaces, cozy terraces, and skylights enhance others. The hotel runs the separate **Casa del Parque,** an exquisitely restored 18th-century hacienda with five guest rooms, a few minutes' walk away. Its restaurant serves refined versions of traditional Mexican dishes and has a sweeping view of Parque Benito Juárez. **Pros:** Old-fashioned. Cooking classes and language school on grounds. **Cons:** Feels a bit stuffy. ✉ *Calle Hospicio 42, El Centro* ☎ *415/154–9704* 🌐 *www.casadesierranevada.com* *17 rooms, 16 suites* *In-room: DVD, a/c (some), safe. In-hotel: 2 restaurants, room service, bar, pool, laundry service, spa, parking (no fee), no elevator* *AE, MC, V*

$$$ **Doña Urraca Suites & Spa.** You may be startled as you step through the plate-glass entrance that transports you from a colonial city to a setting with minimalist decor. Everything is white marble, walls are often substituted by floor-to-ceiling plate glass, black marble is used for countertops, and chairs and sofas are red or white leather. All rooms have kitchenettes. After a day of seeing the sights, you will welcome all the creature comforts offered by this super-modern hotel. **Pros:** Supreme comfort, especially for an extended stay. **Cons:** Minimalist decor can come off as a bit cold. Not in the prettiest part of San Miguel. ✉ *Hidalgo 69, El Centro* ☎ *415/154–9770 through 415/154–9773* 🌐 *www.donaurraca.com.mx* *23 rooms* *In-room: DVD, kitchen, Wi-Fi. In-hotel: Pool, spa, parking (no fee), no elevator* *AE, MC, V.*

$$$ **La Puertecita Boutique Hotel.** An older crowd seeking a tranquil setting also choose La Puertecita for its elegant mix of colonial and modern Mexican design. The hotel is a few minutes from downtown (there's shuttle service), in a private park with waterfalls and flowering trees. The tree-house restaurant (yes, you read that correctly) La Palapa has a view of a 300-year-old aqueduct and offers a romantic setting for intimate lunches and candlelit dinners. Reservations are essential, and upon making them you can create your own menu. **Pros:** Romantic restaurant, tasteful decor. **Cons:** Can't walk to city center and far from nightlife. ✉ *Calle Santo Domingo 75, Col. Los Arcos* ☎ *415/152–5011*

www.lapuertecita.com *34 rooms, 22 suites* *In-room: Dial-up. In-hotel: Restaurant, bar, pools, spa, parking (no fee), no elevator* *AE, MC, V.*

$$$ **Villa Jacaranda.** This cozy hotel in a converted house is three blocks from the Jardín. Rooms aren't very inspired (you'll find some florals and pastels), but are large and do have a few Mexican colonial touches, as well as lovely fireplaces. The Villa restaurant is a popular place to relax on Sunday—there's an excellent champagne brunch on the terrace. You can also enjoy a drink while watching first-run movies in the Cine/bar. And the spa has a range of services, from manicures to massages and facials. **Pros:** Champagne brunches and a Jacuzzi, both with views. **Cons:** Garish decor in rooms. *Calle Aldama 53, El Centro* *415/152–1015* *www.villajacaranda.com* *18 rooms* *In-hotel: Restaurant, bar, spa, parking (no fee), no elevator* *AE, MC, V.*

4

$$–$$$ ★ **Posada Corazón.** One of San Miguel's oldest families has opened their ranch-style home as a hotel, complete with a common area with fireplace and a library full of Mexican and international art books. Only blocks from the action of downtown, rooms here open onto lush gardens and trees. From an ample terrace with sweeping views, you can enjoy an organic breakfast. One of the rooms has its own swimming pool. **Pros:** Incredibly warm and accommodating staff, central location. **Cons:** Breakfast could use some zip, as could room decor. *Aldama 9, El Centro* *415/152–0182 or 415/152–2165* *www.posadacorazon.com.mx* *6 rooms* *In-room: Wi-Fi. In-hotel: Parking (no fee), no elevator* *MC, V* *BP.*

$$–$$$ **Vista Real Hotel.** Located on the upper elevation of San Miguel with sweeping views of the valley, this hotel's ample, elegant, high-ceiling rooms (most with two queen-size beds and ample sofas or chaise longues) all look out onto perfectly manicured gardens. The solar-heated pool is a plus; you can see all of San Miguel lighted up from the overdone restaurant come nighttime—definitely worth the ride up for just the view. **Pros:** Large, heated pool. Spacious rooms. **Cons:** Overly manicured grounds feel sterile. Practically nothing within walking distance. *Callejón de Arias 4, Barrio de La Palmita* *415/152–3996 or 415/152–3984* *www.vistarealhotel.com* *21 suites* *In-room: DVD. In-hotel: Restaurant, bar, pool, parking (no fee), no elevator* *AE, MC, V.*

$$ **Posada Carmina.** This restored 18th-century house stands next to Ignacio Allende's home and opposite the Parroquia. A great location for sure, and the view is spectacular, but be forewarned that La Parroquia's bells might wake you up at all hours. The rooms surround a beautiful courtyard, which has a lovely fountain, umbrella-shaded tables, and a plethora of vines tumbling down the stone walls. Rooms are sparsely decorated—you won't find the profusion of folk art or bold colors that decorate a lot of hotels in the region—but they don't lack comfort or amenities. You might fare better against the ever-chiming bells with one of the newer rooms toward the back. The hotel's restaurant, La Felguera, features live music every night of the week except Sunday. **Pros:** Beautiful courtyard and proximity to city center. **Cons:** Street noise. *Cuna de Allende 7, El Centro* *415/152–0458*

or 415/152–8888 🌐*www.posadacarmina.com* ⇨*24 rooms, 1 suite* ♨*In-hotel: Restaurant, bar, no elevator* ▭*MC, V.*

NIGHTLIFE

Sleepy San Miguel offers a toned-down nightlife that's largely aimed at tourists and expats. The Biblioteca Pública and the Villa Jacaranda have daily screenings of foreign and U.S. films. Concerts, literary readings, theater, art exhibitions, and free dance lessons will keep you busy. Listings appear in the English-language newspaper *Atención* published every Friday.

> **NAME THAT TUNE**
>
> For more than 20 years San Miguel has hosted August's world-class Festival de Musica de Camara, a feast of classical chamber music that has recently included the illustrious Tokyo String Quartet. The Jazz Festival International takes place around the last week in November. You can buy tickets for the concerts, workshops, and after-hour jam sessions individually or for the series. Call the tourist office for dates and details.

You can grab a quiet after-dinner drink any night of the week in El Centro, but nightlife is truly alive only Thursday through Sunday. You can quite easily start (and end) your evening pub crawl on Calle Umarán. **La Azotea** (✉*Umarán 6* ☎*415/152–4977*), inside the Pueblo Viejo restaurant, is the most popular haunt for the well-heeled and well-dressed local crowd, making for supreme people-watching. A slide projector shows amusing images of the city on the wall across the street; cocktails are strong and tasty.

Elegant **La Fragua** (✉*Cuna de Allende 5*) showcases live entertainers singing in Spanish and English.

Next door to La Fragua, **La Felguera** (✉*Cuna de Allende 7* ☎*415/152–8888*) offers two-for-one drinks and live music all week long, all in a beautiful setting.

At **Malagos** (✉*Codo 7* ☎*415/152–0257*) the action changes nightly from tango to salsa to blues.

Pancho & Lefty's (✉*Mesones 99* ☎*415/152–1958*) has all kinds of live music from rock to reggae.

Drop in at **Tapas y 'Tinis** (✉*Umarán 36* ☎*415/154–6276*) for, not surprisingly, a martini and Spanish tapas.

SHOPPING

For centuries San Miguel's artisans have created crafts ranging from straw products to metalwork. Although some boutiques in town may be pricey, you can find good buys on silver, brass, tin, woven cotton goods, and folk art. Hours are erratic, but most stores open daily at around 10, shut their doors for the afternoon siesta (2 to 4 or 5), then

CLOSE UP

Fábrica La Aurora

A 10-minute walk from the center of town, Fábrica La Aurora, which was established in 1902, was the principal source of fine-quality muslin in the region until competition forced its closing. Decades later, it reopened as exhibition spaces for art galleries and antique- and modern-furniture showrooms; also, many local artists have opened studios here.

The concentration of art galleries draws visitors in huge numbers. The **Generator Gallery**, complete with the fábrica's original generator, is the exhibition space for a group of Canadian artists headed by Leonard Brooks, one of the founders of the local artists' colony. **Galería Florencia Riestra** is owned by one of Mexico City's leading galleries. The folks at **Pedro Cerroblanco** are locally revered jewelry designers working with modernistic designs in silver and precious stones.

Planning to decorate? You will find inspiration from the past in the numerous antiques shops, including **Cantadora** and **La Buhardilla,** with their superb collection of Mexican colonial objets d'art. **Finca, Sisal, Atrium,** and **C. DeWayne Youts** are the showrooms of some of San Miguel's most inspired interior designers. **La Bottega di Casa** sells jacquard cottons, fine linens, Capodimonte ceramics, alabaster vases, and traditional pewter from Italy.

Just outside the entrance to the fábrica stands a gigantic tent—*La Carpa*—which is a venue for circus, dance, and theater performances and workshops, as well as a setting for evenings of offbeat and international film screenings.

If you're shopped out and hungry, head for the **Food Factory** with its old-world atmosphere and comfortable sofas under a covered patio. Or pick up a snack at the outdoor **Café de la Aurora** coffee shop. ✉*Calzada de la Aurora s/n, El Centro.*

reopen in the afternoon until 7 or 8. They're usually open for just a half day on Sunday. Most San Miguel shops accept MasterCard and Visa.

ART GALLERIES

Long known as an artists' colony, San Miguel has galleries, museums, and arty shops that line the streets near the Jardín; most close weekdays between 2 and 4 and are open weekends 10 or 11 to 2 or 3. Two salons—at **Bellas Artes** and **Instituto Allende**—feature the work of Mexican artists.

Artes de México (✉*Calz. Aurora 47, at Dolores Hidalgo exit, Col. Guadalupe* ☎*415/152–0764*) has been producing and selling traditional crafts for more than 40 years.

The two collectors behind the regional and international talent of **Galería Atenea** (✉*Calle Jesús 2, El Centro* ☎*415/152–0785*) have a thing for attractive watercolors and Bustamante jewelry.

Lovely **Galería Carlos MuRo** (✉*Zacateros 81A, El Centro* ☎*415/154–8531*) is where you'll find the finest handwrought copper pieces from the Santa Clara del Cobre workshops.

For a taste of contemporary Mexican art, stop by **Galería San Miguel** (✉*Plaza Principal 14, El Centro* ☎*415/152–0454*).

Kunsthaus Santa Fé (✉*Santa Fé 22A, Colonia Allende* ☎*415/152–4608*) is a contemporary art space showing multifaceted installations—it feels more Manhattan than Mexico.

HOME DECOR

Casa María Luisa (✉*Canal 40, El Centro* ☎*415/152–0130*) has contemporary Mexican furniture, frames, household items, and art.

Finca (✉*Fábrica La Aurora, Col. Guadalupe* ☎*415/154–8323*) is a dramatic haven of made-to-order furniture. **Guajuye** (✉*Lupita No. 2, Estacion F.F.C.C.* ☎*415/152–7030* 🌐*www.guajuye.com*), on the road to the railroad station, is the local glass factory, where you can pick up all sorts of handblown glassware. **La Zandunga** (✉*Hernández Macías 129, El Centro* ☎*415/152–4608* 🌐*www.lazandunga.com*) sells high-quality, 100% wool rugs from Oaxaca.

JEWELRY

Check out **Ambar** (✉*Jesús 21B, El Centro* ☎*415/154–4058*) for interesting Chiapas amber pieces.

Established in 1963, **Joyería David** (✉*Zacateros 53, El Centro* ☎*415/152–3446*) has an extensive selection of gold and silver jewelry, all made on the premises. Many pieces contain Mexican opals, amethysts, topazes, malachite, and turquoise.

Platería Cerro Blanco (✉*Canal 21, Int. 109, Plaza Colonial, El Centro* ☎*415/154–9501*) creates and crafts its own silver and gold jewelry and will arrange a visit to its *taller* (workshop) on request.

MARKETS

Spilling out for several blocks behind the Mercado Ignacio Ramírez is the **Mercado de Artesanías** (artisans' market), where you'll find vendors of local work—glass, tin, and papier-mâché—as well as silver jewelry at bargain prices.

Mercado Ignacio Ramírez, a traditional Mexican covered market off Calle Colegio, one block north of Calle Mesones, is a colorful jumble of fresh fruits, flowers, stands, toys, and Mexican-made cassettes. Both markets are open daily from around 8 to 7.

SPORTS & THE OUTDOORS

HEALTH CLUBS & HOT SPRINGS

The **Club de Golf Malanquín** (✉*Celaya Hwy., Km 3* ☎*415/152–0516* ⏲*Closed Monday*) has a heated pool, steam baths, tennis courts, and 9 holes of golf, all of which are open to the public for $50 on weekdays or $67 on weekends.

Escondido Place (✉*Dolores Hidalgo Hwy., Km 10* ☎*415/185–2020*) has several pools, including one with three domed ceilings where the water rushes in directly from the source—great fun for kids. It's open to the public daily for $8. **Taboada** (✉*Dolores Hidalgo Hwy., Km 8*)

CLOSE UP

Outdoorsy in San Miguel

From birding and bathing to mountain biking and golfing, enjoying the outdoors around San Miguel, with its eternal spring climate, is an opportunity not to be missed.

Our favorite outdoor adventures in the region include **mountain biking and hiking,** which may be the most intimate ways to get to know the San Miguel countryside. San Miguel is on the slopes of an ancient volcano called Los Picachos (not active). Riding or walking along narrow mountain paths, you'll find oak and pine forests, bogs, marshes, and streams where migrating birds come to feed. You may come across abandoned chapels, old mining sites, and ancient, solitary haciendas, all testimonies to long-forgotten times. There are several rental outfits specializing in mountain bikes, helmets, and gloves. Expert guides offer various tours for mountain biking and hiking according to your ability. *(⇨ See Sports & the Outdoors for tour and rental information.)*

Whether you have been trekking through the mountains or trudging over cobblestones, a swim in one of San Miguel's **thermal pools** is a welcome way to relax. All the *balnearios* are a short drive out of town, on the Dolores Hidalgo Highway. Balneario Xoté, with its slides and swings, is an ideal place to take kids. Most balnearios have some facilities like snack stands.

4

has three outdoor geothermal pools, one of which is Olympic-size and good for doing laps. The pools are open to the public for $4 from 8 AM to 6 PM every day but Tuesday.

HOT-AIR BALLOON RIDES

Gone with the Wind Balloon Adventures (✉ *Calle Recreo 68, El Centro* ☎ *415/152–6735*) offers hot-air balloon rides over the town and the surrounding countryside with licensed, certified pilots from Napa Valley, California. The one-hour flights depart at 6 or 7 AM, depending on the season, and cost around $160.

OUTDOOR ADVENTURING

Arturo Morales (☎ *415/152–5400* 🌐 *www.tasma.info*) can take you on cultural, mountain-bike, or eco-friendly hiking tours.

BICI–BURRO (✉ *Calle Hospicio 1, El Centro* ☎ *415/152–1526* 🌐 *www.bici-burro.com*) rents bikes and leads various hiking and biking tours.

Coyote Canyon Adventures (☎ *415/154–4193* 🌐 *www.coyotecanyonadventures.com*) offers trail riding and overnight camping on their own ranch. A special weeklong trail ride goes from San Miguel to Guanajuato. For reservations, it's best to contact them through their Web site. **MOTO-RENT** (✉ *Jesus 8, El Centro* ☎ *415/152–4711 or 415/152–1080*) rents various types of equipment, including bikes, ATVs, and scooters.

SIDE TRIPS FROM SAN MIGUEL DE ALLENDE

DOLORES HIDALGO

50 km (31 mi) north of San Miguel de Allende via Rte. 51.

An easy one-hour bus ride from San Miguel de Allende's Central de Autobuses, Dolores Hidalgo is famous for its lovely hand-glazed Talavera-style ceramics, most notably tiles and tableware. The town's numerous stores and factories have reasonable prices. After shopping, have lunch at El Carruaje at Plaza Principal 8, and then cross over to the plaza for possibly the most exotic ice creams you'll ever taste—flavors include mole, avocado, beer, and corn.

HACIENDA HAVEN

If you're looking for a real getaway, far from the madding crowds, book yourself into a real hacienda—Las Trancas—under an hour's drive north of San Miguel (just outside Dolores Hidalgo). Here you can turn back the clock and relax in vast rooms whose walls are 3 feet thick, lounge in the shade of colonnaded porticos, or roam the countryside on a pony. **Hacienda Las Trancas** ✉ *Rte. 51 at Trancas, north of Dolores Hidalgo* ☎ *418/182–9500* 🌐 *www.haciendalastrancas.com.*

It was in Dolores Hildalgo, before dawn on September 16, 1810, that local priest Father Miguel Hidalgo launched Mexico's fight for independence with an impassioned sermon that concluded with the *grito*, "Death to bad government!" Every September 15 at 11 PM, politicians signal the start of Independence Day festivities with a revised version of the grito—"Viva Mexico! Viva Mexico! Viva Mexico!" On September 16 (and only on this day), the bell in Hidalgo's parish church is rung.

EXPLORING

Once Father Hidalgo's home, **Casa Hidalgo** is now a museum. It contains copies of important letters Hidalgo sent or received, and other independence memorabilia. ✉ *Calle Morelos 1* ☎ *418/182–0171* *About $3* ⏲ *Tues.–Sat. 10–5:45, Sun. 10–4:45.*

If you're driving, you might want to make a stop at **Santuario de Atotonilco,** which is a 10-minute drive off the Dolores Hidalgo Highway. This sanctuary and retreat center was built by Father Felipe Neri in the 18th century. The relatively small church is completely covered in authentic paintings by the indigenous people who built it.

POZOS

35 km (21 mi) northeast of San Miguel de Allende.

The captivating, high-desert town of Pozos was a silver-mining center in the late 19th century. Now it's almost a ghost town; you can peek at abandoned buildings or the simple, echoing chapel. Rarely will you see another tourist. The Casa Montana hotel is the hub of information and activity; the owner can arrange a tour of the old mines. It has a collection of photos of Pozos and the surrounding area. Pozos is a 45-minute drive from San Miguel; look for a road marked "Dr. Mora."

WHERE TO STAY

$$ **Casa Montana.** Steep yourself in the town's colonial atmosphere with an overnight stay on its main square. Guest rooms have local artwork, fireplaces, and wonderful deep tubs. Eat on the bougainvillea-filled

terraces; if you get the chance, sip a margarita with the owner and listen to her stories about Pozos. Shuttle service is available to both the Guanajuato and Mexico City airports. **Pros:** Super-stylish rooms and warm staff. **Cons:** Beds aren't the most comfortable. ✉*Jardín Juárez Plaza* ☎*442/293–0032 or 442/293–0033* 🌐*www.casamontanahotel.com.mx* *3 rooms, 2 suites* *In-room: No a/c, no TV. In-hotel: Restaurant, airport shuttle, no elevator* ▭*MC, V* *BP.*

QUERÉTARO

63 km (39 mi; 1 hr by bus) southeast of San Miguel de Allende via Hwy. 111, 220 km (136 mi) northwest of Mexico City via Hwy. 57.

Querétaro is a modern city of more than 1.25 million inhabitants, but it holds its own against the region's other colonial cities, with wide, tree-lined boulevards and beautifully manicured parks adorned with fountains and statues of its heroes. Even the large factories rising around the perimeter manage to look nice.

The city draws more international executives than tourists, but the city is sophisticated, with many restaurants, nightclubs, and theaters. Historically, Querétaro is notable as the former residence of Josefa Ortíz de Domínguez, popularly known as La Corregidora, who warned the conspirators gathered in Dolores Hidalgo and San Miguel that their independence plot had been discovered. It is here that the ill-fated Emperor Maximilian made his last stand and was executed by firing squad on the Cerro de Las Campanas (Hill of Bells), and where eventually the Mexican Constitution was signed in 1917.

The city's relatively small historic center is easily viewed by walking along its *andadores* (pedestrian walkways). When you want to venture farther afield, your best bet is the *tranvías turísticos* operated by the Tourism Department located at Pasteur 4 Norte in the historic center. There are three routes: Ruta A, Maximilian's Empire, tours the city with a stop at the Cerro de Las Campanas where Emperor Maximilian was shot; Ruta B, Foundation of the City, visits historic 18th-century buildings; and Ruta C affords panoramic city views. The trolleys run Tuesday through Sunday, departing at 9, 10, and 11 AM and 4, 5, and 6 PM. The cost is $3. Routes A and B have wheelchair access. Museums close on Monday.

■ TIP→**Querétaro is renowned for its opals, which come in red, green, honey, and fire varieties. Because some street vendors sell opals so full of water that they crumble shortly after purchase, you should make purchases only from reputable dealers.**

GETTING HERE & AROUND

Aeromar flies to Querétaro's new Ignacio Fernando Espinoza Gutiérrez International airport from Mexico City; Continental Airlines, from Houston. ETN has first-class bus service from Mexico City's International Airport direct to Querétaro. The trip takes three hours and costs $22. Omnibus de Mexico and Primera Plus have frequent service from

CLOSE UP

Mexico's Beating Heart

Named for its central position, the Heartland is known for its well-preserved colonial architecture, its fertile farmland and encircling mountains, and its salient role in Mexican history, particularly during the War of Independence (1810–21). The Bajío (ba-*hee*-o), as it is also called, corresponds roughly to the state of Guanajuato and parts of Querétaro and Michoacán states.

Intense Spanish colonization of the Heartland followed the discovery of silver in the area in the 1500s. Guanajuato was the site of the world's largest silver mine, and the Spanish conquistadors wasted no time in founding a network of towns such as Morelia, Zacatecas, and San Miguel de Allende, where they built mansions to fit their lavish lifestyles and protect their interests. Wealthy Creoles (Mexicans of Spanish descent) in Querétaro and San Miguel took the first audacious steps toward independence from Spain three centuries later. When their clandestine efforts were uncovered, two of the early insurgents, Ignacio Allende and Father Miguel Hidalgo, began in earnest the War of Independence.

Another native son, José María Morelos, rallied for independence when Allende and Hidalgo were executed in 1811. This *mestizo* (mixed race) mule skinner-turned-priest-turned-soldier nearly gained control of the land with his army of 9,000 before he was killed in 1815. Thirteen years later the city of Valladolid was renamed Morelia in his honor.

Long after the War of Independence ended in 1821, cities in the Bajío continued to figure prominently in Mexico's history. Three major events occurred in Querétaro alone: in 1848 the Mexican-American War ended with the signing of the Treaty of Guadalupe Hidalgo; in 1867 Austrian Maximilian of Habsburg, whom France's Napoléon III had crowned Emperor of Mexico, was executed in the hills north of town; and in 1917 the Mexican Constitution was signed here.

The Heartland continually honors the events and people that helped shape modern Mexico. In ornate cathedrals or bucolic plazas, down narrow alleyways or atop high hillsides, you'll find monuments—and remnants—of a heroic past. You can savor the region's historic spirit during its numerous fiestas. On a night filled with fireworks, off-key music, and tireless celebrants, it's hard not to be caught up in the vital expression of national pride.

the Central del Norte station for $16. ETN also has first-class service from San Miguel (one hour, $9). Omnibus has frequent service from Querétaro to Zacatecas (five hours, $28). It takes about three hours to get to Querétaro from Mexico City via Highway 57.

ESSENTIALS

Bus Contacts **ETN** (☎ *01800/800–0386 toll-free in Mexico* 🌐 *www.etn.com.mx*). **Omnibus de Mexico** (✉ *Luis Vega Monroy No. 800* ☎ *442/229–0029 or 01800/765–6636 toll-free in Mexico* 🌐 *www.odm.com.mx*). **Primera Plus** (☎ *01800/375–7587 toll-free in Mexico* 🌐 *www.flecha-amarilla.com*).

Medical Assistance **Hospital Angeles de Querétaro** (✉ *Bernardo de Razo 21*

☎442/192–3000 🌐www.hospitalangelesqueretaro.com). **Hospital San José** (✉*Prolongación Constituyentes 302* ☎*442/211–0080* 🌐*www.hospitalsanjose.com*).

Visitor & Tour Info **Dirección de Turismo del Estado** (✉*Plaza de Armas* ☎*442/238–5073*). **Oficina de Turismo de Tequisquiapan** (✉*Andador Independencia 1, Plaza Miguel Hidalgo* ☎*427/273–0295* 🌐*www.tequisquiapan.com.mx*).

EXPLORING

MAIN ATTRACTIONS

2 **Fuente de Neptuno.** Renowned Mexican architect and Bajío native Eduardo Tresguerras originally built this fountain in an orchard of the San Antonio monastery in 1797. According to one story, the monks sold some of their land and the fountain along with it when they were facing serious economic problems. It now stands next to the Templo de Santa Clara. ✉*Allende at Av. Madero.*

4

1 **Jardín de la Corregidora.** This plaza is prominently marked by a statue of its namesake and War of Independence heroine—Josefa Ortiz de Domínguez. Behind the monument stands the Arbol de la Amistad (Tree of Friendship). Planted in 1977 in a mixture of soils from around the world, the tree symbolizes Querétaro's hospitality to all travelers. This is the town's calmest square, with plenty of choices for patio dining. ✉*Corregidora at Av. 16 de Septiembre.*

3 **Museo de Arte de Querétaro.** Focusing on European and Mexican artworks, this baroque 18th-century Augustinian monastery-turned-museum exhibits paintings from the 17th through 19th centuries, as well as rotating exhibits of 20th-century art. Ask about the symbolism of the columns and the figures in conch shells atop each arch on the fascinating baroque patio. ✉*Allende 14 Sur* ☎*442/212–2357 or 442/212–3523* 🌐*www.queretaro-mexico.com.mx/museo-arte* 🎫*About $2* ⏲*Tues.–Sun. 10–6.*

5 **Museo Regional de Querétaro.** This bright, yellow, 17th-century Franciscan monastery displays colonial and European artwork in addition to historic memorabilia. There are early copies of the Mexican Constitution and the table on which the Treaty of Guadalupe Hidalgo was signed. ✉*Corregidora 3* ☎*442/212–4888 or 442/220–2031* 🌐*www.queretaro-mexico.com.mx/coneculta/regional.html* 🎫*About $3* ⏲*Tues.–Sun. 10–7.*

6 **Plaza de la Independencia.** Also known as Plaza de Armas, this immaculate square is bordered by carefully restored colonial mansions and is especially lovely at night, when the central fountain is lighted. Built in 1842, the fountain is dedicated to the Marqués de la Villa del Villar, who constructed

WORD OF MOUTH

"It's not for nothing Querétaro is a UNESCO World Heritage Site; it's a baroque city with a thriving art scene, loads of places to visit, and bars and cafés for all tastes. The people are lovely, and you'll get a taste of Mexican culture, unlike in San Miguel, which, although beautiful, is full of tourists. Enjoy."

–pwilliamson

Querétaro's elegant aqueduct. The old stone aqueduct, with its 74 towering arches, stands at the town's east end. ✉*Bounded by Av. 5 de Mayo on north, Av. Libertad Oriente on south, Pasteur on east, and Vergara Sur on west.*

IF YOU HAVE TIME

❼ **Casa de Ecala.** Long ago, as the story goes, the palace's 18th-century owner elaborately adorned his home in a remodeling war (which he won) with his neighbor. Behind the original facade of this Mexican baroque palace are the offices of DIF, a family-services organization. You can wander the courtyard when the offices are open. ✉*Pasteur Sur 6, at Plaza de la Independencia* ⏲*Weekdays 9–2 and 4–6.*

❹ **Palacio del Gobierno del Estado.** Dubbed La Casa de la Corregidora, this building now houses the municipal government offices, but in 1810 it was home to Querétaro's mayor-magistrate (El Corregidor) and his wife, Josefa Ortíz de Domínguez (La Corregidora). La Corregidora's literary salon was actually a cover for conspirators—including Ignacio Allende and Father Miguel Hidalgo—to plot a course for independence. When he discovered the salon's true nature, El Corregidor imprisoned his wife in her room, but not before she alerted Allende and Hidalgo. Soon after, on September 16, Father Hidalgo tolled the bell of his church to signal the onset of the fight for freedom. A replica of the bell caps this building. ✉ *Northwest corner of Plaza de la Independencia* 🎫 *Free* ⏲ *Weekdays 9–8, Sat. 8–3.* ☎ *No phone*

WHERE TO EAT

$$–$$$$ STEAK ✕ **Restaurante Josecho.** Among the hunting trophies adorning the wood-paneled walls of this highway road stop—next to the bullring at the town's southwest end—are peacocks, elk, bears, and lions. Sports fans stop here for the animated atmosphere as well as the house specialties, which include *filete Chemita* (steak sautéed in butter with onions). Save room for the creamy coconut ice cream. A classical guitarist or pianist performs most evenings. Waiters celebrate birthdays by singing and blasting a red siren. ✉ *Dalia 1, next to Plaza de Toros Santa María* ☎ *442/216–0201* ▭ *AE, MC, V.*

$–$$$ MEXICAN ✕ **Los Laureles.** The flower-filled grand patio in this beautifully restored hacienda just outside the city offers great outdoor dining (shaded by umbrellas). The house specialty is *carnitas,* pieces of pork stewed overnight and served with oodles of guacamole, beans, and homemade tortillas. There's live music *and* mariachis on weekends. ✉ *Carretera Querétaro–San Luis Potosí Km 8* ☎ *442/218–1118* ▭ *AE, MC, V.*

$–$$ MEXICAN ✕ **El Mesón de Chucho el Roto.** This restaurant, named after Querétaro's version of Robin Hood, is on the quiet Plaza de Armas. It's strong on regional dishes like goat-filled tacos and shrimp with nopal (cactus). The restaurant next door, 1810, offers much the same fare. ✉ *Calle Pasteur 16, Plaza de Armas* ☎ *442/212–4295* ▭ *AE, MC, V.*

¢ MEXICAN ✕ **La Mariposa.** A wrought-iron butterfly (*mariposa*) overlooks the entrance of this cafeteria-like local favorite. Despite its plain appearance, it's the spot for coffee and cake or a light Mexican lunch of tacos, tamales, enchiladas, or *tortas* (sandwiches). ✉ *Angela Peralta 7, half a block from Teatro de República* ☎ *442/212–1166* ▭ *No credit cards.*

WHERE TO STAY

$$$–$$$$ Fodor's Choice ★ **Casa de la Marquesa.** A private home in the 18th century, it's now a handsome hotel in Querétaro's center. Each guest room is large and has antiques, tasteful art, parquet floors, and area rugs. The main building's rooms are more elegant and expensive than those in the adjacent La Casa Azul (children under 12 aren't admitted in the main building). The restaurants serve both international and Mexican cuisine. **Pros:** Uniquely decorated rooms and interesting Moorish architecture. **Cons:** Not ideal for traveling families. So-so service. ✉ *Av. Madero 41* ☎ *442/212–0092* 🌐 *www.lacasadelamarquesa.com* *25 suites* *In-hotel: 3 restaurants, room service, bar, public Internet, no elevator* ▭ *AE, MC, V* *BP.*

$$ **Hacienda Jurica.** Families from Mexico City escape to this sprawling 16th-century ex-hacienda, part of the Brisas chain, which has topiary gardens, a horse stable, golf access, and nearly 30 acres of grassy sports fields. Antique horse-drawn carriages dot the grounds and courtyards, and the spacious earth-tone rooms have dark-wood furniture. Jurica is an upscale residential neighborhood 13 km (8 mi) northwest

4

of the city off Highway 57. It's a good alternative to staying in the city. **Pros:** No shortage of activities; romantic restaurant. **Cons:** Need a car to stay here. ✉ *Paseo Jurica at Paseo del Mesón* ☎ *442/218–0022, 888/559–4329 in U.S.* 🌐 *www.brisas.com.mx* *188 rooms, 6 suites* *In-hotel: Restaurant, bar, room service, tennis courts, pool, laundry service, airport shuttle, parking (no fee)* *AE, MC, V.*

$$ **Mesón de Santa Rosa.** On the serene Plaza de la Independencia, this elegant property was a stopover for travelers to the north almost 300 years ago. Rooms are clustered around a placid courtyard. Lace-hung glass doors and wood-beam ceilings preserve the colonial charm in the rooms, but some modern additions like a chrome-colored coffee shop at the entrance detract from the atmosphere. **Pros:** Overall charm of hotel. Views from rooms. **Cons:** Quite old, and could use some renovations. ✉ *Pasteur Sur 1776000* ☎ *442/224–2623 or 442/441–5000* 🌐 *www.mesonsantarosa.com* *21 suites* *In-room: No a/c. In-hotel: Restaurant, bar, pool, gym, no elevator* *AE, MC, V.*

¢–$ **Hotel Hidalgo.** This hotel is one of the best values in the city. It's in a former colonial residence—once host to Santa Ana—just a few doors down from Casa de la Marquesa. The rooms are very simple, but they surround a lovely little courtyard. Restaurant La Llave is small and cute, serving simple Mexican food. **Pros:** Interesting and long history. Low prices. **Cons:** Drab decor. ✉ *Madero 1176000* ☎ *442/212–0081 or 442/212–8102* 🌐 *www.hotelhidalgo.com.mx* *47 rooms* *In-room: No a/c. In-hotel: Restaurant.* *MC, V.*

THE BARD

For a change of pace, go to the **Corral de Comedias** (Venustiano Carranza 39, 442/212–0165), a family-run theater in the round that presents mostly comedies, including Shakespeare in Spanish. It certainly helps if you speak the language, but you still get some laughs if you don't. Purchase your tickets at the entrance.

NIGHTLIFE

Every Sunday evening at 6 there's a band concert in the **Jardín Zenea,** Querétaro's main square at the corner of Corregidora and Juarez. At the tourist office you can pick up a monthly publication called *Tesoro Turístico* (all in Spanish), which provides current information about festivals, concerts, and other events.

The coolest dance club, **La Viejoteca** (✉ *Andador 5 de Mayo 39* ☎ *442/224–2760*), is in the 18th-century Casa de los Cinco Patios.

SIDE TRIPS FROM QUERÉTARO

TEQUISQUIAPAN

58 km (23 mi) southeast of Querétaro via Hwy. 57, then Rte. 120.

Drenched in sun, bougainvillea, and flowering trees, Tequis (as the locals call it) was once famed for its restorative thermal waters. Nowadays, however, the town has experienced a dearth of hot water, reportedly due to a local paper mill's extreme water consumption. As tourism has declined along with the warm-water levels, many spas have turned into recreation areas with swimming pools. That said, Tequis gets crowded on weekends. Check with the tourist office at Andador Independencia 1 on Plaza Miguel Hidalgo for directions to the spas; most are outside of town. Trolleybus tours are offered throughout the day from Plaza Santa Cecilia.

HAPPY HOUR

If you have time, visit the nearby Cavas Freixenet, Carretera San Juan del Río-Cadereyta, Km 40.5, for a tour of the cellars and free samples. ☎ *441/277–0147* ⊕ *www.freixenetmexico.com.mx.*

EXPLORING

Tequis has a well-deserved reputation for high-quality craft work like wicker; head to the **Mercado de Artesanías** (✉ *Calz. de los Misterios s/n* ☎ *No phone*) for woven goods and jewelry.

The town's main plaza, Miguel Hidalgo, has a neoclassical-style temple named **Templo de Santa María de la Asunción,** which was begun in 1874 but not completed until the beginning of the 20th century. This ample plaza is surrounded by restaurants and shops. Tequis hosts a weeklong wine-and-cheese festival in late May or early June.

XILITLA

Approximately 320 km (198 mi) northeast of Querétaro.

Feel the ordinary world fade away with a trip to the decidedly off-the-beaten-path **Las Pozas** *(The Pools)*, the extraordinary sculpture garden of the late, eccentric English millionaire Edward James (1907–84). A friend to artists Dalí and Picasso and rumored to be King Edward VII's illegitimate son, James spent 20 years building 36 Surrealist concrete structures deep in the waterfall-filled Xilitla jungle. These astonishing structures are half-finished fantasy castles, gradually falling to ruin as the rain forest slithers in to claim them. The castles don't have walls, just vine-wrapped pillars, secret passageways, and operatic staircases leading nowhere.

It's a six- to seven-hour thrilling but exhausting mountainous drive to Xilitla, with hairpin turns and spectacular desert, forest, and jungle vistas. On the way to Xilitla it's well worth taking the time to stop at the five Sierra Gorda Missions established by Padre Junípero Serra in the 18th century. They're a mixture of baroque styles and the local imagination of the Indians who worked on them, with angels, saints, and flora and fauna in great profusion. ■ TIP→ **Plan on staying at least two nights, as you'll want time to soak up the jungle magic.** If you choose not to drive, you can take a bus to Ciudad Valles (a 1½-hour drive from Xilitla) or fly to Tampico (a 3½-hour drive from Xilitla), and arrange ahead for the staff of Posada El Castillo to pick you up. ✣ *From Querétaro head north on Hwy. 57 toward Mexico City. Take the peña de bernal turnoff, marked on a bridge overpass and also on a smaller sign at the Cadareyta exit. Continue north through Bernal, after which the road joins Rte. 120. Take 120 through Jalpan and then* *on to Xilitla, just across the border in the state of San Luis Potosí. The turnoff to Las Pozas is just beyond Xilitla on the left after passing a small bridge* *$1.50* *Daily dawn–dusk.*

WHERE TO STAY

$–$$ **Posada El Castillo.** When he wasn't living in his jungle hut, Edward James stayed in town (a 10-minute drive away) in a whimsical house that feels like an extension of the garden structures at Las Pozas—except that it has walls. The house, El Castillo (the Castle), is now a quirky inn run by Lenore and Avery Danziger, who produced an award-winning documentary film about James that they screen for guests. Rooms are adorned with simple wooden furnishings; the best rooms have huge Gothic windows and panoramic mountain views. You can arrange to have meals here; otherwise, there are few dining options in the area. **Pros:** The story behind the place. Proximity to Indian villages and outdoor activities. **Cons:** A little difficult to get to. Requires some degree of "roughing it." ✉ *Ocampo 105, Xilitla, San Luis Potosí,* ☎ *489/365–0038* *www.junglegossip.com/castillo.html* *8 rooms* *In-hotel: Pool, no elevator* *No credit cards.*

GUANAJUATO

100 km (62 mi) west of San Miguel de Allende, 365 km (226 mi) northwest of Mexico City.

Guanajuato is simply beautiful. It spills across cliffs and hillsides down to a series of tree-shaded plazas whose sidewalk cafés and street life are unmatched in any comparably sized town in Mexico. Guanajuato is becoming more known by the day, in part because of how photogenic the colonial town is (you'll go through a lot of film here). The city's street plan is nearly inscrutable—roads never seem to end up where you'd expect, and are intersected by dozens of alleys—but getting lost for a few hours will be an adventure rather than a nuisance. Fewer gringos visit here than San Miguel—the majority of tourists are Mexican—so you'll have no problem remembering that you're in Mexico.

Once the most prominent silver-mining city in colonial Mexico, Guanajuato is in a gorge surrounded by mountains at 6,700 feet. Its cobblestone streets, which are dotted with colorful houses, wind precipitously up the mountainside. The city's other distinguishing feature is a vast subterranean roadway, where a rushing river once coursed through the city.

The city was settled by wealthy land- and mine-owners, and many of its colonial buildings date back to the 18th century. Those buildings around the center of town have become museums, restaurants, hotels, and government offices. Add to this its many imposing churches, plus the green-limestone University of Guanajuato, and it's no wonder the town was named a World Heritage Site in 1988.

One thing you don't need in Guanajuato is a car. Guanajuato's streets are often clogged with traffic, and you can find yourself stuck in an exhaust-filled tunnel for up to an hour waiting for traffic to clear. It's easy and much more practical to stroll along the two main arteries, Avenida Juárez and Positos, from which you can access the main sights.

Start your exploration of Guanajuato with a ride on the funicular (behind the Teatro Juárez) up to the statue of El Pípila to get a great view of this colorful town. If you study your map you'll be able to identify most of the important buildings, like the university, the cathedral, and the Mercado Hidalgo. This perspective may come in handy later when the curving streets spin you around.

> **WORD OF MOUTH**
>
> "I love Guanajuato. It's a wonderful place to stroll around the streets and alleys and just sit in the cafes at the Jardín. The mummy museum is fascinating, and Diego Rivera's house is interesting to visit."
>
> -yestravel

4

A walk around the center of town will take a couple of hours. Remember that most museums and the theater are closed Monday.

GETTING HERE & AROUND

León's Guanajuato International Airport (BJX) is roughly 30 to 45 minutes west of downtown Guanajuato and a 1½-hour drive from San Miguel. It's a small airport, so the check-in desks can have long lines. Taxis to downtown Guanjuato cost about $30. If you're consider going by bus, Primera Plus and ETN have first-class service from Mexico City's Central del Norte to Guanajuato's Central Camionera (5 hours, $28–$30). There is also service from San Miguel (1½ hours, $8–$12) and from San Miguel to León (2½ hours, $12).

ESSENTIALS

Bus Contacts **ETN** (☎ *01800/800–0386 toll-free in Mexico* 🌐 *www.etn.com.mx*). **Primera Plus** (☎ *01800/375–7587 toll-free in Mexico* 🌐 *www.primeraplus.com.mx*).

Internet **Redes Internet** (✉ *Alonso 70, El Centro* ☎ *473/732–0611*).

Medical Assistance **Ambulance–Red Cross** (☎ *473/732–0487*). <**Hospital General** (☎ *473/733–1573*). **Police** (☎ *473/732–0266*).

Visitor Information **Guanajuato tourist office** (✉ *Plaza de la Paz 16, Centro* ☎ *473/732–0086 or 01800/714–1086 toll-free in Mexico* 📠 *473/732–4251*).

EXPLORING

MAIN ATTRACTIONS

❹ **Basílica Colegiata de Nuestra Señora de Guanajuato.** Painted in a striking yellow, the Basílica is a 17th-century baroque church that dominates Plaza de la Paz. Inside is Mexico's oldest Christian statue: a bejeweled 8th-century Virgin. The venerated figure was a gift from King Philip II of Spain in 1557. On the Friday preceding Good Friday, miners, accompanied by floats and mariachi bands, parade to the Basílica to pay homage to the Lady of Guanajuato. ✉*Plaza de la Paz, Centro* ☎*473/732–0314* 🎫*$2* ⏲*Daily 10–6.*

7 **Jardín de la Unión.** Guanajuato's central square is a tree-lined, wedge-shaped plaza bordered by pedestrian walkways. There are musical performances in the plaza's band shell on Tuesday, Thursday, and Sunday evenings; at other times, groups of musicians break into impromptu song along the shaded tile walkways. Strolling mariachis will perform, too—for a price.

8 **Mercado Hidalgo.** Don't miss this 1910 cast-iron-and-glass structure, designed by the one-and-only Gustave Eiffel. **TIP→ T-shirts and cheap plastic toys fill the balcony stalls, but the lower level is full of authentic local wares and colorful basketry, as well as fresh produce, peanuts, and honey-drenched nut candies shaped like mummies.** ✉*Calle Juárez near Mendizabal, Centro* ⏲*Daily 7 AM–9 PM.*

6 ★ **Museo Casa Diego Rivera.** The birthplace of Diego Rivera contains family portraits, furniture, and works by Mexico's foremost muralist; among them are his studies for the controversial mural commissioned for New York City's Rockefeller Center. Completed in 1933, the mural's portrait of Lenin and overall Communist bent prompted Rivera's benefactors to destroy it immediately after it was displayed. The museum's upper galleries show revolving contemporary art exhibitions, often from other countries. ✉*Calle Pozitos 47, El Centro* ☎*473/732–1197* 🎫*$1.50* ⏲*Tues.–Sat. 10–6:30, Sun. 10–2:30.*

10 ★ **Museo de las Momias.** Mummified human corpses—once buried in the municipal cemetery off Calzada del Panteón—are on display in this unique, though run-down, museum at the town's west end; it was most recently renovated in 1972. Until the law was amended in 1858, corpses were removed to make room for new arrivals if the grave site hadn't been paid for after five years. Because of the mineral properties of the local soil, these cadavers (the oldest is over 130 years old) were in astonishingly good condition upon exhumation. You'll need to catch a cab to get here; it's atop a steep hill. ✉*Panteón MunicipalEl Centro* ☎*473/732–0639* 🎫*$5* ⏲*Daily 9–6.*

11 **El Pípila.** A half-hour climb or short funicular ride from downtown is this statue of Juan José de los Reyes Martínez, a young miner and hero of the War of Independence of 1810. Nicknamed El Pípila, de los Reyes crept into the Alhóndiga de Granaditas, where Spanish Royalists were hiding, and set the door ablaze. This enabled Father Hidalgo's army to capture the Spanish troops in this first major military victory for the independence forces. The monument has spectacular city views. Funiculars run daily from 10 AM to 8 PM and cost about $2.50 for the round-trip. ✉*Carretera Panorámica, on bluff above south side of Jardín de la Unión, El Centro.*

2 **Teatro Juárez.** Adorned with bronze lion sculptures and a line of large Greek muses overlooking the Jardín de la Unión from the roof, the theater was inaugurated by Mexican dictator Porfirio Díaz in 1903 with a performance of *Aïda.* It now serves as the principal venue of

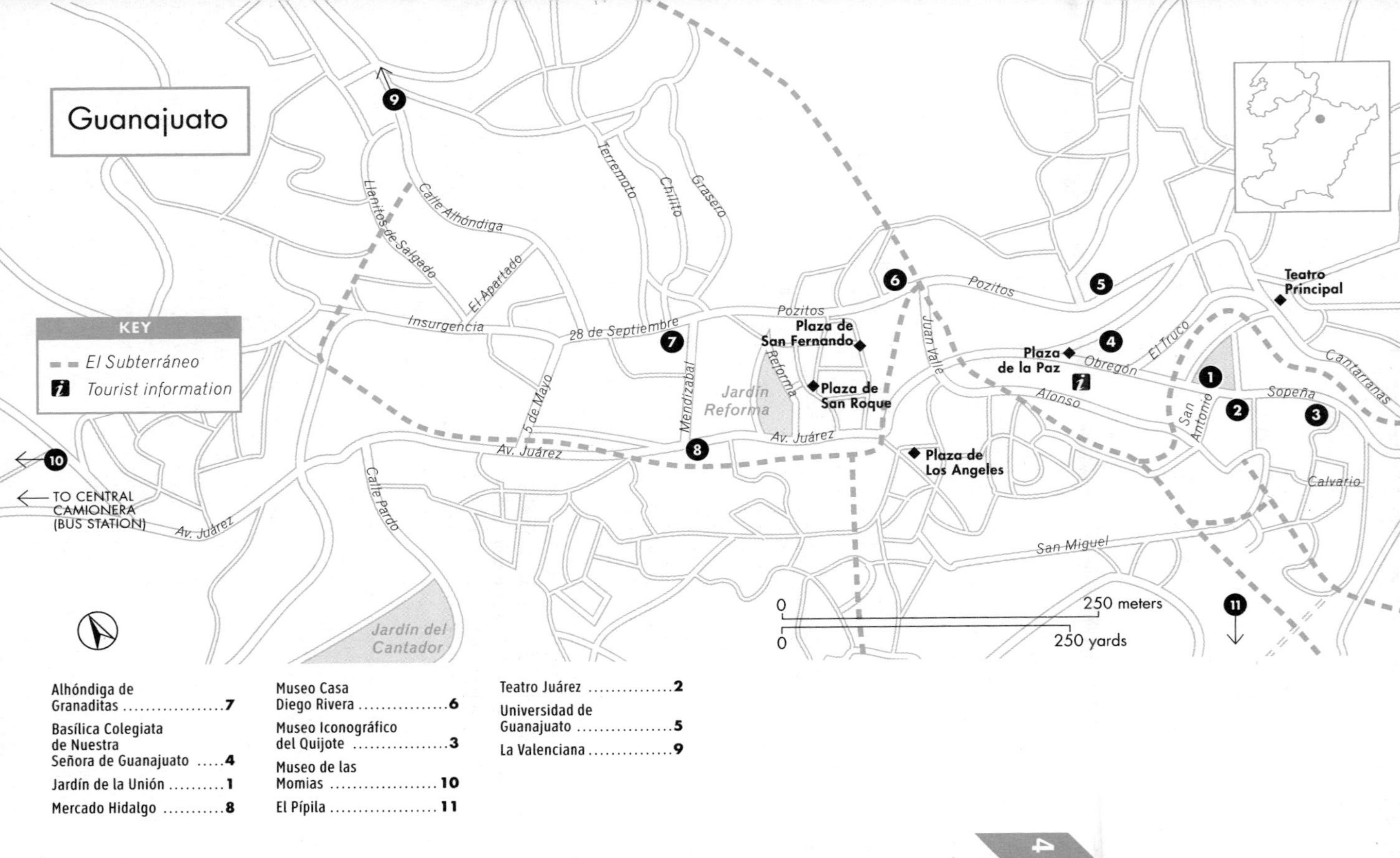

Alhóndiga de Granaditas 7
Basílica Colegiata de Nuestra Señora de Guanajuato 4
Jardín de la Unión 1
Mercado Hidalgo 8
Museo Casa Diego Rivera 6
Museo Iconográfico del Quijote 3
Museo de las Momias 10
El Pípila 11
Teatro Juárez 2
Universidad de Guanajuato 5
La Valenciana 9

4

GO WITH A GUIDE

The following tour operators give half- and full-day tours with English-speaking guides. These tours typically include the Museo de las Momias, the church and mines of La Valenciana, the monument to Pípila, the Panoramic Highway, subterranean streets, and residential neighborhoods. Night tours often begin at El Pípila for a view of the city lights and end at a dance club. The state tourism ministry recommends Juvenal Díaz López. Friendly and full of local knowledge, Díaz tailors tours of Guanajuato and its surrounding areas to your specific needs.

Juvenal Díaz López (☎*473/733-3026 or 473/737-1579*). **Transporte Exclusivo de Turismo** (✉*Av. Juárez at Calle 5 de Mayo, Centro* ☎*473/732-5968*). **Transporte Turísticos de Guanajuato** (✉*Plaza de la Paz 2, by Basílica de Guanajuato, Centro* ☎*473/732-2134 or 473/732-2838*).

the annual International Cervantes Festival. You can take a brief tour of the art deco interior. ✉*Sopeña s/n, Centro* ☎*473/732-0183* *$3* *Tues.–Sun. 9–1:45 and 5–7:45*

5 **Universidad de Guanajuato.** Founded in 1732, the university was formerly a Jesuit seminary. The original Churrigueresque church, **La Compañía,** still stands next door. The facade of the university, built in 1955, was designed to blend in with the town's architecture. ■ TIP→ **If you do wander inside, check the bulletin boards for the town's cultural events.** ✉*Lascurain de Retana 5, ½ block north of Plaza de la Paz, El Centro* ☎*473/732-0006* *www.ugto.mx* *Weekdays 8–3:30.*

9 ★ **La Valenciana.** Officially called La Iglesia de San Cayetano, a 15-minute trek from the city center, this is one of the best-known colonial churches in Mexico. The mid- to late-18th-century pink-stone facade is brilliantly ornate. Inside are three altars, each hand-carved in wood and brightly gilded, in different styles: plateresque, Churrigueresque, and baroque. There are also religious paintings from the viceregal period. ■ TIP→ **Both the mine and church are included in any of Guanajuato's guided tours, and buses (marked** LA VALENCIANA**) frequently make the trip from the city center.** ✉*Carretera Guanajuato–Dolores Hidalgo, Km 5* ☎*No phone* *San Cayetano mine tour about $2.50* *Daily 9–6.*

IF YOU HAVE TIME

7 **Alhóndiga de Granaditas.** Previously this 18th-century grain-storage facility served as a jail under Emperor Maximilian and as a fortress during the War of Independence, where El Pípila helped the revolutionaries overcome the royalists. The hooks on which the Spanish Royalists hung the severed heads of Father Hidalgo, Ignacio Allende, and two other independence leaders still dangle on the exterior of this massive stone structure. It's now a state museum with exhibits on local history, archaeology, and crafts. ✉*Calle 28 de Septiembre 6, El Centro* ☎*473/732-1112 or 473/732-1180* *About $3* *Tues.–Sat. 10–6, Sun. 10–3.*

NEED A BREAK?

Go to the Hotel Museo Posada Santa Fé (✉ *Jardín de la Unión 12, El Centro* ☎ *473/732-0084*) for alfresco dining at the Jardín. Try the *pozole estilo Guanajuato* (hominy soup to which you can add onions, radishes, lettuce, lime, and chile peppers).

MINE EXPLORATIONS

A Valenciana mine near the church has one entrance at **Bocamina de San Ramón** (✉ *Callejón de San Ramón 10*), whose free tour you might call entry-level—you just head down 66 feet, look around, and pop back up.

❸ **Museo Iconográfico del Quijote.** During his imprisonment in a Spanish concentration camp in the 1930s, Spanish writer and journalist Eulalio Ferrer was so uplifted by Miguel de Cervantes's classic novel that he developed a lifelong passion for *Don Quixote.* This restored 19th-century home is a museum displaying Ferrer's collection of over 600 pieces of art, all dedicated to the man of La Mancha. Gathered after he fled Fascist Spain for Mexico, the star-studded collection includes works by Salvador Dalí, Pablo Picasso, Jose Luis Cuevas, and Alfredo Zalce. ✉ *Manuel Doblado 1, Centro* ☎ *473/732–6721 or 473/732–3376* 🌐 *www.guanajuato.gob.mx/museo* 🎟 *$2* ⏲ *Tues.–Sat. 10–6:30, Sun. 10–2:30.*

4

WHERE TO EAT

$$–$$$$ ★ MEXICAN ✕ **El Rincón de los Sabores.** A slight bit out of the scenic city center, this romantic restaurant is worth the trek. The shady patio is a respite from the busy roads, and food is simple and well done. A cream of poblano soup with huitlacoche will have you savoring every spoonful; flavorful parrilladas, the house specialty, feature spicy chorizo and juicy pork. A specialty of the restaurant is camarones huérfanos, shrimp wrapped in bacon and stuffed with cream cheese and fried—they're as heavy as they sound, but they're also delicious. In the evenings, there is often a live guitarist. ✉ *Alhóndiga 84* ☎ *473/731–1984* 💳 *MC, V* ⏲ *No dinner Sun.*

$$–$$$ ECLECTIC ✕ **La Capellina.** This fresh fusion restaurant, set in a 1673 building, is at once minimalist, eclectic, international, French-influenced, and tasty. Each dish is marked on the menu with its own nationality. A recipe for disaster? Not in the case of the shrimp *michelada,* which are beer-marinated with lemon, onion, jicama, carrots, cucumber, and serrano chile; or the *arrachera fusión,* a variation on the classic Mexican marinated steak that features avocado, goat cheese, and a chipotle–red wine salsa. The menu includes a large selection of creative pizzas. Not everything's perfect—guajillo (a type of chile) salmon, for one, is a failure. The wine list is fantastic, and there is often live music. ✉ *Hostería del Frayle, Calle Sopeña 3* ☎ *473/732–7224* 💳 *AE, MC, V* ⏲ *No dinner Sun.* 🌐 *www.lacapellina.com*

$–$$$ ITALIAN ✕ **Frascati.** This bold restaurant overlooking the city's principal plaza takes Italian cooking in Mexico to a new level in an environment that showcases both a city view and a romantic, well-lit interior. Even better are the authentic Italian dishes, from carpaccio to pastas (especially a meaty Bolognese) to thin-crust pizzas to a tender, slow-braised osso buco. Fried appetizers are delicately prepared, and the shrimp are especially delicious. The wine list is surprisingly good for Guanajuato. ✉*Jardín de la Unión 1* ☎*473/732–2851* ▭*AE, MC, V*

$–$$ Fodor's Choice ★ MEXICAN ✕**El Abue.** Don't let Guanajuato's twisted streets deter you from finding this little gem in the middle of the city, near the university. It's got probably the best Mexican food of any upmarket restaurant in the entire region. The interior of the restaurant has a romantic, warmly lit, European feel. Start with the margaritas, and move on to the delicious chiles en nogada; topped with crunchy pomegranate seeds and filled with savory pork, they're one of the best versions in the city. Even better are the enchiladas El Abue, stuffed with dried fruits and covered with Oaxacan red mole. Breakfast is also on offer daily for a mere 15 pesos. ✉*Calle San José 14* ☎*473/732–6242* ▭*MC, V.*

$–$$ MEXICAN ✕**Casa del Conde de la Valenciana.** Across from La Valenciana is this refurbished 18th-century home whose colonial atmosphere goes a long way in enhancing the touristy but serviceable restaurant. Among the highlights are the *crema de aguacate con tequila* (cream of avocado with tequila) served in a bowl made of ice, tender *lomo en salsa de ciruela pasa* (pork shoulder in prune sauce), and *pollo a la flor de calabaza* (chicken with poblano chile slices and squash-blossom sauce). Round out the meal with mango ice cream served in the rind. ✉*Carretera Guanajuato–Dolores Hidalgo, Km 5, La Valenciana* ☎*473/732–2550* ▭*MC, V* ⊗*Closed Sun. No dinner.*

$–$$ ITALIAN ✕**El Gallo Pitagórico.** Huff and puff your way up the 100-plus steps to this restaurant's threshold for an exceptional view of downtown Guanajuato, as well as for the mouthwatering house specialty, *filetto Claudio* (beef fillet with olives, capers, herbs, and garlic). Save room for the velvety tiramisu. Weather permitting, have your aperitif in the top-story bar, which has an even more dazzling view, which is best at sunset, tinting Guanajuato's domes various shades of gold. ✉*Constancia 10, behind Teatro Juárez, El Centro* ☎*473/732–9489* ▭*MC, V.*

$–$$ ★ MEXICAN ✕**México Lindo y Sabroso.** As you sit at umbrella-shaded tables in a gracious courtyard framed by bougainvillea, serenaded by Mexican music you'll be transported back to a simpler Mexico. The margaritas are good and the menu is interesting, from a well-developed *pozole verde* (a rich soup made with hominy) to juicy *cochinita pibíl* (pork baked in banana leaf) with black beans and the traditional pickled onions. The restaurant is out in the quiet residential neighborhood of Presa, above the city center, but it's worth the trip. ✉*San José 17, Presa* ☎*473/731–0529* ▭*MC, V*

$–$$ ★ MEXICAN ✕**Truco 7.** Totally local yet beloved by visitors, this place is the real deal, morning, noon, and night. Multigenerational Mexican families dine amongst a spattering of granola-crunchy tourists, all comfortably ensconced within the warm colors of the walls, wood, and endless bric-a-brac. At breakfast egg dishes reign supreme and enfrijoladas (corn tortillas layered with refried beans, cheese, and sour cream) are an excellent choice. It's also hard to go wrong with the traditional lunch plates: enchiladas, chicken dishes, and such. It's open later than most spots in town. ✉*Truco 7* ☎*473/732–8374* ▭*MC, V.*

¢–$ MEXICAN ✕ **El Claustro.** El Claustro manages to strike a delicate balance: set in a lively plaza, it captures the energy of the city while not feeling like a tourist trap. Walk into the semi-subterranean space and you'll see women making fresh tortillas—always a good sign—and the buzz of locals enjoying simple, authentic Mexican food. The specialty here is enchiladas, and the *enchiladas rojas* are particularly good. Also worth a try is the *pollo a la veracruzana* (chicken stewed with tomatoes and onions). There are three tree-shaded tables out on the plaza. ✉*Jardín de la Reforma 13-B* ☎*473/732–9781* ▭*No credit cards.*

¢ MEXICAN ✕ **El Tapatío.** One of the best-kept secrets in Guanajuato is this hole-in-the-wall across from the university whose bargain *comida corrida* at lunchtime—four courses for about $4—is equally popular with students, faculty, and local workers. It starts with delicious fresh-baked bread, then continues with a starter such as *crema de verduras* (vegetable soup) with green chile, or a chipotle-spiked chicken soup. Tacos and an *antojito* then a meat will follow, plus dessert. The space is cute, with brick archways, knickknacks, and waiters dressed in black and white who are more friendly than attentive. ✉*Lascuráin de Retana 20* ☎*473/732–3291* ▭*MC, V* ⊗*No dinner Sun.*

4

WHERE TO STAY

$$$–$$$$ Fodor'sChoice ★ **Hotel Refugio Casa Colorada.** The spectacular onetime residence of former president Luis Echeverría sits atop one of the highest bluffs in town, with possibly the best views of Guanajuato. The whole building is surrounded by an impressive cactus garden. Each elegantly decorated suite is spacious, with restrained colonial touches; they have bathrooms tiled with local ceramics, floor-to-ceiling windows with views over the town, and small balconies. The Presidential Suite has a sunken tub and a telescope to complement its floor-to-ceiling picture window. The restaurant offers indoor and outdoor dining on a spacious terrace overlooking the town. **Pros:** Relatively new building. Doting service. **Cons:** Not close to city center. A little pricey. ✉*Cerro de San Miguel 13, Col. Loma de Pozuelos,* ☎*473/732–3993 or 473/734–1151* ⊕*www.hotelesrefugio.com* *6 suites* *In-room: Wi-Fi. In-hotel: Restaurant, bar, room service, parking (no fee), no elevator* ▭*AE, MC, V.*

$$$ **Casa Estrella de la Valenciana.** With a panoramic view near the church of La Valenciana, this American-owned house feels like an upmarket bed-and-breakfast—it's one of the most expensive hotels in the city. Some rooms have their own Jacuzzis and all have a terrace with stunning views. The only downside to this place—and it's a big one—is its distance from the city. **Pros:** The views and privacy. **Cons:** Distance from city, which requires cab rides. ✉*Callejón Jalisco 10, La Valenciana, 36240* ☎*473/732–1784, 866/983–8844 toll-free in U.S.* ⊕*www.mexicaninns.com* *7 rooms* *In-room: Safe, DVD. In-hotel: Bar, pool, spa, laundry service, parking (no fee)* ▭*AE* *BP.*

$$$ **Hotel Luna.** Right on the Jardín de la Unión, this hotel is a great bet—as long as you get an exterior-facing room. Those on the interior feel small, dark, and dingy, but the ones facing out are full of life, especially when the light hits their shiny chandeliers. The whole hotel has a quirky, ironic

feel to it, mixing faux-sleazy dim red lights with old colonial grandeur. The lively bar turns into more of a straight-up cantina late at night. **Pros:** Cheeky decor. Supreme people-watching. **Cons:** Some rooms are a bit dark. Not a place for those who like to retire early. ✉*Plaza Principal at Jardín de la Unión 8, El Centro* ☎*473/732–9725* 🌐*www.hotelluna.com.mx* *21 rooms, 2 suites* *In-hotel: Restaurant, bar, laundry service* 💳*AE, MC, V.*

$$$ ★ **Quinta Las Acacias.** It would be hard to argue that the Frida Kahlo suite here, perched as it is above Guanajuato with a full Jacuzzi, relaxing living room, two large-screen TVs, and an enormous bathroom—is not the single best room in Guanajuato. This boutique hotel, which opened in 1998, offers modern, Mexican-style rooms that are beautifully decorated. It's an utterly relaxing place, though you should venture elsewhere for meals. **Pros:** Beautiful and spacious rooms. Incredibly comfortable. **Cons:** The restaurant is not good and it's a bit of a trip to others. ✉*Paseo de la Presa 168 , La Presa* ☎*473/731–1517* 🌐*www.quintalasacacias.com* *17 rooms, 10 suites* *In-room: Safe. In-hotel: Restaurant, room service, library, public Wi-Fi* 💳*AE, MC, V.*

EATING ON THE GO IN PRESA

If you're staying in the Presa neighborhood, you should indulge in walk along Paseo de Presa into the city. You'll pass a number of food carts in Parque Florenceio Antillón, all selling great food at even better prices. Fish ceviche tostadas are astoundingly fresh; you might also find savory tacos al pastor, with tortillas made in front of you on a *comal*, a large, often cast-iron, plate. It's better to make this walk into the city than out—going back to Presa is all uphill, perfect for a taxi.

$$ **Casa del Agua.** The theme here is clearly maritime, with a light-blue color scheme, glass-covered blue tiles, and a bar called Azul. Rooms, however, are decidedly more terrestrial. Somewhat bland, with beige as the dominant color, they're not as exciting as the rest of the hotel. The views are great, though; rooms facing outward have balconies, some with stunning views, and all have a Jacuzzi. Its location just behind Jardín de la Unión puts you right within access of the square's vibrancy, but without the all the noise. **Pros:** Hot tubs in room. Fun bar at hotel. **Cons:** Feels somewhat tired. Management not always present. ✉*Plaza de la Compañía #4, El Centro* ☎*473/731–2257 or 473/734–1974* *15 rooms, 1 suite* *In-room: Safe. In-hotel: Restaurant, bar, room service, laundry service, parking (no fee)* 💳*AE, MC, V.*

$$ ★ **La Casa de Espíritus Alegres Bed and Breakfast.** Folk-art lovers are drawn to this "house of good spirits" for its collection of crafts. Owned by a California artist, the lovingly restored hacienda (circa 1700) has thick stone walls and serene, almost jungle-like grounds covered with bougainvillea and calla lilies. Hand-glazed tile baths, fireplaces, and private terraces are standard with each room, but otherwise, all rooms are unique. Marfil is a 15-minute drive from the center of town—frequent buses are available. Taxi drivers may be unfamiliar with the hotel, so come prepared with directions. **Pros:** Uniquely and creatively decorated

suites. Warm staff and complimentary breakfasts. **Cons:** Hard to find, and driveway is difficult to maneuver. ✉*La Ex-Hacienda La Trinidad 1, Marfil* ☎📠*473/733–1013* 🌐*www.casaspirit.com* *5 rooms, 3 suites* *In-room: No a/c, no TV. In-hotel: Bar, laundry service, parking (no fee), no kids under 13, no elevator* 💳*MC, V* *BP.*

$$ **Hostería del Frayle.** Formerly the Casa de Moneda, where ore was taken to be refined after leaving the mines, this quiet, regal four-story lodging was built in 1673 and turned into a hotel in the mid-1960s. It has whitewashed plaster and wood-beam rooms arranged around a small maze of stairways, landings, and courtyards. Some rooms have excellent views of the Pípila, Teatro Juárez, and Jardín de la Unión, which is a half-block away. Make sure to dine in the adjacent restaurant, La Capellina. **Pros:** In the heart of the city. Great restaurant next door. **Cons:** Lots of noise late at night. Not the newest building. ✉*Calle Sopeña 3, El Centro* ☎📠*473/732–1179* 🌐*www.hosteriadelfrayle.com* *36 rooms, 1 suite* *In-hotel: Restaurant, bar, no elevator* 💳*MC, V.*

$$ **Hotel Museo Posada Santa Fé.** This colonial-style inn at the Jardín de la Unión—the best location in town—has been in operation since 1862. Large historic paintings by local artist Don Manuel Leal hang in the wood-paneled lobby. Rooms are a bit drab, with barely adequate bathrooms. Rooms facing the plaza can be noisy, but boast the best views; quieter rooms face narrow alleyways, and sometimes look onto Guanajuato's twisting roads. The hotel's restaurant is great for late-night snacks. **Pros:** Great location, and not too noisy if you get the right rooms. **Cons:** Some rooms face hallways and have privacy issues. Bathrooms are small and lacking in amenities. ✉*Plaza Principal at Jardín de la Unión 12, El Centro* ☎*473/732–0084* *37 rooms, 7 suites* *In-room: No a/c. In-hotel: Restaurant, bar, laundry service, parking (no fee)* 💳*AE, MC, V* *BP.*

NIGHTLIFE

BARS

There are a number of pricey bars right on the main plazas, such as Jardín de la Unión, that attract more than a few tourists because of their unparalleled people-watching opportunities. One plaza perch is **Bar Luna** (✉*Jardín de la Unión 8* ☎*473/732–9725*), part of the hotel by the same name. It's open late into the evening. Indoors it's got cheeky decor, and outdoors it's got a great crowd. An old-school cantina worth its salt is **Los Barrillitos** (✉*Juárez 180, on corner of Callejón del Cañón Rojo* ☎*No phone*). It's an absolute classic, with long, fluorescent lights and a sign reading "PELIGRO: HOMBRES BEBIENDO" (Danger: Men Drinking). Unusual for a cantina, there's a fine selection of top-end tequila, including the sweet, smooth Cazadores Reposado.

Calle Sopeña hops with nighttime activity, thanks in part to interesting spots like (restaurant by day and bar by night) **La Capellina** (✉*Sopeña 3* ☎*473/732–7224*), which has live music ranging from Latin jazz to blues, and great drinks.

El Corcho de Baco (✉*Plaza San Fernando 8* ☎*473/141–5691*) serves charcuterie, along with a great wine selection, including good Mexican producers like Monte Xanic. Prices on wine are steep, but you can drink it there for only a small fee above the store price.

For an authentic Mexican cantina experience, **El Incendio** (✉*Cantarranas 15* ☎*No phone*) is open until 4 AM and comes complete with swinging doors and gruff old men downing beer after beer. If you're a woman, it's best to come accompanied.

For a bohemian atmosphere, head to **Langolova** (✉*Cantarranas 70* ☎*No phone*).

La Oreja de Van Gogh (✉*San Fernando 24*) has reasonably priced drinks and perfect seating near sidewalks filled with late-night revelers. There's a smaller branch at Plaza San Fernando with similar offerings and a much more relaxed vibe.

Geared toward an older, quieter crowd, **Puerta del Sol** (✉*Sopeña 14* ☎*473/732–7224*) offers a romantic setting complete with *peñas* (traditional folk music performances)—best enjoyed over some tequila.

DANCE CLUBS

Students gather for drinks and salsa dancing at **El Bar** (✉*Sopeña 10, El Centro* ☎*473/732–2566*).

On Friday and Saturday nights there's live music at the **Castillo Santa Cecilia** (✉*Camino a la Valenciana s/n, Km 1, La Valenciana* ☎*473/732–0485*), which is in a hotel, so don't expect to rub elbows with too many locals.

★ Calle Sopeña is one of the hottest streets on weekend nights. **La Dama de las Camelias** (✉*Calle Sopeña 32* ☎*473/732–7587*), with its dingy-hip furnishings and longtime regulars, manages to stay unpretentious while pulling off its dive-bar-meets-vaudeville theme. You'll find everyone from twentysomethings to sixtysomethings hitting the dance floor for salsa and cumbia. It's open until 4 AM.

★ **La Juanita** (✉*Av. Juárez 22*) may be the coolest nightclub in Guanajuato, for young and old alike, with its sleek red-and-black furnishings, great music, and cool but unpretentious crowd. It's equally well suited to drinking, dancing, or just chilling out. Enter through the door for Il Romanico Italian restaurant. Ladies drink free on Wednesday.

Luv Lounge (✉*Jardín de la Unión 4* ☎*473/732–5718*) throbs with music—come prepared to shake it.

The crowd often takes to singing at **Rincón del Beso** (✉*Alhóndiga 84* ☎*473/732–5912*).

Tuesday, Thursday, Friday, and Saturday at 9 PM, **Callejoneadas** (mobile musical parties) begin in front of Teatro Juárez on *Sopeña in the center of town.* These quintessential, traditional tours are led by a group of student-minstrels, in full-out period costumes, who roam the narrowest streets of Guanajuato—the callejones—while strumming stringed instruments and singing folk songs, followed by the mass of paying

FESTIVALS

Guanajuato is completely mobbed each fall for the Festival **Internacional Cervantino** (International Cervantes Festival ✉ *Plaza de San Francisquito 1, El Centro* ☎ *473/731–1150, 473/731–1161 for Ticketmaster* 🌐 *www.guanajuato.gob.mx/ingles/FIC*). For three weeks each October, world-renowned actors, musicians, and dance troupes perform contemporary works nightly at the Teatro Juárez and other local venues. Plaza San Roque, a small square near the Jardín Reforma, hosts a series of Entremeses Cervantinos—swashbuckling one-act farces by classical Spanish writers, such as Cervantes. Grandstand seats require advance tickets, but crowds often gather by the plaza's edge to watch for free. Guanajuato's nightlife also reaches a peak during the festival, and revelers from different parts of Mexico walk through the city streets and display their regional pride by jumping up and down and chanting the name of their hometown. If you're going to be among the hundreds of thousands who attend the festivities annually, contact the Festival Internacional Cervantino office at least six months in advance to secure tickets for top-billed events, or contact Ticketmaster. However, if you're not a fan of elbow-to-elbow crowds morning, noon, and night, then you should avoid the festival.

customers, tourists from both Mexico and abroad. For a small fee you can travel with the group while enjoying an alcoholic beverage of sorts. (It's usually some bad combination of grape drink and firewater—so we recommend bringing your own.) The important thing is to try to get in a smaller group in order to keep up and hear the commentary—which is in Spanish only. You'll see people selling tickets around the theater, and you should ideally pay no more than 100 pesos per person. A fun part of your night will be stopping on the Callejón del Beso, a street so narrow it's said that a kiss could be exchanged between secret lovers on top-floor balconies. Bundle up on cold nights; the tours last up to two hours.

THEATER

Even when it's not festival season, Guanajuato still has dramatic, dance, and musical performances at **Teatro Juárez** (✉ *Sopeña s/n, El Centro* ☎ *473/732–0183*).

SHOPPING

Some jewelry and regional knickknacks are sold at the **Mercado Hidalgo** (✉ *Calle Juárez near Mendizabal, El Centro* ☎ *No phone*). Shops around Plaza de la Paz and Jardín de la Unión sell ceramics, woolen shawls, and sweaters. Book fairs are held on shady Plaza de San Fernando. Street vendors and shops clustered near La Valenciana and La Valencia sell silver.

Casa del Conde de la Valenciana (✉ *Carretera Guanajuato–Dolores Hidalgo, Km 5, La Valenciana* ☎ *473/732–2550*), in addition to being a restaurant, specializes in brass, tin, ceramic, and wrought-iron home decorations from Mexico and Africa. Another good place for ceramics is **La Cruz** (✉ *Cerro de la Cruz* ☎ *473/732–9037*). **Mayólicas Santa Rosa** (✉ *Carretera Guanajuato a Dolores Hidalgo, Km 13* ☎ *473/102–5017*) has lovely Santa Rosa ceramics.

ZACATECAS

300 km (185 mi or 3½ hrs by car) northwest of San Miguel , 250 km (155 mi) northwest of Guanajuato, 350 km (217 mi) northwest of Querétaro, 600 km (375 mi) northwest of Mexico City via Hwy. 57.

Although Zacatecas, nestled high up at 8,000 feet, was once the world's largest silver-producing city, it's relatively undiscovered by foreigners. Designated a UNESCO World Heritage Site in 1993, this extraordinary town is often labeled the "pink city," since most of its 17th- and 18th-century buildings were built of local pink limestone.

As a state capital with a population of 150,000, Zacatecas toes the line between city and small town. There are some good restaurants and museums, and nightlife includes partying in an old silver mine deep beneath the ground. Each year during the Festival Cultural de Zacatecas, the city comes alive with dance, theater, music, and art.

Most town-center attractions are accessible by foot, although you may want a taxi to visit farther-flung sights like the Cerro de la Bufa, a dramatic limestone outcropping visible from most strategic points in town. There's an efficient and inexpensive bus system with clearly marked buses and 30¢ rides. The city's principal avenues such as López Velarde and González Ortega often change names as they proceed through the town and the traffic is divided by islands decorated with carved limestone vases and lampposts, occasional statues, and ornate fountains.

We suggest you get your bearings first on the Tranvía Turístico, a trolleybus that departs daily from 9 to 9 in front of the cathedral. The 40-minute tour costs $3.

GETTING HERE & AROUND

The Zacatecas La Calera airport (ZCL) is 29 km (18 mi) north of town. Aeromar and Aeromexico fly from Mexico City to Zacatecas. Mexicana has direct flights from Chicago. Taxis from the airport into town cost around $17; the Aerotransportes shuttle service costs $5. The Zacatecas bus depot is a couple of miles southwest of the town center. Omnibus de México

GO WITH A GUIDE

Viajes Mazzoco, a well-established travel agency and the local American Express representative, gives tours of the city center, the Eden mine, the Teleférico, and La Bufa, and the Quemada ruins. Ask in advance for an English-speaking guide.

The tourism office recommends **Operadora Zacatecas**, which gives tours of the city center and other sites.

Operadora Zacatecas (✉ *Av. Hidalgo 630* ☎ *492/924–0050* 🌐 *www.operadorazacatecas.com*). **Viajes Mazzoco** (✉ *Calle Lopez Portello 46* ☎📠 *492/922–0859*).

and Estrella Blanca make the five-hour trip between Querétaro and Zacatecas ($27). There are no direct buses from San Miguel de Allende, but you can drive from there on excellent state highways in less than four hours.

LOCAL BREW

Next to Casa Valadez, the popular restaurant opposite the Teatro Juárez, you will find Casa Maximiliano; they sell pretty, blue bottles of local tequila from Pénjamo that make great gifts.

ESSENTIALS

Bus Contacts **Estrella Blanca** (☎*01800/507-5500 toll-free in Mexico* 🌐*www.estrellablanca.com.mx*). **Omnibus de Mexico** (☎*01800/765-6636 toll-free in Mexico* 🌐*www.odm.com.mx*).

Medical Assistance **Farmacia Isstezac** (✉*Tacuba 140* ☎*492/924-0690*). **Hospital General** (✉*Paseo García Salinas s/n* ☎*492/923-3004*). **Police** (☎*492/922-0180*). **Red Cross** (☎*492/922-3005*).

Visitor & Tour Info **Zacatecas Tourist information office** (✉*Av. Hidalgo 403* ☎*492/922-6751 or 492/922-3426* 🌐*www.turismozacatecas.gob.mx*).

4

EXPLORING

MAIN ATTRACTIONS

5 **Catedral de Zacatecas.** This is one of Mexico's finest interpretations of baroque style. It has three facades—the principal one dedicated to the Eucharist is best viewed from 2 to 6 PM when the afternoon sun lights up the deeply sculpted reliefs. ✉*South side of Plaza de Armas on Av. Hidalgo* ☎*No phone* ⏲*Daily 8–2 and 5–9.*

7 **Cerro de la Bufa.** Pancho Villa's definitive battle against dictator Victoriano Huerta occurred on this rugged hill, now a city landmark, in June 1914. The spacious Plaza de la Revolución, paved with the three shades of pink Zacatecas stone, is crowned with three huge equestrian statues of Villa and two other heroes, Felipe Angeles and Panfilo Natera. You can have your photo taken dressed up like Pancho Villa (complete with antique rifle) and a soldadera companion with outfits supplied by an enterprising young man. A walk up to the observatory gets you the best view of Zacatecas. Also on-site are the Sanctuario de la Virgen de Patrocinio, a chapel dedicated to the city's patron, and the **Museo de la Toma de Zacatecas** (☎*492/922-8066* 💵*$1* ⏲*Tues.–Sun. 10–5*), which has nine rooms of historic objects such as guns, newspapers, furniture, and clothing from the days of Pancho Villa. ✉*If driving, follow Av. Hidalgo north from town to Av. Juan de Tolosa; turn right and continue until you come to a fountain; take right off retorno (crossover) onto Calle Mexicapan, which leads to Carretera Panorámica. Turn right to sign-posted Carretera La Bufa, which leads to the top of the hill.*

9 **Mina El Edén.** From 1586 until 1960 this mine supplied Zacatecas with most of its silver. Tours are in Spanish, but you'll have no trouble imagining what life was like for a miner once you're riding in the open mine train down into the underground tunnels. Wear sturdy shoes and bring a sweater. Among the train's stops is a discotheque—Club La Mina—

Catedral de Zacatecas 5
Cerro de la Bufa 7
Mina El Edén 9
Museo Pedro Coronel 1
Museo Rafael Coronel 3
Palacio del Gobierno 6
Palacio de la Mala Noche ...4
Teleférico 8
Templo de Santo Domingo 2

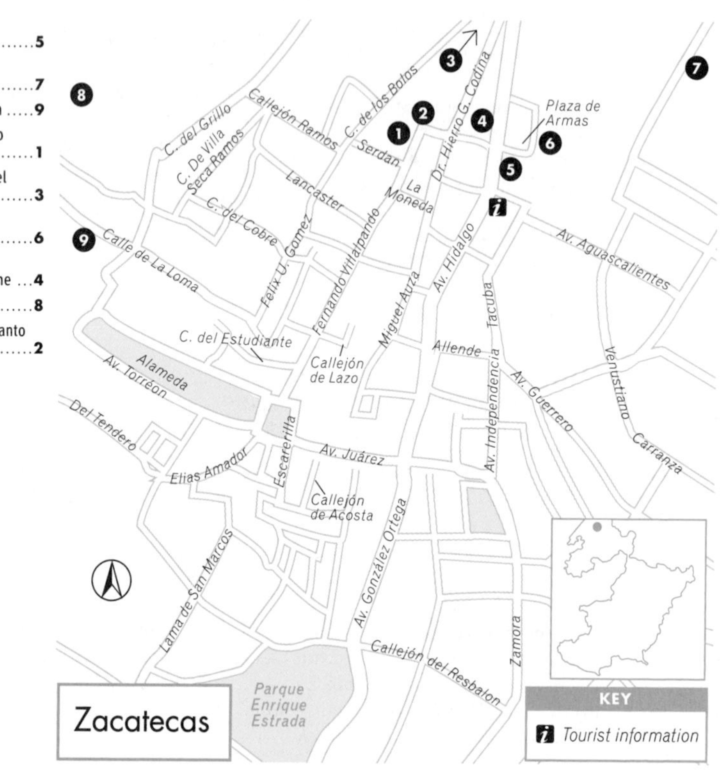

which you should definitely revisit at night during its operating hours. There's a small gift shop at the entrance, and another inside the mine at the museum where you can see examples of different minerals and fossils. ✉*Entrance on Jaime Dovali off Av. Torréon beyond Alameda García de la Cadena* ☎*492/922–3002* 🎟*$6* ⏲*Daily 10–6.*

3 ★ **Museo Rafael Coronel.** Concealed by the Ex-Convento de San Francisco's mellow, pink, 18th-century facade is a rambling structure of open, arched corridors, all leading through garden patios to rooms that exhibit, on a rotating basis, 3,000 of the museum's 10,000 *máscaras* (masks). These representations of saints and devils, wise men and fools, animals and humans were once used in Mexican regional festivals. The museum also has a remarkable display of puppets, pre-Hispanic art, photography, and paintings. It's northeast of the town center, toward Lomas del Calvario. ✉*Off Vergel Nuevo between Chaveño and Garcia Salinas* ☎*492/922–8116* 🎟*About $2* ⏲*Thurs.–Tues. 10–4:30.*

WORD OF MOUTH

"Zacatecas...one of most beautiful 'colonial' cities I've seen... days were sunny and warm in December...several great museums, churches and other sites." -binder40

8 **Teleférico.** The only cable car in the world to cross an entire city, the Teleférico runs from Cerro del Grillo (Cricket Hill) above the Mina Eden to Cerro de la Bufa. Though it crosses at the narrowest point, it showcases the city's magnificent panorama and baroque church domes and spires. It's worth the cost to get the ride up to Cerro de la Bufa, which is quite a climb otherwise. ✉ *Cerro del Grillo station: off Paseo Díaz Ordaz, a steep walk from Plaza de Armas* ☎ *492/922–5494* 🎫 *$2* ⏲ *Daily 10–6, except when there are high winds.*

Fodor's Choice ★

MARCHING MADNESS

Among the charms of Zacatecas is its *tambora*, a musical parade led by a *tamborazo*, a local band that shatters the evening quiet with merriment. It's also known as a *callejoneada* (*callejón* means "alley"), and everyone along the way either joins in or cheers from balconies and doorways. During the December *feria* (festival), the tamborazos serenade the Virgin of Zacatecas by playing night and day.

IF YOU HAVE TIME

1 **Museo Pedro Coronel.** Originally a Jesuit monastery, this building was used as a jail in the 18th century, and is now a museum, which exhibits the work of Zacatecas artist and sculptor Pedro Coronel. Also on display is his extensive collection of works by Picasso, Dalí, Miró, Braque, and Chagall, among others, as well as art from Africa, China, Japan, India, Tibet, Greece, and Egypt. ✉ *Centro s/n at Plaza Santo Domingo* ☎ *492/922–8021 or 492/924–2663* 🎫 *$2* ⏲ *Fri.–Wed. 10–4:30.*

6 **Palacio del Gobierno.** The Governor's Palace is an 18th-century mansion with verdant courtyards and, on the main staircase, a poignant mural by António Pintor Rodríguez that depicts the history of Zacatecas. ✉ *East side of Plaza de Armas* 🎫☎ *No phone Free* ⏲ *Daily 9–9.*

4 **Palacio de la Mala Noche.** Across from the downtown plaza is a national monument: two 18th-century colonial buildings with lacy ironwork balconies and built from native pink stone. One is a municipal building known as the Palace of the Bad Night, which, according to legend, was the home of a silver mine–owner. The owner's mine had failed, so, left with only enough funds to pay his workers' final wages, he went to pray at the cathedral. On the way home he ran into a woman whose son was sick and gave her everything he had. Early the next morning loud banging on the door seemed to herald his doom, but upon opening the door he was instead informed that the mine workers had found the richest gold vein ever seen in these parts. ✉ *Av. Hidalgo 639* ☎ *No phone* 🎫 *Free* ⏲ *Weekdays 9–6.*

2 **Templo de Santo Domingo.** This 18th-century Jesuit church has an ornamented facade and an opulent interior with religious paintings. In the sacristy is an extensive collection of religious art. ✉ *Av. Fernando Villalpando at Plaza Santo Domingo* ☎ *No phone* 🎫 *Free* ⏲ *Daily 10–4:30.*

WHERE TO EAT

GOURMET STOP

San Patricio Caffé on Avenida Hidalgo 403 serves the most elaborate gourmet coffee and tea in Zacatecas. Within an airy, elegant courtyard tucked behind one of the city's most bustling streets, the café is littered with lacquered-wood furniture and delightful imported goodies.

$–$$$ ★ MEXICAN **La Cuija.** "The Gecko," with its high, vaulted ceilings, is a romantic spot. The menu boasts a number of regional specialties, such as *chiles mestizo*—an ancho chile stuffed with huitlacoche and cheese. The wine comes from the owner's Cachola Vineyards in Valle de las Arsinas. ✉ *Tacuba T–5* ☎ *492/922–8275* ▭ *MC, V.*

¢–$ CAFE **Café y Nevería Acrópolis.** This diner is trimmed with paintings and sketches given to the owner by famous people who've eaten here, including a small acrylic by Rafael Coronel. Sip a strong Turkish coffee while watching the locals flood in for breakfast. The *chilaquiles verdes* (fried tortilla strips smothered in tangy green sauce and white cheese) comes with a basket of pastries and bread. Mild *enchiladas zacatecanas* are filled with cheese, onion, and chile, and topped with cream. Traditional café fare like hamburgers, sandwiches, and fruity shakes is available for lunch. ✉ *Av. Hidalgo, in Mercado González Ortega, alongside cathedral* ☎ *492/922–1284* ▭ *MC, V.*

¢–$ MEXICAN **El Recoveco.** There are 25 steaming plates of traditional Mexican dishes to choose from at this rustic, full-buffet diner. Lunch will likely include Spanish rice, beans, *pollo en mole* (chicken in mole sauce), fresh salads, and *aguas frescas* (fruit water). Prices are reasonable: around $5.50 for all-you-can-eat lunch, $4.50 for breakfast. ✉ *Av. Torréon 513, in front of Alameda* ☎ *492/924–2013* ▭ *No credit cards.*

¢ MEXICAN **Gorditas Doña Julia.** Much loved by locals, Doña Julia makes dozens of varieties of *gorditas* day and night—it seems there's nary an hour when the place isn't full of people, in part because of the rock-bottom prices. In the wide-open entrance to the simple shop, you'll watch a woman shaping your fresh tortilla with her hands before putting it on the open fire. Many fillings are available, such as delicious regional specialties like beef tongue, rice with mole, *rajas con queso* (chile strips with cheese), and cactus. There are other locations around the city. ✉ *Hidalgo 409* ☎ *No phone* ▭ *No credit cards.*

WHERE TO STAY

$$$$ Fodor'sChoice ★ **Quinta Real.** This is one of the world's more curious hotels: it's built around Mexico's first *plaza de toros* (bullring), which is the second oldest in the Western Hemisphere. Pastel fabrics complement dark, traditional furniture in the large, bright, and plush rooms. Some of the former bull pens are part of the bar, which is a great place to unwind; candles supply the lighting, and there are cozy corners. Two levels of the spectator area make up an outdoor café. The formal restaurant ($$–$$$) offers Continental cuisine and an awesome view of the bullring and the aqueduct beyond. **Pros:** Bar in a bullring. Decent restaurant. **Cons:** Sometimes the space is overrun by events. Pricey by

Zacatecas standards. ✉*Av. Ignacio Rayón 434, to side of aqueduct* ☎*492/922–9104 through 492/922–9107* 🌐*www.quintareal.com* *49 suites* *In-room: Refrigerator. In-hotel: Restaurant, bar, public Wi-Fi, laundry service, parking (no fee)* ▭*MC, V.*

$$$ **Hotel Emporio.** The 18th-century pink-stone facade of this attractive old colonial building faces the Plaza de Armas and the cathedral. During festival season, rooms looking onto the plaza are within earshot of late-night and early-morning tamborazo music. That said, you'll get a great view of the festivities from your small balcony. **Pros:** Very friendly staff. Within walking distance of sights. **Cons:** Restaurant not the best. Some rooms are noisy. ✉*Av. Hidalgo 703* ☎*492/925–6500* 🌐*www.hotelesemporio.com* *86 rooms, 27 suites* *In-room: Wi-Fi. In-hotel: Restaurant, bar, room service, laundry service, parking (fee)* ▭*AE, MC, V.*

4

$$$ ★ **Hotel Santa Rita.** This shiny, modern newcomer, with its prime location on Avenida Hidalgo, has taken the city by storm. A marble staircase leads up to the first floor, past gleaming glass structures. Rooms are top-of-the-line, simple and sleek, with dark-wood floors, lovely bathrooms, and, in some cases, terraces that open onto terrific views of the city. The restaurant isn't as exciting. **Pros:** Beautiful hardwood floors in rooms. Lots of privacy on balconies. **Cons:** Poor restaurant. ✉*Av. Hidalgo 507* ☎*492/925–4141* *35 rooms* *In-hotel: Restaurant, bar, gym, spa, public Wi-Fi* ▭*AE, MC, V.*

$$ **Mesón de Jobito.** Once an early-19th-century apartment building, this hotel is absolutely sprawling, with courtyard upon courtyard giving way to more rooms than you imagined could exist here. There are two levels of guest rooms, all of which are done in tasteful, if somewhat bland, decor. The Mesón's placement on a little plaza set back from and above the street enhances its tranquil atmosphere. A city tour, dinner, wine, and an American breakfast for two are included in a package. **Pros:** Sprawling, village-like feel. Bright, festive colors. **Cons:** Rooms are a bit drafty. Some steep uphill walking to hotel's plaza. ✉*Jardín Juárez 143* ☎*492/924–1722* 🌐*www.mesondejobito.com* *53 suites* *In-hotel: 2 restaurants, bar, laundry service, parking (fee), public Wi-Fi, no elevator* ▭*AE, MC, V* *BP.*

$ **Hostal del Vasco.** For an authentic Zacatecano hotel, consider this clean, quiet place. The spacious brown-carpeted suites have dark antiques; some are equipped with a small kitchen (but no cookware). Sprawling plants and singing birds—Pepe the parrot leads the choir—enliven the two-story interior courtyard. **There's a breakfast room. Pros:** Kitchens in rooms. Live birds. **Cons:** Rooms are dark and have thin walls. ✉*Alameda and Velasco 1* ☎*492/922–0428* 🌐*www.hostaldelvasco.com.mx* *34 suites* *In-room: No a/c, kitchen (some). In-hotel: Laundry service, parking (no fee), public Wi-Fi* ▭*MC, V.*

NIGHTLIFE

BARS

Fodor'sChoice ★ Stroll along Avenida Hidalgo to survey the bars and dance clubs. Remember—whatever happens in **La Mina Club** (*⊠La Mina Eden ☎492/922–3002*) stays more than 1,000 feet underground. This is the world's only nightclub in a mine. DJs spin modern dance music—don't expect salsa and merengue—while revelers admire the toxic waters deep below through glass floors. It's open Thursday through Saturday nights, with a cover charge of around $9.

★ The **Quinta Real** (*⊠Av. Gonzales Ortega 424 ☎492/922–9104*) is one of Mexico's most unusual and romantic bars, a candlelit haunt literally built into the old bullring.

SIDE TRIP FROM ZACATECAS

ZONA ARQUEOLÓGICA LA QUEMADA

50 km (31 mi) southwest of Zacatecas on Hwy. 54, 3 km (2 mi) off highway.

By the time the Spaniards arrived in the 16th century, this ancient city was already a ruin. The site's original name, Chicomostoc, means "place of the seven tribes." It was previously believed that seven Native American cultures had occupied the area at different times, one community building atop the other. Thin stone slabs wedged into place make up the remaining edifices. The principal draw is a group of rose-colored ruins containing 11 massive round columns built of the same small slabs of rock. Interesting artifacts can be found in the site's impressive museum. To get here, take a bus toward Villanueva, get off at the entrance to La Quemada, and walk 3 km (2 mi). The bus ride takes about an hour. Alternatively, take a taxi or guided tour. *☎492/922–5085 $3 Site and museum daily 10–4:30.*

MORELIA

200 km (125 mi) southwest of San Miguel, 302 km (187 mi) west of Mexico City, 50 km (30 mi) northeast of Pátzcuaro.

Morelia is Michoacán state's capital—its long, wide boulevards and earth-tone colonial mansions earned it its status as a UNESCO World Heritage Site. Founded in 1541 as Valladolid (after the Spanish city), it changed its name in 1828 to honor José María Morelos, the town's most famous son. The legendary mule skinner–turned–priest led the battle for independence after its early leaders were executed in 1811.

Morelia's streets are almost always clogged with traffic, so it's best to see the city on foot—an easy task given the proximity of most sites to the zócalo. The city's well-preserved colonial buildings are today's offices, museums, shops, restaurants, and hotels. The magnificent 17th-century aqueduct, with its 253 arches, still carries water into the city. Recently, the city has become a hotbed for international students.

Finding your way around Morelia can be a a challenge, as street names change frequently, especially on either side of Avenida Madero, the city's main east–west artery. Buses run the length of Avenida Madero.

> **WILLY WONKA WISHES**
>
> Morelia has the delicious distinction of being the candy capital of Mexico. So popular are the sweets that the city has an entire market devoted to candy, called the Mercado de Dulces.

Morelia is always more fun if you start with a trip on the Tranvía Kuanari that departs every half hour Tuesday through Sunday from the Plaza de San Francisco. They offer two daytime tours and an evening tour, "Las Leyendas," to show the city lighted up at night. Tickets are $4, $5.50, and $7, respectively. The Tranvía de la Calle Real departs from the Plaza Valladolid Wednesday through Sunday. It includes a visit to the Museo del Dulce and a demonstration of how the city's delicious confections are made. Tickets are $4.50.

4

GETTING HERE & AROUND

Aeropuerto Internacional Francisco Mujica (MLM) is 24 km (15 mi) north of Morelia. Taxis from the airport into town cost around $15. Aeroméxico and Aeromar fly from Mexico City to Morelia. For bus service, Primera Plus and Herradura de Plata both run to Morelia from Mexico City (4 hours, $23) and Primera Plus goes to San Miguel via Celaya (4½ hours, $15). ETN first-class buses go from Mexico City's Terminal Poniente (also known as Observatorio) to Morelia. Bus trips from Morelia to Pátzcuaro take one hour and cost $4. The drive from Mexico City to Morelia takes about four hours. From San Miguel the trip to Morelia is around 3½ hours. From Morelia it's an easy hour drive on a superhighway to Pátzcuaro.

ESSENTIALS

Bus Contacts **ETN** (☎ *01800/800–0386 toll-free in Mexico* 🌐 *www.etn.com.mx*). **Herradura de Plata** (☎ *443/313–3381*). **Primera Plus** (☎ *01800/375–7587 toll-free in Mexico* 🌐 *www.flecha-amarilla.com*).

Medical Assistance **Ambulance–Red Cross** (☎ *443/314–5151*). **Hospital de la Cruz Roja** (✉ *Ventura Puenta 27* ☎ *443/314–5073*). **Hospital Memorial** (✉ *Paseo de la República 2111* ☎ *443/315–7594*).

Visitor & Tour Info **Secretaría Estatal de Turismo** (✉ *Palacio Clavijero, Calle Nigromante 79* ☎ *443/312–8081* 📠 *443/312–9816*).

EXPLORING

MAIN ATTRACTIONS

❷ **Catedral.** Morelia's cathedral is a majestic structure built between 1640 and 1744. It's known for its 200-foot baroque towers, which are among Mexico's tallest, and its 4,610-pipe organ. ✉ *Av. Madero between Plaza de Armas and Av. Morelos* ☎ *No phone.* 🎟 *Free*

9 **Mercado de Dulces.** If you have a sweet tooth, don't miss Morelia's candy market. All sorts of local sweets are for sale, such as *ate* (a candied fruit) and *cajeta* (heavenly caramel sauce made from goat's milk). Wooden knickknacks, cheap jewelry, and handcrafted acoustic guitars are among the nondigestible regional crafts sold from market stalls. ✉ *Av. Madero Ponente at Av. Valentín Gómez Farías* ☎ *No phone* ⏲ *Daily 10–9.*

10 **Museo de Arte Contemporáneo.** On a beautiful property a stone's throw from both the aqueduct and the Bosque Cuauhtémoc, this late-19th-century summer home is now Michoacán's principal contemporary-art museum. The permanent collection has work by famed muralist, lithographer, and illustrator Alfredo Zalce, a Pátzcuaro native. Some of Mexico's leading contemporary artists have temporary exhibitions here. Dance, cinema, theater, and music performances are held regularly in the small auditorium. ✉ *Av. Acueducto 18* ☎ *443/312–5404* 🎟 *Free* ⏲ *Tues.–Fri. 10–8, weekends 10–6.*

4 **Museo del Estado.** Across from a small plaza with statues of Bishop Vasco de Quiroga and Spanish writer Miguel de Cervantes, this history museum is in a stately mansion that was previously home to the wife of Agustín de Iturbide, Mexico's only native-born emperor. Among the 18th-century home's highlights is a complete Morelia pharmacy from 1868. On display are regional archaeological artifacts and exhibits about mining and indigenous culture. ✉ *Guillermo Prieto 176* ☎ *443/313–0629* 🎟 *Free* ⏲ *Weekdays 9–8, weekends 9–2 and 4–7.*

6 **Museo Regional Michoacano.** Formerly an 18th-century palace, the museum traces Mexico's history from its pre-Hispanic days through the Cardenista period, which ended in 1940. President Lázaro Cárdenas, a native of Michoacán, was one of Mexico's most popular leaders because he nationalized the oil industry and supported other populist reforms. On the ground floor is an art gallery, plus archaeological exhibits from Michoacán. Upstairs is an assortment of colonial objects, including furniture, weapons, and religious paintings. ✉ *Allende 305* ☎ *443/312–0407* 🎟 *$3, free Sun.* ⏲ *Tues.–Sat. 9–5, Sun. 9–4.*

NEED A BREAK?

When you've finished your tour of the Museo Regional Michoacano, walk across the street to the colonial stone *portales* (arcades). On one side of the square, the portales are lined with popular sidewalk cafés. For a sandwich, guacamole with chips, or juices, coffees, and teas, try Hotel Casino (✉ *Portal Hidalgo 229* ☎ *443/313–1328*).

11 **Parque Zoológico Benito Juárez.** This is the largest zoo in Mexico, with more than 3,800 wild animals. It also has the largest aviary in Latin America. This is a great place to take the kids, and there's an especially exciting nighttime tour. ✉ *Calzada Juárez s/n* ☎ *443/299–3522 or 443/299–3610* 🎟 *Entrance $1.60, tour $3.50* ⏲ *Daily 10–6.*

1 **Plaza de Armas.** During the War of Independence, several rebel priests were brutally murdered on this site, and the plaza, known as Plaza de los Mártires, is named after them. Today the square belies its vio-

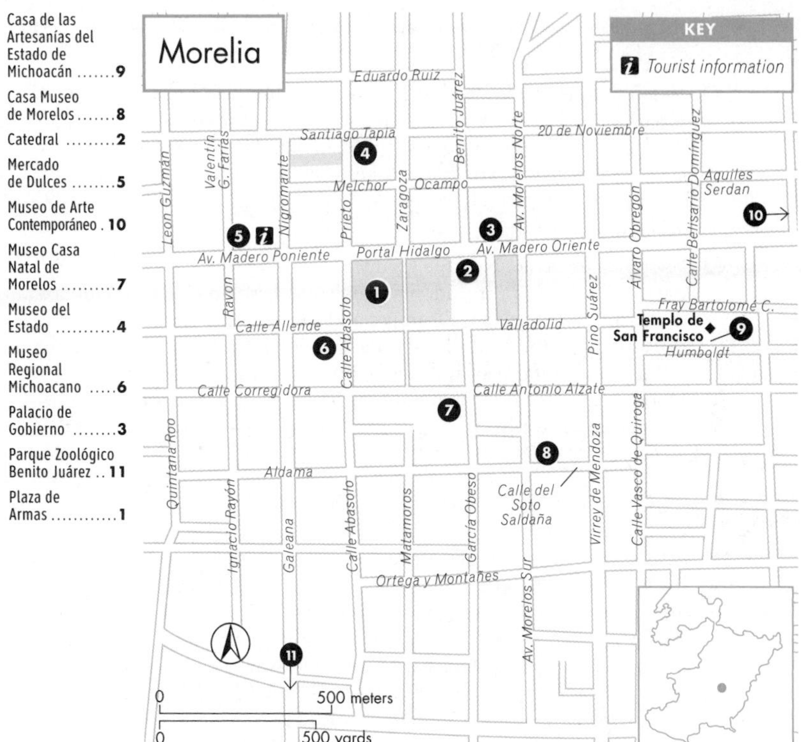

lent past: sweethearts stroll along the tree-lined walks, friends chat under the colossal silver-domed gazebo, and local painters exhibit their work on sunny days. ✉*Bounded on north by Av. Madero, on south by Allende, on west by Abasolo, and on east by cathedral.*

IF YOU HAVE TIME

9 **Casa de las Artesanías del Estado de Michoacán.** In the 16th century, Vasco de Quiroga, the bishop of Michoacán, helped the Purépecha Indians develop artistic specialties so they could be self-supporting. At this two-story museum and store you can see the work that the Purépechas still produce: copper goods from Santa Clara del Cobre, lacquerware from Uruapan, straw items and pottery from Pátzcuaro, guitars from Paracho, fanciful ceramic devil figures from Ocumicho. Some of these items are showcased on the two main floors around the courtyard of the Museo Michoacana de las Artesanías, and artists demonstrate how they are made. ✉*Fray Juan de San Miguel 129* ☎*443/312–2486* *Free* *Daily 10–6.*

8 **Casa Museo de Morelos.** What is now a two-story museum was acquired in 1801 by José María Morelos and was home to generations of the independence leader's family until 1934. Owned by the Mexican government, it exhibits family portraits, various independence movement artifacts (including a camp bed used by Ignacio Allende), and

the blindfold Morelos wore at his execution. ✉ *Av. Morelos Sur 523* ☎ *443/313–2651* 🎫 *$2, free Sun. for children* ⏲ *Daily 9–5.*

7 **Museo Casa Natal de Morelos.** José María Morelos's birthplace is now a national monument and library with mostly literature and history books (as well as two murals by Morelian Alfredo Zalce). Visit the courtyard in back where a marker and an eternal flame honor the fallen hero in a tranquil square. ✉ *Corregidora 113* ☎ *443/312–2793* 🎫 *Free* ⏲ *Daily 9–8.*

3 **Palacio de Gobierno.** Notable graduates of this former Tridentine seminary, built in 1770, include independence hero José María Morelos, social reformer Melchor Ocampo, and Mexico's first emperor, Agustín de Iturbide. In the 1960s local artist Alfredo Zalce painted the striking murals (on the stairway and second floor), which depict dramatic, often bloody scenes from Mexico's history. Zalce is the last of the great modern muralists still living. ✉ *Av. Madero 63* ☎ *443/312–2032* 🎫 *Free* ⏲ *Daily* 7AM–*10*PM.

WHERE TO EAT

$$–$$$ ★ MEXICAN

✕ **La Azotea.** This restaurant overlooking the cathedral might not have the best food in Morelia, but it has the most iconic view, with hip, white lounge cushions to boot. You can dine indoors or out—both boast the panorama. The menu is pricey and a bit stuffy, but not offensively so—its core is formed by Mexican dishes with some fusion touches. The tequila list is overpriced but excellent. ✉ *Hotel Los Juaninos, Morelos Sur 39,* ☎ *443/312–0036* 💳 *AE, D, MC, V.*

$–$$ Fodor'sChoice ★ ECLECTIC

✕ **Fonda Las Mercedes.** A dramatic, narrow entrance lined with stone pillars topped with geodes—round rocks collected from the surrounding countryside—lead into this restored colonial mansion's plant-filled stone patio and covered atrium. The bar and ceiling are covered in vines, and paintings hang everywhere else. Offerings from the eclectic menu include numerous soups plus five kinds of crêpes. The chicken a la portuguesa is stuffed with cheese, rolled in bacon, and cooked in a white wine sauce—it's quite memorable. ✉ *León Guzmán 47* ☎ *443/312–6113* 💳 *MC, V* ⏲ *No dinner Sun.*

$–$$ MEXICAN

✕ **Los Mirasoles.** This restaurant is in a beautifully restored, plant-filled 17th-century mansion. Specialties include the full range of local dishes as well as Argentine-style massive steaks. The bar resembles a cozy living room; copper trays serve as tables and the painted, domed ceilings resemble the sky. The wine list includes a selection of Mexican wines. ✉ *Av. Madero Poniente 549* ☎ *443/317–5775 or 443/317–5777* 🌐 *www.losmirasoles.com* 💳 *MC, V* ⏲ No dinner Sun.

¢–$$ MEXICAN

✕ **La Casa del Portal.** This restaurant overlooking the Plaza de Armas homes has a focus on local dishes. Covered in a red sauce, *corundas* are topped with chopped pork, cream, queso fresco, and chile poblano strips. Don't miss the *arrachera Valladolid,* a slice of skirt steak with *nopales* (sliced and steamed cactus), guacamole, and beans. ✉ *Guillermo Prieto 30* ☎ *443/313–4899* 💳 *AE, MC, V.*

¢ MEXICAN

Taquería Pioneros. Even though it's far from the city center, the tables at this positively plain taco shop are packed at lunch. People come for the delicious grilled meats, prepared Michoacán style, with salsas and mountains of fresh, hot tortillas made on-site. The *pionero* (beef, ham, bacon, onions, and cheese, all grilled) is the only option served in a half portion, which is plenty for most appetites. ⊠*Aquiles Serdán 7, at Morelos Norte* ☎*443/313–4938* ▭*No credit cards.*

TO TASTE

Morelia's restaurants serve some of Michoacán's tastiest dishes: *sopa tarasca* (a black-bean soup with cream and cheese), corn products such as *huchepos* (sweet tamales) and *corundas* (savory triangular tamales with cream and salsa), and game such as rabbit and quail.

4

WHERE TO STAY

$$$–$$$$ ★

Villa Montaña. French count Philippe de Reiset fitted this villa with all the trappings of a wealthy Mexican estate. High above Morelia in the Santa María hills, its 5 impeccably groomed acres are dotted with stone sculptures. Each unit has at least one piece of antique furniture, and most have a fireplace and private patio. The hotel's restaurant serves North American, French, and Mexican cuisine; from its huge windows you'll have a marvelous view of Morelia, especially at night. Children under eight are discouraged from dining in the restaurant. **Pros:** Supreme relaxation and creature comforts. **Cons:** Distance from city. Mediocre restaurant. ⊠*Patzimba 201* ☎*443/314–0231* ⊕*www.villamontana.com.mx* *13 rooms, 22 suites* *In-room: Safe. In-hotel: Restaurant, room service, bar, tennis court, pool, gym, laundry service, airport shuttle, parking (no fee)* ▭*AE, MC, V.*

$$$ Fodor'sChoice ★

Hotel Los Juaninos. This beautiful building is right on Morelia's main plaza. The hotel encapsulates the energy of the city while providing a respite from its traffic and noise. Rooms are spacious and tasteful, avoiding the fluff of some of the older hotels, and generally have great views. On the rooftop is a new bar-restaurant where you can dine—or just sip tequila—while enjoying one of the city's best cathedral views. **Pros:** Superb rooftop bar. Very pleasant and spacious bathrooms and showers. **Cons:** Rooms can get toasty in summer. ⊠*Morelos Sur 3958000* ☎*443/312–0036* ⊕*www.hoteljuaninos.com.mx* *30 rooms* *In-hotel: Restaurant, bar, public Wi-Fi* ▭*AE, MC, V.*

$$$ Fodor'sChoice ★

Hotel Virrey de Mendoza. Built in 1565 for a Spanish nobleman, this downtown hotel radiates the atmosphere of a bygone era. A massive stained-glass skylight casts a warm glow over an elegant lobby lounge fitted with an enormous stone fireplace and cushy black leather couches. Guest rooms have dark colonial-style furnishings, lace curtains, soaring ceilings, creaking hardwood floors, and bathrooms with porcelain tubs. **TIP→Make sure to get a room with a window facing outdoors, as some face only the lobby.** **Pros:** Possible celebrity sightings. Lobby complete with piano player on occasion. **Cons:** It's noisy sometimes and there are problems related to the age of building. ⊠*Av. Madero Ponente*

31058000 ☎443/312–0633 or 443/312–0045 🌐www.hotelvirrey.com 🛏40 rooms, 14 suites ⚓In-hotel: Restaurant, bar, room service, public Wi-Fi, laundry service, parking (no fee) 💳AE, MC, V.

$$ **Hotel Posada de la Soledad.** A private mansion built in the 17th century is now a charming hotel one block from the Plaza de Armas. In the original section, rooms surround an elegant patio with a large fountain and massive bougainvilleas. Smaller, plainer, and quieter rooms are in the newer section. Rooms on Calle Ocampo get loud traffic noise. **Pros:** Inexpensive, with a relaxing patio where you'll forget all about city noise. **Cons:** Tiny bathrooms and showers. Some rooms unacceptably small. *✉Ignacio Zaragoza 9058000 ☎443/312–1888 through 443/312–1890 🌐www.hsoledad.com 🛏49 rooms, 9 suites ⚓In-hotel: Restaurant, bar, public Wi-Fi, laundry service, parking (fee) 💳AE, MC, V.*

FESTIVALS

Each May the **International Organ Festival** is celebrated in the cathedral, giving voice to its outstanding 4,600-pipe organ. The Festival Internacional de Música, featuring baroque and chamber music, is held the last two weeks of July.

NIGHTLIFE

BARS

Don't miss the trendy **Bar de Los Juaninos** (*✉Morelos Sur 39 ☎443/312–0036*), in open air atop the Hotel de Los Juaninos, for the best view of Morelia's cathedral, and proper cocktails to complement it. The bar pushes champagne, too, and they have a great tequila selection—even if it is a bit overpriced.

Salsa is played at **LA Porfiriana** (*✉Calle Corregidora 694 ☎443/312–2663*). Tuesday through Saturday from 7 PM to 3:30 AM.

FOLK MUSIC

Morelia has many lively folk-music clubs in beautiful downtown locations. **Colibrí** (*✉Galeana 36 ☎443/312–2261*) has Latin American folk music every night from 10 PM to 2 AM.

El Rincon de los Sentidos (*✉Av. Madero 548 ☎443/312–2903*) is one of the most-loved places in town for predinner drinks in comfy chairs and is popular with students who like trova music (about love and protest). There are pretty, hanging paper lamps upstairs, and live music downstairs Wednesday through Sunday. Just stay away from hot-tequila-and-mint cocktails. It's open daily from 8 PM to midnight.

SIDE TRIP FROM MORELIA

SANTUARIO DE MARIPOSAS EL ROSARIO

Approximately 115 km (71 mi) east of Morelia.

Fodor'sChoice ★ One hundred million monarch butterflies migrate annually from the United States and Canada to winter in the easternmost part of Michoacán, near Mexico state's border. A visit to the Santuario de Mariposas el Rosario between early November and early March is an awesome sensory experience. The sanctuary's pine forest is so caked with orange-and-black butterflies it looks like it's on fire. Listen closely and you'll hear the rustle of millions of wings beating. **TIP→The hike to the groves is a steep climb, and the high altitude (10,400 feet) will require that you take it slowly.**

This day trip takes about 10 hours, but it's absolutely worth the effort. If you choose not to drive the rough roads, catch a guided tour in Morelia. ✉*Hwy. 15 east to Zitácuaro, then take the marked but unnumbered road north to Angangueo, and on to sanctuary entrance* ☎*No phone* *$3* *Daily 10–5.*

PÁTZCUARO

50 km (30 mi) southwest of Morelia.

Founded in the 16th century on the shores of the tranquil Lake Pátzcuaro, this town remained largely undisturbed for several centuries until it was "discovered" by hordes of international tourists. Nowadays the government has invested in many improvements—streets and parks have been refurbished, and construction is underway for a new artisans' market on the Avenida de Las Américas. Some of the town's historic homes have become first-class hotels, and restaurants serve meals up to discerning tourists' standards.

The town's founder was Bishop Vasco de Quiroga, who implemented a plan whereby each village was assigned a different skill, and to this day their descendants have continued this tradition: artisans in Paracho produce excellent guitars; those in Tzintzuntzán are known for their green-glazed pottery; hand-beaten copper plates and vases come from Santa Clara; lacquerware from Quiroga; fanciful *catrinas* (doll-like figures with skeleton faces) from Capula; and the finest *rebozos* (shawls) are handwoven in Nurío.

Many of Pátzcuaro's principal sights are near the Plaza Vasco de Quiroga and Plaza Bocanegra in the center of town. You can zip through Pátzcuaro's historic center, but Lake Pátzcuaro, which you must surely visit, is a 10-minute cab ride from the center of town. Note that the archaeological areas are closed on Monday. If you want to visit the surrounding villages you can hire taxis. Trails near Pátzcuaro wind up to nearby hilltops for great views across town and the countryside.

TIP→On November 1 the town is inundated with tourists en route to Janítzio, an island in Lake Pátzcuaro,

GO WITH A GUIDE

Several worthy operators conduct tours of Morelia and the butterfly sanctuary. Contact Ayangupani through David Saucedo Ortega at the Villa Montaña front desk.

INFORMATION

Explora Viajes (✉*Av. Madero Oriente 493B* ☎*443/312-7766*). **Kuanari Bus Tours** (☎*443/317-5801*). **Morelia Operadores de Viajes** (✉*Isidro Huarte 481* ☎*443/312-8723 or 443/312-8747*).

where one of Mexico's most elaborate Day of the Dead graveyard ceremonies takes place. Many younger people take the journey to Tzintzuntzán, where Day of the Dead festivities are focused primarily on imbibing.

GETTING HERE & AROUND

Primera Plus has first-class buses to Pátzcuaro from Mexico City (five hours, $24) and Morelia (one hour, $4). From Morelia the excellent, free superhighway to Pátzcuaro takes just over an hour. From Mexico City, the Mexico City–Guadalajara tollway cuts driving time to Pátzcuaro to 4½ or 5 hours. There are no rental outlets in Pátzcuaro.

ESSENTIALS

Bus Contacts **Primera Plus** (☎ *415/152-0084, 01800/849-9001 toll-free in Mexico* 🌐 *www.flecha-amarilla.com.mx*).

Medical Assistance **Hospital Civil** (✉ *Romero 10* ☎ *434/342-0285*). **Police** (☎ *434/342-0004*).

Visitor & Tour Info **Delegación de Turismo** (✉ *Ahumada 9,* ☎📠 *434/342-1214*) **Dirección de Orientación y Fomento al Turismo** (✉ *Portal Hidalgo 1, on Plaza de Quiroga* ☎ *434/344-0289* 📠 *434/342-0967*).

EXPLORING

MAIN ATTRACTIONS

3 **La Basílica de Nuestra Señora de la Salud.** Vasco de Quiroga began this church in 1554, and throughout the centuries others—undaunted by earthquakes and fires—took up the cause and eventually completed it in honor of the Virgin of Health. Near the main altar is a statue of the Virgin made of derivatives of cornstalks and orchids. Several masses are held daily; the earliest begins shortly after dawn. Out front, Purépecha women sell hot tortillas, herbal mixtures for teas, and religious objects. Lake Pátzcuaro is visible in the distance. ✉ *Enseñanza Arciga, near Benigno Serrato* ☎ *434/342-0055.*

8 **Lake Pátzcuaro.** The tranquil shores of Lake Pátzcuaro are a 10-minute cab ride from downtown. There are two different *muelles* (docks) from which you can catch a boat to Janítzio, but you should head to the central *muelle,* which offers far more service. Before or after your trip, stop at one of the lakeside restaurants, which serve fresh *pescado blanco* (white fish) and other local catches. Wooden launches with room for 25 people (but that rarely take that many) depart for Janítzio and the other islands daily 9–6. Purchase round-trip tickets for $3.50 at a dockside office (prices are controlled by the tourist department). If they insist that you need to purchase a private tour in order to visit the other islands, such as Yunuen and La Pacanda, don't believe it: for only about $8 per person, the office is required to sell you a ticket to Janítzio and another island. This rate is not advertised, and be warned that even upon purchasing the ticket, once in Janítzio, you may still have to persuade a begrudging captain to take you.

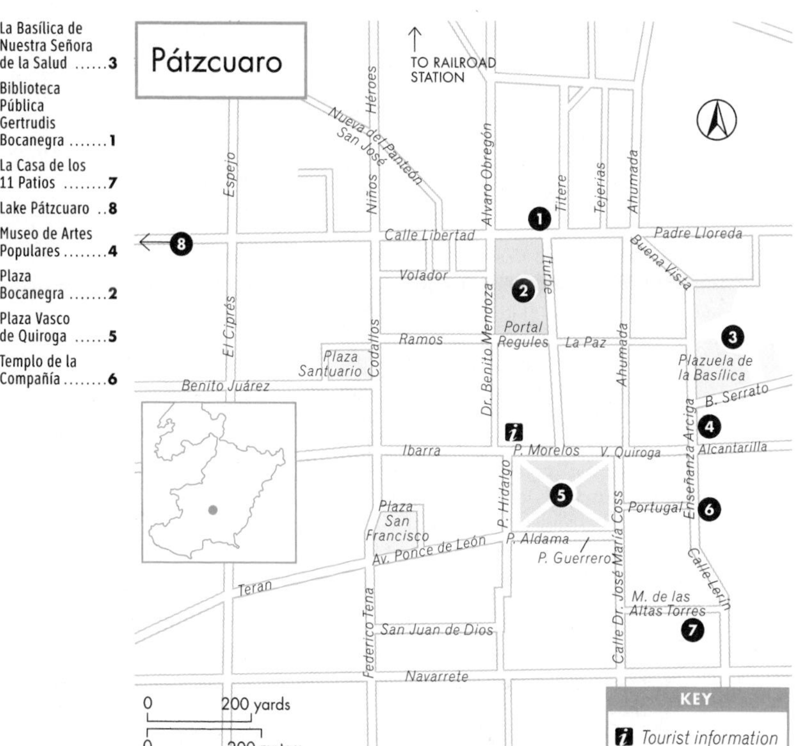

It is absolutely worthwhile to visit La Pacanda—far more worthwhile, in fact, than Janítzio, the largest of Lake Pátzcuaro's five islands. La Pacanda is a quiet and peaceful island: beautiful flowers abound, cows laze about, and the few inhabitants of the island go about their daily activities—which do not include trying to sell you garish souvenirs. La Pacanda might be even more idyllic than tiny Yunuen, but you won't want to stay more than an hour or so. At Yunuen, on the other hand—which also provides a clear picture of island life—you can arrange an overnight stay in simple yet clean visitor cabins.

The ride to Janítzio takes about 30 minutes and is particularly beautiful in late afternoon. Once you're out on the lake, fishermen with butterfly nets may approach your boat in a sad choreographed fishing routine, after which you're expected to give them money.

2 **Plaza Bocanegra.** The smaller of the city's two squares (it's also called Plaza Chica), this is Pátzcuaro's commercial center. Bootblacks, push-cart vendors, and bus and taxi stands are all in the plaza, which is embellished by a statue of the local heroine, Gertrudis Bocanegra. Nearby, a large outdoor mercado sprawls along Libertad and its side streets. At times the road is so crowded with people and their wares—fruit, vegetables, beans, rice, herbs, and other necessities of daily life—that it's difficult to walk. If you press on for about a block,

you'll see an indoor market to your left, filled with more produce; large, hanging slabs of meat; hot food; cheap trinkets; and locally made wool garments. ✉ *Bounded by Av. Libertad on north, Portal Regules on south, Benito Mendoza on west, and Iturbe on east.*

5 Fodor's Choice ★ **Plaza Vasco de Quiroga.** A tranquil courtyard girded by towering, century-old ash and pine trees and 16th-century mansions (since converted into hotels and shops), the larger of the two downtown plazas commemorates the bishop who restored dignity to the Purépecha people. During the Spanish conquest, Nuño de Guzmán, a lieutenant in Hernán Cortés's army, committed atrocities against the local population in his efforts to conquer western Mexico. He was eventually arrested by the Spanish authorities, and in 1537 Vasco de Quiroga was appointed bishop of Michoacán. To regain the trust of the indigenous people, he established model villages in the area and promoted the development of *artesanía* (crafts) commerce among the Purépecha. Quiroga died in 1565 and his remains were consecrated in the Basílica de Nuestra Señora de la Salud. ✉ *Bounded by Quiroga, Av. Ponce de León, Portal Hidalgo, and Dr. José María Coss.*

GO WITH A GUIDE

Guide **Francisco Castilleja** knows a lot about pre-Hispanic philosophy, history, archaeology, and medicinal herbs. He speaks fluent English, German, French, and Spanish. Guide and anthropologist **Miguel Angel Nuñez** specializes in off-the-beaten-path visits to indigenous communities as well as local sights. He speaks Spanish, English, and German.

Francisco Castilleja (✉ *Centro Eronga, Profr. Urueta 105* ☎ *434/344-0167*). **Miguel Angel Nuñez** (☎ *434/344-0108*).

6 **Templo de la Compañía.** Michoacán's first cathedral was begun in 1540 by order of Vasco de Quiroga and completed in 1546. When the state capital was moved to Morelia some 20 years later, the church was taken over by the Jesuits. It remains much as it was in the 16th century. Moss has grown over the crumbling stone steps outside; the dank interior is planked with thick wood floors and lined with bare wood benches. ✉ *Lerín s/n, east end of Portugal* ☎ *434/342-3083.*

IF YOU HAVE TIME

1 **Biblioteca Pública Gertrudis Bocanegra.** Juan O'Gorman painted a vast mural depicting the history of the region and of the Purépecha people in the back of this library in 1942. At the bottom right is Gertrudis Bocanegra, a local heroine who was shot in 1814 for refusing to divulge the revolutionaries' secrets to the Spaniards. The Biblioteca is on a lively plaza. ✉ *North side of Plaza Bocanegra* ☎ *434/342-5441* ⏲ *Daily 9–6:30.*

7 ★ **La Casa de los 11 Patios.** A maze of shops featuring Purépecha handiwork is housed in this former 18th-century convent. As you meander through the shops and courtyards, you'll encounter weavers producing large bolts of cloth, artists working with black lacquerware trimmed with gold, and seamstresses embroidering blouses. ✉ *Madrigal de las Altas Torres s/n* ⏲ *Daily 10–2 and 4–8; some shops close Mon.*

4 **Museo de Artes Populares.** The 16th-century home of the Colegio de San Nicolás Obispo now displays colonial and contemporary crafts, such as ceramics, masks, lacquerware, paintings, and ex-votos in its many rooms. Behind this building is a *troje* (traditional Purépecha wooden house) braced atop a stone platform. ✉*Enseñanza Arciga* ☎*434/342–1029* *About $3* ⊙*Tues.–Sun. 9–6.*

NEED A BREAK?

Before heading to Lake Pátzcuaro, sit in Plaza Vasco de Quiroga and savor the rich Michoacán ice cream available under the portals on the west side of the plaza. Or sip a Doña Paca cappuccino spiked with *rompope* (egg liqueur) at the café in front of Mansión Iturbe.

4

WHERE TO EAT

$–$$ ★ CONTEMPORARY ✕**Cha Cha Cha.** Blackberry tamales are just one of the specialties of this immensely popular, gringo-friendly restaurant, owned partly by Californian Rick Davis, which is locally famous for growing its own leafy greens in a garden out back. You can dine on one of the two beautiful patios, though the interior is comfortable, too (a perk is the open kitchen). For something different, try the *lomo relleno de nuez en salsa de piña y mango* (stuffed beef tenderloin with nuts in a pineapple-and-mango salsa). ✉*Buena Vista 7* ☎*434/342–1627* ⊕*www.restaurantchachacha.com* ▭*MC, V* ⊙*Closed Wed.*

$–$$ CONTEMPORARY ✕**Priscilla's.** Though the prices would suggest a more humble dining experience, this is a first-class restaurant with excellent service in La Mansión de los Sueños. The decor is traditional, with handcrafted wood furnishings made by local artisans. The international menu features numerous fish and pasta dishes. Not to be missed is the cheesecake that melts in your mouth—Priscilla swears it is fat and sugar free! ✉*Ibarra 15* ☎*434/342–5708* ▭*AE, MC, V.*

¢–$$ MEXICAN ✕**Doña Paca.** At this terrific family-run restaurant you'll find some of the best examples of local cuisine. Look for the fish specials and the triangular tamale-like corundas with cream sauce, which are also great for breakfast. There are also several good coffee concoctions. ✉*Hotel Mansión Iturbe, Portal Morelos 59* ☎*434/342–0368* ▭*AE, MC, V.*

$ ★ MEXICAN ✕**El Patio.** It's possible to duck into this low-key restaurant at midday to grab a strong cappuccino or glass of Mexican wine. Try the *pechuga de pollo* (chicken breast) stuffed with *huitlacoche* (corn fungus). For a late-afternoon snack go for a plate of quesadillas with a side

FOOD FOR THOUGHT

Pátzcuaro restaurants specialize in seafood, such as whitefish, *trucha* (trout), and *charales* and *boquerones* (two small, locally caught fish served as appetizers). Many focus on local Purépecha dishes, such as sopa tarasca, a delicious black bean soup. Since lunch is the big meal of the day, many dining establishments are shuttered by 9. For the city's best tortas, tacos, tamales, and carnitas, head straight to the market (called the Mercado, on Calle Libertad, just west of the Biblioteca) and peruse its stalls. Grab one of the simple plaza tables, take in the nighttime bustle, and dig in.

Continued on page 224

The Day of the Dead is celebrated with much fanfare throughout Mexico, but the island of Janítzio in Lake Pátzcuaro has been singled out for its elaborate ceremonies. Although onlookers outnumber mourners, and all-night partying has replaced quiet remembrance, the rituals—both playful and poignant—still shine through. The festivities start on November 1st and end the next day, but half the fun of this holiday is being here for the events leading up to it.

WAKING THE DEAD IN PÁTZCUARO

Well before the last day of October, Pátzcuaro's main plaza is jam-packed with tents selling the candy skulls and other materials needed to decorate graves. There are also concerts and exhibitions in town prior to November 1.

The area's large indigenous population is to thank for making these Day of the Dead celebrations so elaborate and important. Day of the Dead originated with the Tarascan (or P'urhépecha as they're known today) Indians, and the group still has many descendants in the area. The Tarasco people believed that the dead could pay a visit to their loved ones once a year. They also believe that Curicaueri, the fire god, and his brothers founded the towns along the lake and thus they are descended from these ancestor gods.

Sugar skulls to celebrate the Day of the Dead.

THE CEREMONY November 1–November 2

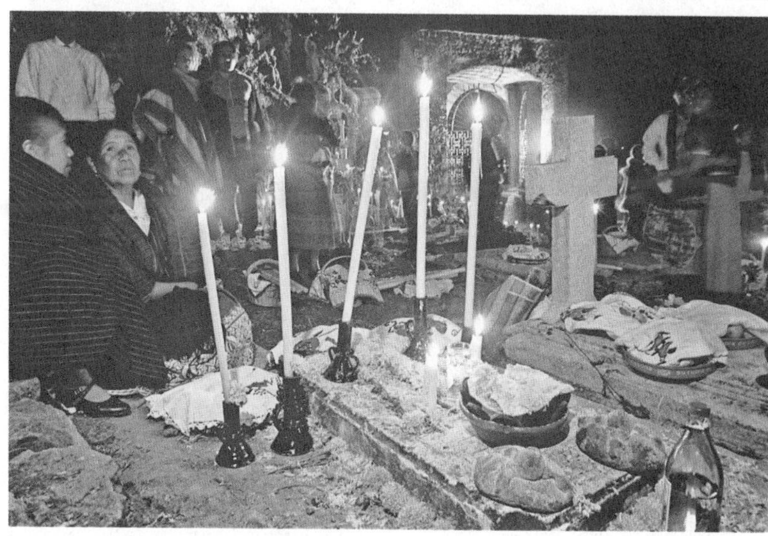
Day of the Dead celebration, Janítzio Island.

Along with decorating the graves, many families display *ofrendas* (offerings) in their homes and businesses. By **October 31st,** nearly all the houses and shops in Pátzcuaro and Janítizio have been decorated in some way. Ofrendas can include candy skulls, papier-mâché skeletons, candles, food and liquor, cigarettes, toys (for deceased children), and *cempasúchil* (yellow marigolds).

On the 31st the docks are packed with families going to and from the island, bringing supplies and decorations to gravesites or picking up items in Pátzcuaro to complete their ofrendas.

The celebration officially gets started at the crack of dawn on November 1st. P'urhépecha Indians have a ceremonial duck hunt; the ducks that are caught are cooked and incorporated into cemetery ofrendas later that night.

From 5 AM to 9 AM, the deceased children are honored in the ceremony of the *angelitos* (little angels). At 5 the church bells start ringing as a call for both the spirits of the children and the relatives honoring them. Mass begins in Janítzio's small chapel at 6. When mass is done, the women and children of the families go to the graveyard, where they clean the tombstones (sometimes no more than a wooden cross) and place their ofrendas around the graves. More people filter into the cemetery. If a family is participating in

Handmade skeletons—a common symbol.

(above) Colorful and haunting figurines.
(left) Townspeople tending to graves.

its first Day of the Dead ceremony, they might bring a band with them as they make their procession from house to graveyard. Prayers, chanting, music, and incense fill the air until the ceremony ends around 9 AM.

The ceremony for deceased adults won't take place until midnight, so the rest of the day is spent preparing for it and setting up a stage for the ceremonial dances that will precede the nighttime festivities.

There are two main dances performed before the **midnight vigil** begins. The *Danza de los Viejitos* (Dance of the Little Old Men), is performed by children dressed up as old peasant men. The children attempt to appear bent over with age as they complete this intricate dance. The *Pescado Blanco* (White Fish) dance is an act of homage to the lake, as fishing is this village's most important source of income.

At midnight, processions head back into the graveyard to honor the adults who have passed away. The church bells ring all night long, while families sit by the graves, some praying and chanting, some just sitting silently. Candles and incense are lit. At dawn the ceremony is concluded with a reading from the Bible, after which families collect their offerings and head home.

THE RITUALS OF DEATH

■ Townspeople will pitch in to decorate the graves of people with no surviving relatives.

■ Incense is burned because the aroma is thought to help guide the spirits to the ofrendas.

■ Ofrendas will often include the deceased's favorite foods, along with traditional foods, the most common of which are *calabaza en tacha,* a sweet pumpkin dessert; some kind of tamal; and *pan de muerto,* a sweet bread that's actually European in origin (though the Spanish never shaped their altar breads into skulls, teardrops, crosses, human figures, and animals).

■ Families often construct wooden arches decorated with cempasúchil as part of their cemetery ofrendas. For the first three years after a person's death, this arch is made by the person's godparents, who present it to the parents of the deceased on November 1.

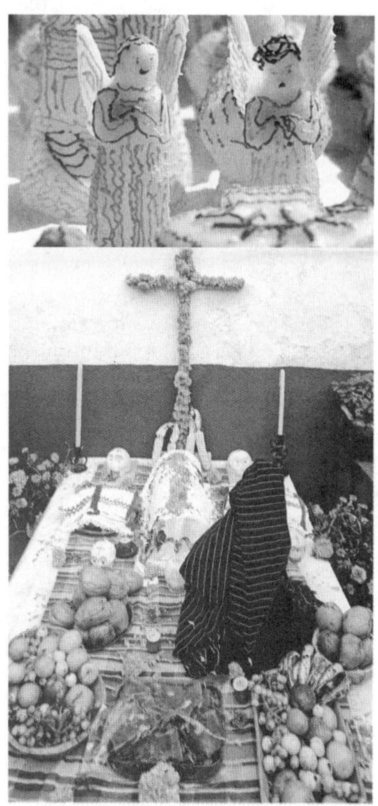

(top) Decorated sugar figurines.
(above) A hearty offering.
(left) Laughing cartoon skeletons.

TIPS

The first rule of attending Day of the Dead ceremonies is to book way in advance. Some hotels are booked solid up to a year early, but booking six months ahead should still leave you with some choices.

If you don't like crowds (or a certain level of commercialism), don't bother with Janítzio. Instead, inquire at the tourist office about other towns in the area that have similar festivities. Note that the lakeside village of Tzintzuntzan will be nearly as crowded as Janítzio, and with a livelier crowd.

order of guacamole or the *sopa tarasca* (black bean soup). ☒*Plaza Vasco de Quiroga 19* ☎*434/342–0484* ▭*MC, V.*

$ ECLECTIC ✕**El Primer Piso.** On warm nights you can watch activities in the Plaza Vasco de Quiroga from a balcony table at this second-floor restaurant. The brightly colored interior is warm and inviting, and the eclectic menu provides a break from typical Pátzcuaro fare: try the pear salad with goat cheese, walnuts, and watercress, or the white-chocolate mousse with blackberries and melon cream. ☒*Plaza Vasco de Quiroga 29* ☎*434/342–0122* ▭ *V* ⊙*Closed Tues.*

$ ★ ARGENTINE ✕**El Viejo Gaucho.** Join the crowd for a festive night of live music from North, Central, and South America. Try the *churrasco Argentino* (seasoned steak) and don't forget to top it with *chimichurri* (an Argentine sauce made with fresh herbs and olive oil). Seasoned chicken on the grill is tasty, too. Most main courses are pseudo-Argentinian, but there are also pizza, hamburgers, and french fries. Live music makes it all taste better. ☒*Iturbe 10* ☎*434/342–0368* ▭*AE, MC, V* ⊙*Closed Sun. No lunch.*

WHERE TO STAY

$$$–$$$$ Fodor'sChoice ★ **La Mansión de los Sueños.** Priscilla Ann Madsen's dream of owning a hotel in Pátzcuaro came true when she found this 17th-century mansion. Now completely restored, each of the rooms and suites is decorated with original hand-painted murals and a mixture of traditional and modern furnishings; fireplaces make some of them extra cozy. One room even has its own patio and Jacuzzi. There are three interior patios and surrounding gardens. **Pros:** Fireplaces in some rooms. Incredibly comfortable beds. **Cons:** Rooms can get very dark at night. ☒*Ibarra 15, 61600* ☎*434/342–5708* ⊕*www.prismas.com.mx* *10 suites, 2 master suites* *In-hotel: 2 restaurants, room service, spa, airport shuttle, public Wi-Fi, parking (fee), no elevator* ▭*AE, MC, V.*

$$–$$$ **Hotel Posada La Basílica.** On some mornings strains from Mass at the neighboring Basílica de Nuestra Señora de la Salud filter softly into this inn. The 17th-century building has comfortable, individually decorated rooms, some with fireplaces. Thick wood shutters cover floor-to-ceiling windows, large wooden beams grace the ceilings, and walls are trimmed in hand-painted colonial designs. **Pros:** Fireplaces in rooms. Wonderful beds. Beautiful view. **Cons:** Staff speaks minimal English. Some noise problems. ☒*Enseñanza Arciga 661600* ☎*434/342–1108* ⊕*www.posadalabasilica.com* *12 rooms* *In-room: No a/c. In-hotel: Restaurant, parking (no fee)* ▭*AE, MC, V.*

$$ Fodor'sChoice ★ **La Casa Encantada.** The charming Casa Encantada is a beautiful hotel built into a 17th-century mansion just off Pátzcuaro's main plaza. The enormous suites, which surround a courtyard with a garden and fountain, are some of the city's biggest. Though rented by the night, they're more like apartments than hotel rooms; most have kitchens and/or dining areas. Note that children under the age of 12 are discouraged from staying at the hotel. **Pros:** Incredibly cheery rooms. Beautiful grounds. **Cons:** Not ideal for families. Not all staff proficient in English. ☒*Dr. Coss 1561600* ☎*434/342–3492* ⊕*www.lacasaencantada.com* *10*

suites *In-room: No a/c. In-hotel: Public Wi-Fi, laundry service, airport shuttle* *No credit cards* *BP.*

$$ ★ **Hacienda Mariposas.** A friendly, bilingual staff and terrific restaurant are just some of the amenities at this getaway just outside of Pátzcuaro; the place is surrounded by tens of acres of forest. They also offer horseback-riding trips, along with other eco-adventures and even a food tour of the Purépecha region. Guest rooms have fireplaces (as well as central heating) and beds topped with down comforters, plus CD players. Transportation to and from Pátzcuaro is included. **Pros:** Comfortable beds. Good for families with young children. **Cons:** Far from city center. Very few luxury amenities. *Santa Clara del Cobre Hwy., Km 3* *443/333–0762 or 434/342–4728* *www.haciendamariposas.com* *12 rooms* *In-room: No TV. In-hotel: Restaurant, spa* *AE, MC, V* *BP.*

$$ ★ **Mansión Iturbe.** Stone archways ring plant-filled courtyards in this 17th-century mansion. Rooms, with large wood-and-glass doors, are partially carpeted. Bicycles are lent to guests for a few hours per stay; every fourth night is free, and breakfast is included—except during high season. The owners are an excellent source of information regarding Pátzcuaro and the surrounding areas. Be sure to check out the restaurant, Doña Paca, and its tasty coffee drinks. **Pros:** Friendly staff. Wonderful coffee bar. **Cons:** Rooms a bit drab. Can get cold. *Portal Morelos 5961600* *434/342–0368* *www.mansioniturbe.com* *12 rooms* *In-room: Safe. In-hotel: 3 restaurants, bicycles, no-smoking rooms, parking (free), laundry service, public Wi-Fi* *AE, MC, V* *BP.*

$–$$ ★ **Hostal Ixhi Xesi Xandesti.** This rustic lodge is up a winding road about 10 minutes outside of Pátzcuaro, but it's worth the bumpy ride for the stunning views of the lake (from atop El Estribo, rising far above the city) and Janítzio island, especially from the dining room's giant glass windows. There's also a small patio strung with hammocks. Some rooms have private terraces and kitchens; all rooms vary in size. This is a great value; reserve well in advance, as yoga groups sometimes take over the entire estate. **Pros:** Breathtaking views of lake. Beautiful communal dining room. **Cons:** Away from city, up a steep road. Can fill up quite easily. *Lomas del Calvario; head out to periférico and follow signs to Estribo* *434/342–6807* *4 rooms, 4 suites* *In-room: No a/c* *No credit cards.*

NIGHTLIFE

FOLK DANCE

The **Danza de los Viejitos** *(Dance of the Old Men)* is a widely known regional dance performed during Saturday dinner at **Hotel Posada de Don Vasco** (*Av. Las Americas 450* *434/342–0227*) for about $15 (includes dinner). It's also performed Saturday night at 8:30 PM at Los Escudos, on Plaza Vasco de Quiroga. On weekends dancers perform for tips in the plaza and outside the boarding area to Janítzio.

4

LIVE MUSIC

For a night of live music, head to **El Viejo Gaucho** (✉*Portal Morelos 59* ☎*434/342–0368)*to hear some covers of American pop tunes as well as Mexican folk songs.

SHOPPING

Pátzcuaro has some of Mexico's finest folk-art shopping. There are good deals at the stalls outside the Basílica and the marketplace off Plaza Bocanegra.

Artesanías Mojiganga (✉*Plaza Vasco de Quiroga 29-2* ☎*434/342–4695*), an intimate group of stores, offers a variety of ceramics, clothing, and folk art.

Since 1898 the family-run **Chocolate Casero Joaquinita** (✉*Enseñanza Arciga 38* ☎*434/342–4514*) has been concocting delectable homemade cinnamon-spiced hot-chocolate tablets.

Don't miss the stands in front of the Basílica and at the daily mercado west of Plaza Chica for inexpensive local crafts. **Mantas Tipicas** (✉*Dr. José María Coss 5* ☎*434/342–1324*) sells hand-loomed tablecloths, place mats, and curtain and cushion fabric.

★ Visit the doorway of Jesús García Zavala at **Plateria García** (✉*Enseñanza Arciga 28* ☎*434/342–2036*) for hand-worked silver Purépecha jewelry in the pre-Columbian tradition.

Santa Teresa Velas y Cirios (✉*Portugal 1* ☎*434/342–4997*) sells handmade candles.

SIDE TRIPS FROM PÁTZCUARO

TZINTZUNTZAN

17 km (10½ mi) northeast of Pátzcuaro.

When the Spanish arrived to colonize the region in the 16th century, some 40,000 Purépecha lived in this lakeshore village, which they called "place of the hummingbirds." The ruins of the pyramid-shape temples, or *yacatas,* found in the ancient capital of the Purépecha kingdom, still stand and are open to the public for $2. There are also vestiges of a 16th-century Franciscan monastery where Spanish friars attempted to convert the Indians to Christianity. The village is still known for the straw and ceramic crafts made by the Purépecha Indians and sold in the market on the main street. The bus marked quiroga takes a half hour to get from Pátzcuaro's Central Camionera to Tzintzuntzan.

SANTA CLARA DEL COBRE

20 km (12½ mi) south of Pátzcuaro.

Even before the conquest, Santa Clara del Cobre was already a center for copper arts. Now the local copper mines are empty, but artisans still make gorgeous vessels, plates, napkin rings, and jewelry using the traditional method of hand-pounding each piece of metal. The bus to Santa Clara del Cobre from Pátzcuaro's Central Camionera takes 40 minutes.

For an introduction to copper work, visit the **Museo del Cobre** before exploring the 50-some little shops and factories in town. ✉ *Calles Morelos and Pino Suárez, near plaza* 50¢ ⏲Tues.–Sun. 10–3 and 5–7.

The friendly owners of **Arte y Cobre** (✉*Pino Suárez 53* ☎*No phone*) speak English.

URUAPAN

64 km (40 mi) west of Pátzcuaro.

The subtropical town of Uruapan is distinctly different from Pátzcuaro: some 2,000 feet lower, although still at an elevation of 5,300 feet, it's a populous commercial center with a warm climate and lush vegetation in its river valley. The town's name is derived from the Purépecha word *urupan,* meaning "where the flowers bloom." ■TIP→**Uruapan celebrates Palm Sunday with a lively procession through the streets, brass bands, and a spectacular bargain-filled crafts market in the central plaza—one of the best in Mexico.**

GETTING HERE & AROUND

You can get to Uruapan from Pátzcuaro by car or bus. Highway 14 and the toll road are the most direct routes between the two cities. There's frequent bus service on the Flecha Amarilla and other major lines; travel time is about 70 minutes. ■TIP→**The high-profile 2006 drug-cartel execution that ended with decapitated heads being rolled into a popular Uruapan nightclub got a lot of press; while tourists won't likely encounter any drug violence, you'll feel the economic hit that the city has taken as a result of such activity.**

EXPLORING

The **Mercado de Antojitos,** an immense, sprawling market, begins in back of the Museo Regional de Arte Popular and extends farther north on Constitución. Along the road, Purépecha Indians sell large mounds of produce, fresh fish, beans, homemade cheese, and cheap manufactured goods. If you travel south along Constitución, you'll come to a courtyard where vendors sell hot food.

The **Museo Regional de Arte Popular,** opposite the north side of Uruapan's Plaza Principal, was a 16th-century hospital before its conversion. It exhibits crafts from the state of Michoacán, including an excellent display of lacquerware made in Uruapan. ☎*452/524–3434* *Free* ⏲*Tues.–Sun. 9:30–1:30 and 3:30–6.*

Parque Nacional Eduardo Ruiz (about six long blocks from the Plaza Principal off Independencia) is an urban park with paved paths that meander through verdant tropical acreage past abundant waterfalls, fountains, and springs to the source of the Río Cupatitzio. There's also a trout farm and a popular playground.

Eleven kilometers (7 mi) south along the Río Cupatitzio is the magnificent waterfall at **Tzaráracua.** The river plunges 150 feet off a sheer rock cliff into a riverbed, often creating a rainbow. Buses marked tzaráracua leave sporadically from the Plaza Principal in Uruapan. You can also take a taxi for about $3, or drive there via Avenida Lázaro Cárdenas.

About 32 km (20 mi) north of Uruapan lies the dormant **Paricutín volcano.** Its initial burst of lava and ashes wiped out the nearby village of San Juan Parangaricútiro in 1943 and only the spire of its church is visible, encased in tons of lava rock. Today travelers can visit this buried site by hiring mountain ponies and a Purépecha guide in the town of Angahuan. You can also hike over surreal gray sands and volcanic rock to the still-steaming crater. The trail isn't clearly marked, so get a guide (plenty of local children are ready to volunteer at the park entrance for a reasonable price). Get an early start and carry lots of water because the round-trip takes all day. Also wear sturdy shoes or hiking boots and be careful on the treacherous volcanic rock. To reach Angahuan, take Los Reyes bus from Uruapan's Central Camionera or go by car via the Uruapan-Carapan highway.

Guadalajara

Palacio de Gobierno, Guadalajara

WORD OF MOUTH

"Guadalajara is very pedestrian-friendly with lots of museums, theaters, and wonderful cafes and restaurants. Not too far from downtown you can go shopping to one of the largest flea markets in the continent."

–juribe31

WELCOME TO GUADALAJARA

TOP REASONS TO GO

★ **The chance to see murals by Orozco:** Titanic works by this distinguished artist adorn several buildings.

★ **Shopping for crafts at the source:** Master craftsmen practice their art in the suburbs of Tonalá and Tlaquepaque.

★ **Experiencing the most Mexican of Mexican traditions:** Jalisco State is the land of tequila, mariachi, and *jarabe tapatío* (the hat dance).

★ **Varied excursions:** Close to the city are Mexico's largest lake and the town of Tequila, the birthplace of the country's famous firewater.

★ **Visiting the site of pre-Hispanic ruins:** Los Guachimontones, in the foothills of Tequila Volcano, is redefining western Mexico's archaeological past.

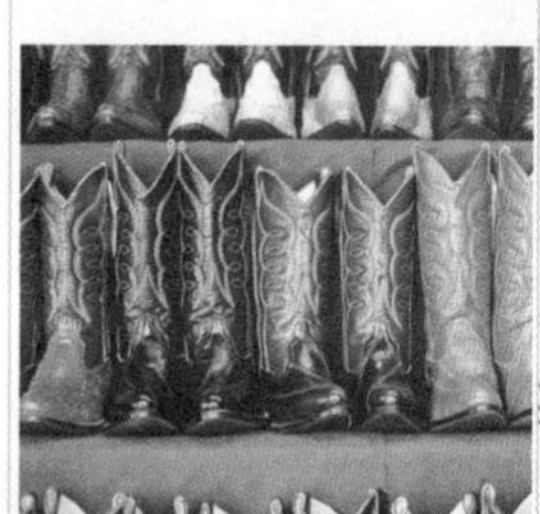

1 Zapopan. Zapopan is a sprawling municipality enveloping Guadalajara's west side. It's a modern suburb of tony shopping malls and residential areas, which sometimes stretches into impoverished fringe neighborhoods. It's also home to Jalisco's most revered religious icon, the four-century-old Virgin of Zapopan.

2 Tonalá. A formerly independent village swallowed by the city, Tonalá retains a small-town aura in its center and is home to some of Mexico's most celebrated claysmiths, many of whom open their workshops to visitors.

3 Tlaquepaque. The metropolitan area's tourist and handicraft magnet is Tlaquepaque, a district of shops, restaurants and bed-and-breakfasts on the southeast side of Guadalajara's sprawl.

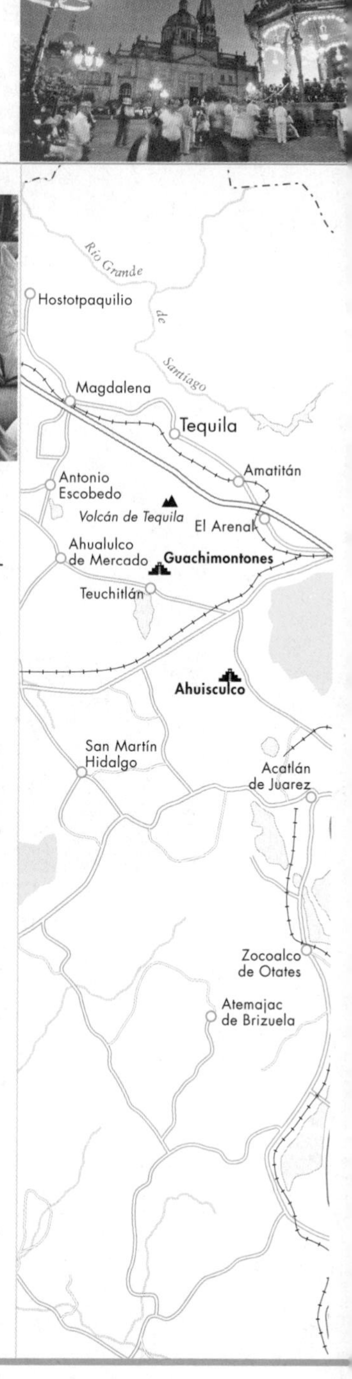

GETTING ORIENTED

Guadalajara rests on a mile-high plain of the Sierra Madre del Occidente, surrounded on three sides by rugged hills and on the fourth by the spectacular Barranca de Oblatos (Oblatos Canyon). Mexico's second-largest city has a population of 4 million and is the capital of the western state of Jalisco. There's a mishmash of terrain here: pine-forest mountain ranges, semideserts, and coastal mangrove swamps.

GUADALAJARA PLANNER

A Hit-and-Run City?

Guadalajara's hotel operators and tourism officials regularly lament the fact that foreign tourists average just two days in their city. Rightly, they point out that visitors can spend at least a week in and around the City of Roses. Unless you've got afterburners on your shoes, it will take at least three days to do justice to the historical district, the artisan hubs of Tonalá and Tlaquepaque, and to savor the region's unique food, drinks, and festivals.

Booking in Advance

Major hotels are rarely booked to capacity, so finding a room at the last minute in Guadalajara is not usually problematic. But plan ahead, just in case. During the winter low season some hotels slash rates considerably, making this cold season an attractive time to visit. Make reservations well in advance if you're planning on staying at a smaller establishment.

Hotel Tips

Many hotels are on busy intersections, in which case rooms higher up or in the interior tend to be less noisy. Some hotels have windows that won't open, so ask for a room with a balcony if fresh air is important to you.

Festivals & Special Events

Guadalajara's major events include a May cultural festival, with a country or region of honor. In September's International Mariachi Festival, local watering holes have even more mariachi performances than usual and distinguished mariachi bands perform nightly with the Jalisco Philharmonic in the Teatro Degollado. The Fiestas de Octubre country fair includes nightly music and cockfights in the *palenque* (fairground). A 10-day book fair starting in November attracts Spanish-speaking literary giants.

To Rent or Not to Rent?

Driving in Guadalajara isn't for the faint of heart. Sure, Tapatío drivers are tamer than those in Mexico City, but traffic can still be wild. Unless you plan on exploring outlying regions by yourself, there's no reason to rent a car.

If the Beach Beckons

Well, you won't find any beaches in Guadalajara, but the city is only a 4½-hour drive (or 5-hour bus ride) from Puerto Vallarta, the hub of the Pacific Coast Resorts. With a little planning, these two very different destinations can be combined into one best-of-both-worlds trip.

Be sure to compare airfares into both cities—depending on where you're flying in from, it might be cheaper to start your journey on the Pacific Coast and work your way inland. If you're driving to PV, the best route is toll Highway 15D to Tepic, followed by Highway 200 (pick it up at the Compostela toll booth).

Safety & Health Concerns

Though considerably less dangerous than Mexico City, Guadalajara still has plenty of crime. If possible, avoid ATMs at night and be watchful of anyone following you from a bank, though the frequency of muggings by so-called *conejeros* (rabbit hunters) has diminished in recent years. In mall parking lots, watch out for scam artists claiming to have broken down cars or no money for rent or a bus ticket home.

At an altitude of one mile, Guadalajara escapes the dengue fever outbreaks that occasionally slap Jalisco's tropical coast (e.g., Puerto Vallarta) in the rainy season. Despite having only a quarter of the capital's traffic, Guadalajara regularly gives it a run for its money as Mexico's most polluted city. Air quality readings reach unsatisfactory levels during the winter months, starting in October and continuing until the winds pick up in February. The pollution can cause raw throats, sore eyes, and sinus irritation.

Where to Stay

Tourists often opt to stay in colonial-style hotels in the Centro, which is convenient to many of Guadalajara's sights. Others choose to stay in Tlaquepaque's modest B&Bs. Modern office spaces in the neighborhood of Avenida López Mateos Sur beckon the business-oriented. For a real treat, stay at the plush Quinta Real near Fuente Minerva. In the same neighborhood is the towering Fiesta Americana. For a lovely stay in Historic Guadalajara, the refined and quiet Hotel de Mendoza is your best bet.

Money Matters

WHAT IT COSTS IN DOLLARS

¢	$	$$	$$$	$$$$
Restaurants				
under $5	$5–$10	$10–$15	$15–$25	over $25
Hotels				
under $50	$50–$75	$75–$150	$150–$250	over $250

Restaurant prices are for a main course excluding tax and tip. Hotel prices are for two people in a standard double room in high season.

How's the Weather?

For most of the year, daytime temperatures hover in the low eighties and the nights are clear and cool. The city is susceptible to bouts of dry heat in April and May, when the mercury surges past 38°C (100°F). Afternoon downpours, occurring June through September, douse the heat (and bring air pollution to its lowest annual levels), but can make streets a flooded nightmare. Temperatures are cooler December to early February (nighttime lows may plunge into the thirties).

Whatever the weather in Guadalajara, the most pleasing pastimes include exploring the city's charms on foot (during the rainy season, bring an umbrella or a rain coat, or simply time it right and plan to be indoors—perhaps sipping margaritas—during the afternoon downpours); shopping for pottery, crafts, jewelry, and even shoes; and discovering local churches, theaters, and public art.

What to Pack

Guadalajara is a casual city, but know that some of the more posh restaurants will demand your Sunday best, so if you're planning on dining out a lot, make sure you bring something presentable.

Updated by Jane Onstott

GUADALAJARA'S SIGHTS ARE DIVIDED INTO five major areas. Guadalajara, Zapopan, Tlaquepaque, and Tonalá are the four primary municipalities. With the exception of Zapopan, they can each be navigated on foot in a few hours, though they deserve at least a day. Zapopan requires more time since it's a sprawling suburb with plenty of shopping and high-end hotels quite a distance from old downtown.

Zona Minerva, the fifth area, is due west of the Centro. Hopping between its shops, cafés, bars, and restaurants is best done by cab. Sample this district by strolling down the Avenida Juarez–Avenida Vallarta corridor, which is shut to vehicular traffic from 8 AM to 2 PM every Sunday.

GETTING HERE & AROUND

If you're flying here, Aeropuerto Internacional Libertador Miguel Hidalgo is 16½ km (10 mi) south of Guadalajara. It's a 30 minute drive to Guadalajara, but the trip can be delayed in either direction by slow-moving caravans of trucks and weekend traffic. The seven- to eight-hour bus ride between Guadalajara and Mexico City usually costs $40 and is generally efficient and comfortable. Estrella Blanca, ETN, Primera Plus, and Transportes al Pacifico have many daily departures. Toll highway 15D is the safest and quickest route between Mexico City and Guadalajara.

ESSENTIALS

Bus Contacts **Estrella Blanca** (☎ *33/3679–0404*). **ETN** (☎ *33/3600–0477, 33/3770–3777, or 01800/360–4200*). **Primera Plus** (☎ *33/3600–0014 or 01800/375–7587*). **Transportes al Pacificio** ☎ *33/3668–5920)*.

Internet **Compu-Flash** (✉ *Calle Priciliano Sánchez 402, Centro Histórico* ☎ *33/3614–7165*).**La Vaca Loca**(✉ *Juárez 145, Tlaquepaque* ☎ *33/3838–6860*).

Medical Assistance **Hospital Angeles del Carmen** (✉ *Calle Tarascos 3435, Zona Minerva* ☎ *33/3813–0025 or 33/3648–0128*). **Hospital México-Americano** (✉ *Calle Colomos 2110, Centro Histórico* ☎ *33/3641–3141*). **Hospital San Javier** (✉ *Av. Pablo Casals 640, Col. Providencia, Zona Minerva* ☎ *33/3669–0222*).

Post Office **Main Post Office** (✉ *Av. Alcalde 500, Centro Histórico* ☎ *33/3614–4770*).

Rental Cars **Alamo** (✉ *Av. Niños Héroes 982, south of Centro Histórico* ☎ *01800/849–8001, 33/3688–8078 at airport* 🌐 *www.alamo-mexico.com.mx*). **Avis** (✉ *Hilton, Av. de las Rosas 2933, Rinconda del Bosque* ☎ *33/3671–3422, 33/3688–5784 at airport*) 🌐www.avis.com.mx). **Budget** (✉ *Av. Niños Héroes 125, at Av. 16 de Septiembre, Centro Histórico* ☎ *01800/700–1700, 33/3688–5216 at the airport* 🌐 *www.budget.com.mx*).

Visitor & Tour Info **Guadalajara Municipal Tourist Office** (✉ *Pedro Morelos 1596, Centro Histórico* ☎ 33/3668–1600). **Jalisco State Tourist Office** (✉ *Calle Morelos 102, Centro Histórico* ☎ *33/3668–1600, 01800/363–2200 toll-free in Mexico* 🌐 *visita.jalisco.gob.mx* ✉ *Palacio de Gobierno, Av. Corona 31Centro Histórico* ☎ *33/3668–1601 Ext. 34730* ✉ *Calle Madero 407-A, 2nd fl., Chapala* ☎ *376/765–3141*)**Tlaquepaque Municipal Tourist Office** (✉ *Calle Morelos 288, Tlaquepaque* ☎ *33/3562–7050 Ext. 2318*). **Tonalá Municipal Tourist Office** (✉ *Av.*

de los Tonaltecas Sur 140, in La Casa de los Artesanos, Tonalá ☎ 33/3284–3092 or 33/3284–3093). **Tourist Board of Zapopan** (✉ *Av. Vallarta 6503, Ciudad Granja, Zona Zapopan* ☎ *33/3110–0754* 🌐 *www.zapopan.gob.mx*).

EXPLORING

CENTRO HISTÓRICO

The downtown core is a mishmash of modern and old buildings connected by a series of large plazas, four of which were designed to form a cross when viewed from the sky, with the cathedral in the middle. Though some remain, many colonial-era structures were razed before authorities got serious about preserving them. Conservation laws, however, merely prohibit such buildings from being altered or destroyed; there are no provisions on upkeep, as plenty of abandoned, crumbling buildings indicate.

5

Must-visit sights include the Palacio del Gobierno and the Instituto Cultural Cabañas; both have phenomenal murals by José Clemente Orozco. Even if you're not in the mood to shop, you should experience the bustling Mercado Libertad. Explore the district in the morning if you dislike crowds; otherwise you'll get a more immediate sense of Mexico's vibrant culture if you wait for street performers and vendors to emerge around the huge Plaza Tapatía in the afternoon.

Allot at least two hours for the Centro, longer if you really want to absorb the main sights. Morning is the best time to visit, but you can spread a walk over several afternoons (when the light is especially beautiful) and reserve your mornings for trips to outlying areas.

MAIN ATTRACTIONS

★ ❶ **Catedral.** Begun in 1561 and consecrated in 1618, this downtown focal point is an intriguing mélange of baroque, Gothic, and other styles. Its emblematic twin towers replaced the originals, felled by the earthquake of 1818. Ten of the silver-and-gold altars were gifts from King Fernando VII for Guadalajara's financial support of Spain during the Napoleonic Wars. Some of the world's most beautiful *retablos* (altarpieces) adorn the walls; above the sacristy (often closed to the public) is Bartolomé Esteban Murillo's priceless 17th-century painting *The Assumption of the Virgin*. In a loft above the main entrance is a magnificent 19th-century French organ. ✉ *Av. Alcalde, between Av. Hidalgo and Calle Morelos, Centro Histórico* ☎ *No phone* 🎟 *Free* ⏲ *Daily 8–8.*

OPEN-AIR BUSES

The **Tranvía Turística** (✉ *Plaza Guadalajara in front of Presidencia Municipal* ☎ *34/1414–0836*) is a convenient and scenic way to get around the city. The open-air, double-decker buses leave about every half hour from Plaza de Armas and cost $11. Buses take you on a route past some of the city's sights to Tlaquepaque, where they drop you off to wander. You can always take a later bus back if you want to stay longer. The scenery is enjoyable, but the narration is mediocre.

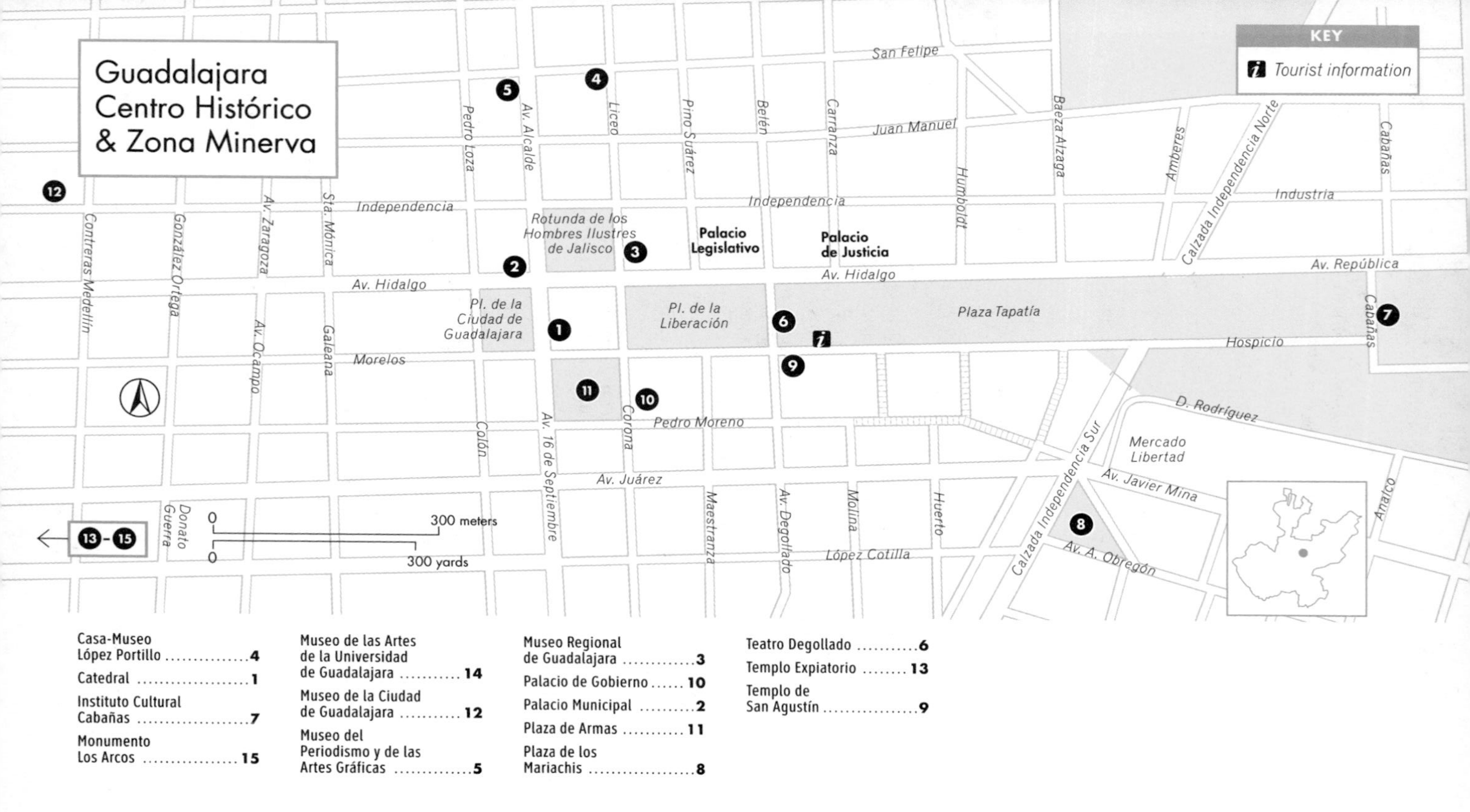

Guadalajara Centro Histórico & Zona Minerva
KEY
Tourist information
San Felipe
Juan Manuel
Pedro Loza
Av. Alcalde
Liceo
Pino Suárez
Belén
Carranza
Humboldt
Baeza Alzaga
Amberes
Calzada Independencia Norte
Cabañas
Industria
Independencia
Rotunda de los Hombres Ilustres de Jalisco
Palacio Legislativo
Palacio de Justicia
Av. República
Contreras Medellín
González Ortega
Av. Zaragoza
Sta. Mónica
Av. Hidalgo
Pl. de la Ciudad de Guadalajara
Pl. de la Liberación
Plaza Tapatía
Hospicio
Av. Ocampo
Galeana
Morelos
Colón
Av. 16 de Septiembre
Corona
Pedro Moreno
D. Rodríguez
Mercado Libertad
Calzada Independencia Sur
Av. Javier Mina
Analco
Av. Juárez
Maestranza
Av. Degollado
Molina
Huerto
López Cotilla
Av. A. Obregón
Donato Guerra
300 meters
300 yards
13-15
Casa-Museo López Portillo 4
Catedral 1
Instituto Cultural Cabañas 7
Monumento Los Arcos 15
Museo de las Artes de la Universidad de Guadalajara 14
Museo de la Ciudad de Guadalajara 12
Museo del Periodismo y de las Artes Gráficas 5
Museo Regional de Guadalajara 3
Palacio de Gobierno 10
Palacio Municipal 2
Plaza de Armas 11
Plaza de los Mariachis 8
Teatro Degollado 6
Templo Expiatorio 13
Templo de San Agustín 9

7 **Instituto Cultural Cabañas.** Spanish architect-sculptor Manuel Tolsá
Fodor's Choice designed this neoclassical-style cultural center. Originally a shelter for widows, the elderly, and orphans, the Instituto's 106 rooms and 23 flower-filled patios now house art exhibitions (ask for an English-speaking guide). The main chapel displays murals by José Clemente Orozco 1938–39, including *The Man of Fire,* his masterpiece. In all, there are 57 murals by Orozco, plus many of his smaller paintings, cartoons, and drawings. Kids can wonder at the murals and investigate the labyrinthine compound. ✉ *Calle Cabañas 8, Centro Histórico* ☎ *33/3668–1647* *$1* *Tues.–Sat. 10:30–5:30, Sun. 10:15–2:30.*

5 **Museo del Periodismo y de las Artes Gráficas.** Guadalajara's first printing press was set up here in 1792; in 1810 it printed the first 2,000 copies of "El Despertador Americano," which impelled would-be Mexicans to join the War of Independence. You can see historic newspapers, printing presses, and recording equipment in this mansion, known as the Casa de los Perros for the two wrought-iron *perros* (dogs) guarding its roof. The permanent collection isn't as exciting as the traveling exhibitions of local and national press, art, and photography, which are usually on the top floor. ✉ *Av. Alcalde 225, between Calle Reforma and Calle San Felipe, Centro Histórico* ☎ *33/3613–9285 or 33/3613–9286* *$1* *Tues.–Sat. 10–6, Sun. 10–3.*

10 **Palacio de Gobierno.** The adobe structure of 1643 was replaced with this churrigueresque and neoclassical stone structure in the 18th century. Within are Jalisco's state offices and two of José Clemente Orozco's most passionate murals. One just past the entrance depicts a gigantic Father Miguel Hidalgo looming amid figures representing oppression and slavery. Upstairs, the other mural (look for a door marked CONGRESO) portrays Hidalgo, Juárez, and other Reform-era figures. Nervous officials routinely lock the main entrance due to the frequent protests in the facing plaza. If that's the case, walk around to the back door. ✉ *Av. Corona between Calle Morelos and Pedro Moreno, Centro Histórico* ☎ *No phone* *Free* *Daily 9–8.*

11

Plaza de Armas. The State Band of Jalisco and the Municipal Band sometimes play at the bandstand on Tuesday around 6:30 PM. ✉ *Av. Corona between Calle Morelos and Pedro Moreno, across from Palacio de Gobierno, Centro Histórico.*

9 **Templo de San Agustín.** One of the city's oldest churches has been remodeled many times since its consecration in 1573, but the sacristy is original. The building to the left of the church, originally an Augustinian cloister, is now the University of Guadalajara's Escuela de Música (School of Music). Free recitals and concerts are held on its patio. ✉ *Calle Morelos 188, at Av. Degollado, Centro Histórico* ☎ *33/3614–5365* *Free* *Daily 8–1 and 5–8.*

IF YOU HAVE TIME

4 **Casa-Museo López Portillo.** For a taste of how the wealthy *jalisciense* (citizens of Jalisco) once lived, visit the former digs of Guadalajara's López Portillo family. The brood included writers and politicians, such as an

5

early-20th-century Jalisco governor and his grandson, José López Portillo, Mexico's president from 1976 to 1982. The stunning collection of 17th- through 20th-century European furniture and accessories is a big hit with antiques lovers. (A former museum administrator was so enamored that she allegedly took home some goblets.) ✉ *Calle Liceo 177, at Calle San Felipe, Centro Histórico* ☎ 33/1201–8720 🎫 *Free* 🕑 *Tues.–Sat. 10–6, Sun. 10–5.*

3 ★ **Museo Regional de Guadalajara.** Constructed as a seminary and public library in 1701, this has been the Guadalajara Regional Museum's home since 1918. First-floor galleries contain artifacts tracing western Mexico's history from prehistoric times through the Spanish conquest. Five 19th-century carriages, including one used by General Porfirio Díaz, are on the second-floor balcony. There's an impressive collection of European and Mexican paintings. ✉ *Calle Liceo 60, Centro Histórico* ☎ *33/3614–9957* 🎫 *$3* 🕑 *Tues.–Sun. 9–5:45.*

GOING UNDERGROUND

Guadalajara's underground *tren ligero* (light-rail train) system is clean, safe, and efficient. Line 1 runs north–south along Avenida Federalismo from the Periférico (city beltway) Sur to Periférico Norte, near the Benito Juárez Auditorium. Line 2 runs east–west along Juárez from Tetlán in eastern Guadalajara to Avenida Federalismo. Lines 1 and 2 form a "T," meeting at the Juárez station at Parque Revolución, at the corner of Avenida Federalismo and Avenida Juárez. Trains run every 10 minutes from 5 AM to midnight; a token good for one trip costs about 35¢.

2 **Palacio Municipal.** Inside City Hall are murals of the city's founding, painted by Guadalajara native Gabriel Flores. Free walking tours of the Centro begin here on weekends at 10 AM (Spanish only). To request tours in English, groups of 10 or more should call the municipal tourism office (☎ *33/3616–9150* or *33/3615–1182*). ✉ *Av. Hidalgo at Av. Alcalde, Centro Histórico* ☎ *No phone* 🎫 *Free* 🕑 *Daily 8 AM–9 PM.*

8 **Plaza de los Mariachis.** This small, triangular plaza south of the Mercado Libertad was once the ideal place to tip up a beer and experience the most Mexican of music. The once placid spot is now boxed in by a busy street, a market, and a run-down neighborhood. It's safest to visit in the day or early evening; mariachi serenades start at about $15 a song. Use the pedestrian overpass from the south side of Plaza Tapatía to avoid heavy traffic. ✉ *Calz. Independencia Sur, Centro Histórico.*

6 ★ **Teatro Degollado.** Inaugurated in 1866, this magnificent theater was modeled after Milan's La Scala. The refurbished theater preserves its traditional red-and-gold color scheme, and its balconies ascend to a multitier dome adorned with Gerardo Suárez's depiction of Dante's *Divine Comedy.* The theater is home to the Jalisco Philharmonic. ✉ *Av. Degollado between Av. Hidalgo and Calle Morelos, Centro Histórico* ☎ *33/3614–4773 or 33/3613–1115* 🎫 *Free; show ticket prices vary* 🕑 *Weekdays 11 AM–midnight.*

ZONA MINERVA

Also known as Zona Rosa (Pink Zone), this district west of the Centro Histórico is arguably the pulse of the city. At night a seemingly endless strip of the region's trendiest (and most touristy) watering holes lights up Avenida Vallarta east of Avenida Enrique Díaz de León. Victorian mansions, art galleries, a striking church, and two emblematic monuments—the Fuente Minerva (Minerva Fountain) and the Monumento Los Arcos—are scattered throughout the tree-lined boulevards.

HORSING AROUND

Calandrias (horse-drawn carriages) tour the area from downtown; it's $20 for an hour-long tour. Tapatío Tour, an open-top, double-decker bus, loops Zona Rosa daily 9 AM–9 PM. You get one day of unlimited rides for about $11; spend the half-hour intervals between rides exploring sights. The bus departs from the west side of the Plaza de Armas.

The best way to get here from the Centro is by cab or on the Par Vial, an electric trolley marked 400 or 500 that runs west on Calle Independencia and Avenida Vallarta, and returns east via Avenida Hidalgo (get off on Hidalgo at either Plaza Guadalajara or Plaza de la Liberación, the plazas in front of and behind the cathedral).

You can cover the relatively small Museo de la Ciudad in an hour. The larger Museo de las Artes, a 10-minute walk west, requires two hours when all its exhibits are open. Budget an hour for the Templo Expiatorio across the street. The Monumento Los Arcos and the Fuente Minerva are quick single-afternoon tours.

MAIN ATTRACTIONS

14 **Museo de las Artes de la Universidad de Guadalajara.** The University of Guadalajara's contemporary-art museum is in this exquisite early-20th-century building. The permanent collection includes several murals by Orozco. Revolving exhibitions have contemporary works from Latin America, Europe, and the United States. ✉*Av. Juarez 975Zona Minerva* ☎*33/3134–1664* 🌐*www.museodelasartes.udg.mx* *Free* ⏲*Tues.–Sat. 10–6, Sun. noon–6.*

13 **Templo Expiatorio.** The striking neo-Gothic Church of Atonement is Guadalajara's most breathtaking church. Modeled after Italy's Orvieto Cathedral, it has phenomenal stained-glass windows—observe the rose window above the choir and pipe organ. Fronted by a large plaza, the church is backed by the Museo de las Artes de la Universidad de Guadalajara. ✉*Calle Díaz de León 930, at Av. López Cotilla, Zona Minerva* ☎*33/3825–3410* *Free* ⏲*Daily 6:30* AM*–10:30* PM.

IF YOU HAVE TIME

15 **Monumento Los Arcos.** The double arches of this monument span Avenida Vallarta, a block east of Fuente Minerva. Reminiscent of the Arc de Triomphe, the neoclassical structure has an intriguing mural inside and a winding stairway to the roof, where there's a view of the fountain and the avenue below. Enter through the south leg, where there's a small

CLOSE UP

Guadalajara Background

The conquistadors had a difficult time founding Guadalajara. A decade of Indian uprisings and Spanish crown interference caused the capital of sprawling Nueva Galicia to shift locations three times before it reached its present perch in 1542. According to popular legend, the founding occurred behind downtown's Teatro Degollado. (A plaza behind the theater commemorates the event.) Guadalajara's name comes from a similarly named Spanish city; the word is Arabic in origin meaning "river of rocks."

Often cut off from the capital during the rainy season, Guadalajara developed independently, with the Catholic Church as its dominant social and political influence. Miguel Hidalgo's final battlefield defeat in the War of Independence from Spain—which eventually ended nearly 300 years of Spanish rule—took place here in 1811. It was briefly the capital of Mexico from 1856 to 1857, during the tumultuous reform period. Later, the city had a tardy start in the Mexican Revolution, taking up arms four years after it began in 1910.

When ultra-right-wing president Plutarco Elías Calles effectively criminalized Catholicism in 1926, Jalisco-area Catholics launched an armed rebellion against the government. During the bitter *La Cristiada* war, many priests were executed. In recent years dozens of *Cristero* martyrs have been canonized by the Vatican, a great source of pride for Guadalajara's Catholics.

tourist office. ✉ *Av. Vallarta 2641, at Lopez Mateos Sur, Zona Minerva* ☎ *33/3616–9150 or 33/3615–1182* 🎟 *Free* ⏲ *Daily 8–7.*

⓬ **Museo de la Ciudad de Guadalajara.** Rooms surrounding the tranquil interior patio of this bi-level colonial mansion contain artwork, artifacts, and documents about the city's development from pre-Hispanic times through the 20th century. Exhibits are labeled in Spanish only; English-language materials should be available at the entrance or in the library upstairs. ✉ *Calle Independencia 684, Zona Minerva* ☎ *33/1201–8712* 🎟 *50¢* ⏲ *Tues.–Sat. 10–5:30, Sun. 10–2:30.*

ZAPOPAN

Mexico's former corn-producing capital is now a municipality of wealthy enclaves, modern hotels, and malls surrounded by hills of poor communities (as is much of metropolitan Guadalajara). Farther out, some farming communities remain. The central district, a good 25-minute cab ride from downtown Guadalajara, has two worthwhile museums, an aged church that's home to the city's most revered religious icon, and a long pedestrian corridor punctuated by watering holes popular with young Tapatíos. The neoclassic city hall building on the north side of the plaza has occasional art exhibitions upstairs.

Zapopan's attractions and its downtown area are far removed from one another and are best reached by taxi. Save money by catching Bus 275 or a northbound Tur. ■ TIP➔ **Catch the Tur at Alcalde and San Felipe for 9 pesos and get off at the corner of Circunvalacion and Avenida Lau-**

reles. Alternatively, take the light-rail to Avila Camacho (Line 1), cross the street, and catch Bus 631.

An afternoon is adequate for downtown Zapopan's major sights. Spend 20 minutes at the basilica, about an hour each at the Huichol Museum and the Art Museum of Zapopan, and 15 minutes at City Hall. If you have more time, check out the market, which is across the plaza and beside City Hall, and a couple of surrounding churches before grabbing a drink or a bite on pedestrian-only Calle 20 de Noviembre.

MAIN ATTRACTIONS

★ **Basílica de la Virgen de Zapopan.** This vast church with an ornate plateresque facade and *mudéjar* (Moorish) tile dome was consecrated in 1730. It's home to the Virgin (or Our Lady) of Zapopan: a 10-inch-high, corn-paste statue venerated as a source of many miracles. Every October 12 more than a million people crowd the streets around the basilica, where the Virgin is returned after a five-month tour of Jalisco's parish churches. It's an all-night fiesta capped by an early-morning procession. ✉ *Av. Hidalgo at Calle Morelos, Zona Zapopan Norte* ☎ *33/3633–0141 or 33/3633–6614* *Free* *Daily* 7AM–9PM.

Museo de Arte de Zapopan. Better known by its initials, MAZ, the large and modern Art Museum of Zapopan is Guadalajara's top contemporary-art gallery. The museum regularly holds expositions of distinguished Latin American painters, photographers, and sculptors, as well as occasional international shows. ✉ *Andador 20 de Noviembre at Calle 28 de Enero* ☎ *33/3818–2575 or 33/3818–2576* *www.mazmuseo.com* *$2.30, free Tues.* *Tues –Sun. 10–6.*

★ **Museo Huichol Wixarica de Zapopan.** The Huichol Indians of northern Jalisco and neighboring states of Zacatecas and Nayarit are famed for their fierce independence and exquisite beadwork and yarn "paintings." This small museum has rather hokey mannequins wearing the intricately embroidered clothing of both men and women. Bilingual placards explain the Huichol religion and worldview. The gift shop sells a small inventory of beaded items, prayer arrows, and god's eyes. ✉ *Av. Hidalgo 152, Centro, Zona Zapopan Norte* ☎ *33/3636–4430* *50¢* *Mon.–Sat. 9:30–1:15 and 3–5:45, Sun. 10–2.*

TLAQUEPAQUE

Tlaquepaque arts and crafts fill the showrooms and stores here; you'll find carved wood furniture, colorful ceramics, and hand-stitched clothing. Pedestrian malls and plazas are lined with more than 300 shops, many run by families with generations of experience. One of Guadalajara's most exceptional museums, which draws gifted artists for its annual ceramics competition in June, is also here.

But there's more to Tlaquepaque than shopping. The downtown area has a pleasant square and many pedestrian-only streets, making this a good place to take a stroll, even if you're not interested in all the crafts for sale. It is touristy, but if you stay in one of the bed-and-

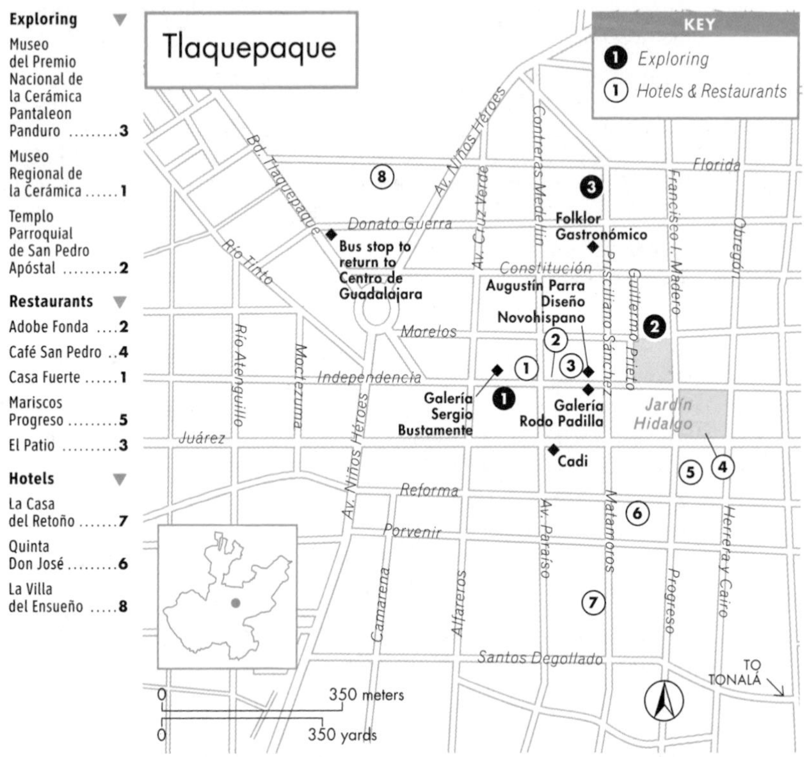

breakfasts here, you'll be able to enjoy some peace in between peak shopping hours.

■TIP→Many tourists come to Tlaquepaque via the Tranvía Turística, an open-air bus that leaves from the Plaza de Armas in Guadalajara's historic center.

MAIN ATTRACTIONS

3 **Museo del Premio Nacional de la Cerámica Pantaleon Panduro.** The museum is named after Pantaleon Panduro, who's considered the father of modern ceramics in Jalisco. On display are prizewinning pieces from the museum's annual ceramics competition, held every June. It's possibly the best representation of modern Mexican pottery under a single roof. You can request an English-speaking guide. ✉ *Calle Priciliano Sánchez 191, at Calle Flórida* ☎ *33/3562–7036* 🎟 *Free* ⏲ *Mon.–Sat. 10–6, Sun. 10–3.*

Fodor's Choice ★

2 **Templo Parroquial de San Pedro Apóstal.** Franciscan friars founded this tiny parish church during the Spanish conquest and named it after the apostle San Pedro de Analco. Adhering to the Mexican custom of adding the name of its patron saint to the town's name, Tlaquepaque was officially changed to San Pedro Tlaquepaque in 1915. The altars of Our Lady of Guadalupe and the Sacred Heart of Jesus are carved in silver

and gold. ✉Calle Guillermo Prieto at Calle Morelos, bordering main plaza ☎33/3635–1001 ⏲Daily 7–1 and 4:30–9.

WORD OF MOUTH

"Tlaquepaque is a living, breathing community, not just a shopper's paradise. There is a magnificent meat and produce market near the Parian. And it is especially charming in the evening, when most of the tourists are in their downtown 4-stars; the families come out to visit in the square, and tons of really good food vendors come out."

–Carolred

IF YOU HAVE TIME

❶ **Museo Regional de la Cerámica.** The frequently changing exhibits at the Regional Museum of Ceramics are in the many rooms surrounding a central courtyard. Track the evolution of ceramic wares in the Atemajac Valley during the 20th century. The presentation isn't always strong, but the Spanish-language displays discuss six common processes used by local ceramics artisans, including *barro bruñido*, which involves polishing large urns with smoothed chunks of the mineral pyrite. Items in the gift shop are surprisingly uninteresting. ✉*Calle Independencia 237* ☎*33/3635–5404* 🌐*www.artesanias.jalisco.gob.mx* 🎫*Free* ⏲ *Tues–Sun. 10–6.*

NEED A BREAK?

For about $20, local mariachis will treat you to a song or two as you sip margaritas at El Parián, an enormous, partly covered conglomeration of 17 cantinas diagonal from the main plaza. Once a marketplace dating from 1883, it has traditional *cazuela* drinks, which are made of fruit and tequila and served in ceramic pots. ✉***Jardín Hidalgo*** ☎***No phone.***

5

TONALÁ

Among the region's oldest pueblos is quiet Tonalá, a place of dusty cobblestone streets and stucco-covered adobe dwellings. Although it's been swallowed by ever-expanding Guadalajara, Tonalá remains independent and industrious; more geared to business than pleasure, it doesn't have the folksy feel of nearby Tlaquepaque. Except for a concentration of shops on Avenida de los Tonaltecas, the main drag into town, most of Tonalá's shops and factories are spread out. Many stores open daily 10–2 and 4–7. Some no longer close for a siesta, but some are closed on Monday. On Thursday and Sunday, bargain-priced merchandise is sold at a street market packed with vendors from 8 AM to 4 PM (Thursday is less crowded than Sunday).

TIP→**The town has unusually long blocks, so wear your most comfortable walking shoes.**

MAIN ATTRACTIONS

❶ **Santuario del Sagrado Corazón.** Moorish arches form the nave, and Stations of the Cross paintings line the walls of the small parish church, which faces the Plaza Principal and neighbors the simple Palacio Municipal (City Hall). ✉*Av. Juárez at Av. Hidalgo* ☎*No phone.*

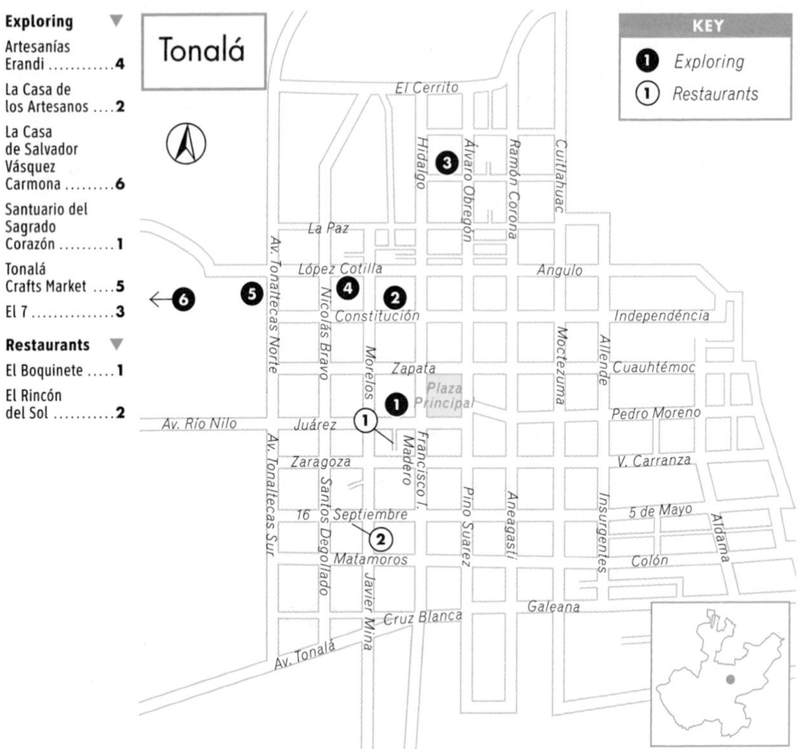

5 **Tonalá crafts market.** This cramped market is *the* place for arts and crafts. Vendors set up ceramics, carved wood, candles, glassware, furniture, metal crafts, and more each Thursday and Sunday (roughly from 9 to 5). Look for *vajilla* (ceramic dining sets), but note that the more high-end ceramic offerings are at government-sponsored Casa de los Artesanos down the street. ✉*Av. Tonaltecas north of Av. Tonalá* ☎*No phone.*

Fodor'sChoice ★

IF YOU HAVE TIME

3 **El 7.** Tonalá native J. Cruz Coldívar Lucano, who signs his work and named his shop El 7 (*el siete*), makes striking hand-painted clay masks and other wall hangings. His work has been exhibited throughout the Americas as well as in Europe, and the Spanish royal family owns some of his pieces. His studio is several long blocks from the plaza on Privado Alvaro Obregón, off the main avenue of the same name. ✉*Privado Alvaro Obregón 28* ☎*33/3683–1122* ⏲*Mon.–Sat. 9–2* and *4–6.*

4 **Artesanías Erandi.** This is the showroom of one of Tonalá's biggest ceramics exporters. If you want to see how the pieces are made, the staff will gladly direct you to one of two nearby workshops. ✉ *Av. López Cotilla 118* ☎*33/3683–0253* 🌐*www.erandi.com* ⏲*Weekdays 10–7, Sat. 9–2.*

2 **La Casa de los Artesanos.** Many of Tonalá's most talented artisans had to disperse when this market relocated to a smaller space. It's still work a look, although the quality and selection are not what they were. Prices are reasonable, and the staff can direct you to nearby studios. ✉ *Calle de la Constitución 104* ☎ *33/3284–3066* 🌐 *www.casadeartesanos.com* ⏲ *Weekdays 9–8, Sat. 9–2.*

6 **La Casa de Salvador Vásquez Carmona.** On a small patio behind his home, Carmona molds enormous ceramic pots and glazes them with intricate designs. Despite posted store hours, the artist's workshop is also his home, and he's willing to receive customers most any time. ✉ *López Cotilla 328, west of Av. de los Tonaltecas* ☎ *33/3683–2896* ⏲ *Weekdays 8–6, Sat. 8–2, Sun. 10–4.*

ELSEWHERE IN GUADALAJARA

North of the Centro is Zona Huentitán, which has a zoo and Barranca de Oblatos. Get to this neighborhood by cab or the northbound Trolley 600 on Calzada Independencia. The zoo is a 20-minute cab ride, more by bus because you have to walk about 1/3 mi to the entrance. To avoid crowds, go to the Barranca de Oblatos in the late morning. South of the Centro, at the confluence of 16 de Septiembre, Calzada de Independencia, and Avenida Washington, is the old train station, where the Tequila Express train departs.

MAIN ATTRACTIONS

Zoológico Guadalajara. On the edge of the jagged Barranca de Huetitán, the city's zoo has more than 1,500 animals representing 360 species. In addition to tropical birds and big cats found in Mexico, you'll see rhinos, polar bears, camels, and other exotic creatures. There are two aviaries, a kids' zoo, and a herpetarium with 130 species of reptiles, amphibians, and fish. For 50¢ you can take a train tour of the grounds. Admission to the adjacent amusement park is $1.30. ✉ *Paseo del Zoológico 600, off Calz. Independencia, Zona Huentitán* ☎ *33/3674–4488* 🌐 *www.zooguadalajara.com.mx* 🎟 *$4.50* ⏲ *Wed.–Sun. 10–6.*

IF YOU HAVE TIME

Barranca de Oblatos. The multipronged 2,000-foot-deep Oblatos Canyon has hiking trails and the narrow Cola de Caballo waterfall, named for its horsetail shape. A portion of the canyon complex called Barranca de Huetitán (Huetitán Canyon) has a steep, winding, 5-km (3-mi) trail to the river below. The trails are less strenuous at the Barranca de Oblatos entrance. Both areas can be crowded on mornings and weekends. Take a northbound electric bus from in front of the Mercado Libertad and get off at Parque Mirador Independencia if you're interested only in the view; alternatively, get off at Periférico and catch any eastbound bus for Huetitán and Oblatos. You can see the Cola de Caballo from the Zoológico Guadalajara, but for a closer look catch an Ixcantantus-bound bus from Glorieta La Normal, a traffic circle 10 blocks north of the cathedral, and ask to be let off at the *mirador de la cascada* (waterfall viewpoint).

CLOSE UP

Slowly Shaking off Stereotypes

Guadalajarans have a tough time shaking their reputation as the most socially conservative people in Mexico. Staunch Catholic moralists are routinely elected into office, and a dominant pharmacy chain refuses to sell contraceptives. Government and church leaders reportedly brush off human rights violations, including allegations of police torture by Amnesty International in 2004. Yet, there are signs of change. A large, vocal gay community is steadily establishing a niche with bars and other establishments. Non-Catholic congregations hold public celebrations with little protest from the public, which is over 90% Catholic.

Called Tapatíos (a name possibly derived from the Nahuatl word *tlapatiotl*, a pre-Hispanic measure of payment), Guadalajarans admit to a long-standing rivalry with *chilangos*, a mildly derogatory term for Mexico City natives. Decades of official neglect from the government have made this derision commonplace in the "provinces, " the term used by capital dwellers to refer to the country outside of Mexico City. The provincial stereotype dogs Guadalajara. Despite having a population of 4.1 million (which locals often exaggerate to six or seven), Guadalajara remains a cultural backwater relative to the capital. Major art expositions rarely open here, in part due to a dearth of galleries and energetic curators, and touring international performing artists usually skip the city.

The **Museo de la Paleontología** (⌧*Av. Dr. R. Michel 520, Centro Histórico* ☎*33/3619–7043*), on the east side of Parque Agua Azul, has plant and animal fossils as well as exhibits on the origin of the planet. Admission is 90¢. The museum is open Tuesday through Saturday 10–6 and Sunday 11–4. (There's no museum entrance inside Agua Azul; you must walk to the park's north side.) ⌧*Calz. Independencia Sur 973, between González Gallo and Las Palmas, south of Centro Histórico* ☎*33/3619–0328 or 33/3619–0333* *40¢* *Tues–Sun. 10–6.*

Parque Agua Azul. This popular park has playgrounds, caged birds, an orchid house, and acres of trees and grass crisscrossed by walking paths. There aren't many butterflies in the huge, geodesic *mariposario* (butterfly sanctuary), but the semitropical garden inside still merits a visit.

WHERE TO EAT

The most popular non-Mexican restaurants are scattered about west Guadalajara, in Zona Minerva; however the best Mexican food is near the main attractions in downtown Guadalajara, Tlaquepaque, and Tonalá.

Reservations are usually required Wednesday through Sunday. A main course usually costs around $10, and alcoholic beverages start at $3 or more, even in cheaper restaurants.

Continued on page 249

With about 5,000 artisans apiece, the suburbs of Tlaquepaque and Tonalá might produce more crafts per square foot than any other place in Mexico. A mere 15–20 minute cab ride from downtown Guadalajara, the twin towns attract droves of shoppers from the city.

POTTERY AND CERAMICS IN TLAQUEPAQUE & TONALÁ

Tonalá Pottery by Antonio Ramirez

Tlaquepaque, which has upscale shops and galleries in converted haciendas, stylish restaurants, and a core of pretty pedestrian-only streets, is the more popular of the two and is actually getting a bit touristy from all the attention. But it hasn't turned into a total theme park just yet and it's still a pleasant place to stroll around and have a leisurely meal in between ducking into stores. Tonalá is less walking-friendly, less wealthy (think dusty cobblestone streets and adobe houses), and less touristy. It does get very busy on Thursday and Sunday, when most of the town is engulfed in a street market. If you can stand the crowds, you'll find bargain prices at these markets. There are more workshops and factories in Tonalá than shops or galleries—a lot of what's produced here ends up in Tlaquepaque—but many are open to the public. Also, the prices are a bit cheaper here, and you'll be able to commission custom work, often directly from the artisans.

Though you might also find glasswork, clothing, leather goods, and hand-carved wood furniture in both towns, they are really known for their pottery and ceramics. The Tonaltecan indians are responsible for Tlaquepaque's craft legacy; they were producing their distinctive decorated pottery as early as the mid-16th century. Tonalá's pre-Hispanic pottery came from the Atemajac Valley indians. Eleven different types of pottery and ceramics are still produced here. Just over 20 molding and firing techniques—most of them centuries old—are used to create the intricately painted flatware and whimsical figures.

Despite the long tradition of art in these towns, many master artisans are struggling to survive, especially in Tonalá. A trip to one of their workshops could be something your grandchildren will only hear about. To arrange studio tours, contact the Municipal Tourist Offices (33/3562–7050, ext. 2318 in Tlaquepaque, 33/3284–3093 in Tonalá) in either town at least a day in advance of your visit.

CLOSE-UP ON CERAMICS

BARRO BRUÑIDO

Polished with pyrite stones, the plates, vases, and figurines typical of this technique are bluish-gray with orange, blue, and white decorations of animals and nature scenes.

BANDERA

Red clay and white and green paint—the three colors of Mexico's *bandera* (flag)—are employed in this nationalistic pottery. However, these days green is missing from many contemporary pieces because the copper oxide used to produce the paint is increasingly rare.

TALAVERA

The colorful tiles and dinnerware of Mexico's best-known ceramics will be among the first things to catch your eye in Tlaquepaque and Tonalá. The technique is actually imported from Puebla, a central Mexican state.

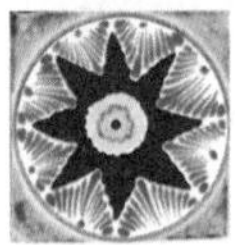

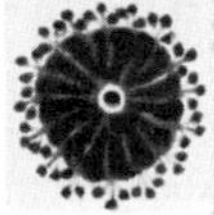

CANELO

Made from dirts that contribute to its cinnamon (*canelo*) coloring, these earth-toned pots are used as water-storing vessels.

PETATILLO

The complexity of this pottery is likened to a handmade *petate* (straw mat). A single piece can require 20 days' labor and may pass through a dozen artisans' hands. Expensive as it is elaborate, *petatillo* is probably Tonalá's most endangered art form.

POLICROMADO

Tlaquepaque's hallmark technique is the centuries-old *policromado* (from "polychrome," made using many colors), in which figurines and nativity scenes are popular.

CENTRO HISTÓRICO

$$ MEXICAN ★ **La Fonda de San Miguel.** La Fonda, in a former convent, is perhaps the Centro's most exceptional eatery. Innovative Mexican eats are presented in a soaring courtyard centered around a stone fountain and hung with a spectacular array of shining tin stars and folk art from Tlaquepaque and Tonalá. Relish the freshly made tortillas with the *molcajete,* a steaming stew of chicken, seafood, or beef that comes in a three-legged stone bowl. *Camarones en mole* (shrimp in mole) is another good dish. There's often a pair of musicians playing on weekday afternoons, and a folkloric show at 9 PM Thursday through Saturday. ✉ *Donato Guerra 25, Centro Histórico* ☎ *33/3613–0809* 💳 *AE, MC, V* ⏲ *No dinner in June.*

TASTE OF THE TOWN

Tapatíos love foreign eats, but homegrown dishes won't ever lose their flavor. The trademark local meal is *torta ahogada,* literally a "drowned sandwich" consisting of pork soaked in tomato sauce and topped with onions and hot sauce—grab a handful of napkins before you dig in. Other steadfast favorites are *carne en su jugo* (beef stew with bacon bits and beans), *birría* (hearty goat or lamb stew), and *pozole* (hominy and pork in tomato broth). Seafood is popular and is available in trendy restaurants as well as at stands.

$$ MEXICAN **La Rinconada.** In a dazzling green-tiled courtyard, this fine restaurant specializes in steak and seafood. The arrachera is good and the *camarones al mojo de ajo* (shrimp with garlic and butter) are even better. Named after the corner building it occupies, the grand old restaurant has appeared in sundry Mexican movies and TV comedies. ✉ *Calle Morelos 86, at Plaza Tapatía, Centro Histórico* ☎ *33/3613–9925* 💳 *MC, V* ⏲ *Closed Sun.*

$ MEXICAN ★ **Birrería las 9 Esquinas.** Mexican families and well-informed travelers come here for specialties like lamb *birría,* which are readied in full view in the vibrantly colored hacienda-style kitchen. The restaurant is on a plaza in one of Guadalajara's oldest neighborhoods, the Nine Corners, so called for its intersecting streets. ✉ *Colon 384, corner of Galeana, Centro Histórico* ☎ *33/3613–6260* 💳 *No credit cards.*

$ MEXICAN **Tacos Providencia del Centro.** This is the source for traditional Guadalajara street-stand fare. Tacos *al pastor* top the clean restaurant's menu, and come with every possible filling, including *trompa* (pig snout). *Tortas ahogadas,* quesadillas, and *gringas* (tortillas filled with cheese and meat) are also available. ✉ *Calle Morelos 84-A, at Plaza Tapatía, Centro Histórico* ☎ *33/3613–9914* 💳 *No credit cards* ⏲ *Closed Wed.*

ZONA MINERVA

$$$ ECLECTIC ★ **Cocina 88.** You won't be the first to discover this indoor/outdoor restaurant along a hip stretch of Avenida Vallarta; it teems with a crowd of well-dressed local yuppies and business travelers every night of the week. They come to soak up the delightful modern feel of the open-air tables or to revel in the equally trendy high-ceilinged interior. Don't miss a trip to the wine cellar, the best in the city. Fresh seafood varies by

5

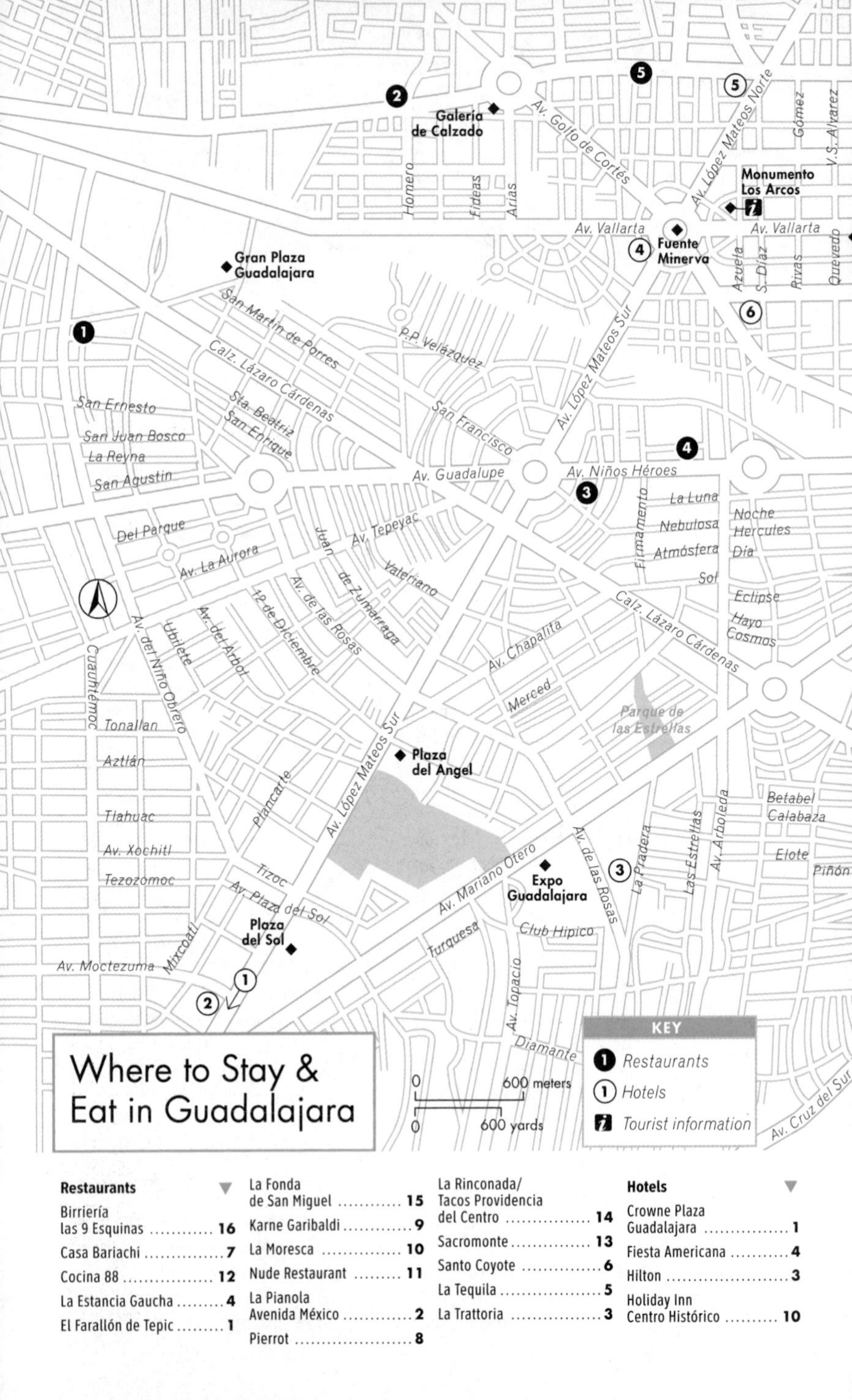

Restaurants

- Birriería las 9 Esquinas **16**
- Casa Bariachi **7**
- Cocina 88 .... **12**
- La Estancia Gaucha **4**
- El Farallón de Tepic **1**
- La Fonda de San Miguel **15**
- Karne Garibaldi **9**
- La Moresca **10**
- Nude Restaurant **11**
- La Pianola Avenida México **2**
- Pierrot **8**
- La Rinconada/ Tacos Providencia del Centro **14**
- Sacromonte **13**
- Santo Coyote **6**
- La Tequila **5**
- La Trattoria **3**

Hotels

- Crowne Plaza Guadalajara **1**
- Fiesta Americana **4**
- Hilton **3**
- Holiday Inn Centro Histórico **10**

Av. México
Justo Sierra
Av. Hidalgo
Morelos
Centro Magno
López Cotilla
Av. de la Paz
Agustín de la Rosa
Av. Américas
Balbuena
Gutiérrez
Amado Nervo
Av. Unión
Simón Bolívar
San Martín
Marsella
Av. Chapultepec
Progreso
Colonias
Ramos Millán
José C. Orozco
Gral Coronado
Ignacia Ramírez
Chilardi
Nicolás Romero
G. Dávila
Frías
Reforma
Av. Hidalgo
Morelos
Av. Juárez
Jesús
Atenas
Miguel Blanco
Libertad
Av. La Paz
Rayón
SEE CENTRO HISTÓRICO INSET BELOW
Independencia
Pedro Moreno
López Cotilla
Madero
Sánchez
Av. Federalismo
Mezquitán
Coronilla
Vega
C. Barca
F.J. Gamboa
Ruiz de Alarcón
Miguel de Cervantes
Circunvalacion Agustín Yáñez
Mexicalizingo
Vidrio
E. Gonzales Montenegro
Colonias
Bruselas
Venezuela
Argentina
Av. Enrique Díaz de León
Fermín Riestra
Av. Mariano Otero
Colón
Fresno
Pino
Tuna
Almendra
Av. Nance
CENTRO HISTÓRICO
Independencia
Av. Alcalde
Nuñez Liceo
Pino Suárez
Carranza
Belén
Humbolt
Alzaga
Baeza
Cabañas
Av. República
Av. Hidalgo
Plaza Tapatía
Instituto Cultural Cabañas
Av. Federalismo
Pavo
8 de julio
Gonzalez Martínez
Donato Guerra
Av. Ocampo
Galeana
Colón
Morelos
Pedro
Moreno
Mercado Libertad
Av. Mina
Av. Juárez
López Cotilla
Av. Corona
Maestranza
Av. Degollado
Molina
Huerto
Calzada Independencia Sur
Av. Obregón
Gigantes
Gómez Farías
Cabañas
V. Guerrero
Madero
Priscilliano Sánchez
Av. 16 de Septiembre
Av. Federalismo Sur
Miguel Blanco
Libertad
Leandro Valle
Madrano
Aldama
Analco
Av. Revolución
0 300 meters
0 300 yards
Hotel Francés 9
Hotel de Mendoza 8
Hotel Morales 11
Hotel Plaza Diana 6
Presidente InterContinental 2
Quinta Real 5
San Francisco Plaza 12
Villa Ganz 7

the day—you can choose it yourself—and be sure to ask what preparations aren't on the menu. Imported steaks are good too, and margaritas come complete with their own miniature bottles of Don Julio. ✉*Av. Vallarta 1342, Zona Minerva* ☎*33/3827–5996* ▭*AE, MC, V.*

$$$ ARGENTINE ✕**La Estancia Gaucha.** Tapatíos adore Argentine cuisine and come to this first-rate steak house for its no-nonsense cuts, including the *churrasco estancia* (rib eye) and the *bife de chorizo* (essentially New York strip steak). Savor the empanadas and Sunday lunch's homemade ravioli. ✉*Av. Niños Héroes 2860, between Arcos and Lopez Mateos, Zona Minerva* ☎*33/3122–6565 or 33/3122–9985* ▭*AE, MC, V* ⏲*No dinner Sun.*

$$$ ECLECTIC ✕**Nude Restaurant.** This soaring bi-level space gleams with enormous panes of glass, bottles, and beautiful people who come to be spotted (which is quite easy, even from the sidewalk). Though the menu is extensive (some would say over-extended—it spans six continents), Nude is as popular for drinks as it is for food. ✉*López Cotilla 1589, Zona Minerva* ☎*33/3616–5248* 🌐*www.nuderestaurant.com.mx* ▭*AE, MC, V.*

$$$ FRENCH ★ ✕**Pierrot.** Nose through this hushed French dining room's extensive wine list for a drink to accompany the mouthwatering pâté, the trout amandine, or the pâté-stuffed chicken breast in tarragon sauce. Wall-mounted lamps and fresh flowers on each table are among the intimate, homey restaurant's gracious touches. In business since the early 1980s, it is very popular with the locals. ✉*Calle Justo Sierra 2355, Zona Minerva* ☎*33/3630–2087* ▭*AE, MC, V* ⏲*Closed Sun.*

$$$ MEXICAN ★ ✕**Sacromonte.** Come here for creative Mexican food, superior service, and warm ambience. You're surrounded by *artesanía* (artwork) in the dining area, and there's jazz and other live music every afternoon from 2 to 5 and on weekend evenings after 9. The kitchen tries to use traditional Mexican ingredients in creative ways. The *San Mateo*, a delicious beef fillet on a bed of cactus with chili sauce, is a winner. So is *La Corona de Reina Isabel*—a crown of intertwined shrimp drowned in lobster bisque with essence of oranges and fried spinach leaves. Don't forget to order margaritas—they're perfect here. ✉*Pedro Moreno 1398, Zona Minerva* ☎*33/3825–5447* ▭*MC, V* ⏲*No dinner Sun.*

$$$ MEXICAN ✕**Santo Coyote.** The food here simply can't compete with the atmosphere, which has so much Disneyesque charm—think faux waterfalls, colorful folk art, and hanging lanterns—that you may forget you're in Guadalajara. Start with chips and a delicious salsa prepared table-side to your spice specification, along with a margarita. Stick to *antojitos (starters),* if possible—you come here to relish the atmosphere, not the food. ✉*Calle Lerdo de Tejada 2379, Zona Minerva* ☎*33/3616–6978* ▭*AE, MC, V.*

$$ MEXICAN ✕**Casa Bariachi.** Beginning at about 9:30 or 10 PM, expect waiters and diners to sing along with the mariachi bands at this touristy restaurant. The party continues until the wee hours of the morning. There's another show during the day, from 3:30 to 5:30. The menu emphasizes steaks, so you can order a T-bone, rib eye, or arrachera (skirt steak) served with guacamole, beans, and grilled chiles. A sizzling molcajete (a hot pot of shrimp, chicken, and panela cheese) is big enough

for two people. Appetizer platters meant to share among two to six people include such exotic items as pickled pigs' feet and head cheese. ✉*Av. Vallarta 2221, Zona Minerva* ☎*33/3616–9900* ▭*AE, MC, V* ⊙*Closed Sun.*

$$ ITALIAN **La Moresca.** Come to eat or just to drink: this modern Italian restaurant in Zona Minerva comes alive at night, when it turns into a hip martini bar. The Tapatíos like to take their dates here for dinner and stick around for the scene that follows. Birthday gatherings are common, too, as are simple be-seen excursions; however you do it, this place is Guadalajara at its trendiest. Luckily, the Italian kitchen is up to the task. ✉*López Cotilla 1835, Zona Minerva* ☎*33/3616–8277* ▭*AE, MC, V* ⊙*Closed Sun.*

$$ MEXICAN **La Tequila.** If you can't make it to the village of Tequila, here's the next best thing: a friendly restaurant–cum–tequila museum that serves decent Mexican fare and 240 varieties of the fiery liquor. Antique photos of tequila distilleries and bilingual plaques explaining tequila's history line the brick walls. Cool contemporary tunes fill the air. The kitchen is uneven—perhaps because the place is so touristy—so you might just want to come for drinks at the upstairs bar, one of the classiest in town. ✉*Av. México 2830, Zona Minerva* ☎*33/3640–3110* ▭*AE, MC, V* ⊙*No dinner Sun.* Bar closed Sun.

5

$$ ITALIAN ★ **La Trattoria.** Guadalajara's top Italian restaurant is a bustling family place. The menu's highlights include spaghetti *frutti di mare* (with seafood), *scaloppine alla Marsala* (beef medallions with Marsala and mushrooms), and fresh garlic bread. All meals include a trip to the salad bar. Make a reservation if you're eating after 8 PM. ✉*Av. Niños Héroes 3051, Zona Minerva* ☎*33/3122–1817* ▭*AE, MC, V.*

$ MEXICAN **Karne Garibaldi.** In the *1996 Guinness Book of World Records,* this Tapatío institution held the record for world's fastest service: 13.5 seconds for a table of six. Lightning service is made possible by the menu's single item: *carne en su jugo,* a combination of finely diced beef and bacon simmered in rich beef broth and served with grilled onions, tortillas, and refried beans mixed with corn. Don't be put off by the somewhat gritty area surrounding the restaurant. The original location on Calle Garibalde is in a less attractive neighborhood than the one on *Mariano Otero*, but the food is equally good at both. ✉*Calle Garibaldi 1306, Zona Minerva* ☎*33/3826–1286* 🌐*www.karnegaribaldi.com.mx* ▭*AE, MC, V* ✉*Mariano Otero 3019, Zona Plaza del Sol* ☎*33/3121–1663.*

$ MEXICAN ★ **La Pianola Avenida México.** Signature piano music and appealing dining areas (view the avenue from the front, or unwind in the airy courtyard out back) provide a soothing backdrop for you to sample specialties from a varied Mexican menu, which includes pozole and *chiles en nogada* (chilies in walnut sauce). For lunch and dinner, half orders are available. ✉*Av. México 3226, Zona Minerva* ☎*33/3813–1385 or 33/3813–2412* ▭*AE, MC, V* ⊙*No dinner Sun.*

ZAPOPAN

$$$ SEAFOOD ★ **El Farallón de Tepic.** Out in the open air and beneath a bright-blue awning, this restaurant specializes in fresh *pescado*—usually red snapper, sea bass, or another equally mild fish—grilled with garlic or butter, in classic tomato sauce, breaded, or stuffed with seafood and cheese. The pescado *sarandeado* (whole barbecued fish stuffed with vegetables) is worth the 30-minute wait. Go with the homemade flan for dessert. ✉*Av. Niño Obrero 560, Zona Zapopan* ☎*33/3121–2616* 💳*AE, MC, V* ⏲*No dinner.*

TLAQUEPAQUE

There are many good restaurants tucked along Tlaquepaque's quaint town center, but be forewarned that almost all of them cater to daytime visitors and close by 8 PM. Don't expect a relaxing late-night meal in this city.

$$ MEXICAN **Adobe Fonda.** Located inside a housewares and textiles shop, Adobe Fonda's strength is its cuteness. The menu consists of hit-or-miss fusion dishes. Try the *chile relleno de camaron con queso brie* (a poblano pepper stuffed with shrimp and Brie) or *taquitos de atún al pastor* (tacos with tuna and pineapple). Lamps supply the low, romantic lighting, while oversized wicker and equipale (pigskin) chairs add some local color. ✉*Francisco de Miranda 27* ☎*33/3657–2792* 💳*MC, V, AE* ⏲*No dinner Sun.–Wed.*

$$ MEXICAN ★ **Casa Fuerte.** Relax with tasty Mexican dishes at the tables along the sidewalk or under the palms and by the fountain on the patio. You'll be tempted by the tables scattered around the sidewalk, but before you decide take a peek at those on the oversize garden patio surrounding a magnificent old tree. Try the house specialty: chicken stuffed with *huitlacoche* (a corn fungus that's Mexico's answer to the truffle) and shrimp in tamarind sauce. Live musicians accompany lunch hours every day except Monday. ✉*Calle Independencia 224* ☎*33/3639–6481 or 33/3639–6474* 💳*AE, MC, V.*

$$ MEXICAN **El Patio.** El Patio is centered around an inviting courtyard dotted with wrought-iron tables. For starters, try the guacamole and powerful margaritas. Order carefully for your mains, as some options are better than others. Sweet, flavorful *chiles en nogada* are a good pick; *mole enchiladas* are a wise choice as well. Don't be tempted by the interesting preparations of fish—they fall short of expectations. Lively mariachi musicians or romantic trios play most days during the midday meal. Note that this is one of a handful of restaurants in Tlaquepaque to serve during dinner hours. ✉*Independencia 186* ☎*33/3635–1108* 🌐*www.elpatio.com.mx* 💳*AE, MC, V*

$ MEXICAN ★ **Mariscos Progreso.** There's always one in every neighborhood: the place all the locals crowd into, leaving everything else deserted. In this case they come for seafood, from wonderfully fresh *ceviche de pescado,* served as a tostada, to a tender octopus cocktail. For your main course don't even look at the menu—go straight for the *huachinango* (red snapper), or other catch of the day, served *a la leña.* This preparation involves coating the fish in butter and heavy spices, wrapping it in foil, and grilling it over an open fire. There's a good tequila selection here, too. ✉*Progreso 80* ☎*33/3639–6149 or 33/3657–4995* ▭*AE, MC, V* ⊙*No dinner.*

¢ CAFÉ ✕**Café San Pedro.** Jazzy music emanates from this popular coffeehouse. Grab a table on the sidewalk or in the cozy dining room. The glass dessert case shows off dozens of different cakes and pies; ask which were made that day, as this huge variety means that some sit for awhile. There's a very long list of coffee drinks (including the Spanish café cortado, which is espresso with a shot of hot milk) and a sandwich maker at the back who will indulge desires beyond sweets and caffeine. ✉ *Av. Juárez 85, Tlaquepaque* ☎ *33/3639–0616* ▭*MC, V.*

TONALÁ

$ MEXICAN ✕**El Boquinete.** Turn down a passageway lined with small shops to be delivered from the market commotion to this tranquil restaurant. Typical Mexican-style chicken and meat dishes are served along with extensive tequila, whiskey, and beer selections. ✉*Passageway between Juárez and Zaragoza, Tonalá* ☎*33/3683–5839* ▭*AE, MC.*

$ MEXICAN ✕**El Rincón del Sol.** A covered patio invites you to sip margaritas while listening to live guitar music (Tuesday to Sunday afternoon). Try one of the steak or chicken dishes or the classic *chiles en nogada* (in walnut sauce) in the colors of the Mexican flag. The staff is friendly and helpful. ✉*Av. 16 de Septiembre 61, Tonalá* ☎*33/3683–1989 or 33/3683–1940* ▭*MC, V.*

WHERE TO STAY

Choosing a place to stay is a matter of location and price; tourists are often drawn to the Centro, where colonial-style hotels are convenient to the historical center and other sights, or to Tlaquepaque's genial B&Bs, like the Quinta Don José. Businesspeople head for the area around Avenida López Mateos Sur, a 16-km (10-mi) strip extending from the Minerva Fountain to the Plaza del Sol shopping center, where they can take advantage of modern office facilities and four-star comforts. Several hotels, like the polished Hilton, are near the Expo Guadalajara convention center.

CENTRO HISTÓRICO

$$$ ★ **Holiday Inn Centro Histórico.** This branch of the reliable international chain sits in the heart of historic Guadalajara. Completely renovated in 2007, the hotel has new mattresses, new bedding—the works. It's all done in a soothing gold-and-white color scheme. Rooms have nice touches like plasma TVs; the bathrooms have glassed-in showers, but no tubs. The breakfast buffet is a good deal, and the restaurant serves national and international dishes. **Pros:** Helpful business center, 24-hour gym, cheerful rooms. **Cons:** No heat, no pool. ✉*Av. Juárez 211, Centro,* ☎*33/3560–1200* 🌐*www.holidaycentrogdl.com* *45 rooms,*

45 suites ♢In-room: Safe, Wi-Fi. In hotel: Restaurant, room service, bar, laundry facilities, laundry service, public Internet, public Wi-Fi, parking (no fee), airport shuttle ▭AE, MC, V.

$$ ★ **Hotel de Mendoza.** Elegant with its postcolonial architecture, this hotel is on a calm side street a block from Teatro Degollado. Hand-carved furniture and doors and wrought-iron railings adorn the public areas and the rooms. Standard rooms are small, making suites worth the extra cost. Balconies overlook the courtyard pool from some rooms. **Pros:** Great location, comfortable rooms. **Cons:** Standard rooms lack tubs, most rooms don't have balconies. ✉*Calle Venustiano Carranza 16, Centro Histórico,* ☎*01800/361–2600 toll-free in Mexico, 33/3942–5151* 🌐*www.demendoza.com.mx* *110 rooms, 17 suites* ♢*In room: Wi-Fi. In-hotel: Restaurant, pool, gym, public Internet, public Wi-Fi, parking (fee)* ▭*AE, MC, V.*

WORD OF MOUTH

"Hotel Mendoza is first class, even if it's a little old. All that's worth doing in Guadalajara is within walking distance. The tip on suites is right on, though "senior" suite is just a large room with iron divider. The hotel dining room is good for breakfast and lunch, but you can get better dinners elsewhere."

–Jerry Holland

$$ ★ **Hotel Morales.** After being abandoned for 30 years, this downtown hotel—originally a 19th-century rooming house—has been transformed into one of the city's most luxurious lodgings. No wonder it's the choice of celebrities ranging from movie stars to soccer heroes. Demure guest rooms have crown molding, blond-wood floors, and gold-and-beige furnishings with an old-world style. Café tables on the rooftop terrace make for a casual retreat. The lobby and restaurant are much more formal. **Pros:** Relaxed elegance, double-paned windows keep out the noise. **Cons:** Lobby restaurant isn't cozy, no Wi-Fi in rooms. ✉*Ave. Ramón Corona 243, Centro* ☎*33/3658–5232* 🌐*www.hotelmorales.com.mx* *59 rooms, 7 suites.* ♢*In-room: Safe, refrigerator (some). In-hotel: Restaurant, public Wi-Fi, parking (free)* ▭ *AE, MC, V.*

$ **Hotel Francés.** Dating from 1610, Guadalajara's oldest hotel is a national monument. Stone columns and colonial arches girdle an attractive three-story atrium lobby and dining area, with a marble fountain. However, the charm ends outside the guest rooms, where threadbare linens, dingy bathrooms, and thin walls are serious drawbacks—music from the downstairs bar will keep you up all night if you're in the wrong room. Rooms facing Calle Maestranza have tiny 17th-century balconies, as well as street noise. **Pros:** Great downtown location, interesting period architecture. **Cons:** On a noisy street, tired furnishings. ✉*Calle Maestranza 35, Centro Histórico,* ☎*33/3613–1190, 01800/718–5309 toll-free in Mexico* 🌐*www.hotelfrances.com* *50 rooms, 10 suites* ♢*In-hotel: Restaurant, bar, public Wi-Fi, parking (no fee)* ▭*AE, MC, V.*

$ **San Francisco Plaza.** On a quiet side street, this appealing two-story colonial-style hotel faces a small triangular plaza. Potted palms and geraniums surround a gurgling stone fountain in the courtyard sitting area. High ceilings and arches, as well as friendly service, make up for somewhat worn furnishings. Rooms facing the San Francisco patio are generally the quietest. **Pros:** Expansive breakfast buffet, double-paned windows to cut down on the noise, friendly staff. **Cons:** Unimpressive room furnishings, cheap plastic showers. ⊠*Calle Degollado 267, Centro Histórico,* ☎*33/3613–8954 or 33/3613–8971* *74 rooms, 2 suites* *In-hotel: restaurant, laundry service, public Wi-Fi, parking (fee)* *AE, MC, V.*

ZONA MINERVA

$$$$ ★ **Quinta Real.** Stone-and-brick walls, colonial arches, and objets d'art fill this luxury hotel's public areas. Suites are plush, though on the small side, with neocolonial-style furnishings, original art, and faux fireplaces. Master suites have separate seating areas with love seats and marble-top desk. For a bit more the Grand Class suites have luxurious touches like round whirlpool tubs. You can arrange in-room massages from one of two nearby spas. The wood-floored gym boasts the latest equipment and plasma-screen TVs. **Pros:** Elegant rooms, stately grounds, in-room spa services. **Cons:** Pricey rates, no on-site spa. ⊠*Av. México 2727, at Av. López Mateos Norte, Zona Minerva,* ☎*33/3669–0600, 01800/500–4000 in Mexico* *www.quintareal.com* *76 suites* *In-room: Safe, dial-up, CD (some). In-hotel: Restaurant, bar, pool, concierge, gym, public Wi-Fi, no-smoking rooms, laundry service* *AE, MC, V.*

$$$ ★ **Fiesta Americana.** The dramatic glass facade of this high-rise faces the Minerva Fountain and Los Arcos monument. Four glass-enclosed elevators ascend dizzyingly above a 14-story atrium lobby to the guest rooms, which have dignified furnishings, small marble bathrooms, and some arresting views (rooms 1211 through 1217 have the best). The lobby bar has live music nightly. On the *piso ejecutivo* (executive floor) rooms come with breakfast, and there's a business center. **Pros:** Nice amenities, ample parking, portable room heaters at no charge. **Cons:** Some rooms have unattractive views, no swimming pool. ⊠*Av. Aurelio Aceves 225, Zona Minerva,* ☎*33/3818–1400* *www.fiesta mericana.com.mx* *387 rooms, 4 suites* *In-room: Wi-Fi. In-hotel: Restaurant, bar, gym, public Internet, concierge, no-smoking rooms, parking (fee)* *AE, DC, MC, V.*

$$$ Fodor'sChoice ★ **Villa Ganz.** Staying in this neighborhood full of restaurants and nightlife yet away from the gritty historic center might be just the ticket. But location is just one of the many virtues of this gracious mansion. We loved the spacious rooms, the hunting-lodge-like sitting area with fireplace, and a candlelit, tree-shaded garden that will make you want to book an extended stay. Private dinners in the garden can be arranged in advance and make for Guadalajara's most romantic dining. **Pros:** Great location, understated elegance, inviting patios. **Cons:** Steep service charge added to your bill. ⊠*López Cotilla 1739, Zona Minerva<zip>44160* ☎*33/3120–1416* *www.villaganz.com* *10 suites* *In-room: Safe. In-hotel: Bar, public Wi-Fi, no kids under 12* *AE, MC, V* *CP.*

$$ ★ **Hotel Plaza Diana.** At this modest hotel two blocks from the Minerva Fountain, the rooms are on the small side, but each has its own rather formal sitting area and two TVs. One suite even has a sauna. Stay on the upper floors in the rear for the quietest rooms. The expansive restaurant specializes in Argentine-style cuts of beef. The huge indoor pool is good for swimming laps. **Pros:** Good location, heated indoor pool, free airport shuttle. **Cons:** Gym is on the small side, bland furnishings. ✉ *Ave. Agustín Yáñez 2760, Zona Minerva,* ☎ *33/3540–9700, 01800/248–1001 in Mexico* ⊕ *www.hoteldiana.com.mx* *127 rooms, 24 suites* *In-room: Safe. In-hotel: Restaurant, room service, bar, pool, gym, airport shuttle* ▭ *AE, DC, MC, V.*

ZONA PLAZA DEL SOL

$$$ ★ **Hilton.** Adjacent to the Expo Guadalajara convention center is the city's top business hotel. Among its many business services are a multilingual staff, a business center, and an executive floor (with free breakfast in a private dining area). There are excellent spa facilities and a fitness center that was renovated in 2007. At breakfast, you'll rub elbows with local business executives at the popular Vitrales restaurant. **Pros:** Good location for business travelers, 24-hour room service. **Cons:** Uninspiring breakfast on executive floor. ✉ *Av. de las Rosas 2933, Zona Plaza del Sol,* ☎ *33/3678–0505, 01800/003–1400 in Mexico, 800/445–8667* ⊕ *www.guadalajara.hilton.com* *432 rooms, 20 suites* *In-room: Ethernet, Wi-Fi. In-hotel: 2 restaurants, bar, pool, gym, spa, executive floor, no-smoking rooms* ▭ *AE, DC, MC, V.*

$$$ **Presidente InterContinental.** With its mirrored facade and 12-story atrium lobby, this bustling hotel attracts a sophisticated business clientele. For the best city view, request a room on an upper floor facing the Plaza del Sol shopping center. A Tane silver shop is one of the many on-site stores, and the 24-hour health club is one of the city's best. **Pros:** 24-hour business center, impressive gym, heated pool. **Cons:** On a busy corner, walking distance to nothing except the mall. ✉ *Av. López Mateos Sur 3515, at Moctezuma, Zona Plaza del Sol,* ☎ *33/3678–1234 or 888/424–6835* ⊕ *www.ichotelsgroup.com* *379 rooms, 30 suites* *In-room: Ethernet, Wi-Fi. In-hotel: 2 restaurants, bar, pool, gym, spa, executive floor, public Internet, public Wi-Fi, parking (fee), laundry service, airport shuttle* ▭ *AE, DC, MC, V .*

$$ **Crowne Plaza Guadalajara.** Gardens encircling the pool add a bit of nature to this family-friendly hotel near Plaza del Sol. A well-chosen mix of reproduction antiques fills the public spaces. Rooms have marble baths and lots of natural light; those in the tower have city views. Plaza Club room rates include a buffet breakfast. The top-floor Jacarandas restaurant—a real '60s throwback with red leatherette booths—has the best panoramic view of Guadalajara. **Pros:** Great views, 24-hour business center. **Cons:** Uninspired room decor, rooms near playground can be noisy. ✉ *Av. López Mateos Sur 2500, Zona Plaza del Sol,* ☎ *33/3634–1034, 01800/009–9900 in Mexico* ⊕ *www.cpguadalajara.com.mx* *291 rooms, 5 suites* *In-room: Wi-Fi (some). In-hotel: 2 restaurants, bar, room service, concierge, pool, gym, executive floor,*

public Wi-Fi, no-smoking rooms, laundry service, parking (fee) ▭*AE, DC, MC, V.*

TLAQUEPAQUE

$$ **Quinta Don José.** One block from Tlaquepaque's main plaza and shopping area, this bed-and-breakfast has a great location. And its amenities make it feel like a small hotel. Natural lighting and room size vary, so look at a few before you choose one. Suites face the pool, and are spacious but a bit dark. There's remarkable tile work in the master suite. Hearty breakfasts are served in an inner courtyard, and tasty pizzas are baked in the brick oven at the Italian restaurant. Inexpensive area tours are offered here, too. **Pros:** Central location, friendly staff, free calls worldwide. **Cons:** Pool is chilly, some rooms are small. ✉*Calle Reforma 139,* ☎*33/3635–7522, 01800/700–2223 in Mexico, 866/629–3753 in U.S. and Canada* 🌐*www.quintadonjose.com* *8 rooms, 7 suites* *In-hotel: bar, pool, laundry service, airport shuttle, public Wi-Fi* ▭*AE, MC, V* *BP.*

$$ **La Villa del Ensueño.** A 10-minute walk from Tlaquepaque's center, this intimate B&B is near lots of shopping. The restored 19th-century hacienda has thick, white adobe walls, exposed-beam ceilings, and plants in huge unglazed pots. Smokers should request a room with private balcony, as smoking isn't allowed inside. A restaurant is in the works. **Pros:** Close to shopping, friendly staff. **Cons:** Only junior suites have bathtubs, for smokers, no smoking inside. ✉*Florida 305,* ☎*33/3635–8792* 🌐*www.villadelensueno.com* *16 rooms, 4 suites* *In-room: refrigerator (some), dial-up, Wi-Fi (some). In-hotel: restaurant, bar, pools, no-smoking rooms, parking (no fee)* ▭*AE, MC, V* *BP.*

$ **La Casa del Retoño.** On a quiet street several blocks from the shopping district is this B&B. Rooms are made of painted cinder block, but are clean and cheerful. Rooms in the back overlook a large garden, while the ones upstairs have private terraces. There's an open-air reading area, and breakfast is served in the courtyard. **Pros:** Quiet neighborhood, private terraces in some rooms. **Cons:** Smallish rooms, lackluster garden. ✉*Matamoros 182,* ☎*33/3587–3989* 🌐*www.lacasadelretono.com.mx* *8 rooms, 1 suite* *In-room: Wi-Fi* ▭*AE, MC, V* *CP.*

NIGHTLIFE

With the exception of a few well-established nightspots like La Maestranza, downtown Guadalajara is mostly asleep by 11 PM. The existing nightlife centers around Avenida Vallarta, favored by the well-to-do under-30 set; Avenida Patria, full of bars for young people who party until early in the morning; or the somewhat seedy Plaza del Sol. Bars in these spots open into the wee hours, usually closing by 3 AM. Dance clubs may charge a $15–$20 cover, which includes an open bar, on Wednesday and Saturday nights. Dress up for nightclubs; highly subjective admission policies hinge on who you know or how you look.

The local music scene centers around Peña Cuicacalli and the Hard Rock Cafe.

BARS

Touristy but fun, **Los Carajos Cantina** (✉*Morelos 79, Centro Histórico* ☎*33/3126–7951*) is a great place to snuggle into a nook on the second floor and have a drink while gazing down over Guadalajara's busiest pedestrian street.

Der Krug Braühaus (✉*Cervantes 15 at Morelos, Col. Americana* ☎*33/1057–8386*) is the newest and most authentic German-style beer hall in the city. It's attracting a young and hip crowd, some of whom stay around to nibble beer-marinated pork chops.

★ Appealing and unpretentious, **La Fuente** (✉*Calle Pino Suarez s/n, Centro Histórico* ☎*No phone*) opened in this location in 1950. The cantina draws business types, intellectuals, and blue-collar workers, all seeking cheap drinks, animated conversation, and live music. Above the bar, look for an old bicycle caked in dust. It's been around since 1957, when, legend has it, one of a long list of famous people (most say it was the father of local newspaper baron Jesús Álvarez del Castillo) left the bike to pay for his drinks. Arrive early to avoid crowds.

One of Guadalajara's hot spots, **I Latina** (✉*Av. Inglaterra at López Mateos*, Col. Vallarta Poniente ☎*33/3647–7774*) is where you will spot a cool international crowd having cocktails.

For some local color, stop at **La Maestranza** (✉*Calle Maestranza 179, between López Cotillo and Madero, Centro Histórico* ☎*33/3613–5878*), a renovated 1940s cantina full of bullfighting memorabilia.

Everyone is talking about **La Matera** (✉*Av. México 2891*, Col. Vallarta Norte ☎*33/3616–1626*). It's an Argentine steak house that attracts late-night drinkers as well.

El Muro (✉*Av. Vallarta 1593*, Col. Americana ☎*33/3616–9043*) is a good place to go hear live music acts in animated surroundings.

After 9 PM Tuesday through Sunday, patrons cluster around the small stage at **La Peña Cuicacalli** (✉*Av. Niños Héroes 1988, Centro Histórico* ☎*33/3825–4690*). There's *rock en español* on Tuesday and folk music from Mexico, Latin America, and Spain other nights.

DANCE CLUBS

Bossé (✉*Av. Patría 1600*, Col. Agraria ☎*33/3848–9395*) keeps people dancing into the wee hours of the night with a rotating selection of top DJs; the crowd is young.

Maxim's (✉*Hotel Francés, Calle Maestranza 35, Centro Histórico* ☎*33/3613–1190 or 33/3613–0936*) stays open quite late and is among downtown's better discos. Cover is $3 Thursday through Sunday, but free otherwise.

Well-dressed professionals over 25 go to the second-floor **El Mito** (✉ *Centro Magno mall, Av. Vallarta 2425, Zona Minerva* ☎ *33/3615–7246*); there's '70s and '80s music Wednesday, Friday, and Saturday 10 PM–4 AM.

OCIO

For the latest listings, grab a *Público* newspaper on Friday and pull out the weekly Ocio cultural guide.

Salón Veracruz (✉ *Calle Manzano 486, behind Hotel Misión Carlton, Centro Histórico* ☎ *33/3613–4422*) is a spartan, old-style dance hall where a 15-piece band keeps hoofers moving to Colombian *cumbia;* Dominican merengue; and *danzón,* a waltzlike dance invented in Cuba. It's open Wednesday to Saturday 9:30 PM–3:30 AM, and Sunday 6 PM–2 AM; cover is about $5, less on Sunday.

You can dance to popular Latin and European music at the multilevel **Tropigala** (✉ *Av. López Mateos Sur 2188, Zona Minerva* ☎ *33/3122–5553 or 33/3122–7903*), across from the Plaza del Sol mall.

5

PERFORMANCES

Ballet Folclórico of the University of Guadalajara. The university's internationally acclaimed troupe performs traditional Mexican folkloric dances and music in Teatro Diana most Sundays at 10 AM. ☎ *33/3614–7072* 🌐 *www.ballet.udg.mx* 🎫 *$3–$25.*

Large-scale theater, dance, and musical performances occasionally take place on a patio at the **Instituto Cultural Cabañas** (✉ *Calle Cabañas 8, Centro Histórico* ☎ *33/3818–2800 Ext. 31016*). The Tolsá Chapel hosts more intimate events. Traveling art exhibitions stop here, and affordable, long-term art courses are offered.

Orquesta Filarmónica de Jalisco. Though it's among Mexico's most poorly paid orchestras, the state-funded philharmonic manages remarkably good performances (usually pieces by Mexican composers mixed with standard orchestral fare). When in season (it varies), the OFJ performs Sunday at 12:30 PM and Friday at 8:30 PM. They perform at Teatro Delgollado, and on the facing plaza, they hold an outdoor year-end performance that helps kick off September's Mariachi Festival. ☎ *No phone* 🌐 *www.ofj.com.mx* 🎫 *$5–$15.*

★ **Teatro Degollado.** Guadalajara's best performing-arts venue is a nearly 150-year-old theater that's subject to constant renovation. If it's open to the public when you're there, however, it's worth a look inside. The popular folkloric dance performances formerly held here have been moved to the newer Teatro Diana. ✉ *Calle Degollado between Av. Hidalgo and Calle Morelos, Centro Histórico* ☎ *33/3614–4773 or 33/3613–1115.*

Affiliated with the University of Guadalajara, **Teatro Diana** (✉ *Av. 16 de Septiembre 710, Centro* ☎ *33/3614–7072* 🌐 *www.teatrodiana.com*) is

Guadalajara's most modern theater. If you don't speak Spanish, see a flamenco show in which actions speak louder than words.

SHOPPING

Tapatíos love shopping at outlet malls *north* of the border. Nevertheless, the city supports a swath of modern malls, and most double as gathering spots with their restaurants and theaters. The *Centro Histórico* is packed with shops as well as ambulatory vendors, who compete with pedestrians for sidewalk space. You'll find the most products under one roof at labyrinthine Mercado Libertad, one of Latin America's largest markets. Tlaquepaque and Tonalá are arts-and-crafts meccas. Shoe stores are ubiquitous in Guadalajara—probably because shoes wear out so fast here.

Stores tend to open Monday–Saturday from 9 or 10 until 8, and Sunday 10–2; some close during lunch, usually 2–4 or 2–5, and others close on Sunday. Bargaining is customary in Mercado Libertad, and you can talk deals with some crafts vendors in Tlaquepaque and Tonalá. The ticketed price sticks just about everywhere else, with the exception of antiques shops.

MARKETS

Tonalá's crafts market and Mercado Libertad are the region's top two marketplaces. Allot yourself plenty of time and energy to explore both. El Trocadero is a weekly antiques market at the north end of Avenida Chapultepec. Feel free to drive a hard bargain at all three.

Antiquers come out of the woodwork every Sunday 10–5 to sell their wares—including European flatware, Mexican pottery, and larger pieces—at El Trocadero in the antiques district. ✉*Av. Mexico at Av. Chapultepec, Zona Minerva* ☎*No phone.*

Mercado Libertad. Better known as San Juan de Dios, this is one of Latin America's largest covered markets. Its three expansive floors, with shops organized thematically, tower over downtown's east side. Fluctuating degrees of government intervention dictate the quantity of contraband electronics available. Avoid the food on the second floor unless you have a stomach of iron. Be wary of fakes in the jewelry stores. The market opens Monday–Saturday 10–8, but some stores close at 6; the few shops open on

LOCAL HAUNTS

Locals stop at the Mercado Corona, due west of the Palacio Municipal, to pick up fresh produce and meat. The streets north of the market have similar goods, dry merchandise, and school supplies. The Medrano district, starting a block south of the Plaza de los Mariachis and continuing east along Calle Obregón into eastern Guadalajara's nether reaches, is a favorite Tapatío shopping haunt. Though they're short on touristy goods, venturing into these parts is like entering the city's central nervous system.

Sunday close by 3. ✉ *Calz. Independencia Sur; use pedestrian bridge from Plaza Tapatía's south side, Centro Histórico* ☎ *No phone.*

SPECIALTY SHOPS

ART & HANDICRAFTS

Influenced by the florid baroque style of 17th-century New Spain, artist Agustín Parra crafts everything from ornate tables and doors to religious icons at **Agustín Parra Diseño Novohispano** (✉ *Calle Independencia 158Tlaquepaque* ☎ *33/3657–8530 or 33/3657–0316*).

The staff at **El antiQuario Magazine** (✉ *Av. Chapultepec Norte 67, interior 32, at Av. Hidalgo, Zona Rosa* ☎ *33/3616–6667* 🌐 *www.elantiquario.com*), particularly Roberto Alvarado, evaluates antiques, art, and folk art. They run personalized buying tours for around $100 a day or more. One week's advance notice is requested.

5

Cadi (✉ *Juárez 174, Tlaquepaque* ☎ *33/3343–3682*) sells awesome stained-glass lamps and other decorative items for the home.

Fodor'sChoice ★ Sergio Bustamante's work is in galleries around the world, but you can purchase his sculptures of human, animal, and fairy-tale creatures in bronze, ceramic. or resin for less at **Galería Sergio Bustamante** (✉ *Calle Independencia 238Tlaquepaque* ☎ *33/3639–5519, 33/3657–8354, or 33/3659–7110*).You'll also find his designs in silver- and gold-plated jewelry. Don't expect a bargain, however; most pieces range from hundreds to thousands of dollars.

The government-run **Instituto de la Artesanía Jalisciense** (✉ *Calz. González Gallo 20, at Calz. Independencia Sur, Centro Histórico* ☎ *33/3030–9090*), on the northeast side of Parque Agua Azul, has exquisite blown glass and hand-glazed pottery typical of Jalisco artisans. Prices are fixed here.

For whimsical statues, head to **Rodo Padilla** (✉ *Independencia 139, CentroTlaquepaque* ☎ *33/3657–3712*). The shop is full of the local artisan's hand-sculpted ceramic and metal pieces. His subjects range from older couples riding bikes to entire families crammed into cars.

CLOTHING

In a stylish Victorian mansion, the boutique of **Alberto Rodríguez** (✉ *Av. Vallarta 1300, Zona Minerva* ☎ *33/3827–2871*) displays wild and refined gowns by one of the region's top designers.

Designer **Alejandro Julian Nuñez** (✉ *Ignacio Ramirez 93, Zona Minerva* ☎ *33/3825–7464*) creates casual and semiformal clothing from *manta* (a sturdy cotton), hand embroidered with Huichol motifs.

Make a splash at Halloween dressed up as a mariachi or charro (Mexican cowboy) with a big leather belt and extra-wide-brim hat. You can thumb through an extensive selection of authentic charro gear at **El Charro** (✉ *Local 30, Av. López Mateos Sur 2375 [Plaza del Sol mall]* ☎ *33/3122–5148* ✉ *Av. Juárez, Centro* ☎ *33/3614–7599*).

SILVER & JEWELRY

Eréndira Contis (✉*La Gran Plaza Mall Av. Vallarta 3959,* Zapopan ☎*33/3123–1254*), specializing in nuptial jewelry, stands out in a city that's rife with jewelry offerings. Contis and Lewis Kant display modern Mexican art, as well as their own sculptures, and craft unique pieces from gold, silver, and precious stones.

Mercado Libertad has silver at great prices, but not everything that glitters there is certifiably silver. A safer, albeit pricier, bet is the shops along Avenida República in downtown Guadalajara, where there are more than 400 jewelers. **Centro Joyero República** (✉*Av. República 28,* Centro ☎*33/3617–7070*) is a safe bet for good authentic silver.Finally, for quality jewelry, check out **Tapatío Centro Joyero** (✉*Av. República 70,* Centro ☎*33/3617–1701*).

> **RUMOR HAS IT**
>
> It's believed that centuries ago the Tiquila, a small Nahuatl-speaking tribe, discovered the fermenting powers of the agave heart's juice. When distilled (an innovation introduced after the Spanish arrived in the 16th century), the fermented liquid turns into the heady liquor, which can be legally named tequila only when cultivated and distilled in this and a few other regions of Mexico.

SPORTS & THE OUTDOORS

BULLFIGHTS

Corridas (bullfights) are held Sunday at 4:30 from October to December at **Plaza Nuevo Progreso** (✉*Calle M. Pirineos 1930 and Calz. Independencia Norte, across from Estadio Jalisco, Zona Huentitán* ☎*33/3637–9982 or 33/3651–8506*), which is 5 km (3 mi) northeast of downtown (Buses 60, 60A, and 600 will get you here). Tickets are sold for the *sol* (sunny) or *sombra* (shady) side of the bullring. Buy tickets ($8–$70) at the bullring or its booth in Plaza México. *Novilleros* (apprentice matadors) often work the cape between 8 AM and 2 PM; it's free to watch them practice.

GOLF

Clubs are less crowded on Wednesday and Thursday; all rent equipment for around $20 to $30. Golf carts typically cost around $40. Guadalajara's top golf clubs—El Cielo and Santa Anita—are technically for members only, but hotels can get you in.

Las Cañadas Country Club (✉*Av. Bosques San Isidro 777, Zapopan* ☎*33/3685–0512 or 33/3685–0412*) is a rolling, 18-hole course in an exclusive area of Zapopan. Greens fees are $60–$80.

The private **El Cielo Country Club** (✉*Paseo del Cello 1* ☎*33/3684–4436*), on a hill outside town, is an 18-hole, 6,765-yard, par-72 course blissfully removed from the city's din and with challenging holes and water features. For nonmembers it's $270 for 18 holes.

Club de Golf Atlas (✉ *Carretera Guadalajara–Chapala, Km 6.5, El Salto* ☎ *33/3689–2620*) is an 18-hole, par-72 course designed by Joe Finger that's on the way to the airport. Greens fees are about $100 on weekdays, and $120 on weekends and holidays.

The **Club de Golf Santa Anita** (✉ *Carretera a Morelia, Km 6.5* ☎ *33/3686–0321 or 33/3686–1192*) is a private club with an 18-hole, 6,872-yard course—the region's longest. Greens fees for nonmembers are $95. Guest passes are necessary at both of these clubs: call ahead or ask your concierge.

HEALTH CLUBS

Gold's Gym (✉ *Av. Vallarta 1791, Zona Minerva* ☎ *33/3630–2220* ✉ *Av. Xóchitl 4203, Zona Plaza del Sol* ☎ *33/3647–0420* ✉ *Av. Niños Héroes 2851, Centro Histórico* ☎ *33/3647–4960*) has three convenient locations. The Vallarta location is close to the Centro and has the best hours (weekdays 6 AM–11 PM, Sat. 8 AM –9 PM and Sun. 8 AM –3 PM). The Xóchitl branch is the best equipped, with a pool, climbing wall, and basketball and squash courts. Xóchitl and Niños Héroes are open until 10 on weekdays and 5 on weekends. Guest passes are $9.50.

5

The health club at **Presidente Inter-Continental** (✉ *Av. López Mateos Sur 3515, Zona Plaza del Sol* ☎ *33/3678–1227*), open daily 5:30 AM–11 PM, admits nonguests for about $15.

TENNIS

The court at the **Camino Real** (✉ *Av. Vallarta 5005, Zona Minerva* ☎ *33/3134–2424*) opens daily 7 AM–10 PM, and costs $14 an hour during the day and $19 at night. Reservations are essential.

SIDE TRIPS FROM GUADALAJARA

An hour's drive in just about any direction from Guadalajara will bring you out of the fray and into the countryside. Due south are Lake Chapala, Mexico's largest lake, and Ajijic, a village of bougainvillea and cobblestone roads. Tequila, where the infamous firewater is brewed, is west of Guadalajara. Teuchitlán, south of Tequila, has the Guachimontones ruins. The placid lakeside area makes for a weeklong (expats would say lifelong) getaway, while Tequila and Teuchitlán are great for day-trippers.

TEQUILA

56 km (35 mi) northwest of Guadalajara.

As you leave the smog of Guadalajara, the entire landscape changes; suddenly, the land is the distinctive blue-green color of agave. As you near Tequila, families are selling pure agave tequila in plastic bottles for astoundingly low prices. For an in-depth look at how Mexico's most

CLOSE UP

The Struggle of the Huichol

The Huichol (WEE-chol) Indians' true name is Wirraritari, or "people who populate places of thorny plants." It's a fitting name for this hardy and reclusive group, whose independence has helped them preserve their traditions better than many of Mexico's native communities. (As a measure of their isolation, some Huichol communities only had electricity installed in 2003.) To outsiders, the most notable among Huichol traditions is the use of peyote, a hallucinogenic cactus fruit, in complex spiritual ceremonies. Huichol artists also create remarkable "paintings" by pressing colorful beads or yarn onto wood molds smeared with sap.

The Huichol fiercely resisted Spanish—and later Mexican—intrusion; nowadays most live in northern Jalisco, southern Nayarit, and Zacatecas, in a remote 592,800-acre reservation established in 1953. In recent years, however, the ownership and boundaries of some Huichol lands, much of it rented out to farmers and cattle breeders, have come under dispute. The conflict hasn't been peaceful, with allegations of human rights violations perpetrated by Nayarit police as well as by the current "tenants." In the mid-1990s, after a long investigation, Mexico's Human Rights Commission (CEDH) corroborated many of the Huichol allegations, and a recent constitutional amendment affirmed the autonomy of the Huichol and other indigenous communities within Mexico. But problems continue—there remains intense pressure to develop some Huichol lands, and the Mexican Army, in its highly visible war on drugs, has arrested Huichol coming back from religious pilgrimages in the San Luis Potosi desert, where they collect peyote.

famous liquor is derived from the spiny blue agave plant that grows in fields alongside the highway, stop by this tiny village.

GETTING HERE & AROUND

The drive to tequila country is a straightforward and easy trip: head west from Guadalajara along Avenida Vallarta for about 25 minutes until you hit the toll road junction (it will say Puerto Vallarta Cuota). The whole trip takes about 1½ hours by car. Either take the toll road (*cuota*) or the free road (*libre*) toward Puerto Vallarta. The toll road is faster, safer, and costs about $10. You can also catch a bus to Tequila from the Antigua Central Camionera (Old Central Bus Station), northeast of the Parque Agua Azul on Avenida Dr. R. Michel, between Calle Los Angeles and Calle 5 de Febrero. Buses marked amatitán–tequila are easy to spot from the entrance on Calle Los Angeles.

EXPLORING

The **Museo Nacional del Tequila** (✉ *Calle Ramon Corona 34* ☎ *374/742–0012*) is open Monday to Sunday 10 to 5 ($1.50). The gallery sometimes hosts exhibits by local artists.

The **Sauza Museum** (✉ *Calle Albino Rojas 22* ☎ *374/742–0247*) has memorabilia from the Sauza family, a tequila-making dynasty second only to the Cuervos. The museum is open weekdays 10 to 2. Admission is $1.

Opened in 1795, the **José Cuervo Distillery** (✉*Calle José Cuervo 73* ☎*374/742–2442*) is the world's oldest tequila distillery. Every day, 150 tons of agave hearts are processed into 80,000 liters of tequila. Hard-hat tours are offered daily every hour from 10 to 4. The tours at noon are normally in English, but English-speakers can often be accommodated at other times. Basic tours, which includes sips of tequila along the way, cost $10. Tours including round-trip transportation are $25. They're a good deal, as they include three tequila tastings and a complimentary margarita. Call ahead.

For a visit to where Herradura tequila is made, go to **San José del Refugio** (✉*Comercio 172, Amatitán* ☎*33/3942–3900* 🌐*www.herradura.com*). It's a spectacular old hacienda where you can see workers' quarters from long ago. The tour ends with a tear-jerking film about the history of tequila, as well as a tasting of some of the different tequilas you can purchase in the gift shop. Tours are scheduled for weekdays on the hour from 9 to 3 and Saturday at 9, 10, and 11, but some are cancelled if there aren't enough customers. Call ahead for reservations.

5

TEUCHITLÁN

50 km (28 mi) west of Guadalajara.

For decades, residents in this sleepy village of sugarcane farmers had a name for the funny-looking mounds in the hills above town, but they never considered the Guachimontones to be more than a convenient source of rocks for local construction projects. Then in the early 1970s an American archaeologist asserted that the mounds were the remnants of a long-vanished, 2,000-year-old community. It took Phil Weigand nearly three decades to convince authorities in far-off Mexico City that he wasn't crazy. Before he was allowed to start excavating and restoring this monumental site in the late 1990s, plenty more houses and roads were produced with Guachimonton rock—and countless tombs were looted of priceless art.

This UNESCO World Heritage Site is most distinctive for its sophisticated concentric architecture—a circular pyramid surrounded by a ring of flat ground, surrounded by a series of smaller platforms arranged in a circle. The "Teuchitlán Tradition," as the concentric circle structures are called, is unique in world architecture. Weigand believes the formations suggest the existence of a pre-Hispanic state in the region, whereas it was previously held that only socially disorganized nomads inhabited the region at the time. Similar ruins are spread throughout the foothills of the extinct Tequila Volcano, but this is the biggest site yet detected.

To get to Teuchitlán from Guadalajara, drive west out along Avenida Vallarta for 25 minutes to the toll road junction to Puerto Vallarta: choose the free (*libre*) road 70 toward Vallarta. Head west along Route 15 for a couple of miles, then turn left onto Route 70 and continue until you reach the town of Tala. One mile past the sugar mill, turn right onto Route 27. Teuchitlán is 15 minutes from the last junction. The ruins are up a dirt road from town; just ask for directions when you arrive. There's a small museum off the main square. If you visit during the dry season you may score a look at a dig or restoration project.

AROUND LAGO DE CHAPALA

48 km (30 mi) southeast of Guadalajara.

Mexico's largest natural lake is a one-hour drive southeast of Guadalajara. Surrounded by jagged hills and serene towns, Lake Chapala is a favorite Tapatío getaway and a haven for thousands of North American retirees. The name probably derives from Chapalac, who was chief of the region's Taltica Indians when the Spaniards arrived in 1538.

The area's main town, Chapala, is flooded with weekend visitors and the pier is packed shoulder-to-shoulder most Sundays. Eight kilometers (5 mi) west is Ajijic, a village that's home to the bulk of the area's expatriates. Farther west is San Juan Cosalá, popular for its thermal-water pools.

WATER LEVELS

Fifty miles wide but less than 30 feet deep when full, Lake Chapala is the vestige of an ancient inland sea. It's at the tail end (in geological terms) of a natural death from millennia of silt accumulation. This drying process has been accelerated in recent decades by overexploitation of the Lerma River feeding the lake. In 2002 Lake Chapala plummeted to an average depth of 4 feet, exposing a mile of lake bed stretching from the Chapala pier. Several years of above-average summer rainfall has the lake on the verge of its former glory—but for its excessive pollution.

GETTING HERE & AROUND

Driving from Guadalajara, take Avenida Lázaro Cárdenas or Dr. R. Michel to Carretera a Chapala. The trip takes about an hour. The Carretera a Chapala is the quickest route to Chapala and Ajijic.

Autotransportes Guadalajara Chapala (☎*33/3619–5675*) serves the lakeside towns for about $4. It's 30 minutes to Chapala and another 15 minutes to Ajijic; there are departures every half hour from 6 AM to 9:30 PM. Make sure you ask for the *directo* (direct) as opposed to *clase segunda* (second-class) bus, which stops at every little pueblo en route.

CHAPALA

45 km (28 mi) south of Guadalajara.

Chapala was a placid weekend getaway for aristocrats in the late 19th century, but when then-president Porfirio Díaz got in on the action in 1904, other wealthy Mexicans followed suit. More and more summer homes were built, and in 1910 the Chapala Yacht Club opened. Avenida Madero, Chapala's main street, is lined with restaurants, shops, and cafés. Three blocks north of the promenade, the plaza at the corner of López Cotilla is a relaxing spot to read a paper or succumb to sweets from surrounding shops. The Iglesia de San Francisco (built in 1528), easily recognized by its blue neon crosses on twin steeples, is two blocks south of the plaza.

On weekends Mexican families flock to the shores of the (for now, at least) rejuvenated lake. Vendors sell refreshments and souvenirs, while lakeside watering holes fill to capacity.

CAUTION

On both ends of the highway are precarious hilly stretches. Care should be taken while returning to Guadalajara from Chapala on Sunday night, when the largely unlighted highway fills with tipsy drivers.

WHERE TO EAT & STAY

$$ MEXICAN **Restaurant Cazadores.** This grandly turreted brick building was once the summer home of the Braniff family, former owners of the defunct airline. The menu includes slightly overpriced seafood and beef dishes. The house specialty is chamorro, pork shank wrapped in banana leaves. A patio overlooks the boardwalk and is inviting in the evening. ⊠*Paseo Ramón Corona 18* ☎*376/765–2162* ▭*AE, MC, V* ⊗*Closed Mon.*

$$ **Hotel Villa Montecarlo.** Built on a Mediterranean-style villa nearly a century old, this hotel has well-maintained grounds dotted with places for picnics or for the kids to play. One of the two swimming pools (the biggest in the area) is filled water from the nearby hot springs; it's usually open only on weekends and holidays. The simple, clean rooms all have patios or terraces. Popular with Mexican families, the hotel has packages that are often good deals. For about $20 more than a standard room you can get a suite with larger terrace or balcony, a kitchenette, and king-size bed. **Pros:** Huge pools, extensive grounds, outdoor dining under a flowering tree. **Cons:** Can be noisy. ⊠*Av. Hidalgo 296, about 1 km (½ mi) west of Av. Madero,* ☎*376/765–2120 or 376/765–2024* *46 rooms, 2 suites* *In-room: no a/c. In-hotel: restaurant, bar, tennis courts, pools, laundry service, parking (no fee)* ▭*AE, MC, V.*

$ ★ **Lake Chapala Inn.** Now that the lake is back, this European-style inn is an especially appealing place to stay. Three of the four rooms in this restored mansion face the shore; all have high ceilings and whitewashed oak furniture. Rates include an English-style breakfast (with a Continental breakfast on Sunday). **Pros:** Solar-heated lap pool, English-speaking host, sunny reading room. **Cons:** Dated furnishings, square tubs not conducive to long soaks. ⊠*Paseo Ramón Corona 23,* ☎*376/765–4786 or 376/765–4809* ⊕*www.mexonline.com/chapalainn.htm* *4 rooms* *In-room: Wi-Fi, no a/c. In-hotel: restaurant, pool, public Wi-Fi, laundry service* ▭*No credit cards* *BP.*

AJIJIC

8 km (5 mi) west of Chapala, 47 km (30 mi) southwest of Guadalajara.

Ajijic has narrow cobblestone streets, vibrantly colored buildings, and a gentle pace—with the exception of the very trafficky main highway through the town's southern end. The foreign influence is unmistakable: English is widely (though not exclusively) spoken and license plates come from far-flung places like British Columbia and Texas.

The Plaza Principal (also known as Plaza de Armas) is a tree- and flower-filled central square at the corner of Avenidas Colón and Hidalgo. The Iglesia de San Andrés (Church of St. Andrew) is on the plaza's north side. In late November the plaza and its surrounding streets fill for the saint's nine-day fiesta. From the plaza, walk down Calle Morelos (the continuation of Avenida Colón) toward the lake and peruse the boutiques. Turn left onto Avenida 16 de Septiembre or Avenida Constitución for art galleries and studios. Northeast of the plaza, along the highway, activity centers around the soccer field, which doubles as a venue for bullfights and concerts.

WHERE TO EAT & STAY

$$ ECLECTIC ✕ **La Bodega de Ajijic.** Eat on a covered patio overlooking a grassy lawn and a small pool at this low-key restaurant. In addition to Mexican standards, the menu has Italian dishes such as pastas; the food here is a bit meager and overpriced. Still, service is friendly, and there's live music—ranging from Mexican pop and rock to jazz, guitar, and harp—most nights. ✉ *Av. 16 de Septiembre 124* ☎ *376/766–1002* ▭ *MC, V.*

$$ GERMAN ✕ **Johanna's.** Come to this intimate bit of Bavaria on the lake for German cuisine like sausages and goose or duck pâté. Main dishes come with soup or salad, applesauce, and cooked red cabbage. For dessert indulge in plum strudel or blackberry-topped torte. ✉ *Carretera Chapala–Jocotepec, Km 6.5* ☎ *376/766–0437* ▭ *No credit cards* ⊙ *Closed Mon. No dinner Sun.*

$ AMERICAN ✕ **Salvador's.** An old mainstay that's showing its years, this cafeteria-like eatery is a popular expat hangout. There's a well-kept salad bar and specialties from both sides of the border. On weekends people flock here for the fish-and-chips lunch special. This is a good place to start your day, as the reasonably prices breakfasts are served beginning at 7:30 AM. ✉ *Carretera Chapala–Jocotepec Oriente 58* ☎ *376/766–2301* ▭ *No credit cards* ⊙ No dinner Sun.

$–$$ ★ ✕ **La Nueva Posada.** The well-kept gardens framed in bougainvillea define this inviting inn. Rooms are large, with high ceilings and local crafts. Villas share a courtyard and have tile kitchenettes. The bar has jazz or Caribbean music most weekend evenings. Out in the garden restaurant ($), strands of tiny white lights set the mood for an evening meal. **Pros:** Unique decor, airy rooms, great restaurant. **Cons:** Small room TVs. ✉ *Calle Donato Guerra 9* *A.P. 30, 45920* ☎ *376/766–1344* 🌐 *www.mexconnect.com/MEX/rest/nueva/posada.html* *19 rooms, 4 villas* *In-hotel: restaurant, bar, pool, laundry service* ▭ *MC, V* *BP.*

$ **Casa Blanca.** This hotel, whose name means White House, brings a hint of the Middle East in the form of gracious gardens, tinkling fountains, and arched windows. Rooms are cheerful and tastefully decorated with blond-wood furnishings. All share a pleasant patio. Each room has plenty of free drinking water. The on-site Internet center offers inexpensive Internet access to guests and others. **Pros:** Charming atmosphere, inexpensive rates, good location near lake and shopping. **Cons:** Small rooms. ✉*Calle 16 de Septiembre 29, Centro,* ☎*376/766–4440, 800/436–0759 in U.S.* 🌐*www.casablancaajijic.com* *8 rooms* *In-room: kitchen (some), Wi-Fi. In-hotel: public Internet, public Wi-Fi, airport shuttle* *AE, MC, V* *CP.*

NIGHTLIFE

La Bodega (✉*Calle 16 de Septiembre 124* ☎*376/766–1002* *$3 cover Fri. and Sun.*) has dancing Friday and Sunday, and live guitar music the rest of the week. It's closed Monday.

The rambling, hacienda-style **Posada Ajijic** (✉*Calle Morelos 1* ☎*376/766–0744*) is a popular weekend dance spot.

SHOPPING

Ajijic's main shopping strip is Calle Morelos, but there are many galleries and shops east of Morelos, on Avenida 16 de Septiembre and Calle Constitución.

5

Artesanía Huichol (✉ *Calle Donato Guerra 18* ☎*376/766–5125*) sells Huichol artwork.

Actually a women's co-op, **Creaciones del Lago**(✉*Calle Ramón Corona 11* ☎376/766–1292 sells knitted, embroidered, and crocheted items.

Mi México (✉*Calle Morelos 8* ☎*376/766–0133*) sells a lovely selection of women's clothing, jewelry, and crafts.

SPORTS & THE OUTDOORS

The **Rojas family** (✉*Paseo Del Lago and Camino Real, 4 blocks east of Los Artistas B&B* ☎*376/766–4261*) has been leading horseback trips for more than 30 years. A ride along the lakeshore or in the surrounding hills costs around $8 an hour.

SAN JUAN COSALÁ

2 km (1 mi) west of Ajijic, 50 km (31mi) southwest of Guadalajara.

San Juan Cosalá is known for its natural thermal-water spas along Lago de Chapala. The spa at the **Hotel Balneario San Juan Cosalá** (✉*Calle La Paz Oriente 420, at Carretera Chapala–Jocotepec, Km 13* ☎*387/761–0302* 🌐*www.hotelspacosala.com*) offers reasonably priced massages. The water park has several large swimming pools and two wading pools; admission is $13. Weekends are crowded.

WHERE TO STAY

$$ **Hotel Villa Bordeaux.** This adults-only hotel is operated by the same people as the Hotel Balneario. Rooms are small but attractive, with brick walls and high ceilings. This is a smaller, more subdued, and more tranquil option than Villas Buenaventura Cosalá. A stay here gets you access to the water park for free.**Pros:** Tranquil setting, good restaurant. **Cons:** Crowded on weekends, small rooms. ✉*Calle La Paz Oriente 418, at Carretera Chapala–Jocotepec, Km 13,* ☎*387/761–0494*

11 rooms In-room: No a/c. In-hotel: Restaurant, pool, gym, spa, no kids under 16 MC, V.

$$ **Villas Buenaventura Cosalá.** You can relax for free in the hotel's outdoor thermal pools or rent time in the private hot tubs or private pools. The large one- and two-bedroom suites are clean, if a bit sterile. The grounds are dotted with sculptures. On many weekends during high season the hotel requires a two- or three-night minimum stay, but likely as not the third night is free, which is a real bonus. Choose a unit with or without Jacuzzi and kitchenette. Spalike atmosphere, easy drive from Guadalajara.Noisy children sometimes disturb the peace. *Carretera Chapala–Jocotepec, Km 13.5, 387/761–0202 www.hotelvbc.com 19 suites In-room: No a/c, kitchen (some). In-hotel: Restaurant, pools MC, V.*

Veracruz

Jarochos, Veracruz Citya

WORD OF MOUTH

"Both Veracruz and Xalapa are clearly closer to traditional culture than Cancun . . . but it will be tough to find a town where life has remained unchanged for hundreds of years . . . even remote villages have satellite TV."

–drdawggy

WELCOME TO VERACRUZ

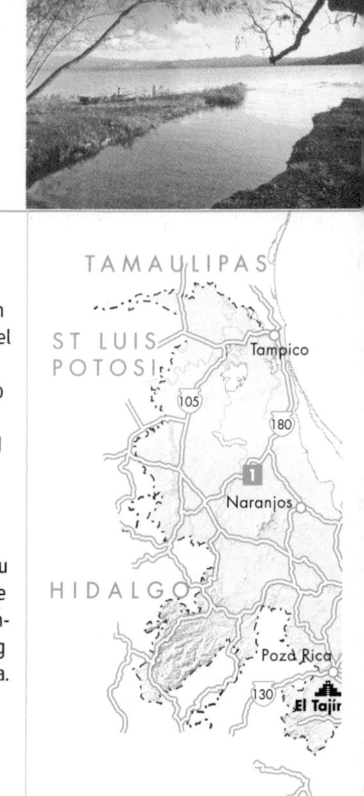

TOP REASONS TO GO

★ **Taking the road less traveled:** Mexicans love to vacation in this state, but it's off the radar for most foreign tourists.

★ **Dining on amazing seafood:** Try it à la *veracruzana,* sautéed with tomatoes, onions, and garlic.

★ **Experiencing little-known ruins:** The ruins of El Tajín, which flourished from the early 9th to the early 13th centuries, are some of the most magnificent in Mexico.

★ **Watching men fly:** Paplanta's *voladores* spin from the top of an 82-foot pole in a breathtaking Totonac ceremony that makes bungee jumping look tame.

★ **Joining in the *danzón*:** This stately dance from Cuba is a cornerstone of Veracruz's eclectic culture.

1 Northern Veracruz. Built by the Totonac, the magnificent ruins of El Tajín are the best reason to travel to Northern Veracruz. The coastal plains that make up this part of the state are filled with vanilla vines and orange and mango groves, giving the city of Papantla its sweet scent.

2 Central Veracruz. If you head inland, you'll meet the Sierra Madre Oriental mountain range, with its stunning 18,400-foot Pico de Orizaba. In the foothills you'll find the state capital Xalapa, a laid-back university town that's also a great base for river-rafting explorations.

3 Veracruz City. Still one of the country's busiest ports, Veracruz City isn't afraid of hard work. But when evening falls the people of this graceful colonial capital let loose and head to the city's parks, which are filled with music and dancing.

4 Southern Veracruz. This is a favorite vacation spot for Mexican families. Along with beaches, you'll find crystalline lakes tucked among gently rolling hills. The most famous is Lago Catemaco, whose shores are lined with small boats waiting to take you out on an excursion.

GETTING ORIENTED

Veracruz State is a long, slim crescent bordering the Gulf of Mexico, about five hours east of Mexico City. The port city of Veracruz is a big draw to the region and the logical jumping-off place. Although the beaches aren't quite the white-sand wonders of the Yucatán, they're cheerful and vibrant. Moreover, the state harbors pockets of colonial history, as well as some fascinating archaeological sites.

VERACRUZ PLANNER

Dancing in the Streets

A great time to visit Veracruz City is during Carnaval, the region's major pre-Lenten bash held the week before Ash Wednesday. There are daily parades; musicians roam the city playing salsa and merengue; and couples literally dance in the streets.

In Tlacotalpan, locals worship the Virgin of the Candelaria. This patron saint of fishermen is officially honored on February 2, but the fiesta, which includes a flotilla of boats and the running of the bulls, begins January 31, lasting 10 days.

Even the smallest of villages has its annual fiestas. A vanilla festival in Papantla draws people every March. Coatepec, in the heart of coffee country, celebrates the bountiful bean in May. Xico is known for its raucous festival celebrating Mary Magdalene, the town's patron saint, that begins on July 16. On July 26 Xalapa celebrates the Fiesta de Santiago Apóstol with an impressive display of fireworks. If you're in Tlacotalpan September 27 to 29, you can take a peek at the Fiesta de San Miguelito, honoring Saint Michael. On September 30, Coatepec marks the Fiesta de San Jerónimo by constructing huge arches decorated with flowers.

Where to Start?

Your first stop will probably be Veracruz City, since it's the state's transportation hub. It's a great base for exploring the region because many of the prettiest colonial-era towns, including La Antigua and Tlacotalpan, are within easy driving distance. There are also a few interesting ruins in the vicinity, such as Cempoala and Tres Zapotes. Veracruz City is about five hours from Mexico City and six hours from Oaxaca, so a trip by car or bus is feasible.

But if you are headed to the fascinating ruins of El Tajín, you might want to choose Xalapa as your base. The state's capital is cool and comfortable throughout the year, unlike most other parts of the region. From here you can also explore atmospheric mountain villages such as Coatepec and Xico and enjoy booming adventure tourism on the rivers of Jalcomulco.

Safari Camp Fun

Based in Jalcomulco, outside of Xalapa, Expediciones Mexico Verde (☎279/832–3730, 01800/362–8800 toll-free in Mexico 🌐www.mexicoverde.com) runs adventure excursions out of their beautiful, riverside ecotourism site. Raft, hike, run the challenge course, or just relax by the pool with good food and a cold cerveza.

Booking in Advance

You'll have to book in advance if you plan on staying in any of the towns during Christmas, Easter, or any festivals, particularly during Veracruz City's Carnaval.

It's always a good idea to do your research when you are planning your trip; check out the online forum at 🌐www.fodors.com, where travelers weigh in on anything from hotel bathrooms to the best ice cream in town.

How's the Weather?

In Veracruz City and along the coast, the weather is hot and humid throughout the year. The rainy season runs from April to November, though the heaviest rains fall between June and September. Most storms are in the afternoon, clearing up by the early evening. There isn't quite as much rain in the arid areas in the northern part of the state.

Xalapa and the surrounding towns are high in the mountains, so they're usually cooler than coastal communities.

Keep in mind the possible range of temperatures if you are planning a trip to Pico de Orizaba, the highest mountain in Mexico, and its surrounding woodlands.

Savoring la Musica de Veracruz

African- and Caribbean-influenced music fills the streets in this port city; the *son jarocho* ("Veracruz sound"), centered on strings and percussion, is a regional variation of Mexican *sones.* To get a sampling of all the types of music in Veracruz, join the crowds swirling about the *zócalo (main plaza)*. Inevitably, strolling mariachis and teams on *marimbas* (wooden xylophones) will be performing for people in the cafés. But for romance, nothing compares to the bands playing late into the night in Parque Zamora. Men blot their brows with crisp handkerchiefs, and women wave fans they had hidden in their bosoms. Everyone is willing to suffer the heat for the spirit of the *danzón,* the sultry dance brought to Mexico in 1879 by Cubans.

Money Matters

WHAT IT COSTS IN DOLLARS

¢	$	$$	$$$	$$$$
Restaurants				
under $5	$5–$10	$10–$15	$15–$25	over $25
Hotels				
under $50	$50–$75	$75–$150	$150–$250	over $250

Restaurant prices are per person for a main course at dinner. Hotel prices are for two people in a standard double room.

Activities & Experiences

Soaking up the atmosphere isn't difficult in Veracruz City. When you take a late-afternoon stroll through the cobblestone streets near the zócalo or along the breezy waterfront walk of the Paseo del Malecón, you'll be joining locals doing just the same. Stopping for an ice-cream cone or a steaming cup of *lechero* (coffee with milk) is a must. If eating seafood is a passion, don't miss the open-air Mariscos Villa Rica Mocamba, arguably one of the best seafood restaurants in the country. The Acuario de Veracruz, one of the largest aquariums in Latin America, displays tiger sharks, manatees, sea turtles, and even offers you a dip with the sharks in their new immersion tank.

Elsewhere in the state, you won't want to miss exploring the ruins at Cempoala and El Tajín (get there in time to see the voladores who entertain the crowds at midday). There are plenty of colonial villages worth exploring, like La Antigua with its narrow rope bridge and Tlacotalpan with its rows of hand-crafted rocking chairs. In Catemaco, a lovely lakefront town, you can ward off evil spirits with a visit to local witches and ward off wrinkles with a mineral mud mask.

VERACRUZ CITY

Updated by Claudia Rosenbaum

THE LIVELY PORT CITY OF VERACRUZ, 345 km (214 mi) east of Mexico City, might not be the city that never sleeps, but it *is* a city that gets very little rest. People listen to music in the squares until late at night, then are found sipping coffee in the sidewalk cafés early the next morning. The exuberance of *jarochos,* as the city's residents are known, does not falter even in the broiling midday heat.

In 1519 Cortés landed in La Antigua, a slip of a place on the Río Huitzilapan some 25 km (16 mi) north, but it was Veracruz that became the major gateway for the Spanish settlement of Mexico. Its name, also given to many other communities throughout Latin America, means "true cross." Pirates frequently attacked the steamy coastal city, and their battles to intercept Spanish goods add a swashbuckling edge to the history of the oldest port in the Americas. The Spanish brought thousands of African slaves to Veracruz; later, Cuban immigrants flooded the town.

Today Veracruz is still one of the most important ports in Mexico, and you'll immediately sense its extroverted character. Huge cargo ships, ocean liners, and fishing vessels crowd its harbor, and the waterfront Paseo del Malecón is always buzzing with strolling couples and sailors with a few hours to kill. In the evening at the zócalo, the sound of marimbas floats through the air.

The city is actually two towns: the historic port of Veracruz and the fishing village of Boca del Río. These communities have fused into one, linked by 10 km (6 mi) of businesses geared toward tourists. The hotels in Veracruz have more charm, but those in Boca del Río, especially along the beaches near Playa Mocambo, have sun and sand. A visit to one of the seafood restaurants in Boca del Río is a must.

GETTING HERE & AROUND

Most flights connect through Mexico City; and there are several daily nonstops flights a day between Veracruz and Monterrey, plus daily flights to Mérida and Cancún. Aeropuerto Internacional Heriberto Jara Corona is a clean, bright facility about 8 km (5 mi) south of downtown Veracruz. A cab ride between the airport and the city center costs $14 and takes roughly half an hour. Buy a ticket inside the airport for a fair price. Though no city bus serves the airport, you can take a bus into and, for the most part, around the city. The most convenient way to purchase bus tickets is through Ticketbus. The bus company ADO has the most buses heading to Veracruz. The trip from Mexico City costs about $24 and takes about five hours. UNO, the deluxe bus line, also serves this route. The highways throughout the state are generally in very good condition, making renting a car a good way to see this long, slender state. From Mexico City you can reach Veracruz in about five hours on Carretera 150-D.

ESSENTIALS

Bus Contacts **Ticketbus** (☎ *800/702–8000* 🌐 *www.ticketbus.com.mx*).

Currency Exchange **Bancomer** (✉ *Av. Juárez at Av. Independencia* ☎ *229/989–8000 or 229/989–8018*). **Casa de Cambio Puebla** (✉ *Av. Juárez 112* ☎ *229/931–2450*).

Internet **NetChatBoys** (✉ *Calle Lerdo 369, between Avs. 5 de Mayo and Madero* ☎ *No phone*).

Mail & Shipping **DHL** (✉ *Calle 3 Lote 3, Col Pedro Quemada* ☎ *55/5345–7000*).

Medical Assistance **Angeles Verdes** (☎ *078*). **For Emergencies** (☎ *066*). **Hospital Regional de Veracruz** (✉ *20 de Noviembre s/n* ☎ *229/931–7857*). **Veracruz Cruz Roja** (☎ *229/937–5500*). **Veracruz Police Department** (☎ *229/938–6599*).

Rental Cars **Alamo** (✉ *Aeropuerto Internacional Heriberto Jara Corona* ☎ *229/938–3700*). **Avis** (✉ *Aeropuerto* ☎ *229/934–9623*). **Budget** (✉ *Aeropuerto* ☎ *229/939–2705*). **Dollar** (✉ *Aeropuerto* ☎ *229/938–7878*).

Visitor & Tour Info **Veracruz Tourist Office** (✉ *Palacio Municipal* ☎ *229/989–8817*).

6

EXPLORING

❻ Fodor's Choice ★ **Acuario de Veracruz.** Veracruz is home to one of the biggest and best aquariums in Latin America. The main exhibits include a tank with 2,000 species of marine life native to the Gulf of Mexico, including manta rays, barracudas, and sea turtles. Other tanks display tiger sharks and gentle manatees that enjoy interacting with the crowds. Kids love the touch tanks. A guided immersion tank ($27 adults; $14 kids) offers daring visitors the chance to go nose to nose with the sharks. ✉ *Plaza Acuario, Blvd. Manuel Avila Camacho s/n* ☎ *229/931–1020 or 229/932–8006* 🌐 *www.acuariodeveracruz.com* 💰 *$6 general, $3 children* ⏲ *Mon.–Thurs. 10–7, Fri.–Sun. 10–7:30.*

❺ **Baluarte de Santiago.** The small fortress is all that's left of the old city walls. Like the Fuerte de San Juan de Ulúa, the colonial-era bulwark was built as a defense against pirates. The 1635 structure is impressively solid from the outside, with cannons pointed toward long-gone marauders. Inside is a tiny museum that has an exquisite exhibition of pre-Hispanic jewelry—Spanish plunder, no doubt—discovered by a fisherman in the 1970s. ✉ *Calle Francisco Canal between Av. Gómez Farías and Av. 16 de Septiembre* ☎ *229/931–1059* 💰 *$2.50* ⏲ *Tues.–Sun. 10–4:30.*

❼ ★ **Fuerte de San Juan de Ulúa.** During the viceregal era, Veracruz was the only east coast port permitted to operate in New Spain and, therefore, was attacked by pirates. This unique coral-stone fort, the last land in Mexico to be held by the Spanish Royalists, is a monument to that era. The moats, ramparts, drawbridges, prison cells, and torture chambers create a miniature city. Fortification began in 1535 under the direction of Antonio de Mendoza, the first viceroy of New Spain. A few centuries later it was used as a prison, housing such prominent figures as Benito Juárez. After independence it was used in unsuccessful attempts to fight off invading French and Americans.

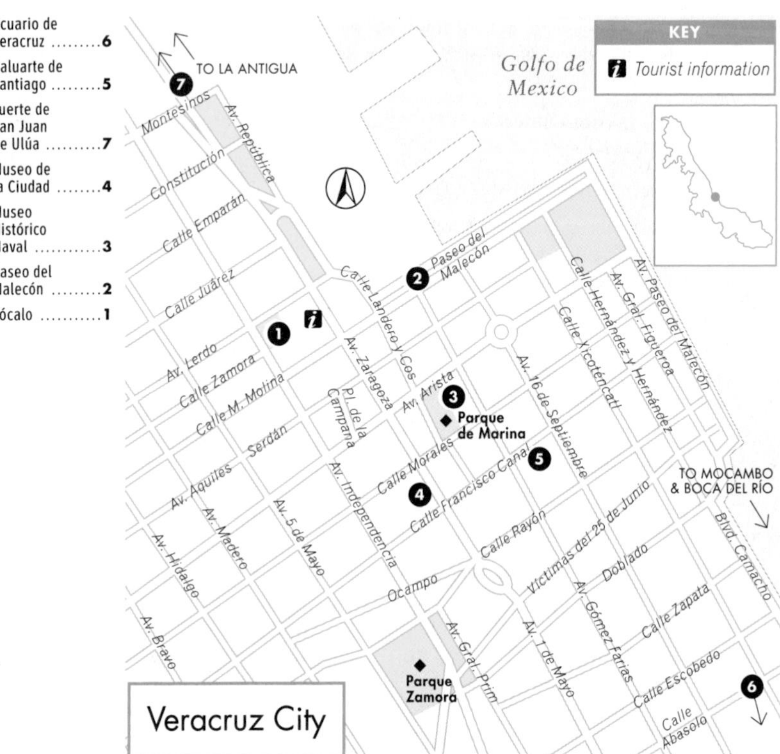

You can explore the former dungeons, climb up on the ramparts, and wander across grassy patios. A tiny museum holds swords, pistols, and cannons, but signs are in Spanish only. Guides wander around in the site until about 3 PM—an English-speaking guide will charge around $25 per group. The fort is connected to the city center by a causeway; a taxi here should cost about $5. ✉ *Via causeway from downtown Veracruz* ☎ *229/938–5151* 🎟 *$3.70* ⏲ *Tues.–Sun. 9–4:30.*

4 **Museo de la Ciudad.** A good place to get oriented, this museum in a lovely colonial-era building tells the city's history through artifacts, displays, and scale models. Also exhibited are copies of pre-Columbian statues and contemporary art. There are no explanatory materials in English, however. ✉ *Av. Zaragoza 397, at Calle Esteban Morales* ☎ *229/989–8872* 🎟 *$3* ⏲ *Tues.–Sat. 10–6, Sun. 10–3.*

3 **Museo Histórico Naval.** In an impressive set of buildings that once housed navy officers, the Naval History Museum tells how the country's history was made on the high seas. Veracruz has been dubbed the city that was *cuatro veces heróica,* or "four times heroic," for its part in defending the country against two attacks by the French and two by the Americans. The museum tells of those wars, as well as the life of revolutionary war hero Venustiano Carranza. Explanatory materials

CLOSE UP

Veracruz Background

Veracruz has been a hub for more than 3,000 years. The Olmec thrived here between 1,200 BC and AD 900, though there are few surviving examples of Olmec architecture. Instead, they're best remembered for the massive carved stone heads, a few of which are in the archaeological museum in Xalapa.

The Olmec were replaced by the Totonac, whose last legacy is the city of El Tajín in the northern part of the state, near present-day Papantla. Although you'll see architectural influences from other cultures—notably the Maya—El Tajín is unlike anywhere else. The style is typified by the hundreds of indentations in the Pyramid of the Niches. This city remained powerful until about AD 1200, when it was abandoned. Archaeologists speculate that it had grown too large to support its population.

Later Totonac cities include Cempoala, which was occupied at the time of the Spanish conquest. Its residents, who had been forced to pay tribute to the more powerful Aztecs, formed an alliance with the Spanish and helped them establish their first town in the New World, called La Villa Rica del la Vera Cruz. It was near present-day Veracruz. The Totonac also embraced Catholicism, and by 1523 the Franciscans were preaching to the population.

During the colonial period, which lasted until the early 19th century, Veracruz was the most important port in the New World. Invaders laid siege to the city time and time again. Veracruz is known as the "city four times heroic" because it repeatedly resisted invasion—first the French during the "Pastry War" in 1838, then the Americans during the Mexican-American War in 1847, the French again in 1866, then the Americans again in 1914.

6

are in Spanish only. ✉ *Av. Arista between Av. 16 de Septiembre and Av. Landero y Coss* ☎ *299/931–4078* *Free* *Tues.–Sun. 10–5.*

❷ **Paseo del Malecón.** Everyone seems to come here at night, from cuddling young couples in search of a secluded bench to parents with children seeking the best place for ice cream. ■ TIP→**Drop by during the day and you'll find boats that will take you out into the harbor for about $5 per person.** ✉ *Northern extension of Calle Molina.*

NEED A BREAK?

There are always lines out the door at Neveria Güero Güero Güera Güera (✉ *Calle Zamora 15, at Av. Landero y Coss* ☎ *229/932-0582*), where you can get a huge cup of *cacahuate* (peanut), *fresa* (strawberry), or more than a dozen other flavors of ice cream for only a buck. Locals say the name came about when the owner used to shout *güero* and *güera*, meaning blond-haired man or woman, to catch the attention of passing foreigners.

❶ **Zócalo.** This park, also known as the Plaza de Armas, is known for its distinctive *portales* (colonnades). Two towers have bells that compete for your attention. The hands-down winner is the deafening Catedral de Nuestra Senora de la Asunción, which sits on the southwest corner of the square. It dates from 1721. The runner-up is the 1635 Palacio Municipal, which has a fainter but no less insistent tune. The tower originally did double duty as a lighthouse for the port. ✉ *Av. Independencia between Calle Lerdo and Calle Zamora.*

BEACHES

Veracruz City's beaches are not particularly inviting, being on the brownish side of gold, with polluted water. Decent beaches with paler, finer sand begin to the south in **Mocambo,** about 7 km (4½ mi) from downtown, and get better even farther down. The beach in front of the Fiesta Americana hotel is particularly well maintained. (Although it may appear to be claimed by the hotel, it's public.) About 4 km (2½ mi) south of Playa Mocambo is **Boca del Río,** a small fishing village at the mouth of the Río Jamapa that is quickly getting sucked into Veracruz's orbit. A taxi from the city center costs about $4. **Mandinga** is a farther 8 km (5 mi) south of Boca del Río and is less frequented by tourists. ■ TIP→ **Tread carefully if you don a pair of flip-flops (chanclas) to do your exploring. If it's wet, the pavement downtown can be dangerous.**

WHERE TO EAT

In addition to the restaurants around the zócalo, you'll want to head to Boca del Río. Many restaurants here are modest but serve some of the finest seafood in this part of the country. If you'd like to eat with the locals, try the Mercado Hidalgo for breakfast or lunch; it's a 10-block walk south from the zócalo. ■ TIP→ **Seafood lovers can get a quick fix at the fish market, a mint-green building at the corner of Avenida Aquiles Serdán and Avenida Landero y Coss.**

CENTRO HISTÓRICO

$$$–$$$$ ARGENTINE ✕ **Che Tango.** For a hearty meal after a day at the aquarium, pop around the corner to this casual yet elegant Argentine restaurant. Select your cut of rib eye, tenderloin, or strip steak from the chilled display case brought to your table and tell your bow-tied waiter how you'd like it cooked. While it sizzles, nibble one of the flaky empanadas topped with *chimichurri* (sauce made with olive oil and parsley). Try the house cocktail, Rosita (made with anise). ✉ *Av. 16 de Septiembre 1938, at Calle Enríquez, Col. Flores Magón* ☎ *229/932–1745 or 229/932–1756* ▭ *AE, MC, V*

$–$$ STEAK ✕ **El Gaucho.** The scent of sizzling steaks and a giant neon cowboy have drawn meat lovers to this cavernous ranch-style restaurant morning, noon, and night. The epic menu lists nearly 100 dishes—from spicy chorizo hot off the grill to tongue sautéed with tomatoes and onions. Or try the shrimp stuffed with peppers and wrapped in bacon. The house specialty drink, *jarra de clericot* (red wine with melon and pineapple), is delicious. The place opens at 7 AM for breakfast. ✉ *Av. Bernal Díaz del Castillo 187, at Calle Colón* ☎ *229/935–0411* 🌐 *www.elgaucho.com.mx* ▭ *AE, MC, V.*

$–$$ CAFÉ ✕ **Gran Café de la Parroquia.** A leisurely stint here in the sun, watching ships unloading their cargo, is what Veracruz is all about. This family restaurant was so popular, it split off into side-by-side establishments run by two brothers. The menus are nearly identical, both boasting renowned *traditional lechero* (coffee with hot milk). The milk is flamboyantly poured from silver jugs at a great height by a server. Visit the Gran Café closest to Hotel Emporio for classic *picadas y gordas* (puffy, deep-fried tortillas with beans, onion, mole, and cheese). ■TIP→**Try for a sidewalk table under the arches, if you can withstand the competing marimbas and the appeals of women selling crafts.** ✉*Paseo de Malecón between Hotel Hawaii and Hotel Emporio* ☎*229/932–2584 or 299/932–1855* ▭*No credit cards.*

$–$$ CAFÉ ★ ✕**Gran Café del Portal.** Sit on a shady terrace, near the live music, or in a dining room with copper columns and beamed ceilings at this famous café, which was opened as a candy shop in 1824. The menu has a wide selection of dishes, including a delicious *huachinango a la veracruzana* (red snapper simmered in tomatoes, onions, garlic, green olives, and capers). The $8 lunch special, available on weekdays, includes a soup or salad and a meat dish. The Gran Café del Portal has an ongoing rivalry with the Gran Café de la Parroquia as to which place serves the real *tradicional lechero*—white-jacketed waiters bring you one kettle of strong coffee and another of hot milk, and let you do the mixing. ✉*Av. Independencia 1187, across from cathedral* ☎*229/931–2759* ▭*No credit cards.*

$–$$ SEAFOOD ✕**Palapa Reyna.** Playa de Hornos, a popular stretch of sand south of the Acuario de Veracruz, is lined with a series of thatch-roofed seafood shacks. They all serve basically the same thing: fish cooked any way you like it. This place, with a giant neon sailfish positioned on the roof, is among the closest to the Acuario and one of the best. Grab a table in the open-air dining room or one under an umbrella along the surf. ✉*Playa de Hornos* ☎*No phone* ▭*No credit cards.*

BOCA DEL RÍO

$$–$$$$ SEAFOOD ✕**Villa Rica.** Though it's tucked away in Boca del Río, this open-air eatery is one of the most popular seafood restaurants in the city. Specialties include mussels, grouper, crab claws, and octopus prepared as you wish. For those who relish spicy food, the *ostiones enchilpayados* (oysters in cream and chipotle chile) are a cut above the rest. ■TIP→**Popular bands play Thursday through Sunday from 3 to 7, so you may need a reservation on those days.** ✉*Calz. Mocambo 527, Boca del Río* ☎*229/922–2113 or 229/922–3743* ▭*AE, DC, MC, V.*

$–$$$ STEAK ✕**Cacharrito.** The cowhides decorating the walls let you know exactly what's on the menu at this longtime favorite. Start off with Argentine-style empanadas (stuffed with beef, of course), then move on to the grilled short ribs. If you have a hankering for the enormous rib eye, call at least three hours ahead. The impressive wine list includes selections from Argentina, Chile, and Spain, as well as a respectable representation from Mexico. ✉*Blvd. Adolfo Ruíz Cortines 15, Boca del Río* ☎*229/935–9246* ▭*MC, V.*

$–$$ SEAFOOD ★ ✕**Pardiño's.** The Guinness Book of World Records honored the founder of this friendly seafood restaurant for dreaming up the world's longest seafood-stuffed fillet of fish, which was once prepared in the street along the waterfront. You can find smaller, but equally scrumptious concoctions and live midday music at this open-air dining room. Espe-

CLOSE UP

Happiness in a Seafood Shack

Some of Mexico's most delicious dishes come from Veracruz. The emphasis is on *pescado* (fish) and *mariscos* (shellfish). Some of the best places to eat in the region are the family-run seafood shacks you often find lining the beaches. Just ask for the *platillo del día*. This "dish of the day" is always fresh and served with a flourish.

Many specialties show the influence of the Spanish and African communities of nearby Cuba, including the state's signature dish, *huachinango a la veracruzana* (red snapper in the Veracruz style, which means it's simmered in tomatoes, onions, garlic, green olives, and capers). Another dish with a similar influence is *salpicón de jaiba*, a spicy crabmeat salad usually prepared with tomatoes, capers, and peppers. Other dishes reflect African ties in their use of beans, plantains, yucca, taro, white sweet potatoes, and especially peanuts, which appear in the classic *puerco encacahuatado* (pork in peanut sauce) and the bracing *salsa macha*, made by grinding peanuts with garlic, chiles, and olive oil.

You'll find peanut ice cream all over the state, as well as other *nieves* made with mangos, papayas, and other local fruits. Another sweet-tooth tempter is *buñuelos veracruzanos*, golden doughnuts that are dipped in a sugar and cinnamon mix. Look out for the charge of *toritos* (little bulls), a heady alcoholic punch made with cane liquor, milk, and tropical fruit pulp or peanuts.

cially popular are the *camarones Pardiños* (juicy shrimp stuffed with queso manchego and wrapped in bacon) and *ostiones a la diabla gratinados* (spicy oysters topped with grated cheese). Dishes like cheese-stuffed plantains satisfy vegetarians. ✉ *Calle Zamora 40, Boca del Río* ☎ *229/986–0135* ▭ *AE, DC, MC, V.*

WHERE TO STAY

CENTRO HISTÓRICO

$$$ **Hotel Emporio.** It's not hard to imagine that the architect had cruise ships in mind when designing the elegantly curved balconies of this waterfront hotel. Many of the immaculate rooms have superb harbor views (for which you pay a premium), as do the gardens on the roof. Dine in the popular restaurant, or under the shade of an umbrella at any of the hotel's three pools. **Pros:** Light-filled rooms. **Cons:** Near the cruise-ship port. ✉ *Paseo del Malecón 244,* ☎ *229/932–2222* 🌐 *www.hotelesemporio.com* *182 rooms, 20 suites* *In-room: Safe, Wi-Fi, Ethernet. In-hotel: Restaurant, room service, bar, pools, gym, laundry service, public Internet, public Wi-Fi, parking (no fee)* ▭ *AE, MC, V.*

$$–$$$ ★ **Gran Hotel Diligencias.** The 2003 renovations of this 18th-century building into a stately hotel transformed the entire Centro Histórico: it lends elegance to the laid-back zócalo. Locals grumble that the decorations in the rooms lack any trace of Veracruz, but all you have to do is throw open the French doors to enjoy warm winds blowing through the palm trees and marimba bands in the square below. The second-floor terrace, which surrounds a small pool, is a great place to

escape the heat. **Pros:** Romantic architecture, nice terrace. **Cons:** Bland decor. ✉*Independencia 1115,* ☎*229/923–0280* 🌐*www.granhotel diligencias.com* *117 rooms, 4 suites* *In-room: Ethernet. In-hotel: Restaurant, room service, bar, pool, gym, public Internet, public Wi-Fi* *AE, DC, MC, V.*

$–$$$ **Hotel Imperial.** Built a century ago, this hotel facing the zócalo has lost little of its charm. The wrought-iron elevator, dating from 1904, was one of the first in Latin America. Though a bit dated, the rooms have a certain elegance and many have balconies on the square. **Pros:** Retains historical charm. **Cons:** Things are looking a bit dated. ✉*Av. Miguel Lerdo 153, near Av. Independencia,* 🌐*www.hotelimperial veracruz.com* ☎*229/932–1204* *54 rooms* *In-hotel: Restaurant, room service, bar* *AE, MC, V.*

$$ **Hawaii Hotel.** You can't miss this hotel, because its profile resembles an arrow pointing straight up. Hotel Hawaii is one of the best deals in town, offering comfort and service at a reasonable rate. Rooms are impeccably maintained. The eager-to-please staff makes sure you have a map of the city and a bag of local coffee to take home. **Pros:** Friendly staff. **Cons:** Slightly tacky architecture. ✉*Paseo del Malecón 458,* ☎*229/938–0088* 🌐*www.hawaiihotel.com.mx* *30 rooms* *In-hotel: Restaurant, room service, pool, laundry service, parking (no fee)* *AE, MC, V.*

6

$$ **Hotel Veracruz.** From the pool on the rooftop patio you have a fantastic view of the mariachis strolling around the zócalo. Guest rooms are spotless. Since this high-rise is a bit removed from the square, the musicians won't keep you awake all night. Sanborns, which occupies the corner of the building, is one of the most popular downtown restaurants. **Pros:** Many rooms have similar views as the rooftop patio. **Cons:** A bit of a walk to the square. ✉*Av. Independencia s/n, at Av. Miguel Lerdo,* ☎*229/989–3800* 🌐*www.hotelescalinda.com.mx* *102 rooms, 14 suites* *In-room: Safe, dial-up. In-hotel: Restaurant, room service, pool, laundry service, public Internet, public Wi-Fi, parking (no fee)* *AE, MC, V.*

$$ **Villa del Mar.** Across from one of the nicer sections of the downtown beach, this hotel lets you enjoy the sun of Veracruz without the scene of Boca del Río. As you might guess when you see the small playground, it caters mostly to families. The spacious rooms surround a garden with a tennis court, swimming pool, and hot tub. **Pros:** Strong air-conditioning, lots of hot water. **Cons:** Motel-like rooms. ✉*Blvd. Manuel Avila Camacho 2431, at Calle Bartolomé de las Casas,* ☎*229/989–6500* 🌐*www.hotel-villadelmar.com* *89 rooms, 4 suites* *In-hotel: Restaurant, bar, tennis court, pool, laundry service, parking (no fee), no elevator* *AE, MC, V* *BP*

$–$$ ★ **Meson del Mar.** In a charming colonial-era building with long corridors and graceful arches, the Meson del Mar is an intimate hotel near the waterfront. A staircase leads up to a breezy patio where you have a view over the rooftops. Exposed-wood beams and tile floors in the guest rooms recall a more gracious era. Rooms facing the busy street have double-paned windows that keep out almost all the noise. Gandara, the open-air seafood restaurant, serves a wide variety of fish dishes. **Pros:** Good restaurant, can be a good value. **Cons:** Many of the staff don't speak English, so learn some Spanish before you go. ✉ *Calle Estaban Morales 543,* ☎ *229/932–5043* 🌐 *www.mesondelmar.com.mx* *13 rooms, 7 suites* *In-room: Safe, Wi-Fi. In-hotel: Restaurant, bar, public Internet, no elevator* ▭ *MC, V.*

BOCA DEL RÍO

$$$ **Crowne Plaza Torremar.** The lobby in this high-rise on Playa Mocambo is adorned with glass sculptures. Many of the rooms face the ocean, and the suites also have small balconies. The poolside fountain and the activities in the play area make this a good bet for families traveling with young children. It's across from the Las Americas mall. **Pros:** Nice pool complex, care taken in decorating. **Cons:** Doesn't feel as if you're in Mexico. ✉ *Blvd. Adolfo Ruíz Cortines 4300, Playa Mocambo,* ☎ *229/989–2100* 🌐 *www.crowneplaza.com* *211 rooms, 18 suites* *In-room: Safe. In-hotel: Restaurant, room service, bar, pools, gym, children's programs (ages 3–11), laundry service, executive floor, public Wi-Fi, parking (no fee)* ▭ *AE, DC, MC, V.*

$$$ **Fiesta Americana.** This splashy luxury hotel reclines on the soft sand at Playa Costa de Oro. The hotel's marble corridors all seem to lead to the giant serpentine pool, maze of bridges, and lush gardens facing the ocean. The brightly colored rooms all overlook the beach. You have access to a 9-hole golf course 20 minutes away. **Pros:** The best business facilities in the state of Veracruz. **Cons:** Expensive for what you get, especially when compared to other more affordable hotels. < ✉ *Blvd. Manuel Avila Camacho s/n, at Fracc. Costa de Oro,* ☎ *229/989–8989 or 800/343–7821* 🌐 *www.fiestaamericana.com.mx* *211 rooms, 23 suites* *In-room: Safe, dial-up. In-hotel: 3 restaurants, room service, bars, tennis court, pool, diving, children's programs (ages 4 and up), public Internet, public Wi-Fi, parking (no fee), no-smoking rooms* ▭ *AE, DC, MC, V.*

$$ **Hotel Lois.** A sophisticated creamy-white facade has replaced the purple exterior; the *Jetsons*–esque lobby is now dressed with leather furniture. Though it's lost its personality, Lois is still a good budget option. Guest rooms have subdued pastels; spend a bit more for one with a hot tub. **Pros:** Bar is the place to go for salsa dancing. **Cons:** Hotel sits on a busy street. ✉ *Blvd. Adolfo Ruíz Cortines 10,* ☎ *229/937–7031 or 229/937–8290* 🌐 *www.hotelluis.com.mx* *107 rooms, 17 suites* *In-room: Safe. In-hotel: Restaurant, room service, bars, pool, gym, children's programs (ages 3–9), public Wi-Fi, parking (no fee)* ▭ *AE, MC, V.*

NIGHTLIFE

It's no surprise that people gravitate toward the **zócalo,** which is full of marimba players, mariachi bands, and guitar players. Grabbing a table at one of the sidewalk cafés along the park's northern edge gives you a front-row seat, but it also means that every musician will offer to play you a song for a few dollars. Friday and Saturday nights at 7 PM locals perform traditional dances on a makeshift stage.

Fodor's Choice ★ A few nights a week, men in dapper hats and women with fans dance the danzón at **Parque Zamora.** It's a magical evening, as the couples swirl around a Victorian bandstand. The types of performances, locations, and times vary every month, so stop by the tourist office in the zócalo for a current schedule. If you'd like to learn a few local steps, the **Instituto Veracruzano de la Cultura** (*[Veracruz Cultural Institute] ✉Calle Canal at Av. Zaragoza ☎229/931–6967*) offers danzón classes.

BARS

Plenty of cantinas are scattered around this port city. Walk down Mario Molina from the Paseo del Malecón to find a handful of the most popular. ■TIP→**Most of the city's nightlife is centered around the beachfront bars of Boca del Río.**

DANCE CLUBS

Dance clubs are plentiful along the waterfront. Most are packed Friday and Saturday nights with a young, largely local crowd. The popular basement club at Hotel Lois offers live music Thursday through Sunday. **Kachimba** (*✉Blvd. Manuel Avila Camacho at Médico Militar, Boca del Río ☎229/927–1980*) is a great spot for live Cuban music. It's open Thursday to Sunday.

6

LIVE MUSIC

For live Latin music, hit the streets and follow your ears: **Plazuela de la Campana** and **Callejón Portal de Miranda,** both just east of the zócalo, are great places to find talented musicians playing to crowds of locals gathered in alleys and plazas to dance the night away. For Cuban rhythms downtown head to the unpretentious **El Rincón de la Trova** (*✉Plazuela de la Lagunilla 59 ☎No phone*), where people of all ages gather Thursday through Saturday.

SHOPPING

The family-run **Guayaberas Fina Cab** (*✉Av. Zaragoza 233, between Calles Arista and Serdán ☎229/931–8427*) has the best-quality goods. Sort through a great selection of hand-stitched shirts and dresses; the embroidery ranges from basic interlocking cables to elaborate floral designs.

Libros y Arte (*✉Callejón Portal de Miranda 9 ☎229/932–6943*), near the zócalo, has a wonderful collection of books, including coffee-table volumes on the art and architecture of Veracruz and plenty of maps and travel guides.

El Mayab (*✉Calle Zamora 78, at Av. Zaragoza ☎229/932–1435*) has a selection of machine-produced guayaberas, which go for less than the hand-embroidered variety.

For a slice of Mexican life, head to the wildly vibrant **Mercado Hidalgo** (*✉Bounded by Calles Cortés, Soto, Madero, and Hidalgo ☎No phone*), where you'll find artful displays of strawberries and chiles beside platters of cow eyeballs and chicken feet.

CLOSE UP

Night Moves

The air is hot and humid, even though the sun has already set on the pretty port city of Veracruz. Elderly couples seated on the wrought-iron benches around Parque Zamora barely move, hoping that inactivity will bring some relief. A conductor lifts a languid baton that rouses a group of musicians to life. The sound they make isn't quite in tune, but it is as rich as honey and as radiant as the summer evening. The couples listen for a few moments, then stroll to the bandstand. Men in crisply ironed shirts and dapper straw hats hold out their hands to women in straight skirts and blouses embroidered with birds and flowers. When they begin to dance, there's barely any movement above the waist, just subtle hip movements and the occasional fancy footwork. It's a dance designed for a tropical night.

This is the *danzón*, a languorous dance brought to Mexico in 1879 by Cubans fleeing their country's Ten Years' War. These refugees ended up living outside the city walls (only aristocrats were allowed to live inside), but the sons of the Mexican elite, looking for thrills, sneaked into the poor neighborhoods at night, and eventually introduced the danzón to high society. Sensuous compared with the stiff dances that were the norm then, the danzón was at first considered scandalous. But soon it won over its detractors and became the most popular dance in Veracruz. It still fills dance halls throughout the city. You can see people of all generations dancing in Parque Zamora every Sunday evening. While their parents and grandparents glide around the bandstand, children practice their steps off to the side.

The city's unique heritage can also be found in its music, swayed by African and Caribbean rhythms. The *son jarocho* (which literally means "Veracruz sound") is one of seven different regional variations of Mexican *sones*. These songs, livelier than the danzón, can be in 4/4 or 6/4 time. Doubtless the best-known one is "La Bamba," which originated here and dates back to the 17th century. Although the most famous version of the song was released by Richie Valens in 1958, there are more than 300 other recordings. Traditionally, the *cantadores* (singers) have been both singers and wordsmiths, creating endless new *coplas* (verses) for well-known songs. Between numbers they continue to entertain the audiences, telling jokes and gently ribbing the other musicians.

The son jarocho centers on strings and percussion. Three instruments are in every ensemble: *arpa* (harp), *jarana* (a 6- or 10-string guitar), and *requinto* (a small rhythm guitar). Musicians energize audiences with their vigorous strumming. A young woman often accompanies them, performing flamenco-like steps in a frilly frock. The *tarima* (wooden dance platform) where dancers pound out the rhythms becomes another essential instrument.

Two other sones are commonly heard. In the son huasteco, named for the region along the northeastern coast of Mexico, violins often take the melody. If trumpets are added, you are probably hearing *son jalisciense*. This type of son hails from Jalisco, a state along the southwestern coast.

–Mark Sullivan

Stands lining the **Paseo del Malecón** sell ocean-related items: seashells and the beauty creams and powders derived from them, black-coral jewelry, and ships in a bottle. You'll also find Coatepec coffee, T-shirts, crucifixes, and tacky stuffed frogs, iguanas, and armadillos.

If you're headed to the Acuario de Veracruz, you enter through a shopping mall called the **Plaza Acuario** (☒*Blvd. Manuel Avila Camacho s/n* ☎*229/932–8311*). It's a good place to pick up gifts for the folks back home.

LOCAL FASHION

Veracruzanos have adopted the fashion of neighboring Yucatán, and its famous embroidered *guayabera* shirts (sometimes called wedding shirts) are as popular here as *mariscos* (shellfish). Guayaberas are comfortable and lightweight, made of either cotton or linen (the linen ones are nicer). Oh, and don't tuck your guayabera into your pants.

The **Plaza de las Artesanías** market on the Paseo de Malecón purveys high-quality goods, including leather and jewelry, with high prices to match. It's open daily 11 to 8.

With its sizable Cuban population, Veracruz does a brisk business in cigars. Around **Plaza de Armas and** throughout the zócalo there are plenty of street-side stands that specialize in both Mexican and Caribbean tobacco. For the largest variety of cigars, try the small kiosk on **Avenida Independencia**, in front of Gran Café del Portal; it sells Cuban Cohibas for less than a buck.

6

SPORTS & THE OUTDOORS

BOATING

You can easily charter a *lancha* (boat) to take you to nearby islands like Isla Verde and Isla de los Sacrificios. **TIP→The best place to find one for a spur-of-the-moment outing is along the Paseo del Malecón.** Expect to pay about $5 per person. Longer trips to nearby Isla Verde (Green Island) and Isla de Enmedio (Middle Island) leave daily from the shack marked paseo en lanchita near Plaza Acuario. If you want to call ahead, contact the friendly folks at **Amphibian** (☒*Calle Lerdo 117* ☎*229/931–0997* ⊕*www.amphibian.com.mx*).

DIVING

The waters near Veracruz are home to nearly two dozen reefs waiting to be explored. **Mundo Submarino** (☒*Blvd. Manuel Avila Camacho 3549* ☎*229/980–6374*) has diving lessons for everyone ranging from newcomers to experts. The company also conducts dives to nearby reefs. **Tridente** (☒*Blvd. Manuel Avila Camacho 165* ☎*229/931–7924*) offers diving trips for around $70 per person; the price includes gear and instruction. If you want to snorkel, the cost is only $23.

WHITE-WATER RAFTING

On trips led by **Rio Aventura** (☒*Calle Urano 784, Boca del Río* ☎*229/130–2759 or 229/121-6942* ⊕*www.rioaventura.com.mx*), you can combine rafting with other sports.

SIDE TRIPS FROM VERACRUZ CITY

LA ANTIGUA

25 km (16 mi) northwest of Veracruz City.

This sleepy little village, given its name ("The Old Town") by the Spaniards after they abandoned it, was the conquistadors' capital for 75 years. They left La Antigua in 1599 after founding Veracruz City. A small community still lives here, however, and they are justifiably proud of the treasures their village holds.

GETTING HERE & AROUND

La Antigua is roughly half an hour north of Veracruz, off Carretera 180. A Xalapa-bound AU bus from the second-class bus station will cost you $1.50 each way; it will drop you off about a 15-minute stroll from La Antigua. Enjoy the walk littered with fat iguanas sunning themselves and speedy lizards darting along the road. Be prepared to flag down a bus on your way back to Veracruz.

EXPLORING

Although locals call it **Casa de Cortés** (✉*Av. Independencia at Calle Ruiz Cortés*), the 16th-century customshouse actually had nothing to do with the Spanish conquistador. Once 22 rooms surrounded a huge courtyard, but little is left. Its crumbling masonry has been reclaimed by clinging vines and massive tree roots.

Heading toward the river on Calle Ruiz Cortés you'll see a tree with tentacle-like branches blocking the road. This is the **Ceiba de la Noche Feliz** *(Tree of the Happy Night)*. It's said the river once extended to this tree and that Cortés tied his boats here when he arrived.

La Antigua also has the first church of New Spain, the diminutive **Ermita del Rosario** (✉*Av. Independencia at Calle Elodia Rosales*). The little white stucco structure has been restored (and enlarged) many times over the years. The oddly placed arch in the middle of the church was actually once the facade. You can see that two windows near the altar were originally doors.

WHERE TO EAT

$–$$ SEAFOOD ✕ **Las Delicias Marinas.** All roads in La Antigua seem to lead to this bustling riverfront restaurant, a favorite for years. The huge arches facing the water are hung with nets full of cardboard fish. Try the shrimp cocktail or the *cazuela de mariscos,* a seafood stew filled with shrimp, crab, octopus, and mussels in a spicy green sauce. Afternoons at 1:30 and 6:30 there's marimba music, and on weekends the musicians are joined by dancers. ✉*On the Río Huitzilapan* ☎*296/971–6038* ▭*MC, V.* ■ TIP→ **Stop by a street stand for a typical treat: cocadas, toasted balls of coconut and pineapple prepared with sugar and vanilla.**

SPORTS & THE OUTDOORS

Day-trippers come to La Antigua to take a leisurely boat ride up the **Río Huitzilapan** *(Hummingbird River)*. There are over a dozen covered boats under the Puente Colgate, a narrow, bouncy rope bridge. Captains charge $5 per person for a cruise up the river while they re-create the scene when La Antigua was the hub of Nueva España. Ask your guide to show you where Cortés kept his ships. Now a valley of sand dunes, it's a fun place for both kids and adults to explore.

CEMPOALA

42 km (26 mi) northwest of Veracruz City.

Cempoala (sometimes spelled "Zempoala") was the capital of the Totonac people. The name means "place of 20 waters," after the sophisticated Totonac irrigation system. When Cortés arrived here under the cover of night, the plaster covering of the massive **Templo Mayor** (Main Temple) and other buildings led him to believe the city was constructed of silver. Cortés placed a cross atop this temple—the first gesture of this sort in New Spain—and had Mass said by a Spanish priest.

The city's fate was sealed in 1519, when Cortés formed an alliance with the Totonac leader. Chicomacatl—dubbed "Fat Chief" by his own people because of his enormous girth—was an avowed enemy of the more powerful Aztec, so he decided to fight them alongside the Spanish. The alliance greatly enlarged Cortés's army and encouraged the Spaniard to march on Mexico City and defeat the Aztec. The strategic move backfired, however. The Totonac could protect themselves against the Spanish swords, but were powerless against the smallpox the invaders brought with them. The population was devastated.

EXPLORING

Upon entering the ruins, you'll see **Circulo de los Gladiadores,** a small circle of waist-high walls to the right of center. This was the site of contests between captured prisoners of war and Totonac warriors: each prisoner was required to fight two armed warriors. One such prisoner, the son of a king from Tlaxcala, won the unfair match and became a national hero. His statue stands in a place of honor in Tlaxcala. Another small structure to the left of the circle marks the spot where an eternal flame was kept lighted during the Totonac sacred 52-year cycle.

At the **Templo de la Luna** (Temple of the Moon), to the far left of Templo Mayor, outstanding warriors were honored with the title "Eagle Knight" or "Tiger Knight" and awarded an obsidian nose ring to wear as a mark of their status. Just to the left of the Moon Temple is the larger **Templo del Sol** (Temple of the Sun), where the hearts and blood of sacrificial victims were placed. Back toward the dirt road and across from it is the **Templo de la Diosa de la Muerte** (Temple of the Goddess of Death), where a statue of the pre-Hispanic deity was found along with 1,700 small idols.

There's a small museum near the entrance that contains some of the minor finds the site has yielded. Well-trained guides offer their services, but tours are mainly in Spanish. Voladores from Papantla usually give a performance here on weekends. To get here from Veracruz, drive 42 km (26 mi) north on Carretera 180, past the turnoff for the town of Cardel. Cempoala is on a clearly marked road a few miles farther on your left. If you are coming by bus, take an ADO bus to Cardel. The terminal for Autotransportes Cempoala buses is at the corner of Calle José Azueta and Avenida Juan Martinez, two blocks from the ADO station. A ride directly to the site costs about 80¢ each way. ☎*No phone* ⊕*www.inah.gob.mx* 🎫*$3* ⊙*Daily 10–6.*

CENTRAL VERACRUZ

The land of Central Veracruz is varied and gorgeous. It's here that you'll find coffee plantations, Mexico's highest mountains, rapids, and even a few sets of ruins. It also holds the state's second-most-important (and talked about) city, Xalapa, a sophisticated university town that's perched on a mountainside. Xalapa is the hub of culture and modernity in this area, and is a good base to explore the small coffee towns of Coatepec and Xico.

XALAPA

100 km (62 mi) northwest of Veracruz City.

A ceremonial center for the Aztec when Cortés swept through the region, Xalapa is still a city of great importance. Take one look at the impressive Palacio de Gobierno and you know this is a political powerhouse. The presence of the Universidad Veracruzana ensures that Xalapa is a cultural capital as well. Its state theater attracts performers from around the world. In addition, Xalapa is also an agricultural center. This mixed background means that in any café you might find farm workers with their machetes, government workers shouting into cell phones, and students tapping away on laptops.

Xalapa is perched on the side of a mountain between the coastal lowlands and the high central plateau. More than 4,000 feet above sea level, the city enjoys cool weather the entire year. But the city also has unpredictable weather changes—sun, rain, and fog are all likely to show themselves over the course of a day. It's a good idea to bring an umbrella and a jacket with you, even if there's not a cloud in the sky.

Much of the city seems to have been built without a plan, and that's the source of its charm. The hills here pose intriguing engineering problems, and major avenues tend to make sharp turns, following the landscape rather than adhering to the strict grid system so beloved by the Spanish. In some places the twisting cobblestone streets are bordered by 6-foot-high sidewalks to compensate for sudden sharp inclines. Locals refer to the city as a *plato roto* (broken dish) because of its layout.

GETTING HERE & AROUND

Xalapa's bus station, called TAXA, is 2 km (1 mi) east of downtown on Avenida 20 de Noviembre. Like the Veracruz station, it houses first-class and second-class companies under the same massive roof. ADO runs several buses an hour between Veracruz and Xalapa. The trip takes two hours and costs about $6. If you're driving, Carretera 140, which branches off Carretera 150-D, leads from Veracruz City to Xalapa. Pay

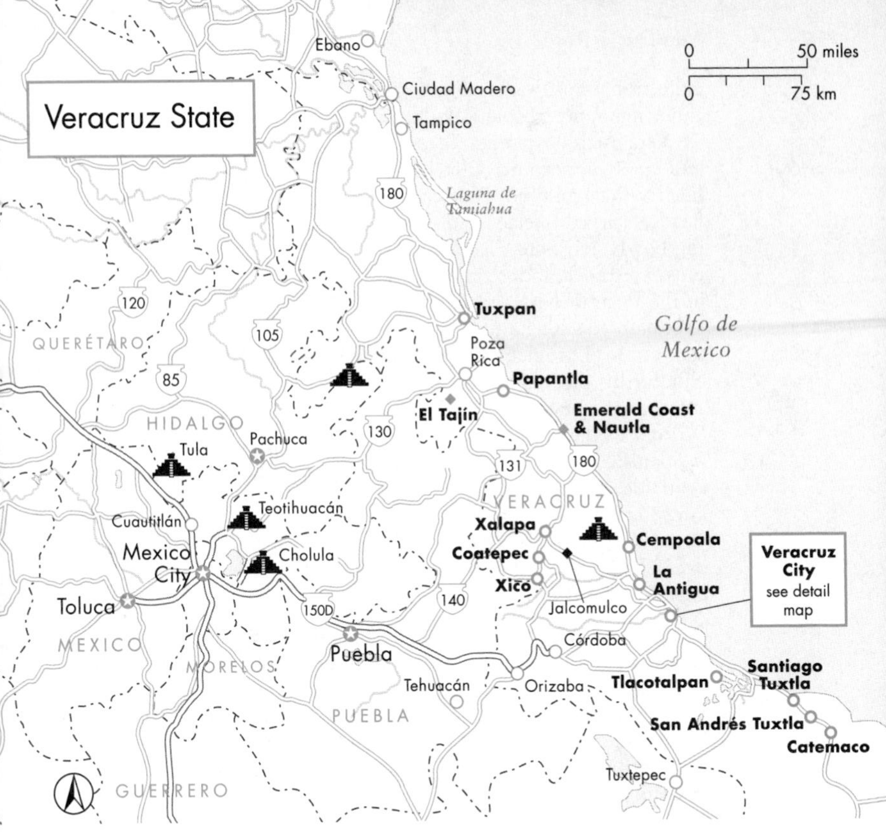

extra attention when driving in Xalapa, since the streets do not follow a traditional grid pattern and getting lost is a real possibility.

ESSENTIALS

Internet **Terra Xalapa** (✉ *Calle 20 de Noviembre 211*).

Mail & Shipping **DHL** (✉ *Av. Ruiz Cortinez 1812* ☎ *228/814–6750 or 228/814–1540*).

Medical Assistance **Angeles Verdes** (☎ *078*). **For Emergencies** (☎ *066*). **Xalapa Cruz Roja** (☎ *228/817–8158*). **Xalapa Police Department** (☎ *228/818–1810*).

Visitor & Tour Info **Xalapa Tourist Office** (✉ *Blvd. Cristóbal Colón 5, Jardines de las Animas* ☎ *228/841–8500 Ext. 4330* 🌐 *www.xalapa.gob.mx*). **Xalapa Tourist Information Booth** (✉ *Calle Enríquez 14* ☎ *No phone*).

EXPLORING

The city's contemporary-art museum, **Galeria de Arte Contemporáneo,** housed in a restored colonial-era building, has temporary exhibits by regional artists. It focuses mainly on paintings. ✉ *Xalapeños Illustres 135 and Arteaga* ☎ *228/817–6374* *Free* ⏲ *Tues.-Sun. 10–7.*

Fodor's Choice ★ The town's prime cultural attraction is the **Museo de Antropología de Xalapa,** second only to the archaeological museum in Mexico City. Its collection of artifacts covers the three main pre-Hispanic cultures of Veracruz: Huasteca, Totonac, and most important, Olmec. It's filled with magnificent Olmec stone heads, carved stelae and offering bowls, terra-cotta jaguars and cross-eyed gods, and cremation urns in the form of bats and monkeys. Especially touching are the life-size sculptures of women who died in childbirth (the ancients elevated them to the status of goddesses). Written explanations appear only in Spanish, but bilingual guides are available. The museum is about 3 km (2 mi) north of Parque Juárez. ✉*Av. Xalapa s/n* ☎*228/815–0920 or 228/815–0708* 🌐*www.uv.mx/max* 🎫*$4* 🕓*Tues.–Sun. 9–5.*

NAME GAMES

As with most places in Mexico, Xalapa (pronounced ha-LA-pa) has had many names over the years. The current name is a slight variation on Xallapan, the name chosen when four neighboring villages decided to pool their otherwise meager resources. You'll sometimes see the name of the city spelled "Jalapa," which is the Hispanic version of the name used by the Nahuatl people, the original inhabitants of the region. Residents of Xalapa call themselves *xalapeños*.

The gorgeous central square, called **Parque Juárez,** has the neoclassical **Palacio de Gobierno** on one side and the neocolonial **Palacio Municipal** on another. At first glance Parque Juárez seems like any park, but a café and art galleries reside below. Between the palaces is the **Catedral de Xalapa,** dating from 1772. If it looks a little crooked from the outside, wait until you step inside. A chapel juts out at an odd angle, making the whole place seem askew.

WHERE TO EAT

$$–$$$ MEXICAN ✕**La Estancia de los Tecajetes.** For fine regional dishes prepared with a dash of creativity, try this rustic restaurant overlooking the tropical Parque Los Tecajetes. Inside it's cozy, always buzzing with diners feasting on *cecina* (paper-thin beef fillet) with slices of avocado and *crepas poblanas* (crepes filled with chicken or spinach and topped with poblano chiles). The restaurant is tucked into a small strip mall, so it's tricky to find. ✉*Plaza Tecajetes, Av. Manuel Avila Camacho 90* ☎*228/818–0732* 💳*MC, V* 🕓*No dinner Sun.*

$–$$ FRENCH ★ ✕**Le Bistrot San José.** You won't need your phrase book to translate such well-known French dishes as *beef Wellington* and *chicken with Roquefort* at this adorable little bistro. Sip a crisp Bordeaux (there are several on the reasonably priced wine list) as you nibble the perfectly prepared pâté. Locals drop by to taste the city's only chocolate mousse and crème brûlée. On the gracefully crumbling walls of this colonial-era building hang etchings of Parisian sights. The back dining room, more intimate than the one facing the street, looks out on a flower-filled courtyard. ✉*Herrera and Miguel Palacios 1* ☎*228/812–8267* 💳*MC, V.*

$–$$ MEXICAN ✕**La Casa de Mamá.** The antique furnishings and lazily turning ceiling fans almost succeed in giving this popular restaurant the feel of an old-fashioned hacienda, but the insistent street noise reminds you that you're in a busy capital city. Never mind: you'll be focusing on the generous portions of charcoal-broiled steaks and the succulent shrimp and fish dishes, served with *frijoles charros* (black beans cooked in a spicy sauce). **TIP→ The place is known for its desserts, which include flan with caramel and bananas flambéed in brandy.** ✉ *Av. Manuel Avila Camacho 113* ☎ *228/817–3144* ▭ *AE, MC, V* ⊙ *No dinner Sun.*

$ MEXICAN ✕ **La Casona del Beaterio.** In contrast to the ho-hum meals served at the other cafeterias lining Avenida Zaragoza, La Casona del Beaterio dishes up fine local fare. The restaurant's two spacious rooms, surrounding a courtyard garden with a fountain, have stained-glass windows and plenty of hanging plants. Breakfast specials are a steal, but the house specialty—*cazuela de mariscos* (stew of shrimp, octopus, and clams cooked with chipotle chiles)—draws the crowds. This is java country, so the menu has a dozen different coffee and espresso concoctions. ✉ *Av. Zaragoza 20* ☎ *228/818–2119* ▭ *AE, MC, V.*

¢–$ MEXICAN ✕ **La Fonda.** The entrance to this second-floor restaurant is hidden on a small pedestrian walkway off Calle Enríquez, a block from Parque Juárez. Bright streamers, baskets of paper flowers, and paintings enliven the little cluster of dining rooms. The lunch is hearty northern Veracruz fare. Delicious *nopales* (cactus strips) and chipotle chiles are essential elements of almost every dish. **TIP→ The three-course lunch special costs about $3—such a deal.** ✉ *Callejón del Diamante 1, at Calle Enríquez* ▭ *No credit cards* ⊙ *Closed Sun. No dinner.*

6

WHERE TO STAY

$$–$$$ **Fiesta Inn Xalapa.** This brick-red hotel is a 10-minute drive from the center of town, but it has hard-to-find (for Xalapa) amenities like a swimming pool. The modern guest rooms in the three-story, colonial-style structure get plenty of morning sunlight. **Pros:** Restaurant buffet has great variety. **Cons:** A bit out of the way. ✉ *Carretera Xalapa–Veracruz, Km 2.5, , Fracc. Las Animas* ☎ *228/841–6800 or 800/504–5000* 🌐 *www.fiestainn.com* *119 rooms, 3 suites* *In-room: Safe, dial-up. In-hotel: Restaurant, room service, bar, pool, gym, laundry service, public Internet, public Wi-Fi, parking (no fee), no elevator* ▭ *AE, DC, MC, V.*

$$–$$$ **Hotel Xalapa.** The lobby full of people shouting into cell phones is a giveaway that this is the city's best business hotel. This hotel sits on a hill high above Parque Los Tecajetes—there's a nice view, but you'll need to take taxis back and forth into town. **Pros:** Rooms are large, sunny, and quiet. **Cons:** Building is less than attractive. ✉ *Victoria at Bustamante, Zona Centro,* ☎ *228/818–2222 or 228/817–7064* 🌐 *www.hotelxalapa.com.mx* *170 rooms, 28 suites, 2 villas* *In-room: Wi-Fi. In-hotel: 2 restaurants, room service, bar, pool, laundry service, parking (no fee), public Wi-Fi* ▭ *AE, DC, MC, V.*

$ ★ **Mesón del Alférez.** A royal lieutenant of the Spanish viceroy lived in this colonial house some 200 years ago. Now it's a gem of a small hotel, restored with earthenware tiles, rustic wood beams, and lime-pigment washes on the walls. Rooms surround three small bougainvillea-covered courtyards and have lovely hand-carved wood headboards, Talavera lamps, and hand-loomed bedspreads. Mesón's friendly, dedicated founders have also opened additional hotels in Xalapa and Coatepec, which can be found at the Web site below. **Pros:** Intriguing history, boutique feel. **Cons:** Some rooms are quite small. ✉*Sebastián Camacho 2, at Av. Zaragoza,* ☎*228/818–6351 or 228/818–0113* 🌐*www.pradodelrio.com* *15 rooms, 6 suites* *In room: Safe. In-hotel: Restaurant, room service, laundry service, public Internet, parking (no fee), no elevator* *MC, V* *CP.*

¢–$ **Posada Del Virrey.** On the plus side, this colonial-style hotel is a short walk north of Parque Juárez. Unfortunately, that walk is mostly uphill, perhaps a reason why the rates are so reasonable. The rooms are quiet, but some are on the small side, so look at a few before you decide. **Pros:** Nicely decorated. **Cons:** Walk uphill wouldn't be easy for certain people. ✉*Dr. Lucio 142, Col. Centro 4,* ☎*228/818–6100* 🌐*www.posadadelvirrey.com.mx* *40 rooms* *In-hotel: Restaurant, room service, bar, laundry service, parking (no fee), public Internet, no elevator* *AE, MC, V.*

¢ **Posada Maria de San Francisco.** Surprisingly plush rooms are set around two flower-filled courtyards at this budget hotel. Its location a few blocks north of Parque Juárez is ideal. **Pros:** Great deal. **Cons:** Steep walk up a hill from the park. ✉*Calle Claviero 17,* ☎*228/818–0039* *21 rooms* *In-hotel: Restaurant, bar, public Wi-Fi, no elevator.* *No credit cards*

NIGHTLIFE

BARS

If you want to go out after dark, there are very few options in the center of the city.

East of the center are many of the city's most popular bars. If you're in the mood for live music, **Barlovento** (✉*Av. 20 de Noviembre Oriente 641* ☎*228/817–8334*) heats up with a salsa beat Wednesday through Saturday.

A coffee shop by day, pretty **Café Lindo** (✉*Primo Verdad 21* ☎*228/841–9166*) transforms itself into a bar at night. There's live music most nights, usually a trio crooning Mexican music.

La Corte de los Milagros (✉*Av. 20 de Noviembre Oriente 522* ☎*228/812–3511*) is a relaxing haunt where you can listen to Cuban-style ballads. It's open Wednesday through Saturday. **Vertice** (✉*Av. Murillo Vidal at Calle Zempoala* ☎*No phone*) is one of the few bars where you can have a conversation. There's music Tuesday through Thursday.

DANCE CLUBS

The major thoroughfares west of Parque Juárez are where you'll find most of the dance clubs.

With music so loud that it rattles the windows of passing cars, the video bar **Boulevard 93** (✉*Av. Manuel Avila Camacho 93* ☎*No phone*) is popular with college students. It's open Tuesday through Sunday.

La Quimera (✉*Blvd. Adolfo Ruíz Cortines 1* ☎*228/812–3277*) throbs with dance music Wednesday through Saturday nights.

PERFORMANCE VENUES

The **Agora de la Ciudad** (✉*Parque Juárez* ☎*228/818–5730*) cultural center has art exhibitions and the occasional folk-music performance, and shows classic and avant-garde films. Stop by during the day to see what's planned; it's closed Monday.

The **Teatro del Estado** (✉*Ignacio de la Llave s/n* ☎*228/817–4177*) is the big, modern state theater of Veracruz. The Orquesta Sinfónica de Xalapa performs here, often giving free concerts during the off-season (early June–mid-August). Check *Diario Xalapa* (Xalapa's Spanish-language newspaper) for dates and times.

SHOPPING

Mexico's finest export coffee is grown in this region, specifically in the highlands around the picturesque colonial towns of Coatepec and Xico, less than 10 km (6 mi) from Xalapa. Shops selling the prized *café de altura* (coffee of the highlands) abound. **Cafécali** (✉*Callejón del Diamante 2* ☎*228/818–1339*) offers a wide selection of excellent coffees at good prices. **Café Colón** (✉*Calle Primo Verdad 15, between Avs. Zaragoza and Enríquez* ☎*228/817–6097* ⏲*Mon.–Sat. 9–8, Sun. 10–1*) sells 20 varieties of coffee for about $2.50 a pound. **Callejón del Diamante,** also known as Calle Antonio M. Rivera, is a charming pedestrian street with vendors hawking inexpensive jewelry, handwoven baskets, and fleece-lined slippers. The **Mercado Jauregui** (✉*Av. Revolución and Calle Altamirano*), open daily, is a wild indoor bazaar with everything from jewelry, blankets, and fresh vegetables to some rather dubious-looking natural "healing" potions and supposedly aphrodisiacal body pastes.

SPORTS & THE OUTDOORS

CLIMBING

An option for climbing is the beautiful **Parque Nacional Cofre de Perote,** where the centerpiece is the 14,022-foot extinct volcano. A road leads almost to the summit, so you can either plan a day trip or stay for several days. The park is about 50 km (31 mi) west of Xalapa. In Xalapa, **Veraventuras** (✉*Santos Degollado 81-8* ☎*228/818-9779* 🌐*www.veraventuras.com.mx*) runs biking and hiking trips in nearby national parks.

NEW HEIGHTS

The 18,400-foot **Pico de Orizaba,** Mexico's highest mountain, will virtually become your traveling companion in Veracruz State—you'll feel as though you see it at every turn. The Aztecs called the volcano Citlaltépetl, or Star Mountain, because under the full moon the snowy peak looks like a star. Woodlands spread along its flanks, with a glacier shining above. Tour operators in Xalapa organize climbs to the summit in the dry season, from November to March. Orizaba is 53 km (33 mi) south of Xalapa.

WHITE-WATER RAFTING

With access to six rivers for white-water rafting, Veracruz is now an established mecca for the sport in Mexico. The rivers drain the steep slopes rising up to the flanks of Pico de Orizaba and are the usual tropical-storm drains: wide valley floors with shoal-like rapids at every twist and turn. The rafting season runs from August to November. The **Río Antigua** has five runs, all classed at level IV or under. Not far from the Río Antigua, the **Río Actopan** is a beautiful Class III stream. For pure white-water fun, the **Río Pescados** is the best run in the area. In the rainy season, it has some rapids on the high side of Class IV, but mostly the rapids are Class III. Tight turns against the towering cliffs make for some great splatting.

Base camps with tents, rafting equipment, and dining facilities are near the river at Jalcomulco, 42 km (26 mi) southeast of Xalapa. With **Amigos del Río** (☒*Calle Chipancingo 205, Xalapa* ☎*228/815–8817* ⊕*www.amigosdelrio.com.mx*) you can choose trips based on skill level, from newcomer to expert. **Expediciones Mexico Verde** (☒*Av. Murillo Vidal 133, Xalapa* ☎*279/832–3734* ⊕*www.mexicoverde.com*) organizes various rafting excursions, from day trips to multiday programs, to Río Pescados, Río Actopan, and other rivers. Most guides speak English. They also offer an array of adventure sports and group programs.

COATEPEC

8 km (5 mi) south of Xalapa on Carretera 7.

The air is cool and refreshing in Coatepec. Residents call their town the "capital mundo del café" (the coffee capital of the world), as the climate is perfect for growing the sought-after *altura pluma* (mountain-grown) coffee. You'll see bushes with bright red berries on every available scrap of land. The heady scent of roasting beans wafts across the main square. Locals are so immersed in coffee culture that many swear they can distinguish a cup made with beans from Coatepac from one made with beans grown in nearby Xico.

Coatepec, from the Nahuatl phrase Coatl-Tepetl ("snake hill"), grew during the coffee boom years of the early 20th century. The mansions along its elegant streets are pinned with ornate balconies; take a peek inside and you'll see gorgeous courtyards overflowing with greenery.

GETTING HERE & AROUND

Getting to Coatepec is easy. Take any of the shuttle buses marked xico that leave from a traffic circle on Calle Allende, a few blocks west of Parque Juárez in Xalapa. The 10-minute ride costs less than $1.

EXPLORING

The wealth of Coatepec town is apparent in its gilt-covered churches. Across from the main square, the 18th-century **Parroquia San Jerónimo** (☒*Calle 5 de Mayo at Calle Jiménez de Capillo*) has low arches trimmed with gold leaf.

The **Santuario de Nuestra Señora de Guadalupe** (☒*Calle Aldama at Calle Hidalgo*) hardly has a surface that isn't covered with some precious metal. Make sure to take a look at the dome, which is cleverly painted to look much taller than it actually is.

WHERE TO EAT & STAY

¢–$ MEXICAN **Arcos de Belem.** Bricked arches beckon you to enter this warm, family-run restaurant where murals of Coatepec's landscape adorn the walls. With simple, classic Mexican dishes, these folks have been drawing fans for more than 50 years. Anticipating your hunger, *totopos* (tortilla chips and salsa) or sweet breads are delivered to your table as you sit down. The *mole* is a specialty and children love the *zopilotas* (fried tortillas topped with beans and cheese). Stop in for breakfast or a big dinner, but don't forget a cup of Coatepec's world-famous coffee. Also keep an eye out for the children's second-floor play area. ■ TIP→ **Ask for the sought-after open-air window seating on the second level.** ✉ *Miguel Lerdo 9* ☎ *228/816–5265* ▭ *MC, V* ⊙ *Closed Sun.*

$$ Fodor's Choice ★ **Posada Coatepec.** Once the home of a coffee baron, this 19th-century mansion—a 15-minute drive from Xalapa—is now a luxury hotel. The lobby, decorated with a fine collection of period antiques, feels like the entrance to a private home. Rooms have original tile floors, beamed ceilings, and heaters for Coatepec's often chilly weather. Stained-glass windows bathe the restaurant in warm reds and yellows. The posada can arrange coffee plantation tours and river excursions. **Pros:** Darling place to stay, coffee plantation tours. **Cons:** Staff can seem uncaring at times. ✉ *Calle Hidalgo 9,* ☎ *228/816–0544* 🌐 *www.posadacoatepec.com.mx* *7 rooms, 15 suites, 1 villa* *In-hotel: Restaurant, room service, bar, pool, laundry service, public Wi-Fi, parking (fee), no elevator* ▭ *AE, MC, V.*

SHOPPING

The friendly folks at the **Café de Avelino** (✉ *Calle Aldama between Calle Constitución and Calle Morelos* ☎ *228/816–3401*) will show you how the experts rate the beans.

XICO

★ *19 km (12 mi) south of Xalapa, 11 km (7 mi) south of Coatepec.*

If you close your eyes and try to imagine the ideal Mexican small town, you'd probably come up with something very close to Xico. In many ways, this village seems untouched by time: donkeys hauling burlap sacks of fresh beans clip-clop along the cobblestone streets followed by local coffee harvesters, machetes tied to their waists with red sashes. Adding to this back-in-time beauty is the fact that the town is often surrounded by mist.

The village is also known for its raucous nine-day festival in July that celebrates the town's patron saint, Mary Magdalene.

GETTING HERE & AROUND

To get to Xico, take one of the shuttle buses marked XICO that leave from a traffic circle on Calle Allende, a few blocks west of Parque Juárez. The 20-minute ride costs less than $1.

6

EXPLORING

Xico is known for its natural wonders, notably the **Cascada de Texolo,** a majestic waterfall set in a deep gorge of tropical greenery. The lush area surrounding the falls is great for exploring; paths lead through forests of banana trees to smaller cascades and crystal-blue pools, perfect for a refreshing swim. There's also a steep staircase that will take you from the observation deck to the base of the falls.

The falls are about 3 km (2 mi) from the center of town. To reach them, start from the red-and-white church where Calle Zaragoza and Calle Matamoros meet and follow the cobblestone street downhill, bearing right when you reach the small roadside shrine to the Virgin Mary. Continue through the coffee plantations, following the signs for la cascada until you reach the main observation deck. ■ TIP→ **It's a long walk, so if it's a hot day you might want to take a taxi from the main square.** Entry is free. There is a small parking fee.

The petite **Parroquia de Santa María Magdalena** (⊠ *Calle Benito Juárez at Calle Lerdo*), at the end of Avenida Hidalgo, was built on the highest spot in town. Behind the altar is a traditional depiction of the crucifixion with Mary Magdalene, showing a bit more shoulder than usual, lying prostrate beneath. A more demure statue of her is dressed in a different outfit for every day of the festival in her honor. The small museum behind the church has a display of her ensembles.

WHERE TO STAY

¢–$ **Hotel Coyopolan.** Overlooking the Río Coyopolan, this two-story hotel couldn't have a better location. From the colonial-style building you can hear the river spill into a few small waterfalls. Rooms are small, but cheerfully decorated with local handicrafts. The open-air restaurant, La Molienda ($), serves up fresh river fish. There's also a satisfying selection of beef and chicken dishes. **Pros:** Fantastic location, pitter-patter of river is totally relaxing. **Cons:** Like many of the hotels around here, rooms are tiny. < ⊠ *Calle Venustiano Carranza Sur s/n,* ☎ *228/813–1266* *14 rooms* *In-room: No phone. In-hotel: Restaurant, no elevator* *MC, V.*

■ TIP→ **Wash down your meals in Xico with a shot of local liquor. Try the creamy *torito de cacahuate* (peanut), *morita* (blackberry), or *verde* (technically this means "green," but in this case signifies herb) varieties.**

SHOPPING

You can find just about anything along Calle Hidalgo, but the one thing not to leave without is mole. **Derivados Acamalín** (⊠ *Av. Hidalgo 150* ☎ *288/813–0713*) is famous for its moles, as you can tell by the photos on the walls of celebrities who have dropped by for a taste.

NORTHERN VERACRUZ

North of Veracruz and Xalapa are a mishmash of sights. The biggest reason to head this way is El Tajín, one of the most impressive sets of ruins in all of Mexico. You can visit El Tajín on side trips from Veracruz (4 hours) or Xalapa (2½ hours), but if you use the hillside vanilla-growing town of Papantla (20 minutes from the ruins) as your base, you'll be able to see the spectacle of the *voladores*. Also nearby, north of El Tajín, is the coastal town of Tuxpán, a peaceful pit stop on the drive up the coast.

PAPANTLA

250 km (155 mi) northwest of Veracruz.

Set on a steep hillside, Papantla is in the center of a vanilla-producing region. Products made from that particular bean, from candies to liqueurs, are sold everywhere; a big vanilla festival draws people to the town every March. The rest of the year, this dusty village goes about its business. Totonac men in flowing white shirts and pants lead their donkeys through the streets, and young couples smooch underneath palm trees that ring the zócalo. Papantla is the home of the *voladores*, who twirl off an 82-foot pole in front of the town's ornate cathedral.

6

GETTING HERE & AROUND

If you're driving, Carretera 130 from Mexico City leads past Poza Rica to Papantla; from Veracruz City, Carretera 180 leads north to Papantla. If you'd prefer the bus, Papantla's station, on Calle Benito Juárez at Calle 20 de Noviembre, is served only by ADO. There's service half a dozen times a day from Veracruz; the ride takes three to four hours and costs $12, and at least four buses a day to Papantla from Xalapa (3¾ to 4¼ hours, $13).

ESSENTIALS

Currency Exchange **Banamex** (✉ *Calle Enríquez 102* ☎ *784/842–1766*).

Medical Assistance **Angeles Verdes** (☎ *078*).**Clínica del Centro Médico** (✉ *Calle 16 de Septiembre 12, Zona Centro* ☎ *784/842–0082*). **For Emergencies** (☎ *066*). **Papantla Cruz Roja** (☎ *784/842–0126*). **Papantla Police Department** (☎ *784/842–0075*).

Visitor & Tour Info **Papantla Tourist Office** (✉ *Calle Azueta at Calle Artes,* ☎ *784/842–3837*).

EXPLORING

★ From the town square you'll see a giant statue honoring the voladores looking down on the city. Whether he's playing to the people below or the gods above is unclear, but he's certainly got the best view in town. Behind this statue and next to the cathedral you'll find Calle Centenario. Following this street, wind your way up to **El Monumento al Volador** to enjoy a lovely mural and a gorgeous view of the city below.

WHERE TO EAT & STAY

$–$$ MEXICAN ✕ **Plaza Pardo.** From the balcony of this cheerful second-story restaurant you'll have a great view of the goings-on in the zócalo. Brightly colored cloths adorn the tables, where house specialties—including *cecina con enchiladas* (salted beef with spicy enchiladas) and *rellenos al gusto* (green chiles stuffed with chicken, cheese, or beef)—are served by the friendly staff. ■ TIP→ **Many people stop here for a breakfast of**

Continued on page 304

THE FLIGHT OF THE VOLADORES

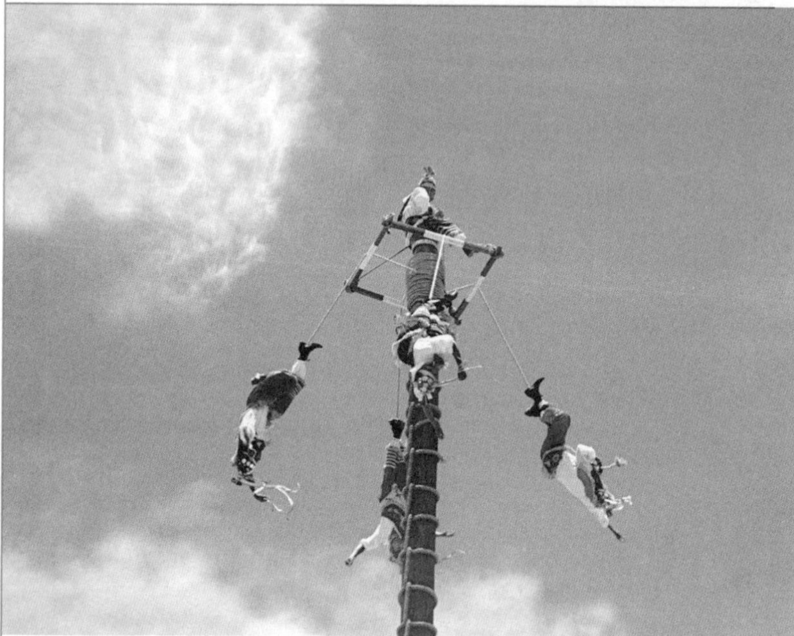

Like most things in Mexico, this story begins with a legend: Centuries ago a long drought had withered the crops of the Totonac people. Some of the elders decided that the only solution was to find a way to send a message to the gods about their plight. But how to attract their attention?

The sages sent five young men out into the woods in search of the tallest tree they could find. When they returned with the tree, its trunk was stripped of branches and stood on end. Four of the young men adorned their bodies with feathers so they would fool the gods into thinking they were birds and whirled around the tree, suspended from vines. The fifth played a song on the flute that resembled a bird's mournful song.

Their plan must have worked, because *voladores* (which means "the ones who fly") continue to perform versions of this ritual all over Mexico. It's a source of pride for the Totonac people, many of whom still live near the town of Papantla, because it's one of the few traditional practices that managed to survive despite the attempts of the Spanish to wipe out all native customs.

The voladores take their task very seriously, studying for years before they can participate. After all, they are learning to fly.

This ritual was originally performed only once every 52 years, to celebrate the beginning of a new calendar. Today it can be witnessed weekly in Papantla and multipe times daily at the archaeological site of El Tajín.

HOW THEY TAKE TO THE SKY

THE RITUAL BEGINS when the *caporal*, or captain, leads the four voladores to the pole which is 82 feet high. Red sashes over their shoulders represent wings; their conical hats resemble the crests of birds.

THE FIVE dance around the pole several times before ascending the pole, keeping their heads down as a sign of respect to the gods.

THE FOUR VOLADORES seat themselves on a square wooden frame suspended from the top of the pole, each facing a different cardinal direction. The caporal stands on top of the 82-foot pole, with nothing to steady himself.

THE CAPORAL JUMPS on the pole several times. He turns to the east, bending so far backward that his torso is parallel to the ground, then he shifts his position and leans forward. He repeats these moves three more times, rotating to face the points of the compass. As if this weren't difficult enough, he accomplishes these feats while playing a hide-covered drum and a three-holed flute.

AFTER THE CAPORAL FINISHES his dance, the wooden frame starts to spin. The voladores each drop backwards from the side of the platform facing east—where the sun rises and the world awakes—held aloft only by a rope tied around their waists. They throw their arms out to their sides, resembling a quartet of birds in flight.

THEY TWIST LEFT for 13 full rotations each. Between them, the flyers circle the pole 52 times, representing the sacred 52-year cycle of the Totonacs (the Maya calendar had the same 52-year cycle).

THE RITUAL takes about 30 minutes. Offering a $2 (per viewer) tip is appropriate.

enchiladas and refried beans before heading to El Tajín. ✉*Enríquez 105, Col. Centro* ☎*784/842–0059* ▭*MC, V.*

¢–$$ MEXICAN ✕**Sorrento.** With dozens of dishes on the menu, this open-air restaurant is the most popular in Papantla. It's always crowded with locals who come to enjoy the reasonably priced seafood and to catch a few minutes of a *telenovela* (soap opera) on the giant TV set. The *platillo mexicano,* a selection of regional appetizers, is big enough for two. ✉*Enríquez 105, Col. Centro* ☎*784/842–0067* ▭*No credit cards.*

¢–$ **Hotel Tajín.** The trick at this hillside hotel is getting the right room; the dozen or so rooms with views of the town are the best, but check the mattress for firmness before you settle in. All rooms are spic-and-span. Although the staff does not speak English, they go out of their way to figure out what you need and deliver it promptly. **Pros:** Thoughtful staff, clean rooms. **Cons:** You might have to do some room testing before you settle. ✉*Domínguez 104, at Nuñez, Col. Centro,* ☎*784/842–0121* *59 rooms, 13 suites* *In-hotel: Restaurant, pool, laundry service, parking (no fee), no elevator* ▭*MC, V.*

¢ **Hotel Provincia Express.** Stay in the heart of things at this hotel, which is up a flight of steps from the main square. Many of the modern rooms have little balconies with views of the mountains. Rooms in front tend to be a bit noisy, so if you're a light sleeper, ask for one in the back. **Pros:** The staff couldn't be friendlier. **Cons:** Some rooms are noisy. ✉*Enríquez 103, Col. Centro,* ☎*784/842–1645 or 784/842–4213* *16 rooms, 4 suites* *In-hotel: Restaurant, bar, laundry service, public Internet, public Wi-Fi, no elevator* ▭*MC, V.*

SHOPPING

The teeming **Mercado Miguel Hidalgo** (✉*Av. 20 de Noviembre*), half a block downhill from the main square, sells Totonac costumes, carvings, baskets, and shoulder bags. It's a daily market, but is much busier on weekends. The real draw is vanilla, the chief product of this region, which is sold in every conceivable form. Especially pretty are flowers made from the dried vanilla pods.

EL TAJÍN

13 km (8 mi) west of Papantla.

Fodor's Choice ★

The extensive ruins of El Tajín—from the Totonac word for "thunder"—express the highest degree of artistry of any ancient city in the coastal area. The city was hidden until 1785, when a Spanish engineer happened upon it. Early theories attributed the complex—believed to be a religious center—to a settlement of Maya-related Huasteca, one of the most important cultures of Veracruz. Because of its immense size and unique architecture, scholars now believe it may have been built by a distinct El Tajín tribe with ties to the Maya. Although much of the site has been restored, many structures are still hidden under jungle.

El Tajín is thought to have reached its peak between AD 600 and 1200. During this time hundreds of structures of native sandstone were built here, including temples, double-storied palaces, ball courts, and hundreds of houses. But El Tajín was already an important religious and administrative center during the first three centuries AD. Its influence is in part attributed to the fact that it had large reserves of cacao beans, used as currency in pre-Hispanic times.

EXPLORING

Evidence suggests that the southern half of the uncovered ruins—the area around the lower plaza—was reserved for ceremonial purposes. Its centerpiece is the 60-foot-high **Pirámide de los Nichoes** (Pyramid of the Niches), one of the finest pre-Columbian buildings in Mexico. The finely wrought seven-level structure has 365 coffers—one for each day of the solar year—built around its seven friezes. The reliefs on the pyramid depict the ruler, 13-Rabbit—all the rulers' names were associated with sacred animals—and allude also to the Tajín tribe's main god, the benign Quetzalcóatl. One panel on the pyramid tells the tale of heroic human sacrifice and of the soul's imminent descent to the underworld, where it is rewarded with the gift from the gods of sacred *pulque,* a milky alcoholic beverage made from cactus.

Just south of the pyramid is the I-shape **Juego de Pelotas Sur** (Southern Ball Court). This is one of more than 15 ball courts—more than at any other site in Mesoamerica—where the sacred pre-Columbian ball game was played. The game is somewhat similar to soccer—players used a hard rubber ball that could not be touched with the hands, and suited up in pads and body protectors—but far more deadly. Intricate carvings at certain ball courts indicate that games ended with human sacrifice. It's believed that the winner of the match won the opportunity to ask a question of the gods in exchange for his sacrifice. Depending on the importance of his question, his sacrifice could be anything from minor body mutilation to his very life. It is surmised that the players involved in these sacrificial games were high-ranking members of the priest or warrior classes.

6

To the north, **El Tajín Chico** (Little El Tajín) is thought to have been the secular part of the city, with mostly administrative buildings and the elite's living quarters. Floors and roofing were made with volcanic rock and limestone. The most important structure here is the **Complejo de los Columnos** (Complex of the Columns). The columns once held up the concrete ceilings, but early settlers in Papantla removed the stones to construct houses. If you're prepared to work your way through the thick jungle, you can see some more recent finds along the dirt paths that lead over the nearby ridges.

You can leave bags at the visitor center at the entrance, which includes a restaurant and a small museum that displays some pottery and sculpture and tells what little is known of the site. Excellent guided tours are available in English and Spanish and cost about $20 per group. A performance by some voladores normally takes place at midday and sometimes up to five times daily. ■ **TIP→Start early to avoid the midday sun, and take water, a hat, and sunblock.** To get here, take a shuttle bus. Head down Calle 20 de Noviembre until you hit Calle Francisco Madero. Cross the street and wait in front of the gas station for an el tajín shuttle bus. The $1 trip takes about 20 minutes. ☎*784/842–8354* 🌐*www.inah.gob.mx* 🎫*$4* ⏲*Daily 9–5.*

COSTA ESMERALDA (EMERALD COAST)

175 km (109 mi) northwest of Veracruz.

Covering 35 km (23 mi) of coastline along the Gulf of Mexico between Nautla and Papantla, Costa Esmeralda's clean, wide beaches and calm waters are popular with beachgoers and fishermen alike. Here Highway 180 is lined with small restaurants and stands selling fresh pineapples, oranges, and cheese. It's also peppered with campgrounds and hotels taking advantage of the beautiful beachfront.

WHERE TO STAY

$$–$$$ ★ **Azúcar.** Azúcar, which opened in 2005, is a hotel specializing in barefoot luxury. Thatched-roof bungalows gather invitingly around a sunken pool overlooking waves crashing 20 feet away. Private open-air seating allows you to take in the ocean view from a daybed of plush pillows or a colorful hammock. Outdoor showers, straw hats, and beach volleyballs lend a sense of fun, while flat-screen TVs and pristine white rooms provide a touch of elegance. An optional package for a minimum of four people includes two nights, one dinner, airport transfers, and round-trip travel from Mexico City on a Cessna 206. The hotel also arranges trips to El Tajín. Note that children under the age of 14 are not allowed. **Pros:** Very nice touches for a reasonable rate (that in other regions would be through the roof), no young children are allowed. **Cons:** Some details that would make your stay more seamless are overlooked, no young children are allowed. ✉*Carretera Federal Nautla-Poza Rica, Km 83.5,* ☎*232/321–0678* 🌐*www.hotelazucar.com* *20 suites* *In-hotel: Restaurant, room service, bar, pool, spa, beachfront, no elevator, laundry service, concierge, airport shuttle, parking (no fee), no-smoking rooms* 💳*AE, MC, V.*

TUXPAN

89 km (55 mi) north of Papantla, 309 km (192 mi) northwest of Veracruz.

A peaceful riverside town with a tangle of twisting streets, Tuxpan—almost as often referred to as Tuxpam—is a pleasant place to stop if you're driving along the coast. The most popular form of public transportation is the fleet of baby-blue *lanchas* (small motorboats) that carry commuters across the Río Tuxpan. A round-trip journey from any of the docks along the river costs about 40¢. In the evening you'll find people strolling along the palm-lined waterfront promenade and watching the sun set over the water. Running parallel to the river, busy Avenida Juárez is lined with restaurants, hotels, and shops.

GETTING HERE & AROUND

ADO buses also shuttle between Veracruz and Tuxpan several times a day; it's a four-hour to six-hour trip and costs about $15. Tuxpan has a small bus terminal east of downtown on Calle Rodriguez.

ESSENTIALS

Currency Exchange **Banamex** (✉ *Av. Juárez at Calle Corregidora, Tuxpan* ☎ *783/834–3868*).

Emergency Numbers **Centro Médico de Tuxpan** (✉ *Av. Cuauhtémoc 82, Col. del Valle* ☎ *783/834–7400*).**Tuxpan Cruz Roja** (☎ *783/834–0158*). **Tuxpan Police Department** (☎ *783/834–0252*).

Visitor & Tour Information **Tuxpan Tourist Office** (✉ *Av. Juárez 20, Tuxpan* ☎ *783/834–0322 Ext. 125*).

6

EXPLORING

Across the river from downtown is the grandly named **Museo Histórico de la Amistad México–Cuba** *(Historical Museum of the Mexico-Cuba Friendship)*. This one-room house, bare save for black-and-white photos and a few threadbare uniforms, is where Fidel Castro lived for a time while planning the overthrow of Fulgencio Batista. To get here from the dock, walk three blocks south to Calle Obregón, then head west for several blocks until you reach the end of the street. ✉ *Calle Obregón* ☎ *No phone* *Free* *Weekdays 9–7.*

Avenida Juárez leads to **Parque Reforma,** where more than 100 tables are set beneath trees clipped into perfect cubes. As the sun goes down, hundreds of noisy birds come here to roost as young couples buy ice cream from carts or slip off to secluded benches. The park has a memorial to Fausto Vega Santander, a member of the 201st Squadron of the Mexican Air Force and the first Mexican to be killed in combat during World War II.

BEACHES

Tuxpan's main attraction are the miles of beaches that begin 7 km (4½ mi) east of town. The first and most accessible beach from Tuxpan is **Playa Tuxpan.** The surf here isn't huge, but there's enough action to warrant breaking out your surf- or Boogie board. Of the open-air restaurants along Playa Tuxpan, the most established is Miramar, which has an extensive menu of freshly caught seafood.

WHERE TO EAT & STAY

$–$$ SEAFOOD ✕ **Antonio's.** Housed in a colonial-style building, this tiled-floor dining room turns out excellent seafood dishes, including *pulpo gallega* (octopus simmered with onions, olive oil, and white wine) and *pez espada bella molineras* (swordfish served with a mushroom-and-shrimp sauce). If you're not in the mood for fish, the kitchen also grills up steaks. On Friday and Saturday nights a trio of musicians swings into action. ✉ *Av. Juárez 25, at Calle Garizurieta* ☎ *783/834–0662* *AE, MC, V.*

¢ SEAFOOD ✕ **Barra de Mariscos.** Don't be fooled by the white plastic tables and chairs—the seafood at this open-air eatery easily rivals that at fancier places in town. Hunker down with a cold beer and a bowl of *sopa* *de ostión* (a spicy oyster stew), then move on to *pulpo encebollado* (octopus cooked with onions, butter, and garlic) or the house specialty, *camarones a la diabla* (a spicy concoction of grilled shrimp and chiles). You may be tempted to make a meal of the chips and salsa. ✉*Av. Juárez 44, at Calle Ortega* 💳*No credit cards.*

$ ★ **Hotel Florida.** This place certainly earns its name—tropical flora tumbles from the balconies. The art deco–style structure, dating from 1940, has gracefully curved windows on the corner overlooking the town's elegant church. The rooms are, for the most part, spacious and sunny. Some have better views than others, so ask to see a few before you decide. El Quijote, which dominates the ground floor, has excellent seafood.**Pros:** Quality restaurant, nice landscaping. **Cons:** Rooms can vary so checking around is a must. ✉*Av. Juárez 23, at Calle Garizurieta,* ☎*783/834–0222 or 783/834–0602* *75 rooms* *In-room: Wi-Fi. In-hotel: Restaurant, room service, bar, laundry service, public Wi-Fi, parking (no fee)* 💳*DC, MC, V.*

$ **Hotel May Palace.** The most luxurious lodgings in Tuxpan are at this modern hotel overlooking Parque Reforma. The five-story building—which qualifies as a high-rise here—is frequented by business executives who meet for drinks in the small video bar or for dinner in the pleasant restaurant. The rooms, all painted in neutral shades, have views of the river. The sparkling rooftop pool is a great place to hang out. **Pros:** A good place to hang out. **Cons:** Geared toward business travelers. ✉*Av. Juárez 44,* ☎*783/834–8882* 🌐*www.hotelmaypalace.com* *70 rooms, 4 suites* *In-room: Wi-Fi. In-hotel: Restaurant, room service, bar, pool, gym, laundry service, public Wi-Fi, parking (no fee).* 💳*AE, MC, V.*

SPORTS & THE OUTDOORS

WATER SPORTS

For scuba diving, head to **Isla Lobos** (Island of the Wolves), a protected eco-reserve that shares its space with a military outpost and a lighthouse. In the shallow water offshore are a few shipwrecks and colorful reefs with puffer fish, parrot fish, damselfish, and barracuda. Generally, the best time to dive is between May and August. **Aqua Sport** (✉*Carretera la Playa, Km 8.5* ☎*783/837–0259*), west of Playa Tuxpan, arranges diving trips to Isla Lobos.

SOUTHERN VERACRUZ

Southern Veracruz has some dramatic sights, both natural and manmade. Tlacotalpan is a tropical port city of waning importance, but its brightly colored buildings and well-preserved colonial architecture make it a lovely place to kick back for a few days. Farther south along the coast the land meets the sea quite dramatically in a trio of towns known as Los Tuxtlas, which cling to the hillside above the water. One of the towns, Catemaco, is also home to an immense lake that is a favorite spot with vacationing Mexicans.

TLACOTALPAN

★ *90 km (56 mi) south of Veracruz.*

The name Tlacotalpan is of Nahuatl origin and means "in the middle of the earth," referring to the settlement's location on what was then an island. Once a prosperous port city, Tlacotalpan, now more run-down, still charms with rustic, century-old houses, all in colors that might have been inspired by a candy shop.

GETTING HERE & AROUND

Getting to Tlacotalpan by car is a snap: simply take Carretera 180 south from Veracruz, then head west on Ruta 175 after you pass Alvarado. If you are traveling by bus, there's a twice-daily ADO bus costing about $7 each way. You can also take the more frequent TRV buses departing from the second-class terminal for a bit less. ■ TIP→**Caution: This can be a painfully slow option, as these also serve as local buses and school buses.**

EXPLORING

The neoclassical **Casa de Cabildo,** which houses all the governmental offices, is painted vivid shades of red and green. The huge arch in the center of the building leads to the old port, and all newcomers once passed through this portal.

The massive orange-trimmed church on the north side of Plaza Zaragoza is the **Capilla de la Candelaria,** constructed in 1779. It houses the town's patron saint, the Virgen de la Candelaria. The saint is honored each year with a festival that runs from January 31 to February 9; a parade with hundreds of horses is followed by the running of the bulls through the streets. The most famous image of the festival is a statue of the Virgin Mary drifting down the river, followed by a flotilla of little boats. The buildings in Plaza Zaragoza are helpfully marked with snippets of history printed in Spanish and English.

Several other churches are scattered around Tlacotalpan, but none are more charming than the diminutive **Iglesia de San Miguel Arcangel.** Known to locals as San Miguelito (Little Saint Michael), the whitewashed structure, constructed in 1785, was once a parish church reached by crossing a little bridge. If you're in town September 27 to 29, you can take a peek at the Fiesta de San Miguelito. The church is about three blocks north of Plaza Zaragoza.

Two tiny museums vie for your attention. On Plaza Hidalgo, diagonally across from Plaza Zaragoza, **Museo Salvador Ferrando** (✉ *Calle Manuel Alegre 6* ☎ *288/884–2385* 🎫 *$1* ⏲ *Tues.–Sun. 10:30–4:30*) displays furniture and other objects from the 19th century.

Museo Casa Lara (✉ *Calle Gonzalo Aguirre Beltrán 6* ☎ *288/884–2166* 🎫 *$1* ⏲ *Daily 9–7*) is filled with photographs and other items that belonged to Augustín Lara, a musician and movie star. Look for stills from films such as *Los Tres Bohemios* and *Los Tres Amores de Lola.* The best reason to visit, though, is the chance to poke around a lovely colonial-era home.

The Casa de Cabildo faces **Plaza Zaragoza,** the town's main square. In the square's shady center you'll find a bandstand decorated with ornamental lyres.

WHERE TO STAY

$–$$ **Posada Doña Lala.** A staircase decorated with hand-painted tiles leads you up to the second-floor rooms at this bright pink hotel. Ask for one of the spacious rooms facing the street so you can look out over the rooftops. Don't miss a meal at the seafood restaurant ($), which has tables in the beamed-ceiling dining room or on a shady porch. **Pros:** No matter where you sit, there's a view of the river. **Cons:** Could use some updating. ✉*Av. Venustiano Carranzo 11,* ☎*288/884–2580* 🌐*hoteldonalala.com* *32 rooms, 5 suites* *In-hotel: Restaurant, public Internet, no elevator* 💳*AE, MC, V*

SHOPPING

The famous *sillón tlacatalpeño*—a wooden rocking chair with a woven seat and back—is one way locals beat the heat. Puchase a full-size love seat or a doll-size miniature at **Casa Artensenal de Tlacotalpan** (✉*Plaza Zaragoza* ☎*288/884–2990*). Doña Rafaela Murillo's shop, housed in a building that once served as the town's prison, also carries various objects made of carved wood, including fanciful animals and birds.

Galeria Vives (✉*Av. Venustiano Carranzo 11* ☎*288/884–3070*) carries lacy garments and monogrammed handkerchiefs.

LOS TUXTLAS

Lush and mysterious, Los Tuxtlas is a hilly region where a small volcanic mountain range, the Sierra de Los Tuxtlas, meets the sea. Crystal-clear lakes, tumbling waterfalls, and relaxing mineral springs make this region a popular stopover for travelers heading south to Oaxaca or east to the Yucatán. The region's three principal towns—Santiago Tuxtla, San Andrés Tuxtla, and Catemaco—are carved into the mountainside more than 600 feet above sea level, lending them a coolness that's the envy of the perspiring masses on the coastal plain.

SANTIAGO TUXTLA

140 km (87 mi) south of Veracruz.

Santiago Tuxtla is most charming of the towns in Los Tuxtlas. The Olmec civilization, the oldest in Mexico, flourished here between 900 and 600 BC. Evidence of Olmec culture is all around you.

EXPLORING

Facing Parque Juárez is the **Museo Regional Tuxteco,** where you'll find another stone head. Housed in a lovely colonial building, the museum is worth a visit to learn about the region's indigenous peoples and contemporary cultures. ✉*Circuito Lic. Angel Carvajal s/n* ☎*294/947–0196* *$2* *Mon.–Sat. 9–6, Sun. 9–3.*

A huge stone head dominates the attractive central square, known as **Parque Juárez.** Called the Cabeza Cobata, or the Cobata Head, for the field west of town where it was discovered, it is by far the largest of these unusual carvings ever discovered. It's also unique because the eyes are clearly closed and the mouth is in a frown.

About 21 km (13 mi) east of Santiago Tuxtla are the ruins of **Tres Zapotes,** once an Olmec ceremonial center. Discovered near here was a stone carving bearing a date that revealed that the Olmec culture is at least as old as that of the Maya. Today there is little to see besides several groups of unreconstructed temples. The site museum, however, holds the first of the massive Olmec heads to have been discovered. To reach Tres Zapotes, head southwest on Carretera 179 and turn north after about 8 km (5 mi). Taxis from Santiago Tuxtla travel this route regularly. Admission to the museum is $2.

WHERE TO STAY

¢ **Hotel Castellanos.** One of the most unusual lodgings in Veracruz, Hotel Castellanos resembles a stack of dishes. In the middle of the cylindrical structure is a seven-story atrium culminating in a domed skylight. Wedge-shape rooms have balconies with views of the surrounding mountains. The small restaurant, which overlooks a sparkling pool, serves regional favorites such as *bistec encebollado* (beef with onions) for extremely reasonable prices. **Pros:** Prices are very reasonable. **Cons:** Looks a little tacky. ✉ *Av. 5 de Mayo at Calle Comonfort,* ☎ *294/947–0300* *53 rooms* *In-hotel: Restaurant, pool* *MC, V.*

6

SAN ANDRÉS TUXTLA

143 km (95 mi) south of Veracruz.

With tobacco fields extending in every direction, Los Tuxtlas is known for its cigars; San Andrés Tuxtla is famous for its hand-rolled variety.

EXPLORING

If you head 3 km (1½ mi) northeast of town, you'll reach the **Laguna Encantada** or Enchanted Lagoon. This lake was thought to be magical because its water level drops during the rainy season and rises again when the weather is dry.

If you'd like to see cigars being made, head to the factory of **Puros Santa Clara** (✉ *Blvd. 5 de Febrero 10* ☎ *294/947–9900*), just outside town on the highway to Catemaco. Workers are happy to explain how they roll the stogies, then place them in wooden holders that force them into a uniform shape. Visit the shop if you'd like to take some home.

WHERE TO STAY

¢–$ **Hotel del Parque.** This hotel in a handsome historic building in the middle of the city has a charm that few others can match. The nicely decorated rooms are by far the most comfortable in San Andrés. You can eat in the colonial-style dining room ($–$$) or outside under the graceful colonnades. **Pros:** They're pretty tuned in to the goings-on about town and can help you plan your itinerary. **Cons:** Modernized to the point of being a little bland. ✉*Calle Madero 5,* ☎*294/942–0198* 🌐*www.hoteldelparque.com* *39 rooms* *In-hotel: Restaurant, room service, bar, laundry service, public Wi-Fi, no elevator* 💳*MC, V.*

CATEMACO

166 km (103 mi) south of Veracruz.

Overlooking an immense blue lake, the town of Catemaco is unquestionably the most popular vacation destination in Los Tuxtlas. Not everyone comes for the breathtaking views, however. The cool, gray fog that slips over the lake provides the perfect setting for the region's most famous attraction: the *brujos* (witches) who claim to be able to cure whatever ails you. Conventional medicine failed to penetrate this jungle area until the 1940s, so the folk traditions have survived, making use of herbal remedies (typically using basil, rosemary, and other ingredients of doubtful origin) to cure diseases and get rid of evil spirits. Catemaco is the place to go for a consultation with a brujo for a ritualistic cleansing. This costs anywhere between $2 and $20, depending on your ailment, which may range from misfortune in love to financial hardships to health problems. The cost also increases according to the brujo's assessment of how much you are able to pay.

EXPLORING

Tours of **Lago Catemaco,** a lake formed from the crater of a volcano, are easy to come by and well worth the $5, but once you've gone you'll be tempted to post a sign on your forehead "Ya fui en lancha" ("I already took the boat"), as dozens of boat drivers lining the waterfront clamor after the business of any nonlocal strolling by. Several small islands are sprinkled across the surface of the deep-blue lake. The most popular is Isla Tanaxpilla, also known as the Island of the Monkeys because it harbors a colorful colony of fish-eating baboons brought here from Thailand by biologists hoping to study them.

A dirt road follows the coast 19 km (12 mi) north of Sontecomapan to the fishing village of **Montepio,** which has a wide beach.

Beyond Catemaco, a dirt road continues over the hills and down to a lovely stretch of undeveloped coastline. About 20 km (12 mi) east from Catemaco is the village of **Sontecomapan,** where you can take a $2 launch across the lagoon to **La Barra,** a quiet village with a beautiful strip of beach sprinkled with palapas and sand dollars.

WHERE TO EAT & STAY

$ SEAFOOD ✕**Jorge's.** You know the fish is fresh when you watch the fishing boats delivering it. At this waterfront restaurant, the staff brings a platter of the day's catch to the table so you can choose one for yourself. If you're brave, try the raw seafood cocktail called *vuelva la vida,* which literally means "returned to life"—it includes octopus tentacles. Dishes such as *camerones enchipotlados* (spicy shrimp) are what make this place popular with both locals and out-of-towners. ✉*Paseo del Malecón* ☎*294/943–1299* 💳*MC, V.*

$$–$$$ **La Finca.** This modern hotel sits on the shore of Lago Catemaco. The builders knew why people were coming here: they designed the low-slung buildings so that all the rooms face the water, and indeed, each room has a balcony with a lovely view. The palm-shaded pool has a pleasant little waterfall. The hotel is popular with Mexican families, so book ahead for summer vacation and other busy times. **Pros:** Fantastic views from the rooms. **Cons:** Can be crowded with local families during certain seasons. < ✉ *Carretera 180, Km 147,* ☎ *294/943–0322* 🌐 *www.lafinca.com.mx* *54 rooms, 3 suites* *In-hotel: Restaurant, bar, pool, beachfront, public Wi-Fi, no elevator* ▭ *AE, MC, V.*

$$ **Hotel Nanciyaga.** A cross between luxury and camping, if there can be one, these rustic, two- and four-person cabins surrounded by jungle are among the most secluded and attractive accommodations on the shores of Lake Catemaco. Enjoy mineral mud baths, kayak expeditions, jungle hikes, and warm, curative *temazcal* steam baths on Saturdays. Dine by candlelight as the sun sets and retire via flashlight to your screened-in, open-air cabin along the water for a peaceful night in your hammock or cozy bed. Consultations with brujos can be arranged. **Pros:** Simply a unique lodging with a wonderful mix of eco and luxe. **Cons:** Might be too rustic for some. ✉ *Carretera Catemaco, Km 7,* ☎ *294/943–0199* 🌐 *www.nanciyaga.com* *10 cabins* *In-room: No a/c, no phone, no TV. In-hotel: Restaurant, bar, no elevator* ▭ *No credit cards.*

Oaxaca

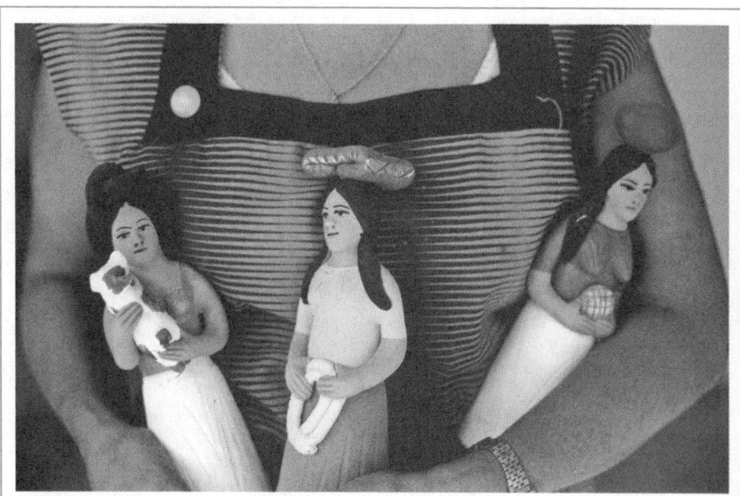

Local handcraft shop, Oaxaca City

7

WORD OF MOUTH

"Oaxaca has a wonderful walkable centro with the best zócalo in Mexico. It is a great craft area, with small villages and markets nearby, and also offers Monte Albán, which is very impressive."

–marilynl

WELCOME TO OAXACA

TOP REASONS TO GO

★ **Sampling a little bit of everything:** The state is a best-of-Mexico sampler: ruins, colonial cities, beaches, crafts, and gorgeous scenery.

★ **Dining on some of the most delicious food the country has to offer:** Oaxaca City's restaurants serve up the tastiest food you'll find in Mexico, hands down. Think cheese, mole, empanadas, tamales, soups, and rich hot chocolates.

★ **Craft-shopping at the source:** The villages around Oaxaca City actually produce many of the crafts you see in markets all over Mexico.

★ **Experiencing Mexico's last coastal frontier:** The Oaxaca Coast is the most unexplored and undeveloped of Mexico's shorelines.

★ **Visiting a striking mountaintop city:** Monte Albán, built by the Zapotecs, is one of the country's most important ruins.

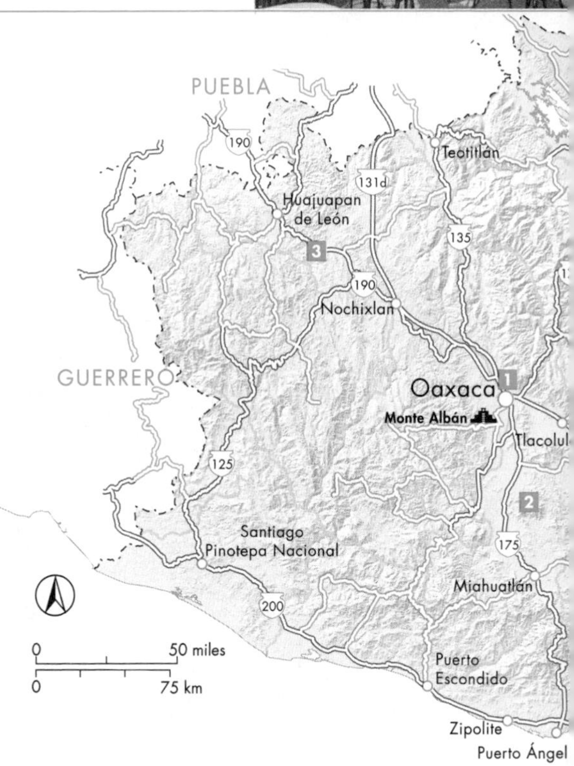

1 Oaxaca City. The capital of the region is one of Mexico's prettiest colonial cities. It has tree-shaded parks, cobblestone streets, and brightly colored buildings, as well as fantastic restaurants. It's a small city—the main sights are easily covered on foot.

2 The Valles Centrales. There are dozens of crafts villages and mezcal makers in the valleys surrounding Oaxaca City. In every direction are archaeological sites, the main ones being Mitla and Monte Albán. The countryside here is simply beautiful: a few main roads take you through miles of farmland.

GETTING ORIENTED

Oaxaca is in one of three adjacent valleys encircled by the majestic Sierra Madre del Sur. Mexico's fifth-largest state, it's bordered by Chiapas to the east, Veracruz and Puebla to the north, and Guerrero to the west. Southern Oaxaca State is blessed with 509 km (316 mi) of Pacific coastline. By the way, it's pronounced *wah-hah-ka*.

3 The Mixteca. This region, northwest of Oaxaca City, is one of the least-explored parts of the state. You'll find pine-covered hills, tiny villages that survive on subsistence farming, and a series of colossal, partially reconstructed monasteries.

4 Oaxaca Coast. The coast is still pretty remote, and it is strikingly beautiful. Puerto Escondido is still surfer territory, though fancier digs are starting to pop up. Bahías de Huatulco is mostly a nature reserve, though the government is trying to transform the rest into another Cancún. Midway between the two are a few tiny beach villages, including the up-and-coming paradise of Zipolite.

OAXACA PLANNER

What's Cooking?

The regional specialties simmering in Oaxaca's kitchens are reason enough to visit the city. Whether you want to master a mole or be an expert on the multicolor chile peppers at the local market, cooking courses offered by some of the city's top chefs are a great way to immerse yourself in Oaxacan culture. Pilar Cabrera (☎951/516–5704 🌐www.laolla.com.mx), proprietor of La Olla restaurant, offers private or group classes in which you prepare a five-course meal. If you take private lessons, you can choose which dishes you'd like to learn and classes usually start with a market visit to select ingredients. The most exclusive course is by Casa de Oaxaca's Alejandro Ruiz (☎951/514–4173 or 951/516–9923 🌐www.casaoaxaca.com.mx), who's take on Nuevo Mexicano cooking is the best in the city. Casa Sagrada (☎951/516–4275 or 310/455–6085 🌐www.casasagrada.com) in the Central Valley town of Teotitlan offers half-day cooking classes or weeklong courses that focus on Zapotec specialties.

How Much Can You Do?

Though the region may not look that big on paper, tackling both city and coast in less than a week isn't possible without exhausting yourself in the process. Driving from Oaxaca City to Puerto Escondido, for example, takes a minimum of seven hours. Flying is time-consuming and expensive. If your time is limited, you should choose either the city and its surroundings, or the coast. If you're going straight to Puerto Escondido or Huatulco, there are connections through Mexico City and direct flights from Houston.

Oaxaca City serves as a great base from which to explore the Oaxaca Valley. Bus tickets and car rentals can usually be arranged at the last minute, and, unless you're visiting during one of Oaxaca City's many festivals, accommodations are usually easy to come by.

Central Valley Excursions

There are dozens of travel agencies scattered around Oaxaca City, and all offer guided trips to outlying archaeological sites and villages. Always available are half- and full-day tours of the city, half-day excursions to Monte Albán, and full-day journeys to Mitla. You can also book trips to villages that coincide with market days. Note that if you enjoy scenic drives and generally taking your time, you'll be happier renting a car or hiring a taxi as packaged tours don't give you much time at the ruins nor the opportunity to spend time wandering from workshop to workshop at the crafts villages.

Booking in Advance

If you have your heart set on a certain hotel, book six months in advance for visits around Easter, Christmas, or the Day of the Dead. Although July and August fall in the rainy season, they're popular travel months with Mexican families. If you visit during the low season, expect prices to drop by 10% or so.

How's the Weather?

Oaxaca City lies in a valley at an altitude of 5,000 feet above sea level, and is surrounded by mountain ranges. The city's easygoing atmosphere is complemented by year-round spring temperatures, although days can get quite hot even in winter. Evenings can be chilly, so make sure to bring a light jacket. The rainy season runs from July to October, with September being the wettest month. Generally you can count on clear mornings, with clouds and showers usually arriving in the late afternoon. The Oaxacan coast lies well within the tropics, so it's always hot and often humid.

Food for the Soul

Oaxaca is known as "the land of seven moles." You may sample a mole made with sesame seeds one day, then a pineapple- or banana-inspired mole the next. Be sure to try Oaxaca's specialty spirit, called *mezcal,* which, like mole, is subject to delicious interpretation. Some varieties can be as high as 120 proof. Other favorites include *jicuatote,* a sweet milky dessert flavored with cloves and cinnamon, and *chapulines,* seasoned and fried grasshoppers, which are said to charm you into returning to Oaxaca. The best complement to an Oaxacan meal is the music that you'll encounter in and out of the restaurants: mariachis, brass bands, and other live music will provide a sound track for your visit.

Money Matters

WHAT IT COSTS IN DOLLARS

¢	$	$$	$$$	$$$$
Restaurants				
under $5	$5–$10	$10–$15	$15–$25	over $25
Hotels				
under $50	$50–$75	$75–$150	$150–$250	over $250

Restaurant prices are per person for a main course at dinner. Hotel prices are for two people in a standard double room.

Safety

Oaxaca City has almost fully recovered from a crippling series of protests that led to high-profile confrontations between demonstrators and police during the second half of 2006. The city's economy suffered dramatically from the protests but a year later most of the damage had been repaired and tourists were slowly returning. The city's still quiet compared to preprotest days—most noticeable in the lack of patrons at high-end restaurants—and though it's not quite its old self behind closed doors, first-time visitors would never guess that it has ever been anything but a city of superlative colonial charm. Do, however, check the latest news. It is always possible that tempers will flare up again.

Driving around the Oaxaca Valley is reasonably safe, with potholes and speed bumps the biggest threats. However, you should stay off the roads at night. Routes 131 and 175, which connect Oaxaca City to the coast, are twisty and desolate and can be dangerous from a road-safety perspective.

Puerto Escondido, Huatulco, and points in between pose no significant threat. Just follow the usual precautions you would anywhere: don't wear flashy and expensive jewelry, show wads of cash, or wander alone after dark.

OAXACA CITY

Updated by Carissa Bluestone

450 km (280 mi) southeast of Mexico City on toll road 135D, 389 km (242 mi) southwest of Veracruz on Hwys. 185 and 190.

WITH ITS MAGICAL CONCOCTION OF sights, smells, and sounds both ancient and new, this mountain-ringed city of about 400,000 people, officially called Oaxaca de Juárez, embodies the bundle of contrasts that is modern Mexico. Here you'll hear the singsong strains of Zapotec, Mixtec, and other native languages in the markets, Spanish rock in the bars and restaurants, and hip-hop in English blaring from passing cars. Affluent families sip tea or tequila in classy restaurants; out on the streets, men, women, and children of significantly more modest means sell pencils, sweets, and ears of delicious grilled elote (corn).

The Centro Histórico is a pastel collage of colonial- and Republican-era mansions, civic edifices, and churches. The colonial heart is laid out in a simple grid, with all the attractions within a few blocks of one another. Most streets change names when they pass the zócalo; for example, Calle Trujano becomes Calle Guerrero as it travels from west to east. Only the two major east–west arteries—Avenida Morelos and Avenida Independencia—keep their names.

GETTING HERE & AROUND

Oaxaca City's Aeropuerto Internacional Benito Juárez, 8 km (5 mi) south of town, is the region's main hub. Note that the airport completely closes at 11 PM no matter what, so try to avoid late-night arrivals, which, if delayed, can sometimes be diverted to other cities because of the policy. At the airport, metered taxis are plentiful—fares to the city center are around $12. Deluxe buses make the six-hour nonstop run from Mexico City to Oaxaca. UNO and Cristóbal Colón also have frequent service to and from regional destinations such as Puebla (4½ hours), Veracruz (7 hours), and Villahermosa (12 hours). There are two bus terminals: the first-class station serves long-distance destinations, while the second-class station serves the Central Valley. There's bus service within the city, but you probably won't need to use it as most major sights are within walking distance of one another and cabs are cheap and easy to come by. You won't need a car to get around Oaxaca City; however, if you're planning several excursions into the countryside then a car is incredibly useful, and you can just park it at your hotel while you're in town.

ESSENTIALS

Bus Contacts **ADO GL** (✉ *Calz. Niños de Chapultepec 1036, Jalatlaco* ☎ *951/515–1248, 01800/702–8000 toll-free in Mexico* 🌐 *www.ticketbus.com.mx*). **Estrella del Valle** (✉ *Calle Armenta y López 721, Centro Histórico, Oaxaca City* ☎ *951/514–5700*). **First-class terminal** (✉ *Calz. Niños Héroes de Chapultepec 1036, at Calle Emilio Carranza* ☎ *951/513–0529*). **Second-class terminal** (✉ *Prolongación de Trujano at the Periférico* ☎ *951/516–1218*).

Medical Assistance **General Emergencies** (☎ *066*). **Hospital Reforma** (✉ *Reforma 613, Centro Histórico* ☎ *951/516–0989, 951/516–6090, or 951/516–6100*).

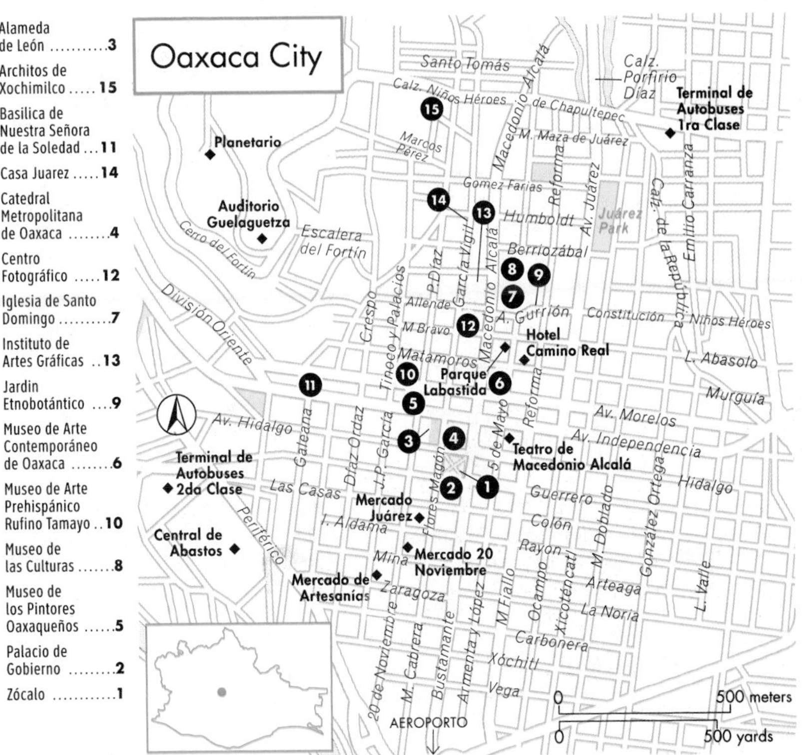

Visitor & Tour Info **State Tourism Office** (✉ *Calle Murguía 206, at Calle 5 de Mayo, Centro Histórico* ☎ *951/516–0123* ✉ *Avenida Juarez 703, Centro Histórico* ☎ *951/516–0123* ✉ *Museo de los Pintores Oaxaqueños, Av. Independencia 607, Centro Histórico* ☎ *951/516–0123*).

EXPLORING

MAIN ATTRACTIONS

❹ **Catedral Metropolitana de Oaxaca.** Begun in 1544, the cathedral was destroyed by earthquakes and fire and not finished until 1733. It honors the Virgin of the Assumption, whose statue can be seen on the facade above the door. The chapel at the back of the church and to the left of the altar houses the revered crucifix of El Señor del Rayo (Our Lord of the Lightning Bolt), the only piece to survive a fire that started when lightning struck the thatch roof of the original structure. There's no clapper in the bell, supposedly because it started to ring on its own accord back in the 18th century. A recent scrubbing has made this a contender for the city's most beautiful church. The inside, however, remains a bit sterile. ✉ *Av. Independencia 700, Centro Histórico* ☎ *951/516–4401* ⏲ *Daily 7* AM–*7* PM.

CLOSE UP

Viva La Fiesta

No matter what the holiday, Oaxaca pulls out all the stops. First and foremost is Guelaguetza, the annual celebration of the state's traditional music and dance, usually held on the last two Mondays in July. It draws delegations of traditional dancers from throughout the region. On these two days people climb up the Cerro del Fortín (Hill of the Fort) to the auditorium built especially to hold the overflow crowds that turn out for the event. Try to see the Danza de las Plumas (Dance of the Feathers), which tells the story of the Spanish conquest.

The Día de los Muertos (Day of the Dead) officially begins on October 31, the eve of All Saints' Day, when both city dwellers and country folk decorate altars for deceased family members. Tradition dictates that they also visit the cemetery with flowers, candles, and the deceased's favorite food and drink. The most frequently visited graveyard is that of Xoxocotlan, a village near Oaxaca City; Atzompa and Xochimilco, and other nearby villages, also have colorful celebrations.

December is full of fiestas, including those for Mexico's patron saint, the Virgen de Guadalupe (December 12), and Oaxaca's patron saint, the Virgen de la Soledad (December 8). The Noche de Rábanos (Night of the Radishes) is on December 23. During this celebration, Oaxaca City's main square is packed with growers and artists displaying their hybrid carved radishes, *flores inmortales* (small, dried "eternal flowers"), and *totomoxtl* (corn husks, pronounced to-to-*mosh*-tl)—all arranged in interesting tableaux. December 24 is the Noche de Calendas, in which locals demonstrate their devotion to the Virgin Mary by bearing heavy baskets of flowers from church to church.

7 Fodor's Choice ★ **Iglesia de Santo Domingo.** With a 17th-century facade framed by two domed bell towers and an interior that's an energetic profusion of white and real gold leaf (typical of the Mexican baroque style), Santo Domingo is Oaxaca's most brilliantly decorated church, and an aesthetic trademark of the city. The interior of the dome is adorned with more than 100 medallions depicting various martyrs. **TIP→ Make sure to look up at the ceiling just inside the front door to see an elaborately gilded rendering of the family tree of Santo Domingo.** ✉ *Plaza Santa Domingo, Macedonio Alcalá at Adolfo Gurrión, Centro Histórico* ☎ *951/516–3720* ⊙ *Mon.–Sat. 7–1 and 4–7:30, Sun. 7–1 and 4–7.*

NEED A BREAK?

Oaxaca is known for its coffee shops, and a stop at one of them is a great way to break up an afternoon of sightseeing. Coffee Beans (✉ ***5 de Mayo 400C, between Absolo and Constitución, Centro Histórico*** ☎ ***951/162–7171*****) is a cozy, two-floor space near Santo Domingo church with yellow walls and local art. The coffee they brew is local, organic, and delicious—it may be the best espresso in town.**

9 **Jardin Etnobotánico.** This sprawling botanical garden inside the massive walls of the Ex-Convento de Santo Domingo was the first of its kind in the Americas. Many plants that are now known throughout the region were first cultivated here. Species found only in Oaxaca are

on display, including many varieties of cactus. Two-hour-long English-language tours are conducted on Tuesday and Thursday at 11 AM. Spanish-language tours are on Friday and Saturday at 10 AM. You must take a tour to gain admission, after which you can roam the grounds. ✉*Calle Gurrión Adolfo and Calle Reforma, enter on Calle Reforma, Centro Histórico* ☎*951/516–7672* 🎫*English tour $9, Spanish tour $5* ⏲*Daily 10–5.*

★ ❻ **Museo de Arte Contemporáneo de Oaxaca.** Although it's in an attractive colonial residence, MACO houses changing exhibitions of contemporary art. Inaugurated by graphic artist Francisco Toledo, the museum has in its collection quite a few of his etchings, though they're not always on display. Be sure to check out the front gallery on the second floor, which displays fragments of frescoes that once decorated the walls of this old mansion. Signs are in Spanish only. ✉*Calle Macedonio Alcalá 202, at Av. Morelos, Centro Histórico* ☎*951/514–2818* 🌐*www.museomaco.com* 🎫*$2; free Sun.* ⏲*Wed.–Mon. 10:30–8.*

❽ **Museo de las Culturas.** This gorgeous museum is laid out in a series of galleries around the cloister of the labyrinthine Ex-Convento de Santo Domingo. On the ground floor are temporary exhibits and a collection of antique books. On the second floor you'll find rooms dedicated to Oaxacan music, medicine, indigenous languages, and pottery. More than a dozen other salons have been organized chronologically. ■TIP→ **Here you'll find such Monte Albán treasures as the stunning gold jewelry from Tomb 7—among the greatest archaeological finds of all time.** Signage is in Spanish only, but English-language audio tours are available. Several lovely second-floor balconies have views of the botanical garden. ✉*Plaza Santa Domingo, Macedonio Alcalá at Adolfo Gurrión, Centro Histórico* ☎*951/516–2991* 🎫*$4.50* ⏲*Tues.–Sun. 10–7, last entrance at 6:15.*

Fodor's Choice ★

❺ **Museo de los Pintores Oaxaqueños.** Even though it occupies a colonial-era building, the Museum of Oaxacan Painters isn't interested in simply reveling in the city's glorious past. Instead, this small gallery finds connections between the past and present, subtly linking Miguel Cabrera's 18th-century religious paintings, which incorporated a few dark-skinned cherubs, to 20th-century portrayals of indigenous people in works by Rodolfo Morales. ✉*Av. Independencia 607, at Calle García Vigil, Centro Histórico* ☎*951/516–5645* 🎫*$2* ⏲*Tues.–Sun. 10–6.*

❶ **Zócalo.** During the day it seems as if everyone passes through Oaxaca's shady main plaza, with its wrought-iron benches and matching bandstand. At night mariachi and marimba bands play under colonial archways or in the bandstand. It's a historic and truly beloved spot: when McDonald's tried to open a branch on its east side in late 2002, grassroots opposition led by painter Francisco Toledo brought the project to a halt. The 2006 protests calling for the removal of the governor started here, although you would never know it today. ✉*Bounded by Portal de Clavería on the north, Portal del Palacio on the south, Portal de Flores on the west, and Portal de Mercaderes on the east, Centro Histórico.*

IF YOU HAVE TIME

3 **Alameda de León.** This shady square, a bit smaller than the zócalo, is bordered by the massive cathedral on one side and the beautifully restored post office on the other. Locals gossip on wrought-iron benches or read the newspaper while their children chase pigeons and blow bubbles. ⊠*Bounded by Av. Indepedencia, Av. Hidalgo, Calle 20 de Noviembre, and Calle Flores Magon, Centro Histórico.*

15 **Architos de Xochimilco.** These stone arches were part of the 18th-century aqueducts that carried water into the city. Through many of the arches you'll find twisting streets or secluded plazas. It's a pretty section of the city for a stroll, far from the crowds in the *Centro Histórico*. The arches are a 5- to 10-minute walk north of Santo Domingo church. Follow Calle Garcia Vigil north; the arches are north of Calle Cosijopi.

11 **Basílica de Nuestra Señora de la Soledad.** The baroque basilica houses the statue of the Virgin of Solitude, Oaxaca's patron saint. According to legend, a mule that had mysteriously joined a mule train bound for Guatemala perished at the site of the church; the statue was discovered in its pack, and the event was construed as a miracle—one commemorated by this church, which was built in 1682. Many Oaxaqueños are devoted to the Virgin, who is believed to have more than the usual facility for healing and miracle working. In the 1980s thieves removed her jewel-studded crown; she now has a replica of the original and a glass-covered shrine. Take a look at the chandeliers inside; they're held aloft by angels. ⊠*Av. Independencia 107, at Calle Victoria, Centro Histórico* ☎*951/516–5067* ⏲*Daily 7–7.*

NEED A BREAK?

In front of the Basílica de Nuestra Señora de la Soledad is a tiny park called Jardín Socrates. Here you'll find half a dozen stands selling some of the best ice cream in Mexico. The hands-down favorite is Nevería La Niagara (⊠*Av. Independencia and Calle Victoria, Centro Histórico* ☎*No phone*). Flavors include *rosas* (roses), *elote* (corn), and the slightly bitter *leche quemada* (burned milk). Wrought-iron tables and chairs and lots of shade make this plaza a great place to get out of the sun for a few minutes.

14 **Casa Juárez.** After he was orphaned, 12-year-old Benito Juárez, the future Mexican president and the first indigenous leader of the country, walked to Oaxaca from his village in the mountains. He was taken in by a bookbinder named Antonio Salanueva, whose colonial-era home is now a small museum honoring the president. A carefully restored workshop as well as a kitchen, dining room, and bedroom give you a peek at Oaxacan life in the 19th century. ⊠*Calle García Vigil 609* ☎*951/516–1860* 🎟*$3* ⏲*Weekdays 10–6, weekends 10–5.*

12 **Centro Fotográfico Álvarez Bravo.** This small gallery and study center is named for the self-taught Mexico City photographer Manuel Alvarez Bravo (he won his first photographic competition here in Oaxaca). Exhibitions change every month or two. ⊠*Calle M. Bravo 116, at Calle García Vigil, Centro Histórico* ☎*951/516–9800* 🌐*www.cfmab.blogspot.com* 🎟 *Free* ⏲*Wed.–Mon. 9:30–8.*

13 **Instituto de Artes Gráficas de Oaxaca.** This small but interesting gallery has constantly changing exhibits of graphic art and design, including some very big names in the national and international communities. ✉ *Calle Macedonio Alcalá 507, Centro Histórico* ☎ *951/516–2045* *Free* *Wed.–Mon. 9:30–8.*

★ 10 **Museo de Arte Prehispánico Rufino Tamayo.** You'll find a beautifully displayed collection of pre-Hispanic pottery and sculpture at this carefully restored colonial mansion. The courtyard, dominated by a fountain guarded by a quartet of stone lions, is shaded with pink and white oleanders. Originally this was the private collection of the painter Rufino Tamayo. Especially interesting are the tiny figurines of women with children from Guerrero, some perhaps dating from more than 3,000 years ago, and the smiling ceramic figures from Veracruz. ✉ *Av. Morelos 503, at Calle Porfirio Díaz, Centro Histórico* ☎ *951/516–4750* *$3* *Mon. and Wed.–Sat. 10–2 and 4–7, Sun. 10–3.*

2 **Palacio de Gobierno.** The 19th-century neoclassical state capitol is on the zócalo's south side. A fresco mural that was completed in 1988 wraps around the stairwell. In it, altars to the dead, painters of codices, fruit sellers, gods, and musicians crowd together to catalog the customs and legends of Oaxaca's indigenous people. At the top, on the left side of the mural, note the *apoala* tree, which, according to Mixtec legend, bore the flowers from which life sprang. If there's a protest in front of the building—and there often is—it will most likely be closed to visitors. ✉ *Portal del Palacio, Centro Histórico* ☎ *951/516–0677* *Daily 9–8.*

7

WHERE TO EAT

CENTRO HISTÓRICO

$$$–$$$$ Fodor's Choice ★ MEXICAN

Casa Oaxaca. Chef Alejandro Ruiz is behind some of the most creative food in southern Mexico—rack of lamb in pineapple and vanilla sauce and venison tamales with mole are just a few examples. Wild game is featured heavily on the menu, though the kitchen also has a way with red snapper. Not one course falls short here: appetizers incorporate local herbs and greens and desserts such as a guava tart with rose-petal sorbet perfectly balance citrus and sweetness. The specialty cocktails are excellent, especially the sangria. The room is modern, open, airy, with white stucco walls, simple wooden tables and chairs, and a beamed ceiling. It's casual and effortlessly romantic. ✉ *Constitución 104A* ☎ *951/516–8889 or 951/516–8531* *AE, MC, V.*

$$–$$$ ★ MEXICAN

Los Danzantes. Named for the dancing figures carved in stone at the nearby ruins of Monte Albán, this restaurant fuses the new and the old with dishes such as *hierba santa asada,* a local leaf stuffed with goat cheese and Oaxaca cheese; and raviolis with *huitlacoche* (corn fungus) in one sauce of squash flower and another of green chile and cream. The three-story-tall walls, consisting of triangular columns of rough stone, are reflected in a pool that takes up about half of the open-air space. The service is perfectly attentive. Expect to dine exclusively in the company of other tourists. ✉ *Calle Macedonio Alcalá*

CLOSE UP

Mezcal's Mysteries

There are two big myths about mezcal, the distilled pride of Oaxaca. The first is that a mezcal bottle contains a worm. (This is true only of the low-grade, mass-produced mezcals, which use the worm as a marketing gimmick.) A second myth is that mezcal is a less-refined version of tequila. Quite the contrary: while tequila is only distilled from the blue agave plant, cooked in steam chambers, and generally made in industrial-sized batches, mezcal is made from dozens of varieties of agave, roasted over a wood fire in a traditional earth pit, distilled, and usually made in small quantities by small producers. The result is a soft, smoky, and complex liquor—one meant to be slowly sipped and savored. Mezcal is an elixir whose renown has been impeded only by the industry's almost comical disorganization and lack of marketing savvy.

To further complicate things, a 2005 law passed by the Mexican government imposed a set of standards on mezcal production for the first time, including the certification process aimed at controlling quality. The law's intent was to weed out the imposters that mixed their product with cane alcohol, but the side effect of the new bureaucratic requirements has been to impose considerable new costs on producers, reducing quantities, and raising prices. That said, you now know just what you're getting when you see a certified *reposado* (aged 2 months–1 year in oak barrels), *añejo* (aged 1–3 years), and *extrañejo* (aged more than 3 years). Some are aged even more than that, like the 10-year-old Joya, which you find at stores in the region.

403 ☎951/501–1184 or 951/501–1187 🌐www.losdanzantes.com.mx ▭AE, MC, V.

$$–$$$ ★ CONTEMPORARY **Temple.** Where did Mexican chefs learn how to make such pillow-soft gnocchi tossed with cherry tomatoes, red cabbage, and Serrano ham? This chic little eatery—more Central Park than Centro Histórico—dares to be different, and actually succeeds in the process. Although you can find some favorite local dishes on the menu, the kitchen's focus is contemporary cuisine with Oaxacan flair, like the squash-blossom soup sprinkled with tangy goat cheese. Tapas are available at the bar all day. *✉Calle García Vigil 409A ☎951/516–8676 🌐www.temple.com.mx ▭AE, MC, V.*

$–$$ MEXICAN **La Biznaga.** The food at this courtyard café is traditional—except a few touches here and there that make it seem you've stumbled on some new cuisine. There's the standard beef smothered with mole, for example, but this version adds the pungent flavor of goat cheese. And the ice cream for dessert comes in tantalizing flavors, such as mezcal or *guanabana*. A retractable screen above the courtyard makes this a great retreat even on a rainy day. The cocktails here are good, too—it's a great place to sample mezcals. *✉Calle García Vigil 512 ☎951/516–1800 ▭MC, V ⊙No dinner Sun.*

$–$$ MEXICAN **Catedral.** This restaurant takes up the entire first floor of a colonial house; you can dine beneath the arches or in the sun next to a fountain. Popular dishes include mushroom soup flavored with *epazote* (a pungent local herb), chicken with *salsa de flor de calabaza* (pumpkin-blossom sauce), and a superbly prepared *lechón* (suckling pig). Sunday sees a buffet from 2:30 to 7. ✉ *Calle García Vigil 105, at Av. Morelos* ☎ *951/516–3285* 🌐 *www.restaurantecatedral.com.mx* ▭ *AE, MC, V* ⊙ *Closed Tues.*

$–$$ MEXICAN ✕ **Como Agua Pa' Chocolate.** Inspired by the book *Like Water For Chocolate,* this second-story restaurant wears its heart on its sleeve. The pale yellow walls are covered with quotations about food, including, "To table and to bed you need call only once." The food is equally romantic, with a whole section of the menu dedicated to foods like quail in rose-petal sauce (a dish inspired by the book and movie). The best choice, however, is the *espejo de moles* (a sampler of five different moles over chicken). The tables on the balcony overlooking the Alameda are the best in the house. ✉ *Calle Hidalgo 612, facing Alameda* ☎ *951/516–2917* 🌐 *www.oaxaca-restaurant.com* ▭ *MC, V.*

$–$$ SEAFOOD ✕ **Marco Polo.** Affluent local families and expats in the know come back to this duo of restaurants to get their seafood fix. The ceviches are delicious, as are the whole-fried-fish platters and the shrimp specials. Margaritas, too, are best-in-class, and a wonderful baked banana dessert comes with condensed milk, cream, and rummy eggnog. The original branch, where you can enjoy your meal out in a lovely, fern-shaded garden, is a breakfast-and-lunch-only place, closing at 6 PM. Another branch on Cinco de Mayo isn't quite as charming, but it is open until 9 PM every day except Sunday. ✉ *Pino Suárez 806, across from Llano* ☎ *951/513–4308* ▭ *AE, DC, MC, V.*

$–$$ MEXICAN ✕ **La Olla.** The service is a bit distracted at chef Pilar Cabrera's combination gallery-café, so you'll have plenty of time to admire the works by local artists that adorn the walls. The food makes up for any shortcomings, however. Start with the *tlayuda azteca,* a Mexican-style pizza topped with chicken, avocados, and stringy Oaxacan cheese. The sampler plate includes everything from strips of beef to seasoned pork to *chapulines* (grasshoppers). They also serve a different *comida corrida* every afternoon for 60 pesos. ✉ *Calle Reforma 402-1* ☎ *951/516–6668* 🌐 *www.laolla.com.mx* ▭ *AE, DC, MC, V* ⊙ *Closed Sun.*

$ MEXICAN ✕ **El Mesón Oaxaqueño.** This storefront restaurant is right off the zócalo, so it's surprising that it doesn't draw more tourists; rather, it's popular with locals who come for the steaks. If you're hungry you can opt for the buffet; otherwise, order à la carte from the many taco options. For a sugar fix, have a cup of Oaxacan hot chocolate and a slice of nut or cheese pie. ✉ *Av. Hidalgo 805, at Calle Valdivieso* ☎ *951/516–2729* ▭ *MC, V.*

★ $ MEXICAN ✕ **Zandunga.** A shabby-chic handful of wooden tables dressed in bright paisley cloths, Zandunga is the quintessential corner café. It fills up with local families who come to sample simple and hearty dishes from the *istmo,* the southeastern part of the state around the town of Tehuantepec. The *estofado,* a savory beef stew, is recommended; start off with the sampler plate of typical regional snacks, which comes with totopos (crunchy tortillas that originated on the isthmus). Daily specials may include a mole for good measure. Wash it all down with a tangy tea made from hibiscus blossoms. ✉ *Calle García Vigil at Calle Jesús Carranza* ☎ *951/516–2265* ▭ *No credit cards* ⊙ *Closed Sun.*

CLOSE UP

On the Menu in Oaxaca

Food isn't taken lightly in Oaxaca. Traditional recipes, many of which predate the arrival of the Spanish, are passed from generation to generation. Sisters argue over who makes the most authentic version of Grandmother's mole.

Oaxacans don't like change, which may be why restaurants like El Naranjo and Los Danzantes that feature updated versions of classic dishes are inundated by foreigners and ignored by locals. You can imagine the outcry when McDonald's announced it was going to open a restaurant on the zócalo. It didn't take long for the company to rethink its plans.

When it comes to sampling Oaxaca's cuisine, do as the locals do. Oaxaca's markets—and inexpensive eateries near them—are among the most interesting places to sample any of the following regional specialties.

Although the name sounds like an elegant dish, **chapulines** are nothing more than fried grasshoppers seasoned with salt, tangy chile, and a pinch of lime. You find them everywhere from the fanciest restaurant to the humblest vendor's cart. All sizes of grasshoppers are available, depending on the season; the large ones go down a bit easier if you remove the legs first. According to local lore, one taste will charm you into returning to Oaxaca.

The sweet, white gelatinous dessert called **jicuatote** is made with milk, cloves, cinnamon, and cornmeal. It's served in tubs or cut into cubes and is usually colored red on top.

Although you'll find versions of this sauce everywhere in Mexico, **mole** is to Oaxaca as baked beans are to Boston. There are seven major kinds of moles, so many restaurants ladle out a different one every day of the week. If you've had mole back home, it was probably *mole oaxaqueña*. Also known as *mole negro*, or black mole, it's the standard-bearer for all moles. It gets its sweetness from chocolate and its fire from peppers. It's found in every kind of dish, both on top of chicken and folded inside enchiladas. Another favorite is *manchamanteles*, which translates as "tablecloth stainer" (it's not as thick as other moles, so it spills easily). Moles are not always a deep, rich brown. *Verde* is green, *amarillo* is a dark, reddish yellow, and *coloradito* can be different shades of red.

Say cheese, or rather **quesillo.** The stringy cheese made in and around Oaxaca is soft and nutty. It makes its way into many dishes, even those that have nothing to do with Mexico. Hint: that's not mozzarella on your pizza.

Made from the flowers and seeds of the cacao tree, **tejate** is sweetened with corn, coconut milk, sugar, and spices. The result—white clumps suspended in brown liquid—is served in a painted gourd bowl. The concoction may look deadly, but it's actually tasty *and* nutritious.

The huge, flat tortillas called **tlayudas** are spread with refried beans and topped with cheese, salsa, and, if you like, strips of chicken or pork. They're halfway between soft tortillas and crispy tostadas, and they're hard to eat delicately. Put away the knife and fork and break off a piece.

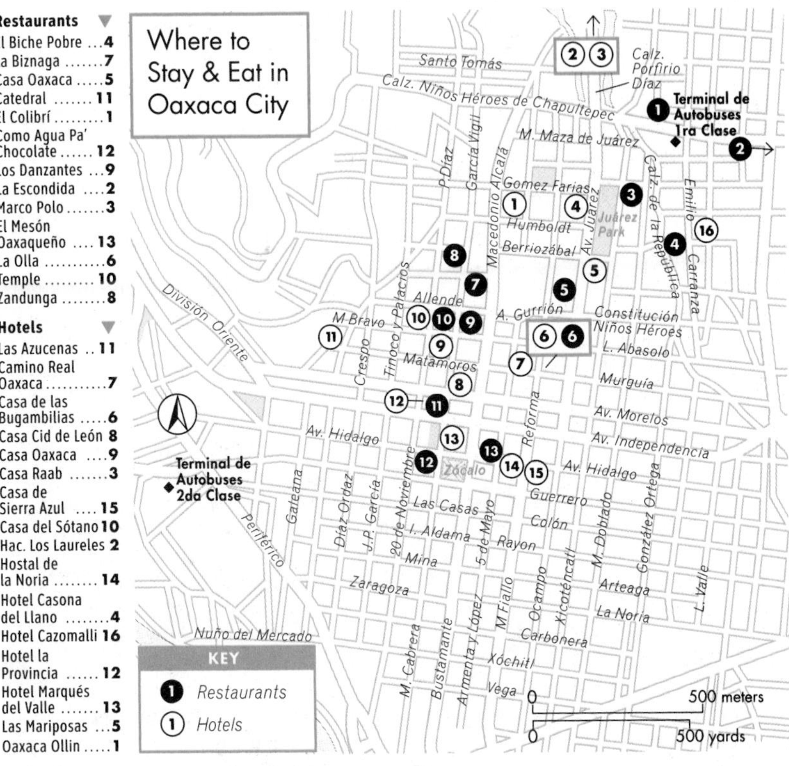

ELSEWHERE IN OAXACA

$–$$ MEXICAN ✕ **El Colibrí.** A neon sign bearing the namesake hummingbird draws you to this little cafeteria. Mothers who have packed their kids off to school and cell-phone-toting business executives favor this place, perhaps for its free refills of super-hot coffee and the extensive menu of Mexican favorites. If you're homesick, you can always order a burger with fries. While you wait, browse in the gift shop. The restaurant is across from the bus station, making it a great escape from the crowded waiting area. ✉ *Calz. Niños Héroes de Chapultepec 903, Colonia Reforma* ☎ *951/515–8087* ▭ *AE, MC, V.*

$ MEXICAN ✕ **El Biche Pobre.** This little restaurant east of Parque Paseo Juárez is packed with locals—sometimes there's not a tourist in sight—who appreciate the traditional fare like *enchiladas suizas* (with sour cream) and the rock-bottom prices. It's a 10-minute walk from the zócalo. You'll know you're there when you spot the huge green eyes on the side of the building. ✉ *Calzado de la República 600, at Calle Hidalgo, Jalatlaco* ☎ *951/513–4636* ▭ *MC, V.*

$ ★ MEXICAN ✕ **La Escondida.** The outdoor lunch buffet, served from 1:30 to 6:30, is a great reason to venture outside the city limits. (It's 3 km [2 mi] east of Oaxaca on the road to Mitla.) Waiters bring you a welcome cocktail and a typical appetizer, such as *taquitos de pollo* (small tacos filled with chicken) or *memelas* (fried discs of corn meal topped with goodies).

7

You then select from more than 70 Mexican dishes, including several kinds of meat fresh from the grill. You can linger here, listening to wandering mariachi and marimba musicians—and let the kids loose on the small playground. ✉ *Carretera a San Agustín Yatareni, Km 7, San Agustín Yatareni* ☎ *951/517–6655* 🌐 *www.restaurantelaescondida.com.mx* 💳 *AE, MC, V* ⊗ *No dinner.*

WHERE TO STAY

CENTRO HISTÓRICO

★ $$$ **Camino Real Oaxaca.** This breathtaking 16th-century building—the former Convento de Santa Catalina de Siena—is one of the city's landmarks. Around every corner is a discovery—a rear patio holds the covered *pileta,* a circle of stone basins where the nuns did laundry. The lavish breakfast buffet is served under the arches in what was the convent's kitchen. The grassy courtyard where mariachis play is a great spot for a margarita. Members of the staff are crisp and professional, and always ready with directions or advice—as you'd hope they would be, given the audacious prices. **Pros:** Historic building, beautiful courtyard and pool area, excellent service. **Cons:** Very pricey, exterior rooms get street noise, some rooms are dark and small. ✉ *Calle 5 de Mayo 300,* ☎ *951/501–6100* 🌐 *www.caminoreal.com/oaxaca* *84 rooms, 7 suites* *In-room: Safe, Ethernet. In-hotel: Restaurant, room service, bars, pool, laundry service, no-smoking rooms, no elevator* 💳 *AE, DC, MC, V*

$$$ **Casa Cid de León.** Your host, poet Lety Ricárdez, lets you know immediately that this mansion in the center of town, furnished with a memorably eclectic collection of objets d'art, is "your home." Pass through a wrought-iron gate to reach two of the suites, then climb a twisting stone staircase to find the other two. Ask for the Bella Epoca suite, where everything seems to come in threes: three rooms with three sets of French doors that lead to three balconies—there are even three crystal chandeliers. The bath has a deep whirlpool tub and towels tied with silk ribbons. The rooftop dining room and café has views of all the city's landmarks. **Pros:** Romantic rooms, central location, friendly owner. **Cons:** On the pricey side. ✉ *Av. Morelos 602, at Calle García Vigil,* ☎ *951/514–1893 or 951/516–0414* 🌐 *www.casaciddeleon.com* *4 suites* *In-hotel: Restaurant, bar, room service* 💳 *AE, MC, V* 🍽 *CP*

$$$ Fodor's Choice ★ **Casa Oaxaca.** A trio of imaginative Europeans poured their hearts and souls into this chic bed-and-breakfast. Their house combines traditional materials like adobe and cantera stone with minimalist sensibilities. The result is a masterpiece where gleaming white colonnades lead you to your room. Each is different; some have little sunrooms overlooking the indigo-tile pool, while others have sitting areas where you can enjoy a cocktail. Put yourself in the hands of a spiritual healer who will guide you through the cleansing experience of *temazcal* (pre-Hispanic steam room). **Pros:** Spacious rooms, unique decor, cooking classes with top chef. **Cons:** Books up quickly, some rooms are a little dark. ✉ *Calle García Vigil 407,* ☎ *951/514–4173 or 951/516–9923*

www.casaoaxaca.com 7 rooms, 2 suites In-hotel: Restaurant, room service, bar, pool, laundry service, airport shuttle, public Internet, parking (no fee) AE, MC, V CP.

$$–$$$ ★ **Hotel La Provincia.** With its classic central courtyard, beamed ceilings, and colonial charm, La Provincia fulfills the expectations of those looking for a bit of old Mexico. But it's also one of the city's most modern hotels, so although rooms have carved-wood furnishings and colorful tile floors they also have modern conveniences like flat-screen TVs. The hotel's location—equidistant from the zócalo and Santo Domingo church—is unbeatable. It's on a busy street, but you'd never know it by the quiet in the courtyard and rooms. **Pros:** Relaxing atmosphere, pretty rooftop terrace, friendly staff. **Cons:** Rooms don't get much natural light, a bit pricey, understated decor. *Calle Porforio Diaz 108, 951/514–0999 www.hotellaprovincia.com.mx 15 rooms, 3 suites In-room: No phone, safe, Wi-Fi. In-hotel: Restaurant, room service, bar, no elevator, public Wi-Fi, laundry service, parking (no fee) AE, MC, V.*

$$ **Casa de las Bugambilias.** This bed-and-breakfast houses La Olla restaurant, and it's run by the same person, chef-personality Pilar Cabrera. Every room is different, but they're all brightly painted and comfortably outfitted. Some rooms have little terraces or patios. **Pros:** Nice roof deck, great breakfasts, beautiful tiled tubs in many rooms. **Cons:** Some rooms are small, a bit expensive, resident cat bad for those with allergies. *Reforma 402, 951/516–1165 www.lasbugambilias.com 8 rooms, 1 suite In-room: Safe. In-hotel: Restaurant, bar, spa, public Wi-Fi, laundry service D, DC, MC, V.*

7

$$ **Casa de Sierra Azul.** The central courtyard in this colonial-era mansion is certainly memorable, with lush vines tumbling down over stone arches. Other touches of note include a wrought-iron gate and leaded-glass windows. Each room is different, so look at a few before you decide; one thing they have in common are the extremely high ceilings. **Pros:** Nice courtyard, good location. **Cons:** A bit pricey. *Av. Hidalgo 1002, at Calle Fiallo, 951/514–8412 www.hotelcasadesierrazul.com.mx 9 rooms, 5 suites In-room: No a/c (some). In-hotel: Restaurant, laundry service AE, MC, V.*

$$ **Casa del Sótano.** From this hillside hotel's sunny terrace you can contemplate one of the city's best views of the Iglesia de Santo Domingo. You can also catch a glimpse from some of the wrought-iron balconies of the top-floor rooms. Inside are arched doorways, vaulted ceilings, and cool tile floors. In secluded courtyards you'll find fountains, gardens, and pools, but the best place in the whole hotel is the terrace, with an amazing city view. **Pros:** Great terrace, friendly staff, nicely decorated rooms. **Cons:** Rooms are dark, attracts many tour groups. *Tinoco y Palacios 414, 951/516–2494 23 rooms, 1 suite In-room: DVD (some). In-hotel: Restaurant, bar, public Internet, public Wi-Fi, parking (no fee) AE, MC, V.*

$$ **Hostal de la Noria.** The rooms in this restored colonial mansion two blocks west of the zócalo have unique, homey touches; in some rooms, it's carved wooden headboards, in others wrought-iron or hammered tin ones. All the rooms wrap around a charming central courtyard

with a flower-filled fountain; surrounding it are tables topped with lacy umbrellas. Chicken mole and fish fillets steamed in a mezcal sauce top the list of favorites at the Restaurante Asunción ($–$$). **Pros:** Nice courtyard, excellent restaurant. **Cons:** A bit pricey, rooms could use some updating, some street noise. ✉*Av. Hidalgo 918,* ☎*951/514–7844* 🌐*www.lanoria.com* *48 rooms, 4 suites* *In-hotel: Restaurant, room service, bar, pool, laundry service, parking (no fee), public Wi-Fi* *AE, MC, V.*

$$ **Hotel Marqués del Valle.** Taking up almost the entire northern edge of the zócalo, this hotel puts Oaxaca at your doorstep, all the while maintaining a polished and classy feel. Many of the rooms have views of the Palacio de Gobierno or the Catedral Metropolitana. If you splurge a bit, you can reserve a room with French doors leading out to a small balcony. Rooms are cozy, although not as atmospheric as at most other hotels in town. The open-air restaurant facing the main square has become extremely popular; you can grab a table right in the middle of the life of the plaza. **Pros:** On the main square, friendly staff, clean and comfortable rooms. **Cons:** Noisy location, pricey rates, utilitarian rooms. ✉*Portal de Clavería s/n,* ☎*951/514–0688* 🌐*www.hotelmarquesdelvalle.com.mx* *95 rooms* *In-room: Safe. In-hotel: Restaurant, bar, room service, laundry service* *AE, MC, V.*

$ **Las Azucenas.** This intimate hotel occupies a charmingly restored old home near the Basilica de la Soledad. You can spot that church, and at least half a dozen others, from the plant-filled terrace. The most private room is secluded on the second floor. The others are just as cozy, but one has a skylight rather than a window. Ask for a tiny *tele* (TV) at the reception desk if you can't bear to miss the evening news. **Pros:** Cheerful rooms, nice roof deck, good value. **Cons:** Out-of-the-way location, booked up far in advance, mediocre breakfasts. ✉*Calle Martiniano Aranda 203, at Matamoros,* ☎*951/514–7918, 800/882–6089 in U.S. and Canada* 🌐*www.hotelazucenas.com* *10 rooms* *In-room: No phone, no TV, Wi-Fi. In-hotel: Public Wi-Fi* *MC, V.*

¢ **Las Mariposas.** María Teresa Villarreal, the owner and operator of this pleasant little place, proudly shows off her restored colonial-style home. It's not fancy, but the lived-in feeling suits most people just fine; in fact, there are a few long-term guests from time to time. You can mingle with other guests on the open patio gladdened with laurel and lemon trees. Those staying in standard rooms share a brightly colored outdoor kitchen, while those who have booked studios have kitchenettes with coffeemakers and other essentials. **Pros:** Great value, helpful hosts. **Cons:** Furnishings are simple, studios are cramped, noise from inner courtyard. ✉*Calle Pino Suárez 517,* ☎*951/515–5854* 🌐*www.lasmariposas.com.mx* *7 rooms, 6 suites* *In-room: No a/c, no phone, kitchen (some), safe. In-hotel: Public Wi-Fi* *MC, V* *CP.*

NORTH OF CENTRO HISTÓRICO

$$ Fodor's Choice ★ **Oaxaca Ollin Bed & Breakfast.** On a quiet street near Santo Domingo church, Oaxaca Ollin feels like a well-kept secret. Two small buildings surround a patio with a pool; those on the top floor have small balconies with wrought-iron furniture. Cheerful rooms have beautiful tiled bathrooms and traditional touches like headboards carved with

elaborate calla lily designs and wooden armoires instead of closets. Breakfast includes plenty of fresh fruit and pastries and tasty regional dishes. The staff is unfailingly friendly and the tours they arrange of the city and crafts villages come highly recommended. **Pros:** Peaceful atmosphere, lovely rooms, relaxing rooftop terrace. **Cons:** Rooms aren't terribly spacious, breakfast isn't lavish, some steps to climb. ✉*Quintana Roo 213, Jalatlaco,* ☎*951/514–9126* 🌐*www.oaxacabedandbreakfast.com* *10 rooms* *In-room: No a/c, no phone, no TV, safe, Wi-Fi. In-hotel: Pool, laundry service, public Internet, public Wi-Fi, no kids under 12, no elevator* ▭*MC, V.*

$–$$ **Hotel Casona del Llano.** This tidy hotel across from Parque Paseo Juarez (El Llano) caters mostly to Mexican travelers. Although part of the hotel is in a converted mansion, the basic rooms are devoid of colonial charm. They are, however, clean and comfortable, and most face a small courtyard garden. The restaurant is popular with locals for lunch and weekend brunch. The staff is very friendly but few of them speak fluent English. **Pros:** Good value, authentic restaurant, off the tourist track. **Cons:** Basic rooms, 10-minute walk to main square, some noise during the day. ✉*Av. Juarez 701, Jalatlaco* ☎*951/514–7719 or 951/514–7703* 28 rooms *In-room: No a/c, Wi-Fi. In-hotel: Restaurant, public Wi-Fi, parking (no fee), laundry service, no elevator* ▭*MC, V.*

$ **Hotel Cazomalli.** Even the baked-earth floor tiles shine at this sleepy little hostelry, whose name means "house of tranquility." It's set in a cobblestone district close to Parque Juárez. Clean, quiet rooms have pale pine furnishings and handwoven fabrics. Sliding doors lead to sunny patios. Friendly owner Marina Flores is happy to help arrange trips to nearby sights. **Pros:** Nice views from rooftop, hosts can help book tours, quiet location. **Cons:** Small bathrooms, 10-minute walk to main square. ✉*Calle El Salto 104, at Calle Aldama, Jalatlaco,* ☎*951/513–8605* 🌐*www.hotelcazomalli.com* *18 rooms* *In-room: No a/c, safe, no TV, Wi-Fi. In-hotel: Public Internet, public Wi-Fi, laundry service* ▭*AE, MC, V.*

ELSEWHERE IN OAXACA

$$$ **Hacienda Los Laureles.** About a 20-minute drive from Oaxaca's historical center, this hotel is a cool, quiet oasis. The spa, which has a hot tub, massage, and traditional *temazcal* steam baths, will help you regain your inner balance. Staff members can assist in arranging horseback excursions, bicycle rides, or ecological tours to the nearby mountains. **Pros:** In a residential neighborhood, beautiful grounds, nice spa. **Cons:** Far from historic center, not many restaurants or shops nearby. ✉*Av. Hidalgo 21, San Felipe del Agua,* ☎*951/501–5300* 🌐*www.hotelhaciendaloslaureles.com* *18 rooms, 9 suites* *In-room: Safe, Wi-Fi. In-hotel: Restaurant, room service, bar, pool, gym, spa, laundry service, parking (no fee)* ▭*AE, MC, V.*

★ $$ **Casa Raab.** A fantasy villa buried in the wooded hills about 30 minutes outside of the city center, Casa Raab is ideal for traveling groups. You can rent rooms in the main house, or take over a casita that's perfect for a family of four. Hiking trails surround the house, which has breathtaking views of the mountains. You'll feel part of the family as you eat meals together in the dining room. Owner Tony Raab produces his own artisanal mezcal, grows his own agave plants, and helps to organize excursions. Otherwise, you'll need a rental car to get into and out of town. **Pros:** Convenient base for excursions into the valley, friendly host, great for families. **Cons:** Far from city center, no meals on Sunday, not great option for single travelers. ✉ *Camino Seminario s/n, San Pablo Etla* ☎ *951/520–4022* *6 rooms* *In-room: Ethernet. In-hotel: Restaurant, bar, pool* ▭ *MC, V.*

NIGHTLIFE

The Centro Histórico has a small but lively nightlife scene, though the crowd at most bars is very young. The streets directly south of Santo Domingo church have plenty of thumping dance clubs, and many people just wander until they find one that's playing music they like. The best place to start any evening is at the zócalo—cafés serve drinks and snacks and mariachis and other performers roam the square, sometimes inspiring revelers to dance.

BARS

The superhip **Café Central** (✉ *Hidalgo 302, Centro Histórico* ☎ *No phone* 🌐 *cafecentraloaxaca.blogspot.com*) screens art flicks, hosts concerts and theater performances, and brings in the occasional DJ for late-night dancing. The music ranges from folk to jazz to hip-hop, and cover charges are up to $5. The bar's open Wednesday through Saturday.

Bring a flashlight to read the menu at the dimly lighted **Comala** (✉ *Allende 109, across from Santo Domingo church, Centro Histórico* ☎ *No phone*) where a mostly young, mostly local crowd sips amusingly titled drinks (try the Dr. Pepe—beer, tequila, amaretto, and coffee liqueur) and chill out to the sounds of Björk and the latest indie-rock sensations. Although the red walls adorned with crosses and gargoyles suggest a goth crowd, it attracts more young professionals than creatures of the night.

Things can get lively at **La Cucaracha** (✉ *Calle Porfirio Díaz 301A, at Matamoros, Centro Histórico* ☎ *951/501–1636*), where for $10 you can taste four tequilas or five mezcals. There's a dark, cool, colonial feel to the cozy performance space, where you'll be serenaded with a romantic *peña* (solo-guitar folk singing); on weekends there's dancing in another room that's so tiny that tables are on a narrow catwalk above.

Freebar (✉ *Calle Matamoros 100, at Calle García Vigil, Centro Histórico* ☎ *No phone*) has some dimly lighted rooms with loud alternative music that is popular with young people who pack the place even during the week.

Fodor's Choice ★ It's about as big as a breadbox, but somehow **La Nueva Babel** (✉ *Calle Porfirio Díaz 224, at Calle Matamoros, Centro Histórico* ☎ *No phone*) squeezes in performers from a lone poet or guitarist to jazz trios or multigenerational son jarocho groups. The crowd, a mix of locals and tourists, is attentive and enthusiastic.

CANTINAS

Bastions of macho men and strong spirits, cantinas traditionally aren't places for women. The cantinas in the Centro Histórico tend to be a bit less rough, but single women should still think twice about going in alone.

Push aside the swinging doors of **La Casa del Mezcal** (✉ *Calle Flores Magón between Calle Las Casas and Calle Aldama, Centro Histórico* ☎ *No phone*), near the Juárez market, for a classic cantina experience that's diminished only slightly by the presence of a large TV (or two). The cantina prides itself on its stock of *tobala,* a cousin of tequila made from wild agave.

A bit calmer than La Casa del Mezcal, but no less classic, is **La Farola** (✉ *Calle 20 de Noviembre between Calle Las Casas and Calle Trujano, Centro Histórico* ☎ *951/516–5352*), which has been serving drinks to locals since 1916—and some of the patrons, it seems, might have been there when the joint opened up.

DANCE CLUBS

Dance to live salsa music every night at the most popular **Candela** (✉ *Calle Murguía 413, at Calle Pino Suárez, Centro Histórico* ☎ *951/514–2010*).

One of the city's most venerable watering holes, **La Tentación** (✉ *Calle Matamoros 101, at Calle García Vigil, Centro Histórico* ☎ *951/514–9521*) is still extremely popular. Salsa, merengue, and cumbia dancing happen on the terrace nightly beginning at 10 PM.

FILM

The **Cinema Pochote** (✉ *Calle García Vigil 817, Centro Histórico* ☎ *951/514–1194 or 951/516–2045*), on the northern edge of the Centro Histórico, offers art films in various languages, often English with Spanish subtitles. On Tuesday, classic films are featured. The folding chairs are a bit hard, but, hey, admission is free. Screenings generally take place at 6 and 8 PM Tuesday through Sunday. Look for posters around town or head up to the theater—each month's schedule is posted on the door.

FOLK MUSIC & DANCE

If you're not in Oaxaca in July, you can still get a taste of Guelaguetza. Some of the best dancers perform all year in several places around town.

Every evening the rather drab **Casa de Cantera** (✉ *Murguiá 102, Centro Histórico* ☎ *951/514–7585 or 951/514–9522* 🌐 *www.casadecantera.com*) transforms itself into the colorful "Casa de Guelaguetza." It's a mesmerizing show, with lots of music and dancing. It starts every night at 8:30 PM, and the cover charge is $10.

CELEBRATE

One of Oaxaca's major celebrations is the Guelaguetza, a Zapotec word for "offering" or "gift." It's generally held on the last two Mondays in July. Delegations of traditional dancers from throughout the state perform in authentic costumes at the Auditorio Guelaguetza.

On Friday nights the **Camino Real Oaxaca** (✉*Calle 5 de Mayo 300, Centro Histórico* ☎*951/501–6100* ⊕*www.caminoreal.com/oaxaca*) hosts a regional dance show that's considered the best in town. The $32 admission includes a buffet dinner (7 PM) and the show (8:30 PM) in the former convent's 16th-century chapel. Make reservations.

The **Hotel Monte Albán** (✉*Alameda de León 1, Centro Histórico* ☎*951/516–2330*) has nightly dance shows beginning at 8:30 PM. Admission is about $8.

THEATER

Centro Cultural Ricardo Flores Magón (✉*Calle Macedonio Alcalá 302, Centro Histórico* ☎*951/514–0395*) hosts performances of music and dance. The French-style, 19th-century **Teatro de Macedonio Alcalá** (✉*Av. Independencia at Calle 5 de Mayo* ☎*951/516–8292*), one of the city's most beautiful buildings, hosts concerts. There are no tours, so you'll need to buy a ticket to a show to see the sumptuous interior. Show times and information are posted at the entrance.

SHOPPING

Don't despair if you can't make it out of town to visit Oaxaca Valley's crafts villages—you'll find all the goods here, in high-end boutiques, artist collectives, and touristy markets. And Oaxaca's art scene isn't just about rural customs—boutiques and galleries clustered around the pedestrian streets south of Santo Domingo church sell modern works from local ceramists and painters.

You'll also find several good books and music shops and quite a few jewelry stores. Several mercados sell packaged foods like Oaxacan chocolate and cheese and jars of mole.

ART GALLERIES

★ Climb the grand staircase to reach **Galería Indigo** (✉*Calle Allende 104, Centro Histórico* ☎*951/514–3889*), a lovely gallery in an enormous restored mansion. Ceramics, graphics, paintings, and other fine art from talented artists from Oaxaca and beyond are for sale.

BOOKSTORES

Amate Books (✉*Calle Macedonia Alcalá 307, Centro Histórico* ☎*951/516–6960*) is the bookstore you wish you had found before your trip. Hundreds of books, most of them in English, cover topics from the country's cuisine to its couture. There's also a great travel-guide section.

Librería Grañén Porrúa (✉*Calle Macedonia Alcalá 104, Centro Histórico* ☎*951/516–9901*) sells books in English as well as Spanish. It also has CDs and high-end gifts.

Libros y Arte (✉ *Calle Macedonia Alcalá s/n, Centro Histórico* ☎*951/514–1398*) has a wonderful collection of books, including coffee-table volumes on the art and architecture of Oaxaca. There are also plenty of maps and travel guides. The shop is inside the Museo de las Culturas in Santo Domingo and closes at 6 PM.

LOCAL LIQUOR

Mezcal is a strong spirit made from agave (maguey) plants; it's similar to tequila, though with a smokier flavor. You can sample varieties of mezcal in many bars, restaurants, and shops. One brand to look for is El Señorio, which makes a nice *reposado* ("rested," meaning aged) mezcal. Tobalá and Del Maguey are small artisan producers. **Benevá,** a large producer, is pretty good, too, and certainly easy to procure—it has several outlets around town (there's one at Calle Macedonio Alcala 402) and a tasting room and shop on the road to Mitla.

La Cava (✉ *Gómez Farías 212-B, 2 blocks east of Calle Alcala, Centro Histórico* ☎ *951/515–2335* 🌐 *www.losdanzantes.com* ⏲ *Closed Sun.*), affiliated with Los Danzantes restaurant, sells a variety of quality mezcals along with regional wines and hand-rolled cigars.

CHOCOLATE

Oaxaca is famous for its chocolate—most of all for its hot chocolate. **Chocolate Mayordomo** (✉ *Calle Colón at Calle Flores Magón, Centro Histórico* ☎ *951/516–3807*), near the market, is arguably the best around; they grind their own chocolate together with the trademark Mexican cinnamon. The shop also sells mole.

7

HANDICRAFTS

Sort through an excellent selection of crafts, including painted copal-wood animals with comical expressions, at **Artesanías Chimalli** (✉ *Calle García Vigil 512-C, Centro Histórico* ☎ *951/514–2101*).

★ Young designers work with local (often organic) materials to create contemporary home accessories at **Blackbox** (✉ *Cinco de Mayo 412, between Absolo and Constitución, Centro Histórico* ☎ *No phone*), the hippest crafts store in the city. Wool rugs from Teotitlan de Valle eschew traditional stripes for paint-splatter designs. Handcrafted paper from Etla is used to create molded lamp shades. The store also sells shirts, bags, and jewelry.

Jarciería El Arte Oaxaqueño (✉ *Calle Mina 317, at J. P. García, Centro Histórico* ☎ *951/516–1581*), in business since 1961, has a small but good assortment of stamped-tin products as well as animals and skeletons carved of featherlight wood. The prices are very reasonable.

★ The magical shop **La Mano Mágica** (✉ *Calle Macedonio Alcalá 203, Centro Histórico* ☎ *951/516–4275* 🌐 *www.lamanomagica.com*) features the works of Arnulfo Mendoza, one of the top weavers in Oaxaca. His rugs, made using hand-dyed silk and wool, have incredibly intricate designs. It's no wonder that some of his larger pieces sell for several thousand dollars. There is also a gallery showing the works of many Oaxacan artists.

★ You'll support the women artists' co-op by shopping at the huge warren of shops that makes up **Mujeres Artesanas de las Regiones de Oaxaca**

(✉Calle 5 de Mayo 204, Centro Histórico ☎951/516–0670), often referred to as MARO. The selection and quality are excellent, the prices are reasonable, and the shop is open daily.

SHOPPING KNOW-HOW

If you think you'll be buying more folk art than you can carry home, get receipts showing that you've paid the 17% sales tax on all purchases. This will allow you to send your purchases home without having to pay extra for them. **Check out the high-end shops on Calle Macedonio Alcalá first; then compare prices and quality with the items you find in the markets or in the pueblos where artisans live and work.** Note that some stores are closed Sunday; many also close for an hour or two at midday.

JEWELRY

The streets west of Mercado 20 de Noviembre between Trujano and Mina are crowded with jewelry shops. Most offer 10- and 12-karat gold. Calle Macedonia Alcalá has become the place for cutting-edge designs. Things can get lively at **La Cucaracha** (*✉Calle Porfirio Díaz 301A, at Matamoros, Centro Histórico ☎951/501–1636*), where for $10 you can taste four tequilas or five mezcals. There's a dark, cool, colonial feel to the cozy performance space, where you'll be serenaded with a romantic *peña* (solo-guitar folk singing); on weekends there's dancing in another room that's so tiny that tables are on a narrow catwalk above.

There are three locations in Centro Histórico of **Oro de Monte Albán** (*✉Calle Macedonio Alcalá 403 ☎951/514–3813 ✉Calle Macedonio Alcalá 503 ☎951/516–4224 ✉Calle Macedonio Alcalá and Calle Bravo ☎951/516–1812*), all within spitting distance of each other. The shops sell gold and silver reproductions of pre-Columbian jewelry found in the tombs of royalty at Monte Albán. There's also a shop at the archaeological site.

SPORTS & THE OUTDOORS

BIKING

Take your pick of trip lengths at **Bicicletas Bravo** (*✉Calle Garcí Vigil 409, at Calle Allende, Centro Histórico ☎951/516–0953*), which leads trips as short as a few hours and as long as a few days into the countryside. You can also rent a bike and set out on your own.

Bicicletas Pedro Martinez (*✉Aldama 418, Centro Histórico ☎951/516–5935 ⊕www.bicicletaspedromartinez.com*) offers hiking and biking tours in the Central Valley as well as trips down to Puerto Escondido. Custom tours are available, too.

HIKING

Expediciones Sierra Norte (*✉Calle M. Bravo 210, Centro Histórico ☎951/514–8271 ⊕www.sierranorte.org.mx*) offers one- to five-day hiking and biking trips into the Central Valley and the mountains of the Sierra Norte. You either camp or stay in simple cabins. Costs start at $40 for one-day excursions. **TierrAventura** (*✉Calle Abasolo 217,*

Centro Histórico ☎*951/501–1363* ⊕*www.tierraventura.com*) has everything from one-day trips to local villages ($55 to $110) to four-day excursions to the coast ($300 to $400). Expect to see some villages far off the beaten path.

SIDE TRIP TO THE VALLES CENTRALES

You could easily fill a week visiting the dozens of villages spreading south and east of Oaxaca City. Looking for colonial-era splendor? There are charming squares dominated by graceful churches in Ocotlán and Santa Ana del Valle, to name but two. Unique crafts? San Bartolo Coyotepec is known for its beautiful *barro negro,* or black pottery, made without the benefit of a pottery wheel, while in Teotitlán del Valle the streets are lined with shops selling *tapetes,* the woven wool rugs that are known all around Mexico. Colorful markets? Take your pick. There are outdoor markets each day of the week, and each is different. In Zaachila, for example, you could pick up some animals—either small carvings or the real thing. Best of all, most markets are geared toward locals, so they don't sell the typical tourist wares, giving you a real sense of each village.

7

And don't forget the striking ruins of cities built by the Zapotec. The must-see on everyone's itinerary is Monte Albán, one of the country's most impressive ancient cities. Its proximity to the city makes it a destination for busloads of tourists. If you want to escape the crowds, head to some of the ruins that are less crowded, especially Dainzú and Yagul, where you'll probably have the place to yourself.

Planning a trip to the Valles Centrales is a snap. Many of the most popular sights are along or just off Carretera 175 (to Ocotlán), Carretera 131 (to Zaachila), or Carretera 190 (to Mitla). This makes it easy to visit two or three villages in a morning or afternoon. Renting a car is an easy and delightful way to cover the distances. Buses bound for Zaachila or other villages along Carretera 131 depart from the terminal run by Añasa on Calle Libertad at Calle Arista; those bound for Ocotlán and other points along Carretera 175 depart from the terminal run by Estrella del Valle on Calle Armenta at Calle Lopez. Distances are short: it takes 20 minutes to get to Monte Albán, San Bartolo Coyotepec, or Atzompa; 30 minutes to Zaachila; 45 minutes to Ocotlán.

■ TIP→Most villages do not have ATMs, so get cash before you leave Oaxaca City. Bring smaller bills as vendors often can't change larger ones.

HIT THE ROAD

An alternative to the bus is a *colectivo* (shared taxi). The fare will be more than what you'd pay for the bus, but the convenience might be worth it. Colectivos leave from Oaxaca City's second-class bus station. Destinations are clearly posted on windshields; if you don't see the village you want, look for a taxi going to the nearest major town on the same route (i.e., Mitla or Ocotlan) and ask the driver if he stops along the way.

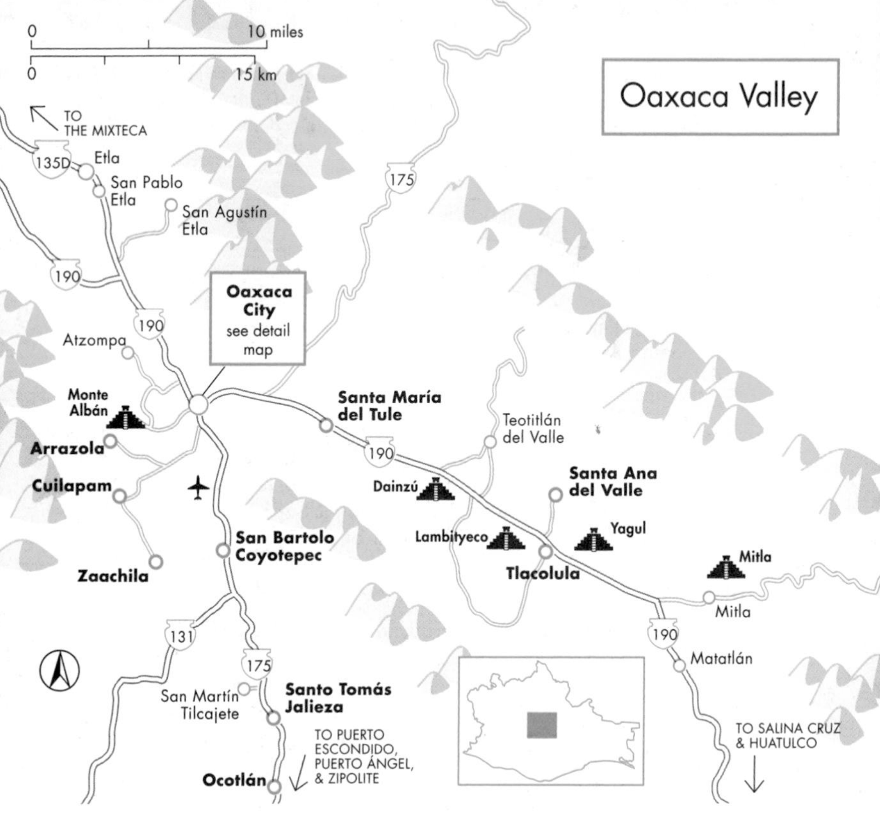

MONTE ALBÁN

10 km (6 mi) southwest of Oaxaca City.

Fodor's Choice ★

Southwest of Oaxaca City, a narrow, twisting road leads up to the mountaintop city of the "cloud people," Monte Albán. Seeing this massive ancient metropolis is a mystical experience, especially if you are lucky enough to find one or more of the tombs open. South of the city lies a string of crafts villages. Atzompa, known for its green-glaze pottery, is a popular stop. It's on the road to Monte Albán, as is San Bartolo Coyotepec, where you'll find gorgeous black pottery.

The massive temples of Monte Albán, perched atop a mesa, make this one of the country's most spectacular archaeological sites. This vast city was home to more than 30,000 Zapotec. Despite its size, experts estimate that only about 10% of the site has been uncovered. Digs are sporadic, taking place whenever the budget permits.

Monte Albán overlooks the Oaxaca Valley from a flattened mountaintop 5,085 feet high; the views are breathtaking. Either the Zapotec or their predecessors leveled the site around 600 BC. The varying heights of the site follow the contours of distant mountains. The oldest of the four temples is the **Galería de los Danzantes,** or the Dancers'

Gallery, so named for the elaborately carved stone figures that once covered the building. Most of the originals are now in the site museum, but some can still be seen in the temple. Experts are unsure whether the nude male figures represent captives, warriors, or some other group; the theory that they were dancers has been discarded because some appear to be bound.

The Zapotec constructed most of the buildings along a north–south axis, except one structure called the **Observatorio** (Observatory). The arrow-shape structure is set at a 45-degree angle, pointing toward the southwest. It's thought to have been an observatory, as it's more closely aligned with the stars than with the Earth's poles.

NAMING IT

Most villages have two-part names, most often names imposed by the Spanish (usually a saint's name) followed by a traditional name. Therefore, a town like Atzompa is actually Santa María Atzompa. It's rare to hear locals use the full name. It might, however, appear on regional maps.

The **Juego de Pelota,** or ball game, was played in the well-excavated court. Hips, shoulders, knees, and elbows were probably used to hit a wooden or rubber ball. The details of these games are sketchy, but there's speculation that they were a means of solving disputes between factions or villages, of celebrating the defeat of a rival, or of worshipping the gods. Although human sacrifice is thought to have been connected with the ball game in certain parts of Mesoamerica, there is no evidence that it happened in Monte Albán.

No one knows for sure whether the Zapotec abandoned the site gradually or suddenly, but by AD 1000 it stood empty. Years afterward the Mixtec used Monte Albán as a lofty necropolis of lavish tombs. More than 200 tombs and 300 burial sites have been explored. The most fantastic of these, **Tumba 7,** yielded a treasure unequaled in North America. Inside were more than 500 priceless Mixtec objects, including gold breastplates; jade, pearl, ivory, and gold jewelry; and fans, masks, and belt buckles of precious stones and metals. The tomb is north of the parking lot, but is seldom open.

At Monte Albán you'll find a small site museum with a gift shop. The cafeteria isn't half bad, and has a great view of the valley; unfortunately, it closes with the rest of the site at 5 PM. Direct buses serve Monte Albán from the Hotel Rivera del Angel (Calle Mina 518, 951/516–6666), departing on the hour from 8:30 to 3:30; the last bus back is at 6 PM. The round-trip fare is about $3.25; to stay longer than two hours you must pay a small surcharge (you can decide once you're on-site). ☎ *951/516–1215* 🎫 *$4.50* ⏲ *Daily 8–5.*

EN ROUTE

Take some time to wander the few main streets of unimposing **Santa María Atzompa,** 8 km (5 mi) northwest of Oaxaca City on the way to Monte Albán. Its inhabitants produce the traditional green-glaze plates, bowls, and cups that people use on a daily basis all over Mexico. Some potters offer fanciful clay pots and vases in an eye-popping range of colors. You can visit workshops, often located in people's homes.

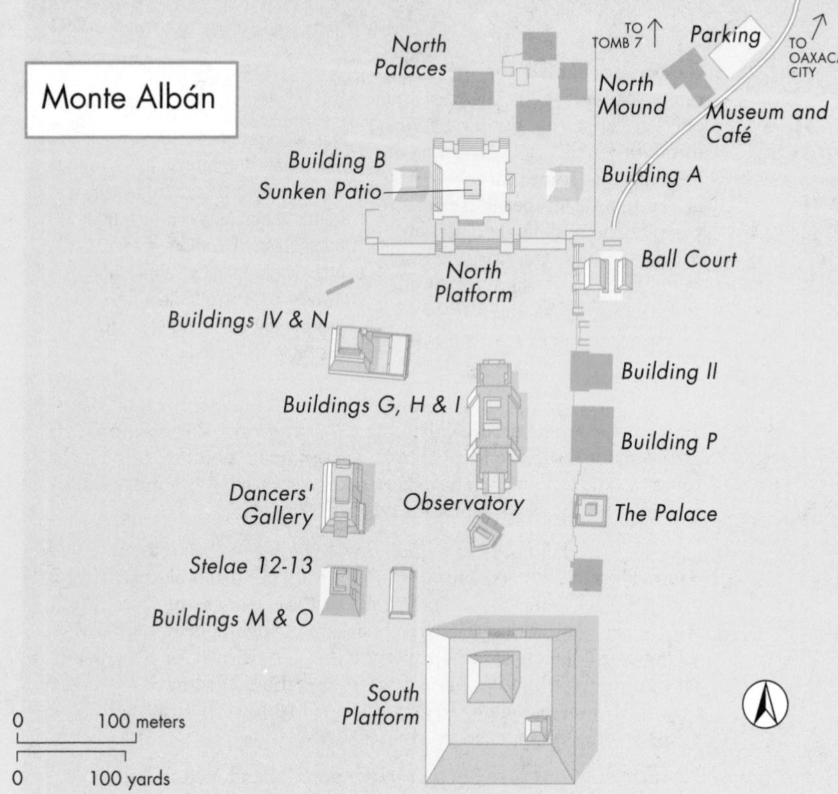

More convenient (although the quality of work can be disappointing) is the Mercado de Artesanías (Handicrafts Market) open daily from 8 to 7. The easiest way to see Atzompa is on a tour of Monte Albán, as it is on the way. You can also take a taxi from anywhere in the city or a bus from Oaxaca's second-class terminal.

ARRAZOLA

A string of villages can be found off Carretera 131, which runs south from Oaxaca City. About 12 km (8 mi) southwest of the city is Arrazola, where you'll find the delightful *alebrijes* (angels, devils, and all sorts of creatures carved out of light, porous copal wood). These brightly colored figures, from tiny to tremendous, are decorated with dots, squiggles, and other artful touches. This craft was developed by Arrazola's best-known artist, Don Manuel Jiménez, and almost everyone in town has jumped on the bandwagon. As you wander along the streets, some people may invite you into their homes to see their work.

CUILAPAM

About 4 km (2½ mi) beyond the turnoff for Arrazola you'll come to the dusty little town of Cuilapam.

The roofless ruins of a church and monastery called the **Ex-Convento de Santiago Apóstol** is Cuilapam's claim to fame. The long, narrow church was begun in 1535 but never finished. Columns that would have supported the roof still stand ready. Vincente Guerrero, one of the heroes of the country's battle for independence, was executed in the adjacent monastery in 1831. A large painting of him is in the room where he was sequestered. Admission to the site, open daily 9–5, is $2.

ZAACHILA

Zaachila was an important center of Zapotec civic and religious authority at the time of the Spanish invasion. On Thursday, oxcarts loaded with alfalfa or hay head for the area's liveliest livestock market. Get here before noon, or there won't be a pig left in the poke. The town, which is 17 km (11 mi) southwest of Oaxaca on Carretera 131, is known for its stately church, the Temple de Santa María Natividad, which sits on the main square.

To get to Zaachila or any of the villages along Carretera 131, take a bus from the second-class terminal or from a terminal for the Añasa bus line at Calle Libertad 1215, at the corner of Calle Arista.

Just behind the Temple de Santa María Natividad is the small **Zona Arqueológica,** with a pair of underground tombs that are fun to explore. A pair of eerie carved owls guards one of the graves containing a noble named Lord Nine Flower. He was buried along with an unidentified young man among riches that rivaled those of Tumba 7 at Monte Albán. These treasures, however, are in the archaeological museum in Mexico City. The site is open daily 9–5. Admission is $2.60.

SAN BARTOLO COYOTEPEC

Three of the most interesting villages in the Valles Centrales lie south of Oaxaca City on Carretera 175. They share a market day on Friday, so it's easy to visit all three. The first you'll reach is San Bartolo Coyotepec, bisected by the highway about 12 km (8 mi) from the city. The name Coyotepec, a Nahuatl word, literally translates as "place of the coyotes." Across from the stately church is a colonnaded square where you can buy the fragile, unglazed black ceramics for which the town is deservedly famous.

Keep an eye out for the **Alfarería Doña Rosa** (✉ *Calle Juárez 24* ☎ *951/551–0011*), a workshop named for the woman who invented the technique for giving the pottery its distinctive gloss. The revered craftsperson died in 1980, but her descendants continue making pottery the old-fashioned way. The workshop, where shelves upon shelves with items for sale line a small courtyard, is open daily 9–6.

SANTO TOMÁS JALIEZA

About 20 km (12 mi) south of Oaxaca City, Santo Tomás Jalieza sits alongside a small road off Carretera 175. Women here make belts, sashes, and other woven goods on small back-strap looms. The prices in the village are quite reasonable.

OCOTLÁN

Revered for its handcrafted knives and machetes, Ocotlán is a large town, 30 km (18 mi) south of Oaxaca on Carretera 175, with a beautifully restored church and monastery on an attractive main plaza. Buses from the second-class station depart for Ocotlán and the surrounding villages every 15 minutes or so. You can also take an Estrella del Valle bus from the terminal at the corner of on Calle Armenta and Calle Lopez. It costs about $1 each way. Or, catch a taxi for about $1.50 each way; the ride is 35 minutes.

In a painstakingly restored monastery is the **Fundación Cultural Rodolfo Morales** (✉*Morelos 108* ☎*951/571–0952 or 951/571–0198* ⏲*Daily 10–2 and 4–8*), funded by the village's most famous resident, artist Rodolfo Morales. There are exhibits of religious art from the monastery, as well as some of the master's own work.

★ Near the entrance to Ocotlán, the **workshops of the Aguilar sisters**—Josefina, Guillermina, Irene, and Concepción—are brimming with distinctive figurines fashioned from red clay. The sisters, now elderly, might be there to show you around their adjoining workshops. If not, one of their children or grandchildren will. Their shops are clustered near each other on the road, so it's easy to go from one to the next. You can find these figures in the markets and shops of Oaxaca City, but at extremely inflated prices.

MITLA & THE TEXTILE VILLAGES

It gets far fewer visitors, but Mitla is, in many ways, as impressive as Monte Albán. Here you'll find splendid stonework that is referred to as *greca* because it resembles that of the ancient Greeks. You'll also see walls painted a striking shade of red, a reminder that when inhabited, these cities were not just the bare stone associated with the ruins. Other worthy archaeological sites along Carretera 190, the newly resurfaced highway to Mitla, are Lambityeco and Yagul.

Carretera 190 is also the road to the great textile town of Teotitlán del Valle, where house after house is set up as a workshop where both men and women work on back-strap looms. Prices can be high, but the workmanship justifies it. Nearby Santa Ana del Valle has weavings at lower prices.

Buses bound for villages east of the city depart from the second-class terminal across the street from the Central de Abastos.

MITLA

Fodor's Choice ★ Mitla, 46 km (27 mi) southeast of Oaxaca, expanded and grew in influence as Monte Albán declined. Like its predecessor, Mitla is a complex of structures started by the Zapotec and later taken over by the Mixtec. The striking architecture, which dates as late as the 1500s, is almost without equal within Mexico thanks to the exquisite *greca* workmanship on the fine local volcanic stone, which ranges in hue from pink to yellow. Unlike Monte Albán, Mitla's attraction lies not in its massive scale, but in its unusual ornamentation; the stonework depicts mesmerizing abstract designs with a powerful harmony. Some of the original red stucco coloring can still be seen.

Continued on page 348

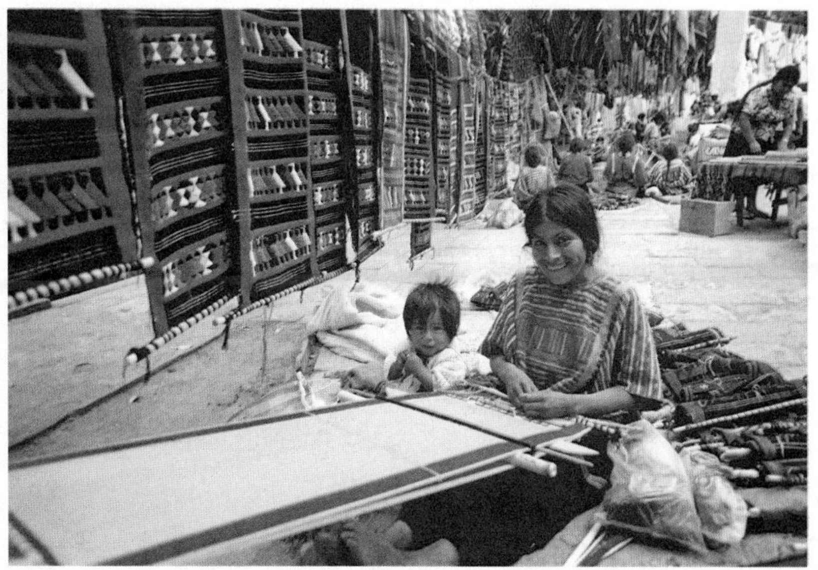

OAXACA VALLEY MARKETS

With markets open most days of the week, choosing which ones to visit may seem like a daunting task. You'll find something interesting at every Oaxaca market; however, there are a few markets you shouldn't miss. Those listed here have the unbeatable combination of beautiful settings and varied, high-quality goods.

Tlacolula, east of Oaxaca City, has a sprawling Sunday market that draws villagers from around the region. Although not specifically targeted at tourists, it has plenty of crafts, including woven blankets from nearby Teotitlán del Valle and Santa Ana del Valle.

On Thursday you should head to **Zaachila**, south of Oaxaca City. Beautiful pottery is on display in outdoor stalls in the shade of a stately church. The neighboring villages of **Ocotlán** and **San Bartolo Coyotepec** have markets on Friday, and it's easy to travel to both. Look for lovely ceramic figurines and black earthenware vases. And on Saturday there's no need to go anywhere—the best market is the Central de Abastos right in **Oaxaca City**. **Mitla** also has a market on Saturday.

Most tour companies offer excursions to the nearby craft villages, often combining them with visits to archaeological sites such as Monte Albán or Mitla. However, being part of a clump of tourists arriving in an air-conditioned bus that's bigger than most local dwellings may make you feel more like an invader than a visitor. Exploring the villages on your own is no problem at all. All are easily reachable by car via well-maintained roads. You can also take one of the frequent local buses that depart from the first- or second-class bus terminals. A round-trip ticket will cost between $1 and $2. Hiring a taxi to take you around is a more expensive option, but you'll still be left with plenty of shopping money.

MARKET SCHEDULE	
Thursday	Zaachila
Friday	Ocotlán and San Bartolo Coyotepec
Saturday	Oaxaca City and Mitla
Sunday	Tlacolula

CITY SHOPPING

There's no need to venture far to find interesting markets. Several are right in Oaxaca City. The largest and oldest market is held at the **Central de Abastos** (literally the "Center of Supplies") on the southwestern edge of downtown. Saturday is the traditional market day, but the enormous covered market swarms daily with thousands of buyers and sellers from Oaxaca and the surrounding villages. Along with mounds of multicolored chiles and herbs, piles of tropical fruit, electronics, and bootleg CDs, you'll find intricately woven straw baskets, fragile green-and-black pottery, and colorful *rebozos* (shawls) of cotton and silk. Don't burden yourself with lots of camera equipment or bags; and keep an eye out for pickpockets and purse-slashers. Polite bargaining is expected.

Close to the zócalo, the spectacular daily **Mercado Benito Juárez** (✉ Between Calles 20 de Noviembre and Miguel Cabrera at Las Calas, Centro Histórico) has stalls selling *moles,* chocolates, fruits and vegetables, and much more. The bulky brick building teems with clothing, arts, and crafts. It's mostly locals that you'll find chowing down amid the lively stalls of the daily **Mercado 20 de Noviembre** (✉ Between Calles 20 de Noviembre and Flores Magón at Calle Aldama, Centro Histórico), across the street from the Mercado Benito Juárez. No prices are listed, but rest assured that this will be your cheapest meal in Oaxaca. For textiles, don't miss the **Mercado de Artesanías** (✉ Calle J.-P. García, near Calle Ignacio Zaragoza, Centro Histórico), a great place to shop for handwoven and embroidered clothing from Oaxaca's seven regions. This is also the place to find the handmade *huipiles* (short, blouses, often made of velveteen) worn in the Isthmus of Tehuantepec.

TYPES OF CRAFTS

ALEBRIJES

Perhaps Oaxaca's most amusing pieces are the angels, devils, Day-of-the-Dead skeletons, and fanciful creatures carved out of light, porous copal wood. These figures, from tiny to tremendous, are decorated with dots, squiggles, and other artful touches. Found in Arrazola.

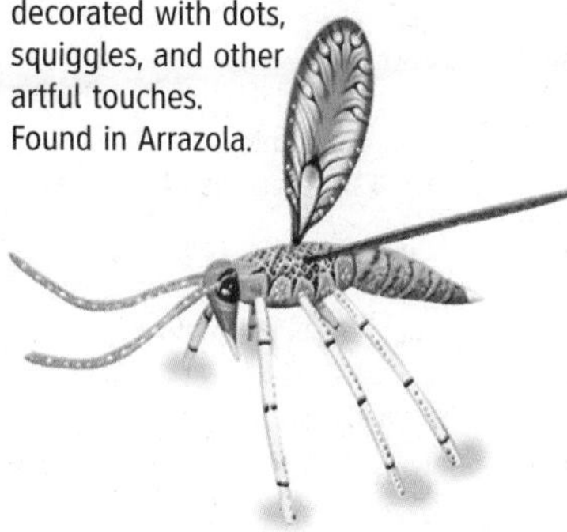

POTTERY

This tan or green-glazed pottery is made with a very simple wheel (a plate balanced on a round rock or overturned saucer). The technique of adding bits of small clay to items as decoration is called *pastillaje*. Though some artists keep their creations plain, others use multicolor glazes to add more flourishes. Found in Aztompa, Ocotlán.

TAPETES

Woven wool rugs (often with geometric patterns) are made on treadle (pedal-operated) looms. Found in Teotitlán del Valle, Santa Ana del Valle, and Tlacolula (on market day).

BARRO NEGRO

Shiny, lightweight black pottery, made without the benefit of a pottery wheel and fired in pit-kilns. Found in Zaachila, San Bartolo Coyotepec, Ocotlán. Pack it with care!

WOVEN GOODS

Though the *tapetes* are more iconic, you'll also find belts, sashes, and other woven items. Unlike the tapetes, these are done on back-strap looms. Found in Santo Tomás Jalieza.

BASKETRY

Woven with palms fronds and reeds, baskets often bear geometric designs in bright colors like magenta, green, and purple. The Mixteca villages produce the most of these crafts, but they're also in abundance in Villa de Etla, northwest of Oaxaca City.

CLOSE UP

Get Out of Town

You can experience village life by staying at a Tourist Yu'u. Developed by the state tourism board, these lodgings are scattered throughout the communities of the Valles Centrales, the Mixteca, and other areas around Oaxaca City. They are the ultimate budget lodging, costing as little as $8 per person, per night.

These *yu'us* aren't all created alike. The older ones, in villages such as Santa Ana del Valle, are housed in concrete-block buildings painted a particularly vivid shade of green. The newer places in villages such as Benito Juárez are much more comfortable—lodging in four rooms in the main building house between three and nine people; six cabins accommodate two or three people. You can cook your own meals, or arrange for a cook (they'll hire someone from a local village) to whip up the delicious dishes typically eaten by the locals. A wide range of activities is available, such as horseback-riding excursions to scenic overlooks or mountain-bike trips over rough terrain. You can even experience a *temazcal*, an adobe sweat lodge used by the indigenous people. Facilities in nearby villages, such as San Antonio Cuajimoloyas, have a similar range of activities.

Volunteers at the **Tourist Yu'u Project** (✉ *Calle Murguía 204, at Calle 5 de Mayo, Centro Histórico* ☎ *951/516–0123*), in the state tourism office, will show you a book with photos of each of the lodgings and give you fact sheets printed in English. They can also make reservations for you. The staff will steer you toward more comfortable facilities unless you specifically request more rustic digs.

The first structure you enter is the **Grupo del Norte,** where the Spanish settlers built Mitla's Catholic cathedral literally on top of the Zapotec structure, integrating the foundation. It's comparable to having the history of Oaxaca laid out before you in one building—truly remarkable. Mitla's name comes from the Nahuatl word *mictlan,* meaning "place of the dead." Don't expect to see anything resembling a graveyard, however; the Zapotec and Mixtec typically buried their dead under the entrance to the structure where the deceased resided. There are a few underground tombs in the impressive **Grupo de las Columnas** (Group of the Columns), the main section of the ruins, that are fun to climb down into. In that group is also the palace that forms the most striking architectural achievement of Mitla.

The journey on Carretera 190 takes about 50 minutes. If you haven't rented a car, you can catch a *colectivo* (collective taxi) at the side of Oaxaca City's second-class bus station or along the road to Mitla—or hire a cab or car through your hotel to take you on a day trip to Mitla (and perhaps a mezcal distillery as well). The ruins are in the midsize town of Mitla, which has many small restaurants along with a beautiful church that practically dwarfs the ruins. There is a small market area adjacent to the parking lot with public restrooms and snack and souvenir vendors. ☎ *951/568–0316* 🎫 *$3.25* 🕒 *Daily 8–5.*

WHERE TO EAT & STAY

$ **Don Cenobio.** What was for a long time just a restaurant and convention center is now the top lodging choice in Mitla. Owner Alfonso Moreno Díz has lovingly restored his grandfather's estate, and it's a remarkable place to stay, complete with an inner courtyard that has a solar-heated pool, an orange-tree-shaded garden bar, and a play structure for kids. Rooms could hardly be cheerier—everything is saturated with color—with intricately carved furniture brightly painted with flowers and fruits. Some doubles have private terraces over the garden—definitely ask for one. Rates are discounted Sunday–Thursday. The restaurant ($) is worthwhile in its own right; don't pass up the *pollo rellena con quesillo y huitlacoche* (chicken stuffed with Oaxacan cheese and corn fungus), or the local version of mole negro. Pros: Great restaurant, good base for exploring the area. Cons: Off the beaten path. *Av. Juárez 3Colonia Centro, 070430 951/568–0330 www.hoteldoncenobio.com 19 rooms, 2 suites In-hotel: Restaurant, bar, pool, public Internet V.*

SANTA MARÍA DEL TULE

About 14 km (9 mi) east of Oaxaca on Carretera 190, the hamlet of Santa María del Tule is known for **El Tule,** the huge cypress tree that towers over the pretty colonial-era church behind it. Thought to be more than 2,000 years old, it's one of the world's largest trees, with roots buried more than 60 feet in the ground and a canopy arcing some 140 feet high. It has an estimated weight of nearly 640,000 tons; it would take 35 adults to embrace the trunk. In front of the church is a pleasant garden with animal-shape topiaries. The fee to enter the grounds 30¢. At informal outdoor eateries in the tree's shadow, local ladies tend large griddles, serving *atole* (a nutritious drink of ground cornmeal or rice), soups, and snacks.

DAINZÚ

The first archaeological site to the east of Oaxaca is Dainzú, about 20 km (12 mi) from the city. It dates as far back as 600 BC. Here you'll find some carvings that may remind you of the Dancers' Gallery at Monte Albán; these, however, depict a ball game. The most spectacular sights are the well-restored ball court and the *Tumba del Jaguar* (Tomb of the Jaguar), with the fearsome head of a jaguar perched above the door. Pre-Columbian pottery shards litter the ground all over, evidence that this is a site that, unlike Monte Albán or Mitla, is still in the earlier stages of excavation. You'll likely have it to yourself, too. The grass-covered ruins are particularly pretty in the late-afternoon light. Note that there are no facilities here. Keep an eye out for the turnoff, because it's poorly marked; arriving from Oaxaca City, it's right before an overpass. *Off Carretera 190 No phone $2.60 Daily 8–6.*

TEOTITLÁN DEL VALLE

Giant rug looms sit in the front rooms of many houses in Teotitlán del Valle, 30 km (18 mi) southeast of Oaxaca, just off Carretera 190. Although many rug shops are clustered right off the highway, be sure to drive all the way into town, where there are many more workshops.

7

Continued on page 354

THE MIXTECA MONASTERIES

Templo y Exconvento de Santo Domingo de Guzmán (16th Century), Yanhuitlán (above and right)

The Mixteca, a rugged region northwest of Oaxaca City, has some of the state's most dramatic scenery. Driving up you'll see more pine-covered hills than people. In the evening, fog creeps into the many valleys here. The Mixteca is a great day trip from Oaxaca City, but the region attracts very few tourists. This may soon change, however, when the extensive restoration of the region's stunning Dominican monasteries is completed. These enormous, ornate structures would be a sight to behold in any city, but are all the more striking here—out in the middle of nowhere—dwarfing the tiny villages that sustain them.

Dominican friars swept through this region soon after the Spanish conquest, employing local labor to construct churches. The Mixteca people were known for their work with gold and precious stones, so these structures are as opulent as any of the churches in Oaxaca City. The same indigenous people that helped build the monasteries were not allowed inside them for worship, so each has *capillas abiertas* (open chapels) that allowed priests to minister to the vast crowds forced to stand outside. The thick, stout walls of the monasteries were built to withstand earthquakes—with mixed success. For several churches, an important part of the restoration process has been reinforcing the original walls with steel supports.

Ironically, smallpox brought to the region by the Spanish eventually killed most of the indigenous Mixteca worshipers, leaving the churchyards empty. Not all monasteries were completely abandoned, though. In many cases, the congregations, too poor to repair the churches themselves, have continued services for years while the churches crumble around them. Today, you'll often find Sunday mass going on amid the construction.

Mexico's National Institute of Anthropology and History (INAH) has been working in conjunction with local conservation groups and outside engineering firms to restore key monasteries since the early 1990s; some projects are still underway and may take years to complete.

TEMPLO DE LA ASUNCIÓN, Nochixtlán

Dominating the town is the 19th-century Templo de la Asunción, in the main square. The interior is especially elegant, with a five-tier chandelier hanging from the dome. Follow the signs to El Centro.

TEMPLO Y EXCONVENTO DE SAN JUAN BAUTISTA, Coixtlahuaca

Coixtlahuaca's monastery may be the most "ruined" of them all, but it has perhaps the best preserved of the Dominican churches in the region. Vivid reds, greens, and blues still cling to the ribs on the vaulted ceiling, wind around the windows, and climb up the columns. Just inside the front doors, you'll find a large chapel dedicated to the Virgen de Guadalupe. The church's patron saint stands guard over the intricately carved retablo, and you can get close enough to the altarpiece to appreciate the delicate work. Outside, the bright red paint that once enlivened the now-demure white facade shows through cracks in the plaster. Be sure to check out the lovely courtyard garden. Though there aren't any set hours, the monastery is often open.

★ TEMPLO Y EXCONVENTO DE SANTO DOMINGO DE GUZMÁN, Yanhuitlán

This towering 16th-century structure and its adjoining monastery appear even larger because they sit on a hill overlooking the village. The massive wooden doors face away from the village's main square.

Where to Eat in Nochixtlán

✕ **Restaurante Claudia.** Half a block from the main square is this no-frills restaurant, which serves up surprisingly good food. Take a seat at one of the long tables as members of the owner's extended family watch soap operas on the tiny television. You can even check your e-mail while you wait. ✉ *Porfirio Díaz between Allende and Benito Juarez* ☎ *No phone* ▭ *No credit cards.*

The church's sheer size is its most stunning feature; its vaulted ceiling soars to almost 25 meters (82 feet). The gold-leaf retablo behind the main altar has five levels, each depicting various saints. Santo Domingo, of course, stands alone at the top. Some of the paintings on this retablo are by the Spanish master Andrés de la Concha. Don't miss the *mudéjar* (Moorish) designs in the wooden ceiling of the choir. The handsome 18th-century pipe organ was restored in 1998.

The site is being restored at a decent clip. At this writing, the church was closed and scaffolded, but the monastery was open—a stunning cobblestoned inner courtyard has been completed and beautifully stuccoed. 🎫 *$2.75 to view the interior* ⏲ *Tues.–Sun. 10–5*

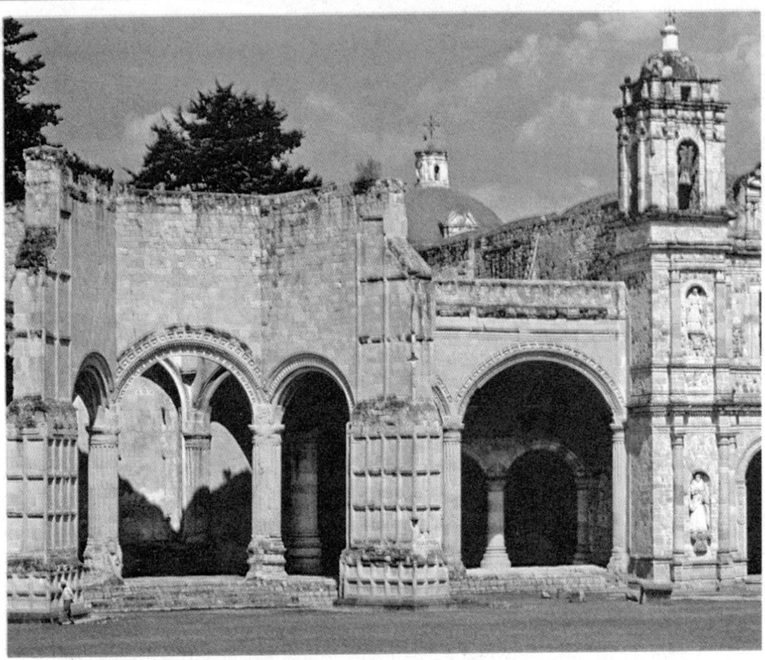

Templo y Exconvento de San Pedro y San Pablo, Teposcolula (1538)

TEMPLO Y EXCONVENTO DE SAN PEDRO Y SAN PABLO, Teposcolula

This sanctuary is one of the most impressive in the region and remains much as it was when it was built in 1538. The only major change is that the gilded retablo behind the main altar has been replaced by one with the neoclassical design that was popular in the 19th century. (You can still see the original to the left side of the main altar.)

The front of the church, which faces away from the town, is the location of its most impressive feature—a meticulously restored open chapel. The roof resembles the vaulted ceiling inside the sanctuary, but between the ribs it's open to the sky. Make sure to take a close look, as the underside is studded with gleaming gold medallions. The sprawling churchyard was meant to hold thousands of Mixteca worshippers.

Inside is a pleasant rose garden ringed by small rooms. Here you'll find many unlabeled paintings by Andrés de la Concha, also responsible for many of the works on the main altar at the Templo y Exconvento de Santo Domingo de Guzmán in Yanhuitlán. Upstairs are a few restored monks' cells. Admission ($2.75) is charged only if someone is at the door. It's open daily from 10–6.

The other interesting structure in Teposcolula is the Casa de la Cacica, which means the "House of the Priestess." The Spanish built this stone building for a Mixteca leader, hoping that her presence would convince others to move to the village. The casa, on the road across from the church's main gate, is currently being restored.

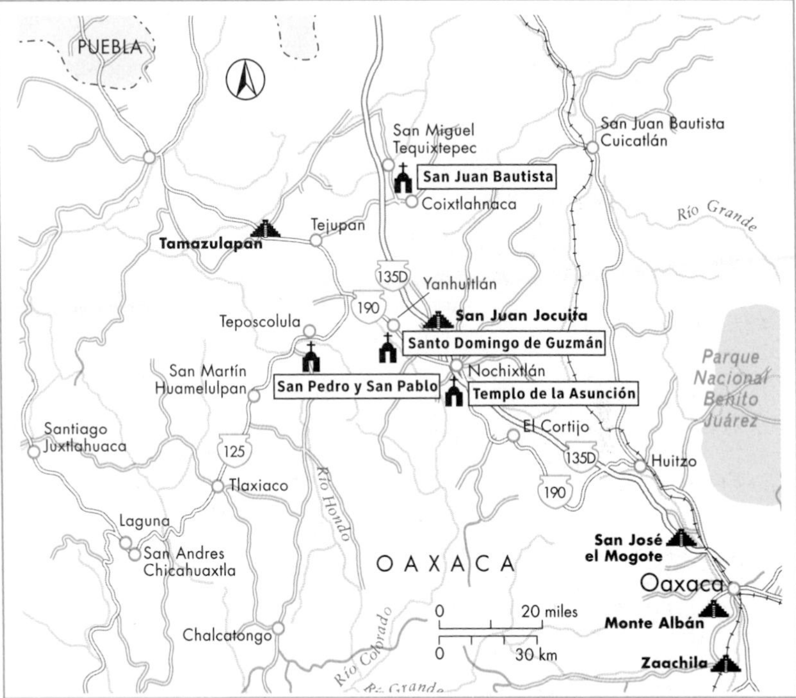

HOW TO GET THERE

BY BUS: Buses bound for Nochixtlán depart daily at 7 AM, 8 AM, and 1 PM from Oaxaca's first-class terminal. From Nochixtlán you can get connections or shared taxis to outlying monasteries, but it's easier to drive. Trips take 1 to 1½ hours.

BY CAR: Carretera 190 has a maddening amount of speed bumps, inexplicably placed in areas where there's nothing for miles but cattle. If you see a sign that says TOPE, slow down immediately or you're in for a nasty jolt. Unfortunately, many aren't marked. You'll do yourself a favor if you spring for the tolls along beautifully paved Carretera 135D. Spending the $6 gets you less traffic, fewer potholes, no speed bumps and a better view of the countryside. Secondary roads have some potholes, but are generally in good shape.

Nochixtlán: Located where Carreterra 190 and Carreterra 135D meet, Nochixtlán is the gateway to the Mixteca. The trip from Oaxaca City takes 1 hour.
Coixtlahuaca: About 35 km (22 mi) north of Nochixtlán; go up main road and turn right on Av. Independencia.
Yanhuitlán: To get to Yanhuitlán, take Carretera 190. It's about 18 km (11 mi) west of Nochixtlán and 37 km (23 mi) south of Tamazulapan.
Teposcolula: About 32 km (20 mi) or 30–40 min. from Yanhuitlán. To get here, head west on Carretera 190, then south on Carretera 125. Bypass the first set of church ruins you on 125—Teposcolula is much farther on.

THE ELIXIR

Mitla and its surroundings are home to dozens of mezcal distilleries, almost all of which sell directly to consumers and some of which offer tours. American Ron Cooper is one of the most accomplished mezcal exporters in the business; his **Del Maguey** (*www.mezcal.com*) bottles contain mezcal sourced from extremely traditional artisanal producers in the countryside. They are prized across America, commanding upward of $70 a bottle. You can visit Cooper's bottling plant and tasting room by appointment, or, for a fee, Ron will take you on a fascinating insider's tasting tour of the region, where you'll meet the old-school producers themselves. **Mezcal Benevá** (*Carretera Oaxaca–Istmo Carretera 190 Km 42.5, San Pablo Villa de Mitla 951/514–7005 www.mezcalbeneva.com*), at the Rancho Zapata restaurant complex, is a short drive out of the town of Mitla toward Oaxaca. Take a guided tour through the mezcal distilling process; during one part, a horse walks around in circles, stomping on the cooked agave. Benevá's mezcals are also notable, especially their five-year-old *Gran Reserva.*

Another American, Doug French, makes **Scorpion Mezcal** (*951/511–5701*). His tasting room is still in development, but his range of mezcals is exported as well.

The 17th-century **Templo de la Precioso Sangre de Cristo** (*Calle Hidalgo, 1 block east of Calle Juárez*) towers over the main square. Some parts of the facade have been scraped away to reveal stones carved with Zapotec designs that were used during the building of the church.

For a peek at the town's past, head to the **Museo Comunitario Balaa Xtee Guech Gulal** (*Calle Hidalgo, 1 block east of Calle Juárez 951/524–9123 $1 Daily 10–6*). The exhibits include Zapotec carvings unearthed in the area. To the right of the museum is a wall from a Zapotec temple that once stood on this site. Look for the geometric patterns similar to those found at Mitla.

WHERE TO EAT

¢ MEXICAN **Tlamanalli.** For a memorable lunch of authentic regional food, head to this eatery in a pretty colonial-style building. Zapotec dishes such as *guisado de pollo* (a rich chicken stew) are so good that Tlamanalli has been featured in several food magazines. Get here early, as it isn't open for dinner. *Av. Juárez 39 951/524–4006 V Closed Mon. No dinner.*

SANTA ANA DEL VALLE

The tiny weaving town of Santa Ana del Valle is less well known than Teotitlán but also worth visiting; prices here are often cheaper. The turnoff is 31 km (19 mi) from Oaxaca on Carretera 190.

The tiny **Museo Shan-Dany** (*Plaza Cívica 951/568–0373 $1 Daily 10–2 and 3–6*) has some interesting exhibits about the archaeological sites scattered around the area. Of particular note are several incense burners bearing the likeness of Cocijo, the Zapotec god honored at a temple in Lambityeco.

TLACOLULA

Although most often visited during its bustling Sunday market, Tlacolula, 31 km (19 mi) east of Oaxaca on Carretera 190, makes an interesting stop midweek. While you're here, visit the baroque-style Capilla del Santo Cristo, a chapel dating from the 16th century. ■ **TIP→There are many inexpensive and tasty places in town, so it's a good place to stop for food on the way between Oaxaca and Mitla.**

LAMBITYECO

Lambityeco, near Ilacolula, was built as the civilization of nearby Mitla was waning. The city flourished until AD 750, when it was abandoned. Many archaeologists believe the inhabitants moved to the better-protected city of Yagul. The *Palacio de los Racoqui,* or Palace of the Lords, is the last of six larger and larger temples built on top of each other. Here you'll see a pair of carvings of a nobleman and his wife. Between these carvings is the tomb where they were buried. Nearby is the Palacio de Cocijo, dedicated to its namesake, a Zapotec god. A pair of carvings depicts the rain god wearing an impressive headdress. The site is clearly visible from the highway, but for some reason there's no sign. ✉ *Off Carretera 190* ☎ *No phone* *$2.60* *Daily 8–5.*

YAGUL

The ruins at Yagul aren't as elaborate as those at Monte Albán or Mitla, but their position atop a hill makes them more than worth a visit. This city, which is 36 km (22 mi) southeast of Oaxaca off Carretera 190, was predominantly a fortress protecting a group of temples. The *Palacio de los Seis Patios* (Palace of the Six Patios), a maze of hallways leading to hidden courtyards, is fun to explore. If you find the eerie *Tumba Triple* (Triple Tomb) locked, give the guard $1 or so to open it for you. He may even let you borrow a flashlight to get a good look at the spooky carved skulls. Follow the steep trail that starts near the parking lot for a good hike and great views over the valley and ruins. The site has restrooms, but no other facilities. ☎ *951/516–0123* *$3.25* *Daily 8–5.*

7

THE OAXACA COAST

Oaxaca's 520-km (322-mi) coastline is one of Mexico's last Pacific frontiers. The town of Puerto Escondido has long been prime territory for international surfers. Its pedestrian walkways, crowded with open-air seafood restaurants, shops, and cafés, are indeed lively, but also incredibly relaxed. Fishing boats pull double duty as water taxis, ferrying folks to lovely scallops of sand up the coast. Across the highway, the "real" town above provides a look at local life and a dazzling view of the coast.

Midway between Puerto Escondido and Huatulco, tiny Puerto Angel has a limited selection of unpolished hotels and funky bungalows tucked into the hills. The growing number of accommodations in nearby beach burgs such as Zipolite—one of the hottest spots on the

Mexican coast—and Mazunte has seduced some of Puerto Angel's previously faithful sun-lovers.

Huatulco covers 51,900 acres, 40,000 of which are dedicated as a nature reserve. The focal point of the development, masterminded in the 1980s by the government's tourism office, is a string of nine sheltered bays that stretches across 35 km (22 mi) of stunning coast. The first in this necklace is Conejos, which has Huatulco's most luxurious private villas and two boutique hotels. The town of La Crucecita, originally built to house the construction crews working on area developments, has the requisite plaza with a Catholic church as well as a thriving market, small shops, budget and moderately priced hotels, and plenty of restaurants.

Bahía Tangolunda is home to Huatulco's most exclusive hotels, whereas Santa Cruz has midrange hotels as well as a marina and a cruise-ship terminal. Development of Bahía Chahué has begun with an 88-slip marina, a luxury spa, and a few small hotels. A parking lot makes the beach accessible, and a public beach club has changing rooms, a restaurant, and a swimming pool. A Best Western and a few other small hotels, bars, and restaurants are near this bay, but most are across the highway on Boulevard Benito Juárez.

No matter where you hole up along Mexico's southern Pacific coast, you'll find that it's all about the beach, the water, and the waves. Surfers and bodysurfers whoop it up at Zicatela and less famous breaks; snorkelers hug rocky coves in search of new and unusual specimens; and divers share the depths with dolphins, rays, eels, and schools of fish instead of shoals of other humans. Friendly locals, superb vistas, and first-rate beaches combine to make Oaxaca's coast a stunner.

PUERTO ESCONDIDO

310 km (192 mi) south of Oaxaca City.

Puerto Escondido was the first beach resort on the *carretera costera* (coastal highway), and it remains the most popular. Playa Zicatela is famous for its waves, drawing surfers from around the world. A few ritzier cliff-top hotels have brought in more of the older set, but the steady presence of the surfing community means that even as the town continues to gentrify, it maintains a relaxed, hippie-ish vibe. Beyond Zicatela's beachfront bars and dreadlocked denizens there are beautiful swimming beaches to the west that are popular with Mexican families. Several nearby nature preserves and a few coffee farms provide the best day-tripping opportunities, as there isn't much else in these parts besides beaches, beaches, and more beaches.

Puerto Escondido is divided into three sections, each attracting a different clientele. El Adoquín, the part of Avenida Pérez Gasga that is reserved for pedestrians, runs right through the center of the town. This area is most popular with Mexican families. You'll find plenty of inexpensive shops, restaurants, and hotels along the four blocks.

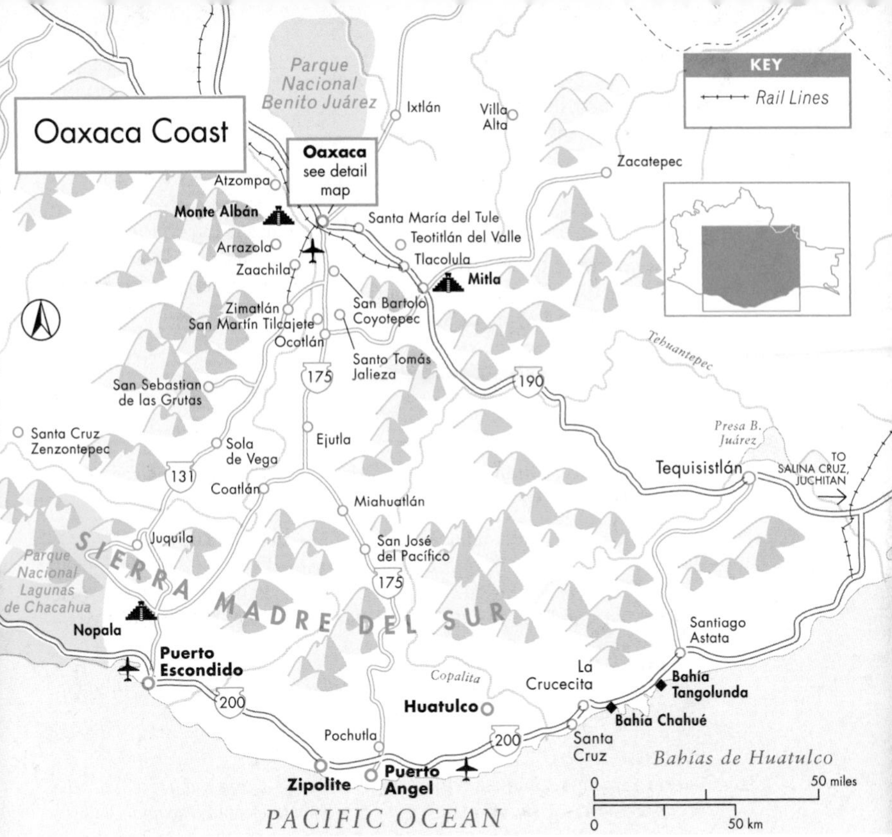

Northwest of El Adoquín, overlooking the sea from atop adobe-colored cliffs, are the Carrizalillo, La Rinconada, and Bacocho neighborhoods. These are the most up-and-coming areas of Puerto Escondido, but for now they are still quiet, and the people who stay here like it that way. The hotels, most of them upscale, cater to families. Along Boulevard Benito Juárez are some of the town's best restaurants. Oh, and if you were wondering why this street is as wide as a runway, it used to be the airport.

GETTING HERE & AROUND

Aeropuerto Puerto Escondido is a 10-minute taxi ride from town; most flights from the states connect in Mexico City. You can fly direct from Oaxaca City, but it's usually pretty pricey. Direct bus service from Oaxaca City is available on several first-class lines. ADO has several first-class buses per day leaving from Oaxaca's first-class bus terminal. Estrella del Valle has buses leaving from Oaxaca City to Puerto Escondido about four or five times daily. If you drive from Oaxaca City, there are two routes. The most direct is Carretera 131 (which turns off Carretera 175 south of Oaxaca City) and goes straight to Puerto Escondido (6½–7 hours). However, it's a winding, narrow, two-lane road. Alternatively, you can take slightly less hair-raising Carretera 190 to Salina Cruz, where you pick up Carretera 200 to Puerto Escondido (8–9 hours). Don't drive either route at night. Taxis in Puerto Escondido start at $2 for a ride from one end of town to another (say, from the Adoquín to Fraccionamiento Bacocho). Renting a car isn't necessary unless you want to explore beaches outside of town. It can be difficult to find a car, as the major agencies aren't well represented. Ask your hotel if it can arrange a rental.

TAKE A TOUR

Lalo Ecotours (☎ *954/582–2468* 🌐 *www.lalo-ecotours.com*)offers guided trips to Laguna Manialtepec including bird-watching tours with Canadian ornithologist Michael Malone.

ESSENTIALS

Bus Contacts **ADO GL** (✉ *Avendia 1a. Norte 207,* ☎ *984/582–1073* 🌐 *www.ticketbus.com.mx*). **Estrella del Valle** (☎ *951/514–5700* ✉ *Av. Hidalgo 400 at Av. 3a Oriente* ☎ *954/582–0050*).

Medical Assistance**International Friends of Puerto Escondido** (☎ *44954/540-3816* 🌐 *www.ifope.com*).**Puerto Escondido Hospital** (✉ *UMQ, Av. Oaxaca 720* ☎ *954/582–1288*) is the town's largest hospital. **Police** (☎ *954/582–0498 in Puerto Escondido*). **Red Cross** (☎ *954/582–0550*). The **Tourist Police** (☎ *954/582–3343*)

Rental Cars **Económica Rent-a-Car** (✉ *Calle Brisas s/n, just off Hwy. 200* ☎ *954/582–2579* 🌐 *www.economica.com.mx*).

VISITOR & TOUR INFO

Puerto Escondido Tourism Office (✉ *Blvd. Benito Juárez s/n, Fracc. Bacocho* ☎ *954/582–0175* ✉ *Av. Pérez Gasga s/n, at Marina Nacional* ☎ *No phone*).**Viajes Dimar** (✉ *Av. Pérez Gasga 905* ☎ *954/582–1551 or 954/582–0734* ✉ *Calle del Morro s/n, Playa Zicatela* ☎ *954/582–2305*).

EXPLORING

MAIN ATTRACTIONS

★ One of the easiest day trips from Puerto Escondido is the wildlife preserve of **Laguna de Manialtepec.** This lagoon about 14 km (9 mi) from the center of town is a birder's paradise, with pelicans, hawks, hummingbirds, and spoonbills in the surrounding mangrove forests. Although an inexpensive half-day tour from Puerto Escondido is the most convenient way to visit, you can also drive or take public transportation and hire a boatman to the lagoon's beaches and restaurants.

If you want a bit of pampering, cleanse your body and soul at **Temazcalli,** a spa that claims its treatments combine the energy of wood, fire, rock, and medicinal herbs. They still use the pre-Columbian techniques, so it's a true cultural experience. Choose a private scented steam (less than $10 each for two people) or a ritualistic group cleansing; the latter involves chants and prayers. Or opt for a good old-fashioned massage with scented oils. ✉ *Av. Infraganti at Calle Temazcalli, Col. Lázaro Cárdenas* ☎📠 *958/582–1023* 🌐 *www.temazcalli.com.*

IF YOU HAVE TIME

Tour operators often combine a trip to Playa Mazunte and its sea turtle center with a visit to **Laguna de Ventanilla** to see resident and migratory species of birds, as well as crocodiles. The cost of the all-day tour starts at $15 to $20 per person. Alternatively, arrange a 1½-hour tour of Laguna de Ventanilla directly from boat owners at the lagoon's entrance about five minutes west of the Centro Mexicano de la Tortuga. Arrive any day between 8 AM and 4 PM and you should be able find someone to take you around.

About 74 km (46 mi) west of Puerto Escondido is the **Parque Nacional Laguna Chacahua** *(Chacahua Lake National Park)*. You can tour the lagoon in a small motor launch, watching the birds that hunt among the mangroves. The bird population is biggest during the winter months, when migratory species arrive from the frozen north. Most tours from Puerto Escondido include a visit to a crocodile farm and an hour or two on the beach at Cerro Hermoso.

BEACHES

Playa Bacocho. High red cliffs serve as the backdrop for this beach west of town. It's ringed by upscale housing and hotel developments as well as some inviting bars, discos, and restaurants. ■TIP→**Although the waves aren't fierce, swimming is risky here because of strong rip currents, especially along the east side of the bay. There aren't any lifeguards.** For most visitors, Playa Bacocho is good for playing in the sand, long walks, and sunsets. Two beach clubs offer restaurant and bar service, swimming pools, showers, and shade; access is about $4. Security guards on three-wheelers patrol during the day, but it's not recommended to walk on this lonely stretch of sand at night.

Fodor's Choice ★ **Playa Carrizalillo.** In a region full of beautiful beaches, Playa Carrizalillo can still take your breath away. The high cliffs that surround it ensure that it's never too crowded. The aquamarine water here is clean, clear, and shallow—perfect for swimming and snorkeling, especially around the rocks that frame the beautiful cove. Sometimes there are waves large enough to be appropriate for beginning surfers. A handful of palm-thatched restaurants rent snorkeling equipment and serve food and drinks. It's a two-minute drive or 35-minute walk from the center of town; a small sign indicates where to turn onto the unpaved road. It's about 150 steps down from the parking area, but the steep stone staircase is well maintained.

Playa Manzanillo. Of Puerto Escondido's seven beaches, Playa Manza-

THE OYSTER GUY

Most days on Playa Manzanillo, from morning until about 5 PM, you can buy a dozen unbelievably fresh oysters on the half shell for about 50 pesos from a purveyor who shucks them for you right out of the bucket. He's usually set up at the far end of the beach (if you're facing the water, walk to your right), next to an elevated fish restaurant, and there's an informal agreement whereby you can eat your oysters at one of their tables, squeezing on lime and chile to your heart's content. There may not be a better food experience in Puerto Escondido.

7

nillo, which rings Puerto Angelito, is one of the safest for swimming. It's also one of the best for snorkeling, with a sandy ocean floor, some rock and coral formations, and calm, clear water. You can reach this beach on foot (a 15-minute walk west of town), by taxi (less than $2 per ride), or by boat ($3 per person one way) from Playa Marinero. There is a short staircase down to the beach that is difficult for some people to navigate. Informal snack shops selling juices, sodas, and beer—and, when available, fresh fish and oysters—rent snorkeling equipment and Boogie boards for $4 per hour. You can use their showers and rustic bathrooms for a small fee. The beach is lined with lounge chairs and can get quite crowded on weekends.

Playa Marinero. This beach abuts Playa Principal; the only thing separating the two is a tiny freshwater lagoon (the mouth of Río Rigadillo), which trickles onto the sand. Skiffs can be hired out for fishing or dolphin- or turtle-seeking expeditions, or as water taxis to nearby beaches. ■ TIP→ **Beginning to intermediate surfers can catch some waves near the east side of the bay.** Lifeguards keep watch from several towers.

Playa Principal. Meeting up with Playa Marinero at the mouth of Río Rigadillo, this strip of medium-coarse beige sand runs parallel to Avenida Pérez Gasga. There are restaurants and hotel bars where you can retreat from the sun and treat yourself to a cool drink. The sand is clean and soft near the shore, but somewhat hard and brown near the palm trees and shrubs that line the beachfront businesses. The beach is popular with Mexican families. Umbrellas can be rented for a minimal daily fee.

Playa Puerto Angelito. Don't confuse the delightful cove of Puerto Angelito, home to both the eponymous beach as well as equally lovely Manzanillo Beach, with the small port town south of Puerto Escondido. Ten steps from the street put you on the white sand of Playa Puerto Angelito, where the shallow depth of the water gives it a luminous, green-blue tint. It's a good spot for swimming, snorkeling, and diving, though the number of boats moored close to shore sometimes shrinks the swimming area considerably. ■ TIP→ **While swimming, beware of water taxis and skiffs offering fishing and sightseeing.** Many thatch-roofed restaurants here offer simple fare and shade and rent snorkels and umbrellas—the latter cost $5 or $6 whether you sit for 10 minutes or all day. Things get quite crowded on holidays and weekends.

★ **Playa Zicatela.** One of the world's top surfing beaches, Zicatela boasts cream-colored sands that are battered by the mighty Mexican Pipeline. In the third week of November, international surfing championships are held here (followed by the even more popular bikini contest). Regardless, the beach is just about always filled with sun-bleached aficionados of both sexes intent on serious surfing. Huts right on the sand serve refreshments sporadically, but Calle del Morro, Zicatela's main street, is lined with hotels and restaurants providing shade and sustenance on a more regular basis. There are often lifeguards on duty. ■ TIP→ **Even when the waters appear calm, the undertows and rip currents can be deadly. If you have any doubts about your prowess, settle for watching the surfers.**

WHERE TO EAT

There are many bars along Playa Zicatela and Playa Principal with beachside tables under palapas; most of those serving food offer a predictable menu of basic shrimp, octopus, and fish dishes. The best choice at these places is usually the whole fried fish, often *mojarra,* generally served with a side of rice and salad. These restaurants change with such frequency that it's best to just scout them out and pick the one that has the most local customers that day.

> **OFF THE BEATEN PATH**
>
> **Playa Agua Blanca** is about 30 minutes east of Puerto Escondido, at Km 172 of the road toward Puerto Angel. You'll see a sign for Agua Blanca pointing down a gravel road. At the end of this road is a pristine beach with soft white sand and a few rocks along the coastline. The only other people here will be locals, and you should join them underneath a palapa to eat fresh oysters. Or enjoy a full lunch at any of the shady *comedores* that dot the beach.

PLAYA ZICATELA

$–$$ MEXICAN ✕**Banana's.** Although this open-air restaurant looks touristy, and its surfer clientele might set off warning bells, the Mexican food is remarkably consistent. Add to that friendly service, and the unusually late opening hours—you can sit down for dinner at 11:45 PM—and you've got a winning formula. *Enfrijoladas,* a satisfying mix of black beans, tortilla, and cheese usually served for breakfast, are served all day. The *chiles rellenos,* stuffed with *picadillo* (ground beef), are undeniably delicious. ✉*Calle del Morro s/n* ☎*954/582–0005* ▭*MC, V.*

$–$$ SPANISH ✕**El Sorbo.** This beachfront restaurant is a bit more upscale than its competition, with its wooden furniture, flickering candlelight, and decent wine list. The focus is on seafood, with various preparations of fish and shrimp, but the Spanish-style paella is the best thing coming out of the kitchen. Try the *paella especiál,* with chicken, chorizo, mussels, shrimp, squid, and crab. Wash it all down with sangria. ✉*Calle del Morro s/n* ☎*954/588–5910* ▭*No credit cards.*

¢–$$ JAPANESE ✕**Sakura.** Sakura may no longer have the area's best sushi (that honor goes to K-Fe), but it still has a loyal following. Skip the complicated combination rolls and go straight for the simple raw-fish *nigiri.* The catch of the day might include delicate dorado along with very fresh tuna or red snapper. Complement your sushi with a delicious juice or *licuado*—the sugary mango version is especially good. If you need a bite between bar hops, there's a sidewalk stand that stays open late. ✉*Calle del Morro s/n, across from Playa Zicatela* ☎*No phone* ▭*No credit cards.*

¢–$ ★ CAFE ✕**El Cafecito.** Not much more than a pair of thatched palapas, this place doesn't look like much. In reality, it's the center of the town; everything you need to know is being passed around by word of mouth here. Oh, and then there's the food: grilled fish or burgers topped with bacon or avocado. The restaurant is best known for its whole-grain breads and fruit-filled pastries. There's another branch on La Rinconada. ✉*Calle del Morro s/n, across from Playa Zicatela* ☎*954/582–0516* ✉*Blvd. Benito Juárez s/n, La Rinconada* ▭*No credit cards.*

7

PLAYA PRINCIPAL & EL ADOQUÍN

$–$$ SEAFOOD **Los Crotos.** This seafood specialist is romantically set right in front of the lapping waves, and the whole fish (mostly red snapper) coming out of the kitchen is fresh and delicious. Throw in cold beer, and it's hard to go wrong. *Av. Pérez Gásga s/n 954/582–0025 AE, MC, V.*

$–$$ ITALIAN **La Galería.** Every inch of wall space at this open-air restaurant on the west end of the Adoquín is filled with paintings. And every inch of your small, square table will be covered by platters of homemade pasta, like tortellini, ravioli, and lasagna. Pizzas are also popular; try the one with eggplant, garlic, mushrooms, and basil. Though the service isn't great, the brick-and-stone floors and red tiles peeking through the rafters make for a pleasant environment. The restaurant features a traditional Mexican breakfast for $4. *Av. Pérez Gasga s/n, across from tourist booth 954/582–2039 Calle del Morro s/n No credit cards.*

¢–$ MEXICAN **Vitamina T.** This is the place where the locals enjoy quick, simple meals right along the main drag. Tables are open to the sidewalk, amidst the hubbub. You won't find frills, but you will find a great *sopa Azteca,* with delicious bits of tasty Oaxacan cheese; the whole fried fish is another good choice. *Av. Pérez Gasga No phone No credit cards.*

LA RINCONADA & BACOCHO

★ $ MEXICAN **La Torre.** This casually elegant place is popular with travelers in the know and locals who would rather keep it a secret. Its location at the far end of Boulevard Benito Juárez doesn't seem to deter anyone. Steaks are available anytime, but the *costillas de cerdo* (pork ribs) are on the menu only on Friday. On pleasant evenings there's no better place to sit than beside the fountain in the garden. *Blvd. Benito Juárez 427, La Rinconada 954/582–1119 No credit cards Closed Mon. No lunch.*

¢–$ ★ ASIAN **K-Fe.** Part of a quickly developing strip in La Rinconada, near Playa Carrizalillo, this bright-orange, minimalist café-restaurant is a transplant from Oaxaca City. Trendy lounge music plays as you peruse the pan-Asian menu that is complete with wonton soup and a number of fusion sushi rolls. The owner also offers Ayurvedic massage by appointment. *308 Amapolas 954/108–0432.*

WHERE TO STAY

PLAYA ZICATELA

$$–$$$ **Hotel Santa Fe.** An impressive archway leads you to the Santa Fe, a hotel that feels more like a small village. A cluster of colonial-style buildings in pastel shades is surrounded by well-tended gardens filled with brilliant red hibiscus. You can catch a glimpse of the surf from the balcony of your room or bungalow. The restaurant ($–$$), known for its vegetarian food, is a great spot to sip a beer and watch the sun set. **Pros:** Good restaurant, pretty pool, excellent location. **Cons:** Standard rooms are pricey, some areas need updating, staff not that helpful. *Calle del Morro s/n, at Blvd. Zicatela, 954/582–0170 or 888/649–6407 www.hotelsantafe.com.mx 59 rooms, 2 suites, 8 bungalows In-room: Kitchen (some), Wi-Fi (some). In-hotel: Res-*

taurant, room service, bar, pool, laundry service, parking (no fee), no-smoking rooms, public Internet, public Wi-Fi ☐*AE, MC, V.*

$–$$ **Arco Iris.** This three-story hotel has something you'll find at few other hotels on Playa Zicatela: private verandas hung with hammocks (available for a small additional fee). The laid-back vibe and easy beach access make up for shortcomings such as the slightly worn furnishings and dated exterior. There's also a large swimming pool, a movie room, and a second-floor restaurant that serves many vegetarian dishes. **Pros:** Nice views, good restaurant, friendly atmosphere. **Cons:** Needs updating, noise from neighboring bars. ☒*Calle del Morro s/n, across from Playa Zicatela,* ☎ *954/582–0432 or 954/582–1494* ⊕*www.hotelarcoiris.com.mx* *32 rooms, 4 suites* *In-room: No a/c, no phone, no TV (some). In-hotel: Restaurant, bar, pools, beachfront, laundry service, public Internet, parking (no fee)* ☐*MC, V.*

$–$$ **Tabachín.** Well-stocked kitchenettes, shelves filled with books, and an assortment of clocks, vases, and other gewgaws make the studios here feel homey. Given the location a block from Playa Zicatela, the spaciousness and comfort of the rooms, and a breakfast from the vegetarian restaurant featuring an astounding array of choices, the room rates are quite low. The English-speaking staff is helpful in aiding guests with travel arrangements. **Pros:** Some rooms have great views, delicious breakfasts, friendly staff. **Cons:** Not right on the beach, no pool. ☒*Calle de Morro s/n, Playa Zicatela,* ☎*954/582–1179* ⊕*www.tabachin.com.mx* *6 apartments* *In-room: Kitchen, safe (some), Wi-Fi. In-hotel: Restaurant, public Wi-Fi, laundry service* ☐*MC, V* *BP.*

$–$$ **Villa Belmar.** The Villa Belmar's array of arches, domes, and cupolas—done in Mediterranean white and blue—give it the appearance of a crazy and secluded castle. The one-bedroom apartments and comfortable double rooms attract a mix of people, although the place has a lonely feel, often with no guests in sight. Many accommodations have balconies from which to admire Playa Zicatela. There you'll find the restaurant and beach club offering an array of shows; it's still a bit of a walk to Calle del Morro. You can rent by the day in high season and by the week or the month at other times. **Pros:** Rooftop pool with views, away from busy Calle Morro. **Cons:** Not right on the beach, rooms are nothing fancy. ☒*Calle Belmar s/n, Playa Zicatela,* ☎*954/582–0244 or 866/751–1440* ⊕*www.villabelmar.com* *32 rooms, 6 suites* *In-room: Refrigerator (some), Wi-Fi. In-hotel: Restaurant, pool, parking (no fee), public Wi-Fi, some pets allowed* ☐*MC, V.*

PLAYA PRINCIPAL & EL ADOQUÍN

$ **Villa Roca Suites.** The only downside here appears to be the absence of a pool. But because the boutique hotel—which looks a little like a sand castle—is right on the beach, you can have your toes in the water in no time. A bright color scheme and minimalist decorating give rooms a spacious tropical feel. Two rooms have two large shaded patios overlooking the beach. Rooms on the street side tend to be noisy. **Pros:** Close to beaches, restaurants and shops, views of Playa Principal. **Cons:** No pool, in a less-than-attractive area. ☒*Av. Pérez Gasga 602,*

7

El Adoquín, ☎*954/582–3525* 🌐*www.prodigyweb.net.mx/villaroca* *6 suites* *In-hotel: Beachfront, parking (no fee)* ▭*MC, V.*

LA RINCONADA & BACOCHO

$$–$$$ **La Hacienda.** These sparkling, French-country–style accommodations, owned by a Parisian interior designer, are pristine and comfortable. Each one- or two-story apartment has fresh flowers, a sprinkling of carefully chosen antiques, and blue-and-white Mexican tiles. The kitchenettes are sizable, and the patio restaurant serves one or two dishes for dinner daily during high season (December–March and Easter) and with advance notice at other times. The hotel is a five-minute walk from Playa Carrizalillo. **Pros:** Beautiful decor, very close to beach. **Cons:** Need car to get around, maximum of three people in a room. ✉*Calle Atunes 15, La Rinconada,* ☎*954/582–0279* 🌐*www.suiteslahacienda.com* *9 apartments* *In-room: Kitchen, Wi-Fi. In-hotel: Restaurant, pool, laundry service* ▭*MC, V.*

★ $$–$$$ **Villas Carrizalillo.** Perfect for those in search of a little solitude, these private, tile-roof villas cling to a cliff above the gorgeous beach for which they were named; you descend to the idyllic beach via a steep staircase. The villas range in size from a small studio to a three-bedroom abode with a private yard. A favorite, called the Puebla, has two bay-view balconies. The road out to the secluded property is dark; this is not the spot for those who want to go into town at night, although the strip of establishments at nearby La Rinconada is burgeoning. **Pros:** Good value, nicely decorated rooms, direct access to one of the area's best beaches. **Cons:** Need a car to get around, no a/c in some rooms. ✉*Av. Carrizalillo 125, Carrizalillo,* ☎📠*954/582–1735* 🌐*www.villascarrizalillo.com* *12 apartments* *In-room: No a/c (some), no phone, kitchen, no TV, Wi-Fi. In-hotel: Restaurant, bar, pool, beachfront, water sports, bicycles, public Wi-Fi, laundry service, parking (no fee)* ▭*MC, V.*

$$ **Hotel Aldea del Bazar.** Like a mirage, this sparkling white hotel sits high on a bluff overlooking the calm waters of Playa Bacocho. The rooms overlook the surf or the manicured lawns. All have tasteful little sitting areas with low couches covered in brightly colored pillows. The Maya temazcal eucalyptus sauna will help you relax before heading to dinner at the restaurant, which is done up like a storybook Moorish palace. It's a bit bizarre, but it's fun, too. **Pros:** Attractive rooms, relaxing sauna, car-rental service. **Cons:** Need a car to get around, design doesn't evoke Mexico. ✉*Blvd. Benito Juárez 7, Fracc. Bacocho,* ☎📠*954/582–0508, 01800/012–3094 toll-free in Mexico* 🌐*www.aldeadelbazar.com* *47 rooms* *In-hotel: Restaurant, room service, bar, pool, spa, laundry service, beachfront, parking (no fee), no elevator* ▭*AE, MC, V.*

NIGHTLIFE

You won't have trouble finding the party in Puerto Escondido. The best part about the whole scene is how low-key it is. Have drinks in the restaurants lining the Adoquín or head to Playa Zicatela and find a beach bar overlooking the ocean.

BARS

Red is the color theme at **Bar Fly** (✉*Calle del Morro s/n* 🌐*www.barfly.com.mx*); grab a seat on a red couch, surrounded by red walls, and relax. It's upstairs from Banana's.

For a lively crowd, head to **Cabo Blanco** (✉*Calle del Morro s/n* ☎*No phone*), where it's always spring break. The young people never seem to stop dancing.

Set under a dramatic dome, **Casa Babylon** (✉*Calle del Morro s/n* ☎*No phone*) is certainly the most beautiful bar near Playa Zicatela. While you nurse your beer, you can challenge friends to a game of Scrabble or Monopoly. It's near Hotel Arco Iris.

La Embajada (✉*Calle del Morro s/n* ☎*No phone*) aptly calls itself "international laid-back territory." Comfortable outdoor seating and chill lounge music set the scene for a beer or a large frozen drink.

For spirited live entertainment, stop by **Son y La Rumba** (✉*Calle del Morro s/n* ☎*954/582–3709*). Owner Mayka sings and plays guitar almost every night, but you never know who will drop in to jam with her—maybe a well-known classical violinist or a flamenco guitarist.

Wipe Out (✉*Av. Pérez Gasga* ☎*954/582–2302*) is a multilevel dance club that goes until the wee hours of the morning.

FILM

On Zicatela Beach, **P.J.'s CineMar** (✉*Calle del Morro s/n, next to La Galería restaurant* ☎*954/582–2288*) shows movies every evening at 5, 7, and 9 PM. Stop by earlier in the day to see what's showing. Besides the basic popcorn, soda, and candy, the concession also sells beer and freshly ground hot chocolate.

SHOPPING

The town's sprawling market, **Mercado Benito Juárez,** is a long walk (but a short cab ride) from the beaches. It's worth checking out, especially on the market days, which are Wednesday and Saturday. Look for black pottery and finely woven textiles.

SPORTS & THE OUTDOORS

Puerto Escondido's pretty coves aren't as deserted as they seem. Fishermen lead angling expeditions as well as sightseeing trips for spotting turtles and dolphins, and the area's not bad for diving and snorkeling.

DIVING & SNORKELING

Puerto Dive Center (✉*El Adoquín and Andador Libertad, at Hotel Mayflower* ☎*954/102–1794* 🌐*www.scuba-diving-mexico.com*) offers diving certification, rentals, and tours.

FISHING

The most common catches off Puerto Escondido are swordfish, marlin, tuna, and dorado. Fiestas de Noviembre, when anglers compete for prizes, is held the entire month of November. Prices for fishing tours run around $35 to $40 an hour, with a minimum of three hours (four people maximum). **TIP→ Many local fishermen expect to keep your**

catch as partial payment for their services, so discuss this with the captain ahead of time. Omar's Sportfishing (✉*Playa Puerto Angelito* ☎*954/559–4406*) will take you out on a four-hour tour of the best fishing spots for about $160 for up to four people.

SURFING

Playa Zicatela is the best place to hang ten in Puerto Escondido. ■TIP→ **If you want to take surfing lessons, one of your best sources of information is the lifeguard at the beach.** You can buy beachwear at **Mexpipe** (✉*Calle del Morro s/n, across from Playa Zicatela* ☎*954/582–2288*). The staff is also happy to give lessons for $30 per hour. Canadian Paul Yacht sells and rents surfboards for $14 a day at **P.J.'s** (✉*Calle del Morro s/n, at Bajada Las Brisas* ☎*954/582–0759*).

ZIPOLITE

Fodor'sChoice ★ *60 km (37 mi) east of Puerto Escondido, 3 km (2 mi) west of Puerto Angel.*

Zipolite-lovers like to brag that this beach is what Puerto Escondido was 20 years ago, but that mantra doesn't even do justice to Zipolite's singular charm. No longer dismissed as just the home of a nudist beach, the town now boasts delicious international food and creative cocktails served in some of Mexico's most beautiful beachfront settings. When you're not sipping a cocktail or soaking up the sun, you can choose from activities such as yoga or fishing on this idyllic stretch of sand just west of Puerto Angel.

The area has displayed a remarkable resistance to any kind of high-rise development, or even any establishments that offer air-conditioning or hot water. Don't expect to use a credit card anywhere, and the nearest ATM is 20 minutes away in Pochutla. Perhaps these are the reasons for the alluring sense of isolation.

GETTING HERE & AROUND

From Puerto Escondido, Zipolite is easily reached via Highway 200. From Puerto Angel, hail a taxi for the 10-minute journey.

EXPLORING

The **Centro Mexicano de la Tortuga** is at Playa Mazunte, west of Zipolite. The local economy was based on catching the *golfina* (olive ridley) turtle until the government put a ban on turtle hunting in 1990. Poachers aside, Mazunte is now devoted to protecting the species. The beach's name derives from the Nahuatl word *Maxonteita*, which means "please come and spawn" and, indeed, four of the world's eight species of marine turtles come to lay their eggs on Oaxaca's shores. A dozen aquariums are filled with the turtles that flourish here. ✉*Playa Mazunte* ☎*958/584 –3376* 🌐*centromexicanodelatortuga.org* 🎫*$2* ⏲*Mon.–Sat. 10–4:30, Sun. 10–2:30.*

BEACHES

■TIP→ **Be careful at the beaches here. The undertow is extremely strong and rip currents are unpredictable.**

★ **Playa Mazunte.** About 8 km (5 mi) west of Zipolite, Mazunte is a stunning stretch of soft sand with a few simple seafood restaurants and low-key accommodations (though there are fewer than at Zipolite). The surf is rougher here than at Playa San Agustanillo, and attracts bodyboarders.

Playa San Agustanillo. This pretty stretch of sand between Zipolite and Playa Mazunte is backed by exuberant vegetation and elegant coconut palms. It's somewhat safe for swimming, although the current is strong. As on neighboring beaches, vendors roam the sand selling cool drinks and grilled fish, and restaurants and rustic accommodations at the back of the beach offer shade from the strong sun.

WHERE TO EAT & STAY

$$–$$$ ★ ITALIAN ✕ **Posada México.** The most romantic atmosphere of any in Zipolite—and arguably on the whole Oaxaca coast—can be found at this beachside extravaganza of warm candles, lounge furniture, and palapas. The Italian chefs do justice to their country's cuisine—a true rarity in Mexico. Most remarkably authentic are the skillfully seared brick-oven pizzas and the addictive bread that comes out of the same oven. ✉ *Colonía Roca Blanca* ☎ *958/584–3194* 🌐 *www.posadamexico.com* 💳 *No credit cards.*

$–$$ MEXICAN ✕ **Pacha Mama.** This candlelit restaurant is set romantically right on the beach. Despite this, you should avoid the seafood main courses, but opt instead for tuna ceviche, which is deliciously fresh and limey. The grilled meats are good, too. Try one of the bartender's legendary herb-infused liquors. ✉ *Playa Zipolite* ☎ *No phone* 💳 *No credit cards.*

¢ 🏨 **Solstice.** Yoga instructor Bridgette Longueville's escapist bungalows, a few steps inland from the beach, are interestingly designed: a ladder from the sleeping area leads to a second-floor loft with hammocks and (in three out of four *cabañas*) water views. Yoga classes, open to the general public, are offered most mornings at 9:30. Bathing facilities consist only of private cold-water washbasins, but such is the rustic charm of Zipolite. **Pros:** Great location, on-site yoga classes. **Cons:** Very rustic accommodations, few amenities. ✉ *Calle del Amor 94* ☎ *No phone* 🌐 *www.solstice-mexico.com* *4 bungalows* *In-room: No a/c, no phone, no TV, safe. In-hotel: Laundry service.* 💳 *No credit cards.*

PUERTO ANGEL

81 km (50 mi) southeast of Puerto Escondido, 48 km (30 mi) west of Huatulco.

The state's leading seaport 100 years ago, Puerto Angel is today simply a tiny town on a small, somewhat buggy bay. The majority of the hotels are away from the beach, either tucked into a canyon or perched above the bay. The town is a good base for visiting smaller communities like Mazunte. It has a few more services, though not many. The beaches in town are unspectacular; there are very pretty beaches in nearby coves, and it's easy to hire water taxis to explore them.

GETTING HERE & AROUND

Puerto Angel is easily reached by car from Huatulco via Highway 200. Frequent, inexpensive second-class buses connect Puerto Escondido, Puerto Angel, and Huatulco, making a pit stop at the inland town of Pochutla. Taxis in Pochutla make the 20-minute ride to Puerto Angel. Some bus and van service from Oaxaca City takes Highway 175 directly to Pochutla, but this trip is far less comfortable than taking first-class service on longer routes to Puerto Escondido or Huatulco.

BEACHES

Playa La Boquilla. About 2 km (1½ mi) east of Puerto Angel, 400-foot-long La Boquilla can be reached by a dirt road from Highway 200 (recommended only if you have a rugged vehicle). It is more easily accessed by boat from Puerto Angel. Shallow and clear water make this a good spot for snorkeling as well as swimming. There are few services on this beach, though there's a restaurant that's open during high season.

Playa Panteón. The most popular swimming and sunning beach in Puerto Angel proper, this 660-foot-long, brown-sand beach has calm, waveless water, which makes it great for swimmers and children. A walkway past the oceanfront *panteón* (cemetery) links it with Playa Principal, Puerto Angel's main beach. Ask about boat services at the informal restaurants along the beach.

Playa Principal. This is Puerto Angel's main beach, closest to the town. It's busy, starting in the morning when fishing boats arrive with the day's catch. There are restaurants running along the beach.

WHERE TO EAT & STAY

$ SEAFOOD **Rincón del Mar.** A few steps from the soft sands of Playa del Panteón, this restaurant is the envy of all the others. From a table in the open-air dining room you can watch as the fishermen return with the catch of the day. Choose your fish (the tuna and pompano are good) and how you want it prepared. Or try the *pescado a la cazuela,* a rich seafood stew. *Playa del Panteón No phone No credit cards.*

$–$$ **Bahía de la Luna.** This collection of thatch-roof bungalows is the only accommodation on beautiful La Boquilla beach, a water-taxi ride away from Puerto Angel. Rooms are very simple, though a tad more chic than the beach huts of Mazunte or Zipolite, with nightstands and bedposts made from found wood. Note that some units are on the hillside, and paths are steep. There's nothing to do here but lie on the beach or snorkel, but the hotel can arrange tours to natural areas and nearby beaches and towns. **Pros:** On a pretty beach with abundant marine life, secluded and quiet location. **Cons:** Need to take expensive water-taxi ride to and from Puerto Angel, no other facilities on beach, basic accommodations (no hot water and limited electricity), kind of pricey in high season. *Playa la Boquilla 958/589–5020 www.bahiadelaluna.com 11 bungalows In-room: No a/c, no phone, no TV. In-hotel: Restaurant No credit cards.*

¢ **Posada Cañón Devata.** The simple bungalows at this eco-friendly hideaway are scattered around a wooded canyon. There are even simpler rooms on several floors of the rambling main house. There's no hot water, but there are nice touches like lamps carved to resemble jaguars and other beasts. Massages and yoga classes are offered—we recommend yoga on a terrace overlooking the ocean. The thatched-roof restaurant is a find for vegetarians, who sometimes hike over from other hotels. **Pros:** Good value, great yoga classes, nice views of bay. **Cons:** Some steep steps to climb, five-minute walk to beach. ✉*Pedro Sainz de Baranza s/n, off Blvd. Virgilio Uribe,* ☎*958/584–3137* 🌐*www.posadapacifico.com* *16 rooms, 6 bungalows* *In-room: No a/c, no phone, no TV. In-hotel: Restaurant, bar* *AE, MC, V.*

¢ **La Buena Vista.** The rooms on the top level of this hillside hotel have great views of the bay, as well as the best breezes. Some have balconies, others have terraces hung with colorful hammocks. None have hot water or much of anything that could be called an amenity; all beds have mosquito netting. The third-floor restaurant has one of the most dependable kitchens in town, although the service lags when there's a crowd. Most rooms are accessed by climbing lots of stairs. **Pros:** Nice views, attractive rooms, pretty pool area. **Cons:** Steep stairs, away from beach. ✉*Calle la Buena Compañía,* ☎*958/584–3104* 🌐*www.labuenavista.com* *23 rooms* *In-room: No a/c, no phone, no TV. In-hotel: Restaurant, pool* *No credit cards.*

HUATULCO

277 km (172 mi) south of Oaxaca City, 111 km (69 mi) east of Puerto Escondido, 48 km (30 mi) east of Puerto Angel.

Development in the beautiful Bahías de Huatulco (Bays of Huatulco) continues to march forward. Four of the nine bays have been developed, but only Bahía Tangolunda, with its golf course and luxury hotels, has the look of a resort.

If you have a car, you can drive to one of several undeveloped bays and play Robinson Crusoe to your heart's content. Boat tours are a good way to explore. Standard four- to eight-hour trips—depending on how many bays you visit—might include a lunch of freshly caught fish. Fishing, diving, and snorkeling tours visit the beaches and reefs.

GETTING HERE & AROUND

Aeropuerto Bahias de Huatulco is 16 km (10 mi) from Bahía Tangolunda. Some U.S. carriers have direct service and there are plenty of domestic connections (though many go through Mexico City). By car from Oaxaca City, take up Carretera 190 to Salina Cruz, where you pick up Carretera 200 to Huatulco. The trip takes 7 to 8 hours. First-class buses follow the same route and depart Oaxaca City daily. Driving to Puerto Escondido takes about two hours. Taxis are plentiful, especially in La Crucecita, and start at $3 from the center of town to the beaches. Many major car-rental agencies have kiosks at the airport, though renting a car isn't necessary unless you want to explore beaches outside of town. Scooter rental is a popular alternative and there are vendors near the large resorts.

ESSENTIALS

Medical Assistance **Central Médica Huatulco** (*CMH, Av. Flamboyan 205 958/587–0104*). **Police** (*958/587–1180*). **Red Cross** (*958/587–1188*).

Rental Cars **Plaza Huatulco Rent** (*Blvd. Benito Juárez s/n, at Hotel Plaza Huatulco, Bahía Tangolunda 958/581–0371*).

Visitor & Tour Info **Asociación de Hoteles** (*Blvd. Benito Juárez 8, Hotel Crown Pacific, Bahía Tangolunda 958/581–0486, 866/416–0555, 01800/224–4279 toll-free in Mexico www.hoteleshuatulco.com.mx*). **Huatulco Tourism Office** (*Blvd. Benito Juárez s/n, Bahía Tangolunda 958/581–0176 or 958/581–0177*).

EXPLORING

La Crucecita, off Carretera 200, is the place in Huatulco that most closely resembles a real Mexican town. Its central plaza has a church whose interior is covered with naive frescoes; on the ceiling is a fresco of what locals claim is the largest Madonna in the world. You can dine, hang out at a bar or sidewalk café, and browse in boutiques. You'll also find a bank, bus station, and Internet cafés here.

Santa Cruz, on the bay of the same name, was the center of a 30-family fishing community until development forced everyone to move elsewhere. Today the bay is a nice spot for swimming and snorkeling, although Jet Skis make a lot of noise on busy weekends and holidays. You can arrange boat tours and fishing trips at the marina. Dine on the beach, mingle with the locals in the central zócalo, or sip a cool drink or cappuccino in Café Huatulco, right in the middle of the plaza where the traditional kiosk should be.

If you're looking for the best fishing and water sports in the area, head to **Playa Entrega,** to the west of Bahía Santa Cruz, where dozens of fishermen aren't shy about offering their services from the moment you set foot in the sand. It's a great place to go out on a fishing boat in the early morning (negotiate a price with one of the captains on the beach); when you come back to Playa Entrega, have one of the little seafood restaurants on the beach, such as Restaurant Arrecife, cook up your catch. Lobster fishing is another option, as are snorkeling and kayaking.

For a day on the beach, head to **Bahía Chahué.** The beach parking lot has a lookout point, and the marina has 88 slips, though other services aren't yet in place. You'll find a swimming pool, changing rooms, a restaurant, and shaded lounge chairs at the public beach

TAKE A TOUR

Bahías Plus (*Calle Carrizal 704, La Crucecita 958/587–0932 www.bahiasplus.com*) has branches in many of the hotels in Huatulco. The company leads tours to Puerto Angel ($19) and to coffee plantations ($36). It is best and offers signature bay cruises ($18). **Paraíso Huatulco** (*Calle Ceiba 202, La Crucecita 958/587–2878 www.paraisohuatulco.com Barceló Hotel, Blvd. Benito Juárez, Bahía Tangolunda 958/581–0051*) offers daylong bay cruises ($20), four-wheeler tours ($45), coffee plantation tours ($40), and overnight tours to Oaxaca City by bus or air ($550). Prices are slightly higher at the Barceló branch.

club. Though several hotels, shops, and restaurants (serving mostly lunch and dinner) are near the main road, Boulevard Benito Juárez, the area is still being developed. Internet access isn't yet available anywhere. The beach itself has a negative reputation: people reportedly drown here more than conditions seem to warrant. **Xquenda Spa** (☒*Blvd. Bugambilia s/n, Bahía Chahué* ☎*958/583–4448*) has a lap pool, tennis court, and gym, and offers massages, facials, and some spa treatments.

The Huatulco of the future is most evident at **Bahía Tangolunda,** where the poshest hotels are in full swing and the sea—in high season—is abob with sightseeing *lanchas* (small motorboats), kayaks, and sailboats. The site was chosen by developers because of its five beautiful beaches. Although there's a small complex with shops and restaurants across from the entrance to the Barceló hotel on Boulevard Benito Juárez, most of the shopping and dining is found in the towns of Santa Cruz and La Crucecita, each about 10 minutes from the hotels by taxi or bus.

WHERE TO EAT

LA CRUCECITA & BAHÍA SANTA CRUZ

★ $$–$$$ SEAFOOD ✕ **Doña Celia.** At this waterfront restaurant, you can sit at a table right on the beach and enjoy the house specialty: lobster burritos. Chef-owner Celia Enriquez Gutiérrez's ceviche is absolutely divine. The service is friendly and informal—this place is more popular with locals than tourists, and as such, has a more authentic feel than some of the competition in the area. ☒*Bahía Santa Cruz* ☎*958/587–0128* ▭*MC, V.*

$–$$ MEXICAN ✕ **Onix.** A second-story restaurant that overlooks the activity of La Crucecita's zócalo, Onix is emblematic of the high-concept development that has sprung up around Huatulco to complement its luxury resorts. Options on the ambitious menu include filet mignon with chipotle on a fried tortilla or tostadas with smoked oysters, chipotle, and guacamole. The wine selection is better than average. ☒*Avendia Bugambilia 603, at corner of Calle Guamuchil, La Crucecita* ☎*958/587–0520* ▭*MC, V.*

$–$$ MEXICAN ✕ **Sabor de Oaxaca.** This narrow, open-fronted but under-ventilated restaurant across from the main plaza is popular with Mexican tourists. Learn the ABCs of Oaxacan cooking by trying one of the massive sampler plates (enough for two or three people). You can go as far as cactus soup or crunchy grasshoppers (in season). The pork *enmolada* (in a chile sauce) is a showstopper, gently spicy and deeply marinated. It's open until 11 PM, so this is a good place for a late-night snack. ☒*Calle Guamuchil 206, La Crucecita* ☎*958/587–0060* ▭*AE, MC, V.*

$ MEXICAN ✕ **Los Portales.** One of the more authentic taquerías in a resort town catering to tourists, Los Portales serves up traditional tacos as well as some more interesting options. Tacos *al pastor* are tasty, especially when accompanied by one of the tropical drinks from the menu. This is also one of the few sit-down restaurants to serve dinner after 10 PM. ☒*Avenida Bugambilia, at corner of Calle Guamuchil, La Crucecita* ☎*958/587–0070* 🌐*www.losportaleshuatulco.com* ▭*MC, V.*

BAHÍA TANGOLUNDA

$$$–$$$$ MEXICAN
Azul Profundo. Sky-high prices are justified by the sky of stars above your head as you dine at this romantic bay-side restaurant. Hanging lanterns, a glowing blue pool, and a sleek lounge complete the scene. The menu is ambitious and international, highlighting lobster, shrimp, and fish tartare. Reservations are essential, but you can also come just for a cocktail without a reservation. *Camino Real Zaashila, Calle Benito Juárez 5 958/581–0460 Reservations essential AE, DC, MC, V.*

$–$$$ MEXICAN
Don Porfirio. You can grab a table in the dining room or out on the covered patio near the busy road. There's a good variety of Mexican dishes, such as grasshoppers fried with chile and garlic, as well as less challenging dishes such as tequila-marinated kebabs. The show is as important as the food here: waiters often dress in costumes and are encouraged to joke and interact with diners. Steaks and shrimp are cooked on the outdoor grill, and several dishes arrive flaming at your table. Because it's popular with groups, it can be noisy, but it's almost always fun. *Calle Benito Juárez s/n, Zona Hotelera Tangolunda, across from Hotel Gala 958/581–0001 AE, MC, V.*

WHERE TO STAY

$ Fodor's Choice ★
Misión de los Arcos. Everything about this hotel is luxurious—except for the rates. Each room of this Mediterannean-style hotel is different, but all have adobe-style rounded walls, a soothing beige-on-bone color scheme, and a minimalist approach to decor. The honeymoon suite has a huge garden patio filled with plants, a wrought-iron table and chairs, and a fountain. The youthful owner works out with half the town in the popular on-site gym. He and his wife cater to their guests, many of them Mexican businesspeople, in a way that virtually guarantees return business. The restaurant is the toast of the town. **Pros:** Great value, air-conditioned rooms, friendly staff. **Cons:** Away from the beaches, rooms are a little sparse, some bathrooms are small. *Calle Gardenia 902, La Crucecita, 958/587–0165 www.misiondelosarcos.com 14 rooms In-room: No phone, no TV, Wi-Fi. In-hotel: Restaurant, pool, gym, laundry service, no elevator AE, MC, V.*

BAHÍA TANGOLUNDA

$$$$
Gala. The emphasis at this resort is on fun; there's a kids' club to entertain the youngsters while the grown-ups play tennis or relax by the pool. The rate includes most outdoor activities—a good deal if you want to do more than just work on your tan. The light-filled guest rooms have plenty of space in which to spread out. During the low season, Gala allows nonguests to spend the day or evening on the property—with unlimited food, drink, and activities—for a per-person rate of $80 all day. **Pros:** Nice beachfront, excellent service, good for families. **Cons:** Not as tranquil as other spots, rooms are nothing special, a bit pricey. *Blvd. Benito Juárez 4, 958/583–0400, 01800/000–4252 toll-free in Mexico www.galaresorts.com 290 rooms, 12 suites In-room: Safe. In-hotel: 4 restaurants, room service, bars, tennis courts, pools, gym, beachfront, children's programs (ages 2–15) AE, MC, V AI.*

$$$$ ★ **Quinta Real.** This hilltop resort, with its trademark double-dome design, takes luxury to almost excessive heights. Each suite has white leather furniture, stained concrete floors, exquisite handwoven tapestries, a hot tub, and a terrace with an ocean view. Eight corner suites have plunge pools, and a few are equipped with telescopes for dolphin- and stargazing. Golf carts take you to and from the beach, which is a long walk from the hotel. **Pros:** Elegant atmosphere, great views, pretty pool area. **Cons:** Very expensive, not directly on beach. ✉*Blvd. Benito Juárez 2,* ☎*958/581–0428, 01800/500–4000 toll-free in Mexico, 866/621–9288* 🌐*www.quintareal.com* *28 suites* *In-room: Safe. In-hotel: 2 restaurants, bars, tennis court, pools, laundry service, parking (fee), no-smoking rooms* *AE, MC, V* *CP.*

$$$ **Barceló.** You'll have bay views from the balcony of any room in this resort, which spans the shore of beautiful Bahía Tangolunda. Red-tile roofs on the low-slung buildings add a touch of Mediterranean elegance. This is an all-inclusive resort, so you'll have free use of most water-sports equipment; dive masters are on hand with all the necessary equipment, for an extra charge. With an excellent beachfront location near the golf course, many activities for kids and adults, and large meeting rooms, this hotel is attractive for both families and corporate events; you'll find you have no reason to leave. At night candles flicker in the glamorous Casa Real restaurant ($–$$). The food is northern Italian; reservations are essential. **Pros:** Great location, lots of amenities, quiet and laid-back. **Cons:** Property is a bit dated, staff can be hard to find. ✉*Blvd. Benito Juárez,* ☎*958/581–0055* 🌐*www.barcelohuatulco.com* *346 rooms, 5 suites* *In-room: Safe, DVD (some), Wi-Fi (some). In-hotel: 4 restaurants, room service, bars, tennis courts, pools, gym, beachfront, diving, water sports, children's programs (ages 5–12), laundry service, parking (no fee), no-smoking rooms* *AE, MC, V* *AI.*

$$$ **Las Brisas.** Only the spacious, minimalist suites of this sprawling complex have balconies, but almost all of the rooms have wonderful views of the ocean. Divided into four different areas that are romantically named for the mountains, stars, clouds, and sea, the rooms are far from the hustle and bustle of the main building. The complex is the size of a small village, and you get around in a fleet of hotel-operated trams. And don't miss the fresh watermelon juice at any one of the several restaurants. **Pros:** Nice beach, good snorkeling, great staff. **Cons:** Property is very spread out, all-white decor is boring, few rooms have balconies. ✉*Blvd. Benito Juárez s/n,* ☎*958/583–0200, 888/559–4329 in U.S. and Canada* 🌐*www.brisas.com.mx* *337 rooms, 149 suites* *In-room: Safe, dial-up. In-hotel: 6 restaurants, room service, bars, public Wi-Fi, tennis courts, pools, gym, spa, laundry service, beachfront, water sports, parking (no fee), no-smoking rooms* *AE, MC, V.*

$$$ ★ **Camino Real Zaashila.** The brilliant blue free-form pool with built-in lounge chairs around its rim creates an irresistible centerpiece for this gleaming white resort. Rooms are an adept mix of modern amenities and more rustic-looking elements like hand-painted bathroom shelves and armoires. Waterfalls punctuate the property's 27 acres, and a dreamy nature walk runs from one end of it to the other. The

7

elegant yet casual Chez Binni ($$–$$$) looks out past the pool to the ocean. Even closer to the water is Azul Profundo, which sits right on the beach. **Pros:** Beautiful beach, pretty pool area, lush grounds. **Cons:** Fewer amenities than bigger resorts, some rooms are noisy, attracts tour groups. ✉ *Blvd. Benito Juárez Lote 5,* ☎ *958/581–0460, 01800/901–2300 toll-free in Mexico, 800/722–6466 in U.S. and Canada* 🌐 *www.caminoreal.com/zaashila* *120 rooms, 28 suites* *In-room: Safe. In-hotel: 3 restaurants, room service, bars, tennis court, pools, beachfront, concierge, parking (no fee), no-smoking rooms* *AE, DC, MC, V* *CP.*

NIGHTLIFE

One of the most intimate and personable bars in the area is also the oldest. **La Crema** (✉ *Av. Carrizal 503, La Crucecita* ☎ *958/587–0702 or 958/587–2182*) offers well-mixed cocktails such as the venerable mai tai. A mix of canned tunes provides the beat: rock, lounge music, ranchera, and other Mexican music. There's dancing after 10 PM.

Noches Oaxaqueños (✉ *Zona Hotelera Tangolunda, across from Hotel Gala* ☎ *958/581–0001*) has a folkloric show with music and dances from Oaxaca and other Mexican states.

Styled after a Miami club, **La Papaya** (✉ *Bahía Chahué* ☎ *958/583–4911*) is an enormous venue open to the stars. Families and singles alike eat, drink, and dance while bathing-suit-clad women swim in giant aquariums up front.

SHOPPING

La Crucecita's **Mercado Municipal** (*[Municipal Market]* ✉ *Calle Guanacaste s/n, between Bugambilia and Carrizal, La Crucecita* ☎ *No phone*) is a fun place to shop for postcards, leather sandals, and souvenirs amid mountains of fresh produce.

Mantelería Escobar (✉ *Av. Cocotillo 217, La Crucecita* ☎ *958/587–0532*) is a family-run workshop where you can purchase bedspreads, curtains, tablecloths, and place mats. Custom items can usually be produced in two to seven days, so plan ahead.

The **Museo de Artesanías Oaxaqueñas** (✉ *Calle Flamboyan 216, La Crucecita* ☎ *958/587–1513*) is really a store, not a museum, where you can find handicrafts produced throughout the state: woven tablecloths, chunky pottery, and colorful rugs. Artisans are occasionally on hand for demonstrations.

SPORTS & THE OUTDOORS

FISHING

Arrange sportfishing trips with the **Sociedad Cooperativa Tangolunda** (✉ *Santa Cruz Marina* ☎ *958/587–0081*), the boat-owners' cooperative at the marina on Santa Cruz Bay. These people are the original inhabitants of this area (they were forceably relocated when the resort was built), so they know the waters well. Prices are more competitive than those of the larger agencies. Fishing costs about $35 an hour (three-hour minimum with a maximum of four people). The group also offers bay tours for about $20 per person. It's also easy to get a fishing expedition going at Playa Entrega.

GOLF

Bahía Tangolunda's challenging 18-hole golf course, the **Campo de Golf Tangolunda** (✉*Blvd. Benito Juárez and Blvd. Tangolunda, Bahía Tangolunda* ☎☎*958/581–0037*), was designed by noted Mexican landscape architect Mario Schjetnan. The greens fees are $73 for 18 holes; carts rent for $34.

SCUBA DIVING

Eagle rays, green moray eels, and, in winter, gray whales are frequently spotted in 13 different dive sites near Huatulco. The average price for area dives is $45 for a one-tank dive, $75 for two tanks. The PADI-certified dive masters at **Hurricane Divers** (✉*Bahía Santa Cruz* ☎*958/587–1107* 🌐*www.hurricanedivers.com*) are well regarded and offer services including equipment repair, diving certification, and safety courses. Night dives and multiple-day packages are also available, as well as snorkeling trips; note that they are closed on Sunday.

Chiapas & Tabasco

Temple of the Assumption, Cupilco, Tabasco

WORD OF MOUTH

"San Cristóbal de las Casas is beautiful but very small, I'd even think about trading in one day and adding it to Tuxtla Gutierrez since the Canon de Sumidero can take up to one full day, especially if you end up going to the park in the middle of the canon (kayaking there is cheap and no feeling will replicate kayaking in the middle of a 400 story canon!)"

–tanita12

www.fodors.com/forums

WELCOME TO CHIAPAS & TABASCO

TOP REASONS TO GO

★ **Taking in mist-covered ruins:** Much of the enormous complex of Palenque has yet to be excavated, so you can see how thoroughly the jungle claimed them.

★ **A pleasant stay in a little-visited colonial town:** Lovely colonial architecture, the excellent Museo Na Bolom, and nearby San Juan Chamula make San Cristóbal de las Casas an important stop.

★ **A Heart of Darkness-like boat trip:** Go by water up the Río Usumacinta to see the Maya city of Yaxchilán surrounded by magnificent 100-year-old ceiba trees.

★ **The chance to see a breathtaking canyon:** Cliffs rise to 1,067 km (3,500 feet) at their highest point in the Cañón del Sumidero.

★ **Convening with history:** Wander through the trees around massive stone heads left behind by the Olmecs at the Parque-Museo La Venta.

1 Villahermosa & Tabasco. Tabasco has lakes, lagoons, caves, and wild rivers that surge through the jungle. Most people who visit Tabasco's capital, Villahermosa, are traveling for business, but the city has an excellent museum and a collection of massive Olmec heads and altars.

2 Tuxtla Gutiérrez & Chiapa de Corzo. The capital of Chiapas, hard-working Tuxtla Gutiérrez isn't a destination in itself. You're better off staying in the village of Chiapa de Corzo closer to the stunning Cañón del Sumidero.

3 Palenque & Environs. One of the jewels of the Maya civilization, the ancient city of Palenque sits shrouded with mist. Nearby are two other equally fascinating ruins, Bonampak and Yaxchilán. Palenque Town makes a good base for all explorations.

4 The Road to Palenque. Winding through the mountains, this road leads to many interesting sights, including waterfalls, the inspiring ruins of Toniná, and small villages where people still wear traditional dress.

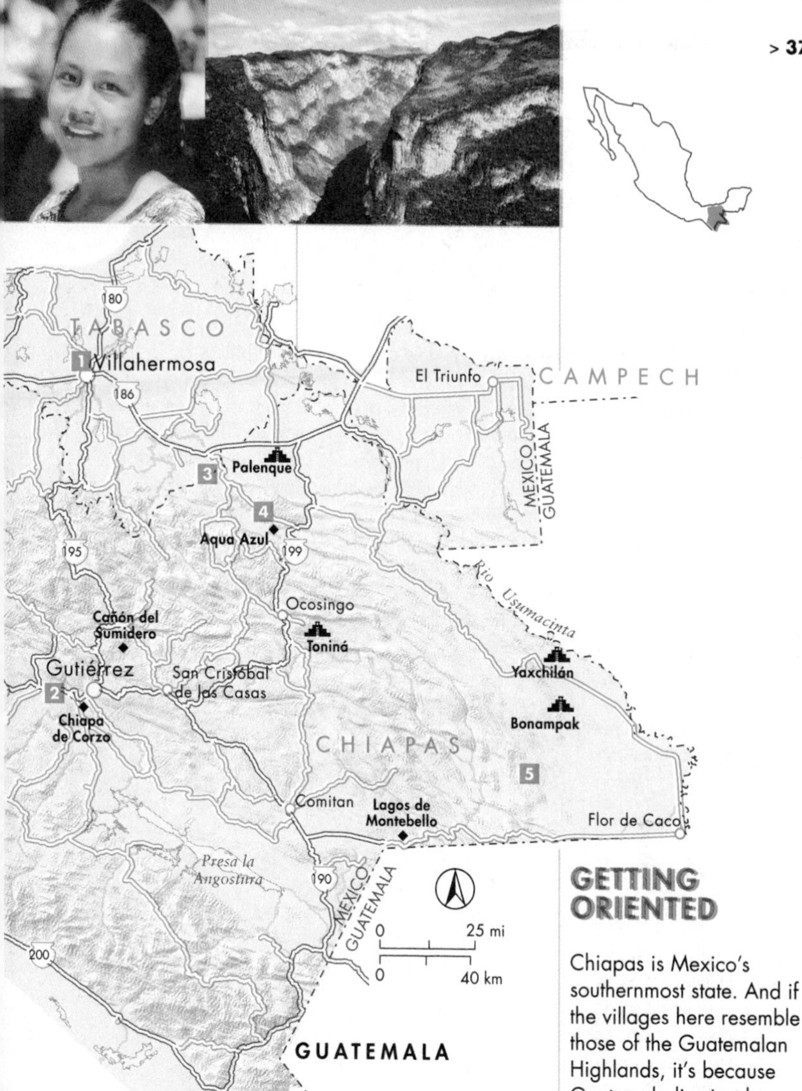

5 Southeastern Chiapas. One of the most beautiful parts of Mexico, Selva Lacandona has the western hemisphere's second-largest remaining rain forest. For centuries this has been the homeland of the Lacandon, a small tribe descended from the Maya.

GETTING ORIENTED

Chiapas is Mexico's southernmost state. And if the villages here resemble those of the Guatemalan Highlands, it's because Guatemala lies just beyond the eastern border. To the west lies Oaxaca, and to the south is one of Mexico's last stretches of relatively undeveloped coastline. Inland, mountain roads are full of hairpin turns hugging the edges of ravines. To the north is the mostly flat, pastoral state of Tabasco.

8

CHIAPAS & TABASCO PLANNER

A Little Reassurance & Advice

Although Chiapas and Tabasco are off-the-beaten path for Americans, they are not for other travelers, so you can be assured of finding the necessary travel services, such as banks, hotels, Internet cafés, and tourist offices. San Cristóbal is especially geared toward travelers. The only places you won't find such businesses are the indigenous villages. Most tourist offices will give you maps that fold up small enough to fit into a pocket or purse.

Bus and car travel throughout the region are options for exploring; use caution, try not to drive after dark, and watch out for slick roads during the rainy season. If twisting mountain roads aren't for you, air travel is an alternative, though it won't take you to the small towns or ruins. Tuxtla and Villahermosa have airports, handling predominantly domestic flights.

If you're looking for the ideal hub for exploring Chiapas, consider San Cristóbal. Whatever you do, you won't want to miss seeing surrounding ruins, notably the Maya city of Palenque.

The Great Outdoors

If you'd rather be climbing ruins than hanging out in colonial cities, you've come to the right place. Fly to Tuxtla Gutiérrez and head first to the impressive Cañón del Sumidero. Then head over to San Cristóbal on the new toll road and use it as your base to explore the nearby villages of San Juan Chamula and Zinacantán and, if you wish, head farther east to Lagos de Montebello for a swim. When you're done in San Cristóbal, start along the Road to Palenque. From your hotel in Ocosingo, you can arrange horseback riding trips to the ruins of Toniná, or you can just hit the stunning jungle waterfalls of Agua Azul before landing in Palenque Town. End with a day or two at Palenque.

The Pros of Hiring a Pro

Even if you usually turn your nose up at the thought of joining a tour group, Chiapas is a place where you should reconsider. If you want to see the isolated ruins at Bonampak and Yaxchilán, it's far easier to take a tour from Palenque Town. (The nearby ruins of Palenque are another matter—there's no need to join a tour.) And if you want to see the villages near San Cristóbal, by all means book a tour with a reputable guide. Going to a village like San Juan Chamula with a local means you'll get an insider's perspective and perhaps even be invited into someone's home. If you show up alone, you may get nothing but suspicious stares.

Regional Specialties

Stopping for a bite to eat or a bit of shopping can be memorable experiences. Favorite dishes include *cochinito horneado* (smoked pork), tamales, delicious white cheese, and *pejelagarto,* a fish that makes up for its unattractive appearance with a sweet flavor. You can also spend time combing open-air markets for hats, leather goods, and embroidered cloth, not to mention beautifully crafted jewelry featuring local amber.

Safety

Although travel in the area is reasonably safe, at this writing the U.S. State Department was advising visitors to exercise caution in Chiapas because of the presence of armed civilian groups in some areas, especially rural areas east of Ocosingo and east of Comitán. Although none of the sporadic confrontations has been near a main tourist destination, armed men did take over one guest ranch near Ocosingo in 2003. There have been no major incidents since that time, however. Review the information on the U.S. State Department Web site at 🌐travel.state.gov/travel/mexico.html for an update on the situation before you go. Always carry your tourist card and passport even on day trips throughout the region. It's best not to stay out after dark. If you're a first-time visitor, you may be more comfortable taking tours of the region—especially if you don't speak Spanish. Throughout all of Chiapas, the number to call in case of emergency is 066. Ask for an operator who speaks English.

What to Pack

Leave room in your luggage for souvenirs. Chiapas is a great place to buy crafts such as embroidered clothing, amber jewelry, and pottery.

Carry your own tissue, as toilets at some of the ruins may not be fully equipped, though most are quite clean.

Money Matters

Many, though not all, hotels quote prices that already include the 17% tax. This is especially true of budget and moderately priced lodgings. Be sure to ask about this when you're quoted a price.

WHAT IT COSTS IN DOLLARS

¢	$	$$	$$$	$$$$
Restaurants				
under $5	$5–$10	$10–$15	$15–$25	over $25
Hotels				
under $50	$50–$75	$75–$150	$150–$250	over $250

Restaurant prices are per person for a main course at dinner. Hotel prices are for two people in a standard double room.

How's the Weather?

In the highlands around San Cristóbal de las Casas the weather is cool and comfortable throughout the year-the average high is 20°C (68°F). Bring a sweater or jacket for the evening as temperatures can fall drastically after the sun sets. (Men in San Juan Chamula wear woolly black cloaks to ward off the cold.) September is the peak of the rainy season, which officially starts in August and can run until early October. In the coastal lowlands, including Palenque and Villahermosa, it is always hot and humid. Temperatures peak in May and June at about 88°F. The sun is extremely strong, so make sure to bring a hat and plenty of sunblock.

Thanks to the warm weather and spectacular landscape, restaurants, cafés, and even hotel lobbies are often outdoors; if not, the doors and windows are wide open. Therefore, a comfortable and casual style reigns at most establishments, and the only rule to live by is long pants—and maybe even some repellent—for evening outings, to help protect you from hungry insects.

SAN CRISTÓBAL DE LAS CASAS

Updated by Claudia Rosenbaum

A PRETTY HIGHLAND TOWN IN a valley where pine forests are interspersed with vegetable fields, San Cristóbal straddles two worlds. Here indigenous women with babies tied tightly in colorful shawls share the main square with teenagers on cell phones. Graceful colonial-era buildings house shops selling DVD players. From the looks of this thoroughly modern city, you'd never know that Chiapas is one of Mexico's poorest regions, or that it was the locus of the 1994 Zapatista rebellion.

In fact, as the city transforms from a quiet mountain village to a requisite stop on the tourist trail, repeat visitors have seen it lose some of its rural charm. But there is no denying the uniqueness of the indigenous villages outside of San Cristóbal, such as San Juan Chamula, that seem utterly disconnected from the rest of Mexico.

San Cristóbal is the perfect hub for exploring the region's villages and towns, lakes and rivers, and archaeological sites; a smart choice would be to base yourself here for a week or longer. In addition to admiring the town's colorful facades, budget some time to visit the market, peek into a few churches, and enjoy a cup of locally grown coffee in a shady courtyard. No itinerary is complete without a trip to the indigenous villages outside of San Cristóbal.

The town's cool climate is a refreshing change from the sweltering heat of the lowlands. On chilly evenings wood smoke scents the air, curling lazily over the red-tile roofs of small, brightly painted stucco houses. The sense of the mystical here is intensified by the fog and low clouds.

San Cristóbal is laid out in a grid pattern centered on the zócalo. When walking around, remember that street names change on either side of this square: Calle Francisco Madero to the east of the square, for example, becomes Calle Diego de Mazariegos to the west. The town was originally divided into *barrios* (neighborhoods), but they now blend together into a city center that's easy to negotiate.

In colonial times Indian allies of the Spaniards were moved onto lands on the outskirts of the nascent city. Each barrio was dedicated to an occupation. There were Tlaxcala fireworks manufacturers in one part of the town and pig butchers from Cuxtitali in another. Although specific divisions no longer exist, some of the local customs have been kept alive. For example, each Saturday certain houses downtown will put out red lamps to indicate that homemade tamales are for sale.

GETTING HERE & AROUND

The region has airports in every major city, but they mostly handle domestic flights. If you want to fly here from the United States, your best bet is the daily flight between Houston and Villahermosa on Continental. Otherwise you're going to connect in Mexico City or another hub. Aeropuerto San Cristóbal, 15 km (9 mi) northwest of downtown, is on the road to Palenque. ADO GL buses travel between San Cristóbal and Tuxtla many times a day; travel time is just under two hours. Chiapas is a big state, but there are few major highways. Carretera 190 goes east from Tuxtla through Chiapa de Corzo to San Cristóbal before continuing southeast to Comitán and the Guatamalan border. There is, however, a new toll road that links Tuxtla and San Cristóbal—it's a much quicker alternative to 190.

> **TRANSPORT TIP**
>
> To avoid bus stations altogether, take one of the Ford Econoline vans directly across from Estación Cristóbal Colón. They leave for Tuxtla, Ocosingo, and Comitán as soon as they fill up, which is about every 20 minutes. A trip should cost less than $4 per person. Note that these vans can be incredibly uncomfortable, as drivers pack in as many people as possible. A van designed to hold 12, for example, might depart with 16 or 18 people.

ESSENTIALS

Bus Contacts **ADO GL** (🌐*www.adogl.com.mx* ✉*Real de Guadalupe 5* ☎*01800/702-8000*). **San Cristóbal Bus Terminal** (*Estación Cristóbal Colón* ✉*Av. Insurgentes and Blvd. Juan Sabines Gutiérrez* ☎*967/678-0291*)

Currency Exchange **Agencia de Cambio Lacantún** (✉*Calle Real de Guadalupe 12-A* ☎*967/678-2587*).**Banamex** (✉*Calle Real de Guadalupe and Plaza 31 de Marzo* ☎*967/678-0277*).

Medical Assistance **Hospital General de San Cristóbal** (✉*Av. Insurgentes 24* ☎*967/678-0770*). **Policía Federal de Caminos (Federal Highway Police)** (✉*Blvd. Juan Sabines Gutiérrez s/n* ☎*967/678-6466*.

Visitor & Tour Info The **San Cristóbal Municipal Tourist Office** (✉*Palacio Municipal, ground fl., on the zócalo* ☎*967/678-0665*) **San Cristóbal State Tourist Office** (✉*Av. Miguel Hidalgo 1, 2nd fl., ½ block from zócalo* ☎*967/678-6570 or 967/678-1467*).

EXPLORING

3 **Arco del Carmen.** San Cristóbal's first skyscraper, this elegant tower was constructed in 1597 in the *mudéjar* (Moorish) style that was popular at the time in Spain. Note the graceful way the three-story-high arch is reflected in the smaller windows on the second and third levels. The tower, which once stood alone, is now connected to the Templo del Carmen. ✉*Av. Hidalgo, at Calle Hermanos Domínguez*

8 **Café Museo Café.** The smell of freshly brewed coffee may be enough to draw you into this three-room museum. The well-executed displays about the local cash crop will be enough to keep you here. Chiapas is the country's biggest producer of coffee, harvesting almost as much as Oaxaca and Veracruz combined. Although indigenous people were exploited for centuries by wealthy landowners, they now produce more than 90% of the region's coffee. The captions are in Spanish, but there are handouts in English. When you're finished with the museum, head to the central café for a taste of rich *cafe chiapaneco.* ✉*Calle María Adelina Flores 10, between Av. General Utrilla and Av. Domínguez* ☎*967/678-7876* 🎫*$1.80* ⏲*Mon.–Sat. 9 AM–9:30 PM. Closed Sun.*

2 **Catedral de San Cristóbal.** Dedicated to San Cristóbal Mártir (St. Christopher the Martyr), this cathedral was built in 1528, then demolished,

CLOSE UP

Chiapas & Tabasco Background

As early as 1000 BC, Chiapas was in the domain of the Maya, along with Guatemala, Belize, Honduras, and much of Mexico. The Maya controlled the region for centuries, constructing colossal cities like Palenque, Toniná, and Yaxchilán in Chiapas. These cities flourished in the 7th and 8th centuries, then were mysteriously abandoned. The rain forest quickly reclaimed its land.

In 1526 the Spaniards, under Diego de Mazariegos, defeated the Chiapan people in a bloody battle. Many were said to have leaped into the Cañón del Sumidero rather than submit to the invaders. Mazariegos founded a city called Villareal de Chiapa de los Españoles two years later. For most of the colonial era, Chiapas, with its capital at San Cristóbal, was a province of Guatemala. Lacking the gold and silver of the north, it was of greater strategic than economic importance.

Under Spanish rule, the region's resources became entrenched in the *encomienda* system, in which wealthy Spanish landowners forced the locals to work as slaves. "In this life all men suffer," lamented a Spanish friar in 1691, "but the Indians suffer most of all." The situation improved only slightly through the efforts of Bartolomé de las Casas, the bishop of San Cristóbal, who in the mid-1500s protested the torture and massacre of the local people; these downtrodden protested in another way, murdering priests and other *ladinos* (Spaniards) in infamous uprisings.

Mexico, Guatemala, and the rest of New Spain declared independence in 1821. Chiapas remained part of Guatemala until electing by plebiscite to join Mexico on September 14, 1824—the date is still celebrated throughout Chiapas as the Día de la Mexicanidad (Day of Mexicanization). In 1892, because of San Cristóbal's allegiance to the Royalists during the War of Independence, the capital was moved to Tuxtla Gutiérrez. Today the state of Chiapas encompasses 45,902 km (28,528 square mi) of mountainous land.

Tabasco was dominated between 1200 and 600 BC by the Olmec, who left behind the massive heads found in Villahermosa and the surrounding area. Cortés landed here in 1519, quickly subduing the local people and taking control of the region. The Maya continued to resist Spanish domination, but they were finally defeated in 1540. One of Mexico's smaller states—only 20,853 square km (12,960 square mi)—Tabasco was of minor importance until the beginning of the 20th century, when oil was discovered off its coast in the Gulf of Mexico. You won't find much evidence of Tabasco's turbulent past today; the spirit that prevails here—at least in modern Villahermosa, Tabasco's capital—is one of commerce.

and rebuilt in 1693, with additions during the 18th and 19th centuries. Note the classic colonial features on the ornate facade: turreted columns, arched windows and doorways, and beneficent-looking statues of saints in niches. The floral embellishments in rust, black, and white accents on the ocher background are unforgettable. Inside, don't miss the painting *Nuestra Señora de Dolores* (*Our Lady of Sorrows*) to the left of the altar, beside the gold-plated *Retablo de los Tres Reyes*

TRAVEL BY TOUR

Gabriela Gudiño Gual (✉ *Calz. México 81, San Cristóbal* ☎📠 *967/678-4223*) is a reliable private tour guide who specializes in history and indigenous peoples. Participants travel by van to local villages.

Pepe Santiago (✉ *Museo Na Bolom, Av. Vicente Guerrero 33, at Calle Comitán, San Cristóbal* ☎ *967/678-1418*), a Lacandon native associated with Museo Na Bolom since childhood, leads tours daily to San Juan Chamula, Zinacantán, and San Nicolás Buenavista. (Pepe's name is a veritable ticket of acceptance in the more remote regions of Chiapas.) The group leaves Museo Na Bolom promptly at 10 AM (they suggest arriving at 9:45) and returns around 3; it's well worth the $18 price. Pepe's sister, Teresa Santiago Hernández, also leads tours.

Raúl and Alex (☎ *967/678-3741 or 967/678-9141*) really know their stuff; their tours leave every day at 9:30 AM from the cross in front of the cathedral in the zócalo, returning around 2 PM FOR $15. You'll visit San Juan Chamula and Zinacantán; the cultural commentary is particularly insightful.

Viajes Chinkultik (✉ *Calle Real de Guadalupe 34, San Cristóbal* ☎ *967/678-0957*) has trips around the city and beyond, but the company's three-day trip to Laguna Miramar is especially recommended. All food, transportation, tents, and even porters (it's a three-hour walk in to the lake) are included in the price of $200 per person.

(*Altarpiece of the Three Kings*); the Chapel of Guadalupe in the rear; and the gold-washed pulpit. ✉ *Calle Guadalupe Victoria at the zócalo* ⏲ *Daily 9–2 and 4–7*

8

★ ❺ **Mercado Municipal.** This municipal market occupies an eight-block area. Best visited early in the morning—especially on the busiest day, Saturday—the market is the social and commercial center for the indigenous groups from surrounding villages. Stalls overflow with medicinal herbs, fresh flowers, and bundles of wool, as well as the best coffee in the region for less than $3 a pound. Be careful here, as robberies are common. If you must bring your camera, ask before photographing people. ✉ *At Avs. General Utrilla, Nicaragua, Honduras, and Belisario Domínguez* ⏲ *Daily 7 AM–3 PM*

⓫ **Museo del Ambar de Chiapas.** Next to the pretty Ex-Convento de la Merced, this museum has exhibits showing how and where amber is mined, as well as its function in Maya and Aztec societies. You'll see samples of everything from fossils to recently quarried pieces to sculptures and jewelry. Labels are in Spanish only; ask for an English-language summary. The volunteer staff can explain how to distinguish between real amber and fake. ✉ *Plazuela de la Merced, Calle Diego de Mazariegos s/n* ☎ *967/678-9716* 🎫 *$2* ⏲ *Tues.–Sun. 10–2 and 4–7*

❾ **Museo del Jade.** Jade was prized as a symbol of wealth and power by Olmec, Teotihuacán, Mixtec, Zapotec, Maya, Toltec, and Aztec nobility, and this museum shows jade pieces from different Mesoamerican

cultures. The most impressive piece is a reproduction of the sarcophagus lid from Pakal's tomb, at Palenque. ✉ *Av. 16 de Septiembre 16* ☎ *967/678–1121* 🎫 *$3* ⏲ *Mon.–Sat. 9AM–9:30PM, Sun. 9–5.*

7 **Museo de la Medicina Maya.** Few travelers venture here—a shame because the Museum of Maya Medicine is fascinating. Displays describe the complex system of medicine employed by the local indigenous cultures. Instead of one healer, they have a team of specialists who are called on for different illnesses. The most interesting display details the role of the midwife, who assists the mother and makes sure the child isn't enveloped by evil spirits. The museum is about 1 km (½ mi) north of the Mercado Municipal. Taxis are plentiful. ✉ *Av. Salomon González Blanco 10 (an extension of Av. General Utrilla)* ☎ *967/678–5438* 🎫 *$2* ⏲ *Weekdays 10–6, weekends 10–5*

6 **Museo Na Bolom.** It's doubtful that any foreigners have made as much of an impact on San Cristóbal as did the European owners of this home-turned-library-museum-restaurant-hotel. Built as a seminary in 1891, the handsome 22-room house was purchased by Frans and Gertrude (Trudi) Blom in 1950. He was a Danish archaeologist, she a Swiss social activist; together they created the Institute for Ethnological and Ecological Advocacy, which carries on today. It got its name, Na Bolom

Fodor's Choice ★

(House of the Jaguar), from the Lacandon Maya with whom Trudi worked: Blom sounds like the Maya word for jaguar. Both Frans and Trudi were great friends of the Lacandon tribe, whose way of life they documented. Their institute is also dedicated to reforestation.

Both Bloms are deceased, but Na Bolom showcases their small collection of religious treasures. Also on display are findings from the Classic Maya site of Moxviquil (pronounced mosh-vee-*keel*), on the outskirts of San Cristóbal, and objects from the daily life of the Lacandon. Trudi's bedroom contains her jewelry, collection of indigenous crafts, and wardrobe of embroidered dresses. A research library holds more than 10,000 volumes on Chiapas and the Maya. Tours are conducted daily in English and Spanish at 11:30 and 4:30.

Across from the museum, the Jardín del Jaguar (Jaguar Garden) store sells crafts and souvenirs. Look for the thatch hut, a replica of local Chiapan architecture. It consists of a mass of woven palm fronds tied to branches, with walls and windows of wooden slats, and high ceilings that allow the heat to rise. The shop here sells Lacandon crafts, as well as black-and-white photos taken by Trudi.

Revenue from Na Bolom supports the work of the institute. You can arrange for a meal at Na Bolom even if you don't stay at the hotel. In addition, the staff is well connected within San Cristóbal and can arrange tours to artisans' co-ops, villages, and nature reserves that are off the beaten path. ⊠*Av. Vicente Guerrero 33, at Calle Comitán* ☎*967/678–1418* ⊕*www.nabolom.org* 🎟*Museum $3.50, tour $4.50* ⏲*Daily 10–6. Tours daily 11:30 and 4:30, library weekdays 10–4, store Mon.–Sat. 9:30–2 and 4–7*

10 ★ **Museo Sergio Castro.** Passing by this slightly ramshackle colonial-era house, you'd never guess it was one of the city's best museums. It's also one of the hardest to get into—you need to call ahead for an appointment. But the effort is well worth it. Sergio Castro's collection of colorful clothing from the villages surrounding San Cristóbal is unparalleled. He explains how different factors—geography, climate, even the crops grown in a certain area—influenced how locals dressed. In explaining their dress, he is explaining their way of life. Each ribbon hanging from a hat, each stitch on an embroidered blouse has a meaning. Castro has spent a lifetime working with indigenous peoples; he currently runs a clinic to treat burn victims. Many of the ceremonial costumes were given to him as payment for his work in the communities. Castro gives tours in English, Spanish, Italian, and French. ⊠*Calle Guadalupe Victoria 47* ☎*967/678–4289* 🎟*Donation suggested* ⏲*Daily* 6 PM–8 PM *by appointment*

4 **Templo de Santo Domingo.** This three-block-long complex houses a church, a former monastery, a regional history museum, and the Templo de la Caridad (Temple of the Sisters of Charity). A two-headed eagle—emblem of the Hapsburg dynasty that once ruled Spain and its American dominions—broods over the pediment of the church, which was built between 1547 and 1569. The pink stone facade (which needs a good cleaning) is carved in an intensely ornamental style known as

Baroque Solomonic: saints' figures, angels, and grooved columns overlaid with vegetation motifs abound. The interior has lavish altarpieces, an exquisitely fashioned pulpit, a sculpture of the Holy Trinity, and wall panels of gilded, carved cedar—one of the precious woods of Chiapas that centuries later lured Tabasco's woodsmen to the highlands surrounding San Cristóbal. At the complex's southeast corner you'll find the tiny, humble Templo de la Caridad, built in 1715 to honor the Immaculate Conception. Its highlight is the finely carved altarpiece. Indigenous groups from San Juan Chamula often light candles and make offerings here. (Do *not* take photos of the Chamulas.)

★ The Ex-Convento de Santo Domingo, adjacent to the Santo Domingo church, now houses **Sna Jolobil,** an Indian cooperative that sells local weavings of a high quality that you won't find elsewhere. These wall hangings and other articles are truly of museum quality, and are priced accordingly. The shop is open Monday–Saturday 9–2 and 4–6. The small **Centro Cultural de los Altos** (*Highlands Cultural Center* ☎*967/678–1609*), also part of the complex, has a permanent exhibition of historical items and documents related to San Cristóbal and the surrounding villages. With the price of admission you can wander around the courtyards of the old monastery. It's open daily 10–5; closed Monday. Admission is $3.70, or free on Sunday. ✉*Av. 20 de Noviembre s/n, near Calle Guatemala*

NEED A BREAK?

On a block closed to traffic, La Casa de Elisa (✉***Av. Hidalgo 11*** ☎***967/674-0880*****) is one of the few cafés with sidewalk seating. You're just a stone's throw from the main square and the coffee's great.**

❶ **Zócalo.** The square around which this colonial city was built has in its center a gazebo used by marimba musicians most weekend evenings at 8 PM. You can have a coffee on the ground floor of the gazebo; expect to be approached by children and women selling bracelets and other wares. Surrounding the square are a number of 16th-century buildings, some with plant-filled central patios. On the facade of the Casa de Diego de Mazariegos, now the Hotel Santa Clara, are a stone mermaid and lions that are typical of the plateresque style—as ornate and busy as the work of a silversmith. The yellow-and-white neoclassical Palacio Municipal (Municipal Palace) on the square's west side was the seat of the state government until 1892. Today it houses a few government offices, including the municipal tourism office. ✉*Between Avs. General Utrilla and 20 de Noviembre and Calles Diego de Mazariegos and Guadalupe Victoria*

WHERE TO EAT

$–$$ MEXICAN

✕**El Fogón de Jovel.** El Fogón de Jovel, spread across a lovely colonial courtyard, strikes a balance: it caters to tourists but is still popular with locals. Order the *parrillada chiapaneca* for a sampling of regional specialties of Chiapas. Also on offer is a large selection of tamales, such as the *tamal untado,* which is stuffed with chicken and mole. In keeping with local ways, they serve a margarita made with *posh* (the local firewater). ✉*Avenida 16 de Septiembre 11* ☎*967/678–1153 or 967/678–2550* ▭*No credit cards*

$–$$ MEXICAN ✕**Na Bolom.** Just off the old-fashioned kitchen, this dining room looks much as it did when Frans and Trudi Blom did their research here in San Cristóbal. Today the communal oak dining table is shared by volunteers, artists, scholars, and travelers. A hearty breakfast is served from 7 AM to 1 PM, while a five-course dinner is served at 7 PM sharp. Don't expect much local cuisine; the menu focuses more on such rib-sticking dishes as beef stew or roasted chicken. Make sure to call several hours ahead for a reservation. ✉*Av. Vicente Guerrero 33, at Calle Comitán* ☎*967/678–1418* ▭*MC, V*

CHIAPAS CHOW

Chiapas cuisine is influenced by the region's heritage, so many of the dishes have been around since the days of the Maya. It's not Mexico's most impressive food region, but some distinctive flavors come from such herbs as *chipilín* and a leaf called *yerba santa* (or *mumu*, as it's known by locals). Don't pass up the *cochinito horneado* (oven-baked pork) or the many local variations of tamales. Wash it all down with *atole* (a cornmeal drink).

$–$$ CAFÉ ✕**La Paloma.** Cozy and relaxing, this café is inside a former home of city founder Diego de Mazariegos. But that doesn't mean it's a musty museum. It's surprisingly modern, with a curved bar surrounded by vegetation. Start with *sopa de flor de calabaza* (squash flower soup) or *ensalada de nopalitos* (cactus salad), then move on to the tongue-twisting *albóndigas enchipotladas* (meatballs in chili sauce). ✉*Calle Hidalgo 3, ½ block south of zócalo* ☎*967/678–1547* ▭*MC, V, AE*

8

$–$$ SWISS ✕**Restaurant L'Eden.** People rave about the dishes—especially the steaks—at this chalet-style restaurant in the Hotel El Paraíso. The interior has eight candlelit tables and a cozy fireplace. Swiss delights include classic *raclette* (melted cheese and potatoes) and several different types of fondue. The service is doting but not distracting. The intimate bar is known for its creative, strong cocktails. ✉*Calle 5 de Febrero 19* ☎*967/678–0085* ▭*AE, MC, V*

$ ★ MEXICAN ✕**Emiliano's Moustache.** It's named for revolutionary hero Emiliano Zapata, which explains why sombreros and rifles are the main decorations. The place is filled with locals, who appreciate the good-natured kitsch, which sometimes includes a sequin-clad entertainer. The tortillas here are made fresh by hand throughout the day, so the taco platters are especially good (try one of the big combinations, or the regional specialties on the table tents). It's a good place to stop for lunch (there are cheap specials), or late in the evening (the dining room is open until 1 AM). Take a seat under the huge wrought-iron chandelier or in the dark upstairs bar. ✉*Av. Crescencio Rosas 7, at Calle Diego de Mazariegos* ☎*967/678–7246* ▭*MC, D, V*

$ ASIAN ✕**Mayambé.** Brightly colored fabrics hang on the walls and from the rafters at this notable, if overrated, pan-Asian restaurant. Grab a seat in the covered courtyard (sit closer to the fireplace if the night is a bit nippy). The expansive menu, which tends to overreach in places, includes the Vietnamese-style *platillo vietnamita* (tofu, shrimp, or chicken sautéed with peanuts, cashews, and bits of chile and coconut and served with sweet coconut rice). *Mayambé* is a good option for vegetarians, who will enjoy the Indian vegetable, rice, and lentil dishes, although sticklers for authentic Thai will be sorely disappointed. Cocktails are weak and overly sweet. ✉*Calle Real de Guadalupe 66* ☎*967/674–6278* ▭*MC, V*

$ MEXICAN ✕**El Titanic.** The name "Titanic" may refer to the amount of food you'll get at this restaurant on the edge of the city. Sit down and just say *surtido,* and you'll be brought a sampling of obscure local specialties, often including unusual parts of the pig. The food doesn't stop coming. You'll enjoy multiple courses in rapid succession, ranging from *lengua* (tongue) to the more pedestrian *pollo en mole (chicken in mole).* The out-of-the-way location has kept the place supremely local (you'll want to go by car or taxi), and you'll probably be the first foreign visitor in weeks. ✉*Calle Tabasco 1* ☎*967/678–4972* ▭*No credit cards*

¢ VEGETARIAN ✕**La Casa del Pan.** The scent of freshly baked bread is the first thing you'll notice, tempting you to skip the restaurant altogether and just grab a few of the warm rolls and a jar of locally made preserves. But the House of Bread serves a fabulous, if leisurely, breakfast. For lunch, try the tasty *tamales chiapanecos* (with a spicy cheese filling) or the mild chiles stuffed with corn and herbs. Round out your meal with bean soup and one of the best salads in town. ✉*Calle Dr. Navarro 10, at Av. Belisario Domínguez* ☎*967/678–5895* 🌐*www.casadelpan.com* ▭*MC, V* ⏲*Closed Mon*

WHERE TO STAY

$$–$$$ **Casa Mexicana.** A pond filled with flowers is one of the many touches that make this hostelry in a restored colonial mansion stand out. Glass ceilings in the lobby and atrium make for beautiful lighting. A lovely newer wing across the street, also in a colonial home, has a colonnaded courtyard and large, quiet rooms painted light colors and filled with tasteful photographs of San Cristóbal. The restaurant, which surrounds a courtyard with banana trees, serves international dishes. **Pros:** Pond and glass ceilings are very cool. **Cons:** Lots of groups stay here and can be better accommodated than other guests. ✉*Calle 28 de Agosto 1, at Av. General Utrilla,* ☎*967/678–0698, 967/678–0683, or 967/678–1348* 🌐*www.hotelcasamexicana.com* *52 rooms, 3 suites* *In-hotel: Restaurant, public Wi-Fi, room service, bar, laundry service, parking (no fee)* ▭*AE, MC, V*

$$ **Casa de los Arcángeles.** This small hotel is beautiful—and feels every bit as new as it is (opened in mid-2006), though its architecture is more of a nod toward tradition. Seven suites surround the evocative open-air restaurant in the hotel's courtyard, which is candlelit by night. Rooms have shiny new hardwood floors and bright colors. **Pros:** Not having to deal with the problems that can be found in older, historic hotels (like shoddy plumbing). **Cons:** Inconveniences aside, there is something to be said about a getting to stay in a hotel that dates from the early 1700s, as this one does not. ✉*Calle Cuauhtémoc 4* ☎*967/678–1531* *7 suites* *In-hotel: Restaurant, bar, room service, spa* ▭*MC, V*

$$ **Casa Felipe Flores.** Breakfast in this restored 18th-century mansion
Fodor's Choice ★ is served in a courtyard or in the antiques-filled dining room. It's such a nice way to start the day that you might find yourself lingering until it's time for lunch. David and Nancy Orr, the friendly owners, are happy to share their knowledge of San Cristóbal. Each guest room has a handsome wardrobe, a fireplace, and an old-fashioned bed with carved headboard. Bathrooms have whimsical hand-painted tiles. The view from the rooftop terrace, to which residents of the cozy and inexpensive Room 5 have access, is one of the city's best. **Pros:** Well-run, wonderful view. **Cons:** Rooms facing the street can be noisy. *Calle Dr. Felipe Flores 36, 967/678–3996 www.felipeflores.com 5 rooms In-hotel: Restaurant, bar, laundry service, airport shuttle No credit cards BP*

$$ ★ **Na Bolom.** The rooms here aren't just named for local indigenous communities; they are filled with pictures and books detailing their lives (and the lives of archaeologists Frans and Trudy Blom), as well as examples of their weavings and pottery. The rooms in the colonial house have touches like corner fireplaces. Na Bolom may be a 15-minute walk from the center of town, but it's so pleasant you might not want to go anywhere. Book well in advance, and ask for a room with a garden view. **Pros:** Much knowledge can be garnered from a simple stay. **Cons:** Bit of a walk into the happening part of town. *Av. Vicente Guerrero 33, at Calle Comitán, 967/678–1418 www.nabolom.org 16 rooms In-room: No a/c, no TV. In-hotel: Restaurant, parking (no fee) AE, MC, V*

$$ **Posada Diego de Mazariegos.** This quaint hotel—really two perfectly preserved 18th-century colonial homes—has beautiful courtyards, gardens, and sunlit nooks throughout. Rooms have high ceilings and wide windows; some have fireplaces. Ask for one of the rooms that number in the 300s, which are in an older wing and have high wood-beam ceilings as well as working charcoal stoves. The bar, reached through a set of swinging doors, stocks more than 175 brands of tequila. **Pros:** Rooms are simple, but many have extra touches. **Cons:** A little more care could be given to such things as the bed linens. *Calle 5 de Febrero 1, at Av. General Utrilla, 967/678–0833 www.diegodemazariegos.com.mx 70 rooms, 6 suites In-hotel: Restaurant, public Internet, room service, bar, laundry service, parking (no fee) AE, MC, V*

$–$$ **Casa Vieja.** Dating from 1740, this colonial-era house has been declared a historical monument. Graceful colonnades separate three interior courtyards. Most of the simple guest rooms have large windows overlooking the courtyard or corridors; a few rooms on the second floor have views of the mountains. The restaurant, Doña Rita, sits among the elegant columns on one of the porches. The hotel is three blocks east of the zócalo. **Pros:** Fantastically historic, reasonably priced. **Cons:** Service can be iffy. *Calle María Adelina Flores 27, 967/678–0385 967/678–6868 www.casavieja.com.mx 37 rooms, 2 suites In-hotel: Restaurant, room service, bar, laundry service, parking (no fee) AE, MC, V*

$–$$ **Hotel El Paraíso.** High, beamed ceilings ennoble the guest rooms in this charming late-19th-century building that once was a hospital.

8

Most of the rooms wind around a central courtyard. For more solitude, request one of two rooms in the exterior courtyard. The lounge overlooks a plant-filled patio where breakfast is served. You're just a block from the town's shopping strip. **Pros:** Good breakfasts, quaint boutique-y feel. **Cons:** Rooms are fairly petite. ✉*Calle 5 de Febrero 19,* ☎*967/678–0085 or 967/678–5382* 🌐*www.hotelposadaparaiso.com* *12 rooms* *In-room: Room service. In-hotel: Restaurant, bar, laundry service* *AE, MC, V*

$ **Hotel Posada Real de Chiapas.** Striking indigenous weavings fill the rooms of this hotel, which is dedicated to the theme of textiles of Chiapas. Rooms here are filled with wrought-iron furniture along with tasteful, colorful weavings, and some even have balconies. **Pros:** If you're into indigenous art, there's no better place for you. **Cons:** Some rooms are better than others, you might have to tour a few before deciding. ✉*Francisco Madero 19* ☎*967/678–0928 or 967/678–0626* 🌐*www.hotelchiapas.com.mx* *30 rooms, 2 suites* *In-hotel: Café, bar, room service, public Internet, parking (free)* *AE, MC, V*

¢–$ **Hotel Santa Clara.** This rambling 16th-century mansion, once the home of city founder Diego de Mazariegos, feels cheap and dark, but it's right on the square. It has a tangible air of past grandeur: beamed ceilings, antique oil paintings, saints in niches, and timeworn hardwood floors. Six of the 10 spacious rooms with balconies overlook the zócalo. The prices are extremely reasonable, given its address. **Pros:** You can book tours through the on-site travel office. **Cons:** You definitely get what you pay for, and not much more. ✉*Av. Insurgentes 1,* ☎*967/678–1140 or 967/678–0871* *37 rooms, 2 suites* *In-room: Room service. In-hotel: Restaurant, bar, pool, parking (no fee)* *MC, V*

¢ **Posada San Cristóbal.** The large rooms in this grand old building a block from the main plaza have high ceilings, antique furniture, and heavy French doors. Most rooms have small balconies. Enjoy the patio, with its cheery walls, blue-and-white tiles, and white wrought-iron furniture. **Pros:** Rooms are spacious. **Cons:** Traffic noise. ✉*Av. Insurgentes 3,* ☎*967/678–6881* *18 rooms* *In-room: No a/c, no phone. In-hotel: Restaurant, room service, bar, laundry service* *No credit cards*

NIGHTLIFE

BARS

Looking for a more sedate scene? Try **Casa Raíz** (✉*Niños Héroes 8* ☎*967/674–6577*), a sophisticated bar two blocks south of the main square. The music here is jazz, and the bands put on quite a show. There's also a menu of light fare.

Someone must have bribed the fire marshal, because **El Circo** (✉*Av. 20 de Noviembre at Calle Primero de Marzo* ☎*No phone*) packs in more people than you'd think possible. The draw at this one-room establishment is the string of excellent rock bands.

In Hotel Santa Clara, **Cocodrilo** (✉*Av. Insurgentes 1* ☎*967/678–0871 or 967/678–1140*) is a laid-back tavern that hosts rock and salsa bands

CLOSE UP

A Voice of Many Voices

In the early hours of January 1, 1994, while most of Mexico was sleeping off the New Year's festivities, the Zapatista National Liberation Army (EZLN) surprised the world when it captured San Cristóbal de las Casas and several surrounding towns, demanding land redistribution and equal rights for Chiapas' indigenous peoples.

The Zapatista triumph was short-lived. The mostly Tzotzil and Tzeltal troops soon departed, and on January 12, President Carlos Salinas de Gortari called for a cease-fire. According to government figures, 145 lives were lost during the 12-day struggle. But hundreds have been killed in years of clashes between rebel supporters and paramilitary groups; thousands have been displaced.

Many factors led to the uprising. Centuries of land appropriation repeatedly uprooted Chiapas' Maya-descended groups. Also, despite its natural resources (Chiapas provides nearly half of Mexico's electricity and has oil and gas reserves), the state's indigenous residents suffer high rates of illiteracy, malnutrition, and infant mortality.

In 1995 President Ernesto Zedillo sent troops into the Lacandon jungle to capture the Zapatista leadership, including charismatic leader Subcomandante Marcos. The ambush failed. The following year negotiations with the rebels resulted in the San Andrés Accords, which called for a constitutional amendment recognizing indigenous cultural rights and limited autonomy. President Zedillo instead pursued a policy of low-intensity warfare—often in the name of "development" or "reforestation." The disastrous results include the massacre of 45 unarmed Zapatista supporters by paramilitary forces in the village of Acteal, Chenalho, in December 1997.

During his presidential campaign, Vicente Fox insisted that he could resolve the Zapatista conflict in 15 minutes; during his inaugural address he announced that he was ordering partial troop withdrawals and would submit legislation based on the San Andrés Accords. In turn, Marcos announced three conditions for the restoration of negotiations—further military withdrawals, the release of Zapatista prisoners, and implementation of the accords. The first two have been achieved. Fox, however, continues to be engaged in a media war with Marcos. In early 2001, a Zapatista caravan traveled to the capital to demand negotiations.

Fox, who welcomed the Zapatistas to the capital, has come under attack from members of the Institutional Revolutionary Party (PRI) as well as members of his own National Action Party (PAN). Not everyone is convinced of the Zapatistas' noble motives. In February 2003 a group of Zapatistas chased out the American owners of a guest ranch not far from the archaeological ruins of Toniná. Even though the resulting publicity continues to put a dent in tourism, the state government continues to decline to intervene, saying a heavy-handed approach would backfire. Around the same time, a group of Zapatistas reportedly detained for a few hours tourists on a kayaking trip along the Río Jatate. Whether these are isolated incidents or a series of ongoing events remains to be seen.

most nights from 9:30 to midnight. Windows in the front overlook the zócalo.

Popular for years, **Latino's** (✉*Calle Francisco Madero 23, corner of Av. Benito Juárez* ☎*967/678–9927*) serves up live salsa, merengue, cumbia, or other tropical music after 8 PM and until 3 AM every night but Sunday; cover is 20 pesos.

You say you want a **Revolución** (✉*Av. 20 de Noviembre at Calle Primero de Marzo* ☎*967/678–6664*)? This bar serves great breakfasts and lunches, then opens the bar for drinks, with a number of good specials. Most nights see live jazz, rock, or ska performances.

Salón Mundial (✉*20 de Noviembre 7*) is where young people come to listen to live jazz music; the cover is 15 pesos, and they are open until 3 AM. Tequila enthusiasts shouldn't miss **Tequilazoo** (✉*Calle 5 de Febrero 1, at Av. General Utrilla* ☎*967/678–0833*)—they have more than 175 tequilas on hand, all served in simple shot glasses.

CAFÉS

At **Namandí Café y Crepas** (✉*Diego de Mazariegos 16/C* ☎*967/678–8054*), the coffee is local and organic.

With more than a dozen organic javas on the menu, it's not surprising that **La Selva Café** (✉*Av. Crescencio Rosas 9, at Calle Cuauhtémoc* ☎*967/678–7244*) is always filled with people. It's a big space, so there are plenty of quiet corners, and there's free Wi-Fi.

FOLK PERFORMANCES

The elegant **Teatro Hermanos Domínguez** (✉*Diagonal Hermanos Paniagua s/n, just outside the city limits* ☎*967/678–3637*) features programs such as folkloric dances from throughout Latin America.

SHOPPING

Look for the elaborately crafted textiles from communities surrounding San Cristóbal; they incorporate designs that have been around for millennia. San Cristóbal's market, although picturesque, generally sells more produce than arts and crafts. The shops on Avenida General Utrilla, south of the market, have a large selection of Guatemalan goods, the price and quality of which may be lower than Mexican wares. Check merchandise carefully.

Shops are generally open Monday–Saturday 9–2 and 4–8. Indian women and children will often approach you on the streets with amber jewelry (mostly fake), woven bracelets, and dolls.

ARTS & CRAFTS

The range of crafts in San Cristóbal extends far beyond those made by indigenous groups. **Arte Sandía** (✉*Calle 20 de Agosto 6* ☎*967/678–4240*) has a wonderful array of housewares, including plates and dishes covered with the store's namesake watermelon. (It's a popular subject in this country, as the watermelon has the three colors of the Mexican flag.)

Artesanías Chiapanecas (✉ *Calle Real de Guadalupe 46C, at Av. Diego Dugelay* ☎ *No phone*) has an excellent selection of embroidered blouses, huipiles, tablecloths, and bags.

The government-run **Casa de las Artesanías** (✉ *Calle Niños Héroes s/n and Av. Hidalgo* ☎ *967/678–1180*) sells wooden toys, ceramics, embroidered blouses, bags, and handwoven textiles from throughout the state. You'll also find honey, marmalade, and locally made liqueurs.

Casa Penagoes (✉ *Calle Real de Guadalupe 50* ☎ *967/678–1126*) has an eye-popping collection of colorful clothing from indigenous groups.

AMBER ADVICE

A good rule of thumb is that stores usually sell real amber, whereas street vendors commonly have the fakes, although there's some crossover. Moreover, amber that looks too perfect—a very smooth finish, uniform background, flora and fauna that are too neatly arranged—is probably fake. If you're about to drop a lot of cash on a piece and you want a foolproof test, rub the stone vigorously with a soft cloth; this should create enough static to pick up a small piece of paper.

Perhaps the most memorable shop is **Nemizapata** (✉ *Calle Real de Guadalupe 57* ☎ *967/678–7487*), which stocks crafts from local villages. Many of these communities were sympathetic to the Zapatista cause, which is reflected in the art. Most interesting are the *servietas* (small pieces of cloth) with hand-embroidered portraits of rebel leaders.

★ Among its excellent selection of wares, **Sna Jolobil** (✉ *Ex-Convento de Santo Domingo, Calz. Lázaro Cárdenas 42* ☎ *967/678–7178*), the regional crafts cooperative, has hand-dyed wool sweaters and tunics, embroidered pillow covers, and pre-Hispanic-design wall hangings. The name means Weaver's House in the Tzotzil language.

8

Taller Leñateros (✉ *Calle Flavio A. Paniagua 54* ☎ *967/678–5174* 🌐 *www.tallerlenateros.com*), a unique indigenous co-op in an old colonial San Cristóbal home, sells top-quality crafts and lets you observe artisans at work. Look for handmade books, boxes, postcards, and writing paper fashioned from plants.

BOOKS

Sharing a courtyard with several other shops, **Chilam Balam** (✉ *Casa Utrilla at Av. General Utrilla 33 and Calle Dr. Navarro* ☎ *967/678–0486*) has travel, archaeology, and art books about Mexico. Just off the main square, **La Pared** (✉ *Av. Hidalgo 3*) is popular with travelers. There are maps and guide books available.

JEWELRY

In the last few years, Calle Real de Guadalupe has transformed itself into the place to go for amber. Nearly a dozen shops line this narrow street off the main square. **Emili Ambar** (✉ *Calle Real de Guadalupe 26* ☎ *967/678–8789*) makes up for its diminutive size with a helpful staff. Here you'll find a small selection of amber with an insect suspended inside. **Tierra del Ambar** (✉ *Calle Real de Guadalupe 16 and*

CLOSE UP

Shopping in Chiapas

The weavers of Chiapas produce striking embroidered blouses, *huipiles* (tunics), bedspreads, and tablecloths. Other artisans create leather goods, homemade paper products, and painted wooden crosses. Lacandon bows and arrows and reproductions of the beribboned ceremonial hats worn by Tzotzil indigenous leaders also make interesting souvenirs.

Chiapas is one of the few places in the world that has amber mines, so finely crafted jewelry made from this prehistoric resin is easy to find in San Cristóbal—as are plastic imitations sold by street vendors. San Cristóbal is also known for the wrought-iron crosses that grace its rooftops. Although many of the iron-working shops have closed, you can still find the crosses in a few old-fashioned stores. Tuxtla Gutiérrez and Palenque, although not known for crafts, have a few shops selling quality folk art from throughout the state.

28 ☎*967/678–0139*) has two storefronts not far from each other. The original pieces by Philippe Catillon are lovely.

But jewelry here isn't limited to amber. For a look at pieces using a certain green stone, visit **Jades y Joyas** (✉*16 de Septiembre* ☎*967/678–2550*). **Sensaciones** (✉*Calle Hidalgo 4* ☎*967/631–5580*) carries jewelry made of turquoise and other stones in funky designs.

SPORTS & THE OUTDOORS

HORSEBACK RIDING

A horseback ride into the neighboring indigenous villages is good exercise for mind and body. Most hotels can arrange trips, or you can contact **Viajes Chinkultik** (✉*Calle Real de Guadalupe 34* ☎*967/678–0957*). Bilingual guides lead five-hour horseback rides to San Juan Chamula and Zinacantán; the cost is about $12 per person.

SIDE TRIPS FROM SAN CRISTÓBAL

Surrounding San Cristóbal are many small villages celebrated for the exquisite colors and embroidery work of their inhabitants' clothing. San Juan Chamula and Zinacantán are traditional villages well worth exploring. Seeing them on your own is a possibility; taxis and colectivos depart from near the market in San Cristóbal. To get the most out of the experience, go with a knowledgeable guide.

SAN JUAN CHAMULA

12 km (7½ mi) northwest of San Cristóbal de las Casas.

Celebrated for its religious and cultural traditions, San Juan Chamula is one of the most fascinating highland villages. The Chamulas, a subgroup of the Tzotzils, are descendants of the Maya. More than 80,000 Chamulas live in hamlets throughout the highlands north and west of San Cristóbal; several thousand of them live in San Juan Chamula. Almost all adults wear traditional dress—men often don dark tunics,

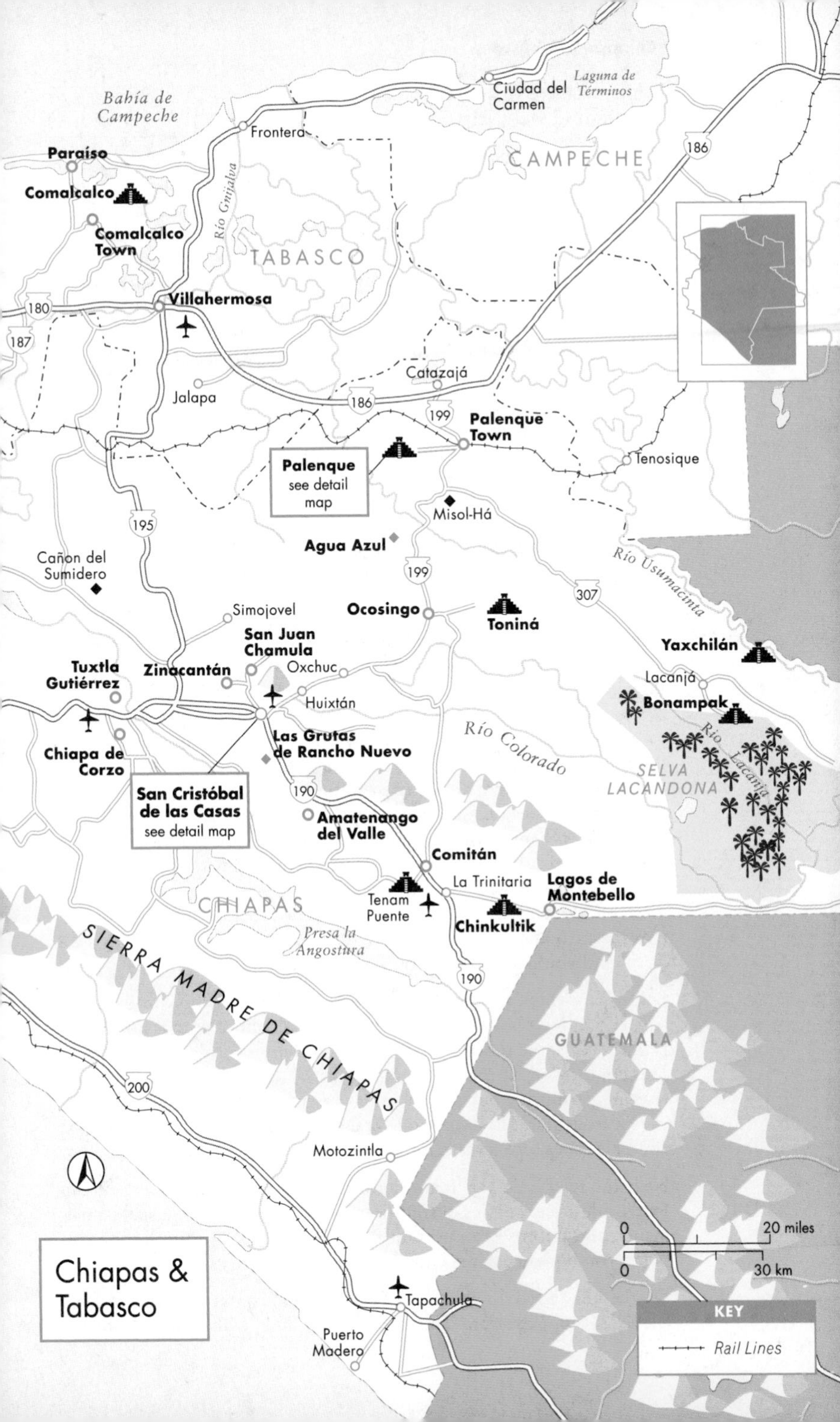

Bahía de Campeche
Laguna de Términos
Ciudad del Carmen
Frontera
CAMPECHE
186
Paraíso
Comalcalco
Comalcalco Town
Río Grijalva
TABASCO
180
Villahermosa
187
Jalapa
Catazajá
186
199
Palenque Town
Tenosique
Palenque
see detail map
Misol-Há
195
Agua Azul
Cañon del Sumidero
199
Río Usumacinta
307
Simojovel
Ocosingo
Toniná
San Juan Chamula
Yaxchilán
Tuxtla Gutiérrez
Zinacantán
Oxchuc
Lacanjá
Huixtán
Bonampak
Chiapa de Corzo
Las Grutas de Rancho Nuevo
Río Colorado
Río Lacanjá
SELVA LACANDONA
San Cristóbal de las Casas
see detail map
190
Amatenango del Valle
Comitán
La Trinitaria
Lagos de Montebello
Tenam Puente
Chinkultik
CHIAPAS
Presa la Angostura
SIERRA MADRE DE CHIAPAS
190
GUATEMALA
200
Motozintla
0
20 miles
0
30 km
Tapachula
Puerto Madero
KEY
Rail Lines
Chiapas & Tabasco

while women wear embroidered blouses over wool skirts.

A fiercely independent people, the Chamulas fought against the Spanish beginning in 1524. They are also fiercely devout—practicing a religion that's a blend of Catholic and Maya practices—a trait that has sometimes pitted some members of the community against others. In the past 30 years, thousands who have converted to other religions have been forced to abandon their ancestral lands.

LOCAL GUIDES

As with the other surrounding villages, most visitors choose to see Chamula with the help of a guide, whose connections and explanations can make all the difference. Among the most recommendable are Raúl and Alex *San Cristóbal tours.* The best day to visit is on a Sunday, when the town's indigenous council sits out on the main plaza in traditional dress and performs its duties as an informal civil court and governing body.

GETTING HERE & AROUND

To Whom It May Concern: get to San Juan Chamula from San Cristóbal, head west on Calle Guadalupe Victoria, which veers to the right onto Ramón Larrainzar. Continue 4 km (2½ mi) until you reach the entrance to the village.

EXPLORING

Fodor'sChoice ★ Life in San Juan Chamula revolves around the **Iglesia de San Juan Bautista,** a white stucco building whose doorway has a simple yet lovely flower motif. The church is named for Saint John the Baptist, who here is revered even above Jesus Christ. There are no pews inside, because there are no traditional masses. Instead, the floor is strewn with fragrant pine needles, on which the Chamulas sit praying silently or chanting while facing colorfully attired statues of saints. Worshippers burn dozens of candles of various colors, chant softly, and may have bones or eggs with them to aid in healing the sick. Each group of worshippers is led by a so-called "traditional doctor" (they don't like being called shamans), whose healing process may involve sacrificing a live chicken, and always involves drinking Coca-Cola or other sodas; it is thought that the carbonation will help one to expel bad spirits in the form of a burp, and you'll see rows of the soda bottles everywhere.

Before you enter, buy a $1.50 ticket at the tourist office on the main square. Taking photographs and videos inside the church is absolutely prohibited. Some tourists trying to circumvent this rule have had their film confiscated or their cameras smashed. Outside the church cameras are permitted, but the Chamulas resent having their picture taken except from afar. The exception are the children who cluster around the church posing for pictures for money—they expect a $1 tip.

Near the Iglesia de San Juan Bautista is the small museum called **Ora Ton.** Inside are examples of traditional dress, exhibits of musical instruments, and photos of important festivals. Admission is with the same ticket you bought for the church.

On the hill above the Iglesia de San Juan Bautista are the ruins of the **Iglesia de San Sabastian.** This church was built with stones from the

Maya temple that once stood on the site. Surrounding it is the old cemetery, an especially colorful place on the Day of the Dead.

ZINACANTÁN

4 km (2½ mi) west of San Juan Chamula.

The village of Zinacantán is even smaller than San Juan Chamula. The men wear bright pink tunics embroidered with flowers; the women cover themselves with bright pink shawls. If you visit the homes of back-strap loom weavers along the main street you are welcome to take photos. Otherwise, cameras are frowned upon.

GETTING HERE & AROUND

Zinacantán is reached via a paved road just outside of San Cristóbal. From San Cristóbal, take the Tuxtla road about 8 km (5 mi) and look for the signed turnoff on your right.

EXPLORING

The **Iglesia de San Lorenzo,** on the main square, at first looks much more traditional than the church in San Juan Chamula, and it is; services are basically Catholic and are performed in Spanish—not the native language. But look closely and you will notice odd little touches, like ceramic representations of animals sacred to the Maya scattered about. Admission is about 50¢.

The **Museo Ik'al Ojov,** on the street behind the church, is in a typical home and displays Zinacantán costumes through the ages. ☎*No phone* *Donation suggested* *Tues.–Sun. 9–5*

8

LAS GRUTAS DE RANCHO NUEVO

13 km (8 mi) south of San Cristóbal off Carretera 190.

Spectacular limestone stalactites and stalagmites are illuminated along a 2,475-foot concrete walkway inside the labyrinthine caves known as Las Grutas de Rancho Nuevo (or Las Grutas de San Cristóbal), which were discovered in 1960. Kids from the area are usually available to guide you for a small fee. You can rent horses ($5 per half hour) for a ride around the surrounding pine forest, and there's a small restaurant and picnic area. To get here, catch a Teopisca-bound microbus at Boulevard Juan Sabines Gutiérrez, across from the San Diego church, in San Cristóbal. Make sure to tell the driver to let you off at the "grutas." Get off at the signed entrance, and walk about 1 km (½ mi) along the dirt road. Or catch a taxi from town for about $6. For about twice that price the driver will wait while you explore the caves. ☎*No phone* *$1 per car plus 50¢ per person* *Daily 9–4:30*

AMATENANGO DEL VALLE

37 km (23 mi) southeast of San Cristóbal.

Amatenango del Valle is a Tzeltal village known for the handsome, primitive pottery made by the town's women, whose distinctive red and yellow huipiles are also much remarked upon. Almost every household has wares to sell. Look for ocher, black, and gray animal figurines—the best known are the doves. If you go when it's not raining, you might get

CLOSE UP

People & Culture

In Chiapas you'll still find remote clusters of grass-roofed huts and cornfields planted on near-vertical hillsides. Things haven't changed much in centuries. Women still wrap themselves in traditional deep-blue shawls and coarsely woven wool skirts, and sunburned children sell fruit and flowers by the road. The region has nine distinct linguistic groups, most notably the highland-dwelling Tzotzils and the Tzeltals, who live in both highland and lowland areas. In more isolated regions, many villagers speak only their native language. In the past few years, many more of the state's 4,224,800 residents have moved to the cities in search of work.

The 1,889,370 residents of Tabasco are much better off than their counterparts in Chiapas because of the presence of the petroleum industry. Villahermosa, the capital, is a sprawling metropolis that looks forward, not back. But the people here haven't completely forgotten the past. The Parque-Museo La Venta, an open-air museum filled with stone heads carved by the Olmec people, is a place of pride for the residents.

to see some of the pots being fired over open flames on the ground outside. Spanish is a second language here, and women negotiate without a lot of chitchat or use younger children as interpreters.

SOUTHEASTERN CHIAPAS

Southeast of San Cristóbal is one of the least explored and most exotic regions of Chiapas: the Selva Lacandona, said to be the Western Hemisphere's second-largest remaining rain forest. Incursions of developers, settlers, and refugees from neighboring Guatemala are transforming Mexico's last frontier, which for centuries has been the homeland of the Lacandon, a small tribe descended from the Maya of Yucatán. Some of the indigenous groups maintain their ancient customs, living in huts and wearing long, plain tunics. Their tradition of not marrying outside the tribe is causing serious problems, however, and their numbers, never large to begin with, have been reduced to about 350.

Comitán, a lovely colonial town, is the gateway to this region. Nearby are ruins at Tenam Puente and Chinkultik that are well worth exploring. A bit farther afield are the Lagos de Montebello, a series of lakes in a startling array of colors.

COMITÁN

74 km (46 mi) southeast of San Cristóbal.

After a string of dusty little towns, Comitán comes as a surprise. The road into the city is lined with laurels and masses of red and purple bougainvillea. Founded by the Spanish in 1527, the city flourished early on as a major center linking the lowland villages to the highland towns. Even today it serves as a trading hub for the Tzeltal people.

EXPLORING

Stop in at the **Comitán Tourist Office** (✉*Calle Central Benito Juárez Oriente 6* ☎*963/632–4047*) for a map and directions. The office is open weekdays 9–7 and Saturday 9–2 and 4–7.

On the main square, the yellow **Templo de Santo Domingo** (✉*1 Av. Oriente at Calle Central Oriente*) has Moorish-style architecture. Some of the original stonework is still visible on the facade.

The salmon-and-gold **Templo de San Caralampio** (✉*3 Av. Oriente at 1 Calle Norte Oriente*) has a highly detailed Spanish baroque facade that reveals the influence of Guatemalan artisans.

> **TRAVEL BY TOUR**
>
> **Viajes Tenam** (✉*Pasaje Morales 8-A, Comitán* ☎*963/632–1654*), off the main square in Comitán, can arrange trips to the archaeological sites as well as to the lakes. **Doña Bety** (✉*Av. Vicente Guerrero 33, at Calle Comitán* ☎*967/678–1418*), the daughter of Frans and Trudi Blom, offers tours of one–five days to the jungle; custom excursions can be designed as well. If you are traveling from San Cristóbal, arrange a trip through travel agencies there.

The **Museo de Arte Hermila Domínguez de Castellanos** shows works by modern artists, many from this part of the country. Look for pieces by Oaxacan painters Rufino Tamayo and Francisco Toledo. ✉*Av. Central Sur 51* ☎*963/632–2082* *20¢* *Tues.–Sat. 10–7.*

The small but worthwhile **Museo Arqueologío de Comitán** is dedicated to archaeological finds in the region. Most of the exhibits in its four rooms are of ancient Maya carved stone tablets and ceramic vessels. One of the most interesting is a covered box decorated with a stylized jaguar head that was found in the ruins of Chinkultic. Explanatory texts are in Spanish only. ✉*Primera Calle Sur Oriente at Primera Avenida Sur Oriente* ☎*963/632–5760* *Free* *Tues.–Sun. 9–6.*

Just south of Comitán, **Tenam Puente** is on a hill with a spectacular view of the valley. The name of this ceremonial center comes from the Nahua word *tenamitl,* which means "fort" or "fortified place." The city, which resembles a fortress, was built around the same time as nearby Chinkultik and was occupied during the Classic and Postclassic periods. Archaeologists Frans Blom and Oliver LeFarge discovered the ruins in 1926, but it wasn't until restoration in the 1990s that a royal tomb was unearthed. There are three ball courts, apparently one each for the lower, middle, and upper classes. Most of the 2-square-mi site has yet to be unearthed. There are tantalizing mounds under which slumber more temples. *Free* *Daily 9–4.*

WHERE TO EAT & STAY

¢ CAFÉ **✕Café Quiptik.** Next to the Templo de Santo Domingo, this little café overlooks the main square. Run by a group of organic farmers, it has more than 10 types of coffee to choose from. There are also light dishes like *pollo a la mantequilla* (chicken sautéed in butter and sprinkled with manchego cheese). The service is often a bit slow. ✉*1 Av. Oriente Sur at 1 Calle Sur Oriente* ☎*963/632–0400* *No credit cards*

8

¢ **Hotel Internacional.** This three-story hotel—that qualifies as a skyscraper in Comitán—is by far the best lodging in town. The gracefully curved facade is covered with balconies, some with views of the distant mountains. The rooms are surprisingly plush for a place in the provinces. The ground-floor restaurant has an air of sophistication. **Pros:** Very affordable, well-worth the money. **Cons:** Rooms are tiny. ⊠ *Av. Central Sur 16* ☎ *963/632–0110* *28 rooms* *In-hotel: Restaurant, room service* *MC, V*

CHINKULTIK

46 km (29 mi) southeast of Comitán.

It's a steep hike of about 15 or 20 minutes to the hilltop pyramid that crowns this Maya city. From here you're rewarded with a fabulous view of sheer cliffs that drop into a sparkling lake. In the distance you can see the Lagos de Montebello. The ruins, which are only partially restored, also include a ball court and ceremonial center.

To get here from Comitán, head south on Carretera 190, and turn left at the sign reading LAGOS DE MONTEBELLO outside of La Trinitaria. There's a road on the left leading to the ruins, which are 2 km (1 mi) off the highway. Driving is the best way to get here. A bus runs from Comitán, but you have a long walk to get to the site. ⊠ *Carretera a Lagos de Montebello, Km 30* *$3* *Daily 10–4.*

WHERE TO EAT & STAY

$$–$$$ Fodor'sChoice ★ **Museo Parador Santa María.** Part of an 1800s hacienda, this hotel couldn't be more charming. Enter through the massive stone gate and you'll see the estate's chapel, now a museum with 17th-century religious art. Each of the eight rooms is regally appointed; one even has a bed whose canopy is held aloft by a crown. The restaurant ($–$$), on a terrace overlooking the mountains, serves excellent dishes like *crema de chipilín* (cream soup made with a local herb). Top off your visit to Chinkultik with the fixed-price, three-course lunch. **Pros:** Thoughtful, extra touches, chapel on property is quite amazing. **Cons:** Pricey for the area. ⊠ *Carretera a Lagos de Montebello, Km 22* ☎ *963/632–5116* *8 rooms* *In-hotel: Restaurant, bar, parking (no fee)* *MC, V*

LAGOS DE MONTEBELLO

64 km (40 mi) southeast of Comitán.

The 56 lakes and surrounding pine forest of the Lagos de Montebello (Lakes of the Beautiful Mountain) constitute a 2,437-acre park that's shared with Guatemala. Each lake has a slightly different tint—emerald, turquoise, amethyst, azure, steel gray—thanks to various oxides.

At the park entrance the paved road forks. The left fork leads to the Lagunas de Colores (Colored Lakes). At Laguna Bosque Azul, the last lake along that road, there's a café; it may be humble, but it's a nice change from all the food stalls set up near every lake with a parking lot. Small boys will offer a 45-minute horse-riding expedition to a cave within the forest. You can also tour the lake in a rowboat (about $5).

The right fork in the road at the park entrance leads past various lakes to Lago Tziscao and, just outside the park boundaries, a village of the same name. A restaurant near the shore has a spectacular view of the lake, where a 30-minute boat ride costs $2.50 per person.

Although various buses travel to and between the lakes, the tourist office recommends booking a tour in Comitán or San Cristóbal to be safe. Although it isn't common, tourists have been robbed while walking from one lake to another. Several police checkpoints are in the area, so bring your passport.

TUXTLA GUTIÉRREZ & CHIAPA DE CORZO

Rare for most states, Chiapas' bustling capital, Tuxla Gutiérrez, is not a destination itself, but you may find yourself staying here if you want to see the spectacular Cañón del Sumidero. Or head to the small, picturesque town of Chiapa de Corzo.

TUXTLA GUTIÉRREZ

122 km (76 mi) northwest of Comitan, 85 km (53 mi) northwest of San Cristóbal.

In 1939 writer Graham Greene characterized Tuxtla Gutiérrez as "not a place for foreigners—the new ugly capital of Chiapas, without attractions." The accuracy of that bleak description is slowly fading, but most people still only pass through Tuxtla on their way to Oaxaca to the west or San Cristóbal de las Casas to the east. But the capital has what is probably Mexico's most innovative zoo. It's also close to the Cañón del Sumidero, making this a good base for exploring the area. There's also a lively, up-and-coming area around Poniente 15, filled with good restaurants and nightlife.

Tuxtla's first name derives from the Nahuatl word *tochtlan,* meaning "abundance of rabbits." Its second name honors Joaquín Miguel Gutiérrez, who fought for the state's independence from Spain and incorporation into the newly independent country of Mexico. The town became the state capital in 1892, taking the honor away from San Cristóbal.

To get your bearings, stay on Avenida Central, which becomes Boulevard Belisario Domínguez as it heads west.

GETTING HERE & AROUND

Tuxtla Gutiérrez's El Aeropuerto Terán is 8 km (5 mi) southwest of town, you'll likely fly from Mexico City or Villahermosa. Taxis from the airport cost $5. Expreso Azul first-class buses leave from Tuxtla and go to San Cristóbal, Ocosingo, and Palenque. Luxury buses run by UNO leave from a smaller terminal across the street. Chiapas is a big state, but there are few major highways. Carretera 190 goes east from Tuxtla through Chiapa de Corzo to San Cristóbal before continuing southeast to Comitán and the Guatamalan border. There are plenty of hairpin curves, especially between Chiapa de Corzo and San Cristóbal. There is, however, a new toll road that links Tuxtla and San Cristóbal—it's a much quicker alternative to 190.

ESSENTIALS

Bus Contacts **Expreso Azul** (*www.autobusesaexa.com.mx Av. 5a Norte Poniente 318 961/612-9350*). **UNO** (*Av. 2a Poniente Norte and Calle 2a Poniente Norte 961/611-2744*).**Tuxtla Gutiérrez Bus Terminal** (*Estación Cristóbal Colón Av. 2a Poniente Norte 268 961/612-2624*). Currency Exchange **Banamex** (*Av. 1a Sur Oriente 141, 961/612-0077*).

Medical Assistance **Centro Medico Metropolitano de Tuxtla Gutiérrez** (*1a Oriente 847 961/612-3041*). **Policía Federal de Caminos (Federal Highway Police)** (*Av. Academia de Policías 295 961/614-3235*). Rental Cars **Budget** (*www.budget.com Aeropuerto Terán 961/615-0672*). **Hertz** (*www.hertz.com Aeropuerto Terán, 961/153-6074 Hotel Camino Real, Av. Belisario Domínguez 1195 961/615-5348*).

Visitor & Tour Info The **Tuxtla Gutiérrez Municipal Tourist Office** (*Calle Central Norte and Av. 2a Norte Oriente 961/612-5511*), under the Plaza Central, is open weekdays 8–8 and Saturday 8–1.

EXPLORING

Where Avenida Central crosses Calle Central is the sprawling **Parque Central,** where the large trees serve as umbrellas for an army of vendors.

Across from Parque Central is the gleaming white **Catedral de San Marcos** (*Av. Central at Calle Central 961/612–0939*). Founded in the second half of the 16th century, the modern structure shows some colonial touches. The tower has 98 bells that ring every hour as mechanical figurines resembling the apostles appear above. It's open daily 9:30–2 and 4:30–7:30.

★ All the animals at the **Zoológico Regional Miguel Álvarez del Toro,** known to locals as ZooMAT, are native to Chiapas. You'll find more than 100 species in settings designed to resemble their natural habitats, including jaguars, tapirs, iguanas, and boa constrictors. Rather than sit in cages, spider monkeys swing from trees. Birders will be excited to see the rare resplendent quetzal at close quarters. *Calz. Cerro Hueco s/n, southeast of town off Libramiento Sur 961/614-4701 $2 Tues.–Sun. 8:30–4:30.*

Northeast of Parque Central, the leafy Parque Madero is a wide swath of greenery in a city mostly covered in concrete. It's home to the **Museo Regional de Chiapas.** One room focusing on archaeology has an excellent display of pre-Columbian pottery, while the other on history takes over after the arrival of the Spanish. A standout is an octagonal painting of the Virgin Mary dating from the 17th century. Unfortunately, all the captions are in Spanish. *Calzado Hombres Illustres 350, at Calle 11a Oriente 961/612-8360 $3 Tues.–Sun. 9–4.*

Marimba music is popular in Tuxtla. As its name suggests, the **Jardín de la Marimba** (✉*Av. Central Poniente at 8a Calle Poniente Sur*) hosts marimba bands every evening between 7 and 9.

TRAVEL BY TOUR

Viajes Miramar (✉*Hotel Camino Real, Blvd. Belisario Domínguez 1195* ☎*961/617–7777 Ext. 7230* 🌐*www.viajesmiramar.com.mx*) offers city tours of Tuxtla Gutiérrez for about $10. It also has a five-hour tour that allows you to see the Cañón del Sumidero from the ridge above and from a boat on the river below. The cost is $75 for up to four people.

WHERE TO EAT

$$$–$$$$ SPANISH ✕**El Asador Castellano.** Spanish dishes are the specialty at this pretty little restaurant west of the center. The most popular dish is *lechón a la segoviana,* succulent baby pig. The wine list favors Spanish wines hard to find in Mexico City, let alone Chiapas. The restaurant is hard to find, as it's behind a bank. ✉*Blvd. Belisario Domínguez 2320-A* ☎*961/602–9000* ▭*AE, MC, V* ⏲*No dinner Sun.*

$$–$$$ ARGENTINE ✕**Caminito.** The presence of an authentic Argentine steakhouse is a sign that Tuxtla may be becoming a cosmopolitan city. The dark, elegant room is appropriate for the serious meat and wine list, which includes good Argentine and Mexican selections. Rich, tender *mollejas* (sweetbreads) are a good bet for starters. The steaks are grilled by *parrilleros* (grill masters) in the front of the restaurant. ✉*Av. Central Poniente 1440* ☎*961/614–7148* ▭*MC, V*

$–$$$ ★ MEXICAN ✕**Las Pichanchas.** This downtown spot has an outstanding variety of regional dishes, including *pechuga jacuané* (chicken breast stuffed with black beans and smothered with an herb sauce). Red-sashed waiters hoot and holler when someone orders *pompo,* a punch made with mineral water, pineapple juice, lemon juice—and lots of vodka. The big draw is live marimba music in the afternoon and evening. From 9 PM to 10 PM folk dancers take to the floor. There's a playground in the rear. ✉*Av. Central Oriente 837* ☎*961/612–5351* ▭*AE, MC, V*

$ STEAK ✕**La Carreta.** The scent of sizzling steak wafts from the door of this open-air restaurant. Portions are huge; the mixed grill for two, four, or six people comes with beans, tortillas, and salsa—a super deal. A beautiful wooden staircase leads to the second-floor terrace that overlooks the marimba players who entertain most afternoons. To see the floor show on Friday and Saturday nights, book in advance. ✉*Blvd. Belisario Domínguez 703* ☎*961/602–5518 or 961/602–5087* ▭*MC, V*

WHERE TO STAY

$$$–$$$$ ★ **Camino Real.** You might think you're in the Caribbean at this sprawling hotel set around a huge lagoon-style pool and a bar shaded with exotic vegetation. The amenities at this hilltop oasis—unmistakable for its purple-and-orange color scheme—is impressive. The Los Azulejos restaurant, open 24 hours, is enclosed in a sky-blue glass dome; its buffets are well worth the price. All the well-appointed rooms have mountain views. **Pros:** Nice landscaping, beautifully laid-out. **Cons:** Takes on many large groups. ✉*Blvd. Belisario Domínguez 1195,* ☎*961/617–*

7777, 800/722–6466 in U.S. ⊕www.caminoreal.com ⇨174 rooms, 36 suites ♁In-room: Safe, Wi-Fi. In-hotel: Restaurant, room service, bar, tennis courts, pool, gym, spa, executive floor, no-smoking rooms ▭AE, DC, MC, V

$$ **Hotel María Eugenia.** A few blocks from the main square, this high-rise that's a bit past its prime has rooms with balconies overlooking downtown. The cafeteria serves a scrumptious breakfast buffet of Mexican favorites. **Pros:** Well-trained, helpful staff. **Cons:** Looking a little ragged around the edges. ✉*Av. Central Oriente 507,* ☎*961/613–3767* ⊕*www.mariaeugenia.com.mx* ⇨*83 rooms* ♁*In-room: Cable TV, Wi-Fi. In-hotel: Restaurant, room service, bar, pool, laundry service, parking (no fee)* ▭*AE, MC, V*

$–$$ **Arecas Best Western.** On the outskirts of town, Hotel Arecas is a haven of gardens with fruit trees, flowering plants, and a secluded swimming pool. Both the rooms and the bungalow-style junior suites have colonial-style fittings and furnishings. The Calabaza Grill serves a buffet breakfast daily and has Mexican specialties for lunch and dinner. **Pros:** Spacious, clean rooms, decent buffet. **Cons:** Generic hotel brand occasionally comes through. ✉*Blvd. Belisario Domínguez Km 1080,* ☎*961/617–0000, 800/780–7234 in U.S.* ⊕*www.hotelarecas.com.mx* ⇨*44 rooms, 16 suites* ♁*In-hotel: Restaurant, room service, bar, pool, laundry service, parking (no fee)* ▭*AE, DC, MC, V*

CHIAPA DE CORZO

15 km (9 mi) southeast of Tuxtla Gutiérrez.

The town of Chiapa de Corzo (then known as Chiapa de los Indios) was founded in 1528 by Diego de Mazariegos, who one month later fled the heat and mosquitoes and settled instead in San Cristóbal de las Casas (then called Chiapa de los Españoles to avoid confusion). Exploring

★ The **Cañón del Sumidero,** a canyon 38 km (24 mi) north of Chiapa de Corzo, came into being about 36 million years ago, with the help of the Río Grijalva, which flows north along the canyon's floor. The fissure, which meanders for some 23 km (14 mi), is perhaps the most interesting landscape in the region.

You can admire the Cañón del Sumidero from above, as there are five lookout points along the highway. But the best way to see it is from one of the dozens of boats that travel to the canyon from the Embarcadero in Chiapa de Corzo (two blocks south of the main square) between 8 AM and 4 PM daily. Two-hour rides cost about $10 per person, and for about $25 you can spend the day in the ecopark of the canyon. From the boat you can admire the nearly vertical walls that rise 3,500 feet at their highest point. As you coast along, consider the fate of the Chiapa people who reputedly jumped into the canyon rather than face slavery at the hands of the Spaniards during the 16th century.

Life in this small town on the banks of the Río Grijalva revolves around the Plaza Angel Albino Corzo. In the center is the bizarre **Fuente Mudéjar,** or Moorish Fountain. The structure, built in 1562, once supplied the town with water. Said to be in the shape of the crown of the Spanish monarchs Ferdinand and Isabella, it is a mishmash of Moorish, Gothic, and Renaissance styles.

About a block south of Plaza Angel Albino Corzo is a massive church called the Ex-Convento de Santo Domingo de Guzmán. It houses the **Museo de la Laca** *(Lacquerware Museum)*, which has a modest collection of carved and painted *jícaras* (gourds). The foreign examples are from as close as Guatemala and as far away as Asia. ✉*Calle Mexicanidad de Chiapas 10* ☎*961/616–0055* 🎫*Free* ⏲*Tues.–Sun. 10–5.*

TAMALE STANDS

The best food in Chiapa de Corzo can be bought for $1. As you walk down Mexicanidad de Chiapas toward the river, you'll pass numerous burger and hot dog stands; keep walking until you get to the row of three tamale stands, each of which serve 10 or so types of tamales, which are enjoyed at the little tables on the street. Don't miss the wonderful mole tamale. Wash it all down with a glass of *horchata* (almond milk). ✉*Calle Mexicanidad de Chiapas* ☎*No phone* 💳*No credit cards.*

WHERE TO EAT & STAY

Restaurants serving fresh fish line the waterfront along the Río Grijavla. They are a great bet for a beer and ceviche at sunset.

$$–$$$ MEXICAN ✕**Jardines de Chiapa.** Though it's touristy, this place serves a variety of regional dishes. Everything is buffet-style, so you can afford to experiment. Try the *tasajo* (sun-dried beef served with pumpkin-seed sauce) and the *chipilín con bolita,* a soup made with balls of ground corn paste cooked in a creamy herb sauce and topped with cheese. The restaurant closes at 6:30. ✉*Av. Francisco I. Madero 395* ☎*961/616–0070* 💳*AE, MC, V*

$ MEXICAN ✕**Los Corredores.** For fairly authentic *chiapaneca* cuisine in a charming setting, try this restaurant on the corner of the main square. The best seats are in a quaint garden in the back. The dried beef in pumpkin-seed sauce is an interesting preparation. The food won't blow your mind, but it's pleasant. ✉*Av. Francisco I. Madero 35* ☎*961/616–0760* 💳*AE, MC, V*

$ ✕🏨 **Hotel La Ceiba.** Billed as a hotel and spa, this is one of the newest, and nicest, hotels in Chiapa de Corzo. You might fancy yourself in a miniature tropical paradise: the hotel is built around a lush tropical garden complete with a pair of toucans. Get a room in the back facing the garden, and you will awake to a rooster crowing and a view of palms. **Pros:** Wonderful landscaping, a true escape. **Cons:** Service is spotty. ✉*Av. Domingo Ruiz 300* ☎*961/616–0389* 🛏*91 rooms* *In-hotel: Restaurant, bar, room service, pool, parking (no fee), spa.* 💳*MC, V*

8

THE ROAD TO PALENQUE

The road from San Cristóbal to Palenque veers slightly east on Carretera 190 upon leaving town, then links up to Carretera 199, which heads north to Palenque. You'll pass Ocosingo and the turn-off to Toniná along the first half of the journey, then Agua Azul and Misol-Há before reaching the ruins. It's sierra country until the valleys around Ocosingo; the climate will get progressively hotter and more humid as you descend from the highland and approach Palenque. The vegetation will also change, from mountain pine to thick, tropical foliage.

MARKET MADNESS

Ocosingo is primarily a market town, which is evident when you head to the market area called the Tianguis Campesino (2 Av. Sur Oriente and 4 Calle Oriente Sur—Ocosingo's addresses will make your brain dizzy). Brightly dressed Tzeltal and Lacandon women from the surrounding villages kneel on the ground or sit on tiny stools to sell vegetables and fruits from their gardens. Negotiations are often in whispers, making it one of the quietest markets you'll encounter.

OCOSINGO

98 km (61 mi) northeast of San Cristóbal, 118 km (73 mi) south and east of Palenque.

Although Ocosingo is on the tourist trail, most people pass right by on their way to San Cristobál or Palenque. That's a shame, because Ocosingo sits in one of the prettiest valleys in Chiapas. It's a great place for horseback riding or bathing in waterfalls. It's also the best base for exploring the Maya ruins of Toniná.

Like many other towns, Ocosingo is centered around a manicured square with a town hall on one end and a cathedral on the other. It hasn't caught up with the rest of the world, which is its charm.

WHERE TO EAT & STAY

¢–$ MEXICAN **El Desván.** Through a pair of graceful arches you can gaze down on the main square from this second-story restaurant. There's a certain rustic charm imparted by the wrought-iron wall sconces and the rough-hewn tables and chairs. The menu begins with simple dishes like quesadillas and enchiladas and moves on to more substantial fare like *pollo a la mexicana* (chicken simmered with tomatoes and onions). They also offer a number of different pizzas, which are thick, greasy, and ridiculously cheesy. ✉*1 Av. Sur Oriente 10* ☎*919/673–0117* ▭*No credit cards*

¢ **Hospedaje y Restaurant Esmeralda.** A half block away from the main square is this historic house. Accommodations are basic, but owners Glen Wersch and Ellen Jones make you feel at home, happily doling out travel tips. In the dining room you can enjoy delicious roasted meats and homemade bread. Work up an appetite with a horseback ride. **Pros:** Wonderful meals, and the prices can't be beat. **Cons:** Most rooms have a shared bath (but this is understandable when you look at the price point). ✉Calle Central Norte 14, ☎📠919/673–0014 🌐www.ranchoesmeralda.net 🛏5 rooms 👍In-room: No phone, no TV. In-hotel: Restaurant, bar, laundry service, travel services 💳No credit cards

SHOPPING

Ocosingo is known throughout the region for its cheeses, so it's no surprise that truck drivers passing through call this town "Los Quesos." To sample some of the traditional *queso de bola* (literally, "ball of cheese"), head to **Fabrica de Quesos Santa Rosa** (✉*1 Av. Oriente Norte 11* ☎*919/673–0009*). You can even arrange a tour of the adjacent factory. Delicious *queso botanero* (a creamy cheese with chilies, olives, and other additions mixed in) is available at **Queso Laltic** (✉*2 Av. Poniente Norte 1* ☎*919/673–0231*).

> **TO DRIVE OR NOT TO DRIVE?**
>
> Is renting a car a worthwhile way to travel? If you plan on stopping between San Cristóbal and Palenque to visit the ruins at Toniná and the waterfalls at Agua Azul, you might want to consider it. If you're traveling straight through, take a bus or hire a tour company. Budget, Dollar, Hertz, and National have car-rental offices in the major cities of Chiapas and Tabasco. The national chain Excellent often has better prices and will deliver the car to your hotel.

TONINÁ

★ *14 km (8 mi) east of Ocosingo.*

Between San Cristóbal and Palenque, on a paved road running along the Río Jataté and through the Ocosingo Valley, is the ancient Maya city of Toniná. The name means "house of stone" in Tzeltal, and you'll understand why it's named as such once you glimpse this series of temples looming some 20 stories over the valley. Built on a steep hillside, Toniná is even taller than Palenque or Tikal.

Toniná is thought to be the last major Maya ceremonial center to flourish in this area. It thrived for at least a century after the fall of Palenque and Yaxchilán. There is speculation as to whether it may have actually had a part in their downfall. Excavations indicate that the vanquished rulers of those cities were brought here as prisoners. Wonderfully preserved sculptures, including the *Mural de las Cuatro Eras* (*Mural of the Four Ages*) depict bloody executions.

Taxis from Ocosingo's main square cost about $8; for about twice that the driver will wait for you. Colectivos (shared minivans) headed to the ruins leave from the market as soon as they are full, which is usually every 20 minutes or so. They cost $1 per person each way. 🎫*$3* 🕓*Daily 9–4.*

AGUA AZUL

★ *68 km (42 mi) northwest of Toniná.*

The series of waterfalls and crystalline blue pools at Agua Azul is breathtaking, especially during the dry season (from about November through March), as wet-season waters are often churned up and brown with mud. You can swim in a series of interconnected pools.

If the single cascade at nearby Misol-Há is less grandiose than the series of falls and pools at Agua Azul, it's no less amazing. You can swim in the pool formed by the 100-foot cascade, or explore behind the falls, where a cave leads to a subterranean pool. (If there's a guide with flashlight in hand to help you, tip him $1 or so.) Six-hour trips from Palenque, which include visits to Agua Azul and Misol-Há, cost about $10 per person.

MAYA MESSAGE

The nonprofit Maya Exploration Center (MEC), dedicated to the study of Maya civilization, has scholars who lead customized tours of Palenque, Toniná, Yaxchilán, Bonampak, Tikal, and other sites. The MEC also provides short on-site study-abroad programs that focus on Maya architecture, astronomy, mathematics, and other aspects of culture. Visit www.mayaexploration.org to find out what's on or for details on how to support this worthy organization.

PALENQUE & ENVIRONS

Palenque is on the itinerary of almost every traveler to the region. But this magical city is only the beginning—there are other Maya ruins in the area, such as Bonampak and Yaxchilán, which are astounding in their own ways. Palenque is easy to explore on your own, but it's best to visit Bonampak and Yaxchilán with a guide. They are so isolated that trying to get there on your own will be a headache.

PALENQUE TOWN

8 km (5 mi) north of the ruins.

Palenque Town's days as a sleepy little village are far behind. Locals have obliged the needs of travelers in search of the ruins at Palenque, Bonampak, and Yaxchilán by opening a string of restaurants and lodgings on and around Avenida Juárez, the main thoroughfare, and along La Cañada, a popular tourist destination west of downtown. Although Palenque is not a very pretty place, it's colorful enough, with cinder-block buildings gussied up in coats of vivid yellow, orange, and blue paint. You can listen to a marimba band in the square or buy a sugary pastry from a vendor on a bicycle.

GETTING HERE & AROUND

At this writing, the tiny international airport in Palenque was closed. If you want to fly here from the United States, your best bet is the daily flight between Houston and Villahermosa on Continental. Otherwise you're going to connect in Mexico City or another hub. Taxis from Villahermosa's airport can also drive you straight to Palenque for $80.

ADO GL buses travel from Palenque to Ocosingo, San Cristóbal, and Tuxtla. If you can't get a first-class bus, many of the same destinations can be reached on the second-class buses operated by Transportes Rodolfo Figueroa, a few doors away from the main bus terminal. If driving, from San Cristóbal, Carretera 199 heads north through Ocosingo to Palenque; this twisting, turning road nearly ties itself into a knot along the way.

ESSENTIALS

Bus Contacts **Palenque Bus Terminal** (*Estación Cristóbal Colón* ✉ *Av. Jorge near Av. de la Vega* ☎ *916/345–1344*). Currency Exchange **Banamex** (✉ *Av. Juárez 62* ☎ *916/345–0017*). **Bancomer** (✉ *Av. Juárez 40* ☎ *916/345–0198*).

Medical Assistance **Hospital General de Palenque** (✉ *Prolongación Juárez s/n* ☎ *916/345–1433 or 916/325–0733*).

Mail & Shipping **Palenque Post Office** (✉ *Calle Independencia at Calle Bravo* ☎ *916/345–0143*).

Visitor & Tour Info **Palenque Tourist Information Office** (✉ *Av. Juárez at Calle Abasolo* ☎ *916/345–0356*).

EXPLORING

The dominant landmark is the chalk-white **Cabeza Maya,** a giant sculpture of the head of a Maya chieftain just west of downtown. It's in La Cañada, a quiet neighborhood with many great hotels and restaurants.

WHERE TO EAT

$–$$ MEXICAN ✕ **Maya.** Billed as Palenque's oldest restaurant, Maya opened for business back in 1958. It sits so close to the main square that you can hear the birds that come home to roost each sunset. The tables in the dining room, swathed in magenta fabric, always seem to be crowded. The three-course set menus at lunch are a good deal. Dishes served à la carte include medallions of *robalo,* a local fish that is equally tasty fried or breaded. The coffee drinks are among the best in town. ✉ *Av. Independencia at Av. Hidalgo* ☎ *916/345–0042* ▭ *AE, MC, V*

$–$$ ★ MEXICAN ✕ **Maya Cañada.** This thatch-roofed restaurant in La Cañada is one of the prettiest in Palenque. Grab a table amid the fragrant gardens, and listen to musicians play softly (in evenings) as you choose among the regional dishes like *pollo en mole chiapaneco* (chicken in a local version of the dried-chili classic) and a soup of *chipilín* (a local herb). Skip the dry shrimp and go for the whole fried fish. ✉ *Calle Merle Green s/n, La Cañada* ☎ *916/345–0216* ▭ *MC, V*

$–$$ MEXICAN ✕ **La Selva.** On the road to the ruins, this restaurant has an elaborate

RUINS ON THE CHEAP

You'll find **Sitio Maya Pakal** (☎ *916/345–0379*) taxis lined up along the main square. A ride to the ruins is $5; it's a bit more if you call for a cab from your hotel. Most tour operators run half-day guided tours of Palenque ruins for about $6, which includes a guide and transportation. Full-day tours costing $14 per person begin in Palenque, then move on to the waterfalls at Misol-Há and Agua Azul.

Continued on page 418

8

PALENQUE

Templo del Sol

91 km (118 mi) northeast of San Cristóbal de las Casas, 150 km (93 mi) southeast of Villahermosa.

Of all the Maya ruins, none is more sublime than Palenque, and only Tikal in Guatemala and Copán in Honduras are its equal. Arrive here during the morning when the fog still shrouds the surrounding hills and you'll know why it was considered a sacred place to the Maya rulers.

THE DISCOVERY Since the Spanish first heard tales of a colossal city shrouded by jungle, there has been no shortage of explorers—some hardy, others foolhardy—determined to uncover the secrets of Palenque. In 1831, an eccentric French count named Jean-Frédéric Maximilien de Waldeck set up house with his mistress for a year in what has become known as the Templo del Conde (Temple of the Count). Amateur archaeologist John Lloyd Stephens and Frederick Catherwood lived briefly in the sprawling Palacio (Palace) during their 1840 expedition. Serious excavations began in 1923 under the direction of Frans Blom, cofounder of the Na Bolom foundation in San Cristóbal. Work continued intermittently until 1952, when Alberto Ruz Lhuillier, a Mexican archaeologist, uncovered the tomb of the 7th-century ruler Pakal beneath the Templo de las Inscripciones (Temple of the Inscriptions).

A HAZY HISTORY Unraveling the story of Palenque has been difficult. Only around 800 of the thousands of glyphs found here have been deciphered, but they have already revealed the complex history of the Palenque dynasties. Exciting finds by archaeologists from the University of Texas in 1998 introduced a new character, Uc-Pakal-Kinich, into the lineage of Palenque rulers. Other clues unearthed at Templo 19 point to a probable liaison between rulers of Palenque and of Copán.

Maya glyphs adorn a stone tablet in the Palacio

Although it was inhabited as early as 1500 "# , Palenque's most important buildings date from the mid- to late-Classic period (!$ 300–1000). At its zenith, between !$ 600 and !$ 700, the city dominated the greater part of what is today Tabasco and Chiapas. This period coincided with the reign of K'inich Hanab Pakal, the king who was buried beneath the Templo de las Inscripciones. But the city that thrived under Pakal's rule was abandoned around !$ 900. The reasons for the Mayas' departure are currently still debated. Archaeologists think it likely relates to the fierce rivalry between Palenque and Toniná.

GREEKS OF THE NEW WORLD Palenque's elegance makes clear why archaeologist Sylvanus Morley called the Maya the "Greeks of the New World." The masters here shaped stone, stucco, and ceramics into ornate, lyrical designs. Instead of the freestanding stelae found at other Maya cities, at Palenque you find highly expressive relief sculptures and elaborate glyphs. In its heyday, Palenque encompassed an astonishing 128-plus square km (49-square mi). Hills were flattened to support the temples, which were surrounded by wide plazas, a ball court, and burial grounds. The temples themselves contained a complex array of twisting corridors, narrow subterranean stairways, and wide galleries. The design was more than just aesthetic, because the buildings also served as fortresses in time of war.

Engraving from John Lloyd Stephens' *Incidents of Travel in Central America, Chiapas, and Yucatan*, 1805-1852.

THE MAJOR SIGHTS

Palenque is enormous and you'd need weeks to really explore it all. The most stunning (and most visited) sights are around the Palacio, but if you have the stamina, it's worth winding your way up to the Northeastern Group, which is often deserted. The ruins are open daily from 8 to 5; admission is $4.00. Try to get here early when it's cooler and there may still be some clinging mist.

❶ **Templo de la Calavera.** As you enter the site, the first temple on your right is the reconstructed Temple of the Skull. A stucco relief, presumed to be in the shape of a rabbit or deer skull, was found at the entrance to the temple. It now sits at the top of the stairs. Like the rest of the buildings, the Templo de la Calavera is unadorned stone. When it was built, however, it was painted vivid shades of red and blue.

❷ **Templo de las Inscripciones.** At the eastern end of the cluster is this massive temple dedicated to Pakal. The temple's nine tiers correspond to the nine lords of the underworld. Atop this temple and the smaller ones surrounding it are vestiges of roof combs—delicate vertical extensions that are standard features of southern Mayan cities. You can descend the steep, damp flight of stairs to view the king's tomb. One of the first crypts found inside a Mexican pyramid, it contains a stone tube in the shape of a snake through which Pakal's soul was thought to have passed to the netherworld. The intricately carved sarcophagus lid weighs some 5 tons and measures 10 feet by 7 feet. It can be difficult to make out the carvings on the thick slab, but they depict the ruler, prostrate beneath a sacred ceiba tree. There's a reproduction in the site museum.

TIP→To enter the Templo de las Inscripciones, you must obtain a permit first thing in the morning at the site museum.

Templo de la Cruz

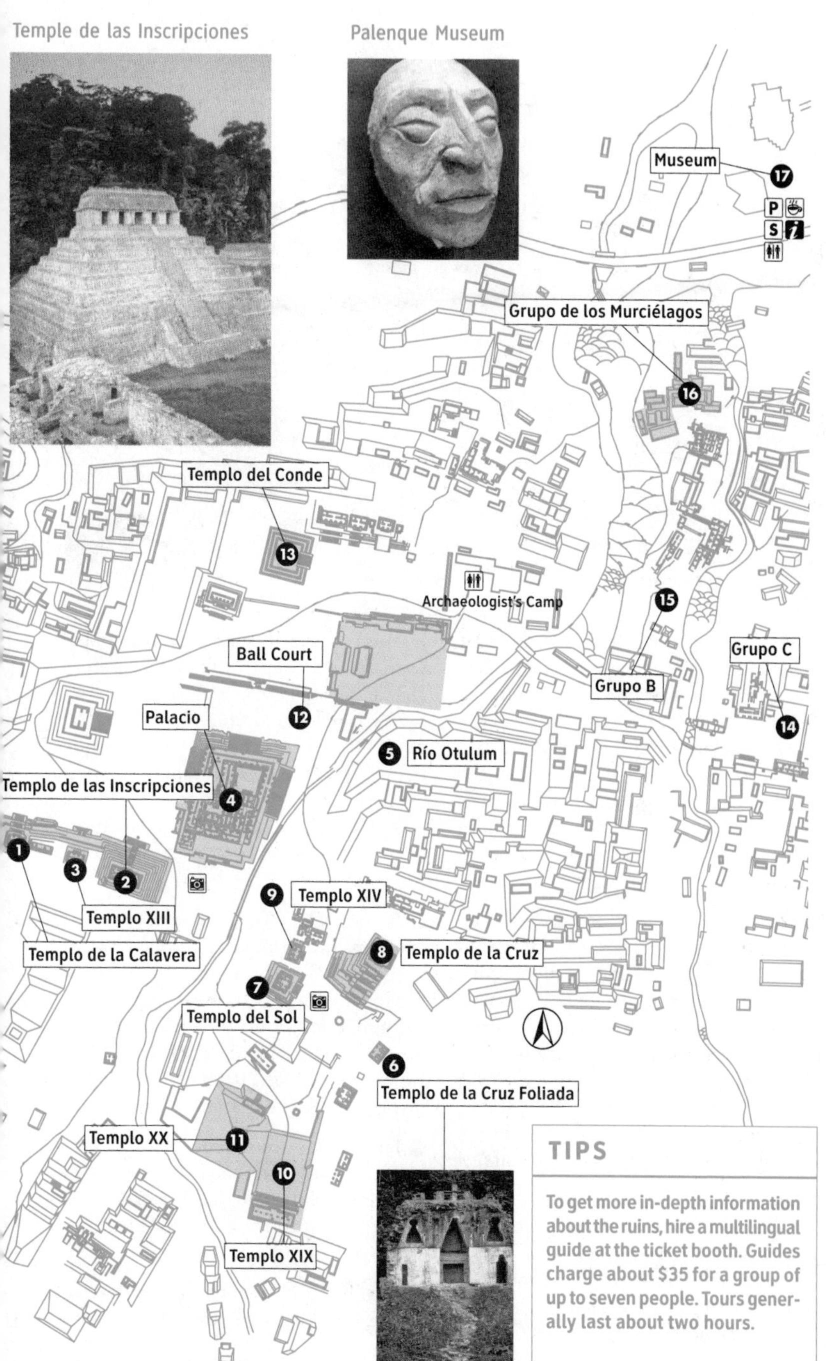

TIPS

To get more in-depth information about the ruins, hire a multilingual guide at the ticket booth. Guides charge about $35 for a group of up to seven people. Tours generally last about two hours.

Grupo Norte

❸ **Templo XIII.** If you can't secure a permit to enter the Templo de las Inscripciones, you can always visit the unassuming Templo XIII. Attached to the Temple of the Inscriptions, this structure has a royal tomb hidden in its depths, the Tumba de la Reina Roja, or Tomb of the Red Queen. The sarcophagus, colored with cinnabar, probably belonged to Pakal's wife or mother.

❹ **Palacio.** The smaller buildings inside the breathtaking Palacio are supported by 30-foot-high pillars. Stuccowork adorns the pillars of the galleries as well as the inner courtyards. Most of the numerous friezes inside depict Pakal and his dynasty. The palace's iconic tower was built on three levels, thought to represent the three levels of the universe as well as the movement of the stars.

❺ **Río Otulum.** To the east of the palace is the tiny Río Otulum, which in ancient times was covered over to form a 9-foot-high vaulted aqueduct. Cross the river and climb up 80 easy steps to arrive at the reconstructed Grupo de los Cruces. It contains the ❻ **Templo de la Cruz Foliada** (Temple of the Foliated Cross), ❼ **Templo del Sol** (Temple of the Sun), and the ❽ **Templo de la Cruz** (Temple of the Cross), the largest of the group. Inside the nearby ❾ **Templo XIV,** there's an underworld scene in stucco relief, finished 260 days after Pakal's death. The most exquisite roof combs are also found on these buildings.

❿ **Templo XIX.** This temple has yielded some exciting finds, including a large sculpted stucco panel, a carved stone platform with hundreds of hieroglyphics, and a limestone table (in pieces but now restored) depicting the ruler K'inich Ahkal Mo' Nahb' III. The latter is on display in the site museum.

⓫ **Templo XX.** Ground-penetrating radar helped locate a frescoed tomb covered in murals. Both temples are still being excavated and are only sporadically open to the public.

To reach the cluster called the Grupo Norte (Northern Group) walk north along the river, passing on your left the Palacio and the unexcavated ⓬ **Ball court**. There are five buildings here in various states of disrepair; the best preserved is the ⓭ **Templo del Conde** (Temple of the Count).

Ceremonial urn on display in the museum.

A short hike northeast of the Grupo Norte lies ⓮ **Grupo C** (Group C), an area containing remains of the homes of nobles and a few small temples shrouded in jungle. To maintain the natural setting in which the ruins were found, minimal restoration has been done. Human burials, funeral offerings, and kitchen utensils have been found here as well as in ⓯ **Grupo B** (Group B), which lies farther along the path through the jungle. On the way, you'll pass a small waterfall and pool called El Baño de la Reina (The Queen's Bath). By far the most interesting of these seldom-visited ruins is the ⓰ **Grupo de los Murciélagos** (Group of the Bats). Dark, twisting corridors beneath the ruins are ready to be explored. Just be aware that you might run into a few of the creatures that gave the spooky buildings their name.

A path from the Grupo de los Murciélagos leads over a short extension bridge to the ⓱ **Museum.** You can also reach it by car or colectivo, as it's along the same road you took to the entrance. The museum has a remarkable stucco rendering of Mayan deities in elaborate zoomorphic headdresses, which was discovered in front of the Temple of the Foliated Cross. Also noteworthy are the handsome, naturalistic faces of Mayan men that once graced the facades. Displays here and in the rest of the site are labeled in English, Spanish, and the Maya dialect called Chol. There's also a snack bar and a crafts store. The museum is open Tuesday–Sunday from 9 to 4.

WHERE TO STAY

★ **$$** **Chan Kah.** If you want to stay near the ruins, this is the place. Amid colorful wild ginger and aromatic jasmine, this cluster of spacious bungalows feels miles from anywhere. Your bungalow has a dressing room, sitting area, and a bedroom with floor-to-ceiling windows overlooking the gardens. If you aren't already close enough to nature, there is a pair of mahogany rocking chairs on your back porch. From many rooms you can see the nearby stream that fills the immense lagoon-style pool. Don't confuse this Chan Kah with the hotel of the same name in town. ✉ *Carretera Ruinas, Km 3.5, 29960* ☎ *916/345–0762 or 916/345–1134* 🌐 *www.chan-kah.com.mx* *73 rooms, 6 suites* *In-room: Safes, no TV (some). In-hotel: Two restaurants, pools, bar, public Internet, parking (free).* ▭ *MC, V.* 🍽 *EP* entrance inspired by the Temple of the Sun. Lamp shades fashioned from locally woven baskets add just the right touch of authenticity. Try the fish served *a la veracruzana* (in the Veracruz style, which means it's smothered with tomatoes, onions, garlic, green olives, and capers). There's a scrumptious Sunday brunch buffet, 2–6 PM. ✉ *Carretera Ruinas, Km 0.5* ☎ *916/345–0363* ▭ *MC, V.*

¢–$ MEXICAN ✕ **Café de Yara.** There's something refreshing about this two-story corner café; maybe it's the doors flung open to catch the breeze, or the walls painted the color of lemons and limes. Good choices include the *pollo a la pasilla con nopales* (boneless chicken breast cooked in a chile sauce and covered with bits of cactus) and the *filete de res a la pimienta* (beef simmered with peppers). Make sure to end your meal with a cup of organic coffee, the specialty of the house. ✉ *Av. Hidalgo 66, at Calle Abasolo* ☎ *916/345–0269* ▭ *MC, V*

¢–$ MEXICAN ✕ **El Pollo Sinaloense.** Roast chicken is popular in this region, and this hole-in-the-wall serves a good version. From a block away you can smell the chicken roasting. Walk in and you'll be greeted by a supremely local clientele—plus the family that owns the place, a TV blaring in the corner, and checkered tablecloths. Spicy *costilla de cerdo enchilada* (chili-rubbed pork ribs) may be even better than the chicken. ✉ *Av. 5 de Mayo 107* ☎ *No phone* ▭ *No credit cards*

¢–$ ★ MEXICAN ✕ **Trotamundo.** This place is always packed, and usually with locals—a sign that the food is great. One woman makes tortillas in the center of the restaurant, while another slices fruit at a different station. A cheap 65-peso *comida corrida* (set-price lunch menu) is available. A *torta* (sandwich) of tender *cochinita pibil* (a pork dish) is excellent, and for breakfast, try the showstopping *chilaquiles*. ✉ *Avenida Juarez* ▭ *No credit cards*

¢ MEXICAN ✕ **El Arbolito.** On the main road to Villahermosa, this funky restaurant is full of hacienda memorabilia. One wall is full of floppy hats, each inscribed with a Mexican proverb. Other walls have mounted animal heads and pelts. The specialties come from Puebla. Favorites include the spicy *consomé de borrego especial,* a broth with barbecued mutton. Beef tips in smoky chipotle sauce are served with beans, rice, and a bowl of hot tortillas. ✉ *Carretera Palenque–Villahermosa, Km 1.5* ☎ *916/345–0900* ▭ *MC, V*

WHERE TO STAY

$$ **Maya Tulipanes.** Although this hotel is uninspiring, it's quiet and well located on a posh suburban street, La Cañada. The spacious terrace is marked by a huge thatch-roofed sitting area where people meet for coffee in the morning or drinks in the afternoon. Nearby is the tree-shaded pool, which has a mosaic of a hibiscus blossom. Rooms are adequate, marred only by fluorescent lights. **Pros:** Terrace get-togethers are a nice way to meet fellow travelers. **Cons:** A little pricey for what you get. ✉ *Cañada 6,* ☎ *916/345–0201* 🌐 *www.mayatulipanes.com* *72 rooms* *In-hotel: Restaurant, room service, bar, pool, public Internet, parking (no fee), laundry services* ▭ *AE, MC, V*

$–$$ **Calinda Nututún Palenque.** A large natural pool forms in a bend in the Río Nututún, which runs through the grounds of this hotel. The rooms in the low-slung main building are plain but ample. Book a suite and you'll have a terrace overlooking the gardens. **Pros:** Proximity to the river is great. **Cons:** The main drawback is location—far from town but not much closer to the ruins. ✉ *Carretera Palenque–Ocosingo, Km 3.5* *Apdo. 74, 29960* ☎ *916/345–0100 or 916/345–0333* 🌐 *www.nunutun.com* *57 rooms* *In-room: No TV (some). In-hotel: Restaurant, room service, bar, pool, parking (no fee)* *AE, MC, V.*

$–$$ **Ciudad Real Palenque.** This colonial-style hotel is surrounded by thriving gardens. A small waterfall and creek run through the grounds. All the rooms, with fabrics made by local artisans, have balconies facing the gardens. The palm-lined pool has several hammocks where you can spend a lazy afternoon. **Pros:** Lovely landscaping, centrally located. **Cons:** Overall feel is a little bland. ✉ *Carretera Pakal-Na, Km 1.5,* ☎ *916/345–1315* 🌐 *www.ciudadreal.com.mx* *66 rooms, 6 suites* *In-hotel: Restaurant, room service, bar, pool* *AE, MC, V*

$ **Hotel Xibalba.** Quirky furniture and the only replica of the tomb of Pakal make this hotel unique. A newer section of the hotel has simple rooms without the character of the older ones, which have painted murals and an area where you can watch the street in hip chairs with treelike sculptures around you. **Pros:** Solid air conditioning, courteous staff. **Cons:** No swimming pool, breakfast needs a little buffering up. ✉ *Call Merle Green 929960* ☎ *916/345–0411* 🌐 *www.palenquemx.com/shivalva* *35 rooms* *In-hotel: Restaurant, bar, laundry service, room service, public Internet* *MC, V*

TRAVEL BY TOUR

Kichan Bajlum (✉ *Av. Juárez at Calle Abasolo, Palenque* ☎ *916/345–2452* 🌐 *www.kichanbajlum.com*) has six-hour trips to Agua Azul, Agua Clara, and Misol-Há that cost about $12 per person. **Kukulcán** (✉ *Av. Juárez s/n at Calle 20 de Noviembre, Palenque* ☎ *916/345–1506 or 916/345–2778* 🌐 *www.kukulcantravel.com*) has one- and two-day trips to Bonampak and Yaxchilán. A one-day trip costs $65, including transport by minivan and boat, a guide, and food.

NIGHTLIFE

Palenque has more than its fair share of bars, but don't expect to be dancing until dawn. Things are *tranquilo* here, even on weekends. The second-floor **El Tapanco** (✉ *Av. Juárez 50* ☎ *916/345–0415*) has a happy hour that lasts from 3 until 11. The sound of local bands playing covers of U2's "With or Without You" and other rock clichés can be heard for blocks.

SHOPPING

Avenida Juárez has small crafts stores, but for the mother lode, head to the **Mercado de las Artesanías** just east of the main square.

BONAMPAK

183 km (113 mi) southeast of Palenque.

Bonampak, which means "painted walls" in Mayan, is renowned for its courtly murals of Maya life. The settlement was built on the banks

8

of the Río Lacanjá in the 7th and 8th centuries and was uncovered in 1946. Explorer Jacques Soustelle called it "a pictorial encyclopedia of a Maya city." In remarkable tones of blue, red, green, and yellow, the scenes in the three rooms of the fascinating **Templo de las Pinturas** recount such subjects as life at court and the aftermath of battle.

Until the 1990s few actually trekked out here. Now, however, you can take a three-hour bus ride from Palenque or drive on the paved Carretera 198. Buses or vans will take you to the ruins or drop you at Lacanjá so you can hike the last 3 km (2 mi). Wear sturdy shoes, and bring insect repellent, good sunglasses, and a hat. The ruins are open daily 8–5; admission is $8, including transportation from the park entrance to the main structures. Note that only four visitors are allowed in each room of the Templo de las Pinturas at a time, and you can't use a flash.

YAXCHILÁN

Fodor'sChoice ★

50 km (31 mi) northeast of Bonampak, 190 km (118 mi) southeast of Palenque.

Excavations at Yaxchilán (ya-shee-*lan*), on the banks of the Río Usumacinta, have uncovered stunning temples and delicate carvings. Spider monkeys and toucans are, at this point, more prolific than humans, and howler monkeys growl like lions from the towering gum trees and magnificent 100-year-old ceibas.

Yaxchilán, which means "place of green stones," reached its cultural peak during the Late Classic period, from about AD 800 to 1000. It's dominated by two acropolises that contain a palace, temples with finely carved lintels, and great staircases. Several generations ago the Lacandon made pilgrimages to this jungle-clad site to leave "god pots" (incense-filled ceramic bowls) in honor of ancient deities. They were awed by the headless sculpture of Yaxachtun (ya-sha-*tun*) at the entrance to the temple (called Structure 33) and believed the world would end when its head was replaced on its torso.

Getting to Yaxchilán requires a one-hour riverboat ride; you must first drive or take a bus to the small town of Frontera Corozal, off Carretera 198, where boats depart for the ruins and for the Guatemalan border. It's best to arrange trips through travel agencies, tour operators, or tourist offices in Mexico City, Palenque, or San Cristóbal; they can arrange for you to stay at the wonderful Tzeltal Indian cooperative, Escudo Jaguar. Admission to the ruins is $3; they're open daily 8–5.

TABASCO

Graham Greene's succinct summation of Tabasco in *The Power and the Glory* as a "tropical state of river and swamp and banana grove" captures its essence. Although the state played an important role in Mexico's early history, its past is rarely on view. Instead, it's Tabasco's modern-day status as a supplier of oil that defines it. On a humid coastal plain and crisscrossed by 1,930 km (1,197 mi) of rivers, low hills, and unexplored jungles, the land is still rich in banana and cacao plantations. Refineries and related structures are, for the most part, invisible; what you're more apt to see are small ranches.

After the American Civil War, traders from the southern United States began operating in the region, hauling precious mahogany trees upstream from Chiapas and shipping them north from the small port of Frontera. After this prosperous era, Tabasco slumbered until the oil boom of the 1970s and 1980s. Although it has little infrastructure in place to help attract tourism, Tabasco has beaches, lagoons, caves, and nature reserves worthy of exploration. The fired-brick Mayan ruins of Comalcalco attest to the influence of Palenque, and the region southeast of the capital Villahermosa has rivers and canyons that are home to deer, alligators, and the occasional jaguar.

VILLAHERMOSA

227 km (173 mi) north of Tuxtla Gutierrez.

The capital city of Villahermosa epitomizes the development of Tabasco, where the airplane arrived before the automobile. Thanks to oil and the money it brought in, the cramped and ugly neighborhoods in the mosquito-ridden town of the 1970s have largely been replaced by spacious boulevards, shady parks, and cultural centers. Running alongside the fast-flowing Río Grijalva, the Zona Luz has been redone as a brick-paved pedestrian zone, with plenty of cafés, coffee shops, and ice-cream parlors.

GETTING HERE & AROUND

Villahermosa's tidy little Aeropuerto Capitán Carlos A. Rovirosa is 15 km (9 mi) south of the city in Ranchería dos Montes. Continental flies here daily from Houston. Aeroméxico, Aviacsa, and Mexicana have daily flights to Villahermosa from Mexico City. The only transportation from Villahermosa's airport is via taxi. A trip downtown costs $15. First-class bus service on ADO GL is available from Mexico City. If you're considering driving, Carretera 199 continues past Palenque until it reaches Carretera 186, which leads west to Villahermosa. There's frequent second-class service to nearby towns from the Central Camionera de Segunga Clase. Trips around Villahermosa are fixed at $1.50 in yellow colectivo taxis; the minimum fare is $2 in the white *especial* (special or private) taxis. **Creatur Transportadora Turística** (☒ *Av. Paseo Tabasco 1404, Villahermosa* ☎ *993/310–9900*) specializes in multiday excursions that take in Misol-Ha, Cañón de Sumidero, and other sights off the beaten path.

ESSENTIALS

Bus Contacts **Villahermosa (first class)** (*Terminal Central de Primera Clase* ☒ *Calle F. J. Mina 297, at Calle Lino Merino* ☎ *993/312–7692 or 993/312–1446*). **Villahermosa (second class)** (*Central Camionera de Segunga Clase* ☒ *Av. Ruíz Cortines s/n at Prolongación de Mina,* ☎ *993/312–0863*).

Currency Exchange **Banco Inverlat** (✉ *Calle Juárez 415* ☎ *993/312–5803*).

Mail & Shipping **Villahermosa Post Office** (✉ *Calle 7a Norte, at Calle Oaxaca* ☎ *954/582–0232*).

Medical Assistance **Hospital Cruz Roja de Villahermosa** (✉ *Av. Sandino 716, Villahermosa* ☎ *993/315–5555 or 993/315–6263*).

Rental Cars **Budget** (🌐 *www.budget.com* ✉ *Aeropuerto Capitán Carlos A. Rovirosa* ☎ *993/356–0118*). **Dollar** (🌐 *www.dollar.com* ✉ *Aeropuerto Villahermosa* ☎ *993/356–0211*). **Hertz** (🌐 *www.hertz.com* ✉ *Aeropuerto Capitán Carlos A. Rovirosa* ☎ *993/356–0200* ✉ *Hotel Camino Real, Paseo Tabasco 1407* ☎ *993/316–0163*).

Visitor & Tour Info **Villahermosa State Tourism Office** (✉ *Av. de los Ríos at Calle 13, Villahermosa* ☎ *993/316–2889* 🌐 *www.etabasco.gob.mx*).

CAUTION

You probably won't want a car in Villahermosa or Tuxtla, as they are sprawling cities with speeding traffic, few signs, and plenty of cheap taxis. If you do drive to Villahermosa, note that the main road, Avenida Ruíz Cortines, is almost a highway; exit ramps are about 1 km (½ mi) apart, and destinations are not clearly marked.

EXPLORING

Many out-of-towners make a beeline for the **Museo Regional de Antropología Carlos Pellicer Cámara.** On the right bank of the Río Grijalva, the museum is named after the man who donated many of its artifacts. Pellicer, who has been called the "poet laureate of Latin America," was constantly inspired by a love of his native Tabasco.

Much of the collection is devoted to Tabasco and the Olmec people, the "inhabitants of the land of rubber" who flourished as early as 1750 BC and disappeared around 100 BC. The Olmec have long been recognized as inventors of the region's numerical and calendrical systems. The pyramid, later copied by the Maya and Aztec cultures, is also attributed to them. Some of the most interesting artifacts on display here are the remnants of their jaguar cult. The jaguar symbolized procreation, and many Olmec sculptures portray half-human, half-jaguar figures or human heads emerging from the mouths of jaguars.

Many artifacts from Mexico's ancient cultures are on the upper two floors, from the red-clay dogs of Colima and the nose rings of the Huichol Indians of Nayarit to the huge burial urns of the Chontal Maya, who built Comalcalco, a Maya city near Villahermosa. All the explanations are in Spanish, but the museum is organized in chronological order and is very easy to follow. ✉ *Carlos Pellicer Cámara 511, an extension of Malecón Madrazo* ☎ *993/312–6344* *$1.50* ⏲ *Tues.–Sun. 9–5.*

Covered with dazzlingly elaborate cobalt tiles, the building housing the **Museo de Historia de Tabasco** was originally called the Casa de los Azulejos (House of the Tiles). The mansion would be over the top even without the cherubs reclining along the roof. The museum's collection is a bit sparse, but the individual pieces—an anchor from the days pirates patrolled the Gulf of Mexico, a carriage from the reign of dictator Porfirio Díaz—help bring the past to life. ✉ *Av. Juárez 402, at Calle 27 de Febrero* ☎ *No phone* 🎫 *$1.50* ⏲ *Tues.–Sun. 10–8.*

Fodor's Choice ★ Giant stone heads and other carvings were salvaged from the oil fields at La Venta, on Tabasco's western edge near the state of Veracruz. They're on display in the 20-acre **Parque-Museo La Venta,** a lush park founded by Carlos Pellicer Cámara in 1958. The views of the misty Lago de las Ilusiones (Lake of Illusions) are stirring, which is probably why young lovers come here to smooch in quiet corners. The 6-foot-tall stone heads, which have bold features and wear what look like helmets, weigh up to 20 tons. The park also contains a zoo displaying animals from Tabasco and neighboring states. The jaguars—including one that is jet black—always elicit screams from children. Sadly, many of the animals housed here are in danger of extinction. ✉ *Blvd. Ruíz Cortines s/n* ☎ *993/314–1652* 🎫 *$4* ⏲ *Daily 8–5; ticket window closes at 4. Zoo closed Mon.*

Parque Yumká, which means "the spirit that looks after the forest" in Chontal Maya, is a nature reserve with jungle, savannah, and wetlands. Guided walking tours take you over a hanging bridge and past free-roaming endangered species such as spider monkeys, crocodiles, and native *tepezcuintles* (giant rodents). Boat tours allow for good bird-watching. The park is about 16 km (10 mi) east of Villahermosa. ✉ *Ranchería Las Barrancas s/n* ☎ *993/356–0107 or 993/356–0119* 🌐 *www.yumka.org* 🎫 *$5* ⏲ *Daily 9–5; ticket window closes at 4.*

WHERE TO EAT

$$$–$$$$ ✕ **Bougainvillea.** Polished wood, crimson carpets, and hanging lanterns are the backdrop here; some entrées, like tamarind duck, have an Asian flair. But the food here is better termed international, especially on Wednesday and Thursday. On ordinary nights start with the paper-thin carpaccio before the garlic shrimp. ✉ *Av. Juárez 106, at Av. Ruíz Cortines* ☎ *993/310–1234* 💳 *AE, DC, MC, V* ⏲ *Closed Sun.*

$$–$$$ SPANISH ✕ **El Mesón del Angel.** You might think you've stumbled into a country inn when you make your way up the blue-tile steps. Inside are cheery lacy curtains and stained-glass windows. The owner is from Madrid, so the menu is full of dishes like *paella a la valenciana* (rice with seafood and sausage) and *arroz negro* (rice with squid ink). There's a wine list with plenty of Spanish vintages. ✉ *Av. Méndez 1604* ☎ *993/352–1138* 💳 *AE, MC, V*

$–$$ MEXICAN ✕ **El Mesón del Duende.** Regional favorites reign at the oddly named House of the Elf. Don't pass up the chance to try *filete en salsa de espinaca y queso* (beef in a spinach-and-cheese sauce) or fried calamari. The plant-filled restaurant, tucked away on a side street, is quieter than most. ✉ *Av. Las Americas 104, at Av. Méndez* ☎ *993/314–7060* 💳 *MC, V* ⏲ *No dinner Sun.*

WHERE TO STAY

$$$ **Camino Real.** A stairway leads directly to the upscale Galería Tabasco, but other than that, this hotel is all work and no play. It's set up for conferences, so the sleek lines of the lobby are often obscured by people fiddling with their BlackBerries. The restaurant, with floor-to-

8

ceiling windows shaded with bamboo, is filled with executives. **Pros:** There's a gorgeous pool that often sits empty. **Cons:** Scads of business travelers. ✉*Paseo Tabasco 1407,* ☎*993/310–020 or 800/722–6466* 🌐*www.caminoreal.com* *243 rooms, 24 suites* *In-room: Safe, dial-up. In-hotel: Restaurant, room service, pool, gym, laundry service, executive floor, parking (no fee), public Internet* 💳*AE, DC, MC, V*

LOCAL EATS

Tabascans eat lots of fresh fish from the sea as well as lakes and rivers. Local specialties include *pejelagarto*, an ugly fish with a head like an alligator's and a strong, sweet flavor. It's often served whole, so be prepared to face the beast. Also try *puchero* (boiled beef and other meats with vegetables and plantains) and *chaya*, a type of green similar to spinach. And make sure to try the region's fresh white cheese.

$$–$$$ **Hyatt Regency Villahermosa.** Although it's stodgy on the outside, this luxury hotel lightens up once you pass through the front doors. The pleasing Ceiba Café serves a superb breakfast buffet, while Bougainvillea is a more formal restaurant. With marble floors and polished wood furnishings, the guest rooms are some of the city's most luxurious. **Pros:** The young staff works hard at making you feel pampered. **Cons:** You don't really feel like you're in Mexico. ✉*Av. Juárez 106,* ☎*993/310–1234* 🌐*www.villahermosa.regency.hyatt.com* *198 rooms, 9 suites* *In-room: Safe, dial-up, cable TV. In-hotel: 2 restaurants, room service, bars, tennis courts, pool, laundry service, executive floor, parking (no fee), no-smoking rooms* 💳*AE, MC, V*

$$ **Calinda Viva Villahermosa.** This hotel is across from Parque-Museo La Venta. After a day exploring, head to the in-house spa. The low-slung building's gleaming white facade is softened by a Spanish tile roof. Rooms are simply furnished, quite comfortable, and complete with a small balcony. The nicest ones overlook the pool. **Pros:** Tasty breakfasts, clean rooms. **Cons:** Many business travelers, the restaurant and bar have bland interiors. ✉*Av. Ruíz Cortines at Paseo Tabasco,* ☎*993/313–6000* 🌐*www.hotelescalinda.com.mx* *239 rooms, 1 suite* *In-room: Safe. In-hotel: Restaurant, bars, pool, gym, spa, laundry service, parking (no fee), public Wi-Fi* 💳*AE, MC, V*

$$ **Olmeca Plaza.** This graceful high-rise sits in the middle of the Zona Luz, not far from downtown. A waterfall sets the mood in the spacious marble lobby. Seemingly dozens of employees are ready at a moment's notice to bring a fresh towel or hail a taxi. The best of the tastefully decorated rooms are in the back. **Pros:** Some rooms have a partial view of the river. **Cons:** Style is a little outdated. ✉*Av. Madero 418, at Calle Lerdo de Tejada,* ☎*993/358–0102* 🌐*www.hotelolmecaplaza.com* *152 rooms* *In-room: Safe, dial-up. In-hotel: Restaurant, room service, bar, pool, gym, laundry service, parking (no fee), public Internet* 💳*AE, MC, V*

$–$$ **Cencali.** Overlooking the sparkling Laguna de las Ilusiones, this hotel is surrounded by coconut-palm, mango, and cacao trees that hide the neighboring hotels. The best ones are in the newest wing beyond the lushly landscaped pool. A buffet breakfast is included in the rate. **Pros:**

Most of the big, cheerful rooms have small balconies. **Cons:** Feels motel-ish. ✉*Av. Juárez 105, at Paseo Tabasco,* ☎*993/313–6611 or 01800/112–5000 toll-free* 🌐*www.cencali.com.mx* *151 rooms, 9 suites* *In-hotel: Restaurant, bar, room service, meeting rooms, laundry service, pool, airport shuttle, parking (free), public Internet* *AE, MC, V* *BP*

$ **Plaza Independencia.** The downtown location—on a quiet street near the main plaza—puts you close to everything in the Zona Luz. The lobby and common areas are painted in eye-popping bright pink, blue, and yellow. Ask for a room overlooking the river on one of the upper floors. **Pros:** The ground-floor restaurant serves regional cuisine and is popular with locals, quirky artsy touches. **Cons:** Popular with conventions and business travelers en masse. ✉*Calle Independencia 123,* ☎*993/312–1299* 🌐*www.hotelesplaza.com.mx* *90 rooms* *In-room: Safe. In-hotel: Restaurant, room service, bars, pool, laundry service, parking (no fee)* *AE, MC, V*

SHOPPING

The pedestrian-only streets of the Zona Luz are great for window-shopping. But when locals want to spend money they head to **Galería Tabasco** (✉*Paseo Tabasco* ☎*993/316–4400*).

Near the main square, **Libros y Arte** (✉*Calle Benito Juárez and Av. 27 de Febrero* ☎*993/312–7323*) has a wonderful collection of books, including coffee-table volumes on the art and architecture of Tabasco. There are also plenty of maps and travel guides, some in English.

COMALCALCO

8

 *3 km (2 mi) northwest of Comalcalco Town.*

The region's abundant cacao trees provided food and a livelihood for a booming Maya population during the Classic period (100 BC to AD 1000). Comalcalco, which was founded in about the 1st century BC, marks the westernmost reach of the Maya; descendants of its builders, the Chontal, still live in the vicinity. Its name means "place of the clay griddles" (bricks) in Nahuatl, and it's Tabasco's most important Maya site, unique for its use of fired brick (made of sand, seashells, and clay), as the area's swamplands lacked the stone for building. The bricks were often inscribed and painted with figures of reptiles and birds, geometric figures, and drawings before being covered with stucco.

The major pyramid on the Gran Acrópolis del Este (Great Eastern Acropolis) is adorned with carvings as well as large stucco masks of the sun god, Kinich Ahau. The burial sites here also depart radically from Maya custom: the dead were placed in cone-shape clay urns, in a fetal position. Some have been left *in situ,* and others are on display in the site museum along with many of the artifacts that were uncovered here. Admission to the site, which is open daily 10–5, is $3.

COMALCALCO TOWN

There's not much to see in this dusty little town, 56 km (31 mi) northwest of Villahermosa, but it's the center of what's called the "Ruta del Cacao," or the Cocoa Route. Call ahead to arrange a free tour of **Hacienda de la Luz** (✉ *Blvd. Zovirosa Wade* ☎ *933/334–1126*), which is quite close to downtown Comalcalco. It's also known as Hacienda Hayer, because a German doctor named Otto Wolter Hayer bought it in the 1930s and turned it into the most profitable hacienda in the region. On the tour you'll learn everything about the production of cacao, from bean to chocolate.

A visit to Comalcalco is pretty much unavoidable if you are visiting the nearby ruins. From here you can take a taxi to the front gate. For about $10 the driver will wait for you while you explore.

PARAÍSO

19 km (12 mi) north of Comalcalco.

As you head toward the Gulf of Mexico coast and Paraíso, stop at one of the cacao plantations and chocolate factories. On the coast you'll get a glimpse of small-town life. Climb the *Cerro Teodomiro* (Teodomiro Hill) for a spectacular view of *Laguna de las Flores* (Las Flores Lagoon) and coconut plantations. Small seafood restaurants and several small hotels dot the shore here.

The region's small, dark-sand beaches are not among Mexico's prettiest; the best place to spend your time is 5 km (3 mi) southeast of Paraíso, in **Puerto Ceiba,** a fishing community whose inhabitants breed and harvest oysters. You can take a two-hour boat tour aboard the *Puerto Ceiba I* around the mangrove-lined Laguna Mecoacán (Mecoacán Lagoon) and the coastal rivers. Tours, which cost about $5 for adults, leave from the small Puerto Ceiba Restaurant.

Sonora

Guaymas marina

9

WORD OF MOUTH

"[In Nogales] you can park your car in a public lot right next to the border crossing and walk over. It is guarded and costs about $8 for the day. It's a quick five-minute walk over the border. Taxis should be no problem. Enjoy."

–M2

www.fodors.com/forums

WELCOME TO SONORA

TOP REASONS TO GO

★ **The chance to visit a colonial city:** Beautifully preserved Alamos has great hotels and restaurants and a friendly community of American expats.

★ **Having a beach all to yourself:** Resort towns provide plenty of creature comforts, but secluded beaches await those with a sense of adventure and a four-wheel drive.

★ **Experiencing ancient traditions:** Several indigenous groups here still live close to their roots—you might get a chance to see Yaqui and Mayo ceremonies.

★ **Going off the grid:** An otherworldly landscape of volcanic craters and towering sand dunes, El Pinacate is isolated, mysterious, and strictly for adventurous sorts.

★ **A drive along the Río Sonora:** Exploring this river route into the sleepy towns in the foothills of the Sierra Madre gives you a glimpse of traditional Mexican cowboy life.

1 El Pinacate. This biosphere reserve has a unique landscape of volcanic cones, lava formations, and desert plants that'll make you feel like you're on another planet.

2 The Sonoran Coast. Most visitors to Sonora come here, where desert collides with shimmering blue water. Puerto Peñasco, San Carlos, and Guaymas are developed, but you'll find miles of secluded beaches along the Mar de Cortés.

3 Nogales. Sonora's major gateway is the most logical border crossing for most of the region's destinations. It's your typical border town, but can be a decent day trip if you have time to linger.

4 Hermosillo. This workaday state capital minds its own business, but is emerging as a major national-airline hub. A new highway runs to beautiful Bahía Kino, about an hour away.

5 Ruta de las Misiones. Just south of Nogales are a string of tiny mission towns that are important to the history of the region.

6 Ruta de Río Sonora. This gorgeous road trip takes you alongside the river and through small, unspoiled towns and old-fashioned ranches.

7 Alamos & Aduana. Northernmost of the major colonial cities, Alamos is the magical antidote to overdeveloped beach resorts. Aduana, a former mining town with one truly outstanding restaurant, is an easy trip from Alamos.

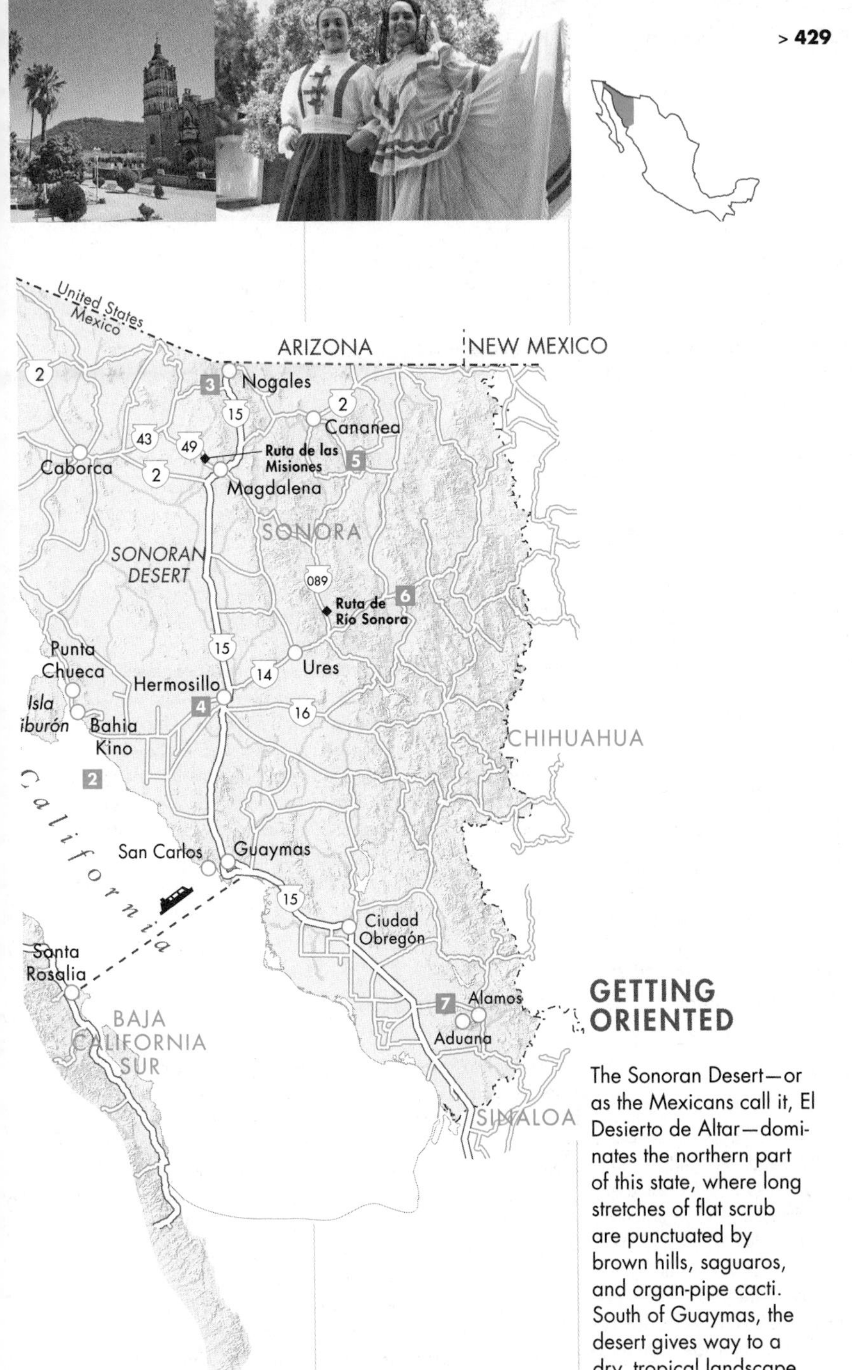

9

GETTING ORIENTED

The Sonoran Desert—or as the Mexicans call it, El Desierto de Altar—dominates the northern part of this state, where long stretches of flat scrub are punctuated by brown hills, saguaros, and organ-pipe cacti. South of Guaymas, the desert gives way to a dry, tropical landscape.

SONORA PLANNER

A Simple Itinerary

Because it's a sprawling region, you'd need eight days to do justice to Sonora. If you have just a few days, start at beachfront San Carlos. (You can drive the entire way, or fly into Hermosillo and drive from there.) The next day, take the easier three-hour drive to lovely Alamos. Spend a night in Hermosillo before taking a leisurely drive along the Río Sonora, stopping for the night in Ures or Arizpe. Make sure to take the 4-km (2½-mi) hike along the rutted road out of Aconchi to soak in the hot springs.

If you only have the weekend, cross the border from the United States and explore the Ruta de los Misiones. Spend the night in Bahía Kino and come back up the Ruta de Río Sonora to catch the ruins of Padre Kino's adobe mission you missed at Imuris and head home.

Sea & Sun

If you want to skip the touristy areas around San Carlos and Puerto Peñasco, seek out the more secluded beaches around Bahía Kino and all along the Mar de Cortés. A coastal highway from Guaymas to Puerto Peñasco is a few years from completion: enjoy the solitude while you can.

Getting Around

Though buses between towns are frequent and inexpensive, by far the easiest way to travel Sonora is by car—towns such as San Carlos and Bahía Kino are very spread out, and some lack taxi service.

Flying is another option—Hermosillo, Guaymas, and Ciudad Obregón all have international airports offering regular flights from the United States—but Sonora's proximity to Arizona means that most visitors, even those in tour groups, enter in private vehicles or buses.

Border Crossings

There are several border crossings, but most people entering Sonora from the United States do so at Nogales, south of Tucson, Arizona. Highway 15 begins at Nogales, continues south through Hermosillo, and reaches the Mar de Cortés at Guaymas, 418 km (261 mi) from the Arizona border. You don't need a car permit unless you are traveling south of Ciudad Obregón. Permits cost $25 if you stay within the state, and $31 if you plan to travel elsewhere in Mexico. Make sure you check in with Mexican immigration before leaving Nogales to get your six-month tourist visa, which will cost $27.

The Baja Car Ferry

An alternative to the Arizona border crossings is to enter Mexico in Baja and take the car ferry from Santa Rosalía to Guaymas. The ferry runs every Wednesday, Friday, and Sunday, departing at 9 AM, from the terminal (☎615/152–1246) on the east side of the transpeninsular highway, near the bus station. Ferries from Guaymas to Santa Rosalía run every Tuesday, Friday, and Saturday at 8 PM, from the ferry terminal on Avenida Serdán (☎622/222–0204). The trip takes approximately 9 hours; the fare is $55 for adults. Cars 10 feet or less in length are $165 and require at least a two-day advance notice. Check the times, too, as these are subject to change. Passenger tickets can be purchased the day of travel.

Safety Concerns

Travel in Sonora is generally not problematic. Roads are good and help is easy to find in the vicinity of populated areas. Care should be taken in Nogales, where common border-town crimes like pickpocketing and petty theft are a concern. Thieves look for easy targets, so remaining alert (and reasonably sober) will lessen your risk of becoming a victim.

Tour Companies

A few companies provide package and customized tours of the region. **South of the Border Tours** (✉7937 East Coronado Rd., Tucson, AZ ☎520/760–4000 ⊕www.southofthebordertours.com) runs mostly senior-citizen package tours to Alamos, San Carlos, Puerto Peñasco, the Mission Route, Baja, and the Copper Canyon. **Solipaso** (✉Calle Obregon 3, Alamos ☎647/428–0466 or 520/241–6682 in the U.S. ⊕www.solipaso.com) is run by an American expat couple based in Alamos; they offer set or custom itineraries and specialize in birding, soft adventure, and natural-history tours throughout Mexico.

MORE INFORMATION?

We list local tourism offices throughout the chapter, but you might want to contact the Sonora Office of Conventions and Visitors (✉El Paseo del Canal at Comonfort, Edificio Sonora, 3rd fl., Hermosillo ☎662/217–0060 or 800/476–6672 ⊕www.sonoraturismo.gob.mx or www.visitasonora.com) while you plan your trip. They'll send you mounds of information and a helpful full-color booklet.

WHAT IT COSTS IN DOLLARS					
¢	$	$$	$$$	$$$$	$$$$
Restaurants					
under $5	$5–$10	$10–$15	$15–$25	over $25	over $25
Hotels					
under $50	$50–$75	$75–$150	$150–$250	over $250	over $250

Restaurant prices are per person for a main course at dinner. Hotel prices are for two people in a standard double room. Hotel rates sometimes include the 17% tax; be sure to check this when you're quoted a price.

How's the Weather?

Summer temperatures in Sonora are as high as they are in southern Arizona, so unless you're prepared to broil, plan your trip for sometime between October and May. Even in winter, daytime temperatures can rise above 27°C (80°F), though at night the temperature does drop considerably. Winter on the coast can also bring strong, steady winds that make temperatures seem much cooler than they actually are. The foothill towns along the Río Sonora and Alamos are generally hot in the summer, but can drop to near freezing in the winter, even during the day. Snow is not unheard of in those places, either.

As the Sonoran weather varies, so does the landscape—from fertile cropland and arid desert to stretches of sandy beaches and mountain ranges.

Filling Up

Sonora is home of the giant flour tortilla, *machaca* (air-dried beef), delicious *carne asada* (grilled and marinated meat), and *coyotas* (sugar cookies).

HERMOSILLO

280 km (175 mi) south of Nogales on Hwy. 15.

HERMOSILLO, THE STATE'S ON-AND-OFF CAPITAL since 1831, is a hardworking city. Manufacturing and agriculture are its main concerns. But a few older plazas and 19th-century buildings hark back to a more gracious past. For travelers to Sonora, it's a transportation hub. Most visitors driving or flying into Sonora pass through this modern city.

GETTING HERE & AROUND

Hermosillo's Aeropuerto Internacional Ignacio Pesqueira is a hub for flights between the United States and the rest of Mexico. It lies 15 minutes outside the city center, a journey that costs $15 by taxi. The Central de Autobuses, located just off Highway 15, serves all the major regional and national bus companies. A bus trip from Nogales, near the border, to Hermosillo takes approximately four hours. Greyhound Mexico has service to Hermosillo. Grupo Estrella Blanca has frequent service to Hermosillo from Nogales, Tijuana, and Mexicali. A taxi downtown should cost $5. Taxis can be flagged from just about anywhere, especially in front of the hotels.

ESSENTIALS

Bus Contacts **Central de Autobuses** (✉ *Blvd. Encinas Luis Johnson 400 at Los Pinos y Jaffa, Colonio El Coloso* ☎ *622/217-1522*).**Greyhound Mexico** (☎ *01800/710-8819 toll-free in Mexico or 800/229-9424* 🌐 *www.greyhound.com.mx*). **Grupo Estrella Blanca** (☎ *662/213-4050* 🌐 *www.estrellablanca.com.mx*).

Currency Exchange **Banco Santander** (✉ *Blvd. Kino 309*, Zona Hotelera ☎ *662/289-0085*).

Medical Assistance **The Green Angels** (☎ *662/212-3253 in Hermosillo, 01800/903-9200 toll-free in Mexico*). **Hospital CIMA de Hermosillo**(✉ *Paseo San Miguel de Río 39, Colonia Vado del Río* ☎ *662/259-0900*). **Red Cross** (☎ *662/214-0010 in Hermosillo, 622/222-5555 in San Carlos, 638/383-2266 in Puerto Peñasco*).

Rental Cars **Hertz** (✉ *Blvd. Garcia Morales 341, Colonia El Llano* ☎ *662/210-1810 or 800/654-3030*).

EXPLORING

MAIN ATTRACTIONS

The best viewpoint in the city is the top of Cerro de la Campana (Hill of Bells), where you'll also find the **Museo de Sonora.** The museum is in a former penitentiary; the cells hold 18 permanent exhibits on astronomy, anthropology, history, geology, geography, and culture, all with a Sonoran slant. The bulk of the exhibits are graphic displays, including charts and maps of trade routes and native populations. Each display has a short summary in English. ✉ *Jesús García Final s/n, Col. La Matanza* ☎ *662/217-0007* 🎫 *$3, free Sun.* ⏲ *Tues.–Sat. 10–5, Sun. 9–4.*

At the center of town, look for charming **Plaza Zaragosa**, a lovely square shaded by towering fig trees. At the center of the plaza stands a turn-of-the-century Florentine wrought-iron gazebo. Flanking the plaza are the contemporaneous **Palacio Gobierno and the Catedral de Nuestra Señora de la Asunción,** which was built between 1877 and 1912.

TOUR BY TROLLEY

Trolebus ☎*662/213-8639* ⊕*www.imcahermosillo.org* *$2.50*), a faux-antique trolley-bus, picks up passengers at Plaza Zaragosa. The trip is an exhilarating plunge into Hermosillo's urban pulse.

IF YOU HAVE TIME

From Plaza Zaragosa, cross the Río Sonora and walk south for several blocks until you reach the odd little neighborhood of **Villa de Seris.** Its small plaza and lovely church have much more charm than the modern city center. The coyota, a sugary dessert cookie, was first baked here. Eat your fill while exploring this elegant neighborhood.

WHERE TO EAT & STAY

$$–$$$ STEAK ✕**Sonora Steak.** Come to this sophisticated steak house for the finest cuts of the famous Sonoran beef. You won't break the bank, as the prices here are quite reasonable. The specialty, rib-eye steak, is aged for 28 days. Vegetarians can graze on a variety of salads or opt for cream of green chile soup or fettuccine with pasillo chiles and garlic. The restaurant is a good spot for a late-night meal—it's open until 1 AM. ✉*Blvd. Kino 914, Zona Hotelera* ☎*662/210–0313* ▭*MC, V.*

$–$$ MEXICAN ✕**Xochimilco.** This large restaurant is rather institutional-looking, but it's a great place to try regional specialties. There's a set menu—meals are designed for two or more, and typically include carne asada, ribs, tripe, vegetable salad, beans, and fresh flour tortillas. It's popular with both locals and visitors from across the border. ✉*Av. Obregón 51, at Gutiérrez, Col. Villa de Seris* ☎*662/250–4089* ▭*MC, V.*

$$ **Fiesta Americana.** Hermosillo's top hotel, Fiesta Americana is especially popular among business executives. The guest rooms, with their tasteful beige-and-forest-green decor, appeal to travelers as well. The adjacent disco is the biggest attraction in the town's sleepy nightlife scene. **Pros:** Friendly staff, tasteful decor, modern gym. **Cons:** On an ugly street, uninspiring exterior. ✉*Blvd. Kino 369, Zona Hotelera,* ☎*662/259–6000 or 800/154-5001* ⊕*www.fiestaamericana.com* *221 rooms* *In-room: Refrigerator, Wi-Fi. In-hotel: Restaurant, bar, tennis court, pool, gym* ▭*AE, MC, V.*

$$ **Holiday Inn Hermosillo.** Most of the attractive rooms in this two-story hotel surround an expansive lawn and a pretty pool. The hotel is a bargain, given the fact that it has some amenities and is in the convenient and generally pricey Zona Hotelera. **Pros:** Friendly staff, convenient location. **Cons:** On an ugly block, chain-hotel feel. ✉*Blvd. Kino and Ramón Corral, Zona Hotelera,* ☎*662/289–1700, 01800/00–9903 toll-free in Mexico* ⊕*www.holidayinn.com* *132 rooms, 9 suites*

9

CLOSE UP

Ruta de Río Sonora

The highways following the Río Sonora are a terrific way to see a less touristy side of Sonora. Between Hermosillo and Cananea, the riverbanks are speckled with small towns, each with its own appeal. Some are known for their thermal springs, others for their rich histories. As is typical of the area, each has a colonial church and a heart-of-town square. People come into town from the surrounding ranches, so you'll see plenty of cowboy boots and hats.

The region is known for its hospitality, and it's common for townspeople to wave as you pass by. The easiest drive is up the valley from Hermosillo, although it's also possible to drive south from Cananea. (This route passes over mountain roads, which are difficult in bad weather.) From Hermosillo, take Sonora 14 east to Mazocahui, where you'll pass through Ures, the first town on the route, and then continue north on Sonora 089. The whole route, without stopping, requires a little over three hours. Driving part it, with stops, makes an easy day trip, especially in autumn.

The land along the Río Sonora was the region's first inhabited area; it was settled by the Pima and Opata people. The route is also linked to the arrival of the Europeans—the Spanish explorer Alvar Núñez Cabeza de Vaca followed the Río Sonora during his travels between central Mexico and what is now the United States in the mid-16th century, and the Coronado expeditions of the 1540s also followed the Río Sonora. The main towns along this route were founded and settled 100 years later. Signs at the entrance to each town give you the exact year.

Heading northeast on Highway 14 from Hermosillo, the first town that you'll come to is **Ures.** The former capital of the state, 45 minutes from Hermosillo, is the largest town on the Río Sonora. Its square is anchored by four bronze statues representing Greek mythological figures. There are some good country-style restaurants, and some of the 19th-century haciendas have been converted into hotels.

Continuing on Route 89, you'll pass through **Baviácora,** with its 19th-century church standing next to the 20th-century church built to replace it. **Aconchi,** about 15 minutes farther down the road, is a good base from which to explore the area. Make sure to visit the local hot springs, which range from tepid to very, very hot.

About two hours from Aconchi is **Arizpe,** the first place in Sonora to bear the title of "city." This was also the first capital of the province of Occidente, which encompassed Sonora and what is now part of California, Arizona, New Mexico, and Texas. Its magnificently worn church, built in 1646, contains the remains of Spanish Captain Juan Francisco de Anza, the founder of San Francisco, California. Arizpe's quiet central square, with its handsome brick clock tower, is a great place to soak up the peace of small-town life. If you decide to stay the night, there are some worthwhile local restaurants and hotels.

In-room: Refrigerator, Wi-Fi. In-hotel: Restaurant, bar, pool, gym, no elevator, airport shuttle, parking (no fee) *AE, MC, V.*

$ **Hotel Bugambilia.** This pleasant small property has a trio of assets: comfortable rooms, convenient location, and a good restaurant. The bougainvillea-covered bungalows facing the parking lot are most popular; other rooms surround the pool. Guests are free to use the facilities at the Holiday Inn across the street. **Pros:** Nice accommodations, pretty pool. **Cons:** On a noisy street. *Blvd. Kino 712, Zona Hotelera,* *662/289–1600* *102 rooms* *In-room: Safe. In-hotel: Restaurant, room service, pool, no elevator, public Wi-Fi, parking (no fee)* *AE, MC, V.*

NIGHTLIFE

This isn't a party town, by any means. More intrepid travelers can pop into any neighborhood cantina and strike up a conversation (provided they know Spanish). There are some downtown clubs catering to the young and hip. Live music will likely consist of Beatles, Pink Floyd, and Led Zeppelin covers.

BARS

Marco n' Charlie's (*Blvd. Abelardo Rodríguez 78, Zona Hotelera* *662/215–3061*) is a watering hole for the town's upper crust.

Open Wednesday through Saturday, **La Negra** (*Revolucion at Zacatecas, Col. Centro* *662/210–3500*) features cover bands and charges a $1 cover.

FOLK MUSIC

La Tequilera (*Pino Suárez 72, Centro* *662/217–5337)* features a wide selection of the namesake beverage that you can enjoy to the strains of norteño (the polka-influenced country music of the region).

NOGALES

100 km (62 mi) south of Tucson via Hwy. 19, on the Arizona-Mexico border, 280 km (175 mi) north of Hermosillo on Hwy. 15.

Sitting on the border of Arizona, Nogales serves as the entry point for most Americans driving into Sonora. While considerably smaller than border cities like Tijuana or Ciudad Juarez, Nogales can be downright chaotic, especially when people pour over the border on weekend evenings. If you're just coming for the day, it's best to park on the Arizona side of the border—you'll see many guarded lots that cost about $8 for the day—and walk across.

Most of the good shopping and dining options are within strolling distance of the border. Head to Avenida Obregón, which begins a few blocks west of the border. Stroll as far south along this thoroughfare as you like; you'll know you have left the tourist strip when the shops are no longer fronted by English-speaking hustlers trying to lure you in the door.

CLOSE UP

Sonora Background

Mexico's second-largest state, Sonora, is also its second richest. Ranch lands here feed Mexico's finest beef cattle, and rivers flowing west from the Sierra Madre are diverted by giant dams to irrigate this area. Sonora's many crops include wheat and other grains, cotton, vegetables, nuts, and fruit—especially melons, citrus, peaches, and apples. Hermosillo, Sonora's capital, bustles with agricultural commerce in the midst of the fertile lands that turn dry again toward the coast.

In 1540 Francisco Vázquez de Coronado, governor of the provinces to the south, became the first Spanish leader to visit the plains of Sonora. More than a century later, Father Eusebio Francisco Kino led a missionary expedition to Sonora and what is now southern Arizona—an area referred to as the Pimería Alta for the band of Pima Indians still living there. The Italian-born, German-educated priest is credited with founding more than 20 missions in what is now northern Sonora and southern Arizona, as well as introducing cattle, citrus, wheat, and peaches—all still important crops—to the region. Although Alamos, in the south of Sonora, boomed with silver-mining wealth in the late 17th century, no one paid much attention to the northern part of the region. When the United States annexed a giant chunk of Mexico's territory after the Mexican-American War (1846–48), northern Sonora suddenly became a border area—and a haven for Arizona outlaws. International squabbles bloomed and faded over the next decades as officials argued over issues such as the right to pursue criminals across the border. Porfirio Díaz, dictator of Mexico for most of the years between 1876 and 1911, finally moved to secure the state by settling it.

Settlers in Sonora, however, proved a hardy and independent bunch ill-suited to accepting the dictates of politicos in faraway Mexico City. Sonorans and their neighbors, the Chihuahenses, were major players in the Mexican Revolution, and the republic was ruled by three Sonorans: Plutarco Elías Calles, Adolfo de la Huerta, and Abelardo Rodríguez. Despite the enormous cost and destruction to railroads and other infrastructure, the Mexican Revolution brought prosperity to Sonora. With irrigation from the state's dams, inhabitants have been able to grow enough wheat and vegetables not only for Mexico but also for export. Today Sonora's economy continues to thrive, partly because of the maquiladoras: American factories that have moved across the border to take advantage of low wages and loose labor and environmental restrictions. State and federal governments are pouring money into tourist-oriented development, making it the fastest-growing part of the economy. Visitors enjoy not only Sonora's abundance of beaches, but also the seclusion and tranquility of its mountains and deserts.

If you want to overnight in the area, it's best to stay on the north side of the border; people going into the country should proceed to the next destination.

WHAT TO BRING BACK

The downtown markets of Hermosillo, particularly along Avenidas Serdán and Monterrey, hawk everything from candles to wedding attire, as well as a terrific selection of handmade cowboy boots. The variety of goods concentrated in this area equals what you'll find in Nogales, and the prices are better. The local sweets, *coyotas*, can be purchased in the Villa de Seris neighborhood.

GETTING HERE & AROUND

Nogales International Airport is about 16 km (10 mi) south of the border. Flights from Nogales tend to be more expensive than from Hermosillo and points further south. A taxi from the airport to downtown Nogales costs about $15. Visitors who'd prefer to drive to Sonora no longer need a car permit to travel south of Nogales. You only need a car permit if you're traveling farther than Ciudad Obregón. They are $25 if you plan to stay in Sonora, $31 if you are going elsewhere in Mexico. Most visitors to Sonora travel by car from Tucson via Interstate 19 to the border in Nogales, Arizona. Mexico's Highway 15, a divided four-lane toll road, begins in Nogales. This highway is the fastest way to get to Hermosillo and Guaymas–San Carlos, but expect to pay approximately $15 in tolls. The alternative *libre* (free) routes are generally slower and not as well maintained, though by no means problematic.

ESSENTIALS

Bus Contacts The **Central de Autobuses** (☎ *631/313–1603*). **Greyhound Mexico** (☎ *01800/710–8819 toll-free in Mexico, 800/229–9424*).

Car Insurance **Arizona Automobile Association** (✉ *8204 E. Broadway, Tucson* ☎ *520/296–7461* ✉ *6950 N. Oracle Rd., Phoenix* ☎ *520/885–0694 or 800/352–5382* 🌐 *www.aaaaz.com*). **Sanborn's Mexico Insurance** (✉ *105 W. Grant, Tucson* ☎ *520/882–5000* 🌐 *www.sanbornsinsurance.com*).

Currency Exchange **Banamex** (✉ *Calle Obregón Ochoa 98, Col. Centro* ☎ *631/312–3234*).

Medical Assistance **Centro Hospitarlo Mexico** (✉ *Patras 123, at the corner of Prigos, Col. El Griego* ☎ *63/319–1637*).

EXPLORING

There's not much to see in Nogales. Besides cheap shopping, the big draw is stepping across the border into a foreign country. Just don't be under the impression you're in the real Mexico, anymore than a Mexican who has only traveled a few hundred feet across the border has a real experience of America.

WHERE TO EAT

$$–$$$ MEXICAN ✕ **Elvira's.** The dining room of this longtime favorite bursts with color and stamped tin stars. Choose from half a dozen different moles, from the *poblano*, rich and dark, to the *manchamanteles,* a sweet stew built around

pineapple, banana, and apple. A free shot of tequila comes with each meal. ✉*Av. Obregón 1, Centro* ☎*631/312–4773* ▭*MC, V.*

$$–$$$ ★ MEXICAN ✕ **La Roca.** You'll find this elegant restaurant within walking distance of the border. The old stone house, built against a cliff, has several dining rooms, some with fireplaces. A balcony overlooks a patio that has a fountain and magnolia trees. Look for the excellent seafood dishes and the *queso la Roca* (seasoned potato slices covered with melted cheese) appetizer. Reservations are suggested weekend nights. ✉*Calle Elias 91, Centro* ☎ *631/312–0760* ▭*MC, V.*

LOCAL FOOD

Sonoran cuisine has all the makings for stellar surf and turf: it's distinguished by its terrific steaks and fresh seafood. Steak is not the only specialty in Sonora; look for *machaca* (air-dried beef), *carne asada* (grilled, marinated beef) and, if you can handle the concept, *tacos de cabeza* (pig's head). Seafood lovers will find shrimp, scallops, octopus, clams, and fish, both freshwater and ocean species, as well as *cahuamanta*, a tasty and filling manta ray now eaten instead of the endangered sea turtles. There's an abundance of enchiladas, tacos, and tamales—the style of Mexican cooking with which most Americans are familiar derives from this region.

NIGHTLIFE

Nightlife in Nogales is strictly for those who like it raw. From north of the border it attracts rowdy college students (and even younger folks) who don't mind—or seek out—crowded bars, blaring Top 40s, and upside-down margaritas. If spilled beer isn't your scene, there are a few places to try.

On the main strip,**Cheves & Munchies'** (✉*Calle Campilo and Av. Obregón, Centro* ☎*631/312–6764)* is a gringo-oriented cantina, a beer hall, featuring classic rock and big plates of familiar, American-style Mexican food.

Pancho Villa (✉*Av. Obregón and Calle Campilo, Centro* ☎*No phone*) is a relatively quiet place decorated with various representations of its namesake, the mustachioed general of the 1917 revolution whose guerilla maneuvers terrorized the border.

SHOPPING

A selection of pottery, fabrics, furnishings, jewelry, and leather wear from all over makes Nogales one of the best shopping strips in Sonora. Along Paseo Miguel Hidalgo, hundreds of vendors compete ferociously for your attention. Bargaining is expected on the street, but stores tend to have fixed prices.

Crafts from San Miguel de Allende and Guanajuato are displayed at **El Cendaro** (✉*Calle Elias 91, Centro* ☎*No phone*).

El Cid (✉*Av. Obregón 1241, Centro* ☎*631/312–1944*) sells silver jewelry.

El Sarape (✉*Av. Obregón 161, Centro* ☎*631/312–0309*) specializes in sterling-silver jewelry from Taxco and pewter crafts from all over Mexico.

For a great selection of leather jackets, belts, wallets, and bags, head to **El Sol de Mayo** (✉*Av. Obregón 147, Centro* ☎*631/312–6367*). They also stock handicrafts like guitars and maracas.

THE SONORAN COAST

Sonora's coastline is mostly known for resort towns such as Puerto Peñasco and San Carlos. Most of Sonora's main beaches have paved access roads, but some of the best—like pristine Playa San Nicolás just south of Bahía Kino—await the adventurous at the end of rutted, washed-out dirt tracks. Your lovable little hatchback isn't going to cut it, so make sure you're driving something sturdy, preferably with four-wheel drive.

PUERTO PEÑASCO

104 km (65 mi) south of the Arizona border at Lukeville on Mexico Hwy. 8.

Puerto Peñasco was dubbed Rocky Point by British explorers in the 18th century, and that's the name most Americans know it by today. The town itself was established about 1927, after Mexican fishermen found abundant shrimp beds in the area and American John Stone built the first hotel. Al Capone was a frequent visitor during the Prohibition era, when he was hiding from U.S. law.

The real appeal of Puerto Peñasco, at the north end of the Mar de Cortés (Sea of Cortes), is the miles of sandy beaches punctuated by stretches of black volcanic rock. A remarkably high tide change—as much as 23 feet—makes for great exploring among countless tide pools. The town itself has already been discovered, as you'll know from all the neon signs advertising Subway, Century 21, and Thrifty. But the newly revamped malecón (waterfront boardwalk), illuminated by night in a wash of color, is a friendly gathering place for locals and travelers.

High-rise developments are already being built which will add an eye-opening skyline to sleepy Puerto Peñasco. Even more dramatic changes to the landscape may result from the forthcoming coastal highway and the town's place at the top of the "Escalera Náutica" (Nautical Ladder), a series of high-end marinas along the coasts.

GETTING HERE & AROUND

Puerto Peñasco doesn't have an airport—yet—but that is sure to change as this part of Sonora expands. If you arrive by bus, remember that the place is pretty spread out. Although cabs are available, you should always set a price with the driver before getting inside. Bus connections can be had from three stations on the main road into town, and buses to the rest of the state and country are plentiful.

CLOSE UP

Ruta de las Misiones

Although most towns in northern Sonora have a link to a nearby mission, those founded by Padre Eusebio Francisco Kino, one of the most prominent figures in the early history of Sonora, seem to hold the most interest for history buffs. Although none of the original missions is still standing—some were destroyed in the Pima Indian uprising of 1695, other were replaced with newer structures by the Franciscans, who took over after the Jesuits were expelled for defending the local people—the so-called "mission route" is still a fascinating bit of local history.

Most of the missions are closed to visitors, but their stolid presence and the atmosphere of these tiny towns, basically unchanged for 400 years, make them worth a visit. The best way to see the mission route is to start on Highway 15 just south of Nogales. It takes around three hours to reach the city of Caborca, a decent-size city with many restaurants and a few hotels. Since most towns don't have much else to see, you could technically tour the missions in one day.

Start at the mission Kino named **Santa María de Magdalena,** in the town of Magdalena de Kino. Padre Kino died here in 1711 while dedicating the town's first church, and the town holds what are alleged to be Kino's surprisingly new-looking remains. (Locals joke that the town has a skeleton of him as a baby, too.) The remains, discovered by archaeologists in 1966, can be viewed inside a special dome constructed for this purpose. The church, on the other side of the **Plaza Colosio**, honors St. Francis the town's patron. Every October 4 the town hosts an extremely rowdy festival in his honor.

Heading south toward Santa Ana, turn west on Highway 2 toward Caborca. Along the way to Caborca detour north on Sonora Highway 43 toward Oquitoa to visit **San Antonio de Oquitoa** (meaning "white woman" in the Opata language) and **San Pedro y San Pablo de Tubutama,** (Opata for "the highest place"), both on sites of missions founded by Kino. The church at Oquitoa has the twin towers typical of the Franciscans, but also the flat roof favored by the Jesuits. Tubutama's façade boasts a working sundial, the church's most striking feature.

Back on Highway 2 you'll come to **San Diego de Pitiquito,** between the towns of Altar and Caborca. The whitewashed church, dating from the 1780s, is most famous for its didactic paintings, which are thought to have been created by the local PapagoIndians in the late 1800s. Once painted over, they were rediscovered and restored in 1966.

The final mission you'll come to on this route is the lovely **La Purísima Concepción de Caborca,** built in 1809. The town is known for beating back the 1857 military expedition of Henry Alexander Crabb, a California state senator. After a six-day battle during which Crabb's 69 men exploded the doors of the church with a keg of dynamite, the Mexican commander, Hilario Gabilondo, offered terms of surrender. Crabb acquiesced, but he and his men were betrayed and executed the next morning. Crabb's was the last of the so-called "filibuster" incursions into Mexico that served as the inspiration for Cormac McCarthy's classic novel Blood Meridian.

Tours of the mission route can be arranged through the compelling and extremely amiable local historian **Valenzuela "Loco" Luna** (☎ *637/372–1989*). The rates, based on your area of interest, range from $45 to $75.

CLOSE UP

El Pinacate

The somewhat difficult trip to El Pinacate, is one of the region's most rewarding. The reserve, midway between Puerto Peñasco and the Arizona border, is famous for volcanic rock formations and thousands of moonlike craters. Highlights include 4,000-foot-high Santa Clara peak, and the mile-wide El Elegante crater, created by a giant steam eruption 150,000 years ago.

With the addition of a solar-powered visitor center, which at this writing was scheduled to open in late 2008, exploring the area wasn't quite as daunting. But you'll still need to plan ahead, bringing your own water, food, and extra gasoline. A high-clearance four-wheel-drive vehicle is also strongly advised. Since an unpopulated stretch of desert is a great place for drug trafficking and illegal border crossings, use common sense. Lastly, be mindful of the heat—summer temperatures can be blistering. The best time to visit is between November and March.

If all the "cons" listed above make you nervous, don't worry. Tours can be arranged through local guide **Antonio Romero** (☎ *637/312-6367*). Romero, a lifetime resident, and can arrange deep-desert excursions with meals. Excellent naturalist-led tours can also be arranged through **La Ruta de Sonora** (☎ *520/792-4693*) in Tucson.

All visitors must register at the park entrance, where a ranger's station provides informative tips for visitors. For current park information, contact the International Sonoran Desert Alliance in Ajo, Arizona, at ☎ *520/387-6823.* ✉ *Hwy. 85 201 Esperanza, near Ejido Nayarit* ☎ 638/384-9007 *Donation requested* *Daily 9–5.*

9

ESSENTIALS

Currency Exchange **Banco Santander** (✉ *Av. Juárez 87, Carretera Internacional* ☎ *638/383-4288*).

Medical Assistance **Dr. Luiz Vasquez** (☎ *638/383 –3024* [available 24 hours a day]).

Visitor & Tour Info **Puerto Peñasco tourism office** (✉ *Blvd. Juárez 320-B at V. Estrella* ☎ *638/388-0444*).

EXPLORING

Though the desert to the north of Puerto Peñasco is one of the most barren looking in the state, there is a complex and delicate ecosystem out in all that sand and scrub. The Gulf of California itself is one of the most vital marine ecosystems in North America, and its deep, nutrient-rich waters make it a breeding ground for whales and produce some of the biggest sportfishing trophies in the world.

The northern Gulf area forms an impressive desert-coast ecosystem, and scientists conduct research programs at the **Intercultural Center for the Study of Desert and Oceans** (known as CEDO, its acronym in Spanish), about 3 km (2 mi) east of town on Fremont Boulevard in the Fraccionamiento Las Conchas neighborhood. You can take an English-language tour of the facility to learn about the ecology of the area and its history, or just pick up a tide calendar (useful if you're planning beach activities) or field guide from the gift shop. Talks and nature outings—including tide-pool walks, Pinacate excursions, and kayaking expeditions of area estuaries—are offered sporadically. ✉*Turn east at municipal building and follow signs for Fremont Rd., where there will be signs for Las Conchas Beach and CEDO* ☎*638/382–0113* 🌐*www.cedointercultural.org* 🎟*Free, donation for tours* 🕒*Mon.–Sat. 9–5, Sun. 10–2; tours Tues. at 2, Sat. at 4.*

Not far from CEDO you'll find the **Acuario Cet–Mar,** which focuses on the Mar de Cortés ecosystem and the local intertidal zone. The tanks, filled with many kinds of fish, invertebrates, and turtles, have information in both Spanish and English. You can buy a bag of feed for the sea lions and turtles. Since all of the sea creatures on display are wild, the displays often change as some animals are released. ✉*Las Conchas* ☎*638/382–0010* 🎟*$3* 🕒*Weekdays 10–3, weekends 10–6.*

WHERE TO EAT

$$–$$$ SEAFOOD ✕ **Point.** So plainly visible that it lacks an address, this three-story landmark stands on its own pier at the northern end of the malecón. Elegant yet affordable, this establishment offers dependable seafood, steaks, and regional cuisine. The house drink is a strawberry and mango concoction you could swim a lap across. ✉ *Malecón Kino, Col. Puerto* ☎*638/383 –6760* ▭*MC, V*

$–$$ MEXICAN ✕ **La Casa del Capitán.** Perched atop Puerto Peñasco's highest point, this restaurant has the best views over the bay and the town below. There's indoor dining, but the long outdoor terrace overlooking the sea is the place to be, especially at sunset, when it can be packed with locals and visitors alike. A wide-ranging menu includes everything from nachos and quesadillas to flaming, brandied, jumbo shrimp. ✉*Av. del Agua 1, Cerro de la Ballena* ☎*638/383–5698* ▭*MC, V.*

$–$$ MEXICAN ✕ **La Curva.** This friendly family restaurant with great Mexican food is easy to spot if you look for the large green-and-yellow building or the mermaid on the sign. Traditional Mexican dishes are the best bargain, but seafood lovers will have plenty to choose from: the menu lists 12 different shrimp dishes, such as Hawaiian-style shrimp wrapped in bacon and served in a sweet apple-and-pineapple sauce. ✉*Blvd. Kino and Comonfort, Centro* ☎*638/383–3470* ▭*MC, V.*

$–$$ SEAFOOD ✕ **Friendly Dolphin.** This bright blue-and-pink palace feels like a home, with its nicely stuccoed ceilings, hand-painted tiles, and upstairs porch with a harbor view. Unique family recipes include foil-wrapped shrimp or fish prepared *estilo delfín*—steamed in orange juice, herbs, and spices. Gaston, the operatic owner, can easily be coaxed into singing traditional rancheras in a baritone as rich and robust as the food. ✉*Calle José Alcantar 44, Col. Puerto* ☎*638/383–2608* ▭*MC, V.*

WHERE TO STAY

$$$–$$$$ **Sonoran Spa Resort.** One of the first megacomplexes in Rocky Point, this massive pink resort operates much like a hotel, but it offers one-, two-, and three-bedroom, fully furnished condominiums in place of standard rooms. The Sonoran Grill ($$–$$$) serves steaks and seafood, as well as a great spicy lasagna made with chipotle chiles. The beach in front is never crowded, and you can do plenty here without leaving

the resort—a good thing since it is a bit far from the center of town. **Pros:** Good service, calm atmosphere, beautiful view. **Cons:** Beach is rocky at low tide, need a car to get around. ✉ *Camino La Cholla, Km 3.6,* ☎ *638/382–8060* 🌐 *www.sonoran-resorts.com* *204 rooms* *In-room: Kitchen, VCR. In-hotel: Restaurant, room service, tennis court, pools, gym, spa, beachfront* *MC, V.*

$$–$$$ **Playa Bonita.** One of the first hotels in Puerto Peñasco, Playa Bonita is beginning to show its age, though rooms are clean and comfortable. Ask for one facing the hotel's broad, sandy beach. An RV park offers 300 hookups at $17–$20 a day. As the name of the Puesta del Sol restaurant ("setting of the sun") implies, this is a perfect place to see the sun set. Don't miss the divine margaritas. **Pros:** Relaxed atmosphere, good security, talented bartender. **Cons:** Pool isn't heated, maintenance is a bit slack. ✉ *Paseo Balboa 100, Playa Hermosa,* ☎ *638/383–2586* 🌐 *www.playabonitaresort.com* *120 rooms, 6 suites* *In-hotel: Restaurant, bar, pool, beachfront* *AE, MC, V.*

$–$$ **Posada la Roca.** The oldest building in town, this 80-year-old stone villa is also the most charming. Constructed by the current proprietor's grandfather, it has plenty of history. This is where gangster Al Capone hid out from the government in 1927, or so it's said. The rooms are small but beautifully restored, with thick wooden doors and castle-like walls. **Pros:** Atmospheric building, good downtown location, cozy rooms. **Cons:** Rooms and bathrooms are quite small, need to make reservations well in advance. ✉ *Primero de Junio 2, Col. Puerto* ☎ *638/383–3199* *18 rooms* *In-room: No phone* *MC, V.*

$–$$ **Viña del Mar.** Overlooking the ocean, this tidy hotel is the kind of place where you want to admire the sweeping views. That would be a shame, as it is steps away from the shops and restaurants of the town's waterfront walk. Rooms here are bright but sparsely decorated; some are excellent places to take in the sunset, but most of them actually don't have views, so take a look around first. **Pros:** Convenient location, great pool area. **Cons:** Not a lot of charm, chilly staff, noise from motor homes coming and going. ✉ *Av. Primer de Junio, Col. Puerto,* ☎ *638/383–0100 or 638/383–3600* 🌐 *www.vinadelmarhotel.com* *110 rooms* *In-hotel: Restaurant, bar, pool, no elevator, beachfront* *MC, V.*

9

NIGHTLIFE

BARS

Puerto Peñasco's nightlife centers around bars rather than big clubs.

The sports bar **Latitude 31** (✉ *Blvd. Benito Juárez, en route to Col. Puerto* ☎ *638/383–4311*) has a great view of the harbor and a host of TVs showing American sports.

The Lighthouse (✉ *Lote 2, Fracc. el Cerro* ☎ *638/383–2389*), a pretty place overlooking the harbor, appeals to a more sophisticated crowd. You can dance to live music between 7 and 10 on weekends.

Popular among the young and those who don't want to put too much distance between the water's edge and their next margarita is **Manny's**

Beach Club (✉ *Blvd. Matamoros s/n, Playa Miramar* ☎ *638/383–3605*). Recorded music blares constantly in this local landmark.

SPORTS & THE OUTDOORS

WATER SPORTS

At **Sun and Fun Dive and Tackle** (✉ *Blvd. Benito Juárez s/n at Calle Lauro Contreras* ☎ *638/383–5450 or 888/381–7720*) you can rent fishing, diving, or snorkeling equipment or receive PADI and NAUI scuba instruction. Sunset cruises, fishing charters, and snorkeling trips can all be booked.

BAHÍA KINO

107 km (64 mi) west of Hermosillo on Sonora Hwy. 100.

On the eastern shore of the Mar de Cortés lies Bahía Kino, home to some of the prettiest beaches in northwest Mexico. For many years, Bahía Kino was undiscovered except by RV owners and other aficionados of the unspoiled. In the past decade or so, great change has come at the hands of North Americans who have been building condos and beach houses here. More change is coming, as land has been acquired and designs submitted for a 100-acre golf course, three marinas, and, eventually, a series of hotels with 50,000 rooms.

The moniker "Bahía Kino" actually refers to twin towns: Kino Viejo (Old Kino, the Mexican village) and Kino Nuevo (New Kino), where facing a long strand of creamy beach you'll find private homes, condos, RV sites, and other tourist facilities.

GETTING HERE & AROUND

If you want to catch a bus from Hermosillo to Bahía Kino, your best bet is La Costa. Public transportation is nearly nonexistent. If you want to stay in Bahía Kino, you pretty much need a car here to get around.

ESSENTIALS

Bus Contacts **La Costa** (☎ *662/212–2556*).

Currency Exchange **Banorte** (✉ *Kino Viejo* ☎ *No phone*).

Medical Assistance **Clinic Kino Viejo** (✉ *Calle Tampico between Blvd. Kino and Calle Acapulco, Kino Viejo* ☎ *662/242–0297*)

Visitor & Tour Info **Bahía Kino tourism office** (✉ *Calle Mar de Cortez at Calle Catalina, Kino Nuevo, Bahía Kino* ☎ *662/242–0447*).

EXPLORING

For a crash ethnography lesson, poke around the interesting—if haphazard—collection of photographs, musical instruments, artwork, baskets, clothing, and dioramas in the **Museo de los Seris.** Be prepared to practice your Spanish, as there are no descriptions in English. ✉ *Blvd. Mar de Cortés at Calle Progreso* ☎ *No phone* 🎫 *$1* ⏲ *Wed.–Sun. 8–5.*

CLOSE UP

Tribe on the Verge

A rustic Seri fishing village perched at the end of a long, bumpy, winding dirt road, Punta Chueca is 27 km (17 mi) north of Bahía Kino. To get there, you'll pass exquisite vistas of the bay, distant empty beaches, and rolling mountains. The inhabitants of this community live a subsistence lifestyle, relying on the sea and desert.

With fewer than 700 remaining members, the Seri tribe represents an ancient culture on the verge of dying out. The Seri love for their natural surroundings is evident in the necklaces that they have traditionally worn and now create to sell. Pretty little shells are wound into the shape of flowers and strung with wild desert seeds and tiny bleached snake vertebrae. Seri women also weave elaborate *canastas* (baskets) of torote grass, which are highly prized and expensive.

As you get out of your car anywhere in town, be prepared to encounter an entourage of Seri women dressed in colorful ankle-length skirts, their heads covered with scarves, and their arms laden with necklaces for sale. The Seri are best known, however, for the carved *palofiero* (ironwood) figurines that represent the animal world around them, including dolphins, turtles, and pelicans. Many Mexican merchants have taken to machine-making large figures out of ironwood for the tourist trade, thereby seriously depleting the supply of the lilac-blossomed tree that grows only in the Sonoran Desert. (If the bottom of the statuette is smooth, it was cut with an electric saw and not made by the Seri.) For this reason, the Seri now carve figures out of several types of stone. In fact, those in the know suggest that very few, if any, ironwood sculptures are being made by the Seri anymore. If you desire an original bit of Seri artwork, you're best off purchasing a necklace or one of the impressive grass baskets.

■ TIP→**This is no place to hang out after dark, as there is some very open drug trafficking on the part of local narcotraficantes.**

9

WHERE TO EAT

$$–$$$ SEAFOOD ✕**Jorge's Restaurant.** This clean, comfortable family restaurant overlooks the bay—a perfect spot for morning coffee and pancakes. At other meals portions tend to be small, but the food is quite good, and the owner and his daughters play the guitar and sing in the evening. The outdoor patio is great for enjoying the giant margaritas that this place is known for. ✉*Near end of Blvd. Mar de Cortés, at Alecantres, Kino Nuevo* ☎*662/242–0049* ▭*No credit cards.*

$$–$$$ SEAFOOD ✕**El Pargo Rojo.** Fishnets and realistic reproductions of the fish you'll be eating decorate this restaurant, whose name means "red snapper." The catch of the day varies, but you can depend on consistent quality. Classics like a brimming shrimp cocktail could be followed by fish stuffed with shrimp, clams, squid, and octopus. Depending on your luck, you'll be serenaded either by Mexican musicians or by the ceaseless wailing of polkalike *norteña* music on MTV. The restaurant also delivers. ✉*Blvd. Mar de Cortés 1426, Kino Nuevo* ☎*662/242–0205* ▭*D, MC, V.*

$–$$ SEAFOOD ✕ **La Palapa del Pescador.** This palm-shaded spot is perched above a beach sprinkled with the thatch-topped palapas that give the place its name. In the summer, when Bahía Kino fills with travelers, the restaurant is the place to be. The kitchen churns out marlin, five kinds of shrimp, and and selection of excellent salads; this is whee those in the know go for a juicy cheeseburger. ✉ *Blvd. Mar de Cortés and Wellington, on way into Kino Nuevo* ☎ *662/242–0210* ▭ *MC, V.*

★ $–$$ SEAFOOD ✕ **Restaurant Marlin.** Though it may be a bit hard to locate, you may well find yourself returning, drawn by the clean, unpretentious atmosphere and congenial service—not to mention margaritas as big as fishbowls. Superb seafood dishes include *sopa de siete mares* (soup of the seven seas) and *jaiba a la diabla* (a spicy hot crab dish). ✉ *Calles Tastiota and Guaymas, Kino Viejo* ☎ *662/242–0111* ▭ *MC, V* ⊗ *Closed Mon.*

WHERE TO STAY

$$ **La Playa Hotel.** This is the only hotel in Kino that's actually on the beach, making it quite a find. The rooms in the Mediterranean-style whitewashed buildings are simple, but tidy and very well maintained: all have views of the water. The owner is mercurial, however: to preserve the peace and quiet, he's likely to turn away young people and families with children. **Pros:** Beachfront location, lovely building. **Cons:** Two-night minimum stay, owner is quirky. ✉ *Blvd. Mar de Cortés and Beirut, Kino Nuevo,* ☎ *662/242–0273* ⊕ *www.laplayarvhotel.com* *20 rooms* *In-room: Kitchen. In-hotel: Pool, no elevator* ▭ *No credit cards.*

$–$$ **Geko Apartments.** The Greek Isles come to mind when you see this small hotel across from the beach. The accommodations aren't luxurious, but they are comfortable and well appointed. The rooms, on two levels, surround a small courtyard. **Pros:** Great location, quiet setting, friendly owners. **Cons:** Resembles an apartment complex. ✉ *1120 Mar de Cortés, Kino Nuevo* ☎ *662/360–1387 or 662/260–1496* *6 rooms, 4 suites* *In-room: Refrigerator. In-hotel: Public Wi-Fi* ▭ *MC.*

GUAYMAS

128 km (79 mi) south of Hermosillo.

The buzz and bustle of Guaymas—one of Mexico's largest ports—has a pleasant backdrop of rusty red, saguaro-speckled bluffs that nudge the deep-blue waters of a sprawling bay on the Mar de Cortés. The Spanish arrived in this "port of ports" by the mid-16th century. In 1701 two Jesuit priests, Father Kino and his colleague Juan María Salvatierra, erected a mission base here intended to convert the native Guaimas, Seri, and Yaqui Indians.

Guaymas was declared a commercial port in 1814, and became an important center of trade. In 1847, during the Mexican-American War, U.S. naval forces attacked and occupied the town for a year. Bumbling filibuster William Walker also managed to take Guaymas for a short time in 1853, and in 1866, during Maximilian's brief reign, the French took control. Today's foreign invaders are mostly travelers passing through on their way somewhere else.

Hardworking Guaymas, unlike its more pristine twin San Carlos, takes Highway 15 right into its gritty heart, and has all the grime, noise, and traffic. But the town is undergoing a major makeover, with a new malecón (waterfront boardwalk) and a cruise-ship terminal set to open in late 2008. The sweeping views across the old harbor are magically suggestive of the town's historic past.

The center of the city is **Plaza 13 de Julio,** a typical main square with thick fig trees, a Moorish-style bandstand, and ornate benches. Facing the park is the 19th-century church **Parroquia de San Fernando.**

GETTING HERE & AROUND

Guaymas has an airport, but flying here can be pricey. Buses bound for other cities stop in Guaymas; the trip here from Nogales is about seven hours. The bus company Grupo Estrella Blanca, which has a network that covers 27 of the 31 states of Mexico, has frequent service to Guaymas from Nogales, Tijuana, and Mexicali. And cabs can be hailed anywhere—a good thing, as the attractions are rather far-flung. The Baja Car Ferry runs to and from Guaymas from Santa Rosalía three times a week.

ESSENTIALS

Bus Contacts **Grupo Estrella Blanca** (☎ *662/213–4050* 🌐 *www.estrellablanca.com.mx*).

Medical Assistance **Hospital General de Guaymas** (✉ *Calle 12 s/n, Centro* ☎ *622/224–0138*).

Visitor & Tour Info **Tourism Office** (✉ *Blvd. Manlio F. Beltrones 37, Sector Creston Norte, San Carlos* ☎ *662/226–0202* 🌐 *www.visitasonora.com*).

EXPLORING

There isn't much to see in Guaymas outside of the old harbor. The hills around the town are dramatic, but the outdoor activities are further south. Relax here and enjoy the sunshine and the simple ambience.

Follow the signs to Playa Miramar and take advantage of the free tours offered by the pearl farm, **Perlas del Mar de Cortéz** (✉ *Bahía de Bacochibampo s/n* ☎ *622/221–0136* 🌐 *www.perlas.com.mx*), which has more than 200,000 native pearl oysters in cultivation—it's the only pearl farm of its scale in the Americas. Tours are conducted on the hour weekdays 9 to 3 and Saturday 9 to 11. After taking the tour, you will have an opportunity to buy jewelry made from the stunningly iridescent pearls they cultivate.

WHERE TO EAT & STAY

$–$$ ✕ **Los Arbolitos.** This palapa-shaded family restaurant is a great stopover on the highway to San Carlos. It has the lazy-day ambience of a more rural setting. It's all seafood here: fish fillets, scallops, oysters, and shrimp cooked to perfection. ✉ *Carretera Internacional, Km. 198.2, Col. Lomalinda* ☎ *622/221–2601* ▭ *MC, V.*

$–$$ ✕ **Colibri Tacos.** If you're curious about the abundance of roadside taco stands, this is the perfect place to see what all the fuss is about. Here you'll find lean grilled beef, fat shrimp, and a delightfully large condi-

9

ment selection featuring the most luscious vegetables you've ever seen in a salad bar. ✉*Corner of El Vigia and Calle La Yoruda, Col. Las Villas* ☎*No phone* ▭*No credit cards.*

$$$ **Playa de Cortes.** Built in 1928, this beachside villa is one of the most romantic lodgings in Sonora. The charming bungalows set amongst bougainvillea-filled gardens have the feel of a film set in the 1920s. The common areas are decorated with antique furniture and heavy wooden chandeliers. The low-walled garden sweeps out to face the rocky shore of beautiful Bahia Bacochibampo. **Pros:** Sweeping views, scenic setting, attentive staff. **Cons:** Beds are hard, isolated location. ✉*Bahia Bacochibampo,* ☎*622/149–622, 01800/623–4400 toll-free in Mexico* 🌐*hermosillovirtual.com/gandara/cortes.htm* *88 rooms, 21 suites, 9 bungalows* *In-room: Wi-Fi. In-hotel: Restaurant, room service, bar, pool, tennis court, public Wi-Fi* ▭*AE, MC, V.*

$ **Hotel Armida.** This hotel has a well-kept pool and a popular coffee shop where locals gather for power breakfasts. At the steak house, El Oeste ($$–$$$), the stuffed and mounted heads of mountain goats, cougars, and buffalo gaze down. Large, bright accommodations are plain but serviceable, with comfortable beds; many have balconies overlooking the pool. Rooms at the back are a great bargain. **Pros:** Excellent restaurants, pretty pool. **Cons:** On the ugliest strip in Guaymas, lots of traffic noise. ✉*Carretera Internacional, Salida Norte,* ☎*622/225–2800* *124 rooms* *In-hotel: 2 restaurants, room service, bar, pool, gym* ▭*AE, MC, V.*

SAN CARLOS

20 km (12 mi) northwest of Guaymas.

Long considered an extension of Guaymas, this resort town—on the other side of the rocky peninsula that separates Bahía de Bacochibampo from Bahía de San Carlos—has a personality of its own. Whitewashed houses with red-tile roofs snuggle together along the water where countless yachts and motorboats are docked. The town is a laid-back favorite among professional anglers, golfers, and the time-share crowd, as well as wealthy Mexican families from Hermosillo and Chihuahua. There are several good hotels, as well as two marinas and a country club with an 18-hole golf course.

The overlapping of desert and semitropical flora and fauna has created a fascinating diversity of species along this coast. More than 650 species of fish exist here, and the marlin and sailfish keep the charter sportfishing business healthy. Dolphins and pelicans frequent the bays, as do blue and gray whales and orcas. The water is calm and warm enough for swimming through October. Scuba, snorkeling, and fishing are popular, too.

The quiet 5-km (3-mi) stretch of sandy beach at **Los Algodones,** where the San Carlos Plaza Hotel and Paradiso are now, was in the 1960s a location for the film *Catch-22.* (In fact, it's still called Catch-22 Beach on many maps.) San Carlos lies in the shadow of the jagged twin-peak **Tetakawi mountain,** a sacred site where native warriors once gathered to

CLOSE UP

The Maquila's March to Modernity

When Mexico began its Border Industrialization Program in 1965, few could have imagined the social and environmental ills that open markets and prosperous free-trade deals would spawn three decades later. Mexico's *maquiladoras* (also known as *maquilas*) are foreign-owned assembly plants that produce cars, electronics, and garments for export to the First World. The passage of the North American Free Trade Agreement (NAFTA), which relaxed tariffs on goods moving across North American borders, made the maquila a profitable tool for U.S. companies. Even prior to NAFTA, repeated recessions and peso devaluations in the 1980s, combined with drought and chronic poverty in many of the northern and central agricultural states, brought both multinational companies and desperate migrant workers to Tijuana and Ensenada in Baja California, Nogales in Sonora, Matamoros in Tamaulipas, and Ciudad Juárez in Chihuahua.

Shantytowns sprang up, most of which are still lacking in clean water, sanitation, electricity, and other basic infrastructure; companies and city governments have had no legal obligation, no financial incentive, and no revenue to provide for inhabitants. With time, the living conditions have improved marginally in some areas, but even with meager allowances for housing or health care, workers here are still exploited. And because NAFTA has only an impotent Commission on Environmental Cooperation (CEC) to evaluate, but not enforce, the safe environmental procedures outlined in the agreement, hundreds of maquilas regularly dump hazardous waste along the border. It's estimated that less than half of American maquilas follow Mexican law and return their toxic waste to the United States.

Though the maquila industry created hundreds of thousands of jobs, it effectively threw a grenade in the midst of rural Mexico's family mores and values—for better and worse. Academic studies chart devastating social disintegration, but Mexican women—who for the first time earn a wage and decide what to do with it—are viewed by many to have finally found some liberation.

Ciudad Juárez sits above anonymous swathes of the huge state of Chihuahua, just over the Río Bravo (or Rio Grande) from El Paso, Texas. Over the last three decades more than a million souls have come to toil in the maquilas. Juárez became a magnet for young women, lured from the interior of the country by plentiful jobs. As it turned out, though, not only was their labor cheap, but so were their lives. Since 1993, there have been more than 370 officially recognized murders of young women. Hundreds of others have disappeared and are presumed dead. The maquila murders in Juárez have become a scandal of international proportions, and although most cases remain unsolved, local, state, and even international protest is beginning to mount.

The maquila zone poses problems with no easy answers, which still look a long way from resolution. Every day hopeful young men and women are carted in from their rank little huts to make gadgets for others, before they can make a life for themselves.

–Barbara Kastelein

gain spiritual strength. The **Mirador Escénico,** or scenic lookout, is the best place in San Carlos to view the Mar de Cortés. Take the steep road up here for a great photo op or just to get an idea of the lay of the land. While you're here you can browse the numerous trinket and souvenir stands set up every day. Just north of the Mirador is Zorro Cove, a great place to snorkel. An interesting day trip (by boat) is the pristine **Isla de San Pedro Nolasco,** an ecological reserve where sea lions claim the rocks.

GETTING HERE & AROUND

The airfield in San Carlos is restricted to charter planes. Most people drive here, and new roads are among the smoothest in the state. To get here by bus, head to nearby Guaymas and take a cab or local bus (you'll see the buses marked "San Carlos" along the main drag).

ESSENTIALS

San Carlos is essentially a suburb of Guaymas. It is less developed in terms of infrastructure, and many essentials are available only in Guaymas.

Visitor & Tour Info **San Carlos Tourism Office** (✉ *Blvd. Manlio F. Beltrones 37, Sector Creston Norte* ☎ *662/226–0202* 🌐 *www.visitasonora.com*).

EXPLORING

Delfinario Sonora. On a pristine bay halfway between Bahia Bacochibampo and San Carlos, this facility offers a chance to interact with dolphins. There isn't much here other than getting close to the animals themselves, but it is a unforgettable experience for the kids. ✉ *Carretera a Las Tinajas Km. 5.5, Nuevo Guaymas* ☎ *662/210–8340* 🌐 *www.delfinariosonora.com.mx* ⏲ *Mon.–Sat. 9–5.*

WHERE TO EAT & STAY

$–$$$ MEXICAN ✕ **Rosa's Cantina.** The walls at this cozy pink restaurant are decorated with historical photos from Mexico's past, including many of Mexican revolutionaries. Ask anyone in town and they'll tell you Rosa's ample breakfasts are the best way to start the day. Try the *machaca* (dried beef) with eggs and salsa; the tortilla soup is great for lunch or dinner. Gringos who miss being pampered will appreciate the no-smoking section, decaf coffee, and a salad bar. ✉ *Calle Aurora 297, Creston* ☎ *622/226–1000* ▭ *MC, V.*

$$–$$$$ **Marinaterra.** This resort overlooks the San Carlos marina and has a commanding view of Cerro Tetakawi. Pastels soften the rooms, most of which have tiny kitchenettes. Some corner rooms have hot tubs on outdoor patios at no extra cost. A shuttle takes guests to the hotel beach club, which is a great place to hang out poolside or take a walk on the beach. El Embarcadero restaurant ($–$$) is a good place to try hearty, traditional Mexican soups like the *caldo Xochitl,* a steaming chicken consommé with white rice and avocado, garnished with chili. **Pros:** Service of a luxury hotel, sophisticated atmosphere, great views. **Cons:** All your fellow guests are Americans. ✉ *Calle Gabriel Estrada s/n, Sector La Herradura,* ☎ *622/225–2020 or 888/688–5353* 🌐 *www.marinaterra.com* ⇨ *94 rooms, 18 suites* ♁ *In-room: Refrigerator, kitchens (some). In-hotel: Restaurant, bar, pool, public Internet* ▭ *AE, DC, MC, V.*

$$$ **San Carlos Plaza Hotel and Resort.** Rising from Bahía de San Carlos, this huge resort is the most luxurious lodging in Sonora. The arresting atrium lobby opens onto a large pool and beach. Attractive rooms—all with at least a partial ocean view—have contemporary, if uninspiring, furnishings. Rooms on the first two floors have balconies overlooking the sea. Children love the swimming-pool slide and horseback riding on beautiful Algodones beach. **Pros:** Elegant public areas, beautiful beach. **Cons:** No flavor of the region, caters to a lot of conventions. ✉ *Paseo Mar Barmejo Norte 4, Los Algodones,* ☎ *622/225–3000 or 800/716–0506* 🌐 *www.sancarlosplazaresort.com* *132 rooms, 41 suites* *In-room: Safe. In-hotel: 3 restaurants, bars, tennis courts, pools, gym, spa, beachfront* *AE, DC, MC, V.*

$$ **Fiesta San Carlos.** Every room in this small, beachfront, family-run hotel soaks up views of the Gulf. The rooms are clean and well maintained, with exceedingly comfortable beds. Some rooms with kitchens are available. **Pros:** Beautiful lawn, beachfront location. **Cons:** On a noisy road, busy singles' bar next door. ✉ *Blvd. Beltrones, Km 8.5, Carretera Escénico,* ☎ *622/226–0229 or 662/226–1318* 🌐 *www.hotel-fiestareal.com* *33 rooms* *In-room: No phone, no TV. In-hotel: Restaurant, bar, pool, parking (no fee), no elevator* *MC, V* *BP.*

$$ **Hacienda Tetakawi.** This hotel and trailer park across from the beach on the town's main street is part of the Best Western chain. Rooms are generic but clean, and each has a balcony or patio, a few with a view of the sea. **Pros:** On one of the nicest stretches of beach in town. **Cons:** Lacks charm. ✉ *Blvd. Beltrones, Km 10* ☎ *622/226–0248* *22 rooms* *In-room: Wi-fi. In-hotel: Restaurant, bar, pool, no elevator* *AE, MC, V.*

NIGHTLIFE

BARS

San Carlos has busy little clusters of bars around the marinas that are frequented by visitors.

Aqua Bar (*Hotel Marinaterra, Calle Gabriel Estrada s/n Sector La Herradura* ☎ *622/225–2020*) has live music weekends until 2 AM.

The hottest new gathering place for younger people is the bar of the restaurant **El Bronco** (✉ *Manlio F. Beltrones 178, Creston* ☎ *622/226–1130*). There's a well-stocked bar at the center of the room.

Stop by the **Galería Bellas Artes** (✉ *Villahermosa 111, Sector Villahermosa* ☎ *622/226–0073*), where artwork is for sale. It's open Monday to Saturday 9:30 to 5.

Every Tuesday the **San Carlos Plaza Hotel** (☎ *622/225–3000*) hosts an evening of folkloric dancing and singing along with dinner buffet and open bar ($18). Reservations are encouraged; transportation from some hotels is provided.

Tequilas Bar (✉ *Gabriel Estrada 1, Marina San Carlos* ☎ *622/226–0545*) is a popular nightspot with a small dance floor, big crowd, and live music on weekends.

SHOPPING

Kiamy's Gift Shop (✉*Blvd. Beltrones, Km 10* ☎*622/226–0400*) is like a bazaar, with something for everyone: silver jewelry, leather bags, ceramics, and Yaqui Indian masks.

Sagitario's Gift Shop (✉*Blvd. Beltrones 132* ☎*622/226–0090*) features clothing and a variety of crafts, including wood carvings, baskets, rugs, and Talavera tile.

SPORTS & THE OUTDOORS

San Carlos may be small, but it's a big destination for anglers. Fishing outfitters are well equipped and knowledgeable about local waters.

WATER SPORTS

Gary's Dive Shop (✉*Blvd. Beltrones, Km 10* ☎*622/226–0049 or 866/356–1236* 🌐*www.garysdivemexico.com*) is run by American owners Gary and Donna Goldstein, who have been residents and business owners here for over 30 years. They run excellent fishing, snorkeling, and PADI-certified diving excursions. You can also book sunset cruises, whale-watching tours, and marine-biology trips.

Ocean Sports (✉*San Carlos Marina #L-7* ☎*622/226–0696* 🌐*www.desertdivers.com*)offers all types of diving and snorkeling equipment, as well as supplies for anglers.

ALAMOS

★ *257 km (160 mi) southeast of Guaymas.*

With its cobblestone streets, charming central plaza, 250-year-old baroque church, and thoughtfully restored haciendas, Alamos is the most authentically restored colonial town in Sonora. Although Sonora has many historical areas from the Spanish colonial period, Alamos once held sway over a vast area and is arguably the most historically important spot in the state. In the ecologically rich zone where the Sonoran Desert meets a dry tropical forest, the entire town is designated a national historic monument.

Coronado camped here in 1540, but Alamos really boomed when silver was discovered in the area during the 1680s. Wealth from the mines financed Spanish expeditions to the north—as far as Los Angeles and San Francisco during the 1770s and '80s—and the town became the capital of the state of Occidente from 1827 to 1832. A government mint was established here in 1864. The mines had closed by the beginning of the Mexican Revolution in 1910. All but abandoned for the first half of the 20th century, it retains it colonial atmosphere.

Points of interest include the impressive **Parroquia de Nuestra Señora de la Concepción,** constructed on the site of a 17th-century adobe church destroyed in an Indian uprising. Fronting the parish church is the beautiful central square, the **Plaza de las Armas;** its ornate Moorish-style wrought-iron gazebo was brought from Mazatlán in 1904. From there head northwest to the rectangular **Alameda,** which is surrounded by promenades and flanked at night by food vendors. If you're in town on Sunday, cross the little arroyo (seasonal riverbed) north of the Alameda to the weekly market. Southeast of the main square is the **Cerro del Perico,** a hill that has awesome views of the city and the craggy forests surrounding it.

Every January Alamos hosts the 10-day **Festival Juan Ortiz Torado,** a celebration of classical music honoring one of its native sons. Named for the 20th century's biggest Latin American opera star, the festival attracts musicians from around the world. Most of the performances are free.

Wealthy American expats who started coming here in the 1950s to restore the enormous haciendas, turned some into luxurious private homes. If possible, time your trip to Alamos to include a Saturday **House and Garden Tour** ($8 suggested donation) of some of the superbly restored mansions and their interior patios and gardens. You can get a tour schedule from the tourist office or any of the local hotels.

GETTING HERE & AROUND

A bus ride from Nogales, near the border, to Alamos will take roughly nine hours. TUFESA and Transportes del Pacifico run to nearby Navajoa, the closest large market town, from where you can catch a TBC bus to Alamos. There is also a TBC bus that runs directly to Tucson and Phoenix nightly from the Alamos bus station.

ESSENTIALS

Bus Contacts **TBC** (☎ *647/428–0096*).

Currency Exchange **Banorte** (✉ *Calle Madero no. 27, Col. Centro* ☎ *647/428–0093 or 647/428–0357*).

Visitor & Tour Info **Alamos tourism office** (✉ *Main Plaza, Calle Juárez 6* ☎ *647/428–0450*).

9

EXPLORING

Don't miss the **Museo Costumbrista de Sonora** for an excellent overview of the history of the state of Sonora. The displays include antique wagons, artifacts from the nearby silver mines, and coins from the mints of Alamos and Hermosillo. There are also examples of the clothing and furnishings of prominent local families. ✉ *Calle Guadalupe Victoria 1, on Plaza de las Armas* ☎ *647/428–0053* *$1* *Wed.–Sun. 9–6.*

WHERE TO EAT

$ ★ MEXICAN

Las Palmeras. This popular Mexican family restaurant sits on the west side of the Alameda. Here you might get homemade *rosca* bread (a sweet, round loaf) with your coffee and an assortment of daily specials. The corn tamales are hard to beat; other specialties include the chiles relleno (cheese-stuffed chile peppers) and the *carne milanesa* (similar to chicken-fried steak). ✉ *Madero 48* ☎ *647/428–0065* *No credit cards.*

WHERE TO STAY

$$$$ Fodor's Choice ★

Hacienda de los Santos. Sonora's swankest hotel rambles across the grounds of five restored colonial mansions; you'll be entirely secluded from the outside world by the walls of these former haciendas. In gracious courtyards and lining long porticos are centuries-old pieces of religious art and hand-carved antique furniture, all collected by the American owners. The spacious bedrooms also have antiques, as well as fireplaces. A 100-year-old bar brought from Cuernavaca presents for your pleasure 400 different varieties of tequila, and a spa offers massage and beauty treatments. **Pros:** Luxury on every level, personalized service, the feeling of complete seclusion. **Cons:** Need a car to get around, noise from a nearby school. ✉ *Calle Molina 8,* ☎ *647/428–0222 or 800/525–4800* 🌐 *www.haciendadelossantos.com* *12 rooms, 13 suites* *In-hotel: 2 restaurants, bar, pools, gym, spa, no kids under 18, no-smoking rooms, no elevator* *AE, MC, V* *BP.*

$$ **Casa de los Tesoros.** This hotel, whose name means the "House of Treasures," is a picturesque and romantic converted 18th-century convent. The rooms were once nuns' cells, but they're no longer austere—they've now got fireplaces, tile baths, antique furnishings, and striking local art. The restaurant is excellent, and the in-house guitar trio provides the mood music. **Pros:** Swanky atmosphere, perfectly located. **Cons:** Austere courtyard, can feel a little too quiet. ✉ *Obregón 10,* ☎ *647/428–0010* 🌐 *www.tesoros-hotel.com* *13 rooms, 2 suites* *In-room: No phone, no TV. In-hotel: Restaurant, bar, pool, no elevator* *MC, V* *BP.*

$$ **La Puerta Roja Inn.** Formerly a private house, this 19th-century structure still gives you the feeling of being a guest in a friend's home. The rooms have high ceilings and are individually decorated; some have handmade tile floors and wooden doors. The postage-stamp pool is a great place to relax with a book from the excellent art library. The owners can hook you up with tours that will satisfy any nature buff. **Pros:** Excellent breakfasts, engaging owners. **Cons:** A bit out of the way, not a lot of privacy. ✉ *Galeana 46,* ☎ *647/428–0142* 🌐 *www.lapuertarojainn.com* *5 rooms, 1 suite* *In-room: No phone, no TV. In-hotel: Restaurant, pool, no elevator* *MC, V* *BP.*

$ **La Posada de Don Andres.** Although it was built in the 1950s, this New Orleans–style hotel feels a century older. Facing the Alameda and just steps from the public market, the hotel's wrought-iron-and-marble courtyard calls to mind a more refined era. The owner, who named the place after his late father, plays acoustic guitar and violin in the comfortable wood-paneled lobby upstairs. **Pros:** Great location, atmospheric building. **Cons:** Decor sometimes resembles a secondhand store, noisy neighbors. ✉ *Calle Rosales 24-A* ☎ *647/428–1110* *10 rooms* *In-room: No phone. In-hotel: Public Internet* *No credit cards.*

$ **Solipaso.** The handful of rooms in this restored hacienda are gorgeous, with antique furnishings and wood-and-glass doors leading outdoors. A small courtyard holds a café and a tiny pool not much bigger than a hot tub. The American owners, a bird expert and a yoga teacher, are building El Pedregal, a 20-acre retreat just outside of town. **Pros:** Cozy yet elegant, good location, on a quiet street. **Cons:** Breakfast is a little pricey. ✉ *Calle Obregon 3,* ☎ *647/428–0466* 🌐 *www.solipaso.com* *4 rooms* *In-room: Wi-Fi, no phone, no TV* *No credit cards.* *Closed Sun. evening, Mon. and most of summer.*

NIGHTLIFE

The nighttime activities in Alamos consist mostly of cruising the Alameda and the Plaza de las Armas and dropping into the town's one cantina.

La Corregidora (✉ *Calle Juárez 6* ☎ *No phone*), named for a heroine of the war for independence, is a comfortable little bar whose prices aren't a bargain, but aren't extortion. You can join locals watching sports on a widescreen TV.

SHOPPING

Small stores lining the **Alameda** sell Mexican sweets, fabrics, belts, and hats, among other items. You'll find *tianguis* (market stalls) lining the **Plaza de las Armas** every day, but Sunday brings artisans and vendors from the surrounding area.

It's worth a peek into the three crowded rooms of **El Nicho Curios** (✉ *Calle Juárez 15* ☎ *647/428–0213*), filled with a storybook assortment of odd treasures and tiny heirlooms ranging from Mexican religious paintings to old jewelry and regional pottery.

ADUANA

10 km (6 mi) west of Alamos, 251 km (156 mi) southeast of Guaymas.

A couple of miles off the main road to Alamos, tiny Aduana was once the site of one of the richest mines in the district. The tiny village is barely more than a church on the humblest of plazas, a country store and two local handicrafts cooperatives, and an abandoned silver mine on a hill. But it's worth a visit for a meal at Sonora's best restaurant.

EXPLORING

On the plaza is the **Iglesia de Nuestra Señora de Balvanera.** A cactus that grows out of one of the church's walls is said to mark the spot where the Virgin appeared to the Yaqui Indians in the 17th century.

WHERE TO STAY & EAT

$$ **Casa la Aduana.** Though it's in an unlikely spot 3 km (2 mi) off the highway into Alamos, the restaurant here has a reputation as the best in the state. The restored 17th-century customhouse presents exceptional four-course, prix-fixe menus ($$$), with entrées such as chicken in an apple-chipotle cream sauce. Although the walls and floors of the B&B here are the restored originals, modern luxuries haven't been overlooked: soft linens, comfortable beds, and thick bath towels add to the charm. Guest rooms have 4-foot-thick walls, which reflect their former duties as vaults for the riches that came from this area's mines. Your stay includes breakfast and four-course dinner. **Pros:** Historic property, great meals. **Cons:** Isolated location. ✉ *Frente a la Placita, 85760* ☎ *647/404–3473, 406/322–3473 in U.S.* 🌐 *www.casaladuana.com* *3 rooms* *In-room: No phone. In-hotel: Restaurant, pool, no kids under 16, no elevator* *No credit cards, cash or U.S. or Mexico check w/ID.*

Fodor's Choice ★

9

Barrancas del Cobre

Paquimé. Casas Grandes

WORD OF MOUTH

"Whatever difficulties there were to get to this place—all forgotten. This one glance at the enormous beauty in front of you is worth all the time to get there."

–FainaAgain

"The train ride was great. If you're going south (Chihuahua to El Fuerte) sit on the left side of the train on the way down."

–Tina

www.fodors.com/forums

WELCOME TO BARRANCAS DEL COBRE

TOP REASONS TO GO

★ **The train ride down:** The Chihuahua al Pacífico railroad allows you to cut a direct path through this dramatic landscape.

★ **Encountering the Tarahumara:** This indigenous community's culture has changed little in the last 1,000 years.

★ **Biking, hiking, or riding to Batopilas and Urique:** The rough roads to these towns are full of switchbacks, with incredible views around each turn.

★ **Communing with nature:** The backcountry Copper Canyon Sierra Lodge is a good place to start with its tranquil setting amid pine trees, lack of electricity, and vegetarian meals.

★ **Exploring an ancient trading center:** The sea of roofless walls at Casas Grandes, the ruins of Paquimé, looks like an adobe maze.

1 Eastern Terminus: Chihuahua City. Most travelers end up in this modern metropolis at the beginning or end of their canyon adventure. With numerous shady plazas, interesting museums, and colorful shops, the congenial city is worth a visit.

2 The Mountain Towns. Most of the important towns in the region are along the train route. Cerocahui is a rugged mountain village with an excellent hotel. Urique is a tiny desert oasis on the floor of the deepest canyon in North America. Posada Barrancas is a whistle-stop minutes from its more photogenic twin, Divisadero. Creel, the largest town, is the hub of most off-road expeditions. Batopilas, in its own canyon, has a storybook colonial center.

3 Western Terminus: Los Mochis. The train line begins at Los Mochis, near the ferry to Baja California, and convenient to the major highway skirting the Pacific coast.

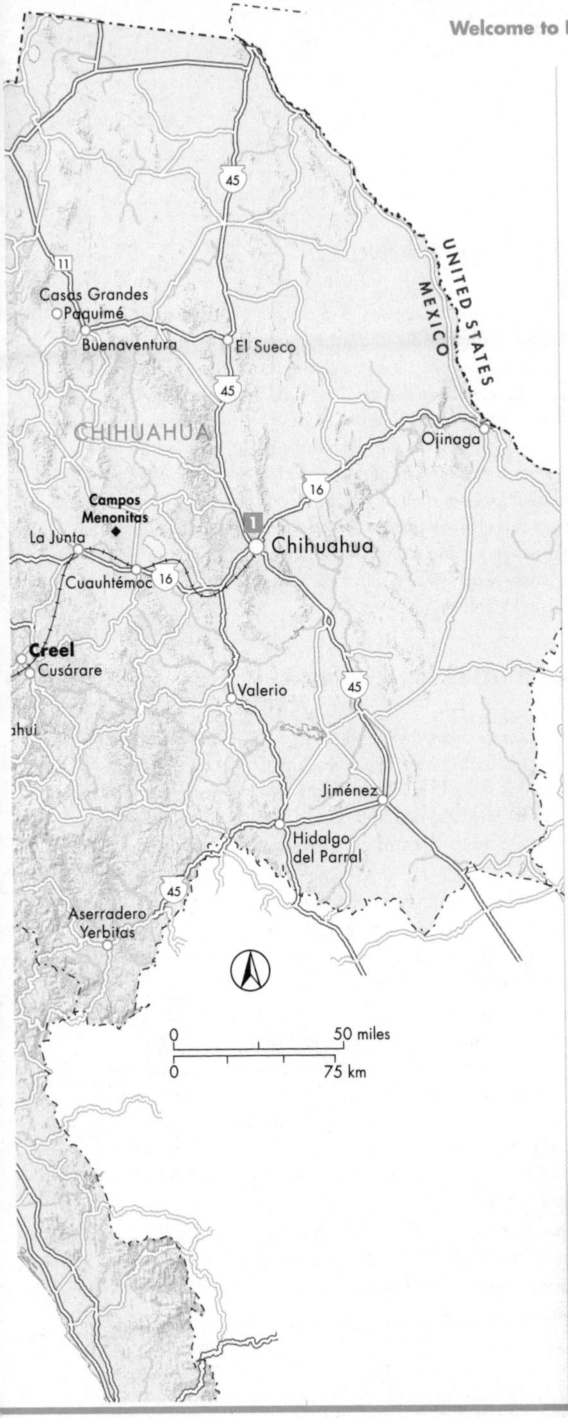

UNITED STATES
MEXICO
45
11
Casas Grandes
Paquimé
Buenaventura
El Sueco
45
CHIHUAHUA
Ojinaga
16
Campos Menonitas
1
La Junta
Chihuahua
Cuauhtémoc
16
Creel
Cusárare
Valerio
45
Jiménez
Hidalgo del Parral
45
Aserradero Yerbitas
0
50 miles
0
75 km

GETTING ORIENTED

The magnificent series of gorges known collectively as las Barrancas del Cobre, or the Copper Canyon, is the real treasure of the Sierra Madre. (The name refers to the tarnished-copper color of the lichen on the canyon walls.) Inaccessible to the casual visitor until the early 1960s and still largely uncharted, the canyons are most frequently visited via one of the most breathtaking train rides in North America.

BARRANCAS DEL COBRE PLANNER

A Little Rough Around the Edges

Imagine, if you will, visiting the Grand Canyon in the days before it was tamed by tourist facilities and you'll have some sense of what it's like to take a trip through the Barrancas del Cobre. And of course it's to be expected that with the opportunity to encounter a relatively untouched natural environment, come some of the discomforts of the rustic experience.

Outside small villages such as Creel and Batopilas, there are few eateries except those connected to lodges; hearty meals are generally included in room rates. In Cerocahui, Divisadero, Posada Barrancas (*posada* means inn), and Creel, most hotels are pine-log types heated by gas furnaces or wood-burning stoves. The lodges send buses or cars to meet the train which is extremely convenient, and for this reason, reservations are recommended.

Booking in Advance

From August to October, and around Christmas and Easter, it's important to book more than a month in advance. Many people come during Easter and Christmas, specifically to see the local take on church holidays. On these and other religious feast days, many Tarahumara communities dance throughout the night, fortified by *tesgüino,* a corn beverage fermented in clay pots. Villages challenge one another in races that can last for days. The men run in small groups for 161 km (100 mi) or more, all the while kicking a small wooden ball. It's not just fun and games—each village places a huge communal wager for this winner-take-all event.

Getting Here & Around

You can fly into either Chihuahua or Los Mochis from many major U.S. and Mexican cities. The Chihuahua airport (CUU) is roughly a 10-minute drive from the city center. The Los Mochis–Topolobampo airport (LMM) is about 30 minutes outside Los Mochis on the road to Topolobampo.

Most people make their way through the canyons by train, on the Ferrocarril Chihuahua al Pacífico, which stops in all the major towns in the region. You can arrange horseback riding or day hikes into the canyon from larger towns, such as Creel.

Bus service is limited, but there are buses between Creel and Chihuahua at the eastern end of the route, and El Fuerte and Los Mochis at the western end. If you're short on time and/or need to fly into Chihuahua to start, you could take the bus to Creel and arrange day hikes from there for an abbreviated trip. (You could also choose to get on the train at Creel, as the best scenery is between Creel and El Fuerte.)

Driving from Chihuahua City to Creel and Divisadero is possible. Beyond Divisadero the roads get rough, especially the dirt road to Bahuichivo, the station for Cerocahui and Urique.

Safety Concerns

Travel in and around the Barrancas del Cobre is generally safe, but off-road trips deep into the canyons should always be done with respectable, local guides who know the terrain. In addition to rock slides and other natural disasters, drug traffickers are sometimes a danger.

The Pros of Hiring a Pro

The complicated logistics of traveling in the region and the dearth of facilities and infrastructure mean that this is one place where a package tour might make sense. But you can rest assured you won't see any mega-tour buses trundling along the canyon's dirt roads. From the United States, the oldest operator in the area is **Pan American Tours** (☎800/876–3942 🌐www.panamericantours.com). Prices for three- to seven-night tours range from $480 to $875 per person. **The California Native** (☎800/926–1140 🌐www.calnative.com) runs small group tours through the canyons. The 4- to 11-day self-guided trips start around $720; group trips last one to two weeks and begin at $1,940. **Copper Canyon Adventures** (☎ 698/893–0915 in El Fuerte, 800/530–8828 🌐www.coppercanyonadventures.com) offers private and group tours ranging from sedate to adventurous. **3 Amigos** (☎ 635/456–0179 or 635/456–0036 🌐www.amigos3.com) will plan tours based on your specific schedule, needs, and interests.

Money Matters

WHAT IT COSTS IN DOLLARS

¢	$	$$	$$$	$$$$
Restaurants				
under $5	$5–$10	$10–$15	$15–$25	over $25
Hotels				
under $50	$50–$75	$75–$150	$150–$250	over $250

Restaurant prices are per person for a main course at dinner. Hotel prices are for two people in a standard double room.

How's the Weather?

The rainy season in this part of Mexico, which runs from late June to September, brings bursts of precipitation every day, but this normally won't interfere with your plans. May, June, and July, the warmest months, are a great time to go hiking in the highlands, though the same doesn't hold true in the canyons, which are often broiling at this time of year.

Overall, the best months to visit are during the fall in September and October, when the weather at the top is starting to cool off the bottom. It's also when the rains of the previous months bring out all the colors of the region's flora.

The middle of winter—December through February—is not the best time to visit the high country. Although the scenery can be breathtaking in the snow, some of the hotels in the region are inadequately prepared for cold weather. However, temperatures on the canyon floors can be ideal for outdoor activities.

EASTERN TERMINUS: CHIHUAHUA CITY

Updated by Grant Cogswell

375 km (233 mi) south of El Paso–Ciudad Juárez border, 1,440 km (893 mi) northwest of Mexico City.

FOR A CITY RINGED WITH highways and pocked by parking lots, Chihuahua has a very pleasant center. Here you'll find a pair of pretty plazas and more trees than you will probably see in any northern city of comparable size. Chihuahua, with a population of 670,000, feels considerably smaller than it is. Its two good museums are tied to key figures in the nation's history: Pancho Villa, the mustachioed revolutionary who helped overthrow Dictator Porfirio Díaz in 1910, and Padre Miguel Hidalgo, the priest known as the father of Mexican independence.

GETTING HERE & AROUND

American and Continental Airlines have daily direct flights to Chihuahua. Aeroméxico and Interjet connect with all major Mexican destinations. The 20-minute taxi ride downtown cost about $16. Most U.S. visitors drive to Chihuahua via Carretera 45. The trip from Ciudad Juárez, just across the border from El Paso, Texas, is about 375 km (233 mi). Parking can be hard to come by. Taxies are safe and can be flagged from anywhere. If you're thinking about taking a bus down, Grupo Estrella Blanca, which includes Chihuahuense and Elite, connects the border cities to Chihuahua City and Creel. Omnibus de México lines run clean, air-conditioned, first-class buses from Ciudad Juárez, just across the border from El Paso, Texas, to Chihuahua City. The intercity bus station is inconveniently located on the ring highway called the Perférico. Getting downtown requires a 10-minute cab ride or a 40-minute journey on Circumvalación 2, a bus that drops you just a block from the train station. (Look for the ominous 1898 state penitentiary, you can't miss it. The station is on the other side.)

ESSENTIALS

Bus Contacts **Estación Central de Chihuahua** (✉ *Boulevard Juan Pablo II, Perférico Oeste* ☎ *614/429–0230*).**Grupo Estrella Blanca** (☎ *614/429–0240 in Chihuahua, 668/812–1757 in Los Mochis, 800/507–5500* 🌐 *www.estrellablanca.com.mx*). **Omnibus de México** (☎ *614/420–1580 in Chihuahua* 🌐 *www.omnibusdemexico.com.mx*).

Medical Assistance **Consultorio Medico** (✉ *Victoria 416, Col. Centro* ☎ *614/415–5994*).**Hospital Central del Estado** (✉ *Calle 33 and Rosales, Col. Obrera* ☎ *614/415–9000*). **Red Cross** (☎ *668/815–0808 in Los Mochis, 614/411–1619 in Chihuahua*).

Rental Cars **Hertz** (✉ *Avenida Revolución 514, Col. Centro* ☎ *614/416–9925*).

Visitor & Tour Info **Chihuahua Tourism Office** (✉ *Palacio de Gobierno, Plaza Hidalgo, Calle Juan Aldama at*

TOURS BY TROLLEY

Sponsored by the state tourism office, the **Trolley Turístico El Tarahumara** (*Palacio de Gobierno, Plaza Hidalgo, Centro, Chihuahua* ☎ *614/429–3596*) stops at every tourist sight in the city. The trolley departs every hour from 9 to 1 and 3 to 7 daily except Monday. The $3 fare allows you to ride four times in the same day.

Venustiano Carranza, Col. Centro ☎01800/508–0111 toll-free in Mexico 🌐www.ah-chihuahua.com)

EXPLORING

MAIN ATTRACTIONS

The regal **Casa Chihuahua** once held the main post office (and before that the telegraph office). All that has changed with a well-funded surge of civic pride that transformed it into this museum. The real treat is the *calabozo,* or dungeon, amazingly preserved despite the fact that the building has been rebuilt three times in the two past centuries. Revolutionary hero Padre Hidalgo was imprisoned by the Spanish prior to his execution. His pistols, trunk, crucifix, and reproductions of his letters are on display. ✉*Av. Juárez between Calles Neri Santos and Carranza, Centro* ☎*614/429–3300* 🎫*40¢* 🕒*Wed.–Mon. 10–5*

Fodor'sChoice ★ Whatever you do, don't miss the **Museo de la Revolución Mexicana,** better known as La Casa de Pancho Villa. Villa lived in this 1909 mansion, also called the Quinta Luz (*quinta* means "manor," or "country house"), with his wife Luz Corral. Although Villa married dozens of women, Corral was considered his only legitimate wife, as the couple was married in both civil and church ceremonies. She lived in this house until her death on June 6, 1986. The 50 small rooms that used to house Villa's bodyguards now hold a vast array of artifacts of Chihuahua's cultural and revolutionary history. Parked in the museum's courtyard is the bullet-ridden 1919 Dodge in which Villa was assassinated in 1923 at the age of 45. Don't be shocked by all the uniformed soldiers, as the museum is run by the Mexican Army. ✉*Calle Décima 3010, near Calle Terrazas, Col. Santa Rosa* ☎*614/416–2958* 🎫*$1* 🕒*Tues.–Sat. 9–1 and 3–7, Sun. and holidays 10–4.*

The **Palacio de Gobierno** was built by the Jesuits as a monastery in 1882. Converted into state government offices in 1891, it was destroyed by a fire and rebuilt in 1947. Murals around the courtyard depict famous episodes from the history of Chihuahua, and a plaque commemorates the spot where Father Hidalgo was executed on the morning of July 30, 1811. In addition, there are a pair of museums. The **Museo de Hidalgo** pays tribute to its namesake and his famous "grito de dolores," the rallying cry for Mexico's War of Independence. The **Galería de Armas** presents an impressive array of weapons from the colonial and independence eras. ✉*Plaza Hidalgo, Centro* ☎*614/429–3596* 🎫*Free* 🕒*Weekdays 9–7, weekends 10–5.*

IF YOU HAVE TIME

Consecrated in 1721, the **Iglesia de San Francisco** is the oldest church in Chihuahua. Father Hidalgo's decapitated body was interred in the chapel until 1827, when it was sent to Mexico City. (His head was publicly displayed for 10 years by Spanish Royalists in Guanajuato on the Alhóndiga de Granaditas.) Although the church's facade is relatively sober, its baroque altarpieces, decorated with 18th-century paintings, are worth studying. ✉*Av. Libertad at Calle 15, Centro* ☎*No phone* 🎫*Free* 🕒*Daily 7–2 and 5–7.*

CLOSE UP

Copper Canyon Train Ride

The Ferrocarril Chihuahua al Pacífico passes through 87 tunnels and crosses 39 bridges on its journey through the canyon. The diverse landscapes include farmland, coastal plains, and the Sierra Madre.

From either direction, first-class trains depart dependably at 6 AM, or you can bypass Los Mochis and depart 1½ hours later from El Fuerte. A ticket costs $156 each way; arrange stopovers when you buy tickets. The first-class train has a restaurant and bar. Reserve ahead a week or more in July, August, and October, and a month or more around Christmas and Easter.

If you're departing on the first-class train from the western terminus of Los Mochis, you can expect to be in El Fuerte at 8 AM, Bahuichivo at 12:30 PM, Posada Barrancas at 1:30 PM, Divisadero at 2 PM, Creel at 3:30 PM, and Chihuahua finally at 9 PM that evening. From Chihuahua, you arrive in Creel at 11:30 AM, Divisadero at 12:45 PM, Posada Barrancas at 1:15 PM, Bahuichivo at 2:30 PM, El Fuerte at 6:15 PM, and Los Mochis at 8 PM that evening.

The departure times for second-class trains are less certain, but they usually pull out of the station about an hour after the first-class trains. They make more stops along the way, arriving at their final destination about three hours after the first-class train. They're rarely crowded and quite comfortable; the cars were used on the first-class route until a few years ago. A snack car sells bad microwave burritos, sandwiches, and soft drinks. No reservations are needed; tickets are half the price of those on the first-class train.

TIP→ Delays of three hours or so aren't unusual, as cargo trains, which share the rails, break down frequently; don't count on reaching the route's scenic end before dark.

TRAIN OPERATORS

The **Ferrocarril Chihuahua al Pacífico** (☎ *01800/367–3900 toll-free in Mexico, 888/484–1623* 🌐 *www.ferromex.com.mx*) runs a first-class and a second-class train daily each way between Chihuahua and Los Mochis.

The Tucson-based **Sierra Madre Express** (☎ *520/747–0346 or 800/666–0346* 🌐 *www.sierramadre-express.com*) runs deluxe trains (with vintage Pullman cars) on eight-day, seven-night excursions about six times a year. Its trips, which combine the charm of sleeping on the train with first-class service, start at $2,895 per person.

TIP→ The most dramatic scenery is between El Fuerte and Creel. As the train ascends almost 6,000 feet from El Fuerte to Bahuichivo, the scenery shifts from cacti to the waterfalls and tropical foliage of the Río Septentrión canyon. Past Témoris, the setting shifts to the oak and pine forest of higher elevations.

The **Nombre de Dios Caverns** are 20 minutes from the city center. An illuminated, 1.6-km (1-mi) path takes you through 17 separate chambers, past rock formations and stalactites and stalagmites, which have been given names such as Christ, the Waterfall, and the Altar. The tour takes about an hour. ✉*H. Colegio Militar s/n, Sector Nombre de Dios* ☎*614/413–0300* *$4* ⏲*Tues.–Sun. 9–4*

GET OUT OF TOWN

Divitur (Rio de Janeiro 310-1, Col. Panamericana, Chihuahua ☎614/414-6046) has kayaking, mountain-biking, and hiking trips. **Turismo Al Mar** (Calle Verna 2202, Col. Mirador, Chihuahua ☎614/416-6589 or 614/416-5950 🌐*www.copper-canyon.net*) offers city tours and canyon sojourns.

Known as the **Parroquia del Sagrado,** the cathedral is also worth a visit. Construction on this stately baroque structure facing the Plaza de Armas was begun by the Jesuits in 1725, but because of local Chichimeca uprisings and the expulsion of the Jesuits it was not completed until 1826. The opulent church has Carrara marble altarpieces, delicate glass chandeliers, and a ceiling studded with 24-karat gold ornaments; the huge German-made pipe organ from the late 18th century is still used on special occasions. In the basement the small but interesting **Museo de Arte Sacro** displays religious art from the 18th century and other artifacts, such as the hand-carved chair used by Pope John Paul II during his visit to Chihuahua in 1990. ✉*Plaza de Armas, Centro* ☎*No phone* *Museum $2* ⏲*Weekdays 10–2 and 4–6.*

Slightly outside the center of town is the cultural center of the Universidad de Chihuahua, known as **Quinta Gameros.** This hybrid French Second Empire–art nouveau palace, with stained-glass windows, ornate staircases, rococo plaster wall panels, and lavish ironwork, was begun in 1907 by Colombian architect Julio Corredor Latorre, for Manuel Gameros, a wealthy mining engineer. The palace is on a fetching, tree-lined boulevard of converted pre-revolutionary mansions. ✉*Calle Bolívar 401, at Calle de la Llave, Centro* ☎*614/416–6684* *$2* ⏲*Tues.–Sun. 11–2 and 4–7.*

A restoration project has made the site of the town's original settlement, **Santa Eulalia,** particularly appealing. The 30-minute drive southeast of town, about $40 one way by taxi, is repaid by the colonial architecture and cobblestone streets of this village, which was founded in 1707 when huge silver deposits were found. The religious artwork in the 18th-century cathedral is noteworthy. Rock hounds will be interested in shopping for specimens of minerals, primarily quartz and calcite, taken from the town's mines. Daily buses bound for the settlement leaves every 15 minutes from 6 AM to 9 PM from the corner of Calle Niños Heroes and Calle Quinta. The fare is 50 cents.

OFF THE BEATEN PATH

Casas Grandes. Some 300 km (186 mi) northwest of Chihuahua, the twin towns of Nuevo Casas Grandes and Casas Grandes are the gateways to the ancient area known as Paquimé, declared a UNESCO World Heritage site in 1998.

Near the aspen-lined Casas Grandes River, Paquimé was inhabited by peoples of the Oasis America culture between AD 700 and 1500. The city was poised between the Pueblo cultures of today's Southwestern United States (to whom they were related) to the north and their Mesoamerican neighbors to the south. Paquimé was a commercial center whose residents manufactured jewelry and raised fowl and macaws from the tropics. Evidence of their engineering and architectural savvy still stands in the form of heat-shielding walls and intricate indoor plumbing systems. The high-tech on-site museum shows Paquimé artifacts and ceramics and has bilingual displays.

Omnibus de México makes the five-hour trip from Chihuahua to Nuevas Casas Grandes (about $20). To get to the ruins, it's easiest to hail a taxi from the bus station in Nuevas Casas Grandes. Once there, head for the *zócalo* (main square). Paquimé is a 10-minute walk from town—follow the PAQUIMÉ sign on Avenida Constitución. ☎ *636/692–4140* *Museum $4* ⏲ *Tues.–Sun. 10–5.*

If you want a quick bite, **Restaurante Constantino** (✉ *Minerva 112, Nuevo Casas Grandes* ☎ *636/694–1005*) makes great enchiladas. Family-style **Hotel Piñon** (✉ *Av. Juárez 605, Nuevo Casas Grandes* ☎ *636/694–0655*) has a swimming pool, restaurant, bar, and a private collection of ancient *ollas* (clay pots) from Paquimé. **Hotel Hacienda** (✉ *Av. Juárez 2603 Norte, Nuevo Casas Grandes* ☎ *636/694–1046*), with a restaurant, bar, and swimming pool, is one of the best places to stay in town. Make reservations in advance.

WHERE TO EAT

$–$$ STEAK ✕ **La Calesa.** With wood paneling and crimson tablecloths and curtains, La Calesa looks every bit the classic steak house. The filet mignon and rib-eye steaks are particularly good; try the former grilled with mushrooms. ✉ *Av. Juárez 3300, Centro* ☎ *614/416–0222* 💳 *AE, MC, V.*

$ ★ MEXICAN ✕ **Casa de los Milagros.** According to legend, the owner of this house fell in love with one of Pancho Villa's "girls." His wife's prayers to Saint Anthony were answered when her husband returned, so the villa was dubbed the "House of Miracles." Today it's *the* place for drinks, with a high-ceilinged room painted in electrifying colors. ✉ *Victoria 812, near Ocampo, Centro* ☎ *614/437–0693* 💳 *MC, V* ⏲ *No lunch.*

$ MEXICAN ✕ **Del Paseo Café.** Two doors down from Quinta Gameros, this casual restaurant is known for its good service. Original art decorates walls painted Santa Fe pinks, peaches, and ochers, and roving musicians sing romantic ballads Wednesday to Sunday after 9 PM. The specialty is *arrachera a la borracha,* tenderized beef marinated in beer and grilled with mushrooms and onions. It's open Sunday to Wednesday 8AM to midnight and Thursday, Friday and Saturday until 2 AM. ✉ *Bolivár 411, Centro* ☎ *614/410–3200* 💳 *MC, V.*

¢–$ MEXICAN ✕ **Café Mandala.** If you need to know your future, or just want to relax and smell the incense, head for this informal New Age eatery high above Chihuahua. (Call ahead to make appointments for card, palm, or coffee-ground readings.) The tables on the outdoor terrace fill up quickly during the summer, with the city lights providing a romantic backdrop. On chilly evenings, move indoors to enjoy the view through the floor-to-ceiling windows. The food—tacos, tostadas, and other standard fare—has a healthful and sometimes vegetarian slant. Try the nontraditional tacos stuffed with grilled green peppers, tomatoes, mushrooms, and cheese. ⊠*Calle Urquidi 905Col. Centro* ☎*614/416–0266* *Reservations not accepted* ▭*No credit cards* ⊗*No lunch.*

WHERE TO STAY

$$–$$$$ **Palacio del Sol.** The high-rise hotel looks faded from the outside, but the rooms and common areas are redecorated on a regular basis. While lacking the luster of some higher-priced hotels, the Palacio del Sol is pleasant and understated. It's within walking distance of most of the downtown sights. The view from the upper floors is amazing. **Pros:** Friendly staff, congenial atmosphere, good mix of guests. **Cons:** Building is charmless, surrounding blocks are desolate at night. ⊠*Independencia 116, Centro,* ☎*614/412–3456* ⊕*www.hotelpalaciodelsol.com* *183 rooms, 25 suites* *In-room: Dial-up. In-hotel: 2 restaurants, bar, gym, laundry service, parking (no fee), public Wi-Fi* ▭*AE, MC, V.*

$$–$$$ **Posada Tierra Blanca.** Across the street from the Palacio del Sol, this modern motel charges considerably less. Rooms surrounding the gated swimming pool have firm mattresses and pseudo-antiques. **Even if you don't stay here, duck inside to see the impressive mural by Chihuahuan painter Aarón Piña Mora.** **Pros:** A swimming pool in an appealing courtyard, nice artwork. **Cons:** Neighborhood is empty after dark, bland atmosphere. ⊠*Niños Héroes 102, Centro,* ☎*614/415–0000* *73 rooms, 2 suites* ⊕*www.posadatierrablanca.com.mx* *In-hotel: Restaurant, room service, bar, pool, parking (no fee), public Wi-Fi, no elevator* ▭*AE, MC, V.*

$$–$$$ ★ **Quality Inn San Francisco.** A favorite of Mexican business travelers, this modern five-story hotel has a prime location behind the Plaza de las Armas. Clean and comfortable rooms have firm mattresses, large televisions, and desks where you can finish that last-minute report. **Pros:** Clean and comfortable, weekend rates are a bargain. **Cons:** No character, neighborhood is intimidating at night. ⊠*Victoria 409, Centro,* ☎*614/416–7550 or 800/847–2546* ⊕*www.qualityinnchihuahua.com* *120 rooms, 20 suites* *In-room: Wi-Fi. In-hotel: Restaurant, bar, gym, parking (no fee) no-smoking rooms* ▭*AE, MC, V.*

10

$$–$$$ **Westin Soberano Chihuahua.** Overlooking the city and surrounding mountains, Chihuahua's most elegant hotel couldn't have a more magnificent view. Designed around an atrium with a cascading waterfall, the sparkling hotel is quite a contrast to the rustic accommodations of the canyons. **Pros:** Rooms are plush yet understated, with richly patterned textiles, televisions hidden in tall chests, and baths with tubs and showers. **Cons:** Far from the downtown attractions, not a lot of charm. ⊠*Barranca del Cobre 3211, Fracc. Barrancas,* ☎*614/429–2929 or 888/625–5144* ⊕*www.starwoodhotels.com* *194 rooms, 10 suites* *In-hotel: 2 restaurants, bars, tennis court, pool, gym, parking (no fee), no-smoking rooms* ▭*AE, MC, V.*

CLOSE UP

Copper Canyon Background

The canyons of the Sierra Tarahumara, as this portion of the Sierra Madre Occidental is known, form part of the Pacific "Ring of Fire," a belt of seismic and volcanic activity ringing the globe. As a result of its massive geologic movement, a large quantity of the earth's buried mineral wealth was shoved toward the surface. The average height of the resulting peaks is 8,000 feet, and some rise to more than 10,000 feet. The canyons were carved over eons by the Urique, Septentrión, Batopilas, and Chínipas rivers and further defined by wind erosion. Totaling more than 1,452 km (900 mi) in length and roughly four times the area of the Grand Canyon, the gorges are nearly a mile deep and wide in places. Four of the major canyons—Cobre, Urique, Sinforosa, and Batopilas—descend deeper than the Grand Canyon.

The unlikely idea of building a railroad line across this forbidding region was first conceived in 1872 by Albert Kinsey Owen, an idealistic American socialist. Owen met with some success initially. More than 1,500 people came from the States to join him in Topolobampo, his utopian colony on the Mexican west coast, and in 1881 he obtained a concession from Mexican president General Manuel Gonzales to build the railroad. Construction on the flat stretches near Los Mochis and Chihuahua presented no difficulties, but eventually the huge mountains of the Sierra Madre got in the way of Owen's dream, along with the twin scourges of typhoid and disillusionment within the community.

Owen abandoned the project in 1893, but it was taken up in 1900 by American railroad magnate and spiritualist Edward Arthur Stilwell. One of Stilwell's contractors in western Chihuahua was Pancho Villa, who ended up tearing up his own work during the Mexican Revolution in order to impede the movement of the government troops chasing him. By 1910, when the revolution began, the Mexican government had taken charge of building the rail line. Progress was painfully slow until 1940, when surveying the difficult Sierra Madre stretch finally began in earnest. Some 90 years and more than $100 million after it was started, the Ferrocarril Chihuahua al Pacífico was dedicated on November 23, 1961. Today the railroad runs between Los Mochis, near the original terminus of Topolobampo, and Chihuahua City.

NIGHTLIFE

This large city is more sedate than one might expect, and its hardworking residents generally wait for the weekends to kick up their heels.

At the neon-bright **Bar La Taberna** (✉*Av. Juárez 3331, Centro* ☎*614/416–8332*) you can play pool, or, on Friday and Saturday nights, dance to a DJ.

La Casa de los Milagros (✉*Victoria 812, Centro* ☎*614/437–0693*), essentially a bar without a bar, starts to groove after 10 PM.

SHOPPING

The streets east of the Plaza de las Armas are chock-full of stores selling Western wear, especially boots in often flamboyant colors. (Neon-blue manta ray skin, anyone?)

In addition to selling gems and geodes found in the area, **Artesanías y Gemas de Chihuahua** (✉*Calle Décima 3015, Col. Santa Rosa* ☎*614/415–2882*) carries exceptional silver jewelry.

Near the jail where Father Hidalgo was held, the **Casa de las Artesanías del Estado de Chihuahua** (✉*Av. Niños Heroes 1101, Centro* ☎*614/437–1292*) carries the city's best selection of Tarahumara and regional crafts, as well as handcrafted wooden furniture and a selection of Mata Ortiz pottery.

The block-long **Mercado de Artesanías** (✉*Calle Victoria 506 [another entrance on Calle Aldama 511], between Calles Quinta and Guerrero, Centro* ☎*614/416–2716*) sells everything from inexpensive jewelry, candy, and T-shirts to mass-produced crafts from all over the region.

For men, **El Norteño** (✉*Calle Victoria 421, Col. Centro* ☎*614/416–8759*) is most likely to carry larger sizes. (Mexican men tend to have smaller feet.) The family that has run the shop for half a century is exceedingly friendly and helpful.

THE MOUNTAIN TOWNS

The towns between Creel and Bahuichivo (the train station for Cerocahui) are in the middle of the Sierra Madre, the reason most people are headed here in the first place. Creel is the largest town and is connected to Chihuahua by a smooth highway that will seem even smoother if you ride it coming out of the canyons. Creel is also the best starting point if you want to take the six-hour trip to Batopilas or if you're intent on seeing high-country attractions such as the Cascada de Basaseachi. Southwest of Creel is Divisadero, the end of the line as far as paved roads are concerned. The view from Divisadero is the most famous in the canyon, and the train stops here for a full 15 minutes to allow passengers time to gaze into the depths of the Barranca de Urique. Beyond lies Posada Barrancas, where three tidy luxury hotels hold their breaths on the precipice.

CREEL

233 km (154 mi) southwest of Chihuahua.

Surrounded by craggy, pine-covered bluffs, Creel is a mining, ranching, and logging town that grew up around the railroad station. The largest settlement in the area, it's also a gathering place for Tarahumara people who come here in search of supplies and to sell their crafts. Creel is in all respects the hub of the Barrancas del Cobre region, with a great tour company, a 24-hour medical clinic, and the only ATM between El Fuerte and Cuauhtemóc.

CLOSE UP

Beyond the Train Ride

Hiking in the Copper Canyon is fantastic if you take the proper precautions. *Mexico's Copper Canyon Country,* by M. John Fayhee, is a good source of information. But even the most experienced trekkers should enlist the help of local guides, who can be contacted through area hotels or through travel agents in Los Mochis, El Fuerte, and Chihuahua. Also, the presence of well-guarded marijuana plantations throughout the canyon makes it safer to travel with a local guide who knows which areas to avoid.

La Barranca de Urique is most easily reached—by horse, bus, truck, or on foot—from Cerocahui. Hotels in Creel, Divisadero, and Posada Barrancas offer tours ranging from easy rim walks to a 27-km (17-mi) descent to the bottom. If you're in Cusárare, a gentle and rewarding hike is the 6-km (4-mi) walk from the Copper Canyon Lodge to 100-foot-high Cusárare Falls. More challenging but also more impressive is a full-day trek to the base of the Cascada de Basaseachi. The descent to Batopilas—not for acrophobes—requires an overnight stay.

Hotels throughout the canyons can arrange for local guides and reasonably gentle horses; however, these trips aren't for couch potatoes. The trails into the canyon are narrow and rocky, also slippery if the weather is icy or wet. At rough spots you might be asked to dismount and walk part of the way. A fairly easy and inexpensive ride is to Wicochic Falls at Cerocahui, about two hours round-trip, including a half-hour hike at the end, where the trail is too narrow for the horses. From Divisadero, horses can be hired to the tiny settlement of Wakajípare, deep within the canyon.

GETTING HERE & AROUND

Creel sits at the crux of the region's highways, making it fairly easy to get around. Bus companies Grupo Estrella Blanca and Noroeste both have terminals immediately across the tracks from the train station.

ESSENTIALS

Currency Exchange **Banco Santander** (✉ *López Mateos, Col. Centro* ☎ *635/456–0060*).**The Banco Santander Serfín is open weekdays 9–4. The ATM sometimes runs out of cash, so use it during bank hours so that you can have a back-up plan. This is the only ATM between Cuauhtémoc and El Fuerte.**

Medical Assistance **Centro de Salud** (✉ *Tarahumara 113, Col. Centro* ☎ *635/456–0905 or 635/456–0132*).

Rental Cars **3 Amigos Tours** (✉ *Av. López Mateos 46, Col. Centro* ☎*635/456–0036* 🌐*www.amigos3.com*)

Visitor & Tour Info **3 Amigos Tours** (✉ *Av. López Mateos 46, Col. Centro* ☎*635/456–0036* 🌐*www.amigos3.com*)

EXPLORING

MAIN ATTRACTIONS

Devoted to the history and philosophy of the Tarahumara people, the **Museo de Paleontologia** (✉ *Av. Ferrocarril 175* ☎*635/456–0080* *$1* ⏲*Mon.–Sat. 9–6, Sun. 9–1*) displays artifacts and replicas of indigenous dwellings, traditional clothing, weapons, and musical instruments. One room is devoted entirely to photos, both historical and recent, of Creel and the Sierra Tarahumara. Descriptions are in English and Spanish. The museum is across from the train station.

Across the tracks from the Museo de Paleontologia, the **Museo de las Tarahumaras** (✉*Av. Ferrocarril 172* ☎*635/456–0080* 💲*$1* ⏲*Mon.–Sat. 9–6, Sun. 9–1*) is actually two museums under one roof. One exhibit focuses on traditional Tarahumara life, including a beautiful exhibit of black-and-white photographs. You'll also find dinosaur bones, Spanish-era artifacts, and mementos from the area's mining days.

IF YOU HAVE TIME

A popular way to spend the day is to hike to the **Balneario Manantial Termal de Recohuata,** or Recohuata Hot Springs. A trip here involves climbing down from the canyon rim into the Barranca de Tararecua. Some tour guides leave their clients at the rim to be guided down to the series of artificial pools by youngsters who station themselves at the trailhead. A little farther down the hill you'll find a series of natural swimming holes.

Worthwhile stops along the way to the colonial town of Batopilas are **Basihuare,** where wide horizontal bands of color cross huge vertical outcroppings of rock, and **La Bufa,** a tiny settlement at the site of a former Spanish silver mine. In the opposite direction, about 73 km (45 mi) northwest of Creel, along an unpaved, winding road, the 806-foot **Cascada de Basaseachi** is among the highest cascades (seasonal waterfalls) in North America.

Don't pass up the easy 6-km (4-mi) hike through a lovely piñon forest to see the **Cascada Cusárare,** a 101-foot waterfall that is most impressive during the rainy months and after the snow melts.

In the middle of the main plaza a collective of tour guides specializes in day trips to areas of interest around Creel. Many half-day tours include a visit to **Cusárare,** whose Tarahumara name means "eagle's nest." Located 26 km (16 mi) from Creel, the village is the site of a Jesuit mission built in 1741, which still serves as a center for religious and community affairs for the Tarahumara people. Inside the simple whitewashed structure men and women stand for the Sunday service, women on one side, men on the other.

One of the most common day tours is a visit to **Lago Arareko,** about 7 km (4 mi) from Creel. The pine-ringed lake merits little more than a quick look. The **Valle de los Hongos** (Valley of the Mushrooms), where rocks perch atop each other precariously, is a scattering of formations among a distressingly poor Tarahumara settlement. In a bit of linguistic imperialism, nearby **Bisabirachi** (Tarahumara for "Valley of the Erect Penises") was renamed by the Spanish as **Valle de los Monjes** (Valley of the Monks). The impressive stone monoliths, set in beautiful rolling countryside, don't care either way.

WHERE TO EAT

¢–$ ★ MEXICAN **Tungar.** "The Hangover Hospital," as it is nicknamed, is a no-nonsense café serving the town's best Mexican food. The shacklike structure may be unnerving, but the food wins over most skeptics. The menu includes traditional morning pick-me-ups—and hangover cures—like *menudo* (tripe soup), *pozole* (hominy soup with chunks of spicy pork), and *ari,* a type of ant excrement that, when mixed with chili, is said to cure many ills. For lunch consider a stingray tostada or a *burro montado* stuffed with cheese, beans, and beef stew. *Calle Francisco Villa s/n, next to train station No phone No credit cards No dinner. No lunch Sun.*

WHERE TO STAY

$$–$$$ **Best Western Lodge at Creel Hotel and Spa.** Door handles fashioned from elk antlers give this hotel, the most luxurious in town, the feel of a hunting lodge. Several wings of rooms resembling log cabins continue the theme. Gas heaters disguised as wood-burning stoves add a bit of atmosphere to the rather plain accommodations. Small pets are allowed. **Pros:** Clean and well-maintained rooms, convenient location. **Cons:** Small and cramped bathrooms, motel-style layout, lacks local feel. *Av. Adolpho López Mateos 61, 635/456–0071 or 888/879–4071 www.thelodgeatcreel.com 38 rooms, 1 suite In-room: No a/c. In-hotel: Restaurant, bar, gym, spa, public Wi-Fi, parking (no fee), no-smoking rooms, no elevator AE, MC, V.*

$$–$$$ **Sierra Bonita.** Perched on a hillside just outside Creel, this self-contained lodging has a restaurant, bar, and even a disco (open on weekends). Rooms and suites have less of a rustic look than most in the canyon area. Vans—reserve one when you check in—make the five-minute jaunt to Creel. **Pros:** Good breakfasts, excellent views, sprawling grounds. **Cons:** Isolated location, need a car to get around. *Carretera Gran Visión s/n, 635/456–0615 www.sierrabonita.com.mx 8 rooms, 10 cabins, 2 suites In-room: No a/c. In-hotel: Restaurant, room service, bar, parking (no fee), no elevator MC, V BP.*

$$ Fodor's Choice ★ **Copper Canyon Sierra Lodge.** On the edge of a peaceful piñon forest near the Cascada Cusárare, this lodge made of pine and stucco is a natural beauty. Rooms are romantically equipped with kerosene lamps and woodstoves or fireplaces. The vegetarian meals are served in a beautiful dining room. This spot is best for those with wheels or who want a night or two of semi-isolation; it's 26 km (16 mi) from Creel. **Pros:** Excellent restaurant, lovely setting. **Cons:** No electricity, cavelike rooms. *Cusárare Nichols Expeditions, 497 N. Main St. Moab, UT 84532 435/259–3999 or 800/648–8488 www.coppercanyonlodges.com 19 rooms In-room: No a/c, no phone, no TV. In-hotel: Restaurant, bar, parking (no fee), no elevator MC, V FAP.*

¢ ★ **Margarita's.** A van awaits backpackers from the second-class train, and then drives them across the street to this international gathering place. The private rooms—with wrought-iron lamps and light-wood furnishings—compare favorably to anything at three times the price. **Pros:** Excellent breakfast and dinner is included, friendly international clientele. **Cons:** Dorm rooms are a little cramped, and fixtures

CLOSE UP

The Tarahumara: People of the Land

Mexico's largest state was once heavily populated by the Tarahumara, close relatives of the Pima Indians of southern Arizona. They are renowned for their running ability and endurance—Tarahumara is a Spanish corruption of their word Rarámuri, which means "running people." Today winners of international marathon races, the Tarahumara in earlier times hunted deer by chasing them to the point of collapse. During festivals they still engage in a game called *rarajípame* in which Tarahumara men run while kicking a hand-carved wooden ball for up to 40 hours.

Like those of other native peoples, the Tarahumara's way of life was totally disrupted by the arrival of the Europeans. The Spanish forced them to labor in the mines, and later both Mexicans and Americans put them to work on the railroads. The threat of slavery and the series of wars that began in the 1600s and continued until the 20th century forced them to retreat deeper into the canyons, where they are still at the mercy of outsiders: nowadays it's loggers and drug lords. Their population has also diminished over the years because of disease, drought, and poverty.

Despite all this, the Tarahumara are also considered to have the most traditional lifestyles of any North American indigenous peoples. They live a life well adjusted to the canyon country—the majority live on small ranches, many of which are seemingly perched on ledges high up on the canyon walls. Housing may be small adobe or log shacks or even caves for at least part of the year. Many Tarahumara still practice transhumance, a form of migration where they live in the relative warmth of the canyon bottoms during the winter and move to cooler altitudes in summer. Primarily subsistence farmers, their diets rely on the corn, beans, and squash that they grow, supplemented with wild game, fish, and seasonal herbs they collect.

In cities you may encounter Tarahumara men wearing more modern clothing, but most of the women—and many of the men—still wear traditional attire. For men this consists of sandals, a white breechcloth, a flowing top cinched with a woven belt, and their ubiquitous headband. Attire for women is sandals, a long skirt, long-sleeved blouse, and a headband, all made of brightly colored printed fabric. The women are mostly encountered selling the crafts they create, which include baskets of pine needles and torote grass, woven belts, and beaded bracelets. Men are known for carving wooden figures and even more for the violins that they make from native woods—an art form they learned from the Spaniards.

Everyone who comes into close contact with Tarahumara culture comes away with a profound respect for these gentle people. That is not to say that all Tarahumara want to interact with you. When approaching their abodes, it is polite to stand at the outer edges of the property and wait quietly. If anyone wishes to greet you, they will eventually come out. If not, then you should move on. This same reserve is appropriate when encountering them in town. You should also take care not to photograph any Tarahumara without their express permission.

are often broken or inappropriately placed. ✉ *Av. López Mateos 11,* ☎ *635/456–0045* *21 rooms, 1 dorm room* *In-room: No a/c, no phone, no TV. In-hotel: Restaurant, bicycles, no elevator* *No credit cards* *MAP.*

¢ **Margarita's Plaza Mexicana.** This two-story hotel set around a courtyard is one of the town's best bargains. Each room has a television, a heater, and a different wall mural. The tequila-and-mariachi parties hosted for tour groups who stay here can get quite noisy, but usually don't run too late. **Pros:** Friendly staff, and Margarita's properties are a magnet for interesting international travelers. **Cons:** The maintenance here is a bit subpar, and for a full-on hotel it's surprising that it still lacks a/c, phone, and the ability to take credit cards. ✉ *Calle Elfido Bautista s/n, off Av. López Mateos,* ☎ *635/456–0245* *26 rooms* *In-room: No a/c, no phone. In-hotel: Restaurant, bar, no elevator* *No credit cards* *MAP.*

NIGHTLIFE

Tia Molca´s (✉ *Avenida López Mateos 35, Col. Centro* ☎ *635/456–0033*) is a small, friendly hole-in-the-wall with a big fireplace. It's popular with expats and travelers.

SHOPPING

Avenida López Mateos, Creel´s main drag, has undergone a considerable transformation, thanks to the influx of trekkers and tourists from the train. There are too many shops selling Tarahumara crafts to count and individual women and children continually approach you with necklaces and baskets on the street.

One of the more established shops is **Artesanías Victoria** (☎ *635/456–0030*), at the far end of town from the train station. The shop sells huge Tarahumara pots and other local handicrafts.

Be sure to pay a visit to **Misión Tarahumara** (☎ *635/456–0097*), on the east side of the plaza. The shop sells only Tarahumara handiwork, including musical instruments, woven belts, and simple pots. Here you'll also find English-language books on the Tarahumara culture. Proceeds benefit the local Jesuit mission hospital.

BATOPILAS

80 km (50 mi) southeast of Creel.

Veins of silver—mined on and off since the time of the conquistadors—made this remote village of fewer than 800 people one of the wealthiest towns in colonial Mexico. At one time it was the only community besides Mexico City that had electricity. Today this town with a population of a few hundred has two postage-stamp plazas, bridges made of rope and river stones, and an aqueduct built in the 19th century by the mayor of Washington, D.C. Most of the entertainment comes from the canciòneros who perform for diners in the town's only restaurant and then sing their hearts out by the river. If this isn't actually the town that inspired Gabriel García Márquez's novel One Hundred Years of Solitude, as some locals claim, it might as well be.

GETTING HERE & AROUND

There are just two ways to get to Batopilas: three days hiking overland from Urique, or four hours by torturous and sometimes frightening back-road switchbacks off Highway 35. 3 Amigos Tours in Creel offers trucks and a guided itinerary for the journey, but this is a route only for fearless drivers. A bus goes comes and goes from Creel daily, taking about six hours.

EXPLORING

The triple-dome 17th-century **Templo de San Miguel Arcangel** is mysteriously isolated in the Satevó Valley, a scenic 16-km (10-mi) round-trip hike from town. Although the mission church still serves the surrounding communities, it is usually locked. Obtain the key from the residents of a cluster of houses located directly behind the church. Ask the townspeople to point you in the right direction.

WHERE TO EAT & STAY

$–$$ ★ MEXICAN **Puente Colgante/Swinging Bridge.** Outdoor dining in the small courtyard over the river is the high point here, and the dinners are pricier than lunch but very good and authentic. The house guitar-and-bass trio is fronted by a terrific singer who could be the Mexican Joe Strummer. ⊠*Negromante and Pablo Ochoa* ☎*649/456–9023* ▭*No credit cards*

$ ★ MEXICAN **Restaurante Carolina.** Snuggled up against tiny Plaza Constitution, this old-fashioned dining room boasts tile floors, thick walls, and glass-panel doors that separate diners from the large kitchen and formal dining room reserved for special occasions. The machaca breakfast is some of the best and heartiest food in the canyons. ⊠*Plaza de la Constitution 10* ☎*649/456–9096* ▭*No credit cards* ⊙*No dinner.*

¢ **Real de Minas.** Owner Martín Alcaraz worked for years as a hotel manager before opening his own small place. It's a charming spot; each room has decent beds and rustic furnishings but no TV or telephone. This is as it should be—guests come here to experience the ambience of this unique place with few distractions. **Pros:** Convenient location, near many restaurants, flower-filled courtyard. **Cons:** The staff consists of the owner's mother. ⊠*Donato Guerra at Pablo Ochoa* ☎*649/456–9045* *8 rooms* *In-room: No a/c, no phone, no TV. In-hotel: No elevator* ▭*No credit cards.*

10

DIVISADERO & POSADA BARRANCAS

60 km (37 mi) southwest of Creel.

At these whistle-stops five minutes apart on the Continental Divide, the views of the Copper Canyon are unforgettable. Three romantic hotels hug the rim of the canyon in Posada Barrancas; in Divisadero, 20 or so cooks working over oil-barrel stoves wait for the train to disgorge hungry travelers.

TIP→If you're staying in Posada Barrancas for one night, your hotel will arrange tours to the Tarahumara Caves that finish in time for you to catch the train. On longer stays you can book hiking or horseback-riding tours of the Copper Canyon.

GETTING HERE & AROUND

Divisadero and Posada Barrancas are connected by a decent road, but it deteriorates as it continues beyond Posada Barrancas to the village of Areponapuchi, a favorite destination for hikers.

WHERE TO STAY

$$$–$$$$ ★ **Mansión Tarahumara.** It may be disconcerting at first to discover a red-turreted castle here in canyon country, but somehow this hotel does not seem out of place. The guest rooms have contemporary pine furnishings, stone walls, and exposed-beam ceilings. **Pros:** Relaxing steam room, palatial common areas, authentic atmosphere. **Cons:** Quite a few stairs to climb, most of the rooms face away from the best views. ✉ *Posada Barrancas* *Reservations: Av. Juárez 1602-A, Col. Centro, Chihuahua City, Chihuahua 31000* ☎ *614/415–4721* 🌐 *www.mansiontarahumara.com.mx* *57 rooms, 1 suite* *In-room: No a/c, no TV (some). In-hotel: Restaurant, bar, pool, no elevator* *MC, V* *FAP.*

$$$–$$$$ ★ **Posada Barrancas Mirador.** On the edge of the canyon, this hotel has an enviable location. It has spectacular views from every room, especially those on the third floor. Although on the small side for a luxury hotel, the rooms are bright and comfortable, with lovely tile floors, old-fashioned chimneys, and small terraces with tables and chairs. The hotel is part of the Balderrama chain, so you can make reservations through Hotel Santa Anita in Los Mochis. **Pros:** Great views, friendly staff, just steps from the train. **Cons:** Smallish rooms, pushy souvenir vendors at the door. ✉ *Posada Barrancas* *Reservations: Hotel Santa Anita, Apdo. 159, Los Mochis 81200* ☎ *668/818–7046 or 800/896–8196* 🌐 *www.mexicoscoppercanyon.com* *51 rooms, 14 suites* *In-room: No a/c, no phone, no TV. In-hotel: Restaurant, bar, no elevator* *AE, MC, V* *FAP.*

$$$ **Posada Barrancas.** The first hotel to be built in the area, Posada Barrancas is a good base from which to explore the canyons. Rooms have stucco walls, tile floors, and colonial-style furniture painted with whimsical designs; some have cozy fireplaces. The lobby has a massive stone mantel, beamed ceiling, and wood furniture. From a rocking chair on one of the long porches you can watch colorful birds in the gardens. Meals are served at the nearby Hotel Posada Barrancas Mirador. Make reservations through Hotel Santa Anita in Los Mochis. **Pros:** Good location, lots of charm. **Cons:** Stairs to climb, bare-bones in-room amenities. ✉ *Posada Barrancas* *Reservations: Hotel Santa Anita, Apdo. 159, 81200Los Mochis* ☎ *668/818–7046 or 800/896–8196* 🌐 *www.mexicoscoppercanyon.com* *24 rooms* *In-room: No a/c, no TV (some). In-hotel: No elevator* *AE, MC, V* *BP, FAP.*

CEROCAHUI

80 km (50 mi) southwest of Divisadero.

Just across the border in the state of Chihuahua, Cerocahui is a quiet mountain village set amid towering pines. It's a 40-minute drive along a bumpy, mostly unpaved road from the train station at Bahuichivo. (Your hotel will send someone to pick you up.) **TIP→ Cerocahui is a**

favorite stop for birders—more than 200 species of birds have been spotted in this part of the Sierras.

GETTING HERE & AROUND

From the station at Bahuichivo, the village of Cerocahui is a 40-minute drive along a bumpy, mostly unpaved road. If you have reservations, a van from your hotel will pick you up. If not, drivers meet each train.

ESSENTIALS

Medical Assistance **Centro de Salud** (*✉Cerocahui ☎635/456-5297*).

Visitor & Tour Info **Albert Lopez Ceniceros** (*☎635/456-5275*).

EXPLORING

It's a lovely ride to **Cerro del Gallego,** with one of the region's most magnificent views. From there you can make out the slim thread of the Río Urique and the old mining town of Urique, a dot on the distant canyon bottom.

In Cerocahui you'll find the **Misión San Francisco Javier,** a graceful little temple established in 1680 by the Jesuits. Although the order arrived in the area in 1680, Tarahumara Indian uprisings and other difficulties delayed construction of the church until 1741. It is said that this was the favorite church of the founder, Padre Juan María de Salvatierra, because the Tarahumara were the most difficult people to convert. Nearby is a boarding school for Tarahumara children.

Paraiso del Oso (*Box 31089, El Paso, TX 79931 ☎800/884–3107 www.mexicohorse.com*) leads horseback tours into the Barranca de Urique. The company, run for more than a decade by Doug Rhodes, also offers day rentals of mountain bikes and ATVs.

At the bottom of the continent's deepest canyon—dropping 6,163 feet—**Urique** enjoys a semitropical climate. Orange, guava, sycamore, and fig trees dot the landscape. The Río Urique, which carved the great canyon, slides lazily along in the dry season but races briskly after the summer rains. Browse in the old general store, El Central, then have lunch at the town's best restaurant, La Plaza, on the main square.

The Tarahumara people eschew life in town, preferring to live in family enclaves scattered throughout the valley or in small communities such as Guadalupe, 7 km (4½ mi) from Urique. The most direct path to this town is across a 400-foot-long suspension bridge that rocks and sways above the river. It's not for the faint of heart.

You can visit Urique as a day trip from Cerocahui, two to three hours each way by car, or ride horses or hike down into the canyon. Tours are offered through Paraíso del Oso Lodge and Hotel Misión in Cerocahui. The best lodgings in Urique are at Hotel Estrella del Río ($36 double), which has large rooms, hot water, and great river views.

WHERE TO STAY

$$$–$$$$ **Misión.** A cross between a ski lodge and a hacienda, the atmospheric main building of this hotel contains the reception area, a small shop, and a combined dining room and bar warmed by two fireplaces. Wide

verandas draw guests outside to sit in leather rocking chairs and sip a glass of house-made wine. The hotel is part of the Balderrama chain, so you can make reservations through Hotel Santa Anita in Los Mochis. **Pros:** Colonial-style rooms, wood-burning stoves, lovely verandas. **Cons:** Staff can be uppity, neighborhood isn't so hot. ✉ *Cerocahui* 📫 *Reservations: Hotel Santa Anita, Apdo. 159, Los Mochis 81200* ☎ *668/818–7046 ot 800/896–8196* 🌐 *www.mexicoscoppercanyon.com* ⇨ *41 rooms* 👍 *In-room: No a/c, no phone, no TV. In-hotel: Public Wi-Fi, restaurant, bars, pool, no elevator* 💳 *AE, MC, V* 🍴 *FAP.*

$$$–$$$$ **Paraíso del Oso Lodge.** This down-to-earth lodge is perfectly situated for bird-watching, walking in the woods, or horseback riding into the canyons. Ranch-style rooms with rough-hewn furniture and wood-burning stoves face a grassy courtyard. A fireplace in the bar and kerosene lamps in the restaurant give the common areas a glow. Room price includes three meals, plus transfer to and from the train. Doug Rhodes, a loquacious U.S. transplant, leads tours. **Pros:** Amazing setting, lots of charm. **Cons:** A little pricey, on a main road. ✉ *5 km (3 mi) outside of Cerocahui* 📫 *Reservations: Box 31089, El Paso, TX 79931* ☎ *644/421–3372 or 800/884–3107* 🌐 *www.mexicohorse.com* ⇨ *21 rooms* 👍 *In-room: No a/c, no phone, no TV. In-hotel: Restaurant, bar, public Wi-Fi, no elevator* 💳 *No credit cards* 🍴 *FAP.*

$$ **Cabañas San Isidro Lodge.** Among the pine-covered hills outside Cerocahui, this cluster of ranch-style cabins feels like it's at the end of the earth. The rustic, wood-paneled rooms are surprisingly comfortable. The family running the place serves tasty meals in their homey kitchen. **Pros:** A romantic hideaway, transportation to and from train, more stars than you have ever seen. **Cons:** Half-hour drive from anywhere else, the only heat is from wood stoves. ✉ *Rancho San Isidro, outside of Cerocahui* ☎ *635/456–5257* 🌐 *www.coppercanyonamigos.com* ⇨ *12 cabins* 👍 *In-room: No a/c, no phone, no TV* 💳 *No credit cards* 🍴 *FAP.*

EL FUERTE

160 km (100 mi) southwest of Cerocahui.

Smart travelers come to El Fuerte, a rather sleepy town of some 45,000 residents, to board the Ferrocarril Chihuahua al Pacífico. But tour operators also use El Fuerte as a base for hiking, birding, or fishing excursions. Some area hotels get in on the action by organizing float trips on the river near town. You'll see herons and egrets, as well as magpies, kingfishers, and many other birds as you drift downstream past willow trees, cacti, and lilac bushes. One popular tour is to Cerro de la Mascara, an interesting archaeological site where hundreds of rock paintings and petroglyphs have been preserved.

Conquistador Don Francisco de Ibarra and a small group of soldiers founded this small town as San Juan Bautista de Carapoa in 1564. It became known as El Fuerte for its 17th-century fort, built by the Spaniards to protect against attacks by the local Mayo, Sinaloa, Zuaque, and Tehueco Indians.

GETTING HERE & AROUND

If you're taking the train bound for Chihuahua, we recommend you depart from El Fuerte. Highway 24 takes you to El Fuerte from Los Mochis. To travel by bus from Los Mochis to El Fuerte, take Alianza de Transportes del Valle del Fuerte. These buses, which depart from in front of the Mercado Independencia, make the trip in 1½ hours. Instead of a terminal, buses pull up to the corner of Avenida Juarez and 16 de Deciembre.

ESSENTIALS

Bus Contacts **Alianza de Transportes del Valle del Fuerte** (*⊠Avs. Independencia and DegolladoCol. Centro ☎No phone*).

Currency Exchange **Banamex** (*⊠212 Juarez, Col. Centro ☎698/893–0151*).

Internet **Cybermail** (*⊠Rodolfo Romero 108, Col. Centro ☎698/893–1558*).

Medical Assistance **Farmacia Cosmos** (*⊠Zaragosa s/n, Col. Centro ☎698/893–1486*).

Rental Cars **3 Amigos Tours** (*⊠Plaza Principal, Col. Centro ☎698/893–5028*).

Visitor & Tour Info **3 Amigos Tours** (*⊠Plaza Principal, Col. Centro ☎698/893–5028*).

EXPLORING

Situated on El Camino Real (literally, the "Royal Road"), El Fuerte was one of the frontier outposts from which the Spanish set out to explore and settle what are today New Mexico, Arizona, and California. For three centuries it was a major trading post for gold and silver miners from the nearby mountains. It was chosen as Sinaloa's capital in 1824, and remained so for several years. Some lovely colonial mansions face the cobblestone streets leading from the central plaza. The plaza itself is extremely appealing, and comes alive at night with food vendors, courting couples, and children playing games.

A replica of the original fort has been built on the Cerro de Las Pilas, not far from the main plaza. It houses the **Museo de El Fuerte** (*☎698/893–1501 50¢ Daily 9–7*), where several rooms have displays on the history of the fort and the regional flora and fauna, and works from local artists, past and present. **TIP→The ramparts of the fort are a great vantage point over the river valley. At dusk you can catch a glimpse of hundreds of bats leaving their homes deep inside the walls of the fort.**

10

WHERE TO EAT & STAY

$–$$ MEXICAN **✕El Mesón del General.** Just a block off the main plaza, the General's Table is the best place to try the *lobina* (black bass) caught in local reservoirs or the *cauque* (crayfish) that thrive in nearby rivers. Beside a plant-filled courtyard, the blue-and-yellow dining room is decorated with pictures and documents from the town's past. If someone in your party is craving Chinese food, there's a restaurant in the back run by the same management. *⊠Juárez 202 ☎698/893–0260 or 698/893–0941 ▭MC, V.*

$$–$$$ Fodor'sChoice ★ **Torres Del Fuerte.** This meticulously appointed hacienda has the style and service of a four-star hotel, minus the stuffy atmosphere. The owner, whose father was born in the house, has an eclectic assortment of furnishings from all over the world. The sometimes eccentrically decorated theme rooms are all unique, and often quite romantic (lovers should ask for the Moroccan Room). The courtyard, with hummingbirds flitting around the fruit trees, is a real charmer. **Pros:** Fabulous decor, romantic rooms. **Cons:** Hard to locate, small rooms, ongoing construction on the premises. ✉ *Rodolfo G. Robles 102,* ☎ *698/893–1974* 🌐 *www.hotelestorres.com* *25 rooms, 4 suites* *In-room: No phone, no TV. In-hotel: Restaurant, bar, no elevator, public Wi-Fi* *No credit cards.*

$$ ★ **El Fuerte.** When hunting guide Robert Brand married a local woman, he and his bride decided to welcome guests to their 380-year-old mansion. Hand-stenciled furniture and antiques here and there add to its considerable charms. *Artesanía* (folk art) decorates the high-ceiling guest rooms; the beds have beautifully carved and painted headboards but somewhat lumpy mattresses. Clusters of chairs and tables on wide verandas invite socializing. **Pros:** Convenient location, lovely rooms. **Cons:** Chilly staff, lumpy mattresses. ✉ *Montesclaro 37,* ☎ *698/893–0226* 🌐 *www.hotelelfuerte.com.mx* *47 rooms* *In-room: No phone. In-hotel: Restaurant, bar, no elevator* *MC, V.*

$$ **Posada del Hidalgo.** With its lovely courtyards and cobblestone paths, this restored hacienda dating from 1895 recalls a more gracious era. It's difficult to choose between the larger rooms with balconies and the slightly more modern rooms that open onto the flower-filled gardens. No matter which you pick you'll find handcrafted furnishings. You can make reservations through Hotel Santa Anita in Los Mochis. **Pros:** Splendid banquet hall, comfortable rooms. **Cons:** Stuffy staff, stairs to climb. ✉ *Hidalgo 101* *Reservations: Hotel Santa Anita, Apdo. 159, Los Mochis, 81200* ☎ *698/893–0242 or 800/896–8196* 🌐 *www.mexicoscoppercanyon.com* *68 rooms, 1 suite* *In-room: No phone, Wi-Fi. In-hotel: Restaurant, bar, pool, no elevator* *AE, MC, V.*

¢–$ **Río Vista Lodge.** On the Cerro de las Pilas, the highest spot in El Fuerte, you'll find this adobe-and-wood posada. It's certainly rustic—the stone wall of one room is actually part of the hillside. Guest rooms are creatively decorated with antiques. Hummingbirds frequent the feeders around the terrace. **Pros:** Best value in the area, lovely views, family-friendly atmosphere. **Cons:** Tiny pool, hard to find. ✉ *Cerro de las Pilas,* ☎ *698/893–0413* 🌐 *www.hotelriovista.com.mx* *18 rooms* *In-room: No phone, no TV. In-hotel: Restaurant, no elevator.* *No credit cards.*

WESTERN TERMINUS: LOS MOCHIS

Los Mochis is 763 km (473 mi) south of Nogales (on the U.S. border) via Hwy. 15, 80 km (50 mi) southwest of El Fuerte, and 650 km (400 mi) from Chihuahua along the Chihuahua al Pacific railway, the only direct route.

At the western end of the railroad line, Los Mochis (population 331,000) sits near the Gulf of California. It is a friendly, but not terribly attractive, town. Unless they are headed to the nearby beach at Topolobampo, most travelers stay here overnight before boarding the morning train. El Fuerte is much smaller, more historic, and more scenic.

GETTING HERE & AROUND

You can fly here from Los Angeles, Tucson, and other U.S. cities. AeroCalifornia has daily flights from Mexico City, Guadalajara, and Tijuana. The Los Mochis–Topolobambo Airport (LMM) is about 30 minutes west of Los Mochis. The cost of a taxi to the city is about $15. The ferry between La Paz, Baja California and Topolobampo leaves daily, weather permitting. If you're driving, Carretera 15, a four-lane toll road, connects the border town of Nogales, south of Tucson, Arizona, with Los Mochis. The trip is about 763 km (473 mi). The bus terminal is in the center of Los Mochis, a few blocks from most hotels.

ESSENTIALS

Bus Contacts **Terminal Los Mochis** (✉ *Zaragosa Sur 800, Col. Centro* ☎ *668/818-0357*).

Currency Exchange **Banamex** (✉ *Av. Guillermo Prieto at Calle Hidalgo,Col. Centro* ☎ *668/812-0116*).

Medical Assistance **Centro Medico** (✉ *Blvd. Castro 30, Col. Centro* ☎ *668/812-0198*).

Rental Cars **Hertz** (✉ *Calle Leyva Norte 171, Col. Centro* ☎ *668/812-1122*).

Visitor & Tour Info **Flamingo Tours** (✉ *Calle Leyva at Av. Hidalgo, Col. Centro* ☎ *668/812-1613*).**Los Mochis Tourism Office** (✉ *Av. Allende at Calle Ordoñez, Col. Centro* ☎ *668/815-1090, 01800/508-0111 toll-free in Mexico*).

EXPLORING

In what was once a doctor's house, the **Museo Regional del Valle del Fuerte** is home to well-researched permanent exhibits covering the area's history. It also hosts rotating exhibits by local, regional, national, and international artists. Placards are in Spanish only, but you can pick up an English-language synopsis at the front office. Occasional music or poetry events are held on an outdoor patio. ✉ *Blvd. Rosales at Av. Obregón, Col. Centro* ☎ *668/812–4692* *50¢, free Sun. and holidays* ⏲ *Tues.–Sat. 9–1 and 4–7, Sun. 10–1.*

Cottonwood trees and bougainvillea line the highway to **Topolobampo.** A century ago this was a socialist utopia built by the same man who dreamed up the railroad across the canyons. Today, this seaside suburb is where travelers arrive on the ferry from La Paz. The beachfront is staked out by a sprinkling of open-air restaurants and budget motels. In the indigenous Mayo language, the name Topolobampo means "watering place of the sea lions"; Isla El Farallón, off the coast, is a breeding ground for the animals that gave the town its name. Tours of the bay, one of the largest in the Americas, can be arranged either through your hotel or tour operators at the dock. Your guide will almost certainly introduce you to Pechocho, the friendly bottlenose dolphin who lives in the bay. The 45-minute bus ride from Los Mochis costs $2; a taxi will take half the time but cost about $15.

WHERE TO EAT

$–$$ SPANISH ✕ **España.** This downtown restaurant's Spanish specialties pull in the local business crowd. The house specialty is a paella with seafood, pork, and chicken that serves at least two people. The $9 breakfast buffet, served until noon, lines up hearty Mexican favorites such as *chilaquiles* (tortilla strips cooked with cheese, mild chiles, and chicken) alongside the usual suspects, such as omelets and eggs cooked *al gusto* (as you like them). ✉ *Av. Obregón 525 Poniente* ☎ *668/812–2221 or 668/812–2335* 💳 *AE, MC, V.*

$–$$ SEAFOOD ✕ **El Farallón.** The food at this nautically themed restaurant has made it a hit for nearly half a century. The taquitos filled with marlin or shrimp are excellent, and you'll also find nigiri sushi and sashimi—rare in Mexico despite the abundance of seafood. For dessert, sample some *pitalla* (cactus-fruit) ice cream. ✉ *Av. Obregón 499 Poniente, at Calle Angel Flores* ☎ *668/812–1428 or 668/812–1273* 💳 *AE, MC, V.*

$–$$ STEAK ✕ **La Fuente.** This unpretentious colonial-style restaurant specializes in local and imported cuts of beef. The local favorite is *cabrería,* a thinly sliced, extremely tender fillet. Yummy *queso fundido* (cheese fondue) is made with fresh flour tortillas. Corn tortillas are made on the premises throughout the day. ✉ *Blvd. López Mateos 1070 Norte, at Jiquilpan* ☎ *668/812–4770* 💳 *AE, MC, V*

WHERE TO STAY

$$$–$$$$ 🏨 **Plaza Inn.** The town's only five-star hotel attracts a mix of business executives and outdoors enthusiasts, many of them taking advantage of the fishing trips offered by the hotel's tour company. The standard rooms are spacious, but suffer from a disconcerting color palette combining various hues of pink, coral, and sea-foam green. Suites have amenities like kitchenettes. This is another link in the Balderrama chain, so the staff can book you into lodgings in their hotels in the canyons. **Pros:** Helpful staff, convenient location. **Cons:** Unattractive decor, neighborhood is deserted at night. ✉ *Calle Leyva at Cárdenas,* ☎ *668/816–0800, 800/862–9026, 01800/672–6677 toll-free in Mexico* 🌐 *www.hotelplazainn.com.mx* 🛏 *122 rooms, 27 suites* 👍 *In-room: Safe, Wi-Fi. In-hotel: 2 restaurants, bar, pool, gym, parking (no fee)* 💳 *AE, DC, MC, V.*

$$–$$$ 🏨 **Best Western Los Mochis.** This business-style hotel has a central location on the Plaza Central, yet it looks down on a large and ugly parking lot. The rooms are clean and comfortable. The American-style restaurant, for many travelers returning from a canyon adventure, is a welcome reminder of home. **Pros:** Helpful staff, on the main square. **Cons:** Bland atmosphere, neighborhood is sketchy at night. ✉ *1 Plaza Central,* ☎ *668/816–3000* 🛏 *112 rooms, 4 suites* 👍 *In-room: Refrig-*

erator, Wi-Fi. In-hotel: Restaurant, pool, room service, bar, gym, parking (no fee) ▭*AE, MC, V.*

$$ **Santa Anita.** The hub of the ubiquitous Balderrama chain, this hotel can secure train tickets, book tours, and arrange accommodations in its sister hotels in El Fuerte, Cerocahui, and Divisadero. Located in the city's commercial district, the hotel is near shops selling everything from cowboy boots to pirated CDs. The restaurant and bar are gathering places for local business executives. **Pros:** Well-appointed rooms, lively neighborhood. **Cons:** Staff can be uppity, labyrinthine public areas. ✉*Calle Leyva at Hidalgo,* ☎*668/818–7046 or 800/896–8196* 🌐*www.santaanitahotel.com* *114 rooms, 5 suites* *In-room: Wi-Fi. In-hotel: Restaurant, bar, parking (no fee)* ▭*AE, MC, V.*

$–$$ **Corintios.** Behind huge white Corinthian columns that give the place its name, this centrally located hotel is a good budget option. The rooms are plain and a bit worn, but have some amenities not often found in this price range, such as marble bathtubs. Junior suites differ from standard rooms only in that they have king-size beds and minibars. **Pros:** Good budget option, some unexpected amenities. **Cons:** Cheesy decor, steps to climb. ✉*Av. Obregón 580 Poniente,* ☎ *668/818–2300* *35 rooms, 6 suites* *In-hotel: Restaurant, room service, bar, gym, laundry service, parking (no fee), no elevator* ▭*AE, D, MC, V.*

NIGHTLIFE

Los Mochis is full of cantinas where only locals will feel comfortable. There are, however, a few places where travelers can belly up to the bar.

Part of the Plaza Inn, **Tabú Ultraclub** (✉*Calle Leyva at Cárdenas* ☎*668/816–0800*) is the city's most popular disco. On Friday and Saturday nights well-dressed locals take to the dance floor. The music, often live, ranges from techno to rock en español.

Live music is the reason people pack into **Yesterday** (✉*Av. Obregón 579 Poniente at Guerrero* ☎*668/815–3810*). Bands from around the region play different types of music (predominantly classic rock in Spanish and English) Wednesday to Sunday from 9 PM to 2 AM.

SHOPPING

The two-block stretch of Avenida Obregón between Calle Leyva and Calle Prieta has a number of small shops that sell everything. Here you can pick up any last-minute items you may need for your journey into the canyon. If you're headed to Divisadero, Creel, or beyond, snacks and reading material can help you survive the long train journey.

Librería Los Mochis (✉*Av. Madero 402 Poniente, at Calle Leyva*) has maps and a small selection of English-language magazines.

Not far from the bus station is the **Mercado Independencia** (✉*Av. Independencia between Calle Degollado and Calle Zapata* ☎*No phone*), a typical Mexican market. Shops along the periphery sell cowboy hats and other apparel, while the stalls inside are piled high with fruits and vegetables, meats, and fish. ■ TIP→**The restaurant stalls toward the back are great places to order cheap, tasty meals. Some are open 24 hours.**

VH (✉*Av. Obregón at Calle Zaragoza* ☎*668/815–7285*) is a large supermarket where you can stock up on provisions for your trip.

Los Cabos & the Baja Peninsula

Cabo San Lucas

WORD OF MOUTH

"Rent a car one day and drive around the lower peninsula, say counterclockwise through San José, East Cape (stopping at one of the fishing hotels), maybe detouring into La Paz for lunch, then to the Pacific side for Todos Santos and then back to Cabo."

–Bill_H

"Baja California is essentially a desert. It offers spectacular scenery and is very popular with many experienced Mexican travelers."

–bajabilly

www.fodors.com/forums

WELCOME TO LOS CABOS & THE BAJA PENINSULA

TOP REASONS TO GO

★ **Driving through starkly beautiful landscapes:** Along the Pacific Coast, south of Tijuana, the Carretera Transpeninsular (Highway 1) makes getting to Baja's historic missions and remote beaches half the fun.

★ **Sampling the other California's finest wines:** The Valle de Guadalupe, near to Ensenada, is a gorgeous valley filled with vineyards and inns with unpretentious hosts.

★ **Making eye contact with a gray whale:** These gentle giants swim to Baja California every winter to mate and calve in three lagoons on the peninsula's west coast.

★ **Catching (and releasing) a feisty marlin:** Sportfishing aficionados flock to Cabo, East Cape, La Paz, Loreto, and San Felipe when temperatures are high, and fish are abundant.

★ **Giving in to sybaritic pleasures:** Indulge in a massage, salt scrub, or seaweed wrap—maybe all three—at a Los Cabos spa.

1 San José del Cabo. Thirty-two kilometers (20 mi) east of Cabo San Lucas, San José, the eldest sister, has remained the smaller, quieter, and more tame of the two siblings. Its 18th-century colonial architecture, artsy vibe, and quality restaurants are great for those who like to be within driving distance of the action.

2 The Corridor. Along this stretch of road, which connects San José to Cabo, exclusive guard-gated resort complexes have taken over much of the waterfront with their sprawling villas, golf courses, and shopping centers.

3 Cabo San Lucas. Cabo holds the sportfishing fleet and the cruise ship terminal. Trendy restaurants and bars line the streets and massive hotels front the beach. Here, you'll find Bahía Cabo San Lucas (Cabo Bay), Land's End Rocks, and the famed El Arco.

4 Baja California Sur. La Paz, the capital of Baja, is a big little city, one of the most authentic on the peninsula, and Loreto, a smaller, charming town beloved by sportfishermen, is developing a new identity as a huge-scale planned community, Loreto Bay, finishes construction. Along the Pacific Coast lie three coves, which fill with birthing gray whales during the months of January to April.

5 Baja California Norte. Border towns Tijuana, Tecate, and Mexicali still retain a hard-nosed grunge and lack the beauty and charm of towns farther south. The beaches and seafood of Rosarito, Ensenada, and San Felipe draw retirees, RVers, and crowds of college kids; the Valle de Guadalupe, however, provides respite and fantastic wine to those willing to stray from Napa.

GETTING ORIENTED

Baja is perfect for both adventurers and hedonists. The narrow peninsula is lapped by the Pacific on one side and by the Sea of Cortez on the other. It has some of the planet's most beautiful terrain: countless bays and coves, mountain ranges, desert as dry as the Sahara, farmlands, vineyards, and last but not least, exclusive resorts rife with swaying palms.

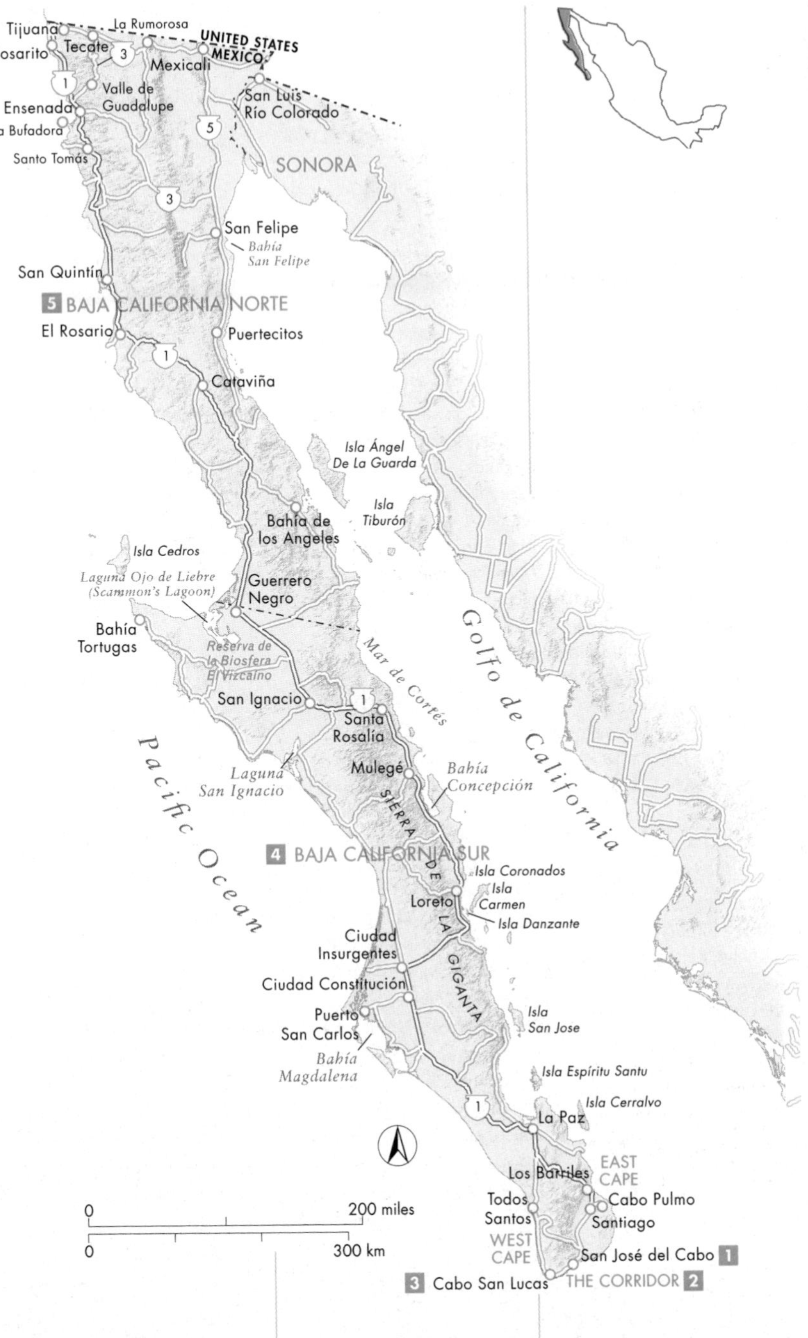

Tijuana
La Rumorosa
UNITED STATES
MEXICO
Rosarito
Tecate
Mexicali
Valle de Guadalupe
San Luis Río Colorado
Ensenada
La Bufadora
Santo Tomás
SONORA
San Felipe
Bahía San Felipe
San Quintín
5 BAJA CALIFORNIA NORTE
El Rosario
Puertecitos
Cataviña
Isla Ángel De La Guarda
Isla Tiburón
Bahía de los Angeles
Isla Cedros
Laguna Ojo de Liebre (Scammon's Lagoon)
Guerrero Negro
Bahía Tortugas
Reserva de la Biosfera El Vizcaíno
Golfo de California
Mar de Cortés
San Ignacio
Santa Rosalía
Pacific Ocean
Laguna San Ignacio
Mulegé
Bahía Concepción
SIERRA DE LA GIGANTA
4 BAJA CALIFORNIA SUR
Isla Coronados
Isla Carmen
Loreto
Isla Danzante
Ciudad Insurgentes
Ciudad Constitución
Puerto San Carlos
Bahía Magdalena
Isla San Jose
Isla Espíritu Santu
Isla Cerralvo
La Paz
Los Barriles
EAST CAPE
Cabo Pulmo
Todos Santos
Santiago
WEST CAPE
San José del Cabo 1
3 Cabo San Lucas
THE CORRIDOR 2
0
200 miles
0
300 km

LOS CABOS & THE BAJA PENINSULA PLANNER

When to Go

Although Los Cabos hotels are often busiest starting in mid-October for the sportfishing season, the high season doesn't technically begin until mid-December, running through the end of Easter week. Spring break is also a particularly crowded and raucous time in Cabo San Lucas and in the beach towns in Baja Norte. Downtown Cabo and the border towns up north are very busy, especially on weekend nights, throughout the year. Whale-watching season from mid-December to April really compounds the situation during high season, though whale-watchers tend to stay in La Paz and Loreto, not Los Cabos.

The Pacific hurricane season mirrors that of the Atlantic and Caribbean, so there is always a slight chance of a hurricane from August through late October. Although hurricanes rarely hit Los Cabos head-on, the effects can reverberate when a large hurricane hits Mexico's Pacific coast. Still, most summer tropical storms pass through quickly, even during the Cape's so-called short "rainy" season, from July through October.

An Active Life

Fishing is a main diversion, whether in *pangas* (small motorized skiffs) or showy yachts. International tournaments fill hotels from Loreto to Los Cabos from September through November. Golf has become equally as important, and some courses are from the drawing boards of such designers as Jack Nicklaus and Tom Weiskopf. Tour companies encourage clients to hike or bike through the Sierra de la Laguna, take ATV (all-terrain vehicle) trips along the beaches and into the desert, or hit the trails on horseback. Every December through March, as many as 6,000 gray whales swim south from Alaska's Bering Strait to Baja, stopping near the shore at several spots to birth their calves. Multiday tours take you to such prime whale-watching places as Bahía Magdalena, Laguna San Ignacio, and Scammon's Lagoon.

A Taste of Baja

Baja's chefs rely on the vegetables and fruits grown in the region's fertile valleys. Beef, pork, and quail are all good here. So is seafood, which is often fried or grilled. You can also eat dorado, tuna, and snapper topped with guajillo and chipotle chiles, tomatillo salsa, or mango and papaya relishes. Mexico's best wines are nurtured in the Santo Tomás and Guadalupe valleys outside Ensenada, and a beloved beer, Tecate, comes from the Baja Norte border town of the same name.

Some say that fish tacos (tacos de pescado) originated in Ensenada, others insist it was San Felipe. No matter. They now appear on menus everywhere, and are made with hunks of battered and fried fish stuffed in a fresh corn tortilla and topped with such fixings as a mayonnaise-based sauce, cilantro, onions, and shredded cabbage.

Lobster gets special treatment in Puerto Nuevo. *Langosta* Puerto Nuevo is typically boiled in oil and served with beans, rice, tortillas, and melted butter.

Try *ceviche,* which is fresh fish marinated in a mixture of lime, onions, and cilantro.

Driving into Mexico

Baja aficionados will tell you that you haven't explored the peninsula unless you've driven its length. Mexico Highway 1 (Carretera 1 or the Carretera Transpeninsular) runs 1,700 km (1,054 mi) from Tijuana to Cabo San Lucas-a major journey, requiring at least a week one way. Few people go the distance. Most are content with day trips to Tijuana from San Diego or long weekends in Rosarito, Ensenada, or San Felipe. A few points to ponder:

Many U.S. rental companies don't allow you to drive their cars into Mexico; those that do often charge fees atop the rental price and restrict how far south you can go.

You must have Mexican auto insurance, available at agencies near the border.

If you're going only as far as Ensenada or San Felipe, you don't need a tourist card unless you stay longer than 72 hours. Cards are available at border customs offices, but you must ask for them.

Bring three copies of the following plus the original: passport, birth certificate, and vehicle registration.

Tours, Mexican auto insurance, and a newsletter are available through the San Diego based **Discover Baja.** (☎619/275–4225 or 800/727–2252 🌐www.discover-baja.com), a club for Baja travelers.

Money Matters

Some restaurants add a 15% service charge to the tab. A few small hotels don't accept credit cards; some lavish places add a 10%–20% service charge. Most properties raise their rates December–April (and raise them even higher around Christmas).

WHAT IT COSTS IN DOLLARS					
¢	$	$$	$$$	$$$$	$$$$
Restaurants					
under $5	$5–$10	$10–$15	$15–$25	over $25	over $25
Hotels					
under $50	$50–$75	$75–$150	$150–$250	over $250	over $250

Restaurant prices are for a main course excluding tax and tip. Hotel prices are for two people in a standard double room in high season.

How's the Weather?

Baja Norte is a desert locale. The heat is tempered by low humidity and cool breezes off the Pacific Ocean and the Sea of Cortez. Temperatures from June through September are searing. Winter can bring chilly, stiff winds.

In Los Cabos rain is rare, except from August to November, when the occasional hurricane brings everything to a halt. Baja Sur's winters are mild. The temperature in Los Cabos from December through April can be chilly at night (horrors—as low as 10°C/50°F). Daytime temperatures rise to 20°C (70°F).

Safety

Be vigilant in border areas and large cities, where purse-snatching, pickpocketing, and hotel-room thefts are common. In Tijuana violent crime is an issue. Stash valuables in room safes, leave jewelry at home, and carry only modest amounts of money. Never leave belongings unattended—anywhere. Although resort areas are generally safe, keep your guard up. There have been reports of people being victimized after imbibing drugged drinks in Cabo San Lucas nightclubs. Like momma always said: don't drink alone or with strangers.

LOS CABOS & BAJA SUR

Updated by Larry Dunmire & Michele Joyce

IF HUMANS PULLED OUT OF Baja it would rapidly regress to its natural dry, brown, uninhabitable state. But man has wrought wonders here. Enormous swaths of desert and coast are carved into exclusive developments, and the demand for more marinas, golf courses, and private homes seems never-ending. In some places hotels command $500 or more a night for their enormous suites, restaurants and spas charge L.A. prices, and million-dollar vacation villas are all the rage.

With the completion in 1973 of the Carretera Transpeninsular (Mexico Carretera 1), travelers gradually found their way down the 1,708-km (1,059-mi) road, drawn by wild terrain and pristine beaches. Baja California Sur became Mexico's 30th state in 1974, and the population and tourism have been growing ever since. Still, Baja Sur remains a rugged, largely undeveloped land. Many people opt to fly to the region rather than brave the often desolate Carretera 1.

Whale-watching in Scammon's Lagoon, San Ignacio Lagoon, Magdalena Bay, and throughout the Mar de Cortés is a main attraction in winter. History buffs enjoy Loreto, where the first mission in the Californias was established. La Paz, today a busy state capital and sportfishing hub, was the first Spanish settlement in Baja. At the peninsula's southernmost tip fishing aficionados, golfers, and sun worshippers gather in Los Cabos, which sits like a sun-splashed movie set where the desert and ocean collide.

San José del Cabo is the government center and traditional Mexican town, albeit with a strong foreign influence. Massive all-inclusives have consumed much of its coastline, making San José the favored destination for families who just want to stay put on a safe, self-contained vacation. Outrageous, excitement-packed Cabo San Lucas is the Cabo you see on MTV, with many of the hotels and restaurants and most of the action. It's spring break here year-round, making it the preferred home base for the let-it-all-hang-out crowd. Connecting the two towns is the Corridor—a strip of designer golf courses and super-luxe resorts set in a desert landscape. Celebrities lounge poolside at Corridor hideaways, their privacy ensured by exorbitant room rates.

CABO SAN LUCAS

28 km (17 mi) southwest of San José del Cabo.

Cabo San Lucas is *in*—for its rowdy nightlife, its slew of trendy restaurants, and its lively beaches. The sportfishing fleet is headquartered here, cruise ships anchor off the marina, and there's a massive hotel on every available plot of waterfront turf. A pedestrian walkway lined with restaurants, bars, and shops anchored by the sleek Puerto Paraíso mall curves around Cabo San Lucas harbor, itself packed with yachts.

A five-story hotel complex at the edge of the harbor blocks the water view and sea breezes from the town's side streets, which are filled with a jarring jumble of structures. The most popular restaurants, clubs, and

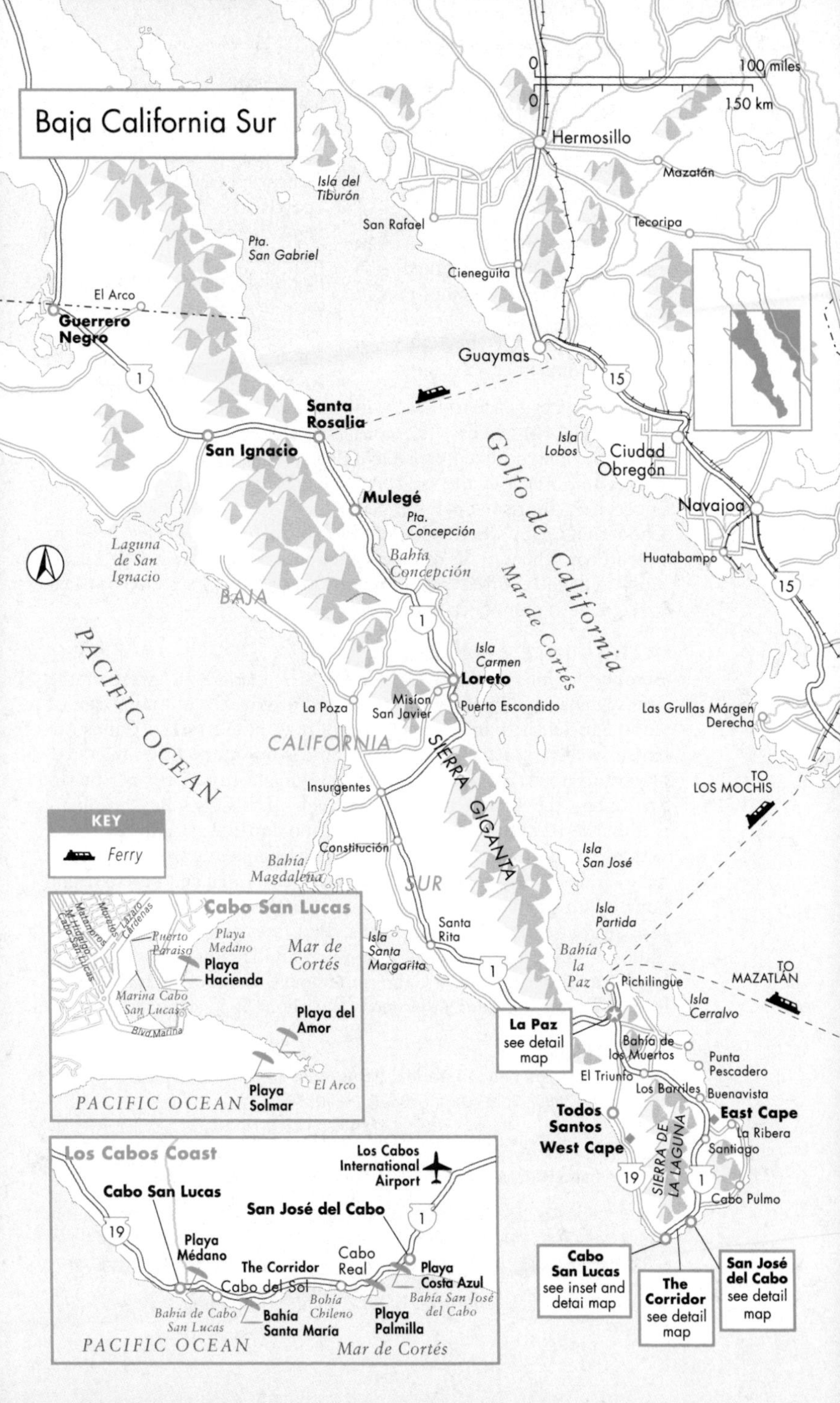
Baja California Sur
0
100 miles
0
150 km
Hermosillo
Mazatán
Isla del Tiburón
San Rafael
Tecoripa
Pta. San Gabriel
Cieneguita
El Arco
Guerrero Negro
Guaymas
15
1
Santa Rosalia
San Ignacio
Isla Lobos
Ciudad Obregón
Golfo de California
Mulegé
Navajoa
Pta. Concepción
Laguna de San Ignacio
Bahía Concepción
Huatabampo
BAJA
Mar de Cortés
PACIFIC OCEAN
Isla Carmen
Loreto
La Poza
Misión San Javier
Puerto Escondido
Las Grullas Márgen Derecha
CALIFORNIA
SIERRA GIGANTA
Insurgentes
TO LOS MOCHIS
KEY
Ferry
Constitución
Bahía Magdalena
Isla San José
SUR
Cabo San Lucas
Matamoros
M. Hidalgo
Cabo San Lucas
Morelos
Lazaro Cardenas
Puerto Paraiso
Playa Medano
Playa Hacienda
Mar de Cortés
Marina Cabo San Lucas
Blvd.Marina
Playa del Amor
El Arco
Playa Solmar
PACIFIC OCEAN
Isla Partida
Santa Rita
Isla Santa Margarita
Bahía la Paz
Pichilingue
TO MAZATLÁN
Isla Cerralvo
La Paz see detail map
Bahía de los Muertos
Punta Pescadero
El Triunfo
Los Barriles
Buenavista
Todos Santos
West Cape
East Cape
SIERRA DE LA LAGUNA
La Ribera
Santiago
Cabo Pulmo
Los Cabos Coast
Los Cabos International Airport
Cabo San Lucas
San José del Cabo
Playa Médano
The Corridor
Cabo Real
Playa Costa Azul
Cabo del Sol
Bahía de Cabo San Lucas
Bahía Santa María
Bahía Chileno
Playa Palmilla
Bahía San José del Cabo
PACIFIC OCEAN
Mar de Cortés
Cabo San Lucas see inset and detai map
The Corridor see detail map
San José del Cabo see detail map

shops are along Avenida Cárdenas (the extension of Highway 1 from the Corridor) and Boulevard Marina, paralleling the waterfront. The side streets closest to the marina are clogged with traffic, and their uneven, crumbling sidewalks front more tourist traps jammed side by side. At Playa Médano, tanned bodies lie shoulder to shoulder on the sand, with every possible form of entertainment close at hand.

> **POOR PITCH**
>
> Unless you want to tour a time-share, ignore the offers for free transfers at the airport in Los Cabos. Representatives from various properties compete vociferously for clients; often you won't realize you've been suckered into a sales presentation until you get in the van. To avoid this, go to the official taxi booths inside the baggage claim or just outside the final customs clearance area and pay for a ticket for a regular shuttle bus.

The short Pacific coast beach in downtown San Lucas is more peaceful, though huge hotels have gobbled up much of the sand. An entire new tourism area dubbed Cabo Pacifica by developers has blossomed on the Pacific, west of downtown. There's talk of a new international airport in San Lucas, along with golf courses and more resorts. San Lucas may soon be Mexico's gaudiest tourism capital.

GETTING HERE & AROUND

Aeropuerto Internacional Los Cabos is 1 km (½ mi) west of the Transpeninsular Highway (Hwy. 1) and 48 km (30 mi) northeast of Cabo San Lucas. Fares from the airport to hotels in Los Cabos are expensive. The least expensive transport is by shuttle buses that stop at various hotels along the route; fares run $12 to $25 per person. In Los Cabos, the main Terminal de Autobus (Los Cabos Bus Terminal) is about a 10-minute drive west of Cabo San Lucas. Express buses with air-conditioning and restrooms travel frequently from the terminal to Todos Santos (one hour), La Paz (three hours), and Loreto (eight hours). SuburBaja can provide private transport for $60 between San José del Cabo and Cabo San Lucas. Taxi fares are exorbitant in Los Cabos, and the taxi union is very powerful. The fare between Cabo San Lucas and San José del Cabo runs about $45—more at night. Cabs from Corridor hotels to either town run about $25 each way.

ESSENTIALS

Bus Contacts **Los Cabos Terminal de Autobus** (✉ *Hwy. 19* ☎ *624/143-5020 or 624/143-7880*). **SuburBaja** (☎ *624/146-0888*).

Currency Exchange **Banamex** (✉ *Av. Cárdenas*).

Internet**Cabo Mail Internet** (✉ *Blvd. Cárdenas* ☎ *624/143-7797*).

Mail & Shipping **Cabo San Lucas Oficina de Correo** (✉ *Av. Lázaro Cárdenas s/n* ☎ *624/143-0048*). **DHL Worldwide Express** (✉ *Hwy. 1, Plaza Copan* ☎ *624/143-5202*). **Mail Boxes Etc.** (✉ *Blvd. Marina, Plaza Bonita Local 44-E* ☎ *624/143-3032*).

Medical Assistance **AmeriMed** (✉ *Blvd. Cárdenas at Paseo Marina* ☎ *624/143-9670*).

Emergency Number for Medical Assistance (☎*Dial 065*). **Police** (☎*624/143–3977*).

WORD OF MOUTH

"What an amazing sight. El Arco takes your breath away. It's so beautiful, and worth every penny to see it up close in a boat! Plus the seals are so cute."

–Christina

EXPLORING

★ **El Arco,** the most spectacular sight in Cabo San Lucas, is a natural rock arch. It's visible from the marina and from some hotels, but it's more impressive from the water. To fully appreciate Cabo, take at least a short boat ride out to the arch and Playa del Amor, the beach underneath it.

Paved walkways run northeast from the busy Boulevard Marina to the hotels and beaches and southeast to the marina's main dock and **Mercado de Artesanías** *(Artisans Market)* that serve as the entryway to town for cruise passengers.

The main downtown street, Avenida Lázaro Cárdenas, passes the **Plaza Amelia Wilkes,** aka Plaza San Lucas, with its white wrought-iron gazebo. The plaza is the loveliest patch of gardens in San Lucas. Many of the older buildings facing the plaza have been renovated as classy restaurants, hotels, and offices.

BEACHES

Fodor'sChoice ★ **Playa del Amor.** Lovers have little chance of finding romantic solitude at Lover's Beach. The azure cove on the Sea of Cortez at the very tip of the peninsula may well be the area's most frequently photographed patch of sand. It's a must-see on every first-timer's list. Water taxis, glass-bottom boats, kayaks, and Jet Skis all make the short trip from Playa Médano to this small beach backed by cliffs streaked white with pelican and seagull guano. Snorkeling around the base of these rocks is fun when the water's calm; you may spot striped sergeant majors and iridescent green and blue parrot fish. Seals hang out on the rocks at the base of the arch. Walk along the sand to the Pacific side to see pounding white surf; just don't dive in. ⊠*Just outside Cabo San Lucas, at El Arco.*

Playa Médano. Foamy plumes of water shoot from Jet Skis and Wave Runners buzzing through the water off Médano, a 3-km (2-mi) span of grainy tan sand that's always crowded. When cruise ships are in town it's mobbed. Bars and restaurants line the sand, waiters deliver ice buckets filled with beers to sunbathers in lounge chairs, and vendors offer everything from fake silver jewelry to henna tattoos. You can even have your hair braided into tiny cornrows or get a pedicure. Swimming areas are roped off to prevent accidents, and the water is calm enough for toddlers. Several hotels line Médano, which is just north of downtown off Paseo del Pescador. Construction is constant on nearby streets, and parking is virtually impossible. ⊠*Paseo del Pescador.*

Playa Solmar. Huge waves crash on the Pacific side of San Lucas. This wide, beautiful beach stretches from land's end north to the cliffs of El Pedregal, where mansions perch on steep cliffs. Swimming is impossible here because of the dangerous surf and undertow; stick to sunbathing

TAKE A TOUR

You may not be able to swim in Cabo's seas, but you can enjoy the sensations of being out on the water. Boat tours range from standard all-you-can-drink booze cruises to pirate-ship trips that kids love. The themes of Los Cabos boat tours vary, but most follow essentially the same route: through Bahía Cabo San Lucas, past El Arco, around Land's End into the Pacific Ocean, and then east through the Sea of Cortez along the Corridor.

Cruises on the remarkable *Buccaneer Queen* are ideal for families with children. The 96-foot-tall ship sails on snorkeling tours ($45) and sunset cruises ($38). The 600-passenger tri-level catamaran *Cabo Rey* sails on a top-notch dinner cruise with lobster and chateaubriand on the menu and a cabaret show on the stage. The cost is $82 per person (Note: no cruises Sunday). Pez Gato has two 42-foot catamarans, *Pez Gato I* and *Pez Gato II*. You can choose the tranquil, romantic sunset cruise or the rowdier booze cruise. Sunset cruises depart from 5 to 7. Costs run about $30–$40 per person, including an open bar.

Tour Operators *Bucaneer Queen* (✉*El Tesoro hotel dock, Cabo San Lucas* ☎*624/144–4217*). *Cabo Rey* (✉*El Tesoro hotel dock, Cabo San Lucas* ☎*624/143–8260*). **Pez Gato** (✉*El Tesoro hotel dock, Cabo San Lucas* ☎*624/143–3797*).

and strolling. From December to March you can spot gray whales spouting just offshore; dolphins leap above the waves year-round. The beach is at the end of Avenida Solmar off Boulevard Marina. ✉*Blvd. Marina to hotel entrances.*

WHERE TO EAT

$$$–$$$$ SEAFOOD ★ ✕ **Edith's Restaurant.** The Caesar salad and flambéed banana crepes are prepared table-side at this colorful, classy, and popular restaurant, where dinners are accompanied by Mexican trios or soft jazz. The Disca de Mariscos, with lobster, shrimp, and fish, is Baja's representative dish. Here even the simplest choices are enhanced: quesadillas are homemade tortillas wrapped around Oaxacan cheese, and meat and fish dishes are doused in chile or tropical fruit sauces. Edith's air-conditioned Wine Cellar offers a large selection of domestic and imported wines, and is ideal for hosting small intimate dinners for up to 10. Families dine in early evening, so come in later if you're looking for a more-romantic atmosphere. ✉*Paseo del Pescador, near Playa Médano* ☎*624/143–0801* 🌐*www.edithscabo.com* ▭*MC, V* ⊗*No lunch.*

$$$–$$$$ SEAFOOD ★ ✕ **Lorenzillo's.** Gleaming hardwood floors and polished brass give a nautical flair to this dining room, where fresh lobster is king. Lorenzillo's has long been a fixture in Cancún, where lobster is raised on the company's farm. That Caribbean lobster is shipped to Los Cabos and served in 12 ways (the simpler preparations—steamed or grilled with lots of melted butter—are best). Menu items are named after pirates and Caribbean marine history, so Sir Francis Drake is their rib-eye steak, El Barbolento is abalone sashimi with spicy "diablo" sauce, and El Doblón is a giant chop on the bone. If you desire a major lobster splurge: a 2-pounder served with spinach puree and linguine or potato sets you back over

$66. Other options—Alaska king crab, conch, coconut shrimp, or beef medallions—are more moderately priced. The dessert list is lengthy and mouthwatering. ✉*Av. Cárdenas at Marina, Centro* ☎*624/105–0212* 🌐*www.lorenzillos.com.mx* ▭*AE, MC, V.*

$$–$$$ MEXICAN ✕**Mi Casa.** One of Cabo's top restaurants is in a cobalt-blue building painted with a mural of a burro. Expanded and renovated, Mi Casa can now seat up to 600. The fresh tuna and dorado, served with tomatillo salsa or Yucatecan achiote, both shine, as does the sophisticated poblano chiles en nogada (stuffed with a meat-and-fruit mixture and covered with white walnut sauce and pomegranate seeds). If you're in the mood for something along the lines of a "Mexican Luau," try the *barbacoa borrego,* or barbecued goat. It's done "á la Hawaiiana," cooked in the ground, luau style. Mi Casa also offers an incredible selection of 20 different fruit margaritas. The large back courtyard glows with candlelight at night, and mariachis provide entertainment. The owners operate several excellent area restaurants, including Mi Casa de Mariscos and Peacocks. ✉*Av. Cabo San Lucas, Centro* ☎*624/143–1933* 🌐*www.micasarestaurant.com* ▭*MC, V.*

$$–$$$ SEAFOOD ✕**Mocambo.** Veracruz—a region known for its seafood preparations—meets Los Cabos in an enormous dining room packed with appreciative locals. The menu has such hard-to-find regional dishes as octopus ceviche, shrimp empanadas, and a heaping mixed seafood platter that includes sea snails, clams, and octopus, with lobster and shrimp. Musicians stroll among the tables and the chatter is somewhat cacophonous, but you're sure to have a great "genuine" and local dining experience here. ✉*Leona Vicario at Calle 20 de Noviembre, Centro* ☎*624/143–2122* ▭*MC, V.*

$$–$$$ ECLECTIC Fodor's Choice ★ ✕**Nick San.** Dare we make such a claim? Nick San may very possibly be Cabo San Lucas's top restaurant. Owner Angel Carbajal is an artist behind the sushi counter (and also has his own fishing boats that collect fish each day). A creative fusion of Japanese and Mexican cuisines truly sets his masterpieces apart. The sauce on the cilantro sashimi is so divine that diners sneak in bread to sop up the sauce (rice isn't the same). You can run up a stiff tab ordering sushi. The mahogany bar and minimalist dining room are packed most nights, but the vibe is upbeat, and many diners eat here so frequently they've become family friends. There's also a second Nick San on the Corridor in the Tiendas de Palmilla shopping center. Reservations are recommended, especially on weekend nights and during high season. Otherwise, get ready to wait. ✉*Blvd. Marina, Plaza de la Danza next to Tesoro Hotel, Centro* ☎*624/143–4484* 🌐*www.nicksan.com* ▭*MC, V.*

$$–$$$ MEXICAN ✕**Pancho's Restaurant & Tequila Bar.** Owner John Bragg has an enormous collection of tequilas, and an encyclopedic knowledge of the stuff. The restaurant is nothing short of a tequila museum, with a colorful display of many hundreds of the world's top historic tequilas, many no longer available, displayed behind the bar. Sample one or two of the nearly 1,000 labels available, and you'll appreciate the Oaxacan tablecloths, murals, painted chairs, and streamers even more than you did when you first arrived. Try regional specialties like tortilla soup, chiles rellenos, or *sopa de mariscos,* seafood soup. The breakfast and lunch specials are a

bargain. Pancho's offers special and private tequila tastings; with them comes a more-appreciative knowledge of this piquant liquor from Jalisco. ✉ *Hidalgo between Zapata and Serdan, Centro* ☎ *624/143–2891 or 624/143–0973* 🌐 *www.panchos.com* 💳 *AE, MC, V.*

WORD OF MOUTH

[At] The Office [you'll] have the best breakfasts ever, with incredible views.

—blamona

$$–$$$ MEDITERRANEAN ✕ **Sancho Panza.** The classy menu, decor, and live Latin rhythms make this small bistro, well stocked with wines, a favorite with sophisticates. Try the steamed mussels, osso buco, Cuban salad, tuna carpaccio, and chicken with sun-dried apricots and walnuts. The menu changes constantly, as does the art in the Dalí-esque bar. To find Sancho Panza, listen for the music emanating from the eastern end of the Tesoro Hotel. ✉ *Blvd. Marina, Centro* ☎ *624/143–3212* 🌐 *www.sanchopanza.com* 💳 *AE, MC, V* ⏲ *No lunch.*

$$ ECLECTIC ✕ **The Office.** Playa Médano is lined with cafés on the sand, some with lounge chairs, others with more-formal settings. At least once during every visit to Los Cabos, you *must* visit the Office, the original breakfast spot on El Médano; with its huge sign and blue umbrellas (the perfect photo backdrop), and great view of Land's End Rocks, the Office is the best. There's no better way to start out the morning in Cabo than enjoying a *sabroso* (tasty) lobster omelet, fresh-fruit smoothie, and powerful cup of Mexican coffee, with your toes comfortably embedded in the sand. Another favorite is their French toast. Here the service is friendly, the menu a bit expensive, but hey, amigo, you're on vacation. Cold beer (later in the day, of course), ceviche, nachos, fish tacos, french fries, and burgers are served in portions that somewhat justify the high prices. You can split most entrées. Dinners of grilled shrimp, fish with garlic, and steaks are popular. ✉ *Playa Médano* ☎ *624/143–3464* ✍ *Reservations essential* 💳 *MC, V.*

$–$$ SEAFOOD Fodor's Choice ★ ✕ **Marisquería Mazatlán.** The crowds of locals lunching at this simple seafood restaurant are a good sign—as are the huge glass cases packed with shrimp, ceviche, and other seafood cocktails. You can dine inexpensively and quickly on wonderful seafood soup, or spend a bit more for tender *pulpo ajillo* (marinated octopus with garlic, chilies, onion, and celery) and have some fun people-watching as you eat. ✉ *Mendoza at Calle 16 de Septiembre, Centro* ☎ *624/143–8565* 💳 *MC, V.*

¢–$ CAFÉ ✕ **Señor Greenberg's Mexicatessen.** Pastrami, chopped liver, knishes, bagels, lox, cheesecake—you can find them all, and much, much more behind the glass counters of this Mexican incarnation of a New York deli. (It's actually a decent impression.) Greenberg's has a couple of locations, serves all three meals, and has an extensive menu that ranges from soups, salads, and sandwiches, to smoothies, steaks, and desserts. Fishermen get their box lunches here, and you can also arrange party platters. The Mexicatessens are no longer open 24 hours, but the air-conditioning, stacks of newspapers, and soft music might pull you back more than once. You'll find this spot in Puerto Paraíso, overlooking Cabo's marina. It has a huge dining room and patio, the entirety of which is outfitted with Wi-Fi, and there several Internet-connected computers set up on dining tables, for a reasonable charge. Another Senor Greenberg's Mexicatessen is now open in the Plaza Gali, in the far northwestern end of the marina, where cruise ship tenders bring their folks ashore. ✉ *Plaza Nautica on Blvd. Marina, Centro* ☎ *624/143–6772 Plaza Gali, 624/144–3804 in Puerto Paraíso* ▭ *MC, V.*

¢ MEXICAN **Gordo's Tortas.** Ready for a floor show along with your *tortas*? Listen for the blaring Beatles' tunes, then watch Javier don his tattered Beatles wig and strum his battered, two-stringed ukulele to "I Wanna Hold Your Hand." You've found Gordo's tiny sidewalk stand. Javier's tacos and *tortas* (sandwiches) are made with loving care, and his fans are loyal enough to chow down on their feet, as there are only two small plastic tables by the stand. You can have two or three ham-and-cheese tortas for the price of one anywhere else. ✉ *Guerrero at Zapata, across street from Cabo Wabo, Centro* ☎ *No phone* ▭ *No credit cards.*

WHERE TO STAY

$$$$ ★ **Pacifica Holistic Retreat & Spa.** Soothing waterfalls, glass-domed ceilings, and pebbled floors bring nature indoors to complement this holistic approach to vacationing. The emphasis here is on health and wellness, peace and tranquillity; a physician who works with natural therapies oversees the Armonia spa, where treatments include *watsu* and an outdoors, beach-side *temazcal*, or native Maya sweat lodge. It's a refreshingly small hotel by Los Cabos standards, and rooms have minimalist decor with cream fabrics, cedar and straw accents, and stunning ocean views. The designers incorporated feng shui elements throughout the resort and grounds, which are stunning with patterned cactus gardens designed by the talented Cacti Mundo. **Pros: No children allowed, which facilitates feelings of calm. Cons: Unexpected extra costs (in-room coffee, gym), no Wi-Fi.** ✉ *Cabo Pacifica s/n* ☎ *624/142–9696 or 866/585–1752 in U.S.* 🌐 *www.pueblobonitopacifica.com* *140 rooms, 14 suites* *In-room: Safe, Internet, refrigerator. In-hotel: 2 restaurants, room service, 2 bars, 2 pools, gym, spa, beachfront, laundry service, public Internet, no kids* ▭ *AE, MC, V* *EP*

$$$$ **Pueblo Bonito Rosé.** Mediterranean-style buildings curve around elegant grounds, imitations of Roman busts guard reflecting pools, and Flemish tapestries adorn the lobby. Not your typical Cabo hotel, but this company never settles for mediocrity. There are two Pueblo Bonito hotels here on El Médano Beach in San Lucas and two new properties, the Pueblo Bonito Pacifica Holistic Resort and Pueblo Bonito Sunset, out on the Pacific coast. A shuttle bus travels between them, and guests have signing privileges at all four. The Pueblo Bonito "secret" for a discount of up to 25% is to book online. **Pros:** Even the Rosé's smallest suites can accommodate four people, and all have private balconies overlooking the grounds. **Cons:** Many suites are time-share units, and the salespeople are sometimes persistent. Just say, nicely and firmly, no. ✉ *Playa Médano,* ☎ *624/142–9898 or 800/990–8250 in U.S.* 🌐 *www.pueblobonito.com* *260 suites* *In-room: Safe, kitchen, refrigerator. In-hotel: 2 restaurants, room service, bars, pools, gym, spa, beachfront, laundry service, public Internet* ▭ *AE, MC, V* *EP*

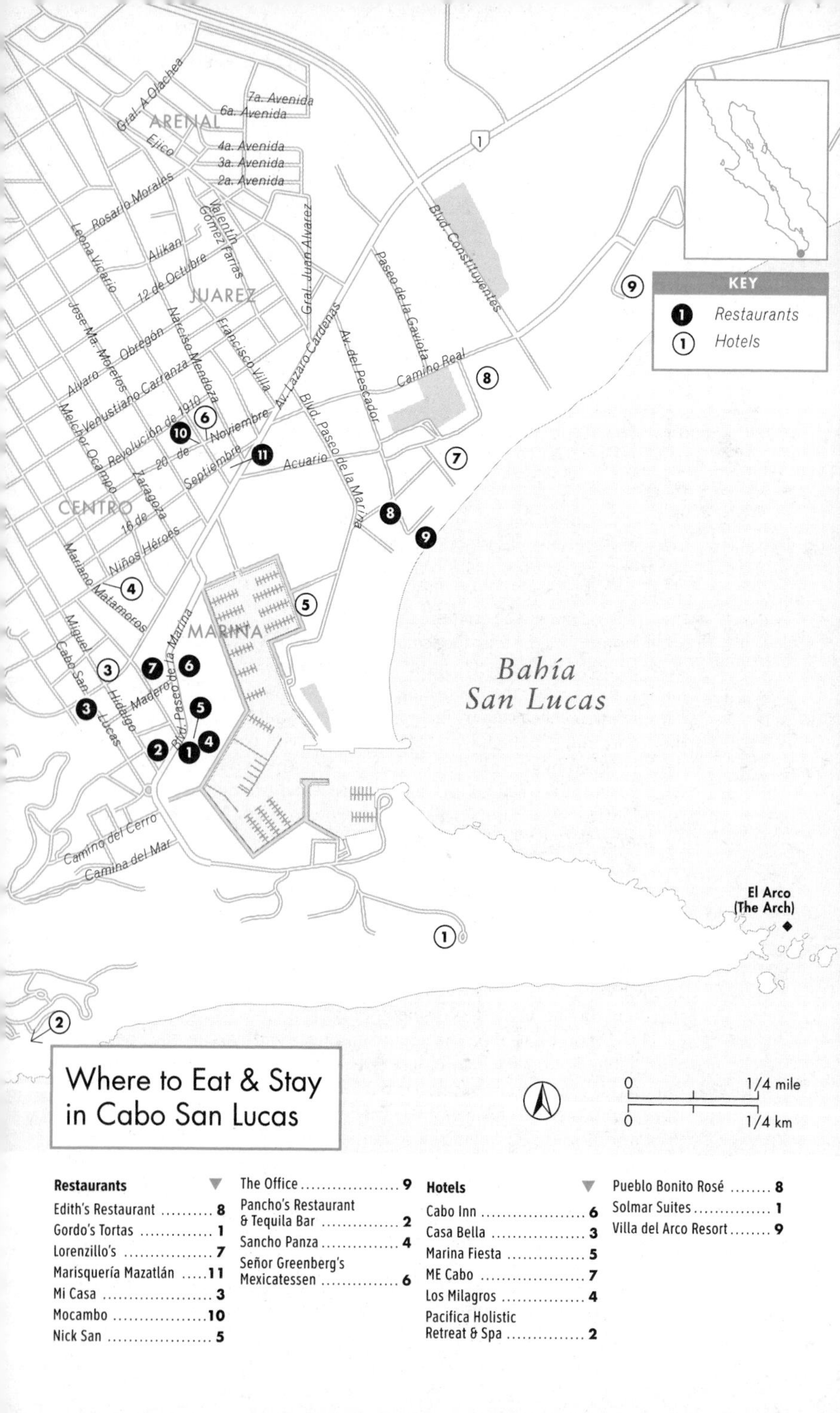

Where to Eat & Stay in Cabo San Lucas

Restaurants

- Edith's Restaurant 8
- Gordo's Tortas 1
- Lorenzillo's 7
- Marisquería Mazatlán 11
- Mi Casa 3
- Mocambo 10
- Nick San 5
- The Office 9
- Pancho's Restaurant & Tequila Bar 2
- Sancho Panza 4
- Señor Greenberg's Mexicatessen 6

Hotels

- Cabo Inn 6
- Casa Bella 3
- Marina Fiesta 5
- ME Cabo 7
- Los Milagros 4
- Pacifica Holistic Retreat & Spa 2
- Pueblo Bonito Rosé 8
- Solmar Suites 1
- Villa del Arco Resort 9

$$$$ **Villa del Arco Resort.** Another resort opened by The Villa Group on El Médano Beach, the Villa del Arco is next to Villa La Estancia. As with its two sister properties, del Arco offers comfortable, stylishly decorated one-, two- and three-bedroom suites and penthouses with all the amenities, including full kitchens. And for spa aficionados, you can't get any better than their 31,000 square foot Desert Spa—the largest in Los Cabos, offering all of treatments that utilize desert plants and herbs, with some authentic Mexico thrown in. Sign up for the Mexican Tequila Body Wrap, or the Organic Succulent Cactus Facial. **Pros:** A on-property deli and market lets you stock up the kitchen, saving some money on meals out. **Cons:** Service is spotty, tendency to overbook. ✉ *Camino Viejo a San José, Km 0.5,* ☎ *624/145–7000, 877/845–5247 U.S.* 🌐 *www.villadelarcoloscabos.com* *221 suites* *In-room: Safe, kitchen (some), Wi-Fi. In-hotel: 3 restaurants, room service, 2 bars, pools, hot tub, elevators* *MC, V* *EP, AI*

$$$–$$$$ **Marina Fiesta.** At this colonial-style building, most rooms have a pleasant view of the cloverleaf-shape pool and out to the yacht-filled marina. Rooms are designed for practicality, with stainproof floral textiles, tile floors, and plenty of space to spread your stuff about. The hotel is on the Golden Zone walkway adjacent to the Puerto Paraiso Mall. **Pros:** The Marina Fiesta is next to popular bars and shops and a quick five-minute walk from the popular beach at Playa Médano. **Cons:** Not ocean side, location can be noisy. ✉ *Marina, Lot 37, Marina,* ☎ *624/145–6020* 🌐 *www.marinafiestaresort.com* *139 rooms, 46 suites* *In-room: Safe, kitchen (some), refrigerator (some). In-hotel: Restaurant, room service, bar, pools, gym, spa, laundry service, public Internet, public Wi-Fi* *AE, MC, V* *EP*

$$$–$$$$ Fodor's Choice ★ **ME Cabo** In the middle of the most popular beach in Los Cabos, El Médano, is where you'll find the ME—Sol Meliá's entrée into this lively W-style hotel brand. With its huge, bustling pool areas, more day beds than you can imagine, hot tubs under the palms, and all the equipment you could need for playing on, and in, the water, the ME Cabo is a playground for adults. The hotel's swim-up pool bar is talked about up and down the beach and throughout town. At poolside is the fun and friendly Nikki Beach Restaurant, serving their culinary blend of Asian and Mediterranean dishes, along with dosages of chill music. Rooms are new, chic, ultra-comfortable, and have easygoing light-wood furnishings with breezy, flowing drapes. A wide range of creatively designed suites are offered, with names like Energy, Chic, and Nikki. The ME's Presidential Suite, located on the top floor, offers a top panoramic view of the hotel pool, El Médano Beach, the bay's cruise ships, Cabo's Land's End Rocks, and VIP parties on the beach, that is, if Presidential Suite guests aren't already down there. Passion Night Club (open only Thursday-Saturday) is *the* place to be seen in Cabo. **Pros:** Happy hour at the pool gives you a break on drink costs, with the restyling of the ME, you'll even find an iPod docking station and plasma TVs in every room. **Cons:** Fills up super quickly, so early reservations are essential; hard-core party atmosphere. ✉ *Playa Médano,* ☎ *624/145–7800 or 800/336–3542 in U.S.* *624/143–0420* 🌐 *www.solmelia.com* *88 rooms, 62 suites*

In-room: Safe, Wi-Fi. In-hotel: 3 restaurants, 4 bars, pools, beachfront, laundry service AE, MC, V EP

$$$ **Solmar Suites.** Like Sinatra's position in the Rat Pack, as far as Cabo hotels go, the whitewashed Solmar was an original. It sits against the rocks at Land's End facing the surging Pacific. Rooms are done in a Mexico–Santa Fe style, with subdued green- and blue-tile baths. The oldest rooms open right onto the sand, and you literally feel the waves breaking on the nearby beach. Newer buildings run up a tiered hillside; it's a little bit of a hike to the beach and pools. Time-share units (also used as hotel rooms) have kitchenettes and a private pool area. Still, be mindful of the waves. The restaurant hosts a Saturday night Mexican fiesta, but the food in the bar is better. Don't miss a stroll along the wide strip of beach. **Pros:** The Solmar's sport-fishing fleet, although slightly subdivided recently, is still first-rate. **Cons:** Surf here is far too dangerous for swimming. *Av. Solmar at Blvd. Marina, Apdo. 8, 624/146–7700 or 800/344–3349 in U.S. www.solmar.com 109 suites, 14 studios In-room: Safe, refrigerator. In-hotel: Restaurant, room service, bar, pools, beachfront, laundry service* MC, V EP

$$–$$$ ★ **Casa Bella.** The Ungson family had been in Cabo for more than four decades before turning their home across from Plaza San Lucas into a spacious, sedate inn. It's by far the classiest and friendliest place in the neighborhood, landscaped with meandering paths leading to the pool, gazebo, and terrace. It is indeed, a *casa bella,* or beautiful house, as they say in Spanish. Room furnishings are handcrafted and thoughtfully arranged. The open showers in the huge tiled bathrooms are works of art—some even have little gardens. **Pros:** The property feels totally secluded, though it's in the middle of town. **Cons:** Pool is quite small, doesn't have amenities of larger properties (a pro for some). *Calle Hidalgo 10, Centro, 624/143–6400 www.casabellahotel.com 11 rooms, 3 suites In-room: No TV. In-hotel: Pool, laundry service, TV room, public Internet, no-smoking rooms, no elevator* MC, V *Closed Aug. and Sept.* CP

$–$$ ★ **Los Milagros.** A mosaic sign (crafted by co-owner Ricardo Rode) near the entrance hints at the beauty inside this small inn. Brilliant purple bougainvillea and orange lipstick vines line the patio, which showcases more of Rode's works by the fountain and small pool. *Bóveda*-style (arched brick) roofs top the rooms, which have terra-cotta tile floors and handmade Guadalajaran furniture. One room is accessible to travelers with disabilities. Checks or cash are accepted at the hotel; to use a credit card, you must pay prior to arrival through PayPal. **Pros:** Co-owner Sandra Scandiber dispenses budget travel tips while visiting with guests in the courtyard, and is always ready to lend books from her huge library. **Cons:** No breakfasts, some rooms are noisy. *Matamoros 116, Centro, 718/928–6647 in U.S. 624/143–4566 www.losmilagros.com.mx 12 rooms In-room: Kitchen (some), Internet. In-hotel: Pool, laundry service, public Internet, public Wi-Fi, no elevator, parking* AE, D, MC, V EP

$ **Cabo Inn.** The small, comfortable rooms at this affordable palapa-roofed, cactus-lined, and jungle-like hotel have tangerine and cobalt sponge-painted walls and stained-glass windows above the headboards. The eight rooms on the lower level have refrigerators; and the two top-floor palapa suites are playful and funky. Palapa #2 has a king bed and hot tub for just $120! A young, hip, international clientele frequents the Cabo Inn, with guests from Argentina, Germany, Ireland, Spain, and Sweden signing in the guest book. Rounding out the fun are shared communal areas that include a kitchen, barbecue and picnic area, small pool, and a television. **Pros:** Conveniently located; guests mingle in common areas, which enlivens your stay. **Cons:** Top-floor suites are a little bit noisy, due to their slightly open-air construction and the hotel's close proximity to downtown Cabo's festivities. ✉*Calle 20 de Noviembre and Vicario, Centro,* ☎📠*624/143–0819, 619/819–2727 in U.S.* 🌐*www.caboinnhotel.com* *20 rooms* *In-room: Refrigerator (some), no TV. In-hotel: No elevator, Wi-Fi* 💳*MC, V* *EP*

WORD OF MOUTH

"What a cool little place! Don't be mistaken: Cabo Inn isn't the Ritz. But it is a wonderful, simple little lodging; a clean place to rest your head that has character."

–Douglas P.

NIGHTLIFE

The latest U.S. rock plays over an excellent sound system at **Cabo Wabo** (✉*Calle Guerrero* ☎*624/143–1188*), but the impromptu jam sessions with appearances by Sammy Hagar—an owner—are the real highlight.

Ronald Valentino plays everything from "*My Way*" to "*Besame Mucho*" at the piano at **El Galeón** (✉*Blvd. Marina* ☎*624/143–0443*). The crowd is generally quiet, though inebriated fans sometimes inspire an impromptu karaoke session.

Giggling Marlin (✉*Blvd. Marina and Matamoros* ☎*624/143–1182 or 624/143–0606*) has been around forever, but its gimmicks remain popular. Watch brave (and inebriated) souls be hoisted upside down at the mock fish-weighing scale or join in an impromptu moonwalk between tables.

Miami meets Cabo at **Nikki Beach** (✉*ME Cabo Hotel by Meliá San Lucas, Playa Médano* ☎*624/145–7800*). With white gauze canopies shading plush white sunbeds and lounge chairs around swimming pools, the club would be the perfect setting for a music video. DJs spin world-beat music while waiters serve salmon and scallop carpaccio and cornmeal-crusted calamari to scantily dressed hipsters.

Local professionals unbutton their shirt collars and gossip over beers at **Nowhere Bar** (✉*Plaza Bonita, Blvd. Marina* ☎*624/143–4493*). Two-for-one drinks are a draw, as is the large dance floor. Sushi and tacos are served from adjacent businesses, and bartenders hand out baskets of popcorn to keep the thirst level high.

Nearby, facing Boulevard Marina and the boats in the water, the aptly named **Margaritaville** (✉*Blvd. Marina* ☎*624/143–0010*) serves frozen margaritas in fishbowl-size glasses at outdoor tables.

WHERE IT'S AT

You may have to run a gantlet of servers waving menus in your face, but the sidewalk bars along the marina between Plaza Bonita and Puerto Paraíso are great places to hang out at happy hour.

If you get an outdoor table at **Sancho Panza Wine Bistro & Jazz Club** (✉*In the eastern end of Tesoro Hotel, Blvd. Marina* ☎*624/143–3212*) you can sip imported wines served by the glass while listening to live Latin bands.

★ **El Squid Roe** (✉*Av. Cárdenas* ☎*624/143–1269*) is packed with young foreigners who work in the local tourist industry and know how to party. Anyone over 18 who loves to dance should check it out.

Las Varitas (✉*About 1 block north of entrance to ME Cabos Hotel by Meliá, on Calle Gomez behind Puerto Paraíso* ☎*624/143–9999*) is a branch of a La Paz rock club favored by young Mexicans.

SHOPPING

★ Boulevard Marina and the side streets between the waterfront and the main plaza are filled with small shops. At the crafts market in the marina you can pose for a photo with an iguana, plan a ride in a glass-bottom boat, or browse through stalls packed with blankets, sombreros, and pottery. Homeowners and restaurateurs from throughout the area shop for furnishings, dishes, and glassware at **Artesanos** (✉*Hwy. 1, Km 4* ☎*624/143–3850*).

★ **El Callejón** (✉*Guerrero between Av. Cárdenas and Madero* ☎*624/143–1139*) has multiple showrooms with gorgeous furniture, lamps, dishes, and pottery.

Cartes (✉*Plaza Bonita, Blvd. Marina* ☎*624/143–1770*) sells handpainted pottery and tableware, pewter frames, handblown glass, and carved furniture. **Dos Lunas** (✉*Plaza Bonita, Blvd. Marina* ☎*624/143–1969* ✉*Puerto Paraíso, Blvd. Marina* ☎*624/143–1969*) is full of trendy, colorful sportswear and straw hats. **Galería Gatemelatta** (✉*Calle Gómez Farias, road to Hotel Hacienda* ☎*624/143–1166*) specializes in colonial furniture and antiques. At **Golden Cactus Gallery** (✉*Calle Guerrero at Madero* ☎*624/143–6399*), owner Marilyn Hurst exhibits paintings and sculptures by local artists. Need a new bathing suit? Check out **H2O de los Cabos** (✉*Av. Madero at Guerrero* ☎*624/143–1219*).

The walk-in humidor at **J&J Casa de los Habanos** (✉*Av. Madero, between Blvd. Marina and Guerrero* ☎*624/143–6160*) is stocked with pricey cigars. The shop also sells expensive tequilas. **Magic of the Moon** (✉*Hidalgo near Blvd. Marina* ☎*624/143–3161*) has handmade women's sundresses, skirts, and lingerie. **Necri** (✉*Blvd. Marina between Av. Madero and Ocampo* ☎*624/143–0283*) sells folk art and furnishings. The palatial entrance of **Puerto Paraíso** (✉*Av. Cárdenas* ☎*624/143–0000*) leads into a three-story marble-and-glass-enclosed mall. Consider visiting Galeria de Kaki Bassi, which has works by one of Baja's leading painters. **Faces of Mexico** (✉ *Cárdenas beside Mar de Cortés hotel* ☎ *624/143–2634*) has masks from Oaxaca and Guerrero.

> **DIVE IN!**
>
> One of the area's diving pioneers was none other than Jacques Cousteau, who explored the Sand Falls. Only 150 feet off Playa de Amor, this underwater sand river cascades off a steep drop-off into a deep abyss. It's just one of several excellent diving and snorkeling spots close to the Cabo San Lucas shore. There are also fantastic coral-reef sites in the Corridor and north of San José at Cabo Pulmo.

SPORTS & THE OUTDOORS

DIVING

The area's oldest and most complete dive shop is **Amigos del Mar** (✉ *Blvd. Marina* ✣ *Near harbor fishing docks* ☎ *624/143–0505, 800/344–3349 or 513/898–0547 in U.S.* 🌐 *www.amigosdelmar.com*). Their dive boats range from a 22-foot panga to a 25-foot runabout and 33- and 36-foot dive catamarans. The staff is courteous and knowledgeable, and all the guides speak English. **Cabo Acuadeportes** (✉ *Playa Médano* ☎ *624/143–0117*) offers dive trips (prices start at $40), rents snorkel gear, and can outfit you for just about every other water sport imaginable. **JT Water Sports** (✉ *Playa Médano* ☎ *624/144–4566 or 624/144–4066* 🌐 *www.jtwatersports.com*) rents all sorts of water- and land-sports equipment, including diving gear ($40), Windsurfers ($60 an hour), and parasails ($40 for roughly 10 minutes).

FISHING

More than 800 species of fish teem in the waters off Los Cabos. Fishing charters can most easily be arranged through hotels or directly from the sportfishing charter companies. They include a captain and crew, tackle, bait, fishing licenses, and drinks. Lunch is usually extra, unless you're quoted an "all-inclusive" charter price. Be sure to ask beforehand. Prices generally start at $375 per half day for a 28-foot cruiser that can carry two or three passengers. A larger cruiser with a head (bathroom) and sunbathing space starts at about $500—from here, the sky's the limit. Private yachts have air-conditioned staterooms, hot-water showers, full kitchens, and every other imaginable amenity. *Pangas* (small motorized skiffs) with a skipper rent for about $250 to $350 for six hours. They're most comfortable with one or two passengers. Companies typically try to help solo anglers hook up with a group to share a boat.

The **Gaviota Fleet** (✉ *Docked between Gates 2 and 3 across from Marina Fiesta Hotel* ☎ *624/145–8165 or 800/521–2281* 🌐 *www.loscabosguide.com/fishing/gaviotasportfishing.htm*) offers charter cruisers and pangas. **Minerva's** (✉ *Av. Madero between Blvd. Marina and Guerrero* ☎ *624/143–1282* 🌐 *www.minervas.com*) is a renowned tackle store. Some of the Corridor's priciest hotels choose the **Pisces Sportfishing Fleet** (✉ *Cabo Maritime Center, Blvd. Marina* ☎ *624/143–1288, 619/819–7983 in U.S.* 🌐 *www.piscessportfishing.com*) for their guests. The fleet includes the usual 31-foot Bertrams and extraordinary 50- to 70-foot

Hatteras cruisers with tuna towers and staterooms. The **Solmar Fleet's** (✉*Blvd. Marina, across from sportfishing dock* ☎*624/122–3440 or 800/344–3349* 🌐*www.solmar.com*) boats and tackle are always in good shape, and many regulars wouldn't fish with anyone else.

> **CAUTION**
>
> Remember that red flags warn of dangerous swimming conditions, yellow flags indicate that you should use caution, and green flags show safe areas.

HORSEBACK RIDING

Cantering down an isolated beach or up a desert trail is one of Baja's great pleasures (as long as the sun isn't beating down on your head). Rates are about $25 per person for a 1¼-hour ride. Horses are available for rent in front of the Playa Médano hotels; contact **Rancho Collins Horses** (☎*624/143–3652 or 624/127–0774*). **Red Rose Riding Stables** (✉*Carretera 1, Km 4* ☎*624/143–4826*) has horses for all levels of riders as well as impressive tack.

WHALE-WATCHING

The gray-whale migration doesn't end at Baja's Pacific lagoons. Plenty of whales of all sizes make it down to the warmer waters off Los Cabos. To watch whales from shore, go to the beach at the Solmar Suites, the Finesterra, or any Corridor hotel, or the lookout points along the Corridor highway. Several companies run trips (about $30–$50, depending on size of boat and length of tour) from Cabo San Lucas. **Cabo Expeditions** (✉*El Tesoro hotel, Blvd. Marina* ☎*624/143–2700*) offers snorkeling and whale-watching tours in rubber boats.

THE CORRIDOR

28 km (17 mi) between San José del Cabo and Cabo San Lucas.

Got a spare million or two in the bank? Cabo's real-estate agents will be delighted to show you around the exclusive developments along the Corridor's wild cliffs. Highway 1 dips into *arroyos* (riverbeds) and climbs onto a floodplain studded with boulders and cacti between San José del Cabo and Cabo San Lucas. This stretch of desert terrain has long been the haunt of the rich and famous. In the 1950s a few fishing lodges and remote resorts with private airstrips attracted adventurers and celebrities. Today the region has gated communities, resorts, posh hotels, and championship golf courses.

BEACHES

The Corridor's coastline edges the Sea of Cortez, with long, secluded stretches of sand, tranquil bays, golf fairways, and hotel beaches. Few areas are safe for swimming. Some hotels have man-made rocky breakwaters that create semi-safe swimming areas when the sea is calm. As a rule, the turnoffs for the beaches aren't well marked. Facilities are extremely limited; lifeguards and public restrooms are nonexistent. **TIP→ The four-lane Highway 1 has well-marked turnoffs for hotels, but it's not well lighted at night. Drivers tend to speed down hills, tempting vigilant traffic officers. Slow buses and trucks seem to appear from nowhere,**

and confused tourists switch lanes with abandon. Wait until you're safely parked to take in Sea of Cortez views.

★ **Bahía Chileno.** A private enclave with golf courses and residences is being developed at Bahía Chileno, roughly midway between San José and San Lucas. The beach skirts a small cove with aquamarine waters that are perfect for snorkeling. At this writing, the dirt access road and parking lot were open, but time will tell how the developers will handle public access—required by law—to the bay. ■TIP→**The turnoff for the beach is at Km 14.5 on Highway 1. Look for the signs whether driving west from San José or at Km 16 when driving east from Cabo San Lucas.**

Fodor's Choice ★ **Bahía Santa María.** Sometimes it feels like the vultures overhead are just waiting for your parched body to drop during the 10-minute walk from the parking lot to Bahía Santa María, a turquoise bay backed by cliffs and lined by a wide, sloping beach. Shade is nonexistent except in the shadows at the base of the cliffs. The bay, part of an underwater reserve, is a great place to snorkel: brightly colored fish swarm through chunks of white coral and golden sea fans. In high season there's usually someone renting snorkeling gear for $10 a day or selling sarongs, straw hats, and soft drinks. It's best to bring your own supplies, though, including lots of drinking water, snacks, and sunscreen. Snorkel and booze-cruise boats from San Lucas visit the bay in midmorning. Come in midafternoon for a Robinson Crusoe feel. A parking lot just off the highway is usually guarded; be sure to tip the guard. The bay is roughly 19 km (11 mi) west of San José and 13 km (8 mi) east of San Lucas. Turn off the highway's east side just north of the Twin Dolphin hotel, at the sign that reads ACCESSO A ZONA FEDERAL (access to federal zone). ✣ *19 km (11 mi) west of San José del Cabo, 13 km (8 mi) east of Cabo San Lucas.*

Playa Costa Azul. Cabo's best surfing beach runs 3 km (2 mi) south from San José's hotel zone along Highway 1. Its Zippers and La Roca breaks (the point where the wave crests and breaks) are world famous. Surfers gather here year-round, but most come in summer, when waves are largest. Several condo complexes line the beach, which is popular with joggers and walkers. Swimming isn't advised unless the waves are small and you're a good swimmer. The turnoff to this beach is sudden; it's on the highway's east side, at Zippers restaurant, which is on the sand by the surf breaks. ✣ *Just over ½ mi southwest of San José.*

Playa Palmilla. Check out the villas on the road to Playa Palmilla, the best swimming beach near San José. The entrance is from the side road through the ritzy Palmilla development; turn off before you reach the guardhouse at the star-studded One & Only Hotel Palmilla. There are signs, but they're not exactly large. The beach is protected by a rocky point, and the water is almost always calm. A few palapas on the sand provide shade; there are trash cans but no restrooms. Panga fishermen have long used this beach as a base, and they're still here, despite the swanky neighbors to the south. Guards patrol the beach fronting the hotel, discouraging nonguests from entering. ✣ *Entrance on Hwy. 1, at Km 27, 8 km (5 mi) southwest of San José del Cabo.*

WHERE TO EAT

$$$–$$$$ AMERICAN Fodor'sChoice ★ ✕ **C.** Famed Chicago chef Charlie Trotter is behind this restaurant in the One & Only Palmilla resort. Cylindrical aquariums separate the open kitchen from the dining room. An open-air bar has seating areas overlooking the rocky coast. A phenomenal wine list will entrance you for hours, if time permits. Trotter's menu emphasizes vegetables—salsify, wax beans, turnips—and pairs short ribs with parsnips and beets, or rabbit with a sweet chile sauce. There's an awesome chocolate soufflé for dessert. The menu changes daily. ✉*One & Only Palmilla, Hwy. 1, Km 27.5* ☎*624/146–7000* 🌐*www.oneandonlyresorts.com* ✍*Reservations essential* 💳*AE, MC, V* ⊗*No lunch.*

$$$–$$$$ AMERICAN ✕ **JC.** Everything's new here at Jacques Chretien's popular bistro. They've undergone a restaurant name change, from French Riviera to merely "JC," and also raised the roof, literally, and added a second floor. If you liked the French Riviera before, you'll love JC all the more, since their view of El Arco and Land's End Rocks is greatly improved. The restaurant is upstairs, and the lounge-bar remain on the ground floor. The menu is airy and eclectic: a spinach, egg, and bacon burrito could be breakfast, and lunch and dinner might consist of a gourmet pizza, Cajun chicken salad, or sushi. For a special treat, ask the restaurant to pack you a picnic meal that you can bring with you to the beach. Though the dinner menu changes every day, look for braised red snapper with Provençale gratin potatoes and zucchini in a basil reduction. Finish with melted chocolate cake with pear puree or strawberries napoleon. ✉*Hwy. 1, Km 6.3* ☎*624/104–3274* 🌐*www.frenchrivieraloscabos.com* 💳*MC, V.*

$$$–$$$$ ASIAN Fodor'sChoice ★ ✕ **Pitahayas.** In this elegant niche above the beach in the resort community Cabo del Sol, chef Volker Romeike blends Thai, Polynesian, and Chinese ingredients into artful, award-winning Asian fusion. He matches lobster with a vanilla-bean sauce, scallops with a sweet chile glaze, and the catch of the day with a Thai curry sauce. Soft jazz plays in the background, and the service is impeccable. The restaurant has been enlarged with a terrace and lounge, and now seats up to 500. With that, they claim to be the largest restaurant in Los Cabos. Pitahayas offers one of the largest wine selections in all of Mexico and, speaking of wine, the restaurant was awarded the Wine Spectator's Award of excellence for the second year in a row in 2007. Speaking of awards, the American Academy of Hospitality Sciences has given Pitahayas their 5 Star Diamond Award for nine consecutive years, from 1999 to 2007. Chef Romeike was also chosen one of the top chefs in the world in 2004. Dress to impress. ✉*Sheraton Hacienda del Mar, Hwy. 1, Km 10* ☎*624/145–8000* 🌐*www.pitahayas.com* 💳*AE, MC, V.*

$$–$$$$ ASIAN Fodor'sChoice ★ ✕ **Nick San–Palmilla.** The sky's the limit here at this out-of-this-world-inventive sushi den in the Tiendas de Palmilla shopping mall. Pair each of your selections with an exceptional wine or liquor, and let Chef Abel and Floor Manager Mauricio help you made the choices. Favorites include the lobster roll (with cilantro, mango, mustard, and roe) with a 2005 Chateau Montalena; lobster *sambal* (marinated in sake with soy, ginger, and garlic) with Kikusi sake; and the Hamachi belly cake and tuna tostadas with a Chilean Casas del Bosque Sauvignon Blanc.

✉ *Las Tiendas de Palmilla mall* ☎ *624/144–6262, 624/144–6263, or 624/144–6264* ▭ *MC, V.*

$$–$$$$ MEXICAN Fodor's Choice ★ ✕ **Trinidad Restaurant.** Owner Angel Carbajal named this restaurant after a woman very dear to his heart, and he has spotlighted a number of her unique recipes on the menu. There's a tostada called Huarache, another name for a Mexican sandal, that is *muy delicioso* and resembles a shoe only by name. There are also many chicken, beef, and seafood dishes spiced up with local ingredients like squash blossoms, chiles, and cheeses. ✉ *Las Tiendas de Palmilla mall* ☎ *624/144–6170* ▭ *MC, V.*

$$–$$$ ECLECTIC ✕ **7 Seas Restaurant & Bar.** It's soothing to sit in this restaurant, in the Cabo Surf Hotel, at the ocean's edge, and smell the sea breezes. Stop off after your morning surf session, to munch on *machaca con huevos* (eggs scrambled with shredded beef) with a fresh fruit smoothie for breakfast; or drop in after you've enjoyed surfing the evening "glass off" to dine on blue crab tostadas and tricolor shrimp ravioli. Your entertainment is simple a wondrous, natural view that never stops changing. ✉ *Cabo Surf Hotel, Km 28* ☎ *624/142–2676* 🌐 *7seasrestaurant.com* ▭ *MC, V.*

$$–$$$ ITALIAN Fodor's Choice ★ ✕ **Sunset Da Mona Lisa Italian Restaurant.** Cocktail tables along the cliffs have full-on views of El Arco, making this the best place to toast to the sunset and another beautiful day in Los Cabos before moving to the candlelit dining room. Or merely remain outside, and enjoy dining alfresco. Italian Chef Emanuele Olivero has paid his dues in Los Cabos, with time at La Dolce in San José, at C in the Palmilla, and also at Pitahayas, before bringing his ideas to full fruition here at the Mona Lisa. The restaurant's four seasonal menus all depend on the ingredients that are in season at that particular time. How about ravioli filled with pumpkin, or La Paz blue crab covered with a cinnamon white sauce? Or seared halibut with crunchy polenta sun-dried tomatoes and asparagus tempura? Or go all out with the Grand Mona Lisa Tasting Menu, and try just about everything on their extensive menu. The restaurant is not really in the Corridor, but not really in town either; just a couple of miles up the hill—a short and relatively inexpensive taxi ride, well worth the trip for a sunset cocktail and dinner. Make sure you appreciate their Mona Lisa tile artwork both close-up and standing back a distance—an interesting optic illusion ensues. ✉ *Carretera 1, Km 5.5* ☎ *624/145–8160* ✍ *Reservations essential* ▭ *MC, V* ⊗ *No lunch.*

$–$$ AMERICAN ✕ **Zippers.** Home to the surfing crowd and those who don't mind a bit of sand in their burgers, this casual *palapa*-roof restaurant is on Costa Azul beach, just south of San José. Come for the sea breezes, the delicious wafting smell of grilling lobster and tacos, and a sound track of surf tunes. Casual doesn't begin to describe the crowd, which can get downright raunchy. But hey, have fun, amigo, you've entered Los Cabos Surf Zone! There's no question that owner "Big Tony" feeds you well for your pesos. Half-pound burgers, slabs of prime rib, or steak and lobster for two at just $40, and you'll leave the beach a glutton, albeit a jolly one. Bring your young kids in the daytime; they'll enjoy running from the dining table to the sand between every couple of bites. Sporting events sometimes blare on the TV. ✉ *Hwy. 1, Km 18.5* ☎ *624/172–6162* ▭ *No credit cards.*

WHERE TO STAY

$$$$ **Cabo Surf Hotel.** Legendary and amateur surfers alike claim the prime break-view rooms in this small hotel on the cliffs above Playa Costa Azul. They mingle by the horizon swimming pool and in the cozy restaurant (which is a great place to enjoy a wonderful meal and stunning views), and they schedule their day's activities around the daily surf report. The hotel offers its own label of Cabo Surf Tequila, a surf school, and surf board rentals. Just recently, owner Mauricio Balderrama has even added the small Sea Spa, adjacent to the lobby, which offers massages developed for overworked surfers, among other types. Book early at this popular spot. **Pros:** Rooms are spacious enough for two wave-hounds to spread out their gear; some have French doors that open to the sea breezes. **Cons:** Some traffic noise, not really possible to walk anywhere off the grounds. ✉*Hwy. 1, Km. 28,* ☎*624/142–2666 or 858/964–5117 in U.S.* 🌐*www.cabosurfhotel.com* *22 rooms* *In-room: Kitchen (some), Internet. In-hotel: Restaurant, bar, pool, public Wi-Fi, no elevator* *MC, V* *EP.*

$$$$ **Casa del Mar Beach, Golf & Spa Resort.** It's all about comfort and privacy at this hacienda-style hotel. An ancient hand-carved door leads into the courtyard-lobby, and stairways curve up to the rooms, spa, and library. Casa del Mar's rooms and Beach Club have just undergone a major renovation. A few steps above the main bedroom, guest quarters have bathrooms with whirlpool bathtubs. Streams, fountains, and gardens lead around the pool to a wide stretch of beach and the restaurant of the Beach Club. **Pros:** Near several of Los Cabos' top courses, on a nice stretch of beach. **Cons:** Car ride into Cabo takes at least 20 minutes if you're looking for nightlife. ✉*Carretera 1, Km. 19.5,* ☎*624/145–7700, 888/227–9621 in U.S.* 🌐*www.casadelmarmexico.com* *31 suites* *In-room: Safe, Wi-Fi, CD. In-hotel: 2 restaurants, Beach Club, room service, bars, tennis courts, pools, gym, spa, beachfront, concierge, laundry service* *AE, MC, V* *EP.*

$$$$ Fodor's Choice ★ **Esperanza.** It's an utterly polished inn with a focus on exquisite privacy. Some suites are right on a secluded beach; and even the smallest is still a heavyweight at 925 square feet. Villas take the luxe even further with private pools and butler service. The brand new Penthouse Suite (as of Dec. 2007) offers one of the most stunning views of El Arco imaginable. What else can we say but: Wow! Californian and Mexican recipes get a Baja twist in the restaurant. New executive chef, new menu. At the spa, they've expanded the comfort level and doubled the size, adding 12 individual and two couples treatment cabins, with small private pools and outdoor showers. Relax with a stone massage or bask in a steam cave. An on-site art gallery showcases local painters and sculptors. **Pros:** All suites have extra touches like handcrafted furnishings, Frette linens, and dual-head showers. **Cons:** Lots of stairs, not a good beach for swimming. ✉*Carretera 1, Km 3.5,* ☎*624/145–6400, 866/311–2226 in U.S.* 🌐*www.esperanzaresort.com* *57 suites* *In-room: Safe, DVD, Wi-Fi. In-hotel: 3 restaurants, pool, gym, spa, beachfront, concierge, laundry service, no elevator* *AE, MC, V* *EP.*

$$$$ Fodor's Choice ★ **Marquis Los Cabos.** Stunning architecture, a property-wide art collection of unique pieces, noticeable attention to detail, and loads of

Where to Eat & Stay Along the Corridor

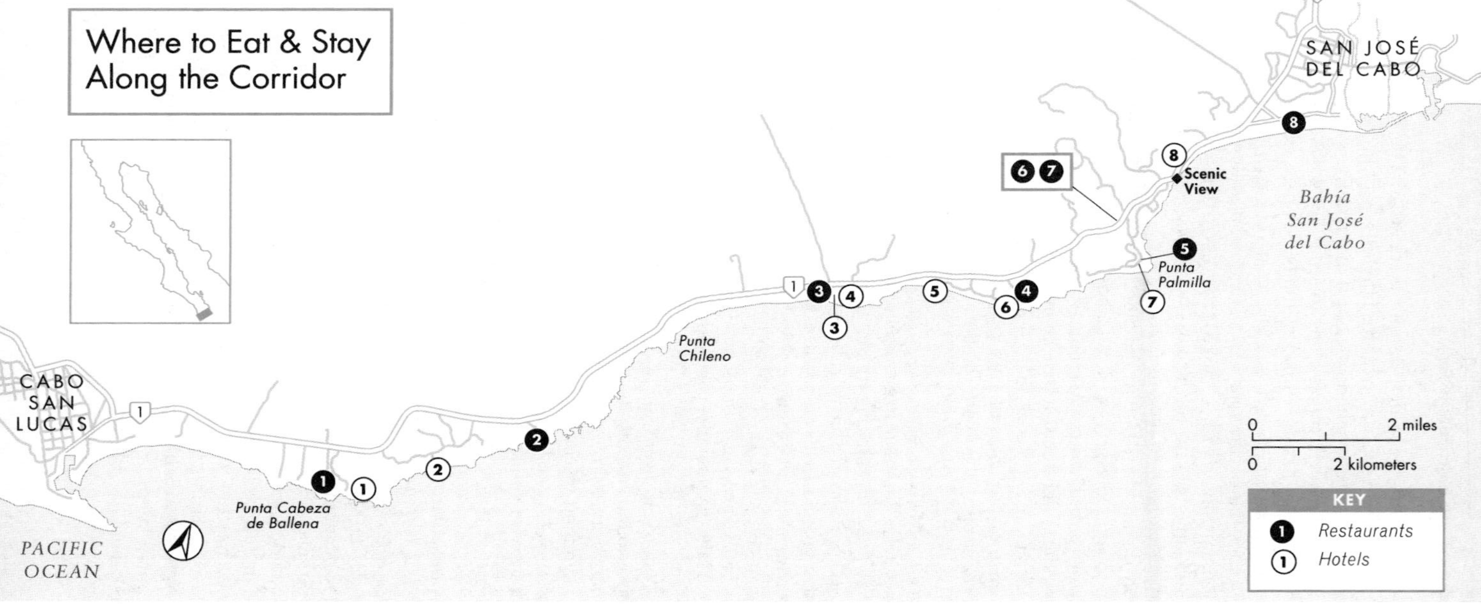

Restaurants	
C	4
JC	3
Nick San-Palmilla	6
Pitahayas	2
7 Seas Restaurant & Bar	8
Sunset Da Mona Lisa Italian Restaurant	1
Trinidad Restaurant	7
Zippers	5

Hotels	
Cabo Surf Hotel	8
Casa del Mar Beach, Golf & Spa Resort	3
Esperanza	1
Fiesta Americana Grand Los Cabos	2
Marquis Los Cabos	5
One&Only Palmilla	7
Las Ventanas al Paraíso	4
Westin Resort & Spa, Los Cabos	6

luxurious touches make the Marquis a standout. The 28 casitas, at 1,600 square feet each, are great for families—with private pools and refrigerators—and are right on the beach. A serpentine swimming pool, the length of the hotel, curves along the edge of the sand. Word is out that the Marquis has developed a number of new and unique custom-tailored packages such an Elopement Package, which includes, among other things, the rental of a Mexican wedding dress and tux, and a Hummer hung with a "Just Married" sign that whisks the newly-married couple back to the airport. Other packages include the Surf & Turf, essentially rounds of golf, cigars, and surfing lessons; and multiday digital photography and painting trips that allow visitors to delve into unique aspects of Los Cabos. **Pros:** Food is excellent and reasonably priced, suites have Bulgari toiletries, reversible mattresses (hard or soft), high-speed Internet connections, and original art. **Cons:** The Marquis recommends that you book packages online, and well in advance of the dates of your planned visit, which can be stifling if you're more of a go-with-the-flow type of person. ✉ *Carretera 1, Km. 21.5,* ☎ *624/144–2000, 877/238–9399 in U.S.* 🌐 *www.marquisloscabos.com* *209 suites, 28 casitas* *In-room: Safe, dial-up, Wi-Fi, refrigerator. In-hotel: 3 restaurants, bar, pool, gym, spa, beachfront, executive floor, no-smoking rooms* *AE, MC, V* *CP.*

$$$$ FodorsChoice ★ **One&Only Palmilla.** This world-class resort has a Charlie Trotter restaurant, a Jack Nicklaus golf course, and a top spa that offers such special treatments as an exclusive O&O Bastien Gonzalez pedicure. The hotel also employs a Director of Celebrations in order to help guests further enjoy their stay. Two pools seem to flow over low cliffs into the sea. Hand-painted tiles edge stairways leading to rooms and suites, where beds are overloaded with pillows, bathtubs are deep, and the water from the shower truly rains down upon you. Your quarters also have Bose sound systems, flat-screen TVs, and wireless Internet access. Some patios and terraces have daybeds and straight-on sea views. **Pros:** From beginning to end, Palmilla has already thought of everything, even offering "Air to Go" meals: quality, custom- made box lunches to take along with you on the flight home. **Cons:** Beach isn't really swimmable. ✉ *Carretera 1, Km. 27.5,* ☎ *624/146–7000, 800/637–2226 in U.S.* 🌐 *www.oneandonlyresorts.com* *61 rooms, 91 junior suites, 20 1-bedroom suites* *In-room: Safe, DVD, dial-up, Wi-Fi, refrigerator. In-hotel: 2 restaurants, bars, golf course, tennis courts, pools, gym, spa, beachfront, water sports, concierge, laundry service, no-smoking rooms* *AE, MC, V* *EP.*

$$$$ FodorsChoice ★ **Las Ventanas al Paraíso.** Despite the high room rates at this ultraprivate, ultraluxe hotel, it's often hard to get a reservation. Late last year it was announced that Las Ventanas had earned the prestigious AAA Five Diamond Award for the sixth consecutive year; this is the only Los Cabos destination to be acclaimed as such. Guests luxuriate in suites that have hot tubs, fireplaces, and telescopes for viewing whales or stars. Newer hotels have attempted to copy such Ventanas touches as handcrafted lamps and doors, inlaid stone floors, and tequila service, but the original is still the best. A knowledgeable butler is assigned to each suite. The spa treatments reflect the latest trends: the three spa

suites (really more like individual villas) have private spa butlers and separate in-suite treatment rooms. **Pros:** Service is sublime, restaurants are outstanding. **Cons:** There's a minimum night stay for weekends depending on the season, see their Web site for details. ✉ *Carretera 1, Km 19.5,* ☎ *624/144–2800, 888/767–3966 in U.S.* 🌐 *www.lasventanas.com* *68 suites, 3 spa suites* *In-room: Safe, VCR, dial-up, refrigerator. In-hotel: 3 restaurants, room service, bar, tennis courts, pools, gym, spa, beachfront, water sports, laundry service, no-smoking rooms, some pets allowed, no elevator* *AE, MC, V* *EP, FAP, MAP.*

WORD OF MOUTH

"I'd sell my mother to be able to go back to Las Ventanas. OK, not really. But my husband and I honeymooned here, and it was the best vacation we've ever been on. We're a little afraid now that we'll never enjoy another vacation again, unless it's at Las Ventanas." –Kate

$$$$ ★ **Westin Resort & Spa, Los Cabos.** The architecturally astounding Westin is a magnificent conglomeration of colors, shapes, and views. The rooms, some set high above a man-made beach, are among the best in this price range and have Westin's trademark "Heavenly Beds," with cushy pillows and comforters. Villas have full kitchens and whirlpool tubs that face the sea. **Pros:** The hotel has so many amenities, including a fabulous spa and gym, you may never need to leave the grounds. **Cons:** It's a trek from the parking lot and lobby to the rooms and pools. ✉ *Hwy. 1, Km 22.5,* ☎ *624/142–9000, 888/625–5144 in U.S.* 🌐 *www.starwood.com/westin* *243 rooms* *In-room: Safe, refrigerator (some). In-hotel: 5 restaurants, room service, 4 bars, 2 tennis courts, 7 pools, gym, spa, beachfront, concierge, children's programs (ages 5–12), laundry service, no-smoking rooms* *AE, MC, V* *EP.*

$$$ **Fiesta Americana Grand Los Cabos.** It's all about the grapes here at the Grand—its newest addition is the SOMMA Wine Spa, a vibrant green center with 15 treatment cabins, opened in late 2007. We've heard of chocolate baths and sugar scrubs, but Vino Therapy? Don't worry so much about the varietal or the bouquet, simply be pampered by your wine wrap or Chardonnay-infused bubble bath. Also available in SOMMA are cutting-edge Kinesis exercise equipment. A "How to Spa" booklet in the rooms provides initial education for those spa-challenged men still a intimidated by the spa experience. Down on the beach, is the Peninsula Restaurant (called "barefoot elegance") where you check your shoes with the shoe valet, stomp grapes and receive a foot massage. Then dine, of course, on Pacific-Rim cuisine. ✉ *Hwy. 1, Km 10.3, Cabo del Sol, 23400* ☎ *624/145–6200, 800/345–5094, or 800/343–7821* 🌐 *www.fiestamericanagrand.com* *250 rooms* *In-room: Refrigerators, safe, Wi-Fi. In-hotel: 3 restaurants, 3 bars, 5 pools, 2 golf courses, spa, beachfront, elevator, children's programs, executive floor, no pets, no-smoking rooms* *AE, DC, MC, V* *EP.*

SPORTS & THE OUTDOORS

ATV TOURS

Desert Park (✉ *Cabo Real* ✣ *Across from Meliá Cabo Real hotel, Corridor* ☎ *624/144–0127* 🌐 *www.desertpark.net*) leads ATV tours through

Continued on page 519

19
1
Cabo
San Lucas
THE
CORRIDOR
San José
del Cabo
Los Cabos
International
Airport
Villa
del Arco
Pacifica Holistic
Retreat & Spa
Playa
Grande
Esperanza
Fiesta
Americana
Grand
Las Ventanas
al Paraíso
Marquis Los
Cabos
Cabo Surf
Hotel
One&Only
Pamilla
PACIFIC OCEAN

BAJA REJUVENATION

A spa vacation—or even a single treatment—is the perfect way to kick-start a healthier lifestyle, slow a hectic routine, or simply indulge in a little pampering. by Larry Dunmire

There are more treatment choices than ever before. Los Cabos, the land of sybaritic pleasures, has no shortage of resorts where you can be smeared with rich mud, plunge into a series of hot and cold baths, or simply enjoy a traditional facial.

Although spas once drew upon European traditions, they now offer treatments from around the globe: Japanese shiatsu, Indonesian jasmine-oil rubdowns, deep-tissue Thai massage, and the *temazcal*, or Maya sweat-lodge experience. Often you can follow an herbal wrap or mud bath with yoga or tension-relieving classes. The small Sea Spa at the Cabo Surf Hotel even offers a Surfer's Massage for those who've overdone themselves in the waves.

Self care is also a growing trend, with custom prescriptions for upkeep between facials and massages and advice on holistic approaches to living to help keep you healthy and sane between spa visits.

All Los Cabos resort spas have packages—whether for a day of beauty or for a long weekend of treatments. Most spas are also open to nonguests of the resorts, and some properties allow you to use the fitness facilities if you've booked a spa treatment. Always call ahead.

RESORT NAME	BODY TREATMENTS	FACIALS	SEASIDE/ SEAVIEW TREATMENTS	TREATMENTS FOR TWO	FITNESS FACILITIES DAY PASS	SAUNA	STEAM ROOM
Cabo Surf Hotel	$65–$330	$95–$135	yes	yes	no	yes	no
Esperanza	$155–$310	$180–$290	yes	yes	no	no	yes
Fiesta Americana Grand	$130–$250	$145–$175	yes	yes	yes	yes	yes
Marquis Los Cabos	$125–$195	$115–$175	yes	yes	$15	yes	yes
One&Only Palmilla	$140–$230	$140–$220	yes	yes	yes*	yes	yes
Pacifica Holistic Retreat & Spa	$100–$170	$70–$300	yes	yes	yes	yes	yes
Playa Grande Resort	$45–$260	$130–$175	yes	yes	no	no	yes
Las Ventanas al Paraíso	$75–$400	$150–$235	yes	yes	yes	yes	yes
Villa del Arco	$55–$259	$95–$125	no	yes	$10	yes	yes

*If you book 60 minutes of treatments, use of facilities is complimentary. If not, cost is $75.

(opposite page) Esperanza Resort; (above) One&Only Palmilla

TOP SPOTS

Esperanza

Luxury continues to soar to great heights at this exclusive 17-acre resort between the towns of Cabo San Lucas and San José del Cabo where the spa doubled its size in 2007. At check in where, you're presented with an *agua fresca*, a healthy drink made with papaya or mango, or other fruits and herbs.

Before your treatment, enjoy the Pasaje de Agua (water passage) therapy, which includes steam caves and a waterfall. Treatments incorporate local ingredients, tropical fruits, and ocean-based products. Look for such pampering as the papaya-mango body polish, the grated coconut and lime exfoliation, and the Corona beer facial. Two free yoga classes at are offered 9:00 and 10:15 each morning.

BODY TREATMENTS. **Massage:** Agua, hot stone, essential oil (stroke techniques vary). **Exfoliation:** Body polish, salt glow. **Wraps/baths:** Aloe wrap, floral bath, herbal bath, mud bath, thalassotherapy. **Other:** Outdoor shower, steam room, warm soaking pool, waterfall rinse.

BEAUTY TREATMENTS. Facials, hair and scalp conditioning, manicure, pedicure.

PRICES. Body Treatments: $155–$310. Facials: $180–$290. Hair/Scalp Conditioning: $70. Manicure/Pedicure: $70–$120.

Carretera 1, Km 3.5. Tel. 624/145–8641. www.esperanzaresort.com. ***Parking:*** *Valet (free, but please tip). AE, MC, V.*

Marquis Los Cabos

Known as the "Resort for All Senses," the Marquis is the only member of Leading Spas of the World in Los Cabos. You'll enjoy the open-air hot tubs that face the Cape's blue sky and overlook the Sea of Cortez. Lounge chairs draped with thick towels tempt you to linger by the hot tubs. Noteworthy is the Quetzalcoatl Oxygenating Experience: a eucalyptus foot bath, marine-salt exfoliation, herbal purification bath, and light massage with cucumber-milk lotion.

A hallway connects the spa with the Marquis' fitness center with its sky-high ceiling and wall-to-wall windows looking out to the pool slithering above the sand along the ocean.

BODY TREATMENTS. **Massage:** Ayurvedic, deep tissue, essential oil, hot stone, reflexology, shiatsu, Thai. **Exfoliation:** salt glow. **Wraps/baths:** herbal bath, mud wrap, thalassotherapy. **Other:** Ayurvedic treatments, hot tub, sauna, steam room.

BEAUTY TREATMENTS. Facials, manicure, pedicure, waxing.

PRICES. Body Treatments: $125–$195. Facials: $115–$175. Manicure/Pedicure: $20–$80. Waxing: $19–$79.

Carretera 1, Km 21.5. Tel. 624/144–0906. www.marquisloscabos.com. ***Parking:*** *Valet (free, but please tip). AE, MC, V.*

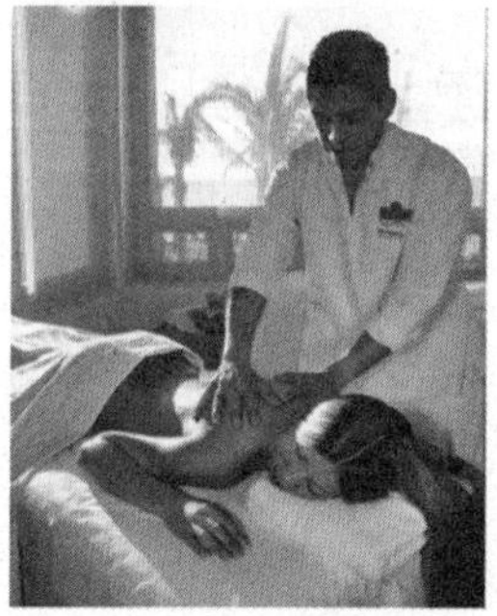

One&Only Palmilla

Treatment villas are tucked behind white stucco walls, ensuring privacy. Therapists lead you through a locked gate into peaceful palm-filled gardens with a bubbling hot tub and a day bed covered with plump pillows.

Treatments blend Mexican, Asian, and other global accents; using cactus, lime, and a variety of Mexican spices. Each session begins with a Floral Footbath—a symbolic Balinese ritual, which represents a cleansing of life's tensions to prepare you for total relaxation. One signature treatment is the Aztec Aromatic Ritual, a spicy body wrap that uses an ancient village recipe of clove, ginger, and cinnamon.

BODY TREATMENTS. **Massage:** Balinese, deep tissue, essential oil, hot stone, pregnancy, reflexology, sports, Swedish, Thai, watsu. **Exfoliation:** Body polish, dry brush, salt glow. **Wraps/baths:** Floral bath, herbal wrap, milk bath. **Other:** Aromatherapy, anticellulite treatments, colon therapy, hot- and warm-water pools, sauna, steam room.

BEAUTY TREATMENTS. Anti-aging treatments, facials, hair/scalp conditioning, hair cutting/styling, makeup, manicure, pedicure, peels, waxing.

PRICES. Body Treatments: $140–$320. Anti-Aging/Facials/Peels: $140–$220. Hair: $40–$90. Makeup: $60–$85. Manicure/Pedicure: $25–$120. Waxing: $20–$80.
Carretera 1, Km 7. S. Tel. 624/146-7000. *www.oneandonlypalmilla.com.* ***Parking:*** *Valet (free, but please tip).* *AE, MC, V.*

Las Ventanas al Paraíso

The resort's bi-level spa is surrounded by serene cactus gardens and has both indoor and outdoor facilities. It's known for innovative treatments—skin resurfacing facials, nopal anticellulite and detox wrap, crystal healing massages, and raindrop therapy.

Some of the eight treatment rooms have private patios; massages are available in a pavilion by the sea; and body wraps and massages are also performed on the hotel's 55-foot yacht.

BODY TREATMENTS. **Massage:** Ayurvedic, deep-tissue, hot stone, reflexology, Reiki, shiatsu, shirodhara, sports, Swedish. **Exfoliation:** Body polish, dry brush, loofah scrub, salt glow. **Wraps/baths:** Herbal wrap, milk bath, mud wrap. **Other:** Acupuncture, anticellulite treatments, aromatherapy, Ayurvedic treatments, crystal therapy, hydrotherapy pool, sauna, steam room.

BEAUTY TREATMENTS. Facials, hair cutting/styling, manicure, pedicure, waxing.

PRICES. Body Treatments: $110–$225. Facials: $115–$175. Hair: $35–$45. Manicure/Pedicure: $35–$60. Waxing: $30–$100.

Carretera 1, Km 19.5. Tel. 624/144-0300. *www.lasventanas.com.* ***Parking:*** *Valet (free, but please tip).* *AE, MC, V.*

Villa del Arco

The Desert Spa on the beach in Los Cabos is also the area's largest, with 17 treatment rooms and two suites comfortably spread through three airy, sunny floors; the entire complex totals 31,000 square feet. With Los Cabos' largest and spacious hydrotherapy "wet" circuit, improve your circulation with dips in hot tubs followed by plunges in cold. The spa has the biggest fitness center in Cabo, and the beauty salon provides a killer view of the sea.

Treatments tend toward the local and authentic, and utilize fruits, plants, and herbs that can be found in the area. Indulge in an organic succulent cactus facial or an after-sun soothing mint and eucalipto treat.

BODY TREATMENTS. **Massage:** Deep tissue, reflexology, aromatherapy, couples. **Exfoliation:** Body scrub, fruit polish. **Wraps/baths:** Tequila wrap, fruit wrap, melon wrap, mineral bath. **Other:** Facials, hot-stone treatments, gentlemen's therapies.

BEAUTY TREATMENTS. Hair/scalp conditioning, hair cutting/styling, manicure, pedicure, waxing.

PRICES. Body Treatments: $55–$259. Facials: $95–$125. Manicure/Pedicure: $42–$53.

Camino Viejo a San José, Km 0.5. Tel. 624/145–7000. www.villadelarcoloscabos.com. ***Parking:*** *Valet (free, but please tip). MC, V.*

Fiesta Americana Grand

Another facility opened under a unique concept is the Fiesta Americana Grand's SOMMA Wine Spa, which uses grapes from the up-and-coming Valle de Guadalupe wine region just outside of Ensenada. It's an unusual experience blended with classical treatments, focusing on the calming, cosmetic, and antioxidant properties of grapes and wine, or vinotherapy.

The Grand's spa is the only one of its kind in Mexico, with only six others throughout the entire world. It towers high above the Sea of Cortez with 15 treatment rooms, both indoor and open-air, and offers more than 30 facial and body treatments from a Champagne Mud Wrap to a Le Vine Massage.

BODY TREATMENTS. **Massage:** Classic, sports, aromatherapy, hot stone, relaxing, foot. **Exfoliation:** Salt body scrub. **Wraps/baths:** Mud wrap, copper wrap, wine wrap, volcanic ash wrap, honey and fruit wrap, seaweed wrap, green coffee wrap, water lily wrap. **Other:** Facials, cellulite firming.

BEAUTY TREATMENTS. Hair/scalp conditioning, hair cutting/styling, manicure, pedicure, waxing.

PRICES. Body Treatments: $130–$250. Facials: $145–$175.

Carretera 1, Km 10.3. Tel. 624/145–6200, or 800/FIESTA. www.fiestaamericanagrand.com. ***Parking:*** *Valet and self parking. MC, V.*

HONORABLE MENTIONS

Pacifica Holistic Retreat & Spa

This small, tranquil hotel on the Pacific side of Cabo is an adults-only property, filled with feng shui design, immaculately kept cactus gardens, and water, water, everywhere. The treatments at their Aromian Spa run the gamut from crystal reiki healing to a yogurt and violet exfoliation, and even an intriguing temazcal (Maya sweat lodge) experience.

BODY TREATMENTS. **Massage:** Hot stone, Swedish, sports, deep tissue, shiatsu, four hands, couples, cranial and foot, personalized, expectant mother, ayurveda abhyanga, shirobyhanga, Thai, back and neck, reflexology, aromatherapy. **Exfoliation:** Honey sugar glow, green tea scrub, damiana/rosemary scrub, coconut/mango scrub, yogurt/violet scrub, chocolate/hazelnut scrub, red-wine scrub, bamboo/alfalfa scrub, lavender scrub, lime scrub, sea-salt scrub. **Wraps/ baths:** Bamboo/alfalfa/aloe/chamomile wrap, detox wrap, Dead Sea mud wrap, revitalizing wrap. **Other:** Shirodhara ritual, facials, firming treatment, antioxidant treatment, Vichy shower, temazcal.

BEAUTY TREATMENTS. Hair/scalp conditioning, hair cutting/styling, manicure, pedicure, waxing.

PRICES. Body Treatments: $130-$250. Facials: $145-$175. Hair: $25-$110. Manicure/ Pedicure: $30-$58. Waxing: $20-$70.

Cabo Pacifica s/n Tel. 624/143–9696. www.pueblobonitopacifica.com. ***Parking:*** *Valet, (free, but please tip). AC, MC, V.*

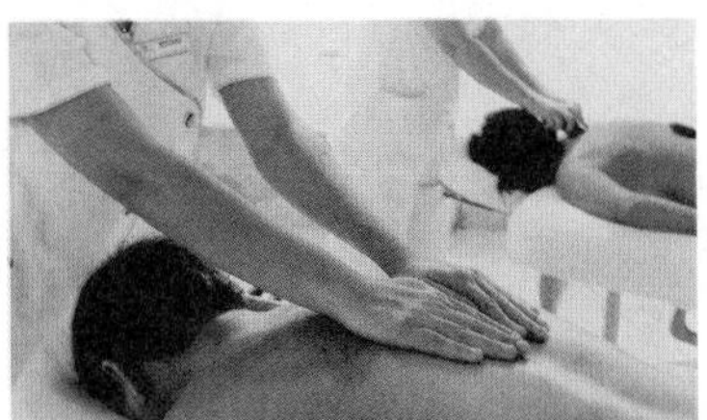

Playa Grande Resort

The meaning of the word thalassotherapy comes from the practice of using seawater baths and seaweed-based treatments for preventive and curative purposes. Playa Grande's spa is said to be the finest thalasso center in North America. They often use combinations of seaweed and seawater and the minerals in both will rejuvenate and renew your skin like you've never experienced.

BODY TREATMENTS. **Massage:** Hot stone, shiatsu, Swedish, four hands, foot reflexology, **Exfoliation:** Honey body polish, sea-salt glow, cinnamon-sugar scrub, pomegranate/cranapple scrub. **Wraps/baths:** Thalassotherapy bath, seaweed bath, hydrotheraphy bath, seaweed body mask, honey/almond/ buttermilk wrap. **Other:** Facials, temazcal, Vichy shower, masks.

BEAUTY TREATMENTS. Hair/scalp conditioning, hair cutting/styling, manicure, pedicure, paraffin, waxing, eyebrow shaping, oxygen bar.

PRICES. Body Treatments: $175-250. Facials: $130-175. Hair: $30-$190. Manicure/Pedicure: $30-$60. Waxing: $20-$60.

Avenida Playa Grande No. 1, Playa Solmar Tel. 624/145–7575 www. playagranderesort.com ***Parking:*** *Valet (free, but please tip). MC, V.*

ALSO WORTH NOTING

The small, boutique Cabo Surf Hotel's Sea Spa caters to its athletic guests with, among others, a Surfer's Sports Package, A Day at the Beach massage and facial, and a Bride's Spa Day. Playa Acapulquito Km 28, San Jose del Cabo Tel. 624/142–2676. www.seaspacabo.com.

GLOSSARY

acupuncture. Painless Chinese medicine during which needles are inserted into key spots on the body to restore the flow of *qi* and allow the body to heal itself.

aromatherapy. Massage and other treatments that use plant-derived essential oils intended to relax the skin's connective tissues and stimulate the flow of lymph fluid.

Ayurveda. An Indian philosophy that uses oils, massage, herbs, and diet and lifestyle modification to restore perfect balance to a body.

body brushing. Dry brushing of the skin to remove dead cells and stimulate circulation.

body polish. Use of scrubs, loofahs, and other exfoliants to remove dead skin cells.

hot-stone massage. Massage using smooth stones heated in water and applied to the skin with pressure or strokes or simply rested on the body.

hydrotherapy. Underwater massage, which alternates hot and cold showers, and other water-oriented treatments.

reflexology. Pressure points massage usually focused on the feet, hands, and head.

Reiki. A Japanese healing method involving the manipulation of universal life energy, with the "laying on" of hands said to result in spiritual balancing. It's intended to relieve acute emotional and physical conditions. Also called radiance technique.

salt glow. Rubbing the body with coarse salt to remove dead skin.

shiatsu. Japanese massage that uses pressure applied with fingers, hands, elbows, and feet.

shirodhara. Ayurvedic massage in which warm herbalized oil is trickled onto the center of the forehead, then gently rubbed into the hair and scalp.

sports massage. A deep-tissue massage to relieve muscle tension and residual pain from workouts.

Swedish massage. Stroking, kneading, and tapping to relax muscles. It was devised at the University of Stockholm in the 19th century by Per Henrik Ling.

Swiss shower. A multijet bath that alternates hot and cold water, often used after mud wraps and other body treatments.

temazcal. Maya meditation in a sauna heated with volcanic rocks.

Thai massage. Deep-tissue massage and passive stretching to ease stiff, tense, or short muscles.

thalassotherapy. Sea-water-based treatments that incorporate seaweed, and algae.

Vichy shower. Treatment in which a person lies on a cushioned, waterproof mat and is showered by overhead water jets.

Watsu. A blend of shiatsu and deep-tissue massage with gentle stretches—all conducted in a warm pool.

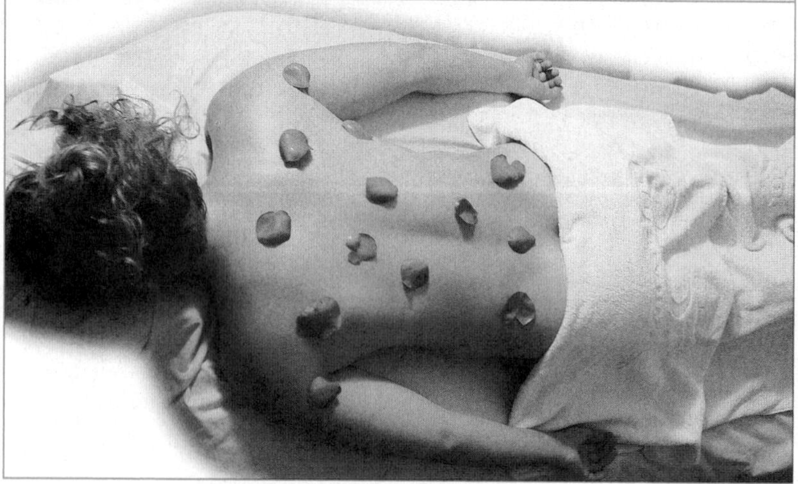

the desert arroyos and canyons on the inland side of the Cabo Real development. Fees start at $50 per person.

FISHING

Some Corridor hotels have fishing fleets anchored at the Cabo San Lucas Marina; all can set up fishing trips. **Victor's Sport Fishing** (☎*624/122–1092*) has a fleet of pangas on the Palmilla resort's beach. Rates start at $180.

GOLF

Los Cabos has become one of the world's top golf destinations, with championship courses that combine lush greens and desert terrain. Greens fees are exorbitant—more than $350 in winter and $220 in summer. **Cabo del Sol** (☎*624/145–8200 or 800/386–2405* ⊕*www.cabodelsol.com*) has an 18-hole Jack Nicklaus course and an 18-hole Tom Weiskopf course. The Robert Trent Jones Jr.–designed **Cabo Real Golf Club** (✉*Meliá Cabo Real hotel* ☎*624/144–0040, 877/795–8727 in U.S.*) has 18 holes on mountainous inland and flat oceanfront terrain.

★ Among the most spectacular golf courses is the 27-hole Jack Nicklaus–designed course at the **One & Only Palmilla Golf Course** (✉*Carretera 1, Km 27.5* ☎*624/146–7000, 954/809–2726 in U.S.*).

HORSEBACK RIDING

★ The **Cuadra San Francisco Equestrian Center** (✉*Carretera 1, Km 19.5, across from Casa del Mar and Las Ventanas al Paraíso hotels* ☎*624/144–0160* ⊕*www.loscaboshorses.com*) offers lessons and trail rides. Treks through back canyons are more interesting than those along the beach, and the horses and guides are both excellent. Reserve at least a day in advance and request an English-speaking guide, and note that you must query them for rates.

SAN JOSÉ DEL CABO

195 km (121 mi) south of La Paz, 28 km (17 mi) northeast of Cabo San Lucas.

San José's downtown is lovely, with adobe houses and jacaranda trees. Entrepreneurs have converted old homes into stylish restaurants and shops, and the government has enlarged the main plaza. An ambitious multiyear beautification process is under way. A 9-hole golf course and residential community are south of Centro (town center); farther south the ever-expanding Zona Hotelera (hotel zone) faces a long beach on the Sea of Cortez. Despite the development—and weekday traffic jams—San José is peaceful. If you want exciting nightlife and rowdy beaches, stay in Cabo San Lucas.

GETTING HERE & AROUND

Aeropuerto Internacional Los Cabos is 1 km (½ mi) west of the Transpeninsular Highway (Hwy. 1), 13 km (8 mi) north of San José del Cabo. Fares from the airport to hotels in Los Cabos are expensive. The least expensive transport is by shuttle buses that stop at various hotels along the route; fares run $12 to $25 per person. SuburBaja can provide private transport for $60 between San José del Cabo and Cabo San Lucas. Taxi fares are exorbitant in Los Cabos, and the taxi union is very powerful. The fare between Cabo San Lucas and San José del Cabo runs about $45—more at night. Cabs from Corridor hotels to either town run about $25 each way.

ESSENTIALS

Bus Contacts **SuburBaja** (☎ *624/146-0888*).

Currency Exchange **Banamex** (✉ *Blvd. Mijares*).

Internet **Trazzo Digital** (✉ *Calle Zaragoza 24* ☎ *624/142-0303*).

Mail & Shipping **DHL Worldwide Express** (✉ *Plaza los Portales, Hwy. 1, Km 31.5* ☎ *624/142-2148*). **Mail Boxes Etc.** (✉ *Plaza las Palmas, Hwy. 1, Km 31* ☎ *624/142-4355*). **San José del Cabo Oficina de Correo** (✉ *Mijares and Margarita Maya de Juárez* ☎ *No phone*).

Medical Assistance **Emergency Number for Medical Assistance** (☎ *Dial 065*). **Highway Patrol** (☎ *624/146-0573*). **Police** (☎ *624/142-2835*).

Visitor & Tour Info **Los Cabos Tourism Board** (✉ *Hwy. 1, Plaza San José,* ☎ *624/146-9628* 🌐 *www.visitloscabos.org*).

EXPLORING

Boulevard Mijares, the main drag, runs roughly perpendicular to the sea. Its north end abuts Avenida Zaragoza, a spot marked by a long fountain and the modest yellow Palacio Municipal (City Hall). The boulevard's south end has been designated a tourist zone, with the Mayan Palace Golf Los Cabos as its centerpiece. A few reasonably priced hotels and large all-inclusives are on a long, beautiful beach with rough surf.

Fires, hurricanes, and neglect have harmed the **Estero San José,** which empties into the sea at the north end of Playa Hotelera, San José's beach. Over the years the estuary has served as a cultural center with a museum (now closed) and a recreational area for kayakers and bird-watchers. This valuable natural resource is now the southern border of Puerto Los Cabos, a marina development that will eventually include several hotels, golf courses, and residential communities. The estuary is gradually coming back to life, and may once again harbor sea and migratory birds as well as all the flora and fauna it once had. ✉ *North end of Paseo Malecón San José* 🎫 *Free.*

Locals and travelers mingle at the central **Plaza Mijares,** on shaded green benches or in the white wrought-iron gazebo. The plaza is often the site of concerts and art shows. Be sure to walk up to the front of the nearby Iglesia San José, the town church, and see the tile mural of a priest being dragged toward a fire by Indians.

BEACHES

Oh, the madness of it all. Here you are in a beach destination with gorgeous weather and miles of clear blue water, yet you dare not dive into the sea. Most of San José's hotels line **Playa Hotelera** on Paseo Malecón San José, and brochures and Web sites gleefully mention beach access.

Although the long, level stretch of coarse brown sand is beautiful, the current is dangerously rough, and the drop-offs are steep and close to shore. Swimming here is extremely dangerous, and signs warn against it all along the way. Feel free to walk along the beach to the Estero San José, or play volleyball on the sand. But for swimming, head to Playa Palmilla along the Corridor.

WORD OF MOUTH

"Had dinner at Mi Cocina in Casa Natalia after walking around. The town is the 'original' Mexico, not commercial as in San Lucas. If you enjoy a cigar you must stop in the Amigos cigar bar."

–T. Buckley, Chicago

WHERE TO EAT

$$$–$$$$ MEXICAN ★ ✕ **La Panga Antigua.** An ancient wooden *panga* (small skiff) hangs above the door at this intriguing restaurant, located just across from San José's historical mission which is hundreds of years old. Tastefully decorated, La Panga has tables on a series of patios, one with a faded mural, another with a burbling fountain. Chef Jacobo Turquie prepares a superb catch of the day, drizzled with basil-infused oil and served with sautéed spinach and mashed potatoes. His regional seafood dishes, *pollo con mole,* gazpacho, and creamed carrot soup are also exceptional. ✉ *Av. Zaragoza 20, Centro* ☎ *624/142–4041* ▭ *AE, MC, V.*

$$–$$$ MEXICAN Fodor'sChoice ★ ✕ **El Chilar.** Set just a few blocks west of mainstream of San José, this spot is worth the search. The fine selection of Mexican wines and tequilas suits the stylish menu at this small, bustling restaurant, where murals of the Virgin of Guadalupe adorn bright orange walls. In his open kitchen, chef Armando Montaño uses chiles from all over Mexico to enhance traditional and Continental dishes (without heating up the spice), coating rack of lamb with ancho chili and perking up lobster bisque with smoky *chiles guajillos*. The management refuses to stagnate however, and changes the menu every month. But one mainstay has been their Oaxacan *tlayudas* (similar to tostadas), possibly the most asked-for item of the last half-dozen years. After dinner, retire to their wine and tequila tasting room, admiring the service that brought them the "Distintivo T" award for tequila knowledge. ✉ *Calle Juárez at Morelos* ☎ *624/142–2544* ▭ *No credit cards* ⏲ *Closed Sun. No lunch.*

$$–$$$ CONTINENTAL ✕ **Damiana.** At this small hacienda beside the San José's town plaza, bougainvillea wraps around tall pines that surround wrought-iron tables, and pink adobe walls glow in the candlelight. Start with mushrooms *diablo* (mushrooms steeped in a fiery-hot sauce), then move on to the tender chateaubriand or the charbroiled lobster. For more-traditional seafood preparations order the shrimp *enfrijolladas* in a creamy black bean sauce, or the shrimp with guajillo and a mild cactus sauce. Or, if you like your dining experiences to come with a side of adventure, Damiana has created a "steak" out of ground shrimp in its signature Imperial Steak Shrimp. During peak season a trio of guitarists serenade the guests. ✉ *Blvd. Mijares 8, Centro* ☎ *624/142–0499* ▭ *AE, MC, V.*

$$–$$$ ECLECTIC Fodor'sChoice ★ ✕ **Mi Cocina.** Traveling foodies, visiting chefs, and locals in the know favor this chic outdoor restaurant at the Casa Natalia, San José del Cabo's loveliest boutique hotel. Torches glow on the dining terrace, and the tables are spaced far enough apart so that you don't have to

share your whispered sweet nothings with a neighbor. Chef-owner Loic Tenoux plays with his ingredients, calling the new approach at Mi Cocina "French Mexican Bistro-style," mixing marinated octopus with Chinese noodles in a to-die-for salad, and stuffing poblano chilies with lamb and Oaxacan cheese. Tenoux also serves classic onion soup, and the homemade fluffy focaccia bread is great for dipping. His fried Camembert goes well with many of the imported wines on the extensive list. ✉ *Casa Natalia, Blvd. Mijares 4, Centro* ☎ *624/142–5100* ▭ *AE, MC, V.*

> **WORD OF MOUTH**
>
> "Baan Thai is a wonderful restaurant. It has many vegetarian options, and the chef was very vegan friendly." –Miz Veg, Portland, OR

$–$$ THAI ★ ✕ **Baan Thai.** The aromas alone are enough to bring you through the door, where you're then greeted with visual and culinary delights. The small comfortable formal dining room has Asian antiques, and a fountain murmurs on a patio in the back. The chef blends Asian spices with aplomb, creating sublime pad thai, lamb curry, Thai lamb shank, and the catch of the day with lemon black-bean sauce. New favorites are mussels in a coconut broth, and wok-seared scallops. Try the Ginger Martini. Prices are reasonable for such memorable food. ✉ *Morelos and Obregon, across from El Encanto Inn, Centro* ☎ *624/142–3344* ▭ *AE, MC, V.*

$–$$ AMERICAN ✕ **Baja Brewing Company.** Now Los Cabos even has its own brewery, right in the middle of San José del Cabo. This fun, upbeat brewpub has great music, and serves up satisfying pub meals. Potpies, burgers, ribs, and pizza should be washed down with a pint of the San José Especial cerveza, brewed within sight of the bar and restaurant. ✉ *Morelos 1277, Comonfort and Obregon, Centro* ☎ *624/142–1292* 🌐 *www.bajabrewingcompany.com* ▭ *MC, V.*

¢–$ MEXICAN ★ ✕ **El Ahorcado Taquería.** By day it looks like a hole in the wall, but when the sun drops down, this open-air eatery really comes to life. It's one of the few area restaurants open late, and it stays packed until closing, usually around 3 AM. And no one cramming into a restaurant at 3 AM gives a damn about the decor. Old pots, baskets, antique irons, sombreros, and the like hang from the walls and rafters. Tacos and enchiladas come with such tasty fillers as *flor de calabaza* (squash blossom), *nopales* (cactus flower), and *rajas* (poblano chilies) or try their empanadas *huitlacoche.* ✉ *Paseo Pescadores and Marinos* ☎ *624/148–2437* ▭ *No credit cards* ⊙ *Closed Mon.*

WHERE TO STAY

$$$$ Fodor'sChoice ★ **Cabo Azul Resort & Spa.** A newcomer on the beach in San José del Cabo, the exceptional Cabo Azul is still partially under construction, but you would never know it. Azul seems destined to be one of Los Cabos' top hotels, with the gorgeous Javier's Cantina & Grill in full operation. A Euro-style nightclub/lounge is planned for later in 2008. This hotel-and-time-share hybrid, despite the sophistication and elegance, has a friendly, relaxed atmosphere with spacious one- to three-bedroom villas and more than a dozen giant penthouses. You'll find that most of the action is centered on the giant asymmetrical pool, with a

swim up bar, and adjacent Flor de Noche Restaurant & Lounge. **Pros:** Pristine grounds, good food. **Cons:** Many timeshare tours walk through property. ✉*Desarrollo Cabo Azul, Paseo Malecon #11. San José del Cabo,* ☎*624/163–5100, 877/216–2226 in U.S.* 🌐*www.caboazulresort.com* *332 villas* *In-room: Safe, kitchen, DVD. In-hotel: 3 restaurants, room service, 2 bars, 5 pools, gym, Spa, laundry service, Internet café, no-smoking rooms, elevators, parking (free)* *AE, MC, V* *EP.*

WORD OF MOUTH

"I've never written a report on a hotel before, and I've stayed at the Plaza Athénée in Paris, the Kempinski in Moscow, the Waldorf-Astoria in New York, and hundreds more. When I tell you that Casa Natalia rocks and that all the details are attended to, it is reflective of my experience. I've been there twice now and will stay there on my next trip."

–Larry, Santa Cruz, CA

$$$$ Fodor'sChoice ★ **Casa Natalia.** A small, graceful boutique hotel, Casa Natalia is on San José's most charming street and opens onto the newly redone zocalo. Rooms are decorated in regional Mexican motifs and have soft robes, king-size beds, remote-controlled air-conditioning, and private patios screened by bamboo and bougainvillea. Suites have hot tubs and hammocks on large terraces. Natalia's cozy little bar offers hotel guests afternoon happy-hour specials, *dos por uno* or two for ones. The in-patio restaurant, Mi Cocina, is fabulous. This is perhaps the top location for those who wish to spend time enjoying the culture of this tranquil town. (Families take note: Children under 13 aren't allowed.) **Pros:** Staffers are helpful and welcoming, a free shuttle takes you to a beach club in the Corridor. **Cons:** Not on the beach, could be considered pricey for what you get. ✉*Blvd. Mijares 4, Centro,* ☎*624/146–7100, 888/277–3814 in U.S.* 🌐*www.casanatalia.com* *14 rooms, 2 suites* *In-room: Safe. In-hotel: Restaurant, bar, pool, concierge, laundry service, no elevator* *AE, MC, V* *CP.*

$$$$ **Presidente InterContinental Los Cabos.** Cactus gardens surround this low-lying hotel, one of the originals in what has become a lineup of massive all-inclusives along the beach. As a result of the hurricane that slammed the southern tip of Baja several years ago, the Presidente went through extensive renovations and has bounded back, and is operating at full capacity. Each of the hotel's three sections is centered on pools and lounging areas, and the ground-floor rooms, which have terraces, are the best. All accommodations have showers but no bathtubs. Try Napa, the property's top restaurant, part of the resort's all-inclusive plan. **Pros:** There's a friendly, old-world Mexican attitude among the staff members, many of whom have been here for decades. **Cons:** The quietest rooms were once next to the estuary, but noise from construction on the nearby Puerto los Cabos development, which is slated to be in the works through 2008, can now be a problem. ✉*Paseo San José, at end of hotel zone, Zona Hotelera,* ☎*624/142–0211, 800/424–6835 in U.S.* 🌐*www.ichotelsgroup.com* *390 rooms, 7 suites* *In-room: Safe, dial-up. In-hotel: 6 restaurants, room service, bars, tennis courts,*

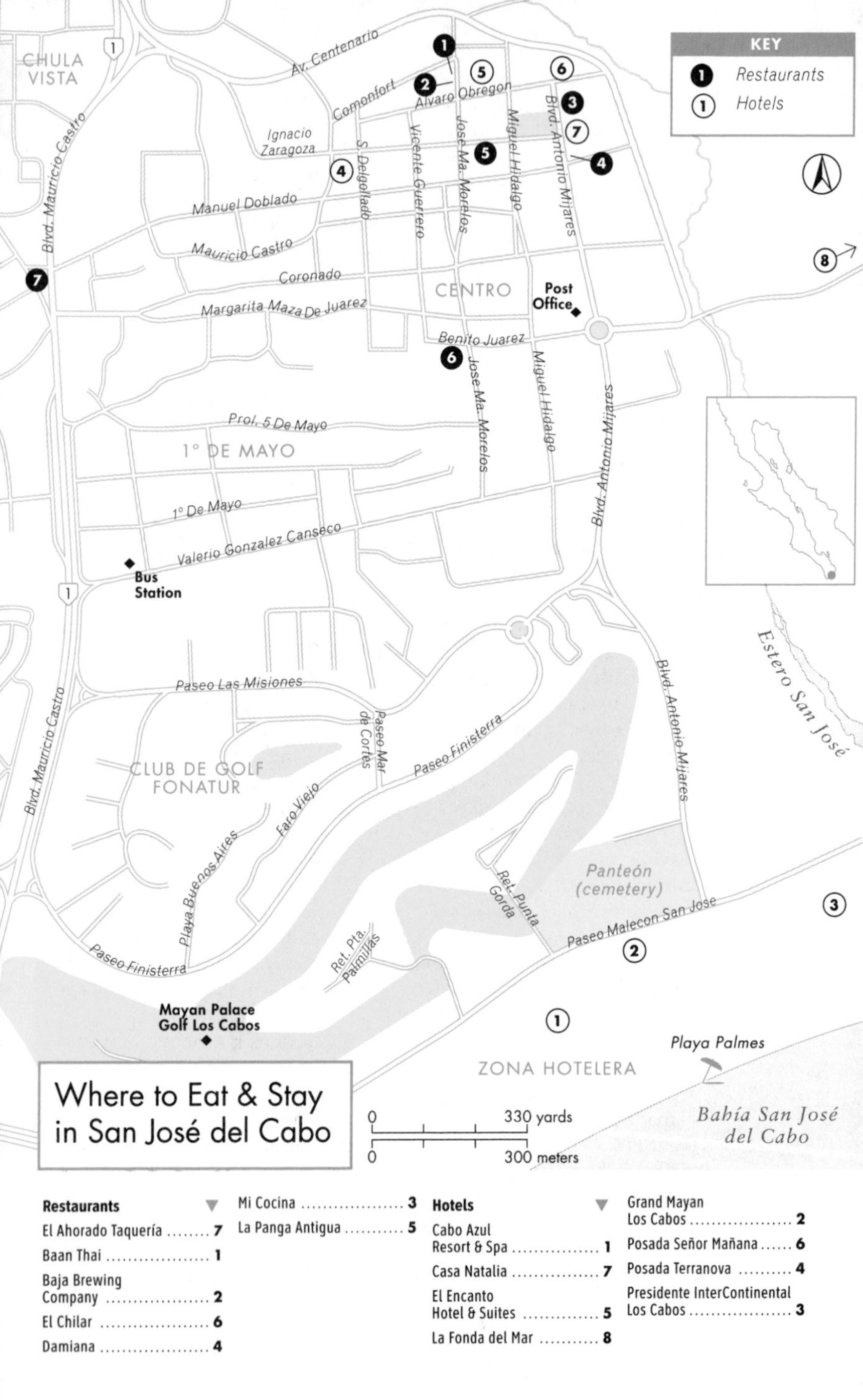

Restaurants

El Ahorado Taquería **7**
Baan Thai **1**
Baja Brewing Company **2**
El Chilar **6**
Damiana **4**
Mi Cocina **3**
La Panga Antigua **5**

Hotels

Cabo Azul Resort & Spa **1**
Casa Natalia **7**
El Encanto Hotel & Suites **5**
La Fonda del Mar **8**
Grand Mayan Los Cabos **2**
Posada Señor Mañana **6**
Posada Terranova **4**
Presidente InterContinental Los Cabos **3**

pools, gym, beachfront, children's programs (ages 5–12), laundry service, no-smoking rooms ☰*AE, MC, V* ꟷ*AI.*

$$$–$$$$ **Grand Mayan Los Cabos** As soon as you see the enormous twin Mayan masks that stand in the dimly lit prelobby entrance you'll feel as if you've entered another world. This ultraglitzy, exotic resort is newly opened and offers vibrant, spacious suites, all with a view of the monstrous pool and the Sea of Cortez beyond. Water flows out of the mouths of giant rattlesnakes into the pool, which is decked out with lights that change colors at night. Early morning yoga classes greet the sunrise near the beach. **Pros:** Size of resort is right on—not too overwhelming, and not so small it feels overrun, free (limited) Internet access. **Cons:** Time-share touts are persistent and everywhere, decor will be considered over the top by some. ✉*Paseo Malecon, San José del Cabo,* ☎*624/1163–4000* 🌐*www.wyndam.com* *172 rooms, 86 suites* *In-room: Safes, kitchen (some), Wi-Fi. In-resort: 2 restaurants, 3 bars, golf course, gym, spa, beachfront, elevators, children's programs, laundry services, concierge, valet parking (free), no-smoking rooms* ☰ *AE, MC, V* *AI.*

$$ ★ **El Encanto Hotel & Suites.** Located near San José's many great restaurants, bars, and galleries, this gorgeous, comfortable inn has two separate buildings—one, the Garden Section, has standard rooms and a second across the street; the Pool Section has suites, some of which have kitchens and patios. All guest quarters are immaculate and are impeccably decorated, and both buildings are surrounded by verdant gardens and adorned with climbing vines. This intimate hotel makes for a great wedding property, and their on-property wedding chapel harkens back to the Mexico of years gone by. **Pros:** Feels safe, walking distance to downtown. **Cons:** Pool section much nicer than suites across the street. ✉*Morelos 133, Centro,* ☎*624/142–0388* 🌐*www.elencantoinn.com* *12 rooms, 14 suites* *In-room: Kitchen (some). In-hotel: Pool, laundry service, no elevator* ☰*AE, MC, V* *EP.*

$$ **La Fonda del Mar.** If you're looking for a peaceful back-to-nature retreat, check out hotel on a long, secluded beach that straddles the line between desert and ocean. And once the diners clear out of the adjacent and very popular Buzzard's Bar & Grill, La Fonda is even more tranquil. The three thatch-roof cabañas and one cabaña/suite are in heavy demand by both surfers and the slightly adventurous in high season. Cabañas have in-suite toilets and sinks but share a hot-water shower; but the suite has all its own in-room facilities. To get here, turn off Boulevard Mijares at the signs for Puerto Los Cabos, continue past PLC and follow the road up the hill, around the minicircle and continue out into the desert; it's about 3 mi and more or less 10 minutes outside town. **Pros:** The whole operation runs on solar power. **Cons:** Shared facilities aren't to everyone's liking. ✉*Old East Cape Rd.,* ☎*624/113–6368 cell, 624/110–6454, 951/303–9384 in U.S.* 🌐*www.vivacabo.com or www.buzzardsbar.com* *3 cabañas, 1 suite* *In-room: No a/c. In-hotel: Restaurant, bar, beachfront, pool* ☰*No credit cards* *Closed Aug.* *BP.*

$–$$ **Posada Terranova.** People return to San José's best inexpensive hotel so frequently they almost become part of the family. The large rooms have two double beds and tile bathrooms. Whether you congregate with other guests at the front patio tables or in the restaurant, it still feels like a private home. **Pros:** Very affordable, especially clean. **Cons:** Must taxi to the beach. ✉*Calle Degollado at Av. Zaragoza, Centro,* ☎*624/142–0534* 🌐*www.hterranova.com.mx* *25 rooms* *In-hotel: Restaurant, room service, bar, no elevator.* ▭*AE, MC, V.*

SHOPPING OPS

San José's shops and galleries carry gorgeous, high-quality folk art, jewelry, and housewares. Serious shoppers should plan on splurging here.

¢–$ **Posada Señor Mañana.** Accommodations at this friendly, funky, eccentric place run the gamut from small no-frills rooms to larger rooms with air-conditioning, fans, cable TV, coffeemakers, and refrigerators. Hammocks hang on an upstairs deck, and you can store food and prepare meals in the communal kitchen. The owners also have inexpensive cabañas by the beach (⇨see 🌐 *www.eldelfinblanco.net* for further information on the cabañas). This posada is just steps away from the new zócalo and fountain in the middle of San José. ✉*Alvaro Obregón #1 L-B, by Casa de la Cultura, Centro,* ☎*624/142–1372* 🌐 *www.srmanana.com* *8 rooms, 1 suite* *In-room: No a/c (some), no TV (some). In-hotel: Kitchen, no elevator* ▭*MC, V* *CP.*

NIGHTLIFE

At **Havana Supper Club,** (✉*Carretera 1, Km 29* ☎*624/142–6203*), the excellent jazz band of owner-singer Sheila Mihevic plays in the hip club Wednesday through Friday.

At the **Tropicana Bar and Grill** (✉*Blvd. Mijares 30* ☎*624/142–1580*), conversation is usually possible on the balcony overlooking the bar and stage, though bands may get you dancing.

If you feel the need to belt out "*Love Shack*" or "*My Way,*" grab the karaoke mike at **Cactus Jack's** (✉*Blvd. Mijares 88* ☎*624/142–5601*), a gringo hangout that's open until the wee hours on weekends.

SHOPPING

Las Tiendas de Palmilla (✉*Hwy. 1, Km 27.5, San José del Cabo* ☎*624/144–6999* 🌐*www.lastiendasdepalmilla.com*), the newest offering on the Corridor shopping scene, is located just across from the posh Palmilla Resort. Your stop here will be rewarded with a selection of tasteful, top-end shops and restaurants, a nice terrace with a peaceful fountain and view of the Palmilla development, and the tranquil turquoise Sea of Cortez beyond.

For fresh produce, flowers, fish, and a sampling of local life in San José, visit the **Mercado Municipal,** off Calle Doblado. Art walks are held by galleries every Thursday night. The architecture at **Galería de Ida Victoria** (✉*Calle Guerrero 1128* ☎*624/142–5772*) is nearly as fascinating as the international art. The two-story building was designed as a gallery, with skylights and domes for natural light. **ADD** (✉*Av. Zaragoza at Hidalgo* ☎*624/143–2055*), an interior-design shop, sells hand-painted dishes from Guanajuato, Talavera pottery signed by the artist, and jewelry with semiprecious stones. **Copal** (✉*Plaza Mijares* ☎*624/142–3070*) has carved animals from Oaxaca, masks from Guerrero Negro, and heavy wooden furnishings. The array of Mexican textiles, pottery, glassware, hammocks, and souvenirs at **Curios Carmela** (✉*Blvd. Mijares 43* ☎*624/142–1117*) is overwhelming, and the prices are reasonable. **El Armario** (✉*Calle Obregon at Calle Morelos* ☎*No phone*) displays modern folk art, frames made from cactus wood, and posters.

An offshoot of a longstanding San Lucas shop, **Necri** (✉*Blvd. Mijares 16* ☎*624/130–7500*) carries ceramics, pottery, and pewter pieces and hot sauce made by the owner.

★ **Galería Veryka** (✉*Blvd. Mijares 418* ☎*624/142–0575*) is associated with galleries in San Miguel de Allende and Oaxaca, two of Mexico's finest art centers. The *huipiles* (embroidered blouses), masks, tapestries, and pottery are coveted by collectors. Prices are high, as is the quality.

SPORTS & THE OUTDOORS

BACKCOUNTRY

★ The folks at **Baja Wild** (✉*Km. 28, Carretera Transpeninsulas, s/n Local 5, Plaza Costa Azul* ☎ *624/172–6300* 🌐*www.bajawild.com*) always come up with adventures that are exciting. Hikes to canyons, hot springs, fossil beds, and caves with rock paintings expose you to the natural side of Cabo. Backcountry Jeep tours run from $95 to $125. Full-day kayak tours at Cabo Pulmo run $95 to $125. ATV tours in the desert with rappelling cost $85. Diving and rock climbing round out the options.

★ Longing to drive a Hummer? Go for it with **Baja Outback** (☎*624/142–9215* 🌐*www.bajaoutback.com*). They have a variety of drive-yourself trips (with a guide in the passenger seat) that range from four hours to several days long. The routes run through Baja backcountry, where you have the opportunity to explore the Cape's rarely seen back roads while learning desert lore from a knowledgeable guide-cum-biologist. Day trips range from $165 to $220 per person.

FISHING

Most hotels in San José can arrange fishing trips. Until the Puerto Los Cabos marina north of San José is completed, you can catch large sportfishing boats only out of the marina in Cabo San Lucas. The *pangas* (small skiffs) of **Gordo Banks Pangas** (✉*La Playa near San José del Cabo* ☎*624/142–1147, 800/408–1199 in U.S.* 🌐*www.gordobanks.com*) are near some of the hottest fishing spots in the Sea of Cortez: the Outer and Inner Gordo Banks. The price for three anglers in a small *panga* runs from $200 to $240. Cruisers, which can accommodate four to six people, are available for $350 to $530 per day.

KAYAKING

Los Lobos del Mar (✉*Brisas del Mar RV park, on south side of San José* ☎*624/142–2983*) rents kayaks and offers tours along the Corridor's peaceful bays. These outings are especially fun in winter when gray whales pass by offshore. Prices start at $30.

SURFING

For good surfing tips, rentals, and lessons, head to **Costa Azul Surf Shop** (✉*Carretera 1, Km 28, along Corridor* ☎*624/142–2771* 🌐*www.costa-azul.com.mx*). Surfboards run $20 a day and lessons are $55 including surfboard rental.

TODOS SANTOS

72 km (45 mi) north of Cabo San Lucas.

Artists from the Southwest (and a few from Mexico) have found a haven in this small town near the Pacific coast north of Los Cabos. Architects and entrepreneurs have restored early-19th-century adobe and brick buildings around the main plaza, and speculators have laid out housing tracts in the rocky hills between the town and the shore, contributing to a rapid rise in real-estate prices. In high season, tour buses on day trips from Los Cabos often clog the streets around the plaza. When the buses leave, the town is a peaceful place to wander.

Los Cabos visitors typically take day trips here, though several small inns provide a peaceful antidote to Cabo's noise and crowds. El Pescadero, the largest settlement before Todos Santos, is home to ranchers and farmers who grow herbs and vegetables. Business hours are erratic, especially in September and October.

GETTING HERE & AROUND

Carretera 19 connects Cabo with Todos Santos. If you're only driving up for the day, be sure to head back to Cabo before dark, because Carretera 19 is unlighted and prone to high winds and flooding. And don't be tempted to try the dirt roads that intersect the highway unless you're in a four-wheel-drive vehicle. Sands on the beach or in the desert stop conventional vehicles in their tracks.

WHERE TO EAT & STAY

$$$–$$$$ ITALIAN ★ ✕**Cafe Santa Fe.** The setting, with tables situated in an overgrown courtyard, is as appealing as the food: salads and soups made from organic vegetables and herbs, homemade pastas, and fresh fish with light sauces. Many Cabo residents lunch here regularly. The marinated seafood salad is a sublime blend of shrimp, octopus, and mussels with olive oil and garlic, with plenty for two to share before dining on lobster ravioli. ✉*Calle Centenario* ☎*612/145–0340* 💳*MC, V* ⊗*Closed Tues. and Sept. and Oct.*

$–$$ MEXICAN ✕**Los Adobes.** Locals swear by the fried, cilantro-studded local cheese and the beef tenderloin with *huitlacoche* (a savory mushroomlike fungus) at this pleasant outdoor restaurant. The menu is ambitious and includes tapas and several organic, vegetarian options—rare in these parts. At night the place sparkles with star-shape lights. The Internet café within the restaurant offers high-speed access. ✉*Calle Hidalgo* ☎*612/145–0203* 🌐*www.losadobesdetodossantos.com* 💳*MC, V* ⊗*No dinner Sun.*

$–$$ ECLECTIC ✕**Caffé Todos Santos.** Omelets, bagels, granola, and whole-grain breads delight the breakfast crowd at this small eatery; deli sandwiches, fresh salads, and an array of tamales, *flautas* (tortillas rolled around savory fillings and fried), and combo plates are lunch and dinner highlights. Check for fresh seafood on the daily specials board. ✉*Calle Centenario 33* ☎*612/145–0300* ▭*No credit cards* ⊙*No lunch or dinner Mon.*

GET THE SCOOP

Be sure to pick up a copy of *El Calendario de Todos Santos,* a free English-language guide with events, available at many hotels and shops, for information on local events. Another good source is the Web site (wwww.todos santos-baja.com), which is maintained by local residents.

$$$–$$$$ **Posada La Poza.** The Swiss owners aim to please with their chic posada next to a bird-filled lagoon that gives way to the open sea. The handsome suites have rust-tone walls, modern furniture, and Swiss linens; a CD player and binoculars are on hand, but there aren't any TVs or phones in the rooms. Even if you're not staying, stop by El Gusto! restaurant ($$–$$$; closed Thursday) for spicy tortilla soup, local scallops, organic salads, and an impressive list of Mexican wines. At the patio dining area, incredible views are included. **Pros:** This is the only Todos Santos property on the water, food is delicious. **Cons:** Beach will be difficult for some to access, town isn't within walking distance. ✉*Follow signs on Carretera 19 and on Benito Juárez to beach,* ☎*612/145–0400* ⊕*www.lapoza.com* *7 suites* *In-room: No phone, safe, refrigerator, no TV. In-hotel: Restaurant, bar, pool, beachfront, no elevator, public Internet, no kids under 12* ▭*MC, V* *BP.*

$$–$$$$ ★ **Hotel California.** This handsome structure with two stories of arched terraces underwent extensive remodeling and design, thanks to the artistic bent of owners John and Debbie Stewart (John passed away a few years ago). A deep-blue-and-ocher scheme runs throughout, and rooms, some with ocean views, are decorated with a funky mix of antiques and folk art. **Pros:** The Coronela restaurant and bar are local hot spots, and the Emporio shop is stuffed with curios. **Cons:** Not all rooms have air-conditioners. ✉*Benito Juárez at Morelos,* ☎*612/145–0525* ⊕*www.hotelcaliforniabaja.com* *11 rooms* *In-room: No a/c (some), no phone, no TV, Wi-Fi. In-hotel: Restaurant, bar, pool, no elevator* ▭*MC, V* *EP.*

$$–$$$ **Todos Santos Inn.** The ambience found in this converted 19th-century house, with only eight guest rooms, is unparalleled in design and comfort. The pool deck is lined with hearty stone and brick; the walls of the foyer are painted with a now fading, dusky scene; and gorgeous antiques are displayed throughout, completing the period feel. The absence of telephones and TVs allow for unencumbered relaxation. The resident Copa Wine Bar is open in the evening, and good restaurants are within easy walking distance. **Pros:** Very beautiful, wonderfully landscaped. **Cons:** Located on a busy street; next to

MUSICAL MYTH

Ignore rumors that the Eagles song originated at this Hotel California. It didn't. It's your call whether to buy the T-shirts and tequila emblazoned with the name that are on sale here.

community basketball hoop, which draws noisy, jubilant kids. ✉ *Calle Legaspi,* ☎📠 *612/145–0040* 🌐 *www.todossantosinn.com* ⇒ *8 rooms* ♁ *In-room: No phone, no TV. In-hotel: Bar, no elevator, public Wi-Fi, no children under 12, no-smoking rooms* ▭ *MC, V* 🍴 *BP.*

SHOPPING

A leader on the art scene is the **Charles Stewart Gallery & Studio** (✉ *Calle Centenario at Calle Obregón* ☎ *612/145–0265*). Stewart moved from Taos, New Mexico, to Todos Santos in 1986, and is credited as one of the founders of the town's artist community. Some of his paintings and art pieces have a Baja or Mexican theme. The gallery is in one of the town's loveliest 19th-century buildings. **Fénix de Todos Santos** (✉ *Calle Juárez at Calle Topete* ☎ *612/145–0666*) has bowls and plates from Tonalá, handblown glassware, Talavera pottery, and cotton clothing by the designer Sucesos.

At **Galería Santa Fé** (✉ *Calle Centenario 4* ☎ *612/145–0340*), in an 1850s adobe building, Paula and Ezio Colombo sell collector-quality folk art, including frames adorned with images of Frida Kahlo and her art, kid-size chairs decorated with bottle caps, Virgin of Guadalupe images, and *milagros* (small tin charms used as offerings to saints). **Galería de Todos Santos** (✉ *Calle Topete and Calle Legaspi* ☎ *612/145–0040*), owned by Michael and Pat Cope, displays Michael's modern art and exhibits works by international artists living in Baja. Filled with gorgeous Guatemalan textiles, Mexican folk art, belts, purses, wood carvings, and Day of the Dead figurines, **Mangos** (✉ *Calle Centenario across from Charles Stewart Gallery* ☎ *612/145–0451*) is an intriguing shop. The best bookstore in the Los Cabos region is **El Tecolote Bookstore** (✉ *Calle Juárez at Calle Hidalgo* ☎ *612/145–0295*). Stop here for Latin American literature, poetry, children's books, current fiction and nonfiction, and books on Baja.

THE EAST CAPE

Los Barriles is 105 km (65 mi) south of La Paz, 34 km (21 mi) north of San José del Cabo.

The Sea of Cortez coast between La Paz and San José del Cabo is a favored hideaway for anglers and adventurers. The area consists of fast-growing gringo communities at Buena Vista and Los Barriles and beloved settlements at Cabo Pulmo and Punta Pescadero. Hotels and small lodges are scattered along the coast. Most offer packages that include meals and activities—a good idea since they're usually isolated. The East Cape is renowned for its rich fishing grounds, good diving, and excellent windsurfing.

There's an outback feel to the East Cape, with a robust group of American "settlers" making their presence known. The East Cape is so Americanized it doesn't even have a Spanish name. It's the East Cape to everybody.

The first coastal settlement of note is Cabo Pulmo, site of one of the few coral reefs in the Sea of Cortez. You'll have to drive about 10 km (6 mi) on a dirt road to reach it. It's a magnet for serious divers, kayakers, and windsurfers. Power comes from solar panels, and drinking water is trucked in over dirt roads. Palapa-shaded restaurants on the sand serve fabulous fish tacos and cold drinks.

North of Cabo Pulmo, Buena Vista has more services and hotels, where you can join fishing and diving excursions. Next in line, Los Barriles has the most amenities, with Internet cafés, restaurants, gift shops, and plenty of eager real-estate agents. Devoted windsurfers roost in Los Barriles when the winter winds are high; anglers are happy year-round. You can rent water-sports equipment and organize boat trips through area hotels. If you're staying here, note that hotel airport transfers typically cost about $90 each way in an eight-person van.

GETTING HERE & AROUND

Intrepid travelers can drive north of San José del Cabo on a dirt washboard road to the East Cape settlements, a dusty drive that takes about three hours to the first major town at Los Barriles. Some car rental agencies don't allow their cars on these roads. Far easier is the drive north on paved Highway 1 through the Sierra de La Laguna.

WHERE TO STAY

You won't find much in the way of dining options in this remote area. Most people come here for the fishing—not the scene—and eat at their hotel's restaurants. If you'd rather cook your own food, you can stock up at **Tio's Tienda** (to get there, take the main road in town toward the beach until it dead-ends and turn left).

$$$ **Hotel Buena Vista Beach Resort.** Flower-lined paths wrap around tile-roof bungalows, pools, fountains, and lawns. The rooms in the bungalows are simply decorated, and some have private terraces. The fishing fleet is excellent, as are other diversions, such as diving, snorkeling, kayaking, horseback riding, and trips to natural springs. But it seems that most guests spend a good part of the day enjoying the pool and the hot tub which is filled with water piped in from the hot springs. Many of the people at the swim-up bar seem to be regulars, swapping stories about Buena Vista's glory days, back when swim-up bars were novel, the furnishings were fashionable, and this was the place to be seen. Things are more laid-back today. Discounts are often available for those who stay for three days or more. The food at the friendly Navegante Restaurant is decent, and they'll cook up the fish you caught earlier in the day. **Pros:** A European plan (without meals) is available from November through March, which cuts the rate considerably. **Cons:** Rooms give you the feeling of stepping back a little in time, to the '80s when colors like bright orange and olive green were in fashion in textiles and furniture. ✉ *Hwy. 1, Km 105, Buena Vista* ☎ *624/141–0033 or 800/752–3555* 🌐 *www.hotelbuenavista.com* *60 rooms* *In-room: No phone (some), no TV. In-hotel: Restaurant, tennis court, pools, beachfront, spa, water sports, no elevator, laundry service.* 💳 *MC, V* *EP, FAP.*

$$$ **Hotel Palmas de Cortez.** Often featured on sportfishing shows, the hotel is near the famed Cortez Banks—a submerged island that is famous for its fishing, diving, and big-wave surfing. Palmas's enor-

mous pool has a swim-up bar, and there's also a 9-hole golf course and driving range where you can dedicate an afternoon or two. Special events, including an arts festival in March and several fishing tournaments, are big draws. **Pros:** Some guest rooms have fireplaces and/or kitchens, the Palmas is the East Cape's social center. **Cons:** Food is OK, some details aren't attended to. ✉ *On beach; take road north through Los Barriles and continue to beach, Los Barriles* ☎ *624/141–0050 or 888/241–1543* 🌐 *www.palmasdecortez.com* *20 rooms, 15 suites, 10 condos* *In-hotel: Restaurant, golf course, tennis court, pool, gym, spa, water sports, no elevator, public Internet* *MC, V* *FAP.*

$–$$$ **Cabo Pulmo Beach Resort.** Solar-powered cottages sit in even rows on the beach, much like in a trailer park. One of these, the Beach House, can accommodate up to eight guests at a time. Owners put their vacation homes up for rent through this back-to-basics resort. The office is next to a PADI facility and a restaurant. It's the largest business in the neighborhood and the best place for newcomers to hang out for a few nights, meet a few people, and have some fun. Reservations are absolutely essential. **Pros:** The setting is idyllic. **Cons:** The long road to get to the hotel is unpaved, and a little bumpy, so driving in before dark is recommended. ✉ *Hwy. 1 at La Ribera turnoff, Cabo Pulmo* ☎ *624/141–0885, 562/366–0398 in U.S.* 🌐 *www.cabopulmo.com* *20 cottages* *In-room: No a/c (some), no phone, kitchen (some), refrigerator (some), no TV. In-hotel: Restaurant, beachfront, diving, water sports, no elevator, public Wi-Fi* *MC, V* *EP.*

$$ **Los Barriles Hotel.** Across the street from beachside businesses, this motel-like inn offers large, comfy rooms. The two-story building wraps around a nicely landscaped central pool and lounging area with a palapa bar and hot tub; water and cold drinks are available at the front desk. Reservations are highly recommended since Los Barriles fills up fast. **Pros:** Front desk arranges tours and fishing trips with ease. **Cons:** Rooms are somewhat basic. ✉ *Take road off Hwy. 1 north through Los Barriles and turn left when it ends at beach, Los Barriles,* ☎ *624/141–0024* 🌐 *www.losbarrileshotel.com* *20 rooms* *In-room: no TV, refrigerator. In-hotel: pool, water sports, no elevator* *MC, V* *EP.*

SPORTS & THE OUTDOORS

Water-sports equipment and boat trips are available through area hotels, although veterans tend to bring their own gear and rent cars to reach isolated spots. Windsurfers take over the East Cape during winter months, when stiff breezes provide ideal conditions. Catch them flying over the waves at Playa Norte in Los Barriles. **VelaWindsurf** (☎ *800/223–5443* 🌐 *www.velawindsurf.com*) offers windsurfing and kite-boarding lessons and trips Los Barriles in winter and fall; their center is located in front of the Hotel Playa del Sol.

Parque Marino Nacional Cabo Pulmo. The 25,000-year-old coral reef here has been legally protected since 1995 and it's home to more than 2,000 different kinds of marine organisms, including 236 species of tropical fish and a dozen kinds of petrified coral. The area is renowned among diving aficionados, whose favorite months to visit are June and July, when visibility is highest. The park isn't too difficult to access. It's just 8 km (5 mi) from the end of the paved road and is bordered by Playa Las Barracas in the north and Bahía Los Frailes to the south.

If you happen to be traveling sans diving gear, you can get everything you need at **Pepe's Dive Center** (⊠*El Camino Rural Costero* ☎*624/141–0001* 🌐*www.cabopulmo.com.mx*). José Luis "Pepe" Murrieta and his knowledgeable crew of dive masters also give tours in English.

Cabo Pulmo Divers (⊠*On beach* 🌐*www.baja.com/cabopulmodivers*) is another option if you want to dive. This family-run shop is right on the beach and offers full diving services but it's most famous for excellent guided fishing trips that run $110 for three people for three hours.

LA PAZ

195 km (121 mi) north of San José del Cabo.

La Paz may be the capital of Baja Sur and home to about 200,000 residents, but it feels like a small town in a time warp. It's the most traditional Mexican city in Baja Sur, the antithesis of the gringolandia developments to the south. Granted, there are plenty of foreigners in La Paz, particularly during snowbird season. But in the slowest part of the off-season, during the oppressive late-summer heat, you can easily see how La Paz aptly translates as "the peace," and its residents can be called *paceños* (peaceful ones). The city sprawls inland from the curve of its malécon along the Bahía La Paz, which, through some strange feat of geography, angles west toward the sunset.

Travelers use La Paz as both a destination in itself and a stopping-off point en route to Los Cabos. There's always excellent scuba diving and sportfishing in the Sea of Cortez. La Paz is the base for divers and fishermen headed for Cerralvo, La Partida, and the Espíritu Santo islands, where parrot fish, manta rays, neons, and angels blur the clear waters by the shore, and marlin, dorado, and yellowtail leap from the sea. Cruise ships are more and more often spotted sailing toward the bay as La Paz emerges as an attractive port.

La Paz officially became the capital of Baja California Sur in 1974, and is the state's largest settlement, though Los Cabos is quickly catching up. There are few chain hotels or restaurants now, but the region, including parts of the coastline south of the city, is slated to have several large-scale, high-end resort developments with golf courses, marinas, and vacation homes.

GETTING HERE & AROUND

Aeropuerto General Manuel Márquez de León serves La Paz. It's 11 km (7 mi) northwest of the Baja California Sur capital, which itself is 188 km (117 mi) northwest of Los Cabos. In La Paz, taxis are readily available and inexpensive. Taxis between the La Paz airport and towns are inexpensive (about $5) and convenient. A ride within town costs under $5; a trip to Pichilingue costs between $7 and $10. In La Paz the main Terminal de Autobus is 10 blocks from the malecón. Bus companies offer service to Los Cabos (three hours), Loreto (five hours), and Guerrero Negro (the buses stop at the highway entrance to town). The Guerrero Negro trip takes anywhere from six to nine hours, and buses stop in Santa Rosalia and San Ignacio.

ESSENTIALS

Bus Contacts **La Paz Terminal de Autobus** (✉ *Calle Jalisco at Calle Gomez Farias* ☎ *612/122-7094*). **SuburBaja** (☎ *624/146-0888*).

Currency Exchange **Banamex** (✉ *Calle 16 de Septiembre* ☎ *No phone*).

Internet**Baja Net** (✉ *Av. Madero 430* ☎ *612/125-9380*).

Mail & Shipping **DHL Worldwide Express** (✉ *Av. Abasolo Edificio 7* ☎ *612/122-6987*). **La Paz Oficina de Correo** (✉ *Av. Revolución at Av. Constitución* ☎ *612/122-0388*).

Medical Assistance **Centro de Especialidades Médicas** (✉ *Calle Delfines 110* ☎ *612/124-0400*). **Emergency Number for Medical Assistance** (☎ *Dial 065*). **Highway Patrol** (☎ *612/122-0369*). **Police** (☎ *612/122-0477*).

Visitor & Tour Info**Baja California Sur State Tourist Office** (✉ *Mariano Abasolo, s/n, La Paz* ☎ *866/733-5272 or 612/122-5939* ⊕ *www.vivalapaz.com*).

EXPLORING

5 The **Biblioteca de las Californias** specializes in the history of Baja California and has an outstanding collection of historical documents. The library has nevertheless been relegated to a small section of the building, which has been turned into a children's cultural center. ✉ *Av. Madero at Calle 5 de Mayo, Centro* ☎ *612/122-0162* ⊙ *Weekdays 9–6.*

4 The downtown church, **Catedral de Nuestra Señora de la Paz,** is a simple stone building with a modest gilded altar. The church was built in 1860 near the site of La Paz's first mission, which was established that same year by Jesuit Jaime Bravo. ✉ *Calle Juárez, Colonia Centro* ☎ *No phone.*

1 ★ The **malecón** is La Paz's seawall, tourist zone, and social center all rolled into one. It runs along Paseo Alvaro Obregón and has a sidewalk as well as several park areas in the sand just off it. Paceños are fond of strolling the malecón at sunset. Teenagers slowly cruise the street in their spiffed-up cars, couples nuzzle on park benches, and grandmothers meander along while keeping an eye on the kids. Marina La Paz, at the malecón's southwest end, is an ever-growing development with condominiums, vacation homes, and a pleasant café-lined walkway.

2 A two-story white gazebo is the focus of **Malecón Plaza,** a small concrete square where musicians sometimes appear on weekend nights. An adjacent street, Calle 16 de Septiembre, leads inland to the city.

6 La Paz's culture and heritage are well represented at the **Museo de Antropología,** which has re-creations of Comondu and Las Palmas Indian villages, photos of cave paintings found in Baja, and copies of Cortés's writings on first sighting La Paz. Many exhibit descriptions are written only in Spanish, but the museum's staff will help you translate. ✉ *Calle*

Altamirano at Calle 5 de Mayo, Centro ☎*612/122–0162* *Donation requested* *Daily 9–6.*

3 **Plaza Constitución,** the true center of La Paz, is a traditional zócalo, which also goes by the name Jardín Velazco. Concerts are held in the park's gazebo and locals gather here for art shows and fairs.

BEACHES

Around the malecón, stick to ambling along the sand while watching local families enjoy the sunset. Just north of town the beach experience is much better; it gets even better north of Pichilingue. Save your swimming and snorkeling energies for this area.

Playa Balandra. A rocky point shelters a clear, warm bay at Playa Balandra, 21 km (13 mi) north of La Paz. Several small coves and pristine beaches appear and disappear with the tides, but there's always a calm area where you can wade and swim. Snorkeling is fair around Balandra's south end where there's a coral reef. You may spot clams, starfish, and anemones. Kayaking and snorkeling tours usually set out from around here. If not on a tour, bring your own gear, as rentals aren't normally available. The beach has a few barbecue pits, trash cans, and palapas for shade. Camping is permitted but there are no hookups. The smallish beach gets crowded on weekends, but on a weekday morning you may have the place to yourself.

Playa Caimancito. La Concha hotel takes up some of the sand at the beach 5 km (3 mi) north of La Paz. But you can enter the beach both north and south of the hotel and enjoy a long stretch of sand facing the bay and downtown. Locals swim laps here, as the water is almost always calm and salty enough for easy buoyancy. There aren't any facilities, but if you wander over to the hotel for lunch or a drink you can use their restrooms and rent water toys.

Playa Pichilingue. Starting in the time of Spanish invaders, Pichilingue, 16 km (10 mi) north of La Paz, was known for its preponderance of oysters bearing black pearls. In 1940 a disease killed them off, leaving the beach deserted. Today it's a pleasant place to sunbathe and watch sportfishing boats haul in their daily catches. Locals set up picnics here on weekend afternoons and linger until the blazing sun settles into the bay. Restaurants consisting of little more than a palapa over plastic tables and chairs serve oysters *diablo,* fresh clams, and plenty of cold beer. Pichilingue curves northeast along the bay to the terminals where the ferries from Mazatlán and Topolobampo arrive and many of the sportfishing boats depart. One downside to this beach: traffic buzzes by on the nearby freeway. The water here, though not particularly clear, is calm enough for swimming.

Playa el Tecolote. Spend a Sunday at Playa el Tecolote, 24 km (15 mi) north of La Paz, and you'll feel like you've experienced the Mexico of old. Families set up house on the soft sand, kids race after seagulls and each other, and *abuelas* (grandmothers) daintily lift their skirts to wade in the water. Vendors rent out beach chairs, umbrellas, kayaks, and small, motorized boats; a couple of restaurants serve up simple

Biblioteca de las Californias ... 5
La Catedral de Nuestra Señora de La Paz 4
Malecón 1
Malecón Plaza ... 2
Museo de Antropología 6
Plaza Constitución 3

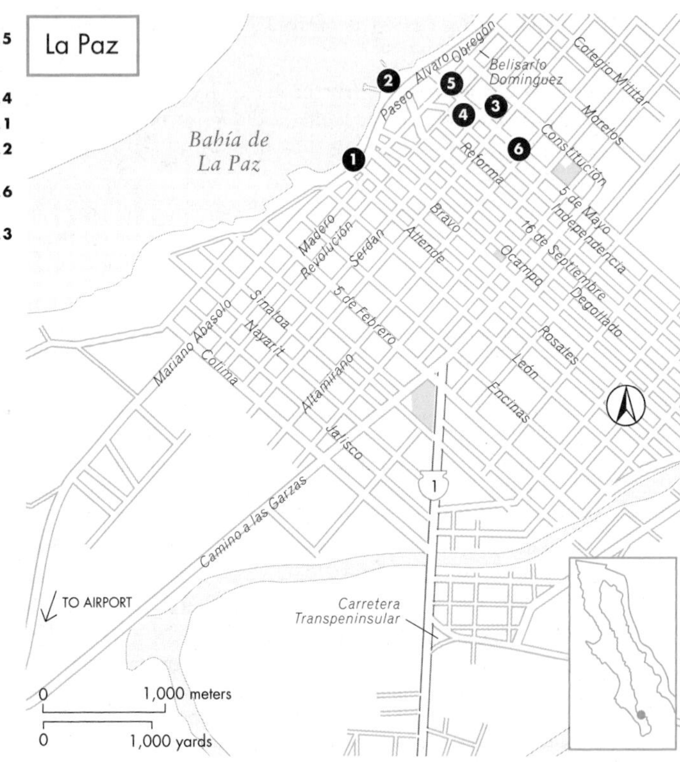

fare such as freshly grilled snapper. These eateries are usually open throughout the week, though they sometimes close on wintery days. Facilities include public restrooms, fire pits, and trash cans. Camping is permitted, but there are no hookups.

WHERE TO EAT

$–$$ SEAFOOD ★ ✕ **La Mar y Peña.** The freshest, tastiest seafood cocktails, ceviches, and clam tacos imaginable are served in this nautical restaurant crowded with locals. If you come with friends, go for the *mariscada,* a huge platter of shellfish and fish for four. The shrimp *albondigas* (meatballs) soup has a hearty fish stock seasoned with cilantro; and the crab *ranchero* is a savory mix of crabmeat, onions, tomatoes, and capers. Portions are huge. ✉ *Calle 16 de Septiembre between Isabel de la Catolica and Albañez, Centro* ☎ *612/122–9949* 💳 *AE, MC, V.*

$–$$ ITALIAN ✕ **La Pazta.** Locals who crave international fare rave about this trattoria with a sleek black-and-white interior and excellent homemade pastas and pizzas. Look for imported cheeses and wines and bracing espresso, though you can't enjoy an early morning coffee here since La Pazta is only open for lunch and dinner. The adjacent café, however, is open for breakfast and lunch and also serves imported Italian *caffe.* Both eateries are at the Hotel Mediterrane, a small inn popular with Europeans.

⊠*Allende 36, at Hotel Mediterrane, Centro* ☎*612/125–1195* 🌐*www.hotelmed.com* ▭*MC, V* ⊗*No dinner Tues.*

¢–$$ MEXICAN ✕**El Bismark.** The original Bismark is a bit out of the way, but it attracts families who settle down for hours at long wood tables, while waitresses divide their attention between patrons and *telenovellas* on the TV above the bar. Tuck into seafood cocktails, enormous grilled lobsters, or carne asada served with beans, guacamole, and homemade tortillas. However, the restaurant is most loved for its seafood tacos, sold out of ice coolers that are set out in front of the restaurant before noon. The smaller Bismark on the malecón, called el Bismark-cito, is also popular. ⊠*Av. Degollado at Calle Altamirano, Centro* ☎*612/122–4854* ⊠*Alvaro Obregón s/n, at malecón* ▭*MC, V.*

¢–$ MEXICAN ✕**Asadero Rancho Viejo.** Everything is delicious, and prices are reasonable at this cheerful little restaurant painted in bright yellow and orange. Meats are the specialty here, but just about everything on the menu is good and choices are abundant. The *tacos de arrachera,* a kind of beef taco, are particularly tasty. You can pop in any time, day or night, since this restaurant is open 24 hours. ⊠*Blvd. Dominguez s/n, at M. de León 228, near malecón* ☎*612/128–4647* ▭*MC, V.*

¢–$ SEAFOOD ✕**Los Laureles.** A small stand that looks as if it might have been rolled along the street by a vendor is just the entryway decoration for this well-established restaurant. Whether you eat at a bench at the stand outside or dine within in the air-conditioning, if you like seafood, you will enjoy Los Laureles. They offer all sorts of fruits de mer served in many different ways, but their seafood cocktails are notable for their freshness (you can even try the shrimp raw) and variety (abalone is an option). ⊠*Paseo Alvaro Obregón s/n* ☎*612/128–8532* ▭*MC, V.*

¢–$ MEXICAN ★ ✕**Taco Hermanos Gonzalez.** La Paz has plenty of great taco shacks, but none is better than the small stand of the Gonzalez brothers who serve up hunks of fresh fish wrapped in corn tortillas and offer bowls of condiments with which to decorate your taco. The top quality draws sizable crowds of satisfied sidewalk munchers. ⊠*Mutualismo at Esquerro, Centro* ☎*No phone* ▭*No credit cards.*

¢ VEGETARIAN ✕**El Quinto Sol Restaurante Vegetariano.** El Quinto's brightly painted exterior is covered with snake symbols and smiling suns. The all-vegetarian menu includes fresh juices and herbal elixirs. The four-course prix-fixe *comida corrida* (daily special) is a bargain; it's served from noon to 4 PM. The back half of this space is a bare-bones store stocked with natural foods. ⊠*Blvd. Domínguez at Av. Independencia, Centro* ☎*612/122–1692* ▭*No credit cards.*

WHERE TO STAY

$$$ **Fiesta Inn La Paz.** As you approach this modern, bright orange hotel, set apart from La Paz, you'll get the feeling that you are in an otherworldly place. From the towering columns that greet you as you drive up to the hotel to the size of the marble-floor lobby as you check in, the proportions in the hotel break from those of the world outside, and although you may feel a little like Alice in Wonderland at first, there is definitely room to put your feet up. Inside the rooms, many of which have views straight out over the water, things are a bit more standard. The decor is somewhat plain, much less shocking than the exte-

rior, but the beige and gray interiors are agreeable. **Pros:** The service, which mainly caters to business travelers, is excellent. **Cons:** Too far out of town to walk. ✉ *Km 5, Carretera a Pichilingue en Marina Costa,* ☎ *612/123–6000* 🌐 *www.fiestamericana.com* *114 rooms, 6 suites* *In room: Wi-Fi, safe, refrigerator. In hotel: Restaurant, room service, bar, pools, gym, beachfront, laundry service* ▭ *D, MC, V* *EP.*

$$–$$$ **La Concha Beach Resort.** On a long beach with calm water, this older resort has a water-sports center and a notable restaurant. Rooms are gradually being renovated with white walls and cheery yellow and blue textiles. If you can, splurge on a condo unit with a separate bedroom and kitchen. These are in a separate apartment-style building with an elevator, within walking distance to the beach. **Pros:** There's also an infrequent shuttle to town. **Cons:** Rooms can be dark and uninviting. ✉ *Carretera a Pichilingue, Km 5, between downtown and Pichilingue,* ☎ *612/121–6344 or 800/999–2252* 🌐 *www.laconcha.com* *107 rooms* *In-room: Refrigerator. In-hotel: Restaurant, room service, bar, pool, beachfront, diving, water sports, no elevator, laundry service, public Internet, public Wi-Fi, no-smoking rooms* ▭ *AE, MC, V* *EP.*

$$ ★ **el ángel azul.** Owner Esther Ammann converted La Paz's historic courthouse into a bed-and-breakfast that's a comfortable retreat in the center of the city. Rooms frame a central courtyard filled with palms and bougainvillea. Walls throughout are painted vivid yellow, coral, and blue and rooms are decorated with original art and Mexican textiles. The rooftop suite overlooks the city. **Pros:** Convenient location that's close to the malecón, free Wi-fi, owner is fantastic. **Cons:** Though the decor is traditional, certain color palettes feel a little dated. ✉ *Av. Independencia 518, at Guillermo Prieto, Centro,* ☎ *612/125–5130* 🌐 *www.elangelazul.com* *10 rooms, 2 suites* *In-room: No TV. In-hotel: Bar, no elevator, public Wi-Fi, no kids under 12, no-smoking rooms* ▭ *MC, V* *CP.*

$$ **Hotel Los Arcos.** This colonial-style 1950s hotel is a beloved La Paz landmark. **Pros:** The relaxed lobby, full of couches and rocking chairs, leads to the courtyard, where the rush of water from the fountain is calming and tranquil. The hotel hosts a good number of conventions and business meetings as well as tourists who return year after year, so expect to find a bustling lobby. Most of the spacious, slightly dated rooms have balconies, some face the bay. The Cabañas de los Arcos next door consist of several small brick cottages surrounded by gardens and a small hotel with a pool. **Cons:** Street noise is a drawback, the Wi-Fi is not consistently up and running. ✉ *Paseo Alvaro Obregón 498, between Rosales and Allende, Malecón,* ☎ *612/122–2744 or 800/347–2252* 🌐 *www.losarcos.com* *Hotel: 115 rooms, 15 suites; Cabañas: 19 rooms, 9 suites, 24 bungalows* *In-room: Refrigerator. In-hotel: Restaurant, bar, pools, public Wi-Fi* ▭ *AE, MC, V* *EP.*

$$ **Hotel Marina.** The full-service marina offers fishing, scuba diving, and kayaking. Private charters are available. Most rooms have terraces or balconies with water views, gardens surround the pool and hot tub. Naturally, it's popular with boaters sailing the Sea of Cortez; they share tall tales and tips at the Dinghy Dock restaurant right on the harbor.

Pros: Seaside promenade that lines the property. **Cons:** Far from downtown, can be noisy. ✉*Carretera a Pichilingue, Km 2.5,* ☎*612/121–6254 or 800/826–1138* 🌐*www.hotelmarina.com.mx* *86 rooms, 5 suites* *In-room: Refrigerator, Wi-Fi. In-hotel: Restaurant, bar, tennis court, pool, spa, no elevator* *AE, MC, V* *EP.*

$$ **Hotel Perla.** The brown low-rise faces the malecón and has been a flurry of activity since 1940, due largely to their nightclub La Cabaña. Rooms are a little kitschy with light-wood furnishings with pink and teal accents; some have king-size beds. **Pros:** The pool is on a second-story sundeck, away from the traffic of the main street. **Cons:** Noise is a factor in the oceanfront rooms, the trade-off being wonderful sunset views, so take your pick. ✉*Paseo Alvaro Obregón 1570, Malecón,* ☎*612/122–0777 or 888/242–3757* 🌐*www.hotelperlabaja.com* *110 rooms* *In-room: Refrigerator, dial-up. In-hotel: restaurant, bar, pool, public Wi-Fi.* *AE, MC, V* *EP*

$$ **Hotel Seven Crown.** This very reasonable, modern, minimalist hotel is perfectly situated to one side of the malecón's action. Take off from your hotel room for nearby cafés and restaurants, and prime people-watching. Other hotels are a little farther off. Hotel Seven Crown's rooms are comfortable, and come complete with a small refrigerator and extra sink. Book your excursions with the travel agency representative in the lobby. **Pros:** There's a small bar on the roof from which you can enjoy a view of the bay; no one ever seems to use the small hot tub next to the bar; and rooms have petite, private balconies. **Cons:** Rooms are a little plain, no pool. ✉*Paseo Alvaro Obregón 1710, Centro* ☎*612/128–7788* 🌐*www.sevencrownhotels.com* *54 rooms, 9 suites* *In-room: Kitchen (some), refrigerator, Wi-Fi. In-hotel: Restaurant, bar* *MC, V* *EP.*

$–$$ **La Casa Mexicana Inn.** Arlaine Cervantes has created a lovely home-like ambience in her small bed-and-breakfast just one block from the malecón. The rooms are exquisite in calming pastels with niches and shelves full of folk art, beds with hand-carved headboards, wrought-iron work, Guatemalean textiles, and custom ceiling and door moldings. Some rooms overlook the bay, while others face the peaceful garden. **Pros:** Guests rave about the breakfasts (for an extra cost) with local fruit, Mexican pastries, crepes, frittatas, and home-baked breads. **Cons:** Charge for continental breakfast (it's a good deal though). ✉*Calle Nicolas Bravo 106, Centro,* ☎*612/125–2748* 🌐*www.casamex.com* *6 rooms* *In-room: No phone, no TV, kitchen (some), Wi-Fi, refrigerator. In-hotel: No kids under 10* *AE, D, MC, V all via PayPal* *EP.*

$–$$ **Hotel Suites Club El Moro.** Possibly the best bargain on the malecón, this vacation-ownership resort has very reasonable suite rentals on a nightly and weekly basis. Within El Moro you'll find a palm-filled garden and a densely landscaped pool area, though the pool itself is a bit shallow for much serious swimming. You can recognize the building by its stark-white turrets and domes. Rooms are Mediterranean in style, with arched windows, Mexican tiles, and private balconies; some have ocean views. A small café serves breakfast and lunch. Fishing packages are available. **Pros:** Convenient, affordable. **Cons:** Facilities are basic.

✉ *Carretera a Pichilingue, Km 2, between downtown and Pichilingue,* ☎ *612/122–4084* 🌐 *www.clubelmoro.com* *28 rooms, 10 suites, 3 studios* *In-room: Wi-Fi, kitchen (some). In-hotel: Restaurant, bar, pool, public Wi-Fi* *AE, MC, V* *CP.*

¢ **Pensión California.** Few budget hotels in Baja feel like those on the mainland. This one has that edgy, almost unacceptable style beloved by those who travel rough. You can nab a bed here for less than $20; and the blue-and-white rooms have baths and are clean. The courtyard has picnic tables and a TV. There is also a public computer in the lobby, and guests are each invited to use it for up to 30 minutes daily. **Pros:** Super-cheap. **Cons:** Hacienda is run-down. ✉ *Av. Degollado 209, Centro,* ☎ *612/122–2896* *25 rooms* *In-room: No a/c, no TV. In-hotel: No elevator* *No credit cards* *EP.*

NIGHTLIFE

El Teatro de la Ciudad (✉ *Av. Navarro 700, Centro* ☎ *612/125–0486*) is La Paz's cultural center. The theater seats 1,500 and stages shows by visiting and local performers. **La Terraza** (✉ *Hotel Perla hotel, Paseo Alvaro Obregón 1570, Malecón* ☎ *612/122–0777*) is the best spot for both sunset- and people-watching along the malecón. The hotel also has a disco called **La Cabaña** where you can dance to Latin music on weekends.

★ **Las Varitas** (✉ *Av. Independencia 111, Centro* ☎ *612/125–2025* 🌐 *www.lasvaritas.com*), a Mexican rock club, heats up after midnight.

SHOPPING

Artesanías la Antigua California (✉ *Paseo Alvaro Obregón 220, Malecón* ☎ *612/125–5230*) has the nicest selection of Mexican folk art in La Paz, including wooden masks and lacquered boxes from Guerrero. It also has a good supply of English-language books on Baja.

Artesanía Cuauhtémoc (✉ *Av. Abasolo between Calles Nayarit and Oaxaca, south of downtown, Centro* ☎ *612/122–4575*) is the workshop of weaver Fortunado Silva, who creates and sells cotton place mats, rugs, and tapestries.

★ Julio Ibarra oversees the potters and painters at **Ibarra's Pottery** (✉ *Guillermo Prieto 625, Centro* ☎ *612/122–0404*). His geometric designs and glazing technique result in gorgeous mirrors, bowls, platters, and cups.

SPORTS & THE OUTDOORS

BOATING & FISHING

The considerable fleet of private boats in La Paz now has room for docking at three marinas: Fidepaz Marina at the north end of town, and the Marina Palmira and Marina La Paz south of town. Most hotels can arrange trips. Tournaments are held in August, September, and October. The **Mosquito Fleet** (☎ *612/121–6120, 612/121–6123, or 877/408–6769*) has cabin cruisers with charters starting around $550 for up to four people, and super *pangas* (skiffs) at $240 for two people.

DIVING & SNORKELING

Popular diving and snorkeling spots include the coral banks off Isla Espíritu Santo, the sea-lion colony off Isla Partida, and the seamount 14 km (9 mi) farther north (best for serious divers).

Baja Expeditions (✉*2625 Garnet Ave., San Diego, CA,* ☎*858/581–3311 or 800/843–6967* 🌐*www.bajaex.com*) runs daylong and multi-day dive packages in the Sea of Cortez. Packages start at about $385 per person (double occupancy) for a three-night, two-day diving package. Seven-day excursions aboard the 80-foot *Don José* dedicated dive boat start at $1,550 for cabin, food, and nearly unlimited diving. Live-aboard trips run from May into October. You may spot whale sharks in May and June.

★ The **Cortez Club** (✉*La Concha Beach Resort, Carretera a Pichilingue, Km 5, between downtown and Pichilingue* ☎*612/121–6120 or 612/121–6121* 🌐*www.cortezclub.com*) is a full-scale water-sports center with equipment rental and scuba, snorkeling, kayaking, and sportfishing tours. A two-tank dive costs about $110.

Fun Baja (✉*Carretera a Pichilingue, Km 2* ☎*612/121–5884* 🌐*www.funbaja.com*) offers scuba and snorkel trips with the sea lions. Two-tank scuba trips start at $130.

KAYAKING

The calm waters off La Paz are perfect for kayaking, and you can take multiday trips along the coast to Loreto or out to the nearby islands.

★ **Baja Expeditions** (✉*2625 Garnet Ave., San Diego, CA* ☎*858/581–3311 or 800/843–6967* 🌐*www.bajaex.com*), one of the oldest outfitters working in Baja, offers several kayak tours, including multinight trips between Loreto and La Paz. A support boat carries all the gear, including ingredients for great meals. The seven-day trip in the Sea of Cortez with camping on remote island beaches starts at $1,225 per person, based on double occupancy.

Baja Quest (✉*Sonora 174, Centro* ☎*612/123–5320*) has day and overnight kakyak trips. Day trips cost about $95 per person. **Fun Baja** (✉*Carretera a Pichilingue, Km 2* ☎*612/121–5884 or 800/667–5362* 🌐*www.funbaja.com*) offers kayak trips around the islands, scuba and snorkel excursions, and land tours. A day of kayaking and snorkeling will run about $130. **Nichols Expeditions** (✉*497 N. Main, Moab, UT* ☎ *800/648–8488* 🌐*www.nicholsexpeditions.com*) arranges kayaking tours to Isla Espíritu Santo and between Loreto and La Paz, with camping along the way. A nine-day trip costs $1,250. It also offers a combination of sea kayaking in the Sea of Cortez with whale-watching in Magdalena Bay. A nine-day trip costs $1,300.

WHALE-WATCHING

La Paz is a good entry point for whale-watching expeditions to **Bahía Magdalena**, 266 km (165 mi) northwest of La Paz on the Pacific coast. Note, however, that such trips entail about six hours of travel from La Paz and back for two to three hours on the water. Only a few tour companies offer this as a daylong excursion, however, because of the time and distance constraints.

Many devoted whale-watchers opt to stay overnight in San Carlos, the small town by the bay. Most La Paz hotels can make arrangements for excursions, or you can head out on your own by renting a car or taking a public bus from La Paz to San Carlos, and then hire a boat captain to take you into the bay. The air and water are cold during whale season from December to April, so you'll need to bring a warm windbreaker and gloves. Captains are not allowed to "chase" whales, but that doesn't keep the whale mamas and their babies from approaching your panga so closely you can reach out and touch them.

An easier expedition is a whale-watching trip in the Sea of Cortez from La Paz, which involves boarding a boat in La Paz and motoring around until whales are spotted. They most likely won't come as close to the boats and you won't see the mothers and newborn calves at play, but it's still fabulous watching the whales breeching and spouting nearby.

Baja Expeditions (✉*2625 Garnet Ave., San Diego, CA* ☎*858/581–3311 or 800/843–6967* 🌐*www.bajaex.com*) runs seven-day trips from La Paz to Magdalena Bay, including boat trips, camping, and meals; prices start at $1,440 per person, based on double occupancy. The company also runs adventure cruises around the tip of Baja between La Paz and Magdalena Bay. The eight-day cruises start at $1,900 per person, based on double occupancy.

Shorter trips including camping at Magdalena Bay are available through **Baja Quest** (✉*Sonora 174, Centro* ☎*612/123–5320* 🌐*www.bajaquest.com.mx*). The two-night camping trip starts at $695 per person; the four-night trip starts at $1,050 per person. The water-sports center **Cortez Club** (✉*La Concha Beach Resort, Carretera a Pichilingue, Km 5, between downtown and Pichilingue* ☎*612/121–6120 or 612/121–6121* 🌐*www.cortezclub.com*) runs extremely popular whale-watching trips in winter. A fishing trip, starting at 6 AM, costs $240 per person with a two-person minimum.

LORETO

354 km (220 mi) north of La Paz.

Loreto's setting on the Sea of Cortez is spectacular: the gold and green hills of the Sierra de la Giganta seem to tumble into cobalt water. According to local promoters, the skies are clear 360 days of the year, and the desert climate harbors few bothersome insects.

The Kikiwa, Cochimi, Cucapa, and Kumiai tribes first inhabited Baja. Jesuit priest Juan María Salvatierra founded the first California mission at Loreto in 1697, and not long after, the indigenous populations were nearly obliterated by disease and war. Seventy-two years later, a Franciscan monk from Mallorca, Spain—Father Junípero Serra—set out from here to establish missions from San Diego to San Francisco, in the land then known as Alta California.

In 1821 Mexico achieved independence from Spain, which ordered all missionaries home. Loreto's mission was abandoned and fell into disrepair. Then in 1829 a hurricane virtually destroyed the settlement, capital of the Californias at the time. The capital was moved to La Paz, and Loreto languished for a century. In the late 1970s, when oil revenue filled government coffers, the area was tapped for development. An international airport was built and a luxury hotel and tennis center opened, followed a few years later by a seaside 18-hole golf course. The infrastructure for a resort area south of town at Nopoló was set up. But the pace of development slowed as the money dried up.

Loreto is once again flush with developments, thanks to an influx of money from Fonatur, the federal government's tourism development fund. The downtown waterfront has a pristine seawall and sidewalk malecón with park benches. Entrepreneurs are opening hotels and restaurants, and investors are buying up land. In Nopoló, an entire resort community is rising. Some say Loreto will be another Los Cabos.

For now Loreto has a population of around 13,000 full-time residents and an increasing number of part-timers. It's still a good place to escape the crowds, relax, and go fishing or whale-watching. The Parque Maritímo Nacional Bahía de Loreto protects much of the Sea of Cortez in this area, but there are a few cruise ships that use Loreto as a port of call, and the marina at Puerto Escondido is central to the government's plans for a series of marinas. With any luck, new developments will be contained in the Nopoló area.

GETTING HERE & AROUND

Loreto's Aeropuerto Internacional Loreto is 7 km (4½ mi) southwest of town. Taxis from the airport into town are inexpensive (about $5) and convenient. Loreto's Terminal de Autobus sits at the entrance to town and has service from La Paz, Los Cabos, and points north. In Loreto taxis are in good supply and fares are inexpensive; it costs $5 or less to get anywhere in town and about $10 from downtown Loreto to Nopoló. Illegitimate taxis aren't a problem in this region.

ESSENTIALS

Bus Contacts **Loreto Terminal de Autobus** (✉ *Calle Salvatierra at Calle Tamaral* ☎ *613/135–0767*). **SuburBaja** (☎ *624/146–0888*).

Mail & Shipping **Loreto Oficina de Correo** (✉ *Palacio Municipal* ☎ *No phone*).

Visitor & Tour Info **Loreto Tourist Information Office** (✉ *Municipal Building on Plaza Principal, Loreto* ☎ *613/135–0411* 🌐 *www.gotoloreto.com*).

EXPLORING

You can arrange picnic trips to **Coronado Island**, inhabited only by sea lions, in Loreto, Nopoló, or Puerto Escondido. The snorkeling and scuba diving near the island are excellent. Danzante and other islands off Loreto are part of the Parque Maritímo Nacional Bahía de Loreto. Commercial fishing boats aren't allowed within the 60-square-km (23-square-mi) park.

Isla Danzante, 5 km (3 mi) southeast of Puerto Escondido, has good reefs and diving opportunities.

The **malecón** along Calle de la Playa (also called Paseo Lopez Mateos) is a pleasant place to walk, jog, or sit on a cast-iron bench watching the sunset. A small marina shelters yachts and the panga fleet; the adjoining beach is popular with locals, especially on Sunday afternoons, when kids hit the playground.

Loreto's main historic sight is **La Misión de Nuestra Señora de Loreto** (☒ *Calle Salvatierra at Calle Misioneros* ☎ *613/135–0005*). The stone church's bell tower is the town's main landmark, rising above the main plaza and reconstructed pedestrian walkway along Salvatierra.

★ A trip to **Misión San Javier,** 32 km (20 mi) southwest of Loreto, shows Baja at its best. A high-clearance vehicle is useful for the two-hour drive to the mission—don't try getting here if the dirt and gravel road is muddy. The road climbs past small ranches, palm groves, and the steep cliffs of the Cerro de la Giganta. Marked trails lead off the road to remnants of a small cluster of Indian cave paintings. The mission village is a remote community of some 50 full-time residents, many of whom come outdoors when visitors arrive.

The mission church (circa 1699), which is amid orchards, is built of blocks of gray volcanic rock and topped with domes and bell towers containing three bells from the 18th and 19th centuries. The side stained-glass windows are framed with wood. Inside, a gilded central altar contains a statue of Saint Javier; side altars have statues of Saint Ignacio and the Virgen de los Dolores. Vestments from the 1700s are displayed in a glass cabinet. The church is often locked; ask anyone hanging about to find the person with the keys. Slip a few pesos into the contribution box as a courtesy to the village's inhabitants, who keep the church well maintained. Loreto residents make pilgrimages to the mission for the patron saint's festival, celebrated December 1–3. Although you can drive to San Javier on your own, it helps to have a guide along to lead you to the caves and Indian paintings. Many hotels and tour companies can arrange trips. In San Javier you can spend the night at **Casa de Ana** (☎ *613/135–1552 or 800/497–3923* 🌐 *www.hoteloasis.com*) in a little bungalow and get a rare view into a small Baja community ($35 per night).

★ **El Museo de los Misiones,** also called the Museo de Historia y Antropologia (Missions Museum or Museum of History and Anthropology), contains religious relics, 19th-century leather saddles, and displays on Baja's history. ☒ *Calle Salvatierra s/n, next to La Misión de Nuestra Señora de Loreto* ☎ *613/135–0441* *$3.40* ⏲ *Tues.–Sun. 9–1 and 3–6.*

A major developer is transforming **Nopoló,** about 8 km (5 mi) south of Loreto, into a truly sustainable resort area called **Loreto Bay** (🌐 *www.loretobay.com*). Mission-style condos and homes with lush vegetation rise on lots laid out in the 1970s. The area will also be home to an estuary and canals, cleaning the water and supporting plant and animal

CLOSE UP

Baja's Gray Whales

A small boat glides through clear waters off Baja, its passengers bundled in jackets and scarves. Suddenly someone spots a dark shape slicing through the water like a submarine. Everyone sits still and silent as the creature moves closer, emitting gusts of air. And then, there she is: a 20-ton mama right by the boat. The interlopers tentatively reach out to touch the gray whale, her skin crusty with mollusks. She opens her enormous eyes, and slowly allows a small form to surface from beneath her fin and nuzzle a human hand. The scene repeats itself as the whale grows comfortable. Cheering and clapping, the enraptured passengers click photos, film videos, and generally perform as they would around any darling new baby.

Every December through March, gray whales swim 8,000 km (5,000 mi) south from Alaska's Bering Strait to the tip of the Baja Peninsula. Up to 6,000 whales swim past and stop close to the shore at several spots to give birth to their calves. These newborns weigh about half a ton and consume nearly 50 gallons of milk a day.

The best places for close encounters are Bahía Magdalena (aka Mag Bay), which is about 266 km (165 mi) northwest of La Paz and 94 km (58 mi) southwest of Loreto, and Laguna San Ignacio, which is about 70 km (43 mi) southwest of San Ignacio. Less accessible is Parque Natural de la Ballena Gris (Gray Whale Natural Park) at Scammon's Lagoon near Guerrero Negro, about 227 km (141 mi) northwest of San Ignacio at the border with Baja Norte. There are no flights into this remote Pacific coast area, which is usually accessed by car or bus from the Tijuana border 720 km (446 mi) north. Several U.S. and Mexican companies offer multiday tours to the various whale-watching areas that include overnight stays in small hotels or camps.

Whale-watching boats—most of them *pangas* (small skiffs)—must get permission from the Mexican government to enter the whale-watching areas. The experience itself entails a trip into the lagoons in a small boat. It's usually chilly, and passengers are bundled up but ready to take off their gloves if a whale comes near. But for a better view, and an easier stay in this rugged country, travel with an outfitter who will arrange your transportation, accommodations, and time on the water. Bring along a telephoto lens and lots of film or a high-capacity memory card if you're shooting digital. Binoculars come in handy as well.

life in the area while also beautifying the town. The nine-court tennis complex and 18-hole golf course have been spiffed up, and the classy and still-affordable Loreto Inn attracts many visitors.

Puerto Escondido, 16 km (10 mi) down Carretera 1 from Nopoló, has an RV park, **Tripui** (☎*613/133–0818* 🌐*www.tripui.com*), with a good restaurant, a few motel rooms, a snack shop, bar, stores, showers, laundry, a pool, and tennis courts. There's a boat ramp at the Puerto Escondido marina close to Tripui; you pay the fee required to launch here to the attendant at the parking lot. The port captain's office (☎*613/135–0656*) is just south of the ramp, but it's rarely open.

WHERE TO EAT

$–$$$ STEAK **El Nido.** If you're hungry for steak, chicken, and hearty Mexican combo plates, then this is your place. It's as close as you'll get to a steak house in these parts. The brass and woodwork and the courteous waiters make this a good place for a special night out or a big, satisfying meal after a hard day's fishing or kayaking. *Calle Salvatierra 154 613/135–2445 No credit cards.*

¢–$ ECLECTIC **Café Olé.** Locals and gringos alike hang out at this casual spot for terrific breakfasts of scrambled eggs with chorizo (sausage), huevos rancheros, and other typical, delicious Mexican breakfasts. Later in the day (they're open until 10 PM) they steer away from Mexican specialties and also serve good burgers, french fries, and ice cream. *Calle Francisco Madero 14 613/135–0496 No credit cards.*

¢–$ ECLECTIC Fodor's Choice ★ **Pachamama.** The owners (she's from Argentina, he's from Mexico City) have combined their cultures and cuisines to create a restaurant worth repeat visits. Nibble on regional cheeses or empanadas, then move on to a salad of goat cheese and sliced homegrown tomatoes or a marinated *arrachera* (skirt) steak. Sandwiches on homemade bread make you wish the place were open for lunch. *Calle Zapata between Calles Salvatierra and Juárez 613/135–2219 MC, V Closed Tues. No lunch.*

¢ MEXICAN ★ **Canipole.** Sofía Rodríguez reigns over the open kitchen of this down-home, open-air Mexican restaurant. The 34 ingredients she uses in her savory mole are displayed in tiny bowls on one table, the ingredients for her homemade Mexican hot chocolate are in bowls on another. Pots of *pozole* (a hominy stew) and tortilla soup simmer over a gas fire on the patio while Sofía pats out fresh tortillas for each order. Specialties include *conejo* (rabbit), quesadillas with *flor de calabaza* (squash blossoms), and unusual carnitas made with lamb. Check out the view of the mission's dome from the restaurant's backyard. *Pino Suárez s/n, beside mission 613/133–0282 No credit cards Closed Sun.*

WHERE TO STAY

$$$$ Fodor's Choice ★ **Danzante Resort.** This hilltop resort facing Isla Danzante is architecturally stunning and ecologically sensitive, and has dramatic views to say the least. Owners Michael and Lauren Farley are Baja experts, writers, and underwater photographers. Guest rooms have bent-twig furnishings, wrought-iron bedsteads, patios with hammocks, and such thoughtful amenities as binoculars and books. Phones and TVs are nonexistent, except for sporadic cellular phone access. There are plenty of activities to pursue, including hiking, kayaking, and bird-watching in an undeveloped area that still feels remote. **Pros:** Wonderfully rustic, many activities, views are to die for. **Cons:** The drive to Loreto to visit restaurants or shops takes about 30 minutes. *32 km (20 mi) south of Loreto off Carretera 1 Box 1166, Los Gatos, CA95031 408/354–0042 in U.S. www.danzante.com 9 suites In-room: No a/c, no phone, no TV. In-hotel: Restaurant, pool, beachfront, diving, water sports, no elevator, no kids under 8, no-smoking rooms MC, V AI.*

$$$ **Hotel Posada de las Flores.** The rose-color walls of this surprisingly chic hotel rise beside downtown's plaza. A glass-bottom pool doubles

as a skylight above the atrium lobby, and the rooftop sundeck and restaurant have huge planters of bougainvillea. Exposed beams and locally crafted tile adorn the lobby and hallways. Guest rooms are also beautifully decorated. There is also a tapas bar that is open in the evenings on the ground level. Sit outside and you can people-watch while you munch. **Pros:** The public areas are its forte, having a drink at the rooftop bar is good for a view of town and the mountains. **Cons:** Rooms can be very dark and noisy, pool is very small. ✉ *Calle Salvatierra at Calle Francisco Madero,* ☎ *613/135–1162* 🌐 *www.posadadelasflores.com* *10 rooms, 5 suites* *In-room: Safe, refrigerator, Wi-Fi. In-hotel: Restaurant (only serves breakfast), bar, pool, laundry service, no elevator, no kids under 12, no-smoking rooms* 💳 *MC, V* 🍽 *BP.*

$$ **Hotel Oasis.** One of the original in-town hostelries, the Oasis remains an ideal base for those who want to be in town and spend plenty of time on the water. The best rooms have coffeemakers, water views, and hammocks on the front terraces. Guests gather in the large bar to wish each other luck over breakfast or exchange fishing tales in the evening. Meal plans vary with the season and with packages. **Pros:** The hotel has its own fleet of skiffs. **Cons:** Rooms vary greatly in size and comfort. ✉ *Calle de la Playa, Apdo. 17,* ☎ *613/135–0112 or 800/497–3923* 🌐 *www.hoteloasis.com* *40 rooms* *In-room: No phone (some), refrigerator (some). In-hotel: Restaurant, bar, pool, no elevator* 💳 *MC, V* 🍽 *BP, EP, FAP.*

$$ **Inn at Loreto Bay.** This fancy resort is surrounded by an entire neighborhood that feels like a ghost town because it's still mostly uninhabited and under development, but even if a walk around the neighborhood is uneventful (though it is becoming more and more beautiful all the time), there is still plenty to do within the hotel and community. There is a nice restaurant, a pool area (though the pool is shallow for those looking for serious swim time), and scuba, snorkeling, and kayak trips depart from the beach. The bright guest rooms have very cozy beds, large closets, double sinks, and marble showers. All rooms look out to the Sea of Cortez; some also face the golf course, which winds around the resort. Most have a balcony or terrace. The rooftop suites, however, have terraces complete with hot tubs. A meal plan is available for $50 per person per day, not including tax and tips. **Pros:** The restaurants are good and reasonably priced. **Cons:** Some terraces too small for chairs. ✉ *Blvd. Misión de Loreto s/n,* ☎ *613/133–0643 or 866/850–0333* 🌐 *www.innatloretobay.com* *137 rooms, 17 suites* *In-room: Safe, dial-up, Wi-Fi. In-hotel: 3 restaurants, room service, bars, pool, beachfront, no elevator, laundry service, no-smoking rooms* 💳 *AE, MC, V* 🍽 *EP.*

$–$$ **Sukasa.** Roomy air-conditioned bungalows with brick and stucco walls, palapa ceilings, and separate bedrooms are clustered in a compound just steps from the malecón. One sturdy, canvas-sided yurt is another affordable and definitely unique option. It's easy to imagine you've moved to Loreto, at least for a while, as you set up housekeeping in the kitchen and wander across the street, coffee in hand, to watch the sun rise and set. **Pros:** The manager is a delight, quick to make guests feel totally at home and set up excursions, kayaks and bikes are on hand for guest use. **Cons:** Yurt can be noisy and cold. ✉ *Calle de la Playa at Calle Jordan,* ☎ *613/135–0490* 🌐 *www.loreto.com/sukasa* *3 bungalows, 1 yurt* *In-room: Kitchen, Wi-Fi. In hotel: Watersports, no elevator* *MC, V* *EP.*

¢ **Motel el Dorado.** Low rates, accessible parking, and a congenial bar are available at this spanking-clean motel. Rooms are classic Baja basic, with thin mattresses, TVs anchored to the walls, and inexpensive darkwood furnishings. The motel also offers rents motorbikes and fishing charters. A seven-hour trip on a 23-foot boat goes for $175. **Pros:** Waterfront is a block away. **Cons:** Missing a pool. ✉ *Paseo Hidalgo at Calle Pipila,* ☎ *613/135–1500 or 888/314–9023* 🌐 *www.moteleldorado.com* *11 rooms* *In-room: No phone. In-hotel: Bar, no elevator, laundry service, public Wi-Fi* *MC, V* *EP.*

SHOPPING

★ Loreto's shopping district is along the pedestrian zone on Calle Salvatierra, where there are several souvenir shops and stands, plus the town's only supermarket. **El Alacrán** (✉ *Calle Salvatierra 47* ☎ *613/135–0029*) has remarkable folk art, jewelry, and sportswear.

SPORTS & THE OUTDOORS

FISHING

Fishing put Loreto on the map. You can catch cabrilla and snapper year-round, yellowtail in spring, and dorado, marlin, and sailfish in summer. If you're a serious angler, bring tackle. Some sportfishing fleets do update their equipment regularly. All Loreto-area hotels can arrange fishing, and many own skiffs. Local anglers congregate with their small boats on the beach at the north and south ends of town.

Arturo's Fishing Fleet (✉ *Paseo Hidalgo between plaza and marina* ☎ *613/135–0766* 🌐 *www.arturosport.com*) has several types of boats and fishing packages and operates the water-sports concession at the Inn at Loreto Bay. The **Baja Big Fish Company** (✉ *Paseo Hidalgo 19, by plaza* ☎ *613/104–0781* 🌐 *www.bajabigfish.com*), which specializes in light tackle and fly-fishing, has packages from the United States that sometimes include free hotel nights and fishing trips from Loreto. Half-day fishing rates start at $150.

GOLF

The 18-hole **Loreto Golf Course** (☎ *613/133–0554*), along Nopoló Bay, was in such bad shape local wags joked it was the only course where golfers turn down free play. The conditions have improved a bit since the Loreto Bay Company, which is developing Nopoló, took over and brought in the international management company Troon Golf to whip things into shape. The setting is gorgeous, with fairways and greens set between the Sea of Cortez and the mountains. Several hotels in Loreto have golf packages and reduced or free greens fees. Greens fees are $25 for 9 holes, and $40 for 18 holes.

WATER SPORTS

Arrange kayaking excursions, whale-watching tours, scuba-certification courses, and dive and snorkeling trips through the **Baja Outpost**

(✉*Blvd. Mateos, near Oasis Hotel* ☎*613/135–1134 or 888/649–5951* 🌐*www.bajaoutpost.com*). The company specializes in sports packages. A three-day, two-night snorkeling package starts at $223 per person based on double occupancy in their hotels; with kayaking, the package starts at $307. The company also offers day tours to Misión San Javier. **Dolphin Dive Center** (✉*Calle Juárez between Calles Davis and Playa* ☎*613/135–1914 in U.S.* 🌐*www.dolphindivebaja.com*) is a PADI shop offering dives around the islands off Loreto and instruction. A two-tank trip costs $89–$110 depending on location; snorkeling excursions run $55. The company also has whale-watching and San Javier tours.

Paddling South Tours (*Box 827, Calistoga, CA 94515* ☎*707/942–4550 or 800/398–6200* 🌐*www.tourbaja.com*) runs guided kayaking trips starting at $995, including meals. The company also offers mountain-biking trips, and multiday mule pack trips with a historic focus. Loreto outdoor specialists **Las Parras Tours** (✉*Calle Salvatierra at Calle Francisco Madero* ☎*613/135–1010*) provides day trips with kayaking, island skiff trips, as well as whale-watching, scuba diving and certification, and visiting San Javier village in the mountains. Day trips in the desert cost $29 and up, and tours to San Javier run $50.

The U.S.–based company **Sea Quest** (☎*360/378–5767 or 888/589–4253* 🌐*www.sea-quest-kayak.com*) has several trips that begin in Loreto. Options include kayaking with gray whales in Magdalena Bay or in the San Ignacio Lagoon. Weeklong trips start at $1,299.

MULEGÉ

134 km (83 mi) north of Loreto.

Mulegé is a popular base for exploring the Sierra de Guadalupe mountains, the site of several prehistoric rock paintings of human and animal figures. Kayaking in Bahía Concepción, Baja's largest protected bay, is spectacular.

Once a mission settlement, this charming town of some 3,500 residents swells in winter, when Americans and Canadians fleeing the cold arrive in motor homes. Amid an oasis of date palms on the banks of the Río Santa Rosalía, Mulegé looks and feels more tropical than other Baja Sur communities. Several narrow streets make up the business district, and dirt roads run from the highway to RV parks south of town.

Access to the rock paintings is good, though you must have a permit and go with a licensed guide. Tours typically involve a bumpy ride followed by an even bumpier climb on burros. **Mulegé Tours** (✉*Hotel Las Casitas, Av. Madero 50* ☎*615/153–0232 or 615/103–5081* 🌐*www.mulegetours.com*) is run by Salvador Castro Drew, a Mulegé native. He leads treks to the cave paintings and to working ranches in the mountains. Cave excursions start at $40.

WHERE TO STAY

$ ★ **Hotel Serenidad.** A Mulegé mainstay for Baja aficionados since the late 1960s, this delightful escape is owned by the Johnson family, longtime residents. The Serenidad's simple rooms in brick and stucco buildings are scattered under bougainvillea vines and fruit trees. Some suiteshave fireplaces and separate bedrooms. **Pros:** The Saturday-night pig roast is a tradition, adjacent RV park for road warriors. **Cons:** Somewhat basic. *2.5 km (1.5 mi) north of Mulegé, Carretera 1, 615/153–0530 www.hotelserenidad.com 50 rooms In-room: No phone. In-hotel: Restaurant, bar, pool, no elevator MC, V EP.*

¢ **Hacienda.** You can read and lounge in rocking chairs by the pool or at the bar in this modest hotel steps from the town plaza. Kayak trips and tours to cave paintings in the mountains can be arranged. Rooms are spartan but work fine for a night or two. **Pros:** Totally affordable. **Cons:** Upkeep can be lacking. *Calle Madero 3, 615/153–0021 or 800/346–3942 615/153–0377 24 rooms In-room: No a/c (some), no phone, no TV. In-hotel: Restaurant, bar, pool, no elevator No credit cards EP.*

SPORTS & THE OUTDOORS

DIVING

Cortez Explorers (*Calle Moctezuma 75A 615/153–0500 www.cortez-explorers.com*) conducts dive trips to the rocky reefs off the Santa Inez Islands. You can rent dive equipment, mountain bikes, and take resort or PADI dive courses and snorkeling trips. A two-tank dive trip with full rented gear costs $180. Bikes rent for $24 a day, ATVs for $40 an hour.

SANTA ROSALIA

64 km (40 mi) north of Mulegé.

The architecture in this dusty mining town is a fascinating mix of French, Mexican, and American Old West styles. It's so different from other architecture in the area that you can easily forget you're in Baja California.

EXPLORING

Santa Rosalia is known for its **Iglesia Santa Barbara** (*Av. Obregón at Calle Altamirano*), a prefabricated iron church designed by Alexandre-Gustave Eiffel, creator of the Eiffel Tower. The iron panels of the little church are brightened by stained-glass windows.

Be sure to stop by **El Boleo** (*Av. Obregón at Calle 4*), where fresh breads tempt customers weekday mornings at 10.

WHERE TO STAY

$ **Hotel Frances.** The glory days of this well-kept 1886 French hillside mansion shine through. The lobby is decorated with framed embroidered flowers, old black-and-white photos of the town, and lace curtains. Many rooms open onto a second-story porch with views of town and the sea. There's a small pool and a classy restaurant in the courtyard. **Pros:** Well-maintained, interesting history, incredibly affordable.

Cons: Amenities obviously aren't the most modern. ✉*Av. 11 de Julio at Calle Jean M. Cousteau,* ☎*615/152–2052* *17 rooms* *In-room: Wi-Fi. In-hotel: Restaurant, pool, no elevator, laundry service, parking (no fee)* *No credit cards* *EP.*

SAN IGNACIO

77 km (48 mi) northwest of Santa Rosalia.

Although San Ignacio is in the Desierto de Vizcaíno, date palms, planted by Jesuit missionaries in the late 1700s, sway gently, in sync with the town's laid-back rhythms. San Ignacio is primarily a place to organize whale-watching and cave-painting tours or to stop and cool off in the shady zócalo (town square).

WHERE TO STAY

$–$$ **Desert Inn.** This simple, functional hotel is a pleasant place to stay on your transpeninsular journey. White arches frame the courtyard and pool, and the rooms are decorated with folk art and wood furnishings. **Pros:** Both the river and town are within walking distance. **Cons:** You may wish for a bit more for the money. ✉*2 km (1 mi) west of Hwy. 1 on unnamed road into San Ignacio,* ☎*615/157–1305, 619/275–4500, or 800/800–9632* *www.desertinns.com* *28 rooms* *In-hotel: Restaurant, room service, bar, no elevator, laundry service, no-smoking rooms, parking (free)* *MC, V* *EP.*

SPORTS & THE OUTDOORS

San Ignacio is the base for trips to Laguna San Ignacio, 59 km (35 mi) from San Ignacio on the Pacific coast. The lagoon is one of the best places to watch the gray-whale migration, and local boat captains will usually take you close enough to pet the new baby whales.

★ Tours arranged through **Baja Discovery** (*Box 152527, San Diego, CA 92195* ☎*619/262–0700 or 800/829–2252* *www.bajadiscovery.com*) include round-trip transport from San Diego to San Ignacio Lagoon, by van to Tijuana and private plane to the company's comfortable camp at the lagoon. Accommodations are in private tents facing the water, and there are solar-heated showers. The cost of a five-day package—including transportation, tours, and meals—is $2,175.

★ **Baja Expeditions** (✉*2625 Garnet Ave., San Diego, CA* ☎*858/581–3311 or 800/843–6967* *www.bajaex.com*) operates a camp at San Ignacio Lagoon and offers five-day tours including air transportation from San Diego. The fee is $2,095 including transport, meals, and tours. **Ecoturísticos Kuyima** (✉*Av. Morelos 23* ☎*615/154–0070* *www.kuyima.com*) in San Ignacio offers transportation between the town and San Ignacio Lagoon, operates a campground at an isolated area of the lagoon, and has adventure tours to caves with prehistoric paintings that include overnights in San Ignacio and at the lagoon. Whale-watching tours with camping and transportation from San Ignacio cost $165 per person per day. Day tours to area cave paintings from San Ignacio cost $50–$70 per person.

GUERRERO NEGRO

227 km (141 mi) northwest of San Ignacio.

Guerrero Negro, near the border with Baja Norte, is a good hub for whale-watching trips to Scammon's Lagoon. Near the Desierto de Vizcaíno (Vizcaíno Desert), on the Pacific Ocean, the area is best known for its salt pans, which produce one-third of the world's salt supply. Salt water collects in some 780 square km (300 square mi) of sea-level ponds and evaporates quickly in the desert heat, leaving great blocks of salt.

EXPLORING

★ **Scammon's Lagoon** is about 27 km (17 mi) south of Guerrero Negro, down a rough but passable sand road that crosses salt flats. The lagoon got its name from U.S. explorer Charles Melville Scammon of Maine, who came here in the mid-1800s. On his first expedition Scammon and his crew collected more than 700 barrels of valuable whale oil, and the whale rush was on. Within 10 years nearly all the whales in the lagoon had been killed, and it took almost a century for the population to increase to what it had been before Scammon arrived. In the 1940s the U.S. and Mexican governments took measures to protect the whales. With a sturdy vehicle you can drive the washboard dirt road to Scammon's Lagoon and arrange a trip for about $25–$40 per person, depending on the type of boat and length of tour. Start early to take advantage of the calmest water and best viewing conditions.

WHERE TO STAY

¢ ★ **Malarrimo Motel.** If you're looking for one-stop shopping, the staff at Malarrimo can wine and dine you, and arrange your whale-watching expedition. The most comfortable place to stay along Boulevard Zapata, the main drag in Guerrero Negro, this motel has 18 rooms and six "Mex" rooms they sometimes call cabañas though they're not freestanding. The "Mex" rooms are a little larger, so they tend to stay cooler when the weather is warm, while the smaller rooms are better in winter. Rooms are spartan, although the hotel's miniature courtyard manages to enliven the ambience a bit. The hotel staff suggests making reservations around six months in advance if you are planning on visiting during whale-watching season. This is the largest, best-established hotel in the area, so rooms go quickly. The restaurant and bar, widely considered the best in town, are a great place to enjoy well-prepared seafood and delicious meats. The walls are covered in bric-a-brac including newspaper articles about the area, and found items like whale bones; buoys hang from the ceilings. The gift shop next door, Casa El Viejo Cactus, offers arts and crafts and a small selection of books. **Pros: Chilaquiles, fresh oysters, convenient**

TRUTH BE TOLD

If it weren't for the whales and the Carretera Transpeninsular, which passes nearby, few would venture into Guerrero Negro, a town of roughly 10,000. It's a dusty, windy, generally unpleasant place, except, it seems, to osprey, which are fond of roosting on area power poles.

tour operator. Cons: Slow wait service, plain hotel rooms. ✉*Blvd. Zapata s/n, 23940* ☎*615/157–0250* 🌐*www.malarrimo.com* *18 rooms, 6 Mex rooms* *In room: No a/c, no phone. In hotel: Public Wi-Fi* *AE, MC, V* *EP.*

SPORTS & THE OUTDOORS

Malarrimo Eco-Tours (✉*Blvd. Zapata s/n* ☎*615/157–0100* 🌐*www.malarrimo.com* *AE, MC, V*) offers the original whale-watching tour in Guerrero Negro. You can arrange for a tour at the Malarrimo Restaurant, but to make sure that you can get a spot, reserve in advance, especially if you want to go out on a weekend. (A 50% deposit is necessary to make the reservation.) Owner Luis Enrique Achoy and his crew offer two tours daily. One leaves at 8 AM and the other at 11 AM. Both tours last about four hours and if the weather won't allow you to see the whales, Malarrimo will reschedule.

BAJA NORTE

Updated by Jonathan J. Levin & Coco Krumme

At turns a land of pristine desert and turquoise beaches, a drunken spring-break hot spot, an up-and-coming wine region, and a patchwork of shantytowns sprawled across dry and barren hills, Baja California Norte truly embodies Mexican border culture. This stretch of land doesn't have so much in common with what lies south: it's a land full of RV parks with California license plates, a society where English is often spoken as freely as Spanish, and a microeconomy in which the U.S. dollar is so prevalent that some vendors only begrudgingly accept pesos.

The border crossing to Tijuana, Baja's largest city, which lies just 29 km (18 mi) south of San Diego, is the busiest in the world—and that's not to mention the millions of Mexicans who would cross to the *otro lado* (the "other side," as the United States is informally called in these parts), if they only could. Meanwhile, although Americans have the luxury of entering and leaving Mexico at will, the sad reality is that Tijuana and the nearby beach town of Rosarito are the only Mexico that many of them ever see. And while this most infamous of border towns is certainly interesting, it can at times represent the worst of its country.

Only a couple of hours farther south along Baja's Pacific coast on the Carretera Transpeninsular (Carretera 1 or Highway 1) you'll find striking seascapes and vineyard-studded countryside. Near the busy port town of Ensenada, which has more Mexican flavor than the nearby cities, Carretera 3 (Highway 3) runs through the starkly beautiful Guadalupe Valley, home to some of the most underappreciated winemakers in the Americas. That same highway also runs southeast of Ensenada, winding past dusty plains and cactus-studded terrain, then climbing the stark foothills of the Sierra San Pedro Mártir to reach the well-traveled fishing port and beach town of San Felipe, on the tranquil waters of the Mar de Cortés (Sea of Cortez).

If you're traveling south, Ensenada is the last major city on the northern section of Mexico Carretera 1. Well south of Ensenada is the turnoff for a paved road to Bahía de los Angeles, a remote bay beloved by fishermen and naturalists that has recently hatched a luxury resort and spa, Los Vientos, along with a marina that is sure to bring further development to the area. It seems the developers are chasing the RVers and motorists who constantly seek the most isolated remaining patches of sand and solitude along the Mar de Cortés. It may take years, but they always catch up eventually.

TIJUANA

29 km (18 mi) south of San Diego.

Over the course of the 20th century, Tijuana grew from a ranch populated by a few hundred Mexicans into a Prohibition retreat for boozing and gambling—then it morphed yet again into an industrial giant infamous for its proliferation of *maquiladoras* (sweat shops). With a documented population of 1.2 million (informal estimates run as high as 2 million), Tijuana has surpassed Ciudad Juárez to become the country's sixth-largest city. Whether the legendary sleazefest is now primary or secondary to Tijuana's economy, the place certainly hasn't shaken its bawdy image; tell someone you're going to Tijuana, and you'll still elicit knowing chuckles all around.

Gone are the glamorous days when Hollywood stars would frequent hot spots like the Agua Caliente Racetrack & Casino, which opened in 1929. When Prohibition was repealed, Tijuana's fortunes began to decline, and, in 1967, when the toll highway to Ensenada was completed, Tijuana ceased to be such a necessary pit stop on the overland route to the rest of Baja. Even the Jai-Alai Palace—which survived into the new millennium as the city's last bastion of gambling—is just a museum now.

That's not to say that the knowing chuckles aren't still deserved, because Tijuana has more recently managed to redefine itself as a hot spot for young Californians in search of the sort of fun not allowed back home, like a lower drinking age, and perhaps some souvenirs, like duty-free tequila, overpriced trinkets, marked-down medicines, and Polaroid photos taken with donkeys painted as zebras (which, we kid you not, are readily available on Avenida Revolución). Even amid the high-profile hotels, casual dining chains, art museums, and Omni movies that have swooped into the city's swankier Zona Río in the last decade, much of Tijuana still represents border culture at its most bleakly opportunistic, from corrupt cops to pharmacies loudly advertising volume discounts on 100mg Viagra tablets (about enough for a horse).

Meanwhile, as the population has mushroomed, driven largely by the *maquiladoras,* the government has struggled to keep up with the growth and demand for services; thousands live without electricity, running water, or adequate housing in villages along the border. And nowhere in Mexico are the realities of commercial sex laid out more starkly. Open prostitution is everywhere: in the Zona Norte, streetwalkers accost passersby as they sidestep pools of vomit; strip bars like Casa Adelita

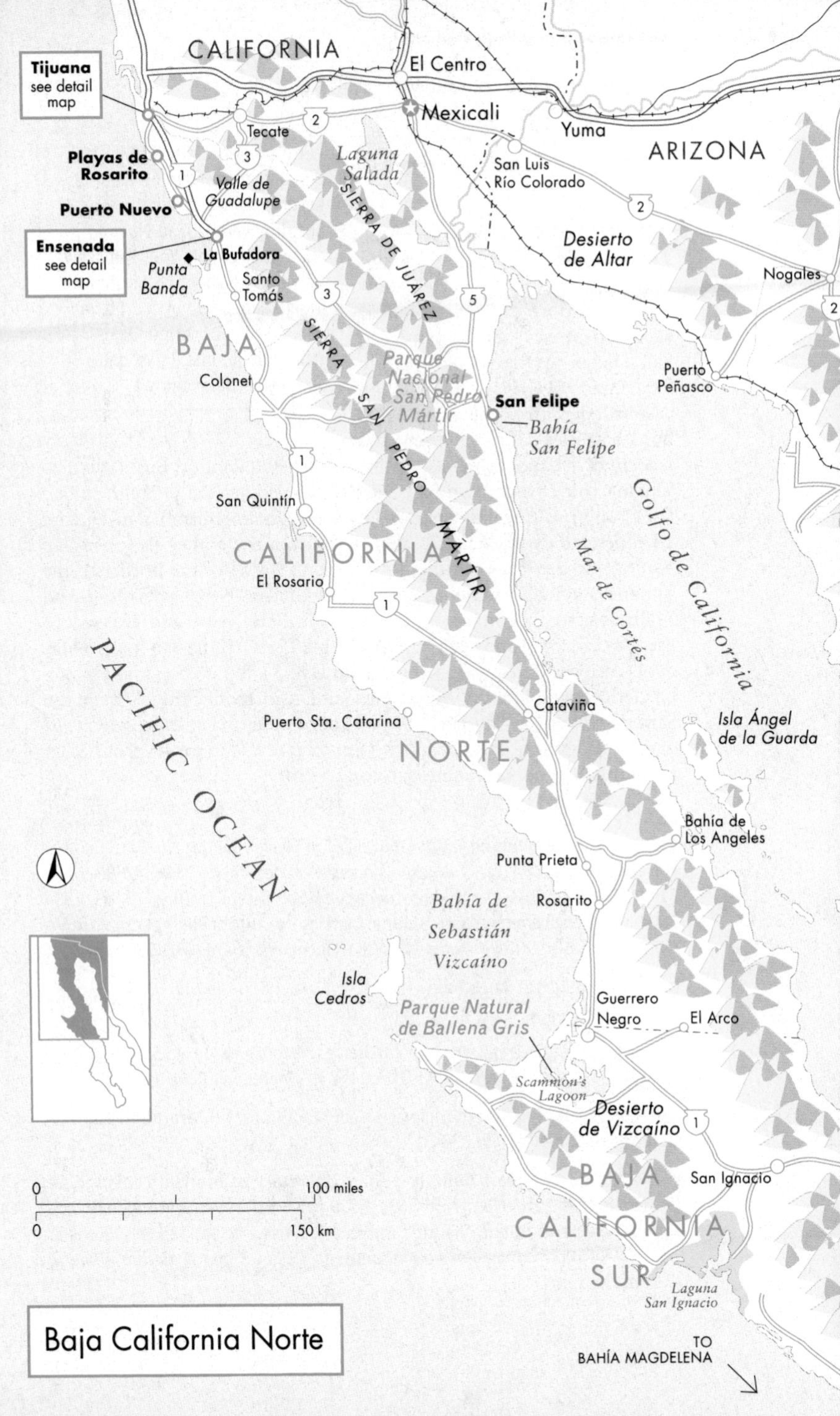

CALIFORNIA
ARIZONA
Tijuana
see detail map
El Centro
Mexicali
Yuma
Tecate
Playas de Rosarito
Laguna Salada
San Luis Río Colorado
Valle de Guadalupe
Puerto Nuevo
SIERRA DE JUÁREZ
Desierto de Altar
Ensenada
see detail map
La Bufadora
Punta Banda
Santo Tomás
Nogales
BAJA
SIERRA SAN PEDRO MÁRTIR
Parque Nacional San Pedro Mártir
Colonet
Puerto Peñasco
San Felipe
Bahía San Felipe
San Quintín
Golfo de California
CALIFORNIA
El Rosario
Mar de Cortés
PACIFIC OCEAN
Cataviña
Puerto Sta. Catarina
Isla Ángel de la Guarda
NORTE
Bahía de Los Angeles
Punta Prieta
Bahía de Sebastián Vizcaíno
Rosarito
Isla Cedros
Parque Natural de Ballena Gris
Guerrero Negro
El Arco
Scammon's Lagoon
Desierto de Vizcaíno
BAJA
San Ignacio
CALIFORNIA
SUR
Laguna San Ignacio
0
100 miles
0
150 km
TO BAHÍA MAGDELENA

Baja California Norte

and Chicago Club also function as giant, multifloor brothels—every single dancer is for sale. Maybe that's why they sell the Viagra in such ludicrous doses.

CAUTION

Petty crime is a significant problem; moreover, the area has become headquarters for serious drug cartels, and violent crime is booming. You're unlikely to witness a shooting or other frightening situation, but be very mindful of your surroundings, stay in the tourist areas, and guard your belongings.

GETTING HERE & AROUND

There are few international flights into Tijuana, Baja Norte's only major airport; most travelers access the area from the border at San Diego. Aeropuerto Alberado Rodriguez (TIJ) is on Tijuana's eastern edge, near the Otay Mesa border crossing. Private taxis and *colectivos* (shared vans) serve the airport. Greyhound buses head to Tijuana from downtown San Diego several times daily. Buses to San Diego and Los Angeles depart from the Greyhound terminal in Tijuana 14 times a day. Mexicoach runs buses from the trolley depot in San Ysidro and the large parking lot on the U.S. side of the border to the Tijuana Tourist Terminal at Avenida Revolución between Calles 6 and 7. Buses actually connect all the towns in Baja Norte and are easy to use. By car from San Diego, U.S. 5 and I–805 end at the San Ysidro border crossing; Highway 905 leads from U.S. 5 and I–805 to the Tijuana border crossing at Otay Mesa. The San Diego Trolley travels from the Santa Fe Depot in San Diego, at Kettner Boulevard and Broadway, to within 100 feet of the border in Tijuana every 15 minutes from 6 AM to midnight. The 45-minute trip costs $2.50.

ESSENTIALS

Bus Contacts **Greyhound** (☎ *664/688–0165 in* Tijuana, *01800/710–8819 toll-free in Mexico, 800/231–2222* ⊕ *www.greyhound.com*). **Mexicoach** (☎ *664/685–1440, 619/428–9517 in U.S.* ⊕ *www.mexicoach.com*). **San Diego Trolley** (☎ *619/233-3004* ⊕ *www.sdcommute.com*).**Tijuana Central de Autobuses** (✉ *Calz. Lázaro Cárdenas, at Blvd. Arroyo Alamar, La Mesa, Tijuana* ☎ *664/621–2987*).

Internet**WorldNet Que Facil Internet Café** (✉ *Calle 2a 8174* ☎ *664/626–1816*).

Mail & Shipping**DHL** (✉ *Paseo de los Heroes #9150Zona Río* ☎ *55/5345–7000 throughout Mexico*). **Tijuana Post Office** (✉ *Av. Negrete, at Calle 11a*).

Medical Assistance **Emergencies** (☎ *Dial 066*). **Tourist Information and Assistance Hotline** (☎ *Dial 078*).

Visitor & Tour Info **Baja California State Secretary of Tourism** (✉ *Paseo de los Héroes 10289, Zona Río* ☎ *664/634–6330* ⊕ *www.discoverbajacalifornia.com*). **Tijuana Convention and Visitor's Bureau** (✉ *Paseo de los Héroes 9365-201* ☎ *664/684–0537* ✉ *Av. Revolución, between Calles 3 and 4, Centro* ⊕ *www.tijuanaonline.org*).

EXPLORING

2 **Avenida Revolución.** This infamous strip, lined with shops and restaurants that cater to uninhibited travelers, has long been Tijuana's main tourism zone, even if the classier side of things has moved over to the Zona Río. Shopkeepers call out from doorways, offering low prices for garish souvenirs and genuine folk-art treasures. Many shopping arcades open onto Avenida Revolución; inside their front doors are mazes of stands with low-priced pottery and other crafts.

3 ★ **Centro Cultural (CECUT).** The cultural center's stark, low-slung, tan buildings and globelike Omnimax Theater are beloved landmarks. The center's Museo de las Californias provides an excellent overview of Baja's history and natural profile, while the Omnimax shows films, some in English. The film *Marine Oasis: The Riches of the Sea of Cortez* has fabulous underwater scenes. ✉ *Paseo de los Héroes and Av. Mina, Zona Río* ☎ *664/687–9600* 🌐 *www.cecut.gob.mx* *Museum: $2; museum and Omnimax Theater: $4* ⏲ *Tues.–Sun. 10–6; Marine Oasis weekends at 3.*

4 **Pueblo Amigo.** This entertainment center resembles a colonial village, with stucco facades and tree-lined paths leading to a domed gazebo. The complex includes a hotel, several restaurants and clubs, a huge grocery store, and a large branch of the Caliente Race Book, where gambling on televised sporting events is legal. Things get lively at night. ✉ *Paseo de Tijuana between Puente Mexico and Calz. Independencia, Zona Río.*

1 **San Ysidro Border Crossing.** Locals and tourists jostle each other along the pedestrian walkway through the Viva Tijuana dining and shopping center and into the center of town. Artisans' stands line the walkway and adjoining streets, offering a quick overview of the wares to be found all over town.

WHERE TO EAT & STAY

$$–$$$ MEXICAN ✕ **La Diferencia.** "The difference" at this gorgeous restaurant in the Zona Río, which features an indoor patio with elegant, relaxing tables that surround a central fountain, is nouvelle Mexican cuisine that completely transcends past notions of Tijuana cuisine. Chef Juan Carlos Rodriguez's creations include a delicious tamarind duck. He also makes liberal use of *huitlacoche* (corn fungus), which is a real treat. ✉ *Blvd. Sánchez Taboada 10611A, Zona Río* ☎ *664/634–3346* 🌐 *www.ladiferencia.com.mx* 💳 *AE, DC, MC, V.*

$–$$ MEXICAN ★ ✕ **La Especial.** At the foot of the stairs that run down to an underground shopping arcade you'll find the best place in the tourist zone for home-style Mexican cooking. The gruff, efficient waiters shuttle around platters of carne asada, enchiladas, and burritos, all with a distinctive flavor found only at this busy, cavernous basement dining room. ✉ *Av. Revolución 718, Centro* ☎ *664/685–6654* 💳 *MC, V.*

$–$$ SEAFOOD ✕ **El Faro de Mazatlán.** Fresh fish prepared simply is the hallmark of one of Tijuana's best seafood restaurants. This is the place to try ceviche, abalone, squid, and lobster without spending a fortune. Frequented by professionals, the dining room is a peaceful spot for a long, lei-

Avenida Revolución 2
Centro Cultural (CECUT) 3
Pueblo Amigo 4
San Ysidro Border Crossing 1

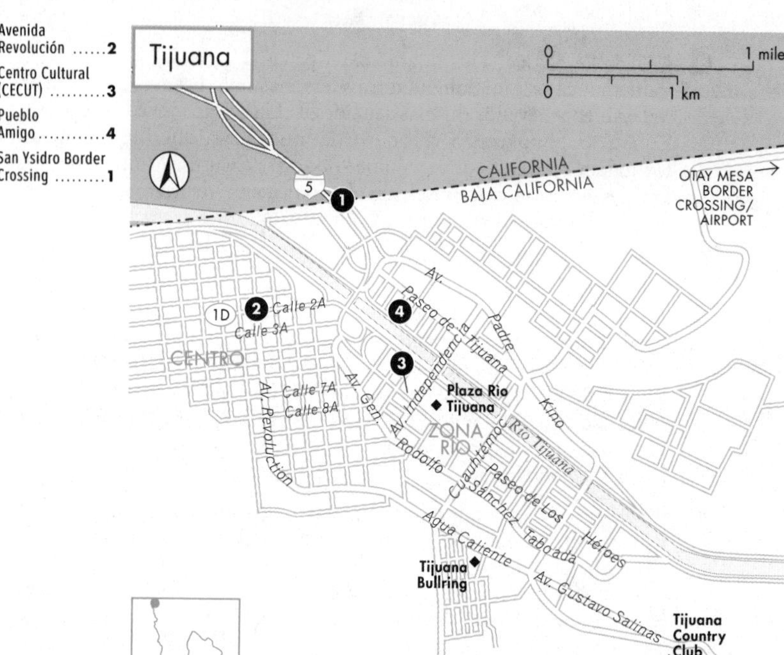

surely lunch. Appetizers and soup are included in the price of the meal. ✉*Blvd. Sánchez Taboada 9542, Zona Río* ☎*664/684–8883* ▭*AE, MC, V.*

$$–$$$ **Lucerna.** Long one of the most charming hotels in Tijuana, the Lucerna has regained its former glory with modern touches like wireless Internet access and a business center. Although the place has American airs, the lovely gardens, large pool surrounded by palms, touches of tile work, and folk art lend the hotel a Mexican character, too. **Pros:** Nicely landscaped. **Cons:** Food so-so, one a busy intersection. ✉*Paseo de los Héroes 10902, at Av. Rodríguez, Zona Río,* ☎*664/633–3900 or 800/582–3762* 🌐*www.lucerna.com.mx* *156 rooms, 9 suites* *In-room: Wi-Fi. In-hotel: Restaurant, room service, pool, gym, laundry service* ▭*AE, MC, V.*

SHOPPING

From the moment you cross the border, people will approach you or call out and insist that you look at their wares. Bargaining is expected in the streets and arcades, but not

> **WORD OF MOUTH**
>
> "We wound up eating at Especial three times. The prices are wonderful and the food is to die for. There's a great leather goods place on the same side of the street, within a few blocks to the right if you're facing the café."
>
> –Catmomma

in the finer shops. If you drive, workers will run out from auto-body shops to place bids on new paint or upholstery for your car.

All along **Avenida Revolución** and its side streets, stores sell everything from tequila to Tiffany-style lamps. This shopping area spreads across Calle 2 to a pedestrian walkway leading from the border. Begin by checking out the stands along this walkway. Beware of fake goods, and above all, beware of higher prices offered to gringos. You may find that the best bargains are closer to the border; you can pick up your piñatas and sarapes on your way out of town. Between Calles 1 and 8, Avenida Revolución is lined with establishments stuffed with crafts and curios.

★ The **Mercado Hidalgo** (✉*Calz. Independencia at Blvd. Sánchez Taboada, 5 blocks east of Av. Revolución, Zona Río*) is Tijuana's municipal market, with rows of fresh produce, some souvenirs, and Baja's best selection of piñatas.

More than 40 stands display crafts from around Mexico at **Bazaar de Mexico** (✉*Av. Revolución at Calle 7, Centro*). Furnishings and art are tastefully displayed at **Mallorca** (✉*Calle 4 at Av. Revolución, Centro* ☎*664/688–3502*). **Sanborns** (✉*Av. Revolución at Calle 8, Centro* ☎*664/688–1462*) has crafts from throughout Mexico, a bakery, and chocolates from Mexico City. The **Tijuana Tourist Terminal** (✉*Av. Revolución between Calles 6 and 7, Centro* ☎*664/683–5681*) is a one-stop center with clean restrooms. The nicest folk-art store, **Tolán** (✉*Av. Revolución 1471, between Calles 7 and 8, Centro* ☎*664/688–3637*), carries everything from antique wooden doors to ceramic miniature village scenes.

ROSARITO

29 km (18 mi) south of Tijuana.

Southern Californians use Rosarito (population 100,000) as a weekend getaway, and during school vacations, especially spring break, the crowd becomes one big raucous party. The police do their best to control the revelers, but spring and summer weekend nights can be outrageously noisy. Off-season, the place becomes a ghost town, which is arguably even less appealing than the frat scene.

The beach, which stretches from the power plant at the north end of town about 8 km (5 mi) south, is long and boasts beautiful sand and sunsets, but it's less romantic for the irritating bar promoters accosting beachwalkers and the amateur explosives that boom every few minutes. Rosarito is a center of fireworks commerce, and some ridiculously powerful blasts are available over-the-counter at the town's several purveyors. Americans and Canadians continue to swell the ranks in vacation developments and gated retirement communities, but they're concealed largely out of sight from charmless downtown Rosarito.

The main drag, alternately known as the Old Ensenada Highway and Boulevard Benito Juárez, is a dirty and depressing eyesore of a strip of cheesy curio shops, mediocre tourist-oriented restaurants, and other assorted signs of the unbridled growth and speculation—this energy might have helped Rosarito's economy, but has certainly ruined its potential charm.

If you do wind up here for a night, head out to the wooden pier that stretches over the ocean in front of the Rosarito Beach Hotel, or hire a horse at the north or south end of Boulevard Juárez for $10 per hour. Whatever you do, come with plenty of U.S. dollars, because many vendors in town don't even accept pesos. That, in itself, should be a hint.

EXPLORING

Foxploration. Fox Studios has expanded its operation to include a film-oriented theme park. You learn how films are made by visiting one set that resembles a New York street scene and another filled with props from *Titanic*. Fox's most famous films are shown in the large state-of-the-art theater. The park includes a children's playroom where kids can shoot thousands of foam balls out of air cannons. ✉ *Old Ensenada Hwy., Km 32.8* ☎ *661/614–9444 or 866/369–2252* 🌐 *www.foxploration.com* 🎟 *$12* ⏲ *Wed.–Fri. 9–5:30, weekends 10–6:30*

WHERE TO EAT & STAY

$$–$$$ STEAK **El Nido Steakhouse.** A dark, wood-paneled restaurant with leather booths and a large central fireplace, this is one of Rosarito's oldest eateries, and the best in town for atmosphere. Diners unimpressed with newer, fancier places come here for mesquite-grilled steaks and grilled quail from the owner's farm in the Baja wine country; just skip the underwhelming frozen lobsters. ✉ *Benito Juárez 67* ☎ *661/612–1430* ▭ *No credit cards.*

$$ **Rosarito Beach Hotel and Spa.** Charm rather than comfort is the main reason for staying here. The rooms in the oldest section have hand-painted wooden beams and heavy dark furnishings. The more modern rooms in the tower have air-conditioning and pastel color schemes. **Pros:** Nice location. **Cons:** Pricey for slightly run-down condition of hotel. ✉ *Blvd. Benito Juárez 1207, south end of town 661/612–0144 or 800/343–8582* 🌐 *www.rosaritobeachhotel.com* *203 rooms, 100 suites* *In-room: no a/c (some), safe. In-hotel: 2 restaurants, bar, tennis court, pools, gym, spa, beachfront, laundry service* ▭ *MC, V.*

NIGHTLIFE

Papas and Beer (✉ *On beach off Blvd. Juárez near Rosarito Beach Hotel* ☎ *661/612–0444*), one of the most popular bars in Baja Norte, draws a young, energetic spring-break crowd for drinking and dancing on the beach and small stages.

PUERTO NUEVO

Old Ensenada Hwy., Km 44, 12 km (7½ mi) south of Rosarito.

Southern Californians regularly cross the border to indulge in the classic Puerto Nuevo meal: lobster fried in hot oil and served with refried beans, rice, homemade tortillas, salsa, and lime. At least 30 restaurants are packed into this village; nearly all offer the same menu, but the quality varies drastically; some establishments cook up live lobsters, while others fly in frozen stuff from the Caribbean. In most places prices are based on size; a medium lobster will cost you about $15.

Though the fried version is the Puerto Nuevo classic, some restaurants also offer steamed or grilled lobsters—why not try one of each and pass 'em around? Each October, to mark the start of the season (which ends in March), the town holds a wine and lobster festival.

WHERE TO EAT & STAY

¢–$$ SEAFOOD **Ortega's Ocean View.** This is one of the cheapest and most unassuming spots on the lobster strip. It's also one of the better ones, serving up lobsters that are fresh, not frozen like many you'll find at the competition. Try the lobster *al ajo* (with garlic), and enjoy it on a rooftop with spectacular sunset views of the Pacific. The quesadillas are also excellent, and the staff is among the friendliest in town. *Calle Anzuelo 15-A* *661/112–5322* *No credit cards.*

¢–$$ SEAFOOD Fodor's Choice ★ **Rosamar.** This two-floor establishment is well patronized by locals, but not so much by tourists. Perhaps it's because of the bright, unromantic lighting. But amble up to the open-air second floor, and you'll be treated to ocean views and fresh lobster at some of the best prices in town. The live lobster here is so fresh (they come in off the fishing boats each morning) that the restaurant sells its B-list lobsters to other places around town. *Calle Anzuelo and Barracuda* *661/614–1210* *No credit cards.*

$$ **Grand Baja Resort.** If you're a lobster fanatic, consider spending a relaxing night just steps away from Puerto Nuevo after your enormous dinner and pitchers of margarita. This resort offers charmingly airy, well-kept "junior suites," which have little living rooms with couches and tables, plus water views; the more-impressive "villas," like little apartments with two floors and kitchenettes, boast even better views. Ground-floor rooms have patios, too. **Pros:** Nice-size rooms, convenient location. **Cons:** Rooms a little spartan. *Carretera Tijuana–Ensenada, Km 44.5, just past Puerto Nuevo in Ensenada direction* *661/614–1488, 661/614–1493, or 877/315–1002* *www.grandbaja.com* *60 villas, 40 suites* *In-hotel: Bars, tennis courts, pool, spa* *AE, DC, MC, V.*

ENSENADA

75 km (47 mi) south of Rosarito.

In 1542 Juan Rodríguez Cabrillo first discovered the seaport that Sebastián Vizcaíno named Ensenada-Bahía de Todos Santos (All Saints' Bay) in 1602. Since then the town has drawn a steady stream of explorers and developers. After playing home to ranchers and gold miners, the harbor gradually grew into a major port for shipping agricultural goods, and today Baja's third-largest city (population 369,000) is one of Mexico's largest sea- and fishing ports.

There are no beaches in Ensenada proper, but sandy stretches north and south of town are satisfactory for swimming, sunning, surfing, and camping. Estero Beach is long and clean, with mild waves; the Estero Beach Hotel takes up much of the oceanfront, but the beach is public. Surfers populate the strands off Carretera 1 north and south of Ensenada, particularly San Miguel, Tres Marías, and Salsipuedes; scuba divers prefer Punta Banda, by La Bufadora. Lifeguards are rare, so be cautious. The tourist office in Ensenada has a map that shows safe diving and surfing beaches.

Both the waterfront and downtown's main street are pleasant places to stroll. If you're driving, be sure to take the Centro exit from the highway, since it bypasses the commercial port area.

WORD OF MOUTH

"The drive to Ensenada has its moments, but what's sure to strike you is the impoverishment and the shanties. And so close to the riches of southern California. Interesting note: every shanty within a 30-mile radius of the border has a satellite dish. Indoor plumbing is a luxury, but TV is an automatic!"

–Johnii

GETTING HERE & AROUND

If you're flying in, Tijuana will be your hub. From Aeropuerto Alberado Rodriguez (TIJ), on Tijuana's eastern edge, you can find buses that also serve Rosarito and Ensenada. Or you can hop on a bus at Tijuana Camionera de la Línea station, just inside the border, with service to Rosarito and Ensenada along with city buses to downtown. To head south from Tijuana by car, follow the signs for Ensenada Cuota, the toll road (i.e., Carretera Transpeninsular or Highway 1) along the coast. Tollbooths accept U.S. and Mexican currency; there are three tolls of about $2.50 each between Tijuana and Ensenada. Ensenada is an hour south of Tijuana on this road. The alternative free road—Carretera 1D or Ensenada Libre—is curvy and difficult to navigate. (Entry to it is on a side street in a congested area of downtown Tijuana.)

Bus Contacts **Tijuana Camionera de la Línea** (✉ *Centro Comercial Viva Tijuana, Vía de la Juventud Oriente 8800, Zona Río, Tijuana* ☎ *No phone*).

Medical Assistance **Emergencies** (☎ *Dial 066*). **Tourist Information and Assistance Hotline** (☎ *Dial 078*).

Mail & Shipping **DHL** (✉ *Blvd. Costero 853, local 1, Zona Centro* ☎ *55/5345–7000 throughout Mexico*). **Ensenada Post Office** (✉ *Av. López Mateos, at Riviera Ensenada*). **Mailboxes Etc.** (✉ *Calzada Las Aguilas #1012, Interior 5, Col. Maestros, Ensenada* ☎ *617/177–3482, 01800/900–1100 in Tijuana*).

Internet **Equinoxio Internet Café** (✉ *Cárdenas 267, Ensenada* ☎ *646/174–0455*).

EXPLORING

❶ **Las Bodegas de Santo Tomás.** One of Baja's oldest wine producers gives tours and tastings at its downtown winery and bottling plant. Take a moment to see the satirical paintings in the main building, depicting the early days of the winery. Santo Tomás' best wines are the Alisio chardonnay, the cabernet, and the Sirocco syrah; avoid the overpriced Unico. The restaurant, La Embotelladora Vieja, is a marvel of modern design,

CLOSE UP

Spa on the Border

More than six decades since its 1940 opening, **Rancho La Puerta**—a pioneer among today's fitness spas—continues to offer personalized service, with more than 350 employees seeing to the needs of up to 150 guests. Equally reliable is the climate, with an average of 341 dry, sunny days a year, and the vegetarian/seafood diet. Newly opened in fall 2007, the Cocina que Canta (kitchen that sings) cooking school teaches guests how to make the spa-cuisine-cum-healthy-Mex specialties for which La Puerta is famous, with both demonstration and hands-on classes taught by the ranch's star chefs.

Still managed by members of its founding family, the spa requires a weeklong stay. Activities can include African dance, back care, spinning, labyrinth meditation, Feldenkrais technique, cardio-boxing, tai chi, and yoga. Mornings begin with guided hikes around the ranch's 40 km (25 mi) of trails at the base of sacred Mt. Kuchumaa. Backed by 3,000 acres of unspoiled foothills, the campus itself is a thoughtful product of locally sourced landscaping, brick paths that meander in and out of secret gardens, and guest residences, which are hidden between yawning oaks and gorgeous swimming pools. An extensive range of à-la-carte spa treatments and salon services offers the chance to be pampering as well as engaged.

One-of-a-kind cottages contain studios and suites decorated with handmade rugs and furniture. Many have tile floors, fireplaces, and kitchenettes. The studios and suites in the villas, which run more than the other cottages, give you the option of in-room massages (for a fee) and breakfast poolside or in-room. There's no air-conditioning or TV, and only the villa studios and suites have phones. ■TIP→ **Inquire about reservations well before your stay; returning guests are known to rebook their same room—for the same week each year—up to a year in advance.**

Spa Services: Aromatherapy, body scrubs, facials, herbal wrap, hydrotherapy, hot-stone massage, manicure, pedicure, reflexology, scalp treatments, salt glow, seaweed wrap, sports massage, trigger-point massage.

Fitness Facilities: 11 gyms total. Elliptical machines, free weights, stair climbers, stationary bikes, treadmills, weight-training circuit; basketball court, labyrinth, Pilates studio, 3 pools, 4 lighted tennis courts, volleyball court; 5 whirlpools, 3 saunas.

Classes & Programs: Aerobics, bird walks, breathing techniques, cooking, crafts classes, dance, drumming, Feldenkrais method, hiking, health lectures, meditation, Pilates, Spanish lessons, spinning, stretching, tai chi, tennis, yoga.

Package: Rates $2,795–$4,375 for a seven-night package, per person, based on double occupancy, excluding tax (some rooms accommodate triples and quads). This includes all meals, classes, and evening programs as well as use of all facilities. Spa treatments and cooking classes are extra. Ground transportation to and from San Diego International Airport is included in the weekly rate.

General Info: ✉ *Carretera Federal Tijuana, Km 5, Tecate,* ☎ *858/764–5500 or 800/443–7565* 🌐 *www.rancholapuerta.com* ⇨ *87 cottages* ▭ *MC, V* 🍽 *AI.*

and pairs dishes with the winery's picks. The winery also operates La Esquina de Bodegas, a café, shop, and gallery in a bright-blue building across the avenue. ✉ *Av. Miramar 666, Centro* ☎ *646/174–0836 or 646/174–0829* 🌐 *www.santo-tomas.com* 🎫 *$5–$10, depending on wines* 🕗 *Tours, tastings daily 9–5; it's best to call first.*

LEGEND SAYS

Legend has it that La Bufadora was created by a whale or sea serpent trapped in an undersea cave; both these stories, and the less-romantic scientific facts, are posted on a roadside plaque.

★ **La Bufadora.** Seawater splashes up to 75 feet in the air, spraying sightseers standing near this impressive tidal blowhole (*la bufadora* means the buffalo snort) in the coastal cliffs at Punta Banda. The road to La Bufadora along Punta Banda—an isolated, mountainous point that juts into the sea—is lined with stands hawking everything from tacos to terra-cotta planters. The drive gives you a sampling of Baja's wilderness. At La Bufadora, expect a small fee to park, and then a half-mile walk past T-shirt hawkers and souvenir stands to the water hole itself. A public bus runs from the downtown Ensenada station to Maneadero, from which you can catch a minibus labeled Punta Banda that goes to La Bufadora. ✉ *Carretera 23, 31 km (19 mi) south of Ensenada, Punta Banda.*

2 ★ **Mercado de Mariscos.** At the northernmost point of Boulevard Costero, the main street along the waterfront, is an indoor-outdoor fish market where row after row of counters display piles of shrimp, tuna, dorado, and other fish caught off Baja's coasts. Outside, stands sell grilled or smoked fish, seafood cocktails, and fish tacos. The smoked salmon is excellent. You can pick up a few souvenirs, eat well for very little money, and take some great photographs. The original fish taco stands line the dirt path to the fish market; around lunchtime, cooks will stand outside to vie for your attention (and your pesos). If your stomach is delicate, try the fish tacos at the cleaner, quieter Plaza de Mariscos in the shadow of the giant beige Plaza de Marina that blocks the view of the traditional fish market from the street.

3 **Paseo Calle Primera.** The renamed Avenida López Mateos is the center of Ensenada's traditional tourist zone. High-rise hotels, souvenir shops, restaurants, and bars line the avenue for eight blocks, from its beginning at the foot of the Chapultepec Hills to the dry channel of the Arroyo de Ensenada. The avenue also has cafés, American-style coffee shops, and most of the town's souvenir stores.

4 **Riviera del Pacífico.** Officially called the Centro Social, Cívico y Cultural de Ensenada, the Riviera is a rambling white hacienda-style mansion built in the 1920s. An enormous gambling palace, hotel, restaurant, and bar, the glamorous Riviera was frequented by wealthy U.S. citizens and Mexicans, particularly during Prohibition. You can tour some of the elegant ballrooms and halls, which occasionally host art shows and civic events. Many of the rooms are locked; check at the main office to see if someone is available to show you around. ✉ *Blvd. Costero*

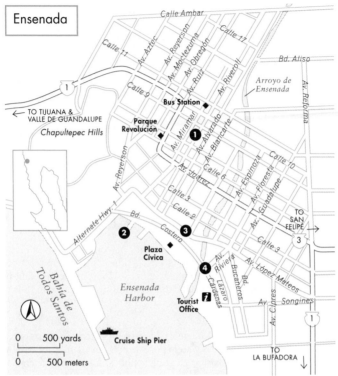

at Av. Riviera, Centro ☎*646/177–0594* *Building and gardens free; museum entry $1* ⏲*Mon.–Sat. 9–5, Sun. 10–5.*

WHERE TO EAT

$$$ FRENCH

✕ **El Rey Sol.** From its chateaubriand *bouquetière* (garnished with a bouquet of vegetables) to the savory chicken chipotle cooked with brandy, port wine, and cream, this French restaurant, family owned since 1947, sets a high standard. Louis XIV–style furnishings and an attentive staff make it both comfortable and elegant. The sidewalk tables are a perfect place to dine and people-watch. The small café in the front sells pastries that are made on the premises. ✉*Av. López Mateos 1000, Centro* ☎*646/178–2351* ▭*AE, MC, V.*

$$–$$$ SEAFOOD

✕ **Manzanilla.** Two of the most exciting chef-owners in Baja Norte, Benito Molina and Solange Muris, are taking a truly modern approach to Mexican cuisine at Manzanilla, integrating the freshest catches from the local waters—oysters, mussels, and clams, for instance—and integrating ingredients like ginger, saffron, smoked tomato marmalade, and *huitlacoche* (corn fungus). The atmosphere is simple and pleasant, if a bit trendy. ✉*Av. Riveroll 122, just after Playitas Club del Mar if you're heading south to Ensenada, Centro* ☎*646/175–7073* 🌐*www.rmanzanilla.com* ▭*AE, DC, MC, V* ⏲*Closed Mon. and Tues. No lunch.*

$$–$$$ STEAK ★ **Sanos.** This elegant restaurant, along the highway heading out from Ensenada toward Tijuana, is the latest extension of the Hussong empire. It's also the best steak house in Baja California. The Sonora beef is juicy, flavorful, and tender, cooked just as beautifully rare (or done) as you order it, and it can be enjoyed on a wonderful outdoor patio. Throw in impeccable service and a wine list that rivals the best in the country, and you can justify the sky-high prices. ✉*Carretera Tijuana–Ensenada, Km 108, just after Playitas Club del Mar if you're heading south to Ensenada, Centro* ☎*646/174–4061* ▭*AE, DC, MC, V.*

WORD OF MOUTH

"The drive to Ensenada has its moments, but what's sure to strike you is the impoverishment and the shanties. And so close to the riches of Southern California. Interesting note: every shanty within a 48-km (30-mi) radius of the border has a satellite dish. Indoor plumbing is a luxury, but TV is an automatic!"

–Johnii

¢–$ MEXICAN Fodor'sChoice ★ **Hacienda Del Charro.** Hungry patrons hover over platters of chiles rellenos, enchiladas, and fresh chips and guacamole at heavy wooden picnic tables. Plump chickens slowly turn over a wood-fueled fire by the front window, and the aroma of simmering beans fills the air. ✉*Av. López Mateos 454, Centro* ☎*646/178–2351* ▭*No credit cards.*

WHERE TO STAY

$$$ **Hotel Coral & Marina.** This all-suites resort is enormous. It has a spa, tennis courts, a water-sports center, and a marina with slips for 350 boats and customs-clearing facilities. All guest quarters have refrigerators and coffeemakers. Suites in the two eight-story towers are done in burgundy and dark green; most have waterfront balconies, seating areas, and international phone service. **Pros:** Affordable, large rooms. **Cons:** Pool can get noisy with kids, so large can feel impersonal. ✉*Hwy. 1, Km 103, Zona Playitas,* ☎*646/175–0000 or 800/862–9020* 🌐*www.hotelcoral.com* *147 suites* *In-room: Refrigerator. In-hotel: Restaurant, room service, bar, tennis courts, pools, gym, spa, laundry service* ▭*MC, V.*

$$$ Fodor'sChoice ★ **Las Rosas Hotel & Spa.** All rooms in this intimate hotel north of Ensenada face the ocean and pool; some have fireplaces and hot tubs, and even the least expensive are lovely. The atrium lobby has marble floors, mint-green-and-pink couches that look out at the sea, and a glass ceiling that glows at night. **Pros:** Boutique, laid-back. **Cons:** Must make reservations far in advance. ✉*Mexico Carretera 1, north of Ensenada, Zona Playitas* ☎*646/174–4320 or 646/174–4360* 🌐*www.lasrosas.com* *48 rooms* *In-hotel: Restaurant, bar, tennis courts, pool, gym, spa, no elevator, laundry service* ▭*MC, V.*

$$ **Estero Beach Resort.** Families love this long-standing resort on Ensenada's top beach. The best rooms (some with kitchenettes) are by the sand. Be sure to check out the outstanding collection of folk art and artifacts in the resort's small museum. Midweek winter rates are a real bargain. There's also an on-site RV park; its 38 sites have hookups for water, sewer, and electricity. **Pros:** Wonderful breakfasts, right on the

beach. **Cons:** Rooms by parking lot aren't great, needs some updating. ✉*Mexico Carretera 1, 10 km (6 mi) south of Ensenada, Estero Beach* ☎*646/176–6235* 📠*646/176–6925* 🌐*www.hotelesterobeach.com* *94 rooms, 2 suites* *In-room: Kitchen (some). In-hotel: Restaurant, bar, tennis courts, pool* 💳*MC, V.*

NIGHTLIFE

★ **Hussong's Cantina** (✉*Av. Ruíz 113, Centro* ☎*646/178–3210*) has been an Ensenada landmark since 1892, and has changed little since then. A security guard stands by the front door to handle the often rowdy crowd—most of all local men. The floor is covered with sawdust, and the noise is usually deafening, pierced by mariachi and ranchera musicians and the whoops and hollers of the pie-eyed. **Papas and Beer** (✉*Av. Ruíz 102, Centro* ☎*646/174–0145*) attracts a collegiate crowd.

SHOPPING

Most of the tourist shops hold court along Avenida López Mateos beside the hotels and restaurants. There are several two-story shopping arcades, some with empty spaces for rent. Dozens of curio shops line the street, all selling similar selections of pottery, sarapes, and the tackier trinkets and T-shirts.

Bazar Casa Ramirez (✉*Av. López Mateos 496, Centro* ☎*646/178–8209*) sells high-quality Talavera pottery and other ceramics, wrought-iron pieces, and papier-mâché figurines. Be sure to check out the displays upstairs.

★ The **Centro Artesenal de Ensenada** (✉*Blvd. Costero 1094–39, Centro* ☎*No phone*) has a smattering of galleries and shops.

La Esquina de Bodegas (✉*Av. Miramar at Calle 6, Centro* ☎*646/178–3557*) is an innovative gallery, shop, and café in a century-old winery building.

Los Globos (✉*Calle 9, 3 blocks east of Av. Reforma, Centro* ☎*No phone*) is a daily open-air swap meet. Vendors and shoppers are most abundant on weekends.

SPORTS & THE OUTDOORS

SPORTFISHING

The best angling is from April through November, with bottom-fishing good in winter. Charter vessels and party boats are available from several outfitters along Avenida López Mateos and Boulevard Costero and off the sportfishing pier. Mexican fishing licenses for the day or year are available at the tourist office or from charter companies.

Sergio's Sportfishing (✉*Sportfishing Pier, Blvd. Costero at Av. Alvarado, Centro* ☎*646/178–2185* 🌐*www.sergios-sportfishing.com*), one of the best sportfishing companies in Ensenada, has charter and group boats as well as boat slips for rent. The fee for a day's fishing is $50 per person on a group boat, including the cost of a license.

VALLE DE GUADALUPE

The Valle de Guadalupe, northeast of Ensenada on Carretera 3, is filled with vineyards, wineries, and rambling hacienda-style estates. Although Mexican wines are still relatively unknown in the United States, the industry is exploding in Mexico, and it's only a matter of time before ordering Baja wines becomes all the rage in the Hollywood crowd. One factor holding back the domestic industry is the staggering 40% winemaker's tax imposed by the Mexican government. Through this policy, the authorities are crushing their own industry by making imports from Chile and Argentina more popular than the domestics at restaurants in Mexico City and the resorts.

Still, Mexican wines are fighting back by growing their exports dramatically, and some truly world-class boutique wineries have developed in the Valle de Guadalupe, most in the past decade. Several of these are open to the public; most require appointments. Baja California Tours (www.bajaspecials.com) conducts tours that include visits to wineries, a historical overview, transportation from the border, and lunch. The cost is about $80 per person. Better yet is visiting the wineries yourself by car, as they all cluster in a relatively small area.

EXPLORING

Fodor'sChoice ★ One of the most up-and-coming small wineries in Baja, **Adobe Guadalupe** (✉*Off Carretera 3, turn at sign and drive 6 km [4 mi], Guadalupe* ☎*646/155–2094, 949/733–2744 in U.S.* 🌐*www.adobeguadalupe.com*) is making an array of fascinating high-end blends named after angels. Don Miller, the American owner of the sprawling villa and wine-making operation, is also a delightful and passionate tour guide (by appointment only). Don't miss the Kerubiel, Don's blockbuster blend; the Serafiel, Gabriel, and Miguel are also excellent. Don and his wife Tru also run a bed-and-breakfast ⇨ *Where to Eat & Stay*.

Casa de Piedra (✉*Carretera Tecate–Ensenada, Km 93.5, San Antonio de las Minas* ☎*646/155–3097 or 646/155–3102* 🌐*www.vinoscasadepiedra.com*) is the brainchild of Hugo D'Acosta, who also consults for Adobe Guadalupe. The space is interesting and modern, designed by the winemaker's architect brother. It would be hard to argue that this isn't one of the best wineries in Mexico.

One of the larger and less personal wineries is **Domecq** (✉*Carretera 3, Km 73.5* ☎*646/165–2264* 🌐*www.vinosdomecq.com.mx*), which offers free wine tastings and tours weekdays 10–4 and Saturday 10–3. Their operation is one of the most corporate of the Baja wineries—they're estranged from the Allied Domecq worldwide liquor empire; don't expect to taste their top wines.

L.A. Cetto (✉*Carretera 3, Km 73.5* ☎*646/155–2179* 🌐*www.cettowines.com*) is another giant, but this is the closest thing to the California wine country experience south of the border. When tasting or buying, avoid the cheaper wines, and go straight for the premiums. Free wine tastings and tours daily 10–5.

★ Call ahead if you want to get in **Monte Xanic** (✉ *Carretera 3, Km 70* ☎ *646/174–6155* 🌐 *www.montexanic.com.mx*). Most impressive is their consistency, right down to the cheapest table wines. Tastings and tours are available by appointment, and be sure to check out the impressively styled cellar.

> **WORD OF MOUTH**
>
> "Quite a few excellent wines are made just south of the border. The hilly terrain between the border and Ensenada is home to several boutique wineries that have done exceptionally well in international tastings and competitions." –TioGringo

★ Within **Vinisterra** (✉ *Carretera Tecate–Ensenada, Km 94.5, San Antonio de las Minas* ☎ *646/178–3350* 🌐 *www.vinisterra.com*), expect to find Tempranillo and cabernet-merlot blends which are big and juicy. Call well ahead.

WHERE TO EAT & STAY

$$$$ MEXICAN Fodor'sChoice ★ ✕**Laja.** One sign that the Valle de Guadalupe has its sights on Napa is this extraordinary restaurant set inside a cozy little house. Celebrity chef Jair Téllez's ambitious prix-fixe menus (there are four-course and seven-course versions) change frequently, but may include cucumber gazpacho, yellowtail tartare, and panna cotta with cold mango soup, all served with excellent regional wines. Polished woods and windows overlooking the valley make the dining room as sleek as the menu. A meal here is well worth the drive. ✉ *Carretera 3, Km 83* ☎ *646/155–2556* 🌐 *www.lajamexico.com* *Reservations essential* ▭ *MC, V* ⊙ *Closed Sun.–Tues. and late Nov.–early Jan. No dinner Wed. Last orders taken at 8:30 PM Thurs.–Sat.*

¢–$ MEXICAN ✕**Los Naranjos.** This pleasant restaurant may be overshadowed by the renowned Laja a few steps away, but it holds to more regular hours. Well respected for its homemade salsas and its *Codorniz Guadalupe* (quail in red wine sauce), it has pleasant seating both indoors and out on a patio in a little orange grove. Prices are reasonable, too. ✉ *Carretera 3, Km 82.5* ☎ *646/155–2522* ▭ *No credit cards.*

$$$ Fodor'sChoice ★ **Adobe Guadalupe.** Brick archways, white-stucco walls, and fountains set a tone of endless pleasure and relaxation at Don and Tru Miller's magnificent country inn surrounded by vineyards. Don has won several awards for his interestingly blended wines, helping to bring outside attention to the valley. The inn's talented chefs do an admirable dinner in their romantic dining room, generously paired with Adobe Guadalupe wines, for $50 per person. Tru's stable of beautiful horses—she'll take you around the valley and to nearby wineries—is yet another draw. **Pros:** Lovely setting, engaging owners. **Cons:** Meal portions can be on the small side. ✉ *Off Carretera 3 through Guadalupe village, 6 km (4 mi) along same road, right turn at small town of Porvenir, Guadalupe,* ☎ *646/155–2094, 949/733–2744 in U.S.* 🌐 *www.adobeguadalupe.com* *6 rooms* *In-room: No phone, no TV. In-hotel: Restaurant, pool* ▭ *MC, V* *CP.*

$$$ **La Villa del Valle.** At this luxury inn in Valle de Guadalupe, the bright, modern rooms have king-size beds and rustic-chic furnishings; some have balconies. The dining room, where you eat breakfast, has been

lovingly done up. It's yet another sign of the emergence of the Baja wine region as a legitimate tourist destination. **Pros:** Attention to detail, charming. **Cons:** A drive to town. ✉*Off Carretera 3, Km 88, between San Antonio de las Minas and Francisco Zarco; exit at Rancho Sicomoro and follow signs* ☎*646/183–9249 or 818/207-7130 in U.S.* 🌐*www.lavilladelvalle.com* *6 rooms* *In-hotel: Restaurant, pool, spa* *MC, V* *CP.*

SAN FELIPE

244 km (151 mi) southeast of Ensenada.

San Felipe (population 25,000) is the quintessential fishing village with one main street (two if you count the highway into town). It's at the edge of the northern Mar de Cortés, which is protected as an ecological reserve in this region. A malecón runs along a broad beach with a swimming area. Taco stands, bars, and restaurants line the sidewalk across the street from the malecón and beach. Impressive shrimping fleets bring in shrimp served all over the peninsula. Shrimp is so important here that there's an annual festival and cooking competition honoring it in November. You can buy fresh shrimp from fishermen along the beach; one of the fish shacks can marinate the shrimp or prepare them as a cocktail.

San Felipe has several campgrounds and modest hotels, which fill up quickly in winter and during spring holidays. Gringo snowbirds populate the RV and trailer parks, making up one-quarter of San Felipe's population; the number is only increasing. But the town itself retains a fishing village flavor, with a few paved streets and dozens of fishing skiffs on the beach. On holiday weekends San Felipe can be boisterous—dune buggies, motorcycles, and off-road vehicles abound—but most of the time it's quiet and relaxing. The town also appeals to sportfishers, especially in spring. It's easy to find launches, bait, and supplies, but even novices can hop onto a fishing excursion by simply asking around the beach at about 7 AM; when you come back, you can have your catch cooked up at a local restaurant—the freshest seafood meal in Mexico. If you catch a few corvina, for example, have the restaurant make one into ceviche and fry up another with garlic.

GETTING HERE & AROUND

I–8 from San Diego connects with U.S. 111 at Calexico—203 km (126 mi) east—and the border crossing to Mexicali. San Felipe is on the coast, 200 km (124 mi) south of Mexicali via Carretera 5.

EXPLORING

The **Bahía San Felipe** has dramatic changes in its tides. They crest at 20 feet, and because the beach is so broad the waterline can move in and out up to 1 km (about ½ mi).

San Felipe's main landmark is the **shrine of the Cerro de la Virgen** *(Virgin of Guadalupe)*, at the north end of the malecón on a hill overlooking the sea. A steep stairway leads to it; fishermen traditionally light a candle to the Virgin here before heading out. There's an awesome view of the bay and beach from the hilltop.

WHERE TO EAT & STAY

¢–$ SEAFOOD ✕ **Maristaco.** This isn't just a single restaurant, but rather a complex full of simple *marisquerías,* small seafood stands, each of which do their own version of the classic San Felipe seafood staples—ceviche, shrimp cocktail, fish tacos, fried whole fish, and so on. Prices are bargain-basement, and the fish usually comes off the boats in the morning. Most places in Maristaco will cook up your fish if you bring it in from a boat after a morning of fishing (or if you buy the catch of the day from a fisherman on the beach). One such spot is **Tacos y Mariscos Liz,** in the middle of the complex; it's open later into the evening than many others, and on request, they'll keep your fish in their fridge until later in the day if you prefer. ✉ *Malecón* ▭ *AE, MC, V.*

¢–$ SEAFOOD ✕ **Rice and Beans.** The name nearly says it all, but the word "fish" should precede it. This is the place to try *mantaraya* (stingray) tacos and fish soup, along with San Felipe's famous shrimp. It's a casual hangout for the expat-retiree gang. ✉ *Malecón at Av. Chetumal* ☎ *686/577–1770* ▭ *AE, MC, V.*

$$ **El Cortéz.** Easily the most popular hotel in San Felipe, El Cortéz, which has been around since 1959, has several types of setups, including moderately priced bungalows and modern hotel rooms. The beachfront and second-floor bars are both enduringly beloved. The hotel is a 15-minute walk from the malecón, but it's preferable to take a taxi at night. **Pros:** Right on beach, laid-back vibe. **Cons:** Rooms a little tired. ✉ *Av. Mar de Cortés s/n,* ☎ *686/577–1055* *80 rooms, 4 suites, 24 bungalows* *In-hotel: Restaurant, room service, bars, pool, laundry facilities* ▭ *MC, V.*

$$ **La Hacienda de la Langosta Roja.** This simple hotel is one block from the waterfront and has the town's fanciest restaurant, though its Italian and Mexican dishes are of uneven quality. Rooms are motel basic: the beds are rather hard, but the heaters are powerful, and the showers have plenty of hot water. The company that owns La Hacienda plans to openthe upscale "Club Havana"—a Cuban-theme hotel and development—in 2008. **Pros:** Friendly staff. **Cons:** Not on beach, rooms are spartan. ✉ *Calz. Chetumal 125,* ☎ *686/577–0483 or 800/967–0005* 🌐 *www.sanfelipelodging.com* *39 rooms* *In-hotel: Restaurant, bar, no elevator* ▭ *MC, V.*

SPORTS & THE OUTDOORS

The northern part of the Mar de Cortés has lots of sea bass, snapper, corvina, halibut, and other game fish. Clamming is good here as well. Simple one-morning tourist fishing excursions can be arranged with the fishermen on the beach; arrive at 7 AM and negotiate. Apply plenty of sunscreen, and bring several bottles of water—and beer, if you like. Prices run about $80–$100 for up to four people, and you can generally keep what you catch (be sure to negotiate that beforehand)—and bring it over to Maristaco or one of the other fish shacks on the malecón for preparation. **Gone to Baja Adventure Tours** (☎ *619/370–4506 in U.S.*)

runs tours to Puertecitos, a small community with natural hot springs south of San Felipe. A three-day tour, including transportation from San Diego to San Felipe, camping on the beach, and fishing, is $700. **Tony Reyes Sportfishing** (☎*714/538–9300 in U.S.*), one of the most reputable companies, has six-day trips that cost about $775.

Puerto Vallarta & the Pacific Coast Resorts

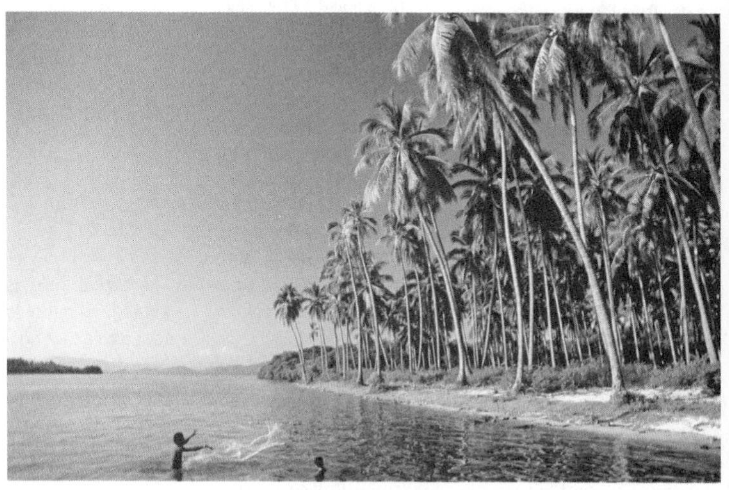

Coyuca de Benitez Lagoon

WORD OF MOUTH

"As for Vallarta, the city center itself is very nice and scenic, just hop a cab from the port to Old Town and wander around with a map or hire a guide. If you want to get out of town and have time there are various tours south to Mismaloya (including what's left of the old movie set), or 'jungle tours' or, much longer, up to San Blas to do a boat trip thru the mangroves (usually called the 'eco tour')."

–Bill_H

www.fodors.com/forums

WELCOME TO PUERTO VALLARTA & THE PACIFIC COAST RESORTS

TOP REASONS TO GO

★ **The chance to scuba dive, snorkel, surf, or kayak:** Zihuatanejo Bay has many opportunities for water sports. And the warm Pacific is as attractive to orcas, humpback whales, and dolphins as it is to humans.

★ **Pitting your will against big-game sport fish:** Sailfish, marlin, tuna, and yellowtail call these waters home. Fish from shore, small skiffs, or comfy cruisers. In November, Mazatlán, Puerto Vallarta, and Manzanillo host tournaments.

★ **Partaking in PV's food scene:** Puerto Vallarta has great chefs in spades—many hailing from Mexico City, the U.S., and Europe. Their delicious dishes are often accompanied by the region's best tequilas and the world's best wines.

★ **Shopping till you drop:** Look for contemporary paintings and sculpture of enduring value as well as for blown-glass items, ceramic tiles, tin lamp shades and frames, distinctive pottery, and Huichol beadwork.

1 Mazatlán. Mazatlán has two distinct sides: many are content to party in the highly developed hotel zone (Zona Dorada), while others choose to stay in the revitalized Centro Histórico, which has brightly painted 19th-century buildings and small museums.

2 Puerto Vallarta. Puerto Vallarta (PV) is Mexico's most popular Pacific resort—picture Cancún with cobblestones. It fronts the big, blue Bahía de Banderas, whose background consists of foothills covered in rain forest. Ecotour opportunities abound, but most people just come here to party.

3 La Costalegre. The "Happy Coast" is the region south of Puerto Vallarta between Cruz de Loreto and Manzanillo. There are a few ultraritzy resorts off Highway 200 but the area is largely undeveloped save for a few tiny villages and the slightly larger beach communities of Barra de Navidad and Melaque.

4 Manzanillo. The twin bays of Manzanillo and Santiago—collectively called Manzanillo—are popular with Mexican families and snowbirds. On one end of town are two beautiful peninsulas; on the other an unattractive working port that brings in the majority of the city's income.

5 Nuevo Vallarta & Nayarit. Just north of PV and across the Jalisco State line is Nuevo Vallarta, on Bahía de Banderas in Nayarit State. This area is dominated by all-inclusives, and golf courses. Dubbed the "Riviera Nayarit" by tourism folk and entrepreneurs, the coast between San Blas and Nuevo Vallarta is being bought, sold, and developed super quickly.

GETTING ORIENTED

The Pacific Coast is 1,609 km (1,000 mi) of lovely real estate that backs up from the ocean rather abruptly into the foothills and mountains of the Sierra Madre Occidental. The shorelines of no fewer than six states make up the Mexican Riviera. The region is mostly remote, with miles of deserted beaches and lonely roads that lead to miniscule villages, though it is heavily punctuated by the rapid development and cruise-ship ports of its four major resorts. At the northern end is Mazatlán, about 1,207 km (750 mi) from the U.S. border; at the southern end is Zihuatanejo, 245 km (152 mi) north of Acapulco. Smack in the middle is Puerto Vallarta.

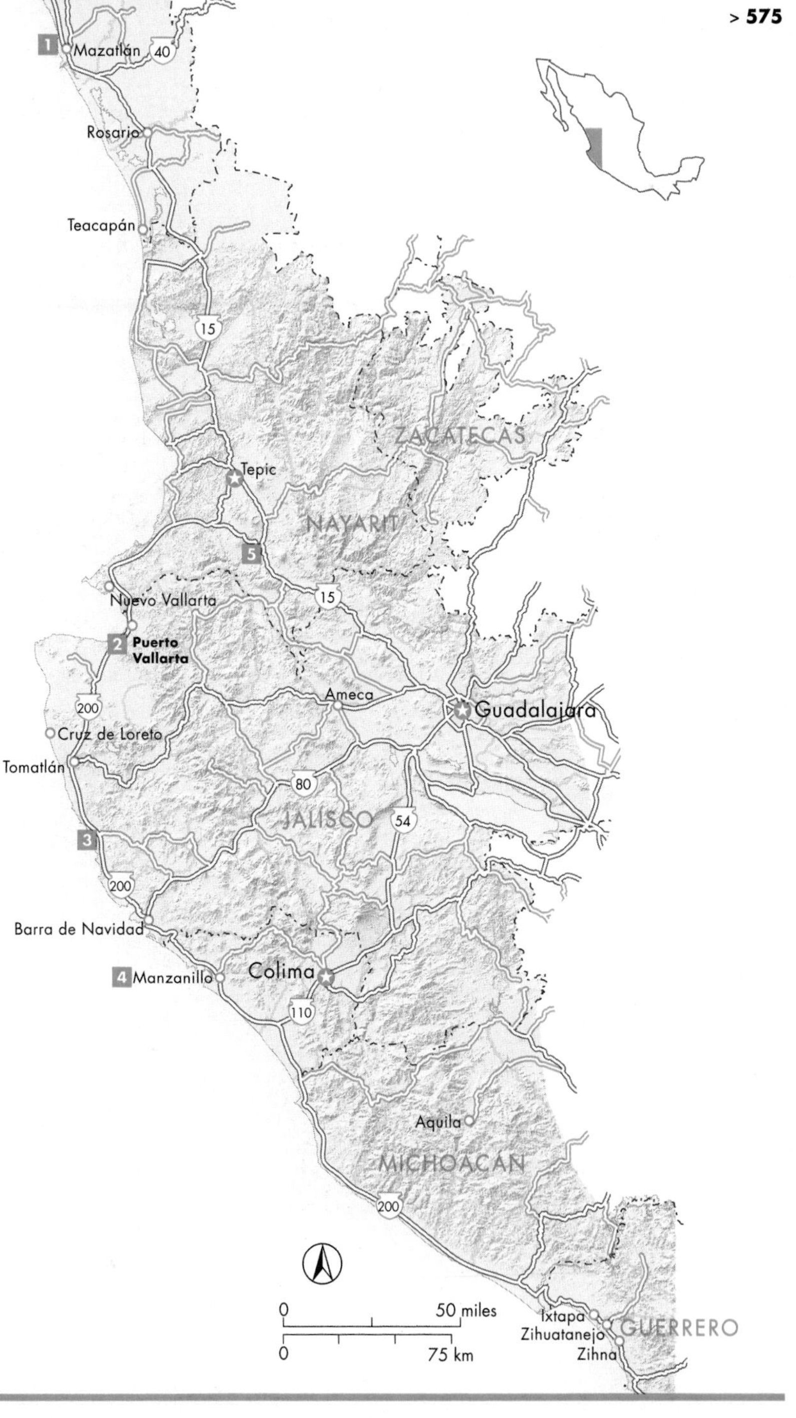

1 Mazatlán
40
Rosario
Teacapán
15
ZACATECAS
Tepic
NAYARIT
5
15
Nuevo Vallarta
2 Puerto Vallarta
200
Ameca
Guadalajara
Cruz de Loreto
Tomatlán
80
JALISCO
54
3
200
Barra de Navidad
4 Manzanillo
Colima
110
Aquila
MICHOACAN
200
0
50 miles
0
75 km
Ixtapa
Zihuatanejo
Zihna
GUERRERO

PUERTO VALLARTA & THE PACIFIC COAST RESORTS PLANNER

Shopping List

In Puerto Vallarta, emporiums selling crafts from throughout Mexico vie with clothing and jewelry boutiques for your attention. Shops filled with home furnishings of carved wood, iron, tin, stone, blown glass, and brass may make you want to buy a house here or open an import–export enterprise. Look for bowls, masks, and less traditional statuettes made by the Huichol Indians. Tiny, colorful beads are embedded in hollowed-out gourds or carved wooden pieces with beeswax and pine resin.

Several Pacific Coast towns are also known for their utilitarian pottery, and you can buy place settings and individual pieces from Mazatlán to Ixtapa.

Throughout the region also look for silver jewelry from Taxco, masks and exquisitely rendered lacquerware from Guerrero, carved-wood animals, hand-dyed woven rugs from Oaxaca, and those ubiquitous embroidered dresses and blouses.

Your Dream Vacation?

Aquamarine swells break upon sandy beaches. Waves are sliced by Boogie-boarders, Jet-Skiers, and surfers. Coves shelter schools of fish followed by curious snorkelers, and mangroves are a haven for birds of all stripes. Fishermen stand thigh deep in the surf, tossing their weighted nets, and each stretch of sand holds the promise of a glorious sunset. Lanky coconut trees shade huts thatched with palm leaves.

A Spot in the Sun

Mazatlán has its share of comfortable beachfront hotels and a few downtown inns. In Puerto Vallarta accommodations range from tiny inns to high-rise international chains to luxury resorts on secluded coves. Many of Manzanillo's properties are laid-back, more functional than elegant, but it does have a few high-end spots. Beachfront high-rises are what's happening in Ixtapa. Zihuatanejo has budget hotels as well as a few exclusive spots on or above the bay. Small beach towns outside Manzanillo and Zihuatanejo offer the best deals, though accommodations are generally very basic. For stays mid-December through New Year's, or mid-March through Easter, reserve rooms up to a year in advance (especially at boutique hotels). The rest of the winter season and July and August are also very busy, so reserve ahead, especially in Puerto Vallarta.

Getting Around

Highway 200 connects most of the coast, starting in Nayarit and creating one doozy of a scenic drive—though the Pacific is an unwavering blue, the landscape around it shifts from rain forest, to pine forest and back again.

Safety

Guard your purse, wallet, and other belongings on the beach as well as in markets and other crowded places. Town squares and seaside promenades are often full of people until the wee hours, making them generally safe. Still, always avoid poorly lit or desolate places at night. Time-share vendors are a hassle—particularly in Puerto Vallarta and Mazatlán—but not a safety concern. Such people often begin their patter with an innocuous topic and then rope you into a sales pitch. Avoid walking on deserted beaches at night, even if they front large resorts.

Who Visits When

Visitors to this part of the country are primarily Americans and Canadians, especially between late November and Easter. Mexicans from Guadalajara, Mexico City, and other inland cities head to the beaches en masse during Christmas, New Year's, Easter, and school holidays in July and August. Europeans make up some 20% to 25% of visitors, and they also tend to visit at Christmastime and in mid- to late summer. The coast has become very popular with the retired set and RVers. Surfers head to the small towns on the Costalegre and around Zihuatanejo.

Money Matters

Some hotel restaurants add 15% IVA (value-added tax) as well as a service charge to your tab. More humble establishments charge neither; check your bill and tip accordingly. Hotel prices drop by as much as 25% in off-season months such as May, June, September, or October; the latter months, sorry to say, are part of hurricane season (late September–early November).

WHAT IT COSTS IN DOLLARS					
¢	$	$$	$$$	$$$$	$$$$
Restaurants					
under $5	$5–$10	$10–$15	$15–$25	over $25	over $25
Hotels					
under $50	$50–$75	$75–$150	$150–$250	over $250	over $250

Restaurant prices represent the median price for a main course excluding tax and tip. Hotel prices are for two people in a standard double room in high season.

How's the Weather?

This coastal stretch is at its best in winter (December through February), with temperatures of 20°C–30°C (70°F–80°F) and a bit higher in Ixtapa and Zihuatanejo. The off-season brings humidity, mosquitoes, and heat, but also emptier beaches, warmer water (about 20°C [70°F]), and less-crowded streets.

Brides who want to glow but not sweat like a sumo wrestler should avoid a June wedding. The rainy season here is June to October, and the heat just before and during it can be stifling.

Surfers, on the other hand, will love the turbulent waters at this time of year. What's more, the countryside, the Sierra Madre Occidental, and the Sierra Madre del Sur turn a brilliant green. Note, though, that hurricane season runs from late September to early November.

MAZATLÁN

Updated by Carissa Bluestone

460 km (286 mi) north of Puerto Vallarta.

MAZATLÁN, THE FIRST MAJOR RESORT town on the Pacific coastline, has a split personality. At the northern end of town is the Zona Dorada (Golden Zone), where the hotels (and the prices) rise high, the pace is frenetic, and the building (mostly luxury condos for the retired set) continues unabated. The streets are jammed with tour buses shuttling cruise-ship passengers to dozens of jewelry shops. At the southern end of the malecón (the seaside promenade) is Viejo Mazatlán (Old Mazatlán), the city's historic center, a beautiful and low-key area of colorful postcolonial buildings—some restored, some still picturesque piles of chipped stucco—where you'll find a few hip restaurants, art galleries, and shops, and a very different scene from the touristy Golden Zone.

Mazatlán's beaches are golden and wide, though they're not nearly as attractive as those south of Puerto Vallarta. There are, however, tons of beach activities here—this is the place for parasailing—and several nearby islands provide alternatives to the crowded sands in town. Overall, the town is a good choice for a quick getaway: it's cheaper than Puerto Vallarta, the party scene is there for those who want to partake, and unlike in many resort towns, the city has some sights to explore beyond the surf and sand.

GETTING HERE & AROUND

Aeropuerto Internacional Rafael Buelna is about 25 km (18 mi) south of town—a good 30-minute drive. A private taxi from the airport will cost about $26. Mazatlán's main bus terminal offers connections north to the U.S. border, inland to Guadalajara and Mexico City, and south along the coast to Puerto Vallarta. When taking city buses, look for "Sabalo Centro" above the front window to get from the Zona Dorada to Viejo Mazatlán. Fares range from 40¢ for the tanklike minibuses to 80¢ for bigger, air-conditioned models (look for the bright green models). Taxis regularly cruise the Zona Dorada strip. Even easier to flag down (though usually more expensive) are the white, open-sided pulmonías; the fare starts at about $3 for a very short trip. It'll cost $6–$10 to get from the Zona Dorada to the Centro Histórico—always negotiate the fare before you get in.

ESSENTIALS

Bus Contacts **Estrella Blanca** (☎ *01800/507–5500 toll-free in Mexico* 🌐 *www.estrellablanca.com.mx*). **Transportes del Pacifico** (☎ *01800/001–1827 toll-free in Mexico* 🌐 *www.tap.com.mx*).

Medical Assistance **Balboa Hospital & Walk-In Clinic** (✉ *Av. Camarón Sábalo 4480, at Plaza Balboa, Zona Dorada* ☎ *669/916–5533*). **General Emergency Number** (☎ *060*). **Red Cross** (✉ *Calle*

WORD OF MOUTH

"We stayed in Mazatlan a few years ago and found very good body surfing right on the beach in front of the hotels. There were good restaurants right on the water too. Not too expensive. Mid-April is the beginning of their season because they are further north than Puerto Vallarta and Ixtapa, etc."

–Otis_B_Driftwood

Zaragoza 1801, Centro Histórico ☎*669/981–1506).* **Sharp Hospital** (✉*Av. Rafael Buelna at Dr. Jesus Kumate, Las Cruces* ☎*669/986–7911).*

Visitor & Tour Info **Sinaloa State Tourism Office** (✉*Calle Mariano Escobedo 1317 at Calle Carnaval, Centro Histórico* ☎*669/981–8883 or 669/981–8889).*

EXPLORING

The Zona Dorada—the start of which is marked by a kitschy white castle that houses a dining and dancing complex—has blocks of high-rise hotels, shops, restaurants, and nightclubs, along with the city's best swimming beaches. The malecón connects this zone with the historic center to the south. The southern part of the city is where all of Mazatlán's charm lies, along with most of the museums and sights. There are some stunning viewpoints from the seaside promenade on this end, but there's virtually no beach access unless you want to do as the locals do and pick your way over rocks to catch the sunset from one of the jetties.

MAIN ATTRACTIONS

2 **Acuario Mazatlán.** A perfect child-pleaser—and a lot of fun for adults, too—Mazatlán's homey little aquarium has more than 50 tanks with sharks, sea horses, and multicolor salt- and freshwater fish. Animal shows featuring kissing sea lions, skating macaws, and penny-pinching parrots are offered three times daily. The grounds aren't very extensive but there are two turtle and crocodile habitats and a small aviary, as well as a gift shop and snack bar. ✉*Av. de los Deportes 111, Olas Altas* ☎*669/981–7815* *$6.50* *Daily 9:30–6.*

4 **Catedral de Mazatlán.** A new lighting scheme gives nighttime drama to the bright yellow spires of the Basilica of the Immaculate Conception, which have towered over downtown for more than a century. Church construction began in 1855 and took nearly 50 years, along the way embracing Moorish, Gothic, baroque, and neoclassical architectural styles. An ongoing restoration has the Italian marble, cedar fixtures, elaborate chandeliers, and Parisian organ shining brighter than ever. ✉*Calles Juárez and 21 de Marzo, Centro Histórico* ☎*No phone.*

3 **Malecón.** A long, gorgeous waterfront makes Mazatlán a great city for walking, biking, or rollerblading. The *malecón,* a sidewalk atop the 10-km-long (6-mi-long) seawall, runs from the Zona Dorada south to Viejo Mazatlán. It bustles, especially in the evenings. The route is dotted with a dozen quirky monuments, from a tribute to the Sinaloa family to a vat from the Pacífico Brewery to a bronzed *pulmonía,* Mazatlán's beloved open-air taxi. The centerpiece is the massive *Monumento del Pescador* (Fisherman's Monument), which seems to portray a man preparing to throw a net over a napping woman. The road turns into Paseo Claussen, which continues past several more statues, including the Monumento a la Continuidad de la Vida (Monument to the Continuity of Life), a large fountain on which a bronze, nude couple stand atop a large conch shell and a school of leaping porpoises. A few steps more bring you to a seaside plaza where you can buy snacks and

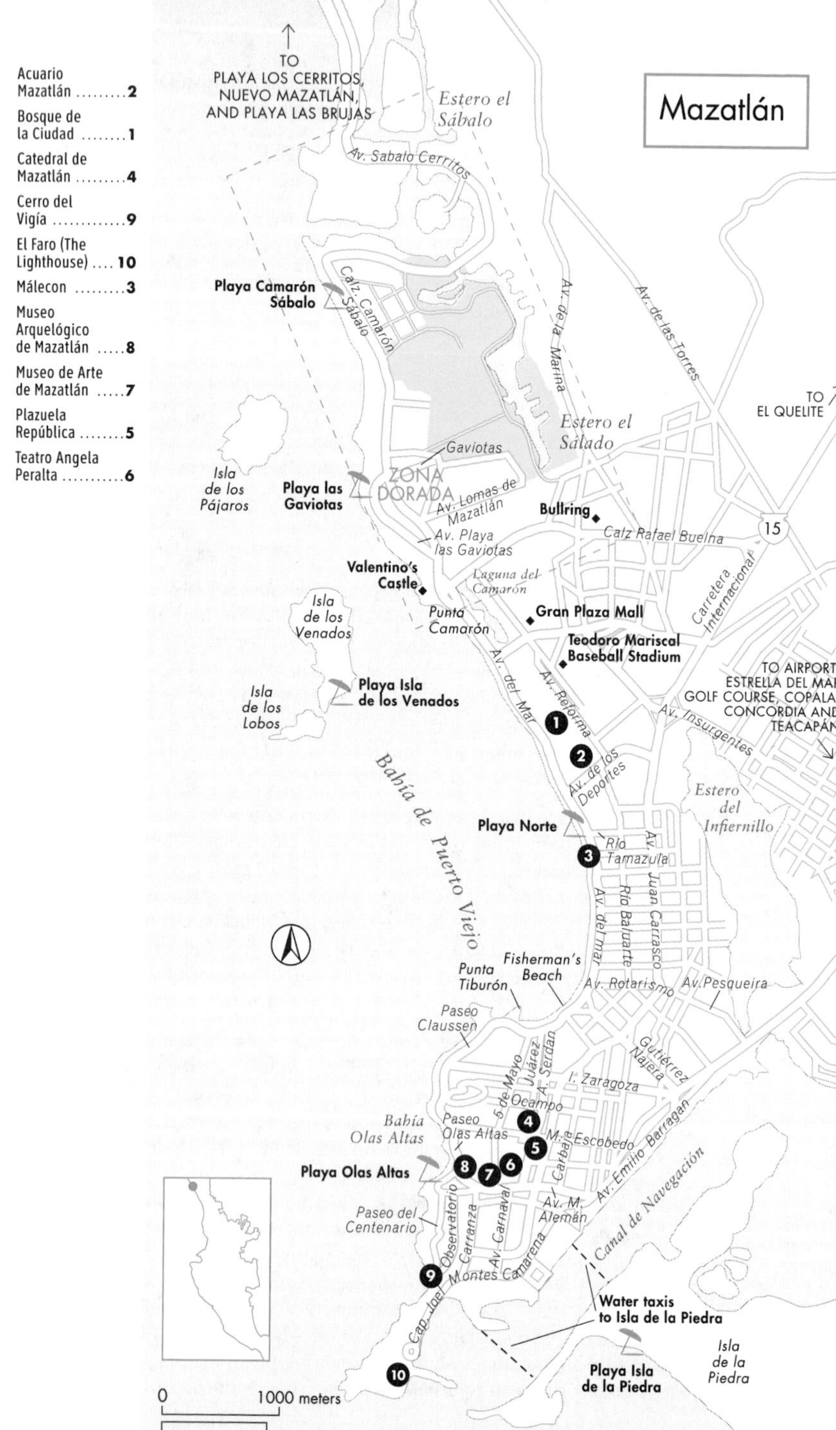
Mazatlán
Acuario Mazatlán 2
Bosque de la Ciudad 1
Catedral de Mazatlán 4
Cerro del Vigía 9
El Faro (The Lighthouse) 10
Málecon 3
Museo Arquelógico de Mazatlán 8
Museo de Arte de Mazatlán 7
Plazuela República 5
Teatro Angela Peralta 6
TO PLAYA LOS CERRITOS, NUEVO MAZATLÁN, AND PLAYA LAS BRUJAS
Estero el Sábalo
Av. Sabalo Cerritos
Playa Camarón Sábalo
Calz. Camarón Sábalo
Av. de la Marina
Av. de las Torres
TO EL QUELITE
Estero el Sálado
Gaviotas
Isla de los Pájaros
Playa las Gaviotas
ZONA DORADA
Av. Lomas de Mazatlán
Bullring
Av. Playa las Gaviotas
Calz Rafael Buelna
15
Valentino's Castle
Laguna del Camarón
Carretera Internacional
Isla de los Venados
Punta Camarón
Gran Plaza Mall
Teodoro Mariscal Baseball Stadium
TO AIRPORT, ESTRELLA DEL MAR GOLF COURSE, COPALA, CONCORDIA AND TEACAPÁN
Playa Isla de los Venados
Isla de los Lobos
Av. del Mar
Av. Reforma
Av. Insurgentes
Av. de los Deportes
Bahía de Puerto Viejo
Estero del Infiernillo
Playa Norte
Río Tamazula
Av. Juan Carrasco
Río Baluarte
Av. del mar
Fisherman's Beach
Punta Tiburón
Av. Rotarismo
Av. Pesqueira
Paseo Claussen
5 de Mayo
Juárez
A. Serdán
Gutiérrez Nájera
I. Zaragoza
Ocampo
Bahía Olas Altas
Paseo Olas Altas
M. Escobedo
Carbajal
Av. Emilio Barragán
Playa Olas Altas
Canal de Navegación
Paseo del Centenario
Av. M. Alemán
Observatorio
Carranza
Av. Carnaval
Camarena
Cap. Joel Montes
Water taxis to Isla de la Piedra
Playa Isla de la Piedra
Isla de la Piedra
0
1000 meters
0
1000 yards

kitschy souvenirs. If the crowd gets big enough, which it usually does when tour buses arrive around 11 am, 3 pm, and sunset, young men will dive into the sea from a high, white platform.

> **GOOD READING**
>
> Mazatlán's English-language monthly magazine, *Pacific Pearl*, has ads and articles of interest to locals and visitors. *Viejo Mazatlán* is a monthly bilingual paper that focuses on art, culture, and activities in Centro Histórico. Both publications are free and widely distributed.

7 **Museo de Arte de Mazatlán.** The revival of the Centro Histórico has injected new relevance into this small museum. Beyond recognized Mexican artists like José Luis Cueva and Arndo Nava, there are also debut exhibits by lesser-known artists in the burgeoning local scene, as well as eclectic concerts, films, and symposiums. ✉ *Calle Sixto Osuna and Av. Venustiano Carranza, Centro Histórico* ☎ *669/985–3502* *$1* *Tues.–Sat. 10–2 and 4–7*, Sun. 10–2.

5 **Plazuela Republica.** Also known as the zócalo or Plaza Revolución, this shaded square at the center of downtown—near the cathedral, city hall, and post office—is the perfect place to relax with a snack from the adjacent ice-cream and pizza shops or shaved-ice stands, get a shoeshine, or mail a letter home. Streets within a couple of blocks in any direction have small restaurants where fast, multicourse lunches (*comida corrida*) cost between $3 and $5. ✉ *Bounded by Calle 21 de Marzo to north, Calle Flores to south, Av. Benito Juárez to east, and Av. Nelson to west, Centro Histórico.*

IF YOU HAVE TIME

1 **Bosque de la Ciudad.** The city's best (read: only) real park is around the corner from the aquarium. With 29 acres of shaded playgrounds, trails, and a train to ride, it's a great place for kids to work off hotel-bound energy. It really gets moving on Sunday, frequently to the beat of a live band. ✉ *Av. Leonismo Internacional and Av. de los Deportes 111,*
9 *Olas Altas* ☎ *No phone* *Free* *Daily dawn–dusk*. **Cerro del Vigía.** The view from Lookout Hill is fantastic, but the road up from Paseo del Centenario is steep and confusing; take a pulmonía. At the top is a rusty cannon, and the Centenario Pégola—built in 1848 to celebrate the end of the U.S. invasion.

10 ★ **El Faro (The Lighthouse).** The best view in Mazatlán gets you some exercise, too—a 30- to 45-minute climb along natural trails and roughhewn stairs to the lighthouse that since 1571 has been warning ships from atop Cerro del Creston, 515 feet above the sea. Wear sturdy shoes, and bring a bottle of water, and, if you go up to watch the sunset, maybe a flashlight for the trip back down. Note that it takes about 20 minutes to walk from the southern terminus of Paseo Claussen (the end of the malecón) to the start of the lighthouse trail, but it's a beautiful route, most of which skirts the water. When Claussen ends just follow the signs for Paseo del Centenario for a few blocks through residential streets until you reemerge on the seaside road. ✉ *Southern terminus of Paseo del Centenario* ☎ *No phone.*

8 **Museo Arqueológico de Mazatlán.** The black-and-red pottery of the Totorame (an indigenous tribe that inhabited the area until 200 years before the Spanish arrived) highlights a small but interesting collection of regional artifacts here. Temporary exhibits fill the small main hall. Little of the information is in English. ✉ *Calle Sixto Osuna 76, at Av. Venustiano Carranza, Centro Histórico* ☎ *669/981–1455* 🎫 *$2.70, free Sun.* 🕙 *Daily 10–6.*

UNCOVERING THE PAST

If you like archaeology, inquire about tours to mysterious petroglyphs and a pyramid. Piedras Labradas (Carved Rocks) is on the beach near Estación Dimas, 74 km (46 mi) north of Mazatlán. El Calón ruins—the site of a 99-foot pyramid made of seashells that probably took the Totorame Indians 100 years to build—are ensconced in a mangrove estuary southward near Rancho Los Angeles.

NEED A BREAK?

The unofficial heart of the old city is Plazuela Machado, next to Teatro Angela Peralta and bounded by calles Libertad, Sixto Osuna, Carnaval, and Frias. Students gossip, locals chat on benches, and tourists tuck into affordable meals at the sidewalk cafés that ring the small, palm-shaded plaza. For a quick bite, check out Ta Café on the quiet southwest corner; it has coffee and sandwiches and comfy orange- and brown-striped armchairs.

6 **Teatro Angela Peralta.** The restoration of this 1860s-era opera house—named for a touring diva who died of yellow fever before she could give her concert—ignited the revival of the Centro Histórico in 1990. Catch a performance by students at the adjacent contemporary dance school (schedule is outside the theater) or take a self-guided tour. ✉ *Plazuela Machado* ☎ *669/982–4446* 🌐 *www.culturamazatlan.com* 🎫 *Varies by performance; tour $2.*

AROUND MAZATLÁN

A pleasant town 48 km (30 mi) east of Mazatlán, **Concordia** is known for its furniture makers, 18th-century church, and unglazed clay pottery. Pose for a photo in the gigantic rocking chair in the town square. The drive into town is lined with organ cactus and mango trees and is especially pretty after the summer rains cover nearby hills and distant mountains in green.

Copala, a tiny former mining town founded in 1565, is at the foot of the Sierra Madre Occidental, 25 km (15 mi) east of Concordia. A single cobblestone street winds to a small plaza and 18th-century church. Locals sell souvenir renditions of the town that they whittle from scraps of bark. Little boys will let your kids ride their burros for a dollar. The plaza has an excellent gift shop. Daniel's restaurant and rooming house serves the locally legendary banana-coconut-cream pie, the perfect way to wrap up delicious meals of hearty Mexican food on a wide veranda with an incredible valley view.

Hardworking farmers and cattle ranchers inhabit the village of **El Quelite** (29 km [18 mi] northeast of Mazatlán, off Carretera 15), which has colorfully painted houses and cobblestone streets. Tours take in livestock, a tortilla factory, a bakery, and a typical country lunch—and

TAKE A TOUR

King David Tours (✉ *Av. Camarón Sábalo 333, Zona Dorada* ☎ *669/914–1444* 🌐 *www.mazinfo.com/jungletour/index.htm*) is one of several operators that offer a bay tour through the harbor and estuary. There's a stop on a sun-drenched beach; a fish lunch with beer or soft drinks is served during a stop at an orchard of fruit trees and coconut palms. The all-inclusive price is $45.

For a look at life beyond Mazatlán's city limits, several tour operators offer trips to the towns listed below. **Olé Tours** (✉ *Av. Camarón Sábalo 7000, Zona Dorada* ☎ *669/916–6288* 🌐 *www.oletours.com*)has tours to Rosario and Copala daily except Sunday for $55, including refreshments and lunch. **Vista Tours** (✉ *Av. Camaron Sabalo 51, Lomas de Mazatlán* ☎ *669/986–8610* 🌐 *www.vistatours.com.mx*)has the most options for seeing Sinaloa State. They go to Concordia and Copala ($42–$50), El Quelite ($35), Rosario ($55), Piedras Labradas ($50), and to either the bird or turtle sanctuaries of Teacapán ($99), among many other destinations. Most tours are offered daily (except for Teacapán), last all day, and include refreshments and lunch. **Pronatours** (✉ *Av. Camarón Sábalo s/n, Centro Comercial El Cid, Zona Dorada* ☎ *669/913–3333 Ext. 3490 or 669/916–7720*) also has tours to Concordia and Copala ($55; Wednesday and Friday), El Quelite ($35; Tuesday and Thursday), and Rosario ($45; Thursday only).

sometimes also a rooster (read: cockfighting) farm, a demonstration of the pre-conquest ball game known as *ulama*, or a traditional riding and roping exhibition called *charrería*.

Accommodations are available at the home of the town's best-known citizen, **Dr. Marcos Osuna** (✉ *Callejón Fco. Bernal 1* ☎ *669/965–4194* ✍ *ruralosuna@hotmail.com*). The cost is roughly $65, including breakfast.

A couple of hours south of Mazatlán, the highway passes serenely through cattle and coconut country. Mazatlán tour companies stop at the 17th-century mining town of **El Rosario,** 72 km (45 mi) from Mazatlán, to see the magnificent church for which the town is named; trips often include stops at a Spanish cemetery and lovely old church and a visit to thermal springs.

Off-the-beaten-trackers can easily spend a few days in **Teacapán,** a tiny, hospitable settlement on the still shores of a huge estuary 59 km (37 mi) south of El Rosario. The joys are simple: beachcombing, bird-watching, kayaking, cycling, strolling the sprawling countryside, eating fresh fish at informal seaside restaurants, and exploring the nearby county seat, nontouristy Escuinapa. After all that simplicity, you can retreat to incongruously marvelous quarters at the **Villas Maria Fernanda** (✉ *Calle Reforma s/n at estuary, Teacapán* ☎ *695/954–5393* 🌐 *www.villasmariafernanda.com*). The compound consists of six homey bungalows, a larger apartment, and a 10-room hotel with cable TV, some kitchenettes, pool, and hot tub, all as tastefully appointed as they are remote.

The restaurant offers room service. Prices range from $55 for a hotel room to $95 for a villa with kitchen.

BEACHES

★ **Playa Camarón Sábalo.** This beach is just north of Playa las Gaviotas on the map but a couple of notches lower on the energy scale. Although hotels and sports concessions back both stretches, there's more room to spread out on this beach. It's also well protected from heavy surf by offshore islands. Most of the hotels have lounge chairs and umbrellas that nonguests can often use if they order drinks.

Playa Escondida. Relentless condo construction is creeping along the 6 km (4 mi) stretch of sand between Marina Mazatlán and Punta Cerritos, so Hidden Beach no longer truly lives up to its name. Still, it is far calmer than the hotel zone. A few small hotel bars and restaurants sell food and drink; otherwise you're on your own. Note that the undertow is strong in places.

Playa las Gaviotas. Seagull Beach, Mazatlán's most popular, parallels the Zona Dorada hotel loop. Streams of vendors sell pottery, lace tablecloths, silver jewelry—even songs. Concessionaires rent boats, Boogie boards, and windsurfers, and tout parasail rides. Food and drink are abundant, either at one of many beachfront hotel restaurants or from more of those vendors, who bear cups of freshly cut fruit, chilled coconuts, and even the odd pastry. If you're looking for relaxation, look elsewhere—between the constant solicitations from vendors and the endless renditions of "YMCA" blasting from the bars, you won't find a moment's peace here.

★ **Playa Isla de la Piedra.** Stone Island is where locals come on weekends and it's a wonderful adventure for visitors—a short trip to a side of Mazatlán that seems worlds away. Stone Island is really a long peninsula and has 16 km (10 mi) of unspoiled sand fronting a coconut plantation and an adjacent village nestled in greenery. There's plenty of space for everyone, although most folks pack the northern end, where bands and boom boxes blare music, restaurants sell seafood, and outfitters rent water-sports gear. There's horseback riding, too. Tour operators sell party-boat trips for $35 and up, but inexpensive water taxis cross the same channel with departures nearly every 15 minutes from dawn to sunset (save your ticket for the return). You can catch them at two small piers: one near the Pacífico Brewery, the other at the La Paz ferry terminal.

★ ☺ **Playa Isla de los Venados.** The most memorable way to get to Deer Island—one of three islands that form a channel off the Zona Dorada—is on an amphibious tank. The World War II relic departs regularly from El Cid hotel, in the Zona Dorada. It's a 20-minute ride. You can also get here on snorkeling and day cruises arranged through area tour operators. The beach is pretty and clean. For even better snorkeling, hike to small, secluded coves covered with shells.

Playa Marlin to Playa Norte. This 6-km (4-mi) arc of sand runs below a seawall walkway along the waterfront road known as Avenida del Mar, from Punta Camerón (Valentino's) to Punta Tiburón (south of the Fisherman's Monument). Palapas selling seafood, tacos, and cold drinks line the way. Fishermen land their skiffs at the sheltered cove at the south end; a bit farther south is Playa los Pinos, a calm inlet popular with families.

Playa Olas Altas. In this small cove, named for its high waves and edged by rocky hills, you can forget that the rest of Mazatlán exists. Three old hotels—La Siesta, Belmar, and Posada Freeman—and several cafés line the waterfront. At the north end, a saltwater swimming pool is filled and drained by the tides. Excluding the one plaza where vendors hawk tacky souvenirs to tourists, this stretch is a favorite spot of locals.

GET OUT OF THE GOLDEN ZONE

To find much greater seclusion than the city's main beaches will allow, head north to Playa los Cerritos or Playa las Brujas. You can negotiate a taxi fare, but it's more economical to take the bus (from the Golden Zone look for ones marked Cerritos Juarez North).

WHERE TO EAT

$$$–$$$$ STEAK & SEAFOOD ★ ✕**Sr. Peppers.** Locals are adamant that this is the best steak-and-shellfish restaurant in Mazatlán, although little about it suggests you're in Mexico. Shrimp, lobster, and mesquite-grilled steak come with north-of-the-border-style soup or salad, pasta or potatoes, steamed vegetable, and Texas toast. The decor is equally gringo: forest-green walls, crystal chandeliers, rattan furnishings, and lots of highly polished brass—all accompanied by a piano soloist. ✉*Av. Camarón Sábalo across from Faro Mazatlán hotel, Zona Dorada* ☎*669/914–0101* ▭*AE, MC, V* ⊙*No lunch.*

$$$ ECLECTIC ✕**La Concha.** It's a waterside palapa as large as a palace, but the ambience doesn't overshadow the menu: fish, beef, and pasta dishes are exquisitely prepared. A few old favorites come with a Mexican twist, perhaps a hint of cilantro or a spark of chile. There's an occasional outright adventure, such as stingray with black butter or calamari in its ink. Breakfast and lunch are served, too. The water views are hard to beat, especially at sunset. ✉*El Cid Moro, Av. Camarón Sábalo s/n, Zona Dorada* ☎*669/913–3333* ▭*AE, MC, V.*

$$–$$$ ITALIAN ✕**Angelo's.** With its fresh flowers, cream-and-beige color scheme, and small rooms flickering with candlelight, this Italian restaurant is truly elegant. A piano-accompanied singer stirs up the romance Thursday through Sunday after 7 PM. Try the veal scaloppine with mushrooms or the capellini with pesto and grilled scallops. The service is impeccable. ✉*Pueblo Bonito hotel, Av. Camarón Sábalo 2121, Zona Dorada* ☎*669/914–3700* ▭*AE, MC, V* ⊙*No lunch.*

$–$$$ SEAFOOD ✕**La Costa Marinera.** The excellent seafood, reasonable prices, and tremendous beachfront view keep this family-owned spot thriving year-round with a clientele that's equal parts visitors and locals. Try the Sinaloa specialty *pescado zarandeado,* in which an entire fish is smothered with vegetables and spices, wrapped, and cooked slowly over a fire until you can strip the meat with a touch of your fork. Request a song and maybe buy a CD from the singing waiter. Turn away the time-share sales pitch with a smile. ✉ *Privada del Camarón, at Privada de la Florida, Zona Dorada* ☎ *669/916–1599* ▭ *MC, V.*

$–$$$ AMERICAN ✕ **El Shrimp Bucket.** A comic sensibility pervades this festive old-town patio restaurant, from the carousel horses outside to the giant sardine can indoors, but the food is no joke. Try the cheese-stuffed jumbo shrimp wrapped in bacon, sautéed, and served with rice and steamed veggies, or the fried shrimp served in clay buckets. Barbecue ribs are also a good bet. It's a nice place for an early breakfast, too, when you'll be joined by Mazatlán businesspeople brokering deals over coffee and eggs. ✉ *Hotel Siesta, Paseo Olas Altas 11–126 Sur, Olas Altas* ☎ *669/981–6350* ▭ *AE, MC, V.*

> **"TACO ALLEY"**
>
> The first three blocks of Calle Gutiérrez Nájera turn into a taco alley every evening after 5 PM, with 15 open-air restaurants serving up all kinds of tacos—including beef, pork, fish, and shrimp. Prices are less than a dollar per taco, depending on ingredients, and four or five make a good meal. It's mostly locals along this stretch, but menus are easy to read and waiters are gregarious as they serve the daily dose of what many call *Vitamina T.* Just head east from the Fisherman's Monument.

$–$$ MEXICAN ✕ **Las Lupitas.** It's only a block from the beach near the heart of the Golden Zone, but this chic and reasonably priced hotel restaurant provides a serene alternative to the ear-splitting beach-bar scene. There's a pleasant patio—if you don't mind looking at busy Avenida Playa Gaviota—or a slightly mod dining room with wood-beam ceilings, polished stone floors, minimally dressed dark-wood tables, and a few red and white accents. At lunch you'll find simple, filling fare like ceviche, hamburgers, and fish tacos; at dinner the Mexican-Mediterranean menu is heavy on fresh fish specialties, like dorado in a honey glaze. ✉ *D'Gala Hotel, Calle Bugambillas 100 at Av. Playa Gaviotas, Zona Dorada* ☎ *669/913–4496* ▭ *MC, V.*

$–$$ MEXICAN ★ ✕ **Pedro & Lola.** Memorializing two local kids who became Mexican legends—movie star Pedro Infante and ranchera singer Lola Beltrán—Pedro & Lola is the best of several fine restaurants that ring the romantic Plazuela Machado. Its seafood dishes are as authentic and creative as the restored 19th-century building it inhabits. Shrimp is the specialty, but try the *papillot,* the day's catch cooked in foil with white wine, shrimp, and mushrooms. Music is also on the menu. There's a piano bar inside and sometimes a harmless rock combo; a guitar soloist serenades diners outside. Reservations are recommended Thursday through Saturday. ✉ *Calle Carnaval 1303, at Plazuela Machado, Centro Histórico* ☎ *669/982–2589* ▭ *AE, MC, V* ⊗ *No lunch.*

$ CAFÉ ★ ✕ **Café Bolero.** This small restaurant and gallery in an old building behind the Posada Freeman in the Centro Histórico allows you to drink and dine, listen and talk so unhurriedly that it's almost meditative. The kitchen, which specializes in grilled meats and fish, serves until about 10:30 PM, but the bar is open long into the night. You're encouraged to listen to the music (nightly after 8 pm), consider the paintings, maybe read something in the small library, and engage in the lost art of conversation. ✉ *Venustiano Carranza 18, Centro Histórico* ☎ *669/985–0003* ⊙ *Closed Mon. and Tues. No lunch.* ▭ *V.*

¢ MEXICAN ✕ **El Túnel.** The Tunnel—named for its long, narrow entrance across from the exit of the Teatro Angela Peralta—has been in business since 1945, and black-and-white photos of classic Mexican stars line the yellow-and-lavender-trimmed walls. You can taste its experience with faithful renditions of such famed regional snacks as *gorditas* (fried rounds of cornmeal topped with garnish), *tostadas,* meat or potato *tacos* and *pozole* (pork-and-hominy stew), and its specialty, *asada de la plaza de res* (chopped beef and cubed potatoes, spiced and smothered in lettuce, carrots, and onions). ✉ *Calle Carnaval 1207, Centro Histórico* ☎ *No phone* ▭ *No credit cards.*

THE OTHER SPRING BREAK

Mazatlán's single most important event is Carnaval, celebrated each spring during the week before Lent. The city fills with music, parades, dances, fireworks, and a beauty pageant to crown the Carnaval queen. Book accommodations far in advance and expect prices to rise significantly during the festival.

12

WHERE TO STAY

$$$–$$$$ **Pueblo Bonito Emerald Bay.** The neoclassical elements of Mazatlán's most remote and luxurious resort feel so close to holy that you may find yourself whispering. Balconies protrude from all 425-square-foot suites, where you can contemplate the sculpted gardens that undulate with the curves of spotless sidewalks, then seem to melt into the shifting sand and rippling ocean beyond. It's easy to enjoy the pillow-top mattresses or 350-foot-long shocking-blue pool. But if you don't like being marooned 10 km (six mi) north of town, then choose another location. **Pros:** Beautiful new property, location far from touristy Golden Zone, great pool areas. **Cons:** Beachfront isn't that impressive, 10-minute cab ride from Golden Zone, obnoxious time-share pitches. ✉ *Av. Ernesto Coppel Campaña 201, Nuevo Mazatlán* ☎ *669/989–0525, 800/990–8250 in U.S. and Canada* ⊕ *www.pueblobonitoemeraldbay.com* *258 suites* *In-room: Safe, kitchen, refrigerator, Wi-Fi. In-hotel: 2 restaurants, room service, bar, pools, gym, spa, beachfront, concierge, children's programs (ages 6–12), laundry service, public Internet, airport shuttle, parking (no fee), no-smoking rooms* ▭ *AE, MC, V.*

$$$ ★ **Pueblo Bonito.** A sense of calm, confident service pervades this all-suites hotel. Colors in the garden are rich: deep terra-cotta, strolling pink flamingos, expansive green palms, pristine white umbrellas, and golden koi ponds. Chandeliers and beveled-glass doors sparkle in the imposing lobby. Guest quarters have cool-aqua-tile floors, built-in sofas with earth-tone upholstery, beds with egg-crate-foam and pillow-top mattress pads, and pillow menus that give you the chance to choose the cushioning that's best for you. Kitchens are well equipped. It all opens out onto a glistening beach. **Pros:** Close to marina and Golden Zone, great beachfront, less of a party scene than at hotels farther down the

strip. **Cons:** So-so restaurants, room decor is starting to look a little dated, street-side rooms are noisy. ☒*Av. Camarón Sábalo 2121, Zona Dorada,* ☎*669/989–8900 or 800/990–8250* ⊕*www.pueblobonito.com* *247 suites* *In-room: Kitchen, refrigerator, safe. In-hotel: 3 restaurants, room service, bar, tennis court, pools, gym, beachfront, water sports, concierge, public Internet, children's programs (ages 6–12), laundry service, airport shuttle, parking (no fee)* *AE, MC, V.*

$$$ **Royal Villas Resort.** Everything feels supersize in this 12-story pyramid in the throbbing heart of the Zona Dorada, from the marble-heavy atrium lobby to the one- and two-bedroom suites that are done in bold blues and oranges. Even the glass elevators that take you to and fro offer amazing views. All rooms have balconies (be sure to request an ocean view, and if possible a room above the third floor). A delicate touch is the bridge to the pool, which spans a fishpond. **Pros:** Good bar and restaurant, nice pool area, comfortable beds. **Cons:** Not a place for a serene getaway (loud clubs nearby, kids at the pool), some of the junior suites are kind of small for the price. ☒*Av. Camarón Sábalo 500, Zona Dorada,* ☎*669/916–6161 or 800/898–3564* ⊕*www.royalvillas.com.mx* *123 suites, 2 penthouses* *In-room: Kitchen, Wi-Fi (some). In-hotel: 2 restaurants, room service, bar, pool, gym, beachfront, water sports, children's programs (ages 5–12), laundry facilities, laundry service, parking (no fee), public Wi-Fi, public Internet, no-smoking rooms* *AE, MC, V* *AI, EP.*

$$–$$$ **El Cid Megaresort.** Named after Spain's legendary medieval leader, Mazatlán's largest resort has four properties, three of which are together in the Zona Dorada. La Castilla (an all-inclusive) and El Moro are the most upscale; the Granada costs less because it's the oldest and has no beachfront. A free shuttle connects these to the upscale, all-inclusive Marina El Cid Hotel and Yacht Club, at the north end of town, overlooking the 100-slip marina. Staying at any El Cid property allows you to use the full-service spa and fitness center, the city's best golf school and course, tennis and racquetball courts, and aquatics center. Among readers, the Marina Beach seems to be the favorite of all the properties for its friendly staff, superior upkeep, and more-serene atmosphere. **Pros:** Tons of activities; several price points, all-inclusive plans, and kitchenette suites make the property more affordable; good restaurants. **Cons:** Time-share reps, about 1 mi from the other resorts, some parts of complex are starting to feel dated. ☒*Av. Camarón Sábalo s/n, Zona Dorada,* ☎*669/913–3333 or 800/525–1925* ⊕*www.elcid.com* *1,320 rooms* *In-room: Safe, kitchen (some), refrigerator (some), Wi-Fi (some). In-hotel: 9 restaurants, room service, bars, golf course, tennis courts, pools, gym, spa, beachfront, diving, water sports, children's programs (ages 4–12), laundry service, concierge, parking (no fee), public Wi-Fi, public Internet, no-smoking rooms* *AE, MC, V* *AI, EP.*

$$ **Casa Contenta.** An oasis of home-style tranquility wedged among Zona Dorada's high-energy high-rises, Casa Contenta consists of two buildings: one with seven one-bedroom apartments (some with waterfront terraces) and the other a house that can accommodate up to eight people with its three bedrooms, three baths, and living-dining room.

The live-like-a-local atmosphere is authentic down to its cheerful Mexican furniture, well-stocked kitchens, and meticulously tended gardens. **Pros:** Full kitchens, lots of space, good value for location, good for long-term stays. **Cons:** Decor could use some updating, no activities or vacation-planning help. ✉*Av. Playa las Gaviotas 224, Zona Dorada,* ☎*669/913–4976* 🌐*www.casacontenta.com.mx* *7 units* *In-room: No phone, kitchen. In-hotel: Pool, beachfront, parking (no fee), no elevator* 💳*MC, V.*

$$ ★ **Casa de Leyendas.** The grand old Centro Histórico home of a prominent Mazatlán doctor and former mayor has been lovingly transformed into this beautiful bed-and-breakfast. Each of its six rooms is dedicated to a different Mexican personage, including Pancho Villa and Frida Kahlo. There's a central courtyard and a rooftop terrace. The location is tops: across the street from two museums, a block from the beach, and three blocks from Plazuela Machado. Rooms have no TVs—more reason to head out and explore—but there's a media center with cable TV, VCR, and DVD. There's a small service fee for paying with a credit card. **Pros:** Beautiful historic building, rooms have tons of personality, great hosts. **Cons:** Some rooms have small bathrooms, strict cancellation policies, far from Golden Zone beaches. ✉*Venustiano Carranza 4, Centro Histórico,* ☎*669/981–6180* 🌐*www.casadeleyendas.com* *6 rooms* *In-room: No phone, no TV. In-hotel: Restaurant, bar, pool, laundry service, public Internet, public Wi-Fi, no elevator, no kids under 12* 💳 *MC, V.*

$$ **Holiday Inn Sunspree Resort.** Not the place for a meditative retreat, the rooms are filled with tour and convention groups that keep up a party mood by the pool and on the beach. The Kid's Spree program provides activities for children; adults can attend tennis clinics and borrow snorkel equipment or Boogie boards. Rooms are done in durable beiges and browns and are set up to facilitate pit stops between activities; all have refrigerators, coffeemakers, irons, hair dryers, and bathrooms with showers (no tubs). Quiet, digitally controlled air-conditioners don't add to the bustle. **Pros:** Family-friendly, nice pool and beachfront, good value. **Cons:** Families tend to takeover the pool area, ugly decor. ✉*Av. Camarón Sábalo 696, Zona Dorada,* ☎*669/913–2222 or 888/465–4329* 🌐*www.sunspreeresorts.com* *186 rooms, 23 suites* *In-room: Kitchen (some), refrigerator, dial-up. In-hotel: Restaurant, room service, bar, tennis court, gym, pools, beachfront, children's programs (ages 5–12), laundry service, laundry facilities, executive floor, public Internet, public Wi-Fi, parking (no fee) no-smoking rooms* 💳*AE, MC, V.*

$$ ★ **Playa Mazatlán.** The founding of this hotel in 1955 laid the cornerstone for the Zona Dorada, and it continues to hold its own. Accommodations are sunny, clean, and tasteful, and most open onto terraces or balconies. The well-kept grounds are mature but not dowdy. The pool is large, and palapas line the beach. When you ask for an ocean-view room, be sure to specify that you want one away from Joe's Oyster Bar. At this writing, many of the rooms were in various stages of renovation, so ask if any of the refurbished ones are available when you book. **Pros:** Beautiful grounds, lots of activities including on-site rock-climbing wall,

good value for location and amenities offered. **Cons:** A lot of noise from area bars, front-desk service has been slipping, in high season pool area doesn't have enough seating. ✉*Av. Playa las Gaviotas 202, Zona Dorada,* ☎*669/989–0555 or 800/762–5816* 🌐*www.playamazatlan.com.mx* *411 rooms* *In-room: Kitchen (some), safe, Wi-Fi (some). In-hotel: Restaurant, room service, bars, pools, gym, beachfront, concierge, children's programs (ages 7–12), laundry service, public Wi-Fi, public Internet, parking (no fee), no-smoking rooms* *AE, MC, V.*

OPEN HOUSE FOR ADULTS

The Centro Histórico's resident artists open up their studios to visitors on the first Friday of every month from 4 to 8 PM. Check out 🌐*www.artwalkmazatlan*.com for information and maps.

$$ **Los Sábalos.** Bring on the partying at this beachfront high-rise just inside the southern entrance to the Zona Dorada. It's home to Joe's Oyster Bar, an open-air dance club–volleyball court that is popular with locals and tourists alike; things really rev up on weekends. Amenities are tasteful, however, with comfortable white-walled rooms highlighted by blue and green fabrics. **Pros:** Great views, good staff. **Cons:** Beachfront is noisy and busy, rooms need updating, rooms get noise from area bars, overpriced. ✉*Av. Playa las Gaviotas 100, Zona Dorada,* ☎*669/983–5333 or 800/528–8760* 🌐*www.lossabalos.com* *155 rooms, 45 suites* *In-room: Safe, kitchen (some), refrigerator (some). In-hotel: 5 restaurants, room service, bars, pool, gym, spa, beachfront, concierge, public Internet, public Wi-Fi, parking (no fee)* *AE, MC, V* *EP.*

$–$$ **Best Western Posada Freeman.** An abandoned husk as recently as 2000, Mazatlán's first high-rise hotel underwent a marvelous restoration, and solidified the comeback of the Centro Histórico. The 12-story Freeman faces the ocean and fronts a charming maze of narrow postcolonial streets that surround nearby Plazuela Machado. Other than the spacious and gleaming tiled bathrooms, the rooms don't deviate from the standard chain hotel look—don't expect colonial charm—but they are bright and up-to-date and have some amenities (like free Wi-Fi and more than two English-language channels) that you won't find in many of the more expensive hotels. The rooftop bar and pool are marvelous spots to watch the sunset. **Pros:** Many rooms have small balconies with ocean or nice city views, cool rooftop bar, great location. **Cons:** On-site restaurant is nothing special, some rooms get noise from creaking elevator, chain hotel decor, far from Golden Zone. ✉*Av. Olas Altas 79 Sur, Centro Histórico,* ☎*669/985–6060, 800/780–7234 in U.S. or Canada* 🌐*www.bestwestern.com* *64 rooms, 8 junior suites* *In-room: Safe, kitchen (some), refrigerator (some), Wi-Fi. In-hotel: Bar, pool, laundry service, parking (no fee), public Wi-Fi, no-smoking rooms* *AE, MC, V* *BP.*

$ **Azteca Inn.** The best bargain in the Zona Dorada, this three-story low-rise is close to everything. Its straightforward accommodations are softened by white-and-yellow walls, colorful bedspreads, and a stand-alone bar called La Capilla (the chapel). Rates bounce up $15–$25 a night during Carnaval, Easter, and school vacations (Christmas through New Year, July, and August). **Pros:** Cheap rates, beach access across the street. **Cons:** No-frills, very small pool area, motel-style configuration, ground floor rooms are noisy. ✉*Av. Playa las Gaviotas 307, Zona Dorada,* ☎*669/913–4477 or 888/777–0705* 🌐*www.aztecainn.com.mx* *74 rooms* *In-room: Wi-Fi (some). In-hotel: Restaurant, room service, bar, pool, laundry service, public Internet, parking (no fee), no elevator* *AE, MC, V* *EP.*

THEY GOT THE BEAT

A plaque at Hotel La Siesta's entrance reports that Jack Kerouac passed through this three-story hotel when he was writing *On The Road* in the 1950s, and there's still something rather Beat generation about the place.

¢–$ **Hotel La Siesta.** This local landmark is a small seaside inn that is rich in history and low on price. Rooms are plain, clean, and comfortable; beds are firm, and the TVs have cable. Exterior halls and stairways are made of romantically creaking wood and surround a sweet-smelling courtyard where dieffenbachias grow to primeval proportions and doves roost in tropical almond trees. The first-floor patio is ringed by such nonaffiliated businesses as a car-rental office and a travel agency. El Shrimp Bucket restaurant provides room service. **Pros:** Nice courtyard, small pool, cheap rates, ocean views from some rooms. **Cons:** Rooms are very basic and not that attractive, far from Golden Zone beaches, no in-room safes. ✉*Paseo Olas Altas 11 Sur, Olas Altas,* ☎*669/981–2640* 🌐*www.lasiesta.com.mx* *57 rooms* *In-room: Wi-Fi. In-hotel: Restaurant, room service, bar, pool, laundry service, public Internet, no elevator* *AE, MC, V* *EP.*

NIGHTLIFE

El Caracol Disco Club (✉*Av. Camarón Sábalo s/n, Zona Dorada* ☎*669/913–3333*), at El Cid Castilla, has a high-tech disco, billiards, board and arcade games, and theme nights. The price of the cover depends on the evening—some nights, it's free and has a two-for-one drink special; others, an $18 cover includes an open bar and games.

★ **Dionisios** (✉*Calle Belisario Domínguez 1406, Centro Histórico* ☎*669/985–0333*) attracts gays and straights to its softly lighted, minimalist lounge adorned with work by local artists and soft DJ beats.

Officially, the weird, white Moorish castle hanging over the water at Punto Camarón is a complex of bars, restaurants, and shops named **Fiesta Land** (✉*Av. Camarón Sábalo at Calz. Rafael Buelna, Zona Dorada* ☎*669/984–1666*). But everybody calls it **Valentino's**—that's the name of its best-known disco, which itself has two dance clubs, one geared to a younger crowd, the other with more tranquil, romantic music, and a karaoke salon. **The Sheik** restaurant delights with waterfalls, ocean views, stained-glass windows, and marble floors, although its best feature may be the inexpensive morning-after breakfasts.

★ The **Fiesta Mexicana** (✉*Playa Mazatlán hotel, Av. Playa las Gaviotas 202, Zona Dorada* ☎*669/989–0555* 🌐*www.laoriginalfiestamexicana.*

BRING ON THE BANDA

Banda, which injects Latin energy into German oompah music, was born in southern Sinaloa when Bavarian immigrants showed up at the turn of the 20th century. It's more popular now than ever.

Mambocafe (✉ *Av. Reforma and Calz. Rafael Buelna, Zona Dorada* ☎ *669/986-6482*) in Mazatlán's **Gran Plaza** mall is modeled after Caribbean-style clubs—it's heavy on the tropical ambience and large, live groups that pump out the best in modern and traditional Latin music. Free salsa lessons happen Thursday through Saturday at 7 pm. There's no cover Monday and ladies enter free Thursday and Sunday; other times expect to pay around $6.

Banda music is everywhere in Mazatlán, including **Toro Bravo** (✉ *Av. del Mar 5500, Zona Costera* ☎ *669/985-0595*), but the mechanical bull is unique. The music starts after 11 PM. It's open Thursday through Sunday, or nightly during holiday seasons.

com) is one of the city's oldest tourist traditions, but the kitschy concept of a trip through Mexican history via a whirlwind of music and dance still draws and deserves big audiences for dinner shows Tuesday, Thursday (in high season), and Saturday from 7 to 10:30 (doors open at 6). The $33 fee covers an all-you-can-eat buffet, open bar, the entertainment, and the chance to do some dancing yourself.

Joe's Oyster Bar (✉ *Los Sábalos hotel, Av. Playa las Gaviotas 100, Zona Dorada* ☎ *669/983-5333*) has become perhaps Mazatlán's most popular club, although it's really not much more than a palapa and a volleyball court. Locals and tourists dance to pop and hip-hop. Get there early and watch the sunset over a couple of drinks, a plate of shrimp, and yes, some oysters.

SHOPPING

Zona Dorada is chockablock with shops, particularly along Avenidas Camarón Sábalo and Playa las Gaviotas, though the area is essentially one big tourist trap, with busloads of cruise-ship passengers and package-tour travelers being dropped off every few minutes. That said, if you're looking for souvenirs, beachwear, delightfully tacky seashell art, and jewelry, you won't have to walk but a few blocks in this area to accomplish all your shopping. ⚠**Be very wary when purchasing jewelry in Mazatlán; stories of tourists paying $800 or more for a ring here only to have it appraised at $300 (or less) at home are all too common. Always demand certificates of authenticity for all pieces.**

The Centro Histórico has fewer shops, but it does have a handful of galleries that sell high-quality crafts that are much more interesting than what you'll find in the Golden Zone. Note that bargaining isn't the norm in shops, no matter where you are in the city, but it's worth a try in markets. Mazatlán's traditional downtown **Mercado Central Pino Suárez** is a gigantic, turn-of-the-20th-century art nouveau structure between Calles Juárez, Ocampo, Serdán, and Leandro Valle. It's open daily and filled with produce, meat, fish, and bustle. The first few rows parallel to Calle Juárez have shell necklaces, huaraches (Mexican sandals), cowhide children's shoes, T-shirts, and gauzy dresses. Then comes the produce and grocery section, and finally the butcher stalls with the inevitable pig heads.

SLICE OF LIFE

Take in the Mercado Central Pino Suarez's frenzy at a serene distance, from a table in one of the inexpensive restaurants upstairs.

CRAFTS

Casa Antigua (✉ *Calle Mariano Escobedo 206, Centro Histórico* ☎ *669/982–5236*), in the former home of Mazatlán's first bishop, sells crafts from throughout Mexico in all price ranges and media—silver, ceramics, black clay, and papier-mâché.

★ **Casa Etnika** (✉ *Sixto Osuna 50, Centro Histórico* ☎ *669/136–0139* ⏲ *Closed Sun.*) sells a funky mélange of non-kitschy Mexican and world crafts, from jewelry to carved wood statuettes to nature photography of Sinaloa state. Some items are even made from recycled materials.

Mexican artist **Elina Chauvet** (✉ *Calle Sixto Osuna 24, Centro Histórico* ☎ *No phone*) sells unique beaded necklaces and bracelets, casual beachwear, Guerrero masks, and embroidered cotton clothing. She's also a renowned painter who sells works by other artists alongside her own.

Part of Hotel Playa, **México México** (✉ *Av. Playa las Gaviotas 202, Zona Dorada* ☎ *669/989–0555*) is a good place to buy resort wear, costume and shell jewelry, and unique ceramic and metal items.

★ The stylish work at **Nidart** (✉ *Calle Libertad 45 and Calle Carnaval, Centro Histórico* ☎ *669/981–0002*) includes leather masks, ceramic sculptures, contemporary black-and-white photos, and other Mexican arts and crafts. Sometimes you can watch artisans in open workshops; it's normally open Monday through Saturday between 10 and 2 only.

★ **La Querencia** (✉ *Calle Belisario Dominguez 1502, Centro Histórico* ☎ *669/981–1036*) is a colorful cavern of Latin American art, clothing, and furniture—from the playful to the sublime and with prices to match.

JEWELRY

Casa Maya (✉ *Av. Playa las Gaviotas 411, across from Hotel Las Flores, Zona Dorada* ☎ *669/914–0491*) has silver and gold jewelry; silver tea sets, platters, and urns; and Talavera place settings. **Rubio Jewelers** (✉ *Costa de Oro hotel, Av. Camarón Sábalo L-1, Zona Dorada* ☎ *669/914–3167*) carries fine gold, silver, and platinum jewelry. It's also Mazatlán's exclusive distributor of Sergio Bustamante's whimsical ceramic and bronze sculptures. The same family owns and runs El Delfin in the Balboa Towers.

SPORTS & THE OUTDOORS

BASEBALL

★ Unlike their counterparts to the south who are soccer mad, sports fans in northwestern Mexico are baseball crazy. The people of Mazatlán are still bragging about how their beloved **Venados** (✉*Blvd. Justo Sierra, Zona Estadio* ☎*669/981–1710* 🌐*www.venadosdemazatlan.com*) captured the 2005 Pacific League title and went on to bring Mexico glory in the Caribbean Series, which was played in their own Teodoro Mariscal Stadium. Rosters consist of Mexico's best players and American minor leaguers trying to stay in shape during the off-season. But it's the energy of the singing, dancing, always-eating-something crowd that makes the experience special. Regular season games are October through December. Purchase tickets at the stadium box office after 1 PM on game day; prices are $1.50–$10.

BULLFIGHTS & CHARREADAS

Bullfights are held most Sunday afternoons at 3:30 from December through April in the bullring—Plaza de Toros Monumental—on Calzada Rafael Buelna near Calle de la Marina. *Charreadas* (rodeos) take place during roughly the same time period, also on Sunday. Tickets (about $10–$20 for charreadas; $30–$35 for bullfights) are available at the bullring, through most hotels and travel agencies, and at **Valentino's** (✉*Fiesta Land complex, Av. Camarón Sábalo, at Calz. Rafael Buelna, Zona Dorada* ☎*669/984–1666*) nightclub.

FISHING

You can arrange deep-sea charters through your hotel, or you can contact the companies directly. Charters include a full day of fishing, bait and tackle, and usually an ice chest with ice. Prices start at about $100 per person on a party boat or from $270 to $470 to charter a boat for one to six passengers.

For bass fishing in El Salto Reservoir, a lake northeast of Mazatlán off Carretera 40, contact **Amazing Outdoors Tours** (✉*El Patio Restaurant, Camarón Sábalo 2601, Zona Dorada* ☎*669/952–1442 or 669/913–1719* 🌐*www.basselsalto.com*). Choose a half- or full-day trip, or stay overnight at their fishing lodge. The reputable **Aries Fleet** (☎*669/916–3468*) is connected with El Cid Hotel and operates from Marina El Cid. The company has shared or charter boats for big-game fishing. **Bill Heimpel's Star Fleet** (☎*669/982–2665 or 888/882–9614* 🌐*www.starfleet.com.mx*), which has fast twin-engine boats, is well regarded.

GOLF

The last 9 holes of the spectacular 27-hole course at **El Cid Golf and Country Club** (☎*669/913–3333 Ext. 3261*) were designed by Lee Trevino. There's a putting green and driving range. Greens fees are $63 (nonguests) for 18 holes, plus $40 for a cart and $20 for a caddy. The **Estrella del Mar Golf Club** (✉*Camino Isla de la Piedra, Km 10* ☎*01800/727–4653 toll-free in Mexico, 800/967–1889 in U.S.* 🌐*www.estrelladelmar.com*) is an 18-hole waterfront course designed by Robert Trent Jones Jr., just south of Mazatlán proper on Isla de la Piedra (Stone Island). Transportation from some of Mazatlán's major hotels is free.

Carts and transportation to and from the course are included in the $75–$110 greens fee.

WATER SPORTS

The two most popular activities are snorkeling tours to Deer Island and parasailing—nearly every hotel offers both, along with kayak and Jet Ski rentals. A few outfitters, including the Aqua Sport Center, offer scuba, but Mazatlán is not a popular diving area.

Aqua Adventures (✉*Hotel Royal Villas, Av. Camarón Sábalo 500, Zona Dorada* ☎*669/916–6161*) rents kayaks ($12–$15 an hour) and WaveRunners ($40 for a half-hour) and offers short parasailing and banana-boat rides.

AquaSport Center (✉*Av. Camarón Sábalo s/n, next to Hotel La Puesta del Sol, Zona Dorada* ☎*669/913–3333 Ext. 3341*) offers banana boat and parasailing rides and rents WaveRunners, kayaks, Boogie boards, and sailboats. Its staffers can also arrange half-day trimaran trips to Isla de los Venados aboard the *Kolonahe,* docked at El Cid Marina.

The 4-acre **Parque Acuático Mazagua** (✉*Av. Sábalo Cerritos and Entronque Habal Cerritos, Nuevo Mazatlán* ☎*669/988–0041* 🌐*www.mazagua.com*) has slides, wading pools, and a wave pool as well as picnic facilities with barbecue grills. Entrance is about $11 per person; the park is open 10 AM–6 PM Wednesday through Sunday for most of the year and daily in July, August, and during school holidays.

> **ECOVENTURING**
>
> **EduVentura** (☎*669/940–8687* 🌐*www.eduventura.com*)at Hotel Playa Mazatlán offers a grab bag of activities and ecotourism opportunities. After trying out the climbing wall and zip line, book a kayaking tour to Deer Island or a whale- or bird-watching excursion through one of several companies committed to sustainable tourism that supports local conservation efforts.

PUERTO VALLARTA

Updated by Jane Onstott

Although Puerto Vallarta (PV) has spread north and south over the years, every attempt has been made to keep the character of the original downtown village intact. City ordinances prohibit neon signs, require houses to be painted white, and dictate other architectural details downtown, where pack mules still occasionally clomp along a few blocks beyond the busy downtown scene.

Puerto Vallarta the destination is much larger than Puerto Vallarta the town. The original town sits smack dab at the center of a 42-km-long (26-mi-long) bay, Bahía de Banderas (Banderas, or Flags, Bay), Mexico's largest. On the same latitude as the Hawaiian Islands, PV is tropical. At Old Vallarta, in the center of the bay, the Sierra Madre foothills practically dive into the sea; numerous mountain-fed rivers and streams nourish tropical deciduous forest as far north as coastal San Blas. South of PV the hills recede from the coast and the drier tropical thorn forest predominates to Barra de Navidad.

The bay provides shelter from storms at sea and has been attracting outsiders since the 16th century. Pirates and explorers paused here to relax—or maybe plunder and pillage—during long trips. Sir Francis Drake apparently stopped here. In the mid-1850s, Don Guadalupe Sánchez Carrillo developed the bay as a port for the silver mines by the Río Cuale. Then it was known as Puerto de Peñas (Rocky Port) and had about 1,500 inhabitants. In 1918 it was made a municipality and renamed for Ignacio L. Vallarta, a governor of Jalisco State.

THE DISH

Although not cast in John Huston's *The Night of the Iguana,* Elizabeth Taylor accompanied Richard Burton during filming, and the gossip about their romance (both were married at the time, but not to each other) brought this tiny fishing village to the public's attention in the early '60s. Considering that Ava Gardner and Deborah Kerr were among the actresses in the film, it's no surprise that Liz felt compelled to be by Richard's side.

In the 1950s Puerto Vallarta was essentially a hideaway for the wealthy and a few hardy escapists. When it first entered the general public's consciousness, with John Huston's 1964 movie *The Night of the Iguana,* it was a quiet fishing and farming community. After the movie was released, tourism began to boom, and today PV has some 300,000 residents. Airports, hotels, and highways have supplanted palm groves and fishing shacks, and about 2 million people visit each year.

El Centro (downtown) rises abruptly from the sea; whitewashed homes and businesses line hilly cobblestone streets. South of the Cuale River, the Zona Romántica (Romantic Zone, aka Col. E. Zapata or South Side), bordering Los Muertos Beach, has the most restaurants and shops. Old Vallarta includes El Centro and the Zona Romántica.

Facing a busy avenue, the Zona Hotelera Norte (Northern Hotel Zone) has malls and businesses in addition to high-rise hotels. More shopping centers and deluxe hotels are found in Marina Vallarta, sandwiched between a golf course and the city's main marina, 15 minutes north of downtown. At the southern edge of Nayarit State, the planned resort of Nuevo Vallarta has lots of all-inclusive hotels but few restaurants and shops outside the Paradise Plaza mall.

The beach towns north of Nuevo Vallarta are steadily gaining in popularity and tourist infrastructure. Once the private stomping grounds of local fishermen and surfers, Punta de Mita is now a super-exclusive gated community, but a sliver of paradise is still accessible to the hoi polloi. Bucerías, Sayulita, and other small communities are attracting more and more travelers while retaining their small-town appeal.

South of PV to Mismaloya, the condos and hotels of the Zona Hotelera Sur straddle the beach or overlook it from cliff-side aeries. Roughly 121 km (75 mi) south of PV en route to the city of Manzanillo, the Costalegre is a mixture of exclusive resorts and earthy little beach hamlets.

To fully explore the beaches and small towns outside downtown PV, it really helps to have a car. However, cars are a serious hindrance in El Centro and the Río Cuale area, and you can see most of the sights there by taxi or on foot—as long as you wear comfortable shoes for the uneven cobblestone streets.

GETTING HERE & AROUND

Many major U.S. airlines have flights to PV; some are nonstop. Private taxis and vans provide transportation from the airport to PV hotels; the airport is about 7½ km (4½ mi) north of downtown. PV's Central Camionero, or Central Bus Station, is 1 km (½ mi) north of the airport, halfway between Nuevo Vallarta and downtown Puerto Vallarta. ETN has the most luxurious service to Guadalajara, Mexico City, and many other destinations. TAP serves Mexico City, Guadalajara, Puerto Vallarta, Tepic, and Mazatlán as well as lesser-known destinations. Basic service, including some buses with marginal or no air-conditioning, is the norm on Transportes Cihuatlán, which connects the Bahía de Banderas and PV with southern Jalisco towns such as Barra de Navidad. City buses, around 50¢ serve downtown, the Zona Hotelera Norte, and Marina VallartaBuses and taxis are the way to get around downtown; rent a car for days when you'll be sightseeing outside the city center.

ESSENTIALS

Bus Contacts **Central Camionero** (✉ *Puerto Vallarta-Tepic Hwy., Km 9, Las Mojoneras* ☎ *322/290-1008*). **ETN** (☎ *01800/800-0386 toll-free in Mexico, 322/290-0996 in PV* 🌐 *www.etn.com.mx*). **Primera Plus** (☎ *322/290-0715 in PV*). **Transporte del Pacifico (TAP)** (☎ *322/290-0119 in PV*).

Currency Exchange **Banamex** (✉ *Plaza Marina, Local 37* ☎ *322/221-0733* ✉ *Calle Juárez, at Calle Zaragoza Centro* ☎ *322/226-6110* ✉ *Paseo de los Cocoteros s/n, Paradise Plaza, Nuevo Vallarta* ☎ *322/297-0688*).

Internet **PV Café** (✉ *Calle Olas Altas 250, Olas Altas* ☎ *322/222-0092*). **PV Net** (✉ *Blvd. Francisco M. Ascencio 1692, across from Sheraton Buganvilias, Zona Hotelera Norte* ☎ *322/223-1127*).

Medical Assistance **Cornerstone Hospital** (✉ *Av. Los Tules 136, across from Plaza Caracol, Zona Hotelera* ☎ *322/226-3700* 🌐 *www.hospitalcornerstone.com*). **Hospital San Javier Marina** (✉ *Blvd. Francisco M. Ascencio 2760, at María Montessori, Zona Hotelera Norte* ☎ *322/226-1010*).

Visitor & Tour Info **Puerto Vallarta Tourism Board & Convention and Visitors Bureau** (✉ *Local 18 Planta Baja, Zona Comercial Hotel Canto del Sol, Zona Hotelera, Las Glorias* ☎ *322/224-1175 or 888/384-6822* 🌐 *www.visitpuertovallarta.com*).

EXPLORING

MAIN ATTRACTIONS

8 The **Zoológico de Vallarta** (✉ *Camino al Edén 700, Mismaloya* ☎ *322/228-0501* 🌐 *www.zoologicodevallarta.com* 🎟 *$10* ⏲ *Daily 10 to 6*)is home to some 450 animals. The zoo's captive breeding programs means you'll see baby emus, kittenlike Bengal tigers, and tiny

little capuchin monkeys, among other species. Native plant species are being cultivated here, too, to be reintroduced in areas damaged by mining or other industries.There's a restaurant on-site, and parking at no additional charge. The $80 VIP tour, available by previous reservation for up to 10 people (English or Spanish), includes face time with interesting animal species, a T-shirt, and a meal chosen off their menu.

7 Located on 20 acres of land, the **Puerto Vallarta Botanical Gardens**(✉ *Carretera a Barra de Navidad Km. 24, Las Juntas y Los Veranos* ☎ *322/223–6182* 🌐 *www.vallartabotanicalgardensac.org* 🎟 *$3* ⏲ Closed Tues.–Sun. 9–6) features more than 3,000 species of plants. Set within the tropical dry forest at 1,300 feet above sea level, its trails lead to palm, agave, and rose gardens as well as a tree fern grotto, orchid house, and displays of Mexican wildflowers and carnivorous plants. You'll find free parking and a lovely, open-sided restaurant. Go to their Web site to arrange a four-hour birding or hiking tour, with lunch, for $85 per person.

4 Fodor's Choice ★ Puerto Vallarta's **malecón** is the Champs Élysées of PV—only shorter, warmer, and less expensive. Every night and weekend along the mile-long concrete walkway bordering the sea is a spectacle, with locals and tourists out to stroll, and vendors and peddlers selling empanadas, corn on the cob, fried bananas, helium balloons, and cotton candy. Clowns, magicians, and musicians entertain in the Los Arcos amphitheater. Even those who have lived here all their lives come out to watch the red sun sink into the gray-blue water beyond the bay. Some of PV's most endearing art pieces are here *en plein air.* Along the sea walk is a series of bronze sculptures—including Puerto Vallarta's well-known sea-horse icon—that are constantly touched, photographed, and climbed on. ✉ *Extending south from Calle 31 de Octubre south to Playa los Muertos Centro.*

IF YOU HAVE TIME

6 The **Centro Cultural Cuale** (✉ *East end of Isla Río Cuale, Aquiles Serdán 437, int. 38, Centro* ☎ *322/223–0095*) sells the work of local artists, has art and dance classes, and hosts free cultural events. Check the free *Bay Vallarta,* available at shops and hotels, for schedules.

2 **La Iglesia de Nuestra Señora de Guadalupe** *(Church of Our Lady of Guadalupe)* is dedicated to the patron saint of Mexico and of Puerto Vallarta. The holy mother's image, by Ignacio Ramírez, is the centerpiece of the cathedral's slender marble altarpiece. The brick bell tower is topped by a lacy-looking crown that replicates the one worn by Carlota, short-lived empress of Mexico. The wrought-iron crown toppled during an earthquake that shook this area of the Pacific Coast in October 1995, but was soon replaced with a fiberglass version, supported, as was the original, by a squadron of stone angels. ✉ *Calle Hidalgo, Centro* ☎ *No phone* ⏲ *7:30* AM*–8* PM.

5 Pre-Columbian and Indian artifacts are on display at the **Museo Arqueológico** *(Archeological Museum).* Most of the exhibits are labeled in English and Spanish. There's a general explanation of Western Pacific cultures and shaft tombs, and abbreviated exhibits of Aztatlán and

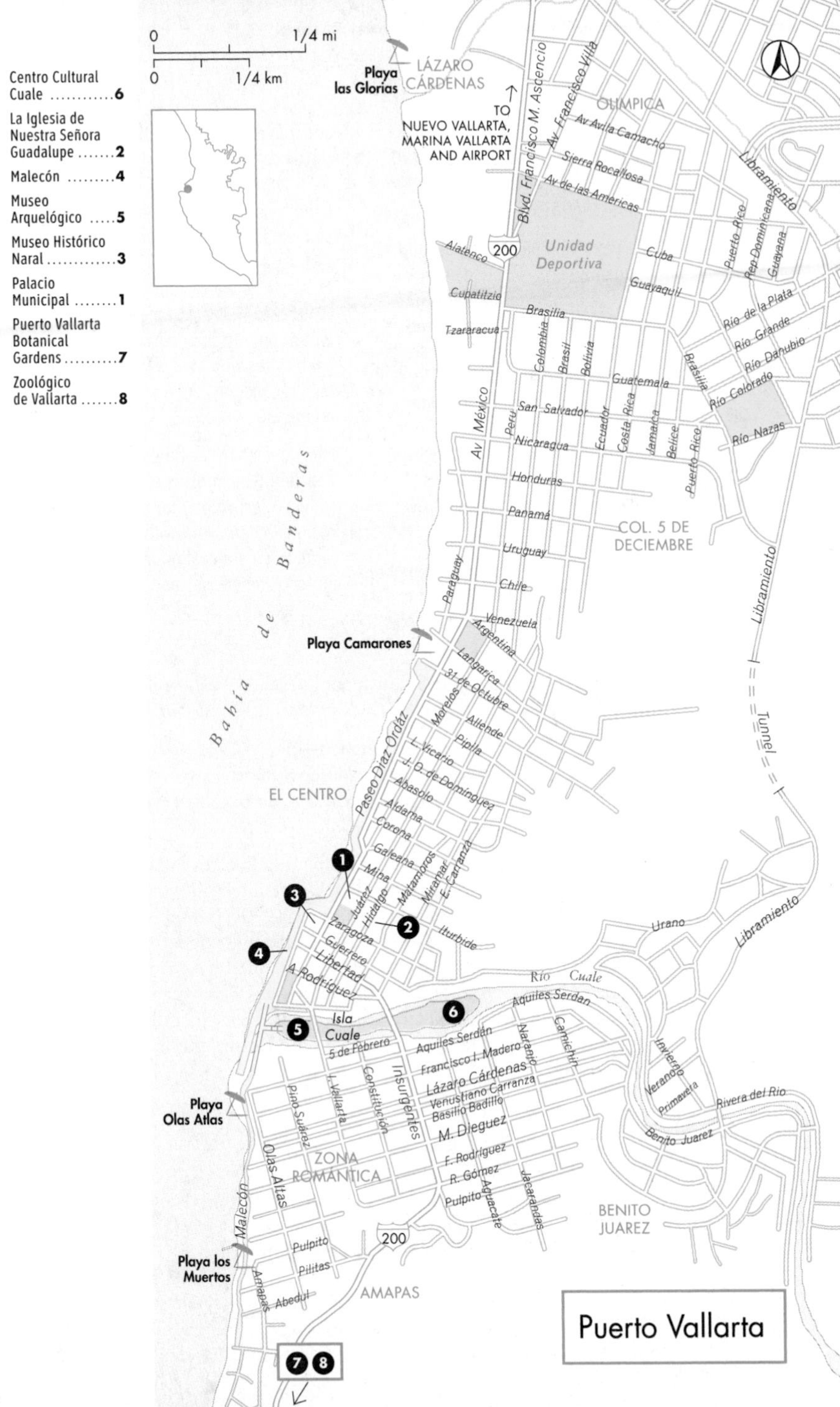

Centro Cultural Cuale 6
La Iglesia de Nuestra Señora Guadalupe 2
Malecón 4
Museo Arquelógico 5
Museo Histórico Naral 3
Palacio Municipal 1
Puerto Vallarta Botanical Gardens 7
Zoológico de Vallarta 8
0 1/4 mi
0 1/4 km
Playa las Glorias
LÁZARO CÁRDENAS
TO NUEVO VALLARTA, MARINA VALLARTA AND AIRPORT
Blvd. Francisco M. Ascencio
Av. Francisco Villa
OLIMPICA
Av Avila Camacho
Sierra Rocallosa
Av de las Americas
Libramiento
Unidad Deportiva
200
Alatenco
Cupatitzio
Tzararacua
Brasilia
Cuba
Guayaquil
Puerto Rico
Rep Dominicana
Guayana
Río de la Plata
Río Grande
Río Danubio
Río Colorado
Río Nazas
Colombia
Brasil
Bolivia
Guatemala
San Salvador
Peru
Av México
Nicaragua
Ecuador
Costa Rica
Jamaica
Belice
Honduras
Panamá
Uruguay
Chile
COL. 5 DE DECIEMBRE
Paraguay
Venezuela
Argentina
Bahía de Banderas
Playa Camarones
Langarica
31 de Octubre
Morelos
Allende
Pipila
I. Vicario
J. O. de Domínguez
Paseo Díaz Ordáz
Abasolo
Aldama
Corona
Galeana
Mina
Juárez
Hidalgo
Matamoros
Miramar
E. Carranza
EL CENTRO
Zaragoza
Iturbide
Guerrero
Libertad
A Rodríguez
Tunnel
Urano
Río Cuale
Aquiles Serdán
Isla Cuale
5 de Febrero
Francisco I. Madero
Naranjo
Camichin
Lázaro Cárdenas
Venustiano Carranza
Basilio Badillo
M. Dieguez
Insurgentes
Constitución
I. Vallarta
Pino Suárez
Invierno
Verano
Primavera
Rivera del Rio
Benito Juarez
Playa Olas Atlas
Olas Altas
ZONA ROMÁNTICA
F. Rodríguez
R. Gómez
Pulpito
Aguacate
Jacarandas
BENITO JUAREZ
Malecón
Playa los Muertos
Pilitas
Amapas
Abedul
AMAPAS
Puerto Vallarta

SAVE THE DATES

Browse nearly 20 open artists' studios during **Old Town artWalk** (☎ *322/222–1982*), the last week of October until late April, 6 PM–10 PM.

The month of March is dedicated to boating activities, beginning with the **Banderas Bay Regatta** (☎ *322/297–2222* 🌐 *www.banderasbayregatta.com*), which starts in San Diego and ends here. The **International Puerto Vallarta Sailfish and Marlin Tournament** (☎ *322/225–5467* 🌐 *www.fishvallarta.com*) in November draws dedicated fishermen from all over the world.

Beginning in late November or early December, the public is invited to see movies of many genres, at reasonable prices, during the five-day **Vallarta Film Festival** (☎ *322/297–1947 or 322/297–1605* 🌐 *www.vallartafilmfestival.com*). Films and seminars are held at the **Cinemark Plaza Caracol** (✉ *Av. Francisco M. Ascencio 2216, Zona Hotelera* ☎ 322/224–8927). Film-industry types come to hobnob and honor each other with awards for best director, picture, cinematographer, and actor.

Mid-November sees the 10-day **Festival Gourmet International** (🌐 *www.festivalgourmet.com*). International chefs work with host restaurants to create custom menus; there are cooking classes and tequila and wine tastings.

Purépecha cultures and the Spanish conquest. ✉ *Western tip of Isla Río Cuale, Centro* ☎ *No phone* 💵 *By donation* ⏲ *Tues.–Sat. 10–7.*

3 Nautical artifacts from around Mexico—photos, old documents, scale models of ships—can be seen at the **Museo Histórico Naval** *(Nautical History Museum).* ✉ *Calle Saragoza 4, Centro, across from the main plaza* ☎ *322/223–5357* 💵 *Free* ⏲ *Tues.–Sun. 10–7.*

1 The late Manuel Lepe's 1981 mural depicting Puerto Vallarta as a fanciful seaside fishing and farming village is painted above the stairs on the second floor of the **Palacio Municipal** (✉ *Av. Juárez, on Plaza de Armas, Centro* ☎ *322/222–4565*), PV's city hall. Lepe is known for his blissful, primitive-style scenes of the city, filled with smiling angels. This one is rather tired, and the naïf work has been surpassed by his devotees. Still, Lepe is considered the father of PV naïf, and the mural is worth a quick look. The tourism office is on the first floor. The Palácio is open weekdays 9–5.

BEACHES

DOWNTOWN PUERTO VALLARTA

★ **Playa los Muertos** is PV's original happenin' downtown beach. Facing Vallarta's South Side (south of the Río Cuale), this flat beach runs about 1½ km (1 mi) south to a rocky point called El Púlpito. Joggers cruise the concrete boardwalk early morning and after sunset; vendors stalk the beach nonstop, hawking kites, jewelry, and serapes as well as hair braiding and alfresco massage. Their parade can range from entertaining (good bargainers can get excellent deals) to downright maddening. Restaurant-bars run the length of the beach; the bright blue umbrellas near the south end of the beach belong to the Blue Chairs resort, the hub of PV's effervescent gay scene.

The surf ranges from mild to choppy with an undertow; the small waves crunching the shore usually discourage mindless paddling. Strapping young men occasionally occupy the lifeguard tower, and local people fish from the small pier at the foot of Calle Francisca Rodríguez or cast nets from waist-deep water near the south end of the beach. Jet Skis zip around, but stay out beyond the small breakers and are not too distracting to bathers and sunbathers. Except during the slow summer months, guys on the beach are usually on hand to offer banana-boat and parasailing rides. ■ TIP→**The steps (more than 100) at Calle Púlpito lead to a lookout with a great view of the beach and the bay.**

PLAYA LOS MUERTOS

There are several versions of how Playa los Muertos got its name. One says that around the time it was founded, Indians attacked a mule train laden with silver and gold from the mountain towns, leaving the bodies of the muleteers on the beach. A version crediting pirates with the same deed seems more plausible. In 1935, anthropologist Dr. Isabel Kelly postulated that the place was an Indian cemetery.

Playa Olas Altas is a few blocks of sand between Daiquiri Dick's restaurant and the Río Cuale. It attracts fewer families than Los Muertos, but is otherwise an extension of that beach. Facing Olas Altas Beach are open-air stands selling beach accessories, small grocery stores, Lázaro Cárdenas Plaza, and easy access to beach-facing bars and restaurants. The waves at the north end are sometimes good for Boogie boarding.

NAYARIT

The beach at **Bucerías,** 8 km (5 mi) north of Nuevo Vallarta, is endless: you could easily walk along its medium-coarse beige sands all the way south to Nuevo Vallarta. The surf is gentle enough for swimming, but also has body-surfable waves, and beginning surfers occasionally arrive with their long boards. The town attracts a loyal flock of snowbirds, and with them, good restaurants and hotels.

Just north of Bucerías and La Cruz de Huanacaxtle is **Playa la Manzanilla,** a crescent of soft, gold sand where kids play in the shallow water while their parents sip cold drinks at one of several seafood shacks. It's somewhat protected by the Piedra Blanca headland to the north.

A few miles north of Piedra Blanca headland, **Playa Destiladeras** is 1½-km (1-mi) long, with white sand and good waves for bodysurfers and Boogie boarders. There's nothing much here except for a couple of seaside *enramadas* (thatch-roof shelters) serving fillets of fish and ceviche. **Punta el Burro,** at the north end of the beach, is a popular surf spot often accessed by boat from Punta de Mita.

Just a few minutes past the entrance to the Four Seasons, the popular beach at **Playa El Anclote,** in Punta de Mita (40 km [25 mi] north of PV) has a string of restaurants of increasing sophistication. This is a primo spot for viewing a sunset. Artificially calmed by several rock jetties and shallow for quite a ways out, it's also a good spot for children and average-to-not-strong swimmers to paddle and play, but there's a long slow wave for surfing, too. **TIP→Sea-life-viewing expeditions set out from El Anclote and Corral de Risco as well as from points up and down Banderas Bay.**

★ Divers favor the fairly clear waters and abundance of fish and coral on the bay side of the **Islas Marietas** about a half-hour offshore from El Anclote. In winter, especially January through March, these same islands are also a good place to spot orcas and humpback whales.

★ The increasingly popular town and beach of **Sayulita** is about 45 minutes north of PV on Carretera 200, just about 19 km (12 mi) north of Bucerías. Some say it's like PV was 40 years ago, apart from the sounds of construction ringing through the narrow streets. Despite the growth, the small-town vibe is still generous, laid-back, and retains its surfer-friendly vibe. Fringed in lanky palms, Sayulita's heavenly beach curves along its small bay. A decent shore break here is good for beginning or novice surfers; the left point break is a bit more challenging. Skiffs on the beach have good rates for surfing or fishing safaris in area waters.

Ten minutes north of Sayulita, **San Francisco** is known to most people by its nickname: San Pancho. Just beginning to boom, it stretches between headlands to the north and south, and is accessed at the end of the town's main road: Avenida Tercer Mundo. You'll see men fishing from shore with nets as you walk the 1½-km-long (1-mi-long) beach of coarse beige sand. There's an undertow sometimes, but otherwise nothing to discourage strong swimmers. Popular with a hip crowd of European artists and intellectuals, San Pancho has just a few hotels but a growing number of good restaurants.

SOUTH OF PUERTO VALLARTA

★ **Playa Conchas Chinas** is a series of rocky coves with crystalline water. Millions of tiny white shells, broken and polished by the waves, form the sand; rocks that resemble petrified cow pies jut into the sea, separating one patch of beach from the next. These individual coves are perfect for reclusive sunbathing and, when the surf is mild, for snorkeling around the rocks; bring your own equipment. It's accessible from Calle Santa Barbara, the continuation of the cobblestone coast road originating at the south end of Los Muertos Beach, and also from Carretera 200 near El Set restaurant. Swimming is best at the cove just north of La Playita de Lindo Mar, below the Hotel Conchas Chinas (where the beach ends), as there are fewer rocks in the water. You can walk—on the sand, over the rocks, or on paths—from Playa los Muertos all the way to Conchas Chinas. Except for the above-mentioned restaurant at the end of the sand, the beach does not have services.

Playa Mismaloya is the cove where *The Night of the Iguana* was made. Unfortunately, the big, tan Hotel La Jolla de Mismaloya looms large over the once-pristine bay, and Hurricane Kenna stole much of Mismaloya's white sand. A couple of full-service seafood restaurants crouch above what's left of the beach on the south side of a wooden bridge over the mouth of the Río Mismaloya. The place retains a certain *cachet* and a pretty view of the famous cove. The tiny village of Mismaloya is on the east side of Carretera 200, about 13 km (8 mi) south of PV.

Boca de Tomatlán is the name of both a small village and a rocky cove that lie at the mouth of the Río Horcones, about 5 km (3 mi) south of Mismaloya and 17 km (10½ mi) south of PV. Water taxis leave from Boca to the southern beaches; you can arrange snorkeling trips to Los Arcos. Five seaside cafés cluster at the water's edge.

TURTLE TALK

In San Pancho, **Grupo Ecológico de la Costa Verde** (*Green Coast Ecological Group* ✉ *Av. Latino América 102, San Pancho* ☎ *311/258–4100* 🌐 *www.project-tortuga.org*) works to save the olive ridley, leatherback, and eastern Pacific green turtles. Encouraged to dedicate two or more months to projects, volunteers patrol beaches, collect eggs, maintain the nursery, tabulate data, and educate the public. Slide shows to raise awareness and funds (buy a T-shirt to support the cause) are held each Thursday at 7 PM at La Casa de Gallo Restaurant.

There's lots to do besides sunbathe at **Playa las Animas,** a largish beach 15 minutes south of Boca de Tomatlán by boat, so it tends to fill up with families on weekends and holidays. The usual seafood eateries line the sand, and you can also rent Jet Skis, ride a banana boat, or soar up into the sky behind a speedboat while dangling from a colorful parachute.

Between the sandy stretches of Las Animas and Majahuitas, and about 20 minutes by boat from Boca de Tomatlán, rocky **Quimixto** has calm, clear waters that attract boatloads of snorkelers. There's just a narrow beach here, with a few seafood eateries. Day-trippers routinely rent horses ($15 round-trip; ask at the restaurants) for the 25-minute ride—or only slightly longer walk—to a large, clear pool under a waterfall. You can bathe at the fall's base, and then have a cool drink at the casual restaurant. There's a fun, fast wave at the reef here, popular with surfers, but because of its inaccessibility, rarely crowded.

Majahuitas—between the beaches of Quimixto and Yelapa and about 35 minutes by boat from Boca de Tomatlán—is the playground of people on day tours and guests of the exclusive Majahuitas Resort. The beach has no services for the average José; the lounge chairs and bathrooms are for hotel guests only. Palm trees shade the white beach of broken, sea-buffed shells. The blue-green water is clear, but tends to break right on shore.

The secluded village and ½-km-long (¼-mi-long) beach of **Yelapa** is about an hour southeast of downtown Puerto Vallarta or half an hour from Boca de Tomatlán. Several seafood *enramadas* (thatch-roof huts) edge its fine, clean, grainy sand. During high season, parasailers float high above it all. From here you can hike 20 minutes into the jungle to see the small Cascada Cola del Caballo (Horse's Tail Waterfall), with a pool at its base for swimming. (The falls are often dry near the end of the dry season, especially April–early June.) A more ambitious expedition of several hours brings you to less-visited, very beautiful Cascada del Catedral (Cathedral Falls).

But, for the most part, Yelapa is *tranquilisimo:* a place to just kick back in a chair on the beach and sip something cold. Seemingly right when you really need them, Cheggy or Agustina, the pie ladies, will show up with their fantastic homemade pies. Phones and electricity arrived in Yelapa around the turn of the 21st century. **TIP→ But bring all the money you'll need, as there is nothing as formal as a bank.**

WORD OF MOUTH

"Yelapa is gorgeous. It's in a cove, protected from wind and waves...and with a small village all around the cove and climbing part way up the mountains. We passed Las Animas, Quimixto, Las Caletas, and Mahajuitas beaches on the way—Yelapa was the prettiest."

-balasteve

COSTALEGRE

The nicest beaches are the private domain of high-end hotels. However, there are some delightful, pristine, and mostly isolated beaches along the Costalegre, most with few services aside from the ubiquitous seafood shacks serving fish fillets and fresh ceviche.

A sylvan beach with no services, **Playa Chalacatepec** is about 82 km (50 mi) south of El Tuito and 115 km (70 mi) south of Puerto Vallarta. The road to the beach is rutted and negotiable only by high-clearance vehicles. The reward for a bone-jarring drive is a beautiful rocky point, Punta Chalacatepec, with a sweep of protected white-sand beach to the north perfect for swimming, bodysurfing, and hunting for shells. The open-ocean beach south of the point, where waves crash more dramatically, discourages swimming. To get here, turn right into the town of José María Morelos (at Km 88). Just after 8 km (5 mi), leave the main road (which bears right) and head to the beach over a smaller track. From there it's less than 1½ km (1 mi) to the beach.

★ Named for the bay on which it is lies, **Playa Tenacatita** is a lovely beach of soft sand about 30 km (18 mi) north of San Patricio Melaque and 176 km (109 mi) south of Puerto Vallarta. Dozens of identical seafood shacks line the shore; birds cruise the miles-long beach, searching for their own fish. Waves crash against clumps of jagged rocks at the north end of the beach, which curves gracefully around to a headland. The water is sparkling blue. There's camping for RVs and tents at Punta Hermanos, where the water is calm, and local men offer fishing excursions. Of the string of restaurants on the beach, La Fiesta Mexicana is especially recommended.

★ On the north end of Playa Tenacatita, **Playa Mora** has a coral reef close to the beach, making it an excellent place to snorkel.

Two-kilometer-long (1-mi-long) **Playa la Manzanilla** is a little more than a kilometer (½ mi) in from the highway, on the southern edge of Bahía de Tenacatita, 193 km (120 mi) south of Puerto Vallarta (at Km 14). Informal hotels and restaurants are interspersed with small businesses and modest houses along the main street of the town. Rocks dot the gray-gold sands and edge both ends of the wide beach. The bay is calm. At the beach road's north end, gigantic, rubbery-looking crocodiles lie heaped together just out of harm's way in a mangrove swamp. The fishing here is excellent; boat owners on the beach can take you fishing for snapper, sea bass, and others for $20–$25 an hour.

WHERE TO EAT

PV's biggest concentration of excellent restaurants is the south side (aka Colonia Emiliano Zapata, or la Zona Romántica). Once called Restaurant Row, Calle Basilio Badillo is now home to at least as many fine shops as restaurants, but on the surrounding streets new eating places are continuously cropping up.

Downtown Vallarta has its fair share of choice eateries, too. All in all, gourmets will be happiest in Old Vallarta, where a delectable appetizer, sunset cocktail, or espresso and dessert is never more than a $3 cab ride away.

Bucerías has a growing cadre of good restaurants in the center of town. Marina Vallarta has a handful of worthwhile eateries, mainly at the high-end resorts and surrounding the marina. In addition to the clutch of beach-facing palapas at El Anclote, Punta de Mita's restaurant scene is diversifying as the area is developed for high rollers.

PUERTO VALLARTA

$$$$ MEXICAN ★

✕**Las Carmelitas.** Hawks soar on updrafts above lumpy, jungle-draped hills. The town and the big blue bay are spread out below in a breathtaking, 200-degree tableau. Under the palapa roof of this small, open restaurant romantic ballads play as waiters start you off with guacamole, fresh and cooked salsas, chopped cactus pad salad, and tostadas. Seared meats—served with grilled green onions and tortillas made on the spot—are the specialty, but you can also order seafood stew or soups. The $10 per person fee you pay to enter (apparently to discourage those wanting to take advantage of the view, but not the food) will be deducted from your tab. Or avoid the hassle altogether—the fee is waved for those who have made reservations. ✉*Camino a la Aguacatera, Km 1.2, Fracc. Lomas de Terra Noble* ☎*322/303–2104* ▭*No credit cards.*

$$$$ ECLECTIC/SEAFOOD

✕**La Palapa.** This large, welcoming, thatch-roof place is open to the breezes of Playa los Muertos and filled with wicker chandeliers, art-glass fixtures, and lazily rotating ceiling fans. The menu meanders among international dishes in modern presentation: roasted stuffed chicken breast, pork loin, or seared yellowfin tuna drizzled in cacao sauce. The seafood enchilada plate is divine. For a pricey but romantic evening, enjoy one of several set menus ($265 for two; reserve with $100 deposit in advance) at a table right on the sand. There's a good breakfast daily after 8 AM, and a guitarist or Latin jazz combo nightly between 8 and 11. ✉*Calle Púlpito 103, Playa los Muertos, Col. E.*

Zapata ☎*322/222–5225* ⊕*www.lapalapapv.com* ▭*MC, V.*

$$$ MEXICAN ★ ✕ **El Arrayán.** The oilcloth table covers, enameled tin plates, exposed rafters, and red roof tiles of this patio-restaurant conjure up nostalgia for the quaint Mexican home of less frenetic times. Carmen Porras, the hip, cute co-owner, masquerades as your waitress, dispensing info about the origins of *chiles en nogada* (first prepared for Emperor Agustín Iturbide—who knew?) and the other Mexican comfort foods on her menu. Here you'll find the things Grandmamá still loves to cook, with a few subtle variations. Try the chicken breasts stuffed with zucchini blossoms or chipotle-chile shrimp with a sauce of citrus juices. Finish with caramel flan, carob-chip cake, or a light, refreshing pumpkin-caramel ice. ✉*Calle Allende 344, at Calle Miramar, Centro* ☎*322/222–7195* ▭*MC, V* ⊗ *Closed Tues. and Aug. No lunch.*

WORD OF MOUTH

"My best suggestion is to take a bus or taxi from the Marina district down to the south-side ("Zona Romantica") one evening (maybe 15-20 mins. away). Get off at the corner of Vallarta and B. Badillo by the Posada de Roger hotel.

From there you can easily walk to: Joe Jacks Fish Shack, Cafe de Olla, Fajita Republic, Roberto's... even Il Torrito sports bar. I have eaten at all of these places solo very comfortably many times. All are reasonably priced."

–suze

$$$ SPANISH ★ ✕ **Barcelona Tapas Bar.** One of the few places in town with both great food and an excellent bay view, Barcelona has traditional Spanish tapas like *patatas alioli* (garlic potatoes), spicy garlic shrimp, and grilled mushrooms, all in both smaller or larger sizes. To start you off, attentive waiters bring a free appetizer, served with delicious homemade bread. There's excellent traditional paella, and a six-course tasting menu allows you to try soup, salad, and dessert as well as tapas—choose your own or follow the chef's suggestions. You can sit in a small, relatively quiet room or the often crowded open-air patio. You'll have to pay for the patio view by walking up a few dozen stairs. Cooking classes ($24) are offered on Wednesday in high season (November through April) and include lunch. ✉*Matamoros at 31 de Octubre, Centro* ☎*322/222–0510* ✍*Reservations essential* ▭*AE.*

$$$ ECLECTIC ★ ✕ **Le Bistro.** Start off with a soup of Mexican or Cuban origin and then on to one of the international main dishes, like the cream of wild spinach soup or mushroom-sherry soup, crepes, duck with blackberry sauce, herbed Cornish hen, or sea scallops with jicama coleslaw. The restaurant overlooks the Cuale River, and its eclectic decor draped in ferns and tropical plants is a knockout, with carved-stone columns, zebra chairs, wicker settees, and other sophisticated touches. During breakfast, the tinkling of the piano keys is a lovely counterpoint to the melody the river. ✉*Isla Río Cuale 16–A, Centro* ☎*322/222–0283* ⊕*www.lebistro.com.mx* ▭*AE, MC, V* ⊗*Closed Sun. and mid-Aug.–mid-Oct.*

$$$ ECLECTIC ✕ **Boca Bento.** This restaurant in the heart of the Romantic Zone represents a fusion of Latin American, Mediterranean, and Caribbean elements. The feeling is simultaneously Eastern and modern, with con-

temporary music and artwork. The small-plates concept has been abandoned in favor of a more traditional menu of appetizers, soups, salads, and entrées with a side of starch and vegetables: try the rib-eye steak, pork ribs with a honey-chile glaze, or the cross-cultural mu shu carnitas with hoisin sauce. It's open daily for breakfast and dinner but closed between 2 and 6 PM. ✉ *Calle Basilio Badillo 180, Col. E. Zapata* ☎ *322/222–9108* 🌐 *www.bocabento.com* ▭ *MC, V* ⏲ Closed June–Oct. *No proper lunch.*

WHAT TO WEAR

We suggest resort casual or at least grunge chic, but the truth is that visitors to PV's best restaurants wear pretty much what they please. As usual, the Mexicans are the best dressed, but even they tone it down in PV, losing jacket and tie in favor of a nice button-down and slacks. Even the most elegant restaurants simply request that men wear shirts with sleeves. But if you enjoy dressing up, don't despair: looking good never goes out of style. The maitre d' *will* take notice.

$$$ STEAK ✕ **Brasil Steakhouse.** One of Vallarta's most popular venues for grilled meat is this all-you-can-eat place, where you're treated to never-ending portions of beef ribs, turkey, several cuts of steak, pork tenderloin, and grilled chicken. Waiters first bring chicken wings and direct you to the salad bar before delivering skewers of meat of your choosing. Lunch begins after 2 PM. ✉ *Venustiano Carranza 210, Col. E. Zapata* ☎ *322/222–2909* ✉ *Calle Mastil s/n, Condominio Marina del Sol, Local 1, Marina Vallarta* ☎ *322/221–5026* ▭ *AE, MC, V.*

$$$ ECLECTIC ★ ✕ **Café des Artistes.** Several sleek dining spaces make up Café des Artistes, the liveliest of which is the courtyard garden with modern sculpture. The main restaurant achieves a modern Casablanca feel with glass raindrops and tranquil music. Thierry Blouet's Cocina de Autor (closed Sunday and September) is a limited-seating restaurant pairing four- to six-course tasting menus with appropriate wines. Decor is restrained, with a waterfall garden behind plate glass taking center stage. Many diners end the night at the clubby cigar bar, but it's open to anyone, as is Constantini Wine Bar, which offers some 50 vintages by the glass as well as distilled spirits, appetizers, and live music most every night of the week. ✉ *Av. Guadalupe Sánchez 740, Centro* ☎ *322/222–3229* ▭ *AE, MC, V* ⏲ *No lunch.*

$$$ ECLECTIC ★ ✕ **Daiquiri Dick's.** Locals come for the reasonably priced breakfasts (the homemade orange-almond granola is great); visitors come (often more than once during a vacation) for the good service and consistent Mexican and world cuisine. The lunch/dinner menu has fabulous appetizers, including superb lobster tacos with a drizzle of béchamel sauce and perfect, tangy jumbo-shrimp wontons. On the menu since the restaurant opened almost 30 years ago is Pescado Vallarta, or grilled fish on a stick. Start with a signature daiquiri; move to the extensive wine list. The tortilla soup is popular, too. The open patio dining room frames a view of Playa los Muertos, creating a beautifully simplistic scene. ✉ *Av. Olas Altas 314, Col. E. Zapata* ☎ *322/222–0566* ▭ *MC, V* ⏲ *Closed Sept. and Tues. May–Aug.*

$$$ CONTINENTAL ★ **Kaiser Maximilian.** Viennese and Continental entrées dominate the menu, which is modified each year when the restaurant participates in PV's culinary festival. One favorite is herb-crusted rack of lamb served with horseradish and pureed vegetables au gratin; another is venison medallions with chestnut sauce served with braised white cabbage. The adjacent café (open 8 AM–midnight) has sandwiches, excellent desserts, and 20 specialty coffees—also available at the main restaurant. To avoid the stream of street peddlers, eat in the European-style dining room, where black-and-white-clad waiters look right at home amid dark-wood framed mirrors, brightly polished brass, and lace curtains. *Av. Olas Altas 380, Col. E. Zapata* *322/223–0760* *AE, MC, V* *Closed Sun. No lunch.*

$$$ ITALIAN ★ **Porto Bello.** Yachties, locals, and other return visitors attest that everything on the menu is good. And if you're not satisfied, the kitchen will give you something else without quibbling. Undoubtedly that's what makes Marina Vallarta's veteran restaurant its most popular. The dining room is diminutive and air-conditioned; the patio over the marina is more elegant, with a white chiffon ceiling drape and ceiling fans. Most folks come in the evening. *Marina del Sol, Local 7, Marina Vallarta* *322/221–0003* *www.portobellovallarta.com* *MC, V.*

$$$ CONTINENTAL Fodor'sChoice ★ **Trio.** Conviviality, hominess, and dedication on the parts of chef-owners Bernhard Güth and Ulf Henriksson have made Trio one of Puerto Vallarta's best restaurants. Fans, many of them members of PV's artsy crowd, marvel at the kitchen's ability to deliver perfect meal after perfect meal. Popular demand guarantees rack of lamb with fresh mint, and, for dessert, the warm chocolate cake. The kitchen often stays open until nearly midnight, and during high season they open the back patio, second floor and rooftop terrace. Waiters are professional yet unpretentious; either the sommelier or the maitre d' can help you with the wine. *Calle Guerrero 264, Centro* *322/222–2196* *www.triopv.com* *AE, MC, V* *No lunch.*

$$$ CONTINENTAL ★ **Vitea.** When chefs Bernhard Güth and Ulf Henriksson of Trio needed a challenge, they cooked up this delightful seaside bistro. So what if your legs bump your partner's at the small tables? This will only make it easier to steal bites off her plate. Tables face the boardwalk outside, and the open, casual venue is as fresh as the food. Appetizers include the smoked salmon roll with crème fraîche and the spicy shrimp tempura; crab manicotti and other entrées are light and delicious. *Libertad 2, near south end of the Malecón, Centro* *322/222–8703* *AE, MC, V* *Closed 1 wk in late Sept.*

$$$ ECLECTIC **Ztai.** Lounge music floats from the cool, dark, modern restaurant to the appealingly spare outdoor garden shaded by bamboo and fig trees. The food is quite good, and portions are large. Try the fresh and oh-so-lightly-fried calamari, the fruity shrimp ceviche or the tender filet mignon. In general, Asian flavors pepper the seafood recipes (pun intended), while the meat dishes lean towards Continental cuisine such as herb-crusted lamb. After dinner you can recline, Roman style, on one of the beds, sofas, or barstools of Ztai's upstairs lounge. *Calle Morelos 737, Centro* *322/222–0306* *AE, MC, V* *No lunch.*

$$ ASIAN ★ **Archie's Wok.** This is the best place on the bay for multiethnic Asian cuisine, including Filipino, Thai, and Chinese. Favorite dishes at the extremely popular South Side restaurant include Thai garlic shrimp, *pancit* (Filipino stir-fry with pasta), and Singapore-style (lightly battered) fish, plus lots of vegetarian dishes. Thursday through Saturday after 7:30 PM the soothing harp music of well-known local musician D'Rachel accompanies your meal. It opens for lunch only after 2 PM. ✉ *Calle Francisca Rodríguez 130, Col. E. Zapata* ☎ *322/222–0411* ▭ *MC, V* ⏲ *Closed Sun.*

$$ MEXICAN ★ **El Brujo.** The street corner on which the small restaurant is tucked means noise on either side. Service is reasonably attentive, though grudging at times. Still, this is an expat (and gay) favorite, and no wonder: the food is seriously good and portions are generous. The *molcajete*—a sizzling black pot of tender flank steak, grilled green onion, and soft white cheese in a delicious homemade sauce of dried red peppers—is served with a big plate of guacamole, refried beans, and made-at-the-moment corn or flour tortillas. ✉ *Venustiano Carranza 510, at Naranjo, Col. Remance* ☎ *322/223–2036* ✍ *Reservations not accepted* ▭ *No credit cards* ⏲ *Closed Mon., 2 wks in late Sept., and early Oct.*

POWER BREAKFAST

The **Pancake House** (✉ *Calle Basilio Badillo 289, Col. E. Zapata*) is the favorite for hotcakes. Ritzier **La Palapa** and **Daiquiri Dick's** (⇨ *above*) are super popular for breakfast at the beach. **Langostino's** (✉ *Los Muertos Beach at Calle Manuel M. Dieguez, Col. E. Zapata*) offers lively canned rock with breakfast. **Playita de Lindo Mar** (✉ *Playa Conchas Chinas*) has an enviable ocean-view location, an excellent brunch, and an extensive menu. In **Bucerías,** head to **Famar** (⇨ *below*) for a typical Mexican breakfast.

$$ SEAFOOD ★ **Cueto's.** Teams of engaging waiters, all family members, squeeze past the trio that croons romantic tunes throughout the day to refill beer glasses, remove empty plates, and bring more fresh tostadas and hot, crusty garlic bread. But don't fill up on nonessentials, as the recommended cream-based and mild-chile casseroles—with crab, clams, fish, shrimp, or mixed seafood—are so delicious you won't want to leave even one bite. The latest menu offering is a shrimp-fest offering a couple dozen crustaceans prepared in seven different styles. You can have a complimentary margarita with dinner or a free digestif later on. Cueto's is a few blocks behind the Unidad Deportivo complex of soccer fields and baseball diamonds. ✉ *Calle Brasilia 469, Col. 5 de Diciembre (Zona Hotelera)* ☎ *322/223–0363* ▭ *No credit cards.*

$$ SEAFOOD ★ **Mariscos 8 Tostadas.** Extremely popular with locals, this large restaurant hums with activity and an upbeat soundtrack, compliments of icons such as Bob Marley and Frank Sinatra. The freshly caught raw tuna, which is thicker than in U.S. sushi houses, but not too thick, is served in a shallow dish with soy sauce, micro-thin cucumber slices, sesame seeds, green onions, chile powder, and lime. Eat with tostadas until fit to burst. Avoid the scallop tostadas, as the shellfish is virtually raw. The ceviche, however, couldn't be better—or fresher. There's a small storefront subsidiary in the parking lot at Plaza Marina; the charming original

venue is behind Blockbuster Video in the Hotel Zone. ✉ *Calle Quilla at Calle Proa, Local 28-29, Marina Vallarta* ☎ *322/221–3124* ▭ *No credit cards* ⏲ *No dinner* ✉ *Calle Río Guayaquil 413 at Calle Ecuador, Col. Versalles (Zona Hotelera)* ✣ *Behind Blockbuster Video store* ☎ *322/222-7691* ▭ *No credit cards* ⏲ *Closed Sun. Closed 2 wks in Sept. No dinner.*

WORD OF MOUTH

"The Red Cabbage is one of the best in town & we have never spent over $18 a plate including salad & desert for dinner. P.S. I have dreams about their incredible carnitas."

–Stewbear

$$ ECLECTIC ✕ **El Repollo Rojo.** Better known as the Red Cabbage (its English name), this restaurant is by—but doesn't overlook—the Cuale River. It's hard to find the first time out. Though recent reviews have been wildly inconsistent, loyal fans say it's the best place in town for international comfort food. Fill up on Frida's Dinner, an aperitif of tequila followed by cream of peanut soup, white or red wine, *chile en nogada* (a stuffed green poblano chile topped with walnut sauce and pomegranate seeds), a main dish from the Yucatán or Puebla, and flan for dessert. Romantic ballads fill the small space decorated with movie posters. ✉ *Calle Rivera del Río 204-A, El Remance* ☎ *322/223–0411* ▭ *No credit cards* ⏲ *Closed Sept. and Sun. May–Oct. No lunch.*

$$ SEAFOOD ★ ✕ **Tino's.** Vine-covered trees poke through the roof of the breeze-blessed, covered outdoor eatery overlooking a placid lagoon. The Carvajal family has worked hard to make this a favorite Nuevo Vallarta restaurant, though the Punta de Mita branch is also nice, on a pretty beach, and the original Pitillal location is popular for a trip back in time to Vallarta's roots. Tino's is full even midweek, mainly with groups of friends or businesspeople leisurely discussing deals. A multitude of solicitous, efficient waiters proffer green-lipped mussels meunière, crab enchiladas, oysters, and the regional specialty, fish *sarandeado* (rubbed with herbs and cooked over a wood fire). Concha de Tino is a dish with seafood, bacon, mushrooms, and spinach prettily presented in three seashells. ✉ *2a Entrada a Nuevo Vallarta, Km 1.2, Las Jarretaderas* ☎ *322/297–0221* ▭ *MC, V* ✉ *Av. El Anclote 64, El Anclote, Punta de Mita* ☎ *329/291–6473* ✉ *Av. 333 at Calle Revolución, Pitillal* ☎ *322/225–2171 or 322/224–5584.*

$ MEXICAN ✕ **El Campanario.** This little jewel is increasingly popular with budget travelers. Egg dishes and chilaquiles are served 9–11 AM, and an inexpensive daily lunch menu is served 2–5 PM. About $5 gets you soup, a main dish, drink, homemade tortillas, and dessert. Drift in between 6 and 10 PM for tacos, *tortas* (Mexican-style sandwiches on crispy white rolls), or pozole. Fans swirl the air, doors are open to the street, and cheerful oilcloths cover wooden tables at this no-frills spot across from the cathedral. ✉ *Calle Hidalgo 339, Centro* ☎ *322/223–1509* ▭ *No credit cards* ⏲ *Closed Sun., and often between 5 and 6 PM.*

$ ECLECTIC ✕ **Fidensio's.** Let the tide lick your toes and the sand caress shoeless feet as simple yet tasty food is brought to your comfortable cloth, palapa-shaded chair right at the ocean's edge. Made when you order them, the

12

shrimp enchiladas—served with rice, a small handful of piping-hot fries, and a miniature salad—are simply delicious. Many expats come for breakfast, or before 6 PM for burgers, nachos, club or tuna sandwiches, or a fresh fish fillet. Service is relaxed and friendly; the only sound track is the sound of the waves. ✉*Pilitas 90, Los Muerto Beach, Col. E. Zapata* ☎*322/222–5457* ▭*No credit cards* ⊙*No dinner.*

$ VEGETARIAN ★ ✕**Planeta Vegetariana.** Partake of the tasty meatless carne asada and a selection of main dishes that changes daily. Choose from at least three delicious main dishes, plus beans, several types of rice, and a daily soup at this buffet-only place. Though the selection of overdressed salads is good, the greens tend to get wilted or soggy pretty quickly. A healthful fruit drink, coffee, or tea, and dessert is included in the reasonable price. Eggs are not used; items containing milk products are labeled as such. It's about a block north of the Church of Guadalupe. ✉*Iturbide 270, Centro* ☎*322/222–3073* ▭*No credit cards.*

> **TIME TRAVEL**
>
> The state of Nayarit (Nuevo Vallarta and points north) is within Mountain Standard Time zone, while Jalisco (Marina Vallarta south to Barra de Navidad) is on Central Standard Time. But because tourism in Bucerías and Nuevo Vallarta has always been linked to that of Puerto Vallarta, many businesses in these Nayarit towns run on Jalisco time. Sayulita and San Pancho businesses run on Nayarit time, generally. When making dinner reservations, ask if the place runs on *hora de Jalisco* (Jalisco time) or *hora de Nayarit.*

NUEVO VALLARTA TO SAN FRANCISCO

$$$ ECLECTIC ✕**Cafe del Mar.** Chefs Eugene of Singapore and Amandine, a Belgian-Mexican, collaborate to create beautiful food focusing on seafood and chicken; the varied and excellent appetizers and desserts are especially recommended. The dishes blend Asian, Mediterranean, and haute Mexican cuisine in simple yet successful dishes. Tiny white lights and soft music accompany individual tables down the side of a hill to a vine-drenched trellis at the bottom. There's usually a guitarist serenading during Friday dinner. ✉*Av. China 9, San Francisco* ☎*311/258–4251* ▭*MC, V* ⊙*Closed Wed. and Aug.–Sept.*

$$$ CONTINENTAL ★ ✕**Don Pedro's.** Sayulita institution Don Pedro's has pizzas baked in a wood-fire oven, prepared by European-trained chef and co-owner Nicholas Parrillo. Also on the menu are consistently reliable seafood dishes, tapenade, delicious ahi tuna, and mesquite-grilled filet mignon—served with baby vegetables and mashed potatoes accompanied by pita bread—which is just about the best around. The pretty second-floor dining room, with the better view, is open when the bottom floor fills up, usually during the high season (November–May). Call to find out about live music—sometimes salsa, sometimes flamenco—which is performed during the week at dinner. This is a good spot for breakfast, too, after 8 AM. ✉*Calle Marlin 2, at beach, Sayulita* ☎*329/291–3090* 🌐 *www.donpedros.com* ▭*MC, V* ⊙*Closed Sept.*

$$$ AMERICAN ★ ✕**Mark's Bar & Grill.** If you're dining alone, the black-granite bar with a TV tuned to sports is a good place to do it. Seemingly a world away is the charming restaurant's dining room known for its delightful

decor and excellent cuisine. Both are best appreciated on the back patio, open to the stars. Standouts include the homemade bread and pizza, salads, and macadamia-crusted fresh fish fillets with mushroom ragout. The lamb is flown in from New Zealand; scallops, oysters and mussels from Baja; and the black Angus beef, from Monterrey. Mixed, organic lettuces, chives, and basil come from the lady down the street. The restaurant is elegant yet warm and inviting, with a golden glow over everything and roving musicians adding to the ambience. Order wine by the glass from the extensive list. ✉*Av. Lázaro Cárdenas 56, Bucerías* ☎*329/298–0303* ▭*MC, V* ⊗*No lunch.*

STREET-FOOD SMARTS

Many think it's madness to eat "street food," but when you see professionals in pinstripes thronging to roadside stands, you've got to wonder why. Stands can be just as hygienic as restaurants, as they are actually tiny exhibition kitchens. Make sure the cook doesn't handle cash, or takes your money with a gloved hand. Ask locals for recommendations, or look for a stand bustling with trade.

$$$ ECLECTIC Fodor'sChoice ★ ✕**La Ola Rica.** Oh. My. God. The food is good. *Really* good. Somehow chef and co-owner Gloria Honan (with Triny Palomera Gil) makes garlic-sautéed mushrooms (a huge portion) into a minor miracle on toast. The cream of poblano-chile soup is simply to die for: not too spicy, but wonderfully flavorful. And these are just the starters. The restaurant is popular, and reservations are encouraged. Locals come for the coconut shrimp, lemon chicken, and medium-crust pizzas. ✉*Av. Tercer Mundo s/n, San Francisco* ☎*311/258–4123* ▭*MC, V* ⊗*CNo lunch. Closed Sun. year-round; closed Mon. –Wed. June and July; completely closed Aug. –Oct.*

$$ ECLECTIC ✕**Sandrina's.** Canadian owner Sandy is as colorful as her wonderful art, which graces this local favorite. Dine on the back patio at night amid dozens of candles and tiny lights. The varied menu has plenty of salads and pasta dishes as well as Greek and Italian dishes like chicken souvlaki, Greek-style (oven-roasted) chicken, and pita bread with hummus or tzatziki. Order an espresso, delicious doctored coffee, or dessert from the bakery counter in the front, which opens at 9 in the morning. The main restaurant opens after 3 PM. ✉*Av. Lázaro Cárdenas 33, Bucerías* ☎*329/298–0273* 🌐*www.sandrinas.com* ▭*MC, V* ⊗*Closed Tues. and 2 wks in Sept.*

$–$$ MEXICAN ✕**Famar.** This unassuming restaurant gets the vote of expats and locals alike. Breakfast in the noisy front room includes chilaquiles, waffles, and omelets. It's more peaceful on the back patio where the top picks are beef fajitas and shrimp Famar: the chef's secret recipe, with shrimp, bacon, cheese, and salsa. Consistency and friendly, familial service is the name of the game. ✉*Héroes de Nacozari 105, Bucerías* ☎*329/298–0113* ▭*No credit cards* ⊗*Closed Sun.*

¢ CAFÉ ✕**Pie in the Sky.** Although the cars on the highway can be noisy, the lure of deliciously decadent mini-cheesecakes, pecan tarts, rich ice cream, and crunchy chocolate cookies exerts a strong gravitational pull. The signature dessert here is the *beso,* a deep chocolate, soft-centered brownie. Cakes, including gorgeous wedding cakes, are decorated by Zulem, a fine artist who excels with frosting as her medium. Chicken potpie, spinach empanadas, and a spinach-and-cheese pizza are also served. Sit a spell and take advantage of the free Wi-Fi, at either location. ✉*Héroes de Nacozari 202, Bucerías* ☎*329/298–0838* ✉*Lázaro Cárdenas 247, at I. Vallarta, Col. E. Zapata* ☎*322/223–8183* ▭*AE, MC, V.*

SOUTH OF PUERTO VALLARTA

$$ FUSION ★ **Maya.** Two Canadian women have teamed up to bring sophistication to San Patricio–Melaque's dining scene. East meets west in contemporary dishes such as tequila-lime prawns and corn, chorizo, and gouda cheese fritters with a smoked jalapeño aioli. Favorite entrées include Szechuan prawns and prosciutto-wrapped chicken. Their hours of operation are complex and subject to change; it's best to check their Web site or confirm by phone. There's often live music; maybe Motown, perhaps jazz or blues. ✉*Calle Alvaro Obregón 1, Villa Obregón, San Patricio–Melaque* ☎*315/102–0775 cell phone* 🌐*www.restaurantmaya.com* ▭*No credit cards* ⊙ *No lunch.*

$ MEXICAN **Cenaduría Flor Morena.** Some folks say these are the best enchiladas they've ever eaten; others call it a "local institution." But everyone pretty much agrees that this hole-in-the-wall on the main square is the best place around to get good, inexpensive Mexican favorites like pozole, tamales, and tacos. ✉*Facing main plaza below Catscan bar, San Patricio–Melaque* ☎*No phone* ▭*No credit cards* ⊙ *Closed Mon. and Tues. No lunch.*

WHERE TO STAY

PUERTO VALLARTA

$$$$ ★ **CasaMagna Marriott.** Hushed and stately in some places, lively and casual in others, CasaMagna is a classy property that nonetheless welcomes children. All of the restaurants—including a sleek Asian restaurant serving Thai, sushi, and teppanyaki and a large, pleasant sports bar—have kids' menus. The meandering grounds boast a large infinity pool as well as indigenous plant and chile gardens. Rooms have an upbeat, classy decor; each has a balcony and most have an ocean view. The hotel has smoke detectors, sprinklers, thrice-filtered water, and other beyond-the-pale safety features. Access to the amazing spa is free with the purchase of a spa service. **Pros:** Lovely new spa, new gym equipment, good Japanese restaurant. **Cons:** Unimpressive beach. ✉*Paseo de la Marina 5, Marina Vallarta,* ☎*322/226–0000, 888/236–2427 in U.S. and Canada* 🌐*www.casamagnapuertovallarta.com* *404 rooms, 29 suites* *In-room: Safe, DVD, Wi-Fi. In-hotel: 4 restaurants, room service, bars, tennis courts, pools, gym, spa, beachfront, concierge, children's programs (ages 4–12), laundry service, public Internet, parking (no fee)* ▭*AE, DC, MC, V* *EP.*

$$$$ Fodor's Choice ★ **Dreams.** Dramatic views of the gorgeous, rock-edged beach are just one reason that this all-inclusive is special. Theme nights go all out, with salsa dancing classes, reggae and circus nights, and for sports night, ball games with hot dogs and beer, and movies on the beach.

Instead of buffet restaurants there are five à la carte eateries. All of the charming suites have fab views but only the newer ones have balconies, some with a hot tub. There are tons of activities for both kids and adults. **Pros:** No wristbands, gorgeous private beach, easy drive or bus to downtown PV. **Cons:** Restaurant doesn't take reservations, which means waiting to eat during busiest seasons. ✉ *Carretera a Barra de Navidad (Carretera 200), at Playa las Estacas, Zona Hotelera Sur,* ☎ *322/226–5000, 866/237–3267 in U.S. and Canada* 🌐 *www.dreamsresorts.com* *337 suites* *In-room: Safe, DVD, refrigerator (some). In-hotel: 5 restaurants, room service, bars, tennis courts, pools, gym, spa, beachfront, water sports, bicycles, concierge, children's programs (ages 4–17), laundry service, parking (no fee), no-smoking rooms* *AE, D, DC, MC, V* *AI.*

$$$$ ★ **Hacienda San Angel.** Each room is unique and elegant at this boutique hotel in the hills six blocks above the malecón. Public spaces also exude wealth and privilege, with 16th- through 19th-century antiques throughout, fountains with Talavera tile–lined basins, and mammoth tables in open dining areas. The Celestial Room has a wondrous view of Bahía de Banderas and the cathedral's tower from its open-air, thatched-roof living room. **Pros:** The only elegant lodgings in downtown PV, excellent bay views, reasonably priced airport transfers. **Cons:** Scary drive up congested cobblestone streets, short but steep walk from the malecón, a bit intimate for some folks. ✉ *Calle Miramar 336, at Iturbide, Col. El Cerro,* ☎ *322/222–2692, 877/815–6594 toll-free in U.S., 866/818–8342 in Canada* 🌐 *www.mexicoboutiquehotels.com* *16 rooms* *In-room: Safe, DVD, VCR. In-hotel: Restaurant, pools, concierge, laundry service, public Internet, public Wi-Fi, airport shuttle, no kids under 16, no elevator* *AE, MC, V* *CP.*

$$$$ **Velas Vallarta Suite Resort & Convention Center.** Silky sheets, cozy down comforters, and large flat-screen TVs are a few of the creature comforts that set Velas apart from the rest. Each large living area has two comfortably wide built-in couches in colorful prints and a round dining table. Huichol cross-stitch and modern Mexican art decorate the walls. Studios and one-, two-, and three-bedroom suites have the same amenities except that the former don't have balconies or beach views. Tall palms, pink bougainvillea, and wild ginger with brilliant red plumes surround the three enormous pools. **Pros:** Large suites, 24-hour room service, pillow menu. **Cons:** Small spa. ✉ *Av. Costera s/n, Marina Vallarta,* ☎ *322/221–0091 or 866/847–4609* 🌐 *www.velasvallarta.com* *339 suites* *In-room: Safe, kitchen, dial-up. In-hotel: 2 restaurants, room service, bars, tennis courts, pools, gym, spa, beachfront, concierge, children's programs (ages 6–12), laundry service, public Wi-Fi, public Internet, parking (no fee), no-smoking rooms* *AE, MC, V* *AI.*

$$$$ **Westin Resort & Spa.** Hot pink! Electric yellow! Color aside, the Westin's buildings evoke ancient temples and are about as mammoth. There's not a bad sightline anywhere—whether you gaze out to the leafy courtyard or down an orange-tiled, brightly painted corridor lined with Mexican art. The spacious, balconied rooms have concrete-and-stone floors and top-of-the-line mattresses and duvets. Guest

quarters above the sixth floor have ocean views; those below face the 600 palm trees surrounding the four beautiful pools. **TIP→ The Westin's Nikki Beach Club is still a classy restaurant/bar/lounge on the beach, although not as in vogue as it was for the first few years.** **Pros:** Fabulous beds and pillows, impressive architecture and landscaping, attentive but not overzealous staff. **Cons:** Small beach, fee for gym, time-share touts make some guests miserable. ✉*Paseo de la Marina Sur 205, Marina Vallarta,* ☎*322/226–1100, 800/228–3000 in U.S. and Canada* 🌐*www.westinvallarta.com* *266 rooms, 14 suites* *In-room: Safe, Wi-Fi. In-hotel: 2 restaurants, room service, bars, tennis courts, pools, gym, spa, beachfront, concierge, children's programs (ages infant–12), laundry service, executive floor, public Wi-Fi, public Internet, parking (no fee), no-smoking rooms, some pets allowed* *AE, DC, MC, V* *BP.*

WORD OF MOUTH

"We loved [Quinta María Cortez] so much that the first night we arrived we didn't even venture into town... Each morning we woke to the sound of the waves crashing against the rocks and the smell of breakfast... The staff was very friendly, we really could not have asked for a better stay." –travel3773

$$–$$$ Fodor'sChoice ★ **Quinta María Cortez.** This B&B has soul. Its seven levels are stacked up a steep hill at Playa Conchas Chinas, about a 20-minute walk along the sand to the Romantic Zone (or a short hop in a bus or taxi). Most rooms have balconies and kitchenettes; all are furnished with antiques and local art. Other draws are the efficient and welcoming staff, the fortifying breakfast (cooked to order) served on a palapa-covered patio, the nearly private beach below, and the views from the rooftop sundeck. It's popular and diminutive, so make reservations early. Minimum stays are five nights in winter, and three nights in summer. **Pros:** Intimate digs, close to PV, above pretty Conchas Chinas beach. **Cons:** Small property, frequently booked solid. ✉*Calle Sagitario 126, Playa Conchas Chinas,* ☎*322/221–5317, 888/640–8100 reservations* 🌐*www.quinta-maria.com* *7 rooms, 3 villas* *In-room: No a/c (some), safe, kitchen (some), refrigerator, no TV. In-hotel: Pool, beachfront, public Internet, no kids under 17, no elevator* *AE, MC, V* *BP.*

$$ **El Pescador.** Fall asleep to the sound of the waves at this modest yet cheerful hotel that's a favorite among Mexican travelers. Balconies are narrow but provide a view of the pool area and beach. The latter has sand but also fist-size rocks in the tidal zone; the curvy, medium-size pool is a nice alternative. Bright white and inexpensive, El Pescador is about five blocks north of the malecón (and a sister property, Hotel Rosita). **Pros:** Near malecón and downtown action, small parking garage, live music during weekend brunch. **Cons:** Summer storms deliver rocks on the narrow, brown sand beach; no ceiling fans. ✉*Calle Paraguay 1117 at Uruguay, Col. 5 de Diciembre,* ☎*322/222–1884, 888/242–9587 in Canada, 877/813–6712 in U.S.* 🌐*www.hotelpescador.com* *103 rooms* *In-hotel: Restaurant, bar, pool, laundry service, public Wi-Fi, public Internet* *MC, V* *EP.*

$$ **Playa Los Arcos.** This hotel is attractive because of its location: right on the beach and in the midst of Zona Romántica's restaurants, bars, and shops. Though the price is right, both service and quality have slipped in recent years. Still, yellow trumpet vines and lacy palms draped in tiny white lights enliven the pool and the bar-restaurant, which has music nightly and a Mexican fiesta on Saturday evening. If you're willing to cross the street, you can get a better deal at Los Arcos Suites, which has larger yet cheaper rooms with kitchenettes; some have balconies, too. **Pros:** Great Zona Romántica location, nightly entertainment with theme-cuisine buffet. **Cons:** Small bathrooms, tired furnishings, tour group noise in high season. ✉ *Av. Olas Altas 380, Col. E. Zapata,* ☎ *322/222–1583, 800/648–2403 in U.S., 888/729–9590 in Canada, 01800/327–7700 toll-free in Mexico* 🌐 *www.playalosarcos.com* *158 rooms, 13 suites* *In-room: Safe (some), kitchen (some). In-hotel: Restaurant, bar, pool, beachfront, parking (no fee), no-smoking rooms* ▭ *MC, V* *AI, EP.*

$$ **Tropicana.** This is a well-groomed, bright-white hotel at the south end of Playa los Muertos for a reasonable price. The one negative is the hard beds. Save $15 a night by booking a standard rather than superior room; except for the size of the TV, they're almost the same. Each has several different areas for sitting or playing cards. Suites have no separate living area, but are larger than other rooms and each has a four-burner stove, blenders, and fridge. **Pros:** Great beach views and access, great Zona Romántica location, nice pool and landscaping. **Cons:** No bathtubs, no Internet access, wristbands required for all guests. ✉ *Calle Amapas 214, Col. E. Zapata,* ☎ *322/226–9696* 🌐 *www.htropicanapv.com* *148 rooms, 12 suites* *In-room: No TV (some), safe (some). In-hotel: Restaurant, bar, pool, beachfront, parking (no fee)* ▭ *MC, V* *EP.*

$ **Los Cuatro Vientos.** Gloria Whiting has owned this Old Vallarta original, which opened in 1955, for about 25 years, and some guests have been coming since then, which explains why most of the guests and staff seem like old friends. The restaurant, Chez Elena, the unadorned rooftop bar, and a few of the rooms have gorgeous views of the bay and of the city's red rooftops. Rooms are plain and without amenities, but homey, with traditional brick ceilings. Come to rub shoulders with Europeans and others who appreciate a bargain and a bit of history. **Pros:** Downtown location overlooking the bay, deep, grottolike pool, free Wi-Fi. **Cons:** Short but steep walk/drive from downtown, no lounge area around pool, no a/c. ✉ *Calle Matamoros 520, Centro,* ☎ *322/222–0161* 🌐 *www.cuatrovientos.com* *14 rooms* *In-room: No a/c, no phone, no TV, Wi-Fi (some). In-hotel: Restaurant, room service, bar, pool, no elevator* ▭ *MC, V* *CP in season.*

$ **Posada de Roger.** Get to know the other guests—many of them savvy budget travelers from Europe and Canada—by hanging around the pool or the small, shared balcony overlooking the street and the bay. A shared, open-air kitchen on the fourth floor has a great view, too. Rooms are spare and vaultlike, the showers are hot, and the beds are comfortable but firm. Freddy's Tucan, the indoor-outdoor bar-restaurant ($; no dinner) is very popular with locals—mainly for breakfast.

The hotel is in a prime part of the Zona Romántica known for its restaurants and shops; Playa los Muertos is a few blocks away. **Pros:** Good Zona Romántica location, tinkling fountain, quiet courtyard, good bar-restaurant next door. **Cons:** Room safes at front desk, many rooms cramped, *Mommy Dearest* wire hangers. *Calle Basilio Badillo 237, Col. E. Zapata, 322/222–0836 or 322/222–0639 www.hotelposadaderoger.com 47 rooms In-hotel: Restaurant, bar, pool, no elevator AE, MC, V EP.*

> **OM AWAY FROM HOME**
>
> **Via Yoga** (*www.viayoga.com*), based in Seattle, Washington, has weeklong packages at Villa Amor that include twice-daily yoga classes with group activities, various disciplines of yoga, and, if you like, surfing classes and excursions.

12

¢ **Yasmín.** Two-story and L-shape, this budget baby has no pool, but it's just a block from the beach and joined at the hip to Café de Olla, the extremely popular Mexican restaurant. Small, ho-hum rooms have low ceilings, firm beds, and open closets but also floor fans and cable TV: not a bad deal for the price, although take note that the front desk staff is consistently grouchy. About six bucks over the base price entitles you to air-conditioning. **Pros:** Inexpensive! Close to Zona Romántica action, pleasant courtyard garden with café tables and chaise lounges. **Cons:** Dark rooms, low ceilings, no pool. *Calle Basilio Badillo, Col. E. Zapata, 322/222–0087 27 rooms In-room: No phone. In-hotel: Restaurant, no elevator No credit cards EP.*

NORTH OF PUERTO VALLARTA

$$$$ ★ **Casa de Mita.** A nook of nonchalant elegance, Las Brisas has updated country furnishings of wicker, leather, and wood, and rock-floor showers without curtains or doors. Mosquito netting lends romance to cozy, quilt-covered beds. Waves crashing onshore, their sound somehow magnified, create white noise that lulls you to sleep. In the morning, settle into a cushy chaise on your private patio; at night watch the sun set behind Punta de Mita. These simple pleasures make this hideaway a winner. It doesn't hurt that the food is truly delicious, the bar is well stocked, and it's all included in the room price. **TIP→ Avoid the 10% surcharge for credit cards by using PayPal.** **Pros:** Delicious food included in price, nearly private beach, free long-distance phone calls. **Cons:** Little if any nightlife in vicinity. *Playa Careyeros, Punta de Mita, Nayarit 329/298–4114 www.mexicoboutiquehotels.com 7 rooms In-room: No phone, safe, refrigerator, no TV, Wi-Fi. In-hotel: Restaurant, bar, pool, water sports, public Wi-Fi, airport shuttle, concierge, parking (no fee), no elevator, no children under 16 AI.*

$$$$ Fodor'sChoice ★ **Four Seasons Punta Mita.** The hotel and its fabulous spa perch above a lovely beach at the northern extreme of Bahía de Banderas, about 45 minutes from the PV airport and an hour north of downtown Puerto Vallarta. Spacious rooms occupy Mexican-style casitas of one, two, and three stories. Each room has elegant yet earthy furnishings and a private terrace or balcony—many with a sweeping sea view. The challenging championship golf course was designed by Jack Nicklaus. The gym is first-rate, and a good variety of sporting and beach equipment

is on hand. Just offshore, the Marietas Islands are great for snorkeling, diving, whale-watching, and fishing. This is the place for indulging golf and spa fantasies, or just staying put and enjoying the luxurious, top-notch facilities. Great for kids, too. **Pros:** Beautiful beach, yoga on the point, great gym equipment, private yacht available for charter. **Cons:** Seemingly each of the 800-plus employees greets you upon passing, very expensive spa treatments, stringent cancellation policy. ✉ *Bahía de Banderas, Punta de Mita, Nayarit* ☎ *329/291–6019, 800/322–3442 in U.S., 800/268–6282 in Canada* 🌐 *www.fshr.com* *141 rooms, 27 suites* *In-room: Safe, DVD, Wi-Fi, refrigerator. In-hotel: 3 restaurants, room service, bars, golf course, tennis courts, pools, gym, spa, beachfront, water sports, concierge, children's programs (ages 5–12), laundry service, public Internet, parking (no fee), no-smoking rooms* *AE, MC, V* *EP, BP.*

$$$$ **Grand Velas.** In scale and majesty, the public areas of this luxury hotel blow other Nuevo Vallarta all-inclusives away. Ceilings soar overhead, and the structure and furnishings are simultaneously minimalist and modern, yet earthy, incorporating stucco, rock, polished teak, and gleaming ecru marble. The spa is excellent, and the views—with the garden-shrouded pool in the foreground and the beach beyond—are striking. Rooms are sleek, with elegant furnishings and appointments. Only the food, in our experience, is not exceptional; for a rack rate of over $1,000 per couple per night, all-inclusive, it should be. **Pros:** Exceptional beauty of rooms and public spaces, lovely spa. **Cons:** Food could be better, Nuevo Vallarta location is far from PV (but 10 minutes by car from Bucerías). ✉ *Paseo de los Cocoteros 98 Sur, Nuevo Vallarta, Jalisco,* ☎ *322/226–8000, 877/398–2784 in U.S., 866/355–3359 in Canada* 🌐 *www.grandvelas.com* *269 suites* *In-room: Safe, DVD, Wi-Fi. In-hotel: 4 restaurants, room service, bars, tennis court, pools, gym, spa, beachfront, children's programs (ages 4–12), laundry service, public Internet, airport shuttle, parking (no fee), some pets allowed* *AE, MC, V* *AI.*

$$–$$$ ★ **Villa Amor.** In the amalgam of unusual, rustic-but-luxurious suites with indoor and outdoor living spaces, the rule is the higher up your room, the more beautiful the view of Sayulita's coast. The trade-off is the walk up a long staircase and the dearth of room phones that make contacting the front desk frustrating. Accommodations range from basic to honeymoon suites with terraces and plunge pools. Details like recessed colored-glass light fixtures, Talavera sinks in bathrooms, brick ceilings, art in wall niches, and colorful concrete floors add a lot of class. The property overlooks a rocky cove where you can fish from shore; a beautiful sandy beach is a few minutes' walk. The restaurant is closed in low season unless occupancy is high. **Pros:** Nice location across bay from Sayulita's main beach; staff arranges tours and tee times, and loans bikes, kayaks, Boogie boards, and snorkeling gear. **Cons:** Tons of stairs, no room phones, open-to-the-elements rooms admit creepy crawlies. ✉ *Playa Sayulita, Sayulita, Nayarit,* ☎ *329/291–3010* 🌐 *www.villaamor.com* *32 villas* *In-room: No a/c (some), no phone, kitchen (some), refrigerator, no TV. In-hotel: Restaurant, bar, water sports, bicycles, laundry service, parking (no fee), no elevator* *MC, V* *EP.*

CLOSE UP

Don't Be (Time-Share) Shark Bait

If the sharks smell interest, you're as good as dead in the water. In Puerto Vallarta, time-share salespeople are as unavoidable as death and taxes. And almost as dreaded. Some people actually enjoy going to one- to four-hour presentations to get freebies that range from Kahlua to free rental cars, but more often, the seemingly endless pitches are just annoying.

Anyone calling you *amigo* as you walk down the street is probably selling. (Vallartenses are friendly, but they don't accost you in public.) Either walk by without a word, or say "No, thanks" as you continue walking. Ignore them when they yell after you. This can be hard to master, but it's a tried and true method.

Even some very nice hotels (like the Westin) allow salespeople in their lobbies disguised as the Welcome Wagon or "information desk." Ask the concierge for the scoop on activities instead. Salespeople might try to guilt-trip you into presentations ("My family relies on the commissions I get," for example) or entice with discounts. The latter can be difficult to redeem, costing more time than they're worth. And while it may be the salesperson's livelihood, remember that this is your vacation, and you have every right to use the time as you wish.

$$ **Costa Azul.** What makes this place attractive are the many activities offered: horseback riding, kayaking, hiking, surfing (with lessons), and excursions to the Marietas Islands or La Tovara mangroves near San Blas. The all-inclusive plan includes activities, but consider not partaking, as the food is mainly mediocre and San Pancho has some excellent restaurants. Although the sandy beach faces the open ocean, it curves around to a spot that's safer for swimming. Some guests have complained of disorganized and unhelpful staff members and a decline in hotel maintenance. **Pros:** Great place to bond with kids of all ages, nice beach, outdoor activities are planned for you, free Wi-Fi in the bar-restaurant. **Cons:** Mediocre food, some frustration with lack of equipment/tours by customers who book the all-inclusive activities package. ✉ *Carretera 200, Km 118, Fracc. Costa Azul, San Francisco, Nayarit,* ☎ *311/258–4210 or 800/365–7613* 🌐 *www.costaazul.com* *24 rooms, 3 villas* *In-room: No phone, kitchen (some), refrigerator (some), no TV. In-hotel: Restaurant, bars, pool, beachfront, water sports, laundry service, public Wi-Fi, airport shuttle, parking (no fee), no elevator* *AE, D, DC, MC, V* *AI, EP, FAP.*

¢–$$ **Palmeras.** This is one of Bucerias' best small hotels. A block from the beach, in an area with lots of good restaurants, Palmeras has small rooms with brightly painted interior walls and modeled-stucco sunflowers serving as a kind of headboard behind the bed. There's plenty of space to socialize around the large, clean, rectangular pool. The more expensive rooms are larger, newer, and have a couch facing satellite TVs and kitchenettes; those on the second floor have partial ocean view. Smaller, older, street-facing rooms are half the price of the newer units. **Pros:** Free Wi-Fi, inexpensive older rooms for bargain hunters. **Cons:** Some rooms have odd layout. ✉ *Lázaro Cárdenas 35, Bucerías, Nayarit* ☎ *329/298–1288, 647/722–4139* in the U.S. 🌐 *www.hotel*

palmeras.com ⇨*21 rooms* ♁*In-room: No phone, kitchen (some), refrigerator, no TV (some), Wi-Fi. In-hotel: Pool, no elevator, no-smoking rooms* ▭*MC, V* 🍽*EP.*

COSTALEGRE

$$$$ ★ **Hotelito Desconocido.** Every inch of the place is painted, tiled, or otherwise decorated with bright Mexican colors and handicrafts. Rooms and suites incorporate local building styles and materials, including plank floors, reed mats, bamboo walls, and palm-frond roofs. They're cooled by battery-powered fans and lighted by lanterns, candles, and low-wattage lamps. Rustic but lovely bathrooms bring the outdoors in through large open windows. Signal for morning coffee by running up the red flag. On a long stretch of beach, this isolated hotel is an idyllic escape for its clientele: about 60% American, 25% European, and 100% laid-back. There's an obligatory meal plan of $184 for two people per day. **Pros:** Completely isolated, unique and charming. **Cons:** Completely isolated, obligatory meal plan is rather pricey. ✉*Playón de Mismaloya s/n, Cruz de Loreto, Jalisco,* ☎*322/281–4010, 01800/013–1313 toll-free in Mexico, 800/851–1143 in U.S.* ⊕*www.hotelito.com* ⇨*16 rooms, 8 suites* ♁*In-room: No a/c, no phone, no TV. In-hotel: 2 restaurants, bar, pool, spa, beachfront, water sports, bicycles, concierge, public Internet, airport shuttle, parking (no fee), no elevator* ▭*AE, MC, V* 🍽*BP, FAP.*

$$$$ Fodor's Choice ★ **El Tamarindo.** More than 2,000 acres of ecological reserve and jungle surround this magical resort along 16 km (10 mi) of private coast. The architecture utilizes simple design elements (with a Mediterranean flavor) and local building materials. Many villas have outdoor living rooms. All have dark-wood floors, king-size beds, wet bars, ample bathrooms, and patios with plunge pools, hammocks, and chaise longues. Sofas are upholstered in rich textured fabrics, and all furnishings and details are spare and classy. At night the staff lights more than 1,500 candles around the villas to create a truly enchanting setting. If you're a golfer, the course may be reason enough to stay here. **Pros:** Individual plunge pools, CD players with music in each room, daily yoga and Pilates classes. **Cons:** 8% service fee on top of 17% sales and hotel taxes, isolated. ✉*Carretera Melaque–Puerto Vallarta (Carretera 200), Km 7.5, Cihuatlán, Jalisco,* ☎*315/351–5032, 888/625–5144 in U.S. or Canada* ⊕*www.mexicoboutiquehotels.com/thetamarindo/* ⇨*32 villas* ♁*In-room: Safe, no TV. In-hotel: Restaurant, room service, bar, gym, spa, golf course, tennis court, pool, beachfront, diving, water sports, bicycles, concierge, laundry service, public Internet, airport shuttle, parking (no fee)* ▭*AE, MC, V* 🍽*EP.*

$$$ ★ **Punta Serena.** Perched on a beautiful headland, this oasis of calm aptly named "Point Serene" enjoys balmy breezes and life-changing views from the infinity hot tub; the beach far below and pool are clothing optional. Spa treatments are inventive: roses and red wine promote moisturizing; carotene and honey contribute to a glowing tan; and the "Mayan Wrap" connects you herbally to the glowing god within. Shamans lead healing steam ceremonies on weekends; mud-and-music therapies are on the beach; and activities like horseback riding and nonmotorized water sports at the adjacent Blue Bay hotel are included

12

in the price. Rooms have lovely furnishings and decor, and shared or private terraces, some with great beach views. **Pros:** Gorgeous views, complimentary horseback ride and mangrove cruise, weekly temazcal, or ritual steam ceremony. **Cons:** Isolated, limited menu, cobblestone walkways and hills make getting around difficult for some folks. ✉ *Carretera 200, Km 20, Tenacatita, Jalisco,* ☎ *315/351–5427 or 315/351–5020* 🌐 *www.puntaserena.com* *12 rooms, 12 suites* *In-room: Safe. In-hotel: Restaurant, bar, pool, gym, spa, beachfront, tennis courts, laundry service, parking (no fee), public Internet, no kids under 18* *AE, MC, V* *AI.*

$$ **La Paloma Oceanfront Retreat.** Room prices are reasonable considering the small studio apartments have almost everything home does, and four of them face a beach that's great for long walks and has good Boogie-boarding waves. Each room is configured differently, but all are uniformly bright and cheerful, with private patios and paintings by the owner (she gives lessons in high season). There's a large pool and patio for outdoor ocean-view barbecuing. Three-day minimum stay; most folks book by the week in high season. La Paloma now offers off-season discounts. **Pros:** Car on-site for rental by the day, located on a beautiful bay, long beach perfect for walking and jogging. **Cons:** Price hike in recent years, although still worth what you pay. ✉ *Av. Las Cabañas 13, San Patricio–Melaque,* ☎ *315/355–5345* 🌐 *www.lapalomamexico.com* *13 studio apartments* *In-room: No a/c (some), no phone, kitchen, refrigerator, DVD (some). In-hotel: Restaurant, pool, beachfront, public Internet, public Wi-Fi, parking (no fee).* *AE, MC, V (through PayPal only)* *CP.*

NIGHTLIFE

BARS

Andale (✉ *Av. Olas Altas 425, Col. E. Zapata* ☎ *322/222–1054*) fills up most nights. Crowds spill out onto the sidewalk as party-hearty men and women shimmy out of the narrow saloon, drinks in hand, to the strains of Chubby Checker and other vintage tunes.

★ **Apaches** (✉ *Av. Olas Altas 439, Col. E. Zapata* ☎ *322/222–4004*) is gay friendly, lesbian friendly, *people* friendly. PV's original martini bar, Apaches is the landing zone for expats reconnoitering after a long day, and a warm-up for late-night types. When the outside tables get jam-packed in high season, the overflow heads into the narrow bar and the adjacent, equally narrow bistro. It opens after 5 PM; happy hour is 5 to 7.

The **Bar Above** (✉ *Av. México at Av. Hidalgo, 2 blocks north of the central plaza, Bucerías* ☎ *329/298–1194*) is a martini bar without a bar (just tables) that also serves desserts like molten chocolate soufflé—the signature dish—or charred pineapple bourbon shortcake. Lights are dim, the music is romantic, and there's an eagle's-eye view of the ocean from the rooftop crow's nest. It's closed every Sunday; in August and September; and Mondays in June, July, and October. At other times, it's open 6 PM–11 PM.

CLOSE UP

Spa Escapes

Puerto Vallarta pamper parlors range from elegant resort spas scented with bergamot to Aztec-inspired day spas. Competition keeps creativity high, with an ever-changing menu of new treatments.

At the **Four Seasons Punta Mita Apuane Spa** service is the hallmark. Treatments are among the most expensive in the area, but the facilities, products, and excellent kid's club allows you to relax thoroughly. Native products are used almost exclusively; the Punta Mita massage combines tequila and sage to excellent effect. ✉ *Punta de Mita, Bahía de Banderas* ☎ *329/291-6000* 🌐 *www.fourseasons.com/puntamita* 💳 *AE, DC, MC, V* ☞ *Body treatments $83–$230; facials $95–$209; hair $44–$95; manicure or pedicure $53–$125; waxing $27–$73.*

The dramatic 16,500-square-foot spa at **Gran Velas** has 23 treatment rooms, and ample steam, sauna, and whirlpools. Highlights are the chocolate, gold, or avocado wraps; Thai massage; European facial; and cinnamon-sage foot scrub. Between or after treatments, sip a cup of hot tea or cold chlorophyll water on comfortable chaises in the "plunge lagoon." ✉ *Av. de los Cocoteros 98 Sur, Nuevo Vallarta* ☎ *322/226-8000* 🌐 *www.grandvelas.com* 💳 *AE, MC, V* ☞ *Body treatments $68–$178; facials $68–$178; manicure/pedicure $20–$89; hair care $48–$89; waxing $18–$58; makeup $78.*

Paradise Village Palenque Spa is a modern Maya temple of glass and marble—a cool oasis with separate wings for men and women, each equipped with private hydrotherapy tubs, whirlpools, saunas, and steam rooms. The reasonably priced therapy selections are extensive, from an anti-cellulite seaweed wrap to milk baths with honey, amaranth, and orange oil or aromatherapy massage. Or choose one of a dozen combined treatment plans, most of which allow you to swap treatments of the same price category. ✉ *Paseo de los Cocoteros 1, Nuevo Vallarta* ☎ *322/226-6727 Ext. 6404 or 6409, 800/995-5714 in U.S. or Canada* 🌐 *www.paradisevillage.com* 💳 *AE, MC, V* ☞ *Body treatments $40–$119; facials $40–$119; manicure/pedicure $23–$63; hair $35–$97; waxing $6–$63.*

El Tamarindo is a *Gilligan's Island*-style spa with no sauna, whirlpool, or fancy extras. What it does have are some of the best treatments and staff in Pacific Mexico, and one of the most authentic temazcals around. Their massages, facials, and scrubs utilize oils, rubs, and lotions made with lemongrass and aloe vera, along with organic mineral-laced, mud-based Miguett products. The vibe here is more convivial warmth than nonchalant New Age. The most popular treatment is the seaside massage. ✉ *Carretera Melaque–Puerto Vallarta (Carretera 200) Km 7.5, Cihuatlán* ☎ *315/351-5032* 🌐 *www.mexicoboutiquehotels.com/thetamarindo* 💳 *AE, MC, V* ☞ *Body treatments $67–$152; facials $86–$95; manicure/pedicure: $38–$48.*

At **El Faro** (✉*Royal Pacific Yacht Club, Marina Vallarta* ☎*322/221–0541*) you can admire the bay and marina from atop a 110-foot lighthouse. There's often live guitar or other romantic music Thursday through Saturday after 11 PM; on Sunday it starts earlier, at 9 PM. It's mainly a baby-boomer crowd, with lots of yachties.

The tallest building around, **Hotel Alondra** (✉*Calle Sinaloa 16, Barra de Navidad* ☎*315/355–8372*), has a rooftop bar that's great for sunset cocktails.

Fodor's Choice ★ Second-story **Memories** (✉*Av. Juárez, at Calle Mina 207, Centro* ☎*322/205–7906*) is darkly romantic and a great place for a date, but still ideal for groups of friends, or singles with a book. The extensive drink list includes "hair of the squirrel," with Frangelica, and lots of specialty alcoholic and nonalcoholic coffees. The classic-rock sound track pays homage to John Lennon, the Eagles, and Bob Marley.

Nikki Beach (✉*Westin hotel, Paseo de la Marina Sur 205, Marina Vallarta* ☎*322/226–1150*) has lost quite a bit of its original glamour-puss reputation among the locals, but the white-on-white, on-the-beach bistro is still chic, and encourages lounging. In the restaurant, sexy waiters deliver dishes from Continental to Mediterranean to Asian, including sushi.

Party Lounge (✉*Av. Mexico 993, across from Parque Hidalgo, Centro* ☎*No phone*) is open daily after 1 PM for stop-and-go drinks: mainly *litros*, that is, 32-ouncers of tequila sunrise, Long Island ice tea, piña colada, and the like. The '70s, '80s, and lounge music appeals to a mixed-ages crowd. It's open 8 PM to 4 AM.

The Wi-Fi flows freely at the chummy **Shamrock** (✉*Avenida México 22, Centro* ☎*329/298–3073* 🌐*www.theshamrockmexico.com*) Open daily after 11 AM, this Irish-owned pub has chips, batter-fried cod, and good cottage pies and burgers. When the amount of trade warrants it during busy seasons, the more sophisticated upstairs lounge opens to those seeking a quieter venue.

Puerto Vallartans decided **Tribu Bar Lounge** (✉*Paseo de la Marina 220, Mayan Palace Marina, Marina Vallarta* ☎*322/226–6000*) was a bit out of the way to become a serious hot spot, but travelers in the Marina district still find it a dark and atmospheric space with two billiards tables. DJ-spun music pulses house, lounge, techno or disco, and '80s. Wednesdays is usually salsa night, though the salsa is canned. It's open 5 PM to 1 AM (closed Mon.), and there's no cover.

DANCE CLUBS

Most dance clubs are open 10 PM to 4 AM but don't get going until midnight. They usually close at least two nights a week (usually Monday and Tuesday). Covers range from around $7 to $20; early birds may get in free.

★ **Christine** (✉*Krystal Vallarta, Av. de las Garzas s/n, Zona Hotelera Norte* ☎*322/224–6990 or 322/224–0202*) has spectacular light shows set to bass-thumping music that ranges from techno and house to disco, rock, and Mexican pop. Most people (young boomers and Gen-Xers) come for the duration (it doesn't close until 6 AM), as this is the top of the food chain for the PV dancing experience.

COCKTAILS TO GO

Stop-and-go bars, where you get your drink in a cardboard cup, are mainly geared toward teens. But it can be fun to sip a cocktail while drinking in the sights along the malecón.

Fodor's Choice ★ A chill mix sets **de Santos** (✉*Calle Morelos 771 at Leona Vicario, Centro* ☎*322/223–3052*) off around 6 PM. By about 9 PM, younger folk show up for DJs spinning disco and house tunes. At the rooftop bar, you and your friends can fling yourselves on the giant futons for some stargazing. Look for art expos, special events, and theme parties. There's no cover, and it's open nightly except Christmas Eve. This is a see-and-be-seen place for locals.

Popular with young (late teens to early thirties), hip *vallartenses,* **Hilo** (✉*Paseo Díaz Ordaz 588, Centro* ☎*322/223–5361*) serves up house, techno, hip-hop, electronic, and Top 40. Enormous bronze-color statues reach up toward the stories-high ceilings in this modern space.

★ **J.B.** (✉*Blvd. Francisco M. Ascencio 2043, Zona Hotelera* ☎*322/224–4616*), pronounced "Hota Bay," is the best club in town for salsa. The age of the crowd varies, but tends toward thirty- and fortysomethings. J.B. is serious about dancing, so it feels young at heart. There's usually a band Thursday through Saturday nights, DJ music the rest of the week. Those with *dos patas zurdas* (two left feet) can attend salsa lessons Thursday and Friday 8 pm–10 PM; or take tango lessons during those times on Monday and Wednesday. Cost is $5 with no additional cover; otherwise, the cover is $9 (except Monday and Tuesday) after 10:30 PM.

FOLK PERFORMANCES

At the Thursday or Sunday dinner show at **La Iguana** (✉*Calle Lázaro Cárdenas 311, Col. E. Zapata* ☎*322/222–0105*), large troupes of professional mariachis entertain, women dance in colorful costumes, kids whack piñatas, and fireworks light up the sky. There's an open bar, and a buffet with 40 different dishes Thursday and Sunday, 7 pm–11 PM. Simulated cockfight notwithstanding (it's supposedly painless for the roosters), most folks deem this party worth the $65-per-person price tag.

El Mariachi Loco (✉*Lázaro Cárdenas 254, Centro* ☎*322/223–2205*) is the place to see silver-studded mariachi musicians. The mariachis begin at 9 PM and the fun continues with various bands and dancing until 6 AM Monday through Wednesday; the rest of the week, warm-up groups play before the mariachis come onstage around 11:30 PM. On weekends a comedian and ranchera group are added to the mix at around 1 AM. Cover is $5.

Playa Los Arcos (✉*Av. Olas Altas 380, Col. E. Zapata* ☎*322/222–1583*) has a theme dinner show ($18) Monday, Wednesday, and Saturday 6 pm–10:30 PM. A buffet and one cocktail are included. Saturday is Mexico Night, with mariachis, a *charro* (cowboy) doing rope tricks, and folkloric dance; other nights they might have a fashion show or other events (prices vary).

FREE INFO

One of the best sources of information for upcoming events is *Bay Vallarta*, published twice a month. The free bilingual publication gets snatched up fast from hotels, restaurants, car-rental agencies, and other places frequented by visitors.

LIVE MUSIC

★ **Blanco y Negro** (✉*Calle Lucerna at Calle Niza, behind Blockbuster Video store, Zona Hotelera Norte* ☎*322/293–2556*) is the place for drinks with friends. The intimate café-bar is comfortable yet rustic, with leather love seats and round cocktail tables. The music is *trova* (think Mexican Cat Stevens) by Latino legends Silvio Rodríguez and Pablo Milanés. There's never a cover. It's closed Sunday and Monday, otherwise open after 8 PM.

La Bodeguita del Medio (✉*Paseo Díaz Ordaz 858, Centro* ☎*322/223–1585*) is a wonderful Cuban bar and restaurant with a friendly vibe. People of all ages come to dance salsa, so the small dance floor fills up as soon as the house sextet starts playing around 9 PM. There's no cover.

SPORTS & THE OUTDOORS

CANOPY TOURS

★ Tours range from about $65 to $80 per person. On the 3½-hour adventure with **Canopy El Edén** (☎*322/222–2516* 🌐*www.canopyeleden.com*), you zip along 10 lines through the trees and above the river. Take the 9 AM tour if you want to leave extra time for swimming. Time enough for a meal at the restaurant or a brief dip is already included in the tour schedule.

★ Vallarta's top canopy tour is **Canopy Tour de Los Veranos** (☎*322/223–0504 or 877/563–4113* 🌐*www.canopytours-vallarta.com*), with the most zip lines (14), the longest line (600 feet), and the highest line (500 feet off the ground). Afterward, you can scale the climbing wall, play in the river, or eat at the restaurant. In Sayulita, **Rancho Mi Chaparrita** (☎*329/291–3112* 🌐*www. michaparrita.com*) runs a 10-zip-line tour on a ranch. Access the ranch on horseback via the beach and backcountry for a complete adventure. The most convenient canopy tour if you're staying in Nuevo Vallarta is **Vallarta Adventures** (☎*322/297–1212, 888/303–2653 in U.S. and Canada* 🌐*www.vallarta-adventures.com*), although it's not the best show in town.

CRUISES

Cruceros Princesa (✉*Terminal Marítima, Marina Vallarta* ☎*322/224–4777*) has sunset cruises, half-day snorkel tours to the Marietas Islands, and full-day trips to the beaches of southern Bahía de Banderas.

MULTISPORT OUTFITTERS

Don't see what you want here? Try one of these outfitters, whose multitude of tours include bird-watching, ATV tours, whale-watching, biking, hot-air ballooning, sailing, and much, much more.

Ecotours (☎ *322/223–3130 or 322/222–6606* 🌐 *www.ecotoursvallarta.com*). **Immersion Adventures** (✉ *La Manzanilla* ☎ *315/351–5341* 🌐 *www.immersionadventures.com*).

Tours Soltero (✉ *San Patricio Melaque* ☎ *315/355–6777* ✉ *raystoursmelaque@yahoo.com*).

Vallarta Adventures (☎ *322/297–1212 Nuevo Vallarta, 322/221–0657 Marina Vallarta, 888/303–2653 in U.S. and Canada* 🌐 *www.vallarta-adventures.com*).

Wild Vallarta (☎ *322/222–8928 and 322/222–8933 or 877/314–9453 toll-free in the U.S.* 🌐 *www.wildvallarta.com*).

A sailing vessel that has circumnavigated the world more than once, the **Marigalante** (✉ *Paseo Diaz Ordaz 770, Centro* ☎ *322/223–0309 or 322/223–1662* 🌐 *www.marigalante.com.mx*) has a pirate crew that keeps things hopping. The adults-only dinner cruise, with open bar and pre-Hispanic show, has some bawdy pirate humor; some women might not enjoy being "kidnapped."

★ **Vallarta Adventures** (☎ *322/221–0657, 888/303–2653 in U.S. and Canada* 🌐 *www.vallarta-adventures.com*) has day or evening cruises to Caletas Beach, its exclusive domain. Daytime cruises include snorkeling, kayaking, hiking, and lunch (scuba or spa treatments available for additional cost). Evening cruises include dinner on the beach and a show at the amphitheater (no kids under 10).

DOLPHIN ENCOUNTERS

Captive-dolphin encounters ($79) with **Dolphin Discovery** (✉ *Sea Life Park, Carretera a Tepic, Km 155, Nuevo Vallarta* ☎ *322/297–0724, 866/393–5158 toll-free in U.S., 866/793–1905 toll-free in Canada* 🌐 *www.sealifeparkvallarta.com*) involve spending about 30 of the 45-minute experience in the water interacting with the mammals.

The only PV encounter with noncaptive dolphins, **Wildlife Connection** (✉ *Calle Francia 140, Dpto. 7, Col. Versalles* ☎ *322/225–3621* 🌐 *www.wildlifeconnection.com*) uses skiffs with listening equipment to find pods of dolphins in the wild blue sea. You can then jump in the water to swim with them (April through December only). The most common destination is around the Marietas Islands. The cost is $65 per person for a three- to four-hour tour, including travel time. There's no guarantee, however, that the dolphins will stick around for the fun. There's also a combined tour searching for whales and dolphins, $80 a pop, December through March only. Turtle, birding, and the new frog tours help finance the group's dolphin and whale research.

12

FISHING

Sportfishing is excellent off Puerto Vallarta, and fisherfolk have landed monster marlin well over 500 pounds. Surf casting from shore nets snook, roosters, and jack crevalles.

CharterDreams (☎*322/221–0690* ⊕*www.charterdreams.com*) has a variety of excursions, from trips with one to three people in skiffs for bass fishing to cruises with up to eight people aboard luxury yachts.

Master Baiter (☎*322/209–0498, 322/209–0499 Marina Vallarta, 322/222–4043 Centro* ⊕*www.mbsportfishing.com*) is a comprehensive fishing outfitter with a solid reputation. An overnight trip ($2,650) allows further exploration, and includes meals and drinks. Both storefronts (downtown Vallarta and Marina Vallarta) sell fishing tackle, although there's a better selection at the Marina store.

At Punta de Mita, **Sociedad Cooperativa de Servicios** (☎*329/291–6298* ⊕*www.prodigyweb.net.mx/cooperativapuntamita*) takes you on fishing trips for up to four people (four-hour minimum). All the guys are local fishermen who know all the hot spots.

GOLF

"Not a bad mango in the bunch" is how one golf aficionado described Puerto Vallarta's courses. Designed by Percy Clifford in 1978, PV's original course, **Los Flamingos Country Club** (✉*Carretera a Bucerías, Km 145, 12 km [8 mi] north of airport, Nuevo Vallarta* ☎*329/296–5006* ⊕*www.flamingosgolf.com.mx*), has been totally renovated. The 18-hole course at the northern extremity of Nuevo Vallarta has new irrigation and sprinkler systems to maintain the rejuvenated greens.**Four Seasons Punta Mita** (✉*Bahía de Banderas, Punta de Mita 329/291–6000* ⊕*www.fourseasons.com*) was designed by Jack Nicklaus. Nonguests are permitted to play the 195-acre, par-72 course, but must pay the hotel's day-use fee of 50% of the room rate: approximately $300 plus 28% taxes and service charge. You'll get the use of the room and the hotel's facilities until about dark. Advance reservations are essential. The club also has perhaps the only natural island-green in golf. Joe Finger designed the 18-hole course at **Marina Vallarta** (✉*Paseo de la Marina s/n, Marina Vallarta* ☎*322/221–0545 or 322/221–0073*), the most convenient for those staying in the Hotel Zone, Old Puerto Vallarta, and Marina Vallarta. It's flat but more challenging than it looks, with lots of water hazards. About two hours south of Vallarta on the
Fodor'sChoice Costalegre is the area's best course, **El Tamarindo** (✉*Carretera Melaque–*
★ *Puerto Vallarta [Carretera 200], Km 7.5, Cihuatlán* ☎*315/351–5032 Ext. 4*). At least six holes on the David Fleming–designed course play along the ocean; some are cliff-side holes with fabulous views, others go right down to the beach. **El Tigre** (✉*Paradise Village, Paseo de los Cocoteros 18, Nuevo Vallarta* ☎*322/297–0773, 866/843–5951 in U.S., 800/214–7758 in Canada* ⊕*www.eltigregolf.com*) is an 18-hole course with 12 water features and a fun island par 3. Some of
★ the best views in the area belong to **Vista Vallarta** (✉*Circuito Universidad 653, Col. San Nicolás* ☎*322/290–0030 or 322/290–0040*). The

course has 18 holes designed by Jack Nicklaus and another 18 by Tom Weiskopf.

SNORKELING SANCTUARY

Protected area **Los Arcos** is an offshore group of giant rocks rising some 65 feet above the water, making the area great for snorkeling and diving. For reasonable fees, local men along the road to Mismaloya Beach run diving, snorkeling, fishing, and boat trips here and as far north as Punta de Mita and Las Marietas or the beach villages of Cabo Corrientes. Restaurants at Playa Mismaloya can also set you up.

SCUBA DIVING & SNORKELING

For PADI or NAUI certification, equipment rentals, and one- or two-tank dives (the latter to farther away destinations like Las Marietas, El Morro, or Chimo), contact **Chico's Dive Shop** (✉*Paseo Díaz Ordáz 772, Centro* ☎*322/222–1895* 🌐*www.chicos-diveshop.com*). Trips to Los Arcos accommodate snorkelers as well as those who want a one- or two-tank dive. The PADI dive masters at **Pacific Scuba** (✉*Blvd. Francisco Medina Ascencio 2486, Zona Hotelera Norte* ☎*322/209–0364* 🌐*www.pacificscuba.com.mx*) teach courses, rent equipment, and arrange trips to Los Arcos, Marietas Islands, Corbeteña, and other areas.

SURFING

On the beach at Sayulita is **Captain Pablo** (☎*329/291–2070 early mornings and evenings only* ✉*pandpsouthworth@hotmail.com*), where you can rent equipment, take surfing lessons with Patricia, or join a four-hour surf tour. n the beach at Sayulita, **Sininen** (✉*Calle Delfín 4–S, Sayulita* ☎*329/291–3186* 🌐 *www.sininen.com.mx*) rents ($20 per day, $30 for 24 hours) and sells surfboards and surf paraphernalia.

TURTLE REPATRIATION

Seven of the world's eight marine turtle species live part time in Mexico. Three hang out in and around Banderas Bay. Turtle repatriation tours involve removing eggs from the sand for safekeeping (from predators) and releasing young turtles to the wild. The usual season is from late summer to fall; that's when females can be seen nesting and hatchlings return to the sea.

Three-hour turtle tours with **Ecotours** (☎*322/223–3130 or 322/222–6606* 🌐*www.ecotoursvallarta.com*) end just after midnight. Trained biologists at **Wildlife Connection** (✉*Calle Francia 140, Col. Versalles* ☎*322/225–3621* 🌐*www.wildlifeconnection.com*) lead turtle repatriation programs that begin by driving ATVs to the beach.

SIDE TRIPS FROM PUERTO VALLARTA

A trip into the Sierra Madre is an excellent way to escape the coastal heat and PV's hordes of vacationers. The air is crisp and clean and scented with pine, the valley and mountain views are spectacular, and the highland towns of San Sebastián and Mascota are earthy, unassuming, and charming.

12

SAN SEBASTIÁN

80 km (50 mi) east of Puerto Vallarta.

This sleepy, friendly town is the Mayberry of Mexico, but a little less lively. The miners who built the town have long gone, and more recently, younger folks are drifting away in search of opportunity. Most of the 800 or so people who remain seem perfectly content with life as it is. The most interesting thing to see in San Sebastián is the town itself. Walk the cobblestone streets and handsome brick sidewalks, admiring the white-faced adobe structures surrounding the plaza.

WHERE TO STAY

$$ **La Galerita de San Sebastián.** A pair of displaced *tapatios* (Guadalajarans) created this cluster of pretty cabins. Double-sided fireplaces heat the bedrooms and adjoining sitting rooms. This is the most modern and stylish place to stay in San Sebastián. **Pros:** Geared toward adults. **Cons:** No a/c. ✉*Camino a Las Galerítas 62, Barrio La Otra Banda,* ☎*322/297–3040* 🌐*www.lagalerita.com.mx* *3 bungalows* *In-room: No a/c, no phone, refrigerator, Wi-Fi. In-hotel: Restaurant, parking (no fee)* *No credit cards* *BP.*

$ **Real de San Sebastián.** Small rooms are dominated by snug king beds in curtained alcoves in this interesting B&B. It has a shared main living space with a cushy plush couch facing a large-screen satellite TV, and more formal round tables where afternoon coffee or hot chocolate is served. In the morning take complimentary coffee and rolls in bed, served through a small service window. **Pros:** The manager, Margarito Salcedo, is friendly and solicitous. **Cons:** Main living space is somewhat cramped. ✉*Calle Zaragoza 41,* ☎*322/297–3224* 🌐*www.sansebastiandeloeste.com* *6 rooms* *In-room: No a/c, no phone, no TV. In-hotel: Restaurant, no elevator* *No credit cards* *CP.*

MASCOTA

85 km (53 mi) east of Puerto Vallarta.

The blue-green hills and valleys surrounding Mascota are lusciously forested; beyond them rise indigo mountains to form a painterly tableau. This former mining town and municipal seat is home to 13,000 people. Its banks, shops, and a hospital serve area villages.

EXPLORING

Mascota's pride is **La Iglesia de la Preciosa Sangre** *(Church of the Precious Blood)*, started in 1909 but unfinished due to the revolution and the ensuing Cristero Revolt. Note the 3-D blood squirting from Jesus's wound in the neighboring seminary chapel.

On one corner of the plaza is the town's white-spired **Iglesia de la Virgen de los Dolores.**

The **Museo de Mascota** (✉*Calle Allende 15* ☎*388/386–0232*) is also worth a look.

Continued on page 636

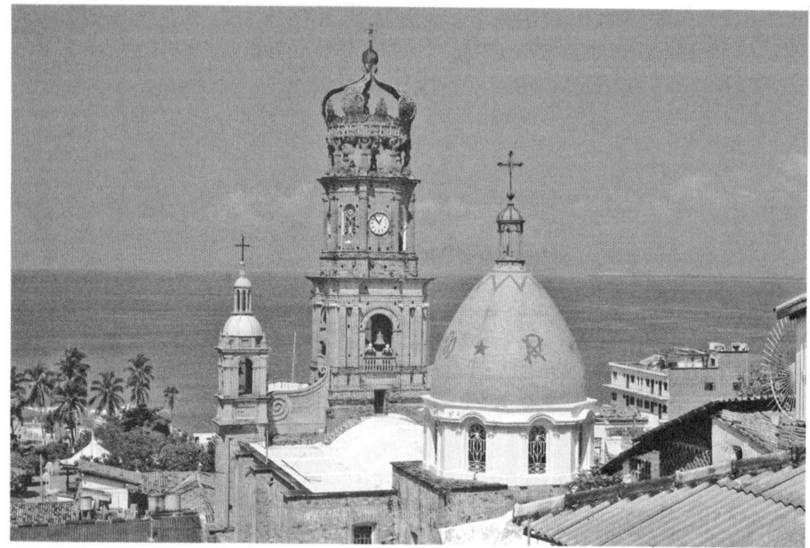

GETTING THE GOODS IN PV

Puerto Vallarta is a shopper's paradise punctuated with hotels and beaches. Masks, pottery, lacquerware, carved-wood animals, hand-dyed woven rugs, Huichol Indian bead art, and embroidered clothing are among the crafts for sale. You can also find great silver; keep in mind that the real stuff carries the designation "0.925." Bottom line? Pack an extra duffle bag or suitcase.

The highest concentration of shops are in Old Vallarta. But specialty stores are now following the construction of hotels north up the bay. More than a half dozen malls line "the airport road," Federico M. Ascencio, which connects downtown with the Hotel Zone, the marina area, Nuevo Vallarta, and towns to the north.

Credit cards are nearly always accepted, and U.S. dollars are almost universally accepted. Prices in shops are theoretically fixed, but bargaining is expected in markets and by beach vendors, who may ask as much as two or three times their bottom line. Then again, they may not; use your best judgment.

Most stores are open Monday through Saturday 10–8. A few close for a two-hour siesta at 1 PM or 2 PM. Many shops close during the low season (August or September through mid-October). We've noted this whenever possible; however, some shops simply close up unexpectedly if things get excruciatingly slow.

Art

★ Fodor's Choice **Gallería Dante** is a 6,000-square-foot gallery (PV's largest) and sculpture garden with classical, contemporary, and abstract works by more than 50 Mexican and American artists.

Galería La Manzanilla has a cadre of more than two dozen fine artists from Mexico, Canada, and the U.S. Their work ranges from photography and portraiture to lovely landscapes and other paintings in various media to pottery and jewelry. It's closed mid-May through mid-October.

Papier-mâché mermaid

You'll find wonderful, varied art in many mediums at **Galería Uno.** National and international artists represented include João Rodriguez, Esaú Andrade, and Daniel Palmer. The owners love to showcase local talent, and individual shows are mounted up to three times a month.

Books & Periodicals

Librería Guadalajara sells magazines and books in English and Spanish, plus a small but respectable selection of educational toys.

Ceramics, Pottery & Tile

The 300 or so potters from the village of Juan Mata Ortiz add their touches to the sometimes-hypnotic geometric designs of their ancestors from Paquimé. The place to peruse this wondrous pottery is **Galería de Ollas.** Pieces range from about \$60 to \$10,000.

Sculpture by Tellosa from Galería Dante

Majolica Antica sells Talavera or tin-glazed pottery. If you purchase, you get a certificate of origin with each piece of beautiful ornamental tile, utilitarian pitcher, plate, or place setting.

Buy machine-made tiles from Monterrey, painted locally, for about 60¢ each at **Mundo de Azulejos.** The handmade tiles (\$1) are slightly sturdier. You can also find mosaic tile scenes (or order your own design), place settings, hand-painted sinks, or any number of soap dishes, cups, plates, and doodads.

★ **Talavera Etc.,** is the exclusive representative of the Uriarte line, the oldest maker of Talavera in Mexico (est. 1805). They sell reproductions of tiles from Puebla churches and made-to-order pieces as well. The shop is closed Sunday, during lunch, and for two weeks in September.

Clothing

La Bohemia is known for elegant clothing, some of it designed by the equally elegant owner, Toody. You'll find unique jewelry, accessories, and the San Miguel shoe—the chic yet comfortable footware designed for walking on cobblestone streets like those of San Miguel and Puerto Vallarta. The store is closed on Sunday.

Caprichoso carries sizes from XS to 2X. This is the only store in PV to stock the Oh My Gauze line of women's resortwear, and also sells Dunes, Juanita Banana, and unusual clothing by Chalí, with cut-out, painted flowers. Most of the inventory is cotton, including a smaller selection of clothing for men.

★ **Mar de Sueños** carries classy Italian threads, including the stylish La Perla brand, as well as silk lingerie and bathing suits. The selection of linen blouses and exquisitely cut linen pants is perfect for PV's sultry climate. Everything is top-notch and priced accordingly. It's closed Sunday.

★ **María de Guadalajara** has inspired jewelry and a fabulous line of women's cotton clothing. It's DIY chic here: you choose the colorful triangular sash of your liking, transforming pretty-but-baggy dresses into flattering and stylish frocks. The color palette is truly inspired.

Painted wood from Lucy's CuCú Cabaña

★ **Ruly's Boutique** has the choicest men's clothing around: nice trousers, shirts, and shorts in a wide selection of handsome yet vibrant colors, as well as accessories, underwear, and hats. The owner designs the clothing sold here and supervises their construction. The color palette and fabrics—blends, linens, cottons, and some synthetics—are superb.

Folk Art & Crafts

Fodor's Choice The American owners of **Banderas Bay**, who also own Daiquiri Dick's restaurant, travel around the country for months in search of antiques, collectibles, handicrafts, and unique household items. The original shop and second location, both of which will pack and ship your purchases, are closed Sunday.

★ **La Hamaca** has a wonderful inventory of folk art and utilitarian handicrafts; each piece is unique. Scoop up masks and pottery from Michoacán, yarn paintings and beaded bowls made by the Huichol, hammocks from the Yucatán, and lacquered boxes from Olinalá, Guerrero.

Shop for inexpensive, one-of-a-kind folk art from Guerrero, Michoacán, Oaxaca, and elsewhere at ★ **Lucy's CuCú Cabana.** Lucy closes during lunch, on Sunday, and in low season (September through mid-October).

Purchase glassware from Jalisco and Guanajuato states at **Mundo de Cristal.** Also available are Talavera place settings and individual platters, pitchers, and decorative pieces. Look in the back for high-quality ceramics with realistic portrayals of fruits and flowers. It's closed Sunday and after 2 PM Saturday.

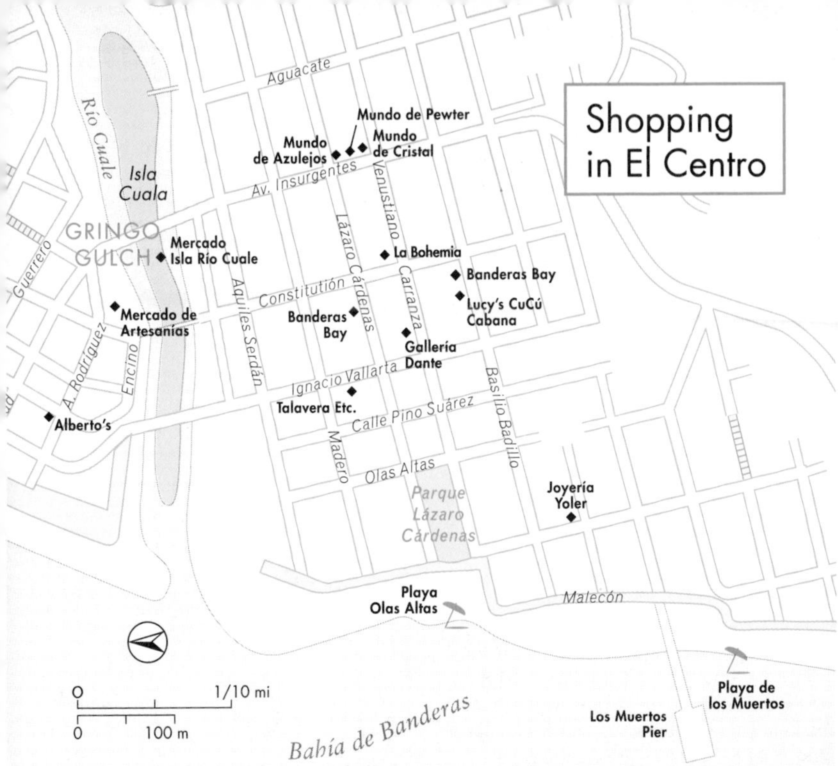

Shopping in El Centro
Aguacate
Río Cuale
Isla Cuala
Mundo de Pewter
Mundo de Azulejos
Mundo de Cristal
Av. Insurgentes
Venustiano
GRINGO GULCH
Mercado Isla Río Cuale
Guerrero
Lázaro Cárdenas
La Bohemia
Banderas Bay
Constitución
Carranza
Lucy's CuCú Cabana
Mercado de Artesanías
Aquiles Serdán
Banderas Bay
Galleria Dante
A. Rodríguez
Encino
Ignacio Vallarta
Basilio Badillo
Talavera Etc.
Calle Pino Suárez
Alberto's
Madero
Olas Altas
Parque Lázaro Cárdenas
Joyería Yoler
Playa Olas Altas
Malecón
0
1/10 mi
0
100 m
Bahía de Banderas
Playa de los Muertos
Los Muertos Pier

Relatives of the owners of Mundo de Cristal and Mundo de Azulejos (⇨ *above*) own **Mundo de Pewter,** which is wedged in between the other two stores. Attractive, lead-free items in modern and traditional designs are sold at reasonable prices. The practical, tarnish-free pieces can go from stovetop or oven to the dining table and be no worse for wear.

Food & Drink

If you crave country-style Texas sausage and other comfort foods from north of the border, try **Agro-Gourmet.** You can find oils (sesame, grapeseed, nut, virgin olive), locally made pastas, homemade spaghetti sauce, lox, real maple syrup, and agave "honey." The Mexican vanilla, in blown-glass containers makes a nice gift for foodies back home.

200
NAYARIT
Bucerías
North Coast
Nuevo Vallarta
Bahía de Banderas
Marina Vallarta
Hotel Zone
El Centro
Conchas Chinas
0
4 miles
0
6 km
South Coast
Los Arcos
Mismaloya
JALISCO
200

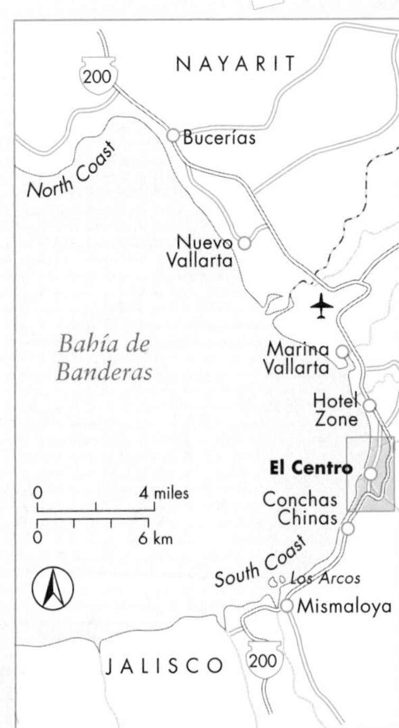

Jewelry

Mexican silver is a good buy in PV, but watch out for *chapa* or *alpaca,* a mix of alloys. Real silver is designated 925 for sterling and 950 for finer pieces.

Spend as little as $5 or as much as $5,000 on anything and everything jade at **Jades Maya.** The shop is open daily until 10 PM in high season. In addition to jewelry made from 20 different colors of jade, there are replicas of ancient Maya masks.

Silver jewelry at **Joyería El Opalo** ranges in price from $3 per gram for simpler pieces to $30 a gram for the finer quality and more complex pieces. Most of the semi-precious stones—amethyst, topaz, malachite, black onyx, and opal in 28 colors—are of Mexican origin. The diamond-cut necklaces are magnificent.

★ **Joyería Yoler** proudly displays its collection of the Los Castillo family's silver jewelry made with lost-wax casting, small silver pitchers with lapis lazuli dragonfly handles, napkin rings, abalone pill boxes, and other lovely utilitarian pieces. The array of silver and semi-precious-stone jewelry is extensive but not overwhelming.

Markets

In the **Mercado de Artesanías,** flowers, piñatas, produce, and plastics share space in indoor and outdoor stands with folk art and lesser-quality crafts. The long-established, family-run restaurants upstairs are local favorites.

Small shops and outdoor market stalls sell an interesting and fun mix of wares at the **Mercado Isla Río Cuale.** Harley-Davidson kerchiefs, Che paintings on velvet, and Madonna icons compete with the usual synthetic lace tablecloths, shell and quartz necklaces, and silver jewelry. A half dozen cafés and restaurants provide sustenance.

ART

Gallería Dante (✉ Calle Basilio Badillo 269, Col. E. Zapata ☎ 322/222–2477).

Galería La Manzanilla (✉ Calle Playa Perula 83, La Manzanilla ☎ 315/351–7099 🌐 www.artinmexico.com).

Galería Uno (✉ Calle Morelos 561, Centro ☎ 322/222–0908).

BOOKS & PERIODICALS

Librería Guadalajara (✉ Plaza Genovesa, Av. Federico M. Ascencio s/n ☎ 322/224–9084).

CERAMICS, POTTERY & TILE

Galería de Ollas (✉ Calle Corona 176, Centro ☎ 322/223–1045).

Majolica Antica (✉ Calle Corona 191, Centro ☎ 322/222–5118).

Mundo de Azulejos (✉ Av. Venustiano Carranza 374, Col. E. Zapata ☎ 322/222–2675 🌐 www.talavera-tile.com).

Talavera Etc. (✉ Av. Ignacio L. Vallarta 266, Col. E. Zapata ☎ 322/222–4100).

CLOTHING

La Bohemia (✉ Calle Constitución, at Calle Basilio Badillo, Col. E. Zapata ☎ 322/222–3164 ✉ Plaza Neptuno, Av. Federico M. Ascencio, Km 7.5, Marina Vallarta ☎ 322/221–2160).

Caprichoso (✉ Plaza Neptuno, Av. Federico M. Ascencio, Km 7.5, Marina Vallarta ☎ 322/221–3067).

Mar de Sueños (✉ Calle Basilio Badillo 277-B, Col. E. Zapata ☎ 322/222–7362).

María de Guadalajara (✉ Puesta del Sol condominiums, Local 15–A, Marina, Marina Vallarta ☎ 322/221–2566 ✉ Calle Morelos 550, Centro ☎ 322/222–2387).

Ruly's Boutique (✉ Paradise Plaza, Local 10, Paseo de los Cocoteros 85 Sur, Nuevo Vallarta ☎ 322/297–1724).

FOLK ART & CRAFTS

Banderas Bay (✉ Lázaro Cárdenas 263, Col. E. Zapata ☎ 322/223–4352 ✉ Constitución 319A, Col. E. Zapata, ☎ 322/223–9871).

La Hamaca (✉ Calle Revolución 110, Sayulita ☎ 329/291–3039).

Lucy's CuCú Cabana (✉ Calle Basilio Badillo 259, Col. E. Zapata ☎ 322/222–1220).

Mundo de Cristal (✉ Av. Insurgentes 333, at Calle Basilio Badillo, Col. E. Zapata ☎ 322/222–1426).

Mundo de Pewter (✉ Av. Venustiano Carranza 358, Col. E. Zapata ☎ 322/222–0503 🌐 www.mundodepewter.com).

FOOD & DRINK

AgroGourmet (✉ Calle Róbalo 79, Corral del Risco, Punta de Mita ☎ 329/291–6721).

JEWELRY

Jades Maya (✉ Leona Vicario 226-A, Col. Centro ☎ 322/222–0371 🌐 www.jadesmaya.com).

Joyería El Opalo (✉ Local 13-A, Plaza Genovesa, Col. Las Glorias ☎ 322/224–6584).

Joyería Yoler (✉ Calle Olas Altas 391, Col. E. Zapata ☎ 322/222–8713 or 322/222–9051).

MARKETS

Mercado de Artesanías (✉ Calle Francisca Rodríguez, between Calles Matamoros and Miramar, at the base of the bridge ☎ No phone).

Mercado Isla Río Cuale (✉ Dividing El Centro from Colonia E. Zapata: access at Calle Morelos (Calle I. Vallarta), Calle Matamoros (Calle Constitución), and Calle Libertad (Av. Insurgentes ☎ No phone).

Tile from Talavera Etc.

WHERE TO STAY

$$ **Rancho La Esmeralda.** Catering to small groups and father-and-son outings, this ranch-style lodging near the entrance to town also accepts individual travelers. All interiors are pinewoods simple, with wood ceiling beams and tile roofs, and plain wood furnishings. The villas have kitchens, most have a porch and fireplace; many sport a king-size bed. This working ranch offers horse riding and rents bicycles and ATVs. Because most business is Guadalajarans on weekends, midweek prices are discounted 30%. **Pros:** Newer construction, fireplaces and king beds, substantial midweek discount. **Cons:** 10-minute drive from town center, bumpy cobblestone entry road. ✉ *Calle Salvador Chavez 47* ☎ *388/386–0953* 🌐 *www.rancholaesmeralda.com.mx* *8 rooms, 6 cabins* *In room: Kitchen (some), refrigerator (some), Wi-Fi. In-hotel: Restaurant (weekends and holidays only), public Wi-Fi, parking (no fee)* *MC, V.*

$ ★ **Mesón de Santa Elena.** Beautiful rooms in this converted 19th-century house have lovely old tile floors, huge windows, and wonderful tiled sinks. Second-floor rooms have views of fields and mountains to the west. **Pros:** Two blocks from the town square, feels like you're a guest in someone's home, Internet café about a block away. **Cons:** Internet intermittent in some rooms, feels like you're a guest in someone's home. ✉ *Hidalgo 155* ☎ *388/386–0313* 🌐 *www.mesondesantaelena.com* *10 rooms, 2 suites* *In-room: No a/c, no phone, no TV. In-hotel: Restaurant (breakfast only), public Wi-Fi, public Internet, no elevator* *No credit cards* *AI, BP, EP.*

> **DAY TRIPPIN'**
>
> **Vallarta Adventures** (☎ *322/297–1212* 🌐 *www.vallarta-adventures.com*) has excellent day tours to these two towns and to Talpa de Allende (a favorite pilgrimage site). The small-plane ride is a wonderful photo op and aerial introduction to the Sierra Madre. From Puerto Vallarta (on a good day), it's a two-hour drive to San Sebastián and 2½ to 3 hours to Mascota. TIP→ **Do not drive these roads after dark.**

MANZANILLO

Updated by Carissa Bluestone

256 km (159 mi) south of Puerto Vallarta via Hwy. 200; 332 km (206 mi) southwest of Guadalajara via the Guadalajara-Colima autopista (toll road).

Manzanillo is the Pacific Coast's strangest resort city. The *Bahías Gemelas* (twin bays)—separated by a huge burl of craggy rocks and lush foliage—offer beaches of black-and-gold volcanic sand, so it ought to be a tourist's dream come true, times two. There's certainly no denying the fantastic quality of its fanciest resorts, nor the quirky cool that permeates some of its out-of-the-way places. But Manzanillo is mostly preoccupied with its other job—that of a working port—so shopping is uneventful, cultural sights are few, and tourism-related building seems to only happen in fits and starts.

Thanks to its geography, Manzanillo feels more like three towns than one. The beautiful Peninsula de Santiago is covered with wealthy enclaves—epitomized by the anachronistic Moorish mini-city of Las Hadas resort—and is worlds away from the tightly packed, bustling downtown where there's nary a gringo in sight. The connective thread between the two is one long stretch of gold sand paralleled by a traffic-clogged road that is alternatively too built-up (if you need an Office Max or Home Depot, have no fear) and seemingly in decline.

With some lovely beaches and a minimum of faux-Mexicana, Manzanillo certainly does have its appeal. But perhaps the best way to enjoy the city is to not be too tied down to it. Along Highway 200 are dozens of low-key beaches easily toured using the city as a base.

GETTING HERE & AROUND

Aeropuerto Internacional Playa de Oro is 32 km (20 mi), or 40 minutes, north of town. Taxis from the airport charge about $40; the shared vans that run to the major resorts are less expensive. First-class and executive-class buses connect Manzanillo's Central Nueva station with other Pacific Coast cities, Guadalajara, and Mexico City. Driving from Guadalajara is a snap on the excellent four-lane toll road (54D), though not much faster than the scenic backcountry route on Highway 80 (via Barra). The trip from Puerto Vallarta on Highway 200 is slightly rough in patches but also very scenic. Having a car is a plus since the city is extremely spread out. Cabs are unmetered and are easy to hail on the streets. Agree on a price beforehand. The minimum fare is a little less than $2.

ESSENTIALS

Bus Contacts **Elite/Estrella Blanca** (☎ *01800/507–5500 toll-free in Mexico, 314/336–7617* 🌐 *www.estrellablanca.com.mx*). **ETN** (☎ *01800/800–0386 toll-free in Mexico, 314/334–1050 in Santiago* 🌐 *www.etn.com.mx*).

Medical Assistance **General Emergencies** (☎ *066 or 060*). **HELP! Manzanillo Foreign Community Assn.** (✉ *Apartado Postal 65, La Villa de Los Pichones, Santiago* ☎📠 *314/334–0977* 🌐 *www.mexicohelp.com*). **Hospital de Manzanillo** (✉ *Blvd. Miguel de la Madrid 444* ☎ *314/336–7272*). **Police/Tourism Police** (☎ *314/332–1004*). **Red Cross** (☎ *314/336–5770*).

Visitor & Tour Info **Colima State Tourism Office** (✉ *Blvd. Costero Miguel de la Madrid 875A, next to Hotel Caracol, Zona Hotelera* ☎ *314/333–3838* 🌐 *www.visitcolima.com.mx*). **Municipal Tourism Office** (✉ *Av. Juárez 100 in Municipal Palace, Centro, Manzanillo* ☎ *314/332–6238*). **Viajes Hectours** (✉ *Blvd. Miguel de la Madrid, Km 15, Zona Hotelera* ☎ *314/333–1707* 🌐 *www.hectours.com*).

EXPLORING

Manzanillo is a practical city geared to function rather than form. The downtown waterfront area isn't so ho-hum anymore, thanks to a face-lift along the malecón (the centerpiece of which is a huge turquoise statue of a leaping sailfish by Chihuahua sculptor Sebastián) and increased cruise-ship travel, but it's not so attractive you'll want to linger there for hours. Most of the services and restaurants used by travelers are strung along the Boulevard Miguel de la Madrid with little sense of connection or community. But to get to know the city's nonresort side, you can stroll the surrounding business district, which is crisscrossed with streets that are safe to explore.

> **LOOKS DECEIVE**
>
> Although it hasn't the look of a colonial city, Manzanillo was founded soon after the Spanish conquest. Hernán Cortés envisioned it as a gateway to the Orient: from these shores Spanish galleons brought in the riches of Cathay to be trekked across the continent to Veracruz, where they filled vessels headed for Spain. But other ports received coveted, exclusive concessions, and Manzanillo was little developed in the colonial period.

Downtown has a few sights, but the beach is the main attraction in Manzanillo, and the prettiest are the rocky coves that cluster at the foot of the Santiago Peninsula, which separates the bays and towns of Bahía de Santiago and Bahía de Manzanillo, and provides the multitiered vistas for Manzanillo's most luxurious resorts. Usually, when visitors decide to leave their hotel's beachfront, they join organized tours or fishing expeditions, or head out of town on their own to explore small beach hamlets like Barra de Navidad or colonial towns like Colima.

Just north of downtown, the **Museo Universitario Arqueológico** is back in business after completing major renovations to repair the damage of a 2003 earthquake. The museum displays thousands of artifacts, which come from the immediate region, along with temporary exhibits from local artists. ✉*San Pedrito traffic circle, Centro* ☎*314/332–2256* *$1* *Tues.–Sat. 10–2 and 5–8, Sun. 10–1.*

At the beginning of the harbor, Carretera 200 jogs around downtown and intersects with Carretera 110 to Colima. Avenida Morelos leads past the shipyards and into town. The zócalo, known as **Jardín de Alvaro Obregón,** is right on the main road by the waterfront. It's sunstruck and shadeless during the day, but can be quite lively in the cool of the evening. A collection of restaurants and bars whip up quick meals and stiff drinks. Streets leading away from the plaza have ice cream and shops selling souvenirs.

BEACHES

★ **Playa la Audiencia.** On the west side of the Península de Santiago, below the Gran Costa Real Resort & Spa and between two rock outcroppings, Playa la Audiencia is small but inviting, with calm water (though be on the lookout for riptides and a steep drop-off) and shade umbrellas for hotel guests and those who order drinks or snacks. Depórtes Aquaticos el Pacifico rents Boogie boards, kayaks, and Jet Skis and has equipment for waterskiing, snorkeling, and diving. Although much of Manzanillo's waters do not have good visibility, this is a good spot for snorkeling, and with its shallow depth and slow current it has several

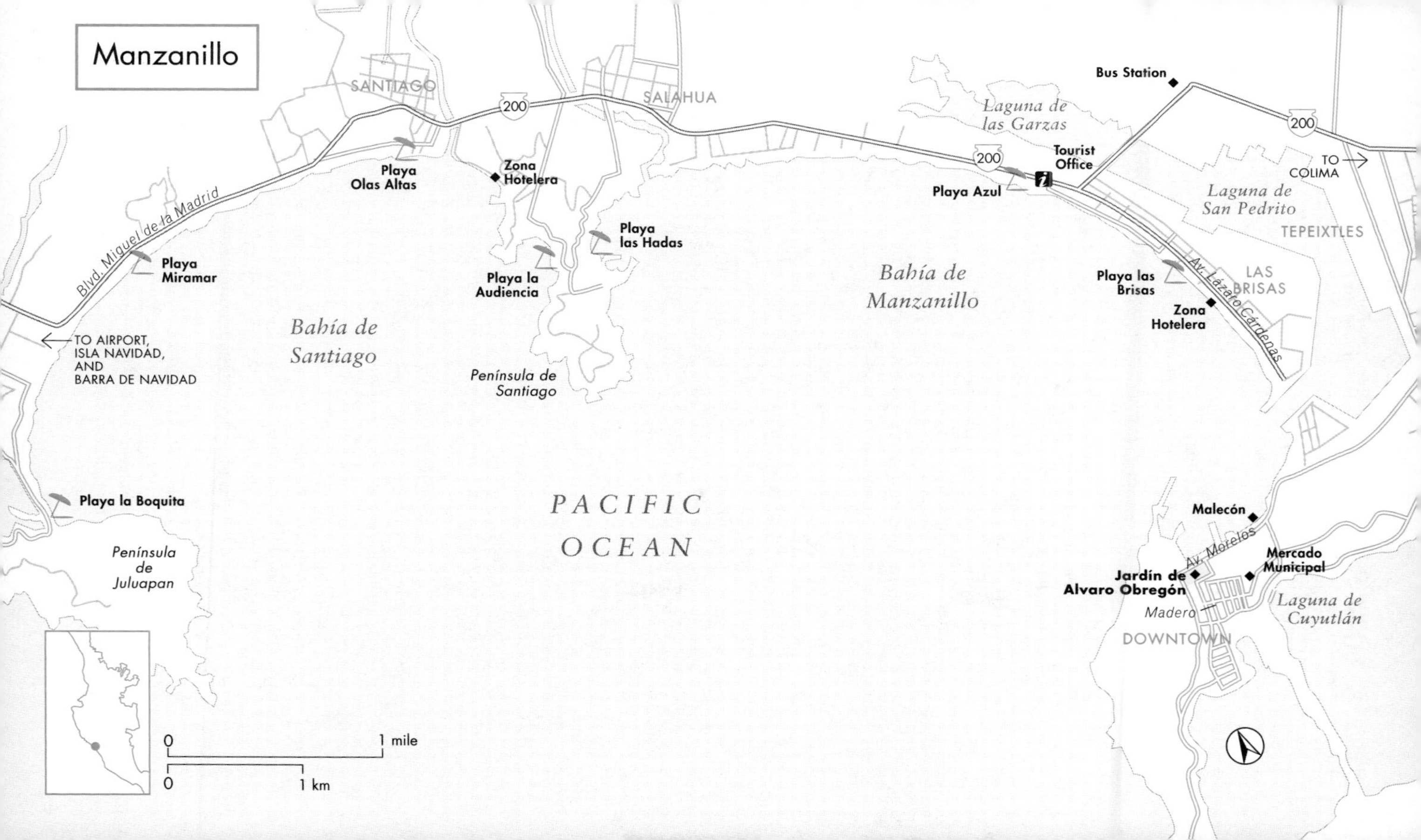
Manzanillo
SANTIAGO
SALAHUA
200
Bus Station
Laguna de las Garzas
Tourist Office
TO COLIMA
Laguna de San Pedrito
TEPEIXTLES
Playa Olas Altas
Zona Hotelera
Playa Azul
Blvd. Miguel de la Madrid
Playa las Hadas
Playa Miramar
Playa la Audiencia
Bahía de Manzanillo
Playa las Brisas
Av. Lázaro Cárdenas
LAS BRISAS
Zona Hotelera
TO AIRPORT, ISLA NAVIDAD, AND BARRA DE NAVIDAD
Bahía de Santiago
Península de Santiago
Playa la Boquita
PACIFIC OCEAN
Malecón
Av. Morelos
Península de Juluapan
Mercado Municipal
Jardín de Alvaro Obregón
Laguna de Cuyutlán
Madero
DOWNTOWN
0
1 mile
0
1 km

good dive spots as well. The cove got its name because local Indians supposedly granted Spanish conquistador Hernán Cortés an audience here. It can get very crowded on weekends and holidays.

Playa la Boquita. A little corner of serenity at the far west end of Bahía de Santiago, this beach offers basic and inexpensive amenities. Sit in the shade of a palm-frond palapa and order seafood or iced coconuts from the informal restaurants. You can rent water toys from vendors on the sand. The calm, waveless water is Manzanillo's safest for kids, perfect for swimming and snorkeling, and an offshore wreck is a good spot for diving. The beach in front of Club Santiago, once the favored hangout for locals, is now accessible only by walking north along the sands from the highway or through the club gates. There's no fee to enter; just stop and let the guard write down your car's license number if you're driving.

PARTYING DAYS & NIGHTS

Manzanillo's biggest local festivals are in the early days of May and December. Fiesta de Mayo begins near the end of April, runs for two weeks, and concludes around May 10. Events include art exhibits, parades, concerts, native dances, and a carnival. Fiesta de Guadalupe celebrates the city's religious patron, the Virgin of Guadalupe, from December 1 through 12. It also has parades and costumed native dancers, as well as tributes to the Virgin.

Playa las Brisas. Long, wide, and often empty, this is a wonderful place to stroll. Swimming is more problematic: although the waves are not generally big, they tend to crash right on the beach. At the south end are most of the modest hotels that make up Manzanillo's Zona Hotelera. An artificial rock jetty divides Playa las Brisas from the boat harbor and creates a place to snorkel, although the water tends to be murky this close to the harbor and the waves that surge against the rocks can surprise. Although this is basically one 6-km-long (4-mi-long) stretch of brown sand, it technically becomes Playa Azul and then Playa Salahua at the bay's west end, just before the Hotel Karmina Palace.

Playa las Hadas. This secluded, nearly private man-made beach is just a tiny crescent of sand on the opposite side of Península de Santiago from the Playa la Audiencia. Framed at both ends by rocks, it's a good snorkeling spot. Expensive restaurants at both Las Hadas and the nearby Karmina Palace serve drinks, snacks, and full meals. Deportes Aquáticos el Pacificio rents Jet Skis and kayaks; it also arranges dive and snorkel trips. Nonguests of the hotels pay $27 per person for use of the beach, pool, and facilities; this fee is credited toward consumption of food or drink at the snack bar or restaurants, which makes it slightly more palatable. You can see the beach from the top of the cobblestone road that leads to the resort's main entrance; take a look to make sure it's your idea of paradise before shelling out the fee.

Playa Miramar. Local families like to enjoy their weekends at Miramar, a long, brown arc of sand that means "Look at the Sea." They camp out for the day in front of beachfront palapa restaurants and rent shade umbrellas and lounge chairs. There are water-sports outfitters and horses for hire, though such concessions are scarce midweek in the off-season. Vendors sell jewelry and beachwear from stalls. Although the waves are a little stronger than at Playa la Boquita, this is still a good spot for swimming.

Playa Olas Altas. Although it's also called Playa de Oro, this beach's alternative name, which means "high waves," is more appropriate. That's what draws the surfers and Boogie-boarders to this comparatively empty stretch between the hotel zone in Playa Santiago and the popular Playa Miramar. They don't mind the lack of services found at more popular stretches.

SUNSET SIGHTINGS

If you're visiting in cetacean season, come to L'Recif at 5 PM, when the restaurant opens, to watch for whales and hope for a glorious sunset.

WHERE TO EAT

$$$–$$$$ ITALIAN ✕ **Legazpi.** Maroon-and-white-stripe cushions adorn dark-wood chairs and banquettes, brass lamps hold thick white candles, and wide windows afford dramatic bay views. The menu is Italian, with an emphasis on Mediterranean dishes. Be sure to check out the cozy bar, where there's a mural depicting the history of Manzanillo. Some claim the food's not worth the high price, despite the dining room's charm. ✉ *Las Hadas Hotel, Av. De los Riscos and Av. Vista Hermosa, Fracc. Península de Santiago* ☎ *314/331–0101 Ext. 3512* ▭ *AE, MC, V* ⊙ *No lunch.*

$–$$$ SEAFOOD ✕ **El Bigotes.** Waitresses in funky meter maid–style hats serve good seafood to canned music and the rhythm of waves at this unpretentious restaurant. Specialties include the Jalisco favorite *pescado sarandeado* (barbecued fish), *camerón mustache* (butterflied shrimp breaded in shredded coconut), and gigantic portions of ceviche. When in doubt, ask for half portions; servers are also flexible about substituting french fries or beans for rice. A smaller branch has the same great food but fewer specials. ✉ *Calle Puesta del Sol 3, Playa Azul* ☎ *314/333–1236* ✉ *Blvd. Miguel de la Madrid 3157, Zona Hotelera* ☎ *314/334–0831* ▭ *MC, V.*

$–$$$ CONTINENTAL ★ ✕ **L'Recif.** Waves crash on the rocks below this lovely cliff-top spot a 15-minute drive from Manzanillo's Zona Hotelera toward Playa la Boquita. There's a little of everything on the menu—seafood, pasta, chicken, beef—but the signature dish is the camerón L'Recif (shrimp stuffed with cheese, wrapped in bacon, and broiled); it's served with mango sauce and sides of mashed potatoes and sautéed corn, zucchini, and carrots. ✉ *Cerro del Cenicero s/n, El Naranjo, Condominio Vida del Mar, Península de Juluapán* ☎ *314/335–0900* ▭ *MC, V* ⊙ *Closed Easter–Oct. No lunch.*

$–$$$ ECLECTIC ✕ **Toscana.** Reviews are good again for this longtime Manzanillo favorite, which has recovered from a stretch of inconsistency in its food and service. Specialties on the eclectic menu include seafood shish kebab served with rice and steamed vegetables, a three-lettuce salad with goat cheese, and a Caesar salad. For dessert, try the tiramisu. Most of the tables sit on the simple outdoor terrace overlooking the beach. People start using the dance floor nightly after 8:30 PM. ✉ *Blvd. Costero Miguel de la Madrid 3177, Zona Hotelera* ☎ *314/333–2515* ▭ *MC, V* ⊙ *No lunch.*

¢–$ AMERICAN ✕ **Juanito's.** Juanito's has been owned by an American since 1976, and the evidence is obvious everywhere from the menu (which includes burgers, milk shakes, fries, barbecued ribs, and fried chicken) to the quick service to the U.S. sporting events on the big-screen TV. But the place has been enthusiastically embraced by the locals, who crowd in every morning for breakfast and stay late into the evening to watch *telenovelas* when there's no game on. The menu features a full range of Mexican food, too, and there are Internet-connected computers, fax machines, and long-distance telephones for rent in the back. ✉ *Blvd. Costero, Km 14, Olas Altas* ☎ *314/333–1388* ✍ *Reservations not accepted* ▭ *AE, MC, V.*

CHAT 'N' CHEW

Check your e-mail or surf the Web for $2.50 per hour on the on-site computer at Juanito's Restaurant; there's also copy, fax, and long-distance phone service.

¢ CAFÉ ✕ **Café Costeno.** A serene tropical garden lies behind the unremarkable facade of this coffee bar on the busy road into the Las Brisas hotel zone. The long list of caffeinated options are Big American Franchise quality at about half the price. It opens at 8 AM for breakfast, which ranges from the healthy (fruit-granola-yogurt combos) to the hearty (chilaquiles). Come back later for the desserts, which span the good (carrot cake), the bad (ice cream), and the wicked (*tres leches* cake). You can score a beer, too. ✉ *Av. Lázaro Cárdenas 1613* ☎ *314/333–9460* ✍ *Reservations not accepted* ▭ *No credit cards.*

WHERE TO STAY

You've got to pick your spots along the two sweeping bays of Manzanillo. Lots of people never leave the grand resorts on the Santiago Peninsula—and don't miss much. But you can secure comfortable waterfront accommodations in a pair of secondary Zonas Hoteleras (hotel zones)—Santiago and Las Brisas. More economical options can be found east along Manzanillo Bay, among a string of hotels on such quiet beaches as Playa Azul and Playa las Brisas. Backed by the Laguna de San Pedrito (San Pedrito Lagoon), this stretch is great for long walks on the beach. However, give the rooms a look before you check in for sure.

$$$$ **Barceló Karmina Palace.** Manzanillo's all-inclusive, all-suites hotel is a short walk from neighboring Las Hadas resort. Cascades, fountains, and multitier lagoons punctuate the grounds, and there's a beautiful palapa restaurant at the ocean's edge. Each junior suite has marble floors, a balcony or terrace, a sofa bed, and a large tub with separate shower facilities. Corner suites have two bedrooms, a bath, a kitchen, and a dining room as well as a balcony with a plunge pool. **Pros:** Lots of space, especially in pool area, many activities for kids, rooms are spacious and quiet. **Cons:** Small restaurant selection for an all-inclusive, lots of families with small kids, beach isn't great for swimming. ✉ *Av. Vista Hermosa 13, Fracc. Península de Santiago,* ☎ *314/334–1313, 888/234–6222 in*

U.S. and Canada *@www.barcelo-karminapalace.com* *324 suites* *In-room: Safe, refrigerator, Wi-Fi (some). In-hotel: 4 restaurants, room service, bars, pools, gym, spa, beachfront, water sports, concierge, children's programs (ages 4–12), laundry service, public Internet, public Wi-Fi, parking (no fee), no-smoking rooms* *AE, MC, V* *AI.*

WORD OF MOUTH

Las Hadas is a lavish retreat built in 1974 by Bolivian tin magnate Antenor Patiño. For a while it and its exclusive clientele were better known than Manzanillo itself.

12

$$$ ★ **Las Hadas Golf & Marina.** The undulating roofs of the Moorish-style buildings glow pink in the afternoon heat, giving an almost hallucinogenic quality to the 15 acres of lacy palms, stylized geometric hedges, flamboyant orange-flowering trees, and white umbrellas on a small but virtually private beach. Las Hadas brought the upscale tourist industry to Manzanillo in the 1970s, when Bo Derek cavorted on its grounds and nearby beaches in the movie *10*. It's not as exclusive as it once was, but it still more than holds its own against the hotels that have followed it to Peninsula Santiago. White-on-white room decoration (even the TVs are white) is elegant and understated; polished marble, fine sheets, and plush towels appear in both standard rooms and suites. The Legazpi restaurant is one of the city's most exclusive. **Pros:** Pretty, semi-private beach, unique design and location, quiet. **Cons:** Starting to show its age in places, understaffed, limited on-site dining options disappoint some all-inclusive customers. *Av. Vista Hermosa s/n and Av. de los Riscos, Fracc. Península de Santiago,* *314/331–0101, 888/559–4329 in U.S. and Canada* *www.brisas.com.mx* *102 rooms, 132 suites* *In-room: Safe, DVD (some), Ethernet. In-hotel: 3 restaurants, room service, bars, golf course, tennis courts, pools, gym, beachfront, diving, water sports, concierge, public Wi-Fi, public Internet, parking (no fee), no-smoking rooms* *AE, MC, V* *EP, AI.*

$$$ **Tesoro Resort & Spa.** For a white-stucco link in a big hotel chain, this resort manages to exude some real personality. The pretty rooms, dizzying activities, and sweet location on La Audiencia beach get the personal touch from people who really seem to like their jobs. The poolside snack bar doubles as a midnight disco; before that, hit the predictable floor show or the lounge, where the piano man sings corny-but-cool Mexican and American standards. All rooms have balconies, but not all have views. Take a look before you bring up the luggage. **Pros:** Beachfront and good activities desk, fun floor shows, great play area for kids. **Cons:** Pool area gets crowded, lackluster restaurants, rooms and some common areas get stuffy. *Av. Audiencia 1, Playa la Audiencia,* *314/333–2000 in U.S.* *www.tesororesorts.com* *289 rooms, 42 suites* *In-room: Safe, refrigerator. In-hotel: 4 restaurants, room service, bars, tennis courts, pool, gym, spa, beachfront, concierge, children's programs (ages 4–12), laundry service, parking (no fee), no-smoking rooms, public Wi-Fi, public Internet* *AE, D, MC, V* *AI, EP.*

$$ **La Posada.** Only one of the famous old iron keys and antique locks remain—they just weren't working anymore—but the special, simple

vibe that permeates this bright-pink beachfront lodging is as sweet as ever. Young hoteliers Lisa and Juan Martinez bought La Posada in 2003, and they've very carefully applied their personal touch to a place that has been a favorite with North Americans since 1957. Rooms have been renovated without losing their kitsch. Same with the large, open-air living-dining-bar area, with its rustic-color walls and *equipale* (pigskin and wood) furnishings. There's 24-hour e-mail access, an honor-system beer and soda bar, and a real sense of community among staff and guests, around the pool and over the complimentary morning breakfast. Only a few rooms have balconies, but all have screened windows. **Pros:** Good value, great staff, beachfront (though not a good swimming beach). **Cons:** Far from swimming beaches, street it's on is unattractive (ask for water view), service might be too informal for some. ✉*Av. Lázaro Cardenas 201, Zona Hotelera, Playa las Brisas,* ☎*314/333–1899* 🌐*www.hotel-la-posada.info* *23 rooms* *In-room: No a/c (some), no phone, kitchen (some), no TV. In-hotel: Bar, pool, beachfront, parking (no fee), public Internet* ▭*MC, V* *BP.*

SIP OF THE PAST

Bar Social has been downtown Manzanillo's main watering hole since 1941, owing to its location at Calle Juarez 101—just across the street from city hall. A circular bar surrounds a huge pedestal in the center of a high-ceiling room whirling with fans, its walls lined with several tables and upholstered booths, and its windows covered in Venetian blinds. An old, red cash register rings up the cheap beers. *Botanas* (plates of tortilla chips with assorted dips) are served free through the afternoon and a pianist plays most evenings.

¢ **Hotel Colonial.** The classic appeal of this four-story, central hotel—frequently used in Mexican movies since its construction in 1944—extends from the stained-glass windows to the intricate curlicues of its brown woodwork to the tarnished little bell that sits on the receptionist's desk. Rooms are small but comfortable and periodically include such architectural surprises as a split-level bathroom. The only downer is the artificial turf in the central courtyard. It's only a block from the waterfront zócalo, and Wi-Fi usually works in the restaurant. **Pros:** Cheap rates, close to local restaurants and shops, away from resort scene, clean and reliable. **Cons:** Very far from beaches, in a busy area, no frills. ✉*Calle Bocanegra 28, at Av. Mexico,* ☎*314/332–1080* *40 rooms* *In-room: Wi-Fi (some). In-hotel: Restaurant, room service, bar, laundry service, public Wi-Fi, parking (no fee), some pets allowed, no elevator* ▭*MC, V.*

NIGHTLIFE

Bar de Félix (✉*Blvd. Miguel de la Madrid 805, Zona Hotelera* ☎*314/333–9277*) is a large bar with crimson faux-velvet settees; a dance floor for Latin tunes, Spanish rock, some American oldies, and electronica; and a giant-screen TV. It's dark on Monday. People of all ages enjoy a night out at the lively **Colima Bay Café** (✉*Blvd. Costero*

921, Fracc. Playa Azul ☎*314/333–1150*), with its whimsical decor, jazzy background music, and variety of seating options—including pigskin barstools.

SHOPPING

Shopping in Manzanillo leaves much to be desired—namely decent shops. Most hotels offer a small selection of folk art and beachwear, and there are souvenir shops around the main square and in Plaza Manzanillo, a shopping center on the coast road between Santiago and Manzanillo. The main market, **Mercado Municipal,** is downtown at Cuauhtémoc and Independencia. The newest shopping center is **Plaza Salagua,** with a Soriana department store and other shops. It's on Boulevard Miguel de la Madrid. Most shops are closed 2–4; many are open Sunday 10–2.

The **Centro Artesenal las Primaveras** (⊠*Av. Juárez 40, Santiago* ☎*314/333–0173*) has a large assortment of handicrafts of so-so quality.

SPORTS & THE OUTDOORS

FISHING

Manzanillo claims to be the world's sailfish capital; the season runs from mid-October through March. The International Sailfish Tournament takes place during the last half of November, and there's another in early February (☎314/333–2770). Blue marlin and dorado are also abundant. Sportfishing boats are available at major hotels and through tour agencies. Contact **Ocean Pacific Adventures** (☎📠*314/335–0605*) to charter a 26-foot boat (one to five people) for $225, or a 40-foot cruiser (1 to 10 people) for $275. Both tours last five hours and include a fishing license and a case each of beer and soda as well as the usual ice, bait, and tackle. A super deal allows fisherpersons and their families to eat their catch, along with side dishes, free at Colima Bay Café or Sunset Lounge, paying for drinks only.

GOLF

★ Robert Von Hagge mapped out the impressive 27-hole **Isla Navidad** (⊠*Paseo Country Club s/n* ☎*315/355–6439* 🌐*www.islanavidad.com*) course in the Grand Bay resort complex, about an hour north of Manzanillo. The expansive clubhouse has a pro shop where you can arrange lessons and a restaurant-bar as well as men's and women's locker rooms with steam, sauna, and whirlpools. Greens fees are $230 for 18 holes, including cart. Caddies are mandatory and charge $30.

La Mantarraya (⊠*Av. De los Riscos and Av. Vista Hermosa, Fracc. Península de Santiago* ☎*314/331–0101*), the 18-hole golf course at Las Hadas hotel, designed by Roy Dye, offers club rentals and caddies. The greens fee is $160, plus $45 for the cart.

WATER SPORTS

Except when the water is rough, the rocky points off Manzanillo's peninsulas and coves make for good snorkeling and scuba diving. You can rent snorkel and scuba gear as well as kayaks, Boogie boards, and Jet Skis at **Deportes Aquáticos el Pacifico** (✉ *Av. Audiencia s/n, Playa las Hadas, Península de Santiago* ☎ *314/331–0101 Ext. 3804* ✉ *Playa la Audiencia, Península de Santiago* ☎ *314/333–1848*).

Underworld Scuba (✉ *Blvd. Miguel de la Madrid, Km 15, near Juanito's restaurant, Santiago* ☎ *314/333–3678*) offers many services. The English-speaking instructors give resort classes and full PADI certification; offer single-day or multiday dive and hotel-dive packages; and rent snorkel and diving equipment.

SIDE TRIP FROM MANZANILLO

COLIMA

98 km (61 mi) northeast of Manzanillo.

Colima, the capital of the eponymous state, is about an hour from Manzanillo via an excellent toll road that continues on to Guadalajara.

EXPLORING

An easygoing provincial city, Colima is most famous for the pre-Hispanic "Colima dog" figurines, which originated in this region and are on display—along with other archaeological pieces—at the **Museo de las Culturas del Occidente** (*[Museum of Western Cultures]* ✉ *Casa de la Cultura, Calz. Galván and Av. del Ejército Nacional* ☎ *312/313–0608 Ext. 15*). It's open Tuesday–Sunday 9–6:30, and admission is $1.50.

The **Museo Universitario de Culturas Populares** (*[University Museum of Popular Culture]* ✉ *Calles Gabino Barreda and Manuel Gallardo* ☎ *312/312–6869*) has pre-Hispanic and contemporary Indian costumes, masks, instruments, and other artifacts. Entry to the museum, which is open Tuesday–Saturday 10–2 and 5–8 and Sunday 10–1, is $1; admission is free on Sunday.

■ TIP→ **The town of Comala, a 15-minute ride north of Colima, is noted for hand-carved furniture and ironwork, and for the charming cafés to which Colima residents flock on holidays and weekends.**

WHERE TO STAY

$$$$ **Hacienda de San Antonio.** If you have to ask the price per night, you probably can't afford it. This stunning hacienda was built as the home of 19th-century German immigrant Arnold Vogel on his 5,000-acre coffee plantation. It was completely refurbished in the 1970s. Palatial rooms have 15-foot beamed ceilings and blend European and American appointments with Mexican handicrafts. Have lunch by the enormous pool, drinks around the fire in the library, and dinner in the courtyard or the dining room. If you're lucky, there will be a nighttime pyrotechnic display by nearby Volcán de Fuego. **Pros:** Good for a romantic getaway, gorgeous setting, excellent meals. **Cons:** Very pricey for the area, twin rooms lack many of the amenities offered in the king rooms. ✉ *San*

Antonio, ☎866/376–7831 in U.S. 🌐www.epoquehotels.com ⇨22 rooms, 3 suites ♿In-room: No a/c, safe (some), Wi-Fi (some). In-hotel: Restaurant, room service, bar, pool, concierge, laundry service, airport shuttle, parking (no fee), public Wi-Fi. ▭AE, MC, V 🍽BP.

12

BARRA DE NAVIDAD

55 km (34 mi) northwest of Manzanillo.

Barra, as the locals call this cobblestoned town perched on a sandbar, isn't the secret it used to be. Periodic flurries of Mexican tourists and a steady trickle of laid-back surfers have been joined by a well-heeled crowd drawn year-round to the luxurious Grand Bay Hotel. But the town somehow handles the traffic, absorbing all who come into its hypnotically easy pace. You really can't take a false step here. Everything can be explored within a few blocks and the choices are few, simple, and without a downside: do a little shopping in family-owned stores on the two main streets, catch a little beach time (waves on the northern ocean beach, no waves on the southern lagoon), and watch the sunset over seafood and a cold beverage. At low tide you can walk along the beach from Barra north to San Patricio Melaque, a distance of about 6 km (4 mi). The key to the easygoing atmosphere is the people, most of them longtime residents, who make this a real town.

Barra is ideally situated between Manzanillo and some beautiful, relatively undeveloped stretches of coast along Highway 200; the only reason more people don't use it as a base for exploring the area is its current lack of midrange accommodations—you either splurge on the Grand Bay Hotel or stay in fairly basic posadas.

Several local tour operators arrange mountain-biking trips, tours of coconut plantations, and day trips to Colima and Cuyutlan. **Sea to Sierra** (✉*Av. Veracruz 204, across the street from the zócalo* ☎*315/355–5790* 🌐*www.seatosierra.com*) is a locally owned, reputable outfitter that offers biking, snorkeling, sportfishing, and horseback-riding tours.

GETTING HERE & AROUND

The closest airport to Barra is Manzanillo's, about 30 minutes away. Barra is easily reached by car via Highway 200. There is a small ETN bus station that connects the town to Puerto Vallarta, Manzanillo, Guadalajara, and many smaller towns along the Pacific Coast. A car is necessary if you intend to explore the area; major rental agencies keep offices in Manzanillo and at the airport. Barra has two ATMs and several Internet cafés.

WHERE TO EAT

$–$$$ SEAFOOD ✕**Mariscos Nacho.** The hand-painted sign declares the cook EL REY DEL PESCADO ASADO (the king of barbecued fish), just in case you couldn't tell from the smoky aroma. People also come to this beachfront family restaurant for delicious breakfasts and strong, wonderful *cafe de olla* (Mexican coffee). If the service seems on the slow side, just ask yourself: what's the rush in Barra? ✉*Calle Legazpi 100* ☎*315/355–5138* ▭*No credit cards.*

¢–$$ ECLECTIC ✕**Los Arcos de Jalisco.** This crossroads of Barra, its walls covered with old photos and its shelves lined with books, is a great place to start your day or wind down an afternoon. Breakfasts focus on Mexican specialties, but you can find basic bacon and eggs as well. Same with lunch, where the chef offers pozole or burgers and fries. Service is fast and friendly, the place is spotless, and did you notice the bar? Yep, what'll it be? ✉*Calle Legazpi 170* ☎*No phone* ▭*No credit cards.*

¢–$ MEXICAN ✕**Mexico Lindo.** Don't let the presence of so many gringos scare you away from this delightful Mexican restaurant—a lot of them are expats who know a thing or two about Barra's restaurants. Head through the narrow entryway to the semi-enclosed courtyard where plants surround the handful of tables that face the bustling open kitchen. The menu is long—you'll find every permutation of quesadilla, enchilada, sope, burrito, and tamale plus salads and fresh fish tacos. Arrachera (skirt steak) and pork in its many incarnations are recommended if you can't figure out which meat to use as a base. ✉*Calle Legazpi 138-A* ☎*No phone* ▭*No credit cards.*

WHERE TO STAY

$$$$ **Grand Bay.** Although actually on a 1,200-acre peninsula between the Pacific Ocean and the Navidad Lagoon, this luxurious yet lonely resort across the bay from Barra de Navidad is more like an island unto itself. It occupies 10 floors replete with Spanish arches, shady patios, cool fountains, and lush gardens, ending with white hammocks strung between the palm trees lining the beach. Tiered swimming pools are connected by slides and waterfalls. There's even a movie theater. If all this indulgence becomes too much, an inexpensive water taxi can take you over to the real world, two minutes away. **Pros:** Only luxury lodging in Barra, excellent service, beautiful rooms and grounds. **Cons:** Need to take water taxi to Barra, very pricey for the area (and lots of added service charges), beachfront is unimpressive. ✉*Isla Navidad,* ☎*315/331–0500 or 877/999–3223* 🌐*www.wyndham.com* *158 rooms, 40 suites* *In-room: Safe, refrigerator, kitchen (some), Wi-Fi, Ethernet. In-hotel: 4 restaurants, room service, bars, golf course, tennis courts, pools, gym, spa, water sports, concierge, public Wi-Fi, public Internet, laundry service, airport shuttle, parking (no fee), no-smoking rooms* ▭*AE, DC, MC, V.*

¢ **Hotel Delfin.** The rooms at this cheerful hotel are very basic and a little dated, but what the hotel lacks in luxury it makes up for in the warmth of its staff and beauty of its common areas, which include a small garden and pool on the ground floor and a roof deck with lounge chairs and panoramic views of Barra, the lagoon, and coconut plantations in the distance. Wide terraces on each floor are lined with cushioned, shaded lounge chairs—request a room on the top floor for the best views. A pair of two-bedroom apartments with fully equipped kitchens can accommodate larger groups or longer stays for $130 a night. A simple breakfast is served daily in the garden. The hotel is a few blocks from the beach. **Pros:** Great roof deck, good value, wonderful hosts, free Wi-Fi, secure parking. **Cons:** Could use new beds (might be too soft for some), rooms get some noise from a local bar (though it's usually quiet by 10 or 11), no elevator. ✉*Calle More-*

los 23, ☎315/355–5068 🌐www.hoteldelfinmx.com 24 rooms, 2 apartments In-room: Kitchen (some), refrigerator (some), no a/c, no TV. In-hotel: Gym, pool, parking (no fee), public Wi-Fi, no elevator ▭MC, V BP.

¢ **Trivento.** With modern rooms as insistently plain as they are impeccably clean, this family operation a couple of blocks from the beach offers reliable accommodations close to restaurants and shops. Most rooms face a pleasant inner courtyard that has palm trees and other greenery and a few white plastic chairs for lounging. A few rooms have balconies overlooking the street, but the Trivento is a low-rise building, so you don't get much of a view. Rooms are motel simple, but they have kitchenettes and a few nice touches like new pedestal sinks in the bathroom. **Pros:** Quieter and newer than Hotel Delfin, pleasant central courtyard, great value. **Cons:** No pool, no extras like Wi-Fi, small bathrooms. *✉Calle Jalisco 75, ☎315/355–7068 🌐www.hoteltrivento.com 22 rooms In-room: Kitchen, refrigerator, no phone. In-hotel: No elevator ▭MC, V.*

12

IXTAPA & ZIHUATANEJO

Updated by Carissa Bluestone

390 km (242 mi) south o f Manzanillo via Hwy. 200, 200 km (124 mi) north of Acapulco via Hwy. 200.

Although they couldn't be more different, Ixtapa (eesh-*tah*-pa) and Zihuatanejo (zee-wha-ta-*NEH*-ho) are marketed together as a single resort destination, and both have gorgeous bays and beaches. Zihua, as it's often called, was a remote fishing village with minimal tourist traffic for hundreds of years. Ixtapa was created in the 1970s when Mexico's National Fund for Tourism Development (FONOTUR) cleared away a coconut plantation. Though both are still very laid-back, they have attracted so much attention (and building) that "purists" are now heading 25 minutes north to the surfing enclave of Troncones or 35 minutes south to the more low-key fishing village of Barra de Potosi.

Although Ixtapa is quite pleasant, and self-sufficient in terms of services, its designers were unable to give it a heart and soul. A pretty marina with a few upscale seafood restaurants at the northern end of town is the only "attraction"; other than that Ixtapa is simply a long line of beachfront resorts. Many visitors head 7 km (4 mi) south to enjoy the more authentic ambience of Zihua. There are plenty of beachfront hotels, and the cluster of pedestrian-only streets close to the marina is very touristy. That said, tourism hasn't completely destroyed Zihua's small-town essence—it's the friendliest of the Pacific Coast's major resort areas.

GETTING HERE & AROUND

Aeropuerto de Zihuatanejo is 12 km (8 mi) southeast of Zihua. Private cab fares range from $22 to $29. The bus station is in Zihua, with service to Manzanillo (8–9 hours), Acapulco (7 hours), Morelia (3½ hours), and Mexico City (7 hours). Driving south from Manzanillo on Carretera 200 is a gorgeous seven-hour trip that twists along mostly undeveloped coast. The four-hour Zihua–Acapulco leg on Carretera 200 passes through small towns and coconut groves. Minibuses run every 10–15 minutes between the Ixtapa hotels and downtown Zihua until 10 PM; the fare is about 50¢. Cabs (unmetered) are easy to hail on the street in Zihua; the fare to Ixtapa is $4–$5. In town, a car only comes in handy if you plan to take day trips, as cab fares can be expensive (as much as $25 one way to Troncones from Ixtapa's resorts).

ESSENTIALS

Bus Contacts **Estrella Blanca** (✉ *Office in Centro Comercial Los Patios, Ixtapa* ☎ *755/554–3474*).**Estrella de Oro** (✉ *Ticket office in Plaza Ixpamar, Ixtapa* ☎ *755/554–2175*).

Medical Assistance **Hospital General de Zihuatanejo** (✉ *Av. Morelos s/n, at Mar Egeo, Zihuatanejo* ☎ *755/554–3965*). **Police** (☎ *755/554–2040*). **Red Cross** (☎ *755/554–2009*). **Tourist Police** (☎ *755/554–2207*).

Visitor & Tour Info **Guerrero State Tourism Office** (✉ *Paseo de las Golondrinas 1-A, Blvd. Ixtapa s/n, Ixtapa* ☎ *755/553–1967*). **Oficina de Convenciones y Visitantes** (*[Convention and Visitors' Bureau]* ✉ *Paseo de las Gaviotas 12, Ixtapa* ☎ *755/553–1570* 🌐 *www.visit-ixtapa-zihuatanejo.org*).

EXPLORING

Ixtapa's primary hotel zone, la Zona Hotelera, extends along a 3-km (2-mi) strip of sandy beach called Playa del Palmar. It's fun to walk along the shore to check out the various hotel scenes and water-sports activities. Swimming is so-so because of how the small waves break close to shore. You can walk the length of the same zone on the landward side of the hotels, along Paseo Ixtapa. This landscaped thoroughfare—essentially, Ixtapa's only main street—is an access road that feeds the hotels on one side and strip malls filled with restaurants on the other. It's nicely landscaped and includes a broad path for pedestrians and cyclists. The Zona Hotelera's southerly end is also home to the 18-hole Palma Real Golf Club; at the resort's northwest end is the anemic Marina Ixtapa development.

Everything in Zihuatenejo radiates out from the main beach. Although this stretch of sand is not the place for swimming, it's the best place to get a sense of the timeless local rhythm. Fishermen still set off in outboard-motorized skiffs and return a few hours later to sell their catch right there on the beach. A few blocks down, companies on and around the municipal pier, or *muelle*, take tourists on half- or full-day fishing adventures of their own, or on a 10-minute trip across the bay to one of the best swimming and snorkeling beaches, Playa las Gatas. The pier also marks the beginning of the Paseo del Pescador (Fishermen's Walk), or malecón. Follow this seaside path, only a third of a mile long, along the main beach which is fronted by small restaurants and shops. Along the way you'll pass the basketball court that doubles as the town square.

The malecón ends at the **Museo Arqueológico de la Costa Grande** (✉ *Paseo del Pescador 7 at Plaza Olof Palme* ☎ *755/554–7552*), a gray stone building identified with a wooden shingle. A permanent display of pre-

Hispanic murals, maps, and archaeological pieces trace the history of the so-called Costa Grande (Grand Coast) through the colonial era. It's open Monday–Saturday 10–6; admission is $1. Beyond the museum, a footpath cut into the rocks leads to Playa la Madera.

BEACHES

IXTAPA

Fodor's Choice ★ **Isla Ixtapa.** The most popular spot on Isla Ixtapa (and the one closest to the boat dock) is Playa Cuachalalate. An excellent swimming beach, it was named for a local tree whose bark has been used as a remedy for kidney ailments since ancient times. A short walk across the island, Playa Varadero hugs a rocky cove. Guides recommend snorkeling here, but watch for coral-covered rocks on both sides of the cove. Just behind is Playa Coral, whose calmer, crystal-clear water is more conducive to swimming. Each of the above beaches is lined with seafood eateries eager to rent snorkel equipment. Playa Carey, toward the island's south end, is small and has no services. Pangas (skiffs; $4 round-trip) run between the boat landings at both Cuachalalate and Varadero beaches and Playa Linda on the mainland, where you'll find a few all-inclusive, high-rise hotels.

Playa del Palmar. Ixtapa's main beach, this broad, 3-km-long (2-mi-long) stretch of soft brown sand runs along the Zona Hotelera. Although you can swim here, small waves break right onshore and currents are sometimes strong. Each hotel offers shaded seating on the sand. Concessions rent Jet Skis ($40 per half hour), Hobie Cats ($50 per day) and arrange banana-boat rides (15 minutes costs $5 per passenger with a four-person minimum) and parasail trips ($25 for a little more than 10 minutes). Licensed guides in white uniforms cruise up and down selling horseback-riding and boating tours. Women offer hair braiding and massage under open-sided tents.

Playa Linda. Thatch-roof restaurants dispense beer, soda, and the catch of the day just north of the Qualton Inn, in the Zona Hotelera II. Mexican families favor this long, coconut-palm-lined beach, which has beautiful views, is perfect for walking, and is bordered at one end by an estuary with birds and gators. You can rent horses (about half as much here as on Playa Ixtapa or from area tour operators), and a warren of identical stalls sells souvenirs and cheap plastic beach toys. Concessions arrange banana-boat rides and rent Jet Skis and Boogie boards. Water taxis depart here for Isla Ixtapa, and land taxis wait in the free parking lot for fares.

Playa Quieta. Club Med occupies the south end of tranquil Playa Quieta; the rest of the lovely cove is empty except for a cluster of tables and chairs that picnicking families rent for the day for a small fee, and the equally unobtrusive Restaurant Neptuno, which sells reasonably priced seafood all week.

WORD OF MOUTH

"Ixtapa is a beautiful beach resort—not as big as Cancún—and Zihuatanejo is a very charming fishing village just a few miles from Ixtapa. The night life is great, and the weather is perfect." –ponchotj

ZIHUATANEJO

★ **Playa las Gatas.** Legend has it that a Tarascan king (from an indigenous, pre-Hispanic community) built the breakwater on Playa las Gatas to create a sheltered area for his daughter's exclusive use. Named for the *gatas* (cat-whiskered nurse sharks) that once lingered here, this beach is bordered by a long row of hewn rocks that create a breakwater. Snorkelers scope out the rocky coves, and surfers spring to life with the arrival of small but fun summer swells. The beach is lined with simple seafood eateries that provide lounge chairs for sunning, as well as kayak and snorkeling-gear rentals, and guiding services. (You really can't go wrong with any of the concessionaires, but La Red del Pescador, at the far end of the beach, has the most attractive setup with the hippest music; ask for Cruz if you need a kayak guide.) Overlooking the beach is *El Faro* (the lighthouse); the view from the top is marvelous but the safe path up can be hard to find—ask any of the waiters to point it out. You can reach Playa las Gatas in about 20 minutes by climbing over the rocks that separate it from Playa la Ropa. But it's much more common and convenient to take one of the skiffs that run from the municipal pier every 10 or 15 minutes between 8 AM and a half hour before sunset. Buy your round-trip ticket (about $4) on the pier, and keep the stub for your return trip.

GIDDYUP!

Most area tour operators arrange guided horseback excursions on Playa Linda and Playa del Palmar. Costs are high ($35–$40 for roughly 1½ hours), but they include transportation and usually a soft drink or beer after the ride.

Playa la Madera. This is a small, flat, dark-sand beach with a sprinkling of restaurants on the sand (which provide just about the only shade, and facilities) and a few more hotels on or just above it. Bobbing boats and the green headlands make for beautiful vistas. Waves are small or nonexistent, and as there's no drop-off it's a great place for the kiddies. Young locals always seem to be kicking a soccer ball around. Get there via a footpath cut into the rocks that separate it from Playa Principal, in downtown Zihua, or by car.

Playa Principal. The less-than-pristine water (water taxis and fishing boats hang out here) may keep you on the sand, but there's plenty going on. Check out the haggling over fish prices, settle into an umbrella-shaded chair with a cool drink and fresh seafood, or shop at makeshift stalls for trinkets and treasures, but save the bulk of your beach-going time for other shores.

Fodor's Choice ★ **Playa la Ropa.** Playa La Ropa (Clothing Beach) apparently got its name hundreds of years ago when a textile-laden ship spilled its silks, which washed up on the sand. The area's most beautiful beach is a 20-minute walk from Playa la Madera and a five-minute taxi ride from town. Parasailers drift above the 1-km (½-mi) stretch of soft light sand; below, concessionaires rent Jet Skis ($40 for 30 minutes) and Hobie Cats (up to $50 an hour, depending on the size). Up and down the beach are open-air restaurants—some with hammocks for post-meal siestas—and a handful of hotels. Kids can splash in the calm, aquamarine water or toss a ball or Frisbee on the shore—but not too close to the little stream

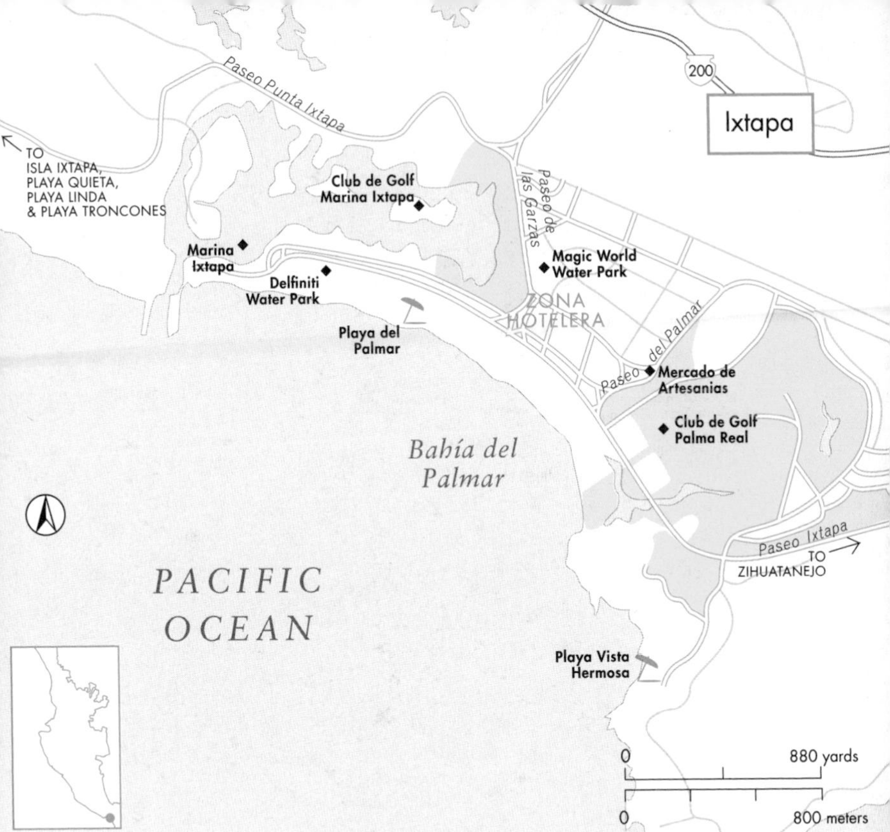

that empties into the southerly end: it's a crocodile refuge! There's free parking in a lot at the south end of the beach.

WHERE TO EAT

IXTAPA

$$$–$$$$ ITALIAN ★ ✕ **Beccofino.** This small, marina-side dining room and cozy bar has been a popular high-season hangout since 1992. Dark polished woods contrast with bright white linens, and bottles of wine are shelved on walls painted with trompe-l'oeil scenes. A canopy-sheltered deck overlooks the marina. Among the best dishes on the northern Italian menu are minestrone soup, *caprese* salad (with tomatoes, basil, and mozzarella), fish fillet (usually red snapper or mahimahi) with a champagne sauce, and chicken cacciatore. Many of the pastas are made in-house, and breakfast is available after 9:30 AM. Enjoy the personalized attention of the owner and all-around excellent service. ✉ *Plaza Marina Ixtapa* ☎ *755/553–1770* ✍ *Reservations essential* ▭ *AE, MC, V.*

$–$$$ MEXICAN ✕ **Casa Morelos.** The wooden bar, ocher walls, and handcrafted furnishings make this tiny restaurant seem like a true cantina, although it's in the middle of a shopping center. Patio tables are more elegant at night than during the day, with potted trees dressed in little white lights and

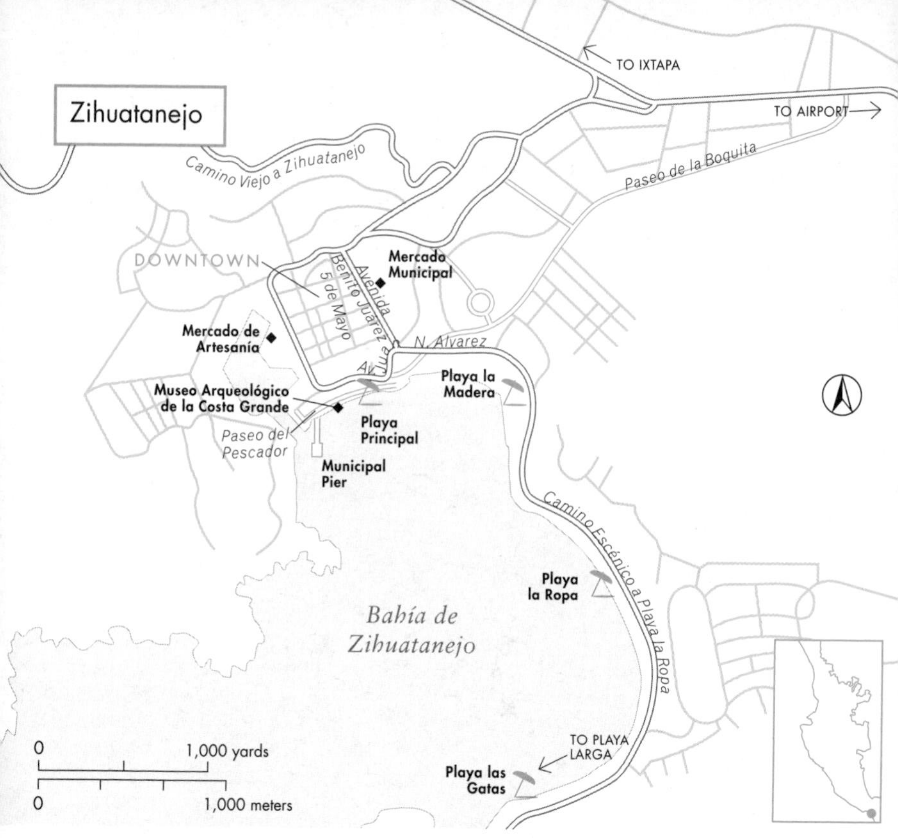

lively tropical music at a level that doesn't drown out conversation. The chiles rellenos de camarón (egg-battered peppers stuffed with shrimp), fajitas, and tuna steak topped with three kinds of chiles are all filling and delicious. Or come early for a generous breakfast; the restaurant opens at 7:30 AM. ✉ *La Puerta shopping center, Blvd. Ixtapa s/n* ☎ *755/553–0578* 💳 *AE, MC, V.*

¢–$ CAFÉ ✕ **Nueva Zelanda.** Although it's open all day, this sparkling little coffee shop is best known for its breakfasts, which some say are the best in town. This branch opened after the success of the original eatery in downtown Zihuatanejo—and it's both more polished and more endearing. Sit at the counter, at the varnished wood tables with six swivel chairs, or in the tiny booths. Options include fresh fruit juices, coconut milk shakes, banana splits, omelets, enchiladas, salads, soup, and *tortas* (sandwiches on large, crusty rolls). ✉ *Centro Comercial El Kiosko, behind bandstand, Blvd. Ixtapa s/n* ☎ *755/553–0838* ✍ *Reservations not accepted* 💳 *No credit cards.*

¢–$ AMERICAN ✕ **Ruben's.** The delicious scent of grilling meats will entrance you from blocks away. Latin music blares from the jukebox inside, so after sundown most clients dine at the white plastic tables on the grassy front yard. The charcoal-grilled burgers, which are made of top sirloin, and the french fries, deep-fried zucchini, and baked potatoes are true-to-the-source American treats. For dessert try the grilled bananas glazed with cinnamon and sugar and served with a dollop of fresh cream. ✉ *Centro Comercial Flamboyant, next to Bancomer bank, Blvd. Ixtapa s/n* ☎ *755/553–0027 or 755/553–0358* ▭ *No credit cards.*

LONG LEGS

To see pink flamingos and other wading birds, head for Barra de Potosí (20–25 minutes south of the airport), where a beautiful *laguna* (lagoon) is an unofficial bird sanctuary. You can go on a tour or take a bus or taxi—you'll pay less for the latter, and you'll be able to linger at one of the casual restaurants lining the beach. Or, hire a fisherman's boat from Zihuatanejo's municipal pier or Playa La Ropa for a trip to the scenic, remote Playa Manzanillo, which is great for snorkeling.

ZIHUATANEJO

$$$–$$$$ ECLECTIC ★ ✕ **Kau-Kan.** When was the last time you enjoyed a plate of stingray in black butter sauce? This unimposing restaurant encases the heart of Zihuatenejo's most deliciously inventive cuisine. Owner-chef Ricardo Rodriguez, who worked in Paris before returning to Mexico, applies deft Mexican and Mediterranean touches to seafood dishes in a beachcomber atmosphere overlooking the bay. The melt-in-your-mouth abalone and exquisite grilled mahimahi under a sweet, spicy pineapple sauce are popular choices, but the house specialty remains *patata rellena*—potatoes stuffed with shrimp and lobster in a fresh basil-and-garlic sauce. ✉ *Carretera Escénica, Lote 7 en route to Playa la Ropa* ☎ *755/554–8446* ▭ *AE, MC, V* ⊙ *Closed last 2 wks of Sept. No lunch.*

$$$ MEXICAN ✕ **Casa Elvira.** This institution is right on the malecón, just a few steps from the fish market. It's not fancy, but the walls radiate bright orange, and a courtyard fountain splashes in a minor key. The staff is helpful yet unobtrusive, and the food habitually good. The fare consists of Mexican dishes and such simple seafood plates as fish steamed in foil and served with rice and french fries. Lobster is a specialty, though it and the well-loved seafood platter will push your tab into the $$$$ category. ✉ *Paseo del Pescador 32* ☎ *755/554–2061* ▭ *MC, V* ⊙ *Closed Tues.*

$$$ SEAFOOD ✕ **Rossy's.** Waterside dining doesn't get any purer than at this spot in the midst of several beachfront eateries. The extensive menu covers all the typical favorites—ceviches, shrimp dishes, and fish fillets served with rice and steamed vegetables. Make a feast of it and choose the mixed-grill selection, which feeds three. For dessert, indulge in the crispy fried bananas served with a scoop of coconut ice cream or bathed in cinnamon-laced cream. Walk it off with a stroll along the sand. The people-watching is great, whether they're wearing swimsuits or business suits. ✉ *South end of Playa la Ropa* ☎ *755/554–4004* ▭ *MC, V.*

$$–$$$ CONTINENTAL ★ ✕ **Coconuts.** Eat at the horseshoe-shape bar—especially if you happen to be by yourself—or out under the sky. Restored by owner Patricia Cumming's architect husband, Zihua's oldest house has a gorgeous patio open to the stars and surrounded by zillions of tiny white lights. The kitchen is consistent: try the roast pork loin, the sweet and zesty coconut shrimp, or one of the vegetarian offerings. Five different dessert coffees are prepared flaming at your table. In the evening a keyboarder or romantic duo playing bossa nova or jazz is sure to entertain.

⊠*Pasaje Agustín Ramírez 1* ☎*755/554–2518* ▭*AE, DC, MC, V* ⊙*Closed June–mid-Oct.*

$$–$$$ SEAFOOD ✕**La Perla.** The slightly more-formal take on the typical toes-in-the-sand dining experience is evident in the fact this popular spot on Playa la Ropa accepts credit cards. Among the seafood specialties here are *filete* La Perla (fish fillet baked with cheese); lobster *thermidor*; and yummy fish or shrimp tacos made with homemade flour or corn tortillas and served with guacamole. There's a nice wine list and Havana cigars for after dinner. And, in fact, you don't have to get your feet wet or sandy at all; you can sit in the palapa-covered restaurant under the trees or take a stool at the corner bar, where there's always a game on satellite TV. But plenty of customers just sit on the beach and sip a drink. ⊠*Playa la Ropa* ☎*755/554–2700* ▭*AE, MC, V.*

¢–$ SEAFOOD ✕**Café America.** This small outdoor café is perfect for soaking up the boho vibe on a walking street lined with shops, small hotels, and huge potted plants. None of its hearty Mexican breakfasts costs more than $4. The lunch menu revolves around seafood plates and appetizers (try the *tiritas,* small strips of raw fish swimming in lime and onion) that don't top $5. Dinner is all about steak and lobster. There's an adjacent bar and rooms to rent upstairs. ⊠*Calle H. Galeana 16* ☎*755/554–4337* ▭*No credit cards.*

¢–$ MEXICAN ✕**Doña Licha.** Come for the authentic Mexican dining experience. Stay for the televised soccer game or beauty pageant. Traditional dishes include barbecued ribs, goat stew, tripe, and—on Thursday as Guerrero State tradition dictates—pozole. The long list of daily specials might include pork chops, tacos, and enchiladas—all come with a drink and either rice or soup. On the extensive regular menu are seafood and breakfast items. ⊠*Calle de los Cocos 8, Centro* ☎*755/554–3933* ▭*No credit cards* ⊙*No dinner.*

¢–$ MEXICAN ★ ✕**Tamales y Atoles Any.** The equivalent of a "soul food" restaurant for Los Guerrerense (the people of Guerrero state), this noisy, fun spot a few blocks from the beach specializes in the traditional cuisine of the deep countryside. Tamales—16 different kinds—are the menu's most popular items. Ingredients ranging from pork and chicken to poblano peppers and squash blossoms are wrapped in *masa,* drenched in rich sauces and baked in corn husks or banana leaves. Pozole, a pork-and-hominy stew that is traditionally eaten on Thursday, is a specialty of the house. There's also a restaurant in Ixtapa at Centro Comercial los Arcos in front of the kiosk. Breakfast is served daily at the downtown Zihua location (in Ixtapa, daily except Sunday). ⊠*Calle Vicente Guerrero 38, at Calle Ejido* ☎*755/554–7373* ▭*MC, V.*

WHERE TO STAY

IXTAPA

Ixtapa is great for getting sticker shock, especially during December and in mid-March, but winter vacationers can get some great deals at its priciest resorts in January after the New Year and most weeks in February. It definitely pays to see what deals sites like Expedia are offering and to get a price quote directly from the hotel to see if they're offering better prices than their Web site might imply. Ixtapa has several gated communities with condo and villa rentals; a good place to start is *www.paradise-properties.com.mx*.

$$$$ **Barceló.** Once you get past its dull exterior, this high-rise turns out to be bright and lively. There's a subdued elegance to its marble-floored lobby and an irresistible cheerfulness to the skylighted inner courtyard—filled with a restaurant and shops—where long vines hang from the balconies of the surrounding rooms. The rooms are nothing special but they are clean and comfortable; most have small balconies with ocean views (be sure to request one and opt for a higher floor to avoid noise from the pool area). The focus is on the outdoors, from the beautiful pool and beach to a sprawling list of recreational options, all facilitated by a helpful staff. There's a quality live show six nights a week and the hotel's Sanca Bar draws a nice crowd for dancing to Latin music. **Pros:** Convenient to other hotels and restaurants, very social, lots of amenities and activities, good service. **Cons:** Rooms need updating, very busy, restaurants aren't spectacular. *Blvd. Ixtapa s/n, 755/555–2000 or 800/227–2356 www.barcelo.com 341 rooms, 5 suites In-room: safe, refrigerator. In-hotel: 4 restaurants, room service, bars, tennis courts, pools, gym, spa, beachfront, concierge, children's programs (ages 5–12), laundry service, parking (no fee), no-smoking rooms, public Wi-Fi, public Internet MC, V AI.*

$$$–$$$$ ★ **Las Brisas Ixtapa.** The balconies of this pyramid-shape resort are reason enough to stay here—sunbathe or sip cocktails from a deck chair during the day and stargaze from your hammock at night (junior-suite balconies also have hot tubs). Las Brisas is at the secluded southern end of Ixtapa away from the main strip, so there's nothing but blue water to gaze at. The resort is built into a hill and has a bit of an awkward layout (it's kind of hike from the main building to the pool complex), but who needs gardens to stroll through when you're on the best stretch of beach in Ixtapa? Recent refurbishments have turned the rooms into the most attractive and modern looking of Ixtapa's resorts. Standard rooms have low ceilings and are a little narrow, but they have heavenly pillow-top beds and small sitting nooks with comfy window-seat-like couches. **Pros:** Great balconies and views, great beachfront, recently remodeled (July 2007), away from the hodgepodge of hotels on the main strip. **Cons:** Lobby area is cavernous and not that inviting, amenities and on-site restaurants are very expensive, not within walking distance of main strip ($4 cab ride away). *Playa Vista Hermosa, 755/553–2121 or 888/559–4329 www.brisas.com.mx 390 rooms, 26 suites In-room: Safe, refrigerator, Wi-Fi. In-hotel: 6 restaurants, room service, bars, pools, gym, beachfront, concierge, laundry service, public Internet, parking (no fee), no-smoking rooms AE, MC, V EP.*

$$–$$$ **Emporio Ixtapa.** Furnishings are an adroit mix of rustic and modern in this midsize, 11-story resort. Rooms are simple but bright, done in mostly white with a few earth-tone accents (be sure to ask for one that's been recently updated). Junior suites have views from both the living room and the bedroom. There aren't any private balconies, but windows that reach nearly from the floor to the ceiling open to the sea breezes. A children's pool with a slide lures kids away from the

palm-shaded main pool, which has a swim-up bar. **Pros:** Calmer than the megaresorts on strip, good value, good spa services. **Cons:** Not all rooms have ocean views, some rooms need to be updated, mediocre restaurants (avoid the all-inclusive plan). ✉*Blvd. Ixtapa s/n,* ☎*755/553–1066 or 866/936–7674* 🌐*www.hotelesemporio.com* *197 rooms, 23 suites* *In-room: Safe, DVD (some), Wi-Fi (some). In-hotel: 3 restaurants, room service, bars, tennis courts, pools, gym, spa, parking (no fee), public Internet, public Wi-Fi, laundry service, no-smoking rooms* 💳*AE, MC, V* *AI, BP.*

CHOICES!

Zihua's singular hotels and gentle pace make for a more authentic Mexican experience. Ixtapa's brand-name resorts and compact hotel zone add up to a more predictable—some might say reassuring—vacation.

TRONCONES

This once-primitive surf spot along the rugged coast is still pretty remote, but a series of very comfortable—in some cases, luxurious—hostelries have sprung up along the road that traces the waterfront. Thankfully, most of these accommodations try to adapt themselves to the gorgeous environment, rather than the other way around. The focus is on the beautiful beaches and lush foliage. There is no high-end shopping district and most of the restaurants are in the hotels.

$$ **Casa Ki.** Each bungalow at this homey haven in the wilds of Troncones has a patio with hammocks, table, and chairs. There's also a house (for $185 a night), with a full kitchen, two bedrooms, two baths, and a long porch looking right onto the sand and waves. All guests have access to a communal kitchen and dining room, as well as barbecue facilities. **Pros:** Cute, colorful bungalows, pleasant beachfront, nice grounds. **Cons:** Three-night minimum stay required, a little overpriced, no a/c in most rooms, which can get stuffy, not many services. ✉*Playa Troncones* *A.P. 405, Zihuatanejo 40880* ☎*755/553–2815* 🌐*www.casa-ki.com* *3 bungalows, 1 house* *In-room: No a/c (some), no phone, Wi-Fi, refrigerator, no TV. In-hotel: Restaurant, beachfront, laundry service, parking (no fee), public Wi-Fi* 💳*No credit cards* *BP, EP.*

$$ ★ **Hacienda Eden.** Gorgeous views of Manzanillo Bay, a beach that has both a nice point break and calmer areas for swimming, and large, cheerful rooms have earned Hacienda Eden a loyal following. The property, which is surrounded by palm trees and gardens, has a two-story house with ocean-view rooms and hammock-filled terraces; one-room ocean-facing bungalows with patios; and newer air-conditioned suites that can accommodate families. Throughout you'll see beamed ceilings, Talavera tile details, and splashes of purple, yellow, and turquoise. The restaurant is one of the best on the beach. **Pros:** Nice beach that is good for swimming, great restaurant, great hosts. **Cons:** Only a few of the suites have a/c and fridges, place books up far in advance, oddly enough, they are closed during peak surfing season. ✉*Camino de la Playa s/n,* ☎*755/553–2802* 🌐*www.edenmex.com* *6 rooms,*

4 suites, 4 bungalows In room: No a/c (some), no phone, no TV, Wi-Fi. In-hotel: Restaurant, bar, beachfront, public Wi-Fi No credit cards Closed May–Nov.

$$ **Inn at Manzanillo Bay.** On a prime surfing point, the inn attracts surfers who are sick of roughing it. Accommodations are small bungalows thatched in palm, with screened windows and mosquito nets over the beds; built-in couches are outside the sliding-wooden doors. A communal eating area is overseen by a chef trained at the California Culinary Academy, who whips up burritos, burgers, and more complex Asian-Mexican fare. A small shop rents snorkel, surf, and Boogie-board gear and arranges fishing and surfing expeditions. Rooms are discounted 20% during surfing season (June to November). **Pros:** Faces a popular point break and has on-site board rentals, beach bum atmosphere without being too rustic, nice pool. **Cons:** Overpriced, some readers have complained about rude staff, strict cancellation policies. *Camino de la Playa s/n, 40880 755/553–2884 www.manzanillobay.com 10 rooms In-room: Safe. In-hotel: 2 restaurants, bar, pool, parking (no fee), public Wi-Fi MC, V EP.*

ZIHUATANEJO

$$$$ **Amuleto.** Local architect Enrique Zozaya has created an unlikely rustic luxury with this five-suite boutique hotel nestled almost undetectably into the hills above Bahía Zihuatenejo. It's as if Gilligan won the lottery. An open-air palapa suite is surrounded by four air-conditioned units, all of them exquisitely appointed with furnishings and decorations of elemental stone, ceramic, and wood. Each room has a small infinity plunge pool if you're not in the mood for the communal pool. The emphasis on tranquillity prohibits intrusive technology; there's no TV, radio, or sound system. **Pros:** Good for a romantic getaway, attentive staff, removed from other major beach resorts. **Cons:** No beachfront (3-minute taxi ride), not many activities. *Calle Escenica 9, 755/544–6222, 213/280–1037 in U.S. www.amuleto.net 5 suites In-room: Safe, refrigerator, Wi-Fi, Ethernet. In-hotel: Restaurant, room service, bar, pool, laundry service, gym, public Wi-Fi, public Internet, no kids under 16, no elevator MC, V BP.*

$$$$ Fodor's Choice ★ **La Casa Que Canta.** The "House That Sings" clings to a cliff above Playa la Ropa. All guest quarters have lovely furnishings and folk art and generous patios with bay views; suites have outdoor living areas. Bathrooms are luxurious, as are such touches as flower petals arranged in intricate mosaics on your bed each day. The infinity pool seems to be airborne; tucked into the cliff below, a saltwater pool overlooks the surf. The restaurant serves guests breakfast and lunch; dinners here are more formal and are open to the public (reservations required). **Pros:** Secluded and quiet with lots of privacy, excellent food, great spa services. **Cons:** No direct access to beach (it's one block

WORD OF MOUTH

"La Casa Que Canta...is small, private, decadent. I was married there, honeymooned there, and can't wait to go back! Get a private pool suite for the ultimate trip; you won't need to leave the room."

–wish

away), no elevator and lots of stairs, overpriced. ✉*Camino Escénico a Playa la Ropa,* ☎*755/555–7000 or 888/523–5050* 🌐*www.lacasaquecanta.com* *21 suites, 2 villas* *In-room: Safe, no TV, Wi-Fi, refrigerator. In-hotel: 2 restaurants, room service, bars, pools, gym, spa, concierge, laundry service, parking (no fee), no kids under 16, no elevator, public Wi-Fi* *AE, MC, V* *EP.*

$$$$ Fodor'sChoice ★ **Tides Zihuatanejo (formerly Villa de Sol).** The main draws are striking rooms, with winning Mediterranean-Mexican architecture, and the spectacular location on perfect Playa la Ropa. Paths meander through gardens, passing coconut palms and fountains en route to the beach. Rooms are artistically and individually designed, with bright but not overpowering textiles and folk art; in some the adobe walls have been left white, while in others they've been painted pale shades of yellow or orange. All rooms have terraces or balconies; suites have private plunge pools. Service is downright deferential, with "beach butlers" delivering everything from sunscreen to pre-programmed iPods to your palapa. **Pros:** Beautiful semiprivate beachfront, outstanding service, standard rooms that actually stack up to the pricier suites. **Cons:** Meal plan required in high season, four-night minimum stay required year-round, hosts a lot of corporate events and weddings, very pricey for the area. ✉*Playa la Ropa,* ☎*755/555–5500, 866/905–9560 in U.S. and Canada* 🌐*www.tideszihuatanejo.com* *35 rooms, 35 suites* *In-room: Safe, DVD (some), Wi-Fi. In-hotel: 2 restaurants, room service, bars, tennis courts, pools, gym, spa, beachfront, no-smoking rooms, public Internet, public Wi-Fi, some pets allowed, no elevator* *AE, MC, V* *EP, MAP.*

$$$ **Hotel Cinco Sentidos.** Perched above La Ropa beach, this intimate property has some of the best views of the bay from its infinity-edge pool. An all-white motif is brightened by colorful throw pillows and terra-cotta accents, as well as a few whimsical touches, like a cactus-shape lamps and sunburst or gecko wall ornaments. All rooms have terraces with ocean views and plunge pools. The Grand Suite has an open-air living room with even more expansive views of the water and surrounding countryside. **Pros:** Similar aesthetic to the Tides at half the price, pillow-top mattresses, very quiet. **Cons:** No direct beach access, no restaurant, no elevator and lots of steps. ✉*C. Escencia 8,* ☎*755/544–8098* 🌐*www.hotelcincosentidos.com* *5 suites* *In-room: Safe, refrigerator. In-hotel: Pool, public Wi-Fi, no kids under 14, no elevator* *AE, MC, V.*

$$–$$$ ★ **Brisas del Mar.** This is almost as enchanting as any of Zihua's luxury hotels at a price that won't haunt you when you get home. Rooms and services are comfortable, not extravagant, but are presented with delightful touches at every turn. And there are many such touches in the property's intricate layout, from the lobby's stone floor and wicker ceiling to the staircases that wander the lush cliff-side grounds. Rooms have Talavera ceramic sinks in wooden surrounds, carved doors and furnishings from Michoacán, molded plastic bathtubs, and large balconies with hammocks; most have fabulous bay views. Situated on the beach, the stone-and-concrete-floored Bistro del Mar ($–$$$) offers simple, delicious Mediterranean food, a wonderful view, and a welcome breeze. **Pros:** All rooms have terraces (some of which have hot tubs) and water views, large bathrooms, nice pool. **Cons:** Some room layouts are cramped, only the junior suites are true bargains, no elevator and some steep stairs. *Calle Eva Sámano de López Mateos s/n, Playa la Madera, 755/554–2142 www.hotelbrisasdelmar.com 28 rooms, 1 villa In-room: Kitchen (some), refrigerator (some), DVD (some). In-hotel: Restaurant, bars, pool, spa, beachfront, parking (no fee), no-smoking rooms, public Wi-Fi, no elevator MC, V EP.*

$–$$ **La Quinta de Don Andrés.** Though the namesake owner of this small, sharp hideaway overlooking Playa Madera passed away in 2005, the family has stayed true to the founder's high standards. Room have pristine white walls and tile floors, and balconies. The little suites still have wonderful sitting areas, bedrooms, minipatios, and small dining areas (toasters, blenders, and coffeemakers available on request). **Pros:** Great views from most rooms, suites have fantastic terraces and are a great value, hotel is equidistant from downtown and Playa la Ropa. **Cons:** Popular with families, so can be noisy; pool is very small. < *Calle Adelita 11, Playa la Madera, 755/554–3794 755/553–8213 www.laquintadedonandres.com 4 rooms, 8 suites In-room: Kitchen (some), no a/c (some), refrigerator (some). In-hotel: Pool, beachfront, parking (no fee), no elevator No credit cards EP.*

NIGHTLIFE

Outside of the resort bars and discos, Ixtapa's nightlife options are limited—unless you like hanging out at Señor Frog's. Zihua's pedestrian-only core is great for barhopping; it has many casual spots and most of the restaurants in this area serve drinks, too.

There's salsa, Cuban, or romantic music at **Bandidos** (*Calle Pedro Ascencio 2, at Calle Cinco de Mayo, Zihuatanejo 755/553–8072*) Monday through Saturday (in low season call to confirm schedule). It's smack in the middle of downtown and almost as popular with locals as with travelers—both foreign and domestic. In the afternoon and early evening you can get drinks, snacks, and full meals at the bar and outdoor patio. The TV is usually tuned to sports, though the volume is turned way down.

Head for **Blue Mamou** (*Paseo Playa la Ropa s/n, near Hotel Irma 755/544–8025*) for live blues, swing, and jazz; it's open nightly except Sunday. The bar, which opens at 7 PM, sometimes hosts private events; call ahead for the schedule. Soak up the booze with some grub: ribs, chicken, fish, sausage, yams, and coleslaw.

Capricho's Grill (*Cinco de Mayo 4, Zihuatanejo 755/554–3019 www.caprichosgrill.com*) has live music Thursday, Friday, and Saturday—usually world, Latin, flamenco, or jazz—and occasionally hosts special events, such as concerts during March's Guitarfest. You can dine in a lovely courtyard with palm trees and hanging lanterns, or enjoy snacks, cocktails, and wine, and a front seat for the performances from the lounge.

Piano Bar Galería (✉*Blvd. Ixtapa s/n, Ixtapa*) in the Hotel Dorado Pacifico, has a wonderful happy-hour pianist playing romantic songs nightly from December to April and July and August.

Sacbé (✉*Calle Ejido at Guerrero, Zihuatanejo* is just far enough outside of the touristy downtown core to attract locals. The crowd at this trendy tri-level club is usually very young (it's a bit more mixed when hosting the odd live-music performance), but there are plenty of couches to lounge on if you're too intimidated to hit the dance floor. The music is a mix of the latest international and Mexican dance and pop hits. The cover is very reasonable (never more than $5).

THE MERMAID'S SONG

Though it's hardly a secret—it's one of the venues that hosts the Guitarfest in March—**El Canto de la Sirena** (✉*Calle Colegio Militar, Zihuatanejo* ☎*No phone*) is something of a hidden gem, if only because of its unlikely location outside of town by the main bus station. This local favorite is owned by a local legend, guitarist José Luis Cobo López, who performs most evenings. There's live music (and sometimes dancing) Tuesday through Saturday starting at 10 pm; jam sessions usually last until the wee hours.

El Sanka Grill (✉*Calle Ejido 22* ☎*755/554–9358*) has musicians playing traditional Mexican songs from 7 pm to 9 PM to finish off a long day of serving delicious grilled meat and seafood.

SHOPPING

IXTAPA

Shopping in Ixtapa lacks traditional Mexican energy. Most stores are relegated to strip malls across from the hotels on Paseo del Palmar. There are boutiques, restaurants, pharmacies, and grocery stores, but everything seems to blend together. A ban on street and beach vendors restricts small merchants to a large handicrafts zone, **Mercado de Artesanía Turístico,** on the right side of Boulevard Ixtapa across from the Hotel Barceló. It's open weekdays 10–9 and has some 150 stands, selling handicrafts, T-shirts, and souvenirs.

★ One of the few stores that stands out from the rest is **La Fuente** (✉*Centro Comercial Los Patios* ☎*755/553–0812* ✉*Centro Comercial a Puerta* ☎*755/553–1733*), with its huge assortment of women's resort wear as well as housewares and gifts. For silver jewelry, check out **Santa Prisca** (✉*Centro Comercial Los Patios* ☎*755/553–0709*).

ZIHUATANEJO

Downtown Zihuatanejo has a compact but fascinating **Mercado Municipal** with a labyrinth of small stands on the east side of the town center, on Avenida Benito Juárez between Avenida Nava and Avenida González.

★ On the western edge is the **Mercado de Artesanía Turístico** (✉*Calle Cinco de Mayo between Paseo del Pescador and Av. Morelos*), with some 250 stands selling jewelry of shell, beads, and quality silver as well as hand-painted bowls and plates, hammocks, gauzy blouses, T-shirts, and souvenirs. **Casa Marina** (⊠*Paseo del Pescador 9, at main plaza* ☎*755/554–2373*) houses a variety of excellent small shops selling Yucatecan hammocks, Oaxacan rugs, and a smattering of folk art. It's generally closed Sunday except when the cruise ships call.

> **JAVA FIX**
>
> The mountains of Guerrero State are home to many coffee plantations, and several shops in Zihuatanejo sell certified-organic, shade-grown blends. **Café Zihuatanejo** (*Cuauhtémoc 170* ⊠ *C. Galeana, between Bravo and Ejido*<) is the best-known retailer in town; the Cuauhtémoc location sells beans, while the Galeana branch is a full café.

Zihua's tiny nucleus has several worthwhile shops; most are closed Sunday. Shop for wonderful silver and gold jewelry at **Alberto's** (⊠*Calle Cuauhtémoc 15, across from Cine Paraíso* ☎*755/554–2161* ⊠*Calle Cuauhtémoc 12, at Calle N. Bravo* ☎*755/554–2162* ⊠*Plaza Galerías across from Hotel Dorado Pacifico* ☎*755/553–1436*). **Arte Mexicano Nopal** (⊠*Av. Cinco de Mayo 56* ☎*755/554–7530*) sells Mexican handicrafts, reproductions of ancient art, candles, incense, and small gifts. **Fruity Keiko** (⊠*C. Guerrero 5a*) has a colorful yet tasteful selection of crafts from local artists, including jewelry and great handbags and beach bags.

In The Tides hotel, **Gala Art** (⊠*Playa la Ropa* ☎*755/554–7774*) exhibits and sells paintings, jewelry, and bronze, wood, and marble sculptures crafted by artists from throughout Mexico. **Lupita's** (⊠*Calle Juan N. Alvarez 5* ☎*755/554–2238*) has been selling colorful women's apparel—including handmade pieces from Oaxaca, Yucatán, Chiapas, and Guatemala—for more than 20 years. **Valentina** (⊠*Paseo del Pescador 18* ☎*755/554–9223*) sells jewelry and pewter pieces.

SPORTS & THE OUTDOORS

DIVING & SNORKELING

More than 30 dive sites in the area range from deep canyons to shallow reefs. The waters teem with sea life, and visibility is generally excellent. Experienced, personable PADI dive masters run trips ($65 for one tank, $80 for two) and teach courses at **Carlo Scuba** (⊠*Playa las Gatas, Zihuatanejo* ☎*755/554–6003* 🌐 *www.carloscuba.com*). **Nautilus Divers** (⊠*Calle Juan N. Alvarez 30, Zihuatanejo* ☎*755/554–9191* 🌐*www.nautilus-divers.com*) is operated by students of famed local NAUI master diver and marine biologist Juan Barnard. They offer one- and two-tank dives and night dives ($65, $75, and $60, respectively), as well as six-day certification courses. **Sunrise Tours** (⊠*Paseo del Pescador 9, Zihuatanejo* ☎*044/755–100–5315 cell*) rents snorkel equipment, surf and Boogie boards, and kayaks, and provides tours to the best places to play with them. **El Vigia** (⊠*South end of Playa la Ropa* ☎*No phone*) rents snorkel gear and arranges boat trips to snorkel spots at Isla Ixtapa or Playa Manzanillo, about an hour's ride south.

FISHING

Right at the pier, **Cooperativo de Pescadores Azueta** (✉*Paseo del Pescador 81, Zihuatanejo* ☎*755/554–2056*) has a large fleet of boats with VHF radios; some have GPS. The outfit charges $150 for trips in small, fast skiffs with up to four passengers or $250 for larger, more comfortable, albeit somewhat slower, craft. **Cooperativo Triángulo del Sol** (✉*Paseo del Pescador 38, Zihuatanejo* ☎*755/554–3758*) offers day trips in boats from 26 to 36 feet. Prices are in the $150 to $350 range. **VIPSA** (✉*Hotel Las Brisas, Paseo Vista Hermosa, Ixtapa* ☎*755/553–2121 Ext. 3469*) is a reliable bet in the Ixtapa area, with boats that can handle four to six passengers; prices range from $300 to $450. **Whiskey Water World** (✉*Paseo del Pescado 20, Zihuatanejo* ☎*755/554–0147, 661/310–3298 in U.S.* 🌐*www.ixtapa-sportfishing.com*) dispatches seven-hour expeditions in pangas ($190 for two people) and cruisers of 32 feet ($250–$350 for three–four people) and 38 feet ($350–$395 for six–eight people). It's run by Ed Garvis, an American expat in business in Zihua since 1997.

GONE FISHING

Anglers revel in the profusion of sailfish (November through March), black and blue marlin (May through January), yellowfin tuna (November through June), and mahimahi (November through January). Light-tackle fishing in the lagoons and just off the beach in *pangas* (skiffs) for *huachinango* (red snapper) is also popular.

GOLF

The **Campo de Golf Ixtapa (formerly Palma Real Golf Club)** (✉*Blvd. Ixtapa s/n, Ixtapa* ☎*755/553–1163 or 755/553–1062*) has an 18-hole, par-72 championship course designed by Robert Trent Jones Jr. It abuts a wildlife preserve that runs from a coconut plantation to the beach; you may glimpse a gator while you play. Greens fees are $75. You must use either a caddy ($19) or a cart ($35). Club rental is available.Part of the Marina Ixtapa complex, the challenging 18-hole, par-72 course at the **Club de Golf Marina Ixtapa** (✉*Ixtapa* ☎*755/553–1410*) was designed by Robert Von Hagge. Greens fees are $94 (including cart). Caddies charge $20, and you can rent clubs.

WATER PARKS

Delfiniti Ixtapa (✉*Blvd. Ixtapa s/n, next to Best Western Posada del Real* ☎*775/553–2707* 🌐*www.delfiniti.com*) showcases dolphins in a huge pool who interact with paying customers—giving "kisses" and "hugs" and short rides (you hang onto their fins as they paddle around on their backs)—in exchange for food treats. Sessions ranging from $50 to $130 are organized and priced by the age of customers (three–adult) and time in the pool (17 minutes–45 minutes). Reservations are highly recommended—you can book online—especially if you have kids under 7, as there are limited time slots available.

13

Acapulco

WITH A SIDE TRIP TO TAXCO

Umbrellas on the beach, Acapulco

WORD OF MOUTH

"We asked our driver where we should go to watch the sunset, and he took us to the Flamingo Hotel. It is up on a cliff with a great view. We invited him to join us for a drink there (he had lemonade, since he was driving), and we had a blast.

–chicgeek

www.fodors.com/forums

WELCOME TO ACAPULCO

TOP REASONS TO GO

★ **Indulging in the most popular activity in town:** Eating out is the all the rage. You can sample cuisines from around the world or feast on classics from throughout Mexico.

★ **The chance to see authentic, small-town life:** Pie de la Cuesta is a laid-back, coastal village northwest of Acapulco with some of the best seafood around.

★ **Standing in the middle of a history lesson:** The old Fort of San Diego overlooking Acapulco Bay houses one of the best museums in Mexico, illustrating the historical importance of this nearly 500-year-old city.

★ **Dancing the night away:** A sleepy village Acapulco is not. With big-city sophistication comes fabulous ocean-side restaurants, flashy hotel lounges, dance clubs with a sleek clientele, and laid-back surfer bars.

★ **Jewelry shopping in a spot where prices are still reasonable:** One of Mexico's prettiest towns, Taxco is also the place to buy silver jewelry.

1 Old Acapulco. Within the *zócalo* (town plaza), banyan and rubber trees provide shade for a wide cast of characters. Surrounding streets are crowded with small businesses and the elusive soul of the city. Local families and fishermen favor the beaches. And magnificient Fuerte de San Diego is also nearby, as are the La Quebrada divers.

2 Acapulco Bay. If Acapulco was an amphitheater, the Bahía de Acapulco would be center stage. From the surrounding hills and beach resorts you can admire the action of in the harbor during the day and experience the lights reflected in the water and salsa music drifting on the breeze at night.

GETTING ORIENTED

The city of Acapulco is on the Pacific coast 433 km (268 mi) south of Mexico City. Warm water, nearly constant sunshine, and balmy year-round temperatures let you plan your day around the beach—whether you want to lounge in a hammock or go snorkeling, parasailing, fishing, or water-skiing. Attractions to lure you away from the sands include crafts markets, cultural institutions, and the amazing cliff divers at La Quebrada.

3 Costera. The heartbeat of Acapulco, Costera pulses with activity. There is nothing quaint or serene about this busy 8-km (5-mi) stretch of commercial bayfront property along Avenida Costera Miguel Alemán. The thoroughfare is lined with resorts, shops, markets, banks, discos—even a park and a golf course. And within walking distance are the bay's golden beaches.

4 Acapulco Diamante. As you head east from Acapulco Bay you enter Acapulco Diamante, which includes the smaller bay of Puerto Marqués and the long wide beaches of Revolcadero. This is where new developments—mostly large, opulent resorts—crop up. Above, the hillside neighborhoods overlooking the water host many of Mexico's most spectacular private villas.

ACAPULCO PLANNER

A Simple Itinerary

Spend the morning of your first day sunning on the beach, perhaps at Playa Caleta or Playa Revolcadero. In the afternoon do a little shopping on the Costera and enjoy an evening cocktail in one of the many bars lining the strip. Have dinner in a restaurant overlooking the bay in Acapulco Diamante. If you want to party afterward, head back to the Costera for the clubs.

The next day, visit Old Acapulco and El Fuerte de San Diego in the morning. In the afternoon visit the aquarium or sign on for some parasailing or waterskiing. In the evening be sure to see the cliff divers at La Quebrada.

On your third day, take a cab or bus to Pie de la Cuesta, a strip of beach west of downtown. Stay long enough to see Acapulco's most brilliant sunset before heading back to town for dinner. Reserve another day for a trip to the beautiful mountain town of Taxco, a 3½-hour drive away, where you can take in a museum and shop for jewelry from some of the world's finest silversmiths.

Getting Around

If you're in town for a long weekend and want to spend most of your time beachside, don't bother renting a car. A small army of taxis and buses is ready to whisk you along the Costera and anywhere else you want to go in town. Taxis are relatively cheap—a ride from Acapulco Diamante to downtown will cost you about $15. If you want to visit the coastal villages and Taxco, however, consider rent-ing a car or open-air jeep, or taking a coach. You can rent a car for $30 per day, including insurance and unlimited miles. And did we mention that the jeeps come in bright pink?

Tours Around Acapulco

One of Acapulco's best tour operators offer guided walking and bus tours of the city and surrounding area. City tours cost $20, while day tours of Taxco cost $80, including lunch. Nightclub tours cost $35 to $40, including transportation and club cover charges.

Acapulco Scuba Center (✉Paseo del Pescador 13 y 14, Old Acapulco ☎744/482–9474 🌐www.acapulcoscuba.com) offers the best off-shore tours.

Viajes Acuario (✉Av. Costera Miguel Alemán 186–3, Costera ☎744/485–6100) is in the center of the action on the Costera strip.

Health

Most tourist hotels and restaurants have high standards of cleanliness, so you can feel safe eating and drinking at their establishments. That said, the United States Centers for Disease Control still recommend drinking only bottled water and sticking to the "boil it, cook it, peel it, or forget it" rule. Refer to the CDC Web site (🌐wwwn.cdc.gov/travel/regionCentralAmerica.aspx) before your trip.

Safety

Crime, especially petty theft and drug trafficking, exists in Acapulco, but it is not obvious and should not deter your trip. Common sense is the best method of prevention: Lock valuables in your hotel safe, and be aware of your belongings when out. At night stay in well-populated areas like the Costera, Las Brisas, and Acapulco Diamante. If you want to minimize contact with aggressive beach vendors don't look at their wares. Just shake your head or politely, but positively, say "no, gracias."

If you have a problem that requires police intervention, contact your embassy first. The local police, recognizable by their blue uniforms, are reputed to be unsympathetic to foreigners. The so-called tourist police that walk the Costera strip in white shirts and dark shorts are generally helpful, however.

If you are looking to buy or rent property in Acapulco, make sure to work with a reliable company; beware of anyone who approaches you claiming to be a real estate agent.

Booking in Advance

Snowbirds from the United States and Canada show up all winter, but the busiest times are Christmas week, Easter week, and during July and August, when the Mexican nationals are on vacation. Most hotels are booked solid during these times, so try to make reservations at least three months in advance. During Christmas week, prices rise 30%–60% above those in low season.

Money Matters

WHAT IT COSTS IN DOLLARS

¢	$	$$	$$$	$$$$
Restaurants				
under $5	$5–$10	$10–$15	$15–$25	over $25
Hotels				
under $50	$50–$75	$75–$150	$150–$250	over $250

Restaurant prices are for a main course excluding tax and tip. Hotel prices are for two people in a standard double room in high season.

How's the Weather?

Hot and humid weather prevails in Acapulco, with temperatures hovering at 30°C (86°F) year-round and sunshine guaranteed virtually every day. During the rainy season, June through October, the late afternoon and nights often bring welcome, cooling showers. Any time of the year is good for a visit, but perhaps the best is in October or November, right after the rainy season. The crowds are small, the prices reasonable, and the hills green from summer rains. As winter and spring roll around, most of the vegetation turns brown. Of course, watching a summer squall over the Pacific from your hotel balcony, cold beverage in hand, is a singular Mexico experience.

Updated by Claudia Rosenbaum

THE CENTER OF ACAPULCO IS on the western edge of the bay. The streets form a grid that's easy to explore on foot. Avenida Costera Miguel Alemán, a wide coastal boulevard, runs the length of the bay and is lined with hotels, restaurants, and malls. You can explore the strip by taxi, bus, or rental car, stopping along the way to shop.

You'll also need a vehicle to get to Acapulco Diamante, farther east along the coast. Running from Las Brisas Hotel to Barra Vieja beach, this 3,000-acre expanse encompasses exclusive Playa Diamante and Playa Revolcadero, with upscale hotels and residential developments, private clubs, beautiful views, and pounding surf.

Pie de la Cuesta, 10 km (6.2 mi) northwest of Acapulco, is famous for its fabulous sunsets, small family-run hotels, and some of the wildest surf in Mexico. The village remains the flip side to the Acapulco coin—a welcome respite from the disco-driven big city. Only the main road is paved, and the town has no major resorts or late-night clubs. A beach chair, a bucket of cold beers, fresh fish and seafood, and a good book is about as much excitement as you'll get here.

For a break from beach life you can travel north 300 km (185 mi) to the old silver-mining town of Taxco, a great place to buy silver from the country's finest metalwork artisans.

GETTING HERE & AROUND

American, Continental, and US Airways have nonstop service to Acapulco. Aeropuerto Internacional Juan N. Alvarez is 20 minutes east of the city. Private taxis aren't permitted to carry passengers from the airport to town, so most people rely on Transportes Aeropuerto, a special airport taxi service. Bus service from Mexico City to Acapulco is excellent. Grupo Estrella Blanca has first-class buses, which leave every hour on the hour from the Taxqueña station. Estrella de Oro also has deluxe service, called Servicio Diamante, which leaves four times a day. Within Acapulco, one of the most useful buses runs from Puerto Marqués to Caleta, making stops along the way. Cabs that cruise the streets usually charge by zone, with a minimum charge of $2. Rent a car if you plan on being in town for a few days and want to take side trips to Taxco and the coastal villages.

ESSENTIALS

Bus Contacts **Estrella de Oro** (✉ *Av. Cuauhtémoc 158, Old Acapulco, Acapulco* ☎ *744/485–8705 or 762/622–0648*). **Grupo Estrella Blanca** (✉ *Calle Ejido 47, Old Acapulco* ☎ *744/469–2028*).

Currency Exchange **Banamex** (✉ *Av. Costera Miguel Alemán 38-A, Costera* ☎ *744/484–3381*). **Casa de Cambio Austral** (✉ *Av. Costera Vieja 3, Old Acapulco* ☎ *744/484–6528*). **Dollar Money Exchange** (✉ *Av. Costera Miguel Alemán 151, Costera* ☎ *744/486–9688*).

Internet **Hostal K3** (✉ *Av. Costera Miguel Alemán 116, in front of Fiesta Americana hotel, Playa Condesa* ☎ *744/481–3111*). **Vid@Net** (✉ *Calle Hidalgo off the zocálo, Old Acapulco*).

Medical Assistance **Hospital del Pacífico** (✉ *Calle Fraile and Calle Nao 4, Cos-*

tera ☎ *744/487-7161).* **Hospital Privado Magallanes** (✉ *Calle Wilfrido Massieu 2, Costera* ☎ *744/485-6194).* **Red Cross** (☎ *744/445-8178 or 744/445-5911).* **Tourist Police** (☎ *744/485-0490).*

Rental Cars **Avis** (☎ *800/288-8888).* **Budget** (☎ *744/481-2433).* **Dollar** (☎ *744/466-9493).* **Hertz** (☎ *744/485-8947).*

Visitor & Tour Info **Procuraduría del Turista** (✉ *Acapulco International Center, Av. Costera Miguel Alemán 4455, Costera* ☎ *744/484-4416* 🌐 *www.visitacapulco.com.mx).* **Taxco Tourism Office** (✉ *Av. de los Plateros 1, Taxco* ☎ *762/622-6616).*

VINTAGE TOURING

Horse-drawn carriage rides, known as *calandrias,* run up and down the Costera in the evenings and can be a fun way to get to a restaurant or club. There are several routes, including one from Parque Papagayo to the *zócalo* (town square) and another from Playa Condesa to the naval base. Rides cost $7.50–$14, depending on the route. Be sure to agree on the price beforehand.

13

EXPLORING

Avenida Costera Miguel Alemán hugs the Bahía de Acapulco from the Carretera Escénica (Scenic Highway) in the east to Playa Caleta (Caleta Beach) in the southwest—a distance of about 8 km (5 mi). Most of the major beaches, shopping malls, and hotels are along or off this avenue, and locals refer to its most exclusive stretch—from El Presidente hotel to Las Brisas—simply as "the Costera." Since many addresses are listed as only "Costera Miguel Alemán," you'll need good directions from a major landmark to find specific shops and hotels.

COSTERA

❶ **Casa de la Cultura.** The city's cultural center has first-class regional and Mexican handicrafts for sale, the Ixcateopan art gallery, and a small sports hall of fame with photos of local athletes. The center also sponsors folk-dancing and theater productions, and offers language workshops. ✉ *Av. Costera Miguel Alemán 4834, Costera* ☎ *744/484–2390* 🎫 *Free* ⏲ *Daily 8* AM*–9* PM.

❷ **CiCi.** A water park for children, the Centro Internacional para Convivencia Infantil, fondly known as CiCi, has dolphin shows, a freshwater pool with a wave machine, a waterslide, the Sky Coaster (a safe, low-key bungee jump for kids), and other attractions. If you book an hour-long swim with the dolphins, CiCi can have you picked up at your hotel. It's easy to catch a cab for the return trip. ✉ *Av. Costera Miguel Alemán, next to Planet Hollywood, Costera* ☎ *744/484–1970* 🎫 *$10* ⏲ *Daily 10–6.*

❸ **Parque Papagayo.** Named for the hotel that formerly occupied the grounds, this park is on 52 acres of prime Costera real estate, just after the underpass that begins at Playa Hornos. It has an aviary, a racetrack with mite-size race cars, a space-shuttle replica, a jogging path, a library, and bumper boats. Find some street food and a shady bench

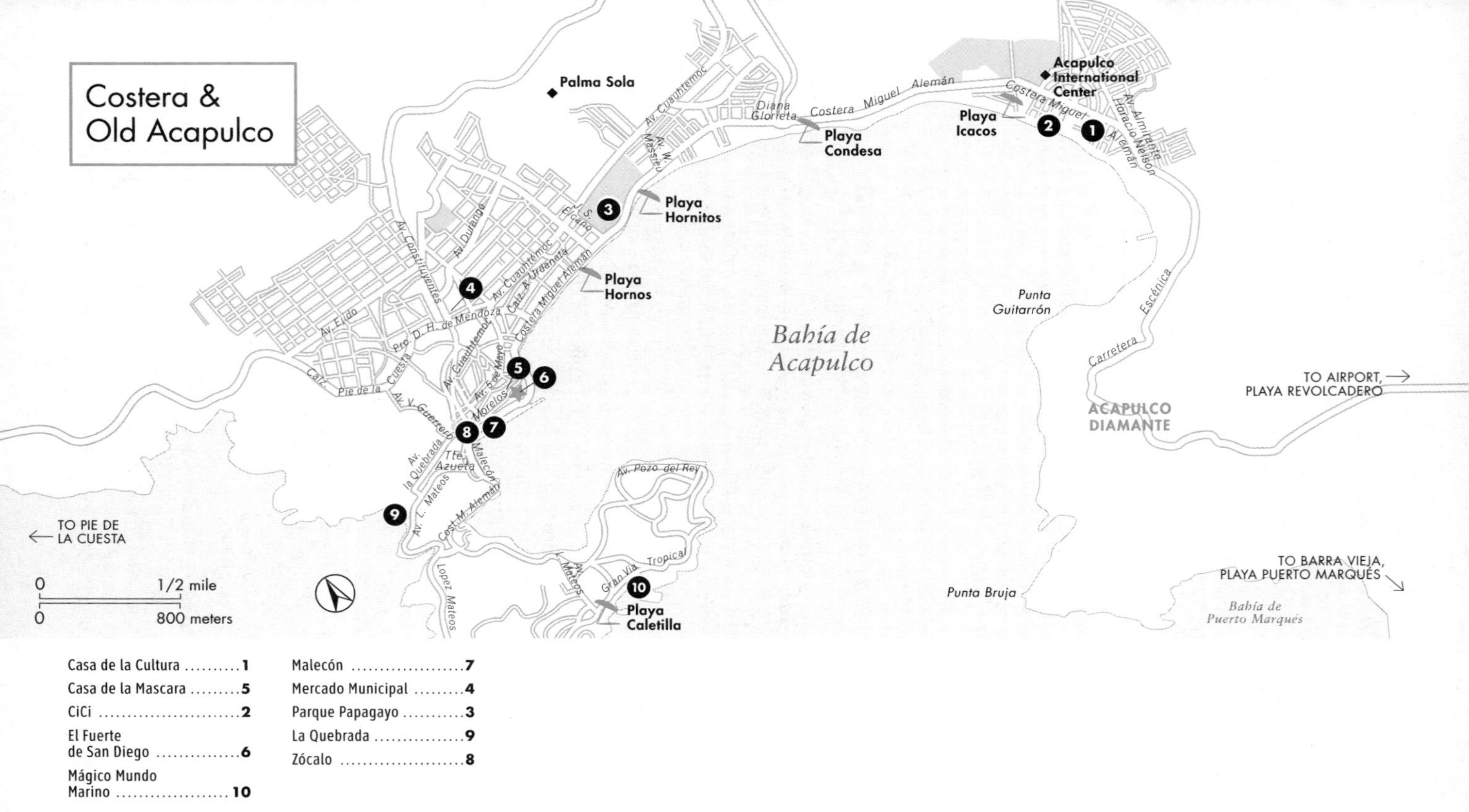

Casa de la Cultura 1
Casa de la Mascara 5
CiCi 2
El Fuerte de San Diego 6
Mágico Mundo Marino 10
Malecón 7
Mercado Municipal 4
Parque Papagayo 3
La Quebrada 9
Zócalo 8

and do some people-watching. ✉ *Av. Costera Miguel Alemán, Costera* ☎ *744/485–6837* 🎫 *No entrance fee; rides $1 each; $5 ride packages available* ⏲ *Park: daily 6 AM–8 PM. Rides section: nightly 4–11.*

OLD ACAPULCO

Old Acapulco, an area that you can easily tour on foot, is where the locals go to dine, enjoy a town festival, run errands, and worship. Also known as El Centro, it's where you'll find the zócalo, the church, and El Fuerte de San Diego. Although a very old city, Acapulco retains little in the way of centuries-old buildings. When development took off here in the '40s and '50s many of the old buildings were razed to make room for resort hotels.

OFF THE BEATEN PATH

Palma Sola. Taking the name of the neighborhood closest to it, this archaeological site juts up a mountainside northeast of Old Acapulco. The area is blanketed with 2,000-year-old petroglyphs executed by the Yopes, Acapulco's earliest known inhabitants. Stone steps with intermittent plazas for viewing the ancient art are set along a path through virgin vegetation. A cave used as a ceremonial center is atop the mountain, more than 1,000 feet above sea level and definitely worth the visit. It's about a 25-minute taxi ride from Old Acapulco. ☎ *744/486–1514 for tours* 🎫 *Free* ⏲ *Daily 8–4.*

5 **Casa de la Mascara.** A private home has been turned into a gallery for a stunning collection of 550 handmade ceremonial masks, most from the state of Guerrero. Some are representative of those still used in such traditional ritualistic dances as "Moors and Christians" and "Battle of the Tigers." Call ahead to book a 30-minute tour in English or Spanish. ✉ *Calle Morelos s/n, Ex-Zona Militar B, a half block from Fuerte de San Diego, Old Acapulco* ☎ *744/485–3944 or 744/485–3404* 🎫 *Free* ⏲ *Tues.–Sat. 10–5.*

6 **El Fuerte de San Diego.** Acapulco's fort was built in 1616 to protect the city's lucrative harbor and wealthy citizens from pirate attacks. Although it was badly damaged by an earthquake in 1776, it was entirely restored by the end of that century. Today the fort houses the excellent **Museo Histórico de Acapulco** *(Acapulco History Museum).* Bilingual videos and text explain exhibits tracing the city's history from the first pre-Hispanic settlements 3,000 years ago through the exploits of pirates like Sir Francis Drake, the era of the missionaries, and up to Mexico's independence from Spain in 1821. There are also displays of precious silks, Talavera tiles, exquisitely hand-tooled wooden furniture, and delicate china. A good multimedia show in Spanish (an English version requires a minimum of 15 people) on the history of Acapulco is staged outside the museum grounds on Thursday, Friday, and Saturday at 8 PM for $10 per person. A visit to the fort is a wonderful way to learn about and appreciate the history of this old port city. ✉ *Calle Hornitos and Calle Morelos, Old Acapulco* ☎ *744/482–3828* 🎫 *$3.60; free on Sun.* ⏲ *Tues.–Sun. 9:30–6.*

Fodor's Choice ★

⑩ **Mágico Mundo Marino.** You can take in Magic Marine World's aquarium and free sea-lion show while the kids splash around in the swimming pools and fly down the waterslides. From Playa Caleta you can take the glass-bottom boat to Isla la Roqueta—about 10 minutes each way—for snorkeling. ✉*Islote de Caleta, Old Acapulco* ☎*744/483–1193 or 744/483–9344* 🎟*$6 for adults, $3 for children. Round-trip boat ride to Isla la Roqueta $5* ⏲*Daily 9–6.*

TAKE THE TROLLEY

An open-air trolley, called the *tranvía,* is convenient for touring the major attractions along the Costera and in Old Acapulco. Operating daily 10–6, the trolley starts at the Parque Papagayo and stops at the Fuerte de San Diego, La Quebrada, Caleta beach, the zócalo, the convention center, and at most hotels along the Costera up until the Hyatt. ($6.50 for unlimited rides in one day.)

⑦ **Malecón.** A stroll by the docks will confirm that Acapulco is a lively port. At night Mexicans bring their children to play on the tree-lined promenade. Farther west, by the zócalo, are docks for yachts and fishing boats. ✉*Av. Costera Miguel Alemán between Calle Escudero on the west and El Fuerte de San Diego on the east, Old Acapulco.*

④ **Mercado Municipal.** Locals come to this municipal market to buy everything from candles and fresh vegetables to plastic buckets and love potions. In addition, you can buy baskets, pottery, hammocks—there's even a stand offering charms, amulets, and talismans. The stalls within the mercado are densely packed together and there's no air-conditioning, but things stay relatively cool. Come early to avoid the crowds. ✉*Calle Diego Hurtado de Mendoza and Av. Constituyentes, a few blocks west of Costera, Old Acapulco* ⏲*Daily 5* AM*–7* PM.

⑨ **La Quebrada.** Just up the hill from Old Acapulco is the southern peninsula, where you'll find La Quebrada and its legendary cliff divers. The peninsula has remnants of Acapulco's golden era, the early- to mid-20th century. Although past its prime, this mostly residential area has been revitalized through the re-openings of the Caleta Hotel and the aquarium at Playa Caleta. And the inexpensive hotels here are still popular with travelers who want good deals and a slower pace. The Plaza de Toros, where bullfights are held on Sunday from the first week of January to Easter, is in the center of the peninsula.

⑧ **Zócalo.** Old Acapulco's hub is this shaded plaza overgrown with dense trees. All day it's filled with vendors, shoe-shine men, and tourists enjoying the culture. After siesta, the locals drift here to socialize. On Sunday evening there's often music in the bandstand. The zócalo fronts Nuestra Señora de la Soledad (Our Lady of Solitude), the town's modern but unusual church, with its stark-white exterior and bulb-shape blue-and-yellow spires. The church hosts the festive Virgin of Guadalupe celebration on December 12. ✉*Bounded by Calle Felipe Valle on north, Av. Costera Miguel Alemán on south, Calle J. Azueta on west, and Calle J. Carranza on east, Old Acapulco.*

NEED A BREAK?

Cafetería Astoria is a little outdoor café on the zócalo where businesspeople stop for breakfast before work or meet midmorning for a cappuccino and a sweet roll. It's always lively, and you can't beat the view of the passing parade of activity.

BEACHES

In the past few years city officials made a great effort to clean up the Bahía de Acapulco, and maintaining it is a priority. Although vending on the beach has been outlawed, you'll probably still be approached by souvenir hawkers. In Acapulco Bay watch for a strong shore break that can knock you off your feet in knee-deep water. It is wise to observe the waves for a few minutes before entering the water.

Barra Vieja. A pleasant drive 27 km (17 mi) east of Acapulco, between Laguna de Tres Palos and the Pacific, brings you to this long stretch of uncrowded beach. Most people make the trip for the solitude and to feast on *pescado à la talla* (red snapper marinated in spices and grilled over hot coals) available at all the seaside outdoor restaurants. The locals flock here on weekends.

Fodor'sChoice ★ **Pie de la Cuesta.** You can reach this relatively unpopulated spot by car, cab, or bus. It's about a 25-minute drive west of downtown. The bus runs every 15 minutes past the zócalo along the Costera, the last one departing at 8 PM. Simple, thatched-roof restaurants and small, rustic inns border the wide beach, with straw palapas (palm frond roofs) providing shade. What attracts people to Pie de la Cuesta, besides the long expanse of beach and spectacular sunsets, is beautiful Laguna Coyuca, a favorite spot for waterskiing, freshwater fishing, and boat rides. Boats ferry you to La Laguna restaurant, where, some people claim, the pescado à la talla is even better than at Barra Vieja.

Playa Caleta. On the southern peninsula in Old Acapulco, this beach and smaller Playa Caletilla (Little Caleta) to the south once rivaled La Quebrada as the main tourist area, and were very popular with the early Hollywood crowd. Today their snug little bays and calm waters make them a favorite with Mexican families. Caleta has the Mágico Mundo Marino entertainment center for children and a large seafood restaurant. Caletilla has many small family-run restaurants serving good, cheap food. On both beaches vendors sell everything from seashells to peeled mangos; boats depart from both to Isla de Roqueta. Spend a day here to get a true taste of Mexico.

Playa Condesa. Referred to as "the strip," this stretch of sand facing the middle of Bahía de Acapulco has more than its share of visitors, especially singles. It's lined with lively restaurants and rockin' bars.

BAY BONANZA

A lovely way to see the bay is to sign up for a cruise on the *Fiesta & Bonanza* (☎744/483-1803). Boats leave from downtown near the zócalo at 11 AM, 4:30 PM, and 10:30 PM. The evening cruise includes live Latin or disco music and dancing, and an open bar with domestic alcohol. Many hotels and shops sell tickets ($31.50), as do waterfront ticket sellers.

Continued on page 678

ACAPULCO'S CLIFF DIVERS

For many people the name Acapulco conjures up images of the *clavadistas,* or cliff-divers, brave local men who make their living by tempting death. The spectacle of these men swan-diving some 130 feet into ❾ **La Quebrada,** literally "gorge," and then splashing into 12 feet of rough surf is a sight not to be missed.

The practice of cliff diving began with local fishermen, who were known to dive from high up on the rocky cliffs in order to propel themselves deep enough into the water to free snagged lines. With the advent of tourism in the 1930s, however, the divers soon discovered that their sensational skill could earn them tips.

This is not a long-term occupation for most divers. New, young divers are trained continually to be accepted into what has become an elite association of daredevils. Amazingly, there have been no reported deaths associated with the dives.

Where to See the Divers

Unless you have recently trained with Sherpas, take a taxi to La Quebrada, high in the hills above downtown Acapulco. You can watch the dives from either the **observation area,** where you will be charged 30 pesos by the divers' union, or from the **Plaza Las Glorias at the El Mirador Hotel,** (☎744/483–1400, 🌐www.hotelelmiradoracapulco.com.mx) for a cover charge of about 35 pesos. The hotel's **La Perla** supper club is the most comfortable viewing spot. Show times are 12, 7:30, 8:30, 9:30, and 10:30 o- . After the show the clavadistas mingle with the audience, posing for photos. This is a good time to offer a tip; most people give 10–50 pesos. Be sure to arrive early to get a spot with a good view. And if you can, try to make it to a night show, which often include hand-held torches carried by the divers—an unforgettable sight.

Clavadistas: 1 Tarzan: 0

A local legend has it that Johnny Weissmuller (1904–1984), the Olympic swimmer and original Hollywood Tarzan, was in attendance in 1947, when one of the divers, Raul Garcia, challenged him to make the dive. As Weissmuller contemplated the offer, the movie company executives called off the stunt, citing insurance risks. Weissmuller was filming *Tarzan and the Mermaids* at the time. He never returned to make the dive, but hey, aren't five Olympic gold medals and 67 world records enough?

The 130-Foot Plunge of the Clavadistas

1. Divers precede their jumps with a prayer at a small shrine on the cliffs.

2. They approach the edge—this is the part when most viewers hold their breath. The divers must time their jumps to coordinate with the wave and tide action below to ensure that they're landing in the maximum amount of water.

3. The dive begins with a beautiful, horizontal takeoff in order to clear the uneven cliff face, and is followed by a plummet past the unforgiving boulders.

4. After surfacing, hopefully without broken bones or dislocated limbs, the divers scale the steep rocky cliffs back to the top.

Showtimes: 12, 7:30, 8:30, 9:30 and 10:30 PM

Playa Hornitos. Running from the Avalon Excalibur west to Las Hamacas, Hornitos (Little Hornos) and adjacent Playa Hornos are shoulder to shoulder with locals and visitors on weekends. Graceful palms shade the sand, and there are scads of casual eateries on the beach, especially on Playa Hornos. A slice of Playa Hornos and Playa Hornitos marks the beginning of the hotel zone to the east. The swimming is generally very safe in this area.

Playa Icacos. Stretching from the naval base to El Presidente hotel, away from the famous strip, this beach is less populated than others on the Costera. The morning surf is especially calm.

Playa Puerto Marqués. Tucked below the airport highway, this protected strand is popular with Mexican tourists, so it tends to get crowded on weekends. Beach shacks here sell fresh fish, and vendors sell silver and other wares.

Playa Revolcadero. This sprawling beach fronts the Fairmont Pierre Marqués and Fairmont Acapulco Princess hotels. People come here to surf and ride horses. The water is shallow, but the waves can be rough, and the rip current can be strong, so be careful swimming.

WHERE TO EAT

Every night Acapulco's restaurants fill up, and every night you can sample a different cuisine, whether you opt for a small, authentic *loncheria* (small, family-run café) serving regional favorites or an establishment with the finest international dishes. On the Costera Miguel Alemán there are dozens of beachside eateries with palapa roofs, as well as wildly decorated rib and hamburger joints full of people of all ages who enjoy a casual, sometimes raucous, time. Most places that cater to visitors and locals purify their drinking and cooking water.

Expect to pay $25 or more for a main course at the best restaurants in town, where views of the ocean are often fantastic. Ties and jackets are out of place, but so are shorts and jeans, except for in the inexpensive places. Unless stated otherwise, all restaurants are open daily for lunch and dinner; dinner-only places open around 6:30 or 7.

ACAPULCO DIAMANTE

$$$–$$$$ ITALIAN
✕ **Casa Nova.** Live piano music lends romance to Casa Nova, which is carved out of a cliff that rises from Bahía de Acapulco. The views, both from the terrace and the air-conditioned dining room, are spectacular, the service is impeccable, and the Italian cuisine is superb. You can choose the fixed-price *menu turístico* for $50 or order à la carte. Favorites include lobster tail, linguine *alle vongole* (with clams, tomato, and garlic), and *costoletta di vitello* (veal chops with mushrooms). ✉ *Carretera Escénica 5256, Las Brisas* ☎ *744/446–6237* ▭ *AE, MC, V* ⊗ *No lunch.*

$$$–$$$$ ★ MEXICAN
✕ **Hacienda.** Personable, efficient waiters dress as classy *charros* (Mexican cowboys with silver-studded outfits) and mariachis entertain at this restaurant in a colonial hacienda, once a millionaire's estate. The menu has such dishes as sautéed oysters from Loreto (Baja California Sur)

served with chili-poblano mousseline. Seafood and chateaubriand made with Black Angus tenderloin are specialties. On Sunday there's a champagne brunch for $30. ✉ *Fairmont Acapulco Princess hotel, Playa Revolcadero, Revolcadero* ☎ *744/469–1000* 🌐 *www.fairmont.com* 💳 *AE, DC, MC, V* ⏲ *Closed Mon. No lunch.*

> **CAUTION**
>
> Acapulco Bay is fairly well protected from the rough Pacific surf, but steep offshore drop-offs can produce waves large enough to knock you off your feet. Pay attention to the wave pattern before you go in. If you are not a strong swimmer, stay close to shore and other people. Some beaches, mostly those outside the bay such as Revolcadero and Pie de la Cuesta, have a strong surf and some have a rip current, so be careful. If you get caught in a rip current, which makes it hard to swim to shore, swim parallel to the sand. Above all, don't panic.

13

$$–$$$$ SEAFOOD ✕ **Pool Bar** On a wharf that juts out into Bahía de Puerto Marqués, this casual open-air dining spot has wooden floors and a dramatic roof that simulates a huge white sail. It's particularly atmospheric after dark, when the lights of Puerto Marqués flicker in the distance. There are several fish and shellfish dishes on the menu, but the specialty is the red snapper *à la talla* (basted with chili and other spices and broiled over hot coals). ✉ *Camino Real Acapulco Diamante, Carretera Escénica, Km 14, Acapulco Diamante* ☎ *744/466–1010* 💳 *AE, DC, MC, V.*

COSTERA

Loud music blares from many restaurants along the Costera, especially those facing Playa Condesa, and proprietors will aggressively try to hustle you inside with offers of drink specials. If you're looking for a more sedate evening, avoid this area or decide in advance where to dine and head straight there.

★ $$–$$$$ CONTEMPORARY ✕ **Baikal.** Modern, ultrachic Baikal is *the* place to see and be seen. The dining room has a white-on-white color scheme and 12-foot-high windows that frame the sparkling bay; sea-theme short films are shown from time to time on drop-down movie screens. The menu is small but select, with dishes that fuse French, Asian, and Mexican preparations and ingredients. Try the cold cream of cucumber soup spiced with mint and mild jalapeño; the sliced abalone with a chipotle (dried, smoked chilies) vinaigrette is also a good bet. Soft bossa nova and jazz play in the background. ✉ *Carretera Escénica 1622, Costera* ☎ *744/446–6867* 🌐 *www.baikal.com.mx* ✍ *Reservations essential* 💳 *AE, DC, MC, V* ⏲ *Closed Mon. May–Nov. No lunch.*

★ $$–$$$$ CONTINENTAL ✕ **Madeiras.** All tables at this elegant restaurant have views of the bay, and the dishes and flatware were created by Taxco silversmiths. In the bar-reception area, groovy glass coffee tables rest on carved wooden animals. Dinner is a four-course, prix-fixe meal, and there are 15 menus from which to choose. Specialties include tasty chilled soups and red snapper baked in sea salt (a Spanish dish); there are also steak choices, lobster tail, chicken, and pork. ✉ *Carretera Escénica 33-Bis, just past*

Restaurants

- El Amigo Miguel **3**
- Baikal **17**
- La Cabaña **1**
- El Cabrito **11**
- La Casa de Tere **5**
- Casa Nova **19**
- Coyuca 22 .... **2**
- Hacienda **21**
- Hard Rock Cafe **9**
- Julio's **6**
- Madeiras **18**
- Mezzanotte **16**
- 100% Natural **8, 13**
- Los Navegantes **14**
- Pipo's **4, 10**
- Pool Bar **20**
- Suntory **12**
- Zapata, Villa y Compañia **15**
- Zorrito's **7**

Hotels

- Alba Suites **1**
- Boca Chica **2**
- Las Brisas **16**
- Camino Real Acapulco Diamante **19**
- Elcano **14**
- Etel Suites **4**
- Fairmont Acapulco Princess **17**
- Fairmont Pierre Marqués **18**
- Fiesta Americana Villas Acapulco **12**
- Los Flamingos **3**
- Hacienda Vayma **9**
- Las Hamacas **10**
- Hyatt Regency Acapulco **15**
- Misión **5**
- El Mirador **6**
- Parador del Sol **7**
- Park Hotel & Tennis Center **11**
- Quinta Real **20**
- Villas Ukae Kim **8**
- Villa Vera **13**

CLOSE UP

A Taste of Acapulco

Most people come to Acapulco for the sun, but dining comes in a close second. Fresh seafood is on every menu, supplied daily by local fisherman. You can also get top-quality beef brought in from the Mexican states of Sonora and Chihuahua.

As for setting, you can have an utterly romantic meal high in the hills, with unparalleled views of the bay, or you can dine in a casual beachside restaurant. Night owls coming out of the clubs can even find a plate of flavorful tacos for less than $2 right before sunrise.

You can dine with the locals in Old Acapulco, or plan a half-day outing to rustic Barra Vieja where you take a boat through the mangroves to one of many dining huts for fish grilled over hot coals. You can also head to Pie de la Cuesta, a laid-back area west of downtown. Here you can have lunch at a seaside eatery, go horseback riding, and then linger on the beach for a spectacular sunset.

La Vista shopping center, Costera ☎*744/446–5636* *Reservations essential* *AE, MC, V* *No lunch.*

$$–$$$$ JAPANESE ✕**Suntory.** You can dine in the delightful Asian-style garden or in an air-conditioned room. Suntory is one of Acapulco's few Japanese restaurants and one of the few deluxe places that's open for lunch. Many diners opt for the *teppanyaki* (thin slices of beef and vegetables seared on a hot grill), prepared at your table by skilled chefs. Rib eye and seafood are also on the menu, but not sushi. ✉*Av. Costera Miguel Alemán 36, across from La Palapa hotel, Costera* ☎*744/484–8088* *AE, MC, V.*

$–$$$$ SEAFOOD ✕**Los Navegantes.** A line often goes out the door at this popular seafood restaurant on the second floor of El Tropicano Hotel. If you get a table by the window, you'll have views of the bustling Costera below. Most dishes, including the popular *filete habañero* (tilapia bathed in a creamy chili sauce), come accompanied with beans or rice and handmade tortillas. ✉*Costera Miguel Alemán 20, Local A, Costera* ☎*744/484–2101* *AE, MC, V.*

$–$$$$ ★ SEAFOOD ✕**Pipo's.** On a rather quiet stretch of the Costera, this old, family-run restaurant doesn't have an especially interesting view, but locals come here for the fresh fish, good service, and reasonable prices for most dishes. Try the huachinango veracruzano (red snapper baked with tomatoes, peppers, onion, and olives) or the fillet of fish in mojo de ajo (garlic butter). The original location downtown is also popular with locals. ✉ *Av. Costera Miguel Alemán and Nao Victoria, across from Acapulco International Center, Costera* ☎ *744/484–0165* ✉*Calle Almirante Bretón 3 Old Acapulco* ☎*744/482–2237* *AE, MC, V.*

$–$$$$ MEXICAN ✕**Zapata, Villa y Compañia.** The music and the food are strictly local, and the memorabilia recall the Mexican Revolution—guns, hats, and photographs of Pancho Villa. Often the evening's highlight is a visit from a sombrero-wearing baby burro, so be sure to bring your camera. The menu includes the ever-popular fajitas, tacos, and grilled meats. ✉*Hyatt Regency Acapulco, Av. Costera Miguel Alemán 1, Costera* ☎*744/469–1234* *AE, DC, MC, V* *No lunch.*

$$–$$$ AMERICAN ✕ **Hard Rock Cafe.** This link in the international Hard Rock chain is one of Acapulco's most popular spots, among locals as well as visitors. The New York–cut steaks, hamburgers, and brownies, as well as the Southern-style fried chicken and ribs are familiar and satisfying. Taped rock music begins at noon, and a live group starts playing at 10 PM on Thursday, Friday, and Saturday. ✉ *Av. Costera Miguel Alemán 37 Costera* ☎ *744/484–6680* 🌐 *www.hardrock.com* 💳 *AE, DC, MC, V.*

> **EXPAT ADVICE**
>
> Check out *wwww.travel-acapulco.com*, a Web site that started as a travelogue by a Texas native named Rick, who moved to Acapulco in early 2003. His reviews, advice, and suggestions for activities are reliable and fun to read.

$–$$$ ITALIAN ✕ **Mezzanotte.** You may end up dancing with your waiter—perhaps atop a table—on a Friday or Saturday evening; you'll definitely end up mixing with the who's who of Acapulco just about any night of the week. The stylish interior has a large sunken dining area, original sculptures, and huge bay windows looking out to sea. Patrons rave about the fettuccine with smoked salmon in avocado sauce and the charcoal-grilled sea bass with shrimp and artichokes in a citrus sauce. For a light ending to your meal, try the gelato. Music videos are projected on large screens on weekends. ✉ *Carretera Escénica 28, L-2, in La Vista shopping center, Costera* ☎ *744/446–5727* 💳 *AE, MC, V* ⏲ *No lunch.*

¢–$$ MEXICAN ✕ **El Cabrito.** As the name implies, young goat—served charcoal-grilled—is a specialty of this restaurant, open since 1963. You can also choose from among such truly Mexican dishes as chicken in *mole* (spicy chocolate-chile sauce); shrimp in tequila; and jerky with egg, fish, and seafood. Wash it down with a cold beer or glass of wine. ✉ *Av. Costera Miguel Alemán 1480, between CiCi and Centro Internacional, Costera* ☎ *744/484–7711* 💳 *MC, V.*

¢–$$ MEXICAN ✕ **La Casa de Tere.** Hidden in a shopping district downtown (signs point the way), this spotless open-air eatery with pink walls is in a league of its own—expect beer-hall tables and chairs, colorful Mexican decorations, and photos of Acapulco of yore. The varied menu includes outstanding *sopa de tortilla* (tortilla soup), chicken mole, and flan. ✉ *Calle Alonso Martín 1721, 2 blocks from Av. Costera Miguel Alemán, Costera* ☎ *744/485–7735* 💳 *No credit cards* ⏲ *Closed Mon.*

¢–$$ ★ MEXICAN ✕ **Zorrito's.** When Julio Iglesias is in town, he heads to this open-air street-side eatery after the discos close. It's open almost all the time, serving Acapulco's famous green-and-white *pozole* (pork and hominy soup) as well as such steak dishes as *filete tampiqueña* (a strip of tender grilled beef), which comes with tacos, enchiladas, guacamole, and beans. ✉ *Av. Costera Miguel Alemán and Calle Anton de Alaminos, next to Banamex, Costera* ☎ *744/485–3735* 💳 *AE, MC, V* ⏲ *Open 24 hrs except Tues., closed 7 AM–3 PM.*

$ ★ SEAFOOD ✕ **Julio's.** The locals rave about Julio's, where they know they'll get a great variety of fresh seafood at an affordable price. There is nothing fancy here except the fresh authentic Mexican dishes served by friendly folks. Try the shrimp tacos or the barbecued whole fish, preceded by a large seafood cocktail. A fish fillet dinner costs about $7. Most tourists haven't found this place yet, so for a great cultural and dining experience that won't empty your wallet, this is the place. ✉*Cristóbal Colón 56, Costera* ☎*744/485–3289* ▭*MC, V.*

¢–$ CONTEMPORARY ✕ **100% Natural.** Along the Costera Miguel Alemán are several of these 24-hour restaurants specializing in quick service and light, healthful food: sandwiches made with whole wheat bread, soy burgers, chicken dishes, yogurt shakes, and fruit salads. You'll recognize these eateries by their green signs with white lettering. The original—and best—is across from the Grand Hotel. ✉*Av. Costera Miguel Alemán 234, near Acapulco Plaza, Costera* ☎*744/485–3982* ✉*Av. Costera Miguel Alemán 3126, in front of Hotel La Palapa, Costera* ☎*744/484–8440* ▭*DC, MC, V.*

13

OLD ACAPULCO

$$–$$$$ Fodor's Choice ★ CONTINENTAL ✕ **Coyuca 22.** This may well be Acapulco's most beautiful restaurant. You sit gazing down on Doric pillars, statuary, an enormous illuminated obelisk, a small pool, and the bay beyond; it's like eating in a partially restored Greek ruin. Choose from two fixed menus or order à la carte; all dishes are artful. Lobster and prime rib are specialties. ✉*Av. Coyuca 22 (10-min taxi ride from zócalo), Old Acapulco* ☎*744/482–3468 or 744/483–5030* ⚠*Reservations essential* ▭*AE, DC, MC, V* ⊗*Closed Apr. 30–Nov. 1. No lunch.*

$–$$$$ SEAFOOD ✕ **La Cabaña.** In the 1950s this local favorite was a bohemian hangout that attracted renowned bullfighters along with Mexican songwriter Agustín Lara and his lady love, María Félix. You can see their photo over the bar and sample the same dishes that made the place famous back then: baby-shark tamales, seafood casserole, or shrimp prepared with sea salt, curry, or garlic. The restaurant is smack in the middle of Playa Caleta, and there are free lockers for diners who want to take a swim, as well as banana and wave-runner rentals. ✉*Playa Caleta Lado Ote. s/n, Fracc. las Playas (5-min taxi ride east of town square), Old Acapulco* ☎*744/482–5007* 🌐*www.lacabanadecaleta.com* ▭*AE, MC, V.*

★ $–$$ SEAFOOD ✕ **El Amigo Miguel.** Locals rave about this lively place. The seafood is fresh, the portions are ample and well priced, and it's in a convenient downtown location right off the zócalo. Feast on fish soup, whole grilled sea bass, fish fillet in a buttery garlic sauce, or lobster. All come with sides of rice and warm bread. ✉*Calle Benito Juarez 31, at Calle Anzueta, Old Acapulco* ☎*744/483–6981* ▭*MC, V.*

WHERE TO STAY

ACAPULCO DIAMANTE

Most of the newer, more expensive resorts are located in Acapulco Diamante and Playa Revolcadero. These are designed to keep you captive by offering the total vacation experience, including restaurants, clubs, spas, expansive grounds, beautiful beaches, and in some cases golf courses. Acapulco proper is a $15 taxi ride away.

$$$$ **Las Brisas.** Perhaps Acapulco's signature resort, this hilltop haven is particularly popular with honeymooners. (The company motto is actually "Where children are seldom seen, but often created.") There are a variety of quarters, from one-bedroom units to deluxe private casitas complete with small private pools. Room interiors are a little dated, but nobody seems to mind because of the enchanting bay views. Since the property is very spread out (all rooms are at ground level), transportation is by pink-and-white Jeeps. The hotel also provides transportation to its private beach club. A continental breakfast is delivered to your room each morning. **Pros:** Astounding views from almost everywhere, service gracious. **Cons:** Room interiors dated, wait for Jeeps can be 20 minutes, pricy for what you get. ⊠*Carretera Escénica Clemente Mejía 5255, Las Brisas,* ☎*744/469–6900, 888/559–4329 in U.S. and Canada* 🌐*www.brisas.com.mx* *300 units* *In-room: Dial-up. In-hotel: 2 restaurants, bars, tennis courts, pools, water sports, concierge, laundry service, public Internet, no elevator* *MC, V* *CP.*

★ $$$$ **Camino Real Acapulco Diamante.** This stunning hotel is at the foot of a lush hill on exclusive Playa Pichilingue, far from the madding crowd. All rooms are done in pastels and have tile floors, luxurious baths, and up-to-date amenities such as laptop-size safes outfitted with chargers; all rooms also have balconies or terraces with a view of peaceful Puerto Marqués bay. Eleven extra-spacious club rooms have their own concierge and extra amenities. **Pros:** Good-size rooms, nice views. **Cons:** Pool can be busy, nothing really within walking distance. ⊠*Calle Baja Catita off Carretera Escénica at Km 14, Acapulco Diamante,* ☎*744/435–1010, 800/722–6466 in U.S.* 🌐*www.caminoreal.com/acapulco* *146 rooms, 11 suites* *In-room: Safe, refrigerator, Wi-Fi. In-hotel: 3 restaurants, room service, bars, pools, gym, spa, beachfront, water sports, concierge, children's programs (ages 5–15), laundry service, no-smoking rooms, Internet.* *AE, DC, MC, V.*

★ $$$$ **Quinta Real.** A member of Mexico's most prestigious hotel chain, this low-slung hillside resort overlooks the sea, about a 15-minute drive from downtown. The 74 suites have balconies, Mexican-made hardwood furniture, and closet door handles shaped like iguanas—a signature motif. Six suites have private hot tubs and small pools on their balconies. **Pros:** Nice facilities, great "world music" in the common areas. **Cons:** Not much to do at night and downtown's a bit of a drive, service is not up to snuff for the price you pay. ⊠*Paseo de la Quinta Lote 6, Acapulco Diamante, Real Diamante,* ☎*744/469–1500, 866/621–9288 in U.S.* 🌐*www.quintareal.com* *74 suites* *In-hotel: Restaurant, room service, bar, pools, gym, spa, beachfront, water sports, concierge, laundry service, WI-FI.* *AE, MC, V.*

$$$–$$$$ ★ **Fairmont Acapulco Princess.** The 17-story Princess lures the rich and famous (Howard Hughes once hid away in a suite here). Near the reception desk, fantastic ponds with waterfalls and a slatted bridge hint at the luxury throughout. Large, airy rooms have cane furniture, marble floors, and wireless Internet access. You can dine in six excellent restaurants, then burn off the calories in a match at the tennis

center, which hosts international tournaments. The superb Willow Stream spa, open to guests and nonguests, has aromatherapy, thalassotherapy, and body wraps, plus a fitness center, Swiss showers, a hair salon, and a Jacuzzi. A shuttle runs frequently to the adjacent Pierre Marqués, where you can use all facilities. **Pros:** Elaborate pools, nice golf course. **Cons:** Caters to conventions, so can be crowded; beach can busy. ✉*Playa Revolcadero, Granjas del Marqués* *AP 1351, 39907* ☎*744/469–1000, 800/441–1414 in U.S., 01800/090–9900 in Mexico* 🌐*www.fairmont.com* *927 rooms, 92 suites* *In-room: Safe, dial-up, Ethernet. In-hotel: 7 restaurants, room service, bars, golf course, tennis courts, pools, gym, spa, beachfront, water sports, concierge, children's programs (ages 3–12), laundry service* *AE, DC, MC, V* *BP, EP.*

13

$$$–$$$$ Fodor's Choice ★ **Fairmont Pierre Marqués.** This boutique-style hotel was built by J. Paul Getty in 1958 as a personal retreat. Longtime employees say that he never used it, instead making it available to his friends before eventually turning it into a hotel. After a multimillion-dollar renovation in 2004, the Pierre Marqués is one of Mexico's finest properties. The hotel offers the serenity and sophistication of a private hacienda but with the first-class services and amenities of an international resort, including a meandering pool overlooking the ocean. You can stay in a room or suite in the tower building or in one of the ultraluxe villas or bungalows, which have private plunge pools. A shuttle runs frequently to the adjacent Princess, where you can use all facilities. **Pros:** High-quality golf course, well-kept grounds. **Cons:** Food is pricey, can't get anywhere without a taxi. ✉*Playa Revolcadero, Granjas del Marqués* *AP 1351, 39907* ☎*744/466–1000, 800/441–1414 in U.S., 01800/090–9900 in Mexico* 🌐*www.fairmont.com* *220 rooms, 74 executive premier rooms, 25 suites, 10 villas, 4 bungalows* *In-room: Safe, refrigerator (some), dial-up, Ethernet. In-hotel: 2 restaurants, room service, bar, golf course, tennis courts, pools, beachfront, concierge, children's programs (ages 3–12), laundry service, public Wi-Fi* *AE, DC, MC, V* *BP, EP.*

THE COSTERA

The 8-km (5-mi) stretch of Avenida Costera Miguel Alemán known as the Costera is lined with beachfront, side-by-side, high-rise hotels. Most were built in the '60s and '70s, forever changing one of the world's most beautiful bays. The hotels are in all price categories, the cheaper properties being on the north side of the avenue. Stay here if you want to be in the middle of the action, surrounded by restaurants, bars, discos, shops, malls, and food stores. For cheap transportation along the Costera, simply jump on one of the local buses that chug up and down the strip (a ride costs 4.50 pesos), or flag one of the many taxis.

$$$$ **Elcano.** Restored to its original 1950s glamour, this perennial favorite has snappy rooms with white-tile floors and modern bathrooms. There's a beachside restaurant with an outstanding breakfast buffet, a more elegant indoor restaurant, and a gorgeous pool that not only seems to float above the bay, but also has whirlpools built into its cor-

ners. **Pros:** Ocean-facing rooms have balconies, located on good stretch of beach. **Cons:** Pool fills up with parents and kids, exercise room very small. ✉ *Av. Costera Miguel Alemán 75, Costera,* ☎ *744/435–1500.* 🌐 *www.hotel-elcano.com* *163 rooms, 17 suites* *In-room: Safe, refrigerator, Wi-Fi. In-hotel: Restaurant, room service, bars, pool, gym, beachfront, water sports, concierge, laundry service* *AE, MC, V.*

$$$–$$$$ **Fiesta Americana Villas Acapulco.** In the thick of the main shopping and restaurant district, this hotel is popular with tour groups and singles. It has a lively lobby bar and is on Playa Condesa, one of the most popular beaches in town. Pastel-colored rooms have light-wood furniture and tile floors. **Pros:** Bar can be loud after hours, good location. **Cons:** Beach can fill up, rooms are average. ✉ *Av. Costera Miguel Alemán 97, Costera,* ☎ *744/435–1600, 800/343–7821 in U.S.* 🌐 *www.fiestaamericana.com* *492 rooms, 8 suites* *In-room: Refrigerator, Wi-Fi (some). In-hotel: 2 restaurants, room service, bar, pools, beachfront, water sports, concierge, children's programs (ages 4–12), laundry service* *AE, MC, V* *EP.*

$$$ **Hyatt Regency Acapulco.** The Hyatt is popular with business travelers, conventioneers, and—thanks to its bold Caribbean color schemes and striking design—TV producers, who have opted to use it as the setting for many a Mexican soap opera. It has four outstanding eateries (one of them a kosher restaurant), a spa, and a deluxe shopping area. It's also the only hotel in Latin America with an on-site synagogue. The west side of the property insulates you from the noise of the nearby naval base. **Pros:** Great service, spacious rooms. **Cons:** Some rooms in need of updating. ✉ *Av. Costera Miguel Alemán 1, Costera,* ☎ *744/469–1234, 800/633–7313 in U.S. and Canada* 🌐 *www.hyatt.com* *640 rooms, 17 suites* *In-room: Refrigerator. In-hotel: 4 restaurants, room service, bars, tennis courts, pools, gym, spa, beachfront, children's programs (ages 8–12; high season only), laundry service, parking (no fee), public Internet* *AE, MC, V.*

★ $$–$$$ **Villa Vera.** A five-minute drive into the hills north of the Costera leads to the place where Elizabeth Taylor married Mike Todd and where Lana Turner settled for three years. This is as close as you can get to the glamour and style of Acapulco when it was Hollywood's retreat. Some villas were once private homes and have their own pools. The excellent Villa Vera Spa and Fitness Center, open to guests and nonguests, has exercise machines, free weights, milk baths, algae treatments, and massages. **Pros:** Architecturally intriguing; extremely comfortable beds. **Cons:** Not on the beach. ✉ *Calle Lomas del Mar 35, Costera* *AP 560, 39690* ☎ *744/484–0333 or 888/554–2361* 🌐 *www.raintreevacationclub.com* *24 rooms, 25 suites, 6 villas* *In-room: Wi-Fi, refrigerator, VCR. In-hotel: Restaurant, bar, tennis courts, pools, gym, spa, concierge, no elevator, laundry service, Internet* *AE, MC, V* *EP.*

$$ **Park Hotel & Tennis Center.** A helpful staff and a prime location make this an appealing place to stay. Rooms, which have colonial-style furnishings, are around a garden with a good-size pool. Some have kitchenettes and balconies; all are spotlessly clean. The Park has a tennis center and is only a block from the beach. **Pros:** Good location, fairly inexpensive. **Cons:** Rooms are "economical," hotel bar is tiny. ✉ *Av. Cos-*

tera Miguel Alemán 127, Costera ✉ *AP 269, 39670* ☎ *744/485–5992* 🌐 *www.parkhotel-acapulco.com* *88 rooms* *In-hotel: bar, tennis courts, pool, no elevator, parking (no fee)* ▭ *AE, MC, V* *EP.*

$–$$ **Las Hamacas.** Rooms at this friendly 1950s Acapulco hotel surround a large inner courtyard. It's across the street from the beach, a 10-minute walk from downtown, and has a lovely garden of coconut palms. The spacious, light-filled rooms have contemporary wood furniture. Junior suites sleep two adults and two children. A stay here gets you access to a beach club. **Pros:** Nice landscaping, good rates. **Cons:** Accommodations basic, hotel near cruise ship terminal. ✉ *Av. Costera Miguel Alemán 239, Costera* ☎ *744/483–7006* 🌐 *www.hamacas.com.mx* *107 rooms, 20 suites* *In-hotel: Restaurant, room service, bar, pools, laundry service, parking (no fee)* ▭ *MC, V* *EP.*

13

OLD ACAPULCO

Old Acapulco is the place to find budget hotels and restaurants.

$$–$$$ **Alba Suites.** This all-white, all-suites hotel is popular with families and comprises seven low-rise buildings—most four or five stories. Units sleep four, six, or eight and have terraces; some also have kitchenettes. There's a cable car to the hotel's beach club, which is on the bay and next to the Club de Yates and its 330-foot-long toboggan run. **Pros:** Considerate service, cable car to beach club. **Cons:** Noisy during the day from kids at pool, decor is basic. ✉ *Grand Via Tropical 35, Caleta* ☎ *744/483–0073, 877/428–1327 in Canada* 🌐 *www.albasuites.com.mx* *300 suites* *In-room: Kitchen (some), refrigerator. In-hotel: Restaurant, bar, pools, beachfront, laundry service* ▭ *AE, MC, V* *EP.*

$$–$$$ **El Mirador.** Another '50s Hollywood hangout, El Mirador exudes nostalgia, with white walls, red-tile roofs, and hand-carved Mexican furnishings. It's on a hill with views of Bahía de Acapulco and La Quebrada, where the cliff divers perform. Many suites have refrigerators, hot tubs, and ocean vistas. **Pros:** Close proximity to divers, nice views. **Cons:** Food inconsistent, sense that its "heyday" has passed. ✉ *Av. Quebrada 74, Old Acapulco* ☎ *744/483–1155, 866/765–0608 in U.S.* 🌐 *www.hotelelmiradoracapulco.com.mx* *133 rooms, 9 suites* *In-room: Refrigerator (some). In-hotel: 2 restaurants, bar, pools, no elevator, children's programs (ages 3–12), laundry service, parking (no fee)* ▭ *AE, MC, V* *EP.*

$–$$$ **Etel Suites.** On Cerro Pinzona (Pinzona Hill), a five-minute walk from La Quebrada, the Etel has outstanding views of Bahía de Acapulco and spacious rooms with sturdy cedar furniture. All accommodations sleep three, and you can rent a full kitchen and dining room to turn your room into a suite. One studio has a kitchenette. There's a garden on the roof and a children's play area by the pool. The owner, gracious Señora Etel Alvarez, is the great-grandniece of John August Sutter, whose gold mine launched the Gold Rush of 1849. **Pros:** Near to cliff divers, reasonably priced, wonderful owner. **Cons:** Accommodations basic. ✉ *Av. Pinzona 92, Old Acapulco* ☎ *744/482–2240* *12 rooms* *In-room: Kitchen (some). In-hotel: Pool, no elevator* ▭ *MC, V* *EP.*

$$ **Boca Chica.** An Old Acapulco mainstay, right down to its antique telephone switchboard, Boca Chica is a few steps from a swimming cove, and the open-air lobby has lovely views of Bahía de Caletilla. Rooms are small and clean. There's also a landscaped jungle garden and a pool. The Mexican breakfasts are ample. **Pros:** Nice views, well-kept gardens. **Cons:** Rooms could use a little TLC. ⊠*Playa Caletilla, across bay from Isla la Roqueta and Mágico Mundo Marino, Old Acapulco* ☎*744/483–6741, 800/346–3942 in U.S.* ⊕*www.acapulco-bocachica.com* *42 rooms, 3 suites* *In-hotel: Restaurant, bar, pool, beachfront, diving, water sports, no elevator, laundry service, parking (no fee)* *MC, V* *BP.*

★ $–$$ **Los Flamingos.** This hot-pink, cliff-side hotel was a favorite hang-out of co-owners John Wayne and Johnny ("Tarzan") Weissmuller. A young busboy at the hotel in those days, Adolfo Santiago, is now the owner. He plays an amazing guitar and, if in the mood, will share some good stories. Today Los Flamingos draws an international clientele for its fine views and its *coco locos,* tequila drinks served in a green coconut. Rooms have bright pink walls and spartan, shower-only baths. Weissmuller liked to stay in the circular two-bedroom master suite. The hotel provides free transportation to the beach and downtown. **Pros:** History is intriguing, epic views. **Cons:** A little wear and tear in rooms, bathrooms need updating. ⊠*Av. López Mateos, Fracc. las Playas, Old Acapulco* ☎*744/482–0690* ⊕*www.hotellosflamingos.com* *46 rooms, 2 suites* *In-room: No a/c (some). In-hotel: restaurant, bar, pool, no elevator, laundry service, parking (no fee)* *AE, MC, V* *EP.*

¢ **Misión.** Two minutes from the zócalo, this charming, colonial-style hotel surrounds a greenery-rich courtyard with an outdoor dining area that's open only for breakfast. Rooms are small and by no means fancy, with painted brick walls, tile floors, wrought-iron beds, and ceiling fans. Every room has a shower, and there's plenty of hot water. The best rooms are on the second and third floors, as you can open the windows and fully appreciate the view; the top-floor room is large but hot in the daytime. **Pros:** Artistic touches, quaint feel. **Cons:** Tiny rooms, no lunch or dinner. ⊠*Calle Felipe Valle 12, Downtown* ☎*744/482–3643* *20 rooms* *In-room: No a/c, no phone, no TV. In-hotel: No elevator* *No credit cards* *EP.*

PIE DE LA CUESTA

To the west of the bay, on the Pacific, is the laid-back beach town of Pie de la Cuesta, home to low- and mid-priced small hotels, usually family-run and on the beach. If you stay here, you'll get a good taste of Mexican beach-village life.

$$$$ **Parador del Sol.** Germans and Canadians favor this low-key, all-inclusive resort's white villas scattered throughout gardens along both the lagoon and the Pacific Ocean sides of Carretera Pie de la Cuesta. The ocean is particularly dramatic here, with towering waves. The spacious rooms have tile floors and fan-cooled terraces with hammocks. In addition to all meals, comprising Guerrero specialties served buffet-style,

including red snapper and tamales, rates include the occasional on-site music and dance performance, aerobics classes, tennis, and nonmotorized water sports. Motorized water sports cost extra. **Pros:** Peaceful, beautiful beach, pricey for what you get. **Cons:** A trek to downtown by car, rough ocean so swimming is limited. ✉ *Carretera Pie de la Cuesta–Barra de Coyuca, Km 5, Pie de la Cuesta* *AP 1070, 39300* ☎ *744/444–4050* 🌐 *www.paradordelsol.com.mx* *150 rooms* *In-hotel: Restaurant, bars, tennis courts, pools, gym, no elevator, laundry service, parking (no fee)* 💳 *MC, V* 🍽 *AI.*

$–$$$ Fodor's Choice ★ **Hacienda Vayma.** White stucco bungalows named for musicians and painters overlook the beach or interior courtyards. The sparse, contemporary rooms accommodate two, three, or five people. The bathrooms are tiny, however, and have no hot water. If you can opt for one of the suites, which have plunge pools, air-conditioning, and terraces, you'll be a lot more comfortable. An excellent outdoor restaurant draws diners from miles around, and on weekends the hotel fills with an interesting array of guests, such as embassy personnel from Mexico City. **Pros:** Animals allowed, some rooms have canopied beds. **Cons:** No credit cards accepted. ✉ *Av. Base Aerea Militar 378, Pie de la Cuesta,* ☎ *744/460–5260* 🌐 *www.vayma.com.mx* *20 rooms, 4 suites* *In-room: No a/c (some), no phone. In-hotel: Restaurant, bar, pool, spa, beachfront, water sports, no elevator, laundry service, parking (no fee), some pets allowed* 💳 *No credit cards* 🍽 *EP.*

$–$$ **Villas Ukae Kim.** You can't miss this colorful, rustic, seaside lodge. The large rooms are painted in bright Mexican hues, and all have terraces and mosquito nets slung over double beds; the honeymoon suite has a private hot tub. **Pros:** Artistic touches. **Cons:** No credit cards accepted. ✉ *Av. Fuerza Aereo Mexicana 356, Pie de la Cuesta,* ☎ *744/440–0486* *21 rooms, 1 suite* *In-room: No a/c (some), no phone, no TV (some). In-hotel: Restaurant, bar, pool, beachfront, water sports, no elevator, laundry service, parking (no fee)* 💳 *No credit cards* 🍽 *EP.*

NIGHTLIFE

Acapulco's clubs are open nearly 365 days a year from about 10:30 PM until they empty out. The minute the sun slips over the horizon, the Costera comes alive. People mill around, window-shopping, choosing restaurants, generally biding their time until the disco hour. Many casual beach restaurants on the strip have live music.

The resorts often have splashy entertainment, sometimes with big-name artists. At the very least such hotels have live music during happy hour, restaurant theme parties, dancing at a beach bar—or all three. For a more informal evening, head for the zócolo, where there's usually a band on weekend evenings.

The more expensive clubs have $20–$60 cover charges, sometimes including drinks and sometimes not. Women usually pay less than men. In general, a higher cover calls for dressier attire, that is, no shorts. The more casual open-air bars are mostly free to enter, and shorts and

T-shirts are common. Drinks cost $2–$5, and two-for-one drink specials during happy hour are common. The waiters depend on tips in the 15%–20% range. Note that Mexico's legal drinking age is 18.

Alebrije (✉*Av. Costera Miguel Alemán 3308, across from Hyatt Regency, Costera* ☎*744/484–5902* 🎫*Cover: $25 women, $35 men, including drinks*) can accommodate 5,000 people in its love seats and booths, and it attracts a younger (late teens, early twenties) crowd. From 10:30 to 11:30, the music is slow and romantic; afterward there's dance music and light shows until dawn. The music ranges from pop to tropical.

★ Frequented primarily by tourists, **Baby Lobster Bar** (✉*Costera Miguel Alemán near Bungee Jump in La Condesa* ☎*744/484–1096* 🎫*No cover*) is a lively open-air bar on the beach. You will get two drinks when you order, and the atmosphere is conducive to meeting other people. Tabletop dancing is not discouraged, especially late at night. There's no cover charge, and there are many other bars in the area.

Small, expensive, and exclusive, **Baby'O** (✉*Av. Costera Miguel Alemán 22, Costera* ☎*744/484–7474* 🎫*Cover: $30 women, $60–$100 men, not including drinks*) caters to the local elite. The club has long had the reputation of being Acapulco's classiest, and the well-dressed clientele lounges and dances in a jungle-inspired interior. It can be hard to get in, and even harder to get a table, but this is *the* place to go to see and be seen. It's closed Sunday and Monday in low season (May through November).

As the name suggests, **Disco Beach** (✉*Playa Condesa, Costera* ☎*744/484–8230* 🎫*Cover: $30, including drinks*)is right on the sands. It's so informal that most people turn up in shorts. The waiters are young and friendly—some people find them overly so, and in fact, this is a legendary pickup spot. Every Wednesday is ladies' night, when all the women receive flowers. Foam parties reign on Friday.

Fodor's Choice ★ A waterfall cascades down from the dance floor of **Palladium** (✉*Carretera Escénica, Costera* ☎*744/446–5490* 🎫*Cover: $16–$26 women, $26–$36 men, including drinks*), considered by many to be Acapulco's best. The dance floor is surrounded by 50-foot-high windows, so dancers have a wraparound view of the city. The club is so popular that it may take a while to get in.

★ At **Paradise,** (✉*Av. Costera Miguel Alemán 101, Costera, near Fiesta Americana Hotel* ☎*744/484–5988* 🎫*No cover*)the restaurant downstairs has beach access, a swimming pool, and lively dance contests at night. The open-air bar upstairs affords a spectacular bay view and it's a great place to watch bungee jumpers as they plunge from the 165-foot platform right next door.

The so-called Cathedral of Salsa, **Salon Q** (✉*Av. Costera Miguel Alemán 3117, Costera* ☎*744/481–0114* 🎫*Cover: $24*)is a combination dance hall and disco, where the bands play salsas, merengues, and other Latin rhythms for young and old. Weekends see shows—mostly impersonations of Mexican entertainers.

★ A snug place on the Las Brisas hill, **Zucca** (✉ *Carretera Escénica 28 Loc. 1, Costera* ☎ *744/446–5690 or 744/466–5691* *Cover: $20–$25, not including drinks*)attracts a 25-and-older crowd, mainly couples. People really dress up here, with the men in well-cut pants and collared shirts and the women in cocktail dresses. The music is from the '60s, '70s, '80s, and '90s. It opens at 11 PM Wednesday to Saturday during high season and Thursday to Saturday in low season.

SPORTS & THE OUTDOORS

BULLFIGHTS

The season runs from about the first week of January to Easter, and *corridas* (bullfights) are held on Sunday at 5:30. Tickets are available through your hotel or at the window in the **Plaza de Toros** (✉ *Av. Circunvalación, Fracc. Las Playas, Playa Caleta* ☎ *744/482–9561*) Monday–Saturday 10–2 and Sunday 10:30–5. Tickets in the shade (*sombra*)—the only way to go—cost about $22. Preceding the fight are performances of Spanish dances and music by the Chili Frito band.

FISHING

Fishing is what originally drew many of the early tourists to Acapulco, and it is still an abundant area. Billfish, striped marlin, pompano, bonito, red snapper, and tuna can be found in the ocean year-round; and carp, mullet, and catfish swim in the freshwater lagoons. You can arrange fishing trips through your hotel or at the Pesca Deportiva near the *muelle* (dock) across from the zócalo. **Acapulco Scuba Center** (✉ *Paseo del Pescador 13 y 14, near zócalo, Old Acapulco* ☎ *744/482–9474* 🌐 *www.acapulcoscuba.com*) is an excellent place to sign up for deep-sea fishing excursions. The center's 40-foot boats accommodate up to six passengers. Trips depart at 7 AM, return at 2 PM, and cost $270 per person.We also recommend **Fish-R-Us** (✉ *Av. Costera Miguel Alemán 100, Fracc. Las Playas, Old Acapulco* ☎ *744/482–8282* 🌐 *www.fish-r-us.com*), which offers charter service for sailfish, tuna, and dorado fishing. Boats depart at 6 AM. You can share a boat for $70 per person, with a maximum of six people, or rent a private yacht for $370 to $440 per day.

For freshwater trips try the companies along Laguna Coyuca. Boats accommodating 4–10 people cost $250–$500 a day, $45–$60 by chair. Excursions leave about 7 AM and return at 1 PM or 2 PM. At the docks you can hire a boat for $40 a day (two lines). You must get a license ($12, depending on the season) from the Secretaría de Pesca; there's a representative at the dock, but note that the office is closed during siesta, between 2 and 4.

GOLF

There's a short, public, well-kept golf course at the **Club de Golf** (✉*Av. Costera Miguel Alemán s/n* ☎*744/484–0781*) on the Costera next to the convention center. Greens fees are $50 for 9 holes, $80 for 18.

Two championship courses—one designed by Ted Robinson, the other remodeled by Robert Trent Jones Sr. and then renovated under the supervision of Robert Trent Jones Jr.—are adjacent to the **Fairmont Acapulco Princess and Pierre Marqués hotels** (✉*Playa Revolcadero* ☎*744/469–1000*). Make reservations well in advance. Greens fees in high season, mid-December to mid-April, are $125 for hotel guests, $140 for nonguests. Fees are lower after noon and in low season.

A round on the 18-hole course at the **Mayan Palace** (✉*Playa Revolcadero, domicilio conocido* ☎*744/469–6000*) time-share condo complex is $70 for guests, $130 for nonguests.

WATER SPORTS

You can arrange to water-ski, rent broncos (one-person Jet Skis), parasail, and windsurf at outfitters on the beaches. Parasailing is an Acapulco highlight developed here in the 1960s; a five-minute trip costs $60. Waterskiing is about $40 an hour; broncos cost $40–$95 for a half hour, depending on the size. You can arrange to windsurf at Playa Caleta and most beaches along the Costera, but the best place to actually do it is at Bahía Puerto Marqués. The main surfing beach is Revolcadero.

Although visibility isn't as good as in the Caribbean, scuba diving is an option. It's best from November through February, when the water is the most transparent. (In summer, from June through October, rains bring mud from the hills down the rivers and into the bay.) A Canadian warship was scuttled in the bay to make a diving trip more appealing.

Acapulco Scuba Center (✉*Paseo del Pescador 13 y 14, near zócalo, Old Acapulco* ☎*744/482–9474* 🌐*www.acapulcoscuba.com*) offers four-hour snorkeling and scuba outings for beginners and certified divers. All tours include gear and round-trip transportation from your hotel. Scuba trips cost $70 with lessons and lunch included; snorkeling costs $35. The center also provides deep-sea fishing excursions.

The **Shotover Jet** (✉*Centro Comerical Plaza Marbella, Local 17 and Av. Costera Miguel Aleman, Costera* ☎*744/484–1154* 🌐 *www.shotoverjet.com.mx*) is a wild boat ride that's an import from the rivers around Queenstown, New Zealand. An air-conditioned bus takes you to the Pierre Marqués Lagoon, about 20 minutes from downtown Acapulco. Twelve-passenger boats provide thrilling 30-minute boat rides on the lagoon, complete with 360-degree turns—one of the Shotover Jet's trademarks—and vistas of local flora and fauna. The cost for the ride and transportation to and from the site is $45. For more thrills, from July through January, you can shoot the rapids on 1½- to 2-hour guided trips for $55; there's a four-person minimum.

SHOPPING

Guerrero State is known for hand-painted ceramics, objects made from *palo de rosa* wood, bark paintings depicting scenes of village life and local flora and fauna, and embroidered textiles. Stands in downtown's sprawling municipal market are piled high with handicrafts, as well as fruit, flowers, spices, herbs, cheeses, seafood, poultry, and other meats. Practice your bargaining skills here or at one of the street-side handicrafts sellers, as prices are usually flexible.

Boutiques selling high-fashion Mexican designs for men and women are plentiful and draw an international clientele. This is a great place to shop for bathing suits, evening wear, and gems from all over the world. Many shops also sell high-quality crafts from throughout the country. Although many of Acapulco's stores carry jewelry and other articles made of silver, aficionados tend to make the three-hour drive to the colonial town of Taxco—one of the world's silver capitals.

Most shops are open Monday–Saturday 10–7. The main strip is along Avenida Costera Miguel Alemán from the Costa Club to El Presidente Hotel. Here you can find Guess, Peer, Aca Joe, Amarras, Polo Ralph Lauren, and other sportswear shops, as well as emporiums like Aurrerá, Gigante, Price Club, Sam's, Wal-Mart, Comercial Mexicana, and the upscale Liverpool department store, Fabricas de Francia. Old Acapulco has inexpensive tailors and lots of souvenir shops.

Sanborns. A countrywide institution, Sanborns is a good place to find English-language newspapers, magazines, and books; basic cosmetics and toiletries; and high-quality souvenirs. All branches are open 7 AM to 1:30 AM in high season and 7:30 AM–11 PM the rest of the year. ✉*Av. Costera Miguel Alemán 1226, Costera* ☎*744/484–4413* ✉*Av. Costera Miguel Alemán 3111, Costera* ☎*744/484–2025* ✉*Av. Costera Miguel Alemán 209, Costera* ☎*744/482–6167* ✉*Av. Costera Miguel Alemán off zócalo, Old Acapulco* ☎*744/482–6168.*

MALLS

Aca Mall, next door to Marbella Mall, is all white and marble and filled with the likes of Tommy Hilfiger, Peer, and Aca Joe.

The multilevel **Marbella Mall,** at the Diana *glorieta* (traffic circle), is home to Martí, a sporting-goods store; a health center (drugstore, clinic, and lab); the Canadian Embassy; Bing's Ice Cream; and several restaurants.

Plaza Bahía, next to the Costa Club hotel, is an air-conditioned mall with boutiques such as Dockers, Nautica, and Aspasia.

MARKETS

One large flea market with a convenient location is **La Diana Mercado de Artesanías,** a block from the Emporio hotel, close to the Diana monument in Costera.

El Mercado de Artesanías El Parazal is a 15-minute walk from Sanborns downtown. Look for fake ceremonial masks, the ever-present onyx chessboards, $20 hand-embroidered dresses, imitation silver, hammocks, and skin cream made from turtles (don't buy it, because turtle harvesting is illegal in both Mexico and the United States, and you won't get it through U.S. Customs). From Sanborns downtown, head away from Avenida Costera to Vásquez de León and turn right one block later. The market is open daily 9–9.

Don't miss the **Mercado Municipal,** where restaurateurs load up on produce early in the morning, and later in the day locals shop for piñatas, serapes, leather goods, baskets, hammocks, amulets to attract lovers or ward off enemies, and velvet paintings of the Virgin of Guadalupe.

SPECIALTY SHOPS

ART GALLERIES

Stop in **Esteban Art Gallery** (✉*Scenic Hwy., Balcones #110-2, next to Madieras restaurant, Costera* ☎*744/446–5719* 🌐 *www.esteban-acapulco.com*)to see the works of renowned international and Mexican artists, including Calder, Dalí, Siqueiros, and Tamayo. Some crafts are also sold.

Galería Rudic (✉*Calle Vicente Yañez Pinzón 9, Costera* ✣*Across from Continental Plaza and adjoining Jardín des Artistes restaurant* ☎*744/484–1004*)sells pieces from contemporary Mexican artists, including Armando Amaya, Gastón Cabrera, Trinidad Osorio, and Casiano García.

The Hungarian artist, **Pal Kepenyes,** (✉*Guitarrón 140, Lomas Guitarrón* ☎*744/484–3738*)who lives in Mexico, gets good press for his jewelry and sculpture (much of it racy and provocative), on display in his workshop.

Guadalajara-based **Sergio Bustamente** (✉*Av. Costera Miguel Alemán 120–9, across from Fiesta American Condesa hotel, Costera* ☎*744/484–4992* ✉*Hyatt Regency Acapulco, Av. Costera Miguel Alemán 1, Costera* ☎*744/469–1234*)is known for his jewelry, whimsical, painted papier-mâché, and giant ceramic sculptures of suns, moons, animals, and people.

CLOTHING

Armando's (✉*Hyatt Regency Acapulco, Av. Costera Miguel Alemán 1, Costera* ☎*744/484–5111* ✉*Av. Costera Miguel Alemán 1252–7, in La Torre de Acapulco, Costera* ☎*744/469–1234*) sells its own line of women's dresses, jackets, and vests with a Mexican flavor. It also has some interesting Luisa Conti accessories.

International celebrities and important local families are among the clientele of **Esteban's**(✉ *Scenic Highway, Balcones #110-2, next to Madiera's restaurant, Costera* ☎*744/446-5719* 🌐*www.esteban-acapulco.com*). Its opulent evening dresses range from $200 to $3,000; daytime dresses average $120. There's a men's clothing section on the second floor. If

CLOSE UP

Acapulco Background

Archaeological evidence indicates that people first inhabited Acapulco around 3000 BC, growing crops and fishing. Around 1500 BC the area was settled by the Nahuas, a tribe related to the Nahuatl, who populated much of southern Mexico. The Nahuatl language provided the name Acapulco, meaning "place of canes" or "reeds." Although it is generally accepted that the first non-natives to reach Acapulco were Spaniards led by Hernán Cortés, some local historians claim that a Chinese monk named Fa Hsein predated Cortés by 100 years.

From 1565 to 1815 the Spanish maintained a thriving port and trading center in Acapulco. Spanish galleons returning from Asia, primarily the Philippines and China, delivered silks, porcelain, jade, jasmine, and spices. These goods were then carried overland on a 6-foot-wide trail to the Mexico gulf coast town of Veracruz for shipment to Spain. Many pirate ships lurked outside Acapulco Bay, making the Pacific voyages a risky business.

Acapulco became a town in 1799, but started to decline with the War of Independence, when locals sided with the Spanish royalists. Insurgent leader José María Morelos showed his displeasure by burning much of the town in 1814. Independence from Spain and a changing world rendered the trade route obsolete.

The town remained in relative obscurity until 1927, when a road was built connecting the port to Mexico City and bringing the first tourists. It wasn't long before Hollywood celebrities and other wealthy world travelers started to arrive, and Acapulco began its transformation. One of the first to recognize the potential of the area was then Mexico President Miguel Alemán, who purchased miles of undeveloped coastline. He in turn sold a portion of the land to billionaire oil magnate J. Paul Getty, who built a lavish getaway for himself and his friends—now the Fairmont Pierre Marqués Hotel on Playa Revolcadero.

By the 1960s it seemed everyone in Hollywood was vacationing in Acapulco: Frank Sinatra, Bob Hope, Leslie Caron, Cary Grant, Lana Turner, John Wayne, Errol Flynn, Brigitte Bardot, Elvis Presley, Elizabeth Taylor…too many names to list. World leaders, artists, and writers were also frequent visitors, including John, Robert, and Edward Kennedy, Dwight Eisenhower, Richard Nixon, Ronald Reagan, the Reverend Billy Graham, Salvador Dalí, Tennessee Williams, and John Huston. To read about the long celebrity history of Acapulco, as well as a great account of how the town has grown, pick up a copy of the book *Mike Oliver's Acapulco*. Oliver, who died in 2004, published the English-language *Acapulco News* for decades, and knew and socialized with them all.

Acapulco today, although not the Hollywood hangout of times past, is still a major tourist destination, especially with Mexican nationals, who make up about 80% of its visitors. Most people will acknowledge that early city planners allowed too much beachfront development, forever changing the visual and aesthetic landscape, but the sun, sand, and culture of this vibrant and historic city still attract fun-seekers by the millions.

you scour the sale racks you can find some items marked down as much as 80%.

SILVER SECRETS

Buy silver and jewelry made from semiprecious stones only in reputable establishments, or you might end up with cleverly painted paste or a silver facsimile called *alpaca.* Make sure that 0.925 is stamped on the silver piece; this verifies its purity.

HANDICRAFTS

A good place for gifts, **Alebrijes & Caracoles** (✉*Plaza Bahía, Costera* ☎*744/485–0490*)consists of two shops designed to look like flea-market stalls. Top-quality merchandise includes papier-mâché fruits and vegetables, Christmas ornaments, wind chimes, and brightly painted wooden animals from Oaxaca.

Arte Para Siempre (✉*Av. Costera Miguel Alemán 4834, near Hyatt Regency Acapulco, Costera* ☎*744/484–2390*), in the Acapulco Cultural Center, sparkles with handicrafts from the seven regions of Guerrero. Look for hand-loomed shawls, painted gourds, hammocks, baskets, Olinalá boxes, and silver jewelry.

SILVER & JEWELRY

You can watch craftsmen at work in **B and B Jewelers** (✉*Parque Papagayo on Av. Costera Miguel Alemán* ☎*744/485–6270*), a huge store and jewelry factory in Papagayo Park. Authentic gold jewelry and fire opals are specialties.

Diamond jewelry of impeccable design by Charles Garnier and Nouvelle Bague is sold at **Minette** (✉*Fairmont Acapulco Princess hotel arcade, Playa Revolcadero, Revolcadero* ☎*744/469–1000*). There's also jewelry set with Caledonia stones from Africa as well as Emilia Castillo's exquisite line of brightly colored porcelainware inlaid with silver fish, stars, and birds.

Tane (✉*Las Brisas hotel, Carretera Escénica 5255, Las Brisas* ☎*744/469–6900*)has exquisite flatware, jewelry, and objets d'art created by one of Mexico's most prestigious (and pricey) silversmiths.

SIDE TRIP TO TAXCO

275 km (170 mi) north of Acapulco.

In Mexico's premier "Silver City," marvelously preserved white-stucco, red-tile-roof colonial buildings hug cobblestone streets that wind up and down the foothills of the Sierra Madre. Taxco (pronounced *tahss*-ko) is a living work of art. For centuries its silver mines drew foreign mining companies. In 1928 the government made it a national monument. And today its charm, abundant sunshine, flowers, and silversmiths make it a popular getaway.

The town's name was derived from the Nahuatl word *tlacho* meaning "the place where ball is played." Spanish explorers first discovered a wealth of minerals in the area in 1524, just three years after Hernán

Cortés entered the Aztec city of Tenochtitlán, present-day Mexico City. Soon Sovácon del Rey, the first mine in the New World, was established on the present-day town square. The first mines were soon depleted of riches, however, and the town went into stagnation for the next 150 years. In 1708 two Frenchmen, Francisco and Don José de la Borda, resumed the mining. Francisco soon died, but José discovered the silver vein that made him the area's wealthiest man. The main square in the town center is named Plaza Borda in his honor.

After the Borda era, however, Taxco's importance again faded, until the 1930s and the arrival of William G. Spratling, a writer-architect from New Orleans. Enchanted by the city and convinced of its potential as a center for silver jewelry, Spratling set up an apprentice shop. His talent and fascination with pre-Columbian design combined to produce silver jewelry and other artifacts that soon earned Taxco its worldwide reputation as the Silver City once more. Spratling's inspiration lives on in his students and their descendants, many of whom are today's famous silversmiths.

Taxco's biggest cultural event is the Jornadas Alarconianos, which honors one of Mexico's greatest dramatists with plays, dance performances, and concerts in the third week of May. Other fiestas provide chances to honor almost every saint in heaven with music, dancing, and fireworks. A refreshing change is the Día del Jumil, which is held each November on the first Monday after the Day of the Dead, when the townsfolk climb the Cerro del Huixteco to capture jumil beetles and fry them up for snacks, or grind them into salsa. Taxco is on the side of a mountain, 5,800 feet above sea level, and many of its narrow, winding streets run nearly vertical. So bring some good walking shoes and be prepared to get some lung-gasping exercise.

GETTING HERE & AROUND

The try by car from Acapulco takes 3½ hours via the toll road and about 45 minutes longer on the more scenic free road. If you can start early, consider taking the scenic road to get there and the toll road to return. Warning: On the toll road there are very few opportunities to turn around. If you'd prefer not to rent a car, Estrella buses leave Acapulco for Taxco five times a day from 7 AM to 6:40 PM from the Terminal Central de Autobuses de Primera Clase (First-Class Bus Terminal). The cost for the approximately 4½-hour ride is about $15 one-way. Grupo Estrella Blanca buses buses depart from Acapulco several times a day from the Terminal de Autobuses. A first-class, one-way ticket is $15. Buses depart from Taxco four times a day.

ESSENTIALS

Bus Contacts First-class **Estrella de Oro** (✉ *Av. Cuauhtémoc 1490, Acapulco* ☎ *744/485–8758* ✉ *Av. de los Plateros 386, Taxco* ☎ *762/485–8705 or 762/622–0648*) **Grupo Estrella Blanca** (✉ *Av. Ejido 47, Old Acapulco, Acapulco* ☎ *744/469–2017* ✉ *Av. de los Plateros 310, Taxco* ☎ *762/622–0131*).

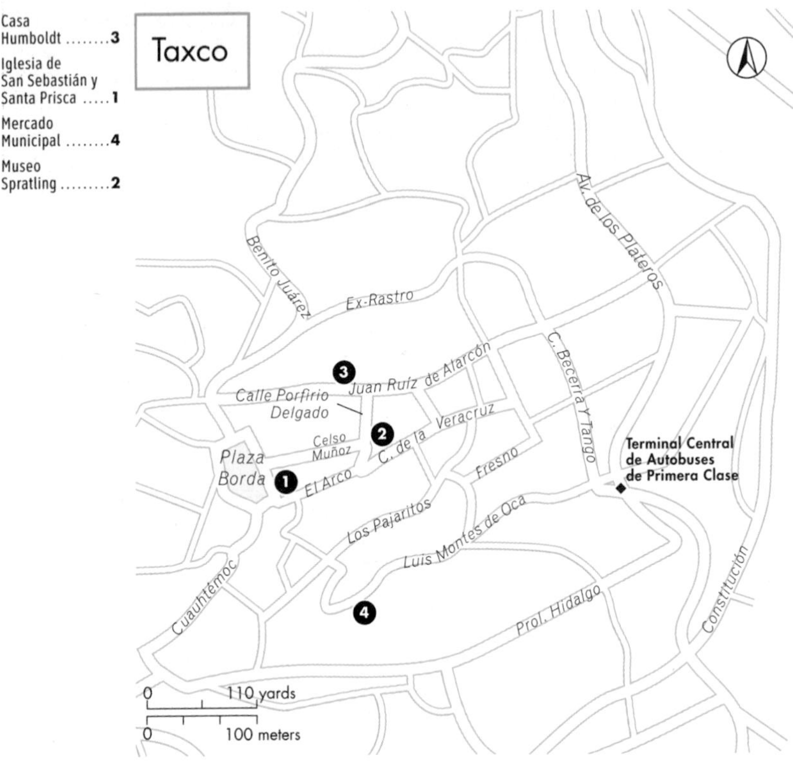

EXPLORING

★ ❶ **Iglesia de San Sebastián y Santa Prisca** has dominated the busy, colorful Plaza Borda since the 18th century. Usually just called Santa Prisca, it was built by French silver magnate José de la Borda in thanks to the Almighty for Borda's having literally stumbled upon a rich silver vein, although the expense nearly bankrupted him. According to legend, St. Prisca appeared to workers during a storm and prevented a wall of the church from tumbling. Soon after, the church was named in her honor. The style of the church—a sort of Spanish baroque known as churrigueresque—and its pale pink exterior have made it Taxco's most important landmark. Its facade, naves, and *bovedas* (vaulted ceilings), as well as important paintings by Mexican Juan Cabrera, are slowly being restored. ✉*Southwest side of Plaza Borda* ☎*No phone* ⏲*Daily* 6 AM–9 PM.

❷ The former home of William G. Spratling houses the **Museo Spratling,** which displays some 140 of the artist's original designs plus his collection of pre-Columbian artifacts. Exhibits also explain the working of colonial mines. ✉*At the Plazuela de Juan Ruíz de Alarcón plaza on Calle Porfirio Delgado 1* ☎*762/622–1660* 🎫*$2.70* ⏲*Tues.–Sun. 9–3.*

3 **Casa Humboldt** or Museo de Arte Virreinal, as it is also known, was named for German naturalist Alexander von Humboldt, who stayed here in 1803. The Moorish-style 18th-century house has a finely detailed facade. It now contains a wonderful little museum of colonial art. ✉ *Calle Juan Ruíz de Alarcón 12* ☎ *762/622–5501* 🎫 *$1.50* ⏲ *Tues.–Sat. 10–6, Sun. 10–4.*

4 Fodor's Choice ★ Weekend mornings locals from surrounding towns come to sell and buy produce, crafts, and everything from peanuts to electrical appliances at the **Mercado Municipal.** It's directly down the hill from Santa Prisca. Look for the market's chapel to the Virgin of Guadalupe.

13

OFF THE BEATEN PATH

Mexico's largest caverns, the Grutas de Cacahuamilpa are about 30 km (19 mi) northeast of Taxco. English-speaking guides will lead you along a 2-km (1 mi) illuminated walkway in large chambers with fascinating geological formations. A tour takes around two hours. 🎫 *$4.50* ☎ *721/104-0155* ⏲ *Daily 9–5.*

WHERE TO EAT

You can find everything from tagliatelle to iguana in Taxco restaurants, and meals are much less expensive than in Acapulco. Taxco has two main types of hotels: small inns nestled in the hills around the zócalo and larger, more modern hotels in the outskirts of town.

$–$$$ SOUTHERN ✕**Señor Costilla.** The Taxco outpost of the zany Carlos Anderson chain, known for joke menus and entertaining waiters, serves barbecued ribs and chops. Get here early for a table on the balcony overlooking the main square. ✉ *Plaza Borda 1* ☎ *762/622–3215* ▭ *MC, V.*

¢–$$ ★ MEXICAN ✕**Hostería el Adobe.** This intimate place has excellent food and hanging lamps and masks. There are meat and fish dishes, but the favorites are garlic-and-egg soup and the *queso adobe,* fried cheese on a bed of potato skins, covered with a green tomatillo sauce. ✉ *Plazuela de San Juan 13* ☎ *762/622–1416* ▭ *MC, V.*

¢–$$ ★ ECLECTIC ✕**El Mural.** You can eat indoors or out on a poolside terrace where there's a view not only of a Juan O'Gorman mural but of the stunning Santa Prisca church. The chef prepares international beef and seafood dishes as well as Mexican specialties like cilantro soup and crepes with *huitlacoche* (corn fungus, a pre-Hispanic delicacy that is counterintuitively delicious). The daily three-course, fixed-price meal is $25. For breakfast try the home-baked sweet rolls and marmalade from the fruit of nearby trees. ✉ *Posada de la Misión, Cerro de la Misión 32* ☎ *762/622–0063* ▭ *AE, MC, V.*

¢–$$ Fodor's Choice ★ MEXICAN ✕**La Parroquia.** The balcony at this pleasant café offers an outstanding view of the plaza and cathedral. Enjoy a too-much-tequila cure—the $4 Mexican breakfast of *huevos parroquia*—and watch the town come to life. Or come in for a beer as the sun sets over the zócalo. ✉ *Plaza Borda* ☎ *762/622–3096* ▭ *MC, V.*

¢–$ MEXICAN ✕**Santa Fe.** Mexican family-type cooking at its best is served in this simple restaurant a few blocks from the main square. Puebla-style mole, Cornish hen in garlic butter, and enchiladas in green or red chile sauce are among the tasty offerings. There's a daily *comida corrida* (fixed-

CLOSE UP

One Man's Metal

In less than a decade after William Spratling arrived in Taxco, he had transformed it into a flourishing silver center, the likes of which had not been seen since colonial times. In 1929 the writer-architect from New Orleans settled in the then sleepy, dusty village because it was inexpensive and close to the pre-Hispanic Mexcala culture that he was studying in Guerrero Valley.

For hundreds of years Taxco's silver was made into bars and exported overseas. No one even considered developing a local jewelry industry. Journeying to a nearby town, Spratling hired a couple of goldsmiths and commissioned them to create jewelry, flatware, trays, and goblets from his own designs. Ever the artist with a keen mind for drawing, design, and aesthetics, Spratling decided to experiment with silver using his designs. Shortly afterward, he set up his own workshop and began producing highly innovative pieces. By the 1940s Spratling's designs were gracing the necks of celebrities and being sold in high-end stores abroad.

Spratling also started a program to train local silversmiths; they were soon joined by foreigners interested in learning the craft. It wasn't long before there were thousands of silversmiths in the town, and Spratling was its wealthiest resident. He moved freely in Mexico's lively art scene, befriending muralists Diego Rivera (Rivera's wife, Frida Kahlo, wore Spratling necklaces) and David Alfaro Siqueiros as well as architect Miguel Covarrubios. The U.S. ambassador to Mexico, Dwight Morrow, father of Anne Morrow who married Charles Lindbergh, hired Spratling to help with the architectural details of his house in Cuernavaca. American movie stars were frequent guests at Spratling's home; once, he even designed furniture for Marilyn Monroe.

When his business failed in 1946, relief came in the form of an offer from the United States Department of the Interior: Spratling was asked to create a program of native crafts for Alaska. This work influenced his later designs. Although he never regained the wealth he once had, he operated the workshop at his ranch and trained apprentices until he died in a car accident in 1969. A friend, Italian engineer Alberto Ulrich, took over the business and replicated Spratling's designs using his original molds. Ulrich died in 2002, and his children now operate the business.

Spratling bequeathed his huge collection of pre-Hispanic art and artifacts to the people of Taxco, and they're now displayed in a museum carrying his name. The grateful citizens also named a street after their much-beloved benefactor and put a bust of him in a small plaza off the main square.

price) meal for $6.50. ✉ *Calle Hidalgo 2* ☎ *762/622–1170* ▭ *No credit cards.*

WHERE TO STAY

$$$–$$$$ ★ **Posada de la Misión.** Laid out like a colonial-style village, this hotel has well-kept doubles with beamed ceilings and two-bedroom suites; some come with fireplaces and terraces as well. The pool area has a mural by noted Mexican artist Juan O'Gorman, and there's a silver

workshop and boutique that sells Spratling-designed silver jewelry. **Pros:** Beautiful view, interesting architecture. **Cons:** Too pricey for what you get, not well up-kept. ✉ *Cerro de la Misión 32* ⓓ *AP 88, 40230* ☎ *762/622–0063* 🌐 *www.posadamision.com* ⇨ *120 rooms, 30 suites* ◊ *In-room: No a/c, kitchen (some). In-hotel: Restaurant, bar, pool, no elevator, parking (no fee)* ▭ *AE, MC, V* |◎| *MAP.*

$$–$$$ **Hotel de la Borda.** It may be a bit worn, but the Borda is still a favorite with tour groups, and the staff couldn't be more hospitable. Ask for a room overlooking town or the suite that John and Jackie Kennedy occupied during their honeymoon in Mexico. **Pros:** View overlooking the Santa Prisca Cathedral. **Cons:** Needs refurbishing. ✉ *Cerro del Pedregal 2* ⓓ *AP 6, 40200* ☎ *762/622–0025* 🌐 *www.taxcohotel.com* ⇨ *110 rooms, 3 suites* ◊ *In-hotel: Restaurant, room service, bar, pool, no elevator, laundry service, parking (no fee)* ▭ *AE, MC, V* |◎| *EP.*

13

$$–$$$ **Monte Taxco.** A colonial style predominates at this full-service hotel, which has a knockout view, a funicular, three restaurants, a disco, and nightly entertainment; it's the fanciest hotel in Taxco.. There are also rooms equipped for guests with disabilities. **Pros:** Funicular is an amazing way to arrive at your digs. **Cons:** A few miles up a mountain from town, so plan to take taxis to get back and forth. ✉ *Lomas de Taxco* ⓓ *AP 8440210* ☎ *762/622–1300* 🌐 *www.montetaxco.com.mx* ⇨ *153 rooms, 6 suites, 32 villas* ◊ *In-hotel: 3 restaurants, golf course, tennis courts, pools, gym, laundry service, parking (no fee)* ▭ *AE, MC, V* |◎| *EP.*

$–$$ **Hotel Victoria.** With its colonial-style architecture, the Victoria is a perfect fit for this charming town. Its simple rooms are attractive and freshly painted. Most have balconies with great views of town and the distant hills. Furniture in the common areas was designed by William Spratling. **Pros:** Dreamy architecture. **Cons:** Sections are in disrepair. ✉ *Calle Carlos J. Nibbi 5* ⓓ *AP 83, 40200* ☎ *762/622–0004* 🌐 *www.victoriataxco.com* ⇨ *63 rooms, 5 suites* ◊ *In-hotel: Restaurant, bar, pool, no elevator, parking (no fee)* ▭ *AE, MC, V* |◎| *EP.*

¢–$$ **Posada San Javier.** The secluded San Javier sprawls haphazardly around a junglelike garden with a pool and a wishing well. In addition to guest rooms, there are seven one-bedroom apartments with living rooms and kitchenettes; however, these are often filled by visiting wholesale silver buyers. **Pros:** Breakfast included, professionally run. **Cons:** No elevator. ✉ *Calle Estacadas 32,* ☎ *762/622–3177* ✉ *posadasanjavier@hotmail.com* ⇨ *18 rooms, 7 apartments* ◊ *In-room: Kitchen (some). In-hotel: restaurant, room service, bar, pool, no elevator, parking (no fee)* ▭ *MC, V* |◎| *EP.*

¢ **Hotel Los Arcos.** This 1620 converted monastery is an island of historical tranquility. Simple, ample-size rooms furnished with colonial hand-carved furniture provide a comfortable stay just a block from the plaza. The hotel doesn't have a restaurant or gift shop, but given its central location they aren't needed. **Pros:** Lovely courtyard, intriguing history. **Cons:** No breakfast, rooms on the street can be noisy. ✉ *Juan Ruíz de Alarcón 4,* ☎ *762/622–1836* 🌐 *www.hotellosarcos.net* ⇨ *21 rooms* ◊ *In-room: No a/c, no phone. In-hotel: No elevator* ▭ *No credit cards.*

Fodor'sChoice ★

¢ **Hotel Emilia Castillo.** Rooms at this straightforward hotel are simple but with carved-wood furniture and Mexican artwork that was clearly chosen with care. The brick and stone lobby has warm red-tile floors, cheerful murals, and its very own silver shop. With a restaurant just outside the front door, and attentive and friendly service, this restaurant is as practical as it is an excellent value. **Pros:** Appealing décor, intimate feeling. **Cons:** Smallish rooms, overall very compact. ✉*Juan Ruíz de Alarcón 7,* ☎*762/622–1396* 🌐*www.hotelemiliacastillo.com* *14 rooms* *In-room: No phone. In-hotel: No elevator* ▭*DC, MC, V* *EP.*

NIGHTLIFE

The **Acerto** (✉*Plaza Borda 12* ☎*762/622–0064*), also called Bar Paco, is a traditional favorite and a great place to meet fellow travelers.

At **Bertha's** (✉*Plaza Borda 9* ☎*762/622–0172*), Taxco's oldest bar, a tequila, lime, and club soda concoction called a Bertha is the specialty. Watch out for Taxco's high curbs and ankle-turning cobblestones after a few Berthas.

La Pachanga (✉*Cerro de la Misión 32* ☎*762/622–5519*), a discotheque at Posada de la Misión, is open Thursday through Sunday and is popular with townsfolk and visitors.

Much of Taxco's weekend nighttime activity is at the Monte Taxco hotel's discotheque, **Windows** (✉*Lomas de Taxco* ☎*762/622–1300*). On Saturday night the hotel has a buffet and a fireworks display.

SHOPPING

Sidewalk vendors sell lacquered gourds and boxes from the town of Olinalá as well as masks, straw baskets, bark paintings, and many other handcrafted items. Sunday is market day, which means that artisans from surrounding villages descend on the town, as do visitors from Mexico City.

Most people come to Taxco with silver in mind. Three types are available: sterling, which is always stamped 0.925 (925 parts in 1,000) and is the most expensive; plated silver; and the inexpensive *alpaca,* which is also known as German or nickel silver. Sterling pieces are usually priced by weight according to world silver prices. Fine workmanship will add to the cost. Bangles start at $4, and bracelets and necklaces cost $10 to $200 and higher.

Many of the more than 600 silver shops carry identical merchandise; a few are noted for their creativity. William Spratling, Andrés Mejía, and Emilia Castillo, daughter of renowned silversmith Antonio Castillo, are among the famous names. Designs range from traditional bulky necklaces (often inlaid with turquoise and other semiprecious stones) to streamlined bangles and chunky earrings.

CRAFTS

Owned by Elsa Ruíz de Figueroa, **D'Elsa** (✉*Plazuela de San Juan 13* ☎*762/622–1683*) carries a selection of native-inspired clothing for women and a well-chosen selection of crafts.

CLOSE UP

People & Culture

Acapulco is home to about 1.5 million people, plus an additional 3.5 million visitors yearly. Many of the locals come from elsewhere, attracted by the job opportunities provided by the port and the businesses that cater to tourism. Despite its size, you will find a more relaxed atmosphere than you would in Guadalajara or Monterrey. As befits a major tourist town, Acapulco has a savvy and sophisticated citizenry. Its diverse economy is anchored by shipping and tourism—the city has the largest convention center in Mexico, along with 18,000 hotel rooms.

The locals are known for being very friendly and helpful to tourists, ever mindful of the many dollars and pesos that are spent in their city. A majority of the tourists are Europeans and Mexicans, so you never feel that you have landed in an Americanized beach resort, as you might in Cancun or Los Cabos. While the city has no major festivals, every week is party week in Acapulco. Many people stay out late at night and wake up closer to noon than sunrise. If you're an early riser, you'll have the town to yourself.

Joyería y Máscaras Arnoldo (⊠*Calle Palma 1* ☎*762/622–1272*) has ceremonial masks; originals come with a certificate of authenticity as well as a written description of origin and use. For $100 per person, Arnoldo will take you on a tour of the villages where the dances using the masks are performed on February 2 and December 12.

SILVER

Fodor's Choice ★ **Emilia Castillo** (⊠*Juan Ruíz de Alarcón 7, in Hotel Emilia Castilla* ☎*762/622–3471*) is one of the most exciting silver shops; it's renowned for innovative designs and for combining silver with porcelain. (Neiman Marcus sells the wares in its U.S. stores.)

The stunning pieces at **Galería de Arte en Plata Andrés** (⊠*Av. de los Plateros 113A, near Posada de la Misión* ☎*762/622–3778* 🌐*www.andresartinsilver.com.mx*) are created by the talented Andrés Mejía. He showcases his own designs and those of such promising young designers as Priscilla Canales, Susana Sanborn, Francisco Diaz, and Daniel Espinosa, whose jewelry has been loved by many a Hollywood celebrity.

★ **Spratling Ranch** (⊠*South of town on Carretera Taxco–Iguala, Km 177* ☎*762/622–6108*) is where the heirs of William Spratling turn out designs using his original molds. You can shop only by appointment.

Cancún & Isla Mujeres

14

Chac Mool, Cancún

WORD OF MOUTH

"As for things to do. Isla Mujeres is a must. Xel-Ha and Tulum are very good. Go to La Isla Mall during the evening. Check out Market 28 downtown Cancún."

–tommy

www.fodors.com/forums

WELCOME TO CANCÚN & ISLA MUJERES

TOP REASONS TO GO

★ **Dancing the night away:** Salsa, cumbia, reggae, mariachi, hip-hop, and electronic music dizzy the air of the Zona Hotelera's many nightclubs.

★ **Exploring the nearby Mayan ruins:** Trips to remarkable sites like Tulum, Cobá, and Chichén Itzá can easily be accomplished in a day.

★ **Getting wild on the water:** Rent Jet Skis, a Windsurfer, or a kayak and skim across the sea or Laguna Nichupté, or diving the caverns off Isla Mujeres to see "sleeping" sharks.

★ **Browsing for Mexican crafts:** The colorful stalls of Mercado Veintiocho will certainly hold something that catches your eye.

1 El Centro. More than 500,000 permanent residents live in Cancún's mainland commercial center; shops and cafés cater mainly to locals. Most hotels here are small and family-operated.

2 The Zona Hotelera Norte. Punta Sam, aka the Northern Hotel Zone, north of Puerto Juárez, is quieter than the main Zona, with smaller hotels and restaurants.

3 The Zona Hotelera. The Hotel Zone barrier island is Cancún's tourist heart, with huge luxury resorts, restaurants, nightclubs, malls, and golf courses—all just a stone's throw from the gorgeous white-sand beach.

4 Playa Norte. Waist-deep turquoise waters and wide soft sands make Isla's most northerly beach its most beautiful. Most of the island's hotels are here, just a short walk from El Pueblo.

5 El Pueblo. Isla's only town, in front of the ferry piers, extends the width of the northern end and is sandwiched between sand and sea to the south, west, and northeast. Its zócalo (main square) is the hub of Isleño life.

6 The Western Coast. Midway along Isla's western coast is lovely Laguna Makax, and to the south, uncrowded Playa Tiburon and Playa Lancheros. At Isla's southernmost tip is El Garrafón National Park.

GETTING ORIENTED

Cancún consists of the Zona Hotelera, a 22½-km (14-mi) barrier island with the Caribbean to the east and lagoons to the west, and El Centro, 4 km (2½ mi) west on the mainland. Sleepy Isla Mujeres is just 8 km (5 mi) long and 1 km (½ mi) wide, with flat sandy beaches in the north and steep rocky bluffs to the south.

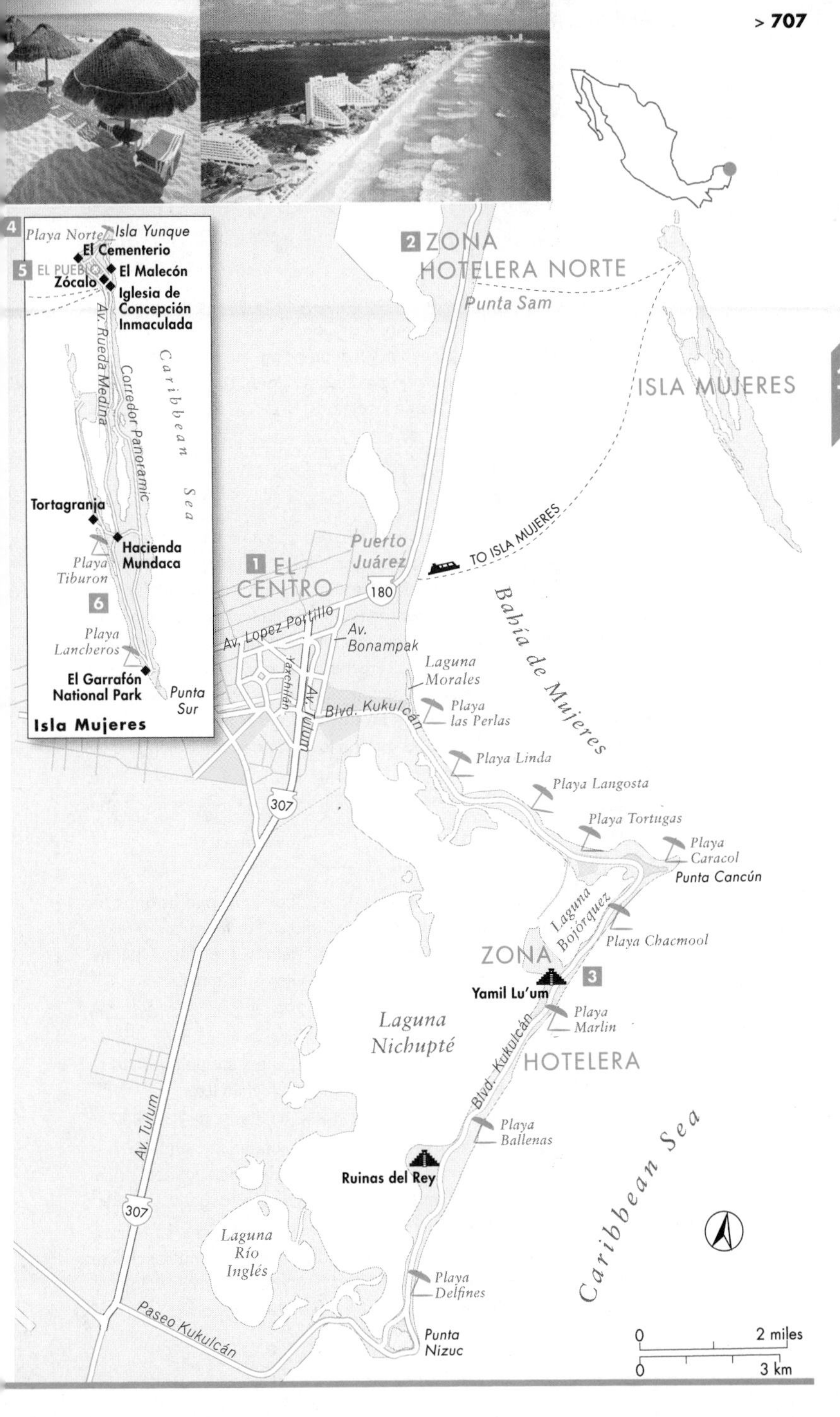

Playa Norte
Isla Yunque
El Cementerio
EL PUEBLO
El Malecón
Zócalo
Iglesia de Concepción Inmaculada
Av. Rueda Medina
Corredor Panoramic
Caribbean Sea
Tortagranja
Hacienda Mundaca
Playa Tiburon
Playa Lancheros
El Garrafón National Park
Punta Sur
Isla Mujeres
ZONA HOTELERA NORTE
Punta Sam
ISLA MUJERES
TO ISLA MUJERES
Puerto Juárez
EL CENTRO
180
Av. Lopez Portillo
Av. Bonampak
Yaxchilán
Av. Tulum
Blvd. Kukulcán
Bahía de Mujeres
Laguna Morales
Playa las Perlas
Playa Linda
Playa Langosta
Playa Tortugas
Playa Caracol
Punta Cancún
Laguna Bojórquez
Playa Chacmool
ZONA HOTELERA
Yamil Lu'um
Playa Marlin
Laguna Nichupté
Blvd. Kukulcán
Playa Ballenas
Ruinas del Rey
Caribbean Sea
307
Av. Tulum
Laguna Río Inglés
Playa Delfines
Paseo Kukulcán
Punta Nizuc
0
2 miles
0
3 km
14

CANCÚN & ISLA MUJERES PLANNER

When to Go, How Long to Stay

There's a lot to see and do in Cancún and Isla Mujeres, though many visitors are happy to spend a week on the beach or at a resort. If you're game for exploring, allow an extra two or three days for day trips to nearby eco-parks and Maya ruins like Tulum, Cobá, or even Chichén Itzá.

High season starts at the end of November and lasts until April. Between December 15 and January 5, hotel prices are highest—often as much as 30%–50% above regular rates. To visit during Christmas, spring break, or Easter, book at least three months in advance.

Getting to Isla

The only way to get to Isla is by ferry from Puerto Juárez on the mainland, just north of Cancún. The trip lasts 30 minutes or less. Buy your ticket on board the boat; the people you see selling them on the docks aren't official ticket sellers, and will charge you more.

On Mexico Time

Mexicans are far more relaxed about time than their counterparts north of the border. Although *mañana* translates as "tomorrow," it is often used to explain why something is not getting done or not ready. In this context, mañana means, "Relax—it'll get taken care of eventually." If you make a date for 9, don't be surprised if everyone else shows up at 9:30. The trick to enjoying life on Mexican time is: don't rush. And be sure to take advantage of the siesta hour between 1 pm and 4 pm. How else are you going to stay up late dancing?

Tour Options

The companies listed here can book tours and arrange for plane tickets and hotel reservations. For more information about specific tour options and details, *see* "Tour Options" in Cancún Essentials *and* Isla Mujeres Essentials.

Intermar Caribe. (✉Av. Tulum 290, at Blvd. Pioneros, Sm 8 ☎998/881–0000 🌐www.travel2mexico.com) offers local tours such as snorkeling at Xel-ha, shopping on Isla Mujeres or exploring the ruins at Chichén Itzá.

Mayaland Tours. (✉Av. Robalo 30, Sm 3 ☎998/887–2450) runs tours to Mérida, the Uxmal ruins, and the flamingo park at Celestún. Self-guided tours to local ruins such as Tulum and Cobá can also be arranged.

Olympus Tours. (✉Av. Yaxchilán, Lote 13, Sm 17, Mza 2 ☎998/881–9030 🌐www.olympustours.com) specializes in tours around Cancún and can book you reservations to Xcaret, Xel-ha, and other local adventure parks.

Booking Your Hotel Online

A growing number of Cancún hotels are encouraging people to make their reservations online. Some allow you to book rooms right on their own Web sites, but even hotels without their own sites usually offer reservations via online booking agencies, such as www.docancun.com, www.cancuntoday.net, and www.travel-center.com. Since hotels customarily work with several different agencies, it's a good idea to shop around online for the best rates before booking with one of them.

Besides being convenient, booking online can often get you a 10%-20% discount on room rates. There are occasional breakdowns in communication, however, between booking agencies and hotels. You may arrive at your hotel to discover that your Spanish-speaking front desk clerk has no record of your Internet reservation, or has reserved a room that's different from the one you specified. To prevent such mishaps, print out copies of all your Internet transactions, including receipts and confirmations, and bring them with you.

Staying Awhile

There are several Internet-based rental agencies that can help you rent a home or apartment on Isla: www.islabeckons.com lists fully equipped properties (and also handles reservations for hotel rooms). www.morningsinmexico.com offers smaller and less expensive properties. Most rental homes have fully equipped kitchens, bathrooms, and bedrooms.

WHAT IT COSTS IN DOLLARS				
¢	$	$$	$$$	$$$$
Restaurants				
under $5	$5–$10	$10–$15	$15–$25	over $25
Hotels				
under $50	$50–$75	$75–$150	$150–$250	over $250

Restaurant prices are per person, for a main course at dinner, excluding tax and tip. Hotel prices are for a standard double room in high season.

When to Go

The sun shines an average of 253 days a year in Cancún. Isla and Cancún have nearly perfect weather between December and April, with daytime temperatures at around 29°C (84°F). May through September are much hotter and more humid; temperatures can reach upwards of 36°C (97°F). The rainy hurricane season starts mid-September and lasts until mid-November, bringing downpours in the afternoons, as well as the occasional hairy tropical storm such as Hurricane Wilma in October 2005.

14

Need More Information?

The Cancún Visitors and Convention Bureau (CVB), (✉Blvd. Kukulcán, Km 9, Zona Hotelera ☎998/881–2745 🌐www.cancun.info) has lots of information about area accommodations, restaurants, and attractions.

The Cancún Travel Agency Association (AMAV), (✉Plaza Mexico, Av. Tulum 200, Sm 4, El Centro ☎998/887–1670) can refer you to local travel agents who'll help plan your visit to Cancún.

The Isla Mujeres tourist office (✉Av. Rueda Medina 130 ☎998/877–0307 🌐www.islamujeres.com.mx) is open weekdays 8–8 and weekends 8–noon and has lots of general information about the island.

CANCÚN

Updated by John Hecht & Marlise Kast

CANCÚN IS A GREAT PLACE to experience 21st-century Mexico. There isn't much that's "quaint" or "historical" in this distinctively modern city; some people living here have eagerly embraced all the accoutrements of urban middle-class life—cell phones, cable TV—that are found all over the world. Most locals live on the mainland, in the part of the city known as El Centro—but many of them work in the posh Zona Hotelera, the barrier island where Cancún's most popular resorts are located.

Boulevard Kukulcán is the main drag in the Zona Hotelera, and because the island is so narrow—less than 1 km (½ mi) wide—you would be able to see both the Caribbean and the Nichupté Lagoon on either side if it weren't for the hotels. The best way to explore Cancún is by hopping on one of the public buses that run between Zona Hotelera and El Centro. The cost is 75¢ no matter the distance you travel.

South of Punta Cancún, Boulevard Kukulcán becomes a busy road, difficult to cross on foot. It's also punctuated by steeply inclined driveways that turn into the hotels, most of which are set at least 100 yards from the road. The lagoon side of the boulevard consists of scrubby stretches of land alternating with marinas, shopping centers, and restaurants. ■ TIP→ **Because there are so few sights, there are no orientation tours of Cancún: just do the local bus circuit to get a feel for the island's layout. The buses run 24 hours a day and you'll rarely have to wait more than five minutes.**

When you first visit El Centro, the downtown layout might not be self-evident. It's not based on a grid but rather on a circular pattern. Initially, tourists may feel out of their comfort zone when moving from Zona Hotelera to the bustle of El Centro. Here locals roam the streets, taking great pride in living in an authentic cultural quarter rather than in a zone of mass tourism. Avenida Tulum is the main street—actually a four-lane road with two northbound and two southbound lanes.

Avenidas Bonampak and Yaxchilán are the other two major north–south streets that parallel Tulum. The three major east–west streets are avenidas Cobá, Uxmal, and Chichén. They are marked along Tulum by huge traffic circles, each set with a piece of sculpture. West of Avenida Tulum to Yaxchilán is where you can find authentic Mexican food at some of the best hole-in-the-wall cantinas. East of Tulum to Avenida Bonampak is considered the more upscale area of El Centro, where business executives tend to roam during lunch hour.

GETTING HERE & AROUND

The Aeropuerto Internacional Cancún is 16 km (9 mi) southwest of the heart of Cancún and 10 km (6 mi) from the Zona Hotelera's southernmost point. While there are direct flights from some major U.S. cities, most flights transfer in Mexico City. Autobuses del Oriente, or ADO, is one of the oldest bus lines in Mexico and offers regular service to Puerto Morelos and Playa del Carmen every 15 minutes from 4 AM until midnight. Playa Express has express buses that leave from a small terminal across from the main bus station every 10 minutes for Puerto Morelos and Playa del Carmen. Mayab Bus Lines has first- and second-class buses leaving for destinations along the Riviera Maya every hour. Although driving in Cancún isn't recommended, exploring the surrounding areas on the peninsula by car is. The roads are excellent within a 100-km (62-mi) radius.

Bus Contacts **Autobuses del Oriente (ADO)** (☎ *998/884–5542*). **Playa Express** (☎ *998/887–6782*). **Mayab Bus Lines** (☎ *998/884–5542*). **Terminal de Autobuses** (✉ *Avs. Tulum and Uxmal, Sm 23* ☎ *998/884–5542* 🌐 *www.ticketbus.com.mx*).

Currency Exchange **Banamex** (✉ *Av. Tulum 19, next to City Hall, Sm 5* ☎ *998/881–6403*). **Banorte** (✉ *Av. Tulum 21, Sm 2* ☎ *998/887–6815* ✉ *Plaza Flamingos, Blvd. Kukulcán, Km 11, Zona Hotelera* ☎ *998/883–1653*). **HSBC** (✉ *Plaza Caracol, Blvd. Kukulcán, Km 8.5, Zona Hotelera* ☎ *998/883–4652*).

14

Internet **Internet B@r** (✉ *Forum-by-the-Sea, Blvd. Kukulcán, Km 9.5, Zona Hotelera* ☎ *998/883–1042*). **Infonet** (✉ *Plaza las Americas, Av. Tulum, Sm 4 and Sm 9* ☎ *998/887–9130*). **Internet Café** (✉ *Av. Tulum 10, behind Comercial Mexicana, across from bus station, Sm 2* ☎ *998/887–3168*) .

Mail & Shipping **Correos (Post Office)** (✉ *Avs. Sunyaxchén and Xel-Há, Sm 26* ☎ *998/884–1418*). **DHL** (✉ *Av. Tulum 29, Sm 5* ☎ *998/892–8449*). **Federal Express** (✉ *Av. Tulum 31, Sm 23* ☎ *998/887–4003*). **Mas Mail Center Inc.** (✉ *Av. Xpuhil 3, behind Mercado 28, Sm 27* ☎ *998/887–4918*).

Medical Assistance **Hospital Amat (emergency hospital)** (✉ *Av. Náder 13, Sm 2* ☎ *998/887–4422*). **Hospital Americano** (✉ *Retorno Viento 15, Sm 4* ☎ *998/884–6133*). **Hospital de las Americas** (✉ *Avs. Bonampak and Nichupté, next to Plaza las Américas, Sm 7* ☎ *998/881–3400, 998/881–3434 for emergencies*). **Red Cross** (✉ *Avs. Xcaret and Labná, Sm 21* ☎ *998/884–1616*). **Tourist Assistance Office** (☎ *998/884–8073*).

Rental Cars **Adocar Rental** (✉ *Plaza Nautilus, Blvd. Kukulcán, Km 3.5, Zona Hotelera* ☎ *998/849–4233* 🌐 *adocarrental.com*). **Buster Renta Car** (✉ *Hotel Holiday Inn Arenas, Blvd. Kukulcán, Km 2.5, Zona Hotelera* ☎ *998/882–2800* 🌐 *www.busterrentacar.com*). **Mónaco Rent a Car** (✉ *Av. Yaxchilán 65, Lote 5, Sm 25* ☎ *998/884–7843* 🌐 *www.monacorentacar.com*).

EXPLORING

MAIN ATTRACTIONS

El Centro. Nearly two decades ago, downtown Cancún was the place to be after a day at the beach. The once barren Hotel Zone had few options in the way of dining, causing many tourists to stroll the active streets of **Avenida Tulum, Xachilan**, and **Parque de las Palapas**. With the emergence of luxury resorts and mass tourism, a major shift brought the focus back to the Hotel Zone. Today many tourists are unaware that the downtown area even exists, while others consider "downtown" to be the string of flea markets near the Convention Center. In reality, El Centro is a combination of markets and malls that offer a glimpse of Mexico's urban lifestyle. Avenida Tulum, the main street, is marked by a huge sculpture of shells and starfish in the middle of a traffic circle.

This iconic Cancún sculpture, which many locals refer to as "el ceviche," is particularly dramatic at night when the lights are turned on. The centro is also home to many restaurants and bars, as well as **Mercado Veintiocho (Market 28)**—an enormous crafts market just off avenidas Yaxchilán and Sunyaxchén. For bargain shopping, hit the stores and small strip malls along Avenida Yaxchilán and Avenida Tulum. As the Hotel Zone becomes increasingly more dense and overcrowded, El Centro is blooming with the development of Puerto Cancún. Construction of this downtown subset has been carefully designed to focus on the resident rather than the tourist. Shopping centers, marinas, golf courses, and over 2,500 condos are taking shape, making El Centro's bustling Avenida Bonampak the next "Blvd. Kukulcán."

Ruinas del Rey. Large signs on the Zona Hotelera's lagoon side, roughly opposite Playa Delfines, point out the small Ruins of the King. Although much smaller than famous archaeological sites like Tulum and Chichén Itzá, this site is worth a visit and makes for an interesting juxtaposition between Mexico's past and present.

First entered into Western chronicles in a 16th-century travelogue, then sighted in 1842 by American explorer John Lloyd Stephens and his draftsman, Frederick Catherwood, the ruins were finally explored by archaeologists in 1910, though excavations didn't begin until 1954. In 1975 archaeologists, along with the Mexican government, began restoration work.

Dating from the 3rd to 2nd century BC, del Rey is notable for having two main plazas bounded by two streets—most other Mayan cities contain only one plaza. The pyramid here is topped by a platform, and inside its vault are paintings on stucco. Skeletons interred both at the apex and at the base indicate that the site may have been a royal burial ground. Originally named Kin Ich Ahau Bonil, Mayan for "king of the solar countenance," the site was linked to astronomical practices in the ancient Mayan culture. ✉ *Blvd. Kukulcán, Km 18.5, Zona Hotelera* ☎ *998/849–2880* 🎫 *$3.50* ⏲ *Daily 8–4:30.*

Yamil Lu'um. Located on Cancún's highest point (the name Yamil Lu'um means "hilly land"), this archaeological site stands on the grounds of the Park Royal Cancún, which means that nonguests can only access the ruins from the beach side. Although it comprises two structures—one probably a temple, the other probably a lighthouse—this is the smallest of Cancún's ruins. Discovered in 1842 by John Lloyd Stephens, the ruins date from the late 13th or early 14th century. ✉ *Blvd. Kukulcán, Km 12, Zona Hotelera* ☎ *No phone* 🎫 *Free.*

IF YOU HAVE TIME

Cancún Convention Center. This strikingly modern venue for cultural events is the jumping-off point for a 1-km (½-mi) string of shopping malls that extends west to the Presidente InterContinental Cancún. Directly adjacent to the Center is Coral Negro Market, famous for its handcrafted souvenirs and black-coral jewelry. Inside the Convention Center itself are remarkable works of art created by Chilean artist Jaime Fierro. Formerly housing the Tourism Offices for both Cancún and Mexico, the Visitor's Bureau for Mexico is now located across from Costco in El Centro's Avenida Yaxchilan.

✉ *Blvd. Kukulcán, Km 9* ☎ *998/881–0400* 🌐 *www.cancuncenter.com* 🎟 *Free* 🕒 *Weekdays 9* AM *–7* PM

Fodor's Choice ★ **La Casa del Arte Popular Mexicano.** This entrancing folk-art museum is a must for anyone interested in Mexican culture and handicrafts. Located on the second floor of El Embarcadero marina, this museum looks fairly small from the outside. But inside it is brimming with original works by the country's finest artisans, which are arranged in fascinating tableaux here. The collection represents all different regions of Mexico—from nativity scenes sculpted out of Oaxaca's clays to the intricate *arbol de la vida* (tree of life) sculptures crafted in Metepec, Estado de México. Children will love the toy room, which includes an impressive display of *alebrijes* (dreamworld animals). In addition to the handicrafts, there are different scenes set up throughout the museum to give visitors an idea of traditional Mexican life. The mannequins used in these re-creations, which include a church and a market setting, were actually modeled on real people that the museum director met during her trips through Mexico. Be sure to visit the museum's shop. **■ TIP→ Other marina complex attractions include the Teatro Cancún, helicopter tours, a small restaurant, and ticket booths for boat tours and other attractions.** ✉ *Blvd. Kukulcán, Km 4.5, Zona Hotelera* ☎ *998/849–4332 or 998/849–5583* 🌐 *www.museoartepopularmexicano.org/main.htm* 🎟 *$5* 🕒 *Weekdays 9* AM*–7* PM*, weekends 11* AM*–6* PM.

14

BEACHES

Cancún Island is one long continuous beach shaped like the number "7." It is virtually impossible to find a bad beach in Cancún; they all have turquoise waters and powdery white sand. Unlike most nontropical beaches that are composed of grainy silica, the sand in Cancún is made up of microscopic star-shape fossils called disco-aster. The light and fluffy texture stays cool underfoot, even when the sun is beating down during prime tanning hours. By law, the entire coast of Mexico is federal property and open to the public. In reality, security guards discourage locals from using the beaches outside hotels. Some all-inclusives distribute neon wristbands to guests; those without a wristband aren't actually prohibited from being on the beach—just from entering or exiting via the hotel. Everyone is welcome to walk along the beach, as long as you get on or off from one of the public points. Although these points are often miles apart, one way around the situation is to find a hotel open to the public, go into the lobby bar for a drink or snack, and afterward go for a swim along the beach. Beaches that are not utilized by hotels all have seaweed on their shores. They can all be reached by public transportation; just let the driver know where you are headed.

In December, strong north winds bring an increase in wave size that often eats away at the sand banks. Unexpected drop-offs along the shoreline can be dangerous, especially when visibility is poor due to

HURRICANE WILMA

Hurricane Wilma struck the northern wedge of the Yucatán Peninsula on October 21, 2005. Wilma was capricious in her attack on Yucatán. She lashed out at Cancún and spared Tulum. The Riviera Maya was hit hard in some places and left virtually unscathed in others. The worst hit were Cancún, Cozumel, and Isla Mujeres. In Cancún sand was washed offshore, winds broke through hotel windows to wreak havoc on countless rooms, and the main road, Boulevard Kukulcán, was covered with downed trees and wires. Wilma then moved south to sit over the island of Cozumel for 24 hours; the delicate reefs so famous with snorkelers were damaged, and the some of the cruise-ship ports were destroyed. Fragile Isla Mujeres, which shielded much of Cancún's Zona Hotelera from the storm, also lost of a lot of sand, and its buildings sustained a lot of damage.

It might have looked like Cancún was dealt a lethal blow when the storm hit. But the whole region is on the mend. Shortly after the storm ended, then president Vicente Fox declared the region would be operational within three months. His prognostications were overly optimistic, but the Mexican government and private businesses poured (and continue to pour) boundless resources into the region's recovery, especially Cancún and Isla Mujeres. Puerto Morelos was severely damaged by Wilma, and recovery was a bit more difficult for this small, tight-knit community.

In the meantime, other attractions to the south that were spared found themselves with more visitors than usual. Sian Ka'an, the ecological reserve two hours south of Cancún, saw more traffic, and tour companies introduced groups to Maya villages and *cenotes* (sinkholes) buried deep in the jungle.

2006 was generally a quiet time for the region, as everyone worked to recover and airlines only slowly resumed their pre-Wilma routes. Hurricane Dean made landfall in August 2007, causing the evacuation of many tourists, but Cancún suffered no major damage. By 2008 things were getting back to normal and tourists were returning. Many hotels had taken advantage of the necessity for renovations to go even further, and either expand their properties or make them more luxurious than ever before.

murky waters. At times the coast guard will "shut down" the ocean due to high winds, causing all water sports to be put on hold. On the flip side, whitecaps are always a pleasant sight for the experienced kiteboarder, sailor, or windsurfer. **TIP→*Don't* swim when the red or black danger flags fly; yellow flags indicate that you should proceed with caution, and green or blue flags mean the waters are calm.**

The listed beaches here are organized by location, beginning on the northwest side of the "7" facing Bahia de Mujeres, and continuing down along the Caribbean side toward Punta Nizuc.

Playa las Perlas is the first beach on the drive heading east from El Centro along Boulevard Kukulcán. Located at Km 2.5, it's a relatively small beach on the protected waters of the Bahía de Mujeres, and is popular with locals. There are several restaurants lining the beach however, most of the water-sports activities are available only to those staying at the nearby resorts such as Imperial las Perlas or the Blue Bay Getaway.

Fodor's Choice ★ Small, placid **Playa Langosta,** which has an entrance at Boulevard Kukulcán's Km 5, has calm waters that make it an excellent place for a swim. There is a dock that juts out in the middle of the water, but swimming areas are marked off with ropes and buoys. Its safe waters and gentle waves make it a popular beach with families as well as Spring Breakers. Next to the beach is a small building with a restaurant, an ice-cream shop, and an ATM.

The calm surf and relaxing shallows of **Playa Pez Volador** make it an aquatic playground for families with young children. Marked by a huge Mexican flag at Km 5.5, the wide beach is popular with locals, as many tourists tend to head to the more active Playa Langosta. Occasionally, sea grass washes ashore here, but by early morning it has already been cleared away by the staff of the neighboring Casa Maya Hotel.

Playa Tortugas, the last "real" beach along the east–west stretch of the Zona Hotelera, eroded greatly after Hurricane Wilma. There's still a small stretch of stand at the entrance located around Km 6.5 (next to Fat Tuesday) on Boulevard Kukulcán. The swimming is excellent, and many people come here to sail, snorkel, kayak, paraglide, and use Wave Runners.

Playa Caracol, the outermost beach in the Zona Hotelera, is a beach only in name. Located at Km 8.5, the whole area has been eaten up by development—in particular the high-rise condominium complex next to the entrance. This beach is also hindered by the rocks that jut out from the water marking the beginning of Punta Cancún, where Boulevard Kukulcán turns south. There are several hotels along here and a few sports rental outfits.

Heading down from Punta Cancún onto the long, southerly stretch of the island, **Playa Chacmool** is the first beach on the Caribbean's open waters. When accessing the beach from Boulevard Kukulcán, walk directly across the street from Señor Frog's. As in the case of Playa Caracol, development has greatly encroached on Chacmool's shores. There are a lot of rocks here and little sand, but it's close to several shopping centers and the party zone, so there are plenty of restaurants nearby. Changing rooms are also available to the public. The shallow clear water makes it tempting to walk far out into the ocean, but be careful—there's a strong current and undertow.

Those who want to be pampered in the sand head to **Playa Cabana Beach Club**. Located at Km 9 behind the City Discotheque, this is a place where tourists can enjoy the full resort experience without booking into a hotel. Facilities include 32 beach cabanas, each equipped with misting machines and a personalized sound system. The $10 entrance fee also includes access to the multi-level swimming pool, sun deck, restaurant, and sushi bar. Craving a dip in the ocean? Just walk down the short flight of stairs that leads directly to the beach. Commonly known as "City Beach," here the waves break up to six feet during the winter months, making it one of the few surfing spots in Cancún. Chances are, you'll never want to leave your cabana. ✉*Blvd. Kukulcán, Km 9, Zona Hotelera* ☎*998/848-8380* 🌐*www.playacabana.com* 🎫*$10* ⏲*9–5:30.*

Playa Marlin, at Km 13 along Boulevard Kukulcán, is in the heart of the Zona Hotelera and is accessible via a road next to Kukulcán Plaza. It's a seductive beach with turquoise waters and silky sands, but like most beaches facing the Caribbean, the waves are strong and the currents are dangerous. Sun umbrellas and beach chairs can be rented at $5 per day. There is also a small tent where one can rent boogie boards, snorkel equipment and motorized sports equipment. Although there are currently no public facilities, you can always walk over to Kukulcán Plaza if you need a restroom.

Playa Ballenas is at Km 14 between Le Meridien Cancún Resort & Spa and Cancún Palace. There's a small stretch of sand between the two hotels. There are often jet-skiers zooming through the water here, and the strong wind makes the surf rough. **Playa Delfines** is the final beach, at Km 20 where Boulevard Kukulcán curves into a hill. There's an incredible lookout over the ocean; on a clear day you can see at least four shades of blue in the water, though swimming is treacherous unless one of the green flags is posted. Here you'll find lots of sand (unlike many of the beaches that were hit by Hurricane Wilma) and surfers. It's one of the few places in Cancún where you can take surfing lessons. Although decent barrels roll in during hurricane season, seldom do waves in Cancún hit "epic" status. At best, you might find choppy, inconsistent surf at Playa Delfines, Playa Chacmool, and City Beach. Those seeking more than just a ripple should avoid the northern beaches, where Isla Mujeres lies just off shore.

WHERE TO EAT

ZONA HOTELERA

$$$$ MEDITERRANEAN Fodor's Choice ★

✕ **Le Basilic.** If heaven had a restaurant, this would be it. Arched bay windows, checkered marble floors, live classical music, and exquisite garden views create the backdrop for this ideal spot for couples. The 14 chestnut tables surround a sunken gazebo where long-stemmed orchids bloom under glass. The dishes here—created by French chef Henri Charvet—are served beneath silver domes by pleasant tuxedoed waiters. The menu changes every four months, but it is always comprised of French-Mediterranean cuisine, from fresh tuna and sea scallops to seared duck and roasted lamb. As a keepsake, guests are presented with a box of French truffles and elegant recipe cards recapping the bill of fare. The dress code is elegant and reservations are recommended. ✉*Fiesta Americana Grand Coral Beach, Blvd. Kukulcán, Km 9.5, Zona Hotelera* ☎*998/881–3200 Ext. 4220, 4221,4223* 💳*AE, D, DC, MC, V* ⏲*Closed Sun. No lunch.*

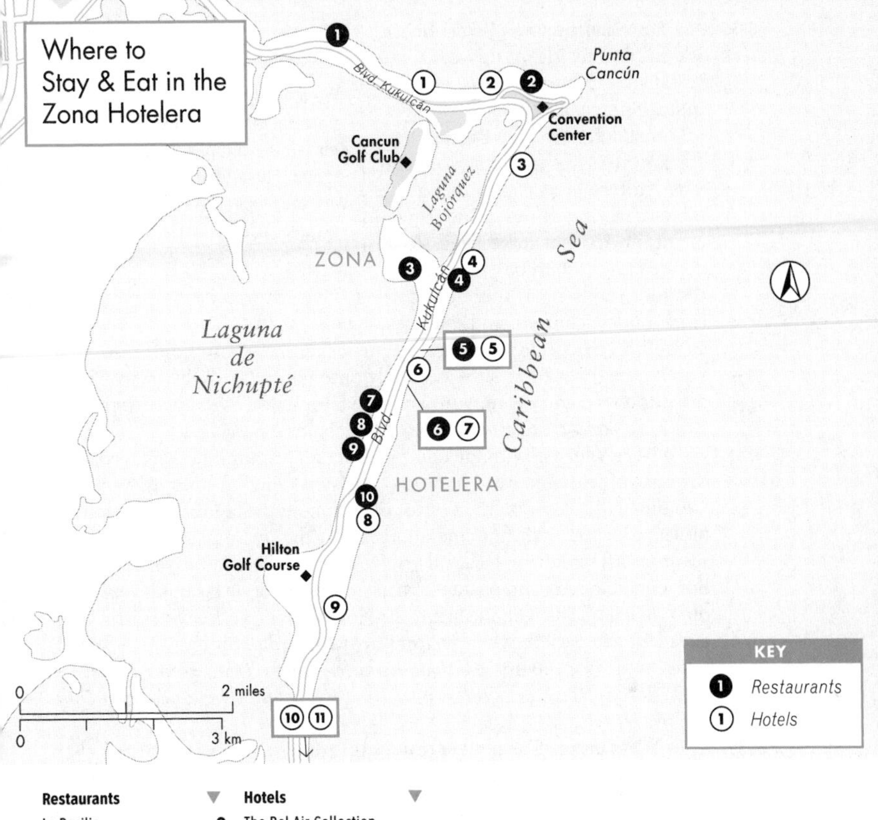

Restaurants	
Le Basilic	2
Cenacolo	4
La Dolce Vita	9
Fantino	5
Grill 14 Cancún	7
Gustino Italian Beachside Grill	6
Laguna Grill	10
Puerto Madero	8
Rio Churrascaria Steak House	1
Thai	3

Hotels	
The Bel Air Collection Cancun	10
Le Blanc Spa Resort	3
Hilton Cancún Golf & Spa Resort	9
JW Marriott Cancún Resort & Spa	7
Me by Melía Cancun	4
Le Meridien Cancún Resort & Spa	6
Omni Cancún Hotel & Villas	8
Presidente InterContinental Cancún Resort	1
The Ritz-Carlton Cancún	5
Riu Palace Las Americas	2
The Westin Resort & Spa Cancún	11

$$$$ STEAK ✕ **Rio Churrascaria Steak House.** It's easy to overlook this Brazilian restaurant because of its generic, unimpressive exterior—but make no mistake, it's one of the best steak houses in the Zona Hotelera. The waiters here walk among the tables carrying different mouthwatering meats that have been slow-cooked over charcoal on skewers (beside Angus beef, there are also cuts of pork, chicken, and sausages, as well as crocodile, ostrich, and quail meat). Simply point out what you'd like; the waiters slice it directly onto your plate. Obviously, if you are not a true carnivore, you won't be happy here. ✉*Blvd. Kukulcán, Km 3.5, Zona Hotelera* ☎*998/849–9040* ▭*AE, MC, V.*

WORD OF MOUTH

"We loved this romantic Italian restaurant [La Dolce Vita]. Our table overlooked the lagoon…beautiful! The waiter was knowledgeable and the food was *delicioso*!"

–Leah

$$$–$$$$ ITALIAN ✕ **La Dolce Vita.** This grande dame of Cancún restaurants delivers on the promise of its name (which means "the sweet life" in Italian). Whether you dine indoors or on the terrace overlooking the lagoon, the candlelit tables adorned with fine linen and china, the live music, and discreet waiters will make you feel as if you've arrived. The Italian fare includes homemade pizzas and pastas such as bolognese-style lasagna, veal ravioli, and calamari steak in shrimp and lobster sauce. The wine list is also excellent. Be patient when waiting for your order, though—good food takes time to prepare. ✉*Blvd. Kukulcán, Km 14.6, Zona Hotelera* ☎*998/885–0161 or 998/885–0150* 🌐*www.ladolchevitacancun.com* ▭*AE, D, DC, MC, V.*

$$$–$$$$ CARIBBEAN Fodor'sChoice ★ ✕ **Grill 14 Cancún.** The newest restaurant from former Ritz-Carlton chef John Gray features gourmet Caribbean cuisine in a beautiful waterfront setting. The signature dishes include roasted duck breast with chipotle chile, tequila, and honey; tender veal cheeks prepared in blackened chile broth; and beef tenderloin and lobster tail with grilled asparagus, mashed potatoes, and toasted garlic butter. The restaurant also has a sushi bar, a martini bar, and a heliport for high rollers. Reservations are highly recommended. ✉ *Blvd. Kukulcán, Km 14 here, Zona Hotelera* ☎*998/840–6146* ▭*AE, MC, V* ⊙*No breakfast.*

$$$–$$$$ ✕ **Laguna Grill.** Intricate tile work adorns this restaurant's floors and walls, and a natural stream divides the open-air dining room, which overlooks the lagoon. Delectable menu options such as an Asian-inspired mojito shrimp entrée and fettuccini with lobster satays match the beautiful setting. Their newly added vegetarian selections include organic soba pasta with teriyaki sautéed vegetables. For dessert there's a Bailey's crème brûlée and a dairy-free fruit dish topped with coconut foam. ✉*Blvd. Kukulcán, Km 15.6, Zona Hotelera* ☎*998/885–0267* 🌐*www.lagunagrill.com.mx* ▭*AE, D, MC, V.*

$$$–$$$$ STEAK Fodor'sChoice ★ ✕ **Puerto Madero.** Modeled after the dock warehouses that have been converted into modern restaurants in the famed Argentine port city Puerto Madero, this steak and seafood house gets rave reviews from locals. The grilled Big Rib Eye generously serves two people. The Alaskan halibut steak, also a crowd pleaser, is prepared with white wine,

shallots, and fresh pepper. If the restaurant is too loud inside, ask for a table outside on the patio overlooking the lagoon. Reservations are recommended on weekends. ✉ *Blvd. Kukulcán, Km 14, Zona Hotelera* ☎ *998/885–2829* ▭ *AE, MC, V.*

WORD OF MOUTH

"You cannot say you have visited Cancún unless you eat at La Habichuela."

–Jim

$$$ ITALIAN ★ ✕ **Cenacolo.** Reliably good pizza and pasta, handmade in full view of patrons, have made this fine Italian restaurant a favorite. Appetizers include a salmon carpaccio that practically melts in your mouth and a light calamari. One of this Italian restaurant's best features is its extensive wine cellar. Although it's located inside a mall, the restaurant's main dining room is elegant, with stained-glass panels on the ceiling and live piano music. ✉ *Kukulcán Plaza, Blvd. Kukulcán, Km 13, Zona Hotelera* ☎ *998/885–3603* ▭ *AE, MC, V.*

14

$$$ ✕ **Fantino.** Reflecting Mexico's rich Spanish heritage, this Mediterranean restaurant lives up to its reputation as one of the country's finest. Grandeur is at its peak in this ballroom setting, with long-stemmed roses and hand-painted ceiling frescos that subtley match the fine English china. Each guest, referred to by name, is treated to the melodious sounds of renowned pianist Mario Patron. Velvet walls mounted with candelabras are only overshadowed by the red satin curtains and ocean views. Each course is paired with its own wine, individually selected by Chef Andreas Schatzschneider. Designed to play with the senses, his appetizers moisten the palate in preparation for the seven-course tasting menu. Divine dishes include foie gras with artichoke hearts, duck prosciutto with truffles, and pesto-crusted lamb with potato-bean timbale. All ingredients are hand selected from local farms or air-freighted to the hotel daily. Just when you think you've seen it all, the waiter wheels over a candy cart, featuring ten glass towers of handmade sweets. Reservations recommended. ✉ *Ritz-Carlton Cancún, Blvd. Kukulcán, Km 14., Zona Hotelera* ☎ *998/881–0808 Ext. 5315* ▭ *AE, MC, V, D, DC* ⊗ *Closed Sun. No lunch.*

$$–$$$ ITALIAN Fodor'sChoice ★ ✕ **Gustino Italian Beachside Grill.** From the moment you walk down the dramatic staircase to enter this restaurant, you know you're in for a memorable dining experience. The dining room has sleek leather furniture, artistic lighting, and views of the wine cellar and open-air kitchen. The *ostriche alla provenzale* (black-shelled mussels in a spicy tomato sauce) appetizer is a standout, as are the salmon-stuffed ravioli and seafood risotto entrées. The service here is impeccable; the saxophone music adds a dash of romance. For those who dare to replicate the exquisite menu, there is a small market where you can purchase all the essential ingredients. ✉ *JW Marriott Resort, Blvd. Kukulcán, Km 14.5, Zona Hotelera* ☎ *998/848–9600 Ext. 6849, 6851* ✍ *Reservations essential* ▭ *AE, MC, V* ⊗ *No lunch.*

$$–$$$ THAI Fodor'sChoice ★ ✕ **Thai.** Expect a truly unique dining experience from the moment you walk into this garden oasis. After all, not many restaurants can boast they have a dolphin aquarium in the bar area. The individual huts with thatched roofs provide an intimate setting to sample spicy Thai dishes

like roasted duck in coconut red curry, and the house favorite, a deep-fried fish fillet prepared with ginger, garlic, and a tamarind chile sauce. Reservations are recommended. ✉ *Plaza la Isla shopping center Blvd. Kukulcán, Km 12.5, Zona Hotelera* ☎ *998/883-1401* ▭ *AE, MC, V* ⏲ *No breakfast or lunch.*

EL CENTRO

$$$–$$$$ CARIBBEAN ★ ✕ **La Habichuela.** Elegant yet cozy, the much-loved Green Bean has an indoor dining room, as well as an outdoor area full of Mayan sculptures and local trees and flowers. Don't miss the famous *crema de habichuela* (a rich, cream-based seafood soup) or the *cocobichuela* (lobster and shrimp in a light curry sauce served inside a coconut). Finish off your meal with Xtabentun, a Mayan liqueur made with honey and anise. ✉ *Av. Margaritas 25, Sm 22* ☎ *998/884–3158* 🌐 *www.lahabichuela.com* ▭ *AE, MC, V.*

$$$ FRENCH ✕ **duMexique.** Discretely located on the bustling Avenida Bonampak, this hidden gem shows no resemblance to a restaurant. Chef Alain Grimond and his wife Sonya have converted their home into an intimate dinner-party setting to create a dining experience unlike any other. Doubling as a gallery, the dining room features modern art, a grand piano, and a crystal chandelier that casts spectrums of light onto the pristine ceiling. Accommodating only 20 guests per evening, the restaurant begins the ritual with martinis in the tropical garden, decorated with tiki torches, dark rattan furniture, glass lanterns, and micro-suede cushions. The French menu (featuring five appetizers, five entrées, and four desserts) changes daily, and is never repeated. Selections might include duckling with risotto or entrecôte with wine sauce. By calling ahead, you can request soufflé de huitlacoche, a delicacy made from mushrooms that grow on cornstalks. A fusion for the eye and palate, each course is a masterpiece of presentation. Be sure to visit the kitchen, where the awards of master chef Alain Grimond are on display. ✉ *Av. Bonampak 109, Sm 3, El Centro* ☎ *998/884–5919* ✍ *Reservations essential* ▭ *MC, V* ⏲ *Closed Mon. No lunch.*

$$$ Fodor'sChoice ★ ASIAN FUSION ✕ **IKI Resto Bar.** Framing the town square of Parque de las Palapas, this chic, Zen-like utopia, from the owners of the renowned Laguna Grill, dares to go where few restaurants have gone before. The thatched temple beckons you into its velvet sanctuary, discretely lit with beaded lamps, Buddha candles, and teardrop crystal globes. The main lounge features a tropical tributary, a glowing cobalt bar, antique Victorian furniture, and a wine wall complete with a sliding ladder. Slow-spinning palm fans twirl overhead while the sounds of chill music ties together this eclectic setting. Those seeking a bit more privacy can hide away in the Balinese cabana, sinfully adorned with overstuffed pillows and bamboo flooring. Blending styles in both decor and cuisine, Iki showcases contemporary Asian-infused dishes like oriental potstickers and coconut cream soup, all with a pinch of Latin flavor. The shrimp siva wrap, rolled in spinach and topped with red curry, is deliciously exotic. The young, hip staff also serves up sweet conclusions like chocolate cake with green-tea ice cream. Here it is about quality, not quantity.

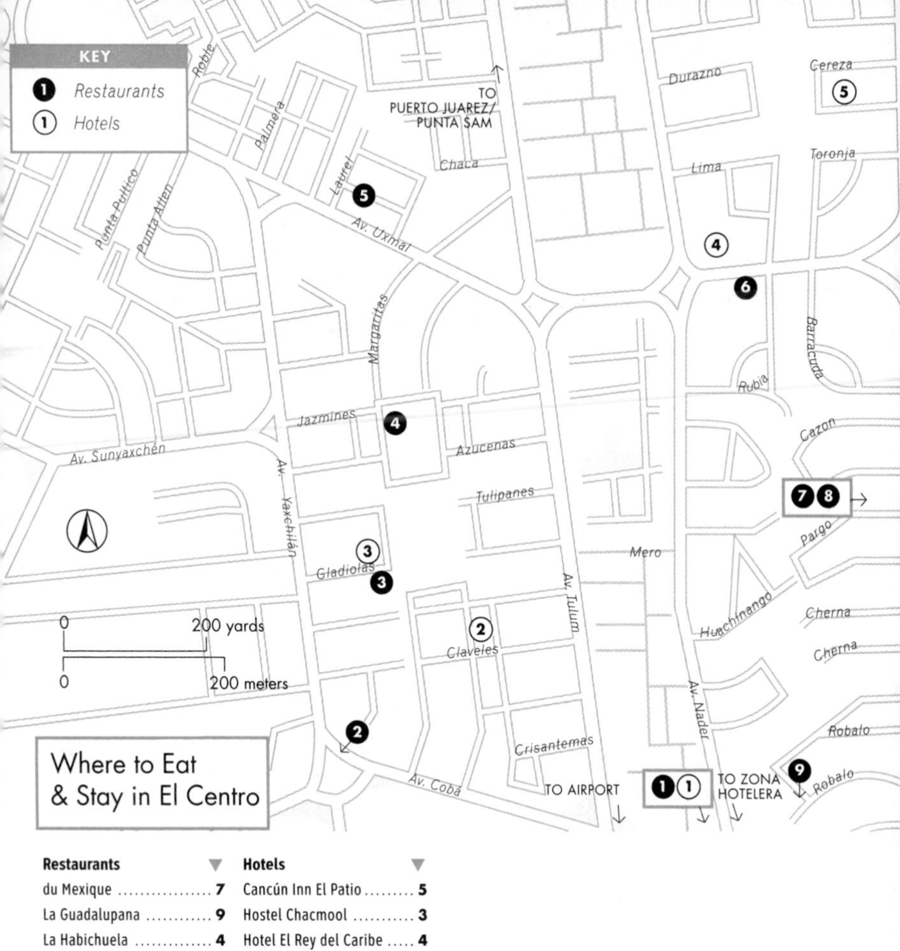

Where to Eat & Stay in El Centro

Restaurants
du Mexique 7
La Guadalupana 9
La Habichuela 4
IKI Resto Bar 3
La Pasteleria-Crepería 2
El Principio 8
El Rincón Yucateco 5
Rolandi's 1
Yamamoto 6

Hotels
Cancún Inn El Patio 5
Hostel Chacmool 3
Hotel El Rey del Caribe 4
Hotel del Sol 2
Suites Sina 1

✉ Alcatraces 39, Sm 22, El Centro ☎ 998/884–7024 ✍ Reservations recommended ▭ AE, MC, V ⏲ Closed Sun. No lunch.

$$$ ITALIAN ✕ **El Principio.** Despite its rather simple decor, this small restaurant is arguably the best place in town to find remarkable pasta. The owner, José Campos Frias, is a thirtysomething cooking genius. His dishes fuse traditional Italian cuisine with his grandmother's Mexican recipes. The salmon and mango salad with cilantro dressing is a meal in itself. Those with hearty appetites should try the exotic oriental spaghetti or the meatball panini in chipotle sauce. The portions here are enormous, and are usually shared by two people. Considered a lunch-hour favorite by Cancún execs, this rustic bistro has just eight tables and can get crowded at times. They also offer takeout for those craving a pasta picnic at the beach. *✉ Ave. Bonampak 227 Sm 4, El Centro ☎ 998/892–8499 ✍ Reservations recommended ▭ No credit cards ⏲ Closed Mon.*

WORD OF MOUTH

"You might want to try some of the little places on the lagoon side of the south end of the hotel zone—they are usually good for grilled fish, fish tacos, grilled shrimp. There are several places in Mercado 28 (again, downtown) in the central food court where you can get the real, economical, all the locals eat their Mexican food at great prices, even seafood.

The Mapchick maps: www.cancunmap.com are a good source of eatery information—check them out. I have found their restaurant picks pretty accurate."

-jw2

$$–$$$ JAPANESE ✕ **Yamamoto.** The sushi here is some of the best in the area, although there's also a menu of traditional Japanese dishes (like chicken teriyaki and tempura) for those who prefer their food cooked. The dining room is tranquil, with Japanese art and bamboo accents—but you can also call for delivery to your hotel room. *✉ Av. Uxmal 31, Sm 3 ☎ 998/887–3366, 998/860–0269 for delivery service ▭ AE, D, DC, MC, V.*

$–$$ MEXICAN ✕ **La Guadalupana.** This lively cantina serves up steak, fajitas, tacos, and other traditional Mexican dishes to an appreciative, if sometimes noisy, local crowd. One wall is decorated with caricatures, mostly of political figures and famous bullfighters—very appropriate since it's on the bottom floor of Cancún's bullring. This is a good place to practice your Spanish, as the menu and staff exhibit no need to practice their English. *✉ Av. Bonampak, Plaza de Toros, Sm 4 ☎ 998/887–0660 ▭ AE, MC, V* ⏲ Closed Sun.

$–$$ CAFE Fodor's Choice ★ ✕ **La Pasteleteria-Crepería.** This small café and bakery has comfortable equipales (rustic Mexican chairs) to plop into as you sample terrific soups, salads, and crepes (the turkey-breast crepe makes a perfect lunch), as well as a variety of sumptuous pastries baked on-site. *✉ Av. Cobá 7, Sm 25 ☎ 998/884–3420 ▭ AE, D, DC, MC, V.*

$–$$ PIZZA ✕ **Rolandi's.** A Cancún landmark for more than 28 years, Rolandi's continues to draw crowds with its scrumptious wood-fired pizzas. There are 20 varieties to choose from—if you can't make up your mind, try the one made with Roquefort cheese. Homemade pasta dishes are also very good. ✉*Av. Cobá 12, Sm 5* ☎*998/884–4047* 🌐*www.rolandi.com* 💳*AE, MC, V.*

¢–$$ MEXICAN ✕ **El Rincón Yucateco.** It's so small that the tables spill out onto the street—but that makes it a great place to people-watch. The traditional Yucatecan dishes here are outstanding; the *panuchos* (puffed corn tortillas stuffed with black beans and topped with shredded pork), the *sopa de lima* (shredded chicken in a tangy broth of chicken stock and lime juice), and the cochinita pibil (a slow-roasted pork dish) should not be missed. ✉*Av. Uxmal 35, Sm 23* ☎*998/892–2459* 💳*No credit cards.*

WHERE TO STAY

14

ZONA HOTELERA

$$$$ Fodor'sChoice ★ **Le Blanc Spa Resort.** An airy and modern hotel with white and beige refined minimalist decor and lots of windows, Le Blanc Spa is the most upscale of the Palace Resorts properties in Cancún. Mainly couples stay in this resort, which is restricted to guests over 18. The spa is one of the largest in Cancún, with 19 indoor treatment rooms and services ranging from aroma foot reflexology to chocolate body wraps. Located along both the ocean and the lagoon, this resort offers some spectacular views. However, only around 40% of the rooms have full ocean views, so availability is limited. **Pros:** The aesthetically pleasing design, excellent spa, butler service. **Cons:** Not even older kids allowed, the price. ✉*Blvd. Kukulcán, Km 10, Zona Hotelera* ☎*998/881–4740* 🌐*www.leblancsparesort.com* *260 rooms* *In-room: Safe, DVD (some), Wi-Fi. In-hotel: 4 restaurants, room service, bars, pools, gym, spa, beachfront, diving, laundry service, concierge, butler service, public Internet, public Wi-Fi, airport shuttle (fee), parking (no fee), no kids under 18, no-smoking rooms* 💳*AE, D, DC, MC, V* *AI.*

$$$$ Fodor'sChoice ★ **JW Marriott Cancún Resort & Spa.** This is the best hotel for experiencing luxury Cancún style and service. Plush is the name of the game at the towering beach resort, where manicured lawns are dotted with an expansive maze of pools, and large vaulted windows let sunlight stream into a lobby decorated with marble floors and beautiful flower arrangements. All rooms have ocean views, private balconies, and wall-to-wall carpeting. Two of the hotel's best features are its 35,000-square-foot spa with indoor pool and its 20-foot dive pool with an artificial reef, where you can practice snorkeling and scuba diving. Like its sister property CasaMagna Marriott Cancún, the majority of guests are here on business travel. **Pros:** Top-notch service, the huge spa and the artificial reef. **Cons:** Some may find this hotel too upscale, seems to lack the festive mood found in other hotels along the strip. ✉*Blvd. Kukulcán, Km 14.5, Zona Hotelera* ☎*998/848–9600 or 888/813–2776* 🌐*www.marriott.com* *448 rooms, 74 suites* *In-room: Safe, kitchen (some), refrigerator (some), Wi-Fi. In-hotel: 3 restaurants, room service, bars, tennis courts, pools, gym, spa, beachfront, diving, water sports, chil-*

> **WORD OF MOUTH**
>
> "What sets [the JW Marriott] apart is the incredible service and attitude of the staff. You are literally treated like royalty."
>
> –Mariah

dren's programs (ages 4–12), laundry service, concierge, executive floor, public Internet, public Wi-Fi, airport shuttle, parking (no fee), no-smoking rooms ▭*AE, MC, V* 🍽*EP.*

WORD OF MOUTH

"The pool is reason enough for staying at [Le Meridien]—it is beautiful."

–Sheree McClure

$$$$ ★ **ME by Meliá Cancún.** The ME takes the chicness of a trendy boutique hotel and blows it up to the grand scale of a large resort. Here all five senses are aroused. For example, guests will find themselves breathing in different soothing scents while listening to electronic lounge music that is played everywhere, including the elevators. This hotel oozes hipness, from the sleek black mermaid sculptures by artist Marie France Porta to the slick bars created by nightlife gurus Rande and Scott Gerber. And if you want to literally bring a piece of ME back home with you, guest-room furnishings and artwork by Yuri Zatarain can be purchased from the on-site gallery. Also, pet owners take note—your furry friends are welcome here. **Pros:** Great spot for young couples, amazing contemporary design, pet-friendly. **Cons:** Not the ideal hotel for kids, very modern, but lacking traditional Mexican flavor. ✉*Blvd. Kukulcán, Km 12, Zona Hotelera* ☎*998/881–2500 or 998/881–2506* 🌐*www.mebymelia.com* *410 rooms, 38 suites* *In-room: Safe, DVD (some), Ethernet (some), Wi-Fi . In-hotel: 4 restaurants, room service, bars, pools, gym, spa, beachfront, laundry service, concierge, executive floor, public Internet, public Wi-Fi, parking (no fee), some pets allowed, no-smoking rooms* ▭*AE, MC, V* 🍽*EP.*

$$$$ ★ **Le Meridien Cancún Resort & Spa.** High on a hill and tucked away from the main boulevard, this refined yet relaxed hotel is an artful blend of art deco and Mayan styles; there's lots of wood, glass, and mirrors. The beach is small, but rooms have spectacular ocean views. The many thoughtful details—such as different temperatures in each of the swimming pools—make a stay here truly special. The Spa del Mar offers the latest European treatments (including seaweed hydrotherapy) in 14 treatment rooms. Business groups are starting to book here, and account for about 40% of the hotel's clientele. **Pros:** Located near one of Cancún's best malls, large fitness center, all rooms with ocean or lagoon views. **Cons:** An expensive stay for a hotel that doesn't offer all-inclusive, small beach. ✉*Blvd. Kukulcán, Km 14, Retorno del Rey, Lote 37, Zona Hotelera* ☎*998/881–2200 or 800/543–4300* 🌐*www.cancun.lemeridien.com* *213 rooms, 26 suites* *In-room: Safe, DVD (some), dial-up, Wi-Fi. In-hotel: 2 restaurants, bar, tennis courts, pools, gym, spa, beachfront, executive floor, public Internet, Wi-Fi, airport shuttle, parking (no fee), children's programs (ages 4–12)* ▭*AE, MC, V* 🍽*BP, EP, CP.*

$$$$ **Presidente InterContinental Cancún Resort.** This landmark hotel boasts arguably the best beach in Cancún. It gained at least 20 feet more sand after Hurricane Wilma. The entire hotel has a contemporary look to it, and the post-Wilma renovation added a swanky new lobby with a tequila bar. Adults looking for even more peace and quiet can take advantage of the adults-only, quiet pool or a beachfront massage. The

atmosphere here is more conservative than at many of the other resorts along the Zona Hotelera, so you're likely to have a quiet, relaxed stay. **Pros:** The Presidente is just a short walk from shops and restaurants; an extremely safe, virtually currentless beach makes it a favorite with families. **Cons:** Definite focus on business travelers and conventions. ✉ *Blvd. Kukulcán, Km 7.5, Zona Hotelera* ☎ *998/848–8700* 🌐 *www.ichotelsgroup.com* *299 rooms, 7 suites* *In-room: Safes, Wi-Fi. In-hotel: 4 restaurants, room service, bars, pools, gym, beachfront, diving, water sports, children's programs (ages 9–12), laundry service, concierge, executive floor, public Wi-Fi, parking (no fee), no-smoking rooms* 💳 *AE, MC, V.*

$$$$ Fodor's Choice ★ **The Ritz-Carlton, Cancún.** Outfitted with crystal chandeliers, beautiful antiques, and elegant oil paintings, this hotel's style is so European that you may well forget you're in Mexico. Rooms are done in understated shades of teal, beige, and rose, with wall-to-wall carpeting, large balconies overlooking the Caribbean, and marble bathrooms with separate tubs and showers. For families with small children, special rooms with cribs and changing tables are available. A great feature of this resort is its Culinary Center, where guests can participate in wine and tequila tastings or join in cooking classes. The resort's overall atmosphere is fairly conservative, and it is one of the few hotels that charges for children's activities ($45 for a half-day program and $65 for a full-day program). **Pros:** One of the city's most elegant hotels, the fine dining experience, tennis center offers private lessons. **Cons:** Conservative atmosphere, expensive rates. ✉ *Blvd. Kukulcán, Km 14, Retorno del Rey 36, Zona Hotelera* ☎ *998/881–0808* 🌐 *www.ritzcarlton.com* *315 rooms, 50 suites* *In-room: Safe, Wi-Fi. In-hotel: 6 restaurants, room service, bar, tennis courts, pools, gym, spa, beachfront, diving, children's programs (ages 4–12), laundry service, concierge, executive floor, public Wi-Fi, airport shuttle, parking (fee), no-smoking rooms* 💳 *AE, D, DC, MC, V* 🍽 *EP.*

$$$$ **Riu Palace Las Americas.** A colossal nine-story property at the north end of the Zona, the Palace is visually stunning and different from the modern, minimalist resorts that dot the Zona Hotelera. Here the decoration is a bit baroque. There are towering columns and cupolas in the lobby, and even the most basic guest rooms (all are suites) have ornate mahogany furniture and Victorian-print bedding. The daily origami ritual of swan towel folding can be rather vexing, as can the boisterous emcee directing poolside games. Each room has its own walk-in closet, sitting room, and four-bottle liquor dispenser. This resort mainly attracts guests over 40. **Pros:** Spacious suites, exchange program allows guests access to sister properties Riu Cancún and Riu Caribe. **Cons:** Pools are fairly small and the beach even tinier, due to the hotel's location, sunbathers will mostly be in the shade by late afternoon. ✉ *Blvd. Kukulcán, Km 8.5, Zona Hotelera* ☎ *998/891–4300* 🌐 *www.riu.com* *372 junior suites* *In-room: Safe, refrigerator, dial-up. In-hotel: 6 restaurants, room service, bars, beachfront, public Internet, water sports, children's programs (ages 4–12), laundry service, pools, gym, spa* 💳 *AE, MC, V* 🍽 *AI.*

14

$$$$ Fodor'sChoice ★ **The Westin Resort & Spa Cancún.** On the southern end of the Zona Hotelera, this hotel is quite secluded—which means you'll get privacy, but you'll also have to drive to get to shops and restaurants. Subtle hints of pampering are what make this hotel so extraordinary, like the white tea mist that periodically sprays in the lobby and the "heavenly beds," so luxurious that many guests purchase them for their homes. Inside the resort, the modern is juxtaposed with the traditional, as sleek dark-wood furniture is offset by brightly colored rugs and the occasional blue or yellow wall. Due to the quiet, isolated nature of the resort, it mainly attracts families with small children and adults in their 30s and 40s. This resort is one of the few in Cancún that allow pets. **Pros:** There are two beaches here—an expansive one on the Caribbean side and a smaller one facing Laguna Nichupté—so guests always have a place to sunbathe. **Cons:** Hidden charges for the use of such amenities as the Internet, gym, and spa. ✉ *Blvd. Kukulcán, Km 20, Zona Hotelera* ☎ *998/848–7400* 🌐 *www.westin.com/Cancún* *362 rooms, 17 suites* *In-room: Safe, DVD (some), Ethernet, dial-up, Wi-Fi. In-hotel: 4 restaurants, room service, bars, tennis courts, pools, gym, spa, beachfront, diving, bicycles, children's programs (ages 4–12), laundry service, concierge, executive floor, public Internet, public Wi-Fi, airport shuttle, parking (no fee), some pets allowed, no-smoking rooms* 💳 *AE, DC, MC, V* *AI, EP.*

$$$–$$$$ Fodor'sChoice ★ **Hilton Cancún Golf & Spa Resort.** The Caribbean plays a central role at this resort, with ocean views offered in all standard guest rooms and junior suites. Set amid 150 lush acres, the tropical setting, with palapa huts and poolside hammocks, is luxurious without seeming overly ostentatious. The landscaping incorporates a series of lavish, interconnected swimming pools that wind through palm-dotted lawns, ending at the beach. Airy and vibrant, the rooms are pristine white with a splash of turquoise to match the sea. Some of the villas, however, only offer garden views, so make sure to specify oceanfront when booking. Guests who want to get more intimate with nature can participate in the resort's turtle release program or work on their swing at the resort's championship 18-hole, par-72 course, where crocodile and peacock sightings are frequent. For the ultimate in pampering, the hotel's renovated spa features a Zen garden hot tub, a bamboo relaxation lounge, poolside yoga, and massages on the beach. There are children's activities here, at a cost of $45 for a full day, $32 for a half-day, or $10 per hour. Pros: Outstanding beachfront villas, tasteful decor without being over the top, multilevel pool, angled pool area offers all-day sunshine. Cons: Food parallels the traditional Hilton brand. ✉ *Blvd. Kukulcán, Km 17, Zona Hotelera* ☎ *998/881–8000* 🌐 *www.hiltoncancun.com* *426 rooms, 23 suites, 82 villas* *In-room: Safe, kitchen (some), DVD, Ethernet (some), dial-up (some), Wi-Fi (some). In-hotel: 5 restaurants, room service, bars, golf course, tennis courts, pools, gym, spa, beachfront, diving, water sports, bicycles, volleyball, soccer, children's programs (ages 4–11), laundry service, concierge, executive floor, public Internet, public Wi-Fi, parking (no fee), no-smoking rooms* 💳 *AE, D, DC, MC, V* *EP.*

$$$–$$$$ ★ **Omni Cancún Hotel & Villas.** After undergoing a $15-million renovation in 2007, this 10-story hotel has definitely moved up a notch or two in Cancún's hotel hierarchy. Each standard room has a balcony with built-in benches, a marble bathroom, flat-screen TV, and radio with an MP3 hookup. And if you decide to splurge on one of the three-floor villas that surround the hotel, you will not be disappointed. They each have a sunken living room, fully equipped kitchen, sun terrace off the third-floor bedroom, and parking space right outside. Your stay here will not be complete without paying a visit to the huge, adults-only hot-tub area with swim-up bar—it is the only one of its kind in the entire Zona Hotelera. If you'd rather be dry when drinking, then grab a table at the lobby bar and try one of the delicious martinis that are the house specialty. There are four handicapped-accessible rooms here. Pros: Refurbished rooms, tons of scheduled activities. Cons: Crowded pool area lined with sun chairs, limited fixed menu. ✉*Blvd. Kukulcán, Km 16.5, Zona Hotelera* ☎*998/881–0600* 🌐*www.omnihotels.com* *312 rooms, 19 suites, 20 villas* *In-room: Safe, kitchen (some), refrigerator (some), DVD (some), Wi-Fi. In-hotel: 3 restaurants, room service, bars, tennis courts, pools, gym, spa, beachfront, children's programs (ages 5–12), laundry service, concierge, public Internet, public Wi-Fi, parking (no fee), no-smoking rooms* *AE, MC, V* *AI, EP.*

$$$ Fodor's Choice ★ **The Bel Air Collection Cancún.** The design scheme at this strikingly chic and tranquil resort is unlike that of any other hotel that lines Boulevard Kukulcán. White furniture is offset by red and black accents, giving the entire hotel a retro futuristic look. Billowing drapery creates a wall-less passage into the open-air lobby. Neon lights in the foil-lined elevators change every two seconds, triggering sensations of peace and relaxation. In addition to the sushi bar, there are two small dining sections where you can actually cool off your feet while eating or enjoying a drink, as the tables and chairs are sitting in a low pool of water. The spa here has a yoga/meditation room, light chambers, and high-tech machines from Europe that are used for aromatherapy and chromotherapy sessions, among other treatments. Children under the age of 12 are not permitted at this hotel, which is targeted at adults looking for a peaceful hideaway. All 19 suites have private, indoor Jacuzzis and ocean views. **Pros:** The luxurious spa, hotel is very aesthetically pleasing. **Cons:** No kids under 12, not close to party zone. ✉*Blvd. Kukulcán, Km 20.5, Zona Hotelera* ☎*998/885–2148 or 998/885–0236* 🌐*www.thebelair.com.mx* *137 rooms, 14 suites* *In-room: Safe, DVD, Wi-Fi (some), minibar. In-hotel: 2 restaurants, room service, bars, pool, gym, spa, beachfront, laundry service, public Wi-Fi, parking (no fee), no kids under 12, no-smoking rooms* *AE, MC, V* *AI, BP, EP.*

EL CENTRO

$–$$$ ★ **Suites Sina.** On a quiet residential street off Boulevard Kukulcán, these economical suites are in front of Laguna Nichupté and close to the Pok-Ta-Pok golf course. The lobby leads out to a lush garden, pool, and a small restaurant at the center. When it comes to accommodations, skip the standard rooms and upgrade to a junior or master suite, as they have lagoon views, kitchenettes, and spacious dining-living rooms. The atmosphere is relaxed and quiet, making it the perfect place to hide away from the craziness that is the Zona Hotelera; the hotel is actually located between the Hotel Zone and El Centro, though they claim to be in the heart of the Hotel Zone. Pros: Ideally situated on the lagoon, affordably priced. Cons: A 10-minute walk to the beach. ✉ *Club de Golf, Calle Quetzal 33, turn right at Km 7.5 after golf course, Zona Hotelera/El Centro* ☎ *998/883–1017 or 877/666–9837* 🌐 *www.cancunsinasuites.com.mx* *4 rooms, 33 suites* *In-room: Kitchen (some), refrigerator (some). In-hotel: Restaurant, room service, bar, pool, no elevator, laundry service, public Internet, parking (fee), no-smoking rooms* ▭ *AE, MC, V* *EP.*

$–$$ ★ **Cancún Inn El Patio.** This traditional, Mexican-style inn has been converted into a charming 15-room guesthouse. An iron gate leads off a busy street into a courtyard, delightfully landscaped with trees, flowers, and a tile fountain, Breakfast is served in a lower-level restaurant, creatively designed with arched doorways, brick walls, and wrought-iron chandeliers, giving it an intimate wine-cellar atmosphere. Upstairs, many of the large, airy rooms have Mexican rustic furniture and Talavera ceramics. Smoking and food are not allowed in the rooms, but are permitted in the outdoor patio areas. The helpful staff embraces the "mi casa es su casa" mentality, and offers expert advice on the area. **Pros:** Clean, safe, and centrally located, this is a great value for seasoned travelers. **Cons:** Ask about the daily exchange rate when paying by credit card, location somewhat of a distance from decent restaurants. ✉ *Av. Bonampak 51, Sm 2* ☎ *998/884–3500* 🌐 *www.cancun-suites.com* *15 rooms* *In-room: No phone, safe. In-hotel: No elevator, parking (no fee), no-smoking rooms* ▭ *MC, V* *CP.*

$ Fodor's Choice ★ **Hotel El Rey del Caribe.** Thanks to the use of solar energy, a water-recycling system, and composting toilets, this unique hotel has very little impact on the environment—and its luxuriant garden blocks the heat and noise of downtown. Hammocks hang poolside, and wrought-iron tables and chairs dot the grounds. There is artwork throughout the property, much of which was painted by the owner herself (who lives on-site). Standard rooms are small but pleasant and have kitchenettes. The newest accommodations, known as the executive rooms, are larger and have wood floors. No smoking allowed in any of the rooms. A great feature is the tiny spa, where you can book honey or chocolate massages that cost a third of what they do in the Zona Hotelera. El Centro's shops and restaurants are within walking distance. **Pros:** Tranquil atmosphere, eco-friendly, affordable spa. **Cons:** No ocean or lagoon view, rooms are simple. ✉ *Av. Uxmal 24 at Náder, Sm 2A* ☎ *998/884–2028* 🌐 *www.reycaribe.com* *33 rooms* *In-room: Safe, kitchen, refrigerator, Wi-Fi. In-hotel: Restaurant, pool, gym, spa, no elevator, public Internet, public Wi-Fi, parking (no fee), no-smoking rooms* ▭ *MC, V* *BP.*

$ Fodor's Choice ★ **Hotel del Sol.** Reminiscent of an upscale European flat, this four-story hotel with tangerine shutters and signature cupolas is one of the jewels of Parque de las Palapas. Bearing names like Nova, Bamboo, Lotus, and Soleil, the theme rooms are uniquely designed to incorporate traces of nature. The artwork here is pure genius, ranging from rustic floor-plank paintings to plaster castings of sea life. Several bathrooms, inlaid with vibrant mosaic tiles, have freestanding stone basins and citrus-infused bath products. A small wooden bridge spans a swimming pool, which separates the main building from the hotel's street-level bistro. Each standard room comes with a private terrace and small lounging area. The three suites tucked in the alcoves are more modern in design with olive-toned walls, micro-suede sofas, and teak furnishings. They also offer stunning views of the town square below. **Pros:** Thoughtful, creative details included for what is really a modest room rate. **Cons:** No elevator, and the hotel's wooden staircase is extremely loud and creaky, so those on lower levels might have restless nights. ✉ *Calle Alcatraces 33, Mza. 9, Sm 22, El Centro* ☎ *998/887–5579* 🌐 *www.solylunahotel.com* *11 rooms, 8 suites* *In-Rooms: Safe, Wi-Fi, refrigerator. In-hotel: Restaurant, concierge, airport shuttle, laundry facilities, parking (free), pool, no elevator* 💳 *AE, V*

14

¢ ★ **Hostel Chacmool.** One of the cheapest and hippest places to stay in downtown Cancún, this family-run hostel offers clean rooms, a complimentary continental breakfast, a trendy lobby bar, and a terrace with a pool table. Live entertainment is just a stone's throw away at the Parque de las Palapas, and there's no curfew if you decide to make it a late night out. Mixed-gender and female-only dorms are available, or if you decide to splurge, opt for the private room with two double beds and a private bath. **Pros:** Excellent location, no curfew, really cool hostel. **Cons:** Not much privacy if you stay in dorm, draws a young crowd party (not ideal if you need some rest). ✉ *Gladiolas 18, Sm 22, in front of Parque de las Palapas, Centro* ☎ *998/887–5873* 🌐 *www.chacmool.com.mx* *30 beds* *In-room: No phone, no TV, a/c. In-hotel: No elevator, laundry facilities, public Internet (free), parking, bar, restaurant* 💳 *MC, V* *CP* .

SPORTS & THE OUTDOORS

BOATING & SAILING

AquaWorld (✉ *Blvd. Kukulcán, Km 15.2, Zona Hotelera* ☎ *998/848–8300* 🌐 *www.aquaworld.com.mx*) rents boats and water toys and offers parasailing and tours aboard a submarine. **El Embarcadero** (✉ *Blvd. Kukulcán, Km 4, Zona Hotelera* ☎ *998/849–7343*), the marina complex at Playa Linda, is the departure point for ferries to Isla Mujeres and several tour boats. **Delta Tours** (✉ *Playa Tortugas, Blvd. Kukulcán, Km 6.5, Zona Hotelera* ☎ *998/849–4995*) has banana boats, snorkeling gear, Wave Runners, and parasails. Willing to match competitive prices, they also offer night cruises, paddy boats, catamarans, and all-inclusive tours to Isla Mujeres.

Marina Barracuda (✉ *Blvd. Kukulcán, Km 14, in front of Ritz-Carlton, Zona Hotelera* ☎ *998/885–3444* 🌐 *www.marinebarracuda.com*), **Marina del Rey** (✉ *Blvd. Kukulcán, Km 15.6, in front of Grand Oasis Cancún, Zona Hotelera* ☎ *998/885–0363*), and **Marina Punta del Este** (✉ *Blvd. Kukulcán, Km 10.3, Zona Hotelera* ☎ *998/883–1210*) all rent out Wave Runners and offer jungle tours that leave several times a day. Marina Punta del Este also has jungle tours that leave every hour from 9 AM to 3 PM.

BULLFIGHTING

The Cancún **bullring** (✉*Av. Bonampak 1, a block from Blvd. Kukulcán, Sm 4* ☎*998/884–8372 or 998/884–8248*), a block south of the Pemex gas station, hosts weekly bullfights. A matador, *charros* (Mexican cowboys), a mariachi band, and flamenco dancers entertain during the hour preceding the bullfight. There are also contests held that involve the spectators, such as playing soccer with a baby bull. Tickets cost about $40. Events begin at 3:30 PM every Wednesday, from December 26 through May 7.

FISHING

Asterix Tours (✉*Blvd. Kukulcán, Km 5.5, Zona Hotelera* ☎*998/886–4847* 🌐*www.contoytours.com*) offers nighttime "party fishing" trips that cost $65 per person and include dinner and drinks. With an emphasis on nature conservation, Asterix is the only tour company permitted to visit Isla Contoy and the underwater gardens of Isla Mujeres. Thirty-minute boat tours cost $65 per person.

Mundo Marino (✉*Blvd. Kukulcán, Km 5.5, Zona Hotelera* ☎*998/849–7257 or 998/849–7258*) is the marina closest to downtown and specializes in diving and fishing, including deep-sea fishing expeditions. Prices range from $380 to $940, depending on the size of the boat and the length of the trip. They also offer small game-fishing trips that cost $220 for four hours or $330 for six hours. **Scuba Cancún** (✉*Blvd. Kukulcán, Km 5, Zona Hotelera* ☎*998/849–7508, 998/849–4736, or 998/849–5225* 🌐*www.scubacancun.com*) also offers deep-sea fishing and diving. Prices range from $550 for a four-hour fishing trip to $800 for an eight-hour expedition.

GOLF

Many hotels offer golf packages that can considerably reduce your greens fees at Cancún golf courses. Cancún's main golf course is at **Cancún Golf Club at Pok-Ta-Pok** (✉*Blvd. Kukulcán, Km 7.5, Zona Hotelera* ☎*998/883–1230* 🌐*www.cancungolfclub.com*). The club has fine views of both sea and lagoon; its 18 holes were designed by Robert Trent Jones Jr. It also has two practice greens, three tennis courts, a pro shop, and a restaurant. The greens fees go from $145 to $175, and include your cart, food, and beverages; club rentals are $40, shoes $18. The 9-hole executive course, **Gran Sol Meliá** (✉*Gran Melia Cancún Resort, Blvd. Kukulcán, Km 16.5, Zona Hotelera* ☎*998/881–1100* 🌐*www.solmelia.com*) forms a semicircle around the property and looks out onto the lagoon. The greens fee is $30, but the course is for the exclusive use of hotel guests. There's an 18-hole championship golf course at the **Hilton** (✉*Hilton Cancún Golf & Spa Resort, Blvd. Kukulcán, Km 17, Zona Hotelera* ☎*998/881–8016* 🌐*www.hiltoncancun.com/golf.htm*). The turf here was replaced in 2006 with Paspalum Sea Isle 1 grass, and all tee boxes were leveled up to USGA standards. The course is located along the Nichupté Lagoon and has a practice facility with driving range and putting green. Greens fees are $199 ($149 for hotel guests), carts included.

The newest course in Cancún is the **Playa Mujeres Golf Club** (✉*Playa Mujeres Beach Resort, Prolongación Bonampak, Punta Sam* ☎*998/887–7322 or 998/892–0874* 🌐*www.playamujeresgolf.com.mx*). Designed by Greg Norman, this 18-hole, par-72 course is located within the 930-acre Playa Mujeres Resort that is currently being developed in Punta Sam. Practice facilities include a driving range, two putting greens, and a short game area. You can also arrange for individual and group instruction. Greens fees run from $185 to $230.

Moon Spa & Golf Club ✉*Carretera Cancún-Chetumal, Km 340, M 18, Sm 40 [about 15 min from airport]*, ☎*998/881–6000* 🌐 *www.palaceresorts.com* has three 9-hole courses. The 18-hole greens fee, which includes a cart, food, and drink service, costs $260. If you're staying at the Moon Palace, inquire about the hotel's all-inclusive golf package.

SNORKELING & SCUBA DIVING

Aqua Fun (✉*Blvd. Kukulcán, Km 16.5, Zona Hotelera* ☎*998/885–2930* 🌐*www.aquafun.com.mx*) offers a two-hour tour of the mangroves that costs $66 per person and includes snorkeling at the Punta Nizuc reef.

AquaWorld (✉*Blvd. Kukulcán, Km 15.2, Zona Hotelera* ☎*998/848–8300* 🌐*www.aquaworld.com.mx*) has a day-trip snorkeling excursion to Isla Mujeres that costs $69 per person. This operation also offers diving; a one-tank dive costs $66 and two-tank dives start at $71. Dive explorations of boat wrecks cost $79, sinkhole expeditions cost $132.

Marina Barracuda (✉*Blvd. Kukulcán, Km 14, Zona Hotelera* ☎*998/885–3444* 🌐*www.marinabarracuda.com*) has a two-hour jungle boat tour through the mangroves, which ends with snorkeling at the Punta Nizuc coral reef. The fee (which starts at $66) includes snorkeling equipment, life jackets, and refreshments.

Marina Punta del Este (✉*Blvd. Kukulcán, Km 10.3, Zona Hotelera* ☎*998/883–1210*) is right in front of the Hyatt Cancún Caribe. They have dives that last from 3½ to 4 hours; $72 if you are certified and $88 for a lesson. Daily lessons begin at 8 AM and 1 PM.

Mundo Marino (✉*Blvd. Kukulcán, Km 5.5, Zona Hotelera* ☎*998/849–7257 or 998/849–7258*) has a 2½-hour snorkeling excursion that costs $28 per person. They also offer a single-tank dive ($55), two-tank dive ($70), night dive ($70), and diving instruction course ($90). **Scuba Cancún** (✉*Blvd. Kukulcán, Km 5, Zona Hotelera* ☎*998/849–7508* 🌐*www.scubacancun.com.mx*) specializes in diving trips and offers NAUI, CMAS, and PADI instruction. It's operated by Tomás Hurtado, who has more than 30 years of experience. A two-tank dive starts at $68. **Solo Buceo** (✉*Blvd. Kukulcán, Km 9.5, Zona Hotelera* ☎*998/883–3979* 🌐*www.solobuceo.com*) charges $55 for one-tank dives, $70 for two-tank dives, and $90 for twilight diving every Tuesday and Thursday. They also have NAUI, FMAS, CMAS, and PADI instruction (lesson prices range from $90 to $240). The outfit also offers a full-day excursion to Cozumel, as well as dive explorations of various cenotes near Akumal. These extended trips are available from $145 every Wednesday and Friday.

NIGHTLIFE

BARS

The Black Pearl (✉*Blvd. Kukulcán, Km 9.1, Zona Hotelera* ☎*998/883–5649)*, a swashbuckler theme bar and grill on the waterfront, is a great place to knock back a few drinks before heading out to the nearby discos. At night, the waiters here toss restaurant leftovers off the bar's deck onto the edge of the lagoon, drawing the attention of fish and a few hungry crocodiles.

Carlos n' Charlie's (✉*Blvd. Kukulcán, Km 9, Forum by the Sea mall, Zona Hotelera* ☎*998/883–4468)* the waiters will occasionally abandon their posts to start singing or performing comical skits. It's not unusual for them to roust everyone from their seats to join in a conga line before going back to serving food and drinks.

Fat Tuesday (✉*Blvd. Kukulcán, Km 6.5, Zona Hotelera* ☎*998/849–7199 or 998/849–7201* 🌐*www.fat-tuesdaycancun.com*), with its large daiquiri bar and live and piped-in disco music, is another place to dance the night away.

Pat O'Brien's (✉*Plaza Flamingo, Blvd. Kukulcán, Km 11.5, Zona Hotelera* ☎*998/883–0832)* brings the New Orleans party scene to the Zona with live rock bands and its famous cocktails balanced on the heads of waiters as they dance through the crowd. The really experienced servers can balance up to four margaritas or strawberry daiquiris at once! It's always Mardi Gras here, so the place is decorated with lots of balloons, banners, and those infamous beads given out to brave patrons.

A relaxing alternative to the loud discos,**Resto-Bar Bling** (✉*Blvd. Kukulcán, Km 13.5, in front of Plaza Kukulcán, Zona Hotelera* ☎*998/840–6015* ⏲*Opens at 7 pm*) has a chic open-air lounge bar with canopy-covered beds overlooking the lagoon. DJs spin house and chillout tunes as the bartenders mix their famous kiwi, cucumber, or coffee martinis. The restaurant inside specializes in Mediterranean cuisine and sushi.

Señor Frog's (✉*Blvd. Kukulcán, Km 9.5, Zona Hotelera* ☎*998/883–1092)* is known for its over-the-top drinks; foot-long funnel glasses are filled with margaritas, daiquiris, or beer, and you can take them home as souvenirs once you've chugged them dry. Needless to say, spring-breakers adore this place and often stagger back night after night.

DANCE CLUBS

Azúcar(✉*Dreams Cancún Resort & SpaBlvd. Kukulcán, Km 9.5, Zona Hotelera* ☎*998/848–7000* 🎫*$15)* showcases the very best Latin American bands. Go just to watch the locals dance (the beautiful people tend to turn up here really late). Proper dress is required—no jeans or sneakers.

The City (✉*Blvd. Kukulcán, Km 9.5, Zona Hotelera* ☎*998/848–8380* 🌐*www.thecitycancun.com*) is a giant party complex with a daytime water park; at night, there's a cavernous dance floor with stadium seating and several large bar selling overpriced drinks. Dancing and live shows are the main draw, as well as a Tuesday night moonlight pool party and bikini contest. This is by far the loudest club in the Zona Hotelera, so don't be surprised if you go home with a ringing in your ears. Doors open at 10 PM.

The wild, wild**Coco Bongo** (✉ *Blvd. Kukulcán, Km 9.5, across street from Dady'O, Zona Hotelera* ☎*998/883–5061* 🌐*www.cocobongo.com.mx* 🎫*$20, $45 for open bar*) has no chairs, but there are plenty of tables that everyone dances on. There's also a popular floor show billed as "Las Vegas meets Hollywood," featuring celebrity impersonators; and an amazing gravity-defying acrobatic show with an accompanying 12-piece orchestra. After the shows the techno gets turned up to full volume and everyone gets up to get down.

14

Dady'O (✉*Blvd. Kukulcán, Km 9.5, Zona Hotelera* ☎*998/883–3333* 🌐*www.dadyo.com.mx* 🎫*$20 cover, $45 for open bar)* has been around for a while but it is still very "in" with the younger set. A giant screen projects music videos about the always-packed dance floor, while laser lights whirl aross the crowd. During spring break, the place gets even livelier during the Hawaiin Bikini contests.

Dady Rock (✉ *Blvd. Kukulcán, Km 9.5, Zona Hotelera* ☎*998/883–3333* 🌐*www.dadyrock.com.mx* 🎫*$20, $45 for open bar*)draws a high-energy crowd that likes entertainment along with their dinner. Live bands usually start off the action, followed by DJs spinning dance tracks into the wee hours of the morning. Wet body contests are on Thursday and hot male contests on Sunday. Winners take home $1,000 in cash and prizes. It's open Thursday through Sunday.

Mambo Café (✉*Blvd. Kukulcán, Km 13.5, Zona Hotelera* ☎*998/840–6498* 🌐*www.mambocafe.com.mx* 🎫*$10, $30 for open bar)*features some of the city's hottest live bands and DJs playing tropical music, making it the ideal disco to practice your salsa and merengue steps.

GAY BARS

Café D' Pa (✉*Parque de las Palapas, Mza. 16, Sm 22, El Centro* ☎*998/884–7615)*is a cheerful bar and restaurant offering a menu of specialty crepes; since it opens at lunchtime, it's a popular place to gather before the city's other gay bars open their doors.

Karamba Bar (✉*Avenida Tulum 1 at Calle Azucenas, Sm 5, El Centro* ☎ *No phone* 🌐*www.karambabar.com)*is a large open-air disco and club that's known for its stage performers. A variety of drag shows with the usual lip-synching and dancing celebrity impersonations are put on every Wednesday and Thursday. On Friday night the Go-Go Boys of Cancún entertain, and strip shows are on weekends. The bar opens at 10:30 pm and the party goes on until dawn. There's no cover charge.

Picante Bar (✉*Plaza Galerias, Av. Tulum 20, Sm 5, El Centro* ☎*No phone* 🌐*www.picantebar.com*), the oldest gay bar in Cancún, has been operating for 15 years. (It survived several raids and closures during less lenient times in the '90s.) The drag shows here tend to reflect local culture; for instance, during Carnival there is a special holiday beauty pageant followed by the crowning of "the Queen." The owner, "Mother Picante," emcees the floor show that includes Las Vegas–type dance revues, singers, and strippers. Doors open at 9 PM and close at 5 AM, and there's no cover.

The Blue Bayou Jazz Club (✉*Blvd. Kukulcán, Km 10.5, Zona Hotelera* ☎*998/884–0044)*, the lobby bar in the Hyatt Cancún Caribe, has nightly jazz ranging from contemporary to Dixieland.

Bulldog Cafe (✉ *Krystal Cancún hotelBlvd. Kukulcán, Km 9, Zona Hotelera* ☎*998/848–9800* 🌐*www.bulldogcafe.com* 🎫*$40)* has an all-you-can-drink bar, live rock groups, the latest dance music, and an impressive laser light show. The stage here is large, and some very well-known bands have played on it, including Guns n' Roses and Radiohead. Another, somewhat bawdier draw is the private hot tub, where you can have "the Jacuzzi bikini girls" scrub your back. Naturally, this place is popular with spring breakers.

To mingle with locals and hear great music for free, head to the**Parque de las Palapas** (✉*Bordered by Avs. Tulum, Yaxchilán, Uxmal and Cobá, Sm 22, El Centro*). Every Friday night at 7:30 there's live music that ranges from jazz to salsa to Caribbean; lots of locals show up to dance. On Sunday afternoons, the Cancún Municipal Orchestra plays.

Sabor Latino (✉ *Plaza Hong KongLoc 31, Sm 20, El Centro* ☎*998/898–4006* 🌐*www.saborlatino.com.mx* ⏲ *Opens at 10 pm, Wed.–Sun.*) has live salsa bands and lots of locals to show you new dance moves. If you want something more structured, you can take dance lessons here.

SHOPPING

GALLERIES

Serious collectors visit **Casa de Cultura** (✉*Prolongación Av. Yaxchilán, Sm 25* ☎*998/884–8364*) for regular art shows featuring Mexican artists. **Dorfman's Art Gallery** (✉*Inside Royal Caribbean hotel, Blvd. Kukulcán, Km 17, Zona Hotelera* ☎*998/881–0100 Ext. 63610*) features Mayan-inspired and environmentally themed sculptures and paintings by local artists and brothers Renato and Adán Dorfman.

El Pabilo (✉*Av. Yaxchilán 3, Sm 7* ☎*998/892–4553*) is a downtown café that showcases Mexican painters and photographers on a rotating basis.

MARKETS & MALLS

ZONA HOTELERA

Coral Negro (✉*Blvd. Kukulcán, Km 9, Zona Hotelera*), next to the Convention Center, is an open-air market that has about 50 stalls selling crafts and souveneirs. It's open daily until late evening. Everything here is overpriced, but bargaining does work. Stalls deeper in the market tend to have better deals than those around the market's periphery.

Forum-by-the-Sea (✉*Blvd. Kukulcán, Km 9.5, Zona Hotelera* ☎*998/883–4428*) is a three-level entertainment and shopping plaza in the Zona. This open-air mall features brand-name restaurants, upscale clothing boutiques, a food court, and chain stores, all in a circuslike atmosphere. For Spring Breakers, the main draws are the nightclubs, Coco Bongo and Hard Rock Café, which are identified by the massive guitar at the mall entrance. The bungee trampolines set up here during high season are especially popular with children.

★ The glittering, ultratrendy, and ultraexpensive **La Isla Shopping Village** (✉*Blvd. Kukulcán, Km 12.5, Zona Hotelera* ☎*998/883–5025*) is on the Laguna Nichupté under chic, white canopies. A series of canals and small bridges is designed to give the place a Venetian look. In addition to more than 200 shops, the mall has a marina, a disco, restaurants, and movie theaters. There is also an interactive aquarium where you can swim with the dolphins and feed the sharks. A fun, inexpensive activity here is the River Ride Tour, a 20-minute boat ride around the canals and out into the lagoon that only costs $4 per person (a great time to go is right at sundown, so you can watch the sun set over the lagoon).

Located north of the Convention Center, the two-story **Plaza Caracol** (✉*Blvd. Kukulcán, Km 8.5, Zona Hotelera* ☎*998/883–4760*) houses chain stores like Sunglass Island, Benetton, and Ultrafemme, along with souvenir and jewelry shops and pharmacies. Making up this contemporary mall are 100 shops, as well as a small food court, an enormous Starbucks, and the fine Italian restaurant Casa Rolandi.

Located in from of the Convention Center, **Plaza la Fiesta** (✉*Blvd. Kukulcán, Km 9, Zona Hotelera* ☎*998/883–2116*) has 20,000 square feet of showroom space, and more than 100,000 different products for sale. This is probably the widest selection of Mexican goods in the Hotel Zone, and includes leather goods, silver and gold jewelry, handicrafts, souvenirs, and swimwear. There are some good bargains here.

Plaza Flamingo (✉*Blvd. Kukulcán, Km 11.5, across from Hotel Flamingo Resort & Plaza, Zona Hotelera* ☎*998/883–2855*) is a small mall that houses around 80 different shops that sell mainly clothing, jewelry, and souvenirs. The main attractions here are the chain restaurants Jimmy Buffet's Margaritaville, Outback Steakhouse, Bubba Gump, and Pat O'Brien's, which fill up with partyers during spring break.

★ **Plaza Kukulcán** (✉*Blvd. Kukulcán, Km 13, Zona Hotelera* ☎*998/193–0161*) is a large, upscale mall with around 100 shops and six restaurants. Some highlights include a bar with a bowling alley and the Luxury Avenue section of the mall, which offers brand names from Cartier, Fendi, Burberry, and Coach. While parents shop, kids can enjoy the game arcade, a play area, and Chocolate City, which features a weekly circus show. The mall hosts art exhibits and other cultural events. If you stop in any night at 8 PM, you can watch the 10-minute, English-language light show (inspired by the ancient text Popol Vuh) under the Mayan stained-glass dome. If you fell in love with the European clothing chain Mango on your last trip to Paris, swing by the branch here.

Plaza El Zocalo (✉ *Blvd. Kuckulcán, Km 9, Zona Hotelera* ☎ *998/883–3698*) may look small from the entrance, but it has about 60 stalls where you can find traditional Mexican handicrafts, silver jewelry, and handmade sandals. El Zocalo also houses four restaurants—including Mextreme, which still sports a banner announcing its claim to fame as a set in the 1980s movie Cocktail.

EL CENTRO

There are lots of interesting shops downtown along Avenida Tulum (between Avenidas Cobá and Uxmal). The oldest and largest of Cancún's crafts markets is **Ki Huic** (✉ *Av. Tulum 17, between Bancomer and Bital banks, Sm 3* ☎ *998/884–3347*). It's open daily 9 AM to 10 PM and houses about 100 vendors. **Mercado Veintiocho** *(Market 28)*, just off Avenidas Yaxchilán and Sunyaxchén, is the largest open-air market in Cancún. In addition to a few small restaurants, here you will find around 100 stalls selling many of the same items found in the Zona Hotelera but at half the price. **Ultrafemme** (✉ *Av. Tulum 111, at Calle Claveles, Sm 21* ☎ *998/884–1402*) is a popular downtown store that carries duty-free perfume, cosmetics, and jewelry. It also has branches in the Zona Hotelera at Plaza Caracol, Plaza las Américas, Plaza Kukulcán, and La Isla Shopping Village. The downtown store is open daily 9:30 AM to 9 PM.

Cancún Gran Plaza (✉ *Av. Nichupté Manzana 18 Lote 1 Locales 24, 30 Y 62A SM 51, El Centro* 77533 ⊙ *9–9*) offers jewelry shops, fashion boutiques and major department stores like Sanborns and Walmart. There are also cinemas, cafés and restaurants in the shopping mall.

Paseo Cancún (✉ *Av. Andrés, Sm 39* ☎ *998/872–3735* 🌐 *www.cabicorp.com.mx*) was developed by the same company that owns La Isla in the Zona Hotelera, so it has the same open-air design with modern white canopies throughout. Here you'll find a small ice-skating rink, a movie theater, a bowling alley, a pet store, a food court, several cafés, and around 60 stores.

Parque Lumpkul (✉ *Between Av. Margaritas and Calle Azucenas, Sm 22*) is a small park with a hippy vibe. Vendors sell their wares here Wednesday through Sunday, but Friday and Saturday are the best nights to go. There are only about 20 tables, but you can find bargains on beautiful handmade jewelry with unusual stones, as well as hand-painted clothes. There are sometimes music and artistic performances on market days.

Plaza las Americas (✉ *Av. Tulum, Sm 4 and Sm 9* ☎ *998/887–3863*) is the largest shopping center in downtown Cancún. Its 50-plus stores, 3 restaurants, 2 movie theaters, video arcade, fast-food outlets, and several large department stores will—for better or worse—make you feel right at home. This mall is intolerably crowded on weekends.

Plaza Las Avenidas (✉*Av. Yaxchilam Sm 35 N.C-2, El Centro* ☎*998/887–7552*) has gift shops, fast-food restaurants, cafés, nightclubs, and a karaoke bar. There are also a drugstore and a bakery on the premises.

Plaza Bonita (✉*Av. Xel Ha 1 and 2, Sm 28* ☎*998/884–6812*) is a small outdoor plaza next door to Mercado Veintiocho (Market 28). It has many wonderful specialty shops carrying Mexican goods and crafts.

Plaza Cancún 2000 (✉*Av. Tulum and Av. López Portillo, Sm 7* ☎*998/884–9988*) is a shopping mall popular with locals. There are some great bargains to be found here on shoes, clothes, and cosmetics. If you need a break from shopping, there is a charming ice-cream parlor nestled in this traditional colonial-town setting.

14

Plaza Chinatown (✉*Sm 35, Mza, 2 Lote 6, between Labná and Av. Xcaret, El Centro* ☎*998/887–6315*) commonly referred to as Plaza Hong Kong, seems strikingly out of place with it massive Pagoda structure. Here you will find Mexican handcrafts, souvenir shops, and a restaurant appropriately named Hong Kong. There is also a babysitting service available in the mall.

Plaza Hollywood (✉*Av. Xcaret esq Rubi Cancún, El Centro* ☎*998/887–4511*) is one of the newest strip malls to join El Centro. Here you will find several small boutiques and restaurants as well as a bank, post office, and Starbucks. For the wine connoisseur, there is La Europe Wine Market, which carries a wide selection of imported cheeses, meats, as well as Mexican reds.

Plaza Nayandei (✉*Av. Bonampak 200, Mz1, Lote 4B-2, Sm 4-A, El Centro* ☎*998/898–3743*) is a local favorite with its bars, cafés, gym, and eight restaurants. This plaza also has several good furniture stores and a yoga club for kids.

ISLA MUJERES

Updated by Michele Joyce

The minute you step off the boat, you'll get a sense of how small Isla is. The sights and properties on the island are strung along the coasts; there's not much to the interior except the two saltwater marshes, Salina Chica and Salina Grande, where Mayan inhabitants harvested salt centuries ago. The main road is Avenida Rueda Medina, which runs the length of the island; southeast of a village known as El Colonia, it turns into Carretera El Garrafón. Smaller street names and other address details don't really matter much here.

GETTING HERE & AROUND

Scooters are the most popular mode of transportation on Isla. Most rental places charge $25 to $35 a day, or $5.50 to $11 per hour, depending on the scooter's make and age. You can also rent bicycles on Isla, but keep in mind that it's hot here and the roads have plenty of speed bumps. **Golf carts are another fun way to get around the island, especially with kids.** Taxis line up by the ferry dock around the clock. Fares run $2 to $3 from the ferry to hotels along Playa Norte. A taxi to the south end of the island should be about $5. You can also hire a taxi for an island tour for about $15 an hour.

ESSENTIALS

Currency Exchange **Cunex Money Exchange** (⊠ *Av. Francisco Madero 12A, at Av. Hidalgo* ☎ *998/877–0474*). **Monex Exchange** (⊠ *Av. Morelos 9, Lote 4* ☎ *No phone*).

Internet **Cafe Internet Isla Mujeres** (⊠ *Av. Francisco Madero 17* ☎ *998/877–0461*). **DigaMe** (⊠ *Av. Guerrero 6, between Avs. Matamoros and Abasolo* ☎ *1/608/467–4202*). **Digit Centre** (⊠ *Av. Juárez between Avs. Mateos and Matamoros* ☎ *998/877–2025*).

Medical Assistance **Centro de Salud** (⊠ *Av. Guerrero de Salud* ☎ *998/877–0017*). **Farmacia Isla Mujeres** (⊠ *Av. Juárez 8* ☎ *998/877–0178*). **Red Cross Clinic** (⊠ *Colonia La Gloria* ☎ *998/877–0280*).

Post Office **Main Post Office** (⊠ *Avs. Guerrero and Lopez Mateos, ½ block from market* ☎ *998/877–0085*).

Rental Cars **Ciro's Motorent** (⊠ *Av. Guerrero Norte 1,at Av. Matamoros* ☎ *998/877–0578*). **David's Bike Rental** (⊠ *Across from Pemex station, Rueda Medina* ☎ *No phone*). **Gomar** (⊠ *Av. Rueda Medina and Nicolas Bravo* ☎ *998/877–0541*). **P'pe's Rentadora** (⊠ *Av. Hidalgo 19* ☎ *998/877–0019*). **Rentadora Ma José** (⊠ *Francisco y Madero No. 25* ☎ *998/877–0130*).

Visitor & Tour Info **Caribbean Realty & Travel Enterprises** (⊠ *Calle Abasolo 6* ☎ *998/877–1371 or 998/877–1372* ⊕ *www.caribbeanrealtytravel.com*). **La Isleña Tours** (⊠ *Av. Morelos, 1 block up from ferry docks* ☎ *998/877–0578*). **Viajes Prisma** (⊠ *Av. Rueda Medina 9C* ☎ *998/877–0938*).

EXPLORING

MAIN ATTRACTIONS

7 **El Garrafón National Park.** Despite participation in the much-publicized "Garrafón Reef Restoration Program," much of the coral reef at this national marine park remains dead (the result of hurricanes, boat anchors, and too many careless tourists). There are still colorful fish, but many of them will only come near if bribed with food. Although there's no longer much for snorkelers, the park does have kayaks and a diving platform, as well as a three-floor facility with restaurants, bathrooms, and gift shops. Be prepared to spend big money here; the basic entry fee doesn't include snorkel gear, lockers, or food, all of which are pretty pricey. However, the park does offer some package deals online that include gear, lunch, and even transportation from Cancún. Another option is Dolphin Discovery, where you can swim with dolphins or bull sharks. ■TIP→ **The Beach Club Garrafón de Castilla next door is a much cheaper alternative; the snorkeling is at least equal to that available in the park. The club is open to everyone and the entrance fee is $4. You can take a taxi from town.**

The park is home to the **Santuario Maya a la Diosa Ixchel,** the sad vestiges of a Mayan temple once dedicated to the goddess Ixchel. A lovely walkway around the area remains, but the natural arch beneath

> **TIMING**
>
> Although it's possible to explore Isla in one day, if you take your time, rent a golf cart, and spend a couple of days, you'll be able to soak up more of the nuances of island life.

the ruin has been blasted open and "repaired" with concrete badly disguised as rocks. The views here are spectacular, though: you can look to the open ocean where waves crash against dramatic cliffs on one side, and the Bahía de Mujeres (Bay of Women) on the other. On the way to the temple there's a cutesy Caribbean-style shopping center selling overpriced jewelry and souvenirs and a park with abstract sculptures painted in bright colors. There's also an old lighthouse, which you can enter for free. Climb to the top for an incredible view to the south; the vista in the other direction is marred by a tower from a defunct amusement-park ride (Ixchel would not be pleased). The ruin, which is open daily 9 to 5:30, is at the point where the road turns northeast into the Corredor Panorámico. To visit just the ruins and sculpture park, the admission is $3. Admission to the village is free. ✉ *Carretera El Garrafón, 2½ km (1½ mi) southeast of Playa Lancheros* ☎ *998/884–9420 in Cancún, 998/877–1100 to park* 🌐 *www.garrafon.com* 🌐 *www.dolphindiscovery.com* 🎫 *Basic entrance fee: $19. Tours from Cancún: $29–$59. Tours from Isla: $44* ⏲ *Daily 8:30 AM–6:30 PM.*

3 **Iglesia de Concepción Inmaculada** *(Church of the Immaculate Conception).* In 1890 local fishermen landed at a deserted colonial settlement known as Ecab, where they found three identical statues of the Virgin Mary, each carved from wood with porcelain face and hands. No one knows for certain where the statues originated, but it's widely believed that they're gifts from the conquistadores during a visit in 1770. One statue went to the city of Izamal in the Yucatán, and another was sent to Kantunikin in Quintana Roo. The third remained on the island. It was housed in a small wooden chapel while this church was being built; legend has it that the chapel burst into flames when the statue was removed. Some islanders still believe the statue walks on the water around the island from dusk until dawn, looking for her sisters. You can pay your respects daily from 10 AM until 11:30 AM and then from 7 PM until 9 PM. ✉ *Avs. Morelos and Bravo, south side of the zócalo.*

NEED A BREAK?

It's a small island, but there are several small shops selling gelato. Gelateria Monte Bianco (✉ ***Av. Matamoros 20*** ☎ ***998/149–3109*** 💳 **No credit cards) is the one to chose. The gelato here is made with the freshest fruit by an Italian couple that has lived on the island for just over a year.**

2 **El Malecón.** To enjoy the drama of Isla's eastern shore while soaking up some rays, stroll along this mile-long boardwalk. It's the beginning of a long-term improvement project and will eventually encircle the island. Currently, it runs from Half Moon Bay to El Colonia, with several benches and lookout points. Visit El Monumento de Tortugas (Turtle Monument) along the way. Food and souvenir vendors run the length of the boardwalk.

CLOSE UP

Who Was Ixchel?

Ixchel (ee-*shell*) is a principal figure in the pantheon of Mayan gods. Originally married to the earth god Voltan, Ixchel fell in love with the moon god Itzamna, considered the founder of the Mayans because he taught them how to read, write, and grow corn. When Ixchel became his consort, she gave birth to four powerful sons known as the Bacabs, who continue to hold up the sky in each of the four directions. Sometimes called Lady Rainbow, Ixchel is the goddess of childbirth, fertility, and healing. She controls the tides and all water on earth.

Often portrayed as a wise crone, she is seen wearing a skirt decorated with crossbones and a crown of serpents while carrying a jug of water. The crossbones are a symbol of her role as the giver of new life and keeper of dead souls. The serpents represent her wisdom and power to rejuvenate. The water jug alludes to her dual role as both a benign and destructive deity. Although she gives mankind the continual gift of water—the most essential element of life—according to Mayan myth, Ixchel also sent floods to cleanse the earth of wicked men who had stopped thanking the gods. She is said to give special protection to those making the sacred pilgrimage to her sites on Cozumel and Isla Mujeres.

5 **Tortugranja** *(Turtle Farm)*. This scientific station is run by the Mexican government in partnership with private funding. Its mission is to continue conservation efforts on behalf of the endangered sea turtle. You can see rescued turtle hatchlings in three large pools or watch the larger turtles in sea pens. There is also a small museum with an excellent display about turtles and the ecosystem. From May through August you can make arrangements to join the staff in collecting and hatching eggs. ✉ *Take Av. Rueda Medina south of town; about a block southeast of Hacienda Mundaca, take right fork (smaller road that loops back north called Sac Bajo); entrance is about ½ km (¼ mi) farther, on left* ☎ *998/877–0595* *$3* *Daily 9–5.*

IF YOU HAVE TIME

1 **El Cementerio.** Isla's unnamed cemetery, with its century-old colorful gravestones, is on Avenida López Mateos, the road that runs parallel to Playa Norte. Many of the tombstones are covered with carved angels and flowers; the most elaborate and beautiful mark the graves of children. Hidden among them is the tomb of the notorious Fermín Mundaca de Marechaja. This 19th-century slave trader—who's often billed more glamorously as a pirate—carved his own skull-and-crossbones gravestone with the ominous epitaph: AS YOU ARE, I ONCE WAS; AS I AM, SO SHALL YOU BE. Mundaca's grave is empty, however; his remains lie in Mérida, where he died. The monument is tough to find—ask a local to point out the unidentified marker.

6 **Hacienda Mundaca.** A dirt drive where vendors sell mobiles, mermaid figurines, and other crafts made out of local shells marks the entrance to what's left of a mansion constructed by 19th-century slave trader–turned–pirate Fermín Mundaca de Marechaja. When the British navy

> **HEAD TO TAIL**
>
> To get your bearings, try thinking of Isla Mujeres as a long, narrow fish, the head being the southeastern tip, the northwest prong the tail.

began cracking down on slavers, Mundaca settled on the island. He fell in love with a local beauty nicknamed La Trigueña (The Brunette). To woo her, Mundaca built a sprawling estate with verdant gardens. Apparently unimpressed, La Trigueña instead married a young islander—and legend has it that Mundaca went slowly mad waiting for her to change her mind. He ended up dying in a brothel in Mérida.

The actual hacienda has vanished. All that remain are a rusted cannon and a ruined stone archway with a triangular pediment carved with the following inscription: HUERTA DE LA HACIENDA DE VISTA ALEGRE (Orchard of the Happy View Hacienda). The gardens are also suffering from neglect, and the animals in a small on-site zoo seem as tired as the rest of the property. Mundaca would, however, approve of the admission charge; considering what little there is to see, it's piracy. ✉ *East of Av. Rueda Medina; take main road southeast from town to S-curve at end of Laguna Makax, turn left onto dirt road* ☎ *No phone* 🎫 *$2* ⏲ *Daily 9–5.*

❹ **Laguna Makax.** Pirates are said to have anchored their ships in this lagoon while waiting to ambush hapless vessels crossing the Spanish Main (the area in which Spanish treasure ships sailed). These days the lagoon houses a local shipyard and provides a safe harbor for boats during hurricane season. It's off Avenida Rueda Medina about 2½ km (1½ mi) south of town, about two blocks south of the naval base and some *salinas* (salt marshes).

BEACHES

★ **Playa Norte** is easy to find: simply head north on any of the north–south streets in town until you hit this superb beach. The turquoise sea is as calm as a lake here, and you can wade out for 40 yards in waist-deep water. The area around the beach has begun to attract developers, so it no longer has an unspoiled feel. Enjoy a drink and a snack at one of the area's palapa bars; **Buho's** is especially popular with locals and tourists who gather to chat, eat fresh seafood, drink cold beer, and watch the sunset. Lounge chairs and hammocks at **Sergio's** are free for customers, but to relax in front of **Maria del Maria** in a lounge chair will cost you $3. **Na Balam** charges a whopping $10 for one chair and umbrella.

There are two beaches between Laguna Makax and El Garrafón National Park. **Playa Lancheros** is a popular spot with an open-air restaurant where locals gather to eat freshly grilled fish. The beach has grittier sand than Playa Norte, but more palm trees. The calm water makes it the perfect spot for children—although it's best if they stay close to shore, since the ocean floor drops off steeply. The souvenir stands here are fairly low-key and run by local families. There is a small pen with domesticated and quite harmless *tiburones gatos*—

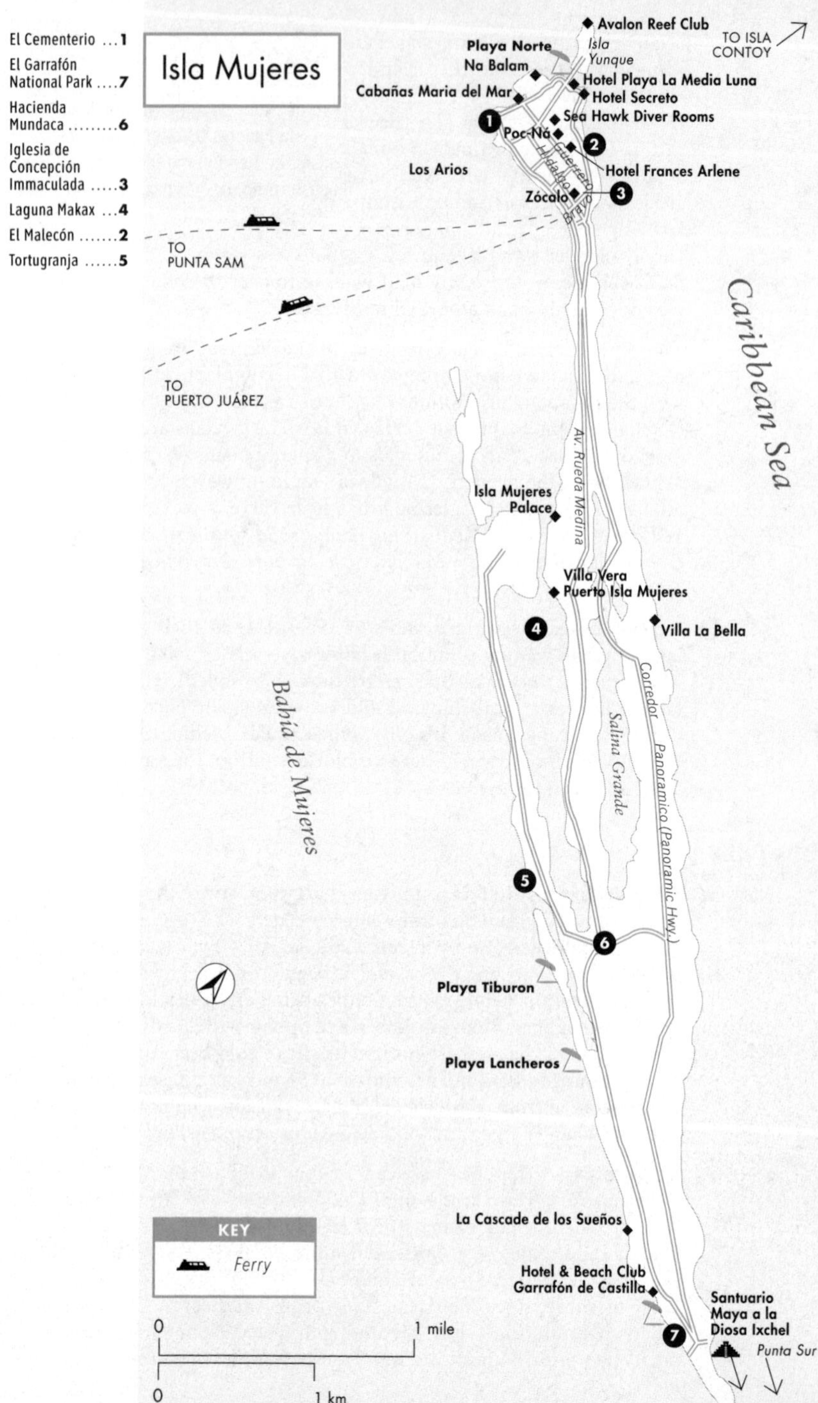
El Cementerio ...1
El Garrafón National Park 7
Hacienda Mundaca 6
Iglesia de Concepción Immaculada 3
Laguna Makax ...4
El Malecón 2
Tortugranja 5
Isla Mujeres
Avalon Reef Club
TO ISLA CONTOY
Playa Norte
Isla Yunque
Na Balam
Hotel Playa La Media Luna
Cabañas Maria del Mar
Hotel Secreto
Sea Hawk Diver Rooms
Poc-Na
Guerrero
Hidalgo
Hotel Frances Arlene
Los Arios
Zócalo
Bravo
TO PUNTA SAM
TO PUERTO JUÁREZ
Caribbean Sea
Av. Rueda Medina
Isla Mujeres Palace
Villa Vera Puerto Isla Mujeres
Villa La Bella
Corredor Panoramico (Panoramic Hwy.)
Salina Grande
Bahía de Mujeres
Playa Tiburon
Playa Lancheros
La Cascade de los Sueños
Hotel & Beach Club Garrafón de Castilla
Santuario Maya a la Diosa Ixchel
Punta Sur
KEY
Ferry
0
1 mile
0
1 km

nurse sharks. (These sharks are much friendlier than the *tintoreras,* or blue sharks, which live in the open seas, have seven rows of teeth, and weigh up to 1,100 lbs.) You can swim with them or get your picture taken with them for $1.

WHERE TO EAT

EL PUEBLO

$$$ MEXICAN ✕ **Fayne's.** The vibe at this brightly painted spot is hip and energetic. Best known for its terrific cocktails (don't dare miss the mango margaritas), this funky restaurant serves good island fare such as garlic shrimp, calamari stuffed with spinach, and grilled snapper. The well-stocked bar has a colorful tile "aquarium" underneath. ✉*Av. Hidalgo 12A, between Avs. Mateos and Guerrero* ☎*No phone* ▭*No credit cards.*

$$ ITALIAN ✕ **Angelo.** Named for Angelo Sanna, its Italian chef, this charming bistro is done up with crisp linens, soft lighting, and a wood-fired oven. The pizzas are decent, but the meat dishes are even tastier. Angelo, who has lived and worked in Isla Mujeres for more than a decade, is also a great source of local information. ✉*Av. Hidalgo 14* ☎*998/877–1273* ▭*MC, V.*

$$ ECLECTIC ✕ **Bamboo.** This casual restaurant, with its bright tablecloths and bamboo-covered walls, has two different chefs. Starting at 7 AM, the first chef cooks up hearty breakfasts of omelets and hash browns with freshly brewed coffee. Later in the day, however, the second chef switches to Asian-fusion-style lunches and dinners, including a knockout shrimp tempura, vegetable stir-fry, and chicken satay in a spicy peanut sauce. During high season two different bands play in the evening, and the place fills with locals until around midnight. This restaurant has the only ATM in the area. ✉*Plaza Los Almendros No. 4* ☎*998/877–1355* ▭*AE, MC, V.*

$$ MEXICAN ✕ **Don Chepo.** Mexican-style grilled meats (tacos, fajitas, and steaks) are the draw at this lively restaurant that resembles a small hacienda. Inside, the focal point is the large and well-stocked bar where you can chat with other visitors or enjoy the (sometimes live) mariachi music. Tables outside are perfect for watching all the downtown action on Hidalgo Street. The *arrachera,* a fine cut of beef grilled to perfection and served with rice, salad, baked potato, warm tortillas, and beans, is a reliably excellent choice. ✉*Avs. Hidalgo and Francisco Madero* ☎*No phone* ▭*MC, V.*

$$ ECLECTIC ✕ **Los Amigos.** This authentic isleño eatery really lives up to its name; once you've settled at one of the

NOT ALL BEACHES ARE FOR SWIMMING!

Although the beaches on the eastern side of the island (often referred to as the Caribe side) are quite beautiful, they're not safe for swimming because of the dangerous undertows; several drownings have occurred at these beaches. Another gorgeous but dangerous beach is found northeast, just kitty-corner to Playa Norte. **Playa Media Luna** (Half Moon beach) is very tempting, but the strong currents make it treacherous for swimmers.

street-side tables, the staff treats you like an old friend. The friendly vibe makes Los Amigos a favorite among locals, so you can expect a taste of real island life. Though it used to be known mainly for its superb pizza, the restaurant serves excellent fish, meat, and vegetarian dishes as well. The garlic shrimp is a good bet, as are desserts like the rich chocolate cake or flambéed crepes. ✉ *Av. Hidalgo between Avs. Matamoros and Abasolo* ☎ *998/877–0624* 💳 *AE, MC, V.*

$$ AMERICAN ✕ **Jax Bar & Grill.** The downstairs of this palapa-roof hot spot is a lively sports bar, which serves up huge, thick, perfectly grilled burgers along with cold beer. The satellite TV is always turned to the big game, and there's usually a competition involving the pool table or dartboard in progress. Upstairs is more elegant; you can enjoy the softly lighted bar and piped-in smooth jazz over fresh grilled seafood while watching the sunset. The friendly staff will cater to the kids with their favorite dishes. ✉ *Av. Adolfo Mateos 42* ☎ *998/887–1218* 🌐 *www.jaxsportfishing.com* 💳 *MC, V.*

$$ SEAFOOD Fodor'sChoice ★ ✕ **Picus Cocktelería.** Kick off your shoes and settle back with a cold beer at this charming beachside restaurant right near the ferry docks. You can watch the fishing boats come and go while you wait for some of the freshest seafood on the island. The grilled fish and grilled lobster with garlic butter are both magnificent, as are the shrimp fajitas—but the real showstopper is the mixed seafood ceviche, which might include conch, shrimp, abalone, fish, or octopus. ✉ *Av. Rueda Medina, 1 block northwest of ferry docks* ☎ *998/129–6011* 💳 *AE.*

$$ MEXICAN Fodor'sChoice ★ ✕ **Sunset Grill.** The perfect place to savor the sunset, this spot has a covered dining terrace with large picture windows that overlook the sea. Soft music and candlelight add to the romantic ambience. Grab a table outside and you can take a dip in the ocean between your appetizer and main course. The dinner menu has a wide range of dishes, including favorites like fried calamari, coconut shrimp, and fried snapper. The kitchen offers a lunch of Mexican favorites like tacos and quesadillas, but also fries up a great burger. The service is very good. ✉ *Av. Rueda Medina, North End, Condominios Nautibeach, Playa Norte* ☎ *998/877–0785* 💳 *AE, V.*

$ CAFE ✕ **Café Cito.** This cheery, seashell-decorated café was one of Isla's first cafés—and it's still one of the best places to breakfast on the island. The breakfast menu includes fresh waffles, fruit-filled crepes, and egg dishes, as well as great cappuccino and espresso; lunch specials are also available daily. After your meal, be sure to head to the Soñadores del Sol shop next door; the proprietor gives great tarot readings. ✉ *Avs. Juárez and Matamoros* ☎ *998/877–1470* 💳 *No credit cards.*

$ CAFE ✕ **Mañana Restaurant & Bookstore.** It's hard to miss this bright fuchsia restaurant with a yellow sun stretching its rays over the front door. But you won't want to miss the great breakfasts, with excellent egg dishes, fresh baguettes, and Italian coffee. Salads, homemade burgers (meat or vegetarian), and fresh fruit shakes are served at lunch. If you're in a hurry, you can grab a quick snack at the outdoor counter with its palapa roof—but since Cosmic Cosas bookstore is also here, you may want to lounge on the couch and read after your meal. ✉ *Av. Guerrero 17* ☎ *998/877–0555* 💳 *No credit cards* ⏲ *No dinner.*

$ MEXICAN ✕ **Sergio's Playa Sol.** Delicious chicken nachos, creamy guacamole, and savory fish kebabs are on the menu at this great beach bar at Playa Norte. You can easily spend the whole day here and stay for the sunset; there are free hammocks, beach chairs, and umbrellas for customers. ✉*North end of Rueda Medina on Playa Norte* ☎*998/130–1924* ▭*No credit cards.*

¢ PIZZA ✕ **Aquí Estoy.** It may have only a few stools to sit on—but what pizza! The thick-crusted pies here are smothered with cheese and spicy tomato sauce, along with toppings like grilled vegetables, pepperoni, and mushrooms. There's a choice of 15 varieties, and everything is fresh and prepared on the spot. For dessert, try a slice of apple pie. This is a great place for a quick snack on your way to the beach. ✉*Av. Matamoros 85* ☎*998/877–1777* ▭*No credit cards.*

14

¢ CAFE ✕ **Color de Verano.** This small café near Playa Norte is one of the cutest on the island. It opens at 8 AM, so it's a good place to start your day. The whole place is done up with an impressive collection of coffee- and teapots, many imported from the owner's native France. The espresso is strong and the desserts are delicious. The *amanacer* crepe, with mango, kiwi, strawberry, and blueberries—served with vanilla ice cream—is a delicious option on a sunny day. ✉*Av. López Mateos 23* ☎*998/877–1264* ▭*MC, V.*

¢ CAFE ✕ **Los Aluxes Cafe.** The perfect spot for an early-morning or late-night cappuccino (it opens at 6:30 AM and closes at 10 PM), this place also has terrific desserts and baked goods. The New York–style cheesecake and triple-fudge brownies are especially decadent. There's also a great selection of exotic teas, and there's locally made jewelry for sale. If you want the café's famous banana bread, get here early—the loaves usually sells out by 10 AM. ✉*Av. Matamoros 87* ☎*998/877–1317* ▭*No credit cards.*

ELSEWHERE ON THE ISLAND

$$$ ECLECTIC Fodor'sChoice ★ ✕ **Casa O's.** This restaurant is more expensive than many of its neighbors—and worth every penny. The magic starts at the footpath, which leads over a small stream before entering the three-tier circular dining room overlooking the bay. As you watch the sunset, you can choose your fish—salmon, tuna, snapper, or grouper—and have the chef prepare it to your individual taste. If you prefer, pick out a lobster from the on-site pond. Be sure to save room for the key lime pie, the house specialty. The restaurant is named for its waiters—all of whose names end in the letter "o." ✉*Carretera El Garrafón s/n* ☎*998/888–0170* ▭*MC, V.*

$$$ ECLECTIC ★ ✕ **Casa Rolandi.** This hotel restaurant is casually sophisticated, with an open-air dining room leading out to a deck that overlooks the water. Tables are done up with beautiful linens, china, and cutlery. The northern Italian menu here includes the wonderful carpaccio *di tonno alla Giorgio* (thin slices of tuna with extra-virgin olive oil and lime juice), along with excellent pastas—even the simplest dishes such as angel-hair pasta in tomato sauce are delicious. For something different, try the saffron risotto or the *costoletto d'agnello al forno* (lamb chops with a thyme infusion). The sunset views are spectacular. ✉*Hotel Villa Rolandi Gourmet & Beach Club, Fracc. Laguna Mar Makax, Sm 7* ☎*998/877–0500* ▭*AE, MC, V.*

$ MEXICAN Fodor'sChoice ★ **Playa Lancheros Restaurant.** If you want to savor one of the island's most authentic meals, take a short taxi ride to this casual eatery under a big palapa roof. It's right on the beach, so it's no surprise that the kitchen takes pride in serving the freshest fish. The house specialty is the Yucatecan *tikinchic* (fish marinated in a sour-orange sauce and cooked in a banana leaf over an open flame). There are also delicious tacos, fresh guacamole, and spicy salsa. The food may take a while to arrive, so bring your swimsuit and take a dip while you wait. On Sunday there's music, dancing, and the occasional shark wrestler. ✉ *Playa Lancheros where Av. Rueda Medina splits into Sac Bajo and Carretera El Garrafón* ☎ *No phone* 💳 *No credit cards.*

WORD OF MOUTH

"As long as you stay on the north end of the island, everything you need is in walking distance: restaurants, shops, moped/golf cart rental places."

–dazzle

WHERE TO STAY

EL PUEBLO

$$$$ **Avalon Reef Club.** This all-inclusive resort sits on a tiny island at the northern tip of Isla Mujeres. The location is gorgeous, and the seaside suites take advantage of this with balconies overlooking the ocean. Regular rooms in the hotel tower are small without balconies. Be warned: this is a time-share resort, and preference is given to those who bought into the "Paradise Found" program. Sales pitches are relentless, but if you can be stalwart in your refusal, you may be able to enjoy this lovely property. You can chose to just pay for your room, or go with the all-inclusive optional. **Pros:** Beautiful location, stunning beaches. **Cons:** Constant sales pitches, some rooms lack views. ✉ *Calle Zacil-Ha s/n, Isla Yunque* ☎ *998/999–2050 or 888/497–4325* 🌐 *www.avalonvacations.com* *83 rooms, 6 suites, 55 villas* *In-room: Kitchen (some). In-hotel: Restaurant, pool, gym, beachfront, public Internet.* 💳 *AE, D, MC, V* *AI.*

$$$$ Fodor'sChoice ★ **Na Balam.** Elegant without being pretentious, this tranquil hotel is a true sanctuary. Each guest room in the main building has a thatched palapa roof, Mexican folk art, a large bathroom, an eating area, and a spacious balcony or patio facing the ocean. The beach here is private, with its own bar serving snacks and drinks. Across the street are eight more spacious rooms surrounding a pool, a garden, and a meditation room where yoga classes are held. **Pros:** Excellent restaurant, beautiful beach. **Cons:** Not all rooms are on the beach. ✉ *Calle Zazil-Ha 118* ☎ *998/877–0279* 🌐 *www.nabalam.com* *31 rooms* *In-room: Safe, no phone, no TV. In-hotel: Restaurant, bar, pool, beachfront, no elevator* 💳 *AE, MC, V.*

$$$ **Hotel Secreto.** It's beautiful. It's famous. It's très, très chic. But if you're looking for a warm, inviting atmosphere, this may not be the place for you. Although the sense of reserve makes it perfect for honeymoon couples that want to be alone, singles may find it too quiet,

and families with children are not made to feel welcome. Rooms have floor-to-ceiling windows, veiled king-size four-poster beds, and balconies overlooking Half Moon Bay. Mexican artwork looks bold against the predominantly white color scheme, and a small, intimate dining room sits alongside a small ocean-side pool. This place isn't much of a secret anymore, so it's sometimes hard to get a reservation. **Pros:** Staff is very accommodating, pool overlooks ocean, plenty of peace and quiet. **Cons:** Not a good place for children, books up in advance. ✉*Sección Rocas, Lote 11, Half Moon Beach* ☎*998/877–1039* 🌐*www.hotelsecreto.com* *9 rooms* *In-room: Safe, refrigerator, Wi-Fi. In-hotel: Bar, pool, water sports, no elevator* *AE, MC, V* *CP.*

WORD OF MOUTH

Not the most luxurious on the island, but my personal favorite is Hotel Playa la Media Luna. It's on the beach, but not a swimmable beach because of the pounding waves on the rocks. Rooms are ok, and the pool is nice. The view is worth a million bucks.

–JeanH

14

$$–$$$ **Hotel Playa la Media Luna.** This breezy palapa-roofed bed-and-breakfast lies along Half Moon Beach, just south of Playa Norte. Guest rooms here are done in bright Mexican colors, with king-sized beds and balconies or terraces that look out over the pool and the ocean beyond. A continental breakfast is served in a sunny dining room. The hotel also has small, spartan rooms, with no view and no breakfast, for $60 per night. **Pros:** Rooms have balconies, nearby beach is calm and shallow. **Cons:** No Internet access. ✉*Sección Rocas, Punta Norte, Lote 9/10* ☎*998/877–0759* 🌐*www.playamedialuna.com* *18 rooms* *In-hotel: Restaurant, pool, beachfront, no elevator* *MC, V* *CP.*

$ ★ **Los Arcos.** In the heart of downtown, this hotel is a terrific value. The comfortable suites are all cheerfully decorated with Mexican-style furnishings. Each has a small kitchenette with a microwave and fridge, a fully tiled bathroom with great water pressure, a small sitting area, and a king-size bed. The large and sunny balconies on the front have views of the street, whereas those at the back are more private. The pleasant and helpful staff is an added bonus. The hotel management encourages online booking. **Pros:** Reasonable rates, spacious rooms, near restaurants and shops. **Cons:** Some linens feel a little worn, sparse furnishings. ✉*Av. Hidalgo 58, between Abasolo and Matamoros* ☎*998/877–1343* 🌐*www.suites-los-arcos.myislamujeres.com* *12 rooms* *In-room: Safe, kitchen. In-hotel: Internet, no elevator* *MC, V.*

$ **Hotel Frances Arlene.** This small hotel is a perennial favorite with visitors. The Magaña family takes great care to maintain the property—signs everywhere remind you to save electricity and keep noise to a minimum. Rooms surround a pleasant courtyard and are outfitted with double beds, bamboo furniture, and refrigerators. Some have kitchenettes. Playa Norte is a few blocks north, and downtown is a block away. This is one of the few hotels that can accommodate wheelchairs. **Pros:** Reasonable rates, friendly staff. **Cons:** Some street noise, not all rooms have balconies. ✉*Av. Guerrero 7* ☎ *998/877–0310* 🌐*www.*

francisarlene.com ⇨*22 rooms* ◊*In-room: No a/c (some), kitchen (some), refrigerator* ▭*MC, V.*

$ **Sea Hawk Divers Rooms.** Catering largely to scuba divers, this hotel is half a block from Playa Norte. Lovely rooms above the dive shop have queen-sized beds, brightly tiled bathrooms, and huge private balconies that face either the ocean or the garden patio. There are also two studio suites with full kitchenettes and large outdoor decks perfect for private breakfasts. The third-floor terrace, open to all, is a great place to watch the sunset. Diving and deep-sea fishing trips are offered at the shop. This hotel encourages online booking. **Pros:** Laid-back atmosphere, lively common areas, great packages. **Cons:** Not the place for non-divers, rooms lack TVs. ✉*Calle Carlos Lazo, just before Buho's restaurant* ☎*998/877–0296* ⊕*www.isla-mujeres.net/seahawkdivers/index.htm* ⇨*4 rooms, 2 studio suites* ◊*In-room: No phone, kitchen (some), no TV. In-hotel: Water sports, no elevator* ▭*MC, V.*

¢ **Poc-Ná.** This coed youth hostel is one of El Pueblo's best deals. Half the dorm-style rooms are shared and have fans, and the others are private with air-conditioning. There's also a camping area and an outdoor garden with hammocks. To promote community spirit, the hostel hosts movie nights, board and card games, and regular parties. It's within walking distance of Playa Norte and all the downtown shops, restaurants, and bars. **Pros:** Convivial atmosphere, unbeatable price. **Cons:** Party atmosphere, basic breakfasts, rooms could use a good cleaning. ✉*Av. Matamoros 15* ☎*998/877–0090 155 beds* ◊*In-room: No a/c (some), no phone, no TV (some). In-hotel: Restaurant, bar, public Internet, no elevator* ▭*MC, V.*

ELSEWHERE ON THE ISLAND

$$$$ **La Casa de los Sueños.** What started out as a B&B is now a high-end spa with New Age aspirations. Rooms are named after celestial concepts like Sun, Moon, Harmony, Peace, and Love, and are tastefully decorated with unique crafts from all over Mexico. A large interior courtyard leads to a sunken, open-air lounge area done in sunset colors; this, in turn, extends to a terrace with a cliff-side swimming pool overlooking the ocean. Spa treatments include massages, body wraps, and facials using herbs and essential oils. **Pros:** Attentive staff, all rooms have ocean views, peaceful setting. **Cons:** One of the priciest properties on the island, not welcoming to families with kids. ✉*Carretera El Garrafón, Fracc. Turqueza, Lotes 9A and 9B* ☎*998/877–0651 or 800/505–0252* ⊕*www.casadelossuenosresort.com* ⇨*8 rooms* ◊*In-room: No phone, no TV. In-hotel: Restaurant, pool, spa, water sports, bicycles, no-smoking rooms, no kids under 18, no elevator* ▭*AE, MC, V* 🍴*CP.*

$$$$ **Isla Mujeres Palace.** At the island's newest all-inclusive hotel you can forget about ever leaving the property, and take advantage of the restaurants, the beach, and the pool. Each of the spacious rooms is done up in a modern Mexican style. All have their own hot tub, either inside the room or on the balcony to take advantage of the wonderful ocean views. The service is excellent, and each building has its own butler who can help with just about anything. If you stay for more than three nights, a tour of the island or a snorkeling trip is included

in the price of your stay. In the evening, there are music and dance performances. **Pros:** Family-friendly environment, comfortable rooms. **Cons:** Far from downtown. ✉*Carrertera Garrafón, Km. 4.5, Manzana 62, Supermanzana 8* ☎*998/999–2020 and 888/774–0040 in the U.S.* 🌐islamujerespalace.com *62 rooms In-room: Refrigerator, safe, Wi-Fi. In-hotel: 2 restaurants, room service, pool, bar, beachfront, spa* *AE, MC, V* *AI.*

$$$–$$$$ **Villa Vera Puerto Isla Mujeres.** Yachties love this hideaway at Isla's main yacht club. Rooms are awash in rose and blue, and have cozy seating areas. The large pool, which has a fountain and swim-up bar, is surrounded by a garden and lawn. Paths lead to the dock and the lagoon, where a shuttle boat ferries you to a beach club that faces Cancún. Families are warmly welcomed. There is a discount when you book online. **Pros:** Family-friendly atmosphere, pretty pool. **Cons:** Restaurant is pricey. ✉*Puerto de Abrigo, Laguna Makax* ☎*998/287–3340 or 800/508–7923* 🌐*www.puertoislamujeres.com* *17 suites, 4 villas In-room: Kitchen (some), VCR. In-hotel: Restaurant, pools, beachfront, no elevator, Wi-Fi* *AE, MC, V* *CP.*

14

$$–$$$ **Villa La Bella.** It can be difficult to get reservations at this romantic hideaway tucked away on the eastern coast—it's often booked up months in advance—but most agree it's worth the effort. All rooms here have funky designs, fantastic sea views, and are equipped with king-sized beds, conch-head showers, ceiling fans, and refrigerators. A restaurant and a small pool mean you don't have to leave the property unless you feel like exploring the island. It's a bit of a hike to downtown, but you can arrange for a taxi or a golf-cart rental. This hotel gets lots of wind! **Pros:** Owners make you feel like part of the family, a great place to relax, tasty breakfasts. **Cons:** Need to take a taxi to get downtown, no kids allowed. ✉*Carretera Perimetral al Garrafón* ☎*998/888–0342* 🌐*www.villalabella.com* *6 rooms In-room: No a/c (some), no phone, no TV, refrigerator. In-hotel: Restaurant, pool, laundry service, no kids under 16, no elevator* *MC, V* *BP.*

$ **Hotel & Beach Club Garrafón de Castilla.** The snorkeling at this small family-owned hotel is better than what you're likely to experience at El Garrafón National Park next door. (The reef is less crowded, and there are more fish.) Rooms have double beds and balconies overlooking the water; some have refrigerators. Decorations are minimal, but the overall effect is bright, cheery, and comfortable. **Pros:** One of the best locations on the island, great for snorkeling and diving. **Cons:** Need a taxi to get downtown. ✉*Carretera Punta Sur, Km 6* ☎*998/877–0107* *12 rooms In-room: No phone, refrigerator (some), no TV. In-hotel: Beachfront, diving, water sports, no elevator* *No credit cards* *CP.*

NIGHTLIFE

BARS

La Adelita (✉*Av. Hidalgo Norte 12A* ☎*998/877–0528*) is a popular spot for enjoying reggae, salsa, and Caribbean music while trying out a variety of tequilas and cigars.

Bar OM (✉*Lote 19, Mza. 15 Av. Matamoros* ☎*998/820–4876*) is an eclectic lounge bar offering wine, organic teas, and self-serve draft-beer taps at each table.

Buho's (✉*Cabañas María del Mar, Av. Arq. Carlos Lazo 1* ☎*No phone*) remains the favorite restaurant on Playa Norte for a relaxing sunset drink—although the drinks have started to become overpriced.

You can dance the night away with the locals at **Nitrox** (✉*Av. Matamoros 87* ☎*998/887–0568*). Wednesday night is salsa night and the weekend is a blend of disco, techno, and house. It's open from 9 PM until 3 AM.

La Peña (✉*Calle Nicolas Bravo, Zona Maritima* ☎*998/845–7384*), just across from the downtown main square, has a lovely terrace bar that serves a variety of sinful cocktails, and a DJ who sets the mood with techno, salsa, reggae, and dance music.

The bar at **El Sombrero de Gomar** (✉*Av. Hidalgo 5* ☎*998/877–0627*) is well stocked with beer and tequila, and its central location makes it a perfect spot for people-watching. The service tends to be hit-or-miss and the food should be avoided.

SPORTS & THE OUTDOORS

BOATING

Villa Vera Puerto Isla Mujeres (✉*Puerto de Abrigo, Laguna Makax* ☎*998/287–3340* 🌐*www.puertoislamujeres.com*) is a full-service marina, for vessels up to 175 feet. Services include a fuel station, a 150-ton lift, customs assistance, 24-hour security, and laundry and cleaning services. If you prefer to sleep on land, the Villa Vera Puerto Isla Mujeres resort is steps away from the docks.

FISHING

Captain Anthony Mendillo Jr. (✉*Av. Arq. Carlos Lazo 1* ☎*998/877–0759*) provides specialized fishing trips aboard his 41-foot vessel, the *Keen M*. He charges $1,000 for a daylong trip for four people. **Sea Hawk Divers** (✉*Av. Arq. Carlos Lazo* ☎*998/877–0296* 🌐*www.sea-hawk-divers.myislamujeres.com*) runs fishing trips—for barracuda, snapper, and smaller fish—that start at $200 for a half day. **Sociedad Cooperativa Turística** (✉*Av. Rueda Medina at Contoy Pier* ☎*No phone*) is a fishermen's cooperative that rents boats for a maximum of four hours and six people ($120). An island tour with lunch costs $20 per person.

SNORKELING & SCUBA DIVING

Isla is a good place for learning to dive, since the snorkeling is close to shore. Offshore, there are excellent

> **THE WHOLE PACKAGE**
>
> **Sea Passion** (☎*998/877–0798* 🌐 www.seapassion.net) offers one-of-a-kind tours that include sailing on a 75-foot catamaran from Cancún to Isla Mujeres, snorkeling, shopping, and lunch at a private beach club. This all-day tour includes food and drink and costs $79–$89 per person. Other packages are also available.

diving and snorkeling at Xlaches (pronounced *ees*-lah-chayss) reef, due north on the way to Isla Contoy. One of Contoy's most alluring dives is the **Cave of the Sleeping Sharks,** east of the northern tip. The cave was discovered by an island fisherman, Carlos Gracía Castilla, and extensively explored by Ramón Bravo, a local diver, cinematographer, and Mexico's foremost expert on sharks. The cave is a fascinating 150-foot dive for experienced divers only.

At 30 feet to 40 feet deep and 3,300 feet off the southwestern coast, the coral reef known as **Los Manchones** is a good dive site. During the summer of 1994 an ecological group hoping to divert divers and snorkelers from El Garrafón commissioned the creation of a 1-ton, 9¾-foot bronze cross, which was sunk here. Named the Cruz de la Bahía (Cross of the Bay), it's a tribute to everyone who has died at sea. Another option is the Barco L-55 and C-58 dive, which takes in sunken World War II boats just 20 minutes off the coast of Isla.

DIVE SHOPS

Most dive shops offer a variety of dive packages with rates variable on the time of day, the reef visited, and the number of tanks.

A PADI-affiliated dive shop, **Aqua Adventures,** (✉ *Plaza Almendros 10* ☎ *998/877 –1615* 🌐 *www.diveislamujeres.com*) offers dives to shipwrecks and sleeping shark caves. A one-tank dive goes for $40 and a two-tank dive costs $64.

Coral Scuba Dive Center (✉ *Av. Matamoros 13A* ☎ *998/877–0763* 🌐 *www.coralscubadivecenter.com*) has a variety of dive packages. Fees start at $29 for one-tank dives and go up to $59 for two-tank dives and shipwreck dives. The PADI-affiliated shop also offers snorkeling trips.

Cruise Divers (✉ *Avs. Rueda Medina and Matamoros* ☎ *998/877–1190*) offers two-tank dives starting at $55 and a resort course (a quickie learn-to-scuba course) for $80. The company also organizes nighttime dives. **Sea Hawk Divers** (✉ *Av. Arq. Carlos Lazo* ☎ *998/877–0296* 🌐 *www.sea-hawk-divers.myislamujeres.com*) runs reef dives from $45 (for one tank) to $60 (for two tanks). Special excursions to the more exotic shipwrecks cost between $75 to $95. The PADI courses taught here are highly regarded. For nondivers there are snorkel trips.

SHOPPING

CRAFTS

Artesanías Arcoiris (✉ *Avs. Hidalgo and Juárez* ☎ *No phone*) has Mexican blankets and other handicrafts. The staffers here also braid hair. Look for Mexican ceramics and onyx jewelry at **Artesanías Lupita** (✉ *Av. Hidalgo 13* ☎ *No phone*). Many local artists display their works at the **Artesanías Market** (✉ *Avs. Matamoros and Arq. Carlos Lazo* ☎ *No phone*), where you can find plenty of bargains. For custom-made clothing, visit **Hortensia:** hers is the last stall on the left after you come through the market entrance. You can choose from bright Mexican fabrics and then pick a pattern for a skirt, shirt, shorts, or a dress; Hortensia will sew it up for you within a day or two. You can also buy

CLOSE UP

Shhh . . . Don't Wake the Sharks

The underwater caverns off Isla Mujeres attract a dangerous species of shark—though nobody knows exactly why. Stranger still, once the sharks swim into the caves they enter a state of relaxed nonaggression seen nowhere else. Naturalists have two explanations, both involving the composition of the water inside the caves—it contains more oxygen, more carbon dioxide, and less salt. According to the first theory, the decreased salinity causes the parasites that plague sharks to loosen their grip, allowing the remora fish (the sharks' personal vacuum cleaner) to eat the parasites more easily. Perhaps the sharks relax in order to facilitate the cleaning, or maybe their deep state of relaxation is a side effect of having been scrubbed clean.

Another theory is that the caves' combination of fresh- and saltwater may produce euphoria, similar to the effect scuba divers experience on extremely deep dives. Whatever the sharks experience while "sleeping" in the caves, they pay a heavy price for it: a swimming shark breathes automatically and without effort (water is forced through the gills as the shark swims), but a stationary shark must laboriously pump water to continue breathing. If you dive in the Cave of the Sleeping Sharks, be cautious: many are reef sharks, the species responsible for the largest number of attacks on humans. Dive with a reliable guide and be on your best diving behavior.

off-the-rack designs. **Casa del Arte Mexicano** (✉*Av. Hidalgo 16* ☎*No phone*) has a large selection of Mexican handicrafts, including ceramics and silver jewelry. **De Corazón** (*Boutique* ✉*Av. Abasolo between Avs. Hidalgo and Guerrero* ☎*998/877–1211*) has a wide variety of jewelry, T-shirts, and personal-care products. **Gladys Galdamez** (✉*Av. Hidalgo 14* ☎*998/877–0320*) carries Isla-designed and -manufactured clothing and accessories for both men and women, as well as bags and jewelry.

JEWELRY

Jewelry on Isla ranges from tasteful creations to junk. Bargains are available, but beware of street vendors—most of their wares, especially the amber, are fake. **Gold and Silver Jewelry** (✉*Av. Hidalgo 58* ☎*No phone*) specializes in precious stones such as sapphires, tanzanite, and amber in a variety of settings. **Joyería Maritz** (✉*Av. Hidalgo between Avs. Morelos and Francisco Madero* ☎*998/877–0526*) sells jewelry from Taxco (Mexico's silver capital) and crafts from Oaxaca at reasonable prices. **Van Cleef & Arpels** (✉*Avs. Juárez and Morelos* ☎*998/877–0331*) stocks rings, bracelets, necklaces, and earrings with precious stones set in 18K gold. Many of the designs are innovative; prices are often lower than in the United States. You can also check out the Van Cleef sister store, **The Silver Factory** (✉*Avs. Juárez and Morelos* ☎*998/877–0331*), which has a variety of designer pieces at reduced prices.

Cozumel & the Riviera Maya

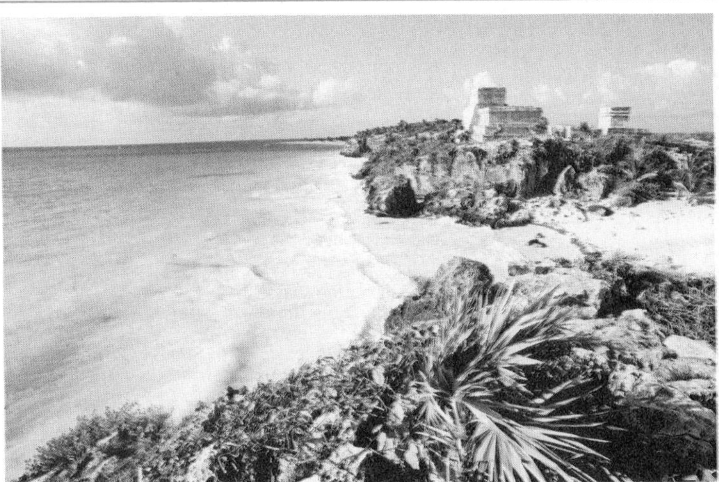
Tulum, Riviera Maya

WORD OF MOUTH

"I've been to many Mex locations and find [Cozumel] to be the best. It has . . . summer breezes, great (the best) snorkeling, great night life, and some nice tours to the mainland Mayan ruins."

–jrstotka

"Tulum and Cobá are close and if you have a car, spend a night and hit one of the resorts (Xelha or Xcaret) as they are fun. I prefer renting the car as you are on your own time schedule."

–blondlady

www.fodors.com/forums

WELCOME TO COZUMEL

TOP REASONS TO GO

★ **Scuba diving along the Great Maya Reef:** A Technicolor profusion of fish, coral, and other creatures resides in this 600-mi-long reef, stretching from Cozumel to Central America.

★ **Indulging in a body treatment:** The Riviera Maya is flush with spa resorts that will make you say ooh and aah.

★ **Tasting local flavor:** On Sunday nights at San Miguel's Plaza Central, on Cozumel, join the people who gather for music and dancing. Visit during Carnival, the spring Fería del Cedral, or any national holiday, and you'll find processions and seasonal treats sold at food stands.

★ **Exploring the inland jungle:** South of Rio Bec, the forests grow thick, and you might glimpse howler monkeys, coatimundi, and Yucatán parrots.

★ **Contemplating the Maya:** Explore the temples dedicated to Ixchel, the Mayan goddess of fertility and the moon, at San Gervasio on Cozumel, and visit Tulum, on the mainland, the only Mayan site that overlooks the Caribbean.

1 San Miguel. Cozumel's only town, where cruise ships loom from the piers and endless souvenir shops line the streets, still retains some of the flavor of a Mexican village. On weekend nights musical groups and food vendors gather in the main square, attracting a lively crowd.

2 Coastal Cozumel. White beaches with calm waters line Cozumel's leeward (western) side. Parque Marino Nacional Arrecifes de Cozumel encompasses the reefs along the southwest edge. The windward (eastern side) facing the Caribbean, has rocky strands and powerful surf. To the northwest broad beaches sometimes give way to limestone shelves over the water.

3 The Riviera Maya. The coastal communities along the Caribbean vary widely: some are sleepy fishing villages, others are filled with glitzy resorts, and one—Tulum—is an ancient Mayan port city. The beaches along this stretch are stunning, and beloved by scuba divers, snorkelers, anglers, birdwatchers, and beachcombers.

GETTING ORIENTED

A 490-square-km (189-square-mi) island 19 km (12 mi) east of the Yucatán peninsula, Cozumel is mostly flat, with an interior covered by parched scrub, low jungle, and marshy lagoons. Beaches, above all else, are what define the Riviera Maya. Powdery white sands embrace clear turquoise Caribbean lagoons and vibrant marine life lies beneath. Inland scrub and jungle are punctuated by Mayan ruins.

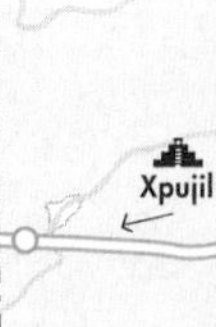

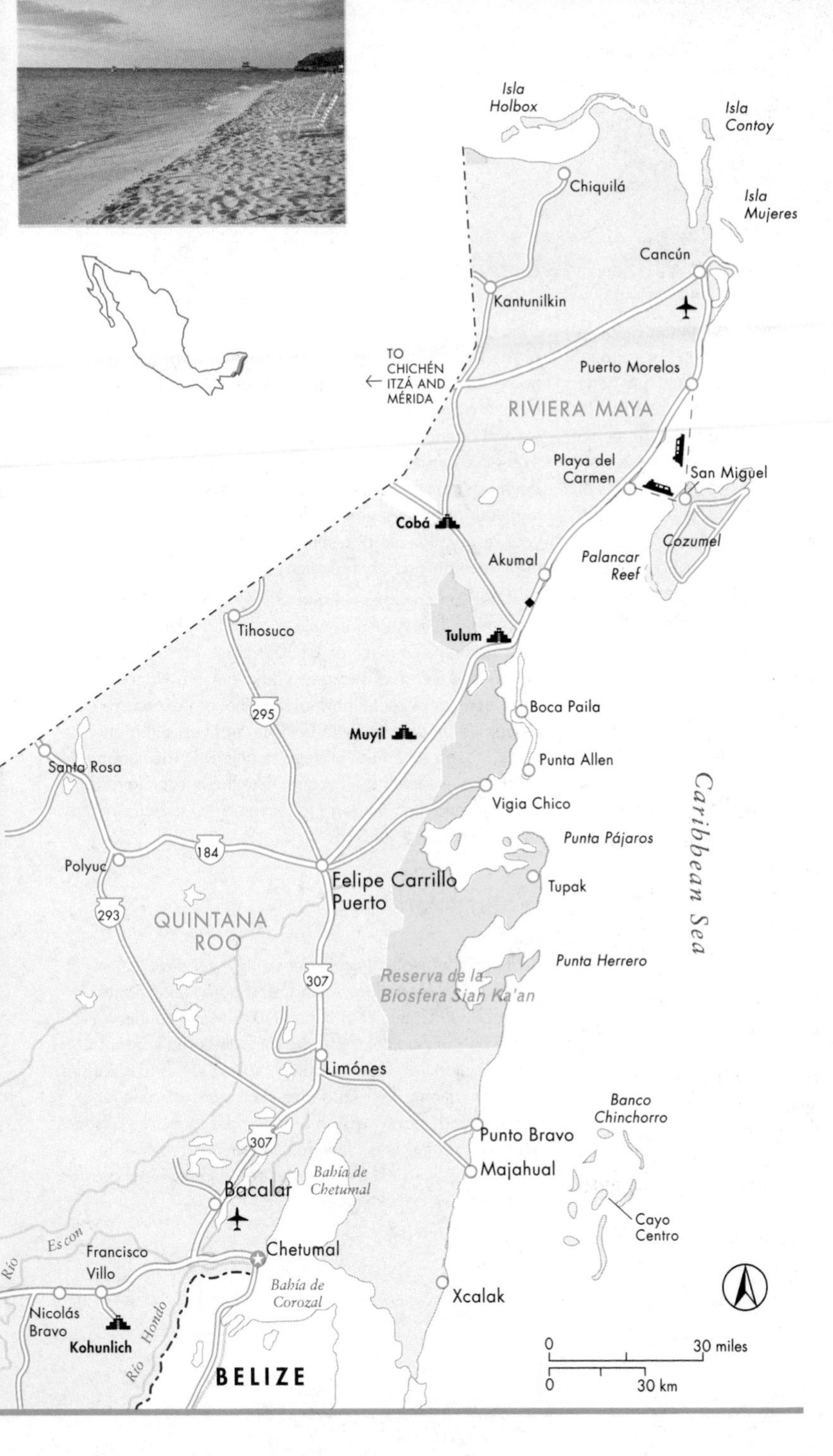

Isla Holbox
Isla Contoy
Chiquilá
Isla Mujeres
Cancún
Kantunilkin
TO CHICHÉN ITZÁ AND MÉRIDA
Puerto Morelos
RIVIERA MAYA
Playa del Carmen
San Miguel
Cobá
Cozumel
Akumal
Palancar Reef
Tihosuco
Tulum
295
Boca Paila
Muyil
Punta Allen
Santa Rosa
Vigia Chico
Caribbean Sea
Punta Pájaros
Polyuc
184
Felipe Carrillo Puerto
Tupak
293
QUINTANA ROO
Punta Herrero
307
Reserva de la Biosfera Sian Ka'an
Limónes
Banco Chinchorro
307
Punto Bravo
Majahual
Bahía de Chetumal
Bacalar
Cayo Centro
Es con
Francisco Villo
Chetumal
Río
Bahía de Corozal
Xcalak
Nicolás Bravo
Kohunlich
Río Hondo
0
30 miles
0
30 km
BELIZE

COZUMEL PLANNER

Stay for a While

Cozumel is perfect for a weeklong vacation—though some people wind up hanging around for months. It's all about the water here—the shimmering, clear-as-glass sea that makes you want to kick off your shoes, slip on your fins, and dive in. Come up for air, though, and you'll find that it's fun to explore on land, too. The island's paved roads are, for the most part, excellent. Dirt roads, however, are too deeply rutted for most rental cars, and flash floods in rainy season make them even tougher to navigate. Many have been closed since Hurricane Wilma in 2005.

Beaches and towns aren't visible from the Riviera Maya's well-paved main highway. The stretch from Cancún to Tulum is 1–2 km (½–1 mi) from the coast, so there's little to see but dense vegetation, billboards, roadside markets, and signs marking hotel entrances. The white-sand beaches and beautiful Maya ruins are here, though. A stay of five to seven days will allow you to visit Tulum and Cobá, spend a day kicking around Playa del Carmen, and still have time to work on your tan.

Booking Hotels

Many Cozumel hotels encourage you to make reservations online though booking agencies such as www.cozumel-hotels.net, www.comeetocozumel.com, or cozumel-mx.com, or their own Web sites. Since hotels customarily work with several agencies, shop around. Booking online can mean 10%–20% discounts. It can also mean occasional breakdowns in communication. You may arrive only to discover that your Spanish-speaking desk clerk has no record of your reservation. To prevent such mishaps, bring printouts of all receipts and confirmations.

Peak season on Cozumel and along the Riviera Maya is November through April, with availability plummeting and rates spiking—as much as $100 a night—at Christmas, Easter, and Carnival seasons. Book well in advance for these periods. Direct flights to Cozumel are expensive year-round. It's cheaper to fly to Cancún and hop a regional flight (though schedules change frequently). The cheapest alternative is to fly into Cancún, take the bus to Playa del Carmen, and then the ferry to Cozumel—a tedious journey that only costs about $16.

Water World

All manner of water sports—jet skiing, scuba diving, snorkeling, waterskiing, sailing, and parasailing—are embraced in Cozumel and the Riviera Maya. Underwater enthusiasts in particular are drawn to the area's clear turquoise waters, abundant tropical marine life, and exquisite coral formations. There are dive excursions suitable for veterans and neophytes—to both famous reefs and offshore wrecks—and currents allow for drift diving. Freshwater cenotes (natural sinkholes) and underwater caverns provide still more dive opportunities.

Tour Options

Tours of Cozumel's sights, including the San Gervasio ruins, El Cedral, Parque Chankanaab, and the Museo de la Isla de Cozumel, cost about $50 a person; you can arrange them through travel agencies. Private taxi tours are also an option; they run about $70 a day. Fiesta Holidays (✉Calle 11 Sur 598, between Avs. 25 and 30 ☎987/872–0923), which has representatives in many hotels, sells several tours.

Although it's easy to visit many of the Riviera Maya's sights on your own, it's also nice to have someone else do everything for you. After all, you're on vacation. Maya Sites Travel Services (☎719/256–5186 or 877/620–8715 ⊕www.mayasites.com) offers inexpensive personalized tours.

Akumal local Hilario Hiller (✉La Jolla, Casa Nai Na, 3rd fl. ☎984/875–9066) is famous for his custom tours of Maya villages, ruins, and the jungle. Trips typically cost about $100 a day, plus transportation expenses, and Hiller is fluent in Spanish, English, and Maya.

Need More Info?

The Web site www.cozumelmycozumel.com, edited by full-time residents of the island, has insider tips on activities, sights, and places to stay and eat. There's a bulletin board, too, where you can post questions.

For additional information on attractions, lodging, dining, and other services in the Caribbean Coast (and the rest of Quintana Roo), these Web sites can be very helpful: www.locogringo.com and www.playamayaews.com.

Money Matters

WHAT IT COSTS IN DOLLARS

¢	$	$$	$$$	$$$$
Restaurants				
under $5	$5–$10	$10–$15	$15–$25	over $25
Hotels				
under $50	$50–$75	$75–$150	$150–$250	over $250

Restaurant prices are per person, for a main course at dinner, excluding tax and tip. Hotel prices are for a standard double room in high season.

How's the Weather?

Cozumel's weather is more extreme than you might expect on a tropical island. *Nortes*—winds from the north—blow through in December, making air and water temperatures drop. If you visit during this time, bring a shawl or jacket for the chilly 18°C (65°F) evenings. Summers, on the other hand, can be beastly hot and humid. The windward side is calmer in winter than the leeward side, and the interior is warmer than the coast. From November to April, the Riviera Maya is heavenly, with temperatures hovering around 27°C (80°F) and near-constant ocean breezes. In July and August the breezes disappear and humidity soars, especially inland, where temperatures reach 35°C (95°F). September and October bring the worst conditions—mosquitos, rains, and the risk of hurricanes.

Updated by Maribeth Mellin

IT'S ALL ABOUT THE WATER here—the shimmering, clear-as-glass aquamarine sea that makes you want to kick off your shoes, slip on your fins, and dive right in. Once you come up for air, though, you'll find that Mexico's largest Caribbean island 53 km (33 mi) long and 15 km (9 mi) wide) is pretty fun to explore on land, too. Despite a severe lashing by Hurricane Wilma in October 2005, by 2008 nearly everything was back to normal.

San Miguel, the main town, is laid out in a grid. *Avenidas* are roads that run north or south; they're numbered in increments of five. A road that starts out as an "avenida norte" turns into an "avenida sur" when it crosses Avenida Juárez. *Calles* are streets that run east–west; those north of Avenida Juárez have even numbers (Calle 2 Norte, Calle 4 Norte), whereas those south have odd numbers (Calle 1 Sur, Calle 3 Sur).

Plaza Central, or *la plaza,* the heart of San Miguel, is directly across from the docks. Residents congregate here in the evening, especially on weekends, when free concerts begin at 8. Shops and restaurants abound in the square. Heading inland (east) takes you away from the tourist zone and toward the residential sections. The heaviest commercial district is concentrated between Calle 10 Norte and Calle 11 Sur to beyond Avenida Pedro Joaquin Coldwell.

GETTING HERE & AROUND

The Aeropuerto Internacional de Cozumel is 3 km (2 mi) north of San Miguel. International airlines serving the island seasonally or year-round include American Airlines from Dallas, American Eagle from Miami, Continental Airlines from Houston and Newark, Delta from Atlanta, Frontier from Denver, and US Airways from Charlotte, North Carolina. At the airport, the *colectivo,* a van that seats up to eight, takes arriving passengers to their hotels; the fare is about $7 to $20 per person. **Passenger-only ferries** to and from Playa del Carmen leave approximately every hour on the hour from early morning until late night. The trip takes 45 minutes and costs about $12 each way. Car ferries leave from Puerto Morelos and Calica.

ESSENTIALS

Currency Exchange **American Express** (✉ *Punta Langosta, Av. Rafael E. Melgar 599* ☎ *987/869–1389*). **Promotora Cambiaria del Centro** (✉ *Av. 5 Sur between Calles 1 Sur and Adolfo Rosado Salas* ☎ *No phone*).

Ferry Contacts **Passenger-only ferry from Playa del Carmen** (☎ *987/872–1508 or 987/872–1588*). **Car ferry from Puerto Morelos** (☎ *987/872–0950*).

Internet **Calling Station** (✉ *Av. Rafael E. Melgar 27, at Calle 3 Sur* ☎ *987/872–1417*). **The Crew Office** (✉ *Av. 5, No. 201, between Calle 3 Sur and Av. Rosada Salas* ☎ *987/869–1485*). **CreWorld Internet** (✉ *Av. Rafael E. Melgar and Calle 11 Sur* ☎ *987/872–6509*).

Mail & Shipping **Correos** (✉ *Calle 7 Sur and Av. Rafael E. Melgar* ☎ *987/872–0106*). **DHL** (✉ *Av. Rafael E. Melgar and Av. 5 Sur* ☎ *987/872–3110*).

Medical Assistance **Air Ambulance** (☎ *987/872–4070*). **Police** (✉ *Anexo del Palacio Municipal* ☎ *987/872–0092*). **Centro Médico de Cozumel** (*Cozumel Medi-*

cal Center) ✉ *Calle 1 Sur 101 and Av. 50* ☎ *987/872–0103 or 987/872–5370).* **Red Cross** *(* ✉ *Calle Adolfo Rosada Salas and Av. 20 Sur* ☎ *987/872–1058, 065 for emergencies).*

Rental Cars **Aguila Rentals** *(* ✉ *Av. Rafael E. Melgar 685* ☎ *987/872–0729).* **CP Rentals** *(* ✉ *Av. 10 Norte, between Calles 2 and 4* ☎ *987/878–4055).* **Fiesta** *(* ✉ *Calle 11, No. 598* ☎ *987/872–4311).*

Visitor & Tour Info **Fidecomiso and the Cozumel Island Hotel Association** *(* ✉ *Calle 2 Norte and Av. 15* ☎ *987/872–7585* 🌐 *www.islacozumel.com.mx).*

EXPLORING

MAIN ATTRACTIONS

★ **Museo de la Isla de Cozumel.** Cozumel's island museum is housed on two floors of a former hotel. It has displays on natural history—with exhibits on the island's origins, endangered species, topography, and coral-reef ecology—as well as the pre-Columbian and colonial periods. The photos of the island's transformation over the 20th and 21st centuries are especially fascinating, as is the exhibit of a typical Mayan home. Guided tours are available. ✉ *Av. Rafael E. Melgar, between Calles 4 and 6 Norte* ☎ *987/872–1434* *$3* *Daily 8–5.*

★ **Parque Chankanaab.** Chankanaab (which means "small sea") is a national park with a saltwater lagoon, an archaeological park, and a botanical garden. Scattered throughout are reproductions of a Mayan village, and of Olmec, Toltec, Aztec, and Mayan stone carvings. The gardens, severely damaged by Hurricane Wilma in 2005, are a testament to nature's ability to recover. You can enjoy a cool walk along pathways leading to the sea, where parrot fish and sergeant majors swarm around snorkelers.

You can swim, scuba dive, or snorkel at the beach. There's plenty to see: underwater caverns, a sunken ship, crusty old cannons and anchors, and a sculpture of la Virgen del Mar (Virgin of the Sea). To preserve the ecosystem, park rules forbid touching the reef or feeding the fish.

Dive shops, restaurants, gift shops, a snack stand, and dressing rooms with lockers and showers are right on the sand. A small museum has exhibits on coral, shells, and the park's history, as well as some sculptures. ✉ *Carretera Sur, Km 9* ☎ *987/872–2940* *$10* *Daily 7–5.*

San Gervasio. Surrounded by a forest, these temples make up Cozumel's largest remaining Mayan and Toltec site. San Gervasio was the island's capital and ceremonial center, dedicated to the fertility goddess Ixchel. Its classic- and postclassic-style buildings and temples were continuously occupied from AD 300 to 1500. Typical architectural features include limestone plazas and arches atop stepped platforms, as well as stelae and bas-reliefs. Be sure to see the temple "Las Manitas," with red handprints all over its altar. Plaques clearly describe each structure in Mayan, Spanish, and English. ✉ *From San Miguel take cross-island* *road (follow signs to airport) east to San Gervasio access road; turn left and follow road 7 km (4½ mi) $ 5.75 Daily 7–4.*

IF YOU HAVE TIME

El Cedral. Spanish explorers discovered this site, once the hub of Mayan life on Cozumel, in 1518. Later it became the island's first official city, founded in 1847. Today it's a farming community with small well-tended houses and gardens. Conquistadors tore down much of the Mayan temple and, during World War II the U.S. Army Corps of Engineers destroyed the rest to make way for the island's first airport. All that remains of the Mayan ruins is one small structure with an arch. Nearby is a green-and-white cinder-block church, decorated inside with crosses shrouded in embroidered lace; legend has it that Mexico's first Mass was held here. Vendors display embroidered blouses, hammocks, and other souvenirs at stands around the main plaza. ⊠ *Turn at Km 17.5 off Carretera Sur or Av. Rafael E. Melgar, then drive 3 km (2 mi) inland to site No phone Free Daily dawn–dusk.*

★ **Discover Mexico.** New to the island in 2007, this ingenious attraction allows visitors to learn about Mexico's archaeological sites, important architectural landmarks, and cultures. A gorgeous film about Mexico runs continuously, and exhibits display collector-quality textiles, pottery, and painted figurines. Outdoors are scale models of temples, pyramids, monasteries, and Mexico City's main square, the Zócalo. An outdoor café serves tasty fruit sorbets and light meals. The gift shop has the island's finest array of Mexican folk art. Expect to spend about two hours to fully experience the entire exhibit. ⊠ *Carretera Sur, Km 5.5 987/875–2820 www.discovermexico.org $14 Mon.–Sat. 8–6.*

Parque Punta Sur. This 247-acre national preserve at Cozumel's southernmost tip is a protected habitat for numerous birds and animals, including crocodiles, flamingos, egrets, and herons. Cars aren't allowed, so you'll need to use park transportation (rented bicycles or park shuttles) to get around here. From observation towers you can spot crocodiles and birds in **Laguna Colombia** or **Laguna Chunchacaab.** Or visit the ancient Mayan lighthouse, **El Caracol,** designed to whistle when the wind blows in a certain direction. At the park's (and the island's) southernmost point is the **Faro de Celarain,** a lighthouse that is now a museum of navigation. Climb the 134 steps to the top; it's a steamy effort, but the views are incredible. Beaches here are wide and deserted, and there's great snorkeling offshore. Snorkeling equipment is available for rent, as are kayaks, and there are restrooms at the museum and by the beach. Without a rental car, expect to pay about $40 for a round-trip taxi ride from San Miguel. ⊠ *Southernmost point of Carretera Sur and coastal road 987/872–2940 or 987/872–8462 $10 Daily 9–5.*

BEACHES

LEEWARD BEACHES

Playa Santa Pilar runs along the northern hotel strip and ends at Punta Norte. Long stretches of sand and shallow water encourage leisurely swims. The privacy diminishes as you swim south past hotels and condos.

Playa San Juan, south of Playa Santa Pilar, has a rocky shore with no easy ocean access. It's usually crowded with guests from nearby hotels. The wind can be strong here, which makes it popular with windsurfers.

A small parking lot on the side of Carretera Sur just south of town marks the entrance to **Playa Caletita.** There's a rock ledge here and fairly easy access into the water.

15

Playa San Francisco was one of the first beach clubs on the coast. The inviting 5-km (3-mi) stretch of sandy beach, which extends along Carretera Sur south of Parque Chankanaab at about Km 14, is among the longest and finest on Cozumel. Encompassing beaches known as Playa Maya and Santa Rosa, it's typically packed with cruise-ship passengers in high season. On Sunday locals flock here to eat fresh fish and hear live music. The abundance of turtle grass in the water, however, makes this a less-than-ideal spot for swimming.

★ South of the resorts lies the mostly ignored (and therefore serene) **Playa Palancar** (✉*Carretera Sur* ☎*987/878–5238*). The deeply rutted and potholed road to the beach is a sure sign you've left tourist hell. Offshore is the famous Palancar Reef, easily accessed by the on-site dive shop. There's also a water-sports center, a bar-café, and a long beach with hammocks hanging under coconut palms. The aroma of grilled fish with garlic butter is tantalizing. Playa del Palancar keeps prices low and rarely feels crowded.

WINDWARD BEACHES

Punta Chiqueros, a half-moon-shape cove sheltered by an offshore reef, is the first popular swimming area as you drive north on the coastal road (it's about 12 km [8 mi] north of Parque Punta Sur). Part of a longer beach that some locals call Playa Bonita, it has fine sand, clear water, and moderate waves. This is a great place to swim, watch the sunset, and eat fresh fish at the restaurant, also called Playa Bonita.

Not quite 5 km (3 mi) north of Punta Chiqueros, a long stretch of beach begins along the Chen Río Reef. Turtles come to lay their eggs on the section known as **Playa de San Martín** (although some locals call it Chen Río, after the reef). During full moons in May and June the beach is sometimes blocked by soldiers or ecologists to prevent poaching of the turtle eggs. Directly in front of the reef is a small bay with clear waters and surf that's relatively mild, thanks to a protective rock formation. This is a particularly good spot for swimming when the water is calm. A restaurant, also called Chen Río, serves cold drinks and decent seafood.

★ Surfers and boogie-boarders have adopted **Punta Morena,** a short drive north of Ventanas al Mar, as their official hangout. The pounding surf creates great waves, and the local restaurant serves typical surfer food (hamburgers, hot dogs, and french fries). Vendors sell hammocks by the side of the road. The owners allow camping here. The beach at **Punta Este** has been nicknamed Mezcalitos, after the much-loved restaurant here. Mezcalito Café serves seafood and beer and can get pretty rowdy. Punta Este is a typical windward beach—great for beachcombing but unsuitable for swimming.

WORD OF MOUTH

"Guido's is the best Italian restaurant on the island! They have a nice patio and I recommend eating there after the sun sets. The sangria with lots of floating fruit in it is the best I've ever had, and the stuffed chicken was surprisingly wonderful!"

–Janabob

WHERE TO EAT

ZONA HOTELERA SUR

$$$ ITALIAN ✕ **Alfredo Di Roma.** The opportunity to dine graciously amid crystal and candlelight (and blessedly cool air-conditioning) is just one reason to book a special dinner at Alfredo's. The pastas are made fresh daily and cheeses are flown in from Italy so the chef can prepare authentic fettuccini Alfredo tableside to rousing music from the accordion player. The octopus salad, pasta puttanesca, and grilled sea bass are all superb, and the wine cellar is the largest on the island. Book a table for early evening and enjoy the sunset view through wall-length windows. ✉*Presidente InterContinental Cozumel, Carretera Chankanaab, Km 6.5* ☎*987/872–9500* *Reservations essential* *AE, MC, V* *No lunch.*

$–$$ MEXICAN ★ ✕ **Coconuts.** The T-shirts and bikinis hanging from the palapa roof at this windward-side hangout are a good indication of its party-time atmosphere. Jimmy Buffett tunes play in the background while crowds down *cervezas* (beers). The scene is more peaceful if you choose a palapa-shaded table on the rocks overlooking the water. The calamari and garlic shrimp are good enough to write home about. Assign a designated driver and hit the road home before dark (remember, there are no streetlights). ✉*East-coast road near junction with Av. Benito Juárez* ☎*No phone* *No credit cards* *No dinner.*

SAN MIGUEL

$$$ ✕ **La Cocay.** This casually sophisticated dining room is one of the most exciting dining venues on the island, thanks to the creative chef. The menu changes frequently, but you can usually order a salad with mixed baby lettuces, an assortment of tapas including hummus and smoked salmon, and entrées like yummy seared sashimi-grade tuna. Such fare may be the norm in L.A. or Honolulu, but is hard to find on Cozumel. Lunch is far more casual, with burgers and *arrachera* (grilled marinated beef) on order. ✉*Calle 8 between Avs. 10 and 15* ☎*987/872–5533* *AE, MC, V* *Closed Sun.*

$$–$$$ ITALIAN ★ **Guido's.** Chef Yvonne Villiger works wonders with fresh fish—if the wahoo with capers and black olives is on the menu, don't miss it. But Guido's is best known for its pizzas baked in a wood-burning oven, which makes sections of the indoor dining room rather warm. Sit in the pleasantly overgrown courtyard instead, and order a pitcher of sangria to go with the puffy garlic bread. *Av. Rafael E. Melgar 23, between Calles 6 and 8 Norte 987/872–0946 AE, D, MC, V Closed Sun.*

WORD OF MOUTH

"Casa Denis is a GREAT little local restaurant—the first on the island. The Mayan food is excellent, the margaritas generous, and the waiters...are humorous and efficient."

–Todd

$$–$$$ MEXICAN ★ **Pancho's Backyard.** Marimbas play beside the bubbling fountain in this gorgeous courtyard behind one of Cozumel's best folk-art shops. Though Pancho's is always busy, the service is excellent and waiters are amazingly patient and helpful. Cruise-ship passengers seeking a taste of Mexico pack the place at lunch; dinner is a bit more serene. The menu is definitely geared toward tourists (written in English with detailed descriptions and prices in dollars), but regional ingredients make even the standard steak stand out when it's flavored with smoky chipotle chile. Other stellar dishes include the cilantro cream soup and shrimp flambéed with tequila. *Av. Rafael Melgar at Calle 8 987/872–2141 AE, MC, V Dinner only on Sun.*

$$ MEXICAN **Casa Mission.** Part private home and part restaurant, this estate evokes a country hacienda in mainland Mexico. The on-site botanical garden has mango and papaya trees, and a small zoo with caged birds. The setting, with tables lining the veranda, outshines the food. Stalwart fans rave about huge platters of fajitas and grilled fish. It's out of the way, so you'll need to take a cab. *Av. Juárez and Calle 55A 987/872–3248 AE, MC, V Closed Sun. No lunch.*

$$ MEXICAN ★ **La Choza.** Purely Mexican in design and cuisine, this family-owned restaurant is a favorite for mole *rojo* (with cinnamon and chiles) and *cochinita pibíl* (marinated pork baked in banana leaves). Leave room for the chilled chocolate pie or the equally intriguing avocado pie. Locals fill the restaurant at lunchtime for the economical fixed-price *comida corrida* (meal of the day). *Calle Adolfo Rosado Salas 198, at Av. 10 987/872–0958 AE, MC, V.*

$ MEXICAN ★ **Casa Denis.** This little yellow house near the plaza has been satisfying cravings for Yucatecan *pollo pibíl* (spiced chicken baked in banana leaves) and other local favorites since 1945. *Tortas* (sandwiches) and tacos are a real bargain, and you'll start to feel like a local if you spend an hour at one of the outdoor tables, watching shoppers dash about. *Calle 1 Sur 132, between Avs. 5 and 10 987/872–0067 No credit cards.*

WHERE TO STAY

WORD OF MOUTH

"One thing that many families love [at the Coral Princess] is that the snorkeling right in front of the resort is easy to access and filled with fish. You can actually sit on the beach and watch your kids snorkel in the ocean."

–TC

ZONA HOTELERA NORTE

$$$ **Coral Princess Hotel & Resort.** Good snorkeling off the rocky shoreline makes this a north coast favorite. The hotel was completely remodeled in 2006 with a new restaurant, bar with karaoke nights, and gym. The suites have one or two bedrooms, a kitchen, and a balcony or terrace. These large rooms are often taken by time-share owners, especially in summer, though there's no pressure to attend a sales demo. Most of the studio-size hotel rooms overlook the jungle; try to get an ocean-view room on an upper floor for the best views and sea breezes. **Pros:** Excellent snorkeling right off the beach, decent, well-priced meals, family-friendly. **Cons:** Can be noisy, some rooms lack bathtubs. ✉ *Carretera Costera Norte, Km 2.5* ☎ *987/872–3200 or 800/253–2702* 🌐 *www.coralprincess.com* *110 rooms, 26 suites* *In-room: Safe, kitchen (some), refrigerator. In-hotel: Restaurant, room service, bar, pools, gym, diving, water sports, laundry service, parking (no fee)* *AE, DC, MC, V* *BP.*

$$$ ★ **Playa Azul Golf and Beach Resort.** This romantic boutique hotel has bright and airy rooms facing the ocean or the gardens. Inside the rooms are mirrored niches, wicker and pale-wood furnishings, and sun-filled terraces. None of the rooms have bathtubs, and the best are the corner suites on the upper floors. Small palapas shade lounge chairs on the beach, and you can arrange snorkeling and diving trips at the hotel's own dock. Golf fees are included in the room rates; some guests hit the course daily. A freestanding spa at the hotel's entrance offers body and beauty treatments. The small Chan Ka'an dinner restaurant is a lovely spot for a quiet evening. Make reservations in advance in case there's a reception or other function taking place. **Pros:** Small and intimate feel, excellent spa, free greens fees. **Cons:** Pool isn't heated, no hot tub. It may be too quiet for those seeking action, and the beach is rocky. ✉ *Carretera Costera Norte, Km 4* ☎ *987/872–0043* 🌐 *www.playa-azul.com* *34 rooms, 16 suites* *In-room: Safe. In-hotel: 2 restaurants, room service, bars, pool, beachfront, diving, water sports, spa, laundry service, parking (no fee)* *AE, MC, V* *BP.*

ZONA HOTELERA SUR

$$$$ **Aura Cozumel Wyndham Grand Bay.** Opened in 2008, this elegant, all-inclusive boutique hotel raises the standard for the southern coast's string of all-inclusive resorts. Four low-rise buildings face a meandering pool with separate areas linked by a lazy river. Swim-up suites have direct patio access to the ground-level pool, while third-story solarium suites have narrow rooftop lap pools. The design throughout the seven suite categories is sleekly contemporary, with dark-wood furnishings and contrasting sea-blue textiles, flat-screen TVs, iPod docks, and Egyptian cotton sheets. The hotel is adjacent to the 402-room

Wyndham Cozumel Resort and Spa (formerly the Reef Club). Both hotels face a long beach and shallow water. **Pros:** High-tech, luxurious suite amenities rare on Cozumel; intimate sophisticated ambience. **Cons:** Far from town, offshore snorkeling not very good. ✉ *Carretera Costera Sur Km 12.9,* ☎ *987/872–9300 or 866/551–2872* 🌐 *www.auraresorts.com* *87 suites* *In-room: Safe, refrigerator, Wi-Fi. In-hotel: 2 restaurants, room service, bars, pool, gym, beachfront, diving, water sports, concierge, laundry service, public Wi-Fi, parking (no fee), no-smoking rooms* ▭ *MC, V* 🍴 *AI.*

$$$$ **Cozumel Palace.** This gorgeous all-inclusive hotel is part of the popular Palace Resorts chain. Within walking distance of San Miguel, the hotel faces the water but lacks a beach. Instead, an infinity pool seems to flow into the sea, and stairs lead from the property into a fairly good snorkeling area. The romantic rooms are airy, white enclaves with double whirlpool tubs and hammocks on the balconies. The chain has vacation ownership and club programs, so you may feel a bit hassled by sellers. Owners can use the facilities at the Palace Resort in Playa del Carmen on the mainland. **Pros:** In-room hot tubs, good honeymoon hideaway. **Cons:** Sales pressure, slow elevators. ✉ *Av. Melgar, Km 1.5* ☎ *987/872–9430 or 800/635–1836* 🌐 *www.palaceresorts.com* *176 rooms* *In-room: Safe, refrigerator. In-hotel: 3 restaurants, room service, bars, pools, gym, spa, diving, water sports, concierge, children's programs (ages 4–12), laundry service, public Wi-Fi, parking (no fee), no-smoking rooms* ▭ *AE, DC, MC, V* 🍴 *AI.*

15

$$$$ **Presidente InterContinental Cozumel Resort & Spa.** Cozumel's loveliest resort is a thoroughly modern, sophisticated property. The expansive lawns and beaches are bordered by a marina to the north and undeveloped jungle to the south, making the hotel feel ultraprivate and secluded. Soft white sand covers the limestone shelf beside a small cove and the shores in front of the two hotel wings. Ground-level suites facing the sea have large terraces, outdoor rain showers, and indoor bathtubs, whereas those in the upper floors have whirlpool tubs with sea views (and separate showers in the large bathrooms). Rooms have sleek dark-wood furnishings and a calm cream and brown color scheme. Special touches include gourmet coffeemakers, iPod docks, and complimentary Wi-Fi. The main palapa-covered restaurant is best for breakfast and lunch by the sea. The Mandara Spa is the island's largest, with sublime treatments and a temazcal (Mayan sweat lodge). Bellmen greet you like an old friend, waiters quickly learn your preferences, and housekeepers are quick to provide whatever you need. **Pros:** Secluded from other hotels, spaciousness in the grounds and beaches, high-quality beds and linens, professional service. **Cons:** May be too quiet for those seeking a party; aggressive vacation-club sales. ✉ *Carretera Chankanaab, Km 6.5* ☎ *987/872–9500 or 800/327–0200* 🌐 *www.intercontinentalcozumel.com* *173 rooms, 47 suites* *In-room: Safe. In-hotel: 2 restaurants, room service, bars, tennis courts, pool, gym, spa, beachfront, diving, water sports, concierge, children's programs (ages 4–12), laundry service, parking (no fee), no-smoking rooms, some pets allowed* ▭ *AE, DC, MC, V* 🍴 *EP.*

Fodor's Choice ★

$$$–$$$$ **El Cid la Ceiba.** A favorite among divers and frequent Cozumel visitors, this compact property was originally built in 1978 beside a shady ceiba (a tree sacred to the Maya). The hotel was completely remodeled in 2006 with an eye to casual comfort (lots of towels, fold-out couches facing TVs, large dining tables). Most rooms overlook the ocean; the best have separate living rooms, kitchenettes, and enormous bathrooms with deep tubs and separate showers. The lobby and a small pool area separate the two towers, one facing a generous beach and the other above a smaller patch of sand bordering a shallow saltwater lagoon with a waterfall. Pros: Great Mexican food in the restaurant and a reasonable all-inclusive plan option, good snorkeling offshore. Cons: Massive cruise ships float near a pier (under reconstruction at this writing) beside the hotel, marring the sea view; the pool scene can be rowdy. ✉ *Carretera Chankanaab Km 4.5* , ☎ *987/872–0844 or 800/525–1925* 🌐 *www.elcid.com* *60 rooms* *In-room: Safe, kitchens (some). In-hotel: Restaurant, room service, bars, tennis, 2 pools, gym, spa, beachfront, diving, water sports* MC, V.

SAN MIGUEL

$$–$$$ **Casa Mexicana.** A dramatic staircase leads up to the windswept lobby, and distinctive rooms are decorated in subtle blues and yellows. Some face the ocean and Avenida Rafael E. Melgar; others overlook the unattractive downtown streets or the terrace. Splurge on a waterfront room if you can, as the balcony is a great place to hang out and enjoy the sea view and street scene. Rooms have bathtubs (hard to find on the island) and are immaculate and comfy. The rate includes a full breakfast buffet, and the lobby bar overlooking the street is a great place for sunset drinks. Two sister properties, Hotel Bahía and Suites Colonial, offer equally comfortable but less expensive suites with kitchenettes (the Bahía has some ocean views; the Colonial is near the square). **Pros:** Great downtown location by restaurants and shops, friendly staff (especially the bartenders), substantial breakfast. **Cons:** No beach, some street noise. ✉ *Av. Rafael E. Melgar Sur 457, between Calles 5 and 7* ☎ *987/872–9090 or 877/228–6747* 🌐 *www.casamexicanacozumel.com* *90 rooms* *In-room: Safe, dial-up. In-hotel: Gym, concierge, laundry service* *AE, D, MC, V* *BP.*

¢ **Hotel Pepita.** Despite being more than 50 years old, the Pepita is one of the best budget hotels on the island. The blue-and-white facade is painted frequently, as are the rooms. Wooden shutters cover screened windows that keep out the bugs (who thrive happily among the courtyard's many plants and shrubs). Cable TV, refrigerators, and air-conditioning are surprising pluses for such low rates. Shelves in the lobby are stacked high with novels in several languages, and German and Dutch are as common as Spanish and English during conversations over free coffee around the long wooden table in the courtyard. There are no kitchen facilities, but plenty of small markets and cafés nearby. **Pros:** Locals' neighborhood with few tourists, amiable staff. **Cons:** Buggy (keep doors closed), no phones in rooms, some staff speak Spanish only. ✉ *Av. 15 Sur 120* ☎ *987/872–0098* *20 rooms* *In-room: refrigerator. In-hotel: No elevator* *No credit cards.*

WINDWARD SIDE

$$ ★ **Ventanas al Mar.** The lights of San Miguel are but a distant glow on the horizon when you look west from the only hotel on the windward coast. Turn east, though, and you can watch shooting stars flash through the nighttime sky over the foaming sea. Escape is complete at this small, ecofriendly inn that runs on solar power; there are no phones, no computer hookups. The rooms are commodious and comfortable, and have microwaves, refrigerators, and coffeemakers. Two-story suites have separate bedrooms, a half-bath downstairs, and a full bath upstairs. Rates ($164 to $184) are significantly higher but a bargain when shared by four people. Full breakfast is served in the open-air lobby, and meals are available at Coconuts, next door, until dusk. Sea turtles nest on the long beach beside the hotel in summer, and tropical fish and anemones gather by the rocky point in front of the rooms. A two-night minimum stay is required. **Pros:** Blissful solitude, long beach great for sunset walks, a sense of escape. **Cons:** Limited food and drink options, driving at night not advisable as coastal road is not lighted. ✉ *East-coast road north of Coconuts* ☎ 987/105–2684 🌐 *www.ventanasalmar.*com.mx *16 rooms* *In-room: No phones, kitchen, refrigerator, no TV. In-hotel: Beachfront, water sports, parking (no fee), no elevator* *No credit cards* *BP.*

> **WORD OF MOUTH**
>
> "I stay at Hotel Pepita often and believe it is an unmatched value in Cozumel. The rooms are clean, well maintained with air and cable TV (rare in this price range) and the staff is friendly and hospitable. Excellent choice!"
>
> –Robert

15

NIGHTLIFE

BARS

Carlos 'n Charlie's and Señor Frog's (✉ *Av. Rafael E. Melgar at Punta Langosta* ☎ *987/872–0191*) are members of the Carlos Anderson chain of rowdy restaurant-bars that attract crowds. The *Animal House* ambience includes loud rock music and a liberated, anything-goes dancing scene that seems to have special allure to the cruising set.

Lively, rowdy **Fat Tuesdays** (✉ *Av. Juárez between Av. Rafael E. Melgar and Calle 3 Sur* ☎ *987/872–5130*) draws crowds day and night for frozen daiquiris, ice-cold beers, and blaring rock.

For a more sophisticated scene with mojitos and great cigars, check out **Havana Blue** (✉ *Av. Rafael E. Melgar and Calle 10 Norte, 2nd fl.* ☎ *987/869–1687*) in the flashy Forum shopping mall.

Viva Mexico (✉ *Av. Rafael E. Melgar* ☎ *987/872–0799*) sometimes has a DJ who spins Latin and American dance music until the wee hours. There's also an extensive snack menu. This place is wildly popular anytime of day or night. The best seats are near the second-story railing overlooking the waterfront.

Martinis and high-end tequilas are on order at **1.5 Tequila Lounge** (✉ *Av. Rafael Melgar at Calle 11 Sur* ☎ *987/872–4421*) on the south end of downtown. The waterfront location and classy lounge ambience set it apart from the rowdier bars, though the scene does get pretty wild here as well.

DANCE CLUBS

Cozumel's oldest disco, **Neptune Dance Club** (✉*Av. Rafael E. Melgar and Av. 11* ☎*987/872–1537*), is the island's classiest nightspot, with a dazzling light-and-laser show. The music varies from disco to salsa, with appearances by Latin-music bands drawing crowds of locals.

SPORTS & OUTDOOR ACTIVITIES

Most people come to Cozumel for the water sports—especially scuba diving, snorkeling, and fishing. Services and equipment rentals are available throughout the island, especially through major hotels and water-sports centers at the beach clubs.

FISHING

The waters off Cozumel swarm with more than 230 species of fish, making this one of the world's best deep-sea fishing destinations. During billfish migration season, from late April through June, world-record catches aren't uncommon. It's illegal to kill certain species within marine reserves, including billfish, so be prepared to return some prize catches to the sea.

CHARTERS

You can charter high-speed fishing boats for about $420 per half-day or $600 per day (with a maximum of six people). Your hotel can help arrange daily charters—some offer special deals, with boats leaving from their own docks. **Albatros Deep Sea Fishing** (☎*987/872–7904 or 888/333–4643*) offers full-day trips that include boat and crew, tackle and bait, and lunch with beer and soda starting at $575 for up to 6 persons. All equipment and tackle, lunch with beer, and the boat and crew are also included in **Ocean Tours'** (☎*987/872–9530 Ext. 8*) full-day rates, which start at $550. **3 Hermanos** (☎*987/872–6417 or 987/876–8931*) specializes in deep-sea and fly-fishing trips. Their rates for a half-day deep-sea fishing trip start at $350; a full day is $450. They also offer scuba-diving trips, and their boats are available for group charters (a great way to snorkel and cruise around at your own pace) for $400 for up to 6 passengers.

GOLF

The **Cozumel Country Club** (✉*Carretera Costera Norte, Km 5.8* ☎*987/872–9570* 🌐*www.cozumelcountryclub.com.mx*) has an 18-hole championship golf course. The gorgeous fairways amid mangroves and a lagoon are the work of the Nicklaus Design Group and have been declared an Audubon nature reserve. The greens fee is $169 ($105 after 1:30 PM), which includes a golf cart. Many hotels offer golf packages here.

If you're not a fan of miniature golf, the challenging **Cozumel Mini-Golf** (✉*Calle 1, Sur 20* ☎*987/872–6570*) might turn you into one. The jungle-theme course has banana trees, birds, two fountains, and a waterfall. You can choose your music from a selection of more than 800 CDs and order your drinks via walkie-talkie; they'll be delivered as you try for that hole in one. Admission is $7 for adults, $5 for kids; it's open Monday through Saturday 10 AM to 11 PM and Sunday 5 PM to 11 PM.

HORSEBACK RIDING

Aventuras Naturales (☒*Av. 35, No. 1081* ☎*987/872–1628 or 858/366–4632* 🌐*www.aventurasnaturalascozumel.com*) runs a two-hour guided horseback tour through the jungle to El Cedral. Prices start at $35. Groups are small and the guides fun and informative. The company also has hiking tours and a full-day action tour combining biking, horseback riding, and snorkeling for $65 per person. **Rancho Buenavista** (☒*Carretera Perimetral, Km 32.5* ☎*987/872–1537*) provides four-hour rides through the jungle starting at $65 per person.

KAYAKING

Located at Uvas beach club, **Clear Kayak** (☒*Carretera Sur, Km 8.5* ☎*987/872–3539*) runs what's called "dry-snorkeling" tours in see-through kayaks (imagine what the fish must be thinking). Paddling around with water seeming to flow past your toes is great fun, and there's time for real snorkeling as well. Tours, which cost $40 for adults and $27 for children, include entrance fee, 2 domestic drinks, and a 45-minute kayak trip; a more-expensive tour includes lunch.

15

SHOPPING

MALLS

Forum Shops (☒*Av. Rafael E. Melgar and Calle 10 Norte* ☎*987/869–1687*) is a flashy marble-and-glass mall with jewels glistening in glass cases and an overabundance of eager salesclerks. Diamonds International and Tanzanite International have shops in the Forum and all over Avenida Rafael E. Melgar, as does Roger's Boots, a leather store. There's a Havana Blue bar upstairs, where shoppers select expensive cigars. **Puerto Maya** (☒*Carretera Sur at southern cruise dock*) is a mall geared to cruise-ship passengers and has branches of many of downtown's most popular shops, restaurants, and bars. It's close to the ships at the end of a huge parking lot.

Punta Langosta (☒*Av. Rafael E. Melgar 551, at Calle 7*), a fancy multi-level shopping mall, is across the street from the cruise-ship dock. An enclosed pedestrian walkway leads over the street from the ships to the center, which houses several jewelry and sportswear stores. The center is designed to lure cruise-ship passengers into shopping in air-conditioned comfort, and has reduced traffic for local businesses.

MARKETS

★ There's a **crafts market** (☒*Calle 1 Sur, behind plaza*) in town, which sells a respectable assortment of Mexican wares. It's the best place to practice your bartering skills while shopping for blankets, T-shirts, hammocks, and pottery. For fresh produce, fish, chilies, and a taste of local life try the **Mercado Municipal** (☒*Calle Adolfo Rosado Salas* *between Avs. 20 and 25 Sur ☎ No phone*), open Monday through Saturday 8 to 5.

SPECIALTY STORES

CLOTHING

Several trendy sportswear stores line Avenida Rafael E. Melgar between Calles 2 and 6. **Exotica** (✉ *Av. Juárez at plaza* ☎ *987/872–5880*) has high-quality sportswear and shirts with nature-theme designs. **Island Outfitters** (✉ *Av. Rafael E. Melgar, at plaza* ☎ *987/872–0132*) has high-quality sportswear, beach towels, and sarongs. **Mr. Buho** (✉ *Av. Rafael E. Melgar between Calles 6 and 8* ☎ *987/869–1601*) specializes in white-and-black clothes and has well-made guayabera shirts and cotton dresses.

CRAFTS

The showrooms at **Anji** (✉ *Av. 5 between Calles Adolfo Rosado Salas and 1 Sur* ☎ *987/869–2623*) are filled with imported lamps, carved animals, and clothing from Bali. At **Balam Mayan Feather** (✉ *Av. 5 and Calle 2 Norte* ☎ *987/869–0548*) artists create intricate paintings on feathers from local birds. **Bugambilias** (✉ *Av. 10 Sur between Calles Adolfo Rosado Salas and 1 Sur* ☎ *987/872–6282*) sells handmade Mexican linens.

★ **Los Cinco Soles** (✉ *Av. Rafael E. Melgar and Calle 8 Norte* ☎ *987/872–0132*) is the best one-stop shop for crafts from around Mexico. Several display rooms, covering almost an entire block, are filled with clothing, furnishings, home-decor items, and jewelry.

El Porton (✉ *Av. 5 Sur and Calle 1 Sur* ☎ *987/872–5606*) has a collection of masks and unusual crafts.

THE RIVIERA MAYA

Updated by Marlise Kast & Michele Joyce

It takes patience to discover the treasures on this part of the coast. Beaches and towns aren't easily visible from the main highway—the road from Cancún to Tulum is 1–2 km (½–1 mi) from the coast. Thus there's little to see but dense vegetation, lots of billboards, many roadside markets, and signs marking entrances to various hotels and attractions.

Still, the treasures—which include spectacular white-sand beaches and some of the peninsula's most beautiful Mayan ruins—are here, and they haven't been lost on resort developers.

PLAYA DEL CARMEN

68 km (42 mi) south of Cancún.

Once upon a time, Playa del Carmen was a fishing village with a ravishing deserted beach. The villagers fished and raised coconut palms, and the only foreigners who ventured here were catching ferries to Cozumel. That was a long time ago, however. These days, although the beach is still delightful—alabaster-white sand, turquoise-blue waters—

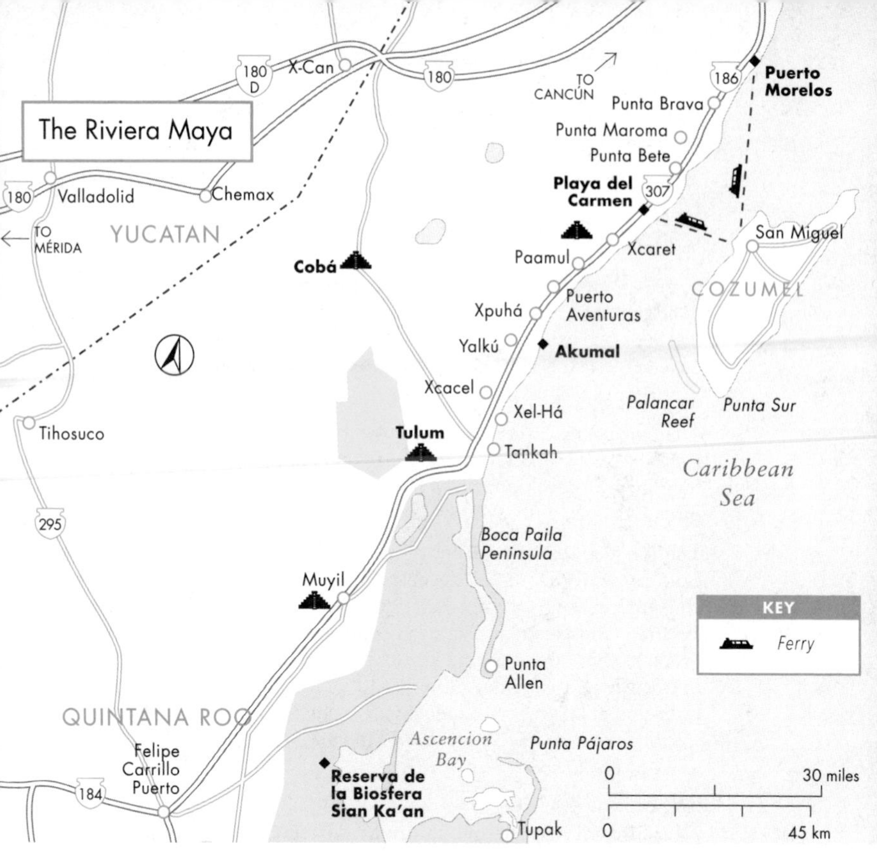

it's far from deserted. In fact, Playa has become one of Latin America's fastest-growing communities, with a population of more than 135,000 and a pace almost as hectic as that of Cancún.

GETTING HERE & AROUND

Almost everyone who arrives by air into this region flies into Cancún, at the Aeropuerto Internacional Cancún. Buses traveling to all points except Cancún stop at Playa del Carmen's bus terminal at Avenida 20 and Calle 12. Buses headed to Cancún use the main bus terminal at Avenida Juárez and Avenida 5. ADO runs express, first-class, and second-class buses to major destinations. You can hire taxis in Cancún to go as far as Playa del Carmen, but the price is steep unless you have many passengers. Fares run about $65.

ESSENTIALS

Bus Contacts **ADO** (☎ *983/832–5110* 🌐 *www.ado.com.mx*).

Currency Exchange **Banamex** (✉ *Av. Juárez between Avs. 20 and 25* ☎ *984/873–0825* ✉ *Av. 10 at 12* ☎ *984/873–2947*). **Bancomer** (✉ *Av. Juárez between Calles 25 and 30* ☎ *984/873–0356*).

Internet **Cyberia Internet Café** (✉ *Calle 4 and Av. 15*).**El Point** (✉ *Av. 5 between 24 and 26 Norte* ☎ *984/803–3412* ✉ *Av. 10 between 12 and 15* ☎ *984/803–0897*

Av 10 between 2 and 4 Norte 984/803–1268). **24 Com Center** (*Av. 24, between Calle 1 and Calle 8 984/803–5778*).

Medical Assistance **Centro de Salud** (*Av. Juárez and Av. 15 984/873–1230 Ext. 147*).

Mail & Shipping **Correos** (*Av. Juárez, next to police station 983/873–0300*).

Visitor & Tour Info **Playa del Carmen tourist information booth** (*Av. Juárez by police station, between Calles 15 and 20 984/873–2804 in Playa del Carmen, 888/955–7155 in U.S., 604/990–6506 in Canada*).**Tierra Maya Tours** (*Av. 5 and Calle 6 984/873–1385*).

EXPLORING

The excellent 32-acre **Xaman Ha Aviary** (*Paseo Xaman-Ha, Playacar 984/873–0235 www.aviarioxamanha.com*), in the middle of the Playacar development, is home to more than 30 species of native birds. It's open daily 9–5, and admission is $15.

The **Tres Ríos Eco Park,** 11 km (7 mi) north of Playa, is a great place to get a sense of this region's ecology and natural wonders. Three rivers converge in the expansive 800-acre property (a lush rarity in the dry Yucatán landscape), and you can explore them by kayaking, canoeing, or snorkeling along them. You can also take horseback rides along the beach or bike rides along jungle paths, keeping an eye out for birds and animals; if you're lucky, you might spot a white-fronted parrot, or even a coati. *Carretera Cancún–Tulum, Km 54 998/850–4849 $18 Daily 9–5.*

WHERE TO EAT

$$$–$$$$ SEAFOOD Fodor's Choice ★ **La Casa Del Agua.** Using nature as a backdrop, this eatery features four separate levels, each with its own atmosphere. From the street-level bistro, a dramatic staircase leads to a small cocktail bar where candelabras drip onto the wooden floors. A stone waterfall is the focal point in the dining rooms illuminated by wrought-iron chandeliers. The open layout provides nearly every table with an ocean breeze. Among the favorites is a seared hamachi served over asparagus and tomato with a sauce of oil, lime, wasabi, jalapeño, and ginger. Those who prefer a local catch should try the fish fillet in a Mediterranean-style vinaigrette. *Av 5 and Calle 2 984/803–0232 www.lacasadelagua.com MC, V.*

$$$–$$$$ MEDITERRANEAN **Negrosal.** An isolated location and alluring atmosphere make "Black Salt" a local favorite. Inspired by the female form, the decor integrates damask chairs cinched by corsets, candles shaded by black lace, and table legs shaped to resemble those of a ballerina. The restaurant's lighting subtlety changes color every few minutes, and a glass flooring allows you to peek down at the extensive wine cellar. Playing with contradictions, the menu features sweet and salty combinations like lobster tail topped with a corn and pineapple sauce. Every dish, including the tequila duck tacos and the grilled sea bass, is served under a silver dome. Be sure to try the house cocktail, black champagne covered

with floating rose pedals. ✉*Calle 16 between Avs. 1 and 5* ☎*984/803–2448* ▭*AE, MC, V* ⊗*No lunch.*

$$$–$$$$ ECLECTIC ✕**Ula-Gula.** As original as its name, this rooftop restaurant boldly experiments with a variety of textures, colors, and flavors. Chef Luis Aguilar puts together such ingenious appetizers as the carrot cannelloni in a warm Brie sauce. Unusual combinations in the entrées include the shrimp tempura with mango sorbet. For dessert, don't miss the liquid chocolate cake with chilled grapefruit—a truly exceptional dish. The decor is just as imaginative. Votive candles embedded in the stucco walls guide you up a wooden staircase. Over the tables are a traditional palapa roof and cone-shaped lamps made of rolled parchment paper. More conspicuous than the secluded restaurant is the street level bar by the same name. ✉*Av. 5 and Calle 10* ☎*984/879–3727* ▭*AE, MC, V* ⊗*No lunch.*

$$–$$$ ECLECTIC ✕**Alux Restaurant & Lounge.** Although this restaurant is 15 to 20 minutes from downtown, its location in an actual underground cavern makes it extremely popular. A rock stairway lighted by candles leads to a setting that's part Carlsbad Caverns, part *The Flintstones.* Some of the "cavernous" rooms are for lounging, some for drinking, some for eating, some for dancing (night club vibe kicks up at night); creative lighting casts the stalactites and stalagmites in pale shades of violet, blue, and pink. Although the food is mediocre compared to the atmosphere, you shouldn't miss this one-of-a-kind place. ✉*Av. Juárez, Colonia Ejidal* ☎*984/803–2936* ▭*MC, V* ⊗*No lunch.*

$$–$$$ SEAFOOD ★ ✕**Blue Lobster.** You can choose your dinner live from a tank here, and if it's grilled, you pay by the weight—a small lobster costs $15, while a monster will set you back $100. At night, the candlelit dining room draws a good crowd. People come not only for the lobster but also for the ceviche, mussels, or jumbo shrimp. Ask for a table on the terrace overlooking the street. ✉*Calle 12 and Av. 5* ☎*984/873–1360* ▭*AE, MC, V.*

$$–$$$ CONTINENTAL ✕**John Gray's Place.** After the success of his restaurant in nearby Puerto Morelos, chef John Gray opened this small place in the heart of Playa del Carmen. Stop in for a drink at the well-stocked downstairs bar or head upstairs to the enjoy some of the finest dining in the city. The pasta in rich cheese sauce with grilled shrimp and truffle oil is an excellent option. The menu is constantly changing, so ask about the daily special. ✉*Calle Corazón, just off Av. 5, between Calles 12 and 14* ☎*984/803–3689* ▭*MC, V* ⊗*Closed Sun. No lunch.*

$$–$$$ MEXICAN ★ ✕**Yaxche.** One of Playa's best restaurants has reproductions of stelae (stone slabs with carved inscriptions) from famous ruins, and murals of Mayan gods and kings. Mayan dishes such as *halach winic* (chicken in a spicy four-pepper sauce) are superb, and you can finish your meal with a Café Maya (made from Kahlúa, brandy, vanilla, and Xtabentun, the local liqueur flavored with anise and honey). Watching the waiter light it and pour it from its silver demitasse is almost as seductive as the drink itself. ✉*Calle 8 and Av. 5* ☎*984/873–2502* ▭*AE, MC, V.*

$–$$ VEGETARIAN ✕**Casa Tucan.** This sidewalk restaurant may be small—it has only 10 tables—but its refined Italian, Swiss, and Greek dishes are top-notch. Everything on the menu is fresh; even the herbs are homegrown. The spanakopita and lasagna are especially good. ✉ *Calle 4 between Avs. 10 and 15* ☎ *984/873–3459* ▭ *No credit cards.*

¢–$ CAFÉ ✕ **Java Joe's.** This is one of Playa's favorite coffee spots, where you can buy your joe by the cup or by the kilo. You can also indulge in Joe's "hangover special"—an English muffin, Canadian bacon, and a fried egg—if you've had a Playa kind of night. There are also 16 types of bagels to choose from, along with other baked goodies and pastries. ✉ *Calle 10 between Avs. 5 and 10* ☎ *984/876–2694* ▭ *No credit cards.*

WHERE TO STAY

$$$$ **Mandarin Oriental Riviera Maya.** Blending Mayan and Asian traditions, the soul of this extraordinary resort is the 25,000-square-foot spa at the center of the property. After settling into a two-story bungalow, you consult with a "lifestyle guru" who recommends a personalized regimen. Shaded by paper parasols, you are escorted to the Mandela Garden, where a circular path blooms with Chinese herbs. There, customized selections are harvested and then infused into aromatic teas and massage oils. Perfect for honeymooners, the spa offers numerous treatments for couples. Extending over the mangroves are winding pathways leading to the bungalows, all rising atop bamboo stilts. Standard rooms have Asian influences like rice-paper walls, onyx sinks, and rain-forest showers. You can explore the property either by boat or by golf cart. **Pros:** Attentive staff, high-tech gadgets in the rooms, innovative architecture. **Cons:** Organized excursions are pricey, murky ocean water strewn with seaweed, overpriced spa treatments. ✉ *Carretera Federal 307, Km 298.8 77710* ☎ *984/877–3888* 🌐 *www.mandarinoriental.com* *128 rooms* *In-room: Safe, kitchen (some), Wi-Fi. In-hotel: 4 restaurants, room service, bar, pools, spa, gym, beachfront, diving, water sports, children's program (4–12), laundry service, public Wi-Fi* ▭ *AE, MC, V.*

$$$$ **Mosquito Blue Hotel and Spa.** Casual, exotic, and elegant, the interiors at this hotel have Indonesian decor, mahogany furniture, and soft lighting. Most rooms have king-size beds and great views. The courtyard bar is a soothing spot—it's sheltered by a thatch roof and pastel walls, near one of the swimming pools. The spa offers services like Mayan healing baths. **Pros:** Access to Mosquito Beach, in the heart of Playa del Carmen, spotless rooms. **Cons:** All-inclusive bracelet must be worn at all times, hotel's billiards area tends to get loud at night. ✉ *Calle 12 between Avs. 5 and 10, 77710* ☎ *984/873–1245* 🌐 *www.mosquitoblue.com* *45 rooms, 1 suite* *In-room: Safe. In-hotel: Restaurant, bar, pools, spa, diving, laundry service, no kids under 16, no elevator* ▭ *AE, MC, V.*

$$$$ **Rosewood Mayakoba.** Marking the entrance to this peaceful oasis is a platinum gate. Meandering trails lead through the 1,600-acre grounds to the main building, where a spiraling limestone staircase descends to a network of lagoons. Here you set sail on a thatch-roofed boat to your private sanctuary. Lily-strewn waters create an exotic labyrinth, leading to 128 suites with jungle or ocean views. In keeping with the contemporary Mexican motif, the villas are crafted from indigenous materials such as wood and limestone. Each features a garden shower, a plunge pool, a private boat dock, and a rooftop sundeck. The golf

course is host to the newest stop on the PGA tour. Despite its elegant atmosphere, the resort is welcoming to families, and offers free accommodations to children under 12. **Pros:** 24-hour butler service, private plunge pools, extraordinary spa. **Cons:** Poor concierge service, limited food options. ✉*Carretera Federal, Km 298,* ☎*984/875–0000 or 998/287–4202* 🌐*www.rosewoodmayakoba.com* *128 suites* *In-room: Safe, DVD, Wi-Fi. In-hotel: 2 restaurants, room service, bar, golf course, pools, spa, gym, beachfront, diving, water sports, children's program (4–11), public Wi-Fi* ▭*MC, V*

$$$ **Hotel Básico.** This ultra-hip hotel has won awards for its innovative design. You'll find imaginatively recycled materials all over the hotel, from the used tires laid down to create the spongy lobby floor to the rooftop lounge chairs made from boxes that were once pickup truck beds. The roof also has two small pools made of recycled oil tanks, and a small bar where Playa's young and hip meet up with hotel guests for late-night drinks. Guest rooms, though equipped with plasma TVs and DVD players, are designed to look very basic, with plain cement walls, exposed plumbing, and floating beds. All come with retro amenities like beach balls, swim fins, and Polaroid cameras. **Pros:** Environmentally friendly, great rooftop lounge, innovative design. **Cons:** Limited storage space, extra charge for in-room amenities, late-night noise. ✉*Av. 5 at Calle 10 Norte, 77710* ☎*984/879–4448* 🌐*www.hotelbasico.com* *In-room: Refrigerator, DVD. In-hotel: Safe, Wi-Fi, restaurant, room service, bar, laundry service* ▭*AE, MC, V.*

$$ **Molcas.** Steps from the ferry docks, this colonial-style hotel has been in business since the early 1980s. Over the past few decades it has aged gracefully. Rooms have dark-wood furniture and face the pool, the sea, or the street. The second-floor pool area is glamorous, with white umbrellas. Although it's in the heart of town, the hotel is well insulated from noise, and the price is reasonable. **Pros:** Affordable rates, near the beach. **Cons:** No-frills rooms, no soap in bathrooms, pool bar seldom open. ✉*Av. 5 and Calle 1 Sur, 77710* ☎*984/873–0070* 🌐*www.molcas.com.mx* *25 rooms* *In-room: Refrigerator. In-hotel: Bar, pool, safe, beachfront, no elevator* ▭*MC, V.*

$–$$ **Hacienda del Caribe.** This hotel evokes an old Yucatecan hacienda—albeit a colorful one—with wrought-iron balconies, stained-glass windows, and Talavera tile work. Rooms have such unique details as headboards with calla-lily motifs and painted tile sinks. The beach is half a block away. **Pros:** Creative architecture, near the beach and bus depot. **Cons:** Street noise, musty bathrooms, breakfast costs extra. ✉*Calle 2 between Avs. 5 and 10, 77710* ☎*984/873–3130* 🌐*www.haciendadelcaribe.com* *29 rooms, 5 suites* *In-room: Safe. In-hotel: Pool, no elevator* ▭*MC, V.*

$ ★ **Casa Tucan.** For the price, it's hard to beat this warm, eclectic, hotel a few blocks from the beach. Mexican fabrics decorate the cheerful rooms and apartments, and the property has a yoga palapa, a TV bar, a book exchange, and a specially designed pool that's used for instruction at the on-site dive center. Cabanas with a shared bathroom are also available for diving students. **Pros:** Multilingual staff, pretty pool, exceptional restaurant. **Cons:** Not all rooms have air-conditioning.

⊠Calle 4 between Avs. 10 and 15, 77710 ☏984/873–0283 ⊕www.casatucan.de ⇨24 rooms, 4 apartments, 7 cabanas ♁In-room: No a/c (some), no phone, no TV. In-hotel: Restaurant, bar, pool, diving, no elevator ▭*MC, V.*

PLAYACAR

$$$$ **Iberostar Tucan and Quetzal.** This unique all-inclusive resort has preserved its natural surroundings—among the resident animals are flamingos, turtles, toucans, and monkeys. Landscaped pool areas surround the open-air restaurant and reception area. Spacious rooms have cheerful color schemes and patios overlooking dense vegetation. **Pros:** Oceanfront rooms, tropical setting, separate areas for families and singles. **Cons:** Restaurants keep serving the same dishes. *⊠Fracc. Playacar, Playacar, ☏984/887–2000 ⊕www.iberostar.com ⇨700 rooms ♁In-room: Safe, refrigerator. In-hotel: 5 restaurants, room service, bars, tennis courts, pools, gym, spa, beachfront, diving, water sports, concierge, children's programs (ages 4–12), laundry service, parking (no fee)* ▭*AE, D, MC, V* ¶◎¶*AI.*

$$$$ ★ **Royal Hideaway.** On a breathtaking stretch of beach, this 13-acre resort has exceptional amenities and superior service. Art and artifacts from around the world fill the lobby, and streams, waterfalls, and fountains dot the grounds. Rooms are in two- and three-story colonial-style villas, each with its own concierge. Gorgeous rooms have two queen-sized beds, sitting areas, and ocean-view terraces. **Pros:** Romantic setting, attentive service, the ultimate in pampering. **Cons:** Not family-friendly, beach never fully recovered from hurricane damage. *⊠Fracc. Playacar, Lote 6, Playacar, ☏984/873–4500 or 800/858–2258 ⊕www.royalhideaway.com ⇨192 rooms, 8 suites ♁In-room: Dial-up. In-hotel: 5 restaurants, bars, tennis courts, pools, spa, beachfront, water sports, bicycles, no elevator, concierge, laundry service, parking (no fee), no kids under 13* ▭*AE, MC, V* ¶◎¶*AI.*

NIGHTLIFE

The area's largest dance club, **Bali** (*⊠Calle 12 Norte, Playa del Carmen ☏984/803–2863*) can accommodate up to 800 people. The multilevel club offers the latest hits mixed by resident spinmaster DJ Carlos. The cover charge is $10.

Bar Ranita (*⊠Calle 10 between Avs. 5 and 10 ☏984/873–0389*), a cozy alcove, is run by a Swedish couple that really knows how to party. The prices are unbeatable, and the margaritas pack a powerful punch.

El Cielo (*⊠Calle 12 between Avs. 1 and 5, Playa del Carmen ☏984/141–3731*) is the area's newest party spot. This trendy venue is divided into a street-level bar, a rooftop terrace, and a dance club. Each section has its own DJ spinning everything from house and hip-hop to disco and techno. The patent-leather sofas are a great place to chill out.

★ DJs spin disco nightly at the **Deseo Lounge** (*⊠Av. 5 at Calle 12, Playa del Carmen ☏984/879–3620 www.hoteldeseo.com*), a rooftop bar and local hot spot.

Diablita (✉ *Calle 12 between Avs. 5 and 1, Playa del Carmen* ☎ *984/803-3695*) is a popular palapa bar. The open-air setting is the perfect place to people-watch while a DJ spins until 3 AM.

Kartabar (✉ *Calle 12 at Av. 1, Playa del Carmen* ☎ *984/873–2228*) has a laid-back vibe. The sweet scent of strawberry, mint, apple, and rose waft from the hookah pipes as belly dancers weave between the tables. The house martini is sinfully divine.

At **Mambo Cafe** (✉ *Calle 6 between Avs. 5 and 10, Playa del Carmen* ☎ *984/879–2304*) a dance review begins at 9:30 every night, followed by live salsa music. A younger crowd of locals and tourists typically fills the dance floor.

SHOPPING

Avenida 5 between Calles 4 and 10 is the best place to shop along the coast. Boutiques sell folk art and textiles from around Mexico, and clothing stores carry lots of sarongs and beachwear made from Indonesian batiks. A shopping area called Calle Corazon, between Calles 12 and 14, has a pedestrian street, art galleries, restaurants, and boutiques.

15

CLOTHING

★ The retro '70s-style fashions at **Blue Planet** (✉ *Av. 5 between Calles 10 and 12* ☎ *984/803–1504*) are great for a day at the beach. **Crunch** (✉ *Av. 5 between Calles 6 and 8* ☎ *984/873–1240*) sells high-style evening gowns, swimsuits, and sportswear for women. **Xbaal** (✉ *Av. 5 and Calle 14* ☎ *984/803–4107*) is filled with attractive men's and women's cotton shirts, woven skirts, and stylish sundresses.

CRAFTS

At **La Hierbabuena Artesania** (✉ Av. 5 between Calles 8 and 10 ☎ *984/873–1741*)owner Melinda Burns offers a collection of fine Mexican clothing and crafts.

★ **La Calaca** (✉ *Av. 5 between Calles 12 and 14* ☎ *984/873–0174*) has an eclectic selection of wooden masks, whimsically carved angels and devils, and other crafts. **Maya Arts Gallery** (✉ *Av. 5 between Calles 6 and 8* ☎ *984/879–3389*) has an extensive collection of *huipiles*, the embroidered cotton dresses worn by Mayan women in Mexico and Guatemala.

JEWELRY

Ambar Mexicano (✉ *Av. 5 between Calles 4 and 6* ☎ *984/873–2357*) has amber jewelry crafted by a local designer who imports the amber from Chiapas. **Lapis** (✉ *Carretera Federal 307, Km 269* ☎ *984/877–4150*) has one of the largest selections of jewelry on the coast.**Opals Mine** (✉ *Av. 5 between Calles 4 and 6* ☎ *984/879–5041* ✉ *Av. 5 and Calle 12* ☎ *984/803–3658*) has fire, white, pink, and orange opals from Jalisco State. You can buy loose stones or commission pieces of custom jewelry. **Santa Prisca** (✉ *Av. 5 between Calles 2 and 4* ☎ *984/873–0960*) has silver jewelry, flatware, trays, and decorative items from the town of Taxco. Some pieces are set with semiprecious stones.

MALLS

Centro Maya (✉ *Carretera Federal 2100* ☎ *984/803–9057*) has Soriana, Mexico's large retail outlet, and more than 50 other stores. **Paseo del Carmen** (✉ *Av 10 and Calle 1* ☎ *984/803–3789*) is an open-air shopping mall with a number of boutiques, including Diesel, Ultrafemme, and American Apparel. Caffeine junkies can get their fix at the Starbucks that dominates the center of the mall. A cobblestone path makes this one of the area's most popular and pleasant shopping destinations. **Plaza Las Americas** (✉ *Carretera Federal* ☎ *984/109–2161*) is a family-friendly mall featuring restaurants, shops, and cinemas.

SPORTS & THE OUTDOORS

ADVENTURE TOURS

Alltournative (✉ *Carretera Federal 307, Km 287, Playa del Carmen* ☎ *984/803–9999* 🌐 *www.alltournative.com*) will have you feeling like Indiana Jones in no time. Ranging in price from $76 to $112, trips offered by this company focus on ecological preservation and Mexican culture. You can kayak through a lagoon, snorkel in a cenote, or zip-line above a lush jungle. The company also organizes trips to Mayan communities.

South of Playa del Camen, **Punta Venado,** (✉ *Carretera Federal 307, Calica* ☎ *998/887–1191 or 800/503–0046* 🌐 *www.puntavenado.com*) offers adventure tours in all-terrain vehicles, on mountain bikes, or in jeeps. The 2.5 mi of isolated coastline are perfect for horseback riding, snorkeling or kayaking. Combined packages range from $57 to $90.

Yucatán Sky Explorer (✉ *Playa del Carmen Airport, Playa del Carmen* ☎ *984/873–1626* 🌐 *www.playatoursdirect.com*) will take you on an exhilarating aerial tour above the Caribbean's turquoise waters. Operated by a licensed pilot, the motorized hang gliders comfortably seat two people. The 25-minute trips cost $99 per person.

GOLF

Playa del Carmen's golf course is an 18-hole, par-72 championship course designed by Robert von Hagge. The greens fee is $180; there's also a special twilight fee of $120. Information is available from the **Casa Club de Golf** (☎ *984/873–0624 or 998/881–6088*). The **Golf Club at Playacar** (✉ *Paseo Xaman-Ha and Mz. 26, Playacar* ☎ *984/873–4990* 🌐 *www.palaceresorts.com)* has an 18-hole course; the greens fee is $190 and the twilight fee $130.

HORSEBACK RIDING

Two-hour horseback rides along beaches and jungle trails are run by **Rancho Loma Bonita** (✉ Carretera Federal 307, Km 49 ☎ *998/887–5465*). The $79 fee includes lunch, drinks, and the use of the property's swimming pool and playground. Children under 5 are free.

SCUBA DIVING

The PADI-affiliated **Abyss** (✉ *Av. 1 between Calles 10 and 12* ☎ *984/873–2164* 🌐 *www.abyssdiveshop.com*) offers introductory courses and dive trips ($50 for one tank, $70 for two tanks).The friendly staff at **Diversity Diving** (✉ *Calle 24, between Avs. 5 and 10, Playa del Carmen*

☎984/803–1042 🌐*www.diversitydiving.com*) takes you out for dives at three different locations: open ocean, cenote, and lagoon. The trips cost $75 per person. The oldest shop in town, **Tank-Ha Dive Shop** (✉*Av. 5 between Calles 8 and 10* ☎*984/873–0302* 🌐*www.tankha.com*), has PADI-certified teachers and runs diving and snorkeling trips to the reefs and caverns. A one-tank dive costs $40; for a two-tank trip it's $70. Dive packages are also available.

★ **Yucatek Divers** (✉*Av. 15 Norte between Calles 2 and 4* ☎*984/803–2836* 🌐*www.yucatek-divers.com*), which is affiliated with PADI, specializes in cenote dives, dive packages, and dives for those with disabilities. Introductory courses start at $90 for a one-tank dive and go as high as $395 for a four-day beginner course in open water.

PUERTO MORELOS

15

7 km (4½ mi) north of Punta Brava.

The sleeping beauty is awakening. For years Puerto Morelos was known only for being the coastal town where the car ferry departed for Cozumel. Over the past decade, this cargo port has morphed into the gateway to the Riviera Maya. About halfway between Cancún and Playa del Carmen, Puerto Morelos makes a great base for exploring the region. The town itself is small but colorful, with a central plaza surrounded by shops and restaurants. The pace is slow, the vibe is relaxed, and the atmosphere bohemian enough to attract a cluster of artists, painters, and poets. Its trademark is a leaning lighthouse. But despite these charms, Puerto Morelos lacks authentic Mexican charm, as do many of the villages throughout the Yucatán.

EXPLORING

The biologists running the **Croco-Cun** (✉*Carretera 307, Km 30* ☎*998/850–3719* 🌐*www.crococunzoo.com*), an animal farm just north of Puerto Morelos, have collected specimens of many of the reptiles and some of the mammals indigenous to the area. They offer immensely informative tours—you may even get to handle a baby crocodile or feed a deer. Be sure to wave hello to the 500-pound crocodile secure in his deep pit. The farm is open daily 9 to 5. Admission is $17.

South of Puerto Morelos, the 150-acre **Jardin Botanico del Dr. Alfredo Barrera Marín** (*[Dr. Alfredo Barrera Marín Botanical Garden]* ✉*Carretera 307, Km 33* ☎*998/206–9233*) is the largest botanical garden in Mexico. Named for a local botanist, the garden exhibits the peninsula's plants and flowers, which are labeled in English, Spanish, and Latin. The park features a 40-meter suspension bridge, three observation towers, and a library equipped with reading hammocks. There's also a tree nursery, a remarkable orchid and epiphyte garden, an authentic Mayan house, and an archaeological site. A nature walk goes directly through the mangroves for some great birding. More than 220 species have been identified here (be sure to bring the bug spray, though). Spider monkeys can usually be spotted in the afternoons, and a treehouse lookout offers a spectacular view—but the climb isn't for those afraid of heights. The park is open Monday to Saturday throughout the year, from 8 to 4 November to April and 9 to 5 May to October. Admission is $7.

A SACRED JOURNEY

In ancient times Puerto Morelos was a point of departure for pregnant Mayan women making pilgrimages by canoe to Cozumel, the sacred isle of the fertility goddess, Ixchel. Remnants of Mayan ruins survive along the coast here, although none of them have been restored.

WHERE TO EAT

$$–$$$$ MEXICAN ★ **John Gray's Kitchen.** The current home for this former Ritz-Carlton chef is set right against the jungle, and his cooking attracts a regular crowd of locals from Cancún and Playa del Carmen. Using only the freshest ingredients—from local fruits and vegetables to seafood right off the pier—Gray works his magic in a comfortable and contemporary setting that feels more Manhattan than Mayan. Don't miss the delicious tender roasted duck breast with tequila, *chipotle,* and honey. When in season, the *boquinete,* a local white fish grilled to perfection and served with mango salsa, is another great option. *Av. Niños Heroes, Lote 6 998/871–0665 MC, V Closed Sun. No lunch.*

$$–$$$$ MEXICAN **El Pirata.** A popular spot for breakfast, lunch, dinner, or just a drink from the bar, this open-air restaurant seats you at the center of the action on Puerto Morelos's town square. If you have a hankering for American food, you can get a good hamburger with fries here; there are also great daily specials. If you're lucky, they might include *pozole,* a broth made from cracked corn, pork, chilies, and bay leaves and served with tostada shells. *Av. Rafael E Melgar, Lote 4 998/871–0489 MC, V.*

$–$$$ MEXICAN ★ **Posada Amor.** This restaurant, the oldest in Puerto Morelos, has retained a loyal clientele for nearly three decades. In the palapa-covered dining room with its picnic-style wooden tables and benches, the gracious staff serves up terrific Mexican and seafood dishes, including a memorable whole fish dinner and a rich seafood bisque. Sunday brunches are also delicious. Live music, including Spanish guitar, can be heard every night at the patio bar. If Rogelio, the founder's congenial son, isn't calling you "friend" by the time you leave, you're probably having an off day. *Avs. Javier Rojo Gómez and Tulum 998/871–0033 AE, MC, V.*

¢ MEXICAN **Loncheria El Tio.** More like a hole in the wall than a restaurant, this short-order eatery is never empty and almost never closed. Yucatecan specialties such as *salbutes* (flour tortillas with shredded turkey, cabbage, tomatoes, and pickled onions) or *panuchos* (beans, chicken, avocado, and pickled onions on flour tortillas) will leave you satisfied, and you'll still have pesos left in your pocket. This is a great place to chuckle at the overdramatic *telenovellas* (soap operas) blaring from the TV in the corner. *Av. Rafael E. Melgar, Lote 2, across from main dock No phone No credit cards.*

WHERE TO STAY

$$$$ Fodor'sChoice ★ **Excellence Riviera Cancún.** A grand entrance leads to a Spanish marble lobby, where bellmen in pith helmets await. Rooms are similarly opulent: all have hot tubs, ornate Italianate furnishings, and private balconies. The property is centered around a luxurious spa and six meandering pools. After a relaxing spa treatment, sip margaritas under a beachside palapa or experience local culture at the traditional temazcal sauna. **Pros:** Caters to honeymooners, plenty of pool lounging space, rooms have private hot tubs for two. **Cons:** Food is bland, far from town. ✉ *Carretera Federal 307, Manzana 7, Lote 1,* ☎ *998/872–8500* 🌐 *www.excellence-resorts.com* *440 rooms* *In-room: Safe, DVD, dial-up. In-hotel: 8 restaurants, room service, bars, tennis courts, pools, gym, spa, beachfront, diving, water sports, concierge, no kids under 18* 💳 *AE, MC, V* *AI.*

¢ **Posada Amor.** In the early 1970s, the founder of this small, cozy downtown hotel dedicated it to the virtues of love *(amor).* Although he's since passed away, the founding philosophy has been upheld by his wife and children, who now run the property. Rooms are clean, small, and simple; all have private baths. The on-site restaurant serves delicious meals, the specialty being fresh fish, and on Sunday the breakfast buffet is not to be missed. The helpful staff makes you feel right at home. **Pros:** Excellent food, friendly staff, family-run business. **Cons:** No towels, rooms can get musty. ✉ *Avs. Javier Rojo Gómez and Tulum, 77580* ☎ *998/871–0033* *13 rooms* *In-room: No phone, no TV. In-hotel: Restaurant, bar, no elevator* 💳 *MC, V.*

SPORTS & THE OUTDOORS

Almost Heaven Adventures(✉ *Javier Rojo Gomez Mz 2, Lote 10* ☎ *998/871–0230* 🌐 *www.almostheavenadventures.com*), the oldest dive shop in the area, is the only one owned and operated by locals. Snorkeling trips cost $30, and reef dives cost $75. Night tours are especially popular in the summer, so book at least a day in advance.

Diving Dog Tours (☎ *998/201–9805 or 998/848–8819* 🌐 *www.puertomorelosfishing.com*) runs snorkeling trips at various sites on the Great Mesoamerican Reef for $25 per person. If you want to fish beyond the reef, a four-hour trip (for up to four people) costs $300.

A downtown restaurant, **Pelicanos** (✉ *Av. Rafael E. Melgar, Lote 2* ☎ *998/871–0014*) offers four-hour tours that include fishing, snorkeling, and cooking up the catch of the day. The tour cost is either $250 for a 27-foot boat or $300 for a 31-foot boat. Drinks and snacks on the boat are included. **Selvática** (✉ *Carretera 307, Km 321, 19 km from turnoff* ☎ *998/849–5510* 🌐 *www.selvatura.com.mx*), just outside the center of Puerto Morelos, offers tours over the jungle on more than 3 km (2 mi) of zip lines. The entire tour will take you a little over two hours, so you'll be glad to have a snack afterward in the on-site cafeteria. Mountain-biking tours are also available. If you want a taste of all the activities Selvática offers, you can go on a four-hour zip-line, biking, and swimming tour for $65. Advance reservations are required.

15

SHOPPING

Alma Libre Bookstore (✉*Av. Tulum* ☎*998/871–0713* 🌐*www.almalibrebooks.com*) has more than 20,000 titles in stock. You can trade in your own books for 25% of their cover prices here and replenish your holiday reading list. It's open October through June, Tuesday through Saturday 10 to 3 and 6 to 9, and on Sunday 4 to 9. Owners Robert and Joanne Birce are also great sources of information on local happenings.

★ The **Collectivo de Artesanos de Puerto Morelos** (*[Puerto Morelos Artists' Cooperative]* ✉*Avs. Javier Rojo Gómez and Isla Mujeres* ☎*No phone*) is a series of palapa-style buildings where local artisans sell their jewelry, hand-embroidered clothes, hammocks, and other items. You can sometimes find real bargains. It's open daily from 8 AM until dusk.

Jungle Market & Spa (✉*Calle 2* ☎*998/208–9148* 🌐*www.mayaecho.com*) is a nonprofit organization that generates income for Mayan women and their families. The Jungle Market features traditional dance, regional foods, and handmade crafts sold by Mayan women dressed in embroidered dresses. Between December and April the market takes place Sunday from 9:30 to 2. The spa offers traditional Mayan treatments such as hot-stone massages and aloe-vera body wraps. It's open Wednesday and Friday from 10:30 to 4.

Rosario & Marco's Art Shoppe (✉*Av. Javier Rojo Gómez 14* ☎*No phone*), close to the ferry docks, is run by the eponymous couple from their living room. They paint regional scenes such as markets, colonial homes, and flora and fauna, as well as portraits. Marco also creates replicas of Spanish galleons.

XCARET

11 km (6½ mi) south of Playa del Carmen.

Fodor'sChoice ★

Once a sacred Mayan city and port, Xcaret (pronounced *ish*-car-et) is now a 250-acre ecological theme park on a gorgeous stretch of coastline. Among its most popular attractions are the Paradise River raft tour that takes you on a winding, watery journey through the jungle; the Butterfly Pavilion, where thousands of butterflies float dreamily through a botanical garden while New Age music plays in the background; and an ocean-fed aquarium where you can see local sea life drifting through coral heads and sea fans without getting wet.

The park has a Wild Bird Breeding Aviary, nurseries for both abandoned flamingo eggs and sea turtles, and a series of underwater caverns that you can explore by snorkeling or snuba (a hybrid of snorkeling and scuba). Riding stables, which have been built to resemble a Mexican hacienda, offer trail rides through the jungle to see Mayan ruins. A replica Mayan village includes a colorful cemetery with catacomb-like caverns underneath; traditional music and dance ceremonies (including performances by the famed *Voladores de Papantla*—the Flying Birdmen of Papantla) are performed here at night. But the star show is the

SHOPPING

Galeria Lamanai Carribean Arts & Crafts (✉ *Carrertera 307, Km 104* ☎ *984/875–9055*) is a laid-back gallery under a palapa roof. There's a real mix of folk art and fine art from Mexican and international artists.

Mexicarte (✉ *Carrertera 307* ☎ *984/875–9115*) is a little shop that sells high-quality crafts from around the country.

SPORTS & THE OUTDOORS

★ The **Akumal Dive Center** (✉ *About 10 min north of Club Akumal Caribe* ☎ *984/875–9025* 🌐 *www.akumaldivecenter.com*) is the area's oldest and most experienced dive operation, offering reef or cenote diving, fishing, and snorkeling. Dives cost from $45 (one tank) to $120 (four tanks); a two-hour fishing trip for up to four people runs $125. Take a sharp right at the Akumal arches, and you'll see the dive shop on the beach.

TSA Travel Agency and Bike Rental (✉ *Carretera 307, Km 104, next to Ecology Center* ☎ *984/875–9030 or 984/875–9031* 🌐 *www.akumal-travel.com*) rents bikes for a 3½-hour jungle-biking adventure. The cost is $35 per person.

15

EN ROUTE

Hidden Worlds Cenotes Park. This park was made semifamous when it was featured in a 2002 IMAX film, *Journey into Amazing Caves,* which was shown at theaters across North America. The park, which was founded by Florida native Buddy Quattlebaum in 1998, contains some of the Yucatán's most spectacular cenotes. You can explore these startlingly clear freshwater sinkholes, which are full of fantastic stalactites, stalagmites, and rock formations, on guided diving or snorkeling tours. A particularly gorgeous cenote, Dream Gate, is also on the property; its underwater topography is so dazzling it's otherworldly. To get to the cenotes, you ride in a jungle buggy through dense tropical forest from the main park entrance. Prices start at $25 for snorkeling tours ($30 for children) and go up to $100 for diving tours. Canopying on the 600 foot zip line will set you back $10. Be sure to bring your bug spray. ✉ *7 km (4½ mi) south of Xel-Há on Carretera 307* ☎ *984/877–8535* 🌐 *www.hiddenworlds.com* ⏲ *Daily 9–5; snorkeling tours at 9, 11, 1, 2, and 3, and diving tours at 9, 11, and 1.*

TULUM

Fodor's Choice ★

61 km (38 mi) southwest of Playa del Carmen.

Tulum is a quickly growing town built near the spectacular ruins that bring most people here in the first place. The ruins are situated on a beach known around world for its sugar-white sand and turquoise water. At the beach you'll find lodgings that claim to be friendly to the environment, if not the wallet.

GETTING HERE & AROUND

You can also hire taxis in Cancún to go as far as Tulum, but the price is steep unless you have many passengers.

ESSENTIALS

Currency Exchange Asesores Turisticos Cambiarios del Caribe (✉ *Av. Tulum s/n* ☎ *984/871–2078*).

Internet El Point (✉ *Avs. Tulum and Alfa* ☎ *984/877–3044*

Mail & Shipping Main Post Office (✉ *Av. Tulum s/n* ☎ *984/871–2001*).

> **WORD OF MOUTH**
>
> "Your biggest problem with taking a collectivo to Tulum ruins and Xel-Há is that it will only drop you off on the highway entrance to these places, and it is quite a walk to the entrances."
>
> –AlwaysDreamin
>
> "For more snorkeling, check out Xel-Há. We were afraid it would be too 'amusement park'-like but it was lovely, with great snorkeling and a fun walk through the "jungle."
>
> –Saugatucker

EXPLORING

Spectacular **Tulum** (pronounced tool-*lum*) is the Yucatán Peninsula's most-visited Mayan ruin, attracting more than 2 million people annually. This means you have to share the site with roughly half of the tourist population of Quintana Roo on any given day, even if you arrive early. Though most of the architecture is of unremarkable postclassic (1000–1521) style, the amount of attention that Tulum receives is not entirely undeserved. Its location by the blue-green Caribbean is breathtaking.

TIP→ At the entrance you can hire a guide, but keep in mind that some of their information is more entertaining than historically accurate. (Disregard that stuff about virgin sacrifices atop the altars.)

Tulum is one of the few Mayan cities known to have been inhabited when the conquistadores arrived in 1518. In the 16th century it functioned as a safe harbor for trade goods from rival Mayan factions; it was considered neutral territory, where merchandise could be stored and traded in peace. The city reached its height when traders, made wealthy through the exchange of goods, for the first time outranked Mayan priests in authority and power. When the Spaniards arrived, they forbade the Mayan traders to sail the seas, and commerce among the Maya died.

Tulum has long held special significance for the Maya. A key city in the League of Mayapán (AD 987–1194), it was never conquered by the Spaniards, although it was abandoned about 75 years after the conquest. For 300 years thereafter it symbolized the defiance of an otherwise subjugated people; it was one of the last outposts of the Maya during their insurrection against Mexican rule in the War of the Castes, which began in 1846. Uprisings continued intermittently until 1935, when the Maya ceded Tulum to the government.

The first significant structure is the two-story **Templo de los Frescos,** to the left of the entryway. The temple's vault roof and corbel arch are examples of classic Mayan architecture. Faint traces of blue-green frescoes outlined in black on the inner and outer walls refer to ancient Mayan beliefs (the clearest frescoes are hidden from sight now that you can't walk into the temple). Reminiscent of the Mixtec style, the frescoes depict the three worlds of the Maya and their major deities, and are decorated with stellar and serpentine patterns, rosettes, and ears of maize and other offerings to the gods. One scene portrays the rain god seated on a four-legged animal—probably a reference to the Spaniards on their horses.

The largest and most famous building, the **Castillo** (Castle), looms at the edge of a 40-foot limestone cliff just past the Temple of the Frescoes. Atop it, at the end of a broad stairway, is a temple with stucco ornamentation on the outside and traces of fine frescoes inside the two chambers. (The stairway has been roped off, so the top temple is inaccessible.) The front wall of the Castillo has faint carvings of the Descending God and columns depicting the plumed serpent god, Kukulcán, who was introduced to the Maya by the Toltecs. To the left of the Castillo is the **Templo del Dios Descendente**—so called for the carving of a winged god plummeting to earth over the doorway.

A few small altars sit atop a hill at the north side of the cove and have a good view of the Castillo and the sea. On the highway about 4 km (2½ mi) south of the ruins is the present-day village of Tulum. As Tulum's importance as a commercial center increases, markets, restaurants, shops, services, and auto-repair shops continue to spring up along the road. Growth hasn't been kind to the pueblo, however: it's rather unsightly, with a wide four-lane highway running down the middle. Despite this blight, it has a few good restaurants. *$9 Daily 8–5.*

WHERE TO EAT

$$–$$$ ITALIAN ★ **Il Giardino Ristorante Italiano.** This cozy café is like an outpost of Italy on the Caribbean Coast. A few tables are nestled under a palapa with a tile floor; there's also outdoor seating in a garden. Many of the dishes contain fresh fish; the grilled calamari in a lemon-and-white-wine sauce is wonderful, as is the spaghetti marinara with mixed seafood. For a Mexican twist, try the risotto with *chaya* (a type of spinach) and cheese. Be sure to leave room for dessert, too: the tiramisu is divine. ✉ *Avs. Satelite and Sagitario, first road to west as you enter Tulum* ☎ *984/806–3601 or 984/114–2103* *No credit cards.*

$$ ARGENTINE **El Pequeño Buenos Aires.** Owner and chef Sergio Patrone serves delicious *parrilladas* (a mixed grill made with marinated chicken, beef, and pork) at this Argentine-inspired restaurant. There are Italian dishes, too, as well as a nice selection of wines. White tablecloths add a sophisticated touch, even though you're eating under a palapa roof. ✉ *Av. Tulum 42* ☎ *984/871–2708* *MC, V.*

$–$$ MEXICAN ★ **Charlie's.** This eatery is a happening spot where local artists display their talents. Wall murals are made from empty wine bottles, and painted chili peppers adorn the dining tables. There's a charming garden in back with a stage for live music. The chicken tacos and black-bean soup are especially good here. ✉ *Avs. Tulum and Jupiter, across from bus station* ☎ *984/871–2573* *MC, V* *Closed Mon.*

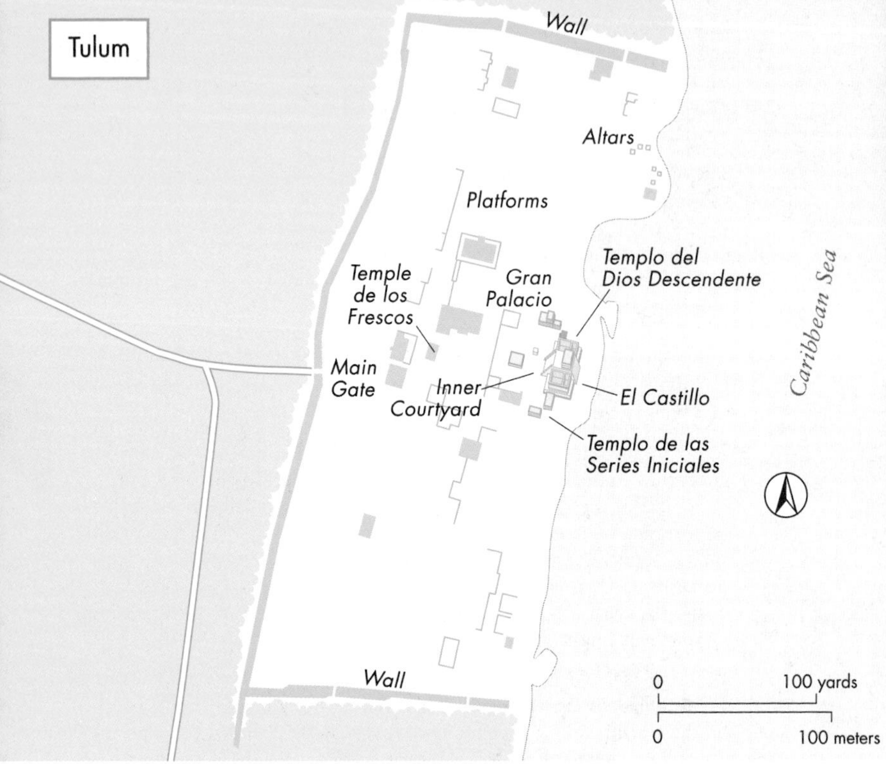

WHERE TO STAY

$$$$ ★ **Eurostars Blue Tulum.** From the lush tropical plants and crashing waterfall at the hotel entrance, to the gorgeous rooms with private hot tubs, this all-inclusive offers luxury and relaxation everywhere you look. There are nearly 100 rooms, but the hotel is divided into smaller buildings that give it a very personal feel. Rooms are spacious and hasve high-tech touches like flat-screen TVs and a DVD player and selection of DVDs (just fill out the request form). The restaurants feature international chefs who are happy to prepare anything you request, whether or not it is on the menu. There are plenty of other things that you can request—including different kinds of pillows and bath products—at no extra cost. **Pros:** Incredible service, attention to detail, beautiful grounds. **Cons:** Not on the beach. ✉ *Carretera Tulum Ruinas, Lote 47,* ☎ *984/871–1000, 866/636–4882 in U.S.* 🌐 *www.eurostarshotels.com* *96 rooms* *In-room: Safe, refrigerator, DVD, Wi-Fi. In-hotel: 4 restaurants, bar, pool, spa, beachfront, no elevator* *AE, MC, V.*

$$$–$$$$ **Mezzanine.** Music lovers will enjoy this small, hip hotel where DJs mix lounge and house music on the patio. On Friday evenings this is the place to be, as guest musicians entertain until 2 AM. Each of the four attractive suites, decorated with dark modern furniture and splashes of bright color, offers an ocean view. The other rooms are on the ground floor. While they are pleasant, they have no view. There's wireless Inter-

net access in the restaurant and lounge. **Pros:** Tasty food, helpful staff. **Cons:** Pool area gets crowded, not all rooms have a view, noisy on weekends. ✉ *Carretera Tulum–Boca Paila, Km 1.5,* ☎ *984/804–1452* 🌐 *www.mezzanine.com.mx* *9 rooms* *In-room: No a/c, no phone, safe. In-hotel: Restaurant, bar, pool, beachfront, water sports, bicycles, public Wi-Fi* *No credit cards.*

WORD OF MOUTH

"In downtown Tulum, Charlie's is a lot of fun, especially on a Saturday night when they have live flamenco."

-zootsi

$$–$$$$ ★ **Las Ranitas.** Built for ecological sustainability, Las Ranitas (the Little Frogs) creates its own power through wind-powered generators and solar panels. Each chic, and very private, room has gorgeous tile and fabric from Oaxaca. Terraces overlook gardens and ocean, and jungle walkways lead to the breathtaking beach. The pièce de résistance is the on-site restaurant's French chef, who whips up tasty French and Mexican cuisine. Yoga classes are also available. **Pros:** On the beach, attractive rooms, lots of privacy. **Cons:** A bit pricey for what you get, inconsistent service. ✉ *Carretera Tulum–Boca Paila, Km 9; last hotel before Reserva de la Biosfera Sian Ka'an,* ☎ *984/877–8554* 🌐 *www.lasranitas.com* *18 rooms, 5 suites* *In-room: No a/c, no phone, no TV. In-hotel: Restaurant, pool, beachfront, water sports, no elevator, public Wi-Fi* *No credit cards.* *CP*

$$–$$$ **Zamas.** On the wild, isolated Punta Piedra (Rock Point), this hotel has ocean views as far as the eye can see. The romantically rustic cabanas—with mosquito nets over comfortable beds, spacious, tile bathrooms, and bright Mexican colors—are nicely distanced from one another. The restaurant, one of the area's best, has an eclectic Italian-Mexican-Yucatecan menu. **Pros:** Great restaurant, unspoiled views. **Cons:** Beach is rocky, on a noisy street. ✉ *Carretera Tulum–Boca Paila, Km 5,* ☎ *984/877–8523, 415/387–9806 in U.S.* 🌐 *www.zamas.com* *15 cabanas* *In-room: No a/c, no phone, safe. In-hotel: Restaurant, bar, beachfront, water sports, no elevator* *No credit cards.*

¢ **Weary Traveler Hostel, Cafe and Bar.** Tulum is backpacker central, and if you're roughing it, this is one of the cheapest, most convenient area spots to hang your hat. Most rooms are shared, with either bunk or twin beds and a private bath. Furnishings are basic but neat. You have use of a communal kitchen, and there are picnic tables in a central area for eating and meeting. A simple but plentiful breakfast is included in the price of the room. There's also a cheap Internet café, and the bus station is across the street. **Pros:** Reasonable rates, friendly atmosphere, great location. **Cons:** Rustic furniture, noise from bar. ✉ *Av. Tulum, between Avs. Jupiter and Acuario,* ☎ *984/871–2390* *10 rooms* *In-room: No a/c, no phone, kitchen, no TV. In-hotel: Restaurant, bar, public Internet, no elevator* *No credit cards* *BP.*

TANKAH

11 km (7 mi) northwest of Tulum.

Although in ancient times Tankah was an important Mayan trading city, over the past few centuries it has lain mostly dormant. That's beginning to change, though; a number of small, reasonably priced hotels have cropped up, and several expats who own villas in the area rent them out year-round. The wonderful ruins of Cobá and the Maya community of Pac Chen are nearby.

EXPLORING

Fodor's Choice ★ Mayan for "water stirred by the wind," **Cobá** flourished from AD 800 to 1100, with a population of as many as 55,000. Now it stands in solitude, and the jungle has overgrown many of its buildings. ■TIP➔**Cobá is often overlooked by visitors who opt for better-known Tulum. This site is less crowded, giving you a chance to immerse yourself in ancient culture.** Cobá exudes stillness, the silence broken by the occasional shriek of a spider monkey or the call of a bird. Processions of huge army ants cross the footpaths as the sun slips through openings between the tall hardwood trees, ferns, and giant palms.

Near five lakes and between coastal watchtowers and inland cities, Cobá (pronounced ko-*bah*) exercised economic control over the region through a network of at least 16 *sacbéob* (white-stone roads), one of which measures 100 km (62 mi) and is the longest in the Mayan world. The city once covered 70 square km (43 square mi), making it a noteworthy sister state to Tikal in northern Guatemala, with which it had close cultural and commercial ties. It's noted for its massive temple-pyramids, one of which is 138 feet tall, the largest and highest in northern Yucatán. The main groupings of ruins are separated by several miles of dense vegetation, so the best way to get a sense of the immensity of the city is to scale one of the pyramids. ■TIP➔**It's easy to get lost here, so stay on the main road; don't be tempted by the narrow paths that lead into the jungle unless you have a qualified guide with you.**

The first major cluster of structures, to your right as you enter the ruins, is the **Cobá Group,** whose pyramids are around a sunken patio. At the near end of the group, facing a large plaza, is the 79-foot-high temple, which was dedicated to the rain god, Chaac; some Mayan people still place offerings and light candles here in hopes of improving their harvests. Around the rear to the left is a restored ball court, where a sacred game was once played to petition the gods for rain, fertility, and other boons.

Farther along the main path to your left is the **Chumuc Mul Group,** little of which has been excavated. The principal pyramid here is covered with the remains of vibrantly painted stucco motifs (*chumuc mul* means "stucco pyramid"). A kilometer (½ mi) past this site is the **Nohoch Mul Group** (Large Hill Group), the highlight of which is the pyramid of the same name, the tallest at Cobá. It has 120 steps—equivalent to 12 stories—and shares a plaza with Temple 10. The Descending God (also seen at Tulum) is depicted on a facade of the temple atop Nohoch Mul, from which the view is excellent.

Beyond the Nohoch Mul Group is the **Castillo,** with nine chambers that are reached by a stairway. To the south are the remains of a ball court, including the stone ring through which the ball was hurled. From the main route follow the sign to **Las Pinturas Group,** named for the still-discernible polychrome friezes on the inner and outer walls of its large, patioed pyramid. An enormous stela here depicts a man standing with his feet on two prone captives. Take the minor path for 1 km (½ mi) to the Macanxoc Group, not far from the lake of the same name. The main pyramid at Macanxoc is accessible by a stairway.

Cobá is a 35-minute drive northwest of Tankah along a pothole-filled road that leads straight through the jungle. Buses depart to and from Cobá for Playa del Carmen and Tulum at least twice daily. Taxis from Tulum are about $16. *$4 Daily 8–5.*

Fodor's Choice ★ **Pac Chen** (pronounced pak chin) is a Mayan jungle settlement of 125 people who still live in round thatch huts; there's no electricity or indoor plumbing, and the roads aren't paved. The inhabitants, who primarily make their living farming pineapple, beans, and plantains, still pray to the gods for good crops. Alltournative also pays them by the number of tourists it brings in, though no more than 80 people are allowed to visit on any given day. This money has made the village self-sustaining, and has given the people an alternative to logging and hunting, which were their main means of livelihood before. **TIP→You can only visit Pac Chen on trips organized by Alltournative, an ecotour company based in Playa del Carmen. The unusual, soft-adventure experience is definitely worth your while.**

15

WHERE TO EAT

$$$ ECLECTIC **Restaurante Oscar y Lalo.** A couple of miles outside Tankah, alone on the pristine Bahía de Punta Soliman, sits this wonderful palapa restaurant with a sandy floor. The seafood is excellent here, although a bit pricey; Lalo's Special, a dish made with local lobster, shrimp, conch, fish, barracuda, and chicken fajitas, prepared for 2 to 10 people, is a standout. The ceviche made of fresh fish, lobster, and caracol with citrus juice is also exceptional. The beachfront here is picture perfect. If you're inspired to sleep on the beach, there are campsites with clean showers and bathrooms. *Carretera 307, north of Tankah, look for faded white sign 984/804–4189 No credit cards.*

¢–$ MEXICAN **El Bocadito.** The restaurant closest to the Cobá ruins is run by a gracious Mayan family that serves simple, traditional cuisine. A three-course fixed-price lunch costs $6. Look for such classic dishes as pollo pibíl and cochinita pibíl. There are also a few bare-bones rooms for $10 a night for those who want to stay close to the ruins. *On road to Cobá ruins, ½ km from ruin-site entrance 987/874–2087 No credit cards No dinner.*

SPORTS & THE OUTDOORS

★ The **Gorgonian Gardens,** an underwater environment that lies just offshore here, have made Tankah a particular destination for divers and snorkelers. From southern Tankah to Bahía de Punta Soliman, the sand-free ocean floor has allowed for the proliferation of Gorgonians, or soft corals—sea fans, candelabras, and fingers that can reach 5 feet in height—as well as a variety of colorful sponges. Fish love to feed here, and so many of them swarm the gardens that some divers have compared the experience to being surrounded by clouds of butterflies. Although this underwater habitat goes on for miles, Tankah is the best place to view it. The **Lucky Fish Dive Center** (☎*984/875–9367 or 984/804–5051* ⊕*www.luckyfishdiving.com*), at the Tankah Inn, runs dive trips to the Gorgonian Gardens, among other sites. Costs start at $40 for a one-tank dive. It also rents equipment.

RESERVA DE LA BIOSFERA SIAN KA'AN

Fodor's Choice ★

15 km (9 mi) south of Tulum to Punta Allen turnoff and within Sian Ka'an, 252 km north of Chetumal.

The Sian Ka'an ("where the sky is born," pronounced see-*an* caan) region is technically within the area known as the Costa Maya. It was first settled by the Maya in the 5th century AD. In 1986 the Mexican government established the 1.3-million-acre Reserva de la Biosfera Sian Ka'an as a protected area. The next year it was named a UNESCO World Heritage Site. The Riviera Maya and Costa Maya split the biosphere reserve; Punta Allen and north belong to the Riviera Maya, and everything south of Punta Allen is part of the Costa Maya.

The Sian Ka'an reserve constitutes 10% of the land in Quintana Roo, and covers 100 km (62 mi) of coast. Hundreds of species of local and migratory birds, fish, other animals and plants, and fewer than 1,000 residents (primarily May) share this area of freshwater and coastal lagoons, mangrove swamps, cays, savannas, tropical forests, and a barrier reef. There are approximately 27 ruins (none excavated) linked by a unique canal system—one of the few of its kind in the Mayan world in Mexico. This is one of the last undeveloped stretches of North American coast. There's a $4 entrance charge. To visit the sites, you must take a guided tour.

Many species of the once-flourishing wildlife have fallen into the endangered category, but the waters here still teem with rooster fish, bonefish, mojarra, snapper, shad, permit, sea bass, and crocodiles. Fishing the flats for wily bonefish is popular, and the peninsula's few lodges also run deep-sea fishing trips.

To explore on your own, follow the road past Boca Paila to the secluded 35-km (22-mi) coastal strip of land that's part of the reserve. You'll be limited to swimming, snorkeling, and camping on the beaches, as there are no trails into the surrounding jungle. The narrow, extremely rough dirt road down the peninsula is filled with monstrous potholes and after a rainfall is completely impassable. Don't attempt it unless you have four-wheel drive. Most fishing lodges along the way close for the rainy season in August and September, and accommodations are hard to come by. The road ends at Punta Allen, a fishing village whose main catch is spiny lobster, which was becoming scarce until ecologists taught the local fishing cooperative how to build and lay special traps to conserve the species. There are several small, expensive guesthouses.

If you haven't booked ahead, start out early in the morning so you can get back to civilization before dark.

Several kinds of tours, including bird-watching by boat and night kayaking to observe crocodiles, are offered on-site through the **Sian Ka'an Visitor Center** (☎ *998/884–3667, 998/884–9580, or 998/871–0709* 🌐 *www.cesiak.org*), which also offers five rooms with shared bath and one private suite for overnight stays. Prices range from $65 to $90, and meals are separate. The visitor center's observation tower offers the best view of the Sian Ka'an Biosphere from high atop their deck and wood bridge.

This photogenic archaeological site at the northern end of the Reserva de la Biosfera Sian Ka'an is underrated. Once known as Chunyaxché, it's now called by its ancient name, **Muyil** (pronounced mool-*hill*). It dates from the late preclassic era, when it was connected by road to the sea and served as a port between Cobá and the Mayan centers in Belize and Guatemala. A 15-foot-wide *sacbé,* built during the postclassic period, extended from the city to the mangrove swamp and was still in use when the Spaniards arrived.

Structures were erected at 400-foot intervals along the white limestone road, almost all of them facing west, but there are only three still standing. At the beginning of the 20th century the ancient stones were used to build a chicle (gum arabic) plantation, which was managed by one of the leaders of the War of the Castes. The most notable site at Muyil today is the remains of the 56-foot **Castillo**—one of the tallest on the Quintana Roo coast—at the center of a large acropolis. During excavations of the Castillo, jade figurines representing the moon and fertility goddess Ixchel were found. Recent excavations at Muyil have uncovered some smaller structures.

The ruins stand near the edge of a deep-blue lagoon, and are surrounded by almost impenetrable jungle—so be sure to bring bug repellent. You can drive down a dirt road on the side of the ruins to swim or fish in the lagoon. The bird-watching is also exceptional here. *$4, free Sun.* *Daily 8–5.*

Mérida & Environs

WITH CHICHÉN ITZÁ

Tourists climbing El Castillo (Pyramid of Kukulcán), Chichén Itzá

16

WORD OF MOUTH

"The best part of Mérida was just getting out and walking downtown. We met some wonderful people, had great food, and found some really interesting and eclectic shops."

–CozAnnie

"Merida en Domingo (Sundays) turns the entire downtown into an open air concert with dancing and many bands playing in different parks and streets."

–Cimbrone

www.fodors.com/forums

WELCOME TO MÉRIDA & ENVIRONS

TOP REASONS TO GO

★ **Visiting spectacular Maya ruins:** Chichén Itzá and Uxmal are two of the largest, most beautiful sites in the region.

★ **Living like a wealthy hacendado:** You can stay in a restored henequen (sisal) plantation-turned-hotel and delight in its old-world charm.

★ **Browsing at fantastic craft markets:** This region is known for its handmade hamacas (hammocks), piñatas, and other local handicrafts.

★ **Swimming in the secluded, pristine freshwater cenotes:** These sinkholes, like portals to the underworld, are scattered throughout the inland landscape.

★ **The chance to taste the diverse flavors of Yucatecan food:** Mérida has 50-odd restaurants, which serve up local specialties like fish stews and Mayan-originated dishes like pollo pibíl (chicken cooked in banana leaves).

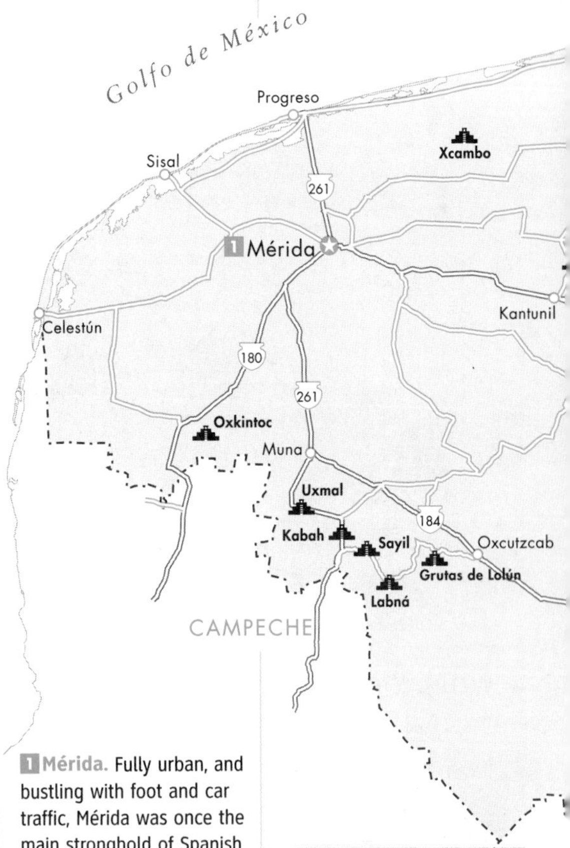

Golfo de México
Progreso
Xcambo
Sisal
261
1 Mérida
Kantunil
Celestún
180
261
Oxkintoc
Muna
Uxmal
184
Kabah
Sayil
Oxcutzcab
Grutas de Lolún
Labná
CAMPECHE

1 Mérida. Fully urban, and bustling with foot and car traffic, Mérida was once the main stronghold of Spanish colonialism in the peninsula. Tucked among the restaurants, museums and markets are grand, old, beautifully ornamented mansions and buildings that recall the city's heyday as the wealthiest capital in Mexico.

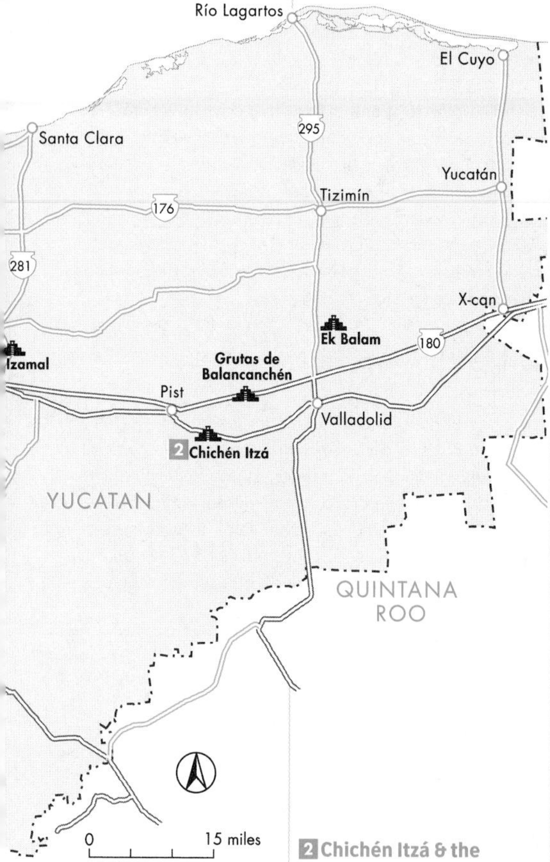

Río Lagartos
El Cuyo
Santa Clara
295
Yucatán
Tizimín
176
281
X-can
Ek Balam
180
Izamal
Grutas de Balancanchén
Pist
Valladolid
2 Chichén Itzá
YUCATAN
QUINTANA ROO
0 15 miles
0 25 km

GETTING ORIENTED

Yucatán State's topography has more in common with that of Florida and Cuba—with which it was probably once connected—than with central Mexico. Exotic plants like wild ginger and spider lilies grow in the jungles; vast flamingo colonies nest at coastal estuaries. Human history is evident everywhere here—in looming Franciscan missions, thatch-roofed adobe huts, and the majestic ruins of ancient Mayan cities.

2 Chichén Itzá & the Mayan Interior. Yucatán's spectacular Mayan ruins are famous all over the world. The best-known, Chichén Itzá, draws thousands of visitors every year. Farther south is the less-known but beautiful site of Uxmal. Many smaller archaeological sites—some hardly visited—lie along the Ruta Puuc south of Mérida.

MÉRIDA & ENVIRONS PLANNER

When to Go

As with many other places in Mexico, the weeks around Christmas and Easter are peak times for visiting Yucatán State. Making reservations up to a year in advance is not over the top.

If you like music and dance, Mérida hosts its Otoño Cultural, or Autumn Cultural Festival, during the last week of October and first week of November. Free and inexpensive classical-music concerts, dance performances, and art exhibits take place almost nightly at theaters and open-air venues around the city.

Thousands of people, from international sightseers to Maya shamans, swarm Chichén Itzá on the vernal equinox (the first day of spring). On this particular day, the sun creates a shadow that looks like a snake—meant to evoke the ancient Maya serpent god, Kukulcán—that moves slowly down the side of the main pyramid. If you're planning to witness it, make your travel arrangements many months in advance.

How Long to Stay

You should plan to spend at least five days in Yucatán. It's best to start your trip with a few days in Mérida; the weekends, when streets are closed to traffic and there are lots of free outdoor performances, are great times to visit. You should also budget enough time to take day trips to the sites of Chichén Itzá and Uxmal; visiting Mérida without traveling to at least one of these sites is like going to the beach and not getting out of the car.

Mérida Carriage Tours

One of the best ways to get a feel for the city of Mérida is to hire a *calesa*—a horse-drawn carriage. You can hail one of these at the main square or, during the day, at Palacio Cantón, site of the archaeology museum on Paseo de Montejo. Some of the horses look dispirited, but others are fairly well cared for. Drivers charge about $13 for an hour-long circuit around downtown and up Paseo de Montejo, and $22 for an extended tour.

How's the Weather?

Rainfall and humidity are greatest between June and October. The coolest months are December–February, when it can get chilly in the evenings. April and May are usually the hottest, as both heat and humidity begin to build unbearably prior to rainy season. Hurricane season is late September through early November.

WHAT IT COSTS IN DOLLARS

¢	$	$$	$$$	$$$$
Restaurants				
under $5	$5–$10	$10–$15	$15–$25	over $25
Hotels				
under $50	$50–$75	$75–$150	$150–$250	over $250

Restaurant prices are per person, for a main course at dinner, excluding tax and tip. Hotel prices are for a standard double room in high season.

MÉRIDA

Updated by Michele Joyce

TRAVELERS TO MÉRIDA ARE A loyal bunch, who return again and again to their favorite restaurants, neighborhoods, and museums. The hubbub of the city can seem frustrating—especially if you've just spent a peaceful few days on the coast or visiting Mayan sites—but as the cultural and intellectual hub of the peninsula, Mérida is rich in art, history, and tradition.

A two- to three-hour group tour of the city, including museums, parks, public buildings, and monuments, costs $20 to $35 per person. Free guided tours are offered daily by the Municipal Tourism Department. These depart from City Hall, on the main plaza, at 9:30 AM.

There have also been recent reports of vendors increasing the prices of their art and crafts by the hundreds, claiming that the value of their wares is far greater than it really is. Most vendors are honest, so just be sure to shop around and acquaint yourself with the kinds of crafts, and the levels of quality, that are available. Once you have an idea of what's out there, you'll be much better able to spot fraud, and you may even have some fun bargaining.

GETTING HERE & AROUND

Mérida's airport, Aeropuerto Manuel Crescencio Rejón, is 7 km (4½ mi) west of the city on Avenida Itzáes. For travel outside the city, ADO and UNO have direct buses to many coastal cities and ruins; they depart from the first-class CAME bus station. Regional bus lines to intermediate or more out-of-the-way destinations leave from the second-class terminal. City buses charge about 40¢ (4 pesos). The minimum fare for a taxi is $3, which should get you from one downtown location to another. A newer fleet of metered taxis has recently started running in Mérida; their prices are usually cheaper than the ones charged by regular cabs. Just look for the "Taximetro" signs on top of the cars. The tourism office recommends these because the price depends exclusively on how far the taxi has traveled, so the rate is fair.

ESSENTIALS

Bus Contacts **Autobuses de Occidente** (✉ *Calles 50 and 67, Centro* ☎ *999/924-8391 or 999/924-9741* 🌐 *www.ado.com.mx*). **CAME** (First Class Terminal)(✉ *Calle 70 No. 555, at Calle 71, Centro* ☎ *999/924-9130*).

Currency Exchange **Banamex** (✉ *Calle 59 No. 485* ☎ *01800/226-2639 toll-free in Mexico* 🌐 *www.banamex.com*). **Banorte** (✉ *Calle 58 No. 524, between Calles 63 and 65, Centro* ☎ *999/926-6060* 🌐 *www.banorte.com*). **HSBC** (✉ *Paseo Montejo 467A, Centro* ☎ *999/942-2378* 🌐 *www.hsbc.com*).

Internet **La Vía Olimpo** (✉ *Calle 62 No. 502, Centro* ☎ *999/923-5843*) .**Café La Habana** (✉ *Calle 59 No. 511-A, at Calle 62, Centro* ☎ *999/928-6502*).

Mail & Shipping **Correo** (✉ *Calles 65 and 56, Centro* ☎ *999/928-5404*).

Medical Assistance **Star Médica** (✉ *Calle 26 No. 199, between Avs. 15 and 16, Alta Brisa* ☎ *999/930-2800* 🌐 *www.starmedica.com*). **Centro Médico de las Américas** (✉ *Calle 54 No. 365, between Calle 33A and Av. Pérez Ponce, Centro*

☎999/926–2111). **Clínica Santa Helena** (✉*Calle 14 No. 81, between Calles 5 and 7, Col. Díz Ordaz* ☎*999/943–1334 or 999/943–1335*).

Rental Cars **Avis** (✉*Fiesta Americana, Calle 60 No. 319-C, near Av. Colón, Centro* ☎*999/925–2525 or 999/920–1101* 🌐*www.avis.com*). **Budget** (✉*Holiday Inn, Av. Colón 498, at Calle 60, Centro* ☎*999/920–4395 or 999/925–6877 Ext. 516* ✉*Airport* ☎*999/946–1323* 🌐*www.budget.com*).

Visitor & Tour Info **Municipal Tourism Department** (✉*Calles 61 and 60, Centro* ☎*999/930–3101*). **Municipal Tourist Information Center** (✉*Calle 62, ground floor of Palacio Municipal, Centro* ☎*999/928–2020 Ext. 133*).

EXPLORING

Every Sunday, from 8 am until 12:30 pm, downtown streets are closed for pedestrians and cyclists. The route begins at the Parque de la Ermita, and travels through the Plaza Grande, out on to the Paseo Montejo (🌐*www.merida.gob.mx/biciruta*).

2 **Casa de Montejo.** Francisco de Montejo—father and son—conquered the peninsula and founded Mérida in 1542; they built their stately "casa" 10 years later. In the late 1970s it was restored by banker Agustín Legorreta, converted to a branch of Banamex bank, and now sits on the south side of the plaza. Built in the French style, it represents the city's finest—and oldest—example of colonial plateresque architecture, which typically has elaborate ornamentation. A bas-relief on the doorway—the facade is all that remains of the original house—depicts Francisco de Montejo the younger, his wife, and daughter, as well as Spanish soldiers standing on the heads of the vanquished Maya. Even if you have no banking to do, step into the building to glimpse the leafy inner patio. ✉*Calle 63, Centro* ⏲*Weekdays 9–5 and Sat. 9–1.*

6 **Catedral de San Ildefonso.** Begun in 1561, St. Ildefonso is believed to be the oldest cathedral in the Americas. It took several hundred Mayan laborers, working with stones from the pyramids of the ravaged Mayan city, 36 years to complete it. Designed in the somber Renaissance style by an architect who had worked on the Escorial in Madrid, its facade is stark and unadorned, with gunnery slits instead of windows, and faintly Moorish spires. Inside, the black Cristo de las Ampollas (Christ of the Blisters)—at 7 meters (23 feet) tall, perhaps the tallest Christ in Mexico—occupies a side chapel to the left of the main altar. The statue is a replica of the original, which was destroyed during the revolution in 1910; this is also when the gold that typically decorated Mexican cathedrals was carried off. According to one of many legends, the Christ figure burned all night yet appeared the next morning unscathed—except that it was covered with the blisters for which it is named. You can hear the pipe organ play at the 11 AM Sunday mass. ✉*Calles 60 and 61, Centro* ☎*No phone* ⏲*Daily 7–11:30 and 4:30–8.*

3 **Centro Cultural de Mérida Olimpo.** Referred to as simply Olimpo, this is the best venue in town for free cultural events. The beautiful porticoed cultural center was built adjacent to City Hall in late 1999, occupying what used to be a parking lot. The marble interior is a showcase for top international art exhibits, classical-music concerts, conferences, and theater

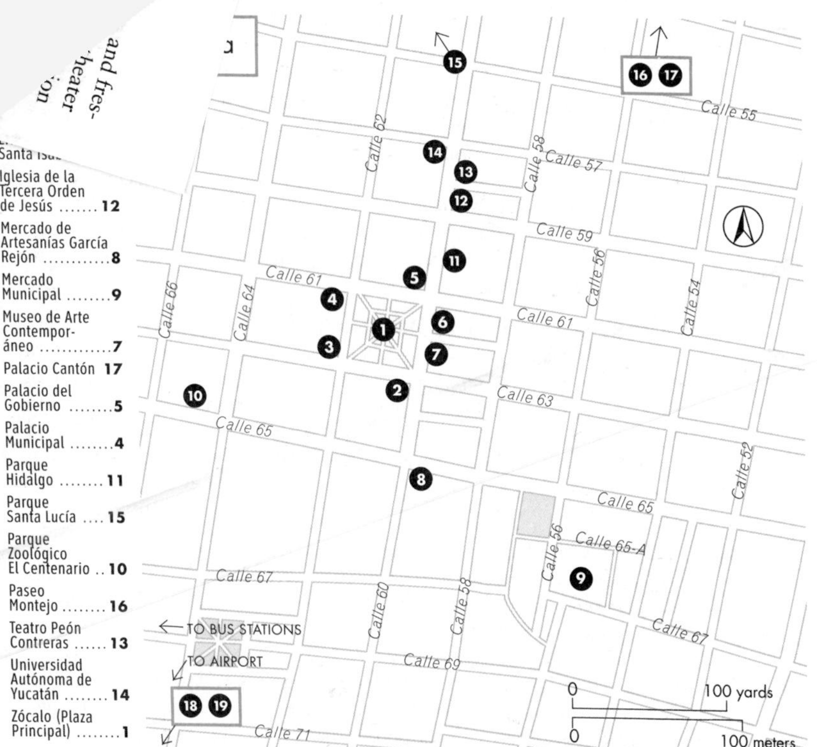

and dance performances. The adjoining 1950s-style movie house shows classic art films by directors like Buñuel, Fellini, and Kazan. There is also a planetarium with 90-minute shows explaining the solar system ($3; Tuesday through Saturday at 5 and 7; Sunday 11 and noon—be sure to be there 15 minutes early, since nobody is allowed to sneak in once the show has begun), a bookstore, and a wonderful cybercafé-restaurant. ✉ *Calle 62 between Calles 61 and 63, Centro* ☎ *999/942–0000* 🌐 *www.merida.gob.mx/planeterio* 🎫 *Free* 🕑 *Tues.–Sun. 10–10.*

16 **Paseo Montejo.** North of downtown, this 10-block-long street was *the* place to reside in the late 19th century, when wealthy plantation owners sought to outdo each other with the opulence of their elegant mansions. Inside, the owners typically displayed imported Carrara marble and antiques, opting for the decorative styles popular in New Orleans, Cuba, and Paris rather than any style from Mexico. The broad boulevard, lined with tamarind and laurel trees, has lost much of its former panache; some of the once-stunning mansions have fallen into disrepair. Others, however, are being restored as part of a citywide, privately funded beautification program, and it's still a lovely place to wander, or to see by horse-drawn carriage.

13 **Teatro Peón Contreras.** This 1908 Italianate theater was built along the same lines as grand turn-of-the-20th-century European theaters and

opera houses. In the early 1980s the marble staircase, don coes were restored. Today, in addition to performing arts th also houses the **Centro de Información Turística** (Tourist Inform Center), which provides maps, brochures, and details about attractions in the city and state. The theater's most popular attraction, however, is the café-bar spilling out into the street facing Parque de la Madre. It's crowded every night with people enjoying the balladeers singing romantic and politically inspired songs. ✉ *Calle 60 between Calles 57 and 59, Centro* ☎ *Tourist Information Center 999/924–9290; theater 999/923–7344 and 999/924–9290* ⊙ *Tourist Information Center daily 8–8; Theater daily 7* AM–*1* AM.

14 **Universidad Autónoma de Yucatán.** Pop into the university's main building—which plays a major role in the city's cultural and intellectual life—to check the bulletin boards just inside the entrance for upcoming cultural events. The folkloric ballet performs on the patio of the main building most Fridays between 9 and 10 PM ($5). You'll easily find this imposing Moorish-inspired building, which dates from 1711, with its crenellated ramparts and arabesque archways. ✉ *Calle 60 between Calles 57 and 59, Centro* ☎ *999/924–8000* 🌐 *www.uady.mx.*

1 **Zócalo.** Méridians traditionally refer to this main square as the Plaza de la Independencia, or the Plaza Principal. Whichever name you prefer, it's a good spot from which to begin a tour of the city, in which to watch music or dance performances, or to chill in the shade of a laurel tree when the day gets too hot. The plaza was laid out in 1542 on the ruins of T'hó, the Mayan city demolished to make way for Mérida, and is still the focal point around which the most important public buildings cluster. *Confidenciales* (S-shape benches) invite intimate tête-à-têtes; lampposts keep the park beautifully illuminated at night. ✉ *Bordered by Calles 60, 62, 61, and 63, Centro.*

IF YOU HAVE TIME

19 **Aké**, a compact archaeological site 35 km (22 mi) southeast of Mérida, offers the unique opportunity to see architecture spanning two millennia in one sweeping vista. Standing atop a ruined Mayan temple built more than a thousand years ago, you can see the incongruous nearby sight of workers processing sisal in a rusty-looking factory, which was built in the early 20th century. To the right of this dilapidated building are the ruins of the old Hacienda and Iglesia de San Lorenzo Aké, both constructed of stones taken from the Mayan temples.

Experts estimate that Aké was populated between around 200 BC and AD 900; today many people in the area have Aké as a surname. The city seems to have been related to the very important and powerful one at present-day Izamal; in fact, the two cities were once connected by a sacbé (white road) 13 meters (43 feet) wide and 33 km (20 mi) long. All that's excavated so far are two pyramids, one with rows of columns (35 total) at the top, very reminiscent of the Toltec columns at Tula, north of Mexico City. 🎫 *$2.20* ⊙ *Daily 9–5.*

18 **Ermita de Santa Isabel.** At the southern end of the city stands the restored and beautiful Hermitage of St. Isabel. Built circa-1748 as part of a Jesuit

monastery also known as the Hermitage of the Good Trip, it served as a resting place for colonial-era travelers heading to Campeche. It is one of the most peaceful places in the city, with an interesting, inlaid-stone facade (although the church itself is almost always closed), and is a good destination for a ride in a horse carriage. Behind the hermitage are its huge and lush tropical gardens, with a waterfall and footpaths; they're usually unlocked during daylight hours. ✉ *Calles 66 and 77, La Ermita* ☎ *No phone* 🎫 *Free* ⏲ *Church open only during mass.*

12 **Iglesia de la Tercera Orden de Jesús.** Just north of Parque Hidalgo is one of Mérida's oldest buildings and the first Jesuit church in the Yucatán. It was built in 1618 from the limestone blocks of a dismantled Mayan temple, and faint outlines of ancient carvings are still visible on the west wall. Although a favorite place for society weddings due to its antiquity, the church interior is not very ornate.

The former convent rooms in the rear of the building now host the **Pinoteca Juan Gamboa Guzmán,** a small but interesting art collection. The most engaging pieces here are the striking bronze sculptures of indigenous Maya crafted by celebrated 20th-century sculptor Enrique Gottdiener. On the second floor are about 20 forgettable oil paintings—mostly of past civic officials of the area. ✉ *Calle 59 between Calles 58 and 60, Centro* ☎ *999/924–5233* 🎫 *$3* ⏲ *Tues.–Sat. 9–5, Sun. 10–5.*

16

8 **Mercado de Artesanías García Rejón.** Although many deal in the same wares, the shops or stalls of the García Rejón Crafts Market sell some quality items, and the shopping experience here can be less of a hassle than at the municipal market. You'll find reasonable prices on palm-fiber hats, hammocks, leather sandals, jewelry, and locally made liqueurs; persistent but polite bargaining may get you even better deals. ✉ *Calles 60 and 65, Centro* ☎ *No phone* ⏲ *Weekdays 9–6, Sat. 9–4, Sun. 9–1.*

9 **Mercado Municipal.** Sellers of chiles, herbs, crafts, trinkets, and fruit fill this pungent and labyrinthine municipal market. In the early morning the first floor is jammed with housewives and restaurateurs shopping for the freshest seafood and produce. The stairs at Calles 56 and 57 lead to the second-floor Bazar de Artesanías Municipales, on either side, where you'll find local pottery, embroidered clothes, men's guayabera dress shirts, hammocks, and straw bags. ✉ *Calles 56 and 67, Centro* ☎ *No phone* ⏲ *Mon.–Sat. dawn–dusk, Sun. 8–3.*

7 **Museo de Arte Contemporáneo.** Originally designed as an art school and used until 1915 as a seminary, this enormous, light-filled building now showcases the works of contemporary Yucatecan artists such as Gabriel Ramírez Aznar and Fernando García Ponce. ✉ *Pasaje de la Revolución 1907, between Calles 58 and 60 on main square, Centro* ☎ *999/928–3236 or 999/928–3258* 🌐 *www.macay.org* 🎫 *Free* ⏲ *Wed., Thurs., 10–5:30, Fri. and Sat. 10–7:30.*

17 **Palacio Cantón.** The most compelling of the mansions on **Paseo Montejo,** this stately palacio was built as the residence for a general between 1909 and 1911. Designed by Enrique Deserti, who also did the blue-

prints for the Teatro Peón Contreras, the building has a grandiose air that seems more characteristic of a mausoleum than a home: there's marble everywhere, as well as Doric and Ionic columns and other Italianate beaux arts flourishes. The building also houses the air-conditioned **Museo de Antropología e Historia,** which introduces visitors to ancient Mayan culture. Temporary exhibits sometimes brighten the standard collection. *Paseo Montejo 485, at Calle 43, Paseo Montejo 999/923–0469 $40 Tues.–Sat. 8–8, Sun. 8–2.*

5 **Palacio del Gobierno.** Visit the seat of state government to see Fernando Castro Pacheco's murals of the bloody history of the conquest of the Yucatán, painted in bold colors in the 1970s and influenced by the Mexican muralists José Clemente Orozco and David Alfaro Siquieros. On the main balcony (visible from outside on the plaza) stands a reproduction of the Bell of Dolores Hidalgo, on which Mexican independence rang out on the night of September 15, 1810, in the town of Dolores Hidalgo in Guanajuato. On the anniversary of the event, the governor rings the bell to commemorate the occasion. *Calle 61 between Calles 60 and 62, Centro 999/930–3101 Free Daily 9–9.*

4 **Palacio Municipal.** The west side of the main square is occupied by City Hall, a 17th-century building trimmed with white arcades, balustrades, and the national coat of arms. Originally erected on the ruins of the last surviving Mayan structure, it was rebuilt in 1735 and then completely reconstructed along colonial lines in 1928. It remains the headquarters of the local government, and houses the municipal tourist office. *Calle 62 between Calles 61 and 63, Centro 999/928–2020 Palacio daily 9–8; Tourist Information Center weekdays 8–8, Sat. 9–1.*

11 **Parque Hidalgo.** A half block north of the main plaza is this small cozy park, officially known as Plaza Cepeda Peraza. Historic mansions, now reincarnated as hotels and sidewalk cafés, line the south side of the park; at night the area comes alive with marimba bands and street vendors. On Sunday the streets are closed to vehicular traffic, and there's free live music performed throughout the day. *Calle 60 between Calles 59 and 61, Centro No phone.*

15 **Parque Santa Lucía.** The rather plain park at Calles 60 and 55 draws crowds with its Thursday-night music and dance performances (shows start at 9); on Sunday, couples also come to dance to a live band, and enjoy food from carts set up in the plaza. The small church opposite the park dates to 1575 and was built as a place of worship for the Maya, who weren't allowed to worship at just any Mérida temple. *Calles 60 and 55, Centro No phone.*

10 **Parque Zoológico El Centenario.** Mérida's greatest children's attraction, this large amusement complex features playgrounds, rides (including ponies and a small train), a rollerblading rink, snack bars, and cages with more than 300 native animals as well as exotics such as lions, tigers, and bears. It also has picnic areas, pleasant wooded paths, and a small lake where you can rent rowboats. The French Renaissance–style arch (1921) commemorates the 100th anniversary of Mexican independence. *Av. Itzáes between Calles 59 and 65,*

entrances on Calles 59 and 65, Centro ☎ *No phone* 🌐 *www.merida.gov.mx/centenario* 🎫 *Free* 🕘 *Zoo daily 8–6.*

NEED A BREAK?

The homemade ice cream and sorbet at El Colón have been a tradition since 1907. It's one way that locals keep cool. The tropical fruit flavors, like chico zapote (a brown fruit that has a flavor a little like cinnamon native to Mexico, from a tree that is used in chewing-gum production), served up in a pyramid-shape scoop are particularly delicious and refreshing. ✉ ***Calle 62 No. 500, at Calle 59Centro*** ☎ ***999/928–1497*** ▭ ***No credit cards.***

WHERE TO EAT

$$$ MEXICAN ★ ✕**Hacienda Teya.** This beautiful hacienda just outside the city serves some of the best regional food in the area. Most patrons are well-to-do Méridians enjoying a leisurely lunch, so you'll want to dress up a bit. Hours are noon to 6 daily (though most Mexicans don't show up until after 3), and a guitarist serenades the tables between 2 and 5 on weekends. After a fabulous lunch of *cochinita pibíl* (pork baked in banana leaves), you can stroll through the surrounding orchards and botanical gardens. If you find yourself wanting to stay longer, the hacienda also has six handsome suites for overnighters. ✉ *13 km (8 mi) east of Mérida on Carretera 180, Kanasín* ☎ *999/988–0800* 🌐 *www.haciendateya.com* ✍ *Reservations essential* ▭ *AE, MC, V* 🕘 *No dinner.*

$$ ITALIAN ✕**Café Lucía.** Opera music floats above black-and-white tile floors in the dining room of this century-old restaurant in the Hotel Casa Lucía near the main plaza. Pizzas and calzones are the linchpins of the Italian menu; luscious pecan pies, cakes, and cookies beckon from behind the glass dessert case. The original art on the walls is for sale, however the paintings by the late Oaxacan artist Rodolfo Morales are not, so don't bother asking. ✉ *Calle 60 No. 474A, Centro* ☎ *999/928–0704* 🌐 *www.casalucia.com.mx* ▭ *AE, MC, V.*

$–$$ ECLECTIC ✕**La Bella Epoca.** The coveted, tiny private balconies at this elegantly restored mansion overlook Parque Hidalgo. (You'll need to call in advance to reserve one for a 7 PM or 10 PM seating.) On weekends, when the street below is closed to traffic and tables are set up outside, it's especially pleasant to survey the park while feasting on Mayan dishes like *sikil-pak* (a dip with ground pumpkin seeds, charbroiled tomatoes, and onions), or succulent *pollo pibíl* (chicken baked in banana leaves). ✉ *Calle 60 No. 497, between Calles 57 and 59, Centro* ☎ *999/928–1928* ▭ *AE, MC, V* 🕘 *No lunch.*

$–$$ MEXICAN ✕**Café La Habana.** A gleaming wood bar, white-jacketed waiters, and the scent of cigarettes contribute to the Old European feel at this overwhelmingly popular café. Overhead, brass-studded ceiling fans swirl the air-conditioned air. Sixteen specialty coffees are offered (some spiked with spirits like Kahlúa or cognac), and the menu has light snacks as well as some entrées, including tamales, fajitas, and enchiladas. The waiters are friendly, and there are plenty of them, although service is not always brisk. Both the café and upstairs Internet joint are open 24 hours a day. ✉ *Calle 59 No. 511A, at Calle 62, Centro* ☎ *999/928–6502* ▭ *MC, V.*

16

$–$$ ECLECTIC Fodor'sChoice ★ **La Casa de Frida.** Chef-owner Gabriela Praget puts a healthful, cosmopolitan spin on Mexican and Yucatecan fare at her restaurant. She prepares all of the dishes, and is usually on hand to greet guests. Traditional dishes like duck in a dark, rich mole sauce (made with chocolate and chiles) share the menu with gourmet vegetarian cuisine: potato and cheese tacos, ratatouille in puff pastry, and crepes made with *cuitlachoche* (a delicious trufflelike corn fungus). The flavors here are so divine that diners have been known to hug Praget after a meal. The dining room, which is open to the stars, is decorated with plants and copies of self-portraits by Frida Kahlo, all of which are for sale. ✉ *Calle 61 No. 526, at Calle 66, Centro* ☎ *999/928–2311* ▭ *No credit cards* ⊙ *Closed Sun. No lunch..*

WORD OF MOUTH

"If you are in Mérida on a weekend—you'd better be used to eating with a LOT of noise—the [restaurants] take their tables to the streets and every one of them has a very loud band playing. We're not fogeys—but we found it hard to have any sort of conversation at any of the restaurants 'on the drag.'"

–TrvlMaven

$ ITALIAN **Ristorante & Pizzería Bologna.** You can dine alfresco or inside at this beautifully restored old mansion, a few blocks off Paseo Montejo. Tables have fresh flowers and cloth napkins; walls are adorned with pictures of Italy, and there are plants everywhere. Most menu items are ordered à la carte; among the favorites are the shrimp pizza and pizza *diabola,* topped with salami, tomato, and chiles. The beef fillet—served solo or covered in cheese or mushrooms—is served with baked potato and a medley of mixed sautéed vegetables. ✉ *Calle 21 No. 117A, near Calle 24, Col. Izimná* ☎ *999/926–2505* ▭ *MC, V.*

¢–$ MIDDLE EASTERN **Alameda.** The waiters are brusque, the building is old, and the decor couldn't be plainer. But you'll find good, hearty, and cheap fare at this always-popular spot. The most expensive main dish here costs about $4—but side dishes are extra. Middle Eastern and standard Yucatecan fare share the menu with vegetarian specialties: meat-free dishes include tabbouleh and spongy, lemon-flavor spinach turnovers. Shopkeepers linger over grilled beef shish kebab, pita bread, and coffee; some old couples have been coming in once a week for decades. An English-language menu, which has explanations as well as translations, is essential even for Spanish speakers. Alameda closes at 5 PM. ✉ *Calle 58 No. 474, near Calle 57, Centro* ☎ *999/928–3635* ▭ *No credit cards* ⊙ *No dinner.*

¢–$ FAST FOOD **Wayan'e.** Friendly owner Mauricio Loría presides over this oasis of carnivorous delights (mostly tortas, Mexico's answer to the sandwich, though tacos are also served) at the crossroads of several busy streets. In addition to ham and cheese tortas, there are pork loin in smoky chipotle-chile sauce, chorizo sausage, turkey strips sautéed with onions and peppers, and several other delicious combos guaranteed to go straight to your arteries. Non-meat-eaters can try some unusual combos, like chopped cactus pads sautéed with mushrooms, or scrambled eggs with chaya or string beans. The place is casual and unassuming, with plastic tables and chairs, but most diners gather around the counter where the food is handed over. The storefront, which is almost always busy but still quick and efficient, closes at 3 PM on weekdays and 2 PM on Saturday. ✉ *Felipe Carrillo Puerto 11A No. 57C, at Calle 4, Col. Itzimná* ☎ *999/938–0676* *Reservations not accepted* ▭ *No credit cards* ⊙ *Closed Sun. No dinner.*

WHERE TO STAY

$$$–$$$$ ★ **Hacienda Xcanatun.** The furnishings at this beautifully restored 18th century henequen hacienda include African and Indonesian antiques, locally made lamps, and oversize comfortable couches and chairs from Puebla. The rooms come with cozy sleigh beds, fine sheets, and fluffy comforters, and are impeccably decorated with art from Mexico, Cuzco, Peru, and other places the owners have traveled. Bathrooms are luxuriously large. There are "Yucatán fusion" dishes in the restaurant, while the hacienda's spa cooks up innovative treatments such as cacao-and-honey massages. **Pros:** Cool and spacious rooms, tasty restaurant, expansive gardens, poolside bar service. **Cons:** A drive from the city, high prices. ✉ *Carretera 261, Km 12, 13 km (8 mi) north of Mérida* ☎ *999/941–0213 or 888/883–3633* 🌐 *www.xcanatun.com* *18 suites* *In-room: No TV, safe. In-hotel: Restaurant, room service, bars, pools, spa, laundry service, airport shuttle, parking (no fee), public Wi-Fi, no elevator* ▭ *AE, MC, V.*

16

$$$–$$$$ **Villa María.** This spacious colonial home was converted to a hotel in 2004. Most rooms are airy and spacious, with loft bedrooms hovering near the 20-foot ceilings. But it's the large patio restaurant ($–$$) that really shines. Stone columns and lacy-looking Moorish arches frame the tables here, along with a lightly spraying central fountain; it's a lovely place to enjoy such European-Mediterranean fare as squash-blossom ravioli garnished with crispy spring potatoes, roast pork loin, or savory French onion soup. For dessert there's crème brûlée, ice cream, or warm apple–almond tart. Breakfast is fine, but less impressive than lunch or dinner. **Pros:** Easy walking distance to downtown sights, romantic architecture and decoration. **Cons:** Street noise can be a problem, the swimming pool is too small for serious swimming. ✉ *Calle 59 No. 553, at Calle 68, Centro* ☎ *999/923–3357* 🌐 *www.villamariamerida.com* *10 rooms, 2 suites* *In-room: Safe, Wi-Fi. In-hotel: Restaurant, room service, bar, parking (no fee), no elevator* ▭ *AE, MC, V.*

$$ **Gran Hotel.** Cozily situated on Parque Hidalgo, this legendary 1901 hotel does look its age, with extremely high ceilings, wrought-iron balcony and stair rails, and ornately patterned tile floors. The period decor is so classic that you expect a mantilla-wearing Spanish señorita to appear, fluttering her fan, at any moment. The old-fashioned sitting room has formal seating areas and lots of antiques and plants. A renovation in 2004 enlarged some guest rooms and replaced tiny twin beds with doubles. Wide interior verandas on the second and third floors provide pretty outside seating. Porfirio Díaz, a former Mexican president, stayed in one of the corner suites, which have small living and dining areas. **Pros:** Beautiful antique decorations (especially in public areas), location in the middle of the downtown bustle, sights, and

shops. **Cons:** Downtown noise, no elevator makes upstairs rooms quite a hike. ✉ *Calle 60 No. 496, Centro* ☎ *999/923–6963* *25 rooms, 7 suites* *In-hotel: Restaurant, room service, laundry service, parking (no fee), some pets allowed, safe, no elevator, no children under 12* ▭ *MC, V.*

$$ ★ **Hyatt Regency Mérida.** The city's first deluxe hotel is still among its most elegant. Rooms are regally decorated, with russet-hue quilts and rugs set off by blond-wood furniture and cream-color walls. There's a top-notch business center, and a beautiful marble lobby. Upper-crust Méridians recommend Spasso Italian restaurant as a fine place to have a drink in the evening; for an amazing seafood extravaganza, don't miss the $20 seafood buffet at Peregrina bistro. **Pros:** Attentive service, reasonable prices (neighboring hotels are more expensive), popular Italian restaurant. **Cons:** Just off the Paseo Montejo, but far from the downtown area. ✉ *Calle 60 No. 344, at Av. Colón, Paseo Montejo* ☎ *999/942–0202, 999/942–1234, or 800/233–1234* ⊕ *merida.regency.hyatt.com.mx* *296 rooms, 4 suites* *In-room: Dial-up, Wi-Fi, safe. In-hotel: 2 restaurants, room service, bars, tennis courts, pool, gym, concierge, laundry service, executive floor, parking (no fee), no-smoking rooms, refrigerator* ▭ *AE, DC, MC, V* *BP, EP.*

$$ ★ **Marionetas.** Attentive proprietors Daniel and Sofija Bosco, who are originally from Argentina and Macedonia, have created this lovely B&B on a quiet street seven blocks from the main plaza. From the Macedonian lace dust ruffles and fine cotton sheets and bedspreads to the quiet, remote-controlled air-conditioning and pressurized showerheads (there are no tubs), every detail and fixture here is of the highest quality. You'll delight in the carefully chosen folk-art decoration throughout. You'll need to book your reservation well in advance. **Pros:** Intimate feel, personal attention from proprietors and their staff, courtyard and pool area are a calm escape from the bustling Mérida streets. **Cons:** Reservations can be hard to come by during high season, no in-room TVs. ✉ *Calle 49 No. 516, between Calles 62 and 64, Centro* ☎ *999/928–3377 or 999/923–2790* ⊕ *www.hotelmarionetas.com* *8 rooms* *In-room: No TV, safe. In-hotel: Restaurant, public Wi-Fi, no elevator* ▭ *MC, V* *BP.*

$–$$ **Casa Mexilio.** Four blocks from the main square is this eclectic B&B. Middle Eastern wall hangings, French tapestries, and colorful tile floors crowd the public spaces; individually decorated rooms have tile sinks and folk-art furniture. Some find this inn private and romantic, although others may find it a bit too intimate for their liking. The grottolike pool is surrounded by ferns, and the light-filled penthouse, up four dozen steps, has an excellent city view from its oversize balcony. A two-night minimum stay is required. **Pros:** Pleasant courtyard, easy walk to places of interest downtown, excellent room prices. **Cons:** Small bathrooms, some of the linens look a little dated, no children allowed, no parking. ✉ *Calle 68 No. 495, between Calles 57 and 59, Centro* ☎ *999/928–2505, 800/538–6802 in U.S. and Canada* ⊕ *www.mexicoholiday.com* *8 rooms, 1 penthouse* *In-room: No a/c (some), no phone, no TV, Wi-Fi (some). In-hotel: Restaurant, bar, pool, no children under 16, no elevator* ▭ *AE, MC, V* *CP.*

¢ **Hostal del Peregrino.** This recently restored old home is now part upscale hostel, part inexpensive hotel. Private rooms downstairs have few amenities but wonderfully restored *piso de pasta*—tile floors with intricate designs. Upstairs are shared coed dorm rooms with separate showers and toilets, and an open-air bar and TV lounge for hanging out in the evening with fellow guests. Hostel staff are open to helping arrange tours, and they also rent out bikes. **Pros:** Really low room prices, easy walk downtown, tours and Spanish tutoring are optional extras. **Cons:** Rooms are spacious, but basic; kitchen and lounge areas can get noisy. ✉*Calle 51 No. 488, between Calles 54 and 56, Centro* ☎*999/924–5491* 🌐*www.hostaldelperegrino.com* *7 private rooms, 3 dorm rooms* *In room: Wi-Fi. In-hotel: Restaurant, bar, bicycles, no elevator* 💳*MC, V* *CP.*

¢ **Posada Toledo.** This beautiful centuries-old house has retained its elegance with high ceilings, floors of patterned tile, and carved, colonial-style furniture. The guest rooms themselves are less impressive, and the furnishings (and their condition) vary more than the rates reflect, so be sure to inspect your shabby-chic room before checking in. Room 5 is an elegant two-room suite that was originally the mansion's master bedroom. Rooms on the second floor are newer and somewhat more modern. If you're a light sleeper, ask for a room away from the courtyard. **Pros:** Great price, friendly staff. **Cons:** Room quality really varies, sound from the courtyard can be heard in nearby rooms, small bathrooms. ✉*Calle 58 No. 487, at Calle 57, Centro* ☎*999/923–1690* *21 rooms, 2 suites* *In-hotel: Restaurant, parking (fee), safe, no elevator* 💳*MC, V.*

16

NIGHTLIFE

Mérida has an active and diverse cultural life, which features free government-sponsored music and dance performances many evenings, as well as sidewalk art shows in local parks. Thursday at 9 PM Méridians enjoy an evening of outdoor entertainment at the **Serenata Yucateca.** At **Parque Santa Lucía** (Calles 60 and 55) you'll see trios, the local orchestra, and soloists performing compositions by Yucatecan composers. On Saturday evenings after 7 PM, the **Noche Mexicana** (corner of Paseo Montejo and Calle 47) hosts different musical and cultural events; more free music, dance, comedy, and regional handicrafts can be found at the **Corazón de Mérida,** on Calle 60 between the main plaza and Calle 55. Between 8 PM and 1 AM, multiple bandstands throughout this area (which is closed to traffic) entertain locals and visitors with an ever-changing playbill, from grunge to classical.

BARS & DANCE CLUBS

Popular with the local *niños fresa* (which translates as "strawberry children," meaning upper-class youth) as well as some middle-age professionals, the indoor-outdoor lounge **El Cielo** (✉*Prolongatión Paseo Montejo between Calles 15 and 17, Col. México* ☎*999/944–5127* 🌐*www.elcielobar.com*) is one of the latest minimalist hot spots where you can drink and dance to party or lounge music videos. It's open

Wednesday through Saturday nights after 9:30 PM. Their first-floor restaurant, Sky, opens at 1 (closed Monday) for sushi.

★ Part bar, restaurant, and stage show, **Eladios** (✉ *Calle 24 No. 101C, at Calle 59, Col. Itzimná* ☎ *999/927–2126* 🌐 *www.eladios.com.mx*), with its peaked palm-thatch room and ample dance floor, is a lively place often crammed with local families and couples. You get free appetizers with your suds (there's a full menu of tasty Yucatecan food served up with fresh tortillas), which makes it a good afternoon pit stop, and there's live salsa, cumbia, and other Latino tunes, punctuated by the live music talent doing plenty of stage-show style talking, between 2 and 6:30 PM. In the evening you can enjoy more stage shows, or dance.

Mambo Café (✉ *Calle 21 No. 327, between Calles 50 and 52, Plaza las Américas, Fracc. Miguel Hidalgo* ☎ *999/987–7533* 🌐 *www.mambocafe.com.mx*) is the best place in town for dancing to DJ-spun salsa, merengue, cumbia, and disco tunes. You might want to hit the john during their raunchy audience-participation acts between sets. It's open from 9 PM until 3 AM Wednesday, Friday, and Saturday.

El Nuevo Tucho (✉ *Calle 60 No. 482, between Calles 55 and 57, Centro* ☎ *999/924–2323*) has cheesy cabaret-style entertainment beginning at 4 PM, with no drink minimum and no cover. In fact, despite the music and comedy, this is not just a place for young people or for dancing. Families dine here as well. There's music for dancing in this cavernous—sometimes full, sometimes empty—venue. Drink orders come with free appetizers.

Pancho's (✉ *Calle 59 No. 509, between Calles 60 and 62, Centro* ☎ *999/923–0942* 🌐 *www.panchosmerida.com*), open daily 6 PM–2:30 AM, has a lively bar and a restaurant. It also has a small dance floor that attracts locals and visitors for a mix of live salsa and English-language pop music.

If dancing to the likes of Los Panchos and other romantic trios of the 1940s is more your style, don't miss this Tuesday-night ritual at **Parque de Santiago** (✉ *Calles 59 and 72, Centro* ☎ *No phone*), where old folks and the occasional young lovers gather for dancing under the stars at 8:30 PM.

Fodor's Choice ★ Enormously popular and rightly so, the red-walled **Slavia** (✉ *Calle 29 No. 490, at Calle 58* ☎ *999/926–6587*) is an exotic Middle Eastern beauty. There are all sorts of nooks where you can be alone yet together with upscale Méridians, most of whom simply call this "the Buddha Bar." Arabian music in the background, low lighting, beaded curtains, embroidered tablecloths, and sumptuous pillows and settees surrounding low tables produce a fabulous Arabian-nights vibe. It's open daily 7 PM–2 AM.

Tequila Rock (✉ *Prolongación Paseo Montejo at Av. Campestre* ☎ *999/883–3147*) is a disco where salsa and Mexican and American pop are played Wednesday through Saturday. It's popular mainly with those between 18 and 25.

FOLKLORIC SHOWS

Paseo Montejo hotels such as the Fiesta Americana, Hyatt Regency, and Holiday Inn stage dinner shows with folkloric dances; check with concierges for schedules.

★ The **Ballet Folklórico de Yucatán** (✉ *Calles 57 and 60, Centro* ☎ *999/923–1198*) presents a combination of music, dance, and theater every Friday at 9 PM at the university; tickets are $5. (Performances are every other Friday in the off-season, and there are no shows from August 1 to September 22 and the last two weeks of December.)

SHOPPING

MALLS

Mérida has several shopping malls, but the largest and nicest, **Gran Plaza** (✉ *Calle 50 Diagonal 460, Fracc. Gonzalo Guerrero* ☎ *999/944–7657* 🌐 *www.granplaza.com.mx*), has more than 90 shops and a multiplex theater. It's just outside town, on the highway to Progreso (called Carretera a Progreso beyond the Mérida city limits). Tiny **Pasaje Picheta** is on the north side of the town square on Calle 61. It has a bus ticket information booth and an upstairs art gallery, as well as souvenir shops and a food court.**Plaza Américas** (✉ *Calle 21 No. 331, Col. Miguel Hidalgo* ☎ *No phone*) is a pleasant mall where you'll find the Cineopolis movie theater complex.

MARKETS

As its name implies, popular art, or handicrafts, are sold at the **Bazar de Artes Populares** (✉ *Parque Santa Lucía, at Calles 60 and 55, Centro*) beginning at 9 AM on Sunday.

Sunday brings an array of wares into Mérida; starting at 9 AM, the Handicrafts Bazaar, or **Bazar de Artesanías** (✉ *At main square, Centro*), sells lots of *huipiles* (traditional, white embroidered dresses) as well as hats and costume jewelry.

If you're interested in handicrafts, **Bazar García Rejón** (✉ *Calles 65 and 62, Centro*) has rows of indoor stalls that sell items like leather goods, palm hats, and handmade guitars.

The **Mercado Municipal** (✉ *Calles 56 and 67, Centro*) has lots of things you won't need, but which are fascinating to look at: songbirds in cane cages, mountains of mysterious fruits and vegetables, dippers made of hollow gourds (the same way they've been made here for a thousand years). There are also lots of crafts for sale, including hammocks, sturdy leather *huaraches,* and piñatas in every imaginable shape and color.

SPECIALTY STORES

CLOTHING

You might not wear a guayabera to a business meeting as some men in Mexico do, but the shirts are cool, comfortable, and attractive; for a good selection, try **Camisería Canul** (✉ *Calle 62 No. 484, between Calles*

CLOSE UP

Hamacas: A Primer

Yucatecan artisans are known for creating some of the finest *hamacas*, or hammocks, in the country. For the most part, the shops of Mérida are the best places in Yucatán to buy these beautiful, practical items—although if you travel to some of the outlying small towns, like Tixkokob, Izamal, and Ek Balam, you may find cheaper prices—and enjoy the experience as well.

One of the first decisions you'll have to make when buying a hamaca is whether to choose one made from cotton or nylon; nylon dries more quickly and is therefore well suited to humid climates, but cotton is softer and more comfortable (though its colors tend to fade faster). You'll also see that hamacas come in both double-threaded and single-threaded weaves; the double-threaded ones are sturdiest because they're more densely woven.

Hamacas come in a variety of sizes, too. A *sencillo* (cen-*see*-oh) hammock is meant for just one person (although most people find it's a rather tight fit); a *doble* (*doh*-blay), on the other hand, is very comfortable for one but crowded for two. *Matrimonial* or king-size hammocks accommodate two; and *familiares* or *matrimoniales especiales* can theoretically sleep an entire family. (Yucatecans tend to be smaller than Anglos are, and also lie diagonally in hammocks rather than end-to-end.)

For a good-quality king-size nylon or cotton hamaca, expect to pay about $35; sencillos go for about $22. Unless you're an expert, it's best to buy a hammock at a specialty shop, where you can climb in to try the size. The proprietors will also give you tips on washing, storing, and hanging your hammock. There are lots of hammock stores near Mérida's municipal market on Calle 58, between Calles 69 and 73.

57 and 59, Centro ☎ *999/923–0158* 🌐 *www.camerisacanul.com*). Custom shirts take a week to construct, in sizes 4 to 52.

Guayaberas Jack (✉ *Calle 59 No. 507A, between Calles 60 and 62, Centro* ☎ *999/928–6002*) has an excellent selection of guayaberas (18 delicious colors to choose from!) and typical women's cotton *filipinas* (house dresses), blouses, dresses, classy straw handbags, and lovely rayon *rebozos* (shawls) from San Luis Potosí. These can be made to order, allegedly in less than a day, to fit anyone from a year-old to a 240-pound man. Everything here is of fine quality, and is often quite different from the clothes sold in neighboring shops. Prices are higher, but they really are in line with the quality of the clothes. The shop has a sophisticated Web site, 🌐 *www.guayaberasjack.com.mx*, which allows online purchasing and browsing. **Mexicanísimo** (✉ *Calle 60 No. 496, at Parque Hidalgo, Centro* ☎ *999/923–8132*) sells sleek, clean-lined clothing made from natural fibers for both women and men.

FOLK ART

A great place to purchase hammocks is **El Aguacate** (✉ *Calle 58 No. 604, at Calle 73, Centro* ☎ *999/928–6429* 🌐 *www.hamacaselaguacate.*

com.mx), a family-run outfit with many sizes and designs. Closed Sundays. Visit the government-run **Casa de las Artesanías Ki-Huic** (✉ *Calle 63 No. 503A, between Calles 64 and 62, Centro* ☎ *999/928–6676*) for folk art from throughout Yucatán. There's a showcase of hard-to-find traditional filigree jewelry in silver, gold, and gold-dipped versions. **Casa de los Artesanos** (✉ *Calle 62 No. 492, between Calles 59 and 61, Centro* ☎ *999/923–4523*), half a block from the main plaza, sells mainly small ceramic pieces, including more modern, stylized takes on traditional designs. The **Casa de Cera** (✉ *Calle 74A No. 430E, between Calles 41 and 43, Centro* ☎ *999/920–0219*) is a small shop selling signed collectible indigenous beeswax figurines. Closed Sunday and afternoons after 3 PM. **El Hamaquero** (✉ *Calle 58 No. 572, between Calles 69 and 71, Centro* ☎ *999/923–2117*) has knowledgeable personnel who let you try out the hammocks before you buy. Closed Sunday. **El Mayab** (✉ *Calle 58 No. 553-A, at Calle 71, Centro* ☎ *999/924–0853*) has a multitude of hammocks and is open on Sundays until 2 PM. **Miniaturas** (✉ *Calle 59 No. 507A, Centro* ☎ *999/928–6503*) sells a delightful and diverse assortment of different crafts, but specializes in miniatures. **El Sombrero Popular** (✉ *Calle 65, between Calles 54 and 56, Centro* ☎ *999/923–9501*) has a good assortment of men's hats—especially *jipis*, better known as Panama hats, which cost between $12 and $65. The elder of this father-and-son team has been in the business for 40 years. Closed Sunday. **Tequilería Ajua** (✉ *Calle 59 No. 506, at Calle 62, Centro* ☎ *999/924–1453*) sells tequila, brandy, and mezcal as well as Xtabentún and thick liqueurs made of local fruit from 10 AM to 9 PM.

16

You can get hammocks made to order—choose from standard nylon and cotton, super-soft processed sisal, Brazilian-style (six stringed), or crocheted—at **El Xiric** (✉ *Calle 57-A No. 15, Pasaje Congreso, Centro* ☎ *999/924–9906*). You can also get *Xtabentún*—a locally made liqueur flavored with anise and honey—as well as jewelry, black pottery, woven goods from Oaxaca, T-shirts, and souvenirs.

JEWELRY

Shop for malachite, turquoise, and other semiprecious stones set in silver at **Joyería Kema** (✉ *Calle 60 No. 502-B, between Calles 61 and 63, at main plaza, Centro* ☎ *999/923–5838*). Beaders and other creative types flock to **Papagayo's Paradise** (✉ *Calle 62 No. 488, between Calles 57 and 59, Centro* ☎ *999/993–0383*), where you'll find loose beads and semiprecious stones; lovely necklaces and earrings; and Brussels-lace-trimmed, hand-embroidered, tatted, and crocheted blouses. This small but exceptional store also sells men's handkerchiefs and place mats. **Tane** (✉ *Hyatt Regency, Calle 60 No. 344, at Av. Colón, Paseo Montejo* ☎ *999/942–0202* 🌐 *www.tane.com.mx*) is an outlet for exquisite (and expensive) silver earrings, necklaces, and bracelets, some incorporating ancient Mayan designs.

SPORTS & THE OUTDOORS

It's possible to either watch or participate in sports, from baseball to bullfights, while you're in town.

BASEBALL

Baseball is played with enthusiasm between February and July at the **Centro Deportivo Kukulcán** (✉ *Calle 6 No. 315, Circuito Colonias, Col. Granjas.* ✣ *Across street from Pemex gas station and next to Santa Clara brewery* ☎ *999/940–0676 or 999/940–4261*). There are also tennis courts, soccer courts, and an Olympic pool. It's most common to buy your ticket at the on-site ticket booth the day of the game. A-league volleyball and basketball games and tennis tournaments are also held here.

BULLFIGHTS

Bullfights are held sporadically from late September through February, though the most famed *matadors* begin their fighting season in November at **Plaza de Toros** (✉ *Av. Reforma near Calle 25, Col. García Ginerés* ☎ *999/925–7996*). Seats in the shade generally go for around $50, but can cost as much as $150, depending on the fame of the bullfighter. You can buy tickets at the bullring or in advance at OXXO convenience stores. Check with the tourism office for the current schedule, or look for posters around town.

GOLF

EN ROUTE

Leaving Mérida, on the way to Chichén Itzá, you'll first come across the beautiful town of **Izamal**, where you may not find too many sights, but you will almost certainly be taken by the town's color and aging architecture. The drive to Izamal (68 km [42 mi] east of Mérida) takes less than an hour; hop on Highway 180 and follow the signs. Although unsophisticated, Izamal is a charming and neighborly alternative to the sometimes frenetic tourism of Mérida. The city has recently been refurbished, and the downtown area shines with remodeled buildings and bright yellow paint that contrasts strikingly with the blue sky.

One of the best examples of a Spanish colonial town in the Yucatán, Izamal is nicknamed *Ciudad Amarilla* (Yellow City), because its most important buildings are painted a golden ocher. It's also sometimes called "the City of Three Cultures," because of its combined pre-Hispanic, colonial, and contemporary influences.

Calesas (horse-drawn carriages) are stationed at the town's large main square, fronting the lovely cathedral, day and night. The drivers charge about $5 an hour for sightseeing; many will also take you on a shopping tour for whichever items you're interested in buying (for instance, hammocks or jewelry). Pick up a brochure at the visitor center for details.

UXMAL

Fodor's Choice ★

78 km (48 mi) south of Mérida on Carretera 261.

If Chichén Itzá is the most expansive Mayan ruin in Yucatán, Uxmal is arguably the most elegant. The architecture here reflects the late classical renaissance of the 7th to 9th century and is contemporary with that of Palenque and Tikal, among other great Mayan cities of the southern highlands.

The site is considered the finest and most extensively excavated example of Puuc architecture, which embraces such details as ornate stone mosaics and friezes on the upper walls, intricate cornices, rows of columns, and soaring vaulted arches.

You could easily spend a couple of days exploring the ruins, though keep in mind that the only entertainment offered outside the ruins is provided by hotels and the odd restaurant.

GETTING HERE & AROUND

There's daily transportation on the ATS bus line to Uxmal. If you plan to drive yourself, take Highway 180 south out of Mérida, and then get on Highway 261 in Uman. This will take you south all the way to Uxmal.

EXPLORING

Although much of Uxmal hasn't been restored, the following buildings in particular merit attention:

At 125 feet high, the **Pirámide del Adivino** is the tallest and most prominent structure at the site. Unlike most other Mayan pyramids, which are stepped and angular, the Temple of the Magician has a softer and more refined round-corner design. This structure was rebuilt five times over hundreds of years, each time on the same foundation, so artifacts found here represent several different kingdoms. The pyramid has a stairway on its western side that leads through a giant open-mouthed mask to two temples at the summit. During restoration work in 2002 the grave of a high-ranking Mayan official, a ceramic mask, and a jade necklace were discovered within the pyramid. Continuing excavations have revealed exciting new finds that are still being studied.

West of the pyramid lies the **Cuadrángulo de las Monjas**, considered by some to be the finest part of Uxmal. The name was given to it by the conquistadores because it reminded them of a convent building (*monjas* means nuns) in Old Spain. You may enter the four buildings; each comprises a series of low, gracefully repetitive chambers that look onto a central patio. Elaborate and symbolic decorations—masks, geometric patterns, coiling snakes, and some phallic figures—blanket the upper facades.

Heading south, you'll pass a small ball court before reaching the **Palacio del Gobernador**, which archaeologist Victor von Hagen considered the most magnificent building ever erected in the Americas. Interestingly, the palace faces east, while the rest of Uxmal faces west. Archaeologists believe this is because the palace was built to allow observation of the planet Venus. Covering five acres and rising over an immense acropolis, it lies at the heart of what may have been Uxmal's administrative center.

Apparently the house of an important person, the recently excavated **Cuadrángalo de los Pájaros** (Quadrangle of the Birds), located between

Continued on page 824

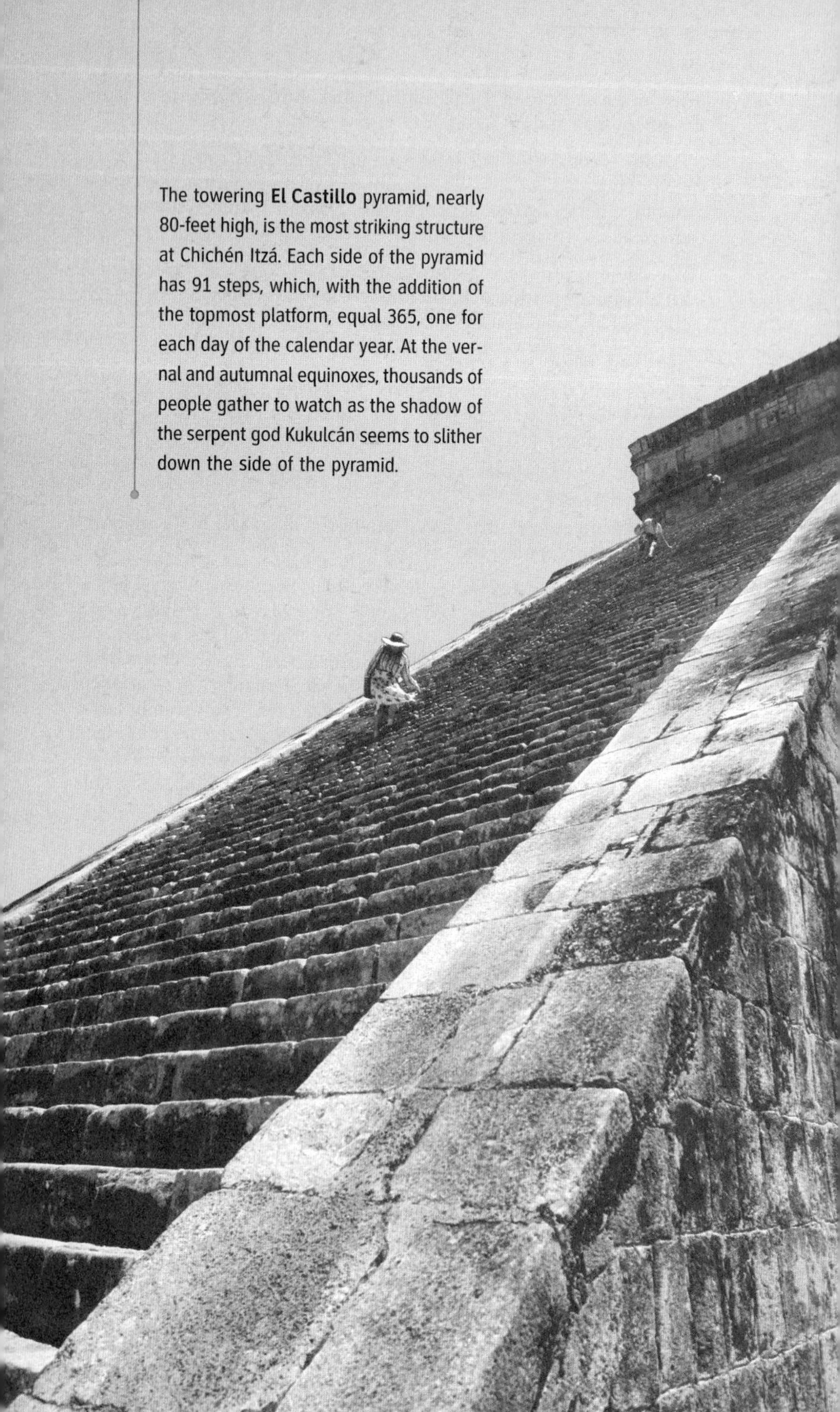

The towering **El Castillo** pyramid, nearly 80-feet high, is the most striking structure at Chichén Itzá. Each side of the pyramid has 91 steps, which, with the addition of the topmost platform, equal 365, one for each day of the calendar year. At the vernal and autumnal equinoxes, thousands of people gather to watch as the shadow of the serpent god Kukulcán seems to slither down the side of the pyramid.

CHICHÉN ITZÁ

Carvings of ball players adorn the walls of the *juego de pelota.*

One of the most dramatically beautiful of the ancient Maya cities, Chichén Itzá draws some 3,000 visitors a day from all over the world. Since the remains of this once-thriving kingdom were discovered by Europeans in the mid 1800s, many of the travelers who make the pilgrimage here have been archaeologists and scholars, who study the structures and glyphs and try to piece together the mysteries surrounding them. While the artifacts here give fascinating insight into the Maya civilization, they also raise many, many unanswered questions.

The name of this ancient city, which means "the mouth of the well of the Itzás," is a mystery in and of itself. Although it likely refers to the valuable water sources at the site (there are several sinkholes here), experts have little information about who might have actually founded the city—some structures, likely built in the 5th century, pre-date the arrival of the Itzás who occupied the city starting around the late 8th and early 9th centuries. The reason why the Itzás abandoned the city, around 1224, is also unknown. The role that this center then took is still being evaluated.

Of course, most of the visitors that converge on Chichén Itzá come to marvel at its beauty, not ponder its significance. This ancient metropolis, which encompasses 6 square km (2½ square mi), is known around the world as one of the most stunning and well-preserved Maya sites in existence.

The sight of the immense ❶ **El Castillo** pyramid, rising imposingly yet gracefully from the surrounding plain, has been known to produce goose pimples on sight. El Castillo (The Castle) dominates the site both in size and in the sym-

CHICHÉN ITZÁ

The spiral staircased El Caracol was used as an astronomical observatory.

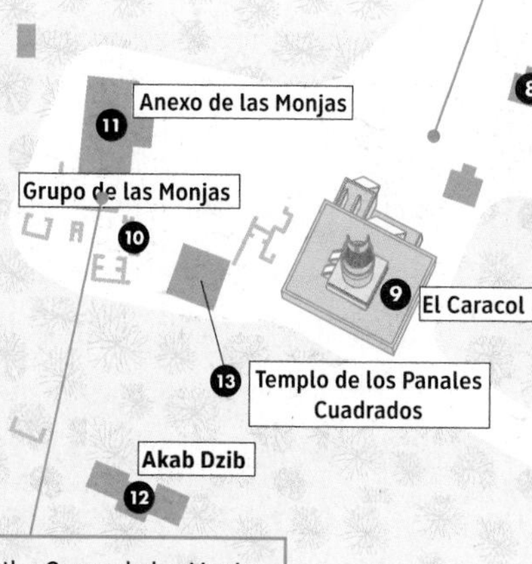

Structures at the Grupo de las Monjas have some of the site's most exquisite carvings and masks.

← TO OLD CHICHÉN ITZÁ

THE CULT OF KUKULCÁN

Although the Maya worshipped many of their own gods, Kukulcán was a deity introduced to them by the Toltecs—who referred to him as Quetzacóatl, or the plumed serpent. The pyramid of El Castillo, along with many other structures at Chichén Itzá, was built in honor of Kukulcán.

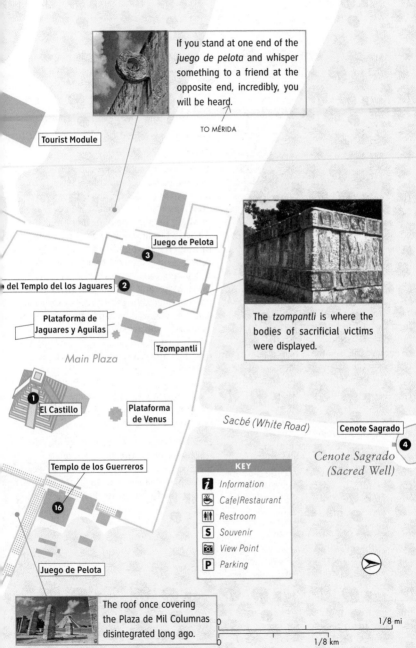

If you stand at one end of the *juego de pelota* and whisper something to a friend at the opposite end, incredibly, you will be heard.

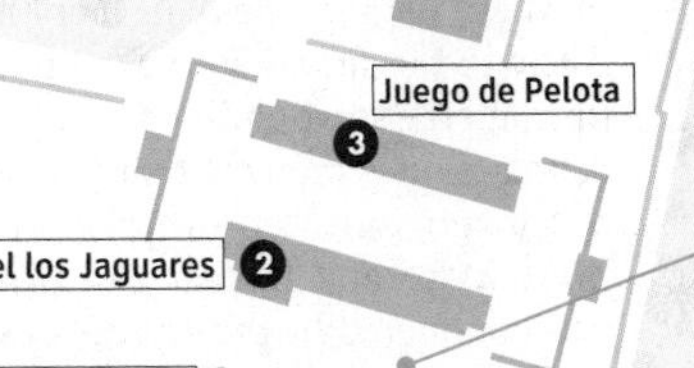

The *tzompantli* is where the bodies of sacrificial victims were displayed.

The roof once covering the Plaza de Mil Columnas disintegrated long ago.

MAJOR SITES AND ATTRACTIONS

Rows of freestanding columns at the site have a strangely Greek look.

metry of its perfect proportions. Open-jawed serpent statues adorn the corners of each of the pyramid's four stairways, honoring the legendary priest-king Kukulcán (also known as Quetzalcóatl), an incarnation of the feathered serpent god. More serpents appear at the top of the building as sculpted columns. At the spring and fall equinoxes, the afternoon light strikes the trapezoidal structure so that the shadow of the snake-god appears to undulate down the side of the pyramid to bless the fertile earth. Thousands of people travel to the site each year to see this phenomenon.

At the base of the temple on the north side, an interior staircase leads to two marvelous statues deep within: a stone jaguar, and the intermediate god Chacmool. As usual, Chacmool is in a reclining position, with a flat spot on the belly for receiving sacrifices. On the ❷ **Anexo del Templo de los Jaguares** (Annex to the Temple of the Jaguars), just west of El Castillo, bas-relief carvings represent more important deities. On the bottom of the columns is the rain god Tlaloc. It's no surprise that his tears represent rain—but why is the Toltec god Tlaloc honored here, instead of the Maya rain god, Chaac?

That's one of many questions that archaeologists and epigraphers have been trying to answer, ever since John Lloyd Stephens and Frederick Catherwood, the first English-speaking explorers to discover the site, first hacked their way through the surrounding forest in 1840. Scholars once thought that the symbols of foreign gods and differing architectural styles at Chichén Itzá proved it was conquered by the Toltecs of central Mexico. (As well as representations of Tlaloc, the site also has a *tzompantli*—a stone platform decorated with row upon row of sculpted human skulls, which is a distinctively Toltec-style structure.) Most experts now agree, however, that Chichén Itzá was only influenced—not conquered—by Toltec trading partners from the north.

Just west of the Anexo del Templo de los Jaguares is another puzzle: the auditory marvel of Chichén Itzá's main ball court. At 490 feet, this ❸ **Juego de Pelota**

The flat part of a reclining Chacmool statue is where sacrificial offerings were laid.

Although the rules of the game that were played on the ball court aren't known, it's thought that players had to pass some sort of ball through high stone loops.

The walls of the ball field are intricately carved.

is the largest in Mesoamerica. Yet if you stand at one end of the playing field and whisper something to a friend at the other end, incredibly, you will be heard. The game played on this ball court was apparently something like soccer (no hands were used), but it likely had some sort of ritualistic significance. Carvings on the low walls surrounding the field show a decapitation, blood spurting from the victim's neck to fertilize the earth. Whether this is a historical depiction (perhaps the losers or winners of the game were sacrificed?) or a symbolic scene, we can only guess.

On the other side of El Castillo, just before a small temple dedicated to the planet Venus, a ruined *sacbé,* or white road leads to the ❹ **Cenote Sagrado** (Holy Well, or Sinkhole), which was also probably used for ritualistic purposes. Jacques Cousteau and his companions recovered about 80 skeletons from this deep, straight-sided, subsurface pond, as well as thousands of pieces of jewelry and figures of jade, obsidian, wood, bone, and turquoise. In direct alignment with this cloudy green cenote, on the other side of El Castillo, the ❺**Xtaloc sinkhole** was kept pristine, undoubtedly for bathing and drinking. Adjacent to this water source

TIPS

To get more in-depth information about the ruins, hire a multilingual guide at the ticket booth. Guides charge about $35 for a group of up to 7 people. Tours generally last about two hours. *$3.50* Ruins daily 8–5, museum Tues.–Sun. 9–4.

is a steam bath, its interior lined with benches along the wall like those you'd see in any steam room today. Outside, a tiny pool was used for cooling down during the ritual.

The older Mayan structures at Chichén Itzá are south and west of Cenote Xtaloc. Archaeologists have been restoring several buildings in this area, including the ❻ **Templo del Osario** (Ossuary Temple), which, as its name implies, concealed several tombs with skeletons and offerings. Behind the smaller ❼ **Casa Roja** (Red House) and ❽ **Casa del Venado** (House of the Deer) are the site's oldest structures, including ❾ **El Caracol** (The Snail), one of the few round buildings built by the Maya, with a spiral staircase within. Clearly built as a celestial observatory, it has eight tiny windows precisely aligned with the points of the compass rose. Scholars now know that Maya priests studied the planets and the stars; in fact, they were able to accurately predict the orbits of Venus and the moon, and the appearance of comets and eclipses. To modern astronomers, this is nothing short of amazing.

The Maya of Chichén Itzá were not just scholars, however. They were skilled artisans and architects as well. South of El Caracol, the ❿ **Grupo de las Monjas** (The Nunnery complex) has some of the site's most exquisite façades. A combination of Puuc and Chenes styles dominates here, with playful latticework, masks, and gargoylelike serpents. On the east side of the ⓫ **Anexo de las Monjas** (Nunnery Annex), the Chenes facade celebrates the rain god Chaac. In typical style, the doorway represents an entrance into the underworld; figures of Chaac decorate the ornate façade above.

The doorway of the Anexo de las Monjas represents an entrance to the underworld.

South of the Nunnery Complex is an area where field archaeologists are still excavating (fewer than a quarter of the structures at Chichén Itzá have been fully restored). If you have more than a superficial interest in the site—and can convince the authorities ahead of time of your importance, or at least your interest in archaeology—you can explore this area, which is generally not open to the public. Otherwise, head back toward El Castillo past the ruins of a housing compound called ⓬ **Akab Dzib** and the ⓭ **Templo de los Panales Cuadrados** (Temple of the Square Panels). The latter of these buildings shows more evidence of Toltec influence: instead of weight-bearing Mayan arches—or "false arches"—that traditionally supported stone roofs, this structure has stone columns but no roof. This means that the building was once roofed, Toltec-style, with perishable materials (most likely palm thatch or wood) that have long since disintegrated.

Beyond El Caracol, Casa Roja, and El Osario, the right-hand path follows an ancient sacbé, now collapsed. A mud-and-straw hut, which the Maya called a **na**, has been reproduced here to show the simple implements used before and after the Spanish conquest. On one side of the room are a typical pre-Hispanic table, seat, fire pit, and reed baskets; on the other, the Christian cross and colonial-style table of the post-conquest Maya.

Behind the tiny oval house, several unexcavated mounds still guard their secrets. The path meanders through a small grove of oak and slender bean trees to the building known today as ⓮ **El Mercado.** This market was likely one end of a huge outdoor market whose counterpart structure, on the other side of the grove, is the ⓯ **Plaza de Mil Columnas.** (Plaza of the Thousand Columns). In typical Toltec-Maya style, the roof once covering the parallel rows of round stone columns in this long arcade has disappeared, giving the place a strangely Greek—and distinctly non-Maya—look. But the curvy-nosed Chaacs on the corners of the adjacent ⓰ **Templo de los Guerreros** are pure Maya. Why their noses are pointing down, like an upside-down "U, " instead of up, as usual, is just another mystery to be solved.

The Templo de los Guerreros shows the influence of Toltec architecture.

WHERE TO STAY AT CHICHÉN ITZÁ

★ **$$$ Mayaland.** This charming property is in a large garden, and close enough to the ruins to have its own entrance (you can even see some of the older structures from the windows). The large number of tour groups that come here, however, will make it less appealing if you're looking for privacy. Colonial-style guest rooms have decorative tiles; ask for one with a balcony, which doesn't cost extra. Bungalows have thatched roofs as well as wide verandas with hammocks. The simple Maya-inspired "huts" near the front of the property, built in the 1930s, are the cheapest option, but are for groups only. *Carretera 180, Km 120 985/851–0100or800/235–4079 985/851–0128 985/851–0129 www.mayaland.com 60 bungalows, 30 rooms, 10 suites 4 restaurants, room service, fans, minibars, cable TV, tennis court, 3 pools, volleyball, 2 bars, shop, laundry service, free parking AE, D, MC, V.*

Fodor's Choice **$$–$$$ Hacienda Chichén.** A converted 16th-century hacienda with its own entrance to the ruins, this hotel once served as the headquarters for the Carnegie expedition to Chichén Itzá. Rustic-chic, soap-scented cottages are simply but beautifully furnished in colonial Yucatecan style, with handwoven bedspreads and dehumidifiers; all of the ground-floor rooms have verandas, but only master suites have hammocks. There's a satellite TV in the library. An enormous (and deep) old pool graces the gardens. Meals are served on the patio overlooking the grounds, or in the air conditioned restaurant. A big plus is the hotel's intimate size; it's a place for honeymoons and silver anniversaries, not tour groups. Carretera 180, Km 120 985/851–0045, 999/924–2150 reservations, 800/624–8451 999/924–5011 www.haciendachichen.com.mx 24 rooms, 4 suites 2 restaurants, fans, some minibars, pool, bar, laundry service, shop, free parking; no room phones, no room TVs AE, DC, MC, V.

the above-mentioned buildings, is composed of a series of small chambers. In one of these chambers, archaeologists found a statue of the royal, by the name of Chac (as opposed to Chaac, the rain god), who apparently dwelt there. The building was named for the repeated pattern of birds, which decorates the upper part of the building's frieze.

Today you can watch a sound-and-light show at the site that recounts Mayan legends. The colored light brings out details of carvings and mosaics that are easy to miss when the sun is shining. The show is performed nightly in Spanish; earphones ($2.50) provide an English translation. ■TIP→**In the summer months, tarantulas are a common sight at the ruins and around the hotels that surround the ruins.** *Site, museum, and sound-and-light show $9.50; parking $1; use of video camera $3 (keep this receipt if visiting other archaeological sites along the Ruta Puuc on the same day) Daily 8–5; sound-and-light show just after dusk (at 7 or 8 PM depending on the time of year).*

WHERE TO EAT & STAY

$ MEXICAN **Cana Nah.** Although this large, recently remodeled roadside spot mainly caters to the groups visiting Uxmal, locals highly recommend it as the most formally established and hygienic eatery in the area, and the friendly owners are happy to serve small parties. The basic menu includes local dishes like lime soup and pollo pibíl, and such universals as fried chicken and vegetable soup. Approach the salsa on the table with a bit of caution: it's made almost purely of habanero chiles. After your meal you can laze in one of the hammocks out back under the trees or dive into the property's large rectangular swimming pool. There's a small shop as well, selling pieces of popular art including figurines of *los aluxes,* the mischievous "lords of the jungle" that Mayan legend says protect farmers' fields. *Carretera Muna–Uxmal, 4 km (2½ mi) north of Uxmal 999/910–3829 No credit cards.*

$$$$ **Lodge at Uxmal.** The outwardly rustic, thatch-roof buildings here have red-tile floors, doors and rocking chairs carved from polished hardwood, and local weavings. The effect is comfortable yet luxuriant; the property feels sort of like a peaceful ranch. All rooms have bathtubs and screened windows; suites have king-size beds and spa baths. **Pros:** Directly across from the entrance to Uxmal, rooms are beautiful in their simplicity, big pools. **Cons:** No room phones, restaurant food could be improved. *Carretera Uxmal, Km 78 997/976–2010 or 800/235–4079 www.mayaland.com 40 suites In-hotel: Safe, 2 restaurants, bar, pools, laundry service, parking (no fee), no elevator AE, MC, V.*

UNDERSTANDING MEXICO

MEXICO AT A GLANCE

FAST FACTS

Name in local language: Mexico
Capital: Mexico City (aka Distrito Federal or Federal District)
National anthem: *Mexicanos, al grito de guerra!* (*Mexicans, to the cry of war!*), by Francisco González Bocanegra and music by Jaime Nunó
Type of government: Federal republic
Administrative divisions: 31 states and 1 federal district
Independence: September 16, 1810 (from Spain)
Constitution: February 5, 1917
Legal system: Mixture of U.S. constitutional theory and civil law system, with judicial review of legislative acts
Suffrage: 18 years of age; universal and compulsory
Legislature: Bicameral National Congress of a Senate (128 seats; 96 elected by popular vote to serve six-year terms, and 32 allocated on the basis of each party's popular vote) and Federal Chamber of Deputies (500 seats; 300 members directly elected by popular vote to serve three-year terms; remaining 200 members allocated on the basis of each party's popular vote, also for three-year terms)
Population: 104.9 million
Population density: 141 people per square mi
Median age: Male 23.7, female 25.5
Life expectancy: Male 72.18, female 77.83
Infant mortality rate: 21.69 deaths per 1,000 live births
Literacy: 92.2%
Language: Spanish (official). Regional indigenous languages include Mayan and Nahuatl
Ethnic groups: Mestizo 60%; Amerindian or predominantly Amerindian 30%; white 9%; other 1%
Religion: Roman Catholic 89%, Protestant 6%, other 5%

In its male, in its public, its city aspect, Mexico is an arch-transvestite, a tragic buffoon. Dogs bark and babies cry when Mother Mexico walks abroad in the light of day. The policeman, the Marxist mayor—Mother Mexico doesn't even bother to shave her mustachios. Swords and rifles and spurs and bags of money chink and clatter beneath her skirts. A chain of martyred priests dangles from her waist, for she is an austere, pious lady. Ay, how much—clutching her jangling bosoms; spilling cigars—how much she has suffered.
–Richard Rodriguez

GEOGRAPHY & ENVIRONMENT

Land area: 1.9 million square km (.7 million square mi), almost three times the size of Texas
Coastline: 9,330 km (3,602 mi) along Pacific and Atlantic oceans, the Gulf of Mexico, and the Gulf of California
Terrain: High, rugged mountains; low coastal plains; high plateaus; desert (highest point is Volcan Pico de Orizaba, 18,400 feet)
Islands: Isla Angel de la Guarda, Isla Cedros, Isla Tiburon, Isla San Jose, Isla del Carmen, Cozumel, Isla Mujeres, Islas Marias, Isla Margarita, Isla Magdalena, Isla Cerralvo, Isla Espiritu Sancto, Isla Guadalupe, Islas Revillagigedos
Natural resources: Copper, gold, lead, natural gas, petroleum, silver, timber, zinc
Natural hazards: Tsunamis along the Pacific coast; volcanoes and earthquakes in the center and south; and hurricanes on the Pacific, Gulf of Mexico, and Caribbean coasts
Environmental issues: Scarcity of hazardous-waste-disposal facilities; natural freshwater resources scarce and polluted in north, inaccessible and poor quality in center and extreme southeast; raw sew-

age and industrial effluents polluting rivers in urban areas; deteriorating agricultural lands, especially groundwater depletion in the Valley of Mexico; serious air and water pollution, especially in the national capital, where pollutants in the city's air exceed World Health Organization guidelines by more than a factor of two, and in urban centers along the U.S.–Mexico border.

ECONOMY

Currency: Peso
Exchange rate: 10.3 pesos = $1
GDP: 7.08 trillion pesos ($637.15 billion)
Per capita income: 69,256 pesos ($6,230)
Inflation: 6%
Unemployment: 3.6%
Work force: 41.4 million
Debt: 1.77 trillion pesos ($159.8 billion)
Economic aid: 13.2 billion pesos ($1.2 billion)
Major industries: Food and beverages, iron and steel, mining, motor vehicles, petroleum, textiles
Agricultural products: Beans, beef, corn, fruit, rice, wheat
Exports: 2.4 trillion pesos ($214 billion)
Major export products: Coffee, cotton, fruits, manufactured goods, oil and oil products, silver, vegetables
Export partners: U.S. 87.6%; Canada 1.8%; Germany 1.2%; other 9.4%
Imports: 2.6 trillion pesos ($234 billion)
Major import products: Agricultural machinery, electrical equipment, car parts for assembly, metalworking machines, repair parts for motor vehicles, aircraft and aircraft parts, steel mill products
Import partners: U.S. 61.8%; China 5.5%; Japan 4.5%; other 28.2%

POLITICAL CLIMATE

Mexico's relationship with the U.S. dominates national politics. The U.S. is Mexico's largest trading partner by far, as well as its largest cultural influence. Both sides are working to improve upon inroads made since the North American Free Trade Agreement (NAFTA) was signed in 1993 and their effects on income and government. In elections in 1997 and 2000, opposition parties defeated the Institutional Revolutionary Party (PRI) for the first time since the 1910 Mexican Revolution. Change has been slow since the upheaval, and it's unclear whether the electorate is happy with the change. Indigenous groups continue to pressure the government for greater rights. An indigenous-rights law passed in 2001 fell short of giving Mexico's Indians political autonomy.

In Mexico an air-conditioner is called a politician because it makes a lot of noise but doesn't work very well.
–Len Deighton

DID YOU KNOW?

Mexico has the greatest number of universities, colleges, and other institutions of higher education in the world, with 10,341.

As you might expect, Mexico holds the record for the world's largest taco. During the 100th-anniversary celebrations of the city of Mexicali in 2003, a 35-foot, 1,654-pound taco was made by residents. Using 1,183 pounds of beef, 186 pounds of dough, 179 pounds of onion, and 106 pounds of cilantro, it took 80 people six hours to finish.

With nearly 105 million people, Mexico is the world's largest Spanish-speaking country by far. Colombia, Spain, and Argentina are next, with about 40 million inhabitants each.

Remittances from Mexicans living in the United States recently passed tourism and foreign investment to become Mexico's second-most-important source of income. Only oil brings in more money.

International law limits the production of tequila to a specific region of Mexico, but most of the tequila distilled there is shipped in bulk to the United States, where it's bottled.

CHRONOLOGY

PRE-COLUMBIAN MEXICO

ca. 40,000 BC Asian nomads cross land bridge over the Bering Strait to North America, gradually migrate south.

ca. 7000 BC–2000 BC Archaic period, which marked the beginnings of agriculture and village life.

ca. 2000 BC–AD 100 Formative or Preclassic period: development of pottery, incipient political structures. (The late Preclassic period runs from 400 bc to ad 100.)

500 BC–900 BC The powerful and sophisticated Olmec civilization develops primarily along the Gulf of Mexico in the present-day states of Veracruz and Tabasco. Olmec culture, the "mother culture" of Mexico, flourishes along Gulf Coast.

AD 100–AD 1000 Classic period: height of Mesoamerican culture. Totonac-speaking people build the city of Teotihuacán (near Mexico City); the powerful and cultured Zapotec rule in Oaxaca, and the Maya advance math and astronomy in the Yucatán. Ruling dynasties produce impressive art and architecture; powerful priests perform elaborate ceremonies based on their interpretation of signs and celestial events. (The Late Classic period runs from 800 to 1000.)

650–900 Fall of Teotihuacán circa 650 leads to competition among other city-states, exacerbated by migrations of tribes from the harsh northern deserts.

ca. 900–1150 The Toltec, a northern tribe, establish a flourishing culture at their capital of Tula under the legendary monarch Topiltzin-Quetzalcóatl.

1000–1521 Postclassic period: with the decline of the monarchy, rule passes to tribal councils. Cultural achievements wane; many once-flourishing cities have by now been abandoned.

1111 The unlettered Aztecs migrate to mainland from island home off the Nayarit coast. They are not welcomed by the peoples of central Mexico.

ca. 1200 Rise of Mixtec culture at Zapotec sites of Monte Albán and Mitla; notable for production of picture codices, which include historical narratives.

1150–1350 Following the fall of Tula, the Chichimec and then the Tepanec assert hegemony over central Mexico. The Tepanec tyrant Tezozómoc (1320–1426), like his contemporaries in Renaissance Italy, establishes his power with murder and treachery.

1320 The Aztec city of Tenochtitlán is built in the middle of Lake Texcoco.

1420–1519 Aztecs extend their rule to much of central and southern Mexico. A warrior society, they build a great city at Tenochtitlán.

1502 Moctezuma II (1502–20) assumes throne at the height of Aztec culture and political power.

1517 Spanish expedition under Francisco Hernandez de Córdoba (1475–1526) lands on Yucatán coast.

1519 Hernán Cortés (1485–1547) lands in Cozumel, founds Veracruz, and is determined to conquer. Steel weapons, horses, and smallpox, combined with a belief that Cortés was the resurrected god Quetzalcóatl, minimize Aztec resistance. Cortés and his men stay for months as somewhat captive guests at Tenochtitlán before taking Moctezuma hostage.

THE COLONIAL PERIOD

1521 Tenochtitlán falls to Cortés after Moctezuma is killed in 1520. The last Aztec emperor, Cuauhtémoc, is tortured to reveal hidden gold; he doesn't, and is later executed.

1528 Juan de Zumárraga (1468–1548) arrives as bishop of Mexico City, gains title "Protector of the Indians"; conversions to Catholicism increase.

1535 First Spanish viceroy arrives in Mexico.

1537 Pope Paul III issues a papal bull declaring that Mesoamerica's indigenous people are indeed human and not beasts. First printing press arrives in Mexico City.

1546–48 Silver deposits discovered at Zacatecas.

1547 Spanish conquest of Aztec Empire—now known as "New Spain"—completed, at enormous cost to native peoples.

1553 Royal and Pontifical University of Mexico, first university in the New World, opens.

1571 The Spanish Inquisition established in New Spain; it is not abolished until 1820.

1609 Northern capital of New Spain established at Santa Fe (New Mexico).

1651 Birth of Sor (Sister) Juana Inés de la Cruz, greatest poet of colonial Mexico (d. 1695).

1718 Franciscan missionaries settle in Texas, which becomes part of New Spain.

1765 Charles III of Spain (1716–88) sends José de Galvez to tour New Spain and propose reforms.

1769 Franciscan Junípero Serra establishes missions in present-day California, extending Spanish hegemony.

1788 Death of Charles III; his reforms improve administration, but also raise social and political expectations among the colonial population that are not fulfilled.

1808 Napoléon invades Spain, leaving a power vacuum in New Spain.

THE WAR OF INDEPENDENCE

1810 September 16: Father Miguel Hidalgo y Costilla (1753–1811) and co-conspirators launch the War of Independence against the Spanish crown.

1811 Hidalgo is captured and executed; leadership of the movement passes to Father José María Morelos y Pavón (1765–1815).

1813 Morelos calls a congress at Chilpancingo, which drafts a Declaration of Independence.

1815 Morelos is captured and executed.

THE EARLY NATIONAL PERIOD

1821 Vicente Guerrero, a rebel leader, and Agustín de Iturbide (1783–1824), a Spanish colonel, sign a peace accord, rejuvenating the independence movement. Spain soon recognizes Mexican independence with the Treaty of Córdoba.

1822 Agustín de Iturbide is named Emperor of Mexico, which stretches from California to Central America.

1823 After 10 months in office, de Iturbide is turned out.

1824 A new constitution creates a federal republic, the Estados Unidos Mexicanos; modeled on the U.S. Constitution, the Mexican version retains the privileges of the Catholic Church and gives the president extraordinary "emergency" powers.

1829 President Vicente Guerrero abolishes slavery. A Spanish attempt at reconquest is halted by General Antonio López de Santa Anna (1794–1876), already a hero for his role in the overthrow of de Iturbide.

1833 Santa Anna is elected president by a huge majority; by 1855, he has held the office for 11 of its 36 changes of hands.

1836 Although voted in as a liberal, Santa Anna abolishes the 1824 constitution. Already dismayed at the abolition of slavery, Texas—whose population is largely American—declares its independence. Santa Anna successfully besieges the Texans at the Alamo. But a month later he is captured by Sam Houston following the Battle of San Jacinto. Texas gains its independence as the Lone Star Republic.

1846 The U.S. decision to annex Texas leads to war.

1848 The treaty of Guadalupe Hidalgo reduces Mexico's territory by half, ceding present-day Texas, New Mexico, Arizona, California, Nevada, Utah, and part of Colorado to the United States.

1853 Santa Anna agrees to the Gadsden Purchase, ceding a further 48,000 square km (18,500 square mi) to the United States.

THE REFORM & FRENCH INTERVENTION

1855 The Revolution of Ayutla topples Santa Anna and leads to the period of the Reform.

1857 The liberal Constitution of 1857 disestablishes the Catholic Church, among other measures.

1858–61 The Civil War of the Reform ends in liberal victory. Benito Juárez (1806–72) is elected president. France, Spain, and Britain agree jointly to occupy the customhouse at Veracruz to force payment of Mexico's huge foreign debt.

1862 Spain and Britain withdraw their forces; the French, seeking empire, march inland. On May 5 General Porfirio Díaz repulses the French at Puebla.

1863 Strengthened with reinforcements, the French occupy Mexico City. Napoléon III of France appoints Archduke Ferdinand Maximilian of Austria (1832–67) as Emperor of Mexico.

1864 Maximilian and his empress, Charlotte, known as Carlotta, land at Veracruz.

1867 With U.S. assistance, Juárez overthrows Mexico's second empire. Maximilian is executed; Carlotta, pleading his case at the Vatican, goes mad.

1872 Juárez dies in office. The Mexico City–Veracruz railway is completed, symbol of the new progressivist mood.

THE PORFIRIATO

1876 Porfirio Díaz (1830–1915) comes to power in the revolution of Tuxtepec; he holds office nearly continuously until 1911. With his advisers, the *científicos,* he forces modernization and balances the budget for the first time in Mexican history. But the social cost is high.

1886 Birth of Diego Rivera (d. 1957).

1890 José Schneider, who is of German ancestry, founds the Cerveceria Cuauhtémoc, brewer of Carta Blanca beer.

1900 Jesús, Enrique, and Ricardo Flores Magón publish the anti-Díaz newspaper *La Regeneración.* Suppressed, the brothers move their campaign to the United States, first to San Antonio, then to St. Louis.

1906 The Flores Magón group publish their Liberal Plan, a proposal for reform. Industrial unrest spreads.

THE SECOND REVOLUTION

1907 Birth of the renowned painter Frida Kahlo (d. 1954).

1910 On the centennial of the Revolution, Díaz wins yet another rigged election. Encouraged by Francisco Madero's campaigning and publications, revolt breaks out.

1911 Rebels under Pascual Orozco and Francisco (Pancho) Villa (1878–1923) capture Ciudad Juárez; Díaz resigns. Francisco Madero is elected president; calling for land reform, Emiliano Zapata (1879–1919) rejects the new regime. Violence continues.

1913 Military coup: Madero is deposed and murdered. In one day Mexico has three presidents, the last being General Victoriano Huerta (1854–1916). Civil war rages.

1914 American intervention leads to dictator Huerta's overthrow. Villa and Zapata briefly join forces at the Convention of Aguascalientes, but the revolution goes on. Birth of poet-critic Octavio Paz.

1916 Villa's border raids lead to an American punitive expedition under Pershing. Villa eludes capture.

1917 Under a new constitution, Venustiano Carranza, head of the Constitutionalist Army, is elected president. Zapata continues his rebellion, which is brutally suppressed.

1918 CROM, the national labor union, is founded.

1919 On order of Carranza, Zapata is assassinated.

1920 Carranza is assassinated; Alvaro Obregón (1880–1928), who helped overthrow dictator Huerta in 1914, is elected president, beginning a period of reform and reconstruction. Schools are built and land is redistributed. In the next two decades, revolutionary culture finds expression in the art of Diego Rivera and José Clemente Orozco (1883–1949), the novels of Martin Luis Guzmán and Gregorio López y Fuentes, and the music of Carlos Chávez (1899–1978).

1923 Pancho Villa is assassinated. The United States finally recognizes the Obregón regime.

1926–28 Catholics react to government anticlericalism in the Cristero Rebellion.

1934–40 The presidency of Lázaro Cárdenas (1895–1970) leads to the fullest implementation of revolutionary reforms.

1938 Cárdenas nationalizes the oil companies, removing them from foreign control.

1940 On August 20, exiled former Soviet leader Leon Trotsky is murdered in his Mexico City home.

OST-REVOLUTIONARY MEXICO

1951 Mexico's segment of the Pan-American Highway is completed, confirming the industrial growth and prosperity of postwar Mexico. Culture is increasingly Americanized; writers such as Octavio Paz and Carlos Fuentes express disillusionment with the post-revolution world.

1968 The Summer Olympics in Mexico City showcase Mexican prosperity, but hundreds of student activists are murdered or jailed during a massive demonstration. The government denies and suppresses this information.

1981–82 Recession and a drop in oil prices severely damage Mexico's economy. The peso is devalued.

1985 Thousands die in the Mexico City earthquake.

1988 American-educated economist Carlos Salinas de Gortari is elected president; for the first time since 1940, support for the PRI, the national political party, seems to be slipping.

1993 North American Free Trade Agreement (NAFTA) is signed with United States and Canada.

1994 Uprising by the indigenous peoples of Chiapas, led by the Zapatista National Liberation Army and their charismatic ski-masked leader, Subcomandante Marcos; election reforms promised as a result. Popular PRI presidential candidate Luis Donaldo Colosio assassinated while campaigning in Tijuana. Ernesto Zedillo, generally thought to be more of a technocrat and "old boy" PRI politician, replaces him and wins the election. Zedillo, blaming the economic policies of his predecessor, devalues the peso in December.

1995 Recession sets in as a result of the peso devaluation. Ex-President Carlos Salinas de Gortari is linked to scandals surrounding the assassinations of Colosio and another high-ranking government official; Salinas moves to the United States.

1996 Mexico's economy, bolstered by a $28 billion bailout program led by the United States, turns upward, but the recovery is fragile. The opposition National Action Party (PAN), which is committed to conservative economic policies, gains strength. New details of scandals of the former administration continue to emerge.

1997 Mexico's top antidrug official is arrested on bribery charges. Nonetheless, the United States recertifies Mexico as a partner in the war on drugs. The Zedillo administration faces midterm party elections.

1998 Death of Octavio Paz.

1999 Raúl Salinas, brother of the former president Carlos Salinas de Gortari, sentenced to prison for the murder of a PRI leader.

2000 Spurning the long-ruling PRI, Mexicans elect opposition candidate Vicente Fox president.

2001 U.S.-Mexico relations take on increased importance as Fox meets repeatedly with George W. Bush to discuss immigration reform and economic programs. President Fox frees imprisoned Zapatista rebel sympathizers and signs into law a controversial Indian rights bill in hopes of bringing peace to southern Chiapas state; however, peace talks remain stalled. Human-rights attorney Digna Ochoa is assassinated, opening the country to accusations of failing to investigate human-rights abuses by the military and police. The case is unsolved.

2002 Under President Fox's orders, the federal Human Rights Commission investigates and confirms that hundreds of people, most suspected leftist rebels, disappeared at the hands of the state after being arrested in the 1960s, '70s, and '80s. Fox also signs into law a freedom of information act and releases nearly 80 million secret intelligence files collected by the government.

2003 High hopes for NAFTA erode as hundreds of factories relocate from Mexico to the Far East, where labor is even cheaper.

2004 In his autobiography *Change of Course,* former president Miguel de la Madrid admits that the government rigged the 1988 presidential election in favor of PRI candidate Carlos Salinas de Gortari and that opposition candidate Cuauhtémoc Cárdenas, son of agrarian reformist Lázaro Cárdenas, was likely to win according to an early count of electronic ballots.

2005 During state elections in February, residents of Guerrero vote in the PRD's favor, dealing a blow to the PRI party, which had been making steady progress since its momentous defeat with the election of President Fox in 2000. Left-wing Mexico City mayor Andrés Manuel López Obrador, a 2006 presidential front-runner, loses his immunity from prosecution by order of congress. The PRD-affiliated mayor faces charges because of a building violation, though he claims it is purely political scheming. The scandal sends Mexico's stock market down 14%.

2006 This was a landmark year for discussions about Mexico–U.S. border security, as well as illegal-immigrant status in the United States. Many people view the issue of closing off the border as a hypocritical move, considering the dependency of the U.S. economy on illegal workers. Others believe that securing the border may help illegal immigrants already in the United States obtain legal status, and also create a more organized system for future immigrants.

2007 Left-wing presidential candidate Andres Manuel Lopez Obrador is defeated by less than one percentage point by Felipe Calderon of the governing National Action Party (PAN). Widespread protests and political unrest ensue. Picturesque Oaxaca City is the site of months-long protests instigated by a teachers' union. Protesters seeking higher wages and the ouster of the state governor take hold of the downtown area of the city, with riot police eventually using drastic tactics to break up the protest. Though the city is calmer and recuperating, lack of tourism to this part of the country was a huge blow to the local economy, while the national economy enjoys great stability.

President Bush visits Mexico in early spring for bilateral talks with President Calderon. Having failed to act on his promise of allowing more guest workers, and for entertaining the idea of constructing a large wall between the United States and Mexico, Bush is met with considerable hostility.

BOOKS & MOVIES

BOOKS

PRE-COLUMBIAN & COLONIAL WORKS & HISTORIES

If the pre-Columbian way of thinking holds any appeal for you, Dennis Tedlock's superb translation of the Maya creation myth, *Popol Vuh,* is essential reading. Good general reference works can deepen your understanding of Mexico's indigenous peoples and enrich your trips to the many marvelous archaeological sites in Mexico. These include *The Conquest of the Yucatán* by celebrated ethnographer and champion of indigenous cultural survival Frans Blom; *The Toltec Heritage,* by Nigel Davies; *Secrets of the Maya* from the editors of *Archaeology* magazine; and the colorful *Ancient Mexico,* by Maria Longhena.

For decades, the standard texts written by scholars for popular audiences have been *A History of Mexico,* by Henry B. Parkes; *Many Mexicos,* by Lesley Byrd Simpson; and *A Compact History of Mexico,* an anthology published by the Colegio de México.

CONTEMPORARY HISTORIES

A number of journalists have made important contributions to the literature on historical and contemporary Mexico. Pulitzer Prize–winning *Miami Herald* Latin American correspondent Andres Oppenheimer's *Bordering on Chaos: Mexico's Roller-Coaster Journey to Prosperity* (1996) chronicles two of the most tumultuous years in recent Mexican history. The book investigates the country's descent into turmoil following the 1994 Zapatista uprising, two shocking 1994 political assassinations, the presidential elections, and the 1995 peso crisis. William Langewiesche's *Cutting for Sign* examines life along the Mexican–U.S. border, and *Los Angeles Times* correspondent Sam Quiñones's *True Tales from Another Mexico: The Lynch Mob, the Popsicle Kings, Chalino, and the Bronx* (2001) recounts engaging stories about everyday Mexican people that manage to reveal the complexities and peculiarities of Mexico's social, economic, and political situations.

Alan Riding's *Distant Neighbors: A Portrait of the Mexicans* is a classic description of Mexican politics, society, and finance from the *New York Times* correspondent who lived there during the 1980s. Another former *New York Times* journalist, Jonathan Kandell, penned *La Capital: The Biography of Mexico City* in 1988, a fascinating and detailed history of the city from pre-Hispanic times to the modern day. Elena Poniatowska, better known in the English-speaking world for her fiction, is one of Mexico's most highly respected journalists. *Massacre in Mexico,* her account of government repression of a demonstration in Mexico City in 1968, is an enlightening and disturbing work.

ETHNOGRAPHY

Excellent ethnographies include Oscar Lewis's classic works on the culture of poverty *The Children of Sanchez* and *Five Families*; *Juan the Chamula,* by Ricardo Pozas, about a small village in Chiapas; *Mexico South: The Isthmus of Tehuantepec,* by Miguel Covarrubias, which discusses Indian life in the early 20th century; Gertrude Blom's *Bearing Witness,* on the Lacandones of Chiapas; and *Maria Sabina: Her Life and Chants,* an autobiography of a shaman in the state of Oaxaca. Beginning in the early 1970s, Carlos Castaneda wrote a series of philosophical, controversial books beginning with *The Teachings of Don Juan: A Yaqui Way of Knowledge.* Each book recounted the author's purported apprenticeship with the wise old shaman from northern Mexico, Don Juan.

FOOD

Perhaps one of the most unusual and delightful books published on Mexican cookery in recent years is *Recipe of Memory: Five Generations of Mexican Cuisine* (1995). Written by Pulitzer Prize–winning food journalist Victor Valle and his wife, Mary Lau Valle, this book reproduces recipes the couple found in an antique chest passed down through the Valle family and in the process weaves an intriguing family and social history. Patricia Quintana's lushly photographed cookbooks, which capture the culinary history and culture of Mexico, include *The Taste of Mexico* (1993). Diana Kennedy's culinary works are also wildly popular, including her classic *The Art of Mexican Cooking* (1989) and *The Essential Cuisines of Mexico* (2000).

Chef Rick Bayless is another staunch champion of Mexican regional cuisine; his books include *Mexico: One Plate at a Time* (2000) and *Mexican Kitchen* (1996). Marita Adair's *The Hungry Traveler Mexico* (1997), with descriptions of Mexican foods and their origins, goes beyond the typical food list. *Frida's Fiestas: Recipes and Recollections of Life with Frida Kahlo* (1994) is a cookbook memoir by the artist's stepdaughter, Guadalupe Rivera Marin. It assembles photos, a personal account of important events in Kahlo's life, and recipes for over 100 dishes Kahlo used to serve to family and friends.

TRAVELOGUES

Alice Adams's *Mexico: Some Travels and Some Travelers There,* which includes an introduction by Jan Morris, is available in paperback; James A. Michener's novel *Mexico* captures the history of the land and the personality of the people. Probably the finest travelogue-cum-guidebook is Kate Simon's *Mexico: Places and Pleasures. Into a Desert Place* chronicles Graham Mackintosh's trek along the Baja coast. So entranced by San Miguel de Allende that he decided to stay, Tony Cohan recounts a gringo's daily life there in *On Mexican Time.* More recently he penned Mexican Days, which describes his later adventures in San Miguel and discoveries other parts of the country. James O'Reilly and Larry Habegger have edited a diverse collection of articles and essays by contemporary writers in *Travelers' Tales Mexico.* Ron Butler's *Dancing Alone in Mexico: From the Border to Baja and Beyond* recounts the author's capricious travels across the country. *Cartwheels in the Sand,* by Ann Hazard, tells of the author's adventures with friends up and down the Baja peninsula.

CONTEMPORARY LITERATURE

The late poet-philosopher Octavio Paz was the dean of Mexican intellectuals. His best works are *Labyrinth of Solitude,* a thoughtful, far-reaching dissection of Mexican culture, and *Sor Juana,* the biography of Sor Juana Inés de la Cruz, a 17th-century nun and poet. For more on Sor Juana, including her own writings, see Alan Trueblood's *A Sor Juana Anthology.* Other top authors include Carlos Fuentes (*The Death of Artemio Cruz* and *The Old Gringo* are among his most popular novels), Juan Rulfo (his classic is *Pedro Páramo*), Jorge Ibarguengoitia (*Two Crimes, The Dead Girls*), Elena Poniatowska (*Dear Diego, Here's to You Jesusa,* and *Tinisima* among others), Rosario Castellanos (*The Nine Guardians* and *City of Kings*), Elena Garros (*Recollections of Things to Come*), Gregorio López y Fuentes (*El Indio*), Angeles Mastretta (*Mexican Bolero*), and José Emilio Pacheco (*Battles in the Desert and Other Stories*).

Recent biographies of Frida Kahlo and Diego Rivera (by Hayden Herrera and Bertram D. Wolfe, respectively) provide glimpses into the Mexican intellectual and political life of the 1920s and '30s. Laura Esquivel's recipe-enhanced novel *Like Water for Chocolate* captures the passions and palates of revolutionary Mexico. Edited by Juana Ponce de León, *Our Word Is Our Weapon* contains writings by the Subcomandante Insurgente Marcos. They range from communiqués made on behalf of the

Zapatista movement to Marcos's own stories and poetry.

D.H. Lawrence's *The Plumed Serpent* is probably the best-known foreign novel about Mexico, although its noble savage theme is quite offensive. Lawrence recorded his travels in Oaxaca in *Mornings in Mexico,* also in a rather condescending tone. A far greater piece of literature is Malcolm Lowry's *Under the Volcano.* Also noteworthy is John Steinbeck's *The Log from the Sea of Cortez. The Reader's Companion to Mexico,* edited by Alan Ryan, includes material by Langston Hughes, D.H. Lawrence, and Paul Theroux. The characters of Cormac McCarthy's *Border Trilogy* weave back and forth across the Texas–Mexico border in the 1940s. The prizewinning *Sky Over El Nido,* by C.M. Mayo, is a collection of contemporary short stories.

MOVIES

Mexican cinema cut its teeth during the Mexican Revolution, when both Mexican and U.S. cameramen braved the battlefields to catch the generals in action. Legend has it that American cameramen helped Pancho Villa "choreograph" the Battle of Celaya for on-screen (and military) success. For an early Hollywood portrayal of the Revolution shot partially in Mexico, check out director Elia Kazan's *Viva Zapata!* (1952), written by John Steinbeck and starring Marlon Brando as Emiliano Zapata.

It wasn't long after Kazan's epic that directors of Hollywood westerns hit on Durango state as a cheap alternative to the usual "Old West" locales north of the border. The quintessential cinema cowboy, John Wayne, made eight movies in the area, including *True Grit* (1969), for which he won an Oscar.

John Huston directed one of the earliest American movies shot in Mexico, the unforgettable prospecting adventure *The Treasure of the Sierra Madre* (1948), filmed in Michoacán state. In 1964, Huston set an adaptation of Tennessee Williams's play *The Night of the Iguana* in Puerto Vallarta. And in 1984, Huston made the beautiful, intense *Under the Volcano,* adapted from Malcolm Lowry's novel. The movie was shot in Morelos, near Cuernavaca, and shows the local Día de los Muertos celebrations.

Hollywood's presence in Mexico continued throughout the 1990s and the early 2000s. After *Titanic* (1997) and parts of *Pearl Harbor* (2001) were filmed in Rosarito, some began referring to the area as "Baja Hollywood." Other recent blockbusters that were shot south of the border include *Frida* (2002), with Salma Hayek as the Mexican artist, and gorgeous settings in Mexico City's Coyoacán neighborhood; Steven Soderbergh's *Traffic* (2001), which trolls some of the tougher areas of Tijuana and other border towns; and Ted Demme's *Blow* (2001), with Johnny Depp and Penélope Cruz, filmed in glitzy Acapulco. *The Mask of Zorro* (1998), starring Antonio Banderas and Anthony Hopkins, gallops across several locations in central Mexico. Robert Rodriguez made his name with his tales of a mariachi musician dragged into a world of crime. The films *El Mariachi* (1992) and *Desperado* (1995) were capped by *Once Upon a Time in Mexico,* starring Antonio Banderas, Johnny Depp, and Salma Hayek, in 2003.

The predominance of Hollywood films in Mexico has not been without controversy. In 1998, Mexico passed a law requiring movie theaters to reserve 10% of their screen time for domestic films. The government also directed funds to support homegrown Mexican cinema, and the effort is already paying off, as recent films gain international attention. Director Carlos Carrera's *El Crimen del Padre Amaro (The Crime of Father Amaro,* 2002) courted scandal with its story of a priest's love affair, becoming Mexico's highest-grossing domestic film in the process. *Y Tu Mamá También*

(And Your Mother Too, 2001) swept film festivals across Europe and Latin America. The funny, very sexual coming-of-age tale of two teenage boys was shot in Mexico City and the Oaxaca coast. *Amores Perros (Love's a Bitch,* 2000) is a Mexico City thriller about intertwining stories of loss and regret. For a delicious romance set in early-20th-century Mexico, see *Como Agua Para Chocolate (Like Water for Chocolate,* 1992), based on the novel by Laura Esquivel.

Less mainstream films that have won critical acclaim include the 2002 films *Amarte Duele (Love Hurts),* a modern love story with a rock-and-roll sound track, and *Asesino en Serio (A Serious Killer),* a sexy murder mystery. Jaime Humberto Hermosillo, Mexico's first openly gay director, made the campy black comedy *El Misterio de los Almendros (Mystery of the Almonds,* 2003).

The undeniably talented threesome Alfonso Cuarón (*Children of Men* director), Alejandro González Iñarritu, and Guillermo del Toro made a splash at the 2007 Academy Awards. González Iñarritu's *Babel* was nominated for best picture and best director, and del Toro's *Pan's Labyrinth* was nominated in the Best Foreign Language Film category, among others.

SPANISH VOCABULARY

BASICS

ENGLISH	SPANISH	PRONUNCIATION
Yes/no	Sí/no	see/no
Please	Por favor	pore fah-**vore**
May I?	¿Me permite?	may pair-**mee**-tay
Thank you (very much)	(Muchas) gracias	(**moo**-chas) **grah**-see-as
You're welcome	De nada	day **nah**-dah
Excuse me	Con permiso	con pair-**mee**-so
Pardon me	¿Perdón?	pair-**dohn**
Could you tell me?	¿Podría decirme?	po-dree-ah deh-**seer**-meh
I'm sorry	Lo siento	lo see-**en**-toh
Good morning!	¡Buenos días!	**bway**-nohs **dee**-ahs
Good afternoon!	¡Buenas tardes!	**bway**-nahs **tar**-dess
Good evening!	¡Buenas noches!	**bway**-nahs **no**-chess
Goodbye! luego!	¡Adiós!/¡Hasta -stah **lwe**-go	ah-dee-**ohss/ah**
Mr./Mrs.	Señor/Señora	sen-**yor**/sen-**yohr**-ah
Miss	Señorita	sen-yo-**ree**-tah
Pleased to meet you	Mucho gusto	**moo**-cho **goose**-toh
How are you?	¿Cómo está usted?	**ko**-mo es-**tah** oo-**sted**
Very well, thank you.	Muy bien, gracias.	**moo**-ee bee-**en**, **grah**-see-as
And you?	¿Y usted?	ee oos-**ted**
Hello (on the telephone)	Diga	**dee**-gah

NUMBERS

ENGLISH	SPANISH	PRONUNCIATION
1	un, uno	oon, **oo**-no
2	dos	dos
3	tres	tress
4	cuatro	**kwah**-tro
5	cinco	**sink**-oh

6	seis	saice
7	siete	see-**et**-eh
8	ocho	**o**-cho
9	nueve	new-**eh**-vey
10	diez	dee-**es**
11	once	**ohn**-seh
12	doce	**doh**-seh
13	trece	**treh**-seh
14	catorce	ka-**tohr**-seh
15	quince	**keen**-seh
16	dieciséis	dee-**es**-ee-**saice**
17	diecisiete	dee-**es**-ee-see-**et**-eh
18	dieciocho	dee-**es**-ee-**o**-cho
19	diecinueve	**dee-es**-ee-new-**ev**-eh
20	veinte	**vain**-teh
21	veinte y uno/veintiuno	**vain**-te-**oo**-noh
30	treinta	**train**-tah
32	treinta y dos	train-tay-**dohs**
40	cuarenta	kwah-**ren**-tah
43	cuarenta y tres	kwah-**ren**-tay-**tress**
50	cincuenta	seen-**kwen**-tah
54	cincuenta y cuatro	seen-**kwen**-tay **kwah**-tro
60	sesenta	sess-**en**-tah
65	sesenta y cinco	sess-**en**-tay **seen**-ko
70	setenta	set-**en**-tah
76	setenta y seis	set-**en**-tay **saice**
80	ochenta	oh-**chen**-tah
87	ochenta y siete	oh-**chen**-tay see-**yet**-eh
90	noventa	no-**ven**-tah
98	noventa y ocho	no-**ven**-tah-**o**-choh
100	cien	see-**en**

101	ciento uno	see-**en**-toh **oo**-noh
200	doscientos	doh-see-**en**-tohss
500	quinientos	keen-**yen**-tohss
700	setecientos	set-eh-see-**en**-tohss
900	novecientos	no-veh-see-**en**-tohss
1,000	mil	meel
2,000	dos mil	dohs meel
1,000,000	un millón	oon meel-**yohn**

COLORS

black	negro	**neh**-groh
blue	azul	ah-**sool**
brown	café	kah-**feh**
green	verde	**ver**-deh
pink	rosa	**ro**-sah
purple	morado	mo-**rah**-doh
orange	naranja	na-**rahn**-hah
red	rojo	**roh**-hoh
white	blanco	**blahn**-koh
yellow	amarillo	ah-mah-**ree**-yoh

DAYS OF THE WEEK

Sunday	domingo	doe-**meen**-goh
Monday	lunes	**loo**-ness
Tuesday	martes	**mahr**-tess
Wednesday	miércoles	me-**air**-koh-less
Thursday	jueves	hoo-**ev**-ess
Friday	viernes	vee-**air**-ness
Saturday	sábado	**sah**-bah-doh

MONTHS

January	enero	eh-**neh**-roh
February	febrero	feh-**breh**-roh
March	marzo	**mahr**-soh
April	abril	ah-**breel**

May	mayo	**my**-oh
June	junio	**hoo**-nee-oh
July	julio	**hoo**-lee-yoh
August	agosto	ah-**ghost**-toh
September	septiembre	sep-tee-**em**-breh
October	octubre	oak-**too**-breh
November	noviembre	no-vee-**em**-breh
December	diciembre	dee-see-**em**-breh

USEFUL PHRASES

Do you speak English?	¿Habla usted inglés?	**ah**-blah oos-**ted** in-**glehs**
I don't speak Spanish	No hablo español	no **ah**-bloh es-pahn-**yol**
I don't understand (you)	No entiendo	no en-tee-**en**-doh
I understand (you)	Entiendo	en-tee-**en**-doh
I don't know	No sé	no seh
I am American/ British	Soy americano (americana)/ inglés(a)	soy ah-meh-ree-**kah**-no (ah-meh-ree-**kah**-nah)/in-**glehs(ah)**
What's your name?	¿Cómo se llama usted?	koh-mo seh **yah**-mah oos-**ted**
My name is . . .	Me llamo . . .	may **yah**-moh
What time is it?	¿Qué hora es?	keh **o**-rah es
It is one, two, three . . . o'clock.	Es la una./Son las dos, tres . . .	es la **oo**-nah/sohn lahs dohs, tress
Yes, please/No, thank you	Sí, por favor/No, gracias	**see** pohr fah-**vor**/no **grah**-see-us
How?	¿Cómo?	**koh**-mo
When?	¿Cuándo?	**kwahn**-doh
This/Next week	Esta semana/ la semana que entra	**es**-teh seh-**mah**-nah/lah seh-**mah**-nah keh **en**-trah
This/Next month	Este mes/el próximo mes	**es**-teh mehs/el **proke**-see-mo mehs
This/Next year	Este año/el año que viene	**es**-teh **ahn**-yo/el **ahn**-yo keh vee-**yen**-ay

Yesterday/today/ tomorrow	Ayer/hoy/mañana	ah-**yehr**/oy/mahn-**yah**-nah
This morning/ afternoon	Esta mañana/ tarde	**es**-tah mahn-**yah**-nah/**tar**-deh
Tonight	Esta noche	**es**-tah **no**-cheh
What?	¿Qué?	keh
What is it?	¿Qué es esto?	keh es **es**-toh
Why?	¿Por qué?	pore **keh**
Who?	¿Quién?	kee-**yen**
Where is . . . ? the train station? the subway station? the bus stop? the post office? the bank? the hotel? the store? the cashier? the museum? the hospital? the elevator? the bathroom?	¿Dónde está . . . ? la estación del tren? la estación del tren subterráneo? la parada del autobus? la oficina de correos? el banco? el hotel? la tienda? la caja? el museo? el hospital? el ascensor? el baño?	**dohn**-deh es-**tah** la es-tah-see-on del trehn la es-ta-see-**on** del trehn la es-ta-see-**on** soob-teh-**rrahn**-eh-oh la pah-**rah**-dah del ow-toh-**boos** la oh-fee-**see**-nah deh koh-**rreh**-os el **bahn**-koh el oh-**tel** la tee-**en**-dah la **kah**-hah el moo-**seh**-oh el ohss-pee-**tal** el ah-**sen**-sohr el **bahn**-yoh
Here/there	Aquí/allá	ah-**key**/ah-**yah**
Open/closed	Abierto/cerrado	ah-bee-**er**-toh/ser-**ah**-doh
Left/right	Izquierda/derecha	iss-key-**er**-dah/dare-**eh**-chah
Straight ahead	Derecho	dare-**eh**-choh
Is it near/far?	¿Está cerca/lejos?	es-**tah** **sehr**-kah/**leh**-hoss
I'd like . . . a room the key a newspaper a stamp	Quisiera . . . un cuarto/una habitación la llave un periódico un sello de correo	kee-see-ehr-ah oon **kwahr**-toh/**oo**-nah ah-bee-tah-see-**on** lah **yah**-veh oon pehr-ee-**oh**-dee-koh oon **seh**-yo deh koh-**reh**-oh

I'd like to buy . . .	Quisiera comprar . . .	kee-see-**ehr**-ah kohm-**prahr**
cigarettes	cigarrillos	ce-ga-**ree**-yohs
matches	cerillos	ser-**ee**-ohs
a dictionary	un diccionario	oon deek-see-oh-**nah**-ree-oh
soap	jabón	hah-**bohn**
sunglasses	gafas de sol	**ga**-fahs deh sohl
suntan lotion	loción bronceadora	loh-see-**ohn** brohn-seh-ah-**do**-rah
a map	un mapa	oon **mah**-pah
a magazine	una revista	**oon**-ah reh-**veess**-tah
paper	papel	pah-**pel**
envelopes	sobres	**so**-brehs
a postcard	una tarjeta postal	**oon**-ah tar-**het**-ah post-**ahl**
How much is it?	¿Cuánto cuesta?	**kwahn**-toh **kwes**-tah
It's expensive/cheap	Está caro/barato	es-**tah kah**-roh/bah-**rah**-toh
A little/a lot	Un poquito/mucho	oon poh-**kee**-toh/**moo**-choh
More/less	Más/menos	mahss/**men**-ohss
Enough/too much/too little	Suficiente/demasiado/muy poco	soo-fee-see-**en**-teh/deh-mah-see-**ah**-doh/**moo**-ee **poh**-koh
Telephone	Teléfono	tel-**ef**-oh-no
Telegram	Telegrama	teh-leh-**grah**-mah
I am ill	Estoy enfermo(a)	es-**toy** en-**fehr**-moh(mah)
Please call a doctor	Por favor llame a un medico	pohr fah-**vor ya**-meh ah oon **med**-ee-koh
Help!	¡Auxilio! ¡Socorro!	owk-see-lee-oh/soh-kohr-roh
Fire!	¡Incendio!	en-sen-dee-oo
Caution!/Look out!	¡Cuidado!	kwee-dah-doh

ON THE ROAD

Avenue	Avenida	ah-ven-**ee**-dah
Broad, tree-lined boulevard	Bulevar	boo-leh-**var**
Fertile plain	Vega	**veh**-gah
Highway	Carretera	car-reh-**ter**-ah

Mountain pass	Puerto	poo-**ehr**-toh
Street	Calle	**cah**-yeh
Waterfront promenade	Rambla	**rahm**-blah
Wharf	Embarcadero	em-bar-cah-**deh**-ro

IN TOWN

Cathedral	Catedral	cah-teh-**dral**
Church	Templo/Iglesia	**tem**-plo/ee-**glehs**-see-ah
City hall	Casa de gobierno	kah-sah deh go-bee-**ehr**-no
Door, gate	Puerta portón	poo-**ehr**-tah por-**ton**
Entrance/exit	Entrada/salida	en-**trah**-dah/sah-**lee**-dah
Inn, rustic bar, or restaurant	Taverna	tah-**vehr**-nah
Main square	Plaza principal	plah-thah prin-see-**pahl**
Market	Mercado	mer-**kah**-doh
Neighborhood	Barrio	**bahr**-ree-o
Traffic circle	Glorieta	glor-ee-**eh**-tah
Wine cellar, wine bar, or wine shop	Bodega	boh-**deh**-gah

DINING OUT

A bottle of . . .	Una botella de . . .	**oo**-nah bo-**teh**-yah deh
A cup of . . .	Una taza de . . .	**oo**-nah **tah**-thah deh
A glass of . . .	Un vaso de . . .	oon **vah**-so deh
Ashtray	Un cenicero	oon sen-ee-**seh**-roh
Bill/check	La cuenta	lah **kwen**-tah
Bread	El pan	el pahn
Breakfast	El desayuno	el deh-sah-**yoon**-oh
Butter	La mantequilla	lah man-teh-**key**-yah
Cheers!	¡Salud!	sah-**lood**
Cocktail	Un aperitivo	oon ah-pehr-ee-**tee**-voh

Dinner	La cena	lah **seh**-nah
Dish	Un plato	oon **plah**-toh
Menu of the day	Menú del día	meh-**noo** del **dee**-ah
Enjoy!	¡Buen provecho!	bwehn pro-**veh**-cho
Fixed-price menu	Menú fijo o turistico	meh-**noo** **fee**-hoh oh too-**ree**-stee-coh
Fork	El tenedor	el ten-eh-**dor**
Is the tip	¿Está incluida la	es-**tah** in-cloo-**ee**-dah
included?	propina?	lah pro-**pee**-nah
Knife	El cuchillo	el koo-**chee**-yo
Large portion of savory snacks	Raciónes	rah-see-**oh**-nehs
Lunch	La comida	lah koh-**mee**-dah
Menu	La carta, el menú	lah **cart**-ah, el meh-**noo**
Napkin	La servilleta	lah sehr-vee-**yet**-ah
Pepper	La pimienta	lah pee-me-**en**-tah
Please give me	Por favor déme	pore fah-**vor** **deh**-meh
Salt	La sal	lah sahl
Savory snacks	Tapas	**tah**-pahs
Spoon	Una cuchara	**oo**-nah koo-**chah**-rah
Sugar	El azúcar	el ah-**thu**-kar
Waiter!/Waitress!	¡Por favor Señor/Señorita!	pohr fah-**vor** sen-**yor**/sen-yor-**ee**-tah

Travel Smart Mexico

WORD OF MOUTH

"On your international flights into Mexico and back into the U.S., you'll need to fill out a customs form that contains your identification and describes what's in your luggage. When you go through customs in Mexico, they'll take one half of your "entry" form and hand back to you the other half—the "exit" form. You'll need to retain this "exit" form for your return to the U.S. If you don't have this "exit" form, you'll have to pay a fee. So it's not like they won't let you leave Mexico if you misplace the form, but your wallet will be a little lighter as a result."

–krbr17

www.fodors.com/forums

GETTING HERE & AROUND

We're really proud of our Web site: www.fodors.com is a great place to begin any journey. Scan Travel News for suggested itineraries, travel deals, restaurant and hotel openings, and other up-to-the-minute info. Check out Book It to research prices and book plane tickets, hotel rooms, rental cars, and vacation packages. Head to Talk for on-the-ground pointers from travelers who frequent our message boards. You can also link to loads of other travel-related resources.

GENERAL REQUIREMENTS FOR MEXICO	
Passport	Required for Americans traveling by air. Not required for entry by land or sea (photo ID and birth certificate or U.S. passport card acceptable)
Visa	Required for stays of longer than 72 hours ($20, included in price of airline or cruise ticket); valid for 180 days
Vaccinations	Typhoid and Hepatitis A recommended by the CDC
Driving	U.S. or Canadian driver's license suffices, no international license is necessary; but Mexican auto insurance is required
Departure Tax	US$18–$29, almost always included in the price of airline ticket

Mexico is a huge country—it's more than a million square miles. Transportation by bus is excellent; routes are extensive, and there are plenty of first-class buses with comfortable seats, air-conditioning, and restrooms. Executive class includes sandwiches and soft drinks, bottled water, movies, and fewer seats per row.

The Baja peninsula, however, at nearly 1,000 mi in length, begs reconnoitering by car or RV. Otherwise, transportation hubs are the airports in the extreme north and south, Tijuana and Los Cabos, respectively. Limited international service is available to Loreto.

Mexico's capital, Mexico City, is the mainland's main hub, with hundreds of national and international flights each day. Located in the south-central part of the country, this is the perfect hub for visiting much of colonial central Mexico. Other transportation centers are the major metropolitan cities such as Guadalajara, four hours from the Pacific Coast in west-central Mexico, and Monterrey, industrial capital of the north.

Beach resorts receive national and international flights; Cancún is the largest, followed by Puerto Vallarta and Mazatlán. Ixtapa/Zihuatanejo and Huatulco are smaller destinations and a lack of direct and international flights keeps them small; however, they are still easily reached with a connection in Mexico City.

Mexico is finally getting onboard with some smaller budget airlines that help connect some cities, precluding the need to fly via Mexico City. This can save you time and money. Of these, Avolar connects cities like Tijuana to Guadalajara, Queretaro, Cuernavaca, and Hermosillo; and some of these to each other.

TRAVEL TIMES FROM MEXICO CITY

To	By Air	By Car or Bus
Guadalajara	1¼ hours	7–8 hours
San Miguel	45 minutes	3½ hours
Veracruz City	1 hour	5 hours
Oaxaca City	1 hour	5½ hours
Puerto Vallarta	1½ hours	12 hours
Acapulco	1 hour	5–6 hours
San Cristóbal	1¼ hours	16 hours
Villahermosa	1½ hours	11 hours
Cancún	2 hours	23 hours
Mérida	1¾ hours	19 hours

BY AIR

Mexico is more accessible than ever; major carriers are offering more direct flights to resorts on both coasts, allowing travelers to bypass Mexico City layovers. On most direct flights, Mexico City is 5 hours from New York, 4½ hours from Chicago, and 3½ hours from Los Angeles. Cancún is 3½ hours from New York and from Chicago, 4½ hours from Los Angeles. Acapulco is 6 hours from New York, 4 hours from Chicago, and 3½ hours from Los Angeles. From London, Mexico City is a 12½-hour flight. From Sydney, you must fly to Los Angeles (13½ hours) and then change planes (and airlines) for Mexico City. Regional flights between all major cities are plentiful, but they are expensive (up to $200 one-way) and they almost always require a lengthy layover in Mexico City.

Most airports in Mexico are easy to navigate. Always find out your carrier's check-in policy. For flights within Mexico originating at Benito Juárez, arrive 1½ hours before the scheduled departure time; for flights originating at small airports, arrive an hour before departure. Many airports elsewhere in the world recommend arriving at the airport about 2 hours before your scheduled departure time for domestic flights and 2½ to 3 hours before international flights. You may need to arrive earlier if you're flying from one of the busier airports, during peak air-traffic times, or during peak seasons.

Note that all flights to and within Mexico are no-smoking.

AIRPORTS

The main gateway to the country is Mexico City's Aeropuerto Internacional Benito Juárez (airport code: MEX), a large, well-equipped, modern airport, though infamous for pickpocketing and taxi scams; be careful with your possessions. You can easily exchange money here as well as buy last-minute gifts (although at high prices) on your way out of the country.

For more information on how to grab a taxi from the airport, see "At the Airport" in the "By Taxi" section. Regional airports vary greatly in size and efficiency, though most coastal hubs are very nice and have plenty of services and facilities catering to tourists.

Airport Information **Aeropuerto Internacional Benito Juárez** (☎55/5571–3600 🌐www.aicm.com.mx).

GROUND TRANSPORTATION

Because Mexico City is famous for renegade taxis, be sure to take an official airport cab: purchase a ticket inside the airport and follow signs to the waiting cabs outside. This is a good rule of thumb for any airport in the country—they all have designated ticketing kiosks offering fixed prices based on your destination.

FLIGHTS

American Airlines has nonstop flights to Mexico City, Guadalajara, Los Cabos, Cancún and Cozumel, and the Pacific Coast resorts. Most nonstops depart from its Dallas/Fort Worth hub, but you can reach Mexico City from New York, Miami, and Chicago; Guadalajara and Puerto Vallarta from Chicago; Los Cabos from Los Angeles; and Cancún and Cozumel from Miami. Continental offers nonstops to most major Mexican cities from its Houston hub (connecting in Houston is a good option for many West Coast and Midwest travelers); from New York, Newark, and Cleveland, it has nonstops to Caribbean coast destinations. JetBlue flies into Cancún from New York or Boston. Aeroméxico and Mexicana also offer many nonstop flights, albeit mostly to Mexico City or Guadalajara. Although the Mexican carriers fly slightly older planes, they still offer such perks as free alcoholic beverages.

Delta serves Cancún, Pacific Coast cities, Mexico City, and Guadalajara, but has few direct flights—most connect through

Atlanta or Houston. United Airlines serves Mexico City and other destinations through hubs in Chicago, Washington, D.C., San Francisco, and Denver. U.S. Airways/America West flies to various Mexican cities from hubs in Phoenix, Las Vegas, and Charlotte. Alaska/Horizon Airlines flies from Los Angeles, San Francisco, and Seattle to Cancún, Loreto, and Los Cabos, as well as to most Pacific Coast cities; flights to Guadalajara and Mexico City originate in Los Angeles.

AeroCalifornia serves Baja California from the west coast of the United States, but many travelers have complained about its service. Northwest has some flights from the United States to Mexico City, most of the Pacific Coast cities, and Monterrey, mostly originating from Detroit and Minneapolis.

Plane travel within Mexico can cost two to four times as much as bus travel, but it may save you considerable time if the inevitable Mexico City layover doesn't add too much time to your journey. AeroCalifornia, Aeroméxico, Aviacsa, and Click Mexicana serve most major cities, though many flights connect in Mexico City. Aerolitoral serves the nation's northeastern reaches and connects a few southern cities to Mexico City, and Aeromar connects the Pacific Coast and the Heartland to Mexico City; make reservations on either line through Mexicana or Aeroméxico. It's easier and sometimes cheaper to buy tickets at travel agencies in Mexico. The budget airline Avolar flies to many of the less touristy destinations, for example between Tijuana and many state capitals, and between Guadalajara and La Paz, Queretaro, Oaxaca, and Cuernavaca. Another new budget airline, Alma de Mexico, is based in Guadalajara. It flies direct between this city and Los Mochis, Monterrey, Queretero, Veracruz, Puerto Vallarta, Puebla, Oaxaca, Zihuatanejo, Mazatlan, and a few other destinations.

TIP→Note: some airline toll-free numbers have an 001800 prefix—two zeroes before the "1"—rather than 01800, like most Mexican toll-free numbers. This is entirely correct: what it means is that your call is actually being routed to the United States and will be charged as an international call.

Airlines & Airports **Airline and Airport Links.com** (www.airlineandairportlinks.com) has links to many of the world's airlines and airports.

Airline Contacts **Aeroméxico** (800/237–6639 in U.S. and Canada, 01800/021–4010 or 55/5133–4010 in Mexico www.aeromexico.com). **American Airlines** (800/433–7300 www.aa.com). **Continental Airlines** (800/523–3273 for U.S. and Mexico reservations, 800/231–0856 for international reservations www.continental.com). **Delta Airlines** (800/221–1212 for U.S. reservations, 800/241–4141 for international reservations www.delta.com). **Mexicana** (800/531–7921 in U.S., 866/281–3049 in Canada, 01800/502–2000 in Mexico www.mexicana.com).

Airline Security Issues **Transportation Security Administration** (www.tsa.gov) has answers for almost every question that might come up.

CHARTER FLIGHTS

Charters mainly serve the beach destinations such as Cancún and Cozumel. Bigger companies like Funjet and Apple Vacations offer either flights or air-and-hotel packages. Funjet specifically serves Cancún, Cozumel, Puerto Vallarta, Vallarta/Nayarit, and the Riviera Maya. Apple Vacations offers air-only and air-and-lodging deals to Acapulco, Cancún, Cozumel, Los Cabos, Puerto Vallarta, Huatulco, and Zihuatanejo from more than 200 U.S. cities.

Contacts **Apple Vacations** (800/828–0639 www.godreamvacations.com). **Funjet** (888/558–6654 www.funjet.com).

BY BOAT

Certain islands in Mexico are connected to the mainland by ferry, such as speedboats that run between Playa del Carmen and Cozumel or from Puerto Juárez, Punta Sam, and Isla Mujeres, all in the Yucatán. Boats also connect Isla Tiburón near Bahía Kino in Northwest Mexico, and car ferries connect Baja California with the mainland on three key routes: Guaymas, Sonora, is connected with Santa Rosalía, Baja California Sur; and La Paz, Baja California Sur, is connected with both Los Mochis and Mazatlán in the state of Sinaloa.

BY BUS

Getting to Mexico by bus is no longer for just the adventurous or budget-conscious. In the past, bus travelers were required to change to Mexican vehicles at the border, and vice versa. Now, however, in an effort to bring more American visitors and their dollars to off-the-beaten-track markets and attractions, the Mexican government has removed this obstacle, and more transborder bus tours are available. If you'll be leaving Mexico for points north by bus, you can buy tickets from the Greyhound representative in Mexico City or Guadalajara.

Within Mexico the bus network is extensive. Though there's a trend toward consolidation, some towns have different stations for each bus line. In Mexico City, there's an ADO luxury bus station at the Mexico City airport, directly across the street from the national arrival terminal.

First-class Mexican buses are generally timely and comfortable, air-conditioned coaches with bathrooms, movies, reclining seats with seat belts, and refreshments (first class or deluxe, known as *primera clase* and *de lujo* or *ejecutivo*). They take the fastest route (usually on safer, well-paved toll roads) and make few stops between points. Second-class vehicles (*segunda clase*) connect smaller, secondary routes; they also run along long-distance routes, often taking slower, local roads. They're tolerable (and air-conditioned), even for long distances, but are usually cramped and make many stops. The class of travel will be listed on your printed ticket—if you see economico printed next to servicio, you've been booked on a second-class bus. At many bus stations, one counter will represent several lines and classes of service and mistakes do happen. For comfort's sake, if you're planning a long-distance haul buy tickets for first class or better when traveling by bus within Mexico. Bring snacks, a sweater, and toilet paper. Smoking is prohibited.

There are several first-class and deluxe bus lines. ADO and ADO GL (deluxe service) travel from Mexico City to southeastern and Gulf Coast destinations, including Cancún, Chiapas, Oaxaca, Tampico, Veracruz, Villahermosa, and Yucatán. Cristóbal Colón goes to Chiapas, Oaxaca, Puebla, and the Guatemala border from Mexico City. Estrella Blanca goes from Mexico City to Manzanillo, Mazatlán, Monterrey, Nuevo Laredo, and other central, Pacific coast, and northern border points. Omnibus de Mexico and Turistar serve the north. ETN and Primera Plus serve Mexico City, Manzanillo, Morelia, Puerto Vallarta, Toluca, and other central and western cities. Estrella de Oro will take you from Mexico City to Acapulco, Cuernavaca, Ixtapa, and Taxco.

For the most part, plan to pay in pesos, although most of the deluxe bus services have started accepting credit cards such as Visa and MasterCard.

Tickets for first-class or better—unlike tickets for the other classes—can be reserved in advance; this is advisable during peak periods or on routes that only have one or two first-class departures each day. You can make reservations for many, though not all, of the first-class bus lines, through the Ticketbus central reservations agency. If you're unable to reserve online, buy your tickets at the station the day before you travel. The day of travel, ask your hotel desk to confirm that your bus still exists—even executive class buses can be canceled at the last minute.

You can also travel by bus from the United States and Canada on Greyhound.

Bus Information ADO and **ADO GL** (☎55/5133–2424, 01800/702–8000 toll-free in Mexico 🌐www.ticketbus.com.mx). **Estrella Blanca/Turistar** (☎01800/507–5500 toll-free in Mexico 🌐www.estrellablanca.com.mx). **Estrella de Oro** (☎55/5549–8520, 01800/900–0105 toll-free in Mexico 🌐www.autobus.com.mx). **ETN** (☎55/5089–9200, 01800/800–0386 toll-free in Mexico 🌐www.etn.com.mx). **Greyhound** (☎01800/010–0600 toll-free in Mexico, 800/231–2222 in U.S., 800/661–8747 in Canada 🌐www.greyhound.com. **Omnibus de México** (☎55/5141–4300, 01800/765–6636 toll-free in Mexico 🌐www.odm.com.mx [Spanish only]). **Primera Plus** (☎55/5567–7176 or 01800/375–7587 toll-free in Mexico 🌐www.flecha-amarilla.com.mx). **Ticketbus** (☎55/5133–2424, 01800/702–8000 toll-free in Mexico 🌐www.ticketbus.com.mx).

BY CAR

There are two absolutely essential points to remember about driving in Mexico. First and foremost is to carry Mexican auto insurance. If you injure anyone in an accident, you could well be jailed unless you have insurance. Second, if you enter Mexico with a car you must leave with it. In recent years the high rate of U.S. vehicles being sold illegally in Mexico has caused the Mexican government to enact stringent regulations on bringing cars into the country.

You must cross the border with the following documents: title or registration for your vehicle; a passport or a certified birth certificate; a credit card (AE, DC, MC, or V); a valid driver's license with a photo. The title holder, driver, and credit-card owner must be one and the same—that is, if your spouse's name is on the title or registration of the car and yours isn't, you cannot be the one to bring the car into the country. For financed, leased, rental, or company cars you must bring a notarized letter of permission from the bank, lien holder, rental agency, or company. When you submit your paperwork at the border and pay the $27 charge on your credit card, you'll receive a car permit and a sticker to put on your vehicle, all valid for up to six months. Be sure to turn in the permit and the sticker at the border prior to their expiration date; otherwise you could incur high fines or even be barred from entering Mexico if you try to visit again.

The fact that you drove in with a car is stamped on your tourist card (visa), which you must give to immigration authorities at departure. If an emergency arises and you must fly home, there are complicated customs procedures to face. If you bring the car into the country you must be in the vehicle at all times when it is driven.

Road conditions vary greatly, from heavy traffic congestion in Mexico City to breezy, piece-of-cake conditions in Ixtapa. Read about the area you plan to visit and decide if renting a car will enhance your visit; sometimes taking reasonably priced, ubiquitous taxis is the better choice. Be prepared for challenging road conditions *(see Road Conditions below)*, and do your best not to drive between cities at night.

AUTO INSURANCE

You must carry Mexican auto insurance, which you can purchase near border crossings on the U.S. side, by mail, or via the Internet. Purchase enough Mexican automobile insurance to cover your estimated trip. It's sold by the day ($10 per day and up), and if your trip is shorter than your original estimate, some companies might issue a prorated refund for the unused time upon application after you exit the country. Baja Bound, Mexico Insurance Professionals, and Instant Mexico Auto Insurance are a few of the many online outfits that allow you to buy the insurance beforehand, but if you're approaching the border at almost any U.S.-Mexico crossing, you'll be overwhelmed by companies where you can buy the insurance on the spot. Sanborn's is a reliable company, has offices in almost every border town, and offers online options, too.

Be sure that you have been provided with proof of such insurance; if you drive without it, you're not only liable for damages, but you're also breaking the law. You could be jailed during investigations after an accident unless you have Mexican insurance. For this reason, after an accident many Mexicans might simply pull over, discuss things, arrive at an impromptu cash settlement on the spot if necessary, and continue on their ways.

Contacts **Baja Bound** (☎888/552-2252 🌐www.bajabound.com).**Instant Mexico Auto Insurance** (☎800/345-4701 in U.S. and Canada 🌐www.instant-mex-auto-insur.com). **Mexico Insurance Professionals** (☎888/467-4639 🌐www.mexpro.com). **Sanborn's Mexican Insurance** (☎800/222-0158 in U.S. and Canada 🌐www.sanbornsinsurance.com).

GASOLINE

Pemex (the government petroleum monopoly) franchises all of Mexico's gas stations, which you'll find at most junctions and in cities and towns. Gas is measured in liters. Some stations accept credit cards and a few have ATMs, but don't count on it—make sure you have pesos handy. Overall, prices run slightly cheaper than in the United States (at this writing, about 63 cents a liter or $2.34 a gallon). Premium unleaded gas (called *premium*), the red pump, and regular unleaded gas (*magna*), the green pump, are available nationwide, but it's still best to fill up whenever you can. Fuel quality is generally lower than that in the United States and Europe, but it has improved enough so that your car will run acceptably.

Gas-station attendants pump the gas for you and will also wash your windshield and check your fluids and tire air pressure, if you ask for these services. A 5- or 10-peso tip is customary, depending on the number of services rendered (even if they just pump the gas). Make sure the attendant resets the pump to "0" and that you're charged the correct price. For a receipt, ask for recibo. To ask the attendant to fill the tank, say "Lleno (YAY-noh), por favor."

PARKING

A circle with a diagonal line superimposed on the letter *E* (for *estacionamiento*) means "no parking." Illegally parked cars are either towed or have wheel blocks placed on the tires, which can require a trip to the traffic-police headquarters for payment of a fine. When in doubt, park in a lot instead of on the street; your car will probably be safer there anyway. Lots are plentiful although not always clearly marked, and fees are reasonable—as little as $1 for a half day or up to $1 or more an hour, depending on where in the country you are. Sometimes you park your own car; more often, though, you hand the keys over to an attendant. There are a few (very few) parking meters in larger cities; the cost is usually about 10¢ per 15 minutes.

RENTAL CAR

Mexico manufactures Chrysler, Ford, General Motors, Honda, Nissan, and Volkswagen vehicles. With the exception of Volkswagen, you can get the same kind of midsize and luxury cars in Mexico that you can rent in the United States. Economy usually refers to a Volkswagen Beetle or another small car barely fitting four passengers, which may or may not come with air-conditioning.

It can really pay to shop around: in Mexico City, rates for a compact car with air-conditioning, manual transmission, and unlimited mileage range from $16 a day and $116 a week to $50 a day and nearly $300 a week, excluding taxes. At resort towns in high season, expect the higher prices from car-rental companies. By far the best option is booking ahead.

Although consolidators like Travelocity.com may offer great deals, it's a good idea to book directly through a major rental company's Web site, as consolidator sites will sometimes allow you to make a booking even when no cars are available. Basic accident insurance averages $18 a day and is compulsory; additional theft and personal injury policies are optional. This doesn't include 10%–15% tax, or the additional 12% concession fee charged at all airport rental facilities. As a general rule, avoid local agencies; stick with the major companies because they tend to be more reliable.

Surcharges for additional drivers are around $5 per day plus tax. Children's car seats run about the same, but not all companies have them. In Mexico the minimum driving age is 18, but most rental-car agencies have a minimum age requirement ranging from 21 to 25; some have a surcharge for drivers under 25. Your own driver's license is acceptable; it's not necessary to get an international driver's license.

Major Agency Contacts **Alamo** (☎800/522–9696 ⊕www.alamo.com). **Avis** (☎800/331–1084 ⊕www.avis.com). **Budget** (☎800/472–3325 ⊕www.budget.com). **Dollar** (☎800/800–3665 ⊕www.dollar.com). **Hertz** (☎800/654–3001 ⊕www.hertz.com). **National Car Rental** (☎800/227–7368 ⊕www.nationalcar.com).**Thrifty** (☎877/283–0898 ⊕www.thrifty.com).

CAR AND DRIVER

You can also hire a car with a driver (who generally doubles as a tour guide) through your hotel. The going rate is about $22–$25 an hour within a given town. Limousine service runs about $65 an hour and up, with a three- to five-hour minimum. Rates for out-of-town trips may be higher. Negotiate a price beforehand if you'll need the service for more than one day. If your hotel can't arrange limousine or car service, ask the concierge to refer you to a reliable *sitio* (cab stand); the rate will be lower.

ROAD CONDITIONS

Mexicans are generally skilled drivers, but they do drive very fast, even on twisting or very dark roads. Most of the newer highways have either designated lanes for slower vehicles or a paved shoulder that is wide enough for you to cruise in while letting the speed demons pass. Big city driving is—as it is in many parts of the world—harrowing, and drivers there are less courteous and more apt to lean on their horns if you hold things up. The worst parts of city driving are negotiating four-way stops (where seemingly no rules except those of machismo apply), and trying to find street signs (which are nearly impossible to spot and hard to read even if you do see them) while keeping up with traffic.

That said, Mexicans are in some ways more courteous than U.S. drivers—it is customary, for example, for drivers to put on their hazard lights to warn the cars behind them of poor road conditions, slow-downs, or upcoming speed bumps; oncoming cars may flash their lights at you for the same reasons. If you are trying to pass a slower-moving vehicle and the driver notices your efforts (you should put on your left blinker), often he or she will signal you with the left blinker when it is safe for you to pass. (When you do pass, just remember to check that none of the cars behind you have gotten the same idea first—it's not uncommon to see someone speed up from the back of a long line of cars as soon as the coast is clear.) However, the lines delineating the various lanes are most often totally ignored; horns are leaned on constantly; and you must either pass or be passed. Yet, the most dangerous thing about driving in Mexico is the actual road conditions—the potholes, inexplicable placement of speed bumps, etc.

Watch out for drunk drivers especially around holidays and late at night. Unless you're very familiar with the terrain, it's best to avoid driving at night outside the city, where you can run into—literally—wandering cows, horses, or dogs, or unforeseen speed bumps at the entrance to small towns. The utter lack of visibility on country roads, even the well-traveled highways, will make even the most confident driver white-knuckled after a few hours. Bandits are generally run off if they start staking out cars or buses along major tourist routes, where tourists with expensive cameras and cash are known to pass by, but their rare presence is another reason to avoid night travel, erring on the side of caution.

There are several well-kept toll roads in Mexico—most of them two lanes wide; a few have four lanes. These *carreteras de cuota* (toll highways) are numbered and connect major cities or border areas. (*Cuota* means "toll road"; *libre* means "free," and such roads are often one lane, slower, and usually not as smooth.) Some excellent roads have opened in the past decade or so, making car travel safer and faster. These include highways connecting Acapulco and Mexico City; Cancún and Mérida; Nogales and Mazatlán; León and Aguascalientes; Guadalajara and Tepic; Mexico City, Morelia, and Guadalajara; Mexico City, Puebla, Teotihuacán, and Oaxaca; Mexico City and Veracruz; and Nuevo Laredo and Monterrey. However, tolls as high as $40 one way (most tolls start at $6–$8) can make using these thoroughfares expensive.

In rural areas roads range from good to poor: use caution, especially during the rainy season, when rock slides, flooding, and potholes may pose problems. Be alert to animals, especially untethered cattle and dogs, and to dangerous, unrailed curves. Note that driving in Mexico's central highlands may also necessitate adjustments to your carburetor. *Topes* (speed bumps, also called reductors) are common and are very large; occasionally, you'll see one that's actually been painted or fitted with reflectors, but usually they're just announced by a single yellow sign. Slow down when approaching a village, where you'll find the most topes, but be aware that you may encounter them in some strange locations, such as on straight stretches of highway where there are no visible hazards or reasons to reduce speed.

ROADSIDE EMERGENCIES

To help motorists on major highways, the Mexican Tourism Ministry operates a fleet of more than 250 pickup trucks, known as the Angeles Verdes, or Green Angels, easily reachable by phone throughout Mexico by simply dialing 078. The bilingual drivers provide mechanical help, first aid, radio-telephone communication, basic supplies and small parts, towing, tourist information, and protection. Services are free, and spare parts, fuel, and lubricants are provided at cost. Tips are always appreciated (figure $5–$10 for big jobs, $3–$5 for minor repairs). The Green Angels patrol fixed sections of the major highways twice daily 8–8 (usually later on holiday weekends). If you break down, pull off the road as far as possible, lift the hood of your car, hail a passing vehicle, and ask the driver to notify the patrol. Most bus and truck drivers will be quite helpful.

Emergency Services **Angeles Verdes** (☎078, nationwide 3-digit Angeles Verdes and tourist emergency line). **Ministry of Tourism hotline** (☎55/3002-6300).

RULES OF THE ROAD

When you sign up for Mexican car insurance, you should receive a booklet on Mexican rules of the road. It really is a good idea to read it to avoid breaking laws that differ from those of your country. If an oncoming vehicle flicks its lights at you in daytime, slow down: it could mean trouble ahead. When approaching a narrow bridge, the first vehicle to flash its lights has right-of-way. One-way streets are common. One-way traffic is indicated by an arrow; two-way, by a double-pointed arrow. Look for these signs in cities and towns; they are sometimes oddly placed or otherwise hard to see. Other road signs follow the widespread system of international symbols.

In Mexico City, watch out for "*Hoy no Circula*" notices. Because of pollution, all cars in the city without a Verification "0" rating (usually those built before 1994) are prohibited from driving one day a week (two days a week during high-alert periods). Posted signs show certain letters or numbers paired with each day of the week, indicating that vehicles with those letters or numbers in their license plates aren't allowed to drive on the corresponding day. Foreigners aren't exempt. Cars with license plate numbers ending in 5 or 6 are prohibited on Monday; 7 or 8 on Tuesday; 3 or 4 on Wednesday; 1 or 2 on Thursday; and 9 or 0 on Friday. Cars whose license plates have only letters, not numerals, can't drive on Fridays.

Mileage and speed limits are given in kilometers: 100 kph and 80 kph (62 mph and 50 mph, respectively) are the most common maximums, which are regularly exceeded by most drivers. A few of the toll roads allow 110 kph (68 mph). However, speed limits can change from curve to curve, so watch the signs carefully. In cities and small towns, observe the posted speed limits, which can be as low as 20 kph (12 mph). Seat belts are required by law throughout Mexico.

Drunk driving laws are fairly harsh in Mexico, and if you're caught you'll go to jail immediately. It's hard to know what the country's blood-alcohol limit really is. Everyone seems to have a different idea about it; this means it's probably being handled in a discretionary way, which is nerve-racking, to say the least. The best way to avoid any problems is to simply not drink and drive. There's no right on red. Foreigners must pay speeding penalties on the spot, which can be steep; sometimes you're better off offering a little *mordida* (bribe, though don't refer to it as such) to the officer—just take out a couple hundred pesos, hold it out inquiringly, and see if the problem goes away.

If you encounter a police checkpoint, stay calm. These are simply routine checks for weapons and drugs; customarily they'll check out the car's registration, look in the backseat, the trunk, and at the undercarriage with a mirror. Basic Spanish does help during these stops, though a smile and polite demeanor will go a long way.

BY CRUISE SHIP

Cozumel and Playa del Carmen have become increasingly popular ports for Caribbean cruises. Most lines—including Carnival, Princess, Royal Caribbean International, Norwegian, Cunard, Holland America, and Silversea Cruises—leave from Miami and/or other Florida ports. Texas passengers can take Royal Caribbean from Galveston and Norwegian from Houston to the Yucatán. Companies offering cruises down the Baja California coast and/or other Pacific Coast routes include Cunard, Celebrity Cruises, Princess, Norwegian, Royal Olympia, Royal Caribbean, and Holland America. Most depart from Los Angeles, Long Beach, or San Diego; some trips originate in Vancouver or San Francisco.

Cruise Lines **Carnival Cruise Line** (☎305/599-2600 or 800/227-6482 🌐www.carnival.com). **Cunard Line** (☎661/753-1000 or 800/728-6273 🌐www.cunard.com). **Holland America Line** (☎206/281-3535 or 877/932-4259 🌐www.hollandamerica.com). **Norwegian Cruise Line** (☎305/436-4000 or 800/327-7030 🌐www.ncl.com). **Princess Cruises** (☎661/753-0000 or 800/774-6237 🌐www.princess.com). **Royal Caribbean International** (☎305/539-6000 or 800/327-6700 🌐www.royalcaribbean.com). **Silversea Cruises** (☎954/522-4477 or 800/722-9955 🌐www.silversea.com).

BY TAXI

Taxis are ubiquitous in Mexico, and thus convenient in both big cities and mid-size towns. The standard taxi is a mid-size, four-door sedan. Drivers generally speak English, either enough to negotiate the fare or, in some cases, excellent enough for a lively discussion of national politics. Because most taxis are unmetered, it's important to negotiate the fare before embarking. (A metered taxi has a taximetro, and the driver, if he has one, should inform you when you ask the fare.) In resort destinations, major hotels often have rate sheets posted, but be sure to reconfirm the fare directly with the driver before setting off. Although these posted rates give you a good baseline (if any cabbie asks for more than the posted fare you'll know you're being grossly overcharged), they're usually somewhat inflated—when you hail a cab back to your hotel, you'll often find that you're able to negotiate a slightly better price. No matter what, always confirm the fare beforehand. Ask a concierge or front-desk person when possible what the rate should be to avoid being overcharged.

If a driver doesn't know the address you give him, he'll radio either a dispatcher or other cabbie to get the info, or drive to the neighborhood and ask around. Because you've negotiated the fare before starting, you needn't pay extra if the cabbie has to drive around a bit to find the address.

A surcharge of 20% to 40% may be added at night, usually after 11 PM. Tipping is not customary, especially since you've just negotiated the rate.

For reasons of security in Mexico City (or any place where you feel unsafe, or locals warn you to take precautions), hire taxis from hotels and taxi stands *(sitios)*, or use those that you have summoned by phone. Street taxis might be the cheapest, but in Mexico City an alarming increase in crime involves street cabs, so don't flag a cab on the street.

In addition to private taxis, many cities have bargain-price collective taxi services using minibuses and sedans. The service is called *colectivo* or *pesero*. Such vehicles run along fixed routes, and you hail them on the street and tell the driver where you are going.

AT THE AIRPORT

From most airports you can take the authorized taxi service only. Whenever possible, purchase the taxi vouchers sold at stands inside or just outside the terminal, which ensure that your fare is established beforehand. Before you purchase your ticket, check the taxi-zone map (it should be posted on or by the ticket stand) and make sure your ticket is properly zoned.

ON THE GROUND

ACCOMMODATIONS

TIP→Find hotel and restaurant price charts in individual chapters.

The price and quality of accommodations in Mexico vary from superluxurious hotels and all-inclusive resorts to modest budget properties, down-at-the-heel places with shared bathrooms, and cabanas. There are far fewer *casas de huéspedes* (guesthouses) and youth hostels in Mexico than, say, Europe, because there are so many options for budget travelers. You may find appealing bargains while you're on the road, but if your comfort threshold is low, look for an English-speaking staff, guaranteed dollar rates, and toll-free reservation numbers. **TIP→Assume that hotels operate on the European Plan (EP, no meals) unless we specify that they use the Breakfast Plan (BP, with full breakfast), Continental Plan (CP, continental breakfast), Full American Plan (FAP, all meals), Modified American Plan (MAP, breakfast and dinner), or are all-inclusive (AI, all meals and most activities).**

APARTMENT & HOUSE RENTALS

Contacts **Akumal Villas** (☎984/875-9088 in Akumal 🌐www.akumal-villas.com).**San Miguel Rentals** (☎415/152-3337 🌐www.sanmiguelrentals.com).**Turquoise Waters** (☎877/254-9791 🌐www.turquoisewater.com). **Vacation Home Rentals Worldwide** (☎201/767-9393 or 800/633-3284 🌐www.vhrww.com). **Villanet** (☎206/417-3444 or 800/964-1891 🌐www.rentavilla.com). **Villas & Apartments Abroad** (☎212/213-6435 or 800/433-3020 🌐www.vaanyc.com). **Villas International** (☎415/499-9490 or 800/221-2260 🌐www.villasintl.com). **Villas of Distinction** (☎707/778-1800 or 800/289-0900 🌐www.villasofdistinction.com). **Wimco** (☎800/449-1553 🌐www.wimco.com).

BOUTIQUE HOTELS & B&BS

Mexico has many unique properties that put you in close touch with the country's essence *and* cater to your need for pampering. Hoteles Boutique de México (Mexico Boutique Hotels) is a private company that represents 45 such properties. Most have fewer than 50 rooms; each is not only selected for its small size, service, and allure, but is inspected annually to ensure it continues to meet the set high standards. The bed-and-breakfast craze hasn't missed Mexico, although there are fewer than in Europe and the United States. San Miguel de Allende and other heartland cities have their share of charming places, as do Mexico City and parts of the Yucatán.

Reservation Services **Bed & Breakfast.com** (☎512/322-2710 or 888/782-9782 🌐www.bedandbreakfast.com/mexico.html) also sends out an online newsletter. **Hoteles Boutique de México** (☎01800/508-7923 toll-free in Mexico, 877/278-8018 in U.S., 866/818-8342 in Canada 🌐www.mexicoboutiquehotels.com). **Internet San Miguel** (🌐www.internetsanmiguel.com/bed_and_breakfasts.html). **Mexperience Guide to Boutique Hotels** (🌐www.mexperience.com/mexicoboutiquehotels). **Oaxaca Bed and Breakfast Association** (🌐www.oaxacabedandbreakfast.org).

HOSTELS

Mexico, while it has many cheap hotels, has few hostels. High school and college students are more often the norm than older travelers at the few hostels that do exist. HI has locations in Acapulco, Guanajuato, Guadalajara, Jalapa, Mexico City, and Puebla.

Information **Hostelling International—USA** (☎301/495-1240 🌐www.hiusa.org).

HOTELS

It's essential to reserve in advance if you're traveling to the resort areas during high season or holiday periods, and it's recommended, though not always necessary to do so elsewhere during high season. Overbooking is a common practice in some parts of Mexico, such as Cancún, Puerto Vallarta, and Acapulco. To protect yourself, get a confirmation in writing, via fax or e-mail. Travelers to remote areas will encounter little difficulty in obtaining rooms on a walk-in basis unless it's during a holiday, yet it's always wise to reserve if the property allows it.

Hotel rates are subject to the 15% value-added tax (it's 10% in the states of Quintana Roo, Baja California, and Baja California Sur, and anywhere within 20 km [12½ mi] of the border). In addition, many states charge a 2% hotel tax. Service charges and meals generally aren't included in the hotel rates.

The Mexican government categorizes hotels, based on qualitative evaluations, into *gran turismo*; five star down to one star. Anything less than two stars generally doesn't advertise the fact, and even budget travelers are unlikely to stay at a one-star lodging. Keep in mind that many hotels that might otherwise be rated higher have opted for a lower category to avoid higher interest rates on loans and financing.

High- versus low-season rates can vary significantly. Hotels in this guide have private bathrooms with showers, unless stated otherwise; bathtubs aren't common in inexpensive hotels in smaller towns. Hotels have private baths, phones, TVs, and air-conditioning unless otherwise noted.

TIP→ **If you're particularly sensitive to noise, you should call ahead to learn if your hotel of choice is on a busy street.**

COMMUNICATIONS

INTERNET

Internet cafés have sprung up all over Mexico, making e-mail by far the easiest and cheapest way to get in touch with people back home. If you're bringing a laptop with you, check with the manufacturer's technical support line to see what service and/or repair affiliates they have in the areas you plan to visit. Larger cities have repair shops that service Compaq, Dell, Macintosh, Sony, Toshiba, and other major brands, though parts tend to be more expensive than in the United States. Carry a spare battery to save yourself the expense and headache of having to hunt down a replacement on the spot.

Connections are fast in major cities and many smaller towns as well. Wi-Fi is widely available in many large hotels, at least in public areas. The cost for in-room connection can run from $15 to $25 per day—quite high, especially when Wi-Fi can sometimes be a free perk at other hotels. Many coffee shops in larger cities offer free Wi-Fi. Most Internet cafés charge 10 to 40 pesos for one hour, though some charge in 10- or 15-minute increments (usually 5 to 10 pesos). Many Internet cafés offer SKYPE connections, too.

Contacts **Cybercafes** (www.cybercafes.com) lists more than 4,000 Internet cafés worldwide.

PHONES

The good news is that you can now make a direct-dial telephone call from virtually any point on earth. The bad news? You can't always do so cheaply. Calling from a hotel is almost always the most expensive option; hotels usually add huge surcharges to all calls, particularly international ones. In some countries you can phone from call centers or even the post office. Calling cards usually keep costs to a minimum, but only if you purchase them locally. And then there are mobile phones (⇨ *below*), which are sometimes more prevalent—particularly in the developing world—than landlines; as expensive as mobile phone calls can be, they are still usually a much cheaper option than calling from your hotel.

LOCAL DO'S AND TABOOS

CUSTOMS OF THE COUNTRY

In the United States and elsewhere in the Western world, being direct, efficient, and succinct is highly valued. But Mexican communication tends to be more subtle, and the direct style of Americans, Canadians, and Europeans is often perceived as curt and aggressive. Mexicans are extremely polite, so losing your temper over delays or complaining loudly will get you branded as rude and make people less inclined to help you.

Remember that things move at a slow pace here and that there's no stigma attached to being late; be gracious about this and other local customs and attitudes. In restaurants, for example, a waiter would never consider bringing you your check before you ask for it; that would be pushy. It's customary to inquire about a colleague's family or general health, and perhaps some other banal subject (such as the beauty of the town you're visiting, or the weather), before launching into a request or mundane business. Mexicans love to discuss politics and ethics, so don't be afraid to ask questions or discuss these issues in friendly and general terms.

Learning basic phrases in Spanish such as *por favor* (please) and *gracias* (thank you) will make a big difference in how people respond to you. Also, being deferential to those who are older than you will earn you lots of points.

GREETINGS

Mexicans are extremely polite and ceremonious. Businesspeople and strangers shake hands upon greeting each other or being introduced, while friends (women to women or women to men) may give a kiss on one cheek, or an "air kiss." Male friends or acquaintances may give each other a stiff hug with a triple pat on the back. When in doubt, shake hands.

It's traditional to use the formal form of you (*usted*) rather than the informal *tu* when addressing elders, subordinates, superiors, and strangers. However, so few gringos speak Spanish that any courteous attempt to speak Spanish is acceptable (although using the correct pronoun is, of course, best). When taking your leave, say "adios" (goodbye) or "hasta luego" (see you later).

SIGHTSEEING

Although shorts are permissible in churches, short shorts and skimpy tops are frowned upon. Don't sightsee during church services, although you can stand at the back and look. If photography and/or flash photography is prohibited, there's usually a sign at the front of the church; otherwise, taking pictures is not a problem. Old women and men or people with disabilities often beg at the entrance to churches; it's common to give them a few coins.

Say *"con permiso"* (pardon me) to get past people in a crowd.

Giving up one's seat on a bus for the elderly, blind, and pregnant women is common courtesy.

OUT ON THE TOWN

Mexicans call waiters joven (literally, young man) no matter how old they are. Call a female waitress señorita (miss) or señora (ma'am). Ask for "la cuenta, por favor" (the check, please) when you want the bill; it's usually considered rude for a server to bring it before a customer asks for it. Mexicans tend to dress nicely for a night out, but in tourist areas, dress codes are mainly upheld only at the more sophisticated discotheques. Some restaurants have separate smoking sections, but in smaller establishments you can usually smoke.

The country code for Mexico is 52. When calling a Mexico number from abroad, dial any necessary international access code, then the country code, and then all of the numbers listed for the entry.

CALLING WITHIN MEXICO

Directory assistance is 040 nationwide. For assistance in English, dial 090 first for an international operator; tell the operator in what city, state, and country you require directory assistance, and he or she will connect you.

For local or long-distance calls, you can use either a standard public pay phone or a *caseta de larga distancia,* a telephone service usually operated out of a small business. To make a direct long-distance or local call from a caseta, tell the person on duty the number you'd like to call, and she or he will give you a rate and dial for you. Rates seem to vary widely, so shop around, but overall they're higher than those of pay phones. If using a pay phone, you'll most often need a prepaid phone card. If you're calling long distance within Mexico, dial 01 before the area code and number. For local calls, just dial the number; no other prefix is necessary.

Sometimes you can make collect calls from casetas, and sometimes you cannot, depending on the individual operator and possibly your degree of visible desperation. Casetas will generally charge 50¢–$1.50 to place a collect call (some charge by the minute); it's usually better to call *por cobrar* (collect) from a pay phone.

CALLING OUTSIDE MEXICO

To make an international call, dial 00 before the country code, area code, and number. The country code for the United States and Canada is 1, the United Kingdom 44, Australia 61, New Zealand 64, and South Africa 27. Be sure to avoid phones near tourist areas that advertise, in English, "Call the U.S. or Canada here!" They charge an outrageous fee per minute. If in doubt, dial the operator and ask for rates. AT&T, MCI, and Sprint calling cards are useful, although infrequently, hotels block access to their service numbers.

Access Codes **AT&T Direct** (☎01800/112-2020 toll-free in Mexico). **MCI WorldPhone** (☎01800/674-7000 toll-free in Mexico). **Sprint International Access** (☎01800/877-8000 toll-free in Mexico).

CALLING CARDS

In most parts of the country, pay phones (predominantly operated by Telmex) accept only prepaid cards (tarjetas Lada), sold in 30-, 50-, or 100-peso denominations at newsstands, pharmacies, minimarkets, or grocery stores; coin-only pay phones are few and far between. There are pay phones are all over the place—on street corners, in bus stations, and so on. They usually have two unmarked slots, one for a Ladatel (a Spanish acronym for "long-distance direct dialing") card and the other for a credit card. These are primarily for Mexican bank cards, but some accept Visa or MasterCard, though *not* U.S. phone credit cards.

To use a Ladatel card, simply insert it in the appropriate slot with the computer chip insignia forward and right-side up, and dial. Credit is deleted from the card as you use it, and your balance is displayed on a small screen on the phone. You'll be charged 1 peso per minute for local calls and more for long-distance and international calls. Most pay phones display a price list and dialing instructions.

A *caseta de larga distancia* is a telephone service usually operated out of a store such as a *papelería* (stationery store) or other small business; look for the phone symbol on the door. Casetas may cost more to use than pay phones, but you tend to be shielded from street noise, as you get your own little cabin. They also have the benefit of not forcing you to buy a prepaid phone card with a specific denomination—you pay in cash according to the calls you make. Operators place the call for you.

MOBILE PHONES

If you have a multiband phone (some countries use different frequencies than what's used in the United States) and your service provider uses the world-standard GSM network (as do T-Mobile, Cingular, and Verizon), you can probably use your phone in Mexico—even semi-remote coastal areas seem to get excellent reception, though don't expect the same to be true in out-of-the-way mountain towns. Roaming fees can be steep, however: 99¢ a minute is considered reasonable. And overseas you normally pay the toll charges for incoming calls. It's almost always cheaper to send a text message than to make a call, since text messages have a very low set fee (often less than 5¢).

If you just want to make local calls, consider buying a new SIM card (note that your provider may have to unlock your phone for you to use a different SIM card) and a prepaid service plan in the destination. You'll then have a local number and can make local calls at local rates. If your trip is extensive, you could also simply buy a new cell phone in your destination, as the initial cost will be offset over time.

TIP→ **If you travel internationally frequently, save one of your old mobile phones or buy a cheap one on the Internet; ask your cell phone company to unlock it for you, and take it with you as a travel phone, buying a new SIM card with pay-as-you-go service in each destination.**

There are now many companies that rent cell phones (with or without SIM cards) for the duration of your trip. Receive the phone, charger, and carrying case in the mail and return it in the mailer. EZ Wireless, Daystar, and other companies rent phones starting at about $3.50 per day or $88 per month. Charges vary for incoming and outgoing calls, depending on the plan you choose.

Contacts **Daystar** (888/908–4100 www.daystarwireless.com) rents cell phones at $6 per day, with incoming calls at 22¢ a minute and outgoing at $1.20.

CUSTOMS & DUTIES

Upon entering Mexico, you'll be given a baggage declaration form—you can fill out one per family. Most airports have a random bag-inspection scheme in place. When you pick up your bags you'll approach something that looks like a stoplight; hand your form to the attendant, press the button, and if you get a green light you (and the rest of your family) may proceed. If you get a red light, you may be subject to further questioning or inspection. Some regional airports have heightened security and all passengers are required to undergo a cursory bag inspection. You're allowed to bring in 3 liters of spirits or wine for personal use; 400 cigarettes, 25 cigars, or 200 grams of tobacco; a reasonable amount of perfume for personal use; one video camera and one regular camera and 12 rolls of film for each; and gift items not to exceed a total of $300. If driving across the U.S. border, gift items must not exceed $50. You aren't allowed to bring firearms or ammunition, meat, vegetables, plants, fruit, or flowers into the country. You can bring in one of each of the following items without paying taxes: a cell phone, a beeper, a radio or tape recorder, a musical instrument, a laptop computer, and portable copier or printer. Compact discs and/or audio cassettes are limited to 20 total and DVDs to five.

Mexico also allows you to bring one cat or dog, if you have two things: 1) a pet health certificate signed by a registered veterinarian in the United States and issued not more than 72 hours before the animal enters Mexico; and 2) a pet vaccination certificate showing that the animal has been treated (as applicable) for rabies, hepatitis, distemper, and leptospirosis. For more information or information on bringing other animals or more than one type of animal, contact a Mexican consulate. Aduana Mexico (Mexican Customs) has an informative Web site, though everything is in Spanish. You can also get customs information from the Mexican consulate, which has branches in many major American cities as well as border towns. To find the consulate nearest you, check the Ministry of Foreign Affairs Web site, http://portal.sre.gob.mx/usa, select Consular Services from the menu on the left, and scroll down.

Information Aduana Mexico (🌐www.aduanas.sat.gob.mx).

U.S. Information U.S. Customs and Border Protection (🌐www.cbp.gov).

EATING OUT

Mexican restaurants run the gamut from humble hole-in-the-wall shacks, street stands, *taquerías,* and American-style fast-food joints to elegant, internationally acclaimed restaurants. Prices, naturally, follow suit. To save money, look for the fixed-menu lunch known as *comida corrida* or *menú del día,* which is served from about 1 to 4 almost everywhere in Mexico. During the day, rely on standard regional dishes served in the hot food area of the local market, or *mercado.* Most of the archaeological sites have a café, at the least, and sometimes, a surprisingly good restaurant.

For information on food-related health issues, see Health below.

MEALS & MEALTIMES

You can get *desayuno* (breakfast) in *cafeterías* (coffee shops), of course, as well as snack bars and other establishments. Choices range from hefty egg-and-chorizo, ham, or beef dishes (the meat is usually shredded in with the scrambled eggs) to *chilaquiles* (a layered casserole with fried tortilla strips, tomato sauce, spices, crumbled white cheese, and sometimes meat or eggs) to lighter fare like bread rolls, yogurt, and fruit. Some cafés don't open until 8 or 8:30, in which case hotel restaurants are the best bets for early risers. Panader*í*as (bakeries) open early and provide the cheapest breakfast you'll find—a bag of assorted rolls and pastries will likely cost less than $1. *Comida* (lunch) is traditionally the big meal of the day, and set menus usually consist of soup and/or salad, bread or tortillas, a main dish, one or two side dishes, and dessert. Restaurants geared toward travelers often serve lighter fare, and cafés and restaurants serve soups, salads, sandwiches, and pizza for those who don't want a full spread. *Cena* (dinner) tends to be lighter; in fact, many people just have milk or hot chocolate and a sweet roll; *tamales* are also traditional evening fare. Many restaurants, however, including both tourist-oriented and local spots serve substantial, multicourse dinners.

Restaurants are plentiful and have long hours. (Note, however, that seafood places often close by late afternoon.) Lunch is usually served from 2 PM to 4 PM; Mexicans rarely go out to dinner before 8 PM, although many types of eateries in different price ranges are open throughout the day, with street vendors filling in the gaps and feeding the late-night crowds. More traditional restaurants may close on Sunday. This isn't a problem in major tourist areas, where plenty of good eateries are open daily. If you're visiting a small town, however, it's best to check with locals or the hotel staff to avoid going hungry.

Unless otherwise noted, the restaurants listed in this guide are open daily for lunch and dinner.

PAYING

Most small restaurants do not accept credit cards. Larger restaurants and those catering to tourists take credit cards, but their prices reflect the fee placed on all credit-card transactions. Credit cards most often accepted are MasterCard and Visa, and to a slightly lesser extent, American Express.

For guidelines on tipping see Tipping below. **TIP→Find hotel and restaurant price charts in individual chapters.**

RESERVATIONS & DRESS

Regardless of where you are, it's a good idea to make a reservation if you can. In some places it's expected. We mention them specifically only when reservations are essential (there's no other way you'll ever get a table) or when they are not accepted.

For popular restaurants, book as far ahead as you can (often two weeks), and reconfirm as soon as you arrive. (Large parties should always call ahead to check the reservations policy.) Some restaurants have online reservations, but it's again wise to call ahead. We mention dress only when men are required to wear a jacket or a jacket and tie.

ELECTRICITY

For U.S. and Canadian travelers, electrical converters aren't necessary because Mexico operates on the 60-cycle, 120-volt system; however, many Mexican outlets have not been updated to accommodate three-prong and polarized plugs (those with one larger prong), so to be safe bring an adapter. Blackouts and brownouts—often lasting an hour or so—are fairly common everywhere, particularly during the rainy season.

Consider making a small investment in a universal adapter, which has several types of plugs in one lightweight, compact unit. Most laptops and mobile phone chargers are dual voltage (i.e., they operate equally well on 110 and 220 volts), so require only an adapter. These days the same is true of small appliances such as hair dryers. Always check labels and manufacturer instructions to be sure. Don't use 110-volt outlets marked FOR SHAVERS ONLY for high-wattage appliances such as hair dryers.

Contacts **Steve Kropla's Help for World Travelers** (www.kropla.com) has information on electrical and telephone plugs around the world.

EMERGENCIES

The emergency number ☎060 works best in Mexico City and environs. In other areas, call ☎080 or ☎066. For roadside assistance contact the Angeles Verdes. If you get into a scrape with the law, you can call your nearest consulate; the U.S. Embassy Web site has links to all consular offices. U.S. citizens can also call the Overseas Citizens Services Center in the United States. The Mexican Ministry of Tourism also has Infotur, a 24-hour toll-free hotline, and local tourist boards may be able to help as well. Two medical emergency evacuation services are Air Ambulance Network and Global Life Flight.

Foreign Embassies **U.S. Embassy** (✉Paseo de la Reforma 305, Col. Cuauhtémoc, Mexico City ☎55/5080–2000 mexico.usembassy.gov/eng).

General Emergency Contacts **Air Ambulance Network** (☎800/327–1966 in U.S. and Canada, 001800/010–0027 in Mexico www.airambulancenetwork.com). **Angeles Verdes, Mexico City** (☎078). **Global Life Flight** (☎01800/305–9400 toll-free in Mexico, 800/831–9307 in U.S and Canada www.globallifeflight.com). **Mexico Ministry of Tourism** (☎800/446–3942 in U.S., 01800/903-9200 toll-free in Mexico www.sectur.gob.mx).**U.S. Overseas Citizens Services Center** (☎202/501–4444 www.travel.state.gov).

HEALTH

In Mexico the major health risk, known as *turista*, or traveler's diarrhea, is caused by eating contaminated fruit or vegetables or drinking contaminated water. In places not geared to foreigners, don't eat raw vegetables that haven't been, or can't be, peeled (e.g., lettuce and raw chile peppers or piles of fresh cilantro, a common cause of turista); ask for your plate *sin ensalada* (without the salad). Avoid uncooked food and unpasteurized milk and milk products. Although fresh *ceviche,* made of raw fish (or scallops or shrimp) cured in lemon juice can be delicious, wary travelers heed the warnings of the Mexican Department of Health, which warns that marinating in lemon juice does not constitute the "cooking" that would make contaminated shellfish safe to eat. Also, if you choose to eat food from street stands, check that utensils and dishes are properly washed and dried (plastic sleeves cover plates at the most hygienic street stalls), and that the food is hot and fresh-looking when you buy it. Although much street food may be healthful and tasty, it's best to err on the side of caution.

Drink only bottled water (or water that has been boiled for at least 10 minutes) even when you're brushing your teeth. *Agua mineral* means mineral water, and *agua purificada* means purified water. Hotels with water-purification systems will post signs to that effect in the rooms; even then, be wary. Restaurants in Cancún and other resort destinations don't want their customers dropping like flies, and take necessary precautions. Stay away from ice, unless you're sure it was made from purified water; commercially made purified ice usually has a uniform shape and a hole in the center. When in doubt, especially when ordering cold drinks at untouristed establishments, skip the ice: *sin hielo*.

Mild cases of *turista* may respond to Imodium (known generically as loperamide), Lomotil, or Pepto-Bismol (not as strong), all of which you can buy over the counter; keep in mind, though, that these drugs can complicate more serious illnesses. You'll need to replace fluids, so drink plenty of purified water or tea; chamomile tea (*te de manzanilla*) is a good folk remedy, and it's readily available in restaurants throughout Mexico. In severe cases, rehydrate yourself with Gatorade or a salt-sugar solution (½ teaspoon salt and 4 tablespoons sugar per quart of water). If your fever and diarrhea last longer than three days, see a doctor—you may have picked up a parasite that requires prescription medication.

Air pollution in Mexico City can pose a health risk. The sheer number of cars and industries in the capital, thermal inversions, and the inability to process sewage have all contributed to the high levels of lead, carbon monoxide, and other pollutants in Mexico City's atmosphere. Children, the elderly, and those with respiratory problems should avoid outdoor activities—including sightseeing—on days of high smog alerts. (Information on smog is often published in the daily papers and mentioned on the radio. If Spanish isn't one of your languages, ask a hotel staffer for an update.) If you have heart problems, keep in mind that Mexico City is, at 7,556 feet, the highest metropolis on the North American continent. This compounded with the smog may pose a serious health risk, so check with your doctor before planning a trip.

In the last few years Mexico has had to make tough choices between much-needed development and protecting the environment. In some places the rate of development has exceeded the government's ability to keep the environment safe. Some cleanup action is under way, after studies released in early 2003 indicated that waters near 16 resort areas contained high levels of pollution from trash, sewage, or industrial waste. Of the resorts—which included Acapulco, Puerto Vallarta, Puerto Escondido, and Huatulco—Zihuatanejo was considered the most polluted. Two factors reportedly contributed to the problem: the waters off its shores are in a bay where pollution is more apt to accumulate than it would in open waters, and this area in particular had difficulties properly treating its wastewater. The cleanup efforts have a long way to go. Polluted waters can give swimmers gastrointestinal and other problems; ask locals about where it's best to swim. The higher you go, the lower the oxygen levels in the air—and the oxygen deficiency in your breathing intake can cause *mal de alturas* (altitude sickness). It usually sets in at 8,000 feet, though some people are affected at 6,000 feet; headache, insomnia, and shortness of breath are the most common symptoms. At 7,556 feet, Mexico City is in the altitude-sickness zone for many travelers. Mild pain relievers, such as aspirin or aspirin substitutes, should help with headaches. Altitude sensitivity varies, but in general you can expect symptoms to abate after two or three days. Stronger drugs, such as acetazolamide, should be taken only after consulting a doctor. More severe symptoms include nausea, vomiting, dry cough, confusion, and difficulty walking a straight line; at worst, altitude sickness can cause pulmonary and cerebral edema. If your symptoms don't go away, get to a lower altitude and consult a doctor. If you're doing any mountain climbing, be especially careful. Stay hydrated (which includes going easy on diuretics, like coffee, tea, and alcoholic beverages) and plan on scaling back your physical activity until you're acclimated.

Caution is advised when venturing out in the Mexican sun. Sunbathers lulled by a slightly overcast sky or the sea breezes can be burned badly in just 20 minutes. To avoid overexposure, use strong sunscreens and avoid the peak sun hours of noon to 2 PM. Sunscreen, including many American brands, can be found in pharmacies, supermarkets, and resort gift shops. Mosquitoes are most prevalent in tropical coastal areas and in the south—particularly in the jungle areas of Campeche, Quintana Roo, and the Yucatán peninsula, where it's best to be cautious and go indoors at dusk (called the "mosquito hour" by locals). An excellent brand of *repelente de insectos* (insect repellent) called Autan is readily available; do not use it on children under age two. Sprays (*aerosoles repelentes contra mosquitos*) don't always have the effective ingredients; make sure they do. If you want to bring a mosquito repellent from home, make sure it has at least 10% DEET or it won't be effective. If you're hiking in the jungle (or near standing water or even a patio restaurant edged in tropical plants), wear repellent and long pants and long sleeves; if you're camping in the jungle, use a mosquito net and invest in a package of *espirales contra mosquitos,* mosquito coils, which are sold in *ferreterías* or *tlalpalerías* (hardware stores) and also in some corner stores. Dengue fever is carried by mosquitoes, so be sure to use enough repellent as necessary to keep mosquitoes away.

You can call International SOS Assistance's U.S.–based phone number collect from Mexico.

OVER-THE-COUNTER REMEDIES

Farmacias (pharmacies) are the most convenient place for such common medicines as *aspirina* (aspirin) or *jarabe para la tos* (cough syrup). You'll be able to find many U.S. brands (e.g., Tylenol, Pepto-Bismol), but don't plan on buying your favorite prescription or nonprescription sleep aid, for example. The same brands and even drugs are not always available. There are pharmacies in all small towns and on practically every corner in larger cities. The Sanborns chain stores also have pharmacies.

SHOTS & MEDICATIONS

According to the U.S. National Centers for Disease Control and Prevention (CDC), there's a limited risk of malaria, dengue fever, and other insect-carried or parasite-caused illnesses in certain rural areas of Mexico (largely, but not exclusively, rural and tropical coastal areas). In most urban or easily accessible areas you need not worry. However, if you plan to visit remote regions or stay for more than six weeks, check with the CDC's International Travelers' Hotline. Malaria and dengue are both carried by mosquitoes; in areas where these illnesses are prevalent, use insect repellent. Also consider taking antimalarial pills if you're doing serious adventure activities in subtropical areas. Don't wait until Mexico to get the pills; ask your doctor for medicine that combats even chloroquine-resistant strains. There's no vaccine to combat dengue. Talk with your health care professional to determine if vaccinations against typhoid, Hepititis A, or Hepititis B are a good idea for you.

TRIP INSURANCE

Consider buying trip insurance with medical-only coverage. Neither Medicare nor some private insurers cover medical expenses anywhere outside of the United States. Medical-only policies typically reimburse you for medical care (excluding that related to preexisting conditions) and hospitalization abroad, and provide for evacuation. You still have to pay the bills and await reimbursement from the insurer, though.

Another option is to sign up with a medical-evacuation assistance company. A membership in one of these companies gets you doctor referrals, emergency evacuation or repatriation, 24-hour hotlines for medical consultation, and other assistance. International SOS Assistance Emergency and AirMed International provide evacuation services and medical referrals. MedjetAssist offers medical evacuation.

Medical Assistance Companies **AirMed International** (w www.airmed.com).**International SOS Assistance Emergency** (🌐www.intsos.com).**MedjetAssist** (🌐www.medjetassist.com).

Medical-Only Insurers **International Medical Group** (🌐www.imglobal.com). **International SOS** (🌐www.internationalsos.com). **Wallach & Company** (🌐www.wallach.com).

HOLIDAYS

Banks and government offices close on January 1, February 5 (Constitution Day), March 21 (Benito Juárez's birthday), May 1 (Labor Day), September 16 (Independence Day), November 20 (Revolution Day), and December 25. They may also close on unofficial holidays, such as Day of the Dead (November 1–2), Virgin of Guadalupe Day (December 12), and during Holy Week (the days leading to Easter Sunday). Government offices usually have reduced hours and staff from Christmas through New Year's Day.

MAIL

The Mexican postal system is notoriously slow and unreliable; avoid sending packages through the postal service and don't expect to receive them, as they may be stolen. It's much better to use a courier service. If you're an American Express cardholder, you may be able to receive packages at a branch office, but check beforehand with customer service to find out if this client mail service is available in your destination.

Post offices (*oficinas de correos*) are found in even the smallest villages. International postal service is all airmail, but even so your letter will take anywhere from 10 days to six weeks to arrive. Service within Mexico can be equally slow.

To receive mail in Mexico, you can have it sent to your hotel or use *poste restante* at the post office. In the latter case, the address must include the words a/c Lista de Correos (general delivery), followed by the city, state, postal code, and country. To use this service, you should first register with the post office at which you wish to receive your mail. The post office posts and updates daily a list of names for whom mail has been received. Mail is generally held for 10 days, and a list of recipients is posted daily.

Information **American Express** (www.americanexpress.com/travel).

SHIPPING PACKAGES

Federal Express, DHL, Estafeta, AeroMexpress, and United Parcel Service are available in major cities and many resort areas. These companies offer office or hotel pickup with 24-hour advance notice (sometimes less, depending on when you call) and are very reliable. From Mexico City to anywhere in the United States, the minimum charge is around $30 for a package weighing about 1 pound.

Express Services **AeroMexpress** (01800/398–2700 toll-free in Mexico, 55/5133–0275 in Mexico City www.aeromexpress.com.mx). **DHL** (01800/765–6345 toll-free in Mexico, 55/5345–7000 in Mexico City www.dhl.com). **Estafeta** (01800/903–3500 toll-free in Mexico, 55/5270–8300 in Mexico City www.estafeta.com). **Federal Express** (01800/900–1100 toll-free in Mexico, 55/228–9904 in Mexico City www.fedex.com). **United Parcel Service** (01800/902–9200 toll-free in Mexico, 55/5228–7900 in Mexico City www.ups.com).

MONEY

The prices given in this book have nearly always been converted to U.S. dollars because high-end hotels and heavily touristed areas often quote prices in U.S. dollars. Admissions and meal prices outside these areas will likely be quoted in pesos.

If you travel only by air or package tour, stay at international hotel-chain properties, and eat at tourist restaurants, you might not find Mexico such a bargain. If you want a closer look at the country and aren't wedded to standard creature comforts you can spend as little as $35 a day on room, board, and local transportation. Speaking Spanish is also helpful in bargaining situations and when asking for dining recommendations.

As a general rule when traveling in Mexico, always pay in pesos. Hotels almost always accept dollars but usually do not offer a good exchange rate. Many businesses, most restaurants (unless they're high-end or in major resort areas), market vendors, and most highway tollbooths do not accept dollars. If you run out of pesos, pay with a credit card or make a withdrawal from an ATM.

TIP→ **Unlike their U.S. counterparts, Mexican banks may refuse torn bills, and for this reason merchants also may refuse them.** Cancún, Cozumel, Isla Mujeres, Playa del Carmen, Puerto Vallarta, Mexico City, Monterrey, Acapulco, Ixtapa, Los Cabos, Manzanillo, and, to a lesser extent, Mazatlán and Huatulco are the most expensive places to visit. All the beach towns, however, offer budget accommodations; lodgings are even less expensive in less accessible areas such as the Chihuahua and Sonora states of northwest Mexico, the Gulf Coast and northern Yucatán parts of Quintana Roo, some of the less-developed spots north and south of Puerto Vallarta in the states of Jalisco and Nayarit, and the smaller Oaxacan coastal towns as well as those of Chiapas and Tabasco.

Probably the best value for your travel dollar is in smaller, inland cities such as Mérida, Morelia, Guanajuato, and Oaxaca. Although upscale lodging can run more than $150 a night, and dinner for two in a high-end restaurant will cost $30–$60, simple colonial-style hotels with adequate accommodations for under $50 can also be found, and most of your meals will cost less than $15.

WHAT IT COSTS	
Cup of Coffee	80¢ to $1.50
Bottle of Beer	$2.50–$5
Sandwich	$1.50–$2.50
One-Mile Taxi Ride	$1.50–$3.50
Museum Admission	Free–$10 (average $8)

Prices throughout this guide are given for adults. Substantially reduced fees are almost always available for children, students, and senior citizens.

TIP→Banks never have every foreign currency on hand, and it may take as long as a week to order. If you're planning to exchange funds before leaving home, don't wait till the last minute.

ATMS & BANKS

Your own bank will probably charge a fee for using ATMs abroad; the foreign bank you use may also charge a fee. Nevertheless, you'll usually get a better rate of exchange at an ATM than you will at a currency-exchange office or even when changing money in a bank. And extracting funds as you need them is a safer option than carrying around a large amount of cash.

TIP→PIN numbers with more than four digits are not recognized at ATMs in many countries. If yours has five or more, remember to change it before you leave.

ATMs (*cajeros automáticos*) are widely available, with Cirrus and Plus the most frequently found networks. Rural towns often lack banking facilities. Unless you're in a major city, treat ATMs as you would gas stations—don't assume you'll be able to find one in a pinch (in smaller towns, even when they're present, machines are often out of order or out of cash). Many, but not all, gas stations have ATMs. All airports have ATMs but many bus stations do not.

Before you leave home, ask what the transaction fee will be for withdrawing money in Mexico (it can be up to $5 a pop), and ask which particular banks offer the lowest fees (Bank of America, for example, advises its customers to use Santander). Be sure to also alert your bank's customer-protection division to let them know you will be using your card in Mexico—otherwise they may assume that the card's been stolen and put a hold on your account. Many Mexican ATMs cannot accept PINs (personal identification numbers, *número de identificación personal* or NIP in Spanish) with more than four digits. If yours is longer, ask your bank about changing your PIN before you leave home. If your PIN is fine yet your transaction still can't be completed, chances are that the computer lines are busy or that the machine has run out of money or is being serviced. Don't give up.

For cash advances, plan to use Visa or MasterCard, as many Mexican ATMs don't accept American Express. Large banks with reliable ATMs include Banamex, HSBC, BBVA Bancomer, Santander Serfín, and Scotiabank Inverlat. *(⇨ Safety, on avoiding ATM robberies.)*

CREDIT CARDS

Throughout this guide, the following abbreviations are used: **AE,** American Express; **D,** Discover; **DC,** Diners Club; **MC,** MasterCard; and **V,** Visa.

If you plan to use your credit card for cash advances, you'll need to apply for a PIN at least two weeks before your trip. Although it's usually cheaper (and safer) to use a credit card abroad for large purchases (so you can cancel payments or be reimbursed if there's a problem), note that some credit-card companies *and* the banks that issue them add substantial percentages to all foreign transactions, whether they're in a foreign currency or not. Check on these fees before leaving home, so there won't be any surprises when you get the bill.

TIP→ Before you charge something, ask the merchant whether or not he or she plans to do a dynamic currency conversion (DCC). In such a transaction the credit-card processor (shop, restaurant, or hotel, not Visa or MasterCard) converts the currency and charges you in dollars. In most cases you'll pay the merchant a 3% fee for this service in addition to any credit-card company and issuing-bank foreign-transaction surcharges.

WORST-CASE SCENARIO

All your money and credit cards have just been stolen. In these days of real-time transactions, this isn't a predicament that should destroy your vacation. First, report the theft of the credit cards. Then get any traveler's checks you were carrying replaced. This can usually be done almost immediately, provided that you kept a record of the serial numbers separate from the checks themselves. If you bank at a large international bank like Citibank or HSBC, go to the closest branch; if you know your account number, chances are you can get a new ATM card and withdraw money right away. **Western Union** (☎ *800/325–6000* 🌐 *www.westernunion.com*) sends money almost anywhere. Have someone back home order a transfer online, over the phone, or at one of the company's offices, which is the cheapest option. The U.S. State Department's **Overseas Citizens Services** (🌐 *www.travel.state.gov/travel* ☎ *202/501–4444*) can wire money to any U.S. consulate or embassy abroad for a fee of $30. Just have someone back home wire money or send a money order or cashier's check to the State Department, which will then disburse the funds as soon as the next working day after it receives them.

Dynamic currency conversion programs are becoming increasingly widespread. Merchants who participate in them are supposed to ask whether you want to be charged in dollars or the local currency, but they don't always do so. And even if they do offer you a choice, they may well avoid mentioning the additional surcharges. The good news is that you *do* have a choice. And if this practice really gets your goat, you can avoid it entirely thanks to American Express; with its cards, DCC simply isn't an option.

Credit cards are accepted in most tourist areas. Smaller, less expensive restaurants and shops, however, tend to take only cash. In general, credit cards aren't accepted in small towns and villages, except in hotels. The most widely accepted cards are MasterCard and Visa. When shopping, you can often get better prices if you pay with cash, particularly in small shops.

At the same time, when traveling internationally you'll receive wholesale exchange rates when you make purchases with credit cards. These exchange rates are usually better than those that banks give you for changing money. (Before you go, it doesn't hurt to ask your credit-card company how it handles purchases in foreign currency.) In Mexico the decision to pay cash or use a credit card might depend on whether the establishment in which you are making a purchase finds bargaining for prices acceptable, as well as whether you want the safety net of your card's purchase protection. To avoid fraud, it's wise to make sure that "pesos" is clearly marked on all credit-card receipts.

CURRENCY & EXCHANGE

Mexican currency comes in denominations of 20-, 50-, 100-, 200-, and 500-peso bills. Coins come in denominations of 1, 2, 5, 10, and 20 pesos, and 10, 20, and 50 centavos (10 and 20 centavos pieces are rarely seen, however). Many of the coins and bills are very similar, so check carefully.

U.S. dollar bills (but not coins) are widely accepted in border towns and in many parts of the Yucatán, particularly in Cancún and Cozumel, where you'll often find prices in shops quoted in dollars. Still, in the majority of the country, even in other resort areas, pesos are the preferred (and many times, only) accepted currency. At this writing, the exchange rate was 10.76 pesos to the U.S. dollar. Check with your bank or the financial pages of your local newspaper for current exchange rates. For quick, rough estimates of how much something costs in U.S. dollar terms, divide prices given in pesos by 10. For example, 50 pesos would be just under $5.

ATM transaction fees may be higher abroad than at home, but ATM currency-exchange rates are the best of all because they're based on wholesale rates offered only by major banks. And if you take out a fair amount of cash per withdrawal, the transaction fee becomes less of a strike against the exchange rate (in percentage terms). However, most ATMs allow only up to $300 a transaction. Banks and *casas de cambio* (money-exchange bureaus) have the second-best exchange rates. The difference from one place to another is usually only a few pesos.

Some banks change money on weekdays only until 3 (though they stay open until 5 or later). Casas de cambio generally stay open until 6 and often operate on weekends also; they usually have competitive rates and much shorter lines. Some hotels exchange money, but for providing you with this convenience they help themselves to a bigger commission than banks.

You can do well at most airport exchange booths, though not as well as at the ATMs. You'll do even worse at rail and bus stations, in hotels, in restaurants, or in stores.

When changing money, count your bills before leaving the bank or casa de cambio, and don't accept any partially torn or taped-together notes as they won't be accepted anywhere. Also, many shop and restaurant owners are unable to make change for large bills. Enough of these encounters may compel you to request *billetes chicos* (small bills) when you exchange money. It's wise to hoard a cache of smaller bills and coins to use at these more humble establishments to avoid having to wait around while the merchant runs off to seek change.

TIP→Even if a currency-exchange booth has a sign promising no commission, rest assured that there's some kind of huge, hidden fee. And as for rates, you're almost always better off getting foreign currency at an ATM or exchanging money at a bank.

Currency Conversion **Google** (www.google.com) **Oanda.com** (www.oanda.com) **XE.com** (www.xe.com)

PACKING

For resorts, bring lightweight sportswear, bathing suits, and cover-ups for the beach. Bathing suits and immodest clothing are inappropriate for shopping and sightseeing, both in cities and, to a lesser extent, in beach resorts. Keep in mind that Mexican men do not generally wear shorts except in beach cities and resorts, even in extremely hot weather. In winter the resort areas along the Pacific Coast can get very cool at night; make sure you have at least one pair of long pants and sweater or light jacket. Mexico City, Queretaro, and the other capital cities are more formal than the resorts, and many are cooler because of their high elevation. Men will want to bring lightweight suits or slacks and blazers; women should pack dresses or pants suits. Many high-end Mexico City restaurants require jacket and tie; jeans are acceptable for shopping and sightseeing, but shorts are rarely worn by local men or women. You'll need a lightweight topcoat for winter and an all-weather coat and umbrella in case of sudden rainstorms. The sun anywhere in Mexico can be fierce; bring a sun hat and sunscreen for the beach and for sightseeing. You'll need a sweater or jacket to cope with hotel and restaurant air-conditioning. TIP→ **It's a good idea to bring along tissue packs in case you hit a place where the toilet paper has run out.**

PASSPORTS & VISAS

A tourist visa is required for all visitors to Mexico. If you're arriving by plane, the standard tourist visa forms will be given to you on the plane. They're also available through travel agents and Mexican consulates, and at the border if you're entering by land. You're supposed to keep a portion of the form. *Be sure that you do.* You'll be asked to present it, your ticket, and your passport at the gate when boarding for departure.

A tourist visa costs about $20. The fee is generally tacked on to the price of your airline ticket; if you enter by land or boat you'll have to pay the fee separately. You're exempt from the fee if you enter by sea and stay less than 72 hours, or by land and do not stray past the 26–30-km (16–18-mi) checkpoint into the interior.

In addition to having your visa form, you must prove your citizenship. U.S. Homeland Security regulations require U.S. citizens of all ages returning by air to have a valid U.S. passport. Those returning by land or sea are required to present either a government-issue photo ID and a certified copy of your birth certificate or a U.S. Passport Card (available as of mid-2008).

Minors traveling with one parent need notarized permission from the absent parent. You're allowed to stay 180 days as a tourist; frequently, though, immigration officials will give you less. Be sure to ask for as much time as you think you'll need up to 180 days; going to a Mexican immigration office to extend a visa can easily take a whole day; plus, you'll have to pay an extension fee.

U.S. Passport Information **U.S. Department of State** (☎877/487-2778 🌐http://travel.state.gov/passport).

U.S. Passport & Visa Expediters **A. Briggs Passport & Visa Expeditors** (☎800/806-0581 or 202/338-0111 🌐www.abriggs.com). **American Passport Express** (☎800/455-5166 or 800/841-6778 🌐www.americanpassport.com). **Passport Express** (☎800/362-8196 🌐www.passportexpress.com). **Travel Document Systems** (☎800/874-5100 or 202/638-3800 🌐www.traveldocs.com). **Travel the World Visas** (☎866/886-8472 🌐www.world-visa.com).

RESTROOMS

Expect to find reasonably clean flushing toilets and running water at public restrooms in the major tourist destinations and at tourist attractions; toilet paper, soap, hot water, and paper towels are not always available, though. Keep a packet of tissues with you at all times. Although many markets, bus and train stations, and the like have public facilities, you usually have to pay about 5 pesos for the privilege. Gas stations have public bathrooms—some tidy and others not so tidy. You're better off popping into a restaurant, buying a little something, and using its restroom, which will probably be simple but clean and adequately equipped. Remember that unless otherwise indicated you should put your used toilet paper in the wastebasket next to the toilet; many plumbing systems in Mexico still can't handle accumulations of toilet paper.

Find a Loo **The Bathroom Diaries** (🌐www.thebathroomdiaries.com) is flush with unsanitized info on restrooms the world over—each one located, reviewed, and rated.

SAFETY

Increased narcotics activity and related violence in the state of Michoacan made the news in late 2007. The states of Sinaloa, Tamaulipas, Guerrero, Baja California, and Nuevo León have had similar troubles in recent years. Tourists are not being targeted—most of the victims are those involved in the drug trade and some Mexican businessmen and officials (as well as some prominent Mexican musicians)—but you should be aware that increased police activity means that you may encounter more roadside checkpoints while driving through these areas, as well as increased security measures in some regional airports. Acapulco has been plagued by increased gang violence in the past year, though police presence in tourist areas of the city has also increased. The U.S. State Department continues to warn of crime against tourists in the border regions of Mexico, especially in Tijuana, Ciudad Juárez, Nogales, and Matamoros.

Mexico City's age-old problem of pickpocketing has been overshadowed by robberies at gunpoint. Other developments have been abductions and robberies in taxicabs hailed from the street (as opposed to hired from a hotel or taxi stand), and even robberies on city buses.

Reports indicate that uniformed police officers have, on occasion, perpetrated nonviolent crimes, and that there's a growing problem with people impersonating police officers, pulling over motorists, and extorting money or robbing them. The patronage system is a well-entrenched part of Mexican politics and industry, and workers in the public sector—notably police and customs officials—are notoriously underpaid. Everyone has heard some horror story about highway assaults, pickpocketing, bribes, or foreigners languishing in Mexican jails. These reports apply in large part to Mexico City and more remote areas of Oaxaca and Chiapas. So far, crime isn't such a problem in the heartland (cities like San Miguel de Allende) and much of the rest of the country. Cancún, which has traditionally been a safe haven, has also seen an increased incidence of taxi robberies and extortion; be particularly careful that your taxi driver from the airport comes from a reputable company.

Use common sense everywhere, but exercise particular caution in Mexico City. Don't wear expensive jewelry, including watches you care about losing, and try not to act too much like a tourist. Keep your passport and all valuables in hotel safes, and carry your own baggage whenever possible.

Avoid driving on desolate streets, and don't travel at night, pick up hitchhikers, or hitchhike yourself. Robberies do occasionally occur on long-distance buses. Use luxury buses whenever possible (rather than second- or third-class vehicles), which take the safer toll roads. In Mexico City, it's best to take only registered hotel taxis or have a hotel concierge call a radio taxi or *sitio* (cab stand)—avoid hailing taxis on the street. Think twice about urges to get away from it all on your own (even as a couple) to go hiking in remote national parks; women in particular shouldn't venture alone onto uncrowded beaches.

Use ATMs during the day and in big, enclosed commercial areas. Avoid the glass-enclosed street variety of banks where you may be more vulnerable to thieves who force you to withdraw money for them. Although this caution is geared mostly to Mexico City, even there, you're reasonably safe if you follow the same standards of safety used in any large, metropolitan city.

Bear in mind that reporting a crime to the police is often a frustrating experience unless you speak excellent Spanish and have a great deal of patience. If you're victimized, contact your local consular agent or the consular section of your country's embassy in Mexico City.

If you're on your own, consider using only your first initial and last name when registering at your hotel. If you carry a purse, choose one with a zipper and a thick strap that you can drape across your body; adjust the length so that the purse sits in front of you at or above hip level. Store only enough money in the purse to cover casual spending. Distribute the rest of your cash and any valuables (including credit cards and your passport) between a deep front pocket, an inside jacket or vest pocket, and a hidden money pouch. Do not reach for the money pouch once in public. Better yet, leave your passport and other valuables you don't need immediately in your hotel's safe-deposit box.

If you're traveling alone or with other women rather than men, you may be subjected to *piropos* (flirtatious comments). Dressing conservatively may deflect some of the attention—at the very least, you won't stand out as much in more traditional rural areas—but don't count on it. This type of harassment is rare in small rural towns; you'll encounter more of it in the big cities, most especially in heavily touristed resort areas. Your best strategy is to ignore the offender.

If you're driving in a big city, especially Mexico City, people selling trinkets, washing windows, and asking for handouts often target drivers at stoplights. If someone approaches your window and will not leave, shake your index finger or your head to indicate that you do not want whatever they are selling. Also be sure to roll up your window and lock your doors.

In big cities like Mexico City, shakedown artists may approach tourists with a convincing sob story. For example, a common ruse is for a woman with multiple children in tow and tears in her eyes to approach a victim saying that she's just been robbed and needs bus fare to get home. It's hard to resist when there are little ones involved, but these and other similar stories are, sadly, often made up.

GOVERNMENT ADVISORIES

As different countries have different world views, look at travel advisories from a range of governments to get more of a sense of what's going on out there. And be sure to parse the language carefully. For example, a warning to "avoid all travel" carries more weight than one urging you to "avoid nonessential travel," and both are much stronger than a plea to "exercise caution." A U.S. government travel warning is more permanent (though not necessarily more serious) than a so-called public announcement.

The U.S. Department of State's Web site has more than just travel warnings. The consular information sheets issued for every country have general safety tips and entry requirements (though be sure to verify these with the country's embassy).

At this writing, crime, murder, and kidnapping are all down in Mexico, and a dozen accused drug lords have been extradited to the United States for prosecution. Only time will tell if these measures are successful. Luckily, travelers are generally unaffected by these troubles, and using the common sense that applies to any metropolitan area should keep you safe.

General Information & Warnings

U.S. Department of State (www.travel.state.gov).

TAXES

Mexico has a value-added tax of 15% (10% in the states of Quintana Roo, Baja California, and Baja California Sur, as well as areas that are up to 20 km, or 12½ mi, from the border), called IVA (*impuesto al valor agregado*). It's often waived for cash purchases, or incorporated into the price. When comparing hotel prices, it's important to know if yours includes or excludes

IVA and any service charge. Other taxes and charges apply for phone calls made from your room. Many states are charging a 2% tax on accommodations that's used for tourism promotion.

TIME

Mexico has three time zones; most of the country falls in Central Standard Time, which includes Mexico City and is in line with Chicago. Baja California is on Pacific Standard Time—the same as California. Baja California Sur, Sonora, Chihuahua, Sinaloa, and most of Nayarit are on Mountain Standard Time. If you're staying in southern Nayarit and flying out of the Puerto Vallarta airport, note that Puerto Vallarta, in Jalisco state, is on Mountain time—an hour later than Nayarit time. Mexico switches to and from daylight saving time on the same schedule as the United States.

TIPPING

When tipping in Mexico, remember that the minimum wage is just under $5 a day and that maids, bellmen, and others in the tourism industry earn minimum wage. Waiters and bellmen in international chain hotels, for example, think in dollars and know that in the United States porters are tipped about $2 a bag; they tend to expect the equivalent. You should always tip using local currency whenever possible so that service personnel aren't stuck going to the bank to exchange dollars for pesos.

What follows are some guidelines. Naturally, larger tips are always welcome: porters and bellhops, 10 pesos per bag at airports and moderate and inexpensive hotels and 20 pesos per person at expensive hotels; maids, 10 pesos per night (all hotels); waiters, 10%–15% of the bill, depending on service, and less in simpler restaurants (anywhere you are, make sure a service charge hasn't already been added, a practice that's particularly common in resorts); bartenders, 10%–15% of the bill, depending on service, or 10 pesos per drink if you're not running a tab; taxi drivers, 5–10 pesos if the driver helps you with your bags only (taxi drivers are not commonly tipped in Mexico, and in any case, commonly overcharge tourists); tour guides and drivers, at least 50 pesos per half day; gas-station attendants, 3–5 pesos unless they check the oil, tires, etc., in which case tip more; parking attendants, 5–10 pesos, even if it's for valet parking at a theater or restaurant that charges for the service. Restroom attendants should be tipped 5–10 pesos. In some cases, this is their only wage.

TIPPING GUIDELINES FOR MEXICO	
Bartender	10 pesos per drink
Bellhop	10–20 pesos per bag
Coat-check Personnel	10 pesos per item checked unless there is a fee
Hotel Concierge	20–50 pesos or more
Hotel Doorman	10 pesos if he helps you get a cab
Hotel Maid	10–20 pesos per day
Hotel Room-Service	10–20 pesos per meal
Parking Attendant	5 to 10 pesos
Porter or Skycap at Airport or Bus Station	10–20 pesos per bag
Restroom Attendant	5 to 10 pesos
Tour Guide	10% of the cost of the tour or 50 pesos per half day
Valet Parking Attendant	10–20 pesos, but only when you get your car
Waiter	10 to 15%

SPECIAL-INTEREST TOURS

ART & ARCHAEOLOGY

Contacts **Far Horizons Archaeological & Cultural Trips** (☎800/552–4575 or 415/842–

8400 www.farhorizons.com). **Maya Sites** (877/620–8715 or 505/255–2279 www.mayasites.com). **The Mayan Traveler** (800/451–8017 or 281/367–3386 www.themayantraveler.com).

BIRD-WATCHING

Contacts **Ecoturismo Yucatán** (999/920–2772 www.ecoyuc.com.mx). **Field Guides** (512/263–7295, 800/728–4953 in U.S. and Canada www.fieldguides.com). **Victor Emanuel Nature Tours** (512/328–5221, 800/328–8368 in U.S. and Canada www.ventbird.com). **Wings** (520/320–9868, 888/293–6443 in U.S. and Canada www.wingsbirds.com).

CULINARY

Seasons of My Heart Cooking School, at Rancho Aurora (about 40 minutes north of Oaxaca), offers cooking and market excursion tours to Veracruz, the Isthmus of Tehuantepec, and the Yucatán peninsula as well as seasonal culinary classes at their Oaxaca ranch.

Contacts **Seasons of My Heart** (951/508–0469 www.seasonsofmyheart.com).

FISHING

Contacts **Fishing International** (800/950–4242 or 707/542–4242 www.fishinginternational.com).

VOLUNTEER PROGRAMS

Contacts **Explorations In Travel** (802/257–0152 www.volunteertravel.com).

WHALE-WATCHING

Contacts **American Cetacean Society** (310/548–7821 www.acsonline.org). **Baja Discovery** (619/262–0700, 800/829–2252 in U.S. www.bajadiscovery.com).

VISITOR INFORMATION

The Mexico Tourism Board has branches in New York, Chicago, Los Angeles, Houston, Miami, Montréal, Toronto, Vancouver, and London.

FODORS.COM CONNECTION

Before your trip, be sure to check out what other travelers are saying in Talk on www.fodors.com.

Mexico Tourism Board **United States** (800/446–3942 [44–MEXICO] in U.S. www.visitmexico.com).

ONLINE TRAVEL TOOLS

Mexico's 31 states and the Federal District (Mexico City) are steadily posting tourism Web sites, though few are in English. A notable exception is the Mexican Tourism Board's official page, which has information about popular destinations, activities, and festivals. Other excellent English-language sites for history, travel information, and news stories include the Mexico Channel, Mexico Connect, Mexico Online, and the United States' Library of Congress Mexico pages. For archaeology, two sites stand above others: Mesoweb and the nonprofit site Ancient Mexico. Mexico's sites have a page on the World Heritage Web site. And Mexico Guru has interactive satellite maps of Mexico linked to destination articles.

All About Mexico **Ancient Mexico** (www.ancientmexico.com), **Mesoweb** (www.mesoweb.com), **The Mexico Channel** (www.trace-sc.com), **Mexico Connect** (www.mexconnect.com), **Mexico Guru** (www.mexicoguru.com), **Mexico Online** (www.mexonline.com), **Mexico Tourism Board** (www.visitmexico.com), **Mexico's World Heritage Sites** (www.worldheritagesite.org/countries/mexico.html), **United States' Library of Congress Mexico pages** (http://lcweb2.loc.gov/frd/cs/mxtoc.html and www.loc.gov/rr/international/hispanic/mexico/mexico.html), the newspaper **El Universal** (in Spanish only, www.eluniversal.com.mx).

INDEX

A

B

H

I

J

T

X

Z

Photo Credits: 5, *José Enrique Molina/age fotostock*. **Chapter 1: Experience Mexico:** 9, *Sexto Sol/Photodisc*. 10, *GUILLERMO ALDANA/Mexico Tourism Board*. 11 (left), *Corbis*. 11 (right), *GUILLERMO ALDANA/Mexico Tourism Board*. 13 (left), *Peter Purchia/viestiphoto.com*. 13 (right), *Corbis*. 15 (left), *Mexico Tourism Board*. 15 (right), *Joe Viesti/Viestiphoto.com*. 18, *Joe Viesti/Viestiphoto.com*. 19 (left), *GUILLERMO ALDANA/Mexico Tourism Board*. 19 (right), *GUILLERMO ALDANA/Mexico Tourism Board*. 20, *S. Murphy-Larronde/age fotostock*. 21, *José Fuste Raga/age fotostock*. 22, *Corbis*. 23 (left), *Juan Carlos Calvin/age fotostock*. 23 (right), *Walter Bibikow/viestiphoto.com*. 24, *CARLOS SANCHEZ/Mexican Tourism Board*. 25, *Doug Scott/age fotostock*. 27 (left), *Corbis*. 27 (right), *Joe Viesti/Viestiphoto.com*. **Chapter 2: Mexico City:** 35, *Martin Siepmann/age fotostock*. 36, *Corbis*. 37 (left), *CARLOS SANCHEZ/Mexican Tourism Board*. 37 (right), *José Fuste Raga/age fotostock*. 37 (bottom), *BRUCE HERMAN/Mexican Tourism Board*. 46-47, *Walter Bibikow/age fotostock*. 49 (top), *Peter Purchia/viestiphoto.com*. 49 (bottom), *George And Audrey DeLange*. 63, *Peter Purchia/viestiphoto.com*. 64 (top), *Yale Collection of American Literature, Beinecke Rare Book and Manuscript Library (Photograph by Carl Van Vechten)*. 64 (bottom), *Planet Art*. 65 (top), *Yale Collection of American Literature, Beinecke Rare Book and Manuscript Library (Photograph by Carl Van Vechten)*. 65 (bottom), *Flat Earth*. 66, *Museo Dolores Olmedo Patiño*. 67 (top left, center, and right), Russell Gordon/viestiphoto.com. 67 (bottom), *George And Audrey DeLange*. **Chapter 3: Around Mexico City:** 125, *Ken Welsh/age fotostock*. 126, *José Fuste Raga/age fotostock*. 127 (top left), *GUILLERMO ALDANA/Mexico Tourism Board*. 127 (top right), *GUILLERMO ALDANA/Mexico Tourism Board*. 127 (bottom), *José Fuste Raga/age fotostock*. 148 (full page), *BRUCE HERMAN/Mexico Tourism Board*. 148 (inset), *José Fuste Raga/age fotostock*. 149 (top), *Marco/viestiphoto.com*. 149 (bottom), *J.D. Heaton/Picture Finders/age fotostock*. 150, *Russell Gordon/age fotostock*. 151, *Toño Labra/age fotostock*. 152, *José Fuste Raga/age fotostock*. **Chapter 4: San Miguel de Allende & the Heartland:** 165, *José Fuste Raga/age fotostock*. 166 (top), *Angelo Cavalli/age fotostock*. 166 (bottom), *Bruno Perousse/age fotostock*. 167 (left), *CARLOS SANCHEZ/Mexico Tourism Board*. 167 (right), PABLO DE AGUINACO/*Mexico Tourism Board*. 220, *Joe Viesti/Viestiphoto.com*. 221 (top), *Joe Viesti/Viestiphoto.com*. 221 (bottom), *Bruno Perousse/age fotostock*. 222 (top), *Joe Viesti/Viestiphoto.com*. 222 (bottom), *Joe Viesti/Viestiphoto.com*. 223 (top), *Joe Viesti/Viestiphoto.com*. 223 (center), *Joe Viesti/Viestiphoto.com*. 223 (bottom), *Corbis*. **Chapter 5: Guadalajara:** 229, *BRUCE HERMAN/Mexico Tourism Board*. 230 (left), *Corbis*. 230 (right), *BRUCE HERMAN/Mexico Tourism Board*. 231 (left and right), *PABLO DE AGUINACO/Mexico Tourism Board*. 247 and 248 (top left), *folkart.com/Sullivan*. 248 (bottom left), *Corbis*. 248 (top right), *Colonial Arts, San Francisco*. 248 (bottom right), *Andrew J. Morris*. **Chapter 6: Veracruz:** 273 and 274 (top), *GUILLERMO ALDANA/Mexico Tourism Board*. 274 (bottom), *NADINE MARKOVA/Mexico Tourism Board*. 275 (top left and top right), *GUILLERMO ALDANA/Mexico Tourism Board*. 275 (bottom), *Joe Viesti/Viestiphoto.com*. 302 and 303 (top and 2nd from top), *Joe Viesti/Viestiphoto.com*. 303 (3rd from top and bottom), *GUILLERMO ALDANA/Mexico Tourism Board*. **Chapter 7: Oaxaca:** 315, S. *Murphy-Larronde/age fotostock*. 316, *BRUCE HERMAN/Mexico Tourism Board*. 317 (top left), *GUILLERMO ALDANA/Mexico Tourism Board*. 317 (top right), *Don Klumpp/age fotostock*. 317 (bottom), *GUILLERMO ALDANA/*

Mexico Tourism Board. 345, *Joe Viesti/Viestiphoto.com*. 346 (top), *Peter Purchia/viestiphoto.com*. 347 (all), *folkart.com/oaxaca*. 350-51, *Oaxaca Ministry of Tourism*. 352, *marco/viestiphoto.com*. **Chapter 8: Chiapas & Tabasco:** 377, *Corbis*. 378 (top), *Jaime Boites/Viestiphoto.com*. 378 (bottom left), *Martin Siepmann/age fotostock*. 378 (bottom right), *GUILLERMO ALDANA/Mexico Tourism Board*. 379 (left), *Sergio Pitamitz/age fotostock*. 379 (right), *Corbis*. 412, *Wojtek Buss/age fotostock*. 413 (top), *SuperStock/age fotostock*. 413 (bottom), *Beinecke Rare Book and Manuscript Library, Yale University*. 414, *Jean Pierre Lebras/Viestiphoto.com*. 415 (left), *GUILLERMO ALDANA/Mexico Tourism Board*. 415 (right), *George & Audrey DeLange*. 415 (bottom), *Philip Baird/www.anthroarcheart.org*. 416, *Sergio Pitamitz/age fotostock*. 417, *GUILLERMO ALDANA/Mexico Tourism Board*. **Chapter 9: Sonora:** 427, *NADINE MARKOVA/Mexico Tourism Board*. 428, *GUILLERMO ALDANA/Mexico Tourism Board*. 429 (left), *Joe Viesti/Viestiphoto.com*. 429 (right), *Ken Ross/Viestiphoto.com Inc*. **Chapter 10: Barrancas del Cobre:** 457, *Gonzalo Azumendi/age fotostock*. 458 (top), *Ann Duncan/viestiphoto.com*. 458 (bottom), *Peter Purchia/viestiphoto.com*. 459, *Peter Purchia/viestiphoto.com*. **Chapter 11: Los Cabos & the Baja Peninsula:** 485, *Mexico Tourism Board*. 486, *Vicki Sills/Casa Del Mar Beach Golf & Spa Resort*. 512, *Esperanza Resort*. 513, *One & Only Palmilla*. 514 (top), *Esperanza Resort*. 514 (bottom), *Marquis Los Cabos*. 515 (top), *One & Only Palmilla*. 515 (bottom), *Las Ventanas Al Paraiso*. 516, *Pueblo Bonito Rosé*. 517, *Westin Regina Golf & Beach Resort*. **Chapter 12: Puerto Vallarta & the Pacific Coast Resorts:** 573, *Corbis*. 574, *Mexico Tourism Board*. 630 (top), *Corbis*. 630 (bottom), *Colonial Arts, San Francisco*. 631 (top), *sergiobustamante.com.mx*. 631 (bottom), *Galleria Dante, Puerto Vallarta*. 632 (left), *sergiobustamante.com.mx*. 632 (right), *Lucy's Cucu Cabana*. 634, *talaveraetc.com*. 635, *Jim Kilpatrick/talaveraetc.com*. **Chapter 13: Acapulco - With a Side Trip to Taxco:** 665, *Corbis*. 666, *Walter Bibikow/age fotostock*. 667 (left), *CARLOS SANCHEZ/Mexico Tourism Board*. 667 (right), Ken Welsh/*age fotostock*. 676, *Everett Collection*. 677 (all), *Joe Viesti/Viestiphoto.com*. **Chapter 14: Cancún & Isla Mujeres:** 705, *Chris Cheadle/age fotostock*. 706 (top), *Jimmy Buffett's Margaritaville*. 706 (bottom), *Frank Lukasseck/age fotostock*. 707 (left), *Philip Coblentz/Brand X Pictures*. 707 (right), *Corbis*. **Chapter 15: Cozumel:** 753, *Bruno Morandi/age fotostock*. 754 (top), *cancuncd.com*. 754 (bottom), *Richard Cummins/viestiphoto.com*. 755, *Robert Winslow/viestiphoto.com*. **Chapter 16: Mérida & Environs - with Chichén Itzá:** 795, *Mark Newman/age fotostock*. 796 (top), *Corbis*. 796 (bottom), *GUILLERMO ALDANA/Mexico Tourism Board*. 797, *J. D. Heaton/Picture Finders/age fotostock*. 816, *Larry Williams/Masterfile*. 817, *Corbis*. 818 (top), *José A. Granados/Cancun CVB*. 818 (bottom), *William Wu*. 819 (top), *Gonzalo Azumendi/age fotostock*. 819 (center), *Philip Baird/anthroarcheart.org*. 819 (bottom), *Mexico Tourism Board*. 820 (top), *Corbis*. 820 (bottom), *Bruno Perousse/age fotostock*. 821 (top inset), *Luis Castañeda/age fotostock*. 821 (top image), *José A. Granados/Cancun CVB*. 821 (bottom), *Joe Viesti/Viestiphoto.com*. 822, *Marco/viestiphoto.com*. 823, *Joe Viesti/viestiphoto.com*.